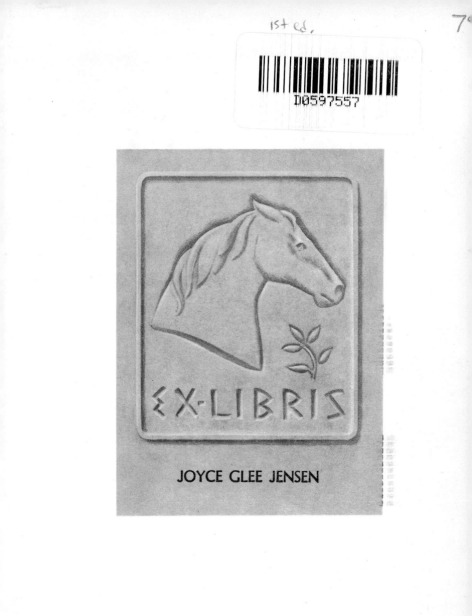

**JOYCE GLEE JENSEN**

# A Johnson Reader

ALSO EDITED BY

E. L. McAdam, Jr., and George Milne

JOHNSON'S DICTIONARY

*A Modern Selection*

# A
# JOHNSON
# READER

EDITED BY

## E. L. McAdam, Jr.
## & George Milne

### PANTHEON BOOKS
A DIVISION OF RANDOM HOUSE
*New York*

TO EDITH AND ALLEN

# Contents

[ vii ]

# Contents

# Introduction

THE OLD STEREOTYPE of Dr. Johnson as a sort of Tory crustacean has begun to crack. It ought to. Any man who could describe Sir Robert Walpole, the great Whig leader, as "a statesman, as able perhaps as any that ever existed" (1753), and in the next sentence refer to the invasion of Bonnie Prince Charlie as "a rebellion, which was not less contemptible in its beginning than threatening in its progress and consequences" should be read out of the party. Neither of these printed comments was known to Boswell or Macaulay, both of whom might have been embarrassed to fit them into a preconceived image of Johnson.

It is the purpose of this volume to give a wide-ranging selection from Johnson's works, deliberately emphasizing that he thought for himself and departed from tradition whenever he thought tradition wrong. We have also tried to present his first, unrevised thoughts, and have therefore reprinted from the first editions of his works, although in later editions he made many changes, mostly stylistic. (As a sample of his revision, we have given all of his changes for the second edition of *Rasselas*.)

Johnson had composed poetry as a schoolboy, and continued to do so at Oxford, but his first extended work was a translation and condensation of Lobo's *Voyage to Abyssinia* (1735), a distant precursor of *Rasselas*. In the spring of 1738 he published *London*, his first imitation of Juvenal, and began to work on Cave's *Gentleman's Magazine*, writing verse, short biographies, and accounts of Parliamentary debates. All of these were anonymous, and, except for *London,* all hack-work, though sometimes hack-work of a superior kind.

In 1744 he published his first major prose work, his *Life of Savage.* The recent biography of Savage by Clarence Tracy is called *The Artificial Bastard,* the story, that is, of a man probably legitimately born who, nevertheless, believed himself a bastard and exerted every effort to prove himself one. It was almost a classical changeling drama. A Lady Macclesfield had an illegitimate child, and put the boy to nurse with a woman who had also just had a baby boy. One child died. The survivor grew up believing that he was Lady Macclesfield's son, and spent his life trying vainly to prove it. He was a minor poet, and managed to elicit some support from Pope, and, even more important, a pension from Queen Caroline. But he would now be forgotten except that he and Johnson became friends in 1738, and in the winter of their discontents paced the streets of London, speaking out for liberty, and, hungry, sometimes slept on the bulks by the river. Johnson believed his story, and wrote a vivid biography, his only life of a close friend. It is here printed in full.

Five years later Johnson published his second imitation of Juvenal, *The Vanity of Human Wishes* (1749). As Pope had done earlier with some of the satires of Horace, Johnson took the basic structure of the Latin poem and generally used modern examples instead of classical ones. (He did, however, retain Xerxes.) The angry violence of Juvenal gives way to a somber tone, and Johnson discards Juvenal's Stoical conclusion for a Christian one. The poem is much more original than *London,* and it is not at all hampered by reference to passing political events. In it Johnson's always competent heroic couplets rise to a noble and moving statement.

In 1746 Johnson had begun to compile a *Dictionary* to challenge those of the French and Italian academies. He had no college degree, but he was backed by the major publishers of England, and by the powerful patronage of Lord Chesterfield. Nine years later, a widower, childless, abandoned by Chesterfield except for belated recommendations, unknown except to a few, he produced his two massive volumes. Their vast comprehensiveness, their wit, their stunning collection of examples from classical

English literature, do not need comment here. But his Preface is a distillation of experience which is worth a new reading. In it Johnson shows his first hope of an authoritative dictionary, then his realization that such a dictionary was not possible, since the language was in a state of flux, bad as that might appear, and finally his statement of what he had accomplished. The great aim, the strong personal tone, the tension of purpose and accomplishment, the stirring, rolling prose, make the Preface unmatched in eighteenth-century literature.

In the decade of the *Dictionary* Johnson also published his two major series of periodical essays, *The Rambler* (1750–52), which appeared separately twice a week, and *The Idler* (1758–60), which appeared once a week in *The Universal Chronicle*. These are generally on moral, occasionally on literary, themes. One of the *Idlers*, No. 22, attacking war, is his most violent satire, so violent that he omitted it from the collected edition of 1761. We reprint it as entirely characteristic of Johnson's attitude toward war. Part of Johnson's admiration for Walpole, mentioned earlier, must stem from Walpole's steady avoidance of war in the face of provocation from abroad and jingoism at home. Another paper on war we have reprinted from Johnson's *Literary Magazine* (1756), and a third from *The British Magazine* (1760). Last among the essays we have included a legal brief which Johnson wrote for Boswell advocating the freeing of a Negro slave.

*The Prince of Abissinia* (1759), soon renamed *Rasselas*, elaborates the themes of some of the essays. According to Sir Joshua Reynolds, it was written in one week to defray the funeral expenses of Johnson's mother, who had died in Lichfield at the age of eighty-nine. But Johnson's translation of Father Lobo's *Voyage to Abyssinia* had been made twenty-four years earlier—that strange, remote land held a strong appeal to a man who was never to travel further from Great Britain than Paris—and his ideas for this book had been developing through *The Vanity of Human Wishes, The Rambler,* and *The Idler.* At some time he read Norden's *Travels into Egypt and Nubia,* and was impelled to note in his diary that Norden saw crocodiles "thirty feet long." But the attraction of *Rasselas* is not only that it is the first long Oriental moral tale in English, but that Johnson uses Abyssinia and Egypt to achieve an appropriate distance, geographical and cultural, for a commentary on human life pertinent to eighteenth-century England. The pertinence, or the liveliness, of the comment may be judged by the fact that the book has appeared in some two hundred editions and translations. The reader will not need to be warned that Johnson has a sly sense of humor; when Imlac becomes pedantic, he is cut short by a bored Rasselas. And not every sentence in the book should be quoted, out of context, as Johnson's last word on literary criticism or the human condition. Sometimes the characters speak for themselves.

Johnson had proposed a new edition of Shakespeare in 1745, but had been put off by publishers claiming a perpetual copyright. In 1756 the dispute was resolved, and Johnson confidently expected to publish in 1757. The eight volumes appeared, after prodigious labor, in 1765. The text of Shakespeare had degenerated steadily since the first folio of 1623, and Johnson attempted to establish a sound text from that volume, with side glances at quartos borrowed from Garrick. The Preface, the text, and the notes were aimed primarily at the reader, since the audience in the theater would hear Shakespeare only as rewritten by Nahum Tate (*King Lear* with a happy ending) or revised by Garrick. To a modern reader, Johnson's common-sense approach forms his greatest appeal. He is not a bardolater, yet he fully recognizes Shakespeare's greatness. He examines, weighs, and finally places the laurel, usually where it belongs. His is the first modern edition of Shakespeare, and has been cited in all subsequent editions. His Preface can stand by itself.

In the twelve years following his *Shakespeare*, Johnson wrote four political pamphlets, *A Journey to the Western Islands*, following his trip to the Hebrides with Boswell, and many shorter works. In 1777 a group of publishers proposed that he write prefaces for a large collection of English poets, and in 1779 the first four volumes appeared: *Prefaces, Biographical and Critical, to the Works of the English Poets* (later called *Lives of the Poets*). Johnson's *Milton* was in the second volume. If Milton had been a conservative, a Royalist, and an undeviating member of the Church of England, Johnson would have treated him with more kindness in his biography. But Milton's advocacy of divorce, his republicanism, and his radicalism in religion insured that Johnson would treat his ideas with rigor, if not abuse. In a little more than a century after his death, his reputation as a poet was steadily growing, but he had not yet been canonized, by Wordsworth, as a leader of free men. Johnson had, however, long admired his poetry. In 1750 he had written a Prologue to *Comus*, for the benefit of Milton's sole surviving granddaughter, and even earlier he had tried, unwisely, to imitate Milton's blank verse in *Irene.*

When he came as a critic to examine Milton's poems, he was not subject to the intimidation of a mass of earlier work. When in college he had translated into Latin Dryden's six-line verse panegyric on Milton, and he had read Addison's appreciative papers in the *Spectator*. But, on the whole, he could read the poems freshly, and he did. Having suffered through innumerable eighteenth-century pastoral poems, however (partly as editor of the *Gentleman's Magazine*), he saw "Lycidas" only as another pastoral, and one disfigured by a combination of Christian elements and pagan myth. He did not see Milton springing through the veils of allusion in his search for identity and fame. He thought *Paradise Lost* a very great poem.

Johnson's biography was attacked immediately after its publication. It is still attacked—and read. It shows much about Milton, and perhaps more about Johnson.

Johnson's *Life of Gray* was published in May 1781, in volume X of his *Prefaces*, just short of ten years after Gray's death. The relatively unsympathetic treatment of some of Gray's poems produced immediate outcries, two books in the same year, another in 1782, and a fourth in 1783. These Johnson characteristically ignored. He did change one word in his criticism ( *or* to *and*) when he revised his *Lives* for the third edition (1783). He made more changes, largely factual, in his biographical account.

A curious blind spot in Johnson's criticism is his tepid reaction to Gray's "Ode on a Favourite Cat." This poem is perhaps the most brilliant self-parody in English literature: Gray takes his own studied poetic diction, and his moralizing, and destroys them. Johnson missed the point. In commenting on "The Bard" and "The Fatal Sisters," Johnson merely reiterates his known position: he wholly approved of resurrecting the old ballads, as Percy had done, but he thought that using such materials for modern poetry was ridiculous. He may have been wrong.

The last three sections of this *Reader* are made up of pieces which Johnson never published, and, indeed, he would not have called them "works." But his light verse, often impromptu, has an ease and sometimes a bite not at all in the stereotype of the Great Cham. His letters range from controlled indignation (to Chesterfield), through suavity (to Bute) and quiet advice (to Susy Thrale) to reckless fury (to Mrs. Thrale on her marriage to Piozzi), and final resignation. Finally we hear Johnson talking. His voice is known in great part from Boswell's biography. Boswell as friend and recorder commemorated Johnson's conversation as no English writer had ever done for anyone. From Boswell, many of Johnson's remarks have become famous, and others deserve to be. We have selected some from the list given by G. B. Hill as "Dicta Philosophiae" at the end of his edition of Boswell's *Life* in 1887, and others from a similar list at the end of his *Johnsonian Miscellanies,* 1892. We have rearranged these and elaborated them from his sources in some instances. That many were spoken in the heat of debate is clear enough; others may have undergone changes in transmission. But the voice still sounds authentic. A few quotations from Johnson's letters are in the same tone.

We do not offer an estimate of Johnson's position as a writer or a thinker. We suggest, instead, that the reader find in this volume a man thinking, and writing with wit, precision, and humanity.

E. L. M. Jʀ.
G. M.

ACKNOWLEDGMENTS

We are grateful for generous help we have received from Dr. Ashley T. Day of the New York University Library, Mr. Herman W. Liebert, Curator of Rare Books at Yale University, and Mr. André Schiffrin, our editor at Pantheon Books.

[ xiv ]

# *A Note on the Text*

WE HAVE printed works published during Johnson's lifetime from the first edition, thinking that a reader would be interested in Johnson's first, unrevised thoughts, and his way of putting them down. For he was, as he said, a man who waited till the printer's boy was waiting for copy, and then wrote in precipitous haste. But he was also an inveterate reviser: few works reprinted during his lifetime, under his supervision, are without changes. Indeed, some six thousand verbal differences have been noted in the 208 numbers of *The Rambler*. Not all of these are improvements, though they tend to greater conciseness, and what Fowler called "elegant variation." For the curious, we have printed the changes Johnson made for the second edition of *Rasselas*, and have noted a few of the significant variants in other works. Except for Dublin piracies, few of these original texts were reprinted during Johnson's life. The Prefaces to the *Dictionary* and to *Shakespeare* have few changes, which may suggest his satisfaction with these two works. He never reprinted *Idler* 22, perhaps because its satire is so bitter, or his *Observations on the Present State of Affairs*, perhaps because he thought it too topical. They are given from the original texts.

We have followed the original spelling and punctuation, except for silently adding quotation marks in *Rasselas* and *Idler* 22 where they are required for conversation. We have throughout reduced capitalization and italics to modern usage.

# A Note on the Text

# A Johnson Reader

# Life of Savage

"*He was a vicious man, but very kind to me. If you call a dog HERVEY, I shall love him.*" *Johnson said this of Henry Hervey, who had befriended him in London, when he was penniless and almost friendless, in 1737. This appears to be the key to Johnson's Life of Savage, for Savage, who was well-known for his poems, as well as his claim to be the illegitimate son of Lady Macclesfield, befriended Johnson in the next year. Johnson believed Savage's story of his birth (Boswell did not), and apparently it was friendship that led him to treat Savage's poems with more kindness than they deserve. But, as with Hervey, Johnson was not deceived as to Savage's character. The biography concludes: "negligence and irregularity, long continued, will make knowledge useless, wit ridiculous, and genius contemptible." Johnson was writing just six months after Savage died.*

*The* Life of Savage *was published, anonymously, in February 1744 in a small octavo volume. It was Johnson's first full-length biography, and his only biography of a close friend. Later he did not use such long footnotes as appear here: they may mark a man who has not yet acquired full mastery of his medium. The* Life *was revised for a second edition in 1745 and was subsequently reprinted in* Prefaces to the Works of the English Poets, *1781, where the long extracts from Savage's poems are omitted, since the collected poems appear in a separate volume. Savage's verse is now largely forgotten, though his anger against his supposed mother gave vigor to* The Bastard, *of which one line is still quoted: "No tenth transmitter of a foolish face."*

*We have put Johnson's notes at the end of the selection, in order to focus attention on his narrative. Reprinted from the first edition.*

# An Account of the Life of Mr. Richard Savage,

## Son of the Earl Rivers

It has been observed in all ages, that the advantages of nature or of fortune have contributed very little to the promotion of happiness; and that those whom the splendor of their rank, or the extent of their capacity, have placed upon the summits of human life, have not often given any just occasion to envy in those who look up to them from a lower station. Whether it be that apparent superiority incites great designs, and great designs are naturally liable to fatal miscarriages, or that the general lot of mankind is misery, and the misfortunes of those whose eminence drew upon them an universal attention, have been more carefully recorded, because they were more generally observed, and have in reality been only more conspicuous than those of others, not more frequent, or more severe.

That affluence and power, advantages extrinsic and adventitious, and therefore easily separable from those by whom they are possessed, should very often flatter the mind with expectations of felicity which they cannot give, raises no astonishment; but it seems rational to hope, that intellectual greatness should produce better effects, that minds qualified for great attainments should first endeavour their own benefit, and that they who are most able to teach others the way to happiness, should with most certainty follow it themselves.

But this expectation, however plausible, has been very frequently disappointed. The heroes of literary as well as civil history have been very often no less remarkable for what they have suffered, than for what they have atchieved; and volumes have been

Because of their length and complexity, the footnotes for the *Life of Savage* will be found grouped together at the end of the selection (pp. 87-105).

written only to enumerate the miseries of the learned, and relate their unhappy lives, and untimely deaths.

To these mournful narratives, I am about to add the life of Richard Savage, a man whose writings entitle him to an eminent rank in the classes of learning, and whose misfortunes claim a degree of compassion, not always due to the unhappy, as they were often the consequences of the crimes of others, rather than his own.

In the year 1697, Anne Countess of Macclesfield having lived for some time upon very uneasy terms with her husband, thought a public confession of adultery the most obvious and expeditious method of obtaining her liberty, and therefore declared, that the child, with which she was then great, was begotten by the Earl Rivers. This, as may be easily imagined, made her husband no less desirous of a separation than herself, and he prosecuted his design in the most effectual manner; for he applied not to the Ecclesiastical Courts for a divorce, but to the Parliament for an Act, by which his marriage might be dissolved, the nuptial contract totally annulled, and the children of his wife illegitimated. This Act, after the usual deliberation, he obtained, tho' without the approbation of some, who considered marriage as an affair only cognizable by ecclesiastical judges;[1] and on March 3d was separated from his wife, whose fortune, which was very great, was repaid her; and who having as well as her husband the liberty of making another choice, was in a short time married to Colonel Bret.

While the Earl of Macclesfield was prosecuting this affair, his wife was, on the tenth of January 1697–8, delivered of a son, and the Earl Rivers, by appearing to consider him as his own, left none any reason to doubt of the sincerity of her declaration; for he was his godfather, and gave him his own name, which was by his direction inserted in the register of St. Andrew's Parish in Holbourn, but unfortunately left him to the care of his mother, whom, as she was now set free from her husband, he probably imagined likely to treat with great tenderness the child that had contributed to so pleasing an event. It is not indeed easy to discover what motives could be found to over-balance that natural affection of a parent, or what interest could be promoted by neglect or cruelty. The dread of shame or of poverty, by which some wretches have been incited to abandon or to murder their children, cannot be supposed to have affected a woman who had proclaimed her crimes and solicited reproach, and on whom the clemency of the legislature had undeservedly bestowed a fortune, which would have been very little diminished by the expences which the care of her child could have brought upon her. It was therefore not likely that she would be wicked without temptation, that she would look upon her son from his birth with a kind of resentment and abhorrence; and instead of supporting, assisting, and defending him, delight to see him struggling with misery, or that she would take every opportunity of aggravating his misfortunes, and obstructing his resources, and with an implacable and restless cruelty continue her persecution from the first hour of his life to the last.

But whatever were her motives, no sooner was her son born, than she discovered a resolution of disowning him; and in a very short time removed him from her sight, by committing him to the care of a poor woman, whom she directed to educate him as her own, and injoined never to inform him of his true parents.

Such was the beginning of the life of Richard Savage: Born with a legal claim to honour and to affluence, he was in two months illegitimated by the Parliament, and disowned by his mother, doomed to poverty and obscurity, and launched upon the ocean of life, only that he might be swallowed by its quicksands, or dashed upon its rocks.

His mother could not indeed infect others with the same cruelty. As it was impossible to avoid the inquiries which the curiosity or tenderness of her relations made after her child, she was obliged to give some account of the measures that she had taken, and her mother, the Lady Mason, whether in approbation of her design, or to prevent more criminal contrivances, engaged to transact with the nurse, to pay her for her care, and to superintend the education of the child.

In this charitable office she was assisted by his godmother Mrs. Loyd, who while she lived always looked upon him with that tenderness, which the barbarity of his mother made peculiarly necessary; but her death, which happened in his tenth year, was another of the misfortunes of his childhood; for though she kindly endeavoured to alleviate his loss by a legacy of three hundred pounds, yet as he had none to prosecute his claim, to shelter him from oppression, or call in law to the assistance of justice, her will was eluded by the executors, and no part of the money was ever paid.

He was however not yet wholly abandoned. The Lady Mason still continued her care, and directed him to be placed at a small grammar school near St. Alban's, where he was called by the name of his nurse, without the least intimation that he had a claim to any other.

Here he was initiated in literature, and passed through several of the classes, with what rapidity or what applause cannot now be known. As he always spoke with respect of his master, it is probable that the mean rank, in which he then appeared, did not hinder his genius from being distinguished, or his industry from being rewarded, and if in so low a state he obtained distinction and rewards, it is not likely that they were gained but by genius and industry.

It is very reasonable to conjecture, that his application was equal to his abilities, because his improvement was more than proportioned to the opportunities which he enjoyed; nor can it be doubted, that if his earliest productions had been preserved, like those of happier students, we might in some have found vigorous sallies of that sprightly humour, which distinguishes the *Author to be let*, and in others, strong touches of that ardent imagination which painted the solemn scenes of *The Wanderer*.

While he was thus cultivating his genius, his father the Earl Rivers was seized with a distemper, which in a short time put an end to his life. He had frequently inquired after his son, and had always been amused with fallacious and evasive answers; but being now in his own opinion on his death-bed, he thought it his duty to provide for him among his other natural children, and therefore demanded a positive account of him, with an importunity not to be diverted or denied. His mother, who could no longer refuse an answer, determined at least to give such as should cut him off for ever from that happiness which competence affords, and therefore declared that he was dead; which is perhaps the first instance of a lie invented by a mother to deprive her son of a provision which was designed him by another, and which she could not expect herself, though he should lose it.

This was therefore an act of wickedness which could not be

defeated, because it could not be suspected; the Earl did not imagine, that there could exist in a human form a mother that would ruin her son without enriching herself, and therefore bestowed upon some other person six thousand pounds, which he had in his will bequeathed to Savage.

The same cruelty which incited his mother to intercept this provision which had been intended him, prompted her in a short time to another project, a project worthy of such a disposition. She endeavoured to rid herself from the danger of being at any time made known to him, by sending him secretly to the American plantations.[2]

By whose kindness this scheme was counteracted, or by what interposition she was induced to lay aside her design, I know not; it is not improbable that the Lady Mason might persuade or compel her to desist, or perhaps she could not easily find accomplices wicked enough to concur in so cruel an action; for it may be conceived, that those who had by a long gradation of guilt hardened their hearts against the sense of common wickedness, would yet be shocked at the design of a mother to expose her son to slavery and want, to expose him without interest, and without provocation; and Savage might on this occasion find protectors and advocates among those who had long traded in crimes, and whom compassion had never touched before.

Being hindered, by whatever means, from banishing him into another country, she formed soon after a scheme for burying him in poverty and obscurity in his own; and that his station of life, if not the place of his residence, might keep him for ever at a distance from her, she ordered him to be placed with a shoemaker in Holbourn, that after the usual time of trial, he might become his apprentice.[3]

It is generally reported, that this project was for some time successful, and that Savage was employed at the awl longer than he was willing to confess; nor was it perhaps any great advantage to him, that an unexpected discovery determined him to quit his occupation.

About this time his nurse, who had always treated him as her own son, died; and it was natural for him to take care of those effects which by her death were, as he imagined, become his own; he therefore went to her house, opened her boxes, and examined her papers, among which he found some letters written to her by the Lady Mason, which informed him of his birth, and the reasons for which it was concealed.

He was now no longer satisfied with the employment which had been allotted him, but thought he had a right to share the affluence of his mother, and therefore without scruple applied to her as her son, and made use of every art to awaken her tenderness, and attract her regard. But neither his letters, nor the interposition of those friends which his merit or his distress procured him, made any impression upon her mind: She still resolved to neglect, though she could no longer disown him.

It was to no purpose that he frequently solicited her to admit him to see her; she avoided him with the most vigilant precaution, and ordered him to be excluded from her house, by whomsoever he might be introduced, and what reason soever he might give for entering it.

Savage was at the same time so touched with the discovery of his real mother, that it was his frequent practice to walk in the dark evenings[4] for several hours before her door, in hopes of seeing her as she might come by accident to the window, or cross her apartment with a candle in her hand.

But all his assiduity and tenderness were without effect, for he could neither soften her heart, nor open her hand, and was reduced to the utmost miseries of want, while he was endeavouring to awaken the affection of a mother: He was therefore obliged to seek some other means of support, and having no profession, became, by necessity, an author.

At this time the attention of all the literary world was engrossed by the Bangorian Controversy, which filled the press with pamphlets, and the coffee-houses with disputants. Of this subject, as most popular, he made choice for his first attempt, and without any other knowledge of the question, than he had casually collected from conversation, published a poem against the bishop.

What was the success or merit of this performance I know not, it was probably lost among the innumerable pamphlets to which that dispute gave occasion. Mr. Savage was himself in a little time ashamed of it, and endeavoured to suppress it, by destroying all the copies that he could collect.

He then attempted a more gainful kind of writing,[5] and in his eighteenth year offered to the stage a comedy borrowed from a Spanish plot, which was refused by the players, and was therefore given by him to Mr. Bullock, who having more interest, made some slight alterations, and brought it upon the stage, under the title of[6] *Woman's a Riddle,* but allowed the unhappy author no part of the profit.

Not discouraged however at his repulse, he wrote two years afterwards *Love in a Veil,* another comedy, borrowed likewise from the Spanish, but with little better success than before; for though it was received and acted, yet it appeared so late in the year, that the author obtained no other advantage from it, than the acquaintance of Sir Richard Steele, and Mr. Wilks; by whom he was pitied, caressed, and relieved.

Sir Richard Steele having declared in his favour with all the ardour of benevolence which constituted his character, promoted his interest with the utmost zeal, related his misfortunes, applauded his merit, took all opportunities of recommending him, and asserted[7] that *the inhumanity of his mother had given him a right to find every good man his father.*

Nor was Mr. Savage admitted to his acquaintance only, but to his confidence, of which he sometimes related an instance too extraordinary to be omitted, as it affords a very just idea of his patron's character.

He was once desired by Sir Richard, with an air of the utmost importance, to come very early to his house the next morning. Mr. Savage came as he had promised, found the chariot at the door, and Sir Richard waiting for him, and ready to go out. What was intended, and whither they were to go, Savage could not conjecture, and was not willing to enquire; but immediately seated himself with Sir Richard; the coachman was ordered to drive, and they hurried with the utmost expedition to Hyde-park Corner, where they stopped at a petty tavern, and retired to a private room. Sir Richard then informed him, that he intended to publish a pamphlet, and that he had desired him to come thither that he might write for him. They soon sat down to the work, Sir Richard dictated, and Savage wrote, till the dinner that had been ordered was put upon the table. Savage was surprised at the meanness of the entertainment, and after some hesitation, ventured to ask for wine, which Sir Richard, not without reluctance, ordered to be brought. They then finished their dinner, and proceeded in their pamphlet, which they concluded in the afternoon.

Mr. Savage then imagined his task over, and expected that Sir Richard would call for the reckoning, and return home; but his expectations deceived him, for Sir Richard told him, that he was without money, and that the pamphlet must be sold before the dinner could be paid for; and Savage was therefore obliged to go and offer their new production to sale for two guineas, which with some difficulty he obtained. Sir Richard then returned home, having retired that day only to avoid his creditors, and composed the pamphlet only to discharge his reckoning.

Mr. Savage related another fact equally uncommon, which, though it has no relation to his life, ought to be preserved. Sir Richard Steele having one day invited to his house a great number of persons of the first quality, they were surprised at the number of liveries which surrounded the table; and after dinner, when wine and mirth had set them free from the observation of rigid ceremony, one of them enquired of Sir Richard, how such an expensive train of domestics could be consistent with his fortune. Sir Richard very frankly confessed, that they were fellows of whom he would very willingly be rid. And being then asked, why he did not discharge them, declared that they were bailiffs who had introduced themselves with an execution, and whom, since he could not send them away, he had thought it convenient to embellish with liveries, that they might do him credit while they staid.

His friends were diverted with the expedient, and by paying the debt discharged their attendance, having obliged Sir Richard to promise that they should never again find him graced with a retinue of the same kind.

Under such a tutor, Mr. Savage was not likely to learn prudence or frugality, and perhaps many of the misfortunes which the want of those virtues brought upon him in the following parts of his life, might be justly imputed to so unimproving an example.

Nor did the kindness of Sir Richard end in common favours. He proposed to have established him in some settled scheme of life, and to have contracted a kind of alliance with him, by marrying him to a natural daughter, on whom he intended to bestow a thousand pounds. But though he was always lavish of future bounties, he conducted his affairs in such a manner, that he was very seldom able to keep his promises, or execute his own intentions; and as he was never able to raise the sum which he had offered, the marriage was delayed. In the mean time he was officiously informed that Mr. Savage had ridiculed him; by which he was so much exasperated, that he withdrew the allowance which he had paid him, and never afterwards admitted him to his house.

It is not indeed unlikely that Savage might by his imprudence expose himself to the malice of a tale-bearer; for his patron had many follies, which as his discernment easily discovered, his imagination might sometimes incite him to mention too ludicrously. A little knowledge of the world is sufficient to discover that such weakness is very common, and that there are few who do not sometimes in the wantonness of thoughtless mirth, or the heat of transient resentment, speak of their friends and benefactors with levity and contempt, though in their cooler moments, they want neither sense of their kindness, nor reverence for their virtue. The fault therefore of Mr. Savage was rather negligence than ingratitude; but Sir Richard must likewise be acquitted of severity, for who is there that can patiently bear contempt from one whom he has relieved and supported, whose establishment he has laboured, and whose interest he has promoted?

He was now again abandoned to fortune, without any other friend than Mr. Wilks; a man, who, whatever were his abilities or skill as an actor, deserves at least to be remembered for his virtues,[8] which are not often to be found in the world, and perhaps less often in his profession than in others. To be humane, generous and candid, is a very high degree of merit in any state; but those qualities deserve still greater praise, when they are found in that condition, which makes almost every other man, for whatever reason, contemptuous, insolent, petulant, selfish, and brutal.

As Mr. Wilks was one of those to whom calamity seldom complained without relief, he naturally took an unfortunate wit into his protection, and not only assisted him in any casual distresses, but continued an equal and steady kindness to the time of his death.

By his interposition Mr. Savage once obtained from his mother[9] fifty pounds, and a promise of one hundred and fifty more; but it was the fate of this unhappy man, that few promises of any advantage to him were performed. His mother was infected among others with the general madness of the South-Sea traffick, and having been disappointed in her expectations, refused to pay what perhaps nothing but the prospect of sudden affluence prompted her to promise.

Being thus obliged to depend upon the friendship of Mr. Wilks, he was consequently an assiduous frequenter of the theatres, and in a short time the amusements of the stage took such possession of his mind, that he never was absent from a play in several years.

This constant attendance naturally procured him the acquaintance of the players, and among others, of Mrs. Oldfield, who was so much pleased with his conversation, and touched with his misfortunes, that she allowed him a settled pension of fifty pounds a year, which was during her life regularly paid.

That this act of generosity may receive its due praise, and that the good actions of Mrs. Oldfield may not be sullied by her general character, it is proper to mention what Mr. Savage often declared in the strongest terms, that he never saw her alone, or in any other place than behind the scenes.

At her death, he endeavoured to shew his gratitude in the most decent manner, by wearing mourning as for a mother, but did not celebrate her in elegies, because he knew that too great profusion of praise would only have revived those faults which his natural equity did not allow him to think less, because they were committed by one who favoured him; but of which, though his virtue would not endeavour to palliate them, his gratitude would not suffer him to prolong the memory, or diffuse the censure.

In his *Wanderer*, he has indeed taken an opportunity of mentioning her, but celebrates her not for her virtue, but her beauty, an excellence which none ever denied her: This is the only encomium with which he has rewarded her liberality, and perhaps he has even in this been too lavish of his praise. He seems to have thought that never to mention his benefactress, would have an appearance of ingratitude, though to have dedicated any particular performance to her memory, would have only betrayed an officious partiality, that without exalting her character, would have depressed his own.

He had sometimes, by the kindness of Mr. Wilks, the advantage of a benefit, on which occasions he often received uncommon marks of regard and compassion; and was once told by the Duke of Dorset, that it was just to consider him as an injured noble-man, and that in his opinion the nobility ought to think themselves obliged without solicitation to take every opportunity of support-ing him by their countenance and patronage. But he had generally the mortification to hear that the whole interest of his mother was employed to frustrate his applications, and that she never left any expedient untried, by which he might be cut off from the possibility of supporting life. The same disposition she endeav-oured to diffuse among all those over whom nature or fortune gave her any influence, and indeed succeeded too well in her design; but could not always propagate her effrontery with her cruelty, for some of those whom she incited against him, were ashamed of their own conduct, and boasted of that relief which they never gave him.

In this censure I do not indiscriminately involve all his rela-tions; for he has mentioned with gratitude the humanity of one lady, whose name I am now unable to recollect, and to whom therefore I cannot pay the praises which she deserves for having acted well in opposition to influence, precept and example.

The punishment which our laws inflict upon those parents who murder their infants, is well known, nor has its justice ever been contested; but if they deserve death who destroy a child in its birth, what pains can be severe enough for her who forbears to destroy him only to inflict sharper miseries upon him; who pro-longs his life only to make it miserable; and who exposes him without care and without pity, to the malice of oppression, the caprices of chance, and the temptations of poverty; who rejoices to see him overwhelmed with calamities; and when his own industry, or the charity of others, has enabled him to rise for a short time above his miseries, plunges him again into his former distress?

The kindness of his friends not affording him any constant sup-ply, and the prospect of improving his fortune, by enlarging his acquaintance, necessarily leading him to places of expence, he found it necessary[1] to endeavour once more at dramatic poetry, for which he was now better qualified by a more extensive knowledge, and longer observation. But having been unsuccessful in comedy, though rather for want of opportunities than genius, he resolved now to try whether he should not be more fortunate in exhibiting a tragedy.

The story which he chose for the subject, was that of Sir Thomas Overbury, a story well adapted to the stage, though perhaps not far enough removed from the present age, to admit properly the fictions necessary to complete the plan; for the mind which naturally loves truth is always most offended with the violation of those truths of which we are most certain, and we of course conceive those facts most certain which approach nearest to our own time.

Out of this story he formed a tragedy, which, if the circumstances in which he wrote it be considered, will afford at once an uncommon proof of strength of genius, an evenness of mind, of a serenity not to be ruffled, and an imagination not to be suppressed.

During a considerable part of the time, in which he was employed upon this performance, he was without lodging, and often without meat; nor had he any other conveniences for study than the fields or the street allowed him, there he used to walk and form his speeches, and afterwards step into a shop, beg for a few moments the use of the pen and ink, and write down what he had composed upon paper which he had picked up by accident.

If the performance of a writer thus distressed is not perfect, its faults ought surely to be imputed to a cause very different from want of genius, and must rather excite pity than provoke censure.

But when under these discouragements the tragedy was finished, there yet remained the labour of introducing it on the stage, an undertaking which to an ingenuous mind was in a very high degree vexatious and disgusting; for having little interest or reputation, he was obliged to submit himself wholly to the players, and admit, with whatever reluctance, the emendations of Mr. Cibber, which he always considered as the disgrace of his performance.

He had indeed in Mr. Hill another critic of a very different class, from whose friendship he received great assistance on many occasions, and whom he never mentioned but with the utmost tenderness and regard.[2] He had been for some time distinguished by him with very particular kindness, and on this occasion it was natural to apply to him as an author of an established character. He therefore sent this tragedy to him with a short copy of verses,[3] in which he desired his correction. Mr. Hill, whose humanity and politeness are generally known, readily complied with his request; but as he is remarkable for singularity of sentiment, and bold experiments in language, Mr. Savage did not think his play much improved by his innovation, and had even at that time the courage to reject several passages which he could not approve, and what is still more laudable, Mr. Hill had the generosity not to resent the neglect of his alterations, but wrote the Prologue and Epilogue, in which he touches on the circumstances of the author with great tenderness.[4]

After all these obstructions and compliances, he was only able to bring his play upon the stage in the summer, when the chief actors had retired, and the rest were in possession of the house for their own advantage. Among these Mr. Savage was admitted to play the part of Sir Thomas Overbury, by which he gained no great reputation, the theatre being a province for which nature seemed not to have designed him; for neither his voice, look, nor gesture, were such as are expected on the stage, and he was himself so much ashamed of having been reduced to appear as a player, that he always blotted out his name from the list, when a copy of his tragedy was to be shown to his friends.

In the publication of his performance he was more successful, for the rays of genius that glimmered in it, that glimmered through all the mists which poverty and Cibber had been able to spread over it, procured him the notice and esteem of many persons eminent for their rank, their virtue, and their wit.

Of this play, acted, printed, and dedicated, the accumulated profits arose to an hundred pounds, which he thought at that time a very large sum, having been never master of so much before.

In the Dedication,[5] for which he received ten guineas, there is nothing remarkable. The Preface contains a very liberal encomium on the blooming excellencies of Mr. Theophilus Cibber, which Mr. Savage could not in the latter part of his life see his friends about to read without snatching the play out of their hands.

The generosity of Mr. Hill did not end on this occasion; for afterwards when Mr. Savage's necessities returned, he encouraged a subscription to a Miscellany of Poems in a very extraordinary manner, by publishing his story in the *Plain Dealer*,[6] with some affecting lines,[7] which he asserts to have been written by Mr. Savage upon the treatment received by him from his mother, but of which he was himself the author, as Mr. Savage afterwards declared. These lines, and the paper in which they were inserted, had a very powerful effect upon all but his mother, whom by making her cruelty more publick, they only hardened in her aversion.

Mr. Hill not only promoted the subscription to the Miscellany, but furnished likewise the greatest part of the poems of which it is composed, and particularly *The Happy Man,* which he published as a specimen.

The subscriptions of those whom these papers should influence to patronise merit in distress, without any other solicitation, were directed to be left at Button's Coffee-house, and Mr. Savage going thither a few days afterwards, without expectation of any effect from his proposal, found to his surprise seventy guineas,[8] which had been sent him in consequence of the compassion excited by Mr. Hill's pathetic representation.

To this Miscellany he wrote a Preface,[9] in which he gives an account of his mother's cruelty in a very uncommon strain of humour, and with a gaiety of imagination, which the success of his subscription probably produced.

The Dedication is addressed to the Lady Mary Wortley Montague, whom he flatters without reserve, and, to confess the truth, with very little[1] art. The same observation may be extended to all his Dedications: his compliments are constrained and violent, heaped together without the grace of order, or the decency of introduction: he seems to have written his panegyrics for the perusal only of his patrons, and to have imagined that he had no other task than to pamper them with praises however gross, and that flattery would make its way to the heart, without the assistance of elegance or invention.

Soon afterwards the death of the King furnished a general subject for a poetical contest, in which Mr. Savage engaged, and is allowed to have carried the prize of honour from his competitors; but I know not whether he gained by his performance any other advantage than the increase of his reputation; though it must certainly have been with farther views that he prevailed upon himself to attempt a species of writing of which all the topics had been long before exhausted, and which was made at once difficult by the multitudes that had failed in it, and those that had succeeded.

He was now advancing in reputation, and though frequently involved in very distressful perplexities, appeared however to be gaining upon mankind, when both his fame and his life were endangered by an event, of which it is not yet determined, whether it ought to be mentioned as a crime or a calamity.

On the 20th of November 1727, Mr. Savage came from Richmond, where he then lodged that he might persue his studies with less interruption, with an intent to discharge another lodging which he had in Westminster, and accidentally meeting two gentlemen his acquaintances, whose names were Merchant and Gregory, he went in with them to a neighbouring coffee-house, and sat drinking till it was late, it being in no time of Mr. Savage's life any part of his character to be the first of the company that desired to separate. He would willingly have gone to bed in the same house, but there was not room for the whole company, and therefore they agreed to ramble about the streets, and divert themselves with such amusements as should offer themselves till morning.

In their walk they happened unluckily to discover light in Robinson's Coffee-house, near Charing-Cross, and therefore went in. Merchant with some rudeness, demanded a room, and was told that there was a good fire in the next parlour, which the company were about to leave, being then paying their reckoning. Merchant not satisfied with this answer, rushed into the room, and was followed by his companions. He then petulantly placed himself between the company and the fire, and soon after kicked down the table. This produced a quarrel, swords were drawn on both sides, and one Mr. James Sinclair was killed. Savage having wounded likewise a maid that held him, forced his way with Merchant out of the house; but being intimidated and confused, without resolution either to fly or stay, they were taken in a back court by one of the company and some soldiers, whom he had called to his assistance.

Being secured and guarded that night, they were in the morning carried before three justices, who committed them to the Gatehouse, from whence, upon the death of Mr. Sinclair, which happened the same day, they were removed in the night to Newgate, where they were however treated with some distinction, exempted from the ignominy of chains, and confined, not among the common criminals, but in the Press-Yard.

When the day of trial came, the court was crouded in a very unusual manner, and the publick appeared to interest itself as in a cause of general concern. The witnesses against Mr. Savage and his friends were, the woman who kept the house, which was a house of ill fame, and her maid, the men who were in the room with Mr. Sinclair, and a woman of the town, who had been drinking with them, and with whom one of them had been seen in bed. They swore in general, that Merchant gave the provocation, which Savage and Gregory drew their swords to justify; that Savage drew first, and that he stabbed Sinclair when he was not in a posture of defence, or while Gregory commanded his sword; that after he had given the thrust he turned pale, and would have retired, but that the maid clung round him, and one of the company endeavoured to detain him, from whom he broke, by cutting the maid on the head, but was afterwards taken in a court.

There was some difference in their depositions; one did not see Savage give the wound, another saw it given when Sinclair held his point towards the ground; and the woman of the town asserted, that she did not see Sinclair's sword at all: This difference however was very far from amounting to inconsistency, but it was sufficient to shew, that the hurry of the dispute was such, that it was not easy to discover the truth with relation to particular circumstances, and that therefore some deductions were to be made from the credibility of the testimonies.

Sinclair had declared several times before his death, that he received his wound from Savage, nor did Savage at his trial deny the fact, but endeavoured partly to extenuate it by urging the suddenness of the whole action, and the impossibility of any ill design, or premeditated malice, and partly to justify it by the necessity of self-defence, and the hazard of his own life, if he had lost that opportunity of giving the thrust: He observed, that neither reason nor law obliged a man to wait for the blow which was threatened, and which, if he should suffer it, he might never be able to return; that it was always allowable to prevent an assault, and to preserve life by taking away that of the adversary, by whom it was endangered.

With regard to the violence with which he endeavoured his escape, he declared, that it was not his design to fly from justice, or decline a trial, but to avoid the expences and severities of a prison, and that he intended to have appeared at the bar without compulsion.

This defence, which took up more than an hour, was heard by the multitude that thronged the court with the most attentive and respectful silence: Those who thought he ought not to be acquitted owned that applause could not be refused him; and those who before pitied his misfortunes, now reverenced his abilities.

The witnesses which appeared against him were proved to be persons of characters which did not entitle them to much credit; a common strumpet, a woman by whom strumpets were entertained, and a man by whom they were supported; and the character of Savage was by several persons of distinction asserted, to be that of a modest inoffensive man, not inclined to broils, or to insolence, and who had, to that time, been only known for his misfortunes and his wit.

Had his audience been his judges, he had undoubtedly been acquitted; but Mr. Page, who was then upon the bench, treated him with his usual insolence and severity, and when he had summed up the evidence, endeavoured to exasperate the jury, as Mr. Savage used to relate it, with this eloquent harangue.

"Gentlemen of the jury, you are to consider, that Mr. Savage is a very great man, a much greater man than you or I, gentlemen of the jury; that he wears very fine clothes, much finer clothes than you or I, gentlemen of the jury; that he has abundance of money in his pocket, much more money than you or I, gentlemen of the jury; but, gentlemen of the jury, is it not a very hard case, gentlemen of the jury, that Mr. Savage should therefore kill you or me, gentlemen of the jury?"

Mr. Savage hearing his defence thus misrepresented, and the men who were to decide his fate incited against him by invidious comparisons, resolutely asserted, that his cause was not candidly explained, and began to recapitulate what he had before said with regard to his condition and the necessity of endeavouring to escape the expences of imprisonment; but the judge having ordered him to be silent, and repeated his orders without effect, commanded that he should be taken from the bar by force.

The jury then heard the opinion of the judge, that good characters were of no weight against positive evidence, though they might turn the scale, where it was doubtful; and that though when two men attack each other, the death of either is only manslaughter; but where one is the aggressor, as in the case before them, and in pursuance of his first attack, kills the other, the law supposes the action, however sudden, to be malicious. They then deliberated upon their verdict, and determined that Mr. Savage and Mr. Gregory were guilty of murder, and Mr. Merchant, who had no sword, only of manslaughter.

Thus ended this memorable trial, which lasted eight hours. Mr. Savage and Mr. Gregory were conducted back to prison, where they were more closely confined, and loaded with irons of fifty pounds weight: Four days afterwards they were sent back to the court to receive sentence; on which occasion Mr. Savage made, as far as it could be retained in memory, the following speech.

"It is now, my Lord, too late to offer any thing by way of defence, or vindication; nor can we expect ought from your Lordships, in this court, but the sentence which the law requires you, as judges, to pronounce against men of our calamitous condition. —But we are also persuaded, that as mere men, and out of this seat of rigorous justice, you are susceptive of the tender passions, and too humane, not to commiserate the unhappy situation of those, whom the law sometimes perhaps—exacts—from you to pronounce upon. No doubt you distinguish between offences, which arise out of premeditation, and a disposition habituated to vice or immorality, and transgressions, which are the unhappy and unforeseen effects of a casual absence of reason, and sudden impulse of passion: We therefore hope you will contribute all you can to an extension of that mercy, which the gentlemen of the jury have been pleased to shew Mr. Merchant, who (allowing facts as sworn against us by the evidence) has led us into this our calamity. I hope, this will not be construed as if we meant to reflect upon that gentleman, or remove any thing from us upon him, or that we repine the more at our fate, because he has no participation of it: No, my Lord! For my part, I declare nothing could more soften my grief, than to be without any companion in so great a misfortune."[2]

Mr. Savage had now no hopes of life, but from the mercy of the Crown, which was very earnestly solicited by his friends, and which, with whatever difficulty the story may obtain belief, was obstructed only by his mother.

To prejudice the Queen against him, she made use of an incident, which was omitted in the order of time, that it might be mentioned together with the purpose which it was made to serve. Mr. Savage, when he had discovered his birth, had an incessant desire to speak to his mother, who always avoided him in publick, and refused him admission into her house. One evening walking, as it was his custom, in the street that she inhabited, he saw the door of her house by accident open; he entered it, and finding no persons in the passage, to hinder him, went up stairs to salute her. She discovered him before he could enter her chamber, alarmed the family with the most distressful outcries, and when she had by her screams gathered them about her, ordered them to drive out of the house that villain, who had forced himself in upon her, and endeavoured to murder her. Savage, who had attempted with the most submissive tenderness to soften her rage, hearing her utter so detestable an accusation, thought it prudent to retire, and, I believe, never attempted afterwards to speak to her.

But shocked as he was with her falshood and her cruelty, he imagined that she intended no other use of her lie, than to set herself free from his embraces and solicitations, and was very far from suspecting that she would treasure it in her memory, as an instrument of future wickedness, or that she would endeavour for this fictitious assault to deprive him of his life.

But when the Queen was solicited for his pardon, and informed of the severe treatments which he had suffered from his judge, she answered, that however unjustifiable might be the manner of his trial, or whatever extenuation the action for which he was condemned might admit, she could not think that man a proper object of the King's mercy, who had been capable of entering his mother's house in the night, with an intent to murder her.

By whom this atrocious calumny had been transmitted to the Queen, whether she that invented, had the front to relate it; whether she found any one weak enough to credit it, or corrupt

enough to concur with her in her hateful design, I know not; but
methods had been taken to persuade the Queen so strongly of the
truth of it, that she for a long time refused to hear any of those
who petitioned for his life.

Thus had Savage perished by the evidence of a bawd, a strumpet, and his mother, had not justice and compassion procured him
an advocate of rank too great to be rejected unheard, and of virtue
too eminent to be heard without being believed. His merit and
his calamities happened to reach the ear of the Countess of Hertford, who engaged in his support with all the tenderness that is
excited by pity, and all the zeal which is kindled by generosity,
and demanding an audience of the Queen, laid before her the
whole series of his mother's cruelty, exposed the improbability of
an accusation by which he was charged with an intent to commit
a murder, that could produce no advantage, and soon convinced
her how little his former conduct could deserve to be mentioned
as a reason for extraordinary severity.

The interposition of this lady was so successful, that he was
soon after admitted to bail, and on the 9th of March 1728, pleaded
the King's pardon.

It is natural to enquire upon what motives his mother could
persecute him in a manner so outragious and implacable; for what
reason she could employ all the acts of malice and all the snares
of calumny, to take away the life of her own son, of a son who
never injured her, who was never supported by her expence, nor
obstructed any prospect of pleasure or advantage; why she
should endeavour to destroy him by a lie; a lie which could not
gain credit, but must vanish of itself at the first moment of examination, and of which only this can be said to make it probable,
that it may be observed from her conduct, that the most execrable
crimes are sometimes committed without apparent temptation.

This mother is still alive, and may perhaps even yet, though her
malice was so often defeated, enjoy the pleasure of reflecting,
that the life which she often endeavoured to destroy, was at least
shortened by her maternal offices; that though she could not
transport her son to the plantations, bury him in the shop of a
mechanick, or hasten the hand of the publick executioner, she has
yet had the satisfaction of imbittering all his hours, and forcing
him into exigencies, that hurried on his death.

It is by no means necessary to aggravate the enormity of this woman's conduct, by placing it in opposition to that of the Countess of Hertford; no one can fail to observe how much more amiable it is to relieve, than to oppress, and to rescue innocence from destruction, than to destroy without an injury.

Mr. Savage, during his imprisonment, his trial, and the time in which he lay under sentence of death, behaved with great firmness and equality of mind, and confirmed by his fortitude the esteem of those, who before admired him for his abilities. The peculiar circumstances of his life were made more generally known by a short Account,[3] which was then published, and of which several thousands were in a few weeks dispersed over the nation; and the compassion of mankind operated so powerfully in his favour, that he was enabled, by frequent presents, not only to support himself, but to assist Mr. Gregory in prison; and when he was pardoned and released he found the number of his friends not lessened.

The nature of the act for which he had been tried was in itself doubtful; of the evidences which appeared against him, the character of the man was not unexceptionable, that of the women notoriously infamous; she whose testimony chiefly influenced the jury to condemn him, afterwards retracted her assertions. He always himself denied that he was drunk, as had been generally reported. Mr. Gregory, who is now Collector of Antegua, is said to declare him far less criminal than he was imagined, even by some who favoured him: And Page himself afterwards confessed, that he had treated him with uncommon rigour. When all these particulars are rated together, perhaps the memory of Savage may not be much sullied by his trial.

Some time after he had obtained his liberty, he met in the street the woman that had sworn with so much malignity against him. She informed him, that she was in distress, and, with a degree of confidence not easily attainable, desired him to relieve her. He, instead of insulting her misery, and taking pleasure in the calamities of one who had brought his life into danger, reproved her gently for her perjury, and changing the only guinea that he had, divided it equally between her and himself.

This is an action which in some ages would have made a saint, and perhaps in others a hero, and which, without any hyperbolical encomiums, must be allowed to be an instance of uncommon generosity, an act of complicated virtue; by which he at once relieved the poor, corrected the vicious, and forgave an enemy; by which he at once remitted the strongest provocations, and exercised the most ardent charity.

Compassion was indeed the distinguishing quality of Savage; he never appeared inclined to take advantage of weakness, to attack the defenceless, or to press upon the falling; whoever was distressed was certain at least of his good-wishes; and when he could give no assistance, to extricate them from misfortunes, he endeavoured to sooth them by sympathy and tenderness.

But when his heart was not softened by the sight of misery, he was sometimes obstinate in his resentment, and did not quickly lose the remembrance of an injury. He always continued to speak with anger of the insolence and partiality of Page, and a short time before his death revenged it by a satire.[4]

It is natural to enquire in what terms Mr. Savage spoke of this fatal action, when the danger was over, and he was under no necessity of using any art to set his conduct in the fairest light. He was not willing to dwell upon it, and if he transiently mentioned it, appeared neither to consider himself as a murderer, nor as a man wholly free from the guilt of blood.[5] How much and how long he regretted it, appeared in a[6] poem which he published many years afterwards. On occasion of a copy of verses in which the failings of good men were recounted, and in which the author had endeavoured to illustrate his position, that *the best may sometimes deviate from virtue,* by an instance of murder committed by Savage in the heat of wine, Savage remarked, that it was no very just representation of a good man, to suppose him liable to drunkenness, and disposed in his riots to cut throats.

He was now indeed at liberty, but was, as before, without any other support than accidental favours and uncertain patronage afforded him; sources by which he was sometimes very liberally supplied, and which at other times were suddenly stopped; so that he spent his life between want and plenty, or what was yet worse, between beggary and extravagance; for as whatever he received was the gift of chance, which might as well favour him at one time as another, he was tempted to squander what he had, because he always hoped to be immediately supplied.

Another cause of his profusion was the absurd kindness of his friends, who at once rewarded and enjoyed his abilities, by treating him at taverns, and habituated him to pleasures which he could not afford to enjoy, and which he was not able to deny himself, though he purchased the luxury of a single night by the anguish of cold and hunger for a week.

The experience of these inconveniences determined him to endeavour after some settled income, which, having long found submission and intreaties fruitless, he attempted to extort from his mother by rougher methods. He had now, as he acknowledged, lost that tenderness for her, which the whole series of her cruelty had not been able wholly to repress, till he found, by the efforts which she made for his destruction, that she was not content with refusing to assist him, and being neutral in his struggles with poverty, but was as ready to snatch every opportunity of adding to his misfortunes, and that she was to be considered as an enemy implacably malicious, whom nothing but his blood could satisfy. He therefore threatened to harass her with lampoons, and to publish a copious narrative of her conduct, unless she consented to purchase an exemption from infamy, by allowing him a pension.

This expedient proved successful. Whether shame still survived, though virtue was extinct, or whether her relations had more delicacy than herself, and imagined that some of the darts which satire might point at her would glance upon them: Lord Tyrconnel, whatever were his motives, upon his promise to lay aside his design of exposing the cruelty of his mother, received him into his family, treated him as his equal, and engaged to allow him a pension of two hundred pounds a year.

This was the golden part of Mr. Savage's life; and for some time he had no reason to complain of fortune; his appearance was splendid, his expences large, and his acquaintance extensive. He was courted by all who endeavoured to be thought men of genius, and caressed by all who valued themselves upon a refined taste. To admire Mr. Savage was a proof of discernment, and to be acquainted with him was a title to poetical reputation. His presence was sufficient to make any place of publick entertainment popular; and his approbation and example constituted the fashion. So powerful is genius, when it is invested with the glitter of affluence; men willingly pay to fortune that regard which they owe to merit, and are pleased when they have an opportunity at once of gratifying their vanity, and practising their duty.

This interval of prosperity furnished him with opportunities of enlarging his knowledge of human nature, by contemplating life from its highest gradations to its lowest, and had he afterwards applied to dramatic poetry, he would perhaps not have had many superiors; for as he never suffered any scene to pass before his eyes without notice, he had treasured in his mind all the different combinations of passions, and the innumerable mixtures of vice and virtue, which distinguish one character from another; and as his conception was strong, his expressions were clear, he easily received impressions from objects, and very forcibly transmitted them to others.

Of his exact observations on human life he has left a proof, which would do honour to the greatest names, in a small pamphlet, called, *The Author to be let,* where he introduces Iscariot Hackney, a prostitute scribler, giving an account of his birth, his education, his disposition and morals, habits of life and maxims of conduct. In the Introduction are related many secret histories of the petty writers of that time, but sometimes mixed with ungenerous reflections on their birth, their circumstances, or those of their relations; nor can it be denied, that some passages are such as Iscariot Hackney might himself have produced.

He was accused likewise of living in an appearance of friendship with some whom he satirised, and of making use of the confidence which he gained by a seeming kindness to discover failings and expose them; it must be confessed, that Mr. Savage's esteem was no very certain possession, and that he would lampoon at one time those whom he had praised at another.

It may be alledged, that the same man may change his principles, and that he who was once deservedly commended, may be afterwards satirised with equal justice, or that the poet was dazzled with the appearance of virtue, and found the man whom he had celebrated, when he had an opportunity of examining him more nearly, unworthy of the panegyric which he had too hastily bestowed; and that as a false satire ought to be recanted, for the sake of him whose reputation may be injured, false praise ought likewise to be obviated, lest the distinction between vice and virtue should be lost, lest a bad man should be trusted upon the credit of his encomiast, or lest others should endeavour to obtain the like praises by the same means.

But though these excuses may be often plausible, and sometimes just, they are very seldom satisfactory to mankind; and the writer, who is not constant to his subject, quickly sinks into contempt, his satire loses its force, and his panegyric its value, and he is only considered at one time as a flatterer, and as a calumniator at another.

To avoid these imputations, it is only necessary to follow the rules of virtue, and to preserve an unvaried regard to truth. For though it is undoubtedly possible, that a man, however cautious, may be sometimes deceived by an artful appearance of virtue, or by false evidences of guilt, such errors will not be frequent; and it will be allowed, that the name of an author would never have been made contemptible, had no man ever said what he did not think, or misled others, but when he was himself deceived.

The[7] *Author to be let* was first published in a single pamphlet, and afterwards inserted in a collection of pieces relating to the *Dunciad*, which were addressed by Mr. Savage to the Earl of Middlesex, in a[8] Dedication, which he was prevailed upon to sign, though he did not write it, and in which there are some positions, that the true author would perhaps not have published under his own name; and on which Mr. Savage afterwards reflected with no great satisfaction.

The enumeration of the bad effects of the *uncontrolled freedom of the press*, and the assertion that the *liberties taken by the writers of journals with their superiors were exorbitant and unjustifiable*, very ill became men, who have themselves not always shewn the exactest regard to the laws of subordination in their writings, and who have often satirised those that at least thought themselves their superiors, as they were eminent for their hereditary rank, and employed in the highest offices of the kingdom. But this is only an instance of that partiality which almost every man indulges with regard to himself; the liberty of the press is a blessing when we are inclined to write against others, and a calamity when we find ourselves overborn by the multitude of our assailants; as the power of the Crown is always thought too great by those who suffer by its influence, and too little by those in whose favour it is exerted; and a standing army is generally accounted necessary by those who command, and dangerous and oppressive by those who support it.

Mr. Savage was likewise very far from believing, that the letters annexed to each species of bad poets in the *Bathos*, were, as he was directed to assert, *set down at random;* for when he was charged by one of his friends with putting his name to such an improbability, he had no other answer to make, than that *he did not think of it*, and his friend had too much tenderness to reply, that next to the crime of writing contrary to what he thought, was that of writing without thinking.

After having remarked what is false in this Dedication, it is proper that I observe the impartiality which I recommend, by declaring what Savage asserted, that the account of the circumstances which attended the publication of the *Dunciad*, however strange and improbable, was exactly true.

The publication of this piece at this time raised Mr. Savage a great number of enemies among those that were attacked by Mr. Pope, with whom he was considered as a kind of confederate, and whom he was suspected of supplying with private intelligence and secret incidents: So that the ignominy of an informer was added to the terror of a satirist.

That he was not altogether free from literary hypocrisy, and that he sometimes spoke one thing, and wrote another, cannot be denied, because he himself confessed, that when he lived in great familiarity with Dennis, he wrote an epigram[9] against him.

Mr. Savage however set all the malice of all the pigmy writers at defiance, and thought the friendship of Mr. Pope cheaply purchased by being exposed to their censure and their hatred; nor had he any reason to repent of the preference, for he found Mr. Pope a steady and unalienable friend almost to the end of his life.

About this time, notwithstanding his avowed neutrality with regard to party, he published a panegyric on Sir Robert Walpole, for which he was rewarded by him with twenty guineas, a sum not very large, if either the excellence of the performance, or the affluence of the patron be considered; but greater than he afterwards obtained from a person of yet higher rank, and more desirous in appearance of being distinguished as a patron of literature.

As he was very far from approving the conduct of Sir Robert Walpole, and in conversation mentioned him sometimes with acrimony, and generally with contempt, as he was one of those who were always zealous in their assertions of the justice of the late opposition, jealous of the rights of the people, and alarmed by the long continued triumph of the Court; it was natural to ask him what could induce him to employ his poetry in praise of that man who was, in his opinion, an enemy to liberty, and an oppressor of his country? He alleged, that he was then dependent upon the Lord Tyrconnel, who was an implicite follower of the ministry, and that being enjoined by him, not without menaces, to write in praise of his leader, he had not resolution sufficient to sacrifice the pleasure of affluence to that of integrity.

On this and on many other occasions he was ready to lament the misery of living at the tables of other men, which was his fate from the beginning to the end of his life; for I know not whether he ever had, for three months together, a settled habitation, in which he could claim a right of residence.

To this unhappy state it is just to impute much of the inconstancy of his conduct; for though a readiness to comply with the inclination of others was no part of his natural character, yet he was sometimes obliged to relax his obstinacy, and submit his own judgment and even his virtue to the government of those by whom he was supported: So that if his miseries were sometimes the consequences of his faults, he ought not yet to be wholly excluded from compassion, because his faults were very often the effects of his misfortunes.

In this gay period[1] of his life, while he was surrounded by affluence and pleasure, he published the *Wanderer,* a moral poem of which the design is comprised in these lines:

> I fly all public care, all venal strife,
> To try the *still* compar'd with *active life,*
> To prove by these, the sons of men may owe
> The fruits of bliss to bursting clouds of woe;
> That even calamity by thought refin'd
> Inspirits and adorns the thinking mind.

and more distinctly in the following passage;

> By woe the soul to daring action swells,
> By woe in plaintless patience it excels;
> From patience prudent, clear experience springs,

And traces knowledge through the course of things.
Thence hope is form'd, thence fortitude, success,
Renown—whate'er men covet and caress.

This performance was always considered by himself as his
master-piece, and Mr. Pope, when he asked his opinion of it, told
him, that he read it once over, and was not displeased with it,
that it gave him more pleasure at the second perusal, and
delighted him still more at the third.

It has been generally objected to the *Wanderer*, that the disposition of the parts is irregular, that the design is obscure, and the
plan perplexed, that the images, however beautiful, succeed each
other without order; and that the whole performance is not so
much a regular fabric as a heap of shining materials thrown
together by accident, which strikes rather with the solemn magnificence of a stupendous ruin, than the elegant grandeur of a
finished pile.

This criticism is universal, and therefore it is reasonable to
believe it at least in a great degree just; but Mr. Savage was
always of a contrary opinion, and thought his drift could only be
missed by negligence or stupidity, and that the whole plan was
regular, and the parts distinct.

It was never denied to abound with strong representations of
nature, and just observations upon life, and it may easily be
observed, that most of his pictures have an evident tendency to
illustrate his first great position, *that good is the consequence of
evil*. The sun that burns up the mountains, fructifies the vales,
the deluge that rushes down the broken rocks with dreadful impetuosity, is separated into purling brooks; and the rage of the
hurricane purifies the air.

Even in this poem he has not been able to forbear one touch
upon the cruelty of his mother,[2] which though remarkably delicate
and tender, is a proof how deep an impression it had made upon
his mind.

This must be at least acknowledged, which ought to be thought
equivalent to many other excellencies, that this poem can promote
no other purposes than those of virtue, and that it is written with
a very strong sense of the efficacy of religion.

But my province is rather to give the history of Mr. Savage's performances, than to display their beauties, or to obviate the criticisms, which they have occasioned, and therefore I shall not dwell upon the particular passages which deserve applause: I shall neither show the excellence of his descriptions,[3] nor expatiate on the terrific portrait of Suicide,[4] nor point out the artful touches,[5] by which he has distinguished the intellectual features of the rebels, who suffer death in his last canto. It is, however, proper to observe, that Mr. Savage always declared the characters wholly fictitious, and without the least allusion to any real persons or actions.

From a poem so diligently laboured, and so successfully finished, it might be reasonably expected that he should have gained considerable advantage; nor can it, without some degree of indignation and concern, be told that he sold the copy for ten guineas, of which he afterwards returned two, that the two last sheets of the work might be reprinted, of which he had in his absence intrusted the correction to a friend, who was too indolent to perform it with accuracy.

A superstitious regard to the correction of his sheets was one of Mr. Savage's peculiarities; he often altered, revised, recurred to his first reading or punctuation, and again adopted the alteration; he was dubious and irresolute without end, as on a question of the last importance, and at last was seldom satisfied; the intrusion or omission of a comma was sufficient to discompose him, and he would lament an error of a single letter as a heavy calamity. In one of his letters relating to an impression of some verses he remarks, that he had with regard to the correction of the proof *a spell upon him,* and indeed the anxiety, with which he dwelt upon the minutest and most trifling niceties, deserved no other name than that of fascination.

That he sold so valuable a performance for so small a price was not to be imputed either to necessity by which the learned and ingenious are often obliged to submit to very hard conditions, or to avarice by which the book-sellers are frequently incited to oppress that genius by which they are supported, but to that intemperate desire of pleasure, and habitual slavery to his passions, which involved him in many perplexities; he happened at that time to be engaged in the pursuit of some trifling gratification, and being without money for the present occasion, sold his poem to the first bidder, and perhaps for the first price that was proposed, and would probably have been content with less, if less had been offered him.

This poem was addressed to the Lord Tyrconnel not only in the first lines,[6] but in a formal dedication filled with the highest strains of panegyric, and the warmest professions of gratitude, but by no means remarkable for delicacy of connection or elegance of stile.

These praises in a short time he found himself inclined to retract, being discarded by the man on whom he had bestowed them, and whom he then immediately discovered not to have deserved them. Of this quarrel, which every day made more bitter, Lord Tyrconnel and Mr. Savage assigned very different reasons, which might perhaps all in reality concur, though they were not all convenient to be alleged by either party. Lord Tyrconnel affirmed, that it was the constant practice of Mr. Savage, to enter a tavern with any company that proposed it, drink the most expensive wines, with great profusion, and when the reckoning was demanded, to be without money: If, as it often happened, his company were willing to defray his part, the affair ended, without any ill consequences; but if they were refractory, and expected that the wine should be paid for by him that drank it, his method of composition was, to take them with him to his own apartment, assume the government of the house, and order the butler in an imperious manner to set the best wine in the cellar before his company, who often drank till they forgot the respect due to the house in which they were entertained, indulged themselves in the utmost extravagance of merriment, practised the most licentious frolics, and committed all the outrages of drunkenness.

Nor was this the only charge which Lord Tyrconnel brought against him: Having given him a collection of valuable books, stamped with his own arms, he had the mortification to see them in a short time exposed to sale upon the stalls, it being usual with Mr. Savage, when he wanted a small sum, to take his books to the pawnbroker.

Whoever was acquainted with Mr. Savage, easily credited both these accusations; for having been obliged from his first entrance into the world to subsist upon expedients, affluence was not able to exalt him above them; and so much was he delighted with wine and conversation, and so long had he been accustomed to live by chance, that he would at any time go to the tavern, without scruple, and trust for his reckoning to the liberality of his company, and frequently of company to whom he was very little known. This conduct indeed very seldom drew upon him those inconveniences that might be feared by any other person, for his conversation was so entertaining, and his address so pleasing, that few thought the pleasure which they received from him dearly purchased by paying for his wine. It was his peculiar happiness, that he scarcely ever found a stranger, whom he did not leave a friend; but it must likewise be added, that he had not often a friend long, without obliging him to become a stranger.

Mr. Savage, on the other hand, declared that Lord Tyrconnel[7] quarrelled with him, because he would not substract from his own luxury and extravagance what he had promised to allow him, and that his resentment was only a plea for the violation of his promise: He asserted that he had done nothing that ought to exclude him from that subsistence which he thought not so much a favour, as a debt, since it was offered him upon conditions, which he had never broken; and that his only fault was, that he could not be supported with nothing.

He acknowledged, that Lord Tyrconnel often exhorted him to regulate his method of life, and not to spend all his nights in taverns, and that he appeared very desirous, that he would pass those hours with him which he so freely bestowed upon others. This demand Mr. Savage considered as a censure of his conduct, which he could never patiently bear; and which in the latter and cooler part of his life was so offensive to him, that he declared it as his resolution, *to spurn that friend who should presume to dictate to him;* and it is not likely, that in his earlier years he received admonitions with more calmness.

He was likewise inclined to resent such expectations, as tending to infringe his liberty, of which he was very jealous when it was necessary to the gratification of his passions, and declared, that the request was still more unreasonable, as the company to which he was to have been confined was insupportably disagreeable. This assertion affords another instance of that inconsistency of his writings with his conversation, which was so often to be observed. He forgot how lavishly he had, in his[8] Dedication to the

*Wanderer,* extolled the delicacy and penetration, the humanity and generosity, the candour and politeness of the man, whom, when he no longer loved him, he declared to be a wretch without understanding, without good-nature, and without justice; of whose name he thought himself obliged to leave no trace in any future edition of his writings; and accordingly blotted it out of that copy of the *Wanderer* which was in his hands.

During his continuance with the Lord Tyrconnel he wrote *The*[9] *Triumph of Health and Mirth,* on the recovery of Lady Tyrconnel from a languishing illness. This performance is remarkable, not only for the gayety of the ideas, and the melody of the numbers, but for the agreeable fiction upon which it is formed. Mirth over-whelmed with sorrow, for the sickness of her favourite, takes a flight in quest of her sister Health, whom she finds reclined upon the brow of a lofty mountain, amidst the fragrance of perpetual spring, with the breezes of the morning sporting about her. Being solicited by her sister Mirth, she readily promises her assistance, flies away in a cloud, and impregnates the waters of Bath with new virtues, by which the sickness of Belinda is relieved.

As the reputation of his abilities, the particular circumstances of his birth and life, the splendour of his appearance, and the distinction which was for some time paid him by Lord Tyrconnel, intitled him to familiarity with persons of higher rank, than those to whose conversation he had been before admitted, he did not fail to gratify that curiosity, which induced him to take a nearer view of those whom their birth, their employments, or their for-tunes, necessarily place at a distance from the greatest part of mankind, and to examine, whether their merit was magnified or diminished by the medium through which it was contemplated; whether the splendour with which they dazzled their admirers, was inherent in themselves, or only reflected on them by the ob-jects that surrounded them; and whether great men were selected for high stations, or high stations made great men.

For this purpose, he took all opportunities of conversing familiarly with those who were most conspicuous at that time, for their power, or their influence; he watched their looser mo-ments, and examined their domestic behaviour, with that acute-ness which nature had given him, and which the uncommon variety of his life had contributed to increase, and that inquisitive-

ness which must always be produced in a vigorous mind by an
absolute freedom from all pressing or domestic engagements. His
discernment was quick, and therefore he soon found in every person, and in every affair, something that deserved attention; he
was supported by others, without any care for himself, and was
therefore at leisure to pursue his observations.

More circumstances to constitute a critic on human life could
not easily concur, nor indeed could any man who assumed from
accidental advantages more praise than he could justly claim from
his real merit, admit an acquaintance more dangerous than that
of Savage; of whom likewise it must be confessed, that abilities
really exalted above the common level, or virtue refined from
passion, or proof against corruption could not easily find an abler
judge, or a warmer advocate.

What was the result of Mr. Savage's enquiry, though he was
not much accustomed to conceal his discoveries, it may not be
entirely safe to relate, because the persons whose characters he
criticised are powerful; and power and resentment are seldom
strangers; nor would it perhaps be wholly just, because what he
asserted in conversation might, though true in general, be heightened by some momentary ardour of imagination, and as it can be
delivered only from memory, may be imperfectly represented; so
that the picture at first aggravated, and then unskilfully copied,
may be justly suspected to retain no great resemblance of the
original.

It may however be observed, that he did not appear to have
formed very elevated ideas of those to whom the administration
of affairs, or the conduct of parties, has been intrusted; who have
been considered as the advocates of the Crown, or the guardians
of the people, and who have obtained the most implicit confidence, and the loudest applauses. Of one particular person, who
has been at one time so popular as to be generally esteemed, and
at another so formidable as to be universally detested, he observed, that his acquisitions had been small, or that his capacity
was narrow, and that the whole range of his mind was from
obscenity to politics, and from politics to obscenity.

But the opportunity of indulging his speculations on great characters was now at an end. He was banished from the table of
Lord Tyrconnel, and turned again adrift upon the world, without

prospect of finding quickly any other harbour. As prudence was not one of the virtues by which he was distinguished, he had made no provision against a misfortune like this. And though it is not to be imagined, but that the separation must for some time have been preceded by coldness, peevishness, or neglect, though it was undoubtedly the consequence of accumulated provocations on both sides, yet every one that knew Savage will readily believe, that to him it was sudden as a stroke of thunder; that though he might have transiently suspected it, he had never suffered any thought so unpleasing to sink into his mind, but that he had driven it away by amusements, or dreams of future felicity and affluence, and had never taken any measures by which he might prevent a precipitation from plenty to indigence.

This quarrel and separation, and the difficulties to which Mr. Savage was exposed by them, were soon known both to his friends and enemies; nor was it long before he perceived, from the behaviour of both, how much is added to the lustre of genius, by the ornaments of wealth.

His condition did not appear to excite much compassion; for he had not always been careful to use the advantages which he enjoyed with that moderation, which ought to have been with more than usual caution preserved by him, who knew, if he had reflected, that he was only a dependant on the bounty of another, whom he could expect to support him no longer than he endeavoured to preserve his favour, by complying with his inclinations, and whom he nevertheless set at defiance, and was continually irritating by negligence or encroachments.

Examples need not be sought at any great distance to prove that superiority of fortune has a natural tendency to kindle pride, and that pride seldom fails to exert itself in contempt and insult; and if this is often the effect of hereditary wealth, and of honours enjoyed only by the merit of others, it is some extenuation of any indecent triumphs to which this unhappy man may have been betrayed, that his prosperity was heightened by the force of novelty, and made more intoxicating by a sense of the misery in which he had so long languished, and perhaps of the insults which he had formerly born, and which he might now think himself entitled to revenge. It is too common for those who have unjustly suffered pain, to inflict it likewise in their turn, with the same

injustice, and to imagine that they have a right to treat others
as they have themselves been treated.

That Mr. Savage was too much elevated by any good fortune
is generally known; and some passages of his introduction to
the *Author to be let* sufficiently shew, that he did not wholly
refrain from such satire as he afterwards thought very unjust,
when he was exposed to it himself; for when he was afterwards
ridiculed in the character of a distressed poet, he very easily discovered, that distress was not a proper subject for merriment, or
topic of invective. He was then able to discern that if misery be
the effect of virtue, it ought to be reverenced; if of ill-fortune, to
be pitied; and if of vice, not to be insulted, because it is perhaps
itself a punishment adequate to the crime by which it was produced. And the humanity of that man can deserve no panegyric,
who is capable of reproaching a criminal in the hands of the
executioner.

But these reflections, though they readily occurred to him in
the first and last parts of his life, were, I am afraid, for a long
time forgotten; at least they were, like many other maxims, treasured up in his mind, rather for shew than use, and operated very
little upon his conduct, however elegantly he might sometimes
explain, or however forcibly he might inculcate them.

His degradation therefore from the condition which he had
enjoyed with such wanton thoughtlessness, was considered by
many as an occasion of triumph. Those who had before paid their
court to him, without success, soon returned the contempt which
they had suffered, and they who had received favours from him,
for of such favours as he could bestow he was very liberal, did
not always remember them. So much more certain are the effects
of resentment than of gratitude: It is not only to many more
pleasing to recollect those faults which place others below them,
than those virtues by which they are themselves comparatively
depressed; but it is likewise more easy to neglect, than to recompense; and though there are few who will practise a laborious
virtue, there will never be wanting multitudes that will indulge
an easy vice.

Savage however was very little disturbed at the marks of contempt which his ill-fortune brought upon him, from those whom
he never esteemed, and with whom he never considered himself

as levelled by any calamities; and though it was not without some uneasiness, that he saw some, whose friendship he valued, change their behaviour; he yet observed their coldness without much emotion, considered them as the slaves of fortune and the worshippers of prosperity; and was more inclined to despise them, than to lament himself.

It does not appear, that after this return of his wants, he found mankind equally favourable to him, as at his first appearance in the world. His story, though in reality not less melancholy, was less affecting, because it was no longer new; it therefore procured him no new friends, and those that had formerly relieved him thought they might now consign him to others. He was now likewise considered by many rather as criminal, than as unhappy; for the friends of Lord Tyrconnel and of his mother were sufficiently industrious to publish his weaknesses, which were indeed very numerous, and nothing was forgotten, that might make him either hateful or ridiculous.

It cannot but be imagined, that such representations of his faults must make great numbers less sensible of his distress; many who had only an opportunity to hear one part, made no scruple to propagate the account which they received; many assisted their circulation from malice or revenge, and perhaps many pretended to credit them, that they might with a better grace withdraw their regard, or withhold their assistance.

Savage however was not one of those, who suffered himself to be injured without resistance, nor was less diligent in exposing the faults of Lord Tyrconnel, over whom he obtained at least this advantage, that he drove him first to the practice of outrage and violence; for he was so much provoked by the wit and virulence of Savage, that he came with a number of attendants, that did no honour to his courage, to beat him at a coffee-house. But it happened that he had left the place a few minutes, and his lordship had without danger the pleasure of boasting, how he would have treated him. Mr. Savage went next day to repay his visit at his own house, but was prevailed on by his domestics, to retire without insisting upon seeing him.

Lord Tyrconnel was accused by Mr. Savage of some actions, which scarcely any provocations will be thought sufficient to justify; such as seizing what he had in his lodgings, and other

instances of wanton cruelty, by which he encreased the distress
of Savage, without any advantage to himself.

These mutual accusations were retorted on both sides for many
years, with the utmost degree of virulence and rage, and time
seemed rather to augment than diminish their resentment; that
the anger of Mr. Savage should be kept alive is not strange, because he felt every day the consequences of the quarrel, but it
might reasonably have been hoped, that Lord Tyrconnel might
have relented, and at length have forgot those provocations,
which, however they might have once inflamed him, had not in
reality much hurt him.

The spirit of Mr. Savage indeed never suffered him to solicite
a reconciliation; he returned reproach for reproach, and insult for
insult; his superiority of wit supplied the disadvantages of his
fortune, and inabled him to form a party, and prejudice great
numbers in his favour.

But though this might be some gratification of his vanity, it
afforded very little relief to his necessities, and he was very frequently reduced to uncommon hardships, of which, however, he
never made any mean or importunate complaints, being formed
rather to bear misery with fortitude, than enjoy prosperity with
moderation.

He now thought himself again at liberty to expose the cruelty
of his mother, and therefore, I believe, about this time, published
*The Bastard*, a poem remarkable for the vivacious sallies of
thought in the beginning,[1] where he makes a pompous enumeration of the imaginary advantages of base birth, and the pathetic
sentiments at the end, where he recounts the real calamities which
he suffered by the crime of his parents.

The vigour and spirit of the verses, the peculiar circumstances
of the author, the novelty of the subject, and the notoriety of the
story, to which the allusions are made, procured this performance
a very favourable reception; great numbers were immediately
dispersed, and editions were multiplied with unusual rapidity.

One circumstance attended the publication, which Savage used
to relate with great satisfaction. His mother, to whom the poem
was *with due reverence* inscribed, happened then to be at Bath,
where she could not conveniently retire from censure, or conceal
herself from observation; and no sooner did the reputation of the

poem begin to spread, than she heard it repeated in all places of concourse, nor could she enter the assembly rooms, or cross the walks, without being saluted with some lines from *The Bastard.*

This was perhaps the first time that ever she discovered a sense of shame, and on this occasion the power of wit was very conspicuous; the wretch who had, without scruple, proclaimed herself an adulteress, and who had first endeavoured to starve her son, then to transport him, and afterwards to hang him, was not able to bear the representation of her own conduct, but fled from reproach, though she felt no pain from guilt, and left Bath with the utmost haste, to shelter herself among the crouds of London.

Thus Savage had the satisfaction of finding, that though he could not reform his mother, he could punish her, and that he did not always suffer alone.

The pleasure which he received from this increase of his poetical reputation, was sufficient for some time to overbalance the miseries of want, which this performance did not much alleviate, for it was sold for a very trivial sum to a bookseller, who, though the success was so uncommon, that five impressions were sold, of which many were undoubtedly very numerous, had not generosity sufficient to admit the unhappy writer to any part of the profit.

The sale of this poem was always mentioned by Mr. Savage with the utmost elevation of heart, and referred to by him as an incontestable proof of a general acknowledgement of his abilities. It was indeed the only production of which he could justly boast a general reception.

But though he did not lose the opportunity which success gave him of setting a high rate on his abilities, but paid due deference to the suffrages of mankind when they were given in his favour, he did not suffer his esteem of himself to depend upon others, nor found any thing sacred in the voice of the people when they were inclined to censure him; he then readily shewed the folly of expecting that the publick should judge right, observed how slowly poetical merit had often forced its way into the world, he contented himself with the applause of men of judgment; and was somewhat disposed to exclude all those from the character of men of judgment, who did not applaud him.

But he was at other times more favourable to mankind, than

to think them blind to the beauties of his works, and imputed the slowness of their sale to other causes; either they were published at a time when the town was empty, or when the attention of the publick was engrossed by some struggle in the Parliament, or some other object of general concern; or they were by the neglect of the publisher not diligently dispersed, or by his avarice not advertised with sufficient frequency. Address, or industry, or liberality, was always wanting; and the blame was laid rather on any other person than the author.

By arts like these, arts which every man practises in some degree, and to which too much of the little tranquillity of life is to be ascribed, Savage was always able to live at peace with himself. Had he indeed only made use of these expedients to alleviate the loss or want of fortune or reputation, or any other advantages, which it is not in man's power to bestow upon himself, they might have been justly mentioned as instances of a philosophical mind, and very properly proposed to the imitation of multitudes, who, for want of diverting their imaginations with the same dexterity, languish under afflictions which might be easily removed.

It were doubtless to be wished, that truth and reason were universally prevalent; that every thing were esteemed according to its real value; and that men would secure themselves from being disappointed in their endeavours after happiness, by placing it only in virtue, which is always to be obtained; but if adventitious and foreign pleasures must be persued, it would be perhaps of some benefit, since that persuit must frequently be fruitless, if the practice of Savage could be taught, that folly might be an antidote to folly, and one fallacy be obviated by another.

But the danger of this pleasing intoxication must not be concealed; nor indeed can any one, after having observed the life of Savage, need to be cautioned against it. By imputing none of his miseries to himself, he continued to act upon the same principles, and to follow the same path; was never made wiser by his sufferings, nor preserved by one misfortune from falling into another. He proceeded throughout his life to tread the same steps on the same circle; always applauding his past conduct, or at least forgetting it, to amuse himself with phantoms of happiness, which were dancing before him; and willingly turned his eyes from the light of reason, when it would have discovered the illusion, and shewn him, what he never wished to see, his real state.

He is even accused, after having lulled his imagination with those ideal opiates, of having tried the same experiment upon his conscience; and having accustomed himself to impute all deviations from the right to foreign causes, it is certain that he was upon every occasion too easily reconciled to himself, and that he appeared very little to regret those practices which had impaired his reputation. The reigning error of his life was, that he mistook the love for the practice of virtue, and was indeed not so much a good man, as the friend of goodness.

This at least must be allowed him, that he always preserved a strong sense of the dignity, the beauty and the necessity of virtue, and that he never contributed deliberately to spread corruption amongst mankind; his actions, which were generally precipitate, were often blameable, but his writings being the productions of study, uniformly tended to the exaltation of the mind, and the propagation of morality and piety.

These writings may improve mankind, when his failings shall be forgotten, and therefore he must be considered upon the whole as a benefactor to the world; nor can his personal example do any hurt, since whoever hears of his faults, will hear of the miseries which they brought upon him, and which would deserve less pity, had not his condition been such as made his faults pardonable. He may be considered as a child *exposed* to all the temptations of indigence, at an age when resolution was not yet strengthened by conviction, nor virtue confirmed by habit; a circumstance which in his *Bastard* he laments in a very affecting manner.

> ——No mother's care
> Shielded my infant ignorance with prayer:
> No father's guardian hand my youth maintain'd,
> Call'd forth my virtues, and from vice restrain'd.

The *Bastard*, however it might provoke or mortify his mother, could not be expected to melt her to compassion, so that he was still under the same want of the necessaries of life, and he therefore exerted all the interest, which his wit, or his birth, or his misfortunes could procure, to obtain upon the death of Eusden the place of Poet Laureat, and prosecuted his application with so much diligence, that the King publickly declared it his intention to bestow it upon him; but such was the fate of Savage, that even the King, when he intended his advantage, was disappointed in his schemes; for the Lord Chamberlain, who has the disposal of the laurel as one of the appendages of his office, either did not know the King's design, or did not approve it, or thought the nomination of the Laureat an encroachment upon his rights, and therefore bestowed the laurel upon Colly Cibber.

Mr. Savage thus disappointed took a resolution of applying to the Queen, that having once given him life, she would enable him to support it, and therefore published a short poem on her birth-day, to which he gave the odd title of *Volunteer Laureat.* The event of this essay he has himself related in the following letter, which he prefixed to the poem, when he afterwards reprinted it in the *Gentleman's Magazine,* from whence I have copied it intire, as this was one of the few attempts in which Mr. Savage succeeded.

"Mr. Urban,

"In your magazine for February you published the last *Volunteer Laureat,* written on a very melancholy occasion, the death of the royal patroness of arts and literature in general, and of the author of that poem in particular; I now send you the first that Mr. Savage wrote under that title. —— This gentleman, notwithstanding a very considerable interest, being, on the death of Mr. Eusden, disappointed of the Laureat's place, wrote the following verses; which were no sooner published, but the late Queen sent to a book-seller for them: The author had not at that time a friend either to get him introduced, or his poem presented at Court; yet such was the unspeakable goodness of that princess, that, notwithstanding this act of ceremony was wanting, in a few days after publication, Mr. Savage received a bank-bill of fifty pounds, and a gracious message from her Majesty, by the Lord North and Guilford, to this effect: 'That her Majesty was highly pleased with the verses; that she took particularly kind his lines there relating to the King; that he had permission to write annually on the same subject; and that he should yearly receive the like present, till something better (which was her Majesty's intention) could be done for him.' After this he was permitted to present one of his annual poems to her Majesty, had the honour of kissing her hand, and met with the most gracious reception.

"Your's, &c."

## The Volunteer Laureat

A Poem: On the Queen's Birth-Day. Humbly
addressed to her Majesty

Twice twenty tedious moons have roll'd away,
Since Hope, kind flatt'rer! tun'd my pensive lay,
Whisp'ring, that you, who rais'd me from despair,
Meant, by your smiles, to make life worth my care;
With pitying hand an orphan's tears to screen,
And o'er the motherless extend the Queen.
'Twill be—the prophet guides the poet's strain!
Grief never touch'd a heart like your's in vain:
Heav'n gave you power, because you love to bless,
And pity, when you feel it, is redress.
     Two fathers join'd to rob my claim of one!
My mother too thought fit to have no son!
The Senate next, whose aid the helpless own,
Forgot my infant wrongs, and mine alone!
Yet parents pitiless, nor peers unkind,
Nor titles lost, nor woes mysterious join'd,
Strip me of hope—by heav'n thus lowly laid,
To find a Pharaoh's daughter in the shade.
     You cannot hear unmov'd, when wrongs implore,
Your heart is woman, though your mind be more;
Kind, like the Pow'r who gave you to our pray'rs,
You would not lengthen life to sharpen cares:
They who a barren leave to live bestow,
Snatch but from death to sacrifice to woe.
Hated by her, from whom my life I drew,
Whence should I hope, if not from heav'n and you?
Nor dare I groan beneath affliction's rod,
My Queen, my mother; and my father, God.
     The pitying muses saw me wit pursue,
A *Bastard Son,* alas! on that side too,
Did not your eyes exalt the poet's fire,
And what the muse denies, the queen inspire;
While rising thus your heavenly soul to view,
I learn, how angels think, by copying you.
     Great Princess! 'tis decreed—once ev'ry year

I march uncall'd your Laureat Volunteer;
Thus shall your poet his low genius raise,
And charm the world with truths too vast for praise.
Nor need I dwell on glories all your own,
Since surer means to tempt your smiles are known;
Your poet shall allot your lord his part,
And paint him in his noblest throne, your heart.
　　Is there a greatness that adorns him best,
A rising wish that ripens in his breast?
Has he fore-meant some distant age to bless,
Disarm oppression, or expel distress?
Plans he some scheme to reconcile mankind,
People the seas, and busy ev'ry wind?
Would he, by pity, the deceiv'd reclaim,
And smile contending factions into shame?
Would his example lend his laws a weight,
And breathe his own soft morals o'er his state?
The muse shall find it all, shall make it seen,
And teach the world his praise, to charm his Queen.
　　Such be the annual truths my verse imparts,
Nor frown, fair *fav'rite* of a people's hearts!
Happy if plac'd, perchance, beneath your eye,
My muse unpension'd might her pinions try,
Fearless to fail, while you indulge her flame,
And bid me proudly boast your Laureat's name;
Renobled thus by wreaths my Queen bestows,
I lose all memory of wrongs and woes.

Such was the performance, and such its reception; a reception which, though by no means unkind, was yet not in the highest degree generous: To chain down the genius of a writer to an annual panegyric, shewed in the Queen too much desire of hearing her own praises, and a greater regard to herself than to him on whom her bounty was conferred. It was a kind of avaricious generosity, by which flattery was rather purchased than genius rewarded.

Mrs. Oldfield had formerly given him the same allowance with much more heroic intention; she had no other view than to enable him to prosecute his studies, and to set himself above the want of assistance, and was contented with doing good without stipulating for encomiums.

Mr. Savage however was not at liberty to make exceptions, but was ravished with the favours which he had received, and probably yet more with those which he was promised; he considered himself now as a favourite of the Queen, and did not doubt but a few annual poems would establish him in some profitable employment.

He therefore assumed the title of *Volunteer Laureat,* not without some reprehensions from Cibber, who informed him, that the title of *Laureat* was a mark of honour conferred by the King, from whom all honour is derived, and which therefore no man has a right to bestow upon himself; and added, that he might with equal propriety stile himself a volunteer lord, or volunteer baronet. It cannot be denied that the remark was just, but Savage did not think any title, which was conferred upon Mr. Cibber, so honourable as that the usurpation of it could be imputed to him as an instance of very exorbitant vanity, and therefore continued to write under the same title, and received every year the same reward.

He did not appear to consider these encomiums as tests of his abilities, or as any thing more than annual hints to the Queen of her promise, or acts of ceremony, by the performance of which he was intitled to his pension, and therefore did not labour them with great diligence, or print more than fifty each year, except that for some of the last years he regularly inserted them in the *Gentleman's Magazine,* by which they were dispersed over the kingdom.

Of some of them he had himself so low an opinion, that he intended to omit them in the collection of poems, for which he printed Proposals, and solicited subscriptions; nor can it seem strange, that being confined to the same subject, he should be at some times indolent, and at others unsuccessful, that he should sometimes delay a disagreeable task, till it was too late to perform it well; or that he should sometimes repeat the same sentiment on the same occasion, or at others be misled by an attempt after novelty to forced conceptions, and far-fetched images.

He wrote indeed with a double intention, which supplied him with some variety, for his business was to praise the Queen for the favours which he had received, and to complain to her of the delay of those which she had promised: In some of his pieces, therefore, gratitude is predominant, and in some discontent; in some he represents himself as happy in her patronage, and in others as disconsolate to find himself neglected.

Her promise, like other promises made to this unfortunate man, was never performed, though he took sufficient care that it should not be forgotten. The publication of his *Volunteer Laureat* procured him no other reward than a regular remittance of fifty pounds.

He was not so depressed by his disappointments as to neglect any opportunity that was offered of advancing his interest. When the Princess Anne was married, he wrote a poem upon her departure, only, as he declared, *because it was expected from him*, and he was not willing to bar his own prospects by any appearance of neglect.

He never mentioned any advantage gain'd by this poem, or any regard that was paid to it, and therefore it is likely that it was considered at Court as an act of duty to which he was obliged by his dependence, and which it was therefore not necessary to reward by any new favour: Or perhaps the Queen really intended his advancement, and therefore thought it superfluous to lavish presents upon a man whom she intended to establish for life.

About this time not only his hopes were in danger of being frustrated, but his pension likewise of being obstructed by an accidental calumny. The writer of the *Daily Courant*, a paper then published under the direction of the ministry, charged him with a crime, which though not very great in itself, would have been remarkably invidious in him, and might very justly have incensed the Queen against him. He was accused by name of influencing elections against the Court, by appearing at the head of a Tory mob; nor did the accuser fail to aggravate his crime, by representing it as the effect of the most atrocious ingratitude, and a kind of rebellion against the Queen, who had first preserved him from an infamous death, and afterwards distinguished him by her favour, and supported him by her charity. The charge, as it was open and confident, was likewise by good fortune very particular. The place of the transaction was mentioned, and the whole series of the rioter's conduct related. This exactness made Mr. Savage's vindication easy, for he never had in his life seen the place which was declared to be the scene of his wickedness, nor ever had been present in any town when its representatives were chosen. This answer he therefore made haste to publish, with all the circumstances necessary to make it credible, and very reasonably demanded, that the accusation should be retracted in the same paper, that he might no longer suffer the imputation of sedition and ingratitude. This demand was likewise pressed by him in a private letter to the author of the paper, who either trusting to the protection of those whose defence he had undertaken, or having entertained some personal malice against Mr. Savage, or fearing lest, by retracting so confident an assertion, he should impair the credit of his paper, refused to give him that satisfaction.

Mr. Savage therefore thought it necessary, to his own vindication, to prosecute him in the King's Bench; but as he did not find any ill effects from the accusation, having sufficiently cleared his innocence, he thought any farther procedure would have the appearance of revenge, and therefore willingly dropped it.

He saw soon afterwards a process commenced in the same court against himself, on an information in which he was accused of writing and publishing an obscene pamphlet.

It was always Mr. Savage's desire to be distinguished, and when any controversy became popular, he never wanted some reason for engaging in it with great ardour, and appearing at the head of the party which he had chosen. As he was never celebrated for his prudence, he had no sooner taken his side, and informed himself of the chief topics of the dispute, than he took all opportunities of asserting and propagating his principles, without much regard to his own interest, or any other visible design than that of drawing upon himself the attention of mankind.

The dispute between the Bishop of London and the Chancellor is well known to have been for some time the chief topic of political conversation, and therefore Mr. Savage, in pursuance of his character, endeavoured to become conspicuous among the controvertists with which every coffee-house was filled on that occasion. He was an indefatigable opposer of all the claims of ecclesiastical power, though he did not know on what they were founded, and was therefore no friend to the Bishop of London. But he had another reason for appearing as a warm advocate for Dr. Rundle, for he was the friend of Mr. Foster and Mr. Thompson, who were the friends of Mr. Savage.

Thus remote was his interest in the question, which however, as he imagined, concerned him so nearly, that it was not sufficient to harangue and dispute, but necessary likewise to write upon it.

He therefore engaged with great ardour in a new poem, called by him, *The Progress of a Divine*, in which he conducts a profligate priest by all the gradations of wickedness from a poor curacy in the country, to the highest preferments of the church, and describes with that humour which was natural to him, and that knowledge which was extended to all the diversities of human life, his behaviour in every station, and insinuates, that this priest thus accomplished found at last a patron in the Bishop of London.

When he was asked by one of his friends, on what pretence he could charge the Bishop with such an action, he had no more to say, than that he had only inverted the accusation, and that he thought reasonable to believe, that he, who obstructed the rise of a good man without reason, would for bad reasons promote the exaltation of a villain.

The clergy were universally provoked by this satire, and Savage, who, as was his constant practice, had set his name to his performance, was censured in the *Weekly Miscellany*[2] with severity, which he did not seem inclined to forget.

But a return of invective was not thought a sufficient punishment. The court of King's Bench was therefore moved against him, and he was obliged to return an answer to a charge of obscenity. It was urged in his defence, that obscenity was criminal when it was intended to promote the practice of vice, but that Mr. Savage had only introduced obscene ideas with the view of exposing them to detestation, and of amending the age by shewing the deformity of wickedness. This plea was admitted, and Sir Philip Yorke, who then presided in that court, dismissed the information with encomiums upon the purity and excellence of Mr. Savage's writings.

The prosecution however answered in some measure the purpose of those by whom it was set on foot, for Mr. Savage was so far intimidated by it, that when the edition of his poem was sold, he did not venture to reprint it, so that it was in a short time forgotten, or forgotten by all but those whom it offended.

It is said, that some endeavours were used to incense the Queen against him, but he found advocates to obviate at least part of their effect; for though he was never advanced, he still continued to receive his pension.

This poem drew more infamy upon him than any incident of his life, and as his conduct cannot be vindicated, it is proper to secure his memory from reproach, by informing those whom he made his enemies, that he never intended to repeat the provocation; and that, though whenever he thought he had any reason to complain of the clergy, he used to threaten them with a new edition of *The Progress of a Divine*, it was his calm and settled resolution to suppress it for ever.

He once intended to have made a better reparation for the folly or injustice with which he might be charged, by writing another poem, called, *The Progress of a Free-Thinker*, whom he intended to lead through all the stages of vice and folly, to convert him from virtue to wickedness, and from religion to infidelity by all the modish sophistry used for that purpose; and at last to dismiss him by his own hand into the other world.

That he did not execute this design is a real loss to mankind, for he was too well acquainted with all the scenes of debauchery to have failed in his representations of them, and too zealous for virtue not to have represented them in such a manner as should expose them either to ridicule or detestation.

But this plan was like others, formed and laid aside, till the vigour of his imagination was spent, and the effervescence of invention had subsided, but soon gave way to some other design which pleased by its novelty for a while, and then was neglected like the former.

He was still in his usual exigencies, having no certain support but the pension allowed him by the Queen, which though it might have kept an exact oeconomist from want, was very far from being sufficient for Mr. Savage, who had never been accustomed to dismiss any of his appetites without the gratification which they solicited, and whom nothing but want of money withheld from partaking of every pleasure that fell within his view.

His conduct with regard to his pension was very particular. No sooner had he changed the bill, than he vanished from the sight of all his acquaintances, and lay for some time out of the reach of all the enquiries that friendship or curiosity could make after him; at length he appeared again pennyless as before, but never informed even those whom he seemed to regard most, where he had been, nor was his retreat ever discovered.

This was his constant practice during the whole time that he received the pension from the Queen: He regularly disappeared and returned. He indeed affirmed, that he retired to study, and that the money supported him in solitude for many months; but his friends declared, that the short time in which it was spent sufficiently confuted his own account of his conduct.

His politeness and his wit still raised him friends, who were desirous of setting him at length free from that indigence by which he had been hitherto oppressed, and therefore solicited Sir Robert Walpole in his favour with so much earnestness, that they obtained a promise of the next place that should become vacant, not exceeding two hundred pounds a year. This promise was made with an uncommon declaration, *that it was not the promise of a minister to a petitioner, but of a friend to his friend.*

Mr. Savage now concluded himself set at ease for ever, and as he observes in a poem[3] written on that incident of his life, *trusted* and *was trusted,* but soon found that his confidence was ill-grounded, and this *friendly* promise was not inviolable. He spent a long time in solicitations, and at last despaired and desisted.

He did not indeed deny that he had given the minister some reason to believe that he should not strengthen his own interest by advancing him, for he had taken care to distinguish himself in coffee-houses as an advocate for the ministry of the last years of Queen Anne, and was always ready to justify the conduct, and exalt the character of Lord Bolingbroke, whom he mentions with great regard in an epistle upon authors, which he wrote about that time, but was too wise to publish, and of which only some fragments[4] have appeared, inserted by him in the *Magazine* after his retirement.

To despair was not, however, the character of Savage, when one patronage failed, he had recourse to another. The Prince was now extremely popular, and had very liberally rewarded the merit of some writers whom Mr. Savage did not think superior to himself, and therefore he resolved to address a poem to him.

For this purpose he made choice of a subject, which could regard only persons of the highest rank and greatest affluence, and which was therefore proper for a poem intended to procure the patronage of a prince; and having retired for some time to Richmond, that he might prosecute his design in full tranquillity, without the temptations of pleasure, or the solicitations of creditors, by which his meditations were in equal danger of being disconcerted, he produced *a Poem on public spirit, with regard to public works.*

The plan of this poem is very extensive, and comprises a multitude of topics, each of which might furnish matter sufficient for a long performance, and of which some have already employed more eminent writers; but as he was perhaps not fully acquainted with the whole extent of his own design, and was writing to obtain a supply of wants too pressing to admit of long or accurate enquiries, he passes negligently over many public works, which, even in his own opinion, deserved to be more elaborately treated.

But though he may sometimes disappoint his reader by transient touches upon these subjects, which have often been considered, and therefore naturally raise expectations, he must be allowed amply to compensate his omissions by expatiating in the conclusion of his work upon a kind of beneficence not yet celebrated by any eminent poet, though it now appears more susceptible of embellishments, more adapted to exalt the ideas, and affect the passions, than many of those which have hitherto been thought most worthy of the ornaments of verse. The settlement of colonies in uninhabited countries, the establishment of those in security whose misfortunes have made their own country no longer pleasing or safe, the acquisition of property without injury to any, the appropriation of the waste and luxuriant bounties of nature, and the enjoyment of those gifts which heaven has scattered upon regions uncultivated and unoccupied, cannot be considered without giving rise to a great number of pleasing ideas, and bewildering the imagination in delightful prospects; and, therefore, whatever speculations they may produce in those who have confined themselves to political studies, naturally fixed the attention, and excited the applause of a poet. The politician, when he considers men driven into other countries for shelter, and obliged to retire to forests and deserts, and pass their lives and fix their posterity in the remotest corners of the world, to avoid those hardships which they suffer or fear in their native place, may very properly enquire why the legislature does not provide a remedy for these miseries, rather than encourage an escape

from them. He may conclude, that the flight of every honest man
is a loss to the community, that those who are unhappy without
guilt ought to be relieved, and the life which is overburthened
by accidental calamities, set at ease by the care of the publick,
and that those, who have by misconduct forfeited their claim to
favour, ought rather to be made useful to the society which they
have injured, than be driven from it. But the poet is employed in
a more pleasing undertaking than that of proposing laws, which,
however just or expedient, will never be made, or endeavouring
to reduce to rational schemes of government societies which were
formed by chance, and are conducted by the private passions of
those who preside in them. He guides the unhappy fugitive from
want and persecution, to plenty, quiet, and security, and seats
him in scenes of peaceful solitude, and undisturbed repose.

Savage has not forgotten amidst the pleasing sentiments which
this prospect of retirement suggested to him to censure those
crimes which have been generally committed by the discoverers
of new regions, and to expose the enormous wickedness of making war upon barbarous nations because they cannot resist, and
of invading countries because they are fruitful; of extending navigation only to propagate vice, and of visiting distant lands only
to lay them waste. He has asserted the natural equality of mankind, and endeavoured to suppress that pride which inclines men
to imagine that right is the consequence of power.[5]

His description of the various miseries which force men to seek
for refuge in distant countries affords another instance of his
proficiency in the important and extensive study of human life,
and the tenderness with which he recounts them, another proof
of his humanity and benevolence.

It is observable, that the close of this poem discovers a change
which experience had made in Mr. Savage's opinions. In a poem
written by him in his youth, and published in his Miscellanies,
he declares his contempt of the contracted views and narrow
prospects of the middle state of life, and declares his resolution
either to tower like the cedar, or be trampled like the shrub; but
in this poem, though addressed to a prince, he mentions this state
of life as comprising those who ought most to attract reward,
those who merit most the confidence of power, and the familiarity
of greatness, and accidentally mentioning this passage to one of

his friends, declared that in his opinion all the virtue of mankind was comprehended in that state.

In describing villas and gardens he did not omit to condemn that absurd custom which prevails among the English of permitting servants to receive money from strangers for the entertainment that they receive, and therefore inserted in his poem these lines:

> But what the flow'ring pride of gardens rare,
> However royal, or however fair:
> If gates which to access should still give way,
> Ope but, like Peter's Paradise, for pay.
> If perquisited varlets frequent stand,
> And each new walk must a new tax demand?
> What foreign eye but with contempt surveys?
> What muse shall from oblivion snatch their praise?

But before the publication of his performance he recollected, that the Queen allowed her garden and cave at Richmond to be shewn for money, and that she so openly countenanced the practice, that she had bestowed the privilege of shewing them as a place of profit on a man whose merit she valued herself upon rewarding, though she gave him only the liberty of disgracing his country.

He therefore thought, with more prudence than was often exerted by him, that the publication of these lines might be officiously represented as an insult upon the Queen to whom he owed his life and his subsistence, and that the propriety of his observation would be no security against the censures which the unseasonableness of it might draw upon him; he therefore suppressed the passage in the first edition, but after the Queen's death thought the same caution no longer necessary, and restored it to the proper place.

The poem was therefore published without any political faults, and inscribed to the Prince, but Mr. Savage having no friend upon whom he could prevail to present it to him, had no other method of attracting his observation than the publication of frequent advertisements, and therefore received no reward from his patron, however generous on other occasions.

This disappointment he never mentioned without indignation,

being by some means or other confident that the Prince was not ignorant of his address to him, and insinuated, that if any advances in popularity could have been made by distinguishing him, he had not written without notice, or without reward.

He was once inclined to have presented his poem in person, and sent to the printer for a copy with that design; but either his opinion changed, or his resolution deserted him, and he continued to resent neglect without attempting to force himself into regard.

Nor was the public much more favourable than his patron, for only seventy-two were sold, though the performance was much commended by some whose judgment in that kind of writing is generally allowed. But Savage easily reconciled himself to mankind without imputing any defect to his work, by observing that his poem was unluckily published two days after the prorogation of the Parliament, and by consequence at a time when all those who could be expected to regard it were in the hurry of preparing for their departure, or engaged in taking leave of others upon their dismission from public affairs.

It must be however allowed, in justification of the public, that this performance is not the most excellent of Mr. Savage's works, and that though it cannot be denied to contain many striking sentiments, majestic lines, and just observations, it is in general not sufficiently polished in the language, or enlivened in the imagery, or digested in the plan.

Thus his poem contributed nothing to the alleviation of his poverty, which was such as very few could have supported with equal patience, but to which it must likewise be confessed, that few would have been exposed who received punctually fifty pounds a year; a salary which though by no means equal to the demands of vanity and luxury, is yet found sufficient to support families above want, and was undoubtedly more than the necessities of life require.

But no sooner had he received his pension, than he withdrew to his darling privacy, from which he return'd in a short time to his former distress, and for some part of the year, generally lived by chance, eating only when he was invited to the tables of his acquaintances, from which the meanness of his dress often excluded him, when the politeness and variety of his conversation would have been thought a sufficient recompence for his entertainment.

He lodged as much by accident as he dined and passed the night, sometimes in mean houses, which are set open at night to any casual wanderers, sometimes in cellars among the riot and filth of the meanest and most profligate of the rabble; and sometimes, when he had not money to support even the expences of these receptacles, walked about the streets till he was weary, and lay down in the summer upon a bulk, or in the winter with his associates in poverty, among the ashes of a glass-house.

In this manner were passed those days and those nights, which nature had enabled him to have employed in elevated speculations, useful studies, or pleasing conversation. On a bulk, in a cellar, or in a glass-house among thieves and beggers, was to be found the author of the *Wanderer*, the man of exalted sentiments, extensive views and curious observations, the man whose remarks on life might have assisted the statesman, whose ideas of virtue might have enlightened the moralist, whose eloquence might have influenced senates, and whose delicacy might have polished courts.

It cannot be imagined [but] that such necessities might sometimes force him upon disreputable practices, and it is probable that these lines in the *Wanderer* were occasioned by his reflections on his own conduct.

> Though mis'ry leads to fortitude and truth,
> Unequal to the load this languid youth,
> (O! let none censure if untried by grief,
> Or amidst woes untempted by relief,)
> He stoop'd, reluctant, to mean acts of shame,
> Which then, ev'n then, he scorn'd, and blush'd to name.

Whoever was acquainted with him, was certain to be solicited for small sums, which the frequency of the request made in time considerable, and he was therefore quickly shunned by those who were become familiar enough to be trusted with his necessities; but his rambling manner of life, and constant appearance at houses of public resort, always procured him a new succession of friends, whose kindness had not been exhausted by repeated requests, so that he was seldom absolutely without resources, but had in his utmost exigences this comfort, that he always imagined himself sure of speedy relief.

It was observed that he always asked favours of this kind without the least submission or apparent consciousness of dependence, and that he did not seem to look upon a compliance with his request as an obligation that deserved any extraordinary acknowledgments, but a refusal was resented by him as an affront, or complained of as an injury; nor did he readily reconcile himself to those who either denied to lend, or gave him afterwards any intimation, that they expected to be repaid.

He was sometimes so far compassionated by those who knew both his merit and his distresses, that they received him into their families, but they soon discovered him to be a very incommodious inmate; for being always accustomed to an irregular manner of life, he could not confine himself to any stated hours, or pay any regard to the rules of a family, but would prolong his conversation till midnight, without considering that business might require his friend's application in the morning; and when he had persuaded himself to retire to bed, was not, without equal difficulty, called up to dinner; it was therefore impossible to pay him any distinction without the entire subversion of all oeconomy, a kind of establishment which, wherever he went, he always appeared ambitious to overthrow.

It must therefore be acknowledged, in justification of mankind, that it was not always by the negligence or coldness of his friends that Savage was distressed, but because it was in reality very difficult to preserve him long in a state of ease. To supply him with money was a hopeless attempt, for no sooner did he see himself master of a sum sufficient to set him free from care for a day, than he became profuse and luxurious. When once he had entered a tavern, or engaged in a scheme of pleasure, he never retired till want of money obliged him to some new expedient. If he was entertained in a family, nothing was any longer to be regarded there but amusements and jollity; wherever Savage entered he immediately expected that order and business should fly before him, that all should thenceforward be left to hazard, and that no dull principle of domestic management should be opposed to his inclination, or intrude upon his gaiety.

His distresses, however afflictive, never dejected him; in his lowest state he wanted not spirit to assert the natural dignity of wit, and was always ready to repress that insolence which superiority of fortune incited, and to trample that reputation which rose upon any other basis than that of merit: He never admitted any gross familiarities, or submitted to be treated otherwise than as an equal. Once when he was without lodging, meat, or cloaths, one of his friends, a man not indeed remarkable for moderation in his prosperity, left a message, that he desired to see him about nine in the morning. Savage knew that his intention was to assist him, but was very much disgusted, that he should presume to prescribe the hour of his attendance, and, I believe, refused to visit him, and rejected his kindness.

The same invincible temper, whether firmness or obstinacy, appeared in his conduct to the Lord Tyrconnel, from whom he very frequently demanded that the allowance which was once paid him should be restored, but with whom he never appeared to entertain for a moment the thought of soliciting a reconciliation, and whom he treated at once with all the haughtiness of superiority, and all the bitterness of resentment. He wrote to him not in a stile of supplication or respect, but of reproach, menace, and contempt, and appeared determined, if he ever regained his allowance, to hold it only by the right of conquest.

As many more can discover, that a man is richer than he is wiser than themselves, superiority of understanding is not so readily acknowledged as that of fortune; nor is that haughtiness, which the consciousness of great abilities incites, borne with the same submission as the tyranny of affluence; and therefore Savage, by asserting his claim to deference and regard, and by treating those with contempt whom better fortune animated to rebel against him, did not fail to raise a great number of enemies in the different classes of mankind. Those who thought themselves raised above him by the advantages of riches, hated him because they found no protection from the petulance of his wit. Those who were esteemed for their writings feared him as a critic, and maligned him as a rival, and almost all the smaller wits were his professed enemies.

Among these Mr. Millar so far indulged his resentment as to introduce him in a farce, and direct him to be personated on the stage in a dress like that which he then wore; a mean insult which only insinuated, that Savage had but one coat, and which was therefore despised by him rather than resented; for though he wrote a lampoon against Millar, he never printed it: and as no other person ought to prosecute that revenge from which the person who was injured desisted, I shall not preserve what Mr. Savage suppressed; of which the publication would indeed have been a punishment too severe for so impotent an assault.

The great hardships of poverty were to Savage not the want of lodging or of food, but the neglect and contempt which it drew upon him. He complained that as his affairs grew desperate he found his reputation for capacity visibly decline, that his opinion in questions of criticism was no longer regarded, when his coat was out of fashion; and that those who in the interval of his prosperity were always encouraging him to great undertakings by encomiums on his genius and assurances of success, now received any mention of his designs with coldness, thought that the subjects on which he proposed to write were very difficult; and were ready to inform him, that the event of a poem was uncertain, that an author ought to employ much time in the consideration of his plan, and not presume to sit down to write in confidence of a few cursory ideas, and a superficial knowledge; difficulties were started on all sides, and he was no longer qualified for any performance but the *Volunteer Laureat*.

Yet even this kind of contempt never depressed him; for he always preserved a steady confidence in his own capacity, and believed nothing above his reach which he should at any time earnestly endeavour to attain. He formed schemes of the same kind with regard to knowledge and to fortune, and flattered himself with advances to be made in science, as with riches to be enjoyed in some distant period of his life. For the acquisition of knowledge he was indeed far better qualified than for that of riches; for he was naturally inquisitive and desirous of the conversation of those from whom any information was to be obtained, but by no means solicitous to improve those opportunities that were sometimes offered of raising his fortune; and he was remarkably retentive of his ideas, which, when once he was in possession of them, rarely forsook him; a quality which could never be communicated to his money.

While he was thus wearing out his life in expectation that the Queen would some time recollect her promise, he had recourse to the usual practice of writers, and published proposals for printing his works by subscription, to which he was encouraged by the success of many who had not a better right to the favour of the public; but whatever was the reason, he did not find the world equally inclined to favour him, and he observed with some discontent, that though he offered his works at half a guinea, he was able to procure but a small number in comparison with those who subscribed twice as much to Duck.

Nor was it without indignation that he saw his Proposals neglected by the Queen, who patronised Mr. Duck's with uncommon ardour, and incited a competition among those who attended the Court, who should most promote his interest, and who should first offer a subscription. This was a distinction to which Mr. Savage made no scruple of asserting that his birth, his misfortunes, and his genius gave him a fairer title, than could be pleaded by him on whom it was conferred.

Savage's applications were however not universally unsuccessful; for some of the nobility countenanced his design, encouraged his Proposals, and subscribed with great liberality. He related of the Duke of Chandos particularly, that, upon receiving his Proposals, he sent him ten guineas.

But the money which his subscriptions afforded him was not less volatile than that which he received from his other schemes; whenever a subscription was paid him he went to a tavern, and as money so collected is necessarily received in small sums, he never was able to send his poems to the press, but for many years continued his solicitation, and squandered whatever he obtained.

This project of printing his works was frequently revived, and as his Proposals grew obsolete, new ones were printed with fresher dates. To form schemes for the publication was one of his favourite amusements, nor was he ever more at ease than when with any friend who readily fell in with his schemes, he was adjusting the print, forming the advertisements, and regulating the dispersion of his new edition, which he really intended some time to publish, and which, as long experience had shewn him the impossibility of printing the volume together, he at last determined to divide into weekly or monthly numbers, that the profits of the first might supply the expences of the next.

Thus he spent his time in mean expedients and tormenting suspense, living for the greatest part in fear of prosecutions from his creditors, and consequently skulking in obscure parts of the town, of which he was no stranger to the remotest corners. But wherever he came his address secured him friends, whom his necessities soon alienated, so that he had perhaps a more numerous acquaintance than any man ever before attained, there being scarcely any person eminent on any account to whom he was not known, or whose character he was not in some degree able to delineate.

To the acquisition of this extensive acquaintance every circumstance of his life contributed. He excelled in the arts of conversation, and therefore willingly practised them: He had seldom any home, or even a lodging in which he could be private, and therefore was driven into public houses for the common conveniences of life, and supports of nature. He was always ready to comply with every invitation, having no employment to withhold him, and often no money to provide for himself; and by dining with one company, he never failed of obtaining an introduction into another.

Thus dissipated was his life, and thus casual his subsistence; yet did not the distraction of his views hinder him from reflection, nor the uncertainty of his condition depress his gaiety. When he had wandered about without any fortunate adventure, by which he was led into a tavern, he sometimes retired into the fields, and was able to employ his mind in study to amuse it with pleasing imaginations; and seldom appeared to be melancholy, but when some sudden misfortune had just fallen upon him, and even then in a few moments he would disentangle himself from his perplexity, adopt the subject of conversation, and apply his mind wholly to the objects that others presented to it.

This life, unhappy as it may be already imagined, was yet imbitter'd in 1738, with new calamities. The death of the Queen deprived him of all the prospects of preferment with which he had so long entertained his imagination; and as Sir Robert Walpole had before given him reason to believe that he never intended the performance of his promise, he was now abandoned again to fortune.

He was, however at that time, supported by a friend; and as it was not his custom to look out for distant calamities, or to feel any other pain than that which forced itself upon his senses, he was not much afflicted at his loss, and perhaps comforted himself that his pension would be now continued without the annual tribute of a panegyric.

Another expectation contributed likewise to support him; he had taken a resolution to write a second tragedy upon the story of Sir Thomas Overbury, in which he preserved a few lines of his former play; but made a total alteration of the plan, added new incidents, and introduced new characters; so that it was a new tragedy, not a revival of the former.

Many of his friends blamed him for not making choice of another subject; but in vindication of himself, he asserted, that it was not easy to find a better; and that he thought it his interest to extinguish the memory of the first tragedy, which he could only do by writing one less defective upon the same story; by which he should entirely defeat the artifice of the booksellers, who after the death of any author of reputation, are always industrious to swell his works, by uniting his worst productions with his best.

In the execution of this scheme however, he proceeded but slowly, and probably only employed himself upon it when he could find no other amusement; but he pleased himself with counting the profits, and perhaps imagined, that the theatrical reputation which he was about to acquire, would be equivalent to all that he had lost by the death of his patroness.

He did not in confidence of his approaching riches neglect the measures proper to secure the continuance of his pension, though some of his favourers thought him culpable for omitting to write on her death; but on her birth day next year, he gave a proof of the solidity of his judgment, and the power of his genius. He knew that the track of elegy had been so long beaten, that it was impossible to travel in it without treading in the footsteps of those who had gone before him; and that therefore it was necessary that he might distinguish himself from the herd of encomiasts, to find out some new walk of funeral panegyric.

This difficult task he performed in such a manner, that his poem may be justly ranked among the best pieces that the death of princes has produced. By transferring the mention of her death to her birth day, he has formed a happy combination of topics which any other man would have thought it very difficult to connect in one view; but which he has united in such a manner, that

the relation between them appears natural; and it may be justly
said that what no other man would have thought on, it now
appears scarcely possible for any man to miss.[6]

The beauty of this peculiar combination of images is so mas-
terly, that it is sufficient to set this poem above censure; and
therefore it is not necessary to mention many other delicate
touches which may be found in it, and which would deservedly be
admired in any other performance.

To these proofs of his genius may be added, from the same
poem, an instance of his prudence, an excellence for which he was
not so often distinguished; he does not forget[7] to remind the King
in the most delicate and artful manner of continuing his pension.

With regard to the success of this address he was for some time
in suspense; but was in no great degree sollicitous about it; and
continued his labour upon his new tragedy with great tranquillity,
till the friend, who had for a considerable time supported him,
removing his family to another place, took occasion to dismiss
him. It then became necessary to enquire more diligently what
was determined in his affair, having reason to suspect that no
great favour was intended him, because he had not received his
pension at the usual time.

It is said, that he did not take those methods of retrieving his
interest which were most likely to succeed; and some of those who
were employed in the Exchequer, cautioned him against too much
violence in his proceedings; but Mr. Savage who seldom regulated
his conduct by the advice of others, gave way to his passion, and
demanded of Sir Robert Walpole, at his levee, the reason of the
distinction that was made between him and the other pensioners
of the Queen, with a degree of roughness which perhaps determined him to withdraw what had been only delayed.

Whatever was the crime of which he was accused or suspected,
and whatever influence was imployed against him, he received
soon after an account that took from him all hopes of regaining
his pension; and he had now no prospect of subsistence but from
his play, and he knew no way of living for the time required to
finish it.

So peculiar were the misfortunes of this man, deprived of an
estate and title by a particular law, exposed and abandoned by
a mother, defrauded by a mother of a fortune which his father

had allotted him, he enter'd the world without a friend; and though his abilities forced themselves into esteem and reputation, he was never able to obtain any real advantage, and whatever prospects arose, were always intercepted as he began to approach them. The King's intentions in his favour were frustrated; his Dedication to the Prince, whose generosity on every other occasion was eminent, procured him no reward; Sir Robert Walpole who valued himself upon keeping his promise to others, broke it to him without regret; and the bounty of the Queen was, after her death, withdrawn from him, and from him only.

Such were his misfortunes, which yet he bore not only with decency, but with cheerfulness, nor was his gaiety clouded even by his last disappointments, though he was in a short time reduced to the lowest degree of distress; and often wanted both lodging and food. At this time, he gave another instance of the insurmountable obstinacy of his spirit; his cloaths were worn out, and he received notice that at a coffee-house some cloaths and linen were left for him; the person who sent them, did not, I believe, inform him to whom he was to be obliged, that he might spare the perplexity of acknowledging the benefit; but though the offer was so far generous, it was made with some neglect of ceremonies, which Mr. Savage so much resented, that he refused the present, and declined to enter the house, till the cloaths that had been designed for him were taken away.

His distress was now publickly known, and his friends, therefore, thought it proper to concert some measures for his relief; and one of them wrote a letter to him, in which he expressed his concern *for the miserable withdrawing of his pension;* and gave him hopes that in a short time, he should find himself supplied with a competence, *without any dependence on those little creatures which we are pleased to call the great.*

The scheme proposed for this happy and independent subsistence, was, that he should retire into Wales, and receive an allowance of fifty pounds a year, to be raised by a subscription, on which he was to live privately in a cheap place, without aspiring any more to affluence, or having any farther care of reputation.

This offer Mr. Savage gladly accepted, tho' with intentions very different from those of his friends; for they proposed, that he should continue an exile from London for ever, and spend all the remaining part of his life at Swansea; but he designed only to take the opportunity, which their scheme offered him, of retreating for a short time, that he might prepare his play for the stage, and his other works for the press, and then to return to London to exhibit his tragedy, and live upon the profits of his own labour.

With regard to his Works, he proposed very great improvements, which would have required much time, or great application; and when he had finish'd them, he designed to do justice to his subscribers, by publishing them according to his Proposals.

As he was ready to entertain himself with future pleasures, he had planned out a scheme of life for the country, of which he had no knowledge but from pastorals and songs. He imagined that he should be transported to scenes of flow'ry felicity, like those which one poet has reflected to another, and had projected a perpetual round of innocent pleasures, of which he suspected no interruption from pride, or ignorance, or brutality.

With these expectations he was so enchanted, that when he was once gently reproach'd by a friend for submitting to live upon a subscription, and advised rather by a resolute exertion of his abilities to support himself, he could not bear to debar himself from the happiness which was to be found in the calm of a cottage, or lose the opportunity of listening without intermission, to the melody of the nightingale, which he believ'd was to be heard from every bramble, and which he did not fail to mention as a very important part of the happiness of a country life.

While this scheme was ripening, his friends directed him to take a lodging in the liberties of the Fleet, that he might be secure from his creditors, and sent him every Monday a guinea, which he commonly spent before the next morning, and trusted, after his usual manner, the remaining part of the week to the bounty of fortune.

He now began very sensibly to feel the miseries of dependence: Those by whom he was to be supported, began to prescribe to him with an air of authority, which he knew not how decently to resent, nor patiently to bear; and he soon discovered from the conduct of most of his subscribers, that he was yet in the hands of *little creatures.*

Of the insolence that he was obliged to suffer, he gave many instances, of which none appeared to raise his indignation to a greater height, than the method which was taken of furnishing him with cloaths. Instead of consulting him and allowing him to send to a taylor his orders for what they thought proper to allow him, they proposed to send for a taylor to take his measure, and then to consult how they should equip him.

This treatment was not very delicate, nor was it such as Savage's humanity would have suggested to him on a like occasion; but it had scarcely deserved mention, had it not, by affecting him in an uncommon degree, shewn the peculiarity of his character. Upon hearing the design that was formed, he came to the lodging of a friend with the most violent agonies of rage; and being asked what it could be that gave him such disturbance, he replied with the utmost vehemence of indignation, "That they had sent for a taylor to measure him."

How the affair ended, was never enquired, for fear of renewing his uneasiness. It is probable that, upon recollection, he submitted with a good grace to what he could not avoid, and that he discovered no resentment where he had no power.

He was, however, not humbled to implicit and universal compliance; for when the gentleman, who had first informed him of the design to support him by a subscription, attempted to procure a reconciliation with the Lord Tyrconnel, he could by no means be prevailed upon to comply with the measures that were proposed.

A letter was written for him to Sir William Lemon, to prevail upon him to interpose his good offices with Lord Tyrconnel, in which he solicited Sir William's assistance, *for a man who really needed it as much as any man could well do;* and informed him, that he was retiring *for ever to a place where he should no more trouble his relations, friends, or enemies;* he confessed, that his *passion* had *betrayed* him to some conduct, with regard to Lord Tyrconnel, *for which he could not but heartily ask his pardon;* and as he imagined Lord Tyrconnel's passion might be yet so high, that he would not *receive a letter from him,* begg'd that Sir William would endeavour to soften him; and expressed his hopes, that he would comply with his request, and that *so small a relation would not harden his heart against him.*

That any man should presume to dictate a letter to him, was not very agreeable to Mr. Savage; and therefore he was, before he had opened it, not much inclined to approve it. But when he read it, he found it contained sentiments entirely opposite to his own, and, as he asserted, to the truth, and therefore instead of copying it, wrote his friend a letter full of masculine resentment and warm expostulations. He very justly observed, that the style was too supplicatory, and the representation too abject, and that he ought at least to have made him complain with *the dignity of a gentleman in distress.* He declared that he would not write the paragraph in which he was to ask Lord Tyrconnel's pardon; for *he despised his pardon, and therefore could not heartily, and would not hypocritically ask it.* He remarked, that his friend made a very unreasonable distinction between himself and him; for, says he, when you mention men of high rank *in your own character,* they are *those little creatures whom we are pleased to call the great;* but when you address them *in mine,* no servility is sufficiently humble. He then with great propriety explained the ill consequences might be expected from such a letter, which his relations would print in their own defence, and which would for ever be produced as a full answer to all that he should allege against them; for he always intended to publish a minute account of the treatment which he had received. It is to be remembered to the honour of the gentleman by whom this letter was drawn up, that he yielded to Mr. Savage's reasons, and agreed that it ought to be suppressed.

After many alterations and delays, a subscription was at length raised which did not amount to fifty pounds a year, though twenty were paid by one gentleman; such was the generosity of mankind, that what had been done by a player without solicitation, could not now be effected by application and interest; and Savage had a great number to court and to obey for a pension less than that which Mrs. Oldfield paid him without exacting any servilities.

Mr. Savage however was satisfied, and willing to retire, and was convinced that the allowance, though scanty, would be more than sufficient for him, being now determined to commence a rigid oeconomist, and to live according to the exactest rules of frugality; for nothing was in his opinion more contemptible than a man, who, when he knew his income, exceeded it, and yet he confessed that instances of such folly, were too common, and lamented, that some men were not to be trusted with their own money.

Full of these salutary resolutions, he left London, in July 1739, having taken leave with great tenderness of his friends, and parted from the author of this narrative with tears in his eyes. He was furnished with fifteen guineas, and informed, that they would be sufficient, not only for the expence of his journey, but for his support in Wales for some time; and that there remained but little more of the first collection. He promised a strict adherence to his maxims of parsimony, and went away in the stage coach; nor did his friends expect to hear from him, till he informed them of his arrival at Swansea.

But when they least expected, arrived a letter dated the four-teenth day after his departure, in which he sent them word, that he was yet upon the road, and without money; and that he there-fore could not proceed without a remittance. They then sent him the money that was in their hands, with which he was enabled to reach Bristol, from whence he was to go to Swansea by water.

At Bristol he found an embargo laid upon the shipping, so that he could not immediately obtain a passage; and being therefore obliged to stay there some time, he, with his usual felicity, in-gratiated himself with many of the principal inhabitants, was invited to their houses, distinguished at their publick feasts, and treated with a regard that gratify'd his vanity, and therefore easily engaged his affection.

He began very early after his retirement to complain of the conduct of his friends in London, and irritated many of them so much by his letters, that they withdrew, however honourably, their contributions; and it is believed, that little more was paid him than the twenty pounds a year, which were allowed him by the gentleman who proposed the subscription.

After some stay at Bristol, he retired to Swansea, the place *originally* proposed for his residence, where he lived about a year very much dissatisfied with the diminution of his salary; but con-tracted, as in other places, acquaintance with those who were most distinguished in that country, among whom he has celebrated Mr. Powel and Mrs. Jones, by some verses which he inserted in the *Gentleman's Magazine*.

Here he completed his tragedy, of which two acts were wanting when he left London, and was desirous of coming to town to bring it upon the stage. This design was very warmly opposed, and he was advised by his chief benefactor to put it into the hands

of Mr. Thomson and Mr. Mallet, that it might be fitted for the
stage, and to allow his friends to receive the profits, out of which
an annual pension should be paid him.

This proposal he rejected with the utmost contempt. He was by
no means convinced that the judgment of those to whom he was
required to submit, was superior to his own. He was now determined, as he expressed it, to be *no longer kept in leading-strings,*
and had no elevated idea of *his bounty,* who proposed to *pension
him out of the profits of his own labours.*

He attempted in Wales to promote a subscription for his Works,
and had once hopes of success; but in a short time afterwards,
formed a resolution of leaving that part of the country, to which
he thought it not reasonable to be confined, for the gratification of
those, who having promised him a liberal income, had no sooner
banished him to a remote corner, than they reduced his allowance
to a salary scarcely equal to the necessities of life.

His resentment of this treatment, which, in his own opinion, at
least, he had not deserved, was such that he broke off all correspondence with most of his contributors, and appeared to consider
them as persecutors and oppressors, and in the latter part of his
life, declared, that their conduct toward him, since his departure
from London, *had been perfidiousness improving on perfidiousness, and inhumanity on inhumanity.*

It is not to be supposed, that the necessities of Mr. Savage did
not sometimes incite him to satirical exaggerations of the behaviour of those by whom he thought himself reduced to them.
But it must be granted, that the diminution of his allowance was
a great hardship, and, that those who withdrew their subscription
from a man, who, upon the faith of their promise, had gone into a
kind of banishment, and abandoned all those by whom he had
been before relieved in his distresses, will find it no easy task to
vindicate their conduct.

It may be alleged, and, perhaps, justly, that he was petulant
and contemptuous, that he more frequently reproached his subscribers for not giving him more, than thanked them for what he
received; but it is to be remembered, that this conduct, and this is
the worst charge that can be drawn up against him, did them no
real injury; and that it, therefore, ought rather to have been pitied
than resented, at least, the resentment that it might provoke ought

to have been generous and manly; epithets which his conduct will hardly deserve, that starves the man whom he has persuaded to put himself into his power.

It might have been reasonably demanded by Savage, that they should, before they had taken away what they promised, have replaced him in his former state, that they should have taken no advantages from the situation to which the appearance of their kindness had reduced him, and that he should have been re-called to London, before he was abandoned. He might justly represent, that he ought to have been considered as a lion in the toils, and demand to be released before the dogs should be loosed upon him.

He endeavoured, indeed, to release himself, and with an intent to return to London, went to Bristol, where a repetition of the kindness which he had formerly found, invited him to stay. He was not only caressed and treated, but had a collection made for him of about thirty pounds, with which it had been happy if he had immediately departed for London; but his negligence did not suffer him to consider, that such proofs of kindness were not often to be expected, and that this ardour of benevolence was in a great degree, the effect of novelty, and might, probably, be every day less; and, therefore, he took no care to improve the happy time, but was encouraged by one favour to hope for another, till at length generosity was exhausted, and officiousness wearied.

Another part of his misconduct was the practice of prolonging his visits, to unseasonable hours, and disconcerting all the families into which he was admitted. This was an error in a place of commerce which all the charms of his conversation could not compensate; for what trader would purchase such airy satisfaction by the loss of solid gain, which must be the consequence of midnight merriment, as those hours which were gained at night, were generally lost in the morning?

Thus Mr. Savage, after the curiosity of the inhabitants was gratified, found the number of his friends daily decreasing, perhaps without suspecting for what reason their conduct was altered, for he still continued to harrass, with his nocturnal intrusions, those that yet countenanced him, and admitted him to their houses.

But he did not spend all the time of his residence at Bristol, in visits or at taverns; for he sometimes returned to his studies, and began several considerable designs. When he felt an inclination to write, he always retired from the knowledge of his friends, and lay hid in an obscure part of the suburbs, till he found himself again desirous of company, to which it is likely that intervals of absence made him more welcome.

He was always full of his design of returning to London to bring his tragedy upon the stage; but having neglected to depart with the money that was raised for him, he could not afterwards procure a sum sufficient to defray the expences of his journey; nor, perhaps, would a fresh supply have had any other effect, than, by putting immediate pleasures in his power, to have driven the thoughts of his journey out of his mind.

While he was thus spending the day in contriving a scheme for the morrow, distress stole upon him by imperceptible degrees. His conduct had already wearied some of those who were at first enamoured of his conversation; but he might, perhaps, still have devolved to others, whom he might have entertained with equal success, had not the decay of his cloaths made it no longer consistent with their vanity to admit him to their tables, or to associate with him in publick places. He now began to find every man from home at whose house he called; and was, therefore, no longer able to procure the necessaries of life, but wandered about the town slighted and neglected, in quest of a dinner, which he did not always obtain.

To complete his misery, he was persued by the officers for small debts which he had contracted; and was, therefore, obliged to withdraw from the small number of friends from whom he had still reason to hope for favours. His custom was to lye in bed the greatest part of the day, and to go out in the dark with the utmost privacy, and after having paid his visit, return again before morning to his lodging, which was in the garret of an obscure inn.

Being thus excluded on one hand, and confined on the other, he suffered the utmost extremities of poverty, and often fasted so long, that he was seized with faintness, and had lost his appetite, not being able to bear the smell of meat, 'till the action of his stomach was restored by a cordial.

In this distress he received a remittance of five pounds from London, with which he provided himself a decent coat, and determined to go to London, but unhappily spent his money at a favourite tavern. Thus was he again confined to Bristol, where he was every day hunted by bailiffs. In this exigence he once more found a friend, who sheltered him in his house, though at the usual inconveniences with which his company was attended; for he could neither be persuaded to go to bed in the night, nor to rise in the day.

It is observable, that in these various scenes of misery, he was always disengaged and cheerful; he at some times persued his studies, and at others continued or enlarged his epistolary correspondence, nor was he ever so far dejected as to endeavour to procure an encrease of his allowance, by any other methods than accusations and reproaches.

He had now no longer any hopes of assistance from his friends at Bristol, who as merchants, and by consequence sufficiently studious of profit, cannot be supposed to have look'd with much compassion upon negligence and extravagance, or to think any excellence equivalent to a fault of such consequence as neglect of oeconomy. It is natural to imagine, that many of those who would have relieved his real wants, were discouraged from the exertion of their benevolence, by observation of the use which was made of their favours, and conviction that relief would only be momentary, and that the same necessity would quickly return.

At last he quitted the house of his friend, and returned to his lodging at the inn, still intending to set out in a few days for London, but on the tenth of January 1742-3, having been at supper with two of his friends, he was at his return to his lodgings arrested for a debt of about eight pounds, which he owed at a coffee-house, and conducted to the house of a sheriff's officer. The account which he gives of this misfortune in a letter to one of the gentlemen with whom he had supped, is too remarkable to be omitted.

"It was not a little unfortunate for me, that I spent yesterday's evening with you; because the hour hindered me from entering on my new lodging; however, I have now got one; but such an one, as I believe nobody would chuse.

"I was arrested at the suit of Mrs. Read, just as I was going up stairs to bed, at Mr. Bowyer's; but taken in so private a manner, that I believe nobody at the White Lyon is apprised of it. Tho' I let the officers know the strength (or rather weakness of my pocket) yet they treated me with the utmost civility, and even when they conducted me to confinement, 'twas in such a manner, that I verily believe I could have escaped, which I would rather be ruined than have done; notwithstanding the whole amount of my finances was but three pence halfpenny.

"In the first place I must insist, that you will industriously conceal this from Mrs. S——s; because I would not have her good nature suffer that pain, which, I know, she would be apt to feel on this occasion.

"Next I conjure you, dear Sir, by all the ties of friendship, by no means to have one uneasy thought on my account; but to have the same pleasantry of countenance and unruffled serenity of mind, which (God be praised!) I have in this, and have had in a much severer calamity. Furthermore, I charge you, if you value my friendship as truly as I do yours, *not* to utter, or even harbour the least resentment against Mrs. Read. I believe she has ruin'd me, but I freely forgive her; and (tho' I will never more have any intimacy with her) would, at a due distance, rather do her an act of good, than ill will. Lastly, (pardon the expression) I *absolutely command* you not to offer me any pecuniary assistance, nor to attempt getting me any from any one of your friends. At another time, or on any other occasion, you may, dear friend, be well assured, I would rather write to you in the submissive stile of a request, than that of a peremptory command.

"However, that my truly valuable friend may not think I am too proud to ask a favour, let me entreat you to let me have your boy to attend me for this day, not only for the sake of saving me the expence of porters; but for the delivery of some letters to people, whose names I would not have known to strangers.

"The civil treatment I have thus far met from those, whose prisoner I am, makes me thankful to the Almighty, that, tho' He has thought fit to visit me (on my birth-night) with affliction; yet (such is His great goodness!) my affliction is not without alleviating circumstances. I murmur not, but am all resignation to the *divine will*. As to the world, I hope that I shall be endued by heaven with that presence of mind, that serene dignity in misfortune, that constitutes the character of a true nobleman; a dignity far beyond that of coronets; a nobility arising from the just principles of philosophy, refined and exalted, by those of Christianity."

He continued five days at the officer's, in hopes that he should be able to procure bail, and avoid the necessity of going to prison. The state in which he passed his time, and the treatment which he received, are very justly expressed by him in a letter which he wrote to a friend; "The whole day," *says he*, "has been employed in various people's filling my head with their foolish chimerical systems, which has obliged me coolly (as far as nature will admit) to digest, and accommodate myself to, every different person's way of thinking; hurried from one wild system to another, 'till it has quite made a chaos of my imagination, and nothing done—promised—disappointed—order'd to send every hour, from one part of the town to the other."——

When his friends, who had hitherto caressed and applauded, found that to give bail and pay the debt was the same, they all refused to preserve him from a prison, at the expence of eight pounds; and therefore after having been for some time at the officer's house, *at an immense expence,* as he observes in his letter, he was at length removed to Newgate.

This expence he was enabled to support, by the generosity of Mr. Nash at Bath, who upon receiving from him an account of his condition, immediately sent him five guineas, and promised to promote his subscription at Bath, with all his interest.

By his removal to Newgate, he obtained at least a freedom from suspense, and rest from the disturbing vicissitudes of hope and disappointment; he now found that his friends were only companions, who were willing to share his gaiety, but not to partake of his misfortunes; and therefore he no longer expected any assistance from them.

It must however be observed of one gentleman, that he offered to release him by paying the debt, but that Mr. Savage would not consent, I suppose, because he thought he had been before too burthensome to him.

He was offered by some of his friends, that a collection should be made for his enlargement, but he *treated the proposal,* and declared,[8] *that he should again treat it, with disdain. As to writing*

*any mendicant letters, he had too high a spirit, and determined
only to write to some Ministers of State, to try to regain his
pension.*

He continued to complain[9] of those that had sent him into the
country, and objected to them, that he had *lost the profits of his
play which had been finished three years,* and in another letter
declares his resolution to publish a pamphlet, that the world might
know how *he had been used.*

This pamphlet was never written, for he in a very short time
recover'd his usual tranquillity, and chearfully applied himself
to more inoffensive studies. He indeed steadily declared, that he
was promised an yearly allowance of fifty pounds, and never received half the sum, but he seemed to resign himself to that as
well as to other misfortunes, and lose the remembrance of it in his
amusements, and employments.

The chearfulness with which he bore his confinement, appears
from the following letter which he wrote Jan. 30th, to one of his
friends in London.

> I now write to you from my confinement in Newgate, where I
> have been ever since Monday last was sev'n-night; and where I
> enjoy myself with much more tranquillity than I have known
> for upwards of a twelve-month past; having a room entirely to
> myself, and persuing the amusement of my poetical studies,
> uninterrupted and agreeable to my mind. I thank the Almighty,
> I am now all collected in myself, and tho' my person is in con-
> finement, my mind can expatiate on ample and useful subjects,
> with all the freedom imaginable. I am now more conversant
> with the Nine than ever; and if, instead of a Newgate bird, I
> may be allowed to be a bird of the muses, I assure you, Sir,
> I sing very freely in my cage; sometimes indeed in the plaintive
> notes of the nightingale; but, at others, in the chearful strains
> of the lark.——

In another letter he observes, that he ranges from one subject to
another without confining himself to any particular task, and that
he was employed one week upon one attempt, and the next upon
another.

Surely the fortitude of this man deserves, at least, to be mentioned with applause, and whatever faults may be imputed to him,

the virtue of *suffering well* cannot be denied him. The two powers which, in the opinion of Epictetus, constituted a wise man, are those of *bearing* and *forbearing*, which it cannot indeed be affirmed to have been equally possessed by Savage, and indeed the want of one obliged him very *frequently* to practise the other.

He was treated by Mr. Dagg, the keeper of the prison, with great humanity; was supported by him at his own table without any certainty of recompense, had a room to himself, to which he could at any time retire from all disturbance, was allowed to stand at the door of the prison, and sometimes taken out into the fields; so that he suffered fewer hardships in the prison, than he had been accustomed to undergo in the greatest part of his life.

The keeper did not confine his benevolence to a gentle execution of his office, but made some overtures to the creditor for his release, but without effect; and continued, during the whole time of his imprisonment to treat him with the utmost tenderness and civility.

Virtue is undoubtedly most laudable in that state which makes it most difficult; and therefore the humanity of a goaler, certainly deserves this publick attestation; and the man whose heart has not been hardened by such an employment, may be justly proposed as a pattern of benevolence. If an inscription was once engraved to the *honest toll-gatherer*, less honours ought not to be paid *to the tender goaler*.

Mr. Savage very frequently received visits, and sometimes presents from his acquaintances, but they did not amount to a subsistence, for the greater part of which he was indebted to the generosity of this keeper; but these favours, however they might endear to him the particular persons, from whom he received them, were very far from impressing upon his mind any advantageous ideas of the people of Bristol, and therefore he thought he could not more properly employ himself in prison, than in writing the following poem.

### *London and Bristol*[1] *delineated*

Two sea-port cities mark Britannia's fame,
And these from commerce different honours claim.
What different honours shall the muses pay,
While one inspires and one untunes the lay?

Now silver Isis bright'ning flows along,
Echoing from Oxford's shore each classic song;
Then weds with Tame; and these, O London, see
Swelling with naval pride, the pride of thee!
Wide deep unsullied Thames meand'ring glides
And bears thy wealth on mild majestic tides.
Thy ships, with gilded palaces that vie,
In glitt'ring pomp, strike wond'ring China's eye;
And thence returning bear, in splendid state,
To Britain's merchants, India's eastern freight.
India, her treasures from her western shores,
Due at thy feet, a willing tribute pours;
Thy warring navies distant nations awe,
And bid the world obey thy righteous law.
Thus shine thy manly sons of lib'ral mind;
Thy Change deep-busied, yet as courts refin'd;
Councils, like senates that enforce debate
With fluent eloquence and reason's weight.
Whose patriot virtue, lawless pow'r controuls;
Their British emulating Roman souls.
Of these the worthiest still selected stand,
Still lead the Senate, and still save the land:
Social, not selfish, here, O learning trace
Thy friends, the lovers of all human race!

In a dark bottom sunk, O Bristol now,
With native malice, lift thy low'ring brow!
Then as some hell-born sprite, in mortal guise,
Borrows the shape of goodness and belies,
All fair, all smug to yon proud hall invite,
To feast all strangers ape an air polite!
From Cambria drain'd, or England's western coast,
Not elegant yet costly banquets boast!
Revere, or seem the stranger to revere;
Praise, fawn, profess, be all things but sincere;
Insidious now, our bosom secrets steal,
And these with sly sarcastic sneer reveal.
Present we meet thy sneaking treach'rous smiles;
The harmless absent still thy sneer reviles;

Such as in thee all parts superior find;
The sneer that marks the fool and knave combin'd.
When melting pity wou'd afford relief,
The ruthless sneer that insult adds to grief.
What friendship can'st thou boast? what honours claim?
To thee each stranger owes an injur'd name.
What smiles thy sons must in their foes excite?
Thy sons to whom all discord is delight;
From whom eternal mutual railing flows;
Who in each others crimes, their own expose;
Thy sons, tho' crafty, deaf to wisdom's call;
Despising all men and despis'd by all.
Sons, while thy cliffs a ditch-like river laves,
Rude as thy rocks, and muddy as thy waves;
Of thoughts as narrow as of words immense;
As full of turbulence as void of sense:
Thee, thee what senatorial souls adorn?
Thy natives sure wou'd prove a senate's scorn.
Do strangers deign to serve thee? what their praise?
Their gen'rous services thy murmurs raise.
What fiend malign, that o'er thy air presides,
Around from breast to breast inherent glides,
And, as he glides, there scatters in a trice
The lurking seeds of ev'ry rank device?
Let foreign youths to thy indentures run!
Each, each will prove, in thy adopted son,
Proud, pert and dull—Tho' brilliant once from schools,
Will scorn all learning's as all virtue's rules;
And, tho' by nature friendly, honest, brave,
Turn a sly, selfish, simp'ring, sharping knave.
Boast petty-courts, where 'stead of fluent ease;
Of cited precedents and learned pleas;
'Stead of sage council in the dubious cause,
Attorneys chatt'ring wild, burlesque the laws.
So shameless quacks, who doctor's rights invade,
Of jargon and of poison form a trade.
So canting coblers, while from tubs they teach,
Buffoon the Gospel they pretend to preach.
Boast petty courts, whence rules new rigour draw;

Unknown to nature's and to statute law;
Quirks that explain all saving rights away,
To give th' attorney and the catch-poll prey.
Is there where law too rig'rous may descend?
Or charity her kindly hand extend?
Thy courts, that shut when pity wou'd redress,
Spontaneous open to inflict distress.
Try misdemeanours!—all thy wiles employ,
Not to chastise the offender but destroy;
Bid the large lawless fine his fate foretell;
Bid it beyond his crime and fortune swell.
Cut off from service due to kindred blood
To private welfare and to public good,
Pitied by all, but thee, he sentenc'd lies;
Imprison'd languishes, imprison'd dies,

❃ ❃ ❃ ❃ ❃ ❃ ❃ ❃ ❃ ❃ ❃ ❃ ❃

Boast swarming vessels, whose plaebeian state
Owes not to merchants but mechanics freight.
Boast nought but pedlar fleets—in war's alarms,
Unknown to glory, as unknown to arms.
Boast thy base[2] Tolsey, and thy turn-spit dogs;
Thy[3] hallier's horses and thy human hogs;
Upstarts and mushrooms, proud, relentless hearts;
Thou blank of sciences! Thou dearth of arts!
Such foes as learning once was doom'd to see;
Huns, Goths, and Vandals were but types of thee.
Proceed, great Bristol, in all-righteous ways,
And let one justice heighten yet thy praise;
Still spare the catamite and swinge the whore,
And be, whate'er Gomorrah was before.

When he had brought this poem to its present state, which, without considering the chasm, is not perfect, he wrote to London an account of his design, and informed his friend, that he was determined to print it with his name; but enjoined him not to communicate his intention to his Bristol acquaintance. The gentleman surprised at his resolution, endeavoured to dissuade him from publishing it, at least, from prefixing his name, and declared, that he could not reconcile the injunction of secrecy with his resolution to own it at its first appearance. To this Mr. Savage returned an answer agreeable to his character in the following terms.

"I received yours this morning and not without a little surprize at the contents. To answer a question with a question, you ask me concerning London and Bristol, *why will I add* delineated? Why did Mr. Woolaston add the same word to his religion of nature? I suppose that it was his will and pleasure to add it in his case; and it is mine to do so in my own. You are pleased to tell me, that you understand not, why secrecy is injoin'd, and yet I intend to set my name to it. My answer is—I have my private reasons; which I am not obliged to explain to any one. You doubt, my friend Mr. S—— would not approve of it—And what is it to me whether he does or not? Do you imagine, that Mr. S—— is to dictate to me? If any man, who calls himself my friend, should assume such an air, I would spurn at his friendship with contempt. You say, I seem to think so by not letting him know it—And suppose I do, what then? Perhaps I can give reasons for that disapprobation, very foreign from what you would imagine. You go on in saying, suppose, I should not put my name to it—My answer is, that I will not suppose any such thing, being determined to the contrary; neither, Sir, would I have you suppose, that I applied to you for want of another press: Nor would I have you imagine, that I owe Mr. S—— obligations which I do not."

Such was his imprudence and such his obstinate adherence to his own resolutions, however absurd. A prisoner! supported by charity! and, whatever insults he might have received during the latter part of his stay in Bristol, once caressed, esteemed, and presented with a liberal collection, he could forget on a sudden his danger, and his obligations, to gratify the petulance of his wit, or the eagerness of his resentment, and publish a satire by which he might reasonably expect, that he should alienate those who then supported him, and provoke those whom he could neither resist nor escape.

This resolution, from the execution of which, it is probable, that only his death could have hindered him, is sufficient to show, how much he disregarded all considerations that opposed his present passions, and how readily he hazarded all future advantages for any immediate gratifications. Whatever was his predominant inclination, neither hope nor fear hinder'd him from complying with it, nor had opposition any other effect than to heighten his ardour and irritate his vehemence.

This performance was however laid aside, while he was employed in soliciting assistance from several great persons, and one interruption succeeding another hinder'd him from supplying the chasm, and perhaps from retouching the other parts, which he can hardly be imagined to have finished, in his own opinion; for it is very unequal, and some of the lines are rather inserted to rhyme to others than to support or improve the sense; but the first and last parts are worked up with great spirit and elegance.

His time was spent in the prison for the most part in study, or in receiving visits; but sometimes he descended to lower amusements, and diverted himself in the kitchen with the conversation of the criminals; for it was not pleasing to him to be much without company, and though he was very capable of a judicious choice, he was often contented with the first that offered; for this he was sometimes reproved by his friends who found him surrounded with felons; but the reproof was on that as on other occasions thrown away; he continued to gratify himself, and to set very little value on the opinion of others.

But here, as in every other scene of his life, he made use of such opportunities as occur'd of benefiting those who were more miserable than himself, and was always ready to perform any offices of humanity to his fellow prisoners.

He had now ceased from corresponding with any of his subscribers except one, who yet continued to remit him the twenty pounds a year which he had promised him, and by whom it was expected, that he would have been in a very short time enlarged, because he had directed the keeper to enquire after the state of his debts.

However he took care to enter his name according to the forms of the court, that the creditor might be obliged to make him some allowance, if he was continued a prisoner, and when on that occasion he appeared in the hall was treated with very unusual respect.

But the resentment of the city was afterwards raised by some accounts that had been spread of the satire, and he was informed that some of the merchants intended to pay the allowance which the law required, and to detain him a prisoner at their own expence. This he treated as an empty menace, and perhaps might have hasten'd the publication, only to shew how much he was superior to their insults, had not all his schemes been suddenly destroyed.

When he had been six months in prison he received from one of his friends in whose kindness he had the greatest confidence, and on whose assistance he chiefly depended, a letter that contained a charge of very atrocious ingratitude, drawn up in such terms as sudden resentment dictated. Mr. Savage returned a very solemn protestation of his innocence, but however appeared much disturbed at the accusation. Some days afterwards he was seized with a pain in his back and side, which as it was not violent was not suspected to be dangerous; but growing daily more languid and dejected, on the 25th of July he confined himself to his room, and a fever seized his spirits. The symptoms grew every day more formidable, but his condition did not enable him to procure any assistance. The last time that the keeper saw him was on July the 31st, when Savage seeing him at his bed-side said, with an uncommon earnestness, *I have something to say to you, Sir,* but after a pause, moved his hand in a melancholy manner, and finding himself unable to recollect what he was going to communicate, said *'Tis gone*. The keeper soon after left him, and the next morning he died. He was buried in the church-yard of St. Peter, at the expence of the keeper.

Such were the life and death of Richard Savage, a man equally distinguished by his virtues and vices, and at once remarkable for his weaknesses and abilities.

He was of a middle stature, of a thin habit of body, a long visage, coarse features, and melancholy aspect; of a grave and manly deportment, a solemn dignity of mien, but which upon a nearer acquaintance softened into an engaging easiness of manners. His walk was slow, and his voice tremulous and mournful. He was easily excited to smiles, but very seldom provoked to laughter.

His mind was in an uncommon degree vigorous and active. His judgment was accurate, his apprehension quick, and his memory so tenacious, that he was frequently observed to know what he had learned from others in a short time better than those by whom he was informed, and could frequently recollect incidents, with all their combination of circumstances, which few would have regarded at the present time; but which the quickness of his apprehension impressed upon him. He had the peculiar felicity, that his attention never deserted him; he was present to every object, and regardful of the most trifling occurrences. He had the art of escaping from his own reflections and accommodating himself to every new scene.

To this quality is to be imputed the extent of his knowledge compared with the small time which he spent in visible endeavours to acquire it. He mingled in cursory conversation with the same steadiness of attention as others apply to a lecture, and, amidst the appearance of thoughtless gayety, lost no new idea that was started, nor any hint that could be improved. He had therefore made in coffee-houses the same proficiency as others in studies; and it is remarkable, that the writings of a man of little education and little reading have an air of learning scarcely to be found in any other performances, but which perhaps as often obscures as embellishes them.

His judgment was eminently exact both with regard to writings and to men. The knowledge of life was indeed his chief attainment, and it is not without some satisfaction, that I can produce the suffrage of Savage in favour of human nature, of which he never appeared to entertain such odious ideas, as some who perhaps had neither his judgment nor experience have published, either in ostentation of their sagacity, vindication of their crimes, or gratification of their malice.

His method of life particularly qualified him for conversation, of which he knew how to practise all the graces. He was never vehement or loud, but at once modest and easy, open and respectful, his language was vivacious and elegant, and equally happy upon grave or humorous subjects. He was generally censured for not knowing when to retire, but that was not the defect of his judgment, but of his fortune; when he left his company he was frequently to spend the remaining part of the night in the street, or at least was abandoned to gloomy reflections, which it is not strange that he delayed as long as he could, and sometimes forgot that he gave others pain to avoid it himself.

It cannot be said, that he made use of his abilities for the direction of his own conduct; an irregular and dissipated manner of life had made him the slave of every passion that happened to be excited by the presence of its object, and that slavery to his passions reciprocally produced a life irregular and dissipated. He was not master of his own emotions, nor could promise any thing for the next day.

With regard to his oeconomy, nothing can be added to the relation of his life: he appeared to think himself born to be supported by others, and dispensed from all necessity of providing for himself; he therefore never prosecuted any scheme of advantage, nor endeavoured even to secure the profits which his writings might have afforded him.

His temper was in consequence of the dominion of his passions uncertain and capricious; he was easily engaged, and easily disgusted; but he is accused of retaining his hatred more tenaciously than his benevolence.

He was compassionate both by nature and principle, and always ready to perform offices of humanity; but when he was provoked, and very small offences were sufficient to provoke him, he would prosecute his revenge with the utmost acrimony till his passion had subsided.

His friendship was therefore of little value; for though he was zealous in the support or vindication of those whom he loved, yet it was always dangerous to trust him, because he considered himself as discharged by the first quarrel, from all ties of honour or gratitude; and would betray those secrets which in the warmth of confidence had been imparted to him. This practice drew upon him an universal accusation of ingratitude; nor can it be denied that he was very ready to set himself free from the load of an obligation; for he could not bear to conceive himself in a state of dependence, his pride being equally powerful with his other passions, and appearing in the form of insolence at one time and of vanity at another. Vanity the most innocent species of pride, was most frequently predominant: he could not easily leave off when he had once began to mention himself or his works, nor ever read his verses without stealing his eyes from the page, to discover in the faces of his audience, how they were affected with any favourite passage.

A kinder name than that of vanity ought to be given to the delicacy with which he was always careful to separate his own merit from every other man's; and to reject that praise to which he had no claim. He did not forget, in mentioning his performances, to mark every line that had been suggested or amended, and was so accurate as to relate that he owed *three words* in *The Wanderer*, to the advice of his friends.

His veracity was questioned but with little reason; his accounts, tho' not indeed always the same, were generally consistent. When he loved any man, he suppress'd all his faults, and when he had been offended by him, concealed all his virtues: but his characters were generally true, so far as he proceeded; tho' it cannot be denied that his partiality might have sometimes the effect of falsehood.

In cases indifferent he was zealous for virtue, truth and justice; he knew very well the necessity of goodness to the present and future happiness of mankind; nor is there perhaps any writer, who has less endeavoured to please by flattering the appetites or perverting the judgment.

As an author, therefore, and he now ceases to influence mankind in any other character, if one piece which he had resolved to suppress be excepted, he has very little to fear from the strictest moral or religious censure. And though he may not be altogether secure against the objections of the critic, it must however be acknowledged, that his works are the productions of a genius truly poetical; and, what many writers who have been more lavishly applauded cannot boast, that they have an original air, which has no resemblance to any foregoing writer; that the versification and sentiments have a cast peculiar to themselves, which no man can imitate with success, because what was nature in Savage would in another be affectation. It must be confessed that his descriptions are striking, his images animated, his fictions justly imagined, and his allegories artfully persued; that his diction is elevated, though sometimes forced, and his numbers sonorous and majestick, though frequently sluggish and encumbered. Of his stile the general fault is harshness, and its general excellence is dignity; of his sentiments the prevailing beauty is sublimity, and uniformity the prevailing defect.

For his life, or for his writings, none who candidly consider his fortune, will think an apology either necessary or difficult. If he was not always sufficiently instructed in his subject, his knowledge was at least greater than could have been attained by others in the same state. If his works were sometimes unfinished, accuracy cannot reasonably be exacted from a man oppressed with want, which he has no hope of relieving but by a speedy publication. The insolence and resentment of which he is accused, were not easily to be avoided by a great mind, irritated by perpetual hardships and constrained hourly to return the spurns of contempt, and repress the insolence of prosperity; and vanity may surely readily be pardoned in him, to whom life afforded no other comforts than barren praises, and the consciousness of deserving them.

Those are no proper judges of his conduct who have slumber'd away their time on the down of affluence, nor will any wise man presume to say, "Had I been in Savage's condition, I should have lived, or written, better than Savage."

This relation will not be wholly without its use, if those, who languish under any part of his sufferings, shall be enabled to fortify their patience by reflecting that they feel only those afflictions from which the abilities of Savage did not exempt him; or those, who in confidence of superior capacities or attainments disregard the common maxims of life, shall be reminded that nothing will supply the want of prudence, and that negligence and irregularity, long continued, will make knowledge useless, wit ridiculous, and genius contemptible.

# NOTES

(*between pp. 5-12*)

1. This year was made remarkable by the dissolution of a marriage solemnized in the face of the Church. *Salmon's Review.*
The following protest is registered in the books of the House of Lords.
*Dissentient.*
Because we conceive that this is the first Bill of that nature that hath passed, where there was not a divorce first obtained in the Spiritual Court; which we look upon as an ill precedent, and may be of dangerous consequence in the future.
HALIFAX. ROCHESTER.
[All notes to the *Life of Savage* are Johnson's unless otherwise indicated.]
2. Savage's Preface to his Miscellany.
3. Preface to Savage's Miscellanies.

4. *Plain Dealer*. See Appendix [to the *Plain Dealer*].
5. Jacob's Lives of Dramatic Poets.
6. This play was printed first in 8vo, and afterwards in 12mo, the fifth edition.
7. *Plain Dealer*.
8. As it is a loss to mankind, when any good action is forgotten, I shall insert another instance of Mr. Wilk's generosity, very little known. Mr. Smith, a gentleman educated at Dublin, being hindered by an impediment in his pronunciation from engaging in Orders, for which his friends designed him, left his own country, and came to London in quest of employment, but found his solicitations fruitless and his necessities every day more pressing. In this distress he wrote a tragedy, and offered it to the players, by whom it was rejected. Thus were his last hopes defeated, and he had no other prospect than of the most deplorable poverty. But Mr. Wilks thought his performance, though not perfect, at least worthy of some reward, and therefore offered him a Benefit. This favour he improved with so much diligence, that the house afforded him a considerable sum, with which he went to Leyden, applied himself to the study of physic, and prosecuted his design with so much diligence and success, that when Dr. Boerhaave was desired by the Czarina to recommend proper persons to introduce into Russia the practice and study of physic, Dr. Smith was one of those whom he selected. He had a considerable pension settled on him at his arrival, and is now one of the chief physicians at the Russian Court.
9. This I write upon the credit of the author of his Life, which was published 1727.

*(between pp. 14-17)*

1. In 1724.
2. He inscribed to him a short poem, called *The Friend*, printed in his Miscellanies, in which he addresses him with the utmost ardour of affection.

> O lov'd, Hillarius! thou by Heav'n design'd
> To charm, to mend, and to instruct mankind:
> To whom my hopes, fears, joys, and sorrows tend,
> Thou brother, father, nearer yet—thou friend——
> —Kind are my wrongs, I thence thy friendship own,
> What state could bless, were I to thee unknown?
> ——While shun'd, obscur'd, or thwarted and expos'd,
> By friends abandon'd, and by foes enclos'd.
> Thy guardian counsel softens ev'ry care,
> To ease sooths anguish, and to hope, despair.

3. To. A. Hill, Esq., with the *Tragedy of Sir Thomas Overbury*.

> As the soul strip'd of mortal clay
>     Shews all divinely fair,
> And boundless roves the Milky Way,
>     And views sweet prospects there.
> This hero clog'd with drossy lines
>     By thee new vigour tries;
> As thy correcting hand refines
>     Bright scenes around him rise.
> Thy touch brings the wish'd stone to pass,
>     So sought, so long foretold;

> It turns polluted lead and brass
>    At once to purest gold.

4.    In a full world our author lives alone,
>    Unhappy, and by consequence unknown;
>    Yet amidst sorrow he disdains complaint,
>    Nor languid in the race of life grows faint:
>    He swims, unyielding, against fortune's stream,
>    Nor to his private sufferings stoops his theme.

5. To —— Tryste, Esq; of Herefordshire.

6. The *Plain Dealer* was a periodical paper written by Mr. Hill and Mr. Bond, whom Mr. Savage called the two contending powers of light and darkness. They wrote by turns each six essays, and the character of the work was observed regularly to rise in Mr. Hill's weeks, and fall in Mr. Bond's.

7.    Hopeless, abandon'd, aimless, and oppress'd,
>    Lost to delight, and, ev'ry way, distress'd;
>    Cross his cold bed, in wild disorder, thrown,
>    Thus sigh'd Alexis, friendless, and alone——

>    Why do I breathe?——What joy can being give?
>    When she, who gave me life, forgets I live!
>    Feels not these wintry blasts;——nor heeds my smart;
>    But shuts me from the shelter of her heart!
>    Saw me expos'd to want! to shame! to scorn!
>    To ills!——which make it *misery*, to be *born!*
>    Cast me, regardless, on the world's bleak wild;
>    And bade me be a wretch, while yet a child!

>    Where can he hope for pity, peace, or rest,
>    Who moves no softness in a mother's breast?
>    Custom, law, reason, *all!* my cause forsake,
>    And Nature *sleeps,* to keep my woes *awake!*
>    Crimes, which the *cruel* scarce believe can be,
>    The *kind* are guilty of, to ruin *me.*
>    Ev'n she, who bore me, blasts me with her hate,
>    And, *meant* my *fortune, makes* herself my *fate.*

>    Yet has this sweet neglecter of my woes,
>    The softest, tend'rest breast, that *pity* knows!
>    Her eyes shed mercy, wheresoe'er they shine;
>    And her soul *melts* at ev'ry woe——but *mine.*
>    Sure then! some secret fate, for guilt unwill'd,
>    Some sentence pre-ordain'd to be fulfill'd!
>    Plung'd me, thus deep, in sorrow's searching flood;
>    And wash'd me from the mem'ry of her blood.

>    But, Oh! whatever cause has mov'd her hate,
>    Let me but sigh, in silence, at my fate;
>    The God, *within,* perhaps may touch her breast;
>    And, when she *pities,* who can be distress'd?

8. The names of those who so generously contributed to his relief, having been mentioned in a former account, ought not to be omitted here. They were the Dutchess of Cleveland, Lady Cheyney, Lady Castlemain, Lady Gower, Lady Lechmere, the Dutchess Dowager, and Dutchess of Rutland. Lady Strafford, the Countess Dowager of Warwick, Mrs.

Mary Floyer, Mrs. Sofuel Noel, Duke of Rutland, Lord Gainsborough, Lord Milsington, Mr. John Savage.

9. This Preface is as follows:

> *Crudelis mater magis, an puer improbus ille?*
> *Improbus ille puer, crudelis tu quoque mater.* Virg.

My readers, I am afraid, when they observe Richard Savage join'd so close, and so constantly, to *son of the late Earl Rivers,* will impute to a ridiculous vanity, what is the effect of an unhappy necessity, which my hard fortune has thrown me under——I am to be pardoned for adhering a little tenaciously to my father, because my mother will allow me to be no-body; and has almost reduced me, among heavier afflictions, to that uncommon kind of want, which the Indians of America complained of at our first settling among them; when they came to beg *names* of the English, because (said they) we are poor men of ourselves, and have none we can lay claim to.

The good nature of those, to whom I have not the honour to be known, would forgive me the ludicrous turn of this beginning, if they knew but how little reason I have to be merry——It was my misfortune to be son of the above-mentioned Earl, by the late Countess of Macclesfield, (now widow of Colonel Henry Bret,) whose divorce, on occasion of the amour which I was a consequence of, has left something on record, which I take to be very remarkable; and it is this: Certain of our great judges, in their *temporal* decisions, act with a *spiritual* regard to *Levitical divinity;* and in particular to the Ten Commandments: Two of which seem in my case, to have visibly influenced their opinions——*Thou shalt not commit adultery,* pointed fullest on my mother: But, as to *The Lord's visiting the sins of the fathers upon the children,* it was considered as what could regard *me* only: And for that reason, I suppose, it had been inconsistent with the rules of sanctity, to assign provision out of my mother's return'd estate, for support of an infant sinner.

Thus, while *legally* the son of one Earl, and *naturally* of another, I am, *nominally,* no-body's son at all: For the lady having given me *too much father,* thought it but an equivalent deduction, to leave me *no mother,* by way of balance——So I am sported into the world, a kind of shuttle-cock, between law and nature——If law had not beaten me back, by the stroke of an Act, on purpose, I had not been *above wit,* by the privilege of a man of quality: Nay, I might have preserved into the bargain, the lives of Duke Hamilton and Lord Mohun, whose dispute arose from the estate of that Earl of Macclesfield, whom (but for the mentioned Act) I must have *called father*——And, if nature had not struck me off, with a stranger blow than law did, the other Earl, who was most *emphatically* my father, could never have been told, I was *dead,* when he was about to enable me, by his *will,* to have lived to some purpose. An unaccountable severity of a mother! whom I was then not old enough to have deserved it from: And by which I am a single unhappy instance, among that nobleman's natural children; and thrown, friendless on the world, without means of supporting *myself;* and without authority to apply to those, whose duty I know it is to support me.

Thus however ill qualified I am to *live by my wits,* I have the best plea in the world for attempting it; since it is too apparent, that I was *born to it*——Having wearied my judgment with fruitless endeavours to be happy, I gave the reins to my fancy, that I might learn, at least, to be *easy.*

But I cease a while to speak of *myself*, that I may say something of my Miscellany——I was furnished, by the verses of my friends, with *wit* enough to deserve a subscription; but I wanted another much more profitable quality, which should have emboldened me to solicite it (another of my wants, that, I hope, may be imputed to my mother!) I had met with little encouragement, but for the endeavours of some few gentlemen, in my behalf, who were generous enough to consider my ill fortune, as a merit that intitled me to their notice.

Among these I am particularly indebted to the author of the *Plain Dealers*, who was pleased, in two of his papers (which I intreat his pardon, for reprinting before my Miscellany) to point out my unhappy story to the world, with so touching a humanity, and so good an effect, that many persons of quality, of all ranks, and of both sexes, distinguished themselves with the promptness he had hinted to the noble minded; and not staying till they were applied to, sent me the honour of their subscriptions, in the most liberal and handsom manner, for encouragement of my undertaking.

I ought here to acknowledge several favours from Mr. Hill, whose writings are a shining ornament of this Miscellany: but I wave detaining my readers, and beg leave to refer them to a copy of verses called the *Friend,* which I have taken the liberty to address to that gentleman.

To return to the lady, my mother——Had the celebrated Mr. Locke been acquainted with her example, it had certainly appeared in his *chapter* against innate practical principles; because it would have completed his instances of enormities: Some of which, though not exactly in the order that he mentions them, are as follow——*Have there not been* (says he) *whole nations, and those of the most civilized people, amongst whom, the exposing their children, to perish by want or wild beasts, has been a practice as little condemned or scrupled as the begetting them?* Were I inclinable to be serious, I could easily prove that I have not been more gently dealt with by Mrs. Bret; but if this is any way foreign to my case, I shall find a nearer example in the whimsical one that ensues.

*It is familiar* (says the afore-cited author) *among the Mengrelians, a people professing Christianity, to bury their children alive without scruple*—— There are indeed sundry sects of Christians, and I have often wondered which could be my *mamma's,* but now I find she piously professes and practises Christianity after the manner of the Mengrelians; she industriously obscured me, when my fortune depended on my being known, and, in that sense, she may be said to have buried me alive; and sure, like a Mengrelian, she must have committed the action without scruple; for she is a woman of spirit, and can see the consequence without remorse——*The Caribbees* (continues my author) *were wont to castrate their children in order to fat and eat them*——Here indeed I can draw no parallel; for to speak justice of the lady, she never contributed ought to have me pampered, but always promoted my being starved: Nor did she, even in my infancy, betray fondness enough to be suspected of a design to devour me; but, on the contrary, not enduring me ever to approach her, offered a bribe to have me shipped off, in an odd manner, to one of the plantations—When I was about fifteen her affection began to awake, and had I but known my interest, I had been handsomly provided for. In short I was solicited to be bound apprentice to a very honest and reputable occupation—a *shoemaker;* an offer which I undutifully rejected. I was, in fine, unwilling to understand her in a literal sense, and hoped, that, like the prophets of old, she might have hinted her mind in a kind of parable, or proverbial way of speaking; as thus—That one time or other I might, on due application, have the honour of *taking the length of her foot.*

Mr. Locke mentions another set of people that dispatch their children, if a pretended astrologer declares them to have unhappy stars——Perhaps my *mamma* has procured some *cunning man* to calculate my nativity; or having had some ominous dream, which preceded my birth, the dire event may have appeared to her in the dark and dreary bottom of a China cup, where coffee-stains are often consulted for prophecies, and held as infallible as were the leaves of the ancient sybils——To be partly serious: I am rather willing to wrong her judgment, by suspecting it to be tainted a little with the tenets of superstition, than suppose she can be mistress of a seared conscience, and act on no principle at all.

*(between pp. 17-29)*

1. This the following extract from it will prove.

——"Since our country has been honour'd with the glory of your wit, as elevated and immortal as your soul, it no longer remains a doubt whether your sex have strength of mind in proportion to their sweetness. There is something in your verses as distinguished as your air——They are as strong as truth, as deep as reason, as clear as innocence, and as smooth as beauty ——They contain a nameless and peculiar mixture of force and grace, which is at once so movingly serene, and so majestically lovely, that it is too amiable to appear any where but in your eyes, and in your writings.

"As fortune is not more my enemy than I am the enemy of flattery, I know not how I can forbear this application to your Ladyship, because there is scarce a possibility that I should say more than I believe, when I am speaking of your excellence."——

2. Mr. Savage's Life.

3. Written by Mr. Beckingham and another gentleman.

4. The satire from which the following lines are extracted was called by Mr. Savage, *An Epistle on Authors:* It was never printed intire, but several fragments were inserted by him in the *Magazine,* after his retirement into the country.

> Were all like *Yorke* of delicate address,
> Strength to discern, and sweetness to express;
> Learn'd, just, polite, born ev'ry heart to gain;
> Like Cummins mild, like[a] Fortescue humane;
> All eloquent of truth, divinely known;
> So deep, so clear, all science is his own.
>    How far unlike such worthies, once a drudge,
> From flound'ring in low causes, rose a *judge.*
> Form'd to make pleaders laugh, his *nonsense* thunders,
> And, on low juries, breathes contagious blunders.
> His brothers blush, because no blush he knows,
> Nor e'er[b] *one uncorrupted finger shows.*
> See, drunk with power, the *Circuit Lord* exprest!
> Full, in his eye, his betters stand confest;

---

[a] The Hon. William Fortescue, Esq; now Master of the Rolls.
[b] When Page one uncorrupted finger shows.

                                              *D. of Wharton.*

Whose wealth, birth, virtue, from a tongue so loose,
'Scape not provincial, vile, buffoon abuse.
Still to what circuit is assign'd his name,
There, swift before him, flies the warner Fame.
Contest stops short, consent yields every cause
To cost, delay, endures them and withdraws.
But how 'scape Pris'ners? To their trial chain'd,
All, all shall stand condemn'd, who stand arraign'd.
Dire Guilt, which else would detestation cause,
Pre-judg'd with insult, wond'rous pity draws.
But 'scapes ev'n Innocence his harsh harangue?
Alas——ev'n Innocence itself must hang;
Must hang to please him, when of spleen possest:
Must hang to bring forth an abortive jest.
     Why liv'd he not ere Star-Chambers had fail'd,
When fine, tax, censure, all, but law, prevail'd;
Or law, subservient to some murd'rous will,
Became a precedent to murder still?
Yet ev'n when patriots did for traytors bleed,
Was e'er the jobb to such a slave decreed;
Whose savage mind wants sophist art to draw,
O'er murder'd virtue, specious veils of law?

          *Gentleman's Magazine*, Sept. 1741.

5. In one of his letters he stiles it, a *fatal quarrel, but too well known.*
6.     Is chance a guilt, that my disast'rous heart,
    For mischief never meant, must ever smart?
    Can self-defence be sin?—Ah! plead no more;
    What though no purpos'd malice stain'd thee o'er;
    Had heav'n befriended thy unhappy side,
    Thou hadst not been provok'd, or then hadst dy'd.
        Far be the guilt of home-shed blood from all
    On whom, unsought, embroiling dangers fall.
    Still the pale Dead revives and lives to me,
    To me, through pity's eye, condemn'd to see.
    Remembrance veils his rage, but swells his fate,
    Griev'd I forgive, and am grown cool too late.
    Young and unthoughtful then, who knows one day
    What rip'ning virtues might have made their way?
    He might perhaps his country's friend have prov'd,
    Been gen'rous, happy, candid and belov'd;
    He might have sav'd some worth now doom'd to fall,
    And I perchance in him have *murder'd* all.

                      *Bastard.*

7. The first edition reads "If the," in error. Eds.
8. *To the right honourable the Earl of Middlesex.*
   My Lord,
   That elegant taste in poetry, which is hereditary to your Lordship, together with that particular regard, with which you honour the author to
whom these papers relate, make me imagine this collection will not be unpleasing to you. And I may presume to say, the pieces themselves are such
as are not unworthy your Lordship's patronage, my own part in it excepted.
I speak only of the *Author to be let,* having no title to any other, not even

the small ones out of the journals. May I be permitted to declare (to the end I may seem not quite so unworthy of your Lordship's favour, as some writers of my *age* and circumstances) that I never was concerned in any journals. I ever thought the exorbitant liberty, which most of those papers take with their superiors, unjustifiable in any rank of men; but detestable in such who do it merely for hire, and without even the bad excuse of *passion* and *resentment*. On the contrary, being once inclined, upon some advantageous proposals, to enter into a *paper of another kind, I immediately desisted, on finding admitted into it (though as the publisher told me purely by an accident) two or three lines reflecting on a *great minister*. Were my life ever so unhappy, it shall not be stained with a conduct, which my birth at least (though neither my *education* nor *good fortune*) should set me above, much less with any ingratitude to that noble person, to whose intercession (next to his Majesty's goodness) I owe in a great measure that *life itself*.

    ——*Nec si miserum Fortuna Sinonem*
    *Finxit, vanum etiam mendacemque improba finget.*

I believe your Lordship will pardon this digression, or any other which keeps me from the stile, you so much hate, of dedication.

I will not pretend to display those rising virtues in your Lordship, which the next age will certainly know without my help, but rather relate (what else it will as certainly be ignorant of) the history of these papers, and the occasion which produced the *War of the Dunces,* (for so it has been commonly called) which begun in the year 1727, and ended in 1730.

When Dr. Swift and Mr. Pope thought it proper, for reasons specified in the Preface to their Miscellanies, to publish such little pieces of theirs as had casually got abroad, there was added to them the treatise of the *Bathos, or the Art of Sinking in Poetry*. It happened that in one chapter of this piece, the several species of bad poets were ranged in classes, to which were prefixed almost all the letters of the alphabet (the greatest part of them at random) but such was the number of poets eminent in *that art,* that some one or other took every letter to himself: All fell into so violent a fury, that for half a year, or more, the common news-papers (in most of which they had some property, as being *hired writers*) were filled with the most abusive falshoods and scurrilities they could possibly devise. A liberty no way to be wondered at in those people, and in those papers, that, for many years during the uncontrolled liberty of the press, had aspersed almost all the great *characters* of the age; and this with impunity, their own *persons* and *names* being utterly secret and obscure.

This gave Mr. Pope the thought, that he had now some opportunity of doing good, by detecting and dragging into light these common enemies of mankind; since to *invalidate* this universal slander, it sufficed to shew what contemptible men were the authors of it. He was not without hopes, that by manifesting the dulness of those who had only malice to recommend them, either the booksellers would not find their account in employing them, or the men themselves when discovered, want courage to proceed in so unlawful an occupation. This it was that gave birth to the *Dunciad,* and he thought it an happiness, that by the late flood of slander on himself, he had acquired such a peculiar right over their *names* as was necessary to this design.

---

    * The paper here meant, was probably the *Grubstreet-Journal,* which Mr. Savage was once invited to undertake, but which he declined, whether for the reason here mentioned is not certain.

On the 12th of March 1729, at St. James's, that poem was presented to the *King* and *Queen* (who had before been pleased to read it) by the right honourable Sir Robert Walpole: And some days after the whole impression was taken and dispersed by several noblemen and persons of the first distinction.

It is certainly a true observation, that no people are so impatient of censure as those who are the greatest slanderers: Which was wonderfully exemplified on this occasion. On the day the book was first vended, a crowd of authors besieged the shop; entreaties, advices, threats of law, and battery, nay cries of treason were all employed to hinder the coming out of the *Dunciad:* On the other side the booksellers and hawkers made as great efforts to procure it: What could a few poor authors do against so great a majority as the publick? There was no stopping a torrent with a finger, so out it came.

Many ludicrous circumstances attended it: The dunces (for by this name they were called) held weekly clubs, to consult of hostilities against the author; one wrote a letter to a great Minister, assuring him Mr. Pope was the greatest enemy the Government had; and another brought his image in clay, to execute him in effigy; with which sad sort of satisfactions the gentlemen were a little comforted.

Some false editions of the book having an owl in their frontispiece, the true one, to distinguish it, fixed in its stead an ass laden with authors. Then another surreptitious one being printed with the same ass, the new edition in octavo returned for distinction to the owl again. Hence arose a great contest of booksellers against booksellers, and advertisements against advertisements; some recommending the *edition of the owl,* and others the *edition of the ass;* by which names they came to be distinguished, to the great honour also of the gentlemen of the *Dunciad.*

Your Lordship will not think these particulars altogether unentertaining; nor are they impertinent, since they clear some passages in the following collection. The whole cannot but be of some use, to shew the *different spirit* with which good and bad authors have ever *acted,* as well as *written;* and to evince a truth, a greater than which was never advanced, that——

> *Each bad author is as bad a friend.*

However, the imperfection of this collection cannot but be owned, as long as it wants that poem with which you, my lord, have honoured the author of the *Dunciad;* but which I durst not presume to add in your absence. As it is, may it please your Lordship to accept of it, as a distant testimony, with what respect and zeal I am,

My Lord,

your most obedient

and devoted servant,

R. SAVAGE.

9. This epigram was, I believe, never published.

> Should Dennis publish you had stabb'd your brother,
> Lampoon'd your Monarch, or debauch'd your mother;
> Say what revenge on Dennis can be had,
> Too dull for laughter, for reply too mad?
> On one so poor you cannot take the law,
> On one so old your sword you scorn to draw:

Uncag'd, then let the harmless monster rage,
Secure in dulness, madness, want, and age.

*(between pp. 30-35)*

1. 1729.
2. False pride! what vices on our conduct steal
   From the world's eye one frailty to conceal.
   Ye cruel mothers—soft! these words command—
   So near should *cruelty* and *mother* stand?
   Can the fond goat, or tender fleecy dam
   Howl like the wolf to tear the kid or lamb?
   Yes, there are mothers——there I fear'd his aim,
   And conscious trembl'd at the coming name:
   Then with a sigh his issuing words oppos'd,
   Straight with a falling tear his speech he clos'd;
   That tenderness which ties of blood deny,
   Nature repaid me from a stranger's eye.
   Pale grow my cheeks——
3. Of his descriptions this specimen may be offered.

   Now, from yon range of rocks, strong rays rebound,
   Doubling the day on flow'ry plains around:
   *Kingcups* beneath far-striking colours glance,
   Bright as th' etherial glows the green expanse.
   Gems of the field!——The topez charms the sight,
   Like these, effulging yellow streams of light.
       From the same rocks fall rills with soften'd force,
   Meet in yon mead, and well a river's source.
   Through her clear channel shine her finny shoals,
   O'er sands like gold the liquid crystal rolls.
   Dim'd in yon coarser moor her charms decay,
   And shape through rustling reeds a ruffled way.
   Near willows short and bushy shadows throw:
   Now lost she seems through nether tracts to flow;
   Yet at yon point winds out in silver state,
   Like virtue from a labyrinth of fate.
   In length'ning rows prone from the mountains run
   The flocks:—Their fleeces glist'ning in the sun;
   Her streams they seek, and, 'twixt her neighb'ring trees,
   Recline in various attitudes of ease:
   Where the herds sip, the little scaly fry,
   Swift from the shore, in scatt'ring myriads fly.
       Each liv'ried cloud, that round th' horizon glows,
   Shifts in odd scenes, like earth from whence it rose.
   The bee hums wanton in yon jess'mine bower,
   And circling settles, and despoils the flower.
   Melodious there the plumy songsters meet,
   And call charm'd Echo from her arch'd retreat.
   Neat, polish'd mansions rise in prospect gay;
   Time-batter'd tow'rs frown awful in decay:
   The sun plays glitt'ring on the rocks and spires,
   And the lawn lightens with reflected fires.
4. Who in the second canto is thus introduced;

Now grief and rage, by gath'ring sighs supprest,
Swell my full heart, and heave my lab'ring breast!
With struggling starts each vital string they strain,
And strike the tott'ring fabric of my brain!
O'er my sunk spirits frowns a vap'ry scene,
Woe's dark retreat! the madding maze of Spleen!
A deep, damp gloom o'erspreads the murky cell;
Here pining Thoughts, and secret Terrors dwell!
Here learn the great unreal wants to feign!
Unpleasing truths here mortify the vain!
Here Learning, blinded first, and then beguil'd,
Looks dark as Ignorance, as Frenzy wild!
Here first Credulity on Reason won!
And here *false* Zeal mysterious rants begun!
Here Love impearls each moment with a tear,
And Superstition owes to Spleen her fear!
——Here the lone hour, a blank of life, displays,
Till now bad thoughts a fiend more active raise;
A fiend in evil moments ever nigh!
Death in her hand, and frenzy in her eye!
Her eye all red, and sunk! A robe she wore,
With life's calamities embroider'd o'er.
A mirror in one hand collective shows,
Varied, and multiplied, that group of woes.
This endless foe to gen'rous toil and pain
Lolls on a couch for ease; but lolls in vain.
She muses o'er her woe-embroider'd vest,
And self-abhorrence heightens in her breast.
To shun her care, the force of sleep she tries,
Still wakes her mind, though slumbers doze her eyes:
She dreams, starts, rises, stalks from place to place,
With restless, thoughtful, interrupted pace:
Now eyes the sun, and curses ev'ry ray,
Now the green ground, where colour fades away.
Dim spectres dance! Again her eyes she rears;
Then from the blood-shot ball wipes purpled tears;
She presses hard her brow, with mischief fraught,
Her brow half bursts with agony of thought!
From me (she cries) pale wretch thy comfort claim,
Born of despair, and Suicide my name!

5. These three rebels are thus described.

Of these were three by different motives fir'd,
Ambition one, and one revenge inspir'd.
The third, O mammon, was thy meaner slave;
Thou idol seldom of the great and brave.
    Florio, whose life was one continued feast,
His wealth diminish'd, and his debts encreas'd,
Vain pomp and equipage his low desires,
Who ne'er to intellectual bliss aspires;
He, to repair by vice what vice has broke,
Durst with bold treasons judgment's road provoke.
His strength of mind, by lux'ry half dissolv'd,

Ill brooks the woe where deep he stands involv'd.
——His genius flies; reflects he now on prayer?
Alas! bad spirits turn those thoughts to air.
What shall he next? What strait relinquish breath,
To bar a public, just and shameful death?
Rash, horrid thought! yet now afraid to live,
Murd'rous he strikes; may Heav'n the deed forgive!
——Why had he thus false spirit to rebel?
And why not fortitude to suffer well?
    ——Where no kind lips the hallow'd dirge resound,
Far from the compass of yon sacred ground;
Full in the center of three meeting ways,
Stak'd through he lies——Warn'd let the wicked gaze!
    Near yonder fane where mis'ry sleeps in peace,
Whose spire fast-lessens, as these shades encrease,
Left to the north, whence oft brew'd tempests roll,
Tempests, dire emblems, Cosmo, of thy soul!
There! mark that Cosmo much for guile renown'd!
His grave by unbid plants of poison crown'd.
When out of pow'r, through him the public good,
So strong his factious tribe, suspended stood.
In power, vindictive actions were his aim,
And patriots perish'd by th' ungenerous flame.
If the best cause he in the senate chose,
Ev'n right in him from some wrong motive rose.
The bad he loath'd, and would the weak despise!
Yet courted for dark ends, and shun'd the wise.
When ill his purpose, eloquent his strain,
His malice had a look and voice humane:
His smile the signal of some vile intent,
A private ponyard, or empoison'd scent;
Proud, yet to popular applause a slave;
No friend he honour'd, and no foe forgave.
His boons unfrequent, or unjust to need,
The hire of guilt, of infamy the meed;
But if they chanc'd on learned worth to fall,
Bounty in him was ostentation all.
No true benevolence his thought sublimes,
His noblest actions are illustrious crimes.
    ——Cosmo, as death draws nigh, no more conceals
That storm of passions, which his nature feels;
He feels much fear, more anger, and most pride;
But pride and anger make all fear subside.
Dauntless he meets at length untimely fate;
A desp'rate spirit! rather fierce, than great.
Darking he glides along the dreary coast,
A sullen, wand'ring, self-tormenting ghost.
    ——Where veiny marble dignifies the ground,
With emblem fair in sculpture rising round,
Just where a crossing, length'ning isle we find,
Full east; whence God returns to judge mankind.
Once lov'd Horatio sleeps, a mind elate!

Lamented shade, ambition was thy fate!
Ev'n angels, wond'ring, oft his worth survey'd;
*Behold a man like one of us!* they said.
Straight heard the Furies, and with envy glar'd,
And to precipitate his fall prepar'd:
First Av'rice came. In vain self-love she press'd;
The poor he pitied still, and still redress'd:
Learning was his, and knowledge to commend,
Of arts a patron, and of want a friend.
Next came Revenge: But her essay, how vain?
Nor hate nor envy in his heart remain:
No previous malice could his mind engage,
Malice the mother of vindictive rage.
No——from his life his foes might learn to live;
He held it still a triumph to forgive.
At length Ambition urg'd his country's weal,
Assuming the fair look of public Zeal;
Still in his breast so gen'rous glow'd the flame,
The vice, when there, a virtue half became.
His pitying eye saw millions in distress,
He deem'd it God-like to have pow'r to bless;
Thus, when unguarded, treason stain'd him o'er,
And virtue and content were then no more.
　　　But when to death by vig'rous justice doom'd,
His genuine spirit saint-like state resum'd.
Oft from soft penitence distill'd a tear;
Oft hope in heav'nly mercy lighten'd fear;
Oft would a drop from struggling nature fall,
And then a smile of patience brighten all.

Canto V.

6.　Fain would my verse, Tyrconnel, boast thy name,
Brownlow at once my subject, and my fame:
O could that spirit which thy bosom warms,
Whose strength surprises, and whose goodness charms.
Thy various worth—could that inspire my lays,
Envy should smile, and censure learn to praise:
Yet though unequal to a soul like thine,
A gen'rous soul approaching to divine;
While bless'd beneath such patronage I write,
Great my attempt, though hazardous my flight.

7. His expression in one of his letters, was, that Lord T——l *had involved his estate, and therefore poorly sought an occasion to quarrel with him.*

8. Part of this poem had the honour of your Lordship's perusal when in manuscript, and it was no small pride to me when it met with approbation. —My intention is to embrace this opportunity of throwing out sentiments that relate to your Lordship's goodness and generosity, which give me leave to say I have lately experienced.

That *I live*, my Lord, is a proof, that dependance upon your Lordship and the present Ministry is an assurance of success. I am persuaded distress in many other instances affects your soul with a compassion that always shews itself in a manner most humane and active, that to forgive injuries, and confer benefits, is your delight, and that to deserve your friendship is

to deserve the countenance of the best of men. To be admitted to the honour
of your Lordship's conversation (permit me to speak but justice) is to be
elegantly introduced into the most instructive as well as entertaining parts
of literature: It is to be furnished with the finest observations upon human
nature, and to receive from the most unassuming, sweet, and winning candour, the worthiest and most polite maxims—such as are always inforced
by the actions of your own life.—If my future morals and writings should
gain any approbation from men of parts and probity, I must acknowledge all
to be the product of your Lordship's goodness.—

9. Of the numbers and sentiments the following lines will afford a specimen.

> Where Thames with pride beholds Augusta's charms,
> And either India pours into her arms,—
> High thron'd appears the laughter-loving dame—
> Goddess of Mirth——
>     O'er the gay world the sweet inspirer reigns,
> Spleen flies, and elegance her pomp sustains;
> Thee, goddess, thee the fair and young obey,
> Wealth, wit, and music, all confess thy sway.—
>     The goddess summons each illustrious name,
> Bids the gay talk, and forms th' amusive game,
> She whose fair throne is fix'd in human souls,
> From joy to joy her eye delighted rolls:
> But where, she cry'd, is she, my fav'rite she,
> Of all my race the dearest far to me—
> Whose life's the source of each refin'd delight,
> She said, but no Belinda glads her sight—
> In kind low murmurs all the loss deplore,
> Belinda droops, and pleasure is no more.
>     The goddess silent paus'd in museful air,
> But Mirth, like Virtue, cannot long despair,—
> Strait wafted on the tepid breeze she flies,
> Where Bath's ascending turrets meet her eyes,
> She flies, her elder sister Health to find,
> She finds her on a mountain's brow reclin'd,
> Around her birds in earliest consort sing,
> Her cheek the semblance of the kindling spring.—
> Loose to the wind her verdant vestments flow,
> Her limbs yet recent from the springs below:
> Thereof she bathes, then peaceful sits secure,
> Where ev'ry breath is fragrant, fresh and pure.—
>     Hail, sister, hail, the kindred goddess cries,
> No common suppliant stands before your eyes—
> Strength, vigour, wit, depriv'd of thee decline,
> Each finer sense that forms delight is thine—
> Bright suns by thee diffuse a brighter blaze,
> And the fresh green a fresher green displays—
> Such thy vast pow'r—the Deity replies,
> Mirth never asks a boon which Health denies;
> Our mingled gifts transcend imperial wealth,
> Health strengthens Mirth, and Mirth inspirits Health.

*(between pp. 40-76)*

1.    In gayer hours, when high my fancy ran,

The muse, exulting, thus her lay began.
    Blest be the Bastard's birth! thro' wondrous ways,
He shines eccentrick like a comet's blaze.
No sickly fruit of faint compliance he;
He! stampt in nature's mint with extasy!
He lives to build, not boast, a gen'rous race:
No tenth transmitter of a foolish face.
His daring hope, no sire's example bounds;
His first-born lights no prejudice confounds.
He, kindling, from within, requires no flame,
He glories, in a bastard's glowing name.
    ——Loos'd to the world's wide range——enjoin'd no aim;
Prescrib'd no duty, and assign'd no name:
Nature's unbounded son he stands alone,
His heart unbiass'd, and his mind his own.
    ——O mother, yet no mother!——'tis to you,
My thanks for such distinguish'd claims are due.
    ——What had I lost, if conjugally kind,
By nature hating, yet by vows confin'd,
——You had *faint-drawn* me with a form alone,
A lawful lump of life by force your own!
    ——I had been born your dull domestick heir;
Load of your life and motive of your care;
Perhaps been poorly rich, and meanly great;
The slave of pomp, a cypher in the state;
Lordly neglectful of a worth unknown,
And slumb'ring in a *seat*, by *chance* my own.
    ——Thus unprophetic, lately uninspir'd,
I sung; gay, flatt'ring hope my fancy fir'd;
Inly secure, thro' conscious scorn of ill;
Nor taught by wisdom how to balance will.
    ——But now expos'd and shrinking from distress,
I fly to shelter while the tempests press.

After the mention of the death of Sinclair, he goes on thus:

    ——Where. shall my hope find rest?——No mother's care
Shielded my infant innocence with pray'r:
No father's guardian hand my youth maintain'd,
Call'd forth my virtues, and from vice restrain'd.

2. A short satire was likewise published in the same paper, in which were
the following lines:

For cruel murder doom'd to hempen death,
Savage, by royal grace, prolong'd his breath.
Well might you think, he spent his *future* years
In prayer, and fasting and repentant tears.
——But, O vain hope!——the truly Savage cries,
"Priests, and their slavish doctrines, I despise.
Shall I————
Who, by free thinking to free action fir'd,
In midnight brawls a deathless name acquir'd,
Now stoop to *learn* of *ecclesiastic men?*——

——No arm'd with rhime, at priests I'll take my aim,
Though prudence bids me murder but their fame."
                                            *Weekly Miscellany.*

An answer was published in the *Gentleman's Magazine,* written by an unknown hand, from which the following lines are selected:

Transform'd by thoughtless rage, and midnight wine,
From malice free, and push'd without *design;*
In equal brawl if Savage lung'd a thrust,
And brought the youth a victim to the dust:
So strong the hand of accident appears,
The royal hand from guilt and vengeance clears.
    Instead of wasting *"all thy future years,*
     *Savage in pray'r and vain repentant tears;"*
Exert thy pen to mend a vicious age,
To curb the priest, and sink his High-Church rage;
To shew what frauds the holy vestments hide,
The nests of av'rice, lust, and pedant pride.
Then change the scene, let merit brightly shine,
And round the patriot twist the wreath divine;
The heav'nly guide deliver down to fame;
In well-tun'd lays transmit a Foster's name.
Touch every passion with harmonious art,
Exalt the genius, and correct the heart.
Thus future times shall royal grace extol;
Thus polish'd lines thy present fame enrol.
    ——But grant————
——Maliciously that Savage plung'd the *steel,*
And made the youth its shining vengeance feel;
My soul abhors the act, the man detests,
But more the bigotry in priestly breasts.
                              *Gentleman's Magazine,* May 1735.

3. The Poet's Dependence on a Statesman, which was published in the
*Gentleman's Magazine,* (Vol. VI. p. 225.) and contained among others
the following passages.

Some seem to hint, and others proof will bring,
That, from neglect, my num'rous hardships spring.
"Seek the *great man,"* they cry——'tis then decreed,
In *him* if I court *fortune,* I succeed.
What friends to second? Who, for *me,* should sue,
Have int'rests, partial to *themselves,* in view.
They own my matchless fate compassion draws,
They all wish well, lament, but drop my cause.
——Say, shall I turn where *lucre* points my views;
At first desert my friends, at length abuse?
But, on less terms, in *promise* he complies;
Years bury years, and hopes on hopes arise;
I trust, am trusted on my fairy gain;
And woes on woes attend an endless train.
    Be posts dispos'd at will!——I have, for these,
No gold to plead, no impudence to teaze.
All secret service from my soul I hate;

All dark intrigues of pleasure, or of state.
———Where these are not what claim to me belongs;
Though mine the *muse* and *virtue, birth* and *wrongs?*
Where lives the *statesman*, so in *honour* clear,
To give where he has nought to hope, nor fear?
No!—there to seek, is but to find fresh pain:
The promise broke, renew'd and broke again;
To be, as humour deigns, receiv'd, refus'd;
By turns affronted, and by turns amus'd;
To lose that time, which worthier thoughts require;
To lose that health, which should those thoughts inspire;
To starve on hope; or, like camelions, fare
On *ministerial faith*, which means but air.
  —A scene *will* shew—(all-righteous vision haste)
The meek exalted, and the proud debas'd!———
Oh! to be there!—to tread that friendly shore;
Where *falsehood, pride* and *statesmen* are no more!

4. From these the following lines are selected as an instance rather of his
impartiality than genius.

Materials which belief in gazettes claim,
Loose strung, run gingling into hist'ry's name.
Thick as Egyptian clouds of raining flies;
As thick as worms where man corrupting lies;
As pests obscene that haunt the ruin'd pile;
As monsters flound'ring in the muddy Nile;
Minutes, memoirs, views and reviews appear,
Where slander darkens each recorded year.
In a past reign is fam'd some am'rous league;
Some ring, or letter, now reveals th' intrigue;
Queens with their minions work unseemly things;
And boys grow dukes, when catamites to kings?
Does a prince die? What poisons they surmise?
No royal mortal sure by nature dies.
Is a prince born? What birth more base believ'd?
Or, what's more strange, his mother ne'er conceiv'd!
Thus slander popular o'er truth prevails,
And easy minds imbibe romantic tales.
  Some usurp names———an English *garreteer,*
From *minutes* forg'd, is *Monsieur Menager.*
  ———Where *hear-say knowledge* sits on public names,
And bold *conjecture* or extols, or blames,
Spring *party libels;* from whose ashes dead,
A *monster,* misnam'd Hist'ry, lifts its head.
Contending factions croud to hear its roar!
But when once heard, it dies to noise no more.
From these no answer, no applause from those,
O'er half they simper, and o'er half they doze.
So when in senate, with egregious pate,
Perks up, Sir —— in some deep debate;
He hems, looks wise, tunes then his lab'ring throat,
To prove black white, postpone or palm the vote;
In sly contempt, some, *hear him! hear him!* cry;

Some yawn, some sneer; none second, none reply.
    But dare such miscreants now rush abroad,
By blanket, cane, pump, pillory, unaw'd?
Dare they imp falshood thus, and plume her wings,
From present characters, and recent things?
Yes, what untruths? Or truths in what disguise?
What Boyers, and what Oldmixons arise?
What *facts* from all but *them* and *slander* screen'd?
Here meets a *council*, no where else conven'd.
There, from *originals*, come, thick as spawn,
*Letters* ne'er wrote, memorials never drawn;
To *secret conf'rence*, never held, they yoke
Treaties ne'er plann'd, and speeches never spoke.
From, Oldmixon, thy brow, too well we know,
Like *sin* from Satan's, far and wide they go.
    In vain may St. John safe in conscience sit,
In vain with truth confute, contemn with wit:
Confute, contemn, amid selected friends;
There sinks the justice, there the satire ends.
Here through a *cent'ry* scarce such leaves unclose,
From mold and dust the slander sacred grows.
Now none reply where all despise the page;
But will dumb scorn deceive no future age?

*Gentleman's Magazine*, Sept. 1741

5.   Learn, future natives of this promis'd land,
What your fore-fathers ow'd my saving hand!
Learn, when *despair* such sudden bliss shall see,
Such bliss must shine from *Oglethorpe* or *me!*
Do you the neighb'ring, blameless Indian aid,
Culture what he neglects, not his invade;
Dare not, oh! dare not, with ambitious view,
Force or demand subjection, never due.
Let by *my* specious name no *tyrants* rise,
And cry, while they enslave, they civilize!
Why must I Afric's sable children see
Vended for slaves, though form'd by nature free,
The nameless tortures cruel minds invent,
Those to subject, whom nature equal meant?
If these you dare, albeit unjust success
Empow'rs you now unpunish'd to oppress,
Revolving empire you and yours may doom;
Rome all subdued, yet Vandals vanquish'd Rome:
Yes, empire may revolve, give them the day,
And yoke may yoke, and blood may blood repay.

6. To exhibit a specimen of the beauties of this poem, the following passages are selected.

    Oft has the muse, on this distinguish'd day,
    Tun'd to glad harmony the vernal lay;
    But, O lamented change! The lay must flow

───────────

* Publick spirit.

From grateful rapture now, to grateful woe.
She, to this day, who joyous lustre gave,
Descends for ever to the silent grave.
She born at once to charm us and to mend,
Of human race the pattern and the friend.
——And, thou, bright Princess! seated now on high,
Next one, the fairest daughter of the sky,
Whose warm-felt love is to all beings known,
Thy sister Charity! next her thy throne;
See at thy tomb the virtues weeping lie!
There in dumb sorrow seem the arts to die.
So were the sun o'er other orbs to blaze,
And from our world, like thee, withdraw his rays,
No more to visit where he warm'd before,
All life must cease, and nature be no more.
Yet shall the *Muse* a heav'nly height essay,
Beyond the weakness mix'd with mortal clay;
Beyond the loss, which, tho' she bleeds to see,
Tho' ne'er to be redeem'd the loss of thee;
Beyond ev'n this, she hails with joyous lay,
Thy better birth, thy first true natal day;
A day, that sees thee born, beyond the tomb,
To endless health, to youth's eternal bloom.
Born to the mighty dead, the souls sublime
Of ev'ry famous age, and ev'ry clime,
To goodness fixed by truth's unvarying laws;
To bliss that knows no period, knows no pause——
Save when thine eye, from yonder pure serene,
Sheds a soft ray on this our gloomy scene.

7. ——Deign one look more! Ah! See thy consort dear!
Wishing all hearts, except his own, to cheer.
Lo! still he bids thy wonted bounties flow
To weeping families of worth and woe.
He stops all tears, however fast they rise,
Save those, that still must fall from grateful eyes:
And spite of griefs, that so usurp his mind,
Still watches o'er the welfare of mankind.

8. In a letter after his confinement.

9. Letter Jan. 15.

*(between pp. 77-80)*

1. The author preferr'd this title to that *of* London *and* Bristol *compared;*
   which, when he began the piece, he intended to prefix to it.

2. A place where the merchants used to meet to transact their affairs before
   the Exchange was erected. See *Gentleman's Magazine.* Vol. XIII. p. 496.

3. *Halliers* are the persons who drive or own the sledges, which are here
   used instead of carts.

*Published in a handsome quarto on January 9, 1749,* The Vanity of Human Wishes *was Johnson's first work to bear his name. Unlike* London, *his earlier imitation of Juvenal, no second separate edition was required. Johnson revised the poem for inclusion in the most popular anthology of the century, Dodsley's* Collection of Poems, IV *(1755), and took the occasion to make his most famous alteration, "garret" to "patron" (l. 160) in a satiric bow to Chesterfield's neglect of the* Dictionary. *Reprinted from the first edition.*

# The Vanity
# of Human Wishes

## The Tenth Satire of Juvenal, Imitated

[a]Let observation with extensive view,
Survey mankind, from China to Peru;
Remark each anxious toil, each eager strife,
And watch the busy scenes of crouded life;
Then say how hope and fear, desire and hate,                    5
O'erspread with snares the clouded maze of fate,
Where wav'ring man, betray'd by vent'rous pride,
To tread the dreary paths without a guide;
As treach'rous phantoms in the mist delude,
Shuns fancied ills, or chases airy good.                        10
How rarely reason guides the stubborn choice,
Rules the bold hand, or prompts the suppliant voice,
How nations sink, by darling schemes oppress'd,

---

[1] Superior letter *a* indicates Johnson's reference to the corresponding lines in Juvenal. These references are listed at the end of the selection, pages 116-17.

When vengeance listens to the fool's request.
Fate wings with ev'ry wish th' afflictive dart, 15
Each gift of nature, and each grace of art,
With fatal heat impetuous courage glows,
With fatal sweetness elocution flows,
Impeachment stops the speaker's pow'rful breath,
And restless fire precipitates on death. 20
   ᵇBut scarce observ'd the knowing and the bold,
Fall in the gen'ral massacre of gold;
Wide-wasting pest! that rages unconfin'd,
And crouds with crimes the records of mankind,
For gold his sword the hireling ruffian draws, 25
For gold the hireling judge distorts the laws;
Wealth heap'd on wealth, nor truth nor safety buys,
The dangers gather as the treasures rise.
   Let hist'ry tell where rival kings command,
And dubious title shakes the madded land, 30
When statutes glean the refuse of the sword,
How much more safe the vassal than the lord,
Low sculks the hind beneath the rage of pow'r,
And leaves the bonny traytor in the Tow'r,
Untouch'd his cottage, and his slumbers sound, 35
Tho' confiscation's vulturs clang around.
   The needy traveller, serene and gay,
Walks the wild heath, and sings his toil away.
Does envy seize thee? crush th' upbraiding joy,
Encrease his riches and his peace destroy, 40
New fears in dire vicissitude invade,
The rustling brake alarms, and quiv'ring shade,
Nor light nor darkness bring his pain relief,
One shews the plunder, and one hides the thief.
   ᶜYet still the gen'ral cry the skies assails 45
And gain and grandeur load the tainted gales;
Few know the toiling statesman's fear or care,
Th' insidious rival and the gaping heir.
   ᵈOnce more, Democritus, arise on earth,

---

[34] *bonny traytor:* a general reference to the Scots lords beheaded after
the Jacobite rebellion of 1745.

With chearful wisdom and instructive mirth,                    50
See motley life in modern trappings dress'd,
And feed with varied fools th' eternal jest:
Thou who couldst laugh where want enchain'd caprice,
Toil crush'd conceit, and man was of a piece;
Where wealth unlov'd without a mourner dy'd;                   55
And scarce a sycophant was fed by pride;
Where ne'er was known the form of mock debate,
Or seen a new-made mayor's unwieldy state;
Where change of fav'rites made no change of laws,
And senates heard before they judg'd a cause;                 60
How wouldst thou shake at Britain's modish tribe,
Dart the quick taunt, and edge the piercing gibe?
Attentive truth and nature to descry,
And pierce each scene with philosophic eye.
To thee were solemn toys or empty shew,                       65
The robes of pleasure and the veils of woe:
All aid the farce, and all thy mirth maintain,
Whose joys are causeless, or whose griefs are vain.
   Such was the scorn that fill'd the sage's mind,
Renew'd at ev'ry glance on humankind;                         70
How just that scorn ere yet thy voice declare,
Search every state, and canvass ev'ry pray'r.
   eUnnumber'd suppliants croud Preferment's gate,
Athirst for wealth, and burning to be great;
Delusive Fortune hears th' incessant call,                    75
They mount, they shine, evaporate, and fall.
On ev'ry stage the foes of peace attend,
Hate dogs their flight, and insult mocks their end.
Love ends with hope, the sinking statesman's door
Pours in the morning worshiper no more;                       80
For growing names the weekly scribbler lies,
To growing wealth the dedicator flies,
From every room descends the painted face,
That hung the bright Palladium of the place,
And smoak'd in kitchens, or in auctions sold,                 85
To better features yields the frame of gold;
For now no more we trace in ev'ry line
Heroic worth, benevolence divine:

The form distorted justifies the fall,
And detestation rids th' indignant wall.        90
　　But will not Britain hear the last appeal,
Sign her foes doom, or guard her fav'rites zeal;
Through Freedom's sons no more remonstrance rings,
Degrading nobles and controuling kings;
Our supple tribes repress their patriot throats,        95
And ask no questions but the price of votes;
With weekly libels and septennial ale,
Their wish is full to riot and to rail.
　　In full-blown dignity, see Wolsey stand,
Law in his voice, and fortune in his hand:        100
To him the church, the realm, their pow'rs consign,
Thro' him the rays of regal bounty shine,
Turn'd by his nod the stream of honour flows,
His smile alone security bestows:
Still to new heights his restless wishes tow'r,        105
Claim leads to claim, and pow'r advances pow'r;
Till conquest unresisted ceas'd to please,
And rights submitted, left him none to seize.
At length his sov'reign frowns—the train of state
Mark the keen glance, and watch the sign to hate.        110
Where-e'er he turns he meets a stranger's eye,
His suppliants scorn him, and his followers fly;
Now drops at once the pride of aweful state,
The golden canopy, the glitt'ring plate,
The regal palace, the luxurious board,        115
The liv'ried army, and the menial lord.
With age, with cares, with maladies oppress'd,
He seeks the refuge of monastic rest.
Grief aids disease, remember'd folly stings,
And his last sighs reproach the faith of kings.        120
　　Speak thou, whose thoughts at humble peace repine,
Shall Wolsey's wealth, with Wolsey's end be thine?
Or liv'st thou now, with safer pride content,
The richest landlord on the banks of Trent?
For why did Wolsey by the steeps of fate,        125

---

[125] *steeps:* misprinted "steps" in the first edition.

On weak foundations raise th' enormous weight?
Why but to sink beneath misfortune's blow,
With louder ruin to the gulphs below?
     ᶠWhat gave great Villiers to th' assassin's knife,
And fix'd disease on Harley's closing life?                    130
What murder'd Wentworth, and what exil'd Hyde,
By kings protected and to kings ally'd?
What but their wish indulg'd in courts to shine,
And pow'r too great to keep or to resign?
     ᵍWhen first the college rolls receive his name,      135
The young enthusiast quits his ease for fame;
Resistless burns the fever of renown,
Caught from the strong contagion of the gown;
O'er Bodley's dome his future labours spread,
And Bacon's mansion trembles o'er his head;                    140
Are these thy views? proceed, illustrious youth,
And virtue guard thee to the throne of Truth,
Yet should thy soul indulge the gen'rous heat,
Till captive Science yields her last retreat;
Should Reason guide thee with her brightest ray,      145
And pour on misty Doubt resistless day;
Should no false kindness lure to loose delight,
Nor Praise relax, nor Difficulty fright;
Should tempting Novelty thy cell refrain,
And Sloth's bland opiates shed their fumes in vain;      150
Should Beauty blunt on fops her fatal dart,
Nor claim the triumph of a letter'd heart;
Should no disease thy torpid veins invade,
Nor Melancholy's phantoms haunt thy shade;
Yet hope not life from grief or danger free,               155
Nor think the doom of man revers'd for thee:

---

¹²⁹ *Villiers:* first Duke of Buckingham, assassinated in 1628.

¹³⁰ *Harley:* Swift's friend, the Earl of Oxford.

¹³¹ *Wentworth:* Earl of Strafford, executed in 1641; *Hyde:* Earl of Clarendon, banished in 1667.

¹³⁹ *Bodley's dome:* the Bodleian Library; "dome" in the old sense of "building."

¹⁴⁰ *Bacon's mansion:* the gatehouse, now demolished, at Folly Bridge in Oxford. In 1755 Johnson added this note: "There is a tradition, that the study of friar Bacon, built on an arch over the bridge, will fall, when a man greater than Bacon shall pass under it."

Deign on the passing world to turn thine eyes,
And pause awhile from learning to be wise;
There mark what ills the scholar's life assail,
Toil, envy, want, the garret, and the jail.     160
See nations slowly wise, and meanly just,
To buried merit raise the tardy bust.
If dreams yet flatter, once again attend,
Hear Lydiat's life, and Galileo's end.

 Nor deem, when learning her lost prize bestows     165
The glitt'ring eminence exempt from foes;
See when the vulgar 'scap'd, despis'd or aw'd,
Rebellion's vengeful talons seize on Laud.
From meaner minds, tho' smaller fines content
The plunder'd palace or sequester'd rent;     170
Mark'd out by dangerous parts he meets the shock,
And fatal Learning leads him to the block:
Around his tomb let Art and Genius weep,
But hear his death, ye blockheads, hear and sleep.

 ʰThe festal blazes, the triumphal show,     175
The ravish'd standard, and the captive foe,
The senate's thanks, the gazette's pompous tale,
With force resistless o'er the brave prevail.
Such bribes the rapid Greek o'er Asia whirl'd,
For such the steady Romans shook the world;     180
For such in distant lands the Britons shine,
And stain with blood the Danube or the Rhine;
This pow'r has praise, that virtue scarce can warm,
Till fame supplies the universal charm.
Yet Reason frowns on War's unequal game,     185
Where wasted nations raise a single name,
And mortgag'd states their grandsires wreaths regret
From age to age in everlasting debt;
Wreaths which at last the dear-bought right convey
To rust on medals, or on stones decay.     190
 ⁱOn what foundation stands the warrior's pride?

---

¹⁶⁰ *garret:* after Johnson's experience with Chesterfield and the *Dictionary,* he replaced "garret" with "patron."
¹⁶⁴ Thomas Lydiat (1572–1646), a needy mathematician of Oxford.
¹⁶⁸ Archbishop Laud was executed by the Puritans in 1645, though not because of his learning.

How just his hopes let Swedish Charles decide;
A frame of adamant, a soul of fire,
No dangers fright him, and no labours tire;
O'er love, o'er force, extends his wide domain,          195
Unconquer'd lord of pleasure and of pain;
No joys to him pacific scepters yield,
War sounds the trump, he rushes to the field;
Behold surrounding kings their pow'r combine,
And one capitulate, and one resign;          200
Peace courts his hand, but spreads her charms in vain;
"Think nothing gain'd," he cries, "till nought remain,
On Moscow's walls till Gothic standards fly,
And all is mine beneath the polar sky."
The march begins in military state,          205
And nations on his eye suspended wait;
Stern Famine guards the solitary coast,
And Winter barricades the realms of Frost;
He comes, nor want nor cold his course delay;——
Hide, blushing Glory, hide Pultowa's day:          210
The vanquish'd hero leaves his broken bands,
And shews his miseries in distant lands;
Condemn'd a needy supplicant to wait,
While ladies interpose, and slaves debate.
But did not Chance at length her error mend?          215
Did no subverted empire mark his end?
Did rival monarchs give the fatal wound?
Or hostile millions press him to the ground?
His fall was destin'd to a barren strand,
A petty fortress, and a dubious hand;          220
He left the name, at which the world grew pale,
To point a moral, or adorn a tale.
    ¹All times their scenes of pompous woes afford,
From Persia's tyrant to Bavaria's lord.
In gay hostility, and barb'rous pride,          225
With half mankind embattled at his side,

---

¹⁹² Charles XII, defeated by Peter the Great at Pultowa (l. 210), was killed in the attack on Frederikshald, Norway, in 1718.
²²⁴ *Bavaria's lord:* Charles Albert, Elector of Bavaria, crowned emperor as Charles VII in 1742, died discredited in 1745.

Great Xerxes comes to seize the certain prey,
And starves exhausted regions in his way;
Attendant Flatt'ry counts his myriads o'er,
Till counted myriads sooth his pride no more;                    230
Fresh praise is try'd till madness fires his mind,
The waves he lashes, and enchains the wind;
New pow'rs are claim'd, new pow'rs are still bestow'd,
Till rude resistance lops the spreading god;
The daring Greeks deride the martial shew,                      235
And heap their vallies with the gaudy foe;
Th' insulted sea with humbler thoughts he gains,
A single skiff to speed his flight remains;
Th' incumber'd oar scarce leaves the dreaded coast
Through purple billows and a floating host.                     240
   The bold Bavarian, in a luckless hour,
Tries the dread summits of Cesarean pow'r,
With unexpected legions bursts away,
And sees defenceless realms receive his sway;
Short sway! fair Austria spreads her mournful charms,           245
The Queen, the beauty, sets the world in arms;
From hill to hill the beacons rousing blaze
Spreads wide the hope of plunder and of praise;
The fierce Croatian, and the wild Hussar,
And all the sons of ravage croud the war;                       250
The baffled prince in honour's flatt'ring bloom
Of hasty greatness finds the fatal doom,
His foes derision, and his subjects blame,
And steals to death from anguish and from shame.
   <sup>k</sup>Enlarge my life with multitude of days,       255
In health, in sickness, thus the suppliant prays;
Hides from himself his state, and shuns to know,
That life protracted is protracted woe.
Time hovers o'er, impatient to destroy,
And shuts up all the passages of joy:                           260
In vain their gifts the bounteous seasons pour,
The fruit autumnal, and the vernal flow'r,
With listless eyes the dotard views the store,

---

[245] *Fair Austria:* Maria Theresa.

He views, and wonders that they please no more;
Now pall the tastless meats, and joyless wines,                265
And Luxury with sighs her slave resigns.
Approach, ye minstrels, try the soothing strain,
And yield the tuneful lenitives of pain:
No sounds alas would touch th' impervious ear,
Though dancing mountains witness'd Orpheus near;               270
Nor lute nor lyre his feeble pow'rs attend,
Nor sweeter musick of a virtuous friend,
But everlasting dictates croud his tongue,
Perversely grave, or positively wrong.
The still returning tale, and ling'ring jest,                 275
Perplex the fawning niece and pamper'd guest,
While growing hopes scarce awe the gath'ring sneer,
And scarce a legacy can bribe to hear;
The watchful guests still hint the last offence,
The daughter's petulance, the son's expence,                  280
Improve his heady rage with treach'rous skill,
And mould his passions till they make his will.
   Unnumber'd maladies each joint invade,
Lay siege to life and press the dire blockade;
But unextinguish'd av'rice still remains,                      285
And dreaded losses aggravate his pains;
He turns, with anxious heart and cripled hands,
His bonds of debt, and mortgages of lands;
Or views his coffers with suspicious eyes,
Unlocks his gold, and counts it till he dies.                 290
   But grant, the virtues of a temp'rate prime
Bless with an age exempt from scorn or crime;
An age that melts in unperceiv'd decay,
And glides in modest innocence away;
Whose peaceful day Benevolence endears,                       295
Whose night congratulating Conscience cheers;
The gen'ral fav'rite as the gen'ral friend:
Such age there is, and who could wish its end?
   Yet ev'n on this her load Misfortune flings,
To press the weary minutes flagging wings:                    300
New sorrow rises as the day returns,
A sister sickens, or a daughter mourns.

Now kindred Merit fills the sable bier,
Now lacerated Friendship claims a tear.
Year chases year, decay pursues decay,                    305
Still drops some joy from with'ring life away;
New forms arise, and diff'rent views engage,
Superfluous lags the vet'ran on the stage,
Till pitying Nature signs the last release,
And bids afflicted worth retire to peace.                 310
   But few there are whom hours like these await,
Who set unclouded in the gulphs of fate.
From Lydia's monarch should the search descend,
By Solon caution'd to regard his end,
In life's last scene what prodigies surprise,            315
Fears of the brave, and follies of the wise?
From Marlb'rough's eyes the streams of dotage flow,
And Swift expires a driv'ler and a show.
   ¹The teeming mother, anxious for her race,
Begs for each birth the fortune of a face:                320
Yet Vane could tell what ills from beauty spring;
And Sedley curs'd the form that pleas'd a king.
Ye nymphs of rosy lips and radiant eyes,
Whom pleasure keeps too busy to be wise,
Whom joys with soft varieties invite                      325
By day the frolick, and the dance by night,
Who frown with vanity, who smile with art,
And ask the latest fashion of the heart,
What care, what rules your heedless charms shall save,
Each nymph your rival, and each youth your slave?         330
An envious breast with certain mischief glows,
And slaves, the maxim tells, are always foes.
Against your fame with fondness hate combines,
The rival batters, and the lover mines.
With distant voice neglected Virtue calls,                335
Less heard, and less the faint remonstrance falls;
Tir'd with contempt, she quits the slipp'ry reign,

---

³¹³ *Lydia's monarch:* Croesus.
³²¹ Anne Vane (1705–36), mistress of Frederick, Prince of Wales.
³²² Catherine Sedley (1657–1717), mistress of the Duke of York, after-wards James II.

And Pride and Prudence take her seat in vain.
In croud at once, where none the pass defend,
The harmless Freedom, and the private Friend.                340
The guardians yield, by force superior ply'd;
By Int'rest, Prudence; and by Flatt'ry, Pride.
Here beauty falls betray'd, despis'd, distress'd,
And hissing Infamy proclaims the rest.
    ᵐWhere then shall Hope and Fear their objects find?     345
Must dull Suspence corrupt the stagnant mind?
Must helpless man, in ignorance sedate,
Swim darkling down the current of his fate?
Must no dislike alarm, no wishes rise,
No cries attempt the mercies of the skies?                  350
Enquirer, cease, petitions yet remain,
Which heav'n may hear, nor deem religion vain.
Still raise for good the supplicating voice,
But leave to heav'n the measure and the choice.
Safe in his pow'r, whose eyes discern afar                  355
The secret ambush of a specious pray'r.
Implore his aid, in his decisions rest,
Secure whate'er he gives, he gives the best.
Yet with the sense of sacred presence prest,
When strong devotion fills thy glowing breast,              360
Pour forth thy fervours for a healthful mind,
Obedient passions, and a will resign'd;
For love, which scarce collective man can fill;
For patience sov'reign o'er transmuted ill;
For faith, that panting for a happier seat,                 365
Thinks death kind Nature's signal of retreat:
These goods for man the laws of heav'n ordain,
These goods he grants, who grants the pow'r to gain;
With these celestial wisdom calms the mind,
And makes the happiness she does not find.                  370

## NOTES

<table>
<tr><td>a.</td><td>Ver. 1–11.</td><td>c.</td><td>Ver. 23–27.</td></tr>
<tr><td>b.</td><td>Ver. 12–22.</td><td>d.</td><td>Ver. 28–55.</td></tr>
</table>

*In 1747, when Johnson addressed his* Plan of a Dictionary of the English Language *to Lord Chesterfield, he was confident he could produce his work in three years. Eight years later the two huge folio volumes appeared. These years had taught Johnson a great deal about the nature of language—and of patrons. Both kinds of learning may be seen in his superb Preface, which is reprinted from the first edition, as are the selections from the* Dictionary *which follow.*

# *Preface to* A Dictionary of the English Language

It is the fate of those who toil at the lower employments of life, to be rather driven by the fear of evil, than attracted by the prospect of good; to be exposed to censure, without hope of praise; to be disgraced by miscarriage, or punished for neglect, where success would have been without applause, and diligence without reward.

Among these unhappy mortals is the writer of dictionaries; whom mankind have considered, not as the pupil, but the slave of science, the pionier of literature, doomed only to remove rubbish and clear obstructions from the paths of Learning and Genius, who press forward to conquest and glory, without bestowing a smile on the humble drudge that facilitates their progress. Every other authour may aspire to praise; the lexicographer can only hope to escape reproach, and even this negative recompense has been yet granted to very few.

I have, notwithstanding this discouragement, attempted a dictionary of the English language, which, while it was employed in the cultivation of every species of literature, has itself been hitherto neglected, suffered to spread, under the direction of chance, into wild exuberance, resigned to the tyranny of time and fashion, and exposed to the corruptions of ignorance, and caprices of innovation.

When I took the first survey of my undertaking, I found our speech copious without order, and energetick without rules: wherever I turned my view, there was perplexity to be disentangled, and confusion to be regulated; choice was to be made out of boundless variety, without any established principle of selection; adulterations were to be detected, without a settled test of purity; and modes of expression to be rejected or received, without the suffrages of any writers of classical reputation or acknowledged authority.

Having therefore no assistance but from general grammar, I applied myself to the perusal of our writers; and noting whatever might be of use to ascertain or illustrate any word or phrase, accumulated in time the materials of a dictionary, which, by degrees, I reduced to method, establishing to myself, in the progress of the work, such rules as experience and analogy suggested to me; experience, which practice and observation were continually increasing; and analogy, which, though in some words obscure, was evident in others.

In adjusting the *orthography*, which has been to this time unsettled and fortuitous, I found it necessary to distinguish those irregularities that are inherent in our tongue, and perhaps coeval with it, from others which the ignorance or negligence of later writers has produced. Every language has its anomalies, which, though inconvenient, and in themselves once unnecessary, must be tolerated among the imperfections of human things, and which require only to be registred, that they may not be increased, and ascertained, that they may not be confounded: but every language has likewise its improprieties and absurdities, which it is the duty of the lexicographer to correct or proscribe.

As language was at its beginning merely oral, all words of necessary or common use were spoken before they were written; and while they were unfixed by any visible signs, must have been spoken with great diversity, as we now observe those who cannot read to catch sounds imperfectly, and utter them negligently. When this wild and barbarous jargon was first reduced to an alphabet, every penman endeavoured to express, as he could, the sounds which he was accustomed to pronounce or to receive, and vitiated in writing such words as were already vitiated in speech. The powers of the letters, when they were applied to a new language, must have been vague and unsettled, and therefore different hands would exhibit the same sound by different combinations.

From this uncertain pronunciation arise in a great part the various dialects of the same country, which will always be observed to grow fewer, and less different, as books are multiplied; and from this arbitrary representation of sounds by letters, proceeds that diversity of spelling observable in the Saxon remains, and I suppose in the first books of every nation, which perplexes or destroys analogy, and produces anomalous formations, which, being once incorporated, can never be afterward dismissed or reformed.

Of this kind are the derivatives *length* from *long, strength* from *strong, darling* from *dear, breadth* from *broad,* from *dry, drought,* and from *high, height,* which Milton, in zeal for analogy, writes *highth; Quid te exempta juvat spinis de pluribus una;*[1] to change all would be too much, and to change one is nothing.

This uncertainty is most frequent in the vowels, which are so capriciously pronounced, and so differently modified, by accident or affectation, not only in every province, but in every mouth, that to them, as is well known to etymologists, little regard is to be shewn in the deduction of one language from another.

Such defects are not errours in orthography, but spots of barbarity impressed so deep in the English language, that criticism can never wash them away; these, therefore, must be permitted to remain untouched: but many words have likewise been altered by accident, or depraved by ignorance, as the pronunciation of the vulgar has been weakly followed; and some still continue to be variously written, as authours differ in their care or skill: of these it was proper to enquire the true orthography, which I have always considered as depending on their derivation, and have therefore referred them to their original languages: thus I write *enchant, enchantment, enchanter,* after the French, and *incantation* after the Latin; thus *entire* is chosen rather than *intire,* because it passed to us not from the Latin *integer,* but from the French *entier.*

---

[1] "What good would it do to remove one out of many errors?" Horace, *Epistles,* 2.2.212.

Of many words it is difficult to say whether they were immediately received from the Latin or the French, since at the time
when we had dominions in France, we had Latin service in our
churches. It is, however, my opinion, that the French generally
supplied us; for we have few Latin words, among the terms of
domestick use, which are not French; but many French, which
are very remote from Latin.

Even in words of which the derivation is apparent, I have been
often obliged to sacrifice uniformity to custom; thus I write, in
compliance with a numberless majority, *convey* and *inveigh*, *deceit* and *receipt*, *fancy* and *phantom*; sometimes the derivative
varies from the primitive, as *explain* and *explanation*, *repeat* and
*repetition.*

Some combinations of letters having the same power are used
indifferently without any discoverable reason of choice, as in
*choak, choke; soap, sope; fewel, fuel,* and many others; which I
have sometimes inserted twice, that those who search for them
under either form, may not search in vain.

In examining the orthography of any doubtful word, the mode
of spelling by which it is inserted in the series of the dictionary,
is to be considered as that to which I give, perhaps not often
rashly, the preference. I have left, in the examples, to every
authour his own practice unmolested, that the reader may balance
suffrages, and judge between us: but this question is not always
to be determined by reputed or by real learning; some men, intent
upon greater things, have thought little on sounds and derivations;
some, knowing in the ancient tongues, have neglected those in
which our words are commonly to be sought. Thus Hammond
writes *fecibleness* for *feasibleness*, because I suppose he imagined
it derived immediately from the Latin; and some words, such as
*dependant, dependent; dependance, dependence,* vary their final
syllable, as one or other language is present to the writer.

In this part of the work, where caprice has long wantoned without controul, and vanity sought praise by petty reformation, I
have endeavoured to proceed with a scholar's reverence for antiquity, and a grammarian's regard to the genius of our tongue.
I have attempted few alterations, and among those few, perhaps
the greater part is from the modern to the ancient practice; and
I hope I may be allowed to recommend to those, whose thoughts
have been, perhaps, employed too anxiously on verbal singularities,

not to disturb, upon narrow views, or for minute propriety, the orthography of their fathers. It has been asserted, that for the law to be *known*, is of more importance than to be *right*. Change, says Hooker, is not made without inconvenience, even from worse to better. There is in constancy and stability a general and lasting advantage, which will always overbalance the slow improvements of gradual correction. Much less ought our written language to comply with the corruptions of oral utterance, or copy that which every variation of time or place makes different from itself, and imitate those changes, which will again be changed, while imitation is employed in observing them.

This recommendation of steadiness and uniformity does not proceed from an opinion, that particular combinations of letters have much influence on human happiness; or that truth may not be successfully taught by modes of spelling fanciful and erroneous: I am not yet so lost in lexicography, as to forget that *words are the daughters of earth, and that things are the sons of heaven.*[2] Language is only the instrument of science, and words are but the signs of ideas: I wish, however, that the instrument might be less apt to decay, and that signs might be permanent, like the things which they denote.

In settling the orthography, I have not wholly neglected the pronunciation, which I have directed, by printing an accent upon the acute or elevated syllable. It will sometimes be found, that the accent is placed by the authour quoted, on a different syllable from that marked in the alphabetical series; it is then to be understood, that custom has varied, or that the authour has, in my opinion, pronounced wrong. Short directions are sometimes given where the sound of letters is irregular; and if they are sometimes omitted, defect in such minute observations will be more easily excused, than superfluity.

In the investigation both of the orthography and signification of words, their *etymology* was necessarily to be considered, and they were therefore to be divided into primitives and derivatives. A primitive word, is that which can be traced no further to any English root; thus *circumspect, circumvent, circumstance, delude,*

---

[2] Paraphrased from a line in Samuel Madden's *Boulter's Monument,* a poem which Johnson was paid to revise before publication.

*concave,* and *complicate,* though compounds in the Latin, are to us primitives. Derivatives, are all those that can be referred to any word in English of greater simplicity.

The derivatives I have referred to their primitives, with an accuracy sometimes needless; for who does not see that *remoteness* comes from *remote, lovely* from *love, concavity* from *concave,* and *demonstrative* from *demonstrate?* but this grammatical exuberance the scheme of my work did not allow me to repress. It is of great importance in examining the general fabrick of a language, to trace one word from another, by noting the usual modes of derivation and inflection; and uniformity must be preserved in systematical works, though sometimes at the expence of particular propriety.

Among other derivatives I have been careful to insert and elucidate the anomalous plurals of nouns and preterites of verbs, which in the Teutonick dialects are very frequent, and, though familiar to those who have always used them, interrupt and embarrass the learners of our language.

The two languages from which our primitives have been derived are the Roman and Teutonick: under the Roman I comprehend the French and provincial tongues; and under the Teutonick range the Saxon, German, and all their kindred dialects. Most of our polysyllables are Roman, and our words of one syllable are very often Teutonick.

In assigning the Roman original, it has perhaps sometimes happened that I have mentioned only the Latin, when the word was borrowed from the French; and considering myself as employed only in the illustration of my own language, I have not been very careful to observe whether the Latin word be pure or barbarous, or the French elegant or obsolete.

For the Teutonick etymologies I am commonly indebted to Junius and Skinner,[3] the only names which I have forborn to quote when I copied their books; not that I might appropriate their labours or usurp their honours, but that I might spare a perpetual repetition by one general acknowledgment. Of these, whom I

---

[3] Francis Junius (d. 1677) author of *Etymologicum Anglicanum,* 1743; Stephen Skinner (d. 1667) author of *Etymologicon Linguae Anglicanae,* 1671.

ought not to mention but with the reverence due to instructors and benefactors, Junius appears to have excelled in extent of learning, and Skinner in rectitude of understanding. Junius was accurately skilled in all the northern languages, Skinner probably examined the ancient and remoter dialects only by occasional inspection into dictionaries; but the learning of Junius is often of no other use than to show him a track by which he may deviate from his purpose, to which Skinner always presses forward by the shortest way. Skinner is often ignorant, but never ridiculous: Junius is always full of knowledge; but his variety distracts his judgment, and his learning is very frequently disgraced by his absurdities.

The votaries of the northern muses will not perhaps easily restrain their indignation, when they find the name of Junius thus degraded by a disadvantageous comparison; but whatever reverence is due to his diligence, or his attainments, it can be no criminal degree of censoriousness to charge that etymologist with want of judgment, who can seriously derive *dream* from *drama,* because *life is a drama, and a drama is a dream;* and who declares with a tone of defiance, that no man can fail to derive *moan* from μόνος, *monos,* who considers that grief naturally loves to be alone.[4]

Our knowledge of the northern literature is so scanty, that of words undoubtedly Teutonick the original is not always to be found in any ancient language; and I have therefore inserted Dutch or German substitutes, which I consider not as radical but parallel, not as the parents, but sisters of the English.

The words which are represented as thus related by descent or cognation, do not always agree in sense; for it is incident to words, as to their authours, to degenerate from their ancestors, and to change their manners when they change their country. It is sufficient, in etymological enquiries, if the senses of kindred words be found such as may easily pass into each other, or such as may both be referred to one general idea.

The etymology, so far as it is yet known, was easily found in the volumes where it is particularly and professedly delivered; and, by proper attention to the rules of derivation, the orthogra-

---

[4] We have omitted a long footnote in which Johnson gives other examples of Junius's "etymological extravagance."

phy was soon adjusted. But to *collect* the *words* of our language was a task of greater difficulty: the deficiency of dictionaries was immediately apparent; and when they were exhausted, what was yet wanting must be sought by fortuitous and unguided excursions into books, and gleaned as industry should find, or chance should offer it, in the boundless chaos of a living speech. My search, however, has been either skilful or lucky; for I have much augmented the vocabulary.

As my design was a dictionary, common or appellative, I have omitted all words which have relation to proper names; such as *Arian, Socinian, Calvinist, Benedictine, Mahometan;* but have retained those of a more general nature, as *Heathen, Pagan.*

Of the terms of art I have received such as could be found either in books of science or technical dictionaries; and have often inserted, from philosophical writers, words which are supported perhaps only by a single authority, and which being not admitted into general use, stand yet as candidates or probationers, and must depend for their adoption on the suffrage of futurity.

The words which our authours have introduced by their knowledge of foreign languages, or ignorance of their own, by vanity or wantonness, by compliance with fashion, or lust of innovation, I have registred as they occurred, though commonly only to censure them, and warn others against the folly of naturalizing useless foreigners to the injury of the natives.

I have not rejected any by design, merely because they were unnecessary or exuberant; but have received those which by different writers have been differently formed, as *viscid,* and *viscidity, viscous,* and *viscosity.*

Compounded or double words I have seldom noted, except when they obtain a signification different from that which the components have in their simple state. Thus *highwayman, woodman,* and *horsecourser,* require an explication; but of *thieflike* or *coachdriver* no notice was needed, because the primitives contain the meaning of the compounds.

Words arbitrarily formed by a constant and settled analogy, like diminutive adjectives in *ish,* as *greenish, bluish,* adverbs in *ly,* as *dully, openly,* substantives in *ness,* as *vileness, faultiness,* were less diligently sought, and many sometimes have been omitted, when I had no authority that invited me to insert them; not that they are not genuine and regular offsprings of English roots, but because their relation to the primitive being always the same, their signification cannot be mistaken.

The verbal nouns in *ing*, such as the *keeping* of the *castle*, the *leading* of the *army*, are always neglected, or placed only to illustrate the sense of the verb, except when they signify things as well as actions, and have therefore a plural number, as *dwelling, living;* or have an absolute and abstract signification, as *colouring, painting, learning.*

The participles are likewise omitted, unless, by signifying rather qualities than action, they take the nature of adjectives; as a *thinking* man, a man of prudence; a *pacing* horse, a horse that can pace: these I have ventured to call *participial adjectives.* But neither are these always inserted, because they are commonly to be understood, without any danger of mistake, by consulting the verb.

Obsolete words are admitted, when they are found in authours not obsolete, or when they have any force or beauty that may deserve revival.

As composition is one of the chief characteristicks of a language, I have endeavoured to make some reparation for the universal negligence of my predecessors, by inserting great numbers of compounded words, as may be found under *after, fore, new, night, fair,* and many more. These, numerous as they are, might be multiplied, but that use and curiosity are here satisfied, and the frame of our language and modes of our combination amply discovered.

Of some forms of composition, such as that by which *re* is prefixed to note *repetition,* and *un* to signify *contrariety* or *privation,* all the examples cannot be accumulated, because the use of these particles, if not wholly arbitrary, is so little limited, that they are hourly affixed to new words as occasion requires, or is imagined to require them.

There is another kind of composition more frequent in our language than perhaps in any other, from which arises to foreigners the greatest difficulty. We modify the signification of many verbs by a particle subjoined; as to *come off,* to escape by a fetch; to *fall on,* to attack; to *fall off,* to apostatize; to *break off,* to stop abruptly; to *bear out,* to justify; to *fall in,* to comply; to *give over,* to cease; to *set off,* to embellish; to *set in,* to begin a continual tenour; to *set out,* to begin a course or journey; to *take off,* to copy; with innumerable expressions of the same kind, of which some appear wildly irregular, being so far distant from the sense of the simple words, that no sagacity will be able to trace the steps by which they arrived at the present use. These I have noted with great care; and though I cannot flatter myself that the collection is complete, I believe I have so far assisted the students of our language, that this kind of phraseology will be no longer insuperable; and the combinations of verbs and particles, by chance omitted, will be easily explained by comparison with those that may be found.

Many words yet stand supported only by the name of Bailey, Ainsworth, Philips,[5] or the contracted *Dict.* for *Dictionaries* subjoined: of these I am not always certain that they are read in any book but the works of lexicographers. Of such I have omitted many, because I had never read them; and many I have inserted, because they may perhaps exist, though they have escaped my notice: they are, however, to be yet considered as resting only upon the credit of former dictionaries. Others, which I considered as useful, or know to be proper, though I could not at present support them by authorities, I have suffered to stand upon my own attestation, claiming the same privilege with my predecessors of being sometimes credited without proof.

The words, thus selected and disposed, are grammatically considered; they are referred to the different parts of speech; traced, when they are irregularly inflected, through their various terminations; and illustrated by observations, not indeed of great or striking importance, separately considered, but necessary to the elucidation of our language, and hitherto neglected or forgotten by English grammarians.

That part of my work on which I expect malignity most frequently to fasten, is the *Explanation;* in which I cannot hope to

---

[5] Nathaniel Bailey (d. 1742) compiled the *English Dictionary,* 1721, which was Johnson's principal reference to check inclusion of words. Robert Ainsworth (d. 1743) was the author of a Latin *Thesaurus,* 1736. Edward Phillips published *A New World of English Words* in 1658.

satisfy those, who are perhaps not inclined to be pleased, since I have not always been able to satisfy myself. To interpret a language by itself is very difficult; many words cannot be explained by synonimes, because the idea signified by them has not more than one appellation; nor by paraphrase, because simple ideas cannot be described. When the nature of things is unknown, or the notion unsettled and indefinite, and various in various minds, the words by which such notions are conveyed, or such things denoted, will be ambiguous and perplexed. And such is the fate of hapless lexicography, that not only darkness, but light, impedes and distresses it; things may be not only too little, but too much known, to be happily illustrated. To explain, requires the use of terms less abstruse than that which is to be explained, and such terms cannot always be found; for as nothing can be proved but by supposing something intuitively known, and evident without proof, so nothing can be defined but by the use of words too plain to admit a definition.

Other words there are, of which the sense is too subtle and evanescent to be fixed in a paraphrase; such are all those which are by the grammarians termed *expletives*, and, in dead languages, are suffered to pass for empty sounds, of no other use than to fill a verse, or to modulate a period, but which are easily perceived in living tongues to have power and emphasis, though it be sometimes such as no other form of expression can convey.

My labour has likewise been much increased by a class of verbs too frequent in the English language, of which the signification is so loose and general, the use so vague and indeterminate, and the senses detorted so widely from the first idea, that it is hard to trace them through the maze of variation, to catch them on the brink of utter inanity, to circumscribe them by any limitations, or interpret them by any words of distinct and settled meaning: such are *bear, break, come, cast, full, get, give, do, put, set, go, run, make, take, turn, throw.* If of these the whole power is not accurately delivered, it must be remembered, that while our language is yet living, and variable by the caprice of every one that speaks it, these words are hourly shifting their relations, and can no more be ascertained in a dictionary, than a grove, in the agitation of a storm, can be accurately delineated from its picture in the water.

The particles are among all nations applied with so great latitude, that they are not easily reducible under any regular scheme of explication: this difficulty is not less, nor perhaps greater, in English, than in other languages. I have laboured them with diligence, I hope with success; such at least as can be expected in a task, which no man, however learned or sagacious, has yet been able to perform.

Some words there are which I cannot explain, because I do not understand them; these might have been omitted very often with little inconvenience, but I would not so far indulge my vanity as to decline this confession: for when Tully owns himself ignorant whether *lessus,* in the twelve tables, means a *funeral song,* or *mourning garment;* and Aristotle doubts whether οὐρεύς[6] in the Iliad, signifies a *mule,* or *muleteer,* I may freely, without shame, leave some obscurities to happier industry, or future information.

The rigour of interpretative lexicography requires that *the explanation, and the word explained, should be always reciprocal;* this I have always endeavoured, but could not always attain. Words are seldom exactly synonimous; a new term was not introduced, but because the former was thought inadequate: names, therefore, have often many ideas, but few ideas have many names. It was then necessary to use the proximate word, for the deficiency of single terms can very seldom be supplied by circumlocution; nor is the inconvenience great of such mutilated interpretations, because the sense may easily be collected entire from the examples.

In every word of extensive use, it was requisite to mark the progress of its meaning, and show by what gradations of intermediate sense it has passed from its primitive to its remote and accidental signification; so that every foregoing explanation should tend to that which follows, and the series be regularly concatenated from the first notion to the last.

This is specious, but not always practicable; kindred senses may be so interwoven, that the perplexity cannot be disentangled, nor any reason be assigned why one should be ranged before the other. When the radical idea branches out into parallel ramifications, how can a consecutive series be formed of senses in their

---

[6] Read οὐρεύς; Aristotle, Poetics, 25.16. Ordinarily *mule,* the word is used by Homer for *guard.*

nature collateral? The shades of meaning sometimes pass imperceptibly into each other; so that though on one side they apparently differ, yet it is impossible to mark the point of contact. Ideas of the same race, though not exactly alike, are sometimes so little different, that no words can express the dissimilitude, though the mind easily perceives it, when they are exhibited together; and sometimes there is such a confusion of acceptations, that discernment is wearied, and distinction puzzled, and perseverance herself hurries to an end, by crouding together what she cannot separate.

These complaints of difficulty will, by those that have never considered words beyond their popular use, be thought only the jargon of a man willing to magnify his labours, and procure veneration to his studies by involution and obscurity. But every art is obscure to those that have not learned it: this uncertainty of terms, and commixture of ideas, is well known to those who have joined philosophy with grammar; and if I have not expressed them very clearly, it must be remembered that I am speaking of that which words are insufficient to explain.

The original sense of words is often driven out of use by their metaphorical acceptations, yet must be inserted for the sake of a regular origination. Thus I know not whether *ardour* is used for *material heat,* or whether *flagrant,* in English, ever signifies the same with *burning;* yet such are the primitive ideas of these words, which are therefore set first, though without examples, that the figurative senses may be commodiously deduced.

Such is the exuberance of signification which many words have obtained, that it was scarcely possible to collect all their senses; sometimes the meaning of derivatives must be sought in the mother term, and sometimes deficient explanations of the primitive may be supplied in the train of derivation. In any case of doubt or difficulty, it will be always proper to examine all the words of the same race; for some words are slightly passed over to avoid repetition, some admitted easier and clearer explanation than others, and all will be better understood, as they are considered in greater variety of structures and relations.

All the interpretations of words are not written with the same skill, or the same happiness: things equally easy in themselves, are not all equally easy to any single mind. Every writer of a long work commits errours, where there appears neither ambiguity to mislead, nor obscurity to confound him; and in a search like this, many felicities of expression will be casually overlooked, many convenient parallels will be forgotten, and many particulars will admit improvement from a mind utterly unequal to the whole performance.

But many seeming faults are to be imputed rather to the nature of the undertaking, than the negligence of the performer. Thus some explanations are unavoidably reciprocal or circular, as *hind, the female of the stag; stag, the male of the hind:* sometimes easier words are changed into harder, as *burial* into *sepulture* or *interment, drier* into *desiccative, dryness* into *siccity* or *aridity, fit* into *paroxysm;* for the easiest word, whatever it be, can never be translated into one more easy. But easiness and difficulty are merely relative, and if the present prevalence of our language should invite foreigners to this dictionary, many will be assisted by those words which now seem only to increase or produce obscurity. For this reason I have endeavoured frequently to join a Teutonick and Roman interpretation, as to *cheer* to *gladden,* or *exhilarate,* that every learner of English may be assisted by his own tongue.

The solution of all difficulties, and the supply of all defects, must be sought in the examples, subjoined to the various senses of each word, and ranged according to the time of their authours.

When first I collected these authorities, I was desirous that every quotation should be useful to some other end than the illustration of a word; I therefore extracted from philosophers principles of science; from historians remarkable facts; from chymists complete processes; from divines striking exhortations; and from poets beautiful descriptions. Such is design, while it is yet at a distance from execution. When the time called upon me to range this accumulation of elegance and wisdom into an alphabetical series, I soon discovered that the bulk of my volumes would fright away the student, and was forced to depart from my scheme of including all that was pleasing or useful in English literature, and reduce my transcripts very often to clusters of words, in which scarcely any meaning is retained; thus to the weariness of copying, I was condemned to add the vexation of expunging. Some passages I have yet spared, which may relieve the labour of verbal searches, and intersperse with verdure and flowers the dusty desarts of barren philology.

The examples, thus mutilated, are no longer to be considered as conveying the sentiments or doctrine of their authours; the word for the sake of which they are inserted, with all its appendant clauses, has been carefully preserved; but it may sometimes happen, by hasty detruncation, that the general tendency of the sentence may be changed: the divine may desert his tenets, or the philosopher his system.

Some of the examples have been taken from writers who were never mentioned as masters of elegance or models of stile; but words must be sought where they are used; and in what pages, eminent for purity, can terms of manufacture or agriculture be found? Many quotations serve no other purpose, than that of proving the bare existence of words, and are therefore selected with less scrupulousness than those which are to teach their structures and relations.

My purpose was to admit no testimony of living authours, that I might not be misled by partiality, and that none of my cotemporaries might have reason to complain; nor have I departed from this resolution, but when some performance of uncommon excellence excited my veneration, when my memory supplied me, from late books, with an example that was wanting, or when my heart, in the tenderness of friendship, solicited admission for a favourite name.

So far have I been from any care to grace my pages with modern decorations, that I have studiously endeavoured to collect examples and authorities from the writers before the restoration, whose works I regard as *the wells of English undefiled,* as the pure sources of genuine diction. Our language, for almost a century, has, by the concurrence of many causes, been gradually departing from its original Teutonick character, and deviating towards a Gallick structure and phraseology, from which it ought to be our endeavour to recal it, by making our ancient volumes the ground-work of stile, admitting among the additions of later times, only such as may supply real deficiencies, such as are readily adopted by the genius of our tongue, and incorporate easily with our native idioms.

But as every language has a time of rudeness antecedent to perfection, as well as of false refinement and declension, I have been cautious lest my zeal for antiquity might drive me into times too remote, and croud my book with words now no longer understood. I have fixed Sidney's work for the boundary, beyond which I make few excursions. From the authours which rose in the time of Elizabeth, a speech might be formed adequate to all the purposes of use and elegance. If the language of theology were extracted from Hooker and the translation of the Bible; the terms of natural knowledge from Bacon; the phrases of policy, war, and navigation from Raleigh; the dialect of poetry and fiction from Spenser and Sidney; and the diction of common life from Shakespeare, few ideas would be lost to mankind, for want of English words, in which they might be expressed.

It is not sufficient that a word is found, unless it be so combined as that its meaning is apparently determined by the tract and tenour of the sentence; such passages I have therefore chosen, and when it happened that any authour gave a definition of a term, or such an explanation as is equivalent to a definition, I have placed his authority as a supplement to my own, without regard to the chronological order, that is otherwise observed.

Some words, indeed, stand unsupported by any authority, but they are commonly derivative nouns or adverbs, formed from their primitives by regular and constant analogy, or names of things seldom occurring in books, or words of which I have reason to doubt the existence.

There is more danger of censure from the multiplicity than paucity of examples; authorities will sometimes seem to have been accumulated without necessity or use, and perhaps some will be found, which might, without loss, have been omitted. But a work of this kind is not hastily to be charged with superfluities: those quotations which to careless or unskilful perusers appear only to repeat the same sense, will often exhibit, to a more accurate examiner, diversities of signification, or, at least, afford different shades of the same meaning: one will shew the word applied to persons, another to things; one will express an ill, another a good, and a third a neutral sense; one will prove the expression genuine from an ancient authour; another will shew it elegant from a modern: a doubtful authority is corroborated by another of more credit; an ambiguous sentence is ascertained by a passage clear and determinate; the word, how often soever repeated, appears with new associates and in different combinations, and every quotation contributes something to the stability or enlargement of the language.

When words are used equivocally, I receive them in either sense; when they are metaphorical, I adopt them in their primitive acceptation.

I have sometimes, though rarely, yielded to the temptation of exhibiting a genealogy of sentiments, by shewing how one authour copied the thoughts and diction of another: such quotations are indeed little more than repetitions, which might justly be censured, did they not gratify the mind, by affording a kind of intellectual history.

The various syntactical structures occurring in the examples have been carefully noted; the licence or negligence with which many words have been hitherto used, has made our stile capricious and indeterminate; when the different combinations of the same word are exhibited together, the preference is readily given to propriety, and I have often endeavoured to direct the choice.

Thus have I laboured to settle the orthography, display the analogy, regulate the structures, and ascertain the signification of English words, to perform all the parts of a faithful lexicographer: but I have not always executed my own scheme, or satisfied my own expectations. The work, whatever proofs of diligence and attention it may exhibit, is yet capable of many improvements: the orthography which I recommend is still controvertible, the etymology which I adopt is uncertain, and perhaps frequently erroneous; the explanations are sometimes too much contracted, and sometimes too much diffused, the significations are distinguished rather with subtilty than skill, and the attention is harrassed with unnecessary minuteness.

The examples are too often injudiciously truncated, and perhaps sometimes, I hope very rarely, alleged in a mistaken sense; for in making this collection I trusted more to memory, than, in a state of disquiet and embarrassment, memory can contain, and purposed to supply at the review what was left incomplete in the first transcription.

Many terms appropriated to particular occupations, though necessary and significant, are undoubtedly omitted; and of the words most studiously considered and exemplified, many senses have escaped observation.

Yet these failures, however frequent, may admit extenuation and apology. To have attempted much is always laudable, even when the enterprize is above the strength that undertakes it: To rest below his own aim is incident to every one whose fancy is active, and whose views are comprehensive; nor is any man satisfied with himself because he has done much, but because he can conceive little. When first I engaged in this work, I resolved to leave neither words nor things unexamined, and pleased myself with a prospect of the hours which I should revel away in feasts of literature, the obscure recesses of northern learning, which I should enter and ransack, the treasures with which I expected every search into those neglected mines to reward my labour, and the triumph with which I should display my acquisitions to mankind. When I had thus enquired into the original of words, I resolved to show likewise my attention to things; to pierce deep into every science, to enquire the nature of every substance of which I inserted the name, to limit every idea by a definition strictly logical, and exhibit every production of art or nature in an accurate description, that my book might be in place of all other dictionaries whether appellative or technical. But these were the dreams of a poet doomed at last to wake a lexicographer. I soon found that it is too late to look for instruments, when the work calls for execution, and that whatever abilities I had brought to my task, with those I must finally perform it. To deliberate whenever I doubted, to enquire whenever I was ignorant, would have protracted the undertaking without end, and, perhaps, without much improvement; for I did not find by my first experiments, that what I had not of my own was easily to be obtained: I saw that one enquiry only gave occasion to another, that book referred to book, that to search was not always to find, and to find was not always to be informed; and that thus to persue perfection, was, like the first inhabitants of Arcadia, to chace the sun, which, when they had reached the hill where he seemed to rest, was still beheld at the same distance from them.

I then contracted my design, determining to confide in myself, and no longer to solicit auxiliaries, which produced more incumbrance than assistance: by this I obtained at least one advantage, that I set limits to my work, which would in time be finished, though not completed.

Despondency has never so far prevailed as to depress me to negligence; some faults will at last appear to be the effects of anxious diligence and persevering activity. The nice and subtle ramifications of meaning were not easily avoided by a mind intent upon accuracy, and convinced of the necessity of disentangling combinations, and separating similitudes. Many of the distinctions which to common readers appear useless and idle, will be found real and important by men versed in the school philosophy, without which no dictionary ever shall be accurately compiled, or skilfully examined.

Some senses however there are, which, though not the same, are yet so nearly allied, that they are often confounded. Most men think indistinctly, and therefore cannot speak with exactness; and consequently some examples might be indifferently put to either signification: this uncertainty is not to be imputed to me, who do not form, but register the language; who do not teach men how they should think, but relate how they have hitherto expressed their thoughts.

The imperfect sense of some examples I lamented, but could not remedy, and hope they will be compensated by innumerable passages selected with propriety, and preserved with exactness; some shining with sparks of imagination, and some replete with treasures of wisdom.

The orthography and etymology, though imperfect, are not imperfect for want of care, but because care will not always be successful, and recollection or information come too late for use.

That many terms of art and manufacture are omitted, must be frankly acknowledged; but for this defect I may boldly allege that it was unavoidable: I could not visit caverns to learn the miner's language, nor take a voyage to perfect my skill in the dialect of navigation, nor visit the warehouses of merchants, and shops of artificers, to gain the names of wares, tools and operations, of which no mention is found in books; what favourable accident, or easy enquiry brought within my reach, has not been neglected; but it had been a hopeless labour to glean up words, by courting living information, and contesting with the sullenness of one, and the roughness of another.

To furnish the academicians della Crusca[7] with words of this

---

[7] The Accademia della Crusca was founded in 1582 to purify and standardize the Italian langauge. Its *Vocabulario* was published in 1612.

kind, a series of comedies called *la Fiera,* or *the Fair,* was professedly written by Buonaroti; but I had no such assistant, and therefore was content to want what they must have wanted likewise, had they not luckily been so supplied.

Nor are all words which are not found in the vocabulary, to be lamented as omissions. Of the laborious and mercantile part of the people, the diction is in a great measure casual and mutable; many of their terms are formed for some temporary or local convenience, and though current at certain times and places, are in others utterly unknown. This fugitive cant, which is always in a state of increase or decay, cannot be regarded as any part of the durable materials of a language, and therefore must be suffered to perish with other things unworthy of preservation.

Care will sometimes betray to the appearance of negligence. He that is catching opportunities which seldom occur, will suffer those to pass by unregarded, which he expects hourly to return; he that is searching for rare and remote things, will neglect those that are obvious and familiar: thus many of the most common and cursory words have been inserted with little illustration, because in gathering the authorities, I forbore to copy those which I thought likely to occur whenever they were wanted. It is remarkable that, in reviewing my collection, I found the word *sea* unexemplified.

Thus it happens, that in things difficult there is danger from ignorance, and in things easy from confidence; the mind, afraid of greatness, and disdainful of littleness, hastily withdraws herself from painful searches, and passes with scornful rapidity over tasks not adequate to her powers, sometimes too secure for caution, and again too anxious for vigorous effort; sometimes idle in a plain path, and sometimes distracted in labyrinths, and dissipated by different intentions.

A large work is difficult because it is large, even though all its parts might singly be performed with facility; where there are many things to be done, each must be allowed its share of time and labour, in the proportion only which it bears to the whole; nor can it be expected, that the stones which form the dome of a temple, should be squared and polished like the diamond of a ring.

Of the event of this work, for which, having laboured it with so much application, I cannot but have some degree of parental fondness, it is natural to form conjectures. Those who have been

persuaded to think well of my design, require that it should fix
our language, and put a stop to those alterations which time and
chance have hitherto been suffered to make in it without opposition. With this consequence I will confess that I flattered myself
for a while; but now begin to fear that I have indulged expectation which neither reason nor experience can justify. When we
see men grow old and die at a certain time one after another,
from century to century, we laugh at the elixir that promises to
prolong life to a thousand years; and with equal justice may the
lexicographer be derided, who being able to produce no example
of a nation that has preserved their words and phrases from mu-
tability, shall imagine that his dictionary can embalm his language,
and secure it from corruption and decay, that it is in his power to
change sublunary nature, or clear the world at once from folly,
vanity, and affectation.

With this hope, however, academies have been instituted, to
guard the avenues of their languages, to retain fugitives, and
repulse intruders; but their vigilance and activity have hitherto
been vain; sounds are too volatile and subtile for legal restraints;
to enchain syllables, and to lash the wind, are equally the undertakings of pride, unwilling to measure its desires by its strength.
The French language has visibly changed under the inspection of
the academy; the stile of Amelot's translation of father Paul is
observed by Le Courayer to be *un peu passé;* and no Italian will
maintain, that the diction of any modern writer is not perceptibly
different from that of Boccace, Machiavel, or Caro.[8]

Total and sudden transformations of a language seldom happen;
conquests and migrations are now very rare: but there are other
causes of change, which, though slow in their operation, and
invisible in their progress, are perhaps as much superiour to human resistance, as the revolutions of the sky, or intumescence of
the tide. Commerce, however necessary, however lucrative, as it
depraves the manners, corrupts the language; they that have fre-

---

[8] Le Courayer made a French translation of Father Paolo Sarpi's *History
of the Council of Trent* in 1736; Amelot had made an earlier one in 1683.
The first edition of the dictionary of the French Academy appeared in 1694.
Boccaccio (d. 1375), Machiavelli (d. 1527), and the poet Annibale Caro
(d. 1566) were too early to benefit from the dictionary published by the
Accademia della Crusca in 1612.

quent intercourse with strangers, to whom they endeavour to accommodate themselves, must in time learn a mingled dialect, like the jargon which serves the traffickers on the Mediterranean and Indian coasts. This will not always be confined to the exchange, the warehouse, or the port, but will be communicated by degrees to other ranks of the people, and be at last incorporated with the current speech.

There are likewise internal causes equally forcible. The language most likely to continue long without alteration, would be that of a nation raised a little, and but a little, above barbarity, secluded from strangers, and totally employed in procuring the conveniencies of life; either without books, or, like some of the Mahometan countries, with very few: men thus busied and unlearned, having only such words as common use requires, would perhaps long continue to express the same notions by the same signs. But no such constancy can be expected in a people polished by arts, and classed by subordination, where one part of the community is sustained and accommodated by the labour of the other. Those who have much leisure to think, will always be enlarging the stock of ideas, and every increase of knowledge, whether real or fancied, will produce new words, or combinations of words. When the mind is unchained from necessity, it will range after convenience; when it is left at large in the fields of speculation, it will shift opinions; as any custom is disused, the words that expressed it must perish with it; as any opinion grows popular, it will innovate speech in the same proportion as it alters practice.

As by the cultivation of various sciences, a language is amplified, it will be more furnished with words deflected from their original sense; the geometrician will talk of a courtier's zenith, or the excentrick virtue of a wild hero, and the physician of sanguine expectations and phlegmatick delays. Copiousness of speech will give opportunities to capricious choice, by which some words will be preferred, and others degraded; vicissitudes of fashion will enforce the use of new, or extend the signification of known terms. The tropes of poetry will make hourly encroachments, and the metaphorical will become the current sense: pronunciation will be varied by levity or ignorance, and the pen must at length comply with the tongue; illiterate writers will at one time or other, by publick infatuation, rise into renown, who, not knowing the original import of words, will use them with colloquial licentiousness, confound distinction, and forget propriety. As politeness increases, some expressions will be considered as too gross and vulgar for the delicate, others as too formal and ceremonious for the gay and airy; new phrases are therefore adopted, which must, for the same reasons, be in time dismissed. Swift, in his petty treatise on the English language, allows that new words must sometimes be introduced, but proposes that none should be suffered to become obsolete. But what makes a word obsolete, more than general agreement to forbear it? and how shall it be continued, when it conveys an offensive idea, or recalled again into the mouths of mankind, when it has once by disuse become unfamiliar, and by unfamiliarity unpleasing.

There is another cause of alteration more prevalent than any other, which yet in the present state of the world cannot be obviated. A mixture of two languages will produce a third distinct from both, and they will always be mixed, where the chief part of education, and the most conspicuous accomplishment, is skill in ancient or in foreign tongues. He that has long cultivated another language, will find its words and combinations croud upon his memory; and haste and negligence, refinement and affectation, will obtrude borrowed terms and exotick expressions.

The great pest of speech is frequency of translation. No book was ever turned from one language into another, without imparting something of its native idiom; this is the most mischievous and comprehensive innovation; single words may enter by thousands, and the fabrick of the tongue continue the same, but new phraseology changes much at once; it alters not the single stones of the building, but the order of the columns. If an academy should be established for the cultivation of our stile, which I, who can never wish to see dependance multiplied, hope the spirit of English liberty will hinder or destroy, let them, instead of compiling grammars and dictionaries, endeavour, with all their influence, to stop the licence of translatours, whose idleness and ignorance, if it be suffered to proceed, will reduce us to babble a dialect of France.

If the changes that we fear be thus irresistible, what remains but to acquiesce with silence, as in the other insurmountable distresses of humanity? it remains that we retard what we cannot

repel, that we palliate what we cannot cure. Life may be lengthened by care, though death cannot be ultimately defeated:
tongues, like governments, have a natural tendency to degenera-
tion; we have long preserved our constitution, let us make some
struggles for our language.

In hope of giving longevity to that which its own nature forbids
to be immortal, I have devoted this book, the labour of years, to
the honour of my country, that we may no longer yield the palm
of philology, to the nations of the continent. The chief glory of
every people arises from its authours: whether I shall add any
thing by my own writings to the reputation of English literature,
must be left to time: much of my life has been lost under the
pressures of disease; much has been trifled away; and much has
always been spent in provision for the day that was passing over
me; but I shall not think my employment useless or ignoble, if by
my assistance foreign nations, and distant ages, gain access to the
propagators of knowledge, and understand the teachers of truth;
if my labours afford light to the repositories of science, and add
celebrity to Bacon, to Hooker, to Milton, and to Boyle.

When I am animated by this wish, I look with pleasure on my
book, however defective, and deliver it to the world with the spirit
of a man that has endeavoured well. That it will immediately become popular I have not promised to myself: a few wild blunders,
and risible absurdities, from which no work of such multiplicity
was ever free, may for a time furnish folly with laughter, and
harden ignorance in contempt; but useful diligence will at last
prevail, and there never can be wanting some who distinguish
desert; who will consider that no dictionary of a living tongue
ever can be perfect, since while it is hastening to publication,
some words are budding, and some falling away; that a whole life
cannot be spent upon syntax and etymology, and that even a
whole life would not be sufficient; that he, whose design includes
whatever language can express, must often speak of what he does
not understand; that a writer will sometimes be hurried by eagerness to the end, and sometimes faint with weariness under a task,
which Scaliger compares to the labours of the anvil and the mine;
that what is obvious is not always known, and what is known is
not always present; that sudden fits of inadvertency will surprize
vigilance, slight avocations will seduce attention, and casual

eclipses of the mind will darken learning; and that the writer shall often in vain trace his memory at the moment of need, for that which yesterday he knew with intuitive readiness, and which will come uncalled into his thoughts tomorrow.

In this work, when it shall be found that much is omitted, let it not be forgotten that much likewise is performed; and though no book was ever spared out of tenderness to the authour, and the world is little solicitous to know whence proceeded the faults of that which it condemns; yet it may gratify curiosity to inform it, that the *English Dictionary* was written with little assistance of the learned, and without any patronage of the great; not in the soft obscurities of retirement, or under the shelter of academick bowers, but amidst inconvenience and distraction, in sickness and in sorrow: and it may repress the triumph of malignant criticism to observe, that if our language is not here fully displayed, I have only failed in an attempt which no human powers have hitherto completed. If the lexicons of ancient tongues, now immutably fixed, and comprised in a few volumes, be yet, after the toil of successive ages, inadequate and delusive; if the aggregated knowledge, and co-operating diligence of the Italian academicians, did not secure them from the censure of Beni, if the embodied criticks of France, when fifty years had been spent upon their work, were obliged to change its oeconomy, and give their second edition another form, I may surely be contented without the praise of perfection, which, if I could obtain, in this gloom of solitude, what would it avail me? I have protracted my work till most of those whom I wished to please, have sunk into the grave, and success and miscarriage are empty sounds: I therefore dismiss it with frigid tranquillity, having little to fear or hope from censure or from praise.

# Selections from the *Dictionary*

**advi′ce.** (4) Intelligence; as, the merchants received *advice* of their loss. This sense is somewhat low, and chiefly commercial.

**agoni′stes.** A prize-fighter; one that contends at any public solemnity for a prize. Milton has so stiled his tragedy, because Sampson was called out to divert the Philistines with feats of strength.

**to ail.** (4) It is remarkable, that this word is never used but with some indefinite term, or the word *nothing;* as, *What ails* him? *What* does he *ail? He ails something: he ails nothing. Something ails* him; *nothing ails* him. Thus we never say, a fever *ails* him, or he *ails* a fever, or use definite terms with this verb.

**to ake.** (2) It is frequently applied, in an improper sense, to the heart; as, *the heart akes;* to imply grief or fear. Shakespeare has used it, still more licentiously, of the soul.

**alamo′de.** According to the fashion: a low word. It is used likewise by shopkeepers for a kind of thin silken manufacture.

**a′lias.** A Latin word, signifying otherwise; often used in the trials of criminals, whose danger has obliged them to change their names; as, Simpson *alias* Smith, *alias* Baker; that is, *otherwise* Smith, *otherwise* Baker.

**alliga′tor.** The crocodile. This name is chiefly used for the crocodile of America, between which, and that of Africa, naturalists have laid down this difference, that one moves the upper, and the other the lower jaw; but this is now known

---

advice. (4) I.e., the fourth definition of this word.

to be chimerical, the lower jaw being equally moved by both.

**amba'ssadress.** (2) In ludicrous language, a woman sent on a message.

**ambide'xter.** (2) A man who is equally ready to act on either side, in party disputes. This sense is ludicrous.

**anthropophagi'nian.** A ludicrous word, formed by Shakespeare from *anthropophagi,* for the sake of a formidable sound.

**aphrodisi'acal, aphrodisi'ack.** Relating to the venereal disease.

**appro'val.** Approbation: a word not much used.

**awa'y.** (6) It is often used with a verb; as, to *drink away* an estate; to *idle away* a manor; that is, to drink or idle till an estate or manor is gone.

**bear-garden.** A word used in familiar or low phrase for *rude* or *turbulent;* as, a *bear-garden* fellow; that is, a man rude enough to be a proper frequenter of the bear-garden. *Bear-garden sport,* is used for gross inelegant entertainment.

**beast.** (3) A brutal savage man, a man acting in any manner unworthy of a reasonable creature.

**bee.** (1) The animal that makes honey, remarkable for its industry and art.

**belda'm.** (1) An old woman; generally a term of contempt, marking the last degree of old age, with all its faults and miseries.

**be'llibone.** A woman excelling both in beauty and goodness. A word now out of use.

**to bethu'mp.** To beat; to lay blows upon; a ludicrous word.

**to bewa're.** (2) It is observable, that it is only used in such forms of speech as admit the word *be:* thus we say, *he may beware, let him beware, he will beware;* but not, *he did beware,* or *he has been ware.*

**bi'lingsgate.** (A cant word, borrowed from *Bilingsgate* in London, a place where there is always a croud of low people, and frequent brawls and foul language.) Ribaldry; foul language.

**blush.** (3) Sudden appearance; a signification that seems barbarous, yet used by good writers.

**bo'mbast.** (This word seems to be derived from Bombastius, one of the names of Paracelsus; a man remarkable for sounding professions, and unintelligible language.) Fustian; big words, without meaning.

**bo'oby.** (A word of no certain etymology; Henshaw thinks it a

corruption of *bull-beef* ridiculously; Skinner imagines it to
be derived from *bobo,* foolish, Span. Junius finds *bowbard*
to be an old Scottish word for a *coward, a contemptible
fellow;* from which he naturally deduces *booby;* but the
original of *bowbard* is not known.) A dull, heavy, stupid
fellow; a lubber.

bo'okish. Given to books; acquainted only with books. It is generally used contemptuously.

bookle'arned. Versed in books, or literature: a term implying some
slight contempt.

bu'lly. (Skinner derives this word from *burly,* as a corruption in
the pronunciation; which is very probably right: or from
*bulky,* or *bull-eyed;* which are less probable. May it not come
from *bull,* the pope's letter, implying the insolence of those
who came invested with authority from the papal court?) A
noisy, blustering, quarrelling fellow: it is generally taken for
a man that has only the appearance of courage.

bum. (1) The buttocks; the part on which we sit.

bu'mpkin. (This word is of uncertain etymology; Henshaw derives it from *pumpkin,* a kind of worthless gourd, or melon.
This seems harsh. *Bump* is used amongst us for a knob, or
lump; may not *bumpkin* be much the same with *clodpate,
loggerhead, block,* and *blockhead.*) An awkward heavy
rustick; a country lout.

bu'tterfly. A beautiful insect, so named because it first appears at
the beginning of the season for butter.

cant. (3) A whining pretension to goodness, in formal and affected terms.

ca'nter. A term of reproach for hypocrites, who talk formally of
religion, without obeying it.

ca'rpet. (4) *Carpet* is used, proverbially, for a state of ease and
luxury; as a *carpet knight,* a knight that has never known the
field, and has recommended himself only at table.

(5) To be on the *carpet,* is the subject of consideration; an
affair in hand.

cat. A domestick animal that catches mice, commonly reckoned
by naturalists the lowest order of the leonine species.

chi'cken. (3) A term for a young girl.

chiru'rgeon. One that cures ailments, not by internal medicines, but outward applications. It is now generally pronounced, and by many written, *surgeon.*

**chit.** (1) A child; a baby. Generally used of young persons in contempt.

**chop-house.** A mean house of entertainment, where provision ready dressed is sold.

**cit.** An inhabitant of a city, in an ill sense. A pert low townsman; a pragmatical trader.

**cli′cker.** A low word for the servant of a salesman, who stands at the door to invite customers.

**cliente′le.** The condition or office of a client. A word scarcely used.

**to coax.** To wheedle; to flatter; to humour. A low word.

**to co′lour.** To blush. A low word, only used in conversation.

**co′nfident.** (5) Bold to a vice; elated with false opinion of his own excellencies; impudent.

**conu′ndrum.** A low jest; a quibble; a mean conceit: a cant word.

**cough.** A convulsion of the lungs, vellicated by some sharp serosity. It is pronounced *coff.*

**cream.** (1) The unctuous or oily part of milk, which, when it is cold, floats on the top, and is changed by the agitation of the churn into butter; the flower of milk.

**cu′ckoo.** (1) A bird which appears in the spring; and is said to suck the eggs of other birds, and lay her own to be hatched in their place; from which practice, it was usual to alarm a husband at the approach of an adulterer by calling *cuckoo,* which, by mistake, was in time applied to the husband. This bird is remarkable for the uniformity of his note, from which his name in most tongues seems to have been formed.

**cu′dden, cu′ddy.** (Without etymology.) A clown; a stupid rustick; a low dolt: a low bad word.

**cu′lprit.** (About this word there is great dispute. It is used by the judge at criminal trials, who, when the prisoner declares himself not guilty, and puts himself upon his trial, answers; *Culprit, God send thee a good deliverance.* It is likely that it is a corruption of *Qu′il paroit, May it so appear,* the wish of the judge being that the prisoner may be found innocent.) A man arraigned before his judge.

**to cu′rtail.** (*curto,* Latin. It was anciently written *curtal,* which perhaps is more proper; but dogs that had their tails cut, being called *curtal* dogs, the word was vulgarly conceived to mean originally *to cut the tail,* and was in time written according to that notion.) (1) To cut off; to cut short; to shorten.

cu'stard. A kind of sweetmeat made by boiling eggs with milk and sugar, 'till the whole thickens into a mass. It is a food much used in city feasts.

a dab. (4) (In low language.) An artist; a man expert at something. This is not used in writing.

da'pper. Little and active; lively without bulk. It is usually spoken in contempt.

da'rkling. (A participle, as it seems, from *darkle,* which yet I have never found.) Being in the dark; being without light: a word merely poetical.

dedica'tion. (2) A servile address to a patron.

dedica'tor. One who inscribes his work to a patron with compliment and servility.

deflora'tion. (2) A selection of that which is most valuable.

demu're. (2) Grave; affectedly modest: it is now generally taken in a sense of contempt.

den. (1) A cavern or hollow running horizontally, or with a small obliquity, under ground; distinct from a hole, which runs down perpendicularly.

dese'rver. A man who merits rewards. It is used, I think, only in a good sense.

de'spot. An absolute prince; one that governs with unlimited authority. This word is not in use, except as applied to some Dacian prince; as, the *despot* of Servia.

devote'e. One erroneously or superstitiously religious; a bigot.

di'ckens. A kind of adverbial exclamation, importing, as it seems, much the same with the *devil;* but I know not whence derived.

To disannu'l. (*dis* and *annul.* This word is formed contrary to analogy by those who not knowing the meaning of the word *annul,* intended to form a negative sense by the needless use

---

dedication. Johnson wrote only two dedications for his own books, his first, and, significantly, the *Plan of a Dictionary,* to Lord Chesterfield. But after he had written this definition, he wrote about twenty dedications for other people, none "servile."

of the negative particle. It ought therefore to be rejected as ungrammatical and barbarous.) To annul; to deprive of authority; to vacate; to make null; to make void; to nullify.

di'sard. A prattler; a boasting talker. This word is inserted both by Skinner and Junius; but I do not remember it.

disciplina'rian. (2) A follower of the presbyterian sect, so called from their perpetual clamour about discipline.

to disgui'se. (4) To deform by liquor: a low term.

to disse'ver. (*dis* and *sever*. In this word the particle *dis* makes no change in the signification, and therefore the word, though supported by great authorities, ought to be ejected from our language.) To part in two; to break; to divide; to sunder; to separate; to disunite.

ditch. (2) Any long narrow receptacle of water: used sometimes of a small river in contempt.

dog. (1) A domestick animal remarkably various in his species; comprising the mastiff, the spaniel, the buldog, the greyhound, the hound, the terrier, the curr, with many others. The larger sort are used as a guard; the less for sports.

(6) *Dog* is a particle added to any thing to mark meanness, or degeneracy, or worthlessness; as *dog* rose.

dose. (3) It is often used of the utmost quantity of strong liquor that a man can swallow. He has his *dose,* that is, he can carry off no more.

dug. (1) A pap; a nipple; a teat: spoken of beasts, or in malice or contempt of human beings.

(2) It seems to have been used formerly of the breast without reproach.

dull. (8) Not exhilarating; not delightful; as, *to make dictionaries is* dull *work.*

eame. Uncle: a word still used in the wilder parts of Staffordshire.

eme'rgence, eme'rgency. (4) Pressing necessity. A sense not proper.

euthu'siasm. (1) A vain belief of private revelation; a vain confidence of divine favour or communication.

e'ssay. (2) A loose sally of the mind; an irregular indigested piece; not a regular and orderly composition.

---

di'sannul. The ungrammatical barbarians quoted by Johnson are Hooker, Bacon, Herbert, and Sandys.

eame. Johnson was born in the Athens of Staffordshire, Lichfield.

**exci'se.** A hateful tax levied upon commodities, and adjudged not by the common judges of property, but wretches hired by those to whom excise is paid.

**eyese'rvant.** A servant that works only while watched.

**fa'ngle.** Silly attempt; trifling scheme. It is never used, or rarely, but in contempt with the epithet *new;* as, *new fangles, new fangleness.*

**fasti'dious.** Disdainful; squeamish; delicate to a vice; insolently nice.

**fa'vourite.** (2) One chosen as a companion by his superiour; a mean wretch whose whole business is by any means to please.

**fib.** (A cant word among children.) A lye; a falsehood.

**to fidge, to fi'dget.** (A cant word.) To move nimbly and irregularly. It implies in Scotland agitation.

**fi'tchat, fi'tchew.** A stinking little beast, that robs the henroost and warren. Skinner calls him the *stinking ferret;* but he is much larger, at least as some provinces distinguish them, in which the polecat is termed a *fitchat,* and the *stinking ferret* a stoat.

**fitz.** A son. Only used in law and genealogy: as *Fitzherbert,* the son of Herbert; *Fitzthomas,* the son of Thomas; *Fitzroy,* the son of the king. It is commonly used of illegitimate children.

**flippa'nt.** (A word of no great authority, probably derived from *flip-flap.*) (1) Nimble; moveable. It is used only of the act of speech.

**flirta'tion.** A quick sprightly motion. A cant word among women.

**to flit.** (2) To remove; to migrate. In Scotland it is still used for removing from one place to another at quarter-day, or the usual term.

**flush.** (2) Affluent; abounding. A cant word.

**foo'tlicker.** A slave; an humble fawner; one who licks the foot.

**fo'pdoodle.** A fool; an insignificant wretch.

**freethi'nker.** A libertine; a contemner of religion.

**fri'ghtful.** (2) A cant word among women for any thing unpleasing.

**fume'tte.** A word introduced by cooks, and the pupils of cooks, for the stink of meat.

**fun.** (A low cant word.) Sport; high merriment; frolicksome delight.

---

excise. Johnson's father had had trouble with the commissioners of excise, in the conduct of his business as a bookseller and maker of parchment.

**fuss.** (A low cant word.) A tumult; a bustle.

**ga'mbler.** (A cant word, I suppose, for *game,* or *gamester.*) A knave whose practice it is to invite the unwary to game and cheat them.

**gang.** A number herding together; a troop; a company; a tribe; a herd. It is seldom used but in contempt or abhorrence.

**gaol.** A prison; a place of confinement. It is always pronounced and too often written *jail,* and sometimes *goal.*

**gazette'er.** (2) It was lately a term of the utmost infamy, being usually applied to wretches who were hired to vindicate the court.

**to gi'ggle.** To laugh idly; to titter; to grin with merry levity. It is retained in Scotland.

**goat.** A ruminant animal that seems a middle species between deer and sheep.

**gob.** A small quantity. A low word.

**to go'spel.** To fill with sentiments of religion. This word in Shakespeare, in whom alone I have found it, is used, though so venerable in itself, with some degree of irony: I suppose from the gospellers, who had long been held in contempt.

**go'speller.** A name of the followers of Wicklif, who first attempted a reformation from popery, given them by the Papists in reproach, from their professing to follow and preach only the gospel.

**gra'vy.** The serous juice that runs from flesh not much dried by the fire.

**to grease.** (2) To bribe; to corrupt with presents.

**gru'bstreet.** Originally the name of a street in Moorfields in London, much inhabited by writers of small histories, dictionaries, and temporary poems; whence any mean production is called grubstreet.

> Χαῖρ᾽ Ἰθάκη μετ᾽ ἄεθλα μετ᾽ ἄλγεα πικρὰ
> Ἀσπασίως τεὸν οὖδας ἱκάνομαι.

**half-seas over.** A proverbial expression for any one far advanced. It is commonly used of one half drunk.

**ha'tchet-face.** An ugly face; such, I suppose, as might be hewn out of a block by a hatchet.

---

grubstreet.   Johnson never lived in Grub Street, but he salutes that home of poor writers like himself with the quotation: "Hail, Ithaca! After toil and bitter woe, I am glad to reach your soil" (*Greek Anthology,* IX. 458).

to hiss. To utter a noise like that of a serpent and some other animals. It is remarkable, that this word cannot be pronounced without making the noise which it signifies.

hop. (3) A place where meaner people dance.

ho'peful. (2) Full of hope; full of expectation of success. This sense is now almost confined to Scotland, though it is analogical, and found in good writers.

ho'rrid. (2) Shocking; offensive; unpleasing: in womens cant.

horse. (1) A neighing quadruped, used in war, and draught and carriage.

hu'swife. (1) A bad manager; a sorry woman. It is common to use *housewife* in a good, and *huswife* or *hussy* in a bad sense.

ice. (3) To break the ice. To make the first opening to any attempt.

immate'rial. (2) Unimportant; without weight; impertinent; without relation. This sense has crept into the conversation and writings of barbarians; but ought to be utterly rejected.

ink. The black liquor with which men write.

irre'gular. (3) Not being according to the laws of virtue. A soft word for *vitious.*

itch. (1) A cutaneous disease extremely contagious, which overspreads the body with small pustules filled with a thin serum, and raised as microscopes have discovered by a small animal. It is cured by sulphur.

ja'ilbird. One who has been in a jail.

je'opardy. Hazard; danger; peril. A word not now in use.

job. (A low word now much in use, of which I cannot tell the etymology.) (1) A low mean lucrative busy affair.

ju'ncate. (3) A furtive or private entertainment. It is now improperly written *junket* in this sense, which alone remains much in use.

to knu'ckle. To submit: I suppose from an odd custom of striking the under side of the table with the knuckles, in confession of an argumental defeat.

lack. (1) Want; need; failure.

(2) *Lack,* whether noun or verb, is now almost obsolete.

la'ntern jaws. A term used of a thin visage, such as if a candle were burning in the mouth might transmit the light.

lass. A girl; a maid; a young woman: used now only of mean girls.

lead. Guidance; first place: a low despicable word.

**le′sser.** A barbarous corruption of *less*, formed by the vulgar from the habit of terminating comparatives in *er;* afterwards adopted by poets, and then by writers of prose.

**lexico′grapher.** A writer of dictionaries; a harmless drudge, that busies himself in tracing the original, and detailing the signification of words.

**lich.** A dead carcase; whence *lichwake*, the time or act of watching by the dead; *lichgate*, the gate through which the dead are carried to the grave; *Lichfield*, the field of the dead, a city in Staffordshire, so named from martyred christians. *Salve magna parens. Lichwake* is still retained in Scotland in the same sense.

**li′ngo.** Language; tongue; speech. A low cant word.

**li′on.** The fiercest and most magnanimous of fourfooted beasts.

**lipla′bour.** Action of the lips without concurrence of the mind; words without sentiments.

**load.** (3) As much drink as one can bear.

**to loll.** (Of this word the etymology is not known. Perhaps it might be contemptuously derived from *lollard*, a name of great reproach before the reformation; of whom one tenet was, that all trades not necessary to life are unlawful.) (1) To lean idly; to rest lazily against any thing.

**lunch, lu′ncheon.** As much food as one's hand can hold.

**magazi′ne.** (2) Of late this word has signified a miscellaneous pamphlet, from a periodical miscellany named the *Gentleman's Magazine*, by Edward Cave.

**ma′udlin.** (*Maudlin* is the corrupt appellation of *Magdelen*, who being drawn by painters with swoln eyes, and disordered look, a drunken countenance, seems to have been so named from a ludicrous resemblance to the picture of *Magdelen*.) Drunk; fuddled.

**meeting-house.** Place where Dissenters assemble to worship.

**me′rrythought.** A forked bone on the body of fowls; so called be-

---

lich.   Johnson's salutation to his birthplace, his "great parent," is, as with many of his most personal remarks, "veiled in the obscurity of a learned language."

magazine.   Johnson had edited the *Gentleman's Magazine* under Cave, the founder and publisher of the first general magazine in English. Cave had died recently, and this reference memorializes a long-time friend.

cause boys and girls pull in play at the two sides, the longest part broken off betokening priority of marriage.

me'thodist. (2) One of a new kind of puritans lately arisen, so called from their profession to live by rules and in constant method.

mo'nsieur. A term of reproach for a Frenchman.

mould. (1) A kind of concretion on the top or outside of things kept, motionless and damp; now discovered by microscopes to be perfect plants.

to mu'cker. To scramble for money; to hoard up; to get or save meanly: a word used by Chaucer, and still retained in conversation.

mum. (Of this word I know not the original: it may be observed, that when it is pronounced it leaves the lips closed.) A word denoting prohibition to speak, or resolution not to speak; silence; hush.

mu'shroom. (2) An upstart; a wretch risen from the dunghill; a director of a company.

ne'twork. Any thing reticulated or decussated, at equal distances, with interstices between the intersections.

oats. A grain, which in England is generally given to horses, but in Scotland supports the people.

ode. A poem written to be sung to musick; a lyrick poem; the ode is either of the greater or less kind. The less is characterised by sweetness and ease; the greater by sublimity, rapture, and quickness of transition.

to owe. (5) A practice has long prevailed among writers, to use *owing*, the active participle of *owe*, in a passive sense, for *owed* or *due*. Of this impropriety Bolinbroke was aware, and, having no quick sense of the force of English words, has used *due*, in the sense of consequence or imputation, which by other writers is only used of *debt*. We say, the money is *due* to me; Bolinbroke says, the effect is *due* to the cause.

pailma'il. (This is commonly written pellmell; nor do I know which of the two is right.) Violent, boisterous.

pamphletee'r. A scribbler of small books.

pa'ramour. (1) A lover or wooer.

(2) A mistress. It is obsolete in both senses, though not inelegant or unmusical.

pa'rasite. One that frequents rich tables, and earns his welcome by flattery.

pa'stern. (1) The knee of an horse.

pat. Fit; convenient; exactly suitable either as to time or place. This is a low word, and should not be used but in burlesque writings.

pa'triot. One whose ruling passion is the love of his country.

pa'tron. (1) One who countenances, supports or protects. Commonly a wretch who supports with insolence, and is paid with flattery.

pe'dant. (2) A man vain of low knowledge; a man awkwardly ostentatious of his literature.

pe'nguin. (1) A bird. This bird was found with this name, as is supposed, by the first discoverers of America; and *penguin* signifying in Welsh a white head, and the head of this fowl being white, it has been imagined, that America was peopled from Wales; whence *Hudibras:*

> British Indians nam'd from *penguins.*

Grew gives another account of the name, deriving it from *pinguis,* Lat. *fat;* but is, I believe, mistaken.

pe'nsion. An allowance made to any one without an equivalent. In England it is generally understood to mean pay given to a state hireling for treason to his country.

pe'nsioner. (2) A slave of state hired by a stipend to obey his master.

picktha'nk. An officious fellow, who does what he is not desired; a whispering parasite.

pi'rate. (2) Any robber; particularly a bookseller who seizes the copies of other men.

to pla'cate. To appease; to reconcile. This word is used in Scotland.

po'sse. An armed power; from *posse comitatus,* the power of the shires. A low word.

---

pastern. (1) In fact, part of the foot of a horse. When a lady asked Johnson how he came to define the word in this way, he answered, "Ignorance, Madam, pure ignorance." But he didn't bother to correct his definition until eighteen years later.

patriot. The fourth edition adds: "It is sometimes used for a factious disturber of the government."

**preca'rious.** Dependent; uncertain, because depending on the will of another; held by courtesy; changeable or alienable at the pleasure of another. No word is more unskilfully used than this with its derivatives. It is used for *uncertain* in all its senses; but it only means uncertain, as dependent on others; thus there are authors who mention the *precariousness* of an *account,* of the *weather,* of a *die.*

**to prejudi'ce.** (3) To injure; to hurt; to diminish; to impair; to be detrimental to. This sense, as in the noun, is often improperly extended to meanings that have no relation to the original sense; who can read with patience of an ingredient that *prejudices* a medicine?

**presbyte'rian.** An abettor of presbytery or calvinistical discipline.

**prig.** (A cant word derived perhaps from *prick,* as he *pricks* up, he is *pert;* or from *prickeared,* an epithet of reproach bestowed upon the presbyterian teachers.) A pert, conceited, saucy, pragmatical, little fellow.

**pro.** For; in defence of; *pro* and *con,* for *pro* and *contra,* for and against. Despicable cant.

**pro'ceed.** Produce: as, *the* proceeds *of an estate. Clarissa.* Not an imitable word, though much used in law writings.

**pu'nster.** A quibbler; a low wit who endeavours at reputation by double meaning.

**pu'rist.** One superstitiously nice in the use of words.

**pu'ritan.** A sectary pretending to eminent purity of religion.

**to refu'nd.** (3) Swift has somewhere the absurd phrase, *to* refund *himself,* for to *reimburse.*

**reli'gionist.** A bigot to any religious persuasion.

**to restri'ct.** To limit; to confine. A word scarce English.

**reti'culated.** Made of network; formed with interstitial vacuities.

**rhino'ceros.** A vast beast in the East Indies armed with a horn in his front.

**to rise.** (1) To change a jacent or recumbent, to an erect posture.

**to roll.** (1) To be moved by the successive application of all parts of the surface to the ground.

---

refund. "The printer has a demand . . . to be fully refunded, both for his disgraces, his losses, and the apparent danger of his life." Swift, letter to Bishop Hort, May 12, 1736, cited by *O.E.D.*

ruse. Cunning; artifice; little stratagem; trick; wile; fraud; deceit. A French word neither elegant nor necessary.

sa'tire. A poem in which wickedness or folly is censured. Proper *satire* is distinguished, by the generality of the reflections, from a *lampoon* which is aimed against a particular person; but they are too frequently confounded.

sco'rpion. (1) A reptile much resembling a small lobster, but that his tail ends in a point with a very venomous sting.

se'nsible. (8) In low conversation it has sometimes the sense of reasonable; judicious; wise.

sha'bby. (A word that has crept into conversation and low writing; but ought not to be admitted into the language.) Mean; paltry.

sheep. (1) The animal that bears wool: remarkable for its usefulness and innocence.

shre'wmouse. A mouse of which the bite is generally supposed venomous, and to which vulgar tradition assigns such malignity, that she is said to lame the foot over which she runs. I am informed that all these reports are calumnious, and that her feet and teeth are equally harmless with those of any other little mouse. Our ancestors however looked on her with such terrour, that they are supposed to have given her name to a scolding woman, whom for her venom they call a *shrew*.

slim. (A cant word as it seems, and therefore not to be used.) Slender; thin of shape.

smu'ggler. A wretch, who, in defiance of justice and the laws, imports or exports goods either contraband or without payment of the customs.

snake. A serpent of the oviparous kind, distinguished from a viper. The snake's bite is harmless. *Snake* in poetry is a general name for a viper.

to sneeze. To emit wind audibly by the nose.

so'nnet. (1) A short poem consisting of fourteen lines, of which the rhymes are adjusted by a particular rule. It is not very suitable to the English language, and has not been used by any man of eminence since Milton.

soup. Strong decoction of flesh for the table.

spa'niel. (2) A low, mean, sneaking fellow; a courtier; a dedicator; a pensioner; a dependant; a placeman.

**spick and span.** (This word I should not have expected to have found authorised by a polite writer. *Span-new* is used by Chaucer, and is supposed to come from *spannan,* to stretch, Sax. *expandere,* Lat. whence *span. Span-new* is therefore originally used of cloath new extended or dressed at the clothiers, and *spick and span* is newly extended on the *spikes* or tenters: it is however a low word.) Quite new; now first used.

**sta'teswoman.** A woman who meddles with publick affairs. In contempt.

**sto'ckjobber.** A low wretch who gets money by buying and selling shares in the funds.

**stu'rdy.** (1) Hardy; stout; brutal; obstinate. It is always used of men with some disagreeable idea of coarseness or rudeness.

**suds.** (1) A lixivium of soap and water.

(2) To be in the suds. A familiar phrase for being in any difficulty.

**swe'arer.** A wretch who obtests the great name wantonly and profanely.

**tail.** (1) That which terminates the animal behind; the continuation of the vertebrae of the back hanging loose behind.

**tale.** (1) A narrative; a story. Commonly a slight or petty account of some trifling or fabulous incident: as, *a* tale *of a tub.*

**tar.** A sailor; a seaman in contempt.

**ta'wdry.** Meanly shewy; splendid without cost; fine without grace; shewy without elegance. It is used both of things and of persons wearing them.

**ti'ny.** Little; small; puny. A burlesque word.

**toad.** An animal resembling a frog; but the frog leaps, the toad crawls: the toad is accounted venomous, I believe truly.

**too.** (1) Over and above; overmuch; more than enough. It is used to augment the signification of an adjective or adverb to a vicious degree.

**to'ry.** (A cant term, derived, I suppose, from an Irish word signifying a savage.) One who adheres to the antient constitution of the state, and the apostolical hierarchy of the church of England, opposed to a whig.

---

tale. Johnson told Boswell that he thought *A Tale of a Tub* too brilliant to have been written by Swift.

**tra'desman.** A shopkeeper. A merchant is called a *trader,* but not a tradesman; and it seems distinguished in Shakespeare from a man that labours with his hands.

**to traipse.** (A low word, I believe, without any etymology.) To walk in a careless or sluttish manner.

**tu'rtle.** It is used among sailors and gluttons for a tortoise.

**to unphilo'sophize.** To degrade from the character of a philosopher. A word made by Pope.

**ve'rdant.** Green. This word is so lately naturalized, that Skinner could find it only in a dictionary.

**vi'sion.** (4) A dream; something shewn in a dream. A dream happens to a sleeping, a vision may happen to a waking man. A dream is supposed natural, a vision miraculous; but they are confounded.

**viz.** (This word is *videlicet,* written with a contraction.) To wit; that is. A barbarous form of an unnecessary word.

**to voluntee'r.** To go for a soldier. A cant word.

**whig.** (2) The name of a faction.

**wi'tticism.** A mean attempt at wit.

**to worm.** (2) To deprive a dog of something, nobody knows what, under his tongue, which is said to prevent him, nobody knows why, from running mad.

**would.** (8) It has the signification of I wish, or I pray; this, I believe, is improper; and formed by a gradual corruption of the phrase, *would God;* which originally imputed, *that God would, might God will, might God decree;* from this phrase ill understood came, *would to God;* thence, *I would to God:* And thence *I would,* or elliptically, *would* come to signify, *I wish:* and so it is used even in good authours, but ought not to be imitated.

**ye'llowboy.** A gold coin. A very low word.

**you'ngster, you'nker.** A young person. In contempt.

---

turtle.  A curious example of Johnson's conservatism: the better classes would speak of "tortoise steak or soup"; vulgarians like sailors or gluttons would talk of "turtle soup."

The Rambler *followed in the tradition of Addison and Steele's* Tatler *and* Spectator. *It was an anonymous, separately published folio of three leaves, appearing on Tuesdays and Saturdays from March 20, 1750, to March 14, 1752. Johnson added a table of contents and translations of the mottoes at the end of the first edition. Even before the end of the original run, Edinburgh and London reprints in small volumes had begun to appear, and about ten more reprints followed during his lifetime. Now reprinted from the first edition.*

# The Rambler

## *No. 4. Saturday, March 31, 1750*

> *Simul et jucunda et idonea dicere Vitae.*
> HOR. [*Ars. Poet.* 334.]

And join both profit and delight in one.
CREECH.

The works of fiction, with which the present generation seems more particularly delighted, are such as exhibit life in its true state, diversified only by the accidents that daily happen in the world, and influenced by those passions and qualities which are really to be found in conversing with mankind.

This kind of writing may be termed not improperly the comedy of romance, and is to be conducted nearly by the rules of comic poetry. Its province is to bring about natural events by easy means, and to keep up curiosity without the help of wonder; it is therefore precluded from the machines and expedients of the heroic romance, and can neither employ giants to snatch away a lady from the nuptial rites, nor knights to bring her back from captivity; it can neither bewilder its personages in desarts, nor lodge them in imaginary castles.

I remember a remark made by Scaliger upon Pontanus, that all his writings are filled with images, and that if you take from him his lillies and his roses, his satyrs and his dryads, he will have nothing left that can be called poetry. In like manner, almost all the fictions of the last age will vanish, if you deprive them of a hermit and a wood, a battle and a shipwreck.

Why this wild strain of imagination found reception so long, in polite and learned ages, it is not easy to conceive; but we cannot wonder, that, while readers could be procured, the authors were willing to continue it: For when a man had, by practice, gained some fluency of language, he had no farther care than to retire to his closet, to let loose his invention, and heat his mind with incredibilities; and a book was produced without fear of criticism, without the toil of study, without knowledge of nature, or acquaintance with life.

The task of our present writers is very different; it requires, together with that learning which is to be gained from books, that experience which can never be attained by solitary diligence, but must arise from general converse, and accurate observation of the living world. Their performances have, as Horace expresses it, *plus oneris quantum veniae minus*, little indulgence, and therefore more difficulty. They are engaged in portraits of which every one knows the original, and can therefore detect any deviation from exactness of resemblance. Other writings are safe, except from the malice of learning; but these are in danger from every common reader; as the slipper ill executed was censured by a shoemaker who happened to stop in his way at the Venus of Apelles.

But the danger of not being approved as just copiers of human manners, is not the most important apprehension that an author of this sort ought to have before him. These books are written chiefly to the young, the ignorant, and the idle, to whom they serve as lectures of conduct, and introductions into life. They are the entertainment of minds unfurnished with ideas, and therefore easily susceptible of impressions; not fixed by principles, and therefore easily following the current of fancy; not informed by experience, and consequently open to every false suggestion and partial account.

That the highest degree of reverence should be paid to youth, and that nothing indecent or unseemly should be suffered to approach their eyes or ears, are precepts extorted by sense and virtue from an ancient writer by no means eminent for chastity of thought. The same kind, tho' not the same degree of caution, is required in every thing which is laid before them, to secure them from unjust prejudices, perverse opinions, and improper combinations of images.

In the romances formerly written every transaction and sentiment was so remote from all that passes among men, that the reader was in very little danger of making any applications to himself; the virtues and crimes were equally beyond his sphere of activity; and he amused himself with heroes and with traitors, deliverers and persecutors, as with beings of another species, whose actions were regulated upon motives of their own, and who had neither faults nor excellencies in common with himself.

But when an adventurer is levelled with the rest of the world, and acts in such scenes of the universal drama, as may be the lot of any other man, young spectators fix their eyes upon him with closer attention, and hope by observing his behaviour and success to regulate their own practices, when they shall be engaged in the like part.

For this reason these familiar histories may perhaps be made of greater use than the solemnities of professed morality, and convey the knowledge of vice and virtue with more efficacy than axioms and definitions. But if the power of example is so great, as to take possession of the memory by a kind of violence, and produce effects almost without the intervention of the will, care ought to be taken that, when the choice is unrestrained, the best examples only should be exhibited; and that which is likely to operate so strongly, should not be mischievous or uncertain in its effects.

The chief advantages which these fictions have over real life is, that their authors are at liberty, tho' not to invent, yet to select objects, and to cull from the mass of mankind, those individuals upon which the attention ought most to be employ'd; as a diamond, though it cannot be made, may be polished by art, and placed in such a situation, as to display that lustre which before was buried among common stones.

It is justly considered as the greatest excellency of art, to imitate nature; but it is necessary to distinguish those parts of nature, which are most proper for imitation: Greater care is still required in representing life, which is so often discoloured by passion, or deformed by wickedness. If the world be promiscuously described, I cannot see of what use it can be to read the account; or why it may not be as safe to turn the eye immediately upon mankind, as upon a mirrour which shows all that presents itself without discrimination.

It is therefore not a sufficient vindication of a character, that it is drawn as it appears; for many characters ought never to be drawn; nor of a narrative, that the train of events is agreeable to observation and experience; for that observation which is called knowledge of the world, will be found much more frequently to make men cunning than good. The purpose of these writings is surely not only to show mankind, but to provide that they may be seen hereafter with less hazard; to teach the means of avoiding the snares which are laid by *treachery* for *innocence,* without infusing any wish for that superiority with which the betrayer flatters his vanity; to give the power of counteracting fraud without the temptation to practise it; to initiate youth by mock encounters in the art of necessary defence, and to increase prudence without impairing virtue.

Many writers for the sake of following nature, so mingle good and bad qualities in their principal personages, that they are both equally conspicuous; and as we accompany them through their adventures with delight, and are led by degrees to interest ourselves in their favour, we lose the abhorrence of their faults, because they do not hinder our pleasure, or, perhaps, regard them with some kindness for being united with so much merit.

There have been men indeed splendidly wicked, whose endowments throw a brightness on their crimes, and whom scarce any villainy made perfectly detestable, because they never could be wholly divested of their excellencies; but such have been in all ages the great corrupters of the world, and their resemblance ought no more to be preserved, than the art of murdering without pain.

Some have advanced, without due attention to the consequences of this notion, that certain virtues have their correspondent faults, and therefore to exhibit either apart is to deviate from probability.

Thus men are observed by Swift to be grateful in the same degree as they are resentful. This principle, with others of the same kind, supposes man to act from a brute impulse, and pursue a certain degree of inclination, without any choice of the object; for, otherwise, though it should be allow'd that gratitude and resentment arise from the same constitution of the passions, it follows not that they will be equally indulged when reason is consulted; and unless that consequence be admitted, this sagacious maxim becomes an empty sound, without any relation to practice or to life.

Nor is it evident, that even the first motions to these effects are always in the same proportion. For pride, which produces quickness of resentment, will frequently obstruct gratitude, by an unwillingness to admit that inferiority which obligation necessarily implies; and it is surely very unlikely, that he who cannot think he receives a favour will ever acknowledge it.

It is of the utmost importance to mankind, that positions of this tendency should be laid open and confuted; for while men consider good and evil as springing from the same root, they will spare the one for the sake of the other, and in judging, if not of others at least of themselves, will be apt to estimate their virtues by their vices. To this fatal error all those will contribute, who confound the colours of right and wrong, and instead of helping to settle their boundaries, mix them with so much art, that no common mind is able to disunite them.

In narratives, where historical veracity has no place, I cannot discover why there should not be exhibited the most perfect idea of virtue; of virtue not angelical, nor above probability; for what we cannot credit we shall never imitate; but of the highest and purest kind that humanity can reach, which, when exercised in such trials as the various revolutions of things shall bring upon it, may, by conquering some calamities, and enduring others, teach us what we may hope, and what we can perform. Vice, for vice is necessary to be shewn, should always disgust; nor should the graces of gaiety, or the dignity of courage, be so united with it, as to reconcile it to the mind. Wherever it appears, it should raise hatred by the malignity of its practices; and contempt, by the meanness of its stratagems; for while it is supported by either parts or spirit, it will be seldom heartily abhorred. The Roman tyrant was content to be hated, if he was but feared; and there are thousands of the readers of romances willing to be thought wicked, if they may be allowed to be wits. It is therefore to be always inculcated, that virtue is the highest proof of a superior understanding, and the only solid basis of greatness; and that vice is the natural consequence of narrow thoughts; that it begins in mistake, and ends in ignominy.

## No. 18. Saturday, May 19, 1750

> *Illic matre carentibus*
>     *Privignis mulier temperat innocens,*
> *Nec dotata regit virum*
>     *Conjux, nec nitido fidit adultero;*
> *Dos est magna parentium*
>     *Virtus, et metuens alterius tori*
> *Certo foedere castitas.*  HOR. [*Odes,* III.xxiv.17.]

> Not there the guiltless stepdame knows
> The baleful draught for orphans to compose;
>     No wife high portion'd rules her spouse,
> Or trusts her essenc'd lover's faithless vows:
>     The lovers there for dowry claim
> The father's virtue, and the spotless fame,
>     Which dares not break the nuptial tie.
>                                           FRANCIS.

There is no observation more frequently made by such as employ themselves in surveying the conduct of mankind, than that marriage, though the dictate of nature, and the institution of providence, is yet very often the cause of misery, and that those who enter into that state can seldom forbear to express their repentance of the folly, and their envy of those, whom either chance, or caution, has withheld from it.

This general unhappiness has given occasion to many sage maxims among the serious, and many smart remarks among the gay; the moralist and the writer of epigrams have equally shown their abilities upon it; some have lamented, and some have ridiculed it; but as the faculty of writing has been, in all ages, chiefly a masculine endowment, the reproach of making the world miserable has been almost always thrown upon the women, and the grave and the merry have equally thought themselves at liberty to conclude either with declamatory complaints, or satyrical censures of female folly or fickleness, ambition or cruelty, extravagance or lust.

Led by such a number of examples, and incited by my share in the common interest, I have sometimes ventured to consider this universal grievance, having endeavoured to divest my heart of all partiality, and place myself as a kind of neutral being between the sexes, whose clamours, if we attend only to the world passing before us, being equally loud, and vented on both sides with all the vehemence of distress, all the apparent confidence of justice, and all the indignation of injured virtue, seem therefore entitled to equal regard. The men have, indeed, by their superiority of writing, been able to collect the evidence of many ages, and raise prejudices in their favour by the venerable testimonies of philosophers, historians and poets. But the pleas of the ladies appeal to passions of more forcible operation than the reverence of antiquity; if they have not so great names on their side, they have stronger arguments; it is to little purpose that Socrates, or Euripides, are produced against the sighs of softness, and the tears of beauty. The most frigid and inexorable judge would, at least, stand suspended between equal powers, as Lucan was perplexed in the determination of the cause, where the deities were on one side, and Cato on the other.

But I, who have long studied the severest and most abstracted philosophy, have now, in the cool maturity of life, arrived to such command over my passions, that I can hear the vociferations of either sex, without catching any of the fire from those that utter them. For I have found, by long experience, that a man will sometimes rage at his wife, when in reality his mistress has offended him; and a lady complain of the cruelty of her husband, when she has no other enemy than bad cards. I do not suffer myself now to be any longer imposed upon by oaths on one side, or fits on the other; nor, when the husband retires to punch, and the lady to citron water, am I always confident that they are driven to it by their miseries; since I have sometimes reason to believe, that they purpose not so much to sooth their sorrows, as to animate their fury. But how little credit soever may be given to particular accusations, the general accumulation of the charge shews, with too much evidence, that married persons are not very often advanced in felicity; and, therefore, it may be no improper enquiry to examine at what avenues so many evils have made their way into the world. With this purpose, I have reviewed the lives of many of my friends, who have been least successful in connubial contracts, and attentively considered by what motives they were incited to marry, and by what principles they regulated their choice.

One of the first of my acquaintances that resolved to quit the unsettled thoughtless condition of a batchelor was Prudentius; a man of slow parts, but not without knowledge, or judgment, in things which he had leisure to consider gradually before he determined them. Whenever we met at a tavern, it was his province to settle the scheme of our entertainment, contract with the cook, and inform us when we had called for wine to the sum originally proposed. This grave considerer found, by deep meditation, that a man was no loser by marrying early, even though he contented himself with a less fortune; for estimating the exact worth of annuities, he found that, considering the constant diminution of the value of life, with the probable fall of the interest of money, it was not worse to have ten thousand pounds at the age of two and twenty years, than a much larger fortune at thirty; for many opportunities, says he, occur of improving money, which if a man misses, he may not afterwards recover.

Full of these reflections he threw his eyes about him, not in search of beauty, or elegance, or dignity, or understanding, but of a woman with ten thousand pounds. Such a woman, in a wealthy part of the kingdom, it was not very difficult to find; and by artful management with her father, whose ambition was to make his daughter a gentlewoman, my friend got her, as he boasted to us in confidence two days after his marriage, for a settlement of seventy three pounds a year less than her fortune might have claimed, and less than he would himself have given, if the fools had been but wise enough to conduct their bargain.

Thus, at once delighted with the superiority of his parts, and the augmentation of his fortune, he carried Furia to his own house, in which he never afterwards enjoyed one hour of happiness. For Furia was a wretch of mean intellects, violent passions, a strong voice, and low education, without any sense of happiness but that which consisted in eating, and counting money. Furia was a scold. They agreed in the desire of wealth, but with this difference, that Prudentius was for growing rich by gain, Furia by parsimony. Prudentius would venture his money with the chances very much in his favour; but Furia very wisely observed, that what they had was, while they had it, *their own,* thought all traffick too great a hazard, and was for putting it out at low interest, upon good security. Prudentius ventured, however, to insure a ship, at a very unreasonable price, but happening to lose his money, was so tormented with the clamours of his wife, that he never durst try a second experiment. He has now grovelled seven and forty years under Furia's direction, who has never mentioned him, since his bad luck, by any other name than that of *the insurer.*

The next that married from our society was Florentius. He happened to see Zephyretta in a chariot at a horse-race, danced with her at night, and was confirmed in his first ardour; waited on her next morning, and declared himself her lover. Florentius had not knowledge enough of the world, to distinguish between the flutter of coquetry, and the sprightliness of wit, or between the smile of allurement, and that of chearfulness. He was soon waked from his rapture by conviction that his pleasure was but the pleasure of a day. Zephyretta had in four and twenty hours spent her stock of repartee, gone round the circle of her airs, and had nothing remaining for him but childish insipidity, or for herself, but the practice of the same artifices upon new men; by which she is every day bringing contempt upon them both.

Melissus was a man of parts, capable of enjoying, and of improving life. He had passed through the various scenes of gayety with that indifference and possession of himself, natural to men who have something higher and nobler in their prospect. He retired to spend the summer in a village little frequented, where happening to lodge in the same house with Ianthe, he was unavoidably drawn to some acquaintance, which her wit and politeness soon invited him to improve. Having no opportunity of any other company, they were always together; and, as they owed their pleasures to each other, they began to forget that any pleasure was enjoyed before their meeting. Melissus from being delighted with her company, quickly began to be uneasy in her absence, and being sufficiently convinced of the merit of her understanding, and finding, as he imagined, such a conformity of temper as declared them formed for each other, he addressed her as a lover, after no very long courtship obtained her for his wife, and brought her next winter to town in triumph.

Now began their infelicity. Melissus had only seen her in one scene, where there was no variety of objects to produce the proper excitements to contrary desires. They had both loved solitude and reflection, where there was nothing but solitude and reflection to be loved. But, when they came into publick life, Ianthe discovered those passions which accident rather than hypocrisy had hitherto concealed. She was, indeed, not without the power of thinking, for that he would have detected, but was wholly without the exertion of that power, when either gayety, or splendour, played on her imagination. She was expensive in her diversions, vehement in her passions, insatiate of pleasure however dangerous to her reputation, and eager of applause by whomsoever it could be given. This was the wife which Melissus the philosopher found in his retirement, and from whom he expected an associate in his studies, and an assistant to his virtues.

Prosapius, upon the death of his younger brother, that the family might not be extinct, married his housekeeper, and has ever since been complaining to his friends, that mean notions are instilled into his children, that he is ashamed to sit at his own table, and that his house is uneasy to him for want of suitable companions.

Avaro, master of a very large estate, took a woman of bad reputation, recommended to him by a rich uncle, who made that marriage the condition on which he should be his heir. Avaro now wonders to perceive his own fortune, his wife's, and his uncle's, insufficient to give him that happiness, which is to be found only with a woman of virtue.

I intend to treat in more papers on this important article of life, to recount the reasons, which influenced not on[ly] others among my friends, but likewise some ladies whom I have known, in the choice of an inseparable companion, and give account of other causes which have disappointed the hope of lovers, I shall, therefore, make no reflexion upon these histories, except that all whom I have mentioned failed to obtain happiness, for want of considering that marriage is the strictest tye of perpetual friendship;

that there can be no friendship without confidence, and no confidence without integrity; and that he, therefore, must expect to be wretched, who pays to beauty, riches, or politeness, that regard which only virtue and piety can justly claim.

## No. 21. Tuesday, May 29, 1750

*Terra salutiferas herbas, eademque nocentes,*
*Nutrit; et urticae proxima saepe rosa est.*

OVID. [*Remedia Amoris*, 45.]

Our bane and physick the same earth bestows,
And near the noisome nettle blooms the rose.

Every man is prompted by the love of himself to imagine, that he possesses some peculiar qualities superior, either in kind or in degree, to those which he sees allotted to the rest of the world; and whatever apparent disadvantages he may suffer in the comparison with others, he has some invisible distinctions, some latent reserve of excellence, which he throws into the balance, and by which he generally fancies that it is turned in his favour.

The studious and speculative part of mankind have always seemed to consider their fraternity, as placed in a state of opposition to those, who are engaged in the tumult of public business; and have pleased themselves, from age to age, with celebrating the felicity of their own condition, and with recounting the perplexity of politics, the dangers of greatness, the anxieties of ambition, and the miseries of riches.

Among the numerous topics of declamation, that their industry has discovered on this subject, there is none which they press with greater efforts, or on which they have more copiously laid out their reason and their imagination, than the instability of high stations, and the uncertainty with which those profits and honours are possessed, that must be acquired with so much hazard, vigilance and labour.

This they appear to consider as an irrefragable argument against the choice of the statesman and the warrior; to this weapon they have always recourse in their rhetorical attacks, and swell with all the confidence of victory, thus furnished by the Muses with the arms which never can be blunted, and which no art or strength of their adversaries can elude or resist.

It was well known by experience to the nations which employed elephants in war, that, though by the terror of their bulk, and the violence of their impression, they often threw the enemy into disorder, yet there was always danger in the use of them, very nearly equivalent to the advantage; for, if their first charge could be supported, they were easily driven back upon their confederates, they broke through the troops behind them, and made no less havock in the precipitation of their retreat, than in the fury of their onset.

I know not whether those, who have so vehemently urged the inconveniences and dangers of an active life, have not made use of arguments that may be retorted with equal force upon themselves; and whether the happiness of a candidate for literary fame be not subject to the same uncertainty, with that of him who governs provinces, or commands armies, presides in the senate, or dictates in the cabinet.

That eminence of learning is not to be gained without labour, at least equal to that which any other kind of greatness can require, will scarcely be denied by those who mean to elevate the character of a scholar; since they cannot but know, that every human acquisition is valuable in proportion to the difficulty implied in its attainment. And that those, who have gained the esteem and veneration of the world, by their knowledge or their genius, are by no means exempt from the solicitude which any other kind of dignity produces, may be conjectured from the innumerable artifices which they make use of to degrade a superior, to repress a rival, or obstruct a follower; artifices so gross and so mean, as to be an evident proof, how easily a man may excel in many kinds of learning, without being either more wise or more virtuous than those, whose ignorance he pities or despises.

Nothing therefore remains, by which the student can gratify his desire of appearing to have built his happiness on a more firm basis than his antagonist, except the security with which literary honours may be enjoyed. The garlands gained by the heroes of literature must be gathered from summits equally difficult to climb with those that bear the civic or triumphal wreaths, they must be worn with equal envy, and guarded with equal care from those hands that are always employed in efforts to tear them away; the only remaining hope is, that their verdure is more lasting, and that they are less likely to fade by time, or less obnoxious to the blasts of accident.

Even this hope will receive very little encouragement from the examination of literary history, or observation of the fate of scholars in the present age. If we look back into past times, we find innumerable names of authors once in high reputation, sung perhaps by the beautiful, quoted by the witty, and commented by the grave; but of whom we now know only that they once existed. If we consider the distribution of literary fame in our own time, we shall find it a possession of very uncertain tenure; sometimes bestowed by a sudden caprice of the public, and again transferred to a new favourite, for no other reason than that he is new; sometimes refused to long labour and eminent desert, and sometimes granted to very slight pretensions; lost sometimes by security and negligence, and sometimes by too diligent endeavours to retain it.

A successful author is equally in danger of the diminution of his fame, whether he continues or ceases to write. The regard of the public is not to be kept but by tribute, and the remembrance of past service will quickly languish, unless some new performance sometimes revives it. Yet in every new attempt there is new hazard, and there are few who do not, at some unlucky time, injure their own characters by attempting to enlarge them.

There are many possible causes of the inequality which we may so frequently observe in the performances of the same man, from the influence of which no ability or industry is sufficiently secured, and which have so often sullied the splendour of genius, that the wit, as well as the conqueror, may be properly cautioned not to indulge his pride with too early triumphs, but to defer to the end of life his estimate of happiness.

> ————————*Ultima semper*
> *Expectanda dies homini, dicique beatus*
> *Ante obitum nemo supremaque funera debet*
> [Ovid. *Metamorphoses*, III. 135.]

But no frail man, however great or high,
Can be concluded blest before he die.
                                        Addison.

Among the motives which urge an author to undertakings that injure his reputation, one of the most frequent is scarcely to be mentioned; because it is not to be counted among his follies, but his miseries. It very often happens that the works of learning or of wit are performed at the direction of those by whom they are to be rewarded; the writer therefore has not always the choice of his subject, but is compelled to accept any task which is thrown before him, without much consideration of his own convenience, and without time to prepare himself for the execution by previous studies.

But miscarriages of this kind are likewise frequently the consequences of that acquaintance with the great, which is generally considered as one of the chief privileges of literature and genius. A man, who has once learned to think himself exalted by familiarity with those, whom nothing but their birth, or their fortunes, or such stations as are seldom gained by moral excellence, set above him, will not be long without submitting his understanding to their conduct, and suffering them to prescribe the course of his studies, and employ him for their own purposes either of diversion or interest. His desire of pleasing those whose favour he has weakly made necessary to himself, will not suffer him always to consider how little he is qualified for the work imposed, his vanity will not allow him to confess his deficiencies, or that cowardice, which always encroaches fast upon such as spend their lives in the company of persons higher than themselves, leaves them not resolution to assert the liberty of choice.

But though we suppose that a man has fortune to avoid the necessity of dependance, and spirit to repel the usurpations of patronage, yet he may easily, by writing long, happen to write ill. There is a general succession of effects, in which contraries are produced by periodical vicissitudes; labour and care are rewarded with success, success produces confidence, confidence relaxes industry, and negligence ruins that reputation which diligence had raised.

He that happens not to be lulled by praise into supineness, may be animated by it to undertakings above his strength, or incited to fancy himself alike qualified for every kind of composition, and able to comply with the public taste through all its variations. From some opinion like this, many men have engaged, at an advanced age, in attempts which they had not time to complete, and, after a few weak efforts, sunk into the grave with vexation to see the rising generation gain ground upon them. That judgment which appears often so penetrating, when it is employed upon the works of others, very often fails when it is applied to performances, where interest or passion can exert their power. We are blinded in examining our own labours by innumerable prejudices. Our juvenile compositions please us, because they bring to our minds the remembrance of youth; our later performances we are ready to esteem, because we are unwilling to think that we have made no improvement; what flows easily from the pen charms us, because we read with pleasure that which flatters our opinion of our own powers; what was composed with great struggles of the mind we are unwilling to reject, because we cannot bear that so much labour should be fruitless. But the reader has none of these prepossessions, and only wonders that the author is so unlike himself, without considering that the same soil will, with different culture, afford different products.

## No. 31. Tuesday, July 3, 1750

*Non ego mendosos ausim defendere mores*
*Falsaque pro vitiis arma tenere meis.*
OVID. [*Amores*, II.iv.1.]

Corrupted manners I shall ne'er defend;
Nor, falsely witty, for my faults contend. ELPHINSTON.

Though the fallibility of man's reason, and the narrowness of his knowledge, be very generally and liberally confessed, yet if an enquiry be made into the conduct of those who so willingly admit the weakness of human nature, there will appear some reason for imagining that this acknowledgment is not altogether sincere, at least, that most make it with a tacit reserve in favour of themselves, and that with whatever ease they give up the claims of their neighbours, they are desirous of being thought exempt from faults in their own conduct, and from error in their opinions.

The certain and obstinate opposition, which we may observe

made to confutation, however clear, and to reproof however tender, is an undoubted argument, that some dormant privilege is thought to be attacked; for as no man can lose what he neither possesses, nor imagines himself to possess, nor be defrauded of that to which he has no right, it is reasonable to suppose that those who break out into fury at the first attacks of contradiction, or the slightest touches of censure, conceive some injury offered to their honour, some antient immunity violated, or some natural prerogative invaded; to be mistaken, if they thought themselves liable to mistake, could not be considered by them as either shameful or wonderful, and they would not surely receive with so much emotion intelligence which could only inform them of that which they knew before, or struggle with so much earnestness against a force that deprives them of nothing to which they thought themselves entitled.

It is related of one of the philosophers, that when an account was brought him of his son's death, he received it only with this reflection, *I knew that my son was subject to death.* He that is convinced of an error, if he had the same knowledge of his own weakness, would, instead of yielding to resentment and indignation, and artifice and malignity, only regard such oversights as the appendages of humanity, and pacify himself with considering that he had always known man to be a fallible being.

If it be true that most of our passions are excited by the novelty of the objects, there is little reason for doubting that to be considered as subject to fallacies of ratiocination, or imperfection of knowledge, is to a very great part of mankind entirely new; for it is impossible to enter any place of general resort, or fall into any company where there is not some regular and established subordination, without finding rage and vehemence produced only by difference of sentiments about things often very trifling, and in which neither of the disputants have any other interest than what proceeds from their mutual unwillingness to give way to any suggestion that may bring upon them the disgrace of being wrong.

I have heard of men that, having advanced some erroneous doctrines in philosophy, have refused to see the experiments by which they were confuted; and the observation of every day will give new proofs with how much industry subterfuges and evasions are sought to decline the pressure of resistless arguments, how often the state of the question is altered, how often the antagonist is wilfully misrepresented, and in how much perplexity the clearest positions are involved by those whom they happen to obstruct in the extension of a pleasing hypothesis.

Of all mortals in every age, none seem to have been more infected with this species of vanity, than the race of writers, whose reputation arising solely from their understanding, has given them a very delicate sensibility of any violence attempted on their literary honour. It is often not unpleasing to remark with what solicitude men of acknowledged abilities will endeavour to palliate absurdities and reconcile contradictions, only to obviate criticisms to which all human performances must ever be exposed, and from which they can never suffer, but when they teach the world by a vain and ridiculous impatience to think them of importance.

Dryden, whose warmth of mind and haste of composition very frequently hurried him into inaccuracies, heard himself sometimes exposed to ridicule for having said in one of his tragedies,

> *I follow fate, which does too fast pursue.*

That no man could at once follow and be followed was, it may be thought, too plain to be long disputed; and the truth is, that Dryden was apparently betrayed into the blunder by the double meaning of the word *fate,* to which in the former part of the verse he had annexed the idea of *fortune,* and in the latter that of *death;* so that the sense only was, *Though persued by* death, *I will not resign myself to despair, but will follow* fortune, *and do and suffer what is appointed.* This however was not completely expressed, and Dryden being determined not to give any way to his critics, never confessed that he had been surprised by an ambiguity; but finding luckily in Virgil an account of a man moving in a circle with this expression,——*Et se sequitur fugitque*—— "Here," says he, "is the passage in imitation of which I wrote the line that my critics were pleased to condemn as nonsense, not but I may sometimes write nonsense, though they have not the fortune to find it."

Every one sees the folly of such mean doublings to escape the persuit of criticism; nor is there a single reader of this poet, who would not have paid him greater veneration, had he shewn consciousness enough of his own superiority to set such cavils at defiance, and owned that he sometimes slipped into errors by the tumult of his imagination, and the multitude of his ideas.

It is however happy when this temper discovers itself only in little things, which may be right or wrong without any influence on the virtue or happiness of mankind; and we may, with very little inquietude, see a man persist in a project, which he himself reckons to be impracticable, live in an inconvenient house because it was contrived by himself, or wear a coat of a particular cut, in hopes by perseverance to bring it into fashion. These are indeed follies, but they are only follies, and, however wild or ridiculous, can very little affect others.

But such pride, once indulged, too frequently operates upon more important objects, and inclines men not only to vindicate their errors, but their vices; to persist in practices which their own hearts condemn, only lest they should seem to feel reproaches, or be made wiser by the advice of others; or to search for sophisms tending to the confusion of all principles, and the evacuation of all duties, that they may not appear to act what they are not able to defend.

Let every man, who finds vanity so far predominant, as to betray him to the danger of this last period of corruption, pause a moment to consider what will be the consequences of the plea which he is about to offer for that to which he knows himself not led at first by reason, but impelled by the violence of desire, surprized by the suddenness of passion, or seduced by the soft approaches of temptation, and by imperceptible gradations of guilt. Let him consider what he is going to commit by forcing his understanding to patronise those appetites, which it is its chief business to hinder and reform.

The cause of virtue requires so little art to defend it, and good and evil, when they have been once shewn, are so easily distinguished, that such apologists very seldom gain over any new proselytes to their party, nor have their fallacies power to deceive any but those whose desires have clouded their discernment, and therefore all that the best faculties thus employed can gain, is, that they may persuade the hearers that the man is hopeless whom they only thought vitious, that corruption has passed from his manners to his principles, that all endeavours for his recovery are without prospect of advantage, and that nothing remains but to avoid him as infectious, or to chase him as destructive.

But if it be supposed that he may impose on his audience by partial representations of consequences, intricate deductions of remote causes, or perplexed combinations of ideas which having various relations appear different as viewed on different sides; that he may sometimes puzzle the weak and well-meaning, and now and then seduce, by the admiration of his abilities, a young mind still fluctuating in unsettled notions, and neither fortified by instruction nor enlightened by experience; yet what must be the event of such a triumph? A man cannot spend all this life in frolick: age, or disease, or solitude will bring some hours of serious consideration, and it will then afford no comfort to think, that he has extended the dominion of vice, that he has loaded himself with the crimes of others, and can never know the extent of his own wickedness, or make reparation for the mischief that he has caused. There is not perhaps in all the stores of ideal anguish, a thought more painful, than the consciousness of having propagated corruption by vitiating the mind, of having not only drawn others from the paths of virtue, but blocked up the way by which they should return, of having blinded them to every beauty but the paint of pleasure, and deafened them to every call but the alluring voice of the syrens of destruction.

There is yet another danger in this practice: men who cannot deceive others, are very often successful in deceiving themselves; they weave their sophistry till they are themselves entangled, and repeat their positions till they credit them; by often contending they grow sincere in the cause, and by long wishing for demonstrative arguments they at last bring themselves to fancy that they have found them. They are then at the uttermost verge of wickedness, and may die without having that light rekindled in their minds, which their own pride and contumacy have extinguished.

The men who can be charged with fewest failings, either with respect to abilities or virtue, are generally most ready to confess them; for not to dwell on things of solemn and awful consideration, the humility of confessors, the tears of saints, and the terrors of persons eminent for piety and innocence, it is well known that Caesar wrote an account of the errors committed by him in his wars of Gaul, and that Hippocrates, a name perhaps in rational estimation greater than Caesar, warned posterity against a mistake into which he had fallen: *So much*, observes Celsus, *does the open and artless confession of an error become a man conscious that he has enough remaining to support his character.*

As all error is meanness, it is incumbent on every man who consults his own dignity, to retract it as soon as he discovers it, without fearing any censure so much as that of his own mind. As justice requires that all injuries should be repaired, it is the duty of him who has seduced others by bad practices, or false notions, to endeavour that such as have adopted his errors should know his retraction, and that those who have learned vice by his example, should by his example be taught amendment.

## No. 60. Saturday, October 13, 1750

*—Quid sit pulchrum, quid turpe, quid utile, quid non,*
*Plenius et melius Chrysippo et Crantore dicit.*

Hor. [*Epistles*, 1.2.3.]

Whose works the beautiful and base contain,
Of vice and virtue more instructive rules,
Than all the sober sages of the schools.          Francis.

All joy or sorrow for the happiness or calamities of others is produced by an act of the imagination, that realises the event however fictitious, or approximates it however remote, by placing us, for a time, in the condition of him whose fortune we contemplate; so that we feel, while the deception lasts, whatever motions would be excited by the same good or evil happening to ourselves.

Our passions are therefore more strongly moved, in proportion as we can more readily adopt the pains or pleasures proposed to our minds, by recognising them as once our own, or considering them as naturally incident to our state of life. It is not easy for the most artful writer to give us an interest in happiness or misery, which we think ourselves never likely to feel, and with which we have never yet been made acquainted. Histories of the downfall of kingdoms, and revolutions of empires are read with great tranquillity; the imperial tragedy pleases common auditors only by its pomp of ornament, and grandeur of ideas; and the man whose faculties have been engrossed by business, and whose heart never fluttered but at the rise or fall of stocks, wonders how the attention can be seized, or the affections agitated by a tale of love.

Those parallel circumstances, and kindred images to which we readily conform our minds, are, above all other writings, to be found in narratives of the lives of particular persons; and there seems therefore no species of writing more worthy of cultivation than biography, since none can be more delightful, or more useful, none can more certainly enchain the heart by irresistible interest, or more widely diffuse instruction to every diversity of condition.

The general and rapid narratives of history, which involve a thousand fortunes in the business of a day, and complicate innumerable incidents in one great transaction, afford few lessons applicable to private life, which derives its comforts and its wretchedness from the right or wrong management of things, that nothing but their frequency makes considerable, *Parva si non fiunt quotidie,* says Pliny, and which can have no place in those relations which never descend below the consultation of senates, the motions of armies, and the schemes of conspirators.

I have often thought that there has rarely passed a life of which a judicious and faithful narrative would not be useful. For, not only every man has in the mighty mass of the world great numbers in the same condition with himself, to whom his mistakes and miscarriages, escapes and expedients would be of immediate and apparent use; but there is such an uniformity in the life of man, if it be considered apart from adventitious and separable decorations and disguises, that there is scarce any possibility of good or ill, but is common to humankind. A great part of the time of those who are placed at the greatest distance by fortune, or by temper, must unavoidably pass in the same manner; and though, when the claims of nature are satisfied, caprice, and vanity, and accident, begin to produce discriminations, and peculiarities, yet the eye is not very heedful, or quick, which cannot discover the same causes still terminating their influence in the same effects, though sometimes accelerated, sometimes retarded, or perplexed by multiplied combinations. We are all prompted by the same motives, all deceived by the same fallacies, all animated by hope, obstructed by danger, entangled by desire, and seduced by pleasure.

It is frequently objected to relations of particular lives, that they are not distinguished by any striking or wonderful vicissitudes. The scholar who passes his life among his books, the merchant who conducted only his own affairs, the priest whose sphere of action was not extended beyond that of his duty, are considered as no proper objects of publick regard, however they might have excelled in their several stations, whatever might have been their learning, integrity, and piety. But this notion arises from false measures of excellence and dignity, and must be eradicated by considering, that, in the eye of uncorrupted reason, what is of most use is of most value.

It is, indeed, not improper to take honest advantages of prejudice, and to gain attention by a great name; but the business of the biographer is often to pass slightly over those performances and incidents, which produce vulgar greatness, to lead the thoughts into domestick privacies, and display the minute details of daily life, where exterior appendages are cast aside, and men excel each other only by prudence, and by virtue. The life of Thuanus is, with great propriety, said by its author to have been written, that it might lay open to posterity the private and familiar character of that man, *cujus ingenium et candorem ex ipsius scriptis sunt olim semper miraturi,* whose candour and genius his writings will to the end of time preserve in admiration.

There are many invisible circumstances, which whether we read as enquirers after natural or moral knowledge, whether we intend to enlarge our science, or encrease our virtue, are more important than publick occurrences. Thus Salust, the great master, has not forgot, in his account of Catiline, to remark that *his walk was now quick, and again slow,* as an indication of a mind revolving something with violent commotion. Thus the story of Melancthon affords a striking lecture on the value of time, by informing us that when he made an appointment, he expected not only the hour, but the minute to be fixed, that life might not run out in the idleness of suspense; and all the plans and enterprizes of De Wit are now of less importance to the world, than that part of his personal character which represents him as careful of his health, and negligent of his life.

But biography has often been allotted to writers who seem very little acquainted with the nature of their task, or very negligent about the performance. They rarely afford any other account than might be collected from publick papers, and imagine themselves writing a life when they exhibit a chronological series of actions or preferments; and so little regard the manners or behaviour of their heroes, that more knowledge may be gained of a man's real character, by a short conversation with one of his servants, than from a formal and studied narrative, begun with his pedigree, and ended with his funeral.

If now and then they condescend to inform the world of particular facts, they are not always so happy as to select those which are of most importance. I know not well what advantage posterity can receive from the only circumstance by which Tickell has distinguished Addison from the rest of mankind, the irregularity of his pulse: nor can I think myself overpaid for the time spent in reading the life of Malherb, by being enabled to relate, after the learned biographer, that Malherb had two predominant opinions; one, that the looseness of a single woman might destroy all the boast of ancient descent; the other, that the French beggers made use very improperly and barbarously of the phrase *noble gentleman*, because either word included the sense of both.

There are, indeed, some natural reasons why these narratives are often written by such as were not likely to give much instruction or delight, and why most accounts of particular persons are barren and useless. If a life be delayed till all interest and envy are at an end, and all motives to calumny or flattery are suppressed, we may hope for impartiality, but must expect little intelligence; for the incidents which give excellence to biography are of a volatile and evanescent kind, such as soon escape the memory, and are rarely transmitted by tradition. We know how few can portray a living acquaintance, except by his most prominent and observable particularities, and the grosser features of his mind; and it may be easily imagined how much of this little knowledge may be lost in imparting it, and how soon a succession of copies will lose all resemblance of the original.

If the biographer writes from personal knowledge, and makes haste to gratify the publick curiosity, there is danger lest his interest, his fear, his gratitude, or his tenderness, overpower his fidelity, and tempt him to conceal, if not to invent. There are many who think it an act of piety to hide the faults or failings of their friends, even when they can no longer suffer by their detection; we therefore see whole ranks of characters adorned with uniform panegyrick, and not to be known from one another, but by extrinsick and casual circumstances. "Let me remember," says Hale, "when I find myself inclined to pity a criminal, that there is likewise a pity due to the country." If there is a regard due to the memory of the dead, there is yet more respect to be paid to knowledge, to virtue, and to truth.

## No. 144. Saturday, August 3, 1751

—————*Daphnidis arcum*
*Fregisti et calamos: quae tu, perverse Menalca,*
*Et cum vidisti puero donata, dolebas;*
*Et si non aliqua nocuisses, mortuus esses.*

                              VIRG. [*Eclogues*, III.12.]

The bow of Daphnis and the shafts you broke;
When the fair boy receiv'd the gift of right;
And but for mischief, you had dy'd for spite.   DRYDEN.

It is impossible to mingle in any conversation without observing the difficulty with which a new name makes its way into the world. The first appearance of any excellence unites multitudes against it, unexpected opposition rises up on every side, the celebrated and the obscure join in the confederacy, subtilty furnishes arms to impudence, and invention leads on credulity.

The strength and unanimity of this alliance is not easily conceived. It might be expected that no man should suffer his heart to be enflamed with malice, but by injuries, that none should busy himself in contesting the pretensions of another, but where some right of his own was involved in the question, and that at least hostilities commenced without cause, should quickly cease, that the armies of malignity should soon disperse, when no common interest could be found to hold them together, and that the attack upon a rising character should be left entirely to those who had something to hope or fear from the event.

The hazards of those that aspire to eminence would be much diminished if they had none but acknowledged rivals to encounter. Their enemies would then be few, and, what is of yet greater importance, would be known. But what caution is sufficient to ward off the blows of invisible assailants, or what force can stand against unintermitted violence, and a continual succession of enemies? Yet such is the state of the world, that no sooner can any man emerge from the crowd, and fix the eyes of the publick upon him, than he stands as a mark to the arrows of lurking calumny, and receives, in the tumult of hostility, from distant and from nameless hands, wounds not always easy to be cured.

It is indeed probable that the first onset against the candidates for renown, is originally incited by those who imagine themselves in danger of suffering by their success, but when war is once declared, volunteers flock to the standard, multitudes follow the camp only for want of employment, and flying squadrons are dispersed to every part, so pleased with an opportunity of mischief, that they toil without prospect of praise, and pillage without hope of profit.

When any man has endeavoured to deserve distinction, he may easily convince himself how long his claim is likely to remain unacknowledged, by wandering for a few days from one place of resort to another. He will be surprised to hear himself censured where he could not expect to have been named; he will find himself persecuted with the utmost acrimony of malice, by those whom he never could have offended, and perhaps may be invited to an association against himself, or appealed to as a witness of his own infamy.

As there are commonly to be found in the service of envy men of every diversity of temper and degree of understanding, calumny is diffused by every art and method of propagation. Nothing is too gross or too refined, too cruel or too trifling to be practised; very little regard is had to the rules of honourable hostility, but every weapon is accounted lawful, and those that cannot make a thrust at life are content to keep themselves in play with petty malevolence, to teaze with feeble blows and impotent disturbance.

But as the industry of observation has divided the most miscellaneous and confused assemblages into proper classes, and ranged the insects of the summer, that torment us with their drones or stings, by their several tribes; the persecutors of merit notwithstanding their number may be likewise commodiously distinguished into Roarers, Whisperers and Moderators.

The Roarer is an enemy rather terrible than dangerous; he has commonly no other qualifications for a champion of controversy than a hardened front and strong voice. He seldom has so much desire to confute as to silence, he depends, therefore, rather upon vociferation than argument, and has very little care to adjust one part of his accusation to another, to preserve decency in his language or probability in his narratives. He has always a store of reproachful epithets and contemptuous appellations, ready to be produced as occasion may require, which by constant use he pours out with resistless volubility. If the wealth of a trader is mentioned, he without hesitation devotes him to bankruptcy; if the beauty and elegance of a lady be commended, he wonders how the town can fall in love with rustick deformity; if a new performance of a rising genius happens to be celebrated, he pronounces the writer a hopeless ideot, without knowledge of books or life, and without the understanding by which it must be acquired. His exaggerations are generally without effect upon those whom he compels to hear them, and though it will sometimes happen that the timorous are awed by his violence, and that the credulous mistake his confidence for knowledge, yet the opinions which he endeavours to suppress commonly recover their former strength, as the trees that bend to the tempest erect themselves again when its force is past.

The Whisperer is more dangerous. He easily gains attention by a soft address, and excites curiosity by an air of importance. As secrets are not to be made cheap by promiscuous publication, he calls a select audience about him, and gratifies their vanity with an appearance of trust by communicating his intelligence in a low voice. Of the trader he can tell that though he seems to manage a very extensive commerce, talks in high terms of the funds, and has a counting-house crowded with clerks and porters, yet his wealth is not equal to his reputation; he has lately suffered much by the miscarriage of an expensive project, and had a greater share than is publickly acknowledged in the rich ship that perished by the storm. Of the beauty he has little to say, but that they who see her in a morning do not discover all the graces which are admired in the park. Of the writer he can tell with great certainty, that, though the excellence of the work be incontestable, he can justly claim but a small part of the reputation;

that he owed most of the shining images and elevated sentiments to the kindness of a secret friend, and that the accuracy and equality of the stile was produced by the successive correction of the chief criticks of the age.

Every man is pleased with imagining that he knows something not yet commonly divulged, and therefore secret history easily gains credit, but it is for the most part believed only while it is circulated in whispers, and when once it comes to be openly told is openly confuted.

The most pernicious enemy is the man of Moderation. Without any interest in the question, or any motive but honest curiosity this impartial and zealous enquirer after truth, is ready to hear whatever can be urged on either side, and always disposed to kind interpretations and favourable opinions. He has indeed heard the trader's affairs reported with great variation, and after a diligent comparison of the evidence, concludes it most probable that the splendid superstructure of business and credit being originally built upon a narrow basis, has lately been found to totter, but between dilatory payment and bankruptcy there is a great distance; many merchants have supported themselves by expedients for a time, without any final injury to their creditors; what is lost by one adventure may be recovered by another, and no man however prudent, can secure himself against the failure of correspondents. He believes that a young lady pleased with admiration, and desirous to make perfect what is already excellent, may heighten some of her charms by artificial improvements, but surely most of her beauties must be genuine, and who can say that he is wholly what he endeavours to appear? The author he knows to be a man of application, and though perhaps he does not sparkle with the fire of Homer, yet he has the judgment to discover his own deficiencies, and to supply them by the help of others; and in his opinion modesty is a quality so amiable and so rare that [it] ought to find a patron wherever it appears, and may justly be preferred by the publick suffrage to petulant wit and ostentatious literature.

He who thus discovers failings with unwillingness, and extenuates the faults which cannot be denied, puts an end at once to doubt or vindication; his hearers repose upon his candour and veracity, and admit the charge without allowing the excuse.

Such are the arts by which the envious, the idle, the peevish, and the thoughtless obstruct that worth which they cannot equal, and by artifices thus easy, thus sordid, and thus detestable is industry defeated, beauty blasted, and genius depressed.

## No. 208. Saturday, March 14, 1752

'Ηράκλειτος ἐγώ· τί με ὦ κάτω ἕλκετ' ἄμουσοι;
Οὐχ ὑμῖν ἐπόνουν, τοῖς δέ μ' ἐπισταμένοις.
Εἷς ἐμοὶ ἄνθρωπος τρισμύριοι· οἱ δ' ἀνάριθμοι
Οὐδείς· ταῦτ' αὐδῶ καὶ παρὰ Περσεφόνη.

DIOG. LAERT. [IX. 1. 16.]

Begone ye blockheads, Heraclitus cries,
And leave my labours to the learn'd and wise:
By wit, by knowledge, studious to be read,
I scorn the multitude, alive and dead.

Time, which puts an end to all human pleasures and sorrows, has likewise concluded the labours of the *Rambler*. Having supported for two years the anxious employment of a periodical writer, and multiplied my essays to six volumes, I have now determined to desist.

What are the reasons of this resolution, it is of little importance to declare, since no justification is necessary when no objection is made. I am far from supposing, that the cessation of my performances will raise any inquiry; for I have never been much a favourite of the publick, nor can boast that, in the progress of my undertaking, I have been animated by the rewards of the liberal, the caresses of the great, or the praises of the eminent.

I have, however, no intention to gratify pride by submission, or malice by lamentation, nor think it reasonable to complain of neglect from those whose attention I never solicited. If I have not been distinguished by the distributers of literary honours, I have seldom descended to any of the arts by which favour is obtained. I have seen the meteors of fashion rise and fall, without any attempt to add a moment to their duration; I have never complied with temporary curiosity, nor furnished my readers with abilities to discuss the topic of the day; I have seldom exemplified my assertions by living characters from my papers; therefore no man could hope either censures of his enemies, or praises of himself, and they only could be expected to peruse them, whose passions left them leisure for the contemplation of abstracted truth, and whom virtue could please by her native dignity, without the assistance of modish ornaments.

To some, however, I am indebted for encouragement, and to others for assistance; the number of my friends was never great, but they have been such as would not suffer me to think I was writing in vain, and I therefore felt very little uneasiness at the want of popularity.

As my obligations have not been frequent, my acknowledgements may be soon dispatched. I can restore to all my correspondents their productions, with very little diminution of the bulk of my volumes, tho' not without the loss of some pieces to which particular honours have been paid.

The parts, from which I can claim no other praise than that of having given them an opportunity of appearing, are the four billets in the tenth paper, the second letter in the fifteenth; the thirtieth, the forty-fourth, the ninety-seventh, and the hundredth papers; and the second letter in the hundred and seventh.

Having thus deprived myself of many excuses, which candor might have admitted for the inequality of my compositions, being no longer able to allege the necessity of gratifying my correspondents, the importunity with which publication was solicited, or the obstinacy with which correction was rejected, I must now remain accountable for all my faults, and submit without subterfuge to the censures of criticism; which, however, I shall not endeavour to soften by a formal deprecation, or to overbear by the influence of a patron; for the supplications of an author never yet reprieved him a moment from oblivion; and, though greatness has sometimes sheltered guilt, it can afford no protection to ignorance or dulness. Having hitherto attempted only the propagation of truth, I will not at last violate it by the confession of terrors which I do not feel: Having laboured to maintain the dignity of virtue, I will not now degrade it by the meanness of dedication.

The seeming vanity with which I have sometimes spoken of myself, would perhaps require an apology, were it not extenuated by the example of all those who have published essays before me, and by the privilege which a nameless writer has been hitherto allowed. "A mask," says Castiglione, "confers a right of acting and speaking with less restraint, even when the wearer is known to the whole company." He that is discovered without his own consent, may claim some indulgence, and cannot be rigorously called to justify those sallies or frolicks which his disguise is a proof that he wishes to conceal.

But I have been cautious lest this offence should be very frequently or grossly committed; for as one of the philosophers directs us to live with a friend, as with one that is sometime to become an enemy, I have always thought it the duty of an anonymous author to write, as if he expected to be hereafter known.

I am willing to flatter myself with hopes, that, by collecting these papers, I am not preparing for my future life either shame or repentance. That they are all happily imagined, or accurately polished; that the same sentiment will not sometimes recur, or the same form of expression be too frequently repeated, I have not confidence in my abilities sufficient to promise. He that condemns himself to compose on a stated day, will often bring to his task, an attention dissipated, a memory overwhelmed, an imagination embarrassed, a mind distracted with anxieties, and a body languishing with disease: He will sometimes labour on a barren topic, till it is too late to change it; and sometimes, in the ardour of invention, diffuse his thoughts into wild exuberance, which the pressing hour of publication will not suffer judgment to examine or reduce.

Whatever shall be the final sentence of mankind, I have at least endeavoured to deserve their kindness; I have laboured to refine our language to grammatical purity, and to clear it from colloquial barbarisms, licentious idioms, and irregular combinations. Something, perhaps, I have added to the elegance of its construction, and something to the harmony of its cadence. When common words were less pleasing to the ear, or less distinct in their signification, I have familiarized the terms of philosophy, by applying them to known objects and popular ideas, but have rarely admitted any word, not authorized by former writers; for I believe, that whoever knows the English tongue in its present extent, will be able to express all his thoughts without farther help from other nations.

As it has been always my principal design to inculcate wisdom or piety, I have allotted few papers to the idle sports of wild imagination; and though some, perhaps, may be found, of which the highest excellence is harmless merriment, yet scarcely any man will be so steadily serious, as not rather to complain, that the severity of dictatorial instruction is too seldom relieved, and that he is driven by the sternness of philosophy to more chearful and airy companions.

Next to the excursions of fancy are the disquisitions of criticism, which, in my opinion, is to be ranked only among the subordinate and instrumental arts. The common practice of arbitrary decision and general exclamation, I have carefully avoided. I have asserted nothing without a reason; and have established all my principles of judgment on unalterable and evident truth.

In the pictures of life I have never been so studious of novelty or surprize, as to depart wholly from all resemblance; a fault which some writers, deservedly celebrated, frequently commit, only that they may raise, as the occasion requires, either mirth or abhorrence. Some enlargement may be allowed to declamation, and some exaggeration to burlesque; but as they deviate farther from life, they are less useful, because their lessons will fail of application. The mind of the reader is carried away from the contemplation of his own manners; he finds in himself no likeness to the phantom before him, and though he laughs or rages, he is not reformed.

The essays professedly serious, if I have been able to execute my own intentions, will be found exactly conformable to the precepts of Christianity, without any accommodation to the licentiousness and levity of the present age. I therefore look back on this part of my work with pleasure, which no blame or praise of man shall diminish or augment; I shall never envy the honours which wit and learning obtain in any other cause, if I can be numbered among the writers, who have given ardour to virtue, and confidence to truth.

Αὐτῶν ἐκ μακάρων ἀντάξιος εἴη ἀμοιβή.
[Dionysius, *Periegesis*, 1186.]

Celestial pow'rs! that piety regard,
From you my labours wait their last reward.

*First published in* The Literary Magazine, *which Johnson was editing, in No. IV, July 15–August 15, 1756, this article is representative of Johnson's attitude toward the Seven Years' War, and particularly of his opinions of the relations between the American colonists and the Indians.*

# Observations on the Present State of Affairs

The time is now come in which every Englishman expects to be informed of the national affairs, and in which he has a right to have that expectation gratified. For whatever may be urged by ministers, or those whom vanity or interest make the followers of ministers, concerning the necessity of confidence in our governors, and the presumption of prying with profane eyes into the recesses of policy, it is evident, that this reverence can be claimed only by counsels yet unexecuted, and projects suspended in deliberation. But when a design has ended in miscarriage or success, when every eye and every ear is witness to general discontent, or general satisfaction, it is then a proper time to disentangle confusion and illustrate obscurity; to shew by what causes every event was produced, and in what effects it is likely to terminate; to lay down with distinct particularity, what rumour always huddles in general exclamations, or perplexes by undigested narratives; to shew whence happiness or calamity is derived, and whence it may be expected, and honestly to lay before the people what inquiry can gather of the past, and conjecture can estimate of the future.

The general subject of the present war is sufficiently known. It is allowed on both sides, that hostilities began in America, and that the French and English quarrelled about the boundaries of their settlements, about grounds and rivers to which, I am afraid, neither can shew any other right than that of power, and which neither can occupy but by usurpation, and the dispossession of the natural lords and original inhabitants. Such is the contest that no honest man can heartily wish success to either party.

It may indeed be alleged, that the Indians have granted large tracts of land both to one and to the other; but these grants can add little to the validity of our titles, till it be experienced how they were obtained: for if they were extorted by violence, or induced by fraud; by threats, which the miseries of other nations had shewn not to be vain, or by promises of which no performance was ever intended, what are they but new modes of usurpation, but new instances of cruelty and treachery?

And indeed what but false hope, or resistless terror can prevail upon a weaker nation to invite a stronger into their country, to give their lands to strangers whom no affinity of manners, or similitude of opinion, can be said to recommend, to permit them to build towns from which the natives are excluded, to raise fortresses by which they are intimidated, to settle themselves with such strength, that they cannot afterwards be expelled, but are for ever to remain the masters of the original inhabitants, the dictators of their conduct, and the arbiters of their fate?

When we see men acting thus against the precepts of reason, and the instincts of nature, we cannot hesitate to determine, that by some means or other they were debarred from choice; that they were lured or frighted into compliance; that they either granted only what they found impossible to keep, or expected advantages upon the faith of their new inmates, which there was no purpose to confer upon them. It cannot be said, that the Indians originally invited us to their coasts; we went uncalled and unexpected to nations who had no imagination that the earth contained any inhabitants so distant and so different from themselves. We astonished them with our ships, with our arms, and with our general superiority. They yielded to us as to beings of another and higher race, sent among them from some unknown regions, with power which naked Indians could not resist, and which they were therefore, by every act of humility, to propitiate, that they, who could so easily destroy, might be induced to spare.

To this influence, and to this only, are to be attributed all the cessions and submissions of the Indian princes, if indeed any such cessions were ever made, of which we have no witness but those who claim from them, and there is no great malignity in suspecting, that those who have robbed have also lied.

Some colonies indeed have been established more peaceably than others. The utmost extremity of wrong has not always been practised; but those that have settled in the new world on the fairest terms, have no other merit than that of a scrivener[1] who ruins in silence over a plunderer that seizes by force; all have taken what had other owners, and all have had recourse to arms, rather than quit the prey on which they had fastened.

The American dispute between the French and us is therefore only the quarrel of two robbers for the spoils of a passenger, but, as robbers have terms of confederacy, which they are obliged to observe as members of the gang, so the English and French may have relative rights, and do injustice to each other, while both are injuring the Indians. And such, indeed, is the present contest: they have parted the northern continent of America between them, and are now disputing about their boundaries, and each is endeavouring the destruction of the other by the help of the Indians, whose interest it is that both should be destroyed.

Both nations clamour with great vehemence about infraction of limits, violation of treaties, open usurpation, insidious artifices, and breach of faith. The English rail at the perfidious French, and the French at the encroaching English; they quote treaties on each side, charge each other with aspiring to universal monarchy, and complain on either part of the insecurity of possession near such turbulent neighbours.

Through this mist of controversy it can raise no wonder, that the truth is not easily discovered. When a quarrel has been long carried on between individuals, it is often very hard to tell by whom it was begun. Every fact is darkened by distance, by interest, and by multitudes. Information is not easily procured from far; those whom the truth will not favour, will not step voluntarily forth to tell it; and where there are many agents, it is easy for every single action to be concealed.

---

[1] scrivener: "One whose business is to place money at interest." Johnson's *Dictionary.*

All these causes concur to the obscurity of the question, by whom were hostilities in America commenced? Perhaps there never can be remembered a time in which hostilities had ceased. Two powerful colonies enflamed with immemorial rivalry, and placed out of the superintendence of the mother nations, were not likely to be long at rest. Some opposition was always going forward, some mischief was every day done or meditated, and the borderers were always better pleased with what they could snatch from their neighbours, than what they had of their own.

In this disposition to reciprocal invasion a cause of dispute never could be wanting. The forests and desarts of America are without land-marks, and therefore cannot be particularly specified in stipulations; the appellations of those wide extended regions have in every mouth a different meaning, and are understood on either side as inclination happens to contract or extend them. Who has yet pretended to define how much of America is included in Brazil, Mexico, or Peru? It is almost as easy to divide the Atlantic ocean by a line, as clearly to ascertain the limits of those uncultivated, uninhabitable, unmeasured regions.

It is likewise to be considered, that contracts concerning boundaries are often left vague and indefinite without necessity, by the desire of each party, to interpret the ambiguity to its own advantage when a fit opportunity shall be found. In forming stipulations, the commissaries are often ignorant, and often negligent; they are sometimes weary with debate, and contract a tedious discussion into general terms, or refer it to a former treaty, which was never understood. The weaker part is always afraid of requiring explanations, and the stronger always has an interest in leaving the question undecided: thus it will happen without great caution on either side, that after long treaties solemnly ratified, the rights that had been disputed are still equally open to controversy.

In America it may easily be supposed, that there are tracts of land not yet claimed by either party, and therefore mentioned in no treaties, which yet one or the other may be afterwards inclined to occupy; but to these vacant and unsettled countries each nation may pretend, as each conceives itself intitled to all that is not expressly granted to the other.

Here then is a perpetual ground of contest, every enlargement of the possessions of either will be considered as something taken from the other, and each will endeavour to regain what had never been claimed, but that the other occupied it.

Thus obscure in its original is the American contest. It is difficult to find the first invader, or to tell where invasion properly begins; but I suppose it is not to be doubted, that after the last war, when the French had made peace with such apparent superiority, they naturally began to treat us with less respect in distant parts of the world, and to consider us as a people from whom they had nothing to fear, and who could no longer presume to contravene their designs, or to check their progress.

The power of doing wrong with impunity seldom waits long for the will, and it is reasonable to believe, that in America the French would avow their purpose of aggrandising themselves with at least as little reserve as in Europe. We may therefore readily believe, that they were unquiet neighbours, and had no great regard to right which they believed us no longer able to enforce.

That in forming a line of forts behind our colonies, if in no other part of their attempt, they had acted against the general intention, if not against the literal terms of treaties, can scarcely be denied; for it never can be supposed, that we intended to be inclosed between the sea and the French garrisons, or preclude ourselves from extending our plantations backwards to any length that our convenience should require.

With dominion is conferred every thing that can secure dominion. He that has the coast, has likewise the sea to a certain distance; he that possesses a fortress, has the right of prohibiting another fortress to be built within the command of its cannon. When therefore we planted the coast of North-America we supposed the possession of the inland region granted to an indefinite extent, and every nation that settled in that part of the world, seems, by the permission of every other nation, to have made the same supposition in its own favour.

Here then, perhaps, it will be safest to fix the justice of our cause; here we are apparently and indisputably injured, and this injury may, according to the practice of nations, be justly resented. Whether we have not in return made some incroachments upon them, must be left doubtful, till our practices on the Ohio shall be stated and vindicated. There are no two nations confining on each other, between whom a war may not always be kindled

with plausible pretences on either part, as there is always passing
between them a reciprocation of injuries and fluctuation of incroachments.

From the conclusion of the last peace perpetual complaints of
the supplantations and invasions of the French have been sent to
Europe from our colonies, and transmitted to our ministers at
Paris, where good words were sometimes given us, and the practices of the American commanders were sometimes disowned;
but no redress was ever obtained, nor is it probable that any
prohibition was sent to America. We were still amused with such
doubtful promises as those who are afraid of war are ready to
interpret in their own favour, and the French pushed forward
their line of fortresses, and seemed to resolve that before our
complaints were finally dismissed, all remedy should be hopeless.

We, likewise, endeavour'd at the same time to form a barrier
against the Canadians by sending a colony to New-Scotland, a
cold uncomfortable tract of ground, of which we had long the
nominal possession before we really began to occupy it. To this
those were invited whom the cessation of war deprived of employment, and made burdensome to their country, and settlers
were allured thither by many fallacious descriptions of fertile
vallies and clear skies. What effects these pictures of American
happiness had upon my countrymen I was never informed, but
I suppose very few sought provision in those frozen regions,
whom guilt or poverty did not drive from their native country.
About the boundaries of this new colony there were some disputes; but as there was nothing yet worth a contest, the power
of the French was not much exerted on that side; some disturbance was however given and some skirmishes ensued. But perhaps being peopled chiefly with soldiers, who would rather live by
plunder than by agriculture, and who consider war as their best
trade, New-Scotland would be more obstinately defended than
some settlements of far greater value, and the French are too well
informed of their own interest, to provoke hostility for no advantage, or to select that country for invasion, where they must hazard
much, and can win little. They therefore pressed on southward
behind our ancient and wealthy settlements, and built fort after
fort at such distances that they might conveniently relieve one
another, invade our colonies with sudden incursions, and retire to

places of safety before our people could unite to oppose them.

This design of the French has been long formed, and long known, both in America and Europe, and might at first have been easily repressed had force been used instead of expostulation. When the English attempted a settlement upon the Island of St. Lucia, the French, whether justly or not, considering it as neutral and forbidden to be occupied by either nation, immediately landed upon it, and destroyed the houses, wasted the plantations, and drove or carried away the inhabitants. This was done in the time of peace, when mutual professions of friendship were daily exchanged by the two courts, and was not considered as any violation of treaties, nor was any more than a very soft remonstrance made on our part.

The French therefore taught us how to act, but an Hanoverian quarrel with the house of Austria for some time induced us to court, at any expence, the alliance of a nation whose very situation makes them our enemies. We suffered them to destroy our settlements, and to advance their own, which we had an equal right to attack. The time however came at last, when we ventured to quarrel with Spain, and then France no longer suffered the appearance of peace to subsist between us, but armed in defence of her ally.

The events of the war are well known, we pleased ourselves with a victory at Dettingen, where we left our wounded men to the care of our enemies, but our army was broken at Fontenoy and Val; and though after the disgrace which we suffered in the Mediterranean we had some naval success, and an accidental dearth made peace necessary for the French, yet they prescribed the conditions, obliged us to give hostages, and acted as conquerors, though as conquerors of moderation.

In this war the Americans distinguished themselves in a manner unknown and unexpected. The New English raised an army, and under the command of Pepperel took Cape-Breton, with the assistance of the fleet. This is the most important fortress in America. We pleased ourselves so much with the acquisition, that we could not think of restoring it, and among the arguments used to inflame the people against Charles Stuart, it was very clamorously urged, that if he gained the kingdom, he would give Cape-Breton back to the French.

The French however had a more easy expedient to regain Cape-

Breton than by exalting Charles Stuart to the English throne, they took in their turn Fort St. George, and had our East-India company wholly in their power, whom they restored at the peace to their former possessions, that they may continue to export our silver.

Cape-Breton therefore was restored, and the French were re-established in America, with equal power and greater spirit, having lost nothing by the war which they had before gained.

To the general reputation of their arms, and that habitual superiority which they derive from it, they owe their power in America, rather than to any real strength, or circumstances of advantage. Their numbers are yet not great; their trade, though daily improved, is not very extensive; their country is barren, their fortresses, though numerous, are weak, and rather shelters from wild beasts, or savage nations, than places built for defence against bombs or cannons. Cape-Breton has been found not to be impregnable; nor, if we consider the state of the places possessed by the two nations in America, is there any reason upon which the French should have presumed to molest us; but that they thought our spirit so broken that we durst not resist them, and in this opinion our long forbearance easily confirmed them.

We forgot, or rather avoided to think, that what we delayed to do must be done at last, and done with more difficulty, as it was delayed longer; that while we were complaining, and they were eluding, or answering our complaints, fort was rising upon fort, and one invasion made a precedent for another.

This confidence of the French is exalted by some real advantages. If they possess in those countries less than we, they have more to gain, and less to hazard; if they are less numerous, they are better united.

The French compose one body with one head. They have all the same interest, and agree to pursue it by the same means. They are subject to a governor commission'd by an absolute monarch, and participating the authority of his master. Designs are therefore formed without debate, and executed without impediment. They have yet more martial than mercantile ambition, and seldom suffer their military schemes to be entangled with collateral projects of gain: they have no wish but for conquest, of which they justly consider riches as the consequence.

Some advantages they will always have as invaders. They make war at the hazard of their enemies: the contest being carried on in our territories we must lose more by a victory than they will suffer by a defeat. They will subsist, while they stay, upon our plantations, and perhaps destroy them when they can stay no longer. If we pursue them and carry the war into their dominions, our difficulties will encrease every step as we advance, for we shall leave plenty behind us, and find nothing in Canada, but lakes and forests barren and trackless, our enemies will shut themselves up in their forts, against which it is difficult to bring cannon through so rough a country, and which if they are provided with good magazines will soon starve those who besiege them.

All these are the natural effects of their government, and situation; they are accidentally more formidable as they are less happy. But the favour of the Indians which they enjoy, with very few exceptions, among all the nations of the northern continent, we ought to consider with other thoughts; this favour we might have enjoyed, if we had been careful to deserve it. The French by having these savage nations on their side, are always supplied with spies, and guides, and with auxiliaries, like the Tartars to the Turks or the Hussars to the Germans, of no great use against troops ranged in order of battle, but very well qualified to maintain a war among woods and rivulets, where much mischief may be done by unexpected onsets, and safety be obtained by quick retreats. They can waste a colony by sudden inroads, surprise the straggling planters, frighten the inhabitants into towns, hinder the cultivation of lands, and starve those whom they are not able to conquer.

*Unlike* The Rambler, The Idler *appeared in a weekly newspaper,* The Universal Chronicle, *as the first piece of the eight pages. The first* Idler *appeared in the second number, April 8, 1758, and the rest followed to No. 104, April 5, 1760. They were reprinted in two small volumes in 1761, and again in 1767; in both instances Johnson suppressed No. 22, perhaps because of its violence. Reprinted from* The Universal Chronicle, *with the original numbering.*

# The Idler

## *No. 22. Saturday, September 9, 1758*

Many naturalists are of opinion, that the animals which we commonly consider as mute, have the power of imparting their thoughts to one another. That they can express general sensations is very certain; every being that can utter sounds, has a different voice for pleasure and for pain. The hound informs his fellows when he scents his game; the hen calls her chickens to their food by her cluck, and drives them from danger by her scream.

Birds have the greatest variety of notes; they have indeed a variety, which seems almost sufficient to make a speech adequate to the purposes of a life, which is regulated by instinct, and can admit little change or improvement. To the cries of birds, curiosity or superstition has been always attentive, many have studied the language of the feathered tribes, and some have boasted that they understood it.

The most skilful or most confident interpreters of the silvan dialogues have been commonly found among the philosophers of the East, in a country where the calmness of the air, and the mildness of the seasons, allow the student to pass a great part of the year in groves and bowers. But what may be done in one place by peculiar opportunities, may be performed in another by peculiar diligence. A shepherd of Bohemia has, by long abode in the forests, enabled himself to understand the voice of birds, at least he relates with great confidence a story of which the credibility may be considered by the learned.

"As I was sitting, (said he) within a hollow rock, and watching my sheep that fed in the valley, I heard two vultures interchangeably crying on the summit of the cliff. Both voices were earnest and deliberate. My curiosity prevailed over my care of the flock; I climbed slowly and silently from crag to crag, concealed among the shrubs, till I found a cavity where I might sit and listen without suffering, or giving disturbance.

"I soon perceived, that my labour would be well repaid; for an old vulture was sitting on a naked prominence, with her young about her, whom she was instructing in the arts of a vulture's life, and preparing, by the last lecture, for their final dismission to the mountains and the skies.

" 'My children,' said the old vulture, 'you will the less want my instructions because you have had my practice before your eyes; you have seen me snatch from the farm the houshold fowl, you have seen me seize the leveret in the bush, and the kid in the pasture, you know how to fix your talons, and how to balance your flight when you are laden with your prey. But you remember the taste of more delicious food; I have often regaled you with the flesh of man.' 'Tell us,' said the young vultures, 'where man may be found, and how he may be known; his flesh is surely the natural food of a vulture. Why have you never brought a man in your talons to the nest?' 'He is too bulky,' said the mother; 'when we find a man, we can only tear away his flesh and leave his bones upon the ground.' 'Since man is so big,' said the young ones, 'how do you kill him. You are afraid of the wolf and of the bear, by what power are vultures superior to man, is man more defenseless than a sheep?' 'We have not the strength of man,' returned the mother, 'and I am sometimes in doubt whether we have the subtilty; and the vultures would seldom feast upon his flesh, had not nature, that devoted him to our uses, infused into him a strange ferocity, which I have never observed in any other being that feeds upon the earth. Two herds of men will often meet and shake the earth with noise, and fill the air with fire. When you hear noise and see fire which flashes along the ground, hasten to the place with your swiftest wing, for men are surely destroying one another; you will then find the ground smoking with blood and covered with carcasses, of which many are dismembered and mangled for the convenience of the vulture.' 'But when men have killed their prey,' said the pupil, 'why do they not eat it? When the wolf has killed a sheep he suffers not the vulture to touch it till he has satisfied himself. Is not man another kind of wolf?' 'Man,' said the mother, 'is the only beast who kills that which he does not devour, and this quality makes him so much a benefactor to our species.' 'If men kill our prey and lay it in our way,' said the young one, 'what need shall we have of labouring for ourselves.' 'Because man will, sometimes,' replied the mother, 'remain for a long time quiet in his den. The old vultures will tell you when you are to watch his motions. When you see men in great numbers moving close together, like a flight of storks, you may conclude that they are hunting, and that you will soon revel in human blood.' 'But still,' said the young one, 'I would gladly know the reason of this mutual slaughter. I could never kill what I could not eat.' 'My child,' said the mother, 'this is a question which I cannot answer, tho' I am reckoned the most subtile bird of the mountain. When I was young I used frequently to visit the ayry of an old vulture who dwelt upon the Carpathian rocks; he had made many observations; he knew the places that afforded prey round his habitation, as far in every direction as the strongest wing can fly between the rising and setting of the summer sun; he had fed year after year on the entrails of men. His opinion was, that men had only the appearance of animal life, being really vegetables with a power of motion; and that as the boughs of an oak are dashed together by the storm, that swine may fatten upon the falling acorns, so men are by some unaccountable power driven one against another, till they lose their motion, that vultures may be fed. Others think they have observed something of contrivance and policy among these mischievous beings, and those that hover more closely round them, pretend, that there is, in every herd, one that gives directions to the rest, and seems to be more eminently delighted with a wide carnage. What it is that intitles him to such pre-eminence we know not;

he is seldom the biggest or the swiftest, but he shews by his eagerness and diligence that he is, more than any of the others, a friend
to vultures.'"

## No. 23. *Saturday, September 16, 1758*

### To the Idler

Sɪʀ,

As I was passing lately under one of the gates of this city, I was
struck with horror by a rueful cry, which summoned me *to
remember the poor debtors.*

The wisdom and justice of the English laws are, by Englishmen
at least, loudly celebrated; but scarcely the most zealous admirers
of our institutions can think that law wise, which, when men are
capable of work, obliges them to beg; or just, which exposes the
liberty of one to the passions of another.

The prosperity of a people is proportionate to the number of
hands and minds usefully employed. To the community sedition
is a fever, corruption is a gangrene, and idleness an atrophy.
Whatever body, and whatever society, wastes more than it ac-
quires, must gradually decay; and every being that continues to
be fed, and ceases to labour, takes away something from the
public stock.

The confinement, therefore, of any man in the sloth and darkness of a prison, is a loss to the nation, and no gain to the creditor.
For of the multitudes who are pining in those cells of misery, a
very small part is suspected of any fraudulent act by which they
retain what belongs to others. The rest are imprisoned by the
wantonness of pride, the malignity of revenge, or the acrimony of
disappointed expectation.

If those who thus rigorously exercise the power, which the law
has put into their hands, be asked, why they continue to imprison
those whom they know to be unable to pay them: One will
answer, that his debtor once lived better than himself; another,
that his wife looked above her neighbours, and his children went
in silk cloaths to the dancing school; and another, that he pretended to be a joker and a wit. Some will reply, that if they were
in debt they should meet with the same treatment; some, that

they owe no more than they can pay, and need therefore give no account of their actions. Some will confess their resolution, that their debtors shall rot in jail; and some will discover, that they hope, by cruelty, to wring the payment from their friends.

The end of all civil regulations is to secure private happiness from private malignity; to keep individuals from the power of one another; but this end is apparently neglected, when a man, irritated with loss, is allowed to be the judge of his own cause, and to assign the punishment of his own pain; when the distinction between guilt and unhappiness, between casualty and design, is intrusted to eyes blind with interest, to understandings depraved by resentment.

Since poverty is punished among us as a crime, it ought at least to be treated with the same lenity as other crimes; the offender ought not to languish, at the will of him whom he has offended, but to be allowed some appeal to the justice of his country. There can be no reason, why any debtor should be imprisoned, but that he may be compelled to payment; and a term should therefore be fixed, in which the creditor should exhibit his accusation of concealed property. If such property can be discovered, let it be given to the creditor; if the charge is not offered, or cannot be proved, let the prisoner be dismissed.

Those who made the laws have apparently supposed, that every deficiency of payment is the crime of the debtor. But the truth is, that the creditor always shares the act, and often more than shares the guilt of improper trust. It seldom happens that any man imprisons another but for debts which he suffered to be contracted, in hope of advantage to himself, and for bargains in which he proportioned his profit to his own opinion of the hazard; and there is no reason, why one should punish the other, for a contract in which both concurred.

Many of the inhabitants of prisons may justly complain of harder treatment. He that once owes more than he can pay, is often obliged to bribe his creditor to patience, by encreasing his debt. Worse and worse commodities, at a higher and higher price, are forced upon him; he is impoverished by compulsive traffick, and at last overwhelmed, in the common receptacles of misery, by debts, which, without his own consent, were accumulated on his head. To the relief of such distress, and to the redress of such misery, no other objection can be made, but that by such easy dissolution of debts, fraud will be left without punishment, and imprudence without awe, and that when insolvency shall become no longer punishable, credit will cease.

The motive to credit, is the hope of advantage. Commerce can never be at a stop, while one man wants what another can supply; and credit will never be denied, while it is likely to be repaid with profit. He that trusts one whom he designs to sue, is criminal by the act of trust; the cessation of such insidious traffick is to be desired, and no reason can be given, why a change of the law should impair any other.

We see nation trade with nation, where no payment can be compelled. Mutual convenience produces mutual confidence, and the merchants continue to satisfy the demands of each other, though they have nothing to dread but the loss of trade.

It is vain to continue an institution, which experience shews to be ineffectual. We have now imprisoned one generation of debtors after another, but we do not find that their numbers lessen. We have now learned, that rashness and imprudence will not be deterred from taking credit; let us try whether fraud and avarice may be more easily restrained from giving it.

I am, Sir, &c.

## No. 61. Saturday, June 9, 1759

Criticism is a study by which men grow important and formidable at a very small expence. The power of invention has been conferred by nature upon few, and the labour of learning those sciences which may, by mere labour, be obtained, is too great to be willingly endured; but every man can exert such judgment as he has upon the works of others, and he whom nature has made weak and idleness keeps ignorant, may yet support his vanity by the name of a critick.

I hope it will give comfort to great numbers who are passing thro' the world in obscurity, when I inform them how easily distinction may be obtained. All the other powers of literature are coy and haughty, they must be long courted, and at last are not always gained; but criticism is a goddess easy of access and forward of advance, who will meet the slow and encourage the timorous; the want of meaning she supplies with words, and the want of spirit with malignity.

This profession has one recommendation peculiar to itself, that it gives vent to malignity without real mischief. No genius was ever blasted by the breath of criticks. The poison, which, if confined, would have burst the heart, fumes away in empty hisses, and malice is set at ease with very little danger to merit. The critick is the only man whose triumph is without another's pain, and whose greatness does not rise upon another's ruin.

To a study at once so easy and so reputable, so malicious, and so harmless, it cannot be necessary to invite my readers by a long or laboured exhortation; it is sufficient, since all would be criticks if they could, to shew by one eminent example that all can be criticks if they will.

Dick Minim, after the common course of puerile studies, in which he was no great proficient, was put apprentice to a brewer, with whom he had lived two years, when his uncle died in the city, and left him a large fortune in the stocks. Dick had for six months before used the company of the lower players, of whom he had learned to scorn a trade, and being now at liberty to follow his genius, he resolved to be a man of wit and humour. That he might be properly initiated in his new character, he frequented the coffee-houses near the theatres, where he listned very diligently day after day to those who talked of language and sentiments, and unities and catastrophes, till by slow degrees he began to think that he understood something of the stage, and hoped in time to talk himself.

But he did not trust so much to natural sagacity as wholly to neglect the help of books. When the theatres were shut, he retired to Richmond with a few select writers, whose opinion he impressed upon his memory by unwearied diligence; and when he returned with other wits to the town, was able to tell in very proper phrases that the chief business of art is to copy nature; that a perfect writer is not to be expected, because genius decays as judgment increases; that the great art is the art of blotting, and that according to the rule of Horace every piece should be kept nine years.

Of the great authors he now began to display the characters, laying down as an universal position that all had beauties and defects. His opinion was, that Shakespeare committing himself wholly to the impulse of nature wanted that correctness which learning would have given him; and that Johnson, trusting to learning, did not sufficiently cast his eye on nature. He blamed the stanza of Spenser, and could not bear the hexameters of Sidney. Denham and Waller he held the first reformers of English numbers, and thought that if Waller could have obtained the strength of Denham, or Denham the sweetness of Waller, there had been nothing wanting to compleat a poet. He often expressed his commiseration of Dryden's poverty, and his indignation at the age which suffered him to write for bread; he repeated with rapture the first lines of *All for Love*, but wondered at the corruption of taste which could bear any thing so unnatural as rhyming tragedies. In Otway he found uncommon powers of moving the passions, but was disgusted by his general negligence, and blamed him for making a conspirator his hero. He never concluded his disquisition without remarking how happily the sound of the clock is made to alarm the audience. Southerne would have been his favourite, but that he mixes comic with tragic scenes, intercepts the natural course of the passions, and fills the mind with a mild confusion of mirth and melancholy. The versification of Rowe he thought too melodious for the stage, and too little varied in different passions. He made it the great fault of Congreve, that all his persons were wits, and that he always wrote with more art than nature. He considered *Cato* rather as a poem than a play, and allowed Addison to be the complete master of allegory and grave humour, but paid no great deference to him as a critic. He thought the chief merit of Prior was in his easy tales and lighter poems, though he allowed that his *Solomon* had many noble sentiments elegantly expressed. In Swift he discovered an inimitable vein of irony, and an easiness which all would hope and few would attain. Pope he was inclined to degrade from a poet to a versifier, and thought his numbers rather luscious than sweet. He often lamented the neglect of *Phaedra and Hippolitus,* and wished to see the stage under better regulations.

These assertions passed commonly uncontradicted, and if now and then an opponent started up, he was quickly repressed by the suffrages of the company, and Minim went away from every dispute with elation of heart, and encrease of confidence.

He now grew conscious of his abilities, and began to talk of the present state of dramatic poetry, wondered what was become of the comick genius which supplied our ancestors with wit and pleasantry, and why no writer could be found that durst now venture beyond a farce. He saw no reason for thinking that the vein of humour was exhausted, since we live in a country where liberty suffers every character to spread itself to its utmost bulk, and which therefore produces more originals than all the rest of the world together. Of tragedy he concluded business to be the soul, and yet often hinted that love predominates too much upon the modern stage.

He was now an acknowledged critick, and had his own seat in the coffee-house, and headed a party in the pit. Minim has more vanity than ill-nature, and seldom desires to do much mischief; he will, perhaps, murmur a little in the ear of him that sits next him, but endeavours to influence the audience to favour, by clapping, when an actor exclaims *ye Gods,* or laments the misery of his country.

By degrees he was admitted to rehearsals, and many of his friends are of opinion, that our present poets are indebted to him for their happiest thoughts; by his contrivance the bell was rung twice in *Barbarossa,* and by his persuasion the author of *Cleone* concluded his play without a couplet; for what can be more absurd, said Minim, than that part of a play should be rhymed, and part written in blank verse? and by what acquisition of faculties is the speaker who never could find rhymes before, enabled to rhyme at the conclusion of an act?

He is the great investigator of hidden beauties, and is particularly delighted when he finds *the sound an echo to the sense.* He has read all our poets with particular attention to this delicacy of versification, and wonders at the supineness with which their works have been hitherto perused, so that no man has found the sound of a drum in this distich,

> When pulpit, drum ecclesiastic,
> Was beat with fist instead of a stick;

and that the wonderful lines upon honour and a bubble have hitherto passed without notice,

> Honour is like the glassy bubble,
> Which costs philosophers such trouble,
> Where one part crack'd, the whole does fly,
> And wits are crack'd to find out why.

In these verses, says Minim, we have two striking accommodations of the sound to the sense. It is impossible to utter the two lines emphatically without an act like that which they describe; *bubble* and *trouble* causing a momentary inflation of the cheeks by the retention of the breath which is afterwards forcibly emitted as in the practice of *blowing bubbles*. But the greatest excellence is in the third line which is *cracked* in the middle to express a crack, and then shivers into monosyllables. Yet has [this] diamond lain neglected with common stones, and among the innumerable admirers of *Hudibrass* the observation of this superlative passage has been reserved for the sagacity of Minim.

## No. 62. Saturday, June 16, 1759

Mr. Minim had now advanced himself to the zenith of critical reputation; when he was in the pit, every eye in the boxes was fixed upon him, when he entered his coffee-house, he was surrounded by circles of candidates who passed their noviciate of literature under his tuition; his opinion was asked by all who had no opinion of their own, and yet loved to debate and decide, and no composition was supposed to pass in safety to posterity, till it had been secured by Minim's approbation.

Minim professes great admiration of the wisdom and munificence, by which the academies are formed on the continent, and often wishes for some standard of taste, for some tribunal, to which merit might appeal from caprice, prejudice, and malignity. He has formed a plan for an academy of criticism, where every work of imagination may be read before it is printed, and which shall authoritatively direct the theatres what pieces to receive or reject, to exclude or to revive.

Such an institution would, in Dick's opinion, spread the fame of English literature over Europe, and make London the metropolis of elegance and politeness, the place to which the learned and ingenious of all countries would repair for instruction and improvement, and where nothing would any longer be applauded or endured that was not conformed to the nicest rules, and finished with the highest elegance.

Till some happy conjunction of the planets shall dispose our princes or ministers to make themselves immortal by such an academy, Minim contents himself to preside four nights in a week in a critical society selected by himself, where he is heard without contradiction, and whence his judgment is disseminated through the great vulgar and the small.

When he is placed in the chair of criticism, he declares loudly for the noble simplicity of our ancestors, in opposition to the petty refinements, and ornamental luxuriance. Sometimes he is sunk in despair, and perceives false delicacy daily gaining ground, and sometimes brightens his countenance with a gleam of hope, and predicts the revival of the true sublime. He then fulminates his loudest censures against the monkish barbarity of rhime; wonders how beings that pretend to reason can be pleased with one line always ending like another; tells how unjustly and unnaturally sense is sacrificed to sound, how often the best thoughts are mangled by the necessity of confining or extending them to the dimensions of a couplet, and rejoices that genius has in our days shaken off the shackles which had encumbered it so long. Yet he allows that rhyme may sometimes be borne, if the lines be often broken, and the pauses judiciously diversified.

From blank verse he makes an easy transition to Milton, whom he produces as an example of the slow advance of lasting reputation. Milton is the only writer whose books Minim can read for ever without weariness. What cause it is that exempts this pleasure from satiety he has long and diligently enquired, and believes it to consist in the perpetual variation of the numbers, by which the ear is gratified, and the attention awakened. The lines that are commonly thought rugged and unmusical he conceives to have been written to temper the melodious luxury of the rest, or to express things by a proper cadence: for he scarcely finds a verse that has not this favourite beauty; he declares that he could shiver in a hothouse when he reads that

the ground

Burns frore, and cold performs th' effect of fire;

and that when Milton bewails his blindness, the verse

So thick a drop serene has quench'd these orbs,

has, he knows not how, something that strikes him with an obscure sensation like that which he fancies would be felt from the sound of darkness.

Minim is not so confident of his rules of judgment as not very eagerly to catch new light from the name of the author. He is commonly so prudent as to spare those whom he cannot resist, unless, as will sometimes happen, he finds the public combined against them. But a new pretender to fame he is strongly inclined to censure, till his own honour requires that he commend him. 'Till he knows the success of a new production, he intrenches himself in general terms; there are some new thoughts, and beautiful passages, but there is likewise much which he would have advised the author to expunge. He has several favourite epithets, of which he has never settled the meaning, but which are very commodiously applied to books which he has not read, or cannot understand. One is *manly,* another is *dry,* another *stiff,* and another *flimzy;* sometimes he discovers delicacy of stile, and sometimes meets with *strange expressions.*

He is never so great, or so happy, as when a youth of promising parts is brought to receive his advice for the prosecution of his studies. He then puts on a very serious air; he advises the pupil to read none but the best authors, and when he finds one congenial to his own mind, to study his beauties, to avoid his faults, and, when he sits down to write, to consider how his favourite author would think at the present time on the present occasion. He directs him to catch those moments when he finds his thoughts expanded, and his genius exalted, but to take care lest his imagination hurry him beyond the bounds of nature. He holds diligence the mother of success, yet enjoins him, with great earnestness, not to read more than he can digest, and not to confuse his mind by pursuing studies of contrary tendencies. He tells him, that every man has his genius, and that Cicero could never be a poet. The boy retires illuminated, resolves to follow his genius, and to think how Milton would have thought; and Minim feasts upon his own beneficence till another day brings another pupil.

*Printed anonymously in the first number of* The British Magazine,
*edited by Smollett (January 1760, pp. 37–39). In the same issue,*
Idler *No. 89 was reprinted, "by permission of the author, whose
great genius and extensive learning may be justly numbered
among the most shining ornaments of the present age." This is
quite unexpected praise from Smollett, who a few months earlier
had called Johnson "that great CHAM of literature." Reprinted,
without revision, at the end of the third edition of* The Idler, *1767.*

# The Bravery of the English Common Soldiers

By those who have compared the military genius of the English
with that of the French nation, it is remarked, that *the French
officers will always lead, if the soldiers will follow;* and that *the
English soldiers will always follow, if their officers will lead.*

In all pointed sentences some degree of accuracy must be sacrificed to conciseness; and, in this comparison, our officers seem to
lose what our soldiers gain. I know not any reason for supposing
that the English officers are less willing than the French to lead;
but it is, I think, universally allowed, that the English soldiers are
more willing to follow. Our nation may boast, beyond any other
people in the world, of a kind of epidemick bravery, diffused
equally through all its ranks. We can shew a peasantry of heroes,
and fill our armies with clowns, whose courage may vie with that
of their general.

There may be some pleasure in tracing the causes of this plebeian
magnanimity. The qualities which commonly make an army formidable, are long habits of regularity, great exactness of discipline,

and great confidence in the commander. Regularity may, in time, produce a kind of mechanical obedience to signals and commands, like that which the perverse Cartesians impute to animals: discipline may impress such an awe upon the mind, that any danger shall be less dreaded than the danger of punishment; and confidence in the wisdom or fortune of the general, may induce the soldiers to follow him blindly to the most dangerous enterprize.

What may be done by discipline and regularity, may be seen in the troops of the Russian empress, and Prussian monarch. We find that they may be broken without confusion, and repulsed without flight.

But the English troops have none of these requisites, in any eminent degree. Regularity is by no means part of their character: they are rarely exercised, and therefore shew very little dexterity in their evolutions as bodies of men, or in the manual use of their weapons as individuals: they neither are thought by others, nor by themselves, more active or exact than their enemies, and therefore derive none of their courage from such imaginary superiority.

The manner in which they are dispersed in quarters over the country, during times of peace, naturally produces laxity of discipline: they are very little in sight of their officers; and, when they are not engaged in the slight duty of the guard, are suffered to live every man his own way.

The equality of English privileges, the impartiality of our laws, the freedom of our tenures, and the prosperity of our trade, dispose us very little to reverence of superiors. It is not to any great esteem of the officers that the English soldier is indebted for his spirit in the hour of battle; for perhaps it does not often happen that he thinks much better of his leader than of himself. The French Count,[1] who has lately published the *Art of War*, remarks how much soldiers are animated, when they see all their dangers shared by those who were born to be their masters, and whom they consider as beings of a different rank. The Englishman despises such motives of courage: he was born without a master;

---

[1] Maurice, Comte de Saxe (1696–1750), Marshal of France, author of *Rêveries, ou Mémoires sur l'art de la Guerre* (1756–58), an important work in the history of warfare, though described by Carlyle as "a strange military farrago, dictated, as I should think, under opium."

and looks not on any man, however dignified by lace or titles, as deriving from nature any claims to his respect, or inheriting any qualities superior to his own.

There are some, perhaps, who would imagine that every Englishman fights better than the subjects of absolute governments, because he has more to defend. But what has the English more than the French soldier? Property they are both commonly without. Liberty is, to the lowest rank of every nation, little more than the choice of working or starving; and this choice is, I suppose, equally allowed in every country. The English soldier seldom has his head very full of the constitution; nor has there been, for more than a century, any war that put the property or liberty of a single Englishman in danger.

Whence then is the courage of the English vulgar? It proceeds, in my opinion, from that dissolution of dependance which obliges every man to regard his own character. While every man is fed by his own hands, he has no need of any servile arts: he may always have wages for his labour; and is no less necessary to his employer, than his employer is to him. While he looks for no protection from others, he is naturally roused to be his own protector; and having nothing to abate his esteem of himself, he consequently aspires to the esteem of others. Thus every man that crowds our streets is a man of honour, disdainful of obligation, impatient of reproach, and desirous of extending his reputation among those of his own rank; and as courage is in most frequent use, the fame of courage is most eagerly persued. From this neglect of subordination I do not deny that some inconveniences may from time to time proceed: the power of the law does not always sufficiently supply the want of reverence, or maintain the proper distinction between different ranks: but good and evil will grow up in this world together; and they who complain, in peace, of the insolence of the populace, must remember, that their insolence in peace is bravery in war.

*Joseph Knight, a Negro who had been kidnapped as a child, was sold to a Scottish gentleman, who gave him sixpence a week. After marriage he found this inadequate and left. His case was brought to the Court of Session, which freed him. Johnson dictated the following argument to Boswell on September 23, 1777, for the use of Knight's counsel* (Life, III. 202-3).

# Freeing a Negro Slave

It must be agreed that in most ages many countries have had part of their inhabitants in a state of slavery; yet it may be doubted whether slavery can ever be supposed the natural condition of man. It is impossible not to conceive that men in their original state were equal; and very difficult to imagine how one would be subjected to another but by violent compulsion. An individual may, indeed, forfeit his liberty by a crime; but he cannot by that crime forfeit the liberty of his children. What is true of a criminal seems true likewise of a captive. A man may accept life from a conquering enemy on condition of perpetual servitude; but it is very doubtful whether he can entail that servitude on his descendants; for no man can stipulate without commission for another. The condition which he himself accepts, his son or grandson perhaps would have rejected. If we should admit, what perhaps may with more reason be denied, that there are certain relations between man and man which may make slavery necessary and just, yet it can never be proved that he who is now suing for his freedom ever stood in any of those relations. He is certainly subject by no law, but that of violence, to his present master; who pretends no claim to his obedience, but that he bought him from a merchant of slaves, whose right to sell him never was examined. It is said that, according to the constitutions of Jamaica, he was legally enslaved; these constitutions are merely positive; and apparently injurious to the rights of mankind, because whoever is exposed to sale is condemned to slavery without appeal; by whatever fraud or violence he might have been originally brought into the merchant's power. In our own time Princes have been sold, by wretches to whose care they were entrusted, that they might have an European education; but when once they were brought to a market in the plantations, little would avail either their dignity or their wrongs. The laws of Jamaica afford a Negro no redress. His colour is considered as a sufficient testimony against him. It is to be lamented that moral right should ever give way to political convenience. But if temptations of interest are sometimes too strong for human virtue, let us at least retain a virtue where there is no temptation to quit it. In the present case there is apparent right on one side, and no convenience on the other. Inhabitants of this island can neither gain riches nor power by taking away the liberty of any part of the human species. The sum of the argument is this:—No man is by nature the property of another: The defendant is, therefore, by nature free: The rights of nature must be some way forfeited before they can be justly taken away: That the defendant has by any act forfeited the rights of nature we require to be proved; and if no proof of such forfeiture can be given, we doubt not but the justice of the court will declare him free.

Rasselas *appeared anonymously in two small volumes in April 1759 as* The Prince of Abissinia. *(The first page of the text of each volume is headed "The History of Rasselas, Prince of Abissinia," and that is the title ordinarily used.) A second edition followed at once, and by 1773 an edition had been printed in the American colonies, as well as translations into Dutch, French, German, and Italian. It is Johnson's most famous work. Reprinted from the first edition.*

# The History of Rasselas

## Prince of Abissinia

## I

### DESCRIPTION OF A PALACE IN A VALLEY

Ye who listen with credulity to the whispers of fancy, and pursue with eagerness the phantoms of hope; who expect that age will perform the promises of youth, and that the deficiencies of the present day will be supplied by the morrow; attend to the history of Rasselas[1] prince of Abissinia.

Rasselas was the fourth son of the mighty emperour, in whose dominions the Father of waters begins his course; whose bounty pours down the streams of plenty, and scatters over half the world the harvests of Egypt.

According to the custom which has descended from age to age among the monarchs of the torrid zone, he[2] was confined in a private palace, with the other sons and daughters of Abissinian royalty, till the order of succession should call him to the throne.

---

[1] Rasselas: "Ratz" is explained as "viceroy" in Johnson's translation of Lobo's *Abyssinia*, 1735, p. 48.

[2] he: *changed to* Rasselas *in the second edition; hereafter such changes are marked* 2.

The place, which the wisdom or policy of antiquity had destined for the residence of the Abissinian princes, was a spacious valley in the kingdom of Amhara, surrounded on every side by mountains, of which the summits overhang the middle part. The only passage, by which it could be entered, was a cavern that passed under a rock, of which it has long been disputed whether it was the work of nature or of human industry. The outlet of the cavern was concealed by a thick wood, and the mouth which opened into the valley was closed with gates of iron, forged by the artificers of ancient days, so massy that no man could, without the help of engines, open or shut them.

From the mountains on every side, rivulets descended that filled all the valley with verdure and fertility, and formed a lake in the middle inhabited by fish of every species, and frequented by every fowl whom nature has taught to dip the wing in water. This lake discharged its superfluities by a stream which entered a dark cleft of the mountain on the northern side, and fell with dreadful noise from precipice to precipice till it was heard no more.

The sides of the mountains were covered with trees, the banks of the brooks were diversified with flowers; every blast shook spices from the rocks, and every month dropped fruits upon the ground. All animals that bite the grass, or brouse the shrub, whether wild or tame, wandered in this extensive circuit, secured from beasts of prey by the mountains which confined them. On one part were flocks and herds feeding in the pastures, on another all the beasts of chase frisking in the lawns; the spritely kid was bounding on the rocks, the subtle monkey frolicking in the trees, and the solemn elephant reposing in the shade. All the diversities of the world were brought together, the blessings of nature were collected, and its evils extracted and excluded.

The valley, wide and fruitful, supplied its inhabitants with the necessaries of life, and all delights and superfluities were added at the annual visit which the emperour paid his children, when the iron gate was opened to the sound of musick; and during eight days every one that resided in the valley was required to propose whatever might contribute to make seclusion pleasant, to fill up the vacancies of attention, and lessen the tediousness of time. Every desire was immediately granted. All the artificers of pleasure were called to gladden the festivity; the musicians exerted the

power of harmony, and the dancers shewed their activity before
the princes, in hope that they should pass their lives in this blisful
captivity, to which these only were admitted whose performance
was thought able to add novelty to luxury. Such was the appearance of security and delight which this retirement afforded, that
they to whom it was new always desired that it might be perpetual; and as those, on whom the iron gate had once closed,
were never suffered to return, the effect of longer experience could
not be known. Thus every year produced new schemes of delight,
and new competitors for imprisonment.

The palace stood on an eminence raised about thirty paces
above the surface of the lake. It was divided into many squares or
courts, built with greater or less magnificence according to the
rank of those for whom they were designed. The roofs were
turned into arches of massy stone joined with a cement that grew
harder by time, and the building stood from century to century,
deriding the solstitial rains and equinoctial hurricanes, without
need of reparation.

This house, which was so large as to be fully known to none
but some ancient officers who successively inherited the secrets
of the place, was built as if suspicion herself had dictated the
plan. To every room there was an open and secret passage, every
square had a communication with the rest, either from the upper
stories by private galleries, or by subterranean passages from the
lower apartments. Many of the columns had unsuspected cavities,
in which successive[3] monarchs reposited their treasures. They
then closed up the opening with marble, which was never to be
removed but in the utmost exigencies of the kingdom; and recorded their accumulations in a book which was itself concealed
in a tower not entered but by the emperour, attended by the
prince who stood next in succession.

## II

### THE DISCONTENT OF RASSELAS IN THE HAPPY VALLEY

Here the sons and daughters of Abissinia lived only to know the
soft vicissitudes of pleasure and repose, attended by all that were

---

[3] successive monarchs: a long race of monarchs had 2

skilful to delight, and gratified with whatever the senses can enjoy. They wandered in gardens of fragrance, and slept in the fortresses of security. Every art was practised to make them pleased with their own condition. The sages who instructed them, told them of nothing but the miseries of publick life, and described all beyond the mountains as regions of calamity, where discord was always raging, and where man preyed upon man.

To heighten their opinion of their own felicity, they were daily entertained with songs, the subject of which was the *happy valley*. Their appetites were excited by frequent enumerations of different enjoyments, and revelry and merriment was the business of every hour from the dawn of morning to the close of even.

These methods were generally successful; few of the princes had ever wished to enlarge their bounds, but passed their lives in full conviction that they had all within their reach that art or nature could bestow, and pitied those whom fate had excluded from this seat of tranquility, as the sport of chance, and the slaves of misery.

Thus they rose in the morning, and lay down at night, pleased with each other and with themselves, all but Rasselas, who, in the twenty-sixth year of his age, began to withdraw himself from their pastimes and assemblies, and to delight in solitary walks and silent meditation. He often sat before tables covered with luxury, and forgot to taste the dainties that were placed before him: he rose abruptly in the midst of the song, and hastily retired beyond the sound of musick. His attendants observed the change and endeavoured to renew his love of pleasure: he neglected their endeavours,[4] repulsed their invitations, and spent day after day on the banks of rivulets sheltered with trees, where he sometimes listened to the birds in the branches, sometimes observed the fish playing in the stream, and anon cast his eyes upon the pastures and mountains filled with animals, of which some were biting the herbage, and some sleeping among the bushes.

This singularity of his humour made him much observed. One of the Sages, in whose conversation he had formerly delighted, followed him secretly, in hope of discovering the cause of his disquiet. Rasselas, who knew not that any one was near him,

---

[4] endeavours: officiousness 2, avoiding the repetition of the word.

having for some time fixed his eyes upon the goats that were brousing among the rocks, began to compare their condition with his own.

"What," said he, "makes the difference between man and all the rest of the animal creation? Every beast that strays beside me has the same corporal necessities with myself; he is hungry and crops the grass, he is thirsty and drinks the stream, his thirst and hunger are appeased, he is satisfied and sleeps; he rises again and is hungry, he is again fed and is at rest. I am hungry and thirsty like him, but when thirst and hunger cease I am not at rest; I am, like him, pained with want, but am not, like him, satisfied with fulness. The intermediate hours are tedious and gloomy; I long again to be hungry that I may again quicken my attention. The birds peck the berries or the corn, and fly away to the groves where they sit in seeming happiness on the branches, and waste their lives in tuning one unvaried series of sounds. I likewise can call the lutanist and the singer, but the sounds that pleased me yesterday weary me to day, and will grow yet more wearisome to morrow. I can discover within me no power of perception which is not glutted with its proper pleasure, yet I do not feel myself delighted. Man has surely some latent sense for which this place affords no gratification, or he has some desires distinct from sense which must be satisfied before he can be happy."

After this he lifted up his head, and seeing the moon rising, walked towards the palace. As he passed through the fields, and saw the animals around him, "Ye," said he, "are happy, and need not envy me that walk thus among you, burthened with myself; nor do I, ye gentle beings, envy your felicity; for it is not the felicity of man. I have many distresses from which ye are free; I fear pain when I do not feel it; I sometimes shrink at evils recollected, and sometimes start at evils anticipated: surely the equity of providence has ballanced peculiar sufferings with peculiar enjoyments."

With observations like these the prince amused himself as he returned, uttering them with a plaintive voice, yet with a look that discovered him to feel some complacence in his own perspicacity, and to receive some solace of the miseries of life, from consciousness of the delicacy with which he felt, and the eloquence with which he bewailed them. He mingled cheerfully in the diversions of the evening, and all rejoiced to find that his heart was lightened.

## III

### THE WANTS OF HIM THAT WANTS NOTHING

On the next day his old instructor, imagining that he had now made himself acquainted with his disease of mind, was in hope of curing it by counsel, and officiously sought an opportunity of conference, which the prince, having long considered him as one whose intellects were exhausted, was not very willing to afford: "Why," said he, "does this man thus intrude upon me; shall I be never suffered to forget those lectures which pleased only while they were new, and to become new again must be forgotten?" He then walked into the wood, and composed himself to his usual meditations; when, before his thoughts had taken any settled form, he perceived his persuer at his side, and was at first prompted by his impatience to go hastily away; but, being unwilling to offend a man whom he had once reverenced and still loved, he invited him to sit down with him on the bank.

The old man, thus encouraged, began to lament the change which had been lately observed in the prince, and to enquire why he so often retired from the pleasures of the palace, to loneliness and silence. "I fly from pleasure," said the prince, "because pleasure has ceased to please; I am lonely because I am miserable, and am unwilling to cloud with my presence the happiness of others." "You, Sir," said the sage, "are the first who has complained of misery in the *happy valley*. I hope to convince you that your complaints have no real cause. You are here in full possession of all that the emperour of Abissinia can bestow; here is neither labour to be endured nor danger to be dreaded, yet here is all that labour or danger can procure.[5] Look around and tell me which of your wants is without supply: if you want nothing, how are you unhappy?"

"That I want nothing," said the prince, "or that I know not what I want, is the cause of my complaint; if I had any known want, I

---

[5] procure: procure or purchase 2, completing the third member of a triplet.

should have a certain wish; that wish would excite endeavour, and I should not then repine to see the sun move so slowly towards the western mountain, or lament when the day breaks and sleep will no longer hide me from myself. When I see the kids and the lambs chasing one another, I fancy that I should be happy if I had something to persue. But, possessing all that I can want, I find one day and one hour exactly like another, except that the latter is still more tedious than the former. Let your experience inform me how the day may now seem as short as in my childhood, while nature was yet fresh, and every moment shewed me what I never had observed before. I have already enjoyed too much; give me something to desire."

The old man was surprised at this new species of affliction, and knew not what to reply, yet was unwilling to be silent. "Sir," said he, "if you had seen the miseries of the world, you would know how to value your present state." "Now," said the prince, "you have given me something to desire; I shall long to see the miseries of the world, since the sight of them is necessary to happiness."


# IV

### THE PRINCE CONTINUES TO GRIEVE AND MUSE

At this time the sound of musick proclaimed the hour of repast, and the conversation was concluded. The old man went away sufficiently discontented to find that his reasonings had produced the only conclusion which they were intended to prevent. But in the decline of life shame and grief are of short duration; whether it be that we bear easily what we have born long, or that, finding ourselves in age less regarded, we less regard others; or, that we look with slight regard upon afflictions, to which we know that the hand of death is about to put an end.

The prince, whose views were extended to a wider space, could not speedily quiet his emotions. He had been before terrified at the length of life which nature promised him, because he considered that in a long time much must be endured; he now rejoiced in his youth, because in many years much might be done.

This first beam of hope, that had been ever darted into his mind, rekindled youth in his cheeks, and doubled the lustre of his eyes. He was fired with the desire of doing something, though he knew not yet with distinctness, either end or means.

He was now no longer gloomy and unsocial; but, considering himself as master of a secret stock of happiness, which he could enjoy only by concealing it, he affected to be busy in all schemes of diversion, and endeavoured to make others pleased with the state of which he himself was weary. But pleasures never can be so multiplied or continued, as not to leave much of life unemployed; there were many hours, both of the night and day, which he could spend without suspicion in solitary thought. The load of life was much lightened: he went eagerly into the assemblies, because he supposed the frequency of his presence necessary to the success of his purposes; he retired gladly to privacy, because he had now a subject of thought.

His chief amusement was to picture to himself that world which he had never seen; to place himself in various conditions; to be entangled in imaginary difficulties, and to be engaged in wild adventures: but his benevolence always terminated his projects in the relief of distress, the detection of fraud, the defeat of oppression, and the diffusion of happiness.

Thus passed twenty months of the life of Rasselas. He busied himself so intensely in visionary bustle, that he forgot his real solitude; and, amidst hourly preparations for the various incidents of human affairs, neglected to consider by what means he should mingle with mankind.

One day, as he was sitting on a bank, he feigned to himself an orphan virgin robbed of her little portion by a treacherous lover, and crying after him for restitution and redress. So strongly was the image impressed upon his mind, that he started up in the maid's defence, and run forward to seize the plunderer with all the eagerness of real persuit. Fear naturally quickens the flight of guilt. Rasselas could not catch the fugitive with his utmost efforts; but, resolving to weary, by perseverance, him whom he could not surpass in speed, he pressed on till the foot of the mountain stopped his course.

Here he recollected himself, and smiled at his own useless impetuosity. Then raising his eyes to the mountain, "This," said he, "is the fatal obstacle that hinders at once the enjoyment of pleasure, and the exercise of virtue. How long is it that my hopes and wishes have flown beyond this boundary of my life, which yet I never have attempted to surmount!"

Struck with this reflection, he sat down to muse, and remembered, that since he first resolved to escape from his confinement, the sun had passed twice over him in his annual course. He now felt a degree of regret with which he had never been before acquainted. He considered how much might have been done in the time which had passed, and left nothing real behind it. He compared twenty months with the life of man. "In life," said he, "is not to be counted the ignorance of infancy, or imbecility of age. We are long before we are able to think, and we soon cease from the power of acting. The true period of human existence may be reasonably estimated as forty years, of which I have mused away the four and twentieth part. What I have lost was certain, for I have certainly possessed it; but of twenty months to come who can assure me?"

The consciousness of his own folly pierced him deeply, and he was long before he could be reconciled to himself. "The rest of my time," said he, "has been lost by the crime or folly of my ancestors, and the absurd institutions of my country; I remember it with disgust, but[6] without remorse: but the months that have passed since new light darted into my soul, since I formed a scheme of reasonable felicity, have been squandered by my own fault. I have lost that which can never be restored: I have seen the sun rise and set for twenty months, an idle gazer on the light of heaven: In this time the birds have left the nest of their mother, and committed themselves to the woods and to the skies: the kid has forsaken the teat, and learned by degrees to climb the rocks in quest of independant sustenance. I only have made no advances, but am still helpless and ignorant. The moon, by more than twenty changes, admonished me of the flux of life; the stream that rolled before my feet upbraided my inactivity. I sat feasting on intellectual luxury, regardless alike of the examples of the earth, and the instructions of the planets. Twenty months are past, who shall restore them!"

These sorrowful meditations fastened upon his mind; he past four months in resolving to lose no more time in idle resolves,

---

[6] but: yet 2

and was awakened to more vigorous exertion by hearing a maid, who had broken a porcelain cup, remark, that what cannot be repaired is not to be regretted.

This was obvious; and Rasselas reproached himself that he had not discovered it, having not known, or not considered, how many useful hints are obtained by chance, and how often the mind, hurried by her own ardour to distant views, neglects the truths that lie open before her. He, for a few hours, regretted his regret, and from that time bent his whole mind upon the means of escaping from the valley of happiness.

## V

### THE PRINCE MEDITATES HIS ESCAPE

He now found that it would be very difficult to effect that which it was very easy to suppose effected. When he looked round about him, he saw himself confined by the bars of nature which had never yet been broken, and by the gate, through which none that once had passed it were ever able to return. He was now impatient as an eagle in a grate. He passed week after week in clambering the mountains, to see if there was any aperture which the bushes might conceal, but found all the summits inaccessible by their prominence. The iron gate he despaired to open; for it was not only secured with all the power of art, but was always watched by successive sentinels, and was by its position exposed to the perpetual observation of all the inhabitants.

He then examined the cavern through which the waters of the lake were discharged; and, looking down at a time when the sun shone strongly upon its mouth, he discovered it to be full of broken rocks, which, though they permitted the stream to flow through many narrow passages, would stop any body of solid bulk. He returned discouraged and dejected; but, having now known the blessing of hope, resolved never to despair.

In these fruitless searches he spent ten months. The time, however, passed cheerfully away: in the morning he rose with new hope, in the evening applauded his own diligence, and in the night slept sound after his fatigue. He met a thousand amusements which beguiled his labour, and diversified his thoughts. He discerned the various instincts of animals, and properties of plants, and found the place replete with wonders, of which he purposed to solace himself with the contemplation, if he should never be able to accomplish his flight; rejoicing that his endeavours, though yet unsuccessful, had supplied him with a source of inexhaustible enquiry.

But his original curiosity was not yet abated; he resolved to obtain some knowledge of the ways of men. His wish still continued, but his hope grew less. He ceased to survey any longer the walls of his prison, and spared to search by new toils for interstices which he knew could not be found, yet determined to keep his design always in view, and lay hold on any expedient that time should offer.

# VI

### A DISSERTATION ON THE ART OF FLYING

Among the artists that had been allured into the happy valley, to labour for the accommodation and pleasure of its inhabitants, was a man eminent for his knowledge of the mechanick powers, who had contrived many engines both of use and recreation. By a wheel, which the stream turned, he forced the water into a tower, whence it was distributed to all the apartments of the palace. He erected a pavillion in the garden, around which he kept the air always cool by artificial showers. One of the groves, appropriated to the ladies, was ventilated by fans, to which the rivulet that run through it gave a constant motion; and instruments of soft musick were placed at proper distances, of which some played by the impulse of the wind, and some by the power of the stream.

This artist was sometimes visited by Rasselas, who was pleased with every kind of knowledge, imagining that the time would come when all his acquisitions should be of use to him in the open world. He came one day to amuse himself in his usual manner, and found the master busy in building a sailing chariot: he saw that the design was practicable upon a level surface, and with expressions of great esteem solicited its completion. The workman was pleased to find himself so much regarded by the prince, and resolved to gain yet higher honours. "Sir," said he, "you have seen but a small part of what the mechanick sciences can perform. I have been long of opinion, that, instead of the tardy conveyance of ships and chariots, man might use the swifter migration of wings; that the fields of air are open to knowledge, and that only ignorance and idleness need crawl upon the ground."

This hint rekindled the prince's desire of passing the mountains; and[7] having seen what the mechanist had already performed, he was willing to fancy that he could do more; yet resolved to enquire further before he suffered hope to afflict him by disappointment. "I am afraid," said he to the artist, "that your imagination prevails over your skill, and that you now tell me rather what you wish than what you know. Every animal has his element assigned him; the birds have the air, and man and beasts the earth." "So," replied the mechanist, "fishes have the water, in which yet beasts can swim by nature, and men by art. He that can swim needs not despair to fly: to swim is to fly in a grosser fluid, and to fly is to swim in a subtler. We are only to proportion our power of resistance to the different density of the matter through which we are to pass. You will be necessarily upborn by the air, if you can renew any impulse upon it, faster than the air can recede from the pressure."

"But the exercise of swimming," said the prince, "is very laborious; the strongest limbs are soon wearied; I am afraid the act of flying will be yet more violent, and wings will be of no great use, unless we can fly further than we can swim."

"The labour of rising from the ground," said the artist, "will be great, as we see it in the heavier domestick fowls; but, as we mount higher, the earth's attraction, and the body's gravity, will be gradually diminished, till we shall arrive at a region where the man will float in the air without any tendency to fall: no care will then be necessary, but to move forwards, which the gentlest impulse will effect. You, Sir, whose curiosity is so extensive, will easily conceive with what pleasure a philosopher, furnished with wings, and hovering in the sky, would see the earth, and all its inhabitants, rolling beneath him, and presenting to him successively, by its diurnal motion, all the countries within the same

[7] and having: having 2

parallel. How must it amuse the pendent spectator to see the moving scene of land and ocean, cities and desarts! To survey with equal security the marts of trade, and the fields of battle; mountains infested by barbarians, and fruitful regions gladdened by plenty, and lulled by peace! How easily shall we then trace the Nile through all his passage; pass over to distant regions, and examine the face of nature from one extremity of the earth to the other!"

"All this," said the prince, "is much to be desired, but I am afraid that no man will be able to breathe in these regions of speculation and tranquility. I have been told, that respiration is difficult upon lofty mountains, yet from these precipices, though so high as to produce great tenuity of the air, it is very easy to fall: and[8] I suspect, that from any height, where life can be supported, there may be danger of too quick descent."

"Nothing," replied the artist, "will ever be attempted, if all possible objections must be first overcome. If you will favour my project I will try the first flight at my own hazard. I have considered the structure of all volant animals, and find the folding continuity of the bat's wings most easily accommodated to the human form. Upon this model I shall begin my task to morrow, and in a year expect to tower into the air beyond the malice or pursuit of man. But I will work only on this condition, that the art shall not be divulged, and that you shall not require me to make wings for any but ourselves."

"Why," said Rasselas, "should you envy others so great an advantage? All skill ought to be exerted for universal good; every man has owed much to others, and ought to repay the kindness that he has received."

"If men were all virtuous," returned the artist, "I should with great alacrity teach them all to fly. But what would be the security of the good, if the bad could at pleasure invade them from the sky? Against an army sailing through the clouds neither walls, nor mountains, nor seas, could afford any security. A flight of northern savages might hover in the wind, and light at once with irresistible violence upon the capital of a fruitful region that was rolling under them. Even this valley, the retreat of princes, the abode of

---

[8] and: therefore 2

happiness, might be violated by the sudden descent of some of the naked nations that swarm on the coast of the southern sea."

The prince promised secrecy, and waited for the performance, not wholly hopeless of success. He visited the work from time to time, observed its progress, and remarked the[9] ingenious contrivances to facilitate motion, and unite levity with strength. The artist was every day more certain that he should leave vultures and eagles behind him, and the contagion of his confidence seized upon the prince.

In a year the wings were finished, and, on a morning appointed, the maker appeared furnished for flight on a little promontory: he waved his pinions a while to gather air, then leaped from his stand, and in an instant dropped into the lake. His wings, which were of no use in the air, sustained him in the water, and the prince drew him to land, half dead with terrour and vexation.

## VII

### THE PRINCE FINDS A MAN OF LEARNING

The prince was not much afflicted by this disaster, having suffered himself to hope for a happier event, only because he had no other means of escape in view. He still persisted in his design to leave the happy valley by the first opportunity.

His imagination was now at a stand; he had no prospect of entering into the world; and, notwithstanding all his endeavours to support himself, discontent by degrees preyed upon him, and he began again to lose his thoughts in sadness, when the rainy season, which in these countries is periodical, made it inconvenient to wander in the woods.

The rain continued longer and with more violence than had been ever known: the clouds broke on the surrounding mountains, and the torrents streamed into the plain on every side, till the cavern was too narrow to discharge the water. The lake overflowed its banks, and all the level of the valley was covered with the inundation. The eminence, on which the palace was built, and some other spots of rising ground, were all that the eye could

---

[9] the: many 2

now discover. The herds and flocks left the pastures, and both the wild beasts and the tame retreated to the mountains.

This inundation confined all the princes to domestick amusements, and the attention of Rasselas was particularly seized by a poem, which Imlac recited,[1] upon the various conditions of humanity. He commanded the poet to attend him in his apartment, and recite his verses a second time; then entering into familiar talk, he thought himself happy in having found a man who knew the world so well, and could so skilfully paint the scenes of life. He asked a thousand questions about things, to which, though common to all other mortals, his confinement from childhood had kept him a stranger. The poet pitied his ignorance, and loved his curiosity, and entertained him from day to day with novelty and instruction, so that the prince regretted the necessity of sleep, and longed till the morning should renew his pleasure.

As they were sitting together, the prince commanded Imlac to relate his history, and to tell by what accident he was forced, or by what motive induced, to close his life in the happy valley. As he was going to begin his narrative, Rasselas was called to a concert, and obliged to restrain his curiosity till the evening.

# VIII

### THE HISTORY OF IMLAC

The close of the day is, in the regions of the torrid zone, the only season of diversion and entertainment, and it was therefore midnight before the musick ceased, and the princesses retired. Rasselas then called for his companion and required him to begin the story of his life.

"Sir," said Imlac, "my history will not be long: the life that is devoted to knowledge passes silently away, and is very little diversified by events. To talk in publick, to think in solitude, to read and to hear, to inquire, and answer inquiries, is the business of a scholar. He wanders about the world without pomp or terrour, and is neither known nor valued but by men like himself.

"I was born in the kingdom of Goiama, at no greater distance

---

[1] recited: rehearsed 2

from the fountain of the Nile. My father was a wealthy merchant, who traded between the inland countries of Africk and the ports of the red sea. He was honest, frugal and diligent, but of mean sentiments, and narrow comprehension: he desired only to be rich, and to conceal his riches, lest he should be spoiled by the governours of the province."

"Surely," said the prince, "my father must be negligent of his charge, if any man in his dominions dares take that which belongs to another. Does he not know that kings are accountable for injustice permitted as well as done? If I were emperour, not the meanest of my subjects should be oppressed with impunity. My blood boils when I am told that a merchant durst not enjoy his honest gains for fear of losing[2] by the rapacity of power. Name the governour who robbed the people, that I may declare his crimes to the emperour."

"Sir," said Imlac, "your ardour is the natural effect of virtue animated by youth: the time will come when you will acquit your father, and perhaps hear with less impatience of the governour. Oppression is, in the Abissinian dominions, neither frequent nor tolerated; but no form of government has been yet discovered, by which cruelty can be wholly prevented. Subordination supposes power on one part and subjection on the other; and if power be in the hands of men, it will sometimes be abused. The vigilance of the supreme magistrate may do much, but much will still remain undone. He can never know all the crimes that are committed, and can seldom punish all that he knows."

"This," said the prince, "I do not understand, but I had rather hear thee than dispute. Continue thy narration."

"My father," proceeded Imlac, "originally intended that I should have no other education, than such as might qualify me for commerce; and discovering in me great strength of memory, and quickness of apprehension, often declared his hope that I should be some time the richest man in Abissinia."

"Why," said the prince, "did thy father desire the increase of his wealth, when it was already greater than he durst discover or enjoy? I am unwilling to doubt thy veracity, yet inconsistencies cannot both be true."

---

[2] losing: losing them 2

"Inconsistencies," answered Imlac, "cannot both be right, but, imputed to man, they may both be true. Yet diversity is not inconsistency. My father might expect a time of greater security. However, some desire is necessary to keep life in motion, and he, whose real wants are supplied, must admit those of fancy."

"This," said the prince, "I can in some measure conceive. I repent that I interrupted thee."

"With this hope," proceeded Imlac, "he sent me to school; but when I had once found the delight of knowledge, and felt the pleasure of intelligence and the pride of invention, I began silently to despise riches, and determined to disappoint the purpose of my father, whose grossness of conception raised my pity. I was twenty years old before his tenderness would expose me to the fatigue of travel, in which time I had been instructed, by successive masters, in all the literature of my native country. As every hour taught me something new, I lived in a continual course of gratifications; but, as I advanced towards manhood, I lost much of the reverence with which I had been used to look on my instructors; because, when the lesson was ended, I did not find them wiser or better than common men.

"At length my father resolved to initiate me in commerce, and, opening one of his subterranean treasuries, counted out ten thousand pieces of gold. 'This, young man,' said he, 'is the stock with which you must negociate. I began with less than the fifth part, and you see how diligence and parsimony have increased it. This is your own to waste or to improve. If you squander it by negligence or caprice, you must wait for my death before you will be rich: if, in four years, you double your stock, we will thenceforward let subordination cease, and live together as friends and partners; for he shall always be equal with me, who is equally skilled in the art of growing rich.'

"We laid our money upon camels, concealed in bales of cheap goods, and travelled to the shore of the red sea. When I cast my eye on the expanse of waters my heart bounded like that of a prisoner escaped. I felt an unextinguishable curiosity kindle in my mind, and resolved to snatch this opportunity of seeing the manners of other nations, and of learning sciences unknown in Abissinia.

"I remembered that my father had obliged me to the improvement of my stock, not by a promise which I ought not to violate, but by a penalty which I was at liberty to incur; and therefore determined to gratify my predominant desire, and by drinking at the fountains of knowledge, to quench the thirst of curiosity.

"As I was supposed to trade without connexion with my father, it was easy for me to become acquainted with the master of a ship, and procure a passage to some other country. I had no motives of choice to regulate my voyage; it was sufficient for me that, wherever I wandered, I should see a country which I had not seen before. I therefore entered a ship bound for Surat, having left a letter for my father declaring my intention.

# IX

## THE HISTORY OF IMLAC CONTINUED

"When I first entered upon the world of waters, and lost sight of land, I looked round about me with pleasing terrour, and thinking my soul enlarged by the boundless prospect, imagined that I could gaze round for ever without satiety; but, in a short time, I grew weary of looking on barren uniformity, where I could only see again what I had already seen. I then descended into the ship, and doubted for a while whether all my future pleasures would not end like this in disgust and disappointment. Yet, surely, said I, the ocean and the land are very different; the only variety of water is rest and motion, but the earth has mountains and vallies, desarts and cities: it is inhabited by men of different customs and contrary opinions; and I may hope to find variety in life, though I should miss it in nature.

"With this hope[3] I quieted my mind, and amused myself during the voyage; sometimes by learning from the sailors the art of navigation, which I have never practised, and sometimes by forming schemes for my conduct in different situations, in not one of which I have been ever placed.

"I was almost weary of my naval amusements when we landed safely at Surat. I secured my money, and purchasing some commodities for show, joined myself to a caravan that was passing

---

[3] hope: thought 2

into the inland country. My companions, for some reason or other, conjecturing that I was rich, and, by my inquiries and admiration, finding that I was ignorant, considered me as a novice whom they had a right to cheat, and who was to learn at the usual expence the art of fraud. They exposed me to the theft of servants, and the exaction of officers, and saw me plundered upon false pretences, without any advantage to themselves, but that of rejoicing in the superiority of their own knowledge."

"Stop a moment," said the prince, "is there such depravity in man, as that he should injure another without benefit to himself? I can easily conceive that all are pleased with superiority; but your ignorance was merely accidental, which, being neither your crime nor your folly, could afford them no reason to applaud themselves; and the knowledge which they had, and which you wanted, they might as effectually have shewn by warning you,[4] as betraying you."

"Pride," said Imlac, "is seldom delicate, it will please itself with very mean advantages; and envy feels not its own happiness, but when it may be compared with the misery of others. They were my enemies because they thought[5] me rich, and my oppressors because they delighted to find me weak."

"Proceed," said the prince: "I doubt not of the facts which you relate, but imagine that you impute them to mistaken motives."

"In this company," said Imlac, "I arrived at Agra, the capital of Indostan, the city in which the great Mogul commonly resides. I applied myself to the language of the country, and in a few months was able to converse with the learned men; some of whom I found morose and reserved, and others easy and communicative; some were unwilling to teach another what they had with difficulty learned themselves; and some shewed that the end of their studies was to gain the dignity of instructing.

"To the tutor of the young princes I recommended myself so much, that I was presented to the emperour as a man of uncommon knowledge. The emperour asked me many questions concerning my country and my travels; and though I cannot now recollect any thing that he uttered above the power of a common

---

[4] warning you: warning 2
[5] thought: grieved to think 2

man, he dismissed me astonished at his wisdom, and enamoured of his goodness.

"My credit was now so high, that the merchants, with whom I had travelled, applied to me for recommendations to the ladies of the court. I was surprised at their confidence of solicitation, and gently reproached them with their practices on the road. They heard me with cold indifference, and shewed no tokens of shame or sorrow.

"They then urged their request with the offer of a bribe; but what I would not do for kindness I would not do for money; and refused them, not because they had injured me, but because I would not enable them to injure others; for I knew they would have made use of my credit to cheat those who should buy their wares.

"Having resided at Agra, till there was no more to be learned, I travelled into Persia, where I saw many remains of ancient magnificence, and observed many new accommodations[6] of life. The Persians are a nation eminently social, and their assemblies afforded me daily opportunities of remarking characters and manners, and of tracing human nature through all its variations.

"From Persia I passed into Arabia, where I saw a nation at once pastoral and warlike; who live without any settled habitation; whose only wealth is their flocks and herds; and who have yet carried on, through all ages, an hereditary war with all mankind, though they neither covet nor envy their possessions.

# X

### IMLAC'S HISTORY CONTINUED. A DISSERTATION UPON POETRY

"Wherever I went, I found that Poetry was considered as the highest learning, and regarded with a veneration somewhat approaching to that which man would pay to the Angelick Nature. And it yet fills me with wonder, that, in almost all countries, the most ancient poets are considered as the best: whether it be that every other kind of knowledge is an acquistion gradually attained, and poetry is a gift conferred at once; or that the first poetry of

---

[6] accommodations: "conveniencies." Johnson's *Dictionary*.

every nation surprised them as a novelty, and retained the credit by consent which it received by accident at first: or whether[7] the province of poetry is to describe Nature and Passion, which are always the same, and[8] the first writers took possession of the most striking objects for description, and the most probable occurrences for fiction, and left nothing to those that followed them, but transcription of the same events, and new combinations of the same images. Whatever be the reason, it is commonly observed that the early writers are in possession of nature, and their followers of art: that the first excel in strength and invention, and the latter in elegance and refinement.

"I was desirous to add my name to this illustrious fraternity. I read all the poets of Persia and Arabia, and was able to repeat by memory the volumes that are suspended in the mosque of Mecca. But I soon found that no man was ever great by imitation. My desire of excellence impelled me to transfer my attention to nature and to life. Nature was to be my subject, and men to be my auditors: I could never describe what I had not seen: I could not hope to move those with delight or terrour, whose interests and opinions I did not understand.

"Being now resolved to be a poet, I saw every thing with a new purpose; my sphere of attention was suddenly magnified: no kind of knowledge was to be overlooked. I ranged mountains and deserts for images and resemblances, and pictured upon my mind every tree of the forest and flower of the valley. I observed with equal care the crags of the rock and the pinnacles of the palace. Sometimes I wandered along the mazes of the rivulet, and sometimes watched the changes of the summer clouds. To a poet nothing can be useless. Whatever is beautiful, and whatever is dreadful, must be familiar to his imagination: he must be conversant with all that is awfully vast or elegantly little. The plants of the garden, the animals of the wood, the minerals of the earth, and meteors of the sky, must all concur to store his mind with inexhaustible variety: for every idea is useful for the inforcement or decoration of moral or religious truth; and he, who knows most, will have most power of diversifying his scenes, and of gratifying his reader with remote allusions and unexpected instruction.

---

[7] whether: whether, as 2
[8] same, and: same, 2

"All the appearances of nature I was therefore careful to study, and every country which I have surveyed has contributed something to my poetical powers."

"In so wide a survey," said the prince, "you must surely have left much unobserved. I have lived, till now, within the circuit of these mountains, and yet cannot walk abroad without the sight of something which I had never beheld before, or never heeded."

"The business of a poet," said Imlac, "is to examine, not the individual, but the species; to remark general properties and large appearances: he does not number the streaks of the tulip, or describe the different shades in the verdure of the forest. He is to exhibit in his portraits of nature such prominent and striking features, as recal the original to every mind; and must neglect the minuter discriminations, which one may have remarked, and another have neglected, for those characteristicks which are alike obvious to vigilance and carelessness.

"But the knowledge of nature is only half the task of a poet; he must be acquainted likewise with all the modes of life. His character requires that he estimate the happiness and misery of every condition; observe the power of all the passions in all their combinations, and trace the changes of the human mind as they are modified by various institutions and accidental influences of climate or custom, from the spriteliness of infancy to the despondence of decrepitude. He must divest himself of the prejudices of his age or country; he must consider right and wrong in their abstracted and invariable state; he must disregard present laws and opinions, and rise to general and transcendental truths, which will always be the same: he must therefore content himself with the slow progress of his name; contemn the applause of his own time, and commit his claims to the justice of posterity. He must write as the interpreter of nature, and the legislator of mankind, and consider himself as presiding over the thoughts and manners of successive[9] generations; as a being superiour to time and place. His labour is not yet at an end: he must know many languages and many sciences; and, that his stile may be worthy of his thoughts, must, by incessant practice, familiarize to himself every delicacy of speech and grace of harmony."

---

[9] successive: future 2

# XI

### IMLAC'S NARRATIVE CONTINUED. A HINT ON PILGRIMAGE

Imlac now felt the enthusiastic fit, and was proceeding to aggrandize his own profession, when the prince cried out, "Enough! Thou hast convinced me, that no human being can ever be a poet. Proceed now with thy narration."

"To be a poet," said Imlac, "is indeed very difficult." "So difficult," returned the prince, "that I will at present hear no more of his labours. Tell me whither you went when you had seen Persia."

"From Persia," said the poet, "I travelled through Syria, and for three years resided in Palestine, where I conversed with great numbers of the northern and western nations of Europe; the nations which are now in possession of all power and all knowledge; whose armies are irresistible, and whose fleets command the remotest parts of the globe. When I compared these men with the natives of our own kingdom, and those that surround us, they appeared almost another order of beings. In their countries it is difficult to wish for any thing that may not be obtained: a thousand arts, of which we never heard, are continually labouring for their convenience and pleasure; and whatever their own climate has denied them is supplied by their commerce."

"By what means," said the prince, "are the Europeans thus powerful? or why, since they can so easily visit Asia and Africa for trade or conquest, cannot the Asiaticks and Africans invade their coasts, plant colonies in their ports, and give laws to their natural princes? The same wind that carries them back would bring us thither."

"They are more powerful, Sir, than we," answered Imlac, "because they are wiser; knowledge will always predominate over ignorance, as man governs the other animals. But why their knowledge is more than ours, I know not what reason can be given, but the unsearchable will of the Supreme Being."

"When," said the prince with a sigh, "shall I be able to visit Palestine, and mingle with this mighty confluence of nations? Till that happy moment shall arrive, let me fill up the time with such representations as thou canst give me. I am not ignorant of the motive that assembles such numbers in that place, and cannot but consider it as the center of wisdom and piety, to which the best and wisest men of every land must be continually resorting."

"There are some nations," said Imlac, "that send few visitants to Palestine; for many numerous and learned sects in Europe, concur to censure pilgrimage as superstitious, or deride it as ridiculous."

"You know," said the prince, "how little my life has made me acquainted with diversity of opinions: it will be too long to hear the arguments on both sides; you, that have considered them, tell me the result."

"Pilgrimage," said Imlac, "like many other acts of piety, may be reasonable or superstitious, according to the principles upon which it is performed. Long journies in search of truth are not commanded. Truth, such as is necessary to the regulation of life, is always found where it is honestly sought. Change of place is no natural cause of the increase of piety, for it inevitably produces dissipation of mind. Yet, since men go every day to view the places[1] where great actions have been performed, and return with stronger impressions of the event, curiosity of the same kind may naturally dispose us to view that country whence our religion had its beginning; and I believe no man surveys those awful scenes without some confirmation of holy resolutions. That the Supreme Being may be more easily propitiated in one place than in another, is the dream of idle superstition; but that some places may operate upon our own minds in an uncommon manner, is an opinion which hourly experience will justify. He who supposes that his vices may be more successfully combated in Palestine, will, perhaps, find himself mistaken, yet he may go thither without folly: he who thinks they will be more freely pardoned, dishonours at once his reason and religion."

"These," said the prince, "are European distinctions. I will consider them another time. What have you found to be the effect of knowledge? Are those nations happier than we?"

"There is so much infelicity," said the poet, "in the world, that scarce any man has leisure from his own distresses to estimate the comparative happiness of others. Knowledge is certainly one of the means of pleasure, as is confessed by the natural desire which

---

[1] places: fields 2

every mind feels of increasing its ideas. Ignorance is mere privation, by which nothing can be produced: it is a vacuity in which the soul sits motionless and torpid for want of attraction; and, without knowing why, we always rejoice when we learn, and grieve when we forget. I am therefore inclined to conclude, that, if nothing counteracts the natural consequence of learning, we grow more happy as our minds take a wider range.

"In enumerating the particular comforts of life we shall find many advantages on the side of the Europeans. They cure wounds and diseases with which we languish and perish. We suffer inclemencies of weather which they can obviate. They have engines for the despatch of many laborious works, which we must perform by manual industry. There is such communication between distant places, that one friend can hardly be said to be absent from another. Their policy removes all publick inconveniencies: they have roads cut through their mountains, and bridges laid upon their rivers. And, if we descend to the privacies of life, their habitations are more commodious, and their possessions are more secure."

"They are surely happy," said the prince, "who have all these conveniencies, of which I envy none so much as the facility with which separated friends interchange their thoughts."

"The Europeans," answered Imlac, "are less unhappy than we, but they are not happy. Human life is every where a state in which much is to be endured, and little to be enjoyed."

## XII

### THE STORY OF IMLAC CONTINUED

"I am not yet willing," said the prince, "to suppose that happiness is so parsimoniously distributed to mortals; nor can believe but that, if I had the choice of life, I should be able to fill every day with pleasure. I would injure no man, and should provoke no resentment: I would relieve every distress, and should enjoy the benedictions of gratitude. I would choose my friends among the wise, and my wife among the virtuous; and therefore should be in no danger from treachery, or unkindness. My children should, by my care, be learned and pious, and would repay to my age what their childhood had received. What would dare to molest him who might call on every side to thousands enriched by his bounty, or assisted by his power? And why should not life glide quietly away in the soft reciprocation of protection and reverence? All this may be done without the help of European refinements, which appear by their effects to be rather specious than useful. Let us leave them and persue our journey."

"From Palestine," said Imlac, "I passed through many regions of Asia; in the more civilized kingdoms as a trader, and among the Barbarians of the mountains as a pilgrim. At last I began to long for my native country, that I might repose after my travels, and fatigues, in the places where I had spent my earliest years, and gladden my old companions with the recital of my adventures. Often did I figure to myself those, with whom I had sported away the gay hours of dawning life, sitting round me in its evening, wondering at my tales, and listening to my counsels.

"When this thought had taken possession of my mind, I considered every moment as wasted which did not bring me nearer to Abissinia. I hastened into Egypt, and, notwithstanding my impatience, was detained ten months in the contemplation of its ancient magnificence, and in enquiries after the remains of its ancient learning. I found in Cairo a mixture of all nations; some brought thither by the love of knowledge, some by the hope of gain, and many by the desire of living after their own manner without observation, and of lying hid in the obscurity of multitudes: for, in a city, populous as Cairo, it is possible to obtain at the same time the gratifications of society, and the secrecy of solitude.

"From Cairo I travelled to Suez, and embarked on the Red sea, passing along the coast till I arrived at the port from which I had departed twenty years before. Here I joined myself to a caravan and re-entered my native country.

"I now expected the caresses of my kinsmen, and the congratulations of my friends, and was not without hope that my father, whatever value he had set upon riches, would own with gladness and pride a son who was able to add to the felicity and honour of the nation. But I was soon convinced that my thoughts were vain. My father had been dead fourteen years, having divided his wealth among my brothers, who were removed to some other provinces. Of my companions the greater part was in the grave, of the rest some could with difficulty remember me, and some considered me as one corrupted by foreign manners.

"A man used to vicissitudes is not easily dejected. I forgot, after a time, my disappointment, and endeavoured to recommend myself to the nobles of the kingdom: they admitted me to their tables, heard my story, and dismissed me. I opened a school, and was prohibited to teach. I then resolved to sit down in the quiet of domestick life, and addressed a lady that was fond of my conversation, but rejected my suit, because my father was a merchant.

"Wearied at last with solicitation and repulses, I resolved to hide myself for ever from the world, and depend no longer on the opinion or caprice of others. I waited for the time when the gate of the *happy valley* should open, that I might bid farewell to hope and fear: the day came; my performance was distinguished with favour, and I resigned myself with joy to perpetual confinement."

"Hast thou here found happiness at last?" said Rasselas. "Tell me without reserve; art thou content with thy condition? or, dost thou wish to be again wandering and inquiring? All the inhabitants of this valley celebrate their lot, and, at the annual visit of the emperour, invite others to partake of their felicity."

"Great prince," said Imlac, "I shall speak the truth: I know not one of all your attendants who does not lament the hour when he entered this retreat. I am less unhappy than the rest, because I have a mind replete with images, which I can vary and combine at pleasure. I can amuse my solitude by the renovation of the knowledge which begins to fade from my memory, and with the[2] recollection of the accidents of my past life. Yet all this ends in the sorrowful consideration, that my acquirements are now useless, and that none of my pleasures can be again enjoyed. The rest, whose minds have no impression but of the present moment, are either corroded by malignant passions, or sit stupid in the gloom of perpetual vacancy."

"What passions can infest those," said the prince, "who have no rivals? We are in a place where impotence precludes malice, and where all envy is repressed by community of enjoyments."

"There may be community," said Imlac, "of material posses-

---

[2] with the. by 2

sions, but there can never be community of love or of esteem. It must happen that one will please more than another; he that knows himself despised will always be envious; and still more envious and malevolent, if he is condemned to live in the presence of those who despise him. The invitations, by which they allure others to a state which they feel to be wretched, proceed from the natural malignity of hopeless misery. They are weary of themselves, and of each other, and expect to find relief in new companions. They envy the liberty which their folly has forfeited, and would gladly see all mankind imprisoned like themselves.

"From this crime, however, I am wholly free. No man can say that he is wretched by my persuasion. I look with pity on the crowds who are annually soliciting admission to captivity, and wish that it were lawful for me to warn them of their danger."

"My dear Imlac," said the prince, "I will open to thee my whole heart, that[3] I have long meditated an escape from the happy valley. I have examined the mountains on every side, but find myself insuperably barred: teach me the way to break my prison; thou shalt be the companion of my flight, the guide of my rambles, the partner of my fortune, and my sole director in the *choice of life*."

"Sir," answered the poet, "your escape will be difficult, and, perhaps, you may soon repent your curiosity. The world, which you figure to yourself smooth and quiet as the lake in the valley, you will find a sea foaming with tempests, and boiling with whirlpools: you will be sometimes overwhelmed by the waves of violence, and sometimes dashed against the rocks of treachery. Amidst wrongs and frauds, competitions and anxieties, you will wish a thousand times for these seats of quiet, and willingly quit hope to be free from fear."

"Do not seek to deter me from my purpose," said the prince: "I am impatient to see what thou hast seen; and, since thou art thyself weary of the valley, it is evident, that thy former state was better than this. Whatever be the consequence of my experiment, I am resolved to judge with my own eyes of the various conditions of men, and then to make deliberately my *choice of life*."

---

[3] heart, that: heart. 2

"I am afraid," said Imlac, "you are hindered by stronger restraints than my persuasions; yet, if your determination is fixed, I do not counsel you to despair. Few things are impossible to diligence and skill."

# XIII

### RASSELAS DISCOVERS THE MEANS OF ESCAPE

The prince now dismissed his favourite to rest, but the narrative of wonders and novelties filled his mind with perturbation. He revolved all that he had heard, and prepared innumerable questions for the morning.

Much of his uneasiness was now removed. He had a friend to whom he could impart his thoughts, and whose experience could assist him in his designs. His heart was no longer condemned to swell with silent vexation. He thought that even the *happy valley* might be endured with such a companion, and that, if they could range the world together, he should have nothing further to desire.

In a few days the water was discharged, and the ground dried. The prince and Imlac then walked out together to converse without the notice of the rest. The prince, whose thoughts were always on the wing, as he passed by the gate, said, with a countenance of sorrow, "Why art thou so strong, and why is man so weak?"

"Man is not weak," answered his companion; "knowledge is more than equivalent to force. The master of mechanicks laughs at strength. I can burst the gate, but cannot do it secretly. Some other expedient must be tried."

As they were walking on the side of the mountain, they observed that the conies, which the rain had driven from their burrows, had taken shelter among the bushes, and formed holes behind them, tending upwards in an oblique line. "It has been the opinion of antiquity," said Imlac, "that human reason borrowed many arts from the instinct of animals; let us, therefore, not think ourselves degraded by learning from the coney. We may escape by piercing the mountain in the same direction. We will begin where the summit hangs over the middle part, and labour upward till we shall issue out beyond the prominence."

The eyes of the prince, when he heard this proposal, sparkled with joy. The execution was easy, and the success certain.

No time was now lost. They hastened early in the morning to chuse a place proper for their mine. They clambered with great fatigue among crags and brambles, and returned without having discovered any part that favoured their design. The second and the third day were spent in the same manner, and with the same frustration. But, on the fourth, they found a small cavern, concealed by a thicket, where they resolved to make their experiment.

Imlac procured instruments proper to hew stone and remove earth, and they fell to their work on the next day with more eagerness than vigour. They were presently exhausted by their efforts, and sat down to pant upon the grass. The prince, for a moment, appeared to be discouraged. "Sir," said his companion, "practice will enable us to continue our labour for a longer time; mark, however, how far we have advanced, and you will find that our toil will some time have an end. Great works are performed, not by strength, but perseverance: yonder palace was raised by single stones, yet you see its height and spaciousness. He that shall walk with vigour three hours a day will pass in seven years a space equal to the circumference of the globe."

They returned to their labour[4] day after day, and, in a short time, found a fissure in the rock, which enabled them to pass far with very little obstruction. This Rasselas considered as a good omen. "Do not disturb your mind," said Imlac, "with other hopes or fears than reason may suggest: if you are pleased with prognosticks of good, you will be terrified likewise with tokens of evil, and your whole life will be a prey to superstition. Whatever facilitates our work is more than an omen, it is a cause of success. This is one of those pleasing surprises which often happen to active resolution. Many things difficult to design prove easy to performance."

## XIV

### RASSELAS AND IMLAC RECEIVE AN UNEXPECTED VISIT

They had now wrought their way to the middle, and solaced their labour[5] with the approach of liberty, when the prince, coming

---

[4] labour: work 2
[5] labour: toil 2

down to refresh himself with air, found his sister Nekayah standing before the mouth of the cavity. He started and stood confused, afraid to tell his design, and yet hopeless to conceal it. A few moments determined him to repose on her fidelity, and secure her secrecy by a declaration without reserve.

"Do not imagine," said the princess, "that I came hither as a spy: I had often[6] observed from my window, that you and Imlac directed your walk every day towards the same point, but I did not suppose you had any better reason for the preference than a cooler shade, or more fragrant bank; nor followed you with any other design than to partake of your conversation. Since then not suspicion but fondness has detected you, let me not lose the advantage of my discovery. I am equally weary of confinement with yourself, and not less desirous of knowing what is done or suffered in the world. Permit me to fly with you from this tasteless tranquility, which will yet grow more loathsome when you have left me. You may deny me to accompany you, but cannot hinder me from following."

The prince, who loved Nekayah above his other sisters, had no inclination to refuse her request, and grieved that he had lost an opportunity of shewing his confidence by a voluntary communication. It was therefore agreed that she should leave the valley with them; and that, in the mean time, she should watch, lest any other straggler should, by chance or curiosity, follow them to the mountain.

At length their labour was at an end; they saw light beyond the prominence, and, issuing to the top of the mountain, beheld the Nile, yet a narrow current, wandering beneath them.

The prince looked round with rapture, anticipated all the pleasures of travel, and in thought was already transported beyond his father's dominions. Imlac, though very joyful at his escape, had less expectation of pleasure in the world, which he had before tried, and of which he had been weary.

Rasselas was so much delighted with a wider horizon, that he could not soon be persuaded to return into the valley. He informed his sister that the way was open, and that nothing now remained but to prepare for their departure.

---

[6] often: long 2

# XV

## THE PRINCE AND PRINCESS LEAVE THE VALLEY, AND SEE
## MANY WONDERS

The prince and princess had jewels sufficient to make them rich whenever they came into a place of commerce, which, by Imlac's direction, they hid in their cloaths, and, on the night of the next full moon, all left the valley. The princess was followed only by a single favourite, who did not know whither she was going.

They clambered through the cavity, and began to go down on the other side. The princess and her maid turned their eyes towards every part, and, seeing nothing to bound their prospect, considered themselves as in danger of being lost in a dreary vacuity. They stopped and trembled. "I am almost afraid," said the princess, "to begin a journey of which I cannot perceive an end, and to venture into this immense plain where I may be approached on every side by men whom I never saw." The prince felt nearly the same emotions, though he thought it more manly to conceal them.

Imlac smiled at their terrours, and encouraged them to proceed; but the princess continued irresolute till she had been imperceptibly drawn forward too far to return.

In the morning they found some shepherds in the field, who set milk and fruits before them. The princess wondered that she did not see a palace ready for her reception, and a table spread with delicacies; but, being faint and hungry, she drank the milk and eat the fruits, and thought them of a higher flavour than the products of the valley.

They travelled forward by easy journeys, being all unaccustomed to toil or difficulty, and knowing, that though they might be missed, they could not be persued. In a few days they came into a more populous region, where Imlac was diverted with the admiration which his companions expressed at the diversity of manners, stations and employments.

Their dress was such as might not bring upon them the suspicion of having any thing to conceal, yet the prince, wherever he came, expected to be obeyed, and the princess was frighted, because those that came into her presence did not prostrate themselves before her. Imlac was forced to observe them with great vigilance, lest they should betray their rank by their unusual behaviour, and detained them several weeks in the first village to accustom them to the sight of common mortals.

By degrees the royal wanderers were taught to understand that they had for a time laid aside their dignity, and were to expect only such regard as liberality and courtesy could procure. And Imlac, having, by many admonitions, prepared them to endure the tumults of a port, and the ruggedness of the commercial race, brought them down to the sea-coast.

The prince and his sister, to whom every thing was new, were gratified equally at all places, and therefore remained for some months at the port without any inclination to pass further. Imlac was content with their stay, because he did not think it safe to expose them, unpractised in the world, to the hazards of a foreign country.

At last he began to fear lest they should be discovered, and proposed to fix a day for their departure. They had no pretensions to judge for themselves, and referred the whole scheme to his direction. He therefore took passage in a ship to Suez; and, when the time came, with great difficulty prevailed on the princess to enter the vessel. They had a quick and prosperous voyage, and from Suez travelled by land to Cairo.

# XVI

## THEY ENTER CAIRO, AND FIND EVERY MAN HAPPY

As they approached the city, which filled the strangers with astonishment, "This," said Imlac to the prince, "is the place where travellers and merchants assemble from all the corners of the earth. You will here find men of every character, and every occupation. Commerce is here honourable: I will act as a merchant, and you shall live as strangers, who have no other end of travel than curiosity; it will soon be observed that we are rich; our reputation will procure us access to all whom we shall desire to know; you will see all the conditions of humanity, and enable yourself at leisure to make your *choice of life*."

They now entered the town, stunned by the noise, and offended by the crowds. Instruction had not yet so prevailed over habit, but that they wondered to see themselves pass undistinguished along the street, and met by the lowest of the people without reverence or notice. The princess could not at first bear the thought of being levelled with the vulgar, and, for some days, continued in her chamber, where she was served by her favourite[7] as in the palace of the valley.

Imlac, who understood traffick, sold part of the jewels the next day, and hired a house, which he adorned with such magnificence, that he was immediately considered as a merchant of great wealth. His politeness attracted many acquaintance, and his generosity made him courted by many dependants. His table was crowded by men of every nation, who all admired his knowledge, and solicited his favour. His companions, not being able to mix in the conversation, could make no discovery of their ignorance or surprise, and were gradually initiated in the world as they gained knowledge of the language.

The prince had, by frequent lectures, been taught the use and nature of money; but the ladies could not, for a long time, comprehend what the merchants did with small pieces of gold and silver, or why things of so little use should be received as equivalent to the necessaries of life.

They studied the language two years, while Imlac was preparing to set before them the various ranks and conditions of mankind. He grew acquainted with all who had any thing uncommon in their fortune or conduct. He frequented the voluptuous and the frugal, the idle and the busy, the merchants and the men of learning.

The prince, being now able to converse with fluency, and having learned the caution necessary to be observed in his intercourse with strangers, began to accompany Imlac to places of resort, and to enter into all assemblies, that he might make his *choice of life.*

For some time he thought choice needless, because all appeared to him equally happy. Wherever he went he met gayety and kindness, and heard the song of joy, or the laugh of carelessness. He began to believe that the world overflowed with universal plenty,

---

[7] favourite: favourite Pekuah 2

and that nothing was withheld either from want or merit; that every hand showered liberality, and every heart melted with benevolence: "and who then," says he, "will be suffered to be wretched?"

Imlac permitted the pleasing delusion, and was unwilling to crush the hope of inexperience, till one day, having sat a while silent, "I know not," said the prince, "what can be the reason that I am more unhappy than any of our friends. I see them perpetually and unalterably chearful, but feel my own mind restless and uneasy. I am unsatisfied with those pleasures which I seem most to court; I live in the crowds of jollity, not so much to enjoy company as to shun myself, and am only loud and merry to conceal my sadness."

"Every man," said Imlac, "may, by examining his own mind, guess what passes in the minds of others: when you feel that your own gaiety is counterfeit, it may justly lead you to suspect that of your companions not to be sincere. Envy is commonly reciprocal. We are long before we are convinced that happiness is never to be found, and each believes it possessed by others, to keep alive the hope of obtaining it for himself. In the assembly, where you passed the last night, there appeared such spriteliness of air, and volatility of fancy, as might have suited beings of an higher order, formed to inhabit serener regions inaccessible to care or sorrow: yet, believe me, prince, there was not one who did not dread the moment when solitude should deliver him to the tyranny of reflection."

"This," said the prince, "may be true of others, since it is true of me; yet, whatever be the general infelicity of man, one condition is more happy than another, and wisdom surely directs us to take the least evil in the *choice of life*."

"The causes of good and evil," answered Imlac, "are so various and uncertain, so often entangled with each other, so diversified by various relations, and so much subject to accidents which cannot be foreseen, that he who would fix his condition upon incontestable reasons of preference, must live and die enquiring and deliberating."

"But surely," said Rasselas, "the wise men, to whom we listen with reverence and wonder, chose that mode of life for themselves which they thought most likely to make them happy."

"Very few," said the poet, "live by choice. Every man is placed in his present condition by causes which acted without his foresight, and with which he did not always willingly co-operate; and therefore you will rarely meet one who does not think the lot of his neighbour better than his own."

"I am pleased to think," said the prince, "that my birth has given me at least one advantage over others, by enabling me to determine for myself. I have here the world before me; I will review it at leisure: surely happiness is somewhere to be found."

## XVII

### THE PRINCE ASSOCIATES WITH YOUNG MEN OF SPIRIT AND GAIETY

Rasselas rose next day, and resolved to begin his experiments upon life. "Youth," cried he, "is the time of gladness: I will join myself to the young men, whose only business is to gratify their desires, and whose time is all spent in a succession of enjoyments."

To such societies he was readily admitted, but a few days brought him back weary and disgusted. Their mirth was without images, their laughter without motive; their pleasures were gross and sensual, in which the mind had no part; their conduct was at once wild and mean; they laughed at order and at law, but the frown of power dejected, and the eye of wisdom abashed them.

The prince soon concluded, that he should never be happy in a course of life of which he was ashamed. He thought it unsuitable to a reasonable being to act without a plan, and to be sad or chearful only by chance. "Happiness," said he, "must be something solid and permanent, without fear and without uncertainty."

But his young companions had gained so much of his regard by their frankness and courtesy, that he could not leave them without warning and remonstrance. "My friends," said he, "I have seriously considered our manners and our prospects, and find that we have mistaken our own interest. The first years of man must make provision for the last. He that never thinks never can be wise. Perpetual levity must end in ignorance; and intemperance, though it may fire the spirits for an hour, will make life short or miserable. Let us consider that youth is of no long duration, and that in maturer age, when the enchantments of fancy shall cease, and phantoms of delight dance no more about us, we shall have no comforts but the esteem of wise men, and the means of doing good. Let us, therefore, stop, while to stop is in our power: let us live as men who are sometime to grow old, and to whom it will be the most dreadful of all evils not to count their past years but by follies, and to be reminded of their former luxuriance of health only by the maladies which riot has produced."

They stared a while in silence one upon another, and, at last, drove him away by a general chorus of continued laughter.

The consciousness that his sentiments were just, and his intentions kind, was scarcely sufficient to support him against the horrour of derision. But he recovered his tranquility, and persued his search.

## XVIII

### THE PRINCE FINDS A WISE AND HAPPY MAN

As he was one day walking in the street, he saw a spacious building which all were, by the open doors, invited to enter: he followed the stream of people, and found it a hall or school of declamation, in which professors read lectures to their auditory. He fixed his eye upon a sage raised above the rest, who discoursed with great energy on the government of the passions. His look was venerable, his action graceful, his pronunciation clear, and his diction elegant. He shewed, with great strength of sentiment, and variety of illustration, that human nature is degraded and debased, when the lower faculties predominate over the higher; that when fancy, the parent of passion, usurps the dominion of the mind, nothing ensues but the natural effect of unlawful government, perturbation and confusion; that she betrays the fortresses of the intellect to rebels, and excites her children to sedition against reason their lawful sovereign. He compared reason to the sun, of which the light is constant, uniform, and lasting; and fancy to a meteor, of bright but transitory lustre, irregular in its motion, and delusive in its direction.

He then communicated the various precepts given from time

to time for the conquest of passion, and displayed the happiness of those who had obtained the important victory, after which man is no longer the slave of fear, nor the fool of hope; is no more emaciated by envy, inflamed by anger, emasculated by tenderness, or depressed by grief; but walks on calmly through the tumults or the privacies of life, as the sun persues alike his course through the calm or the stormy sky.

He enumerated many examples of heroes immovable by pain or pleasure, who looked with indifference on those modes or accidents to which the vulgar give the names of good and evil. He exhorted his hearers to lay aside their prejudices, and arm themselves against the shafts of malice or misfortune, by invulnerable patience; concluding, that this state only was happiness, and that this happiness was in every one's power.

Rasselas listened to him with the veneration due to the instructions of a superiour being, and, waiting for him at the door, humbly implored the liberty of visiting so great a master of true wisdom. The lecturer hesitated a moment, when Rasselas put a purse of gold into his hand, which he received with a mixture of joy and wonder.

"I have found," said the prince, at his return to Imlac, "a man who can teach all that is necessary to be known, who, from the unshaken throne of rational fortitude, looks down on the scenes of life changing beneath him. He speaks, and attention watches his lips. He reasons, and conviction closes his periods. This man shall be my future guide: I will learn his doctrines, and imitate his life."

"Be not too hasty," said Imlac, "to trust, or to admire, the teachers of morality: they discourse like angels, but they live like men."

Rasselas, who could not conceive how any man could reason so forcibly without feeling the cogency of his own arguments, paid his visit in a few days, and was denied admission. He had now learned the power of money, and made his way by a piece of gold to the inner apartment, where he found the philosopher in a room half darkened, with his eyes misty, and his face pale. "Sir," said he, "you are come at a time when all human friendship is useless; what I suffer cannot be remedied, what I have lost cannot be supplied. My daughter, my only daughter, from whose tenderness I expected all the comforts of my age, died last night of a fever. My views, my purposes, my hopes are at an end: I am now a lonely being disunited from society."

"Sir," said the prince, "mortality is an event by which a wise man can never be surprised: we know that death is always near, and it should therefore always be expected." "Young man," answered the philosopher, "you speak like one that has never felt the pangs of separation." "Have you then forgot the precepts," said Rasselas, "which you so powerfully enforced? Has wisdom no strength to arm the heart against calamity? Consider, that external things are naturally variable, but truth and reason are always the same." "What comfort," said the mourner, "can truth and reason afford me? of what effect are they now, but to tell me, that my daughter will not be restored?"

The prince, whose humanity would not suffer him to insult misery with reproof, went away convinced of the emptiness of rhetorical sound, and the inefficacy of polished periods and studied sentences.

## XIX

### A GLIMPSE OF PASTORAL LIFE

He was still eager upon the same enquiry; and, having heard of a hermit, that lived near the lowest cataract of the Nile, and filled the whole country with the fame of his sanctity, resolved to visit his retreat, and enquire whether that felicity, which publick life could not afford, was to be found in solitude; and whether a man, whose age and virtue made him venerable, could teach any peculiar art of shunning evils, or enduring them.

Imlac and the princess agreed to accompany him, and, after the necessary preparations, they began their journey. Their way lay through fields, where shepherds tended their flocks, and the lambs were playing upon the pasture. "This," said the poet, "is the life which has been often celebrated for its innocence and quiet: let us pass the heat of the day among the shepherds tents, and know whether all our searches are not to terminate in pastoral simplicity."

The proposal pleased them, and they induced the shepherds, by small presents and familiar questions, to tell their opinion of their own state: they were so rude and ignorant, so little able to compare the good with the evil of the occupation, and so indistinct in their narratives and descriptions, that very little could be learned from them. But it was evident that their hearts were cankered with discontent; that they considered themselves as condemned to labour for the luxury of the rich, and looked up with stupid malevolence toward those that were placed above them.

The princess pronounced with vehemence, that she would never suffer these envious savages to be her companions, and that she should not soon be desirous of seeing any more specimens of rustick happiness; but could not believe that all the accounts of primeval pleasures were fabulous, and was yet in doubt whether life had any thing that could be justly preferred to the placid gratifications of fields and woods. She hoped that the time would come, when, with a few virtuous and elegant companions, she should gather flowers planted by her own hand, fondle the lambs of her own ewe, and listen, without care, among brooks and breezes, to one of her maidens reading in the shade.

## XX

### THE DANGER OF PROSPERITY

On the next day they continued their journey, till the heat compelled them to look round for shelter. At a small distance they saw a thick wood, which they no sooner entered than they perceived that they were approaching the habitations of men. The shrubs were diligently cut away to open walks where the shades were darkest; the boughs of opposite trees were artificially interwoven; seats of flowery turf were raised in vacant spaces, and a rivulet, that wantoned along the side of a winding path, had its banks sometimes opened into small basons, and its stream sometimes obstructed by little mounds of stone heaped together to increase its murmurs.

They passed slowly through the wood, delighted with such unexpected accommodations, and entertained each other with conjecturing what, or who, he could be, that, in those rude and unfrequented regions, had leisure and art for such harmless luxury.

As they advanced, they heard the sound of musick, and saw youths and virgins dancing in the grove; and, going still further, beheld a stately palace built upon a hill surrounded with woods. The laws of eastern hospitality allowed them to enter, and the master welcomed them like a man liberal and wealthy.

He was skilful enough in appearances soon to discern that they were no common guests, and spread his table with magnificence. The eloquence of Imlac caught his attention, and the lofty courtesy of the princess excited his respect. When they offered to depart he entreated their stay, and was the next day still more unwilling to dismiss them than before. They were easily persuaded to stop, and civility grew up in time to freedom and confidence.

The prince now saw all the domesticks chearful, and all the face of nature smiling round the place, and could not forbear to hope that he should find here what he was seeking; but when he was congratulating the master upon his possessions, he answered with a sigh, "My condition has indeed the appearance of happiness, but appearances are delusive. My prosperity puts my life in danger; the Bassa of Egypt is my enemy, incensed only by my wealth and popularity. I have been hitherto protected against him by the princes of the country; but, as the favour of the great is uncertain, I know not how soon my defenders may be persuaded to share the plunder with the Bassa. I have sent my treasures into a distant country, and, upon the first alarm, am prepared to follow them. Then will my enemies riot in my mansion, and enjoy the gardens which I have planted."

They all joined in lamenting his danger, and deprecating his exile; and the princess was so much disturbed with the tumult of grief and indignation, that she retired to her apartment. They continued with their kind inviter a few days longer, and then went forward to find the hermit.

## XXI

### THE HAPPINESS OF SOLITUDE. THE HERMIT'S HISTORY

They came on the third day, by the direction of the peasants, to the hermit's cell: it was a cavern in the side of a mountain, overshadowed with palm-trees; at such a distance from the cataract, that nothing more was heard than a gentle uniform murmur, such as composed the mind to pensive meditation, especially when it was assisted by the wind whistling among the branches. The first rude essay of nature had been so much improved by human labour, that the cave contained several apartments, appropriated to different uses, and often afforded lodging to travellers, whom darkness or tempests happened to overtake.

The hermit sat on a bench at the door, to enjoy the coolness of the evening. On one side lay a book with pens and papers, on the other mechanical instruments of various kinds. As they approached him unregarded, the princess observed that he had not the countenance of a man that had found, or could teach, the way to happiness.

They saluted him with great respect, which he repaid like a man not unaccustomed to the forms of courts. "My children," said he, "if you have lost your way, you shall be willingly supplied with such conveniencies for the night as this cavern will afford. I have all that nature requires, and you will not expect delicacies in a hermit's cell."

They thanked him, and, entering, were pleased with the neatness and regularity of the place. The hermit set flesh and wine before them, though he fed only upon fruits and water. His discourse was chearful without levity, and pious without enthusiasm.[8] He soon gained the esteem of his guests, and the princess repented of her hasty censure.

At last Imlac began thus: "I do not now wonder that your reputation is so far extended; we have heard at Cairo of your wisdom, and came hither to implore your direction for this young man and maiden in the *choice of life*."

"To him that lives well," answered the hermit, "every form of life is good; nor can I give any other rule for choice, than to remove from all apparent evil."

"He will remove most certainly from evil," said the prince, "who shall devote himself to that solitude which you have recommended by your example."

---

[8] enthusiasm: "A vain belief of private revelation; a vain confidence of divine favour or communication." Johnson's *Dictionary*.

"I have indeed lived fifteen years in solitude," said the hermit, "but have no desire that my example should gain any imitators. In my youth I professed arms, and was raised by degrees to the highest military rank. I have traversed wide countries at the head of my troops, and seen many battles and sieges. At last, being disgusted by the preferment of a younger officer, and finding my vigour[9] beginning to decay, I resolved to close my life in peace, having found the world full of snares, discord, and misery. I had once escaped from the persuit of the enemy by the shelter of this cavern, and therefore chose it for my final residence. I employed artificers to form it into chambers, and stored it with all that I was likely to want.

"For some time after my retreat, I rejoiced like a tempest-beaten sailor at his entrance into the harbour, being delighted with the sudden change of the noise and hurry of war, to stillness and repose. When the pleasure of novelty went away, I employed my hours in examining the plants which grow in the valley, and the minerals which I collected from the rocks. But that enquiry is now grown tasteless and irksome. I have been for some time unsettled and distracted: my mind is disturbed with a thousand perplexities of doubt, and vanities of imagination, which hourly prevail upon me, because I have no opportunities of relaxation or diversion. I am sometimes ashamed to think that I could not secure myself from vice, but by retiring from the practice[1] of virtue, and begin to suspect that I was rather impelled by resentment, than led by devotion, into solitude. My fancy riots in scenes of folly, and I lament that I have lost so much, and have gained so little. In solitude, if I escape the example of bad men, I want likewise the counsel and conversation of the good. I have been long comparing the evils with the advantages of society, and resolve to return into the world to morrow. The life of a solitary man will be certainly miserable, but not certainly devout."

They heard his resolution with surprise, but, after a short pause, offered to conduct him to Cairo. He dug up a considerable treasure which he had hid among the rocks, and accompanied them to the city, on which, as he approached it, he gazed with rapture.

---

[9] finding my vigour: feeling that my vigour was 2
[1] practice: exercise 2

# XXII

## THE HAPPINESS OF A LIFE LED ACCORDING TO NATURE

Rasselas went often to an assembly of learned men, who met at stated times to unbend their minds, and compare their opinions. Their manners were somewhat coarse, but their conversation was instructive, and their disputations acute, though sometimes too violent, and often continued till neither controvertist remembered upon what question they began. Some faults were almost general among them: every one was desirous to dictate to the rest, and every one was pleased to hear the genius or knowledge of another depreciated.

In this assembly Rasselas was relating his interview with the hermit, and the wonder with which he heard him censure a course of life which he had so deliberately chosen, and so laudably followed. The sentiments of the hearers were various. Some were of opinion, that the folly of his choice had been justly punished by condemnation to perpetual perseverance. One of the youngest among them, with great vehemence, pronounced him an hypocrite. Some talked of the right of society to the labour of individuals, and considered retirement as a desertion of duty. Others readily allowed, that there was a time when the claims of the publick were satisfied, and when a man might properly sequester himself, to review his life, and purify his heart.

One, who appeared more affected with the narrative than the rest, thought it likely, that the hermit would, in a few years, go back to his retreat, and, perhaps, if shame did not restrain, or death intercept him, return once more from his retreat into the world: "For the hope of happiness," says[2] he, "is so strongly impressed, that the longest experience is not able to efface it. Of the present state, whatever it be, we feel, and are forced to confess, the misery, yet, when the same state is again at a distance, imagination paints it as desirable. But the time will surely come, when desire will be no longer our torment, and no man shall be wretched but by his own fault."

"This," said a philosopher, who had heard him with tokens of

---

[2] says: said 2

great impatience, "is the present condition of a wise man. The time is already come, when none are wretched but by their own fault. Nothing is more idle, than to enquire after happiness, which nature has kindly placed within our reach. The way to be happy is to live according to nature, in obedience to that universal and unalterable law with which every heart is originally impressed; which is not written on it by precept, but engraven by destiny, not instilled by education, but infused at our nativity. He that lives according to nature will suffer nothing from the delusions of hope, or importunities of desire: he will receive and reject with equability of temper; and act or suffer as the reason of things shall alternately prescribe. Other men may amuse themselves with subtle definitions, or intricate raciocination. Let them learn to be wise by easier means: let them observe the hind of the forest, and the linnet of the grove: let them consider the life of animals, whose motions are regulated by instinct; they obey their guide and are happy. Let us therefore, at length, cease to dispute, and learn to live; throw away the incumbrance of precepts, which they who utter them with so much pride and pomp do not understand, and carry with us this simple and intelligible maxim, That deviation from nature is deviation from happiness."

When he had spoken, he looked round him with a placid air, and enjoyed the consciousness of his own beneficence. "Sir," said the prince, with great modesty, "as I, like all the rest of mankind, am desirous of felicity, my closest attention has been fixed upon your discourse: I doubt not the truth of a position which a man so learned has so confidently advanced. Let me only know what it is to live according to nature."

"When I find young men so humble and so docile," said the philosopher, "I can deny them no information which my studies have enabled me to afford. To live according to nature, is to act always with due regard to the fitness arising from the relations and qualities of causes and effects; to concur with the great and unchangeable scheme of universal felicity; to co-operate with the general disposition and tendency of the present system of things."

The prince soon found that this was one of the sages whom he should understand less as he heard him longer. He therefore bowed and was silent, and the philosopher, supposing him satisfied, and the rest vanquished, rose up and departed with the air of a man that had co-operated with the present system.

# XXIII

## THE PRINCE AND HIS SISTER DIVIDE BETWEEN THEM THE
## WORK OF OBSERVATION

Rasselas returned home full of reflexions, doubtful how to direct his future steps. Of the way to happiness he found the learned and simple equally ignorant; but, as he was yet young, he flattered himself that he had time remaining for more experiments, and further enquiries. He communicated to Imlac his observations and his doubts, but was answered by him with new doubts, and remarks that gave him no comfort. He therefore discoursed more frequently and freely with his sister, who had yet the same hope with himself, and always assisted him to give some reason why, though he had been hitherto frustrated, he might succeed at last.

"We have hitherto," said she, "known but little of the world: we have never yet been either great or mean. In our own country, though we had royalty, we had no power, and in this we have not yet seen the private recesses of domestick peace. Imlac favours not our search, lest we should in time find him mistaken. We will divide the task between us: you shall try what is to be found in the splendour of courts, and I will range the shades of humbler life. Perhaps command and authority may be the supreme blessings, as they afford most opportunities of doing good: or, perhaps, what this world can give may be found in the modest habitations of middle fortune; too low for great designs, and too high for penury and distress."

# XXIV

## THE PRINCE EXAMINES THE HAPPINESS OF HIGH STATIONS

Rasselas applauded the design, and appeared next day with a splendid retinue at the court of the Bassa. He was soon distinguished for his magnificence, and admitted, as a prince whose curiosity had brought him from distant countries, to an intimacy with the great officers, and frequent conversation with the Bassa himself.

He was at first inclined to believe, that the man must be pleased with his own condition, whom all approached with reverence, and heard with obedience, and who had the power to extend his edicts to a whole kingdom. "There can be no pleasure," said he, "equal to that of feeling at once the joy of thousands all made happy by wise administration. Yet, since, by the law of subordination, this sublime delight can be in one nation but the lot of one, it is surely reasonable to think that there is some satisfaction more popular and accessible, and that millions can hardly be subjected to the will of a single man, only to fill his particular breast with incommunicable content."

These thoughts were often in his mind, and he found no solution of the difficulty. But as presents and civilities gained him more familiarity, he found that almost every man that[3] stood high in employment hated all the rest, and was hated by them, and that their lives were a continual succession of plots and detections, stratagems and escapes, faction and treachery. Many of those, who surrounded the Bassa, were sent only to watch and report his conduct; every tongue was muttering censure, and every eye was searching for a fault.

At last the letters of revocation arrived, the Bassa was carried in chains to Constantinople, and his name was mentioned no more.

"What are we now to think of the prerogatives of power," said Rasselas to his sister; "is it without any efficacy to good? or, is the subordinate degree only dangerous, and the supreme safe and glorious? Is the Sultan the only happy man in his dominions? or, is the Sultan himself subject to the torments of suspicion, and the dread of enemies?"

In a short time the second Bassa was deposed. The Sultan, that had advanced him, was murdered by the Janisaries, and his successor had other views and different favourites.

## XXV

### THE PRINCESS PERSUES HER ENQUIRY WITH MORE DILIGENCE THAN SUCCESS

The princess, in the mean time, insinuated herself into many families; for there are few doors, through which liberality, joined with good humour, cannot find its way. The daughters of many houses were airy and chearful, but Nekayah had been too long

---

[3] that: who 2

accustomed to the conversation of Imlac and her brother to be much pleased with childish levity and prattle which had no meaning. She found their thoughts narrow, their wishes low, and their merriment often artificial. Their pleasures, poor as they were, could not be preserved pure, but were embittered by petty competitions and worthless emulation. They were always jealous of the beauty of each other; of a quality to which solicitude can add nothing, and from which detraction can take nothing away. Many were in love with triflers like themselves, and many fancied that they were in love when in truth they were only idle. Their affection was seldom fixed on sense or virtue, and therefore seldom ended but in vexation. Their grief, however, like their joy, was transient; every thing floated in their mind unconnected with the past or future, so that one desire easily gave way to another, as a second stone cast into the water effaces and confounds the circles of the first.

With these girls she played as with inoffensive animals, and found them proud of her countenance, and weary of her company.

But her purpose was to examine more deeply, and her affability easily persuaded the hearts that were swelling with sorrow to discharge their secrets in her ear: and those whom hope flattered, or prosperity delighted, often courted her to partake their pleasures.

The princess and her brother commonly met in the evening in a private summer-house on the bank of the Nile, and related to each other the occurrences of the day. As they were sitting together, the princess cast her eyes upon the river that flowed before her. "Answer," said she, "great father of waters, thou that rollest thy floods through eighty nations, to the invocations of the daughter of thy native king. Tell me if thou waterest, through all thy course, a single habitation from which thou dost not hear the murmurs of complaint?"

"You are then," said Rasselas, "not more successful in private houses than I have been in courts." "I have, since the last partition of our provinces," said the princess, "enabled myself to enter familiarly into many families, where there was the fairest show of prosperity and peace, and know not one house that is not haunted by some fiend[4] that destroys its quiet.

"I did not seek ease among the poor, because I concluded that

---

[4] fiend: fury 2

there it could not be found. But I saw many poor whom I had supposed to live in affluence. Poverty has, in large cities, very different appearances: it is often concealed in splendour, and often in extravagance. It is the care of a very great part of mankind to conceal their indigence from the rest: they support themselves by temporary expedients, and every day is lost in contriving for the morrow.

"This, however, was an evil, which, though frequent, I saw with less pain, because I could relieve it. Yet some have refused my bounties; more offended with my quickness to detect their wants, than pleased with my readiness to succour them: and others, whose exigencies compelled them to admit my kindness, have never been able to forgive their benefactress. Many, however, have been sincerely grateful without the ostentation of gratitude, or the hope of other favours."

## XXVI

### THE PRINCESS CONTINUES HER REMARKS UPON PRIVATE LIFE

Nekayah perceiving her brother's attention fixed, proceeded in her narrative.

"In families, where there is or is not poverty, there is commonly discord: if a kingdom be, as Imlac tells us, a great family, a family likewise is a little kingdom, torn with factions and exposed to revolutions. An unpractised observer expects the love of parents and children to be constant and equal; but this kindness seldom continues beyond the years of infancy: in a short time the children become rivals to their parents. Benefits are allayed[5] by reproaches, and gratitude debased by envy.

"Parents and children seldom act in concert: each child endeavours to appropriate the esteem or fondness of the parents, and the parents, with yet less temptation, betray each other to their children; thus some place their confidence in the father, and some in the mother, and, by degrees, the house is filled with artifices and feuds.

"The opinions of children and parents, of the young and the

---

[5] allayed: i.e., alloyed.

old, are naturally opposite, by the contrary effects of hope and despondence, of expectation and experience, without crime or folly on either side. The colours of life in youth and age appear different, as the face of nature in spring and winter. And how can children credit the assertions of parents, which their own eyes show them to be false?

"Few parents act in such a manner as much to enforce their maxims by the credit of their lives. The old man trusts wholly to slow contrivance and gradual progression: the youth expects to force his way by genius, vigour, and precipitance. The old man pays regard to riches, and the youth reverences virtue. The old man deifies prudence: the youth commits himself to magnanimity and chance. The young man, who intends no ill, believes that none is intended, and therefore acts with openness and candour: but his father, having suffered the injuries of fraud, is impelled to suspect, and too often allured to practice it. Age looks with anger on the temerity of youth, and youth with contempt on the scrupulosity of age. Thus parents and children, for the greatest part, live on to love less and less: and, if those whom nature has thus closely united are the torments of each other, where shall we look for tenderness and consolation?"

"Surely," said the prince, "you must have been unfortunate in your choice of acquaintance: I am unwilling to believe, that the most tender of all relations is thus impeded in its effects by natural necessity."

"Domestick discord," answered she, "is not inevitably and fatally necessary; but yet is not easily avoided. We seldom see that a whole family is virtuous: the good and evil cannot well agree; and the evil can yet less agree with one another: even the virtuous fall sometimes to variance, when their virtues are of different kinds, and tending to extremes. In general, those parents have most reverence who most deserve it: for he that lives well cannot be despised.

"Many other evils infest private life. Some are the slaves of servants whom they have trusted with their affairs. Some are kept in continual anxiety to the caprice of rich relations, whom they cannot please, and dare not offend. Some husbands are imperious, and some wives perverse: and, as it is always more easy to do evil than good, though the wisdom or virtue of one can very rarely make many happy, the folly or vice of one may often make many miserable."

"If such be the general effect of marriage," said the prince, "I shall, for the future, think it dangerous to connect my interest with that of another, lest I should be unhappy by my partner's fault."

"I have met," said the princess, "with many who live single for that reason; but I never found that their prudence ought to raise envy. They dream away their time without friendship, without fondness, and are driven to rid themselves of the day, for which they have no use, by childish amusements, or vicious delights. They act as beings under the constant sense of some known inferiority, that fills their minds with rancour, and their tongues with censure. They are peevish at home, and malevolent abroad; and, as the out-laws of human nature, make it their business and their pleasure to disturb that society which debars them from its privileges. To live without feeling or exciting sympathy, to be fortunate without adding to the felicity of others, or afflicted without tasting the balm of pity, is a state more gloomy than solitude: it is not retreat but exclusion from mankind. Marriage has many pains, but celibacy has no pleasures."

"What then is to be done?" said Rasselas; "the more we enquire, the less we can resolve. Surely he is most likely to please himself that has no other inclination to regard."

## XXVII

### DISQUISITION UPON GREATNESS

The conversation had a short pause. The prince, having considered his sister's observations, told her, that she had surveyed life with prejudice, and supposed misery where she did not find it. "Your narrative," says he, "throws yet a darker gloom upon the prospects of futurity: the predictions of Imlac were but faint sketches of the evils painted by Nekayah. I have been lately convinced that quiet is not the daughter of grandeur, or of power: that her presence is not to be bought by wealth, nor enforced by conquest. It is evident, that as any man acts in a wider compass, he must be more exposed to opposition from enmity or miscarriage from chance; whoever has many to please or to govern, must use the ministry of many agents, some of whom will be wicked, and some ignorant; by some he will be misled, and by others betrayed. If he gratifies one he will offend another: those that are not favoured will think themselves injured; and, since favours can be conferred but upon few, the greater number will be always discontented."

"The discontent," said the princess, "which is thus unreasonable, I hope that I shall always have spirit to despise, and you, power to repress."

"Discontent," answered Rasselas, "will not always be without reason under the most just or vigilant administration of publick affairs. None, however attentive, can always discover that merit which indigence or faction may happen to obscure; and none, however powerful, can always reward it. Yet, he that sees inferiour desert advanced above him, will naturally impute that preference to partiality or caprice; and, indeed, it can scarcely be hoped that any man, however magnanimous by nature, or exalted by condition, will be able to persist for ever in fixed and inexorable justice of distribution: he will sometimes indulge his own affections, and sometimes those of his favourites; he will permit some to please him who can never serve him; he will discover in those whom he loves qualities which in reality they do not possess; and to those, from whom he receives pleasure, he will in his turn endeavour to give it. Thus will recommendations sometimes prevail which were purchased by money, or by the more destructive bribery of flattery and servility.

"He that has much to do will do something wrong, and of that wrong must suffer the consequences; and, if it were possible that he should always act rightly, yet when such numbers are to judge of his conduct, the bad will censure and obstruct him by malevolence, and the good sometimes by mistake.

"The highest stations cannot therefore hope to be the abodes of happiness, which I would willingly believe to have fled from thrones and palaces to seats of humble privacy and placid obscurity. For what can hinder the satisfaction, or intercept the expectations, of him whose abilities are adequate to his employments, who sees with his own eyes the whole circuit of his influence, who chooses by his own knowledge all whom he trusts, and whom none are tempted to deceive by hope or fear? Surely he has nothing to do but to love and to be loved, to be virtuous and to be happy."

"Whether perfect happiness would be procured by perfect goodness," said Nekayah, "this world will never afford an opportunity of deciding. But this, at least, may be maintained, that we do not always find visible happiness in proportion to visible virtue. All natural and almost all political evils, are incident alike to the bad and good: they are confounded in the misery of a famine, and not much distinguished in the fury of a faction; they sink together in a tempest, and are driven together from their country by invaders. All that virtue can afford is quietness of conscience, a steady prospect of a happier state; this may enable us to endure calamity with patience; but remember that patience must suppose pain."

## XXVIII

### RASSELAS AND NEKAYAH CONTINUE THEIR CONVERSATION

"Dear princess," said Rasselas, "you fall into the common errours of exaggeratory declamation, by producing, in a familiar disquisition, examples of national calamities, and scenes of extensive misery, which are found in books rather than in the world, and which, as they are horrid, are ordained to be rare. Let us not imagine evils which we do not feel, nor injure life by misrepresentations. I cannot bear that querelous eloquence which threatens every city with a siege like that of Jerusalem, that makes famine attend on every flight of locusts, and suspends pestilence on the wing of every blast that issues from the south.

"On necessary and inevitable evils, which overwhelm kingdoms at once, all disputation is vain: when they happen they must be endured. But it is evident, that these bursts of universal distress are more dreaded than felt: thousands and ten thousands flourish in youth, and wither in age, without the knowledge of any other than domestick evils, and share the same pleasures and vexations whether their kings are mild or cruel, whether the armies of their country persue their enemies, or retreat before them. While courts are disturbed with intestine competitions, and ambassadours are negotiating in foreign countries, the smith still plies his anvil, and the husbandman drives his plow forward; the necessaries of life are required and obtained, and the successive business of the seasons continues to make its wonted revolutions.

"Let us cease to consider what, perhaps, may never happen, and what, when it shall happen, will laugh at human speculation. We will not endeavour to modify the motions of the elements, or to fix the destiny of kingdoms. It is our business to consider what beings like us may perform; each labouring for his own happiness, by promoting within his circle, however narrow, the happiness of others.

"Marriage is evidently the dictate of nature; men and women were made to be companions of each other, and therefore I cannot be persuaded but that marriage is one of the means of happiness."

"I know not," said the princess, "whether marriage be more than one of the innumerable modes of human misery. When I see and reckon the various forms of connubial infelicity, the unexpected causes of lasting discord, the diversities of temper, the oppositions of opinion, the rude collisions of contrary desire where both are urged by violent impulses, the obstinate contests of disagreeing virtues, where both are supported by consciousness of good intention, I am sometimes disposed to think with the severer casuists of most nations, that marriage is rather permitted than approved, and that none, but by the instigation of a passion too much indulged, entangle themselves with indissoluble compacts."

"You seem to forget," replied Rasselas, "that you have, even now, represented celibacy as less happy than marriage. Both conditions may be bad, but they cannot both be worst. Thus it happens when wrong opinions are entertained, that they mutually destroy each other, and leave the mind open to truth."

"I did not expect," answered the princess, "to hear that imputed to falshood which is the consequence only of frailty. To the mind, as to the eye, it is difficult to compare with exactness objects vast in their extent, and various in their parts. Where we see or conceive the whole at once we readily note the discriminations and decide the preference: but of two systems, of which neither can be surveyed by any human being in its full compass of magnitude and multiplicity of complication, where is the wonder, that judging of the whole by parts, I am affected by one or[6] the other as either presses on my memory or fancy? We differ from ourselves just as we differ from each other, when we see only part of the question, as in the multifarious relations of politicks and morality: but when we perceive the whole at once, as in numerical computations, all agree in one judgment, and none ever varies his opinion."

"Let us not add," said the prince, "to the other evils of life, the bitterness of controversy, nor endeavour to vie with each other in subtilties of argument. We are employed in a search, of which both are equally to enjoy the success, or suffer by the miscarriage. It is therefore fit that we assist each other. You surely conclude too hastily from the infelicity of marriage against its institution. Will not the misery of life prove equally that life cannot be the gift of heaven? The world must be peopled by marriage, or peopled without it."

"How the world is to be peopled," returned Nekayah, "is not my care, and needs not be yours. I see no danger that the present generation should omit to leave successors behind them: we are not now enquiring for the world, but for ourselves."

## XXIX

### THE DEBATE ON MARRIAGE CONTINUED

"The good of the whole," says Rasselas, "is the same with the good of all its parts. If marriage be best for mankind it must be evidently best for individuals, or a permanent and necessary duty must be the cause of evil, and some must be inevitably sacrificed to the convenience of others. In the estimate which you have made of the two states, it appears that the incommodities of a single life are, in a great measure, necessary and certain, but those of the conjugal state accidental and avoidable.

"I cannot forbear to flatter myself that prudence and benevolence will make marriage happy. The general folly of mankind is the cause of general complaint. What can be expected but dis-

---

[6] affected by one or: alternately affected by one and 2

appointment and repentance from a choice made in the immaturity of youth, in the ardour of desire, without judgment, without foresight, without enquiry after conformity of opinions, similarity of manners, rectitude of judgment, or purity of sentiment.

"Such is the common process of marriage. A youth and maiden meeting by chance, or brought together by artifice, exchange glances, reciprocate civilities, go home, and dream of one another. Having little to divert attention, or diversify thought, they find themselves uneasy when they are apart, and therefore conclude that they shall be happy together. They marry, and discover what nothing but voluntary blindness had before concealed; they wear out life in altercations, and charge nature with cruelty.

"From those early marriages proceeds likewise the rivalry of parents and children: the son is eager to enjoy the world before the father is willing to forsake it, and there is hardly room at once for two generations. The daughter begins to bloom before the mother can be content to fade, and neither can forbear to wish for the absence of the other.

"Surely all these evils may be avoided by that deliberation and delay which prudence prescribes to irrevocable choice. In the variety and jollity of youthful pleasures life may be well enough supported without the help of a partner. Longer time will increase experience, and wider views will allow better opportunities of enquiry and selection: one advantage, at least, will be certain; the parents will be visibly older than their children."

"What reason cannot collect," said Nekayah, "and what experiment has not yet taught, can be known only from the report of others. I have been told that late marriages are not eminently happy. This is a question too important to be neglected, and I have often proposed it to those, whose accuracy of remark, and comprehensiveness of knowledge, made their suffrages worthy of regard. They have generally determined, that it is dangerous for a man and woman to suspend their fate upon each other, at a time when opinions are fixed, and habits are established; when friendships have been contracted on both sides, when life has been planned into method, and the mind has long enjoyed the contemplation of its own prospects.

"It is scarcely possible that two travelling through the world under the conduct of chance, should have been both directed to the same path, and it will not often happen that either will quit the track which custom has made pleasing. When the desultory levity of youth has settled into regularity, it is soon succeeded by pride ashamed to yield, or obstinacy delighting to contend. And even though mutual esteem produces mutual desire to please, time itself, as it modifies unchangeably the external mien, determines likewise the direction of the passions, and gives an inflexible rigidity to the manners. Long customs are not easily broken: he that attempts to change the course of his own life, very often labours in vain; and how shall we do that for others which we are seldom able to do for ourselves?"

"But surely," interposed the prince, "you suppose the chief motive of choice forgotten or neglected. Whenever I shall seek a wife, it shall be my first question, whether she be willing to be led by reason?"

"Thus it is," said Nekayah, "that philosophers are deceived. There are a thousand familiar disputes which reason never can decide; questions that elude investigation, and make logick ridiculous; cases where something must be done, and where little can be said. Consider the state of mankind, and enquire how few can be supposed to act upon any occasions, whether small or great, with all the reasons of action present to their minds. Wretched would be the pair above all names of wretchedness, who should be doomed to adjust by reason every morning all the minute detail of a domestick day.

"Those who marry at an advanced age, will probably escape the encroachments of their children; but, in diminution of this advantage, they will be likely to leave them, ignorant and helpless, to a guardian's mercy: or, if that should not happen, they must at least go out of the world before they see those whom they love best either wise or great.

"From their children, if they have less to fear, they have less also to hope, and they lose, without equivalent, the joys of early love, and the convenience of uniting with manners pliant, and minds susceptible of new impressions, which might wear away their dissimilitudes by long cohabitation, as soft bodies, by continual attrition, conform their surfaces to each other.

"I believe it will be found that those who marry late are best pleased with their children, and those who marry early with their partners."

"The union of these two affections," said Rasselas, "would produce all that could be wished. Perhaps there is a time when marriage might unite them, a time neither too early for the father, nor too late for the husband."

"Every hour," answered the princess, "confirms my prejudice in favour of the position so often uttered by the mouth of Imlac, 'That nature sets her gifts on the right hand and on the left.' Those conditions, which flatter hope and attract desire, are so constituted, that, as we approach one, we recede from another. There are goods so opposed that we cannot seize both, but, by too much prudence, may pass between them at too great a distance to reach either. This is often the fate of long consideration; he does nothing who endeavours to do more than is allowed to humanity. Flatter not yourself with contrarieties of pleasure. Of the blessings set before you make your choice, and be content. No man can taste the fruits of autumn while he is delighting his scent with the flowers of the spring: no man can, at the same time, fill his cup from the source and from the mouth of the Nile."

## XXX

### IMLAC ENTERS, AND CHANGES THE CONVERSATION

Here Imlac entered, and interrupted them. His look was clouded with thought.[7] "Imlac," said Rasselas, "I have been taking from the princess the dismal history of private life, and am almost discouraged from further search."

"It seems to me," said Imlac, "that while you are making the choice of life, you neglect to live. You wander about a single city, which, however large and diversified, can now afford few novelties, and forget that you are in a country, famous among the earliest monarchies for the power and wisdom of its inhabitants; a country where the sciences first dawned that illuminate the world, and beyond which the arts cannot be traced of civil society or domestick life.

"The old Egyptians have left behind them monuments of industry and power before which all European magnificence is confessed to fade away. The ruins of their architecture are the

---

[7] His . . . thought: *omitted* 2

schools of modern builders, and from the wonders which time has spared we may conjecture, though uncertainly, what it has destroyed."

"My curiosity," said Rasselas, "does not very strongly lead me to survey piles of stone, or mounds of earth; my business is with man. I came hither not to measure fragments of temples, or trace choaked aqueducts, but to look upon the various scenes of the present world."

"The things that are now before us," said the princess, "necessarily require attention, and sufficiently deserve it.[8] What have I to do with the heroes or the monuments of ancient times? with times which never can return, and heroes, whose form of life was different from all that the present condition of mankind requires or allows."

"To know any thing," returned the poet, "we must know its effects; to see men we must see their works, that we may learn what reason has dictated, or passion has incited, and find what are the most powerful motives of action. To judge rightly of the present we must oppose it to the past; for all judgment is comparative, and of the future nothing can be known. The truth is, that no mind is much employed upon the present: recollection and anticipation fill up almost all our moments. Our passions are joy and grief, love and hatred, hope and fear. Of joy and grief the past is the object, and the future of hope and fear; even love and hatred respect the past, for the cause must have been before the effect.

"The present state of things is the consequence of the former, and it is natural to inquire what were the sources of the good that we enjoy, or of the evil that we suffer. If we act only for ourselves, to neglect the study of history is not prudent: if we are entrusted with the care of others, it is not just. Ignorance, when it is voluntary, is criminal; and he may properly be charged with evil who refused to learn how he might prevent it.

"There is no part of history so generally useful as that which relates the progress of the human mind, the gradual improvement of reason, the successive advances of science, the vicissitudes of

---

[8] necessarily require attention, and sufficiently deserve it: require attention, and deserve it 2

learning and ignorance, which are the light and darkness of thinking beings, the extinction and resuscitation of arts, and all the revolutions of the intellectual world. If accounts of battles and invasions are peculiarly the business of princes, the useful or elegant arts are not to be neglected; those who have kingdoms to govern have understandings to cultivate.

"Example is always more efficacious than precept. A soldier is formed in war, and a painter must copy pictures. In this, contemplative life has the advantage: great actions are seldom seen, but the labours of art are always at hand for those who desire to know what art has been able to perform.

"When the eye or the imagination is struck with any uncommon work the next transition of an active mind is to the means by which it was performed. Here begins the true use of such contemplation; we enlarge our comprehension by new ideas, and perhaps recover some art lost to mankind, or learn what is less perfectly known in our own country. At least we compare our own with former times, and either rejoice at our improvements, or, what is the first motion towards good, discover our defects."

"I am willing," said the prince, "to see all that can deserve my search." "And I," said the princess, "shall rejoice to learn something of the manners of antiquity."

"The most pompous monument of Egyptian greatness, and one of the most bulky works of manual industry," said Imlac, "are the pyramids; fabricks raised before the time of history, and of which the earliest narratives afford us only uncertain traditions. Of these the greatest is still standing, very little injured by time."

"Let us visit them to morrow," said Nekayah. "I have often heard of the pyramids, and shall not rest, till I have seen them within and without with my own eyes."

## XXXI

### THEY VISIT THE PYRAMIDS

The resolution being thus taken, they set out the next day. They laid tents upon their camels, being resolved to stay among the pyramids till their curiosity was fully satisfied. They travelled gently, turned aside to every thing remarkable, stopped from time to time and conversed with the inhabitants, and observed the various appearances of towns ruined and inhabited, of wild and cultivated nature.

When they came to the great pyramid they were astonished at the extent of the base, and the height of the top. Imlac explained to them the principles upon which the pyramidal form was chosen for a fabrick intended to co-extend its duration with that of the world: he showed that its gradual diminution gave it such stability, as defeated all the common attacks of the elements, and could scarcely be overthrown by earthquakes themselves, the least resistible of natural violence. A concussion that should shatter the pyramid would threaten the dissolution of the continent.

They measured all its dimensions, and pitched their tents at its foot. Next day they prepared to enter its interiour apartments, and having hired the common guides climbed up to the first passage, when the favourite of the princess, looking into the cavity, stepped back and trembled. "Pekuah," said the princess, "of what art thou afraid?" "Of the narrow entrance," answered the lady, "and of the dreadful gloom. I dare not enter a place which must surely be inhabited by unquiet souls. The original possessors of these dreadful vaults will start up before us, and, perhaps, shut us up[9] for ever." She spoke, and threw her arms round the neck of her mistress.

"If all your fear be of apparitions," said the prince, "I will promise you safety: there is no danger from the dead; he that is once buried will be seen no more."

"That the dead are seen no more," said Imlac, "I will not undertake to maintain against the concurrent and unvaried testimony of all ages, and of all nations. There is no people, rude or learned, among whom apparitions of the dead are not related and believed. This opinion, which, perhaps, prevails as far as human nature is diffused, could become universal only by its truth: those, that never heard of one another, would not have agreed in a tale which nothing but experience can make credible. That it is doubted by single cavillers can very little weaken the general evidence, and some who deny it with their tongues confess it by their fears.

---

[9] up: in 2

"Yet I do not mean to add new terrours to those which have already seized upon Pekuah. There can be no reason why spectres should haunt the pyramid more than other places, or why they should have power or will to hurt innocence and purity. Our entrance is no violation of their privileges; we can take nothing from them, how then can we offend them?"

"My dear Pekuah," said the princess, "I will always go before you, and Imlac shall follow you. Remember that you are the companion of the princess of Abissinia."

"If the princess is pleased that her servant should die," returned the lady, "let her command some death less dreadful than enclosure in this horrid cavern. You know I dare not disobey you: I must go if you command me; but, if I once enter, I never shall come back."

The princess saw that her fear was too strong for expostulation or reproof, and embracing her, told her that she should stay in the tent till their return. Pekuah was yet not satisfied, but entreated the princess not to persue so dreadful a purpose as that of entering the recesses of the pyramid. "Though I cannot teach courage," said Nekayah, "I must not learn cowardise; nor leave at last undone what I came hither only to do."

## XXXII

### THEY ENTER THE PYRAMID

Pekuah descended to the tents, and the rest entered the pyramid: they passed through the galleries, surveyed the vaults of marble, and examined the chest in which the body of the founder is supposed to have been reposited. They then sat down in one of the most spacious chambers to rest a while before they attempted to return.

"We have now," said Imlac, "gratified our minds with an exact view of the greatest work of man, except the wall of China.

"Of the wall it is very easy to assign the motives. It secured a wealthy and timorous nation from the incursions of Barbarians, whose unskilfulness in arts made it easier for them to supply their wants by rapine than by industry, and who from time to time poured in upon the habitations of peaceful commerce, as vultures descend upon domestick fowl. Their celerity and fierceness made the wall necessary, and their ignorance made it efficacious.

"But for the pyramids no reason has ever been given adequate to the cost and labour of the work. The narrowness of the chambers proves that it could afford no retreat from enemies, and treasures might have been reposited at far less expence with equal security. It seems to have been erected only in compliance with that hunger of imagination which preys incessantly upon life, and must be always appeased by some employment. Those who have already all that they can enjoy, must enlarge their desires. He that has built for use, till use is supplied, must begin to build for vanity, and extend his plan to the utmost power of human performance, that he may not be soon reduced to form another wish.

"I consider this mighty structure as a monument of the insufficiency of human enjoyments. A king, whose power is unlimited, and whose treasures surmount all real and imaginary wants, is compelled to solace, by the erection of a pyramid, the satiety of dominion and tastelesness of pleasures, and to amuse the tediousness of declining life, by seeing thousands labouring without end, and one stone, for no purpose, laid upon another. Whoever thou art, that, not content with a moderate condition, imaginest happiness in royal magnificence, and dreamest that command or riches can feed the appetite of novelty with successive[1] gratifications, survey the pyramids, and confess thy folly!"

## XXXIII

### THE PRINCESS MEETS WITH AN UNEXPECTED MISFORTUNE

They rose up, and returned through the cavity at which they had entered, and the princess prepared for her favourite a long narrative of dark labyrinths, and costly rooms, and of the different impressions which the varieties of the way had made upon her. But, when they came to their train, they found every one silent and dejected: the men discovered shame and fear in their countenances, and the women were weeping in the tents.

What had happened they did not try to conjecture, but imme-

---

[1] successive: perpetual 2

diately enquired. "You had scarcely entered into the pyramid," said one of the attendants, "when a troop of Arabs rushed upon us: we were too few to resist them, and too slow to escape. They were about to search the tents, set us on our camels, and drive us along before them, when the approach of some Turkish horsemen put them to flight; but they seized the lady Pekuah with her two maids, and carried them away: the Turks are now persuing them by our instigation, but I fear they will not be able to overtake them."

The princess was overpowered with surprise and grief. Rasselas, in the first heat of his resentment, ordered his servants to follow him, and prepared to persue the robbers with his sabre in his hand. "Sir," said Imlac, "what can you hope from violence or valour? the Arabs are mounted on horses trained to battle and retreat; we have only beasts of burthen. By leaving our present station we may lose the princess, but cannot hope to regain Pekuah."

In a short time the Turks returned, having not been able to reach the enemy. The princess burst out into new lamentations, and Rasselas could scarcely forbear to reproach them with cowardice; but Imlac was of opinion, that the escape of the Arabs was no addition to their misfortune, for, perhaps, they would have killed their captives rather than have resigned them.

## XXXIV

### THEY RETURN TO CAIRO WITHOUT PEKUAH

There was nothing to be hoped from longer stay. They returned to Cairo repenting of their curiosity, censuring the negligence of the government, lamenting their own rashness which had neglected to procure a guard, imagining many expedients by which the loss of Pekuah might have been prevented, and resolving to do something for her recovery, though none could find any thing proper to be done.

Nekayah retired to her chamber, where her women attempted to comfort her, by telling her that all had their troubles, and that lady Pekuah had enjoyed much happiness in the world for a long time, and might reasonably expect a change of fortune. They hoped that some good would befal her wheresoever she was, and that their mistress would find another friend who might supply her place.

The princess made them no answer, and they continued the form of condolence, not much grieved in their hearts that the favourite was lost.

Next day the prince presented to the Bassa a memorial of the wrong which he had suffered, and a petition for redress. The Bassa threatened to punish the robbers, but did not attempt to catch them, nor, indeed, could any account or description be given by which he might direct the persuit.

It soon appeared that nothing would be done by authority. Governors, being accustomed to hear of more crimes than they can punish, and more wrongs than they can redress, set themselves at ease by indiscriminate negligence, and presently forget the request when they lose sight of the petitioner.

Imlac then endeavoured to gain some intelligence by private agents. He found many who pretended to an exact knowledge of all the haunts of the Arabs, and to regular correspondence with their chiefs, and who readily undertook the recovery of Pekuah. Of these, some were furnished with money for their journey, and came back no more; some were liberally paid for accounts which a few days discovered to be false. But the princess would not suffer any means, however improbable, to be left untried. While she was doing something she kept her hope alive. As one expedient failed, another was suggested; when one messenger returned unsuccessful, another was despatched to a different quarter.

Two months had now passed, and of Pekuah nothing had been heard; the hopes which they had endeavoured to raise in each other grew more languid, and the princess, when she saw nothing more to be tried, sunk down inconsolable in hopeless dejection. A thousand times she reproached herself with the easy compliance by which she permitted her favourite to stay behind her. "Had not my fondness," said she, "lessened my authority, Pekuah had not dared to talk of her terrours. She ought to have feared me more than spectres. A severe look would have overpowered her; a peremptory command would have compelled obedience. Why did foolish indulgence prevail upon me? Why did I not speak and refuse to hear?"

"Great princess," said Imlac, "do not reproach yourself for your virtue, or consider that as blameable by which evil has accidentally been caused. Your tenderness for the timidity of Pekuah was generous and kind. When we act according to our duty, we commit the event to him by whose laws our actions are governed, and who will suffer none to be finally punished for obedience. When, in prospect of some good, whether natural or moral, we break the rules prescribed us, we withdraw from the direction of superiour wisdom, and take all consequences upon ourselves. Man cannot so far know the connexion of causes and events, as that he may venture to do wrong in order to do right. When we persue our end by lawful means, we may always console our miscarriage by the hope of future recompense. When we consult only our own policy, and attempt to find a nearer way to good, by overleaping the settled boundaries of right and wrong, we cannot be happy even by success, because we cannot escape the consciousness of our fault; but, if we miscarry, the disappointment is irremediably embittered. How comfortless is the sorrow of him, who feels at once the pangs of guilt, and the vexation of calamity which guilt has brought upon him?

"Consider, princess, what would have been your condition, if the lady Pekuah had intreated to accompany you, and, being compelled to stay in the tents, had been carried away; or how would you have born the thought, if you had forced her into the pyramid, and she had died before you in agonies of terrour."

"Had either happened," said Nekayah, "I could not have endured life till now: I should have been tortured to madness by the remembrance of such cruelty, or must have pined away in abhorrence of myself."

"This at least," said Imlac, "is the present reward of virtuous conduct, that no unlucky consequence can oblige us to repent it."

## XXXV

### THE PRINCESS CONTINUES TO LAMENT[2] PEKUAH

Nekayah, being thus reconciled to herself, found that no evil is insupportable but that which is accompanied with consciousness of wrong. She was, from that time, delivered from the violence of

---

[2] continues to lament: languishes for want of 2

tempestuous sorrow, and sunk into silent pensiveness and gloomy tranquillity. She sat from morning to evening recollecting all that had been done or said by her Pekuah, treasured up with care every trifle on which Pekuah had set an accidental value, and which might recal to mind any little incident or careless conversation. The sentiments of her, whom she now expected to see no more, were treasured up[3] in her memory as rules of life, and she deliberated to no other end than to conjecture on any occasion what would have been the opinion and counsel of Pekuah.

The women, by whom she was attended, knew nothing of her real condition, and therefore she could not talk to them but with caution and reserve. She began to remit her curiosity, having no great care to collect notions which she had no convenience of uttering. Rasselas endeavoured first to comfort and afterwards to divert her; he hired musicians, to whom she seemed to listen, but did not hear them, and procured masters to instruct her in various arts, whose lectures, when they visited her again, were again to be repeated. She had lost her taste of pleasure and her ambition of excellence. And her mind, though forced into short excursions, always recurred to the image of her friend.

Imlac was every morning earnestly enjoined to renew his enquiries, and was asked every night whether he had yet heard of Pekuah, till not being able to return the princess the answer that she desired, he was less and less willing to come into her presence. She observed his backwardness, and commanded him to attend her. "You are not," said she, "to confound impatience with resentment, or to suppose that I charge you with negligence, because I repine at your unsuccessfulness. I do not much wonder at your absence; I know that the unhappy are never pleasing, and that all naturally avoid the contagion of misery. To hear complaints is wearisome alike to the wretched and the happy; for who would cloud by adventitious grief the short gleams of gaiety which life allows us? or who, that is struggling under his own evils, will add to them the miseries of another?

"The time is at hand, when none shall be disturbed any longer by the sighs of Nekayah: my search after happiness is now at an end. I am resolved to retire from the world with all its flatteries

---

[3] treasured up: treasured 2

and deceits, and will hide myself in solitude, without any other care than to compose my thoughts, and regulate my hours by a constant succession of innocent occupations, till, with a mind purified from all earthly desires, I shall enter into that state, to which all are hastening, and in which I hope again to enjoy the friendship of Pekuah."

"Do not entangle your mind," said Imlac, "by irrevocable determinations, nor increase the burthen of life by a voluntary accumulation of misery: the weariness of retirement will continue or increase when the loss of Pekuah is forgotten. That you have been deprived of one pleasure is no very good reason for rejection of the rest."

"Since Pekuah was taken from me," said the princess, "I have no pleasure to reject or to retain. She that has no one to love or trust has little to hope. She wants the radical principle of happiness. We may, perhaps, allow that what satisfaction this world can afford, must arise from the conjunction of wealth, knowledge and goodness: wealth is nothing but as it is bestowed, and knowledge nothing but as it is communicated.[4] Goodness affords the only comfort which can be enjoyed without a partner, and goodness may be practised in retirement."

"How far solitude may admit goodness, or advance it, I shall not," replied Imlac, "dispute at present. Remember the confession of the pious hermit. You will wish to return into the world, when the image of your companion has left your thoughts." "That time," said Nekayah, "will never come. The generous frankness, the modest obsequiousness, and the faithful secrecy of my dear Pekuah, will always be more missed, as I shall live longer to see vice and folly."

"The state of a mind oppressed with a sudden calamity," said Imlac, "is like that of the fabulous inhabitants of the new created earth, who, when the first night came upon them, supposed that day never would return. When the clouds of sorrow gather over us, we see nothing beyond them, nor can imagine how they will be dispelled: yet a new day succeeded to the night, and sorrow is never long without a dawn of ease. But they who restrain them-

---

[4] communicated: 2 *adds* they must therefore be imparted to others, and to whom could I now delight to impart them?

selves from receiving comfort, do as the savages would have done, had they put out their eyes when it was dark. Our minds, like our bodies, are in continual flux; something is hourly lost, and something acquired. To lose much at once is inconvenient to either, but while the vital powers remain uninjured, nature will find the means of reparation. Distance has the same effect on the mind as on the eye, and while we glide along the stream of time, whatever we leave behind us is always lessening, and that which we approach increasing in magnitude. Do not suffer life to stagnate; it will grow muddy for want of motion: commit yourself again to the current of the world; Pekuah will vanish by degrees; you will meet in your way some other favourite, or learn to diffuse yourself in general conversation."

"At least," said the prince, "do not despair before all remedies have been tried: the enquiry after the unfortunate lady is still continued, and shall be carried on with yet greater diligence, on condition that you will promise to wait a year for the event, without any unalterable resolution."

Nekayah thought this a reasonable demand, and made the promise to her brother, who had been advised by Imlac to require it. Imlac had, indeed, no great hope of regaining Pekuah, but he supposed, that if he could secure the interval of a year, the princess would be then in no danger of a cloister.

## XXXVI

### PEKUAH IS STILL REMEMBERED BY THE PRINCESS[5]

Nekayah, seeing that nothing was omitted for the recovery of her favourite, and having, by her promise, set her intention of retirement at a distance, began imperceptibly to return to common cares and common pleasures. She rejoiced without her own consent at the suspension of her sorrows, and sometimes caught herself with indignation in the act of turning away her mind from the remembrance of her, whom yet she resolved never to forget.

She then appointed a certain hour of the day for meditation on the merits and fondness of Pekuah, and for some weeks retired constantly at the time fixed, and returned with her eyes swollen

---

[5] remembered by the princess: remembered. The progress of sorrow 2

and her countenance clouded. By degrees she grew less scrupulous, and suffered any important and pressing avocation to delay
the tribute of daily tears. She then yielded to less occasions;
sometimes forgot what she was indeed afraid to remember, and,
at last, wholly released herself from the duty of periodical
affliction.

Her real love of Pekuah was yet not diminished. A thousand
occurrences brought her back to memory, and a thousand wants,
which nothing but the confidence of friendship can supply, made
her frequently regretted. She, therefore, solicited Imlac never to
desist from enquiry, and to leave no art of intelligence untried,
that, at least, she might have the comfort of knowing that she did
not suffer by negligence or sluggishness. "Yet what," said she, "is
to be expected from our persuit of happiness, when we find the
state of life to be such, that happiness itself is the cause of misery?
Why should we endeavour to attain that, of which the possession
cannot be secured? I shall henceforward fear to yield my heart
to excellence, however bright, or to fondness, however tender, lest
I should lose again what I have lost in Pekuah."

## XXXVII

### THE PRINCESS HEARS NEWS OF PEKUAH

In seven months, one of the messengers, who had been sent away
upon the day when the promise was drawn from the princess,
returned, after many unsuccessful rambles, from the borders of
Nubia, with an account that Pekuah was in the hands of an Arab
chief, who possessed a castle or fortress on the extremity of Egypt.
The Arab, whose revenue was plunder, was willing to restore her,
with her two attendants, for two hundred ounces of gold.

The price was no subject of debate. The princess was in extasies
when she heard that her favourite was alive, and might so cheaply
be ransomed. She could not think of delaying for a moment
Pekuah's happiness or her own, but entreated her brother to send
back the messenger with the sum required. Imlac, being consulted,
was not very confident of the veracity of the relator, and was still
more doubtful of the Arab's faith, who might, if he were too
liberally trusted, detain at once the money and the captives. He

thought it dangerous to put themselves in the power of the Arab, by going into his district, and could not expect that the Arab[6] would so much expose himself as to come into the lower country, where he might be seized by the forces of the Bassa.

It is difficult to negotiate where neither will trust. But Imlac, after some deliberation, directed the messenger to propose that Pekuah should be conducted by ten horsemen to the monastry of St. Antony, which is situated in the deserts of Upper-Egypt, where she should be met by the same number, and her ransome should be paid.

That no time might be lost, as they expected that the proposal would not be refused, they immediately began their journey to the monastry; and, when they arrived, Imlac went forward with the former messenger to the Arab's fortress. Rasselas was desirous to go with them, but neither his sister nor Imlac would consent. The Arab, according to the custom of his nation, observed the laws of hospitality with great exactness to those who put themselves into his power, and, in a few days, brought Pekuah with her maids, by easy journeys, to their place appointed, where he received the stipulated price, and, with great respect, restored her[7] to liberty and her friends, and undertook to conduct them back towards Cairo beyond all danger of robbery or violence.

The princess and her favourite embraced each other with transport too violent to be expressed, and went out together to pour the tears of tenderness in secret, and exchange professions of kindness and gratitude. After a few hours they returned into the refectory of the convent, where, in the presence of the prior and his brethren, the prince required of Pekuah the history of her adventures.

## XXXVIII

### THE ADVENTURES OF THE LADY PEKUAH

"At what time, and in what manner, I was forced away," said Pekuah, "your servants have told you. The suddenness of the

---

[6] Arab: Rover 2

[7] he received the stipulated price, and, with great respect, restored her: receiving the stipulated price, he restored her with great respect 2

event struck me with surprise, and I was at first rather stupified than agitated with any passion of either fear or sorrow. My confusion was encreased by the speed and tumult of our flight while we were followed by the Turks, who, as it seemed, soon despaired to overtake us, or were afraid of those whom they made a shew of menacing.

"When the Arabs saw themselves out of danger they slackened their course, and, as I was less harassed by external violence, I began to feel more uneasiness in my mind. After some time we stopped near a spring shaded with trees in a pleasant meadow, where we were set upon the ground, and offered such refreshments as our masters were partaking. I was suffered to sit with my maids apart from the rest, and none attempted to comfort or insult us. Here I first began to feel the full weight of my misery. The girls sat weeping in silence, and from time to time looked up to[8] me for succour. I knew not to what condition we were doomed, nor could conjecture where would be the place of our captivity, or whence to draw any hope of deliverance. I was in the hands of robbers and savages, and had no reason to suppose that their pity was more than their justice, or that they would forbear the gratification of any ardour of desire, or caprice of cruelty. I, however, kissed my maids, and endeavoured to pacify them by remarking, that we were yet treated with decency, and that, since we were now carried beyond pursuit, there was no danger of violence to our lives.

"When we were to be set again on horseback, my maids clung round me, and refused to be parted, but I commanded them not to irritate those who had us in their power. We travelled the remaining part of the day through an unfrequented and pathless country, and came by moonlight to the side of a hill, where the rest of the troop was stationed. Their tents were pitched, and their fires kindled, and our chief was welcomed as a man much beloved by his dependants.

"We were received into a large tent, where we found women who had attended their husbands in the expedition. They set before us the supper which they had provided, and I eat it rather to encourage my maids than to comply with any appetite of my

---

[8] up to: on 2

own. When the meat was taken away they spread the carpets for
repose. I was weary, and hoped to find in sleep that remission of
distress which nature seldom denies. Ordering myself therefore
to be undrest, I observed that the women looked very earnestly
upon me, not expecting, I suppose, to see me so submissively attended. When my upper vest was taken off, they were apparently
struck with the splendour of my cloaths, and one of them
timorously laid her hand upon the embroidery. She then went
out, and, in a short time, came back with another woman, who
seemed to be of higher rank, and greater authority. She did, at her
entrance, the usual act of reverence, and, taking me by the hand,
placed me in a smaller tent, spread with finer carpets, where I
spent the night quietly with my maids.

"In the morning, as I was sitting on the grass, the chief of the
troop came towards me: I rose up to receive him, and he bowed
with great respect. 'Illustrious lady,' said he, 'my fortune is better
than I had presumed to hope; I am told by my women, that I have
a princess in my camp.' 'Sir,' answered I, 'your women have deceived themselves and you; I am not a princess, but an unhappy
stranger who intended soon to have left this country, in which I
am now to be imprisoned for ever.' 'Whoever, or whencesoever,
you are,' returned the Arab, 'your dress, and that of your servants,
show your rank to be high, and your wealth to be great. Why
should you, who can so easily procure your ransome, think yourself in danger of perpetual captivity? The purpose of my incursions is to encrease my riches, or more properly to gather
tribute. The sons of Ishmael are the natural and hereditary lords
of this part of the continent, which is usurped by late invaders,
and low-born tyrants, from whom we are compelled to take by the
sword what is denied to justice. The violence of war admits no
distinction; the lance that is lifted at guilt and power will sometimes fall on innocence and gentleness.'

" 'How little,' said I, 'did I expect that yesterday it should have
fallen upon me.'

" 'Misfortunes,' answered the Arab, 'should always be expected.
If the eye of hostility could have learned to spare,[9] excellence like
yours had been exempt from injury. But the angels of affliction

---

[9] have learned to spare: learn reverence or pity 2

spread their toils alike for the virtuous and the wicked, for the mighty and the mean. Do not be disconsolate; I am not one of the lawless and cruel rovers of the desart; I know the rules of civil life; I will fix your ransome, give a pasport to your messenger, and perform my stipulation with nice punctuality.'

"You will easily believe that I was pleased with his courtesy; and finding that his predominant passion was desire of money, I began now to think my danger less, for I knew that no sum would be thought too great for the release of Pekuah. I told him that he should have no reason to charge me with ingratitude, if I was used with kindness, and that any ransome, which could be expected for a maid of common rank, would be paid, but that he must not persist to rate me as a princess. He said, he would consider what he should demand, and then, smiling, bowed and retired.

"Soon after the women came about me, each contending to be more officious[1] than the other, and my maids themselves were served with reverence. We travelled onward by short journeys. On the fourth day the chief told me, that my ransome must be two hundred ounces of gold, which I not only promised him, but told him, that I would add fifty more, if I and my maids were honourably treated.

"I never knew the power of gold before. From that time I was the leader of the troop. The march of every day was longer or shorter as I commanded, and the tents were pitched where I chose to rest. We now had camels and other conveniencies for travel, my own women were always at my side, and I amused myself with observing the manners of the vagrant nations, and with viewing remains of ancient edifices with which these deserted countries appear to have been, in some distant age, lavishly embellished.

"The chief of the band was a man far from illiterate: he was able to travel by the stars or the compass, and had marked in his erratick expeditions such places as are most worthy the notice of a passenger. He observed to me, that buildings are always best preserved in places little frequented, and difficult of access: for, when once a country declines from its primitive splendour, the

---

[1] officious: in the old sense, "kind; doing good offices." Johnson's *Dictionary*.

more inhabitants are left, the quicker ruin will be made. Walls supply stones more easily than quarries, and palaces and temples will be demolished to make stables of granate, and cottages of porphyry.

# XXXIX

### THE ADVENTURES OF PEKUAH CONTINUED

"We wandered about in this manner for some weeks, whether, as our chief pretended, for my gratification, or, as I rather suspected, for some convenience of his own. I endeavoured to appear contented where sullenness and resentment would have been of no use, and that endeavour conduced much to the calmness of my mind; but my heart was always with Nekayah, and the troubles of the night much overbalanced the amusements of the day. My women, who threw all their cares upon their mistress, set their minds at ease from the time when they saw me treated with respect, and gave themselves up to the incidental alleviations of our fatigue without solicitude or sorrow. I was pleased with their pleasure, and animated with their confidence. My condition had lost much of its terrour, since I found that the Arab ranged the country merely to get riches. Avarice is an uniform and tractable vice: other intellectual distempers are different in different constitutions of mind; that which sooths the pride of one will offend the pride of another; but to the favour of the covetous there is a ready way, bring money and nothing is denied.

"At last we came to the dwelling of our chief, a strong and spacious house built with stone in an island of the Nile, which lies, as I was told, under the tropick. 'Lady,' said the Arab, 'you shall rest a few weeks after your journey[2] in this place, where you are to consider yourself as sovereign. My occupation is war: I have therefore chosen this obscure residence, from which I can issue unexpected, and to which I can retire unpersued. You may now repose in security: here are few pleasures, but here is no danger.' He then led me into the inner apartments, and seating me in the place of honour,[3] bowed to the ground. His women,

---

[2] a few weeks after your journey: after your journey a few weeks 2
[3] in the place of honour: on the richest couch 2

who considered me as a rival, looked on me with malignity; but being soon informed that I was a great lady detained only for my ransome, they began to vie with each other in obsequiousness and reverence.

"Being again comforted with new assurances of speedy liberty, I was for some days diverted from impatience by the novelty of the place. The turrets overlooked the country to a great distance, and afforded a view of many windings of the stream. In the day I wandered from one place to another as the course of the sun varied the splendour of the prospect, and saw many things which I had never seen before. The crocodiles and river-horses were[4] common in this unpeopled region, and I often looked upon them with terrour, though I knew that they could not hurt me. For some time I expected to see mermaids and tritons, which, as Imlac has told me, the European travellers have stationed in the Nile, but no such beings ever appeared, and the Arab, when I enquired after them, laughed at my credulity.

"At night the Arab always attended me to a tower set apart for celestial observations, where he endeavoured to teach me the names and courses of the stars. I had no great inclination to this study, but an appearance of attention was necessary to please my instructor, who valued himself for his skill, and, in a little while, I found some employment requisite to beguile the tediousness of time, which was to be passed always amidst the same objects. I was weary of looking in the morning on things from which I had turned away weary in the evening: I therefore was at last willing to observe the stars rather than do nothing, but could not always compose my thoughts, and was very often thinking on Nekayah when others imagined me contemplating the sky. Soon after the Arab went upon another expedition, and then my only pleasure was to talk with my maids about the accident by which we were carried away, and the happiness that we should all enjoy at the end of our captivity."

"There were women in your Arab's fortress," said the princess, "why did you not make them your companions, enjoy their conversation, and partake their diversions? In a place where they found business or amusement, why should you alone sit corroded

---

[4] river-horses were: river-horses are 2. Johnson also translated "hippopotami" thus in his Lobo's *Abyssinia*.

with idle melancholy? or why could not you bear for a few months that condition to which they were condemned for life?"

"The diversions of the women," answered Pekuah, "were only childish play, by which the mind accustomed to stronger operations could not be kept busy. I could do all which they delighted in doing by powers merely sensitive,[5] while my intellectual faculties were flown to Cairo. They ran from room to room as a bird hops from wire to wire in his cage. They danced for the sake of motion, as lambs frisk in a meadow. One sometimes pretended to be hurt that the rest might be alarmed, or hid herself that another might seek her. Part of their time passed in watching the progress of light bodies that floated on the river, and part in marking the various forms into which clouds broke in the sky.

"Their business was only needlework, in which I and my maids sometimes helped them; but you know that the mind will easily straggle from the fingers, nor will you suspect that captivity and absence from Nekayah could be much solaced by[6] silken flowers.

"Nor was much satisfaction to be hoped from their conversation: for of what could they be expected to talk? They had seen nothing; for they had lived from early youth in that narrow spot: of what they had not seen they could have no knowledge, for they could not read. They had no ideas but of the few things that were within their view, and had hardly names for any thing but their cloaths and their food. As I bore a superiour character, I was often called to terminate their quarrels, which I decided as equitably as I could. If it could have amused me to hear the complaints of each against the rest, I might have been often detained by long stories, but the motives of their animosity were so small that I could not listen long[7] without intercepting the tale."

"How," said Rasselas, "can the Arab, whom you represented as a man of more than common accomplishments, take any pleasure in his seraglio, when it is filled only with women like these. Are they exquisitely beautiful?"

"They do not," said Pekuah, "want that unaffecting and ignoble

---

[5] sensitive: "having sense or perception, but not reason." Johnson's *Dictionary*.

[6] be much solaced by: receive solace from 2

[7] listen long: listen 2

beauty which may subsist without spriteliness or sublimity, without energy of thought or dignity of virtue. But to a man like the Arab such beauty was only a flower casually plucked and carelessly thrown away. Whatever pleasures he might find among them, they were not those of friendship or society. When they were playing about him he looked on them with inattentive superiority: when they vied for his regard he sometimes turned away disgusted. As they had no knowledge, their talk could take nothing from the tediousness of life: as they had no choice, their fondness, or appearance of fondness, excited in him neither pride nor gratitude; he was not exalted in his own esteem by the smiles of a woman who saw no other man, nor was much obliged by that regard, of which he could never know the sincerity, and which he might often perceive to be exerted not so much to delight him as to pain a rival. That which he gave, and they received, as love, was only a careless distribution of superfluous time, such love as man can bestow upon that which he despises, such as has neither hope nor fear, neither joy nor sorrow."

"You have reason, lady, to think yourself happy," said Imlac, "that you have been thus easily dismissed. How could a mind, hungry for knowledge, be willing, in an intellectual famine, to lose such a banquet as Pekuah's conversation?"

"I am inclined to believe," answered Pekuah, "that he was for some time in suspense; for, notwithstanding his promise, whenever I proposed to dispatch a messenger to Cairo, he found some excuse for delay. While I was detained in his house he made many incursions into the neighbouring countries, and, perhaps, he would have refused to discharge me, had his plunder been equal to his wishes. He returned always courteous, related his adventures, delighted to hear my observations, and endeavoured to advance my acquaintance with the stars. When I importuned him to send away my letters, he soothed me with professions of honour and sincerity; and, when I could be no longer decently denied, put his troop again in motion, and left me to govern in his absence. I was much afflicted by this studied procrastination, and was sometimes afraid that I should be forgotten; that you would leave Cairo, and I must end my days in an island of the Nile.

"I grew at last hopeless and dejected, and cared so little to entertain him, that he for a while more frequently talked with my maids. That he should fall in love with them, or with me, might have been equally fatal, and I was not much pleased with the growing friendship. My anxiety was not long; for, as I recovered some degree of chearfulness, he returned to me, and I could not forbear to despise my former uneasiness.

"He still delayed to send for my ransome, and would, perhaps, never have determined, had not your agent found his way to him. The gold, which he would not fetch, he could not reject when it was offered. He hastened to prepare for our journey hither, like a man delivered from the pain of an intestine conflict. I took leave of my companions in the house, who dismissed me with cold indifference."

Nekayah, having heard her favourite's relation, rose and embraced her, and Rasselas gave her an hundred ounces of gold, which she presented to the Arab for the fifty that were promised.

# XL

### THE HISTORY OF A MAN OF LEARNING

They returned to Cairo, and were so well pleased at finding themselves together, that none of them went much abroad. The prince began to love learning, and one day declared to Imlac, that he intended to devote himself to science, and pass the rest of his days in literary solitude.

"Before you make your final choice," answered Imlac, "you ought to examine its hazards, and converse with some of those who are grown old in the company of themselves. I have just left the observatory of one of the most learned astronomers in the world, who has spent forty years in unwearied attention to the motions and appearances of the celestial bodies, and has drawn out his soul in endless calculations. He admits a few friends once a month to hear his deductions and enjoy his discoveries. I was introduced as a man of knowledge worthy of his notice. Men of various ideas and fluent conversation are commonly welcome to those whose thoughts have been long fixed upon a single point, and who find the images of other things stealing away. I delighted him with my remarks, he smiled at the narrative of my travels, and was glad to forget the constellations, and descend for a moment into the lower world.

"On the next day of vacation I renewed my visit, and was so fortunate as to please him again. He relaxed from that time the severity of his rule, and permitted me to enter at my own choice. I found him always busy, and always glad to be relieved. As each knew much which the other was desirous of learning, we exchanged our notions with great delight. I perceived that I had every day more of his confidence, and always found new cause of admiration in the profundity of his mind. His comprehension is vast, his memory capacious and retentive, his discourse is methodical, and his expression clear.

"His integrity and benevolence are equal to his learning. His deepest researches and most favourite studies are willingly interrupted for any opportunity of doing good by his counsel or his riches. To his closest retreat, at his most busy moments, all are admitted that want his assistance: 'For though I exclude idleness and pleasure, I will never,' says he, 'bar my doors against charity. To man is permitted the contemplation of the skies, but the practice of virtue is commanded.'"

"Surely," said the princess, "this man is happy."

"I visited him," said Imlac, "with more and more frequency, and was every time more enamoured of his conversation: he was sublime without haughtiness, courteous without formality, and communicative without ostentaticn. I was at first, Madam,[8] of your opinion, thought him the happiest of mankind, and often congratulated him on the blessing that he enjoyed. He seemed to hear nothing with indifference but the praises of his condition, to which he always returned a general answer, and diverted the conversation to some other topick.

"Amidst this willingness to be pleased, and labour to please, I had always[9] reason to imagine that some painful sentiment pressed upon his mind. He often looked up earnestly towards the sun, and let his voice fall in the midst of his discourse. He would sometimes, when we were alone, gaze upon me in silence with the air of a man who longed to speak what he was yet resolved to suppress.

[8] Madam: great princess 2
[9] always: quickly 2

He would sometimes[1] send for me with vehement injunctions of haste, though, when I came to him, he had nothing extraordinary to say. And sometimes, when I was leaving him, would call me back, pause a few moments and then dismiss me.

## XLI

### THE ASTRONOMER DISCOVERS THE CAUSE OF HIS UNEASINESS

"At last the time came when the secret burst his reserve. We were sitting together last night in the turret of his house, watching the emersion of a satellite of Jupiter. A sudden tempest clouded the sky, and disappointed our observation. We sat a while silent in the dark, and then he addressed himself to me in these words: 'Imlac, I have long considered thy friendship as the greatest blessing of my life. Integrity without knowledge is weak and useless, and knowledge without integrity is dangerous and dreadful. I have found in thee all the qualities requisite for trust, benevolence, experience, and fortitude. I have long discharged an office which I must soon quit at the call of nature, and shall rejoice in the hour of imbecility and pain to devolve it upon thee.'

"I thought myself honoured by this testimony, and protested that whatever could conduce to his happiness would add likewise to mine.

"'Hear, Imlac, what thou wilt not without difficulty credit. I have possessed for five years the regulation of weather, and the distribution of the seasons: the sun has listened to my dictates, and passed from tropick to tropick by my direction; the clouds, at my call, have poured their waters, and the Nile has overflowed at my command; I have restrained the rage of the dog-star, and mitigated the fervours of the crab. The winds alone, of all the elemental powers, have hitherto refused my authority, and multitudes have perished by equinoctial tempests which I found myself unable to prohibit or restrain. I have administered this great office with exact justice, and made to the different nations of the earth an impartial dividend of rain and sunshine. What must have been the misery of half the globe, if I had limited the clouds to particular regions, or confined the sun to either side of the equator?'

---

[1] sometimes: often 2

# XLII

### THE ASTRONOMER JUSTIFIES HIS ACCOUNT OF HIMSELF[2]

"I suppose he discovered in me, through the obscurity of the room, some tokens of amazement and doubt, for, after a short pause, he proceeded thus:

" 'Not to be easily credited will neither surprise nor offend me; for I am, probably, the first of human beings to whom this trust has been imparted. Nor do I know whether to deem this distinction a reward or punishment; since I have possessed it I have been far less happy than before, and nothing but the consciousness of good intention could have enabled me to support the weariness of unremitted vigilance.'

" 'How long, Sir,' said I, 'has this great office been in your hands?'

" 'About ten years ago,' said he, 'my daily observations of the changes of the sky led me to consider, whether, if I had the power of the seasons, I could confer greater plenty upon the inhabitants of the earth. This contemplation fastened on my mind, and I sat days and nights in imaginary dominion, pouring upon this country and that the showers of fertility, and seconding every fall of rain with a due proportion of sunshine. I had yet only the will to do good, and did not imagine that I should ever have the power.

" 'One day as I was looking on the fields withering with heat, I felt in my mind a sudden wish that I could send rain on the southern mountains, and raise the Nile to an inundation. In the hurry of my imagination I commanded rain to fall, and, by comparing the time of my command, with that of the inundation, I found that the clouds had listned to my lips.'

" 'Might not some other cause,' said I, 'produce this concurrence? the Nile does not always rise on the same day.'

" 'Do not believe,' said he with impatience, 'that such objections could escape me: I reasoned long against my own conviction, and laboured against truth with the utmost obstinacy. I sometimes suspected myself of madness, and should not have dared to im-

---

[2] The astronomer justifies his account of himself: The opinion of the astronomer is explained and justified 2

part this secret but to a man like you, capable of distinguishing the wonderful from the impossible, and the incredible from the false.'

" 'Why, Sir,' said I, 'do you call that incredible, which you know, or think you know, to be true?'

" 'Because,' said he, 'I cannot prove it by any external evidence; and I know too well the laws of demonstration to think that my conviction ought to influence another, who cannot, like me, be conscious of its force. I, therefore, shall not attempt to gain credit by disputation. It is sufficient that I feel this power, that I have long possessed, and every day exerted it. But the life of man is short, the infirmities of age increase upon me, and the time will soon come when the regulator of the year must mingle with the dust. The care of appointing a successor has long disturbed me; the night and the day have been spent in comparisons of all the characters which have come to my knowledge, and I have yet found none so worthy as thyself.

# XLIII

### THE ASTRONOMER LEAVES IMLAC HIS DIRECTIONS

" 'Hear therefore, what I shall impart, with attention, such as the welfare of a world requires. If the task of a king be considered as difficult, who has the care only of a few millions, to whom he cannot do much good or harm, what must be the anxiety of him, on whom depend the action of the elements, and the great gifts of light and heat!——Hear me therefore with attention.

" 'I have diligently considered the position of the earth and sun, and formed innumerable schemes in which I changed their situation. I have sometimes turned aside the axis of the earth, and sometimes varied the ecliptick of the sun: but I have found it impossible to make a disposition by which the world may be advantaged; what one region gains, another loses by any imaginable alteration, even without considering the distant parts of the solar system with which we are unacquainted. Do not, therefore, in thy administration of the year, indulge thy pride by innovation; do not please thyself with thinking that thou canst make thyself renowned to all future ages, by disordering the seasons. The memory of mischief is no desirable fame. Much less will it become thee to let kindness or interest prevail. Never rob other countries of rain to pour it on thine own. For us the Nile is sufficient.'

"I promised that when I possessed the power, I would use it with inflexible integrity, and he dismissed me, pressing my hand. 'My heart,' said he, 'will be now at rest, and my benevolence will no more destroy my quiet: I have found a man of wisdom and virtue, to whom I can chearfully bequeath the inheritance of the sun.' "

The prince heard this narration with very serious regard, but the princess smiled, and Pekuah convulsed herself with laughter. "Ladies," said Imlac, "to mock the heaviest of human afflictions is neither charitable nor wise. Few can attain this man's knowledge, and few practise his virtues; but all may suffer his calamity. Of the uncertainties of our present state, the most dreadful and alarming is the uncertain continuance of reason."

The princess was recollected, and the favourite was abashed. Rasselas, more deeply affected, enquired of Imlac, whether he thought such maladies of the mind frequent, and how they were contracted.

## XLIV

### THE DANGEROUS PREVALENCE OF IMAGINATION

"Disorders of intellect," answered Imlac, "happen much more often than superficial observers will easily believe. Perhaps, if we speak with rigorous exactness, no human mind is in its right state. There is no man whose imagination does not sometimes predominate over his reason, who can regulate his attention wholly by his will, and whose ideas will come and go at his command. No man will be found in whose mind airy notions do not sometimes tyrannise, and force him to hope or fear beyond the limits of sober probability. All power of fancy over reason is a degree of insanity; but while this power is such as we can controll and repress, it is not visible to others, nor considered as any depravation of the mental faculties: it is not pronounced madness but when it comes ungovernable, and apparently influences speech or action.

"To indulge the power of fiction, and send imagination out upon the wing, is often the sport of those who delight too much in silent speculation. When we are alone we are not always busy; the labour of excogitation is too violent to last long; the ardour of enquiry will sometimes give way to idleness or satiety. He who has nothing external that can divert him, must find pleasure in his own thoughts, and must conceive himself what he is not; for who is pleased with what he is? He then expatiates in boundless futurity, and culls from all imaginable conditions that which for the present moment he should most desire, amuses his desires with impossible enjoyments, and confers upon his pride unattainable dominion. The mind dances from scene to scene, unites all pleasures in all combinations, and riots in delights which nature and fortune, with all their bounty, cannot bestow.

"In time some particular train of ideas fixes the attention, all other intellectual gratifications are rejected, the mind, in weariness or leisure, recurs constantly to the favourite conception, and feasts on the luscious falsehood whenever she is offended with the bitterness of truth. By degrees the reign of fancy is confirmed; she grows first imperious, and in time despotick. Then fictions begin to operate as realities, false opinions fasten upon the mind, and life passes in dreams of rapture or of anguish.

"This, Sir, is one of the dangers of solitude, which the hermit has confessed not always to promote goodness, and the astronomer's misery has proved to be not always propitious to wisdom."

"I will no more," said the favourite, "imagine myself the queen of Abissinia. I have often spent the hours, which the princess gave to my own disposal, in adjusting ceremonies and regulating the court; I have repressed the pride of the powerful, and granted the petitions of the poor; I have built new palaces in more happy situations, planted groves upon the tops of mountains, and have exulted in the beneficence of royalty, till, when the princess entered, I had almost forgotten to bow down before her."

"And I," said the princess, "will not allow myself any more to play the shepherdess in my waking dreams. I have often soothed my thoughts with the quiet and innocence of pastoral employments, till I have in my chamber heard the winds whistle, and the sheep bleat; sometimes freed the lamb entangled in the thicket, and sometimes with my crook encountered the wolf. I have a dress like that of the village maids, which I put on to help my imagination, and a pipe on which I play softly, and suppose myself followed by my flocks."

"I will confess," said the prince, "an indulgence of fantastick delight more dangerous than yours. I have frequently endeavoured to image the possibility of a perfect government, by which all wrong should be restrained, all vice reformed, and all the subjects preserved in tranquility and innocence. This thought produced innumerable schemes of reformation, and dictated many useful regulations and salutary edicts. This has been the sport and sometimes the labour of my solitude; and I start, when I think with how little anguish I once supposed the death of my father and my brothers."

"Such," says Imlac, "are the effects of visionary schemes: when we first form them we know them to be absurd, but familiarise them by degrees, and in time lose sight of their folly."

# XLV

## THEY DISCOURSE WITH AN OLD MAN

The evening was now far past, and they rose to return home. As they walked along the bank of the Nile, delighted with the beams of the moon quivering on the water, they saw at a small distance an old man, whom the prince had often heard in the assembly of the sages. "Yonder," said he, "is one whose years have calmed his passions, but not clouded his reason: let us close the disquisitions of the night, by enquiring what are his sentiments of his own state, that we may know whether youth alone is to struggle with vexation, and whether any better hope remains for the latter part of life."

Here the sage approached and saluted them. They invited him to join their walk, and prattled a while as acquaintance that had unexpectedly met one another. The old man was chearful and talkative, and the way seemed short in his company. He was pleased to find himself not disregarded, accompanied them to their house, and, at the prince's request, entered with them. They placed him in the seat of honour, and set wine and conserves before him.

"Sir," said the princess, "an evening walk must give to a man of learning, like you, pleasures which ignorance and youth can hardly conceive. You know the qualities and the causes of all that you behold, the laws by which the river flows, the periods in which the planets perform their revolutions. Every thing must supply you with contemplation, and renew the consciousness of your own dignity."

"Lady," answered he, "let the gay and the vigorous expect pleasure in their excursions, it is enough that age can obtain ease. To me the world has lost its novelty: I look round, and see what I remember to have seen in happier days. I rest against a tree, and consider, that in the same shade I once disputed upon the annual overflow of the Nile with a friend who is now silent in the grave. I cast my eyes upwards, fix them on the changing moon, and think with pain on the vicissitudes of life. I have ceased to take much delight in physical truth; for what have I to do with those things which I am soon to leave?"

"You may at least recreate yourself," said Imlac, "with the recollection of an honourable and useful life, and enjoy the praise which all agree to give you."

"Praise," said the sage, with a sigh, "is to an old man an empty sound. I have neither mother to be delighted with the reputation of her son, nor wife to partake the honours of her husband. I have outlived my friends and my rivals. Nothing is now of much importance; for I cannot extend my interest beyond myself. Youth is delighted with applause, because it is considered as the earnest of some future good, and because the prospect of life is far extended: but to me, who am now declining to decrepitude, there is little to be feared from the malevolence of men, and yet less to be hoped from their affection or esteem. Something they may yet take away, but they can give me nothing. Riches would now be useless, and high employment would be pain. My retrospect of life recalls to my view many opportunities of good neglected, much time squandered upon trifles, and more lost in idleness and vacancy. I leave many great designs unattempted, and many great attempts unfinished. My mind is burthened with no heavy crime, and therefore I compose myself to tranquility; endeavour to abstract my thoughts from hopes and cares, which, though reason knows them to be vain, still try to keep their old possession of the heart; expect, with serene humility, that hour which nature cannot long delay; and hope to possess in a better state that happiness which here I could not find, and that virtue which here I have not attained."

He rose and went away, leaving his audience not much elated with the hope of long life. The prince consoled himself with remarking, that it was not reasonable to be disappointed by this account; for age had never been considered as the season of felicity, and, if it was possible to be easy in decline and weakness, it was likely that the days of vigour and alacrity might be happy: that the noon of life might be bright, if the evening could be calm.

The princess suspected that age was querulous and malignant, and delighted to repress the expectations of those who had newly entered the world. She had seen the possessors of estates look with envy on their heirs, and known many who enjoy pleasure no longer than they can confine it to themselves.

Pekuah conjectured, that the man was older than he appeared, and was willing to impute his complaints to delirious dejection; or else supposed that he had been unfortunate, and was therefore discontented: "For nothing," said she, "is more common than to call our own condition, the condition of life."

Imlac, who had no desire to see them depressed, smiled at the comforts which they could so readily procure to themselves, and remembered, that at the same age, he was equally confident of unmingled prosperity, and equally fertile of consolatory expedients. He forbore to force upon them unwelcome knowledge, which time itself would too soon impress. The princess and her lady retired; the madness of the astronomer hung upon their minds, and they desired Imlac to enter upon his office, and delay next morning the rising of the sun.

## XLVI

### THE PRINCESS AND PEKUAH VISIT THE ASTRONOMER

The princess and Pekuah having talked in private of Imlac's astronomer, thought his character at once so amiable and so strange, that they could not be satisfied without a nearer knowledge, and Imlac was requested to find the means of bringing them together.

This was somewhat difficult; the philosopher had never received any visits from women, though he lived in a city that had in it many Europeans who followed the manners of their own countries, and many from other parts of the world that lived there with European liberty. The ladies would not be refused, and several schemes were proposed for the accomplishment of their design. It was proposed to introduce them as strangers in distress, to whom the sage was always accessible; but, after some deliberation, it appeared, that by this artifice, no acquaintance could be formed, for their conversation would be short, and they could not decently importune him often. "This," said Rasselas, "is true; but I have yet a stronger objection against the misrepresentation of your state. I have always considered it as treason against the great republick of human nature, to make any man's virtues the means of deceiving him, whether on great or little occasions. All imposture weakens confidence and chills benevolence. When the sage finds that you are not what you seemed, he will feel the resentment natural to a man who, conscious of great abilities, discovers that he has been tricked by understandings meaner than his own, and, perhaps, the distrust, which he can never afterwards wholly lay aside, may stop the voice of counsel, and close the hand of charity; and where will you find the power of restoring his benefactions to mankind, or his peace to himself?"

To this no reply was attempted, and Imlac began to hope that their curiosity would subside; but, next day, Pekuah told him, she had now found an honest pretence for a visit to the astronomer, for she would solicit permission to continue under him the studies in which she had been initiated by the Arab, and the princess might go with her either as a fellow-student, or because a woman could not decently come alone. "I am afraid," said Imlac, "that he will be soon weary of your company: men advanced far in knowledge do not love to repeat the elements of their art, and I am not certain, that even of the elements, as he will deliver them connected with inferences, and mingled with reflections, you are a very capable auditress." "That," said Pekuah, "must be my care: I ask of you only to take me thither. My knowledge is, perhaps, more than you imagine it, and by concurring always with his opinions I shall make him think it greater than it is."

The astronomer, in pursuance of this resolution, was told, that a foreign lady, travelling in search of knowledge, had heard of his reputation, and was desirous to become his scholar. The uncommonness of the proposal raised at once his surprise and curiosity, and when, after a short deliberation, he consented to admit her, he could not stay without impatience till the next day.

The ladies dressed themselves magnificently, and were attended by Imlac to the astronomer, who was pleased to see himself approached with respect by persons of so splendid an appearance. In the exchange of the first civilities he was timorous and bashful; but, when the talk became regular, he recollected his powers, and justified the character which Imlac had given. Enquiring of Pekuah what could have turned her inclination towards astronomy, he received from her a history of her adventure at the pyramid, and of the time passed in the Arab's island. She told her tale with ease and elegance, and her conversation took possession of his heart. The discourse was then turned to astronomy: Pekuah displayed what she knew: he looked upon her as a prodigy of genius, and intreated her not to desist from a study which she had so happily begun.

They came again and again, and were every time more welcome than before. The sage endeavoured to amuse them, that they might prolong their visits, for he found his thoughts grow brighter in their company; the clouds of solicitude vanished by degrees, as he forced himself to entertain them, and he grieved when he was left at their departure to his old employment of regulating the seasons.

The princess and her favourite had now watched his lips for several months, and could not catch a single word from which they could judge whether he continued, or not, in the opinion of his preternatural commission. They often contrived to bring him to an open declaration, but he easily eluded all their attacks, and on which side soever they pressed him escaped from them to some other topick.

As their familiarity increased they invited him often to the house of Imlac, where they distinguished him by extraordinary respect. He began gradually to delight in sublunary pleasures. He came early and departed late; laboured to recommend himself by assiduity and compliance; excited their curiosity after new arts, that they might still want his assistance; and when they made any excursion of pleasure or enquiry, entreated to attend them.

By long experience of his integrity and wisdom, the prince and his sister were convinced that he might be trusted without danger; and, lest he should draw any false hopes from the civilities which he received, discovered to him their condition, with the motives of their journey, and required his opinion on the choice of life.

"Of the various conditions which the world spreads before you, which you shall prefer," said the sage, "I am not able to instruct you. I can only tell that I have chosen wrong. I have passed my time in study without experience; in the attainment of sciences which can, for the most part, be but remotely useful to mankind. I have purchased knowledge at the expence of all the common comforts of life: I have missed the endearing elegance of female friendship, and the happy commerce of domestick tenderness. If I have obtained any prerogatives above other students, they have been accompanied with fear, disquiet, and scrupulosity; but even of these prerogatives, whatever they were, I have, since my thoughts have been diversified by more intercourse with the world, begun to question the reality. When I have been for a few days lost in pleasing dissipation, I am always tempted to think that my enquiries have ended in errour, and that I have suffered much, and suffered it in vain."

Imlac was delighted to find that the sage's understanding was breaking through its mists, and resolved to detain him from the planets till he should forget his task of ruling them, and reason should recover its original influence.

From this time the astronomer was received into familiar friendship, and partook of all their projects and pleasures: his respect kept him attentive, and the activity of Rasselas did not leave much time unengaged. Something was always to be done; the day was spent in making observations which furnished talk for the evening, and the evening was closed with a scheme for the morrow.

The sage confessed to Imlac, that since he had mingled in the gay tumults of life, and divided his hours by a succession of amusements, he found the conviction of his authority over the skies fade gradually from his mind, and began to trust less to an opinion which he never could prove to others, and which he now found subject to variation from causes in which reason had no part. "If I am accidentally left alone for a few hours," said he, "my inveterate persuasion rushes upon my soul, and my thoughts are chained down by some irresistible violence, but they are soon disentangled by the prince's conversation, and instantaneously released at the entrance of Pekuah. I am like a man habitually afraid of spectres, who is set at ease by a lamp, and wonders at the dread which harrassed him in the dark, yet, if his lamp be extinguished, feels again the terrours which he knows that when it is light he shall feel no more. But I am sometimes afraid lest I indulge my quiet by criminal negligence, and voluntarily forget the great charge with which I am intrusted. If I favour myself in a known errour, or am determined by my own ease in a doubtful question of this importance, how dreadful is my crime!"

"No disease of the imagination," answered Imlac, "is so difficult of cure, as that which is complicated with the dread of guilt: fancy and conscience then act interchangeably upon us, and so often shift their places, that the illusions of one are not distinguished from the dictates of the other. If fancy presents images not moral or religious, the mind drives them away when they give it pain, but when melancholick notions take the form of duty, they lay hold on the faculties without opposition, because we are afraid to exclude or banish them. For this reason the superstitious are often melancholy, and the melancholy almost always superstitious.

"But do not let the suggestions of timidity overpower your better reason: the danger of neglect can be but as the probability of the obligation, which, when you consider it with freedom, you find very little, and that little growing every day less. Open your heart to the influence of the light, which, from time to time, breaks in upon you: when scruples importune you, which you in your lucid moments know to be vain, do not stand to parley, but fly to business or to Pekuah, and keep this thought always prevalent, that you are only one atom of the mass of humanity, and have neither such virtue nor vice, as that you should be singled out for supernatural favours or afflictions."

## XLVII

### THE PRINCE ENTERS AND BRINGS A NEW TOPICK

"All this," said the astronomer, "I have often thought, but my reason has been so long subjugated by an uncontrolable and

overwhelming idea, that it durst not confide in its own decisions.
I now see how fatally I betrayed my quiet, by suffering chimeras
to prey upon me in secret; but melancholy shrinks from communication, and I never found a man before, to whom I could impart my troubles, though I had been certain of relief. I rejoice to
find my own sentiments confirmed by yours, who are not easily
deceived, and can have no motive or purpose to deceive. I hope
that time and variety will dissipate the gloom that has so long
surrounded me, and the latter part of my days will be spent in
peace."

"Your learning and virtue," said Imlac, "may justly give you
hopes."

Rasselas then entered with the princess and Pekuah, and enquired whether they had contrived any new diversion for the
next day. "Such," said Nekayah, "is the state of life, that none are
happy but by the anticipation of change: the change itself is
nothing; when we have made it, the next wish is to change again.
The world is not yet exhausted; let me see something to morrow
which I never saw before."

"Variety," said Rasselas, "is so necessary to content, that even
the happy valley disgusted me by the recurrence of its luxuries;
yet I could not forbear to reproach myself with impatience, when
I saw the monks of St. Anthony support without complaint, a life,
not of uniform delight, but uniform hardship."

"Those men," answered Imlac, "are less wretched in their silent
convent than the Abissinian princes in their prison of pleasure.
Whatever is done by the monks is incited by an adequate and
reasonable motive. Their labour supplies them with necessaries;
it therefore cannot be omitted, and is certainly rewarded. Their
devotion prepares them for another state, and reminds them of its
approach, while it fits them for it. Their time is regularly distributed; one duty succeeds another, so that they are not left open
to the distraction of unguided choice, nor lost in the shades of
listless inactivity. There is a certain task to be performed at an
appropriated hour; and their toils are cheerful, because they consider them as acts of piety, by which they are always advancing
towards endless felicity."

"Do you think," said Nekayah, "that the monastick rule is a
more holy and less imperfect state than any other? May not he
equally hope for future happiness who converses openly with

mankind, who succours the distressed by his charity, instructs the ignorant by his learning, and contributes by his industry to the general system of life; even though he should omit some of the mortifications which are practised in the cloister, and allow himself such harmless delights as his condition may place within his reach?"

"This," said Imlac, "is a question which has long divided the wise, and perplexed the good. I am afraid to decide on either part. He that lives well in the world is better than he that lives well in a monastery. But, perhaps, every one is not able to stem the temptations of publick life; and, if he cannot conquer, he may properly retreat. Some have little power to do good, and have likewise little strength to resist evil. Many are weary of their conflicts with adversity, and are willing to eject those passions which have long busied them in vain. And many are dismissed by age and diseases from the more laborious duties of society. In monasteries the weak and timorous may be happily sheltered, the weary may repose, and the penitent may meditate. Those retreats of prayer and contemplation have something so congenial to the mind of man, that, perhaps, there is scarcely one that does not purpose to close his life in pious abstraction with a few associates serious as himself."

"Such," said Pekuah, "has often been my wish, and I have heard the princess declare, that she should not willingly die in a croud."

"The liberty of using harmless pleasures," proceeded Imlac, "will not be disputed; but it is still to be examined what pleasures are harmless. The evil of any pleasure that Nekayah can image is not in the act itself, but in its consequences. Pleasure, in itself harmless, may become mischievous, by endearing to us a state which we know to be transient and probatory, and withdrawing our thoughts from that, of which every hour brings us nearer to the beginning, and of which no length of time will bring us to the end. Mortification is not virtuous in itself, nor has any other use, but that it disengages us from the allurements of sense. In the state of future perfection, to which we all aspire, there will be pleasure without danger, and security without restraint."

The princess was silent, and Rasselas, turning to the astronomer, asked him, whether he could not delay her retreat, by shewing her something which she had not seen before.

"Your curiosity," said the sage, "has been so general, and your pursuit of knowledge so vigorous, that novelties are not now very easily to be found: but what you can no longer procure from the living may be given by the dead. Among the wonders of this country are the catacombs, or the ancient repositories, in which the bodies of the earliest generations were lodged, and where, by the virtue of the gums which embalmed them, they yet remain without corruption."

"I know not," said Rasselas, "what pleasure the sight of the catacombs can afford; but, since nothing else is offered, I am resolved to view them, and shall place this with many other things which I have done, because I would do something."

They hired a guard of horsemen, and the next day visited the catacombs. When they were about to descend into the sepulchral caves, "Pekuah," said the princess, "we are now again invading the habitations of the dead; I know that you will stay behind; let me find you safe when I return." "No, I will not be left," answered Pekuah; "I will go down between you and the prince."

They then all descended, and roved with wonder through the labyrinth of subterraneous passages, where the bodies were laid in rows on either side.

## XLVIII

### IMLAC DISCOURSES ON THE NATURE OF THE SOUL

"What reason," said the prince, "can be given, why the Egyptians should thus expensively preserve those carcasses which some nations consume with fire, others lay to mingle with the earth, and all agree to remove from their sight, as soon as decent rites can be performed?"

"The original of ancient customs," said Imlac, "is commonly unknown; for the practice often continues when the cause has ceased; and concerning superstitious ceremonies it is vain to conjecture; for what reason did not dictate reason cannot explain. I have long believed that the practice of embalming arose only from tenderness to the remains of relations or friends, and to this opinion I am more inclined, because it seems impossible that this care should have been general: had all the dead been embalmed, their repositories must in time have been more spacious than the dwellings of the living. I suppose only the rich or honourable were secured from corruption, and the rest left to the course of nature.

"But it is commonly supposed that the Egyptians believed the soul to live as long as the body continued undissolved, and therefore tried this method of eluding death."

"Could the wise Egyptians," said Nekayah, "think so grosly of the soul? If the soul could once survive its separation, what could it afterwards receive or suffer from the body?"

"The Egyptians would doubtless think erroneously," said the astronomer, "in the darkness of heathenism, and the first dawn of philosophy. The nature of the soul is still disputed amidst all our opportunities of clearer knowledge: some yet say, that it may be material, who, nevertheless, believe it to be immortal."

"Some," answered Imlac, "have indeed said that the soul is material, but I can scarcely believe that any man has thought it, who knew how to think; for all the conclusions of reason enforce the immateriality of the[3] mind, and all the notices of sense and investigations of science concur to prove the unconsciousness of matter.

"It was never supposed that cogitation is inherent in matter, or that every particle is a thinking being. Yet, if any part of matter be devoid of thought, what part can we suppose to think? Matter can differ from matter only in form, density, bulk, motion, and direction of motion: to which of these, however varied or combined, can consciousness be annexed? To be round or square, to be solid or fluid, to be great or little, to be moved slowly or swiftly one way or another, are modes of material existence, all equally alien from the nature of cogitation. If matter be once without thought, it can only be made to think by some new modification, but all the modifications which it can admit are equally unconnected with cogitative powers."

"But the materialists," said the astronomer, "urge that matter may have qualities with which we are unacquainted."

"He who will determine," returned Imlac, "against that which he knows, because there may be something which he knows not; he that can set hypothetical possibility against acknowledged

---

[3] of the: of 2

certainty, is not to be admitted among reasonable beings. All that we know of matter is, that matter is inert, senseless and lifeless; and if this conviction cannot be opposed but by referring us to something that we know not, we have all the evidence that human intellect can admit. If that which is known may be over-ruled by that which is unknown, no being, not omniscient, can arrive at certainty."

"Yet let us not," said the astronomer, "too arrogantly limit the Creator's power."

"It is no limitation of omnipotence," replied the poet, "to suppose that one thing is not consistent with another, that the same proposition cannot be at once true and false, that the same number cannot be even and odd, that cogitation cannot be conferred on that which is created incapable of cogitation."

"I know not," said Nekayah, "any great use of this question. Does that immateriality, which, in my opinion, you have sufficiently proved, necessarily include eternal duration?"

"Of immateriality," said Imlac, "our ideas are negative, and therefore obscure. Immateriality seems to imply a natural power of perpetual duration as a consequence of exemption from all causes of decay: whatever perishes, is destroyed by the solution of its contexture, and separation of its parts; nor can we conceive how that which has no parts, and therefore admits no solution, can be naturally corrupted or impaired."

"I know not," said Rasselas, "how to conceive any thing without extension: what is extended must have parts, and you allow, that whatever has parts may be destroyed."

"Consider your own conceptions," replied Imlac, "and the difficulty will be less. You will find substance without extension. An ideal form is no less real than material bulk: yet an ideal form has no extension. It is no less certain, when you think on a pyramid, that your mind possesses the idea of a pyramid, than that the pyramid itself is standing. What space does the idea of a pyramid occupy more than the idea of a grain of corn? or how can either idea suffer laceration? As is the effect such is the cause; as thought is, such is the power that thinks; a power impassive and indiscerptible."

"But the Being," said Nekayah, "whom I fear to name, the Being which made the soul, can destroy it."

"He, surely, can destroy it," answered Imlac, "since, however unperishable in itself, it receives from a higher[4] nature its power of duration. That it will not perish by any inherent cause or principle of corruption, may be collected from[5] philosophy; but philosophy can tell no more. That it will not be annihilated by him that made it, we must humbly learn from higher authority."

The whole assembly stood a while silent and collected. "Let us return," said Rasselas, "from this scene of mortality. How gloomy would be these mansions of the dead to him who did not know that he shall never die; that what now acts shall continue its agency, and what now thinks shall think on for ever. Those that lie here stretched before us, the wise and the powerful of antient times, warn us to remember the shortness of our present state: they were, perhaps, snatched away while they were busy, like us, in the choice of life."

"To me," said the princess, "the choice of life is become less important; I hope hereafter to think only on the choice of eternity."

They then hastened out of the caverns, and, under the protection of their guard, returned to Cairo.

## XLIX

### THE CONCLUSION, IN WHICH NOTHING IS CONCLUDED

It was now the time of the inundation of the Nile: a few days after their visit to the catacombs, the river began to rise.

They were confined to their house. The whole region being under water gave them no invitation to any excursions, and, being well supplied with materials for talk, they diverted themselves with comparisons of the different forms of life which they had observed, and with various schemes of happiness which each of them had formed.

Pekuah was never so much charmed with any place as the convent of St. Anthony, where the Arab restored her to the princess, and wished only to fill it with pious maidens, and to be made

---

[4] in itself, it receives from a higher: it receives from a superiour 2

[5] cause or principle of corruption, may be collected from: cause of decay, or principle of corruption, may be shown by 2

prioress of the order: she was weary of expectation and disgust, and would gladly be fixed in some unvariable state.

The princess thought, that of all sublunary things, knowledge was the best: She desired first to learn all sciences, and then purposed to found a college of learned women, in which she would preside, that, by conversing with the old, and educating the young, she might divide her time between the acquisition and communication of wisdom, and raise up for the next age models of prudence, and patterns of piety.

The prince desired a little kingdom, in which he might administer justice in his own person, and see all the parts of government with his own eyes; but he could never fix the limits of his dominion, and was always adding to the number of his subjects.

Imlac and the astronomer were contented to be driven along the stream of life without directing their course to any particular port.

Of these wishes that they had formed they well knew that none could be obtained. They deliberated a while what was to be done, and resolved, when the inundation should cease, to return to Abissinia.

*Like the Preface to the* Dictionary, *Johnson's Preface to his eight-volume edition of Shakespeare is the distillation of many years of work—twenty, in this instance. It was published with the edition in October 1765, separately published shortly thereafter, reprinted with the edition within a few weeks, and at least three more times before Johnson's death. It is now reprinted from the first edition.*

# Preface to Shakespeare

That praises are without reason lavished on the dead, and that the honours due only to excellence are paid to antiquity, is a complaint likely to be always continued by those, who, being able to add nothing to truth, hope for eminence from the heresies of paradox; or those, who, being forced by disappointment upon consolatory expedients, are willing to hope from posterity what the present age refuses, and flatter themselves that the regard which is yet denied by envy, will be at last bestowed by time.

Antiquity, like every other quality that attracts the notice of mankind, has undoubtedly votaries that reverence it, not from reason, but from prejudice. Some seem to admire indiscriminately whatever has been long preserved, without considering that time has sometimes co-operated with chance; all perhaps are more willing to honour past than present excellence; and the mind contemplates genius through the shades of age, as the eye surveys the sun through artificial opacity. The great contention of criticism is to find the faults of the moderns, and the beauties of the ancients. While an authour is yet living we estimate his powers by his worst performance, and when he is dead we rate them by his best.

To works, however, of which the excellence is not absolute and definite, but gradual and comparative; to works not raised upon principles demonstrative and scientifick, but appealing wholly to observation and experience, no other test can be applied than length of duration and continuance of esteem. What mankind have long possessed they have often examined and compared, and if they persist to value the possession, it is because frequent comparisons have confirmed opinion in its favour. As among the works of nature no man can properly call a river deep or a mountain high, without the knowledge of many mountains and many rivers; so in the productions of genius, nothing can be stiled excellent till it has been compared with other works of the same kind. Demonstration immediately displays its power, and has nothing to hope or fear from the flux of years; but works tentative and experimental must be estimated by their proportion to the general and collective ability of man, as it is discovered in a long succession of endeavours. Of the first building that was raised, it might be with certainty determined that it was round or square, but whether it was spacious or lofty must have been referred to time. The Pythagorean scale of numbers was at once discovered to be perfect; but the poems of Homer we yet know not to transcend the common limits of human intelligence, but by remarking, that nation after nation, and century after century, has been able to do little more than transpose his incidents, new name his characters, and paraphrase his sentiments.

The reverence due to writings that have long subsisted arises therefore not from any credulous confidence in the superior wisdom of past ages, or gloomy persuasion of the degeneracy of mankind, but is the consequence of acknowledged and indubitable positions, that what has been longest known has been most considered, and what is most considered is best understood.

The poet, of whose works I have undertaken the revision, may now begin to assume the dignity of an ancient, and claim the privilege of established fame and prescriptive veneration. He has long outlived his century, the term commonly fixed as the test of literary merit. Whatever advantages he might once derive from personal allusions, local customs, or temporary opinions, have for many years been lost; and every topick of merriment or motive of sorrow, which the modes of artificial life afforded him, now only obscure the scenes which they once illuminated. The effects of favour and competition are at an end; the tradition of his friendships and his enmities has perished; his works support no opinion with arguments, nor supply any faction with invectives; they can neither indulge vanity nor gratify malignity, but are read without any other reason than the desire of pleasure, and are therefore praised only as pleasure is obtained; yet, thus unassisted by interest or passion, they have past through variations of taste and changes of manners, and, as they devolved from one generation to another, have received new honours at every transmission.

But because human judgment, though it be gradually gaining upon certainty, never becomes infallible; and approbation, though long continued, may yet be only the approbation of prejudice or fashion; it is proper to inquire, by what peculiarities of excellence Shakespeare has gained and kept the favour of his countrymen.

Nothing can please many, and please long, but just representations of general nature. Particular manners can be known to few, and therefore few only can judge how nearly they are copied. The irregular combinations of fanciful invention may delight a-while, by that novelty of which the common satiety of life sends us all in quest; but the pleasures of sudden wonder are soon exhausted, and the mind can only repose on the stability of truth.

Shakespeare is above all writers, at least above all modern writers, the poet of nature; the poet that holds up to his readers a faithful mirrour of manners and of life. His characters are not modified by the customs of particular places, unpractised by the rest of the world; by the peculiarities of studies or professions, which can operate but upon small numbers; or by the accidents of transient fashions or temporary opinions: they are the genuine progeny of common humanity, such as the world will always supply, and observation will always find. His persons act and speak by the influence of those general passions and principles by which all minds are agitated, and the whole system of life is continued in motion. In the writings of other poets a character is too often an individual; in those of Shakespeare it is commonly a species.

It is from this wide extension of design that so much instruction is derived. It is this which fills the plays of Shakespeare with practical axioms and domestick wisdom. It was said of Euripides,[1] that every verse was a precept; and it may be said of Shake-

---

[1] By Cicero.

speare, that from his works may be collected a system of civil and oeconomical prudence. Yet his real power is not shewn in the splendour of particular passages, but by the progress of his fable, and the tenour of his dialogue; and he that tries to recommend him by select quotations, will succeed like the pedant in Hierocles, who, when he offered his house to sale, carried a brick in his pocket as a specimen.[2]

It will not easily be imagined how much Shakespeare excells in accommodating his sentiments to real life, but by comparing him with other authours. It was observed of the ancient schools of declamation, that the more diligently they were frequented, the more was the student disqualified for the world, because he found nothing there which he should ever meet in any other place. The same remark may be applied to every stage but that of Shakespeare. The theatre, when it is under any other direction, is peopled by such characters as were never seen, conversing in a language which was never heard, upon topicks which will never arise in the commerce of mankind. But the dialogue of this authour is often so evidently determined by the incident which produces it, and is pursued with so much ease and simplicity, that it seems scarcely to claim the merit of fiction, but to have been gleaned by diligent selection out of common conversation, and common occurrences.

Upon every other stage the universal agent is love, by whose power all good and evil is distributed, and every action quickened or retarded. To bring a lover, a lady and a rival into the fable; to entangle them in contradictory obligations, perplex them with oppositions of interest, and harrass them with violence of desires inconsistent with each other; to make them meet in rapture and part in agony; to fill their mouths with hyperbolical joy and outrageous sorrow; to distress them as nothing human ever was distressed; to deliver them as nothing human ever was delivered, is the business of a modern dramatist. For this probability is violated, life is misrepresented, and language is depraved. But

---

[2] The story appears in Dacier's "Life of Hierocles," an Alexandrian philosopher, c. A.D. 430, translated in Rowe's *Life of Pythagoras*, etc., 1707, p. 146: "Another [scholar], who was desirous to sell his house, took a stone of it out of the wall, and carry'd it to the market for a sample." Attributed to a follower of Hierocles.

love is only one of many passions, and as it has no great influence upon the sum of life, it has little operation in the dramas of a poet, who caught his ideas from the living world, and exhibited only what he saw before him. He knew, that any other passion, as it was regular or exorbitant, was a cause of happiness or calamity.

Characters thus ample and general were not easily discriminated and preserved, yet perhaps no poet ever kept his personages more distinct from each other. I will not say with Pope, that every speech may be assigned to the proper speaker,[3] because many speeches there are which have nothing characteristical; but perhaps, though some may be equally adapted to every person, it will be difficult to find, any that can be properly transferred from the present possessor to another claimant. The choice is right, when there is reason for choice.

Other dramatists can only gain attention by hyperbolical or aggravated characters, by fabulous and unexampled excellence or depravity, as the writers of barbarous romances invigorated the reader by a giant and a dwarf; and he that should form his expectations of human affairs from the play, or from the tale, would be equally deceived. Shakespeare has no heroes; his scenes are occupied only by men, who act and speak as the reader thinks that he should himself have spoken or acted on the same occasion: Even where the agency is supernatural the dialogue is level with life. Other writers disguise the most natural passions and most frequent incidents; so that he who contemplates them in the book will not know them in the world: Shakespeare approximates the remote, and familiarizes the wonderful; the event which he represents will not happen, but if it were possible, its effects would probably be such as he has assigned; and it may be said, that he has not only shewn human nature as it acts in real exigences, but as it would be found in trials, to which it cannot be exposed.

This therefore is the praise of Shakespeare, that his drama is the mirrour of life; that he who has mazed his imagination, in following the phantoms which other writers raise up before him, may here be cured of his delirious extasies, by reading human

---

[3] Pope's Preface to his edition of Shakespeare, 1725.

sentiments in human language; by scenes from which a hermit may estimate the transactions of the world, and a confessor predict the progress of the passions.

His adherence to general nature has exposed him to the censure of criticks, who form their judgments upon narrower principles. Dennis and Rhymer[4] think his Romans not sufficiently Roman; and Voltaire censures his kings as not completely royal. Dennis is offended, that Menenius, a senator of Rome, should play the buffoon; and Voltaire perhaps thinks decency violated when the Danish usurper is represented as a drunkard. But Shakespeare always makes nature predominate over accident; and if he preserves the essential character, is not very careful of distinctions superinduced and adventitious. His story requires Romans or kings, but he thinks only on men. He knew that Rome, like every other city, had men of all dispositions; and wanting a buffoon, he went into the senate-house for that which the senate-house would certainly have afforded him. He was inclined to shew an usurper and a murderer not only odious but despicable, he therefore added drunkenness to his other qualities, knowing that kings love wine like other men, and that wine exerts its natural power upon kings. These are the petty cavils of petty minds; a poet overlooks the casual distinction of country and condition, as a painter, satisfied with the figure, neglects the drapery.

The censure which he has incurred by mixing comick and tragick scenes, as it extends to all his works, deserves more consideration. Let the fact be first stated, and then examined.

Shakespeare's plays are not in the rigorous and critical sense either tragedies or comedies, but compositions of a distinct kind; exhibiting the real state of sublunary nature, which partakes of good and evil, joy and sorrow, mingled with endless variety of proportion and innumerable modes of combination; and expressing the course of the world, in which the loss of one is the gain of another; in which, at the same time, the reveller is hasting to his wine, and the mourner burying his friend; in which the malignity of one is sometimes defeated by the frolick of another; and many mischiefs and many benefits are done and hindered without design.

---

[4] John Dennis (d. 1734), whose *Essay on the Genius and Writings of Shakespear*, 1712, Johnson cites; and Thomas Rymer (d. 1713), whose *Short View of Tragedy*, 1693, is referred to.

Out of this chaos of mingled purposes and casualties the ancient poets, according to the laws which custom had prescribed, selected some the crimes of men, and some their absurdities; some the momentous vicissitudes of life, and some the lighter occurrences; some the terrours of distress, and some the gayeties of prosperity. Thus rose the two modes of imitation, known by the names of *tragedy* and *comedy*, compositions intended to promote different ends by contrary means, and considered as so little allied, that I do not recollect among the Greeks or Romans a single writer who attempted both.

Shakespeare has united the powers of exciting laughter and sorrow not only in one mind but in one composition. Almost all his plays are divided between serious and ludicrous characters, and, in the successive evolutions of the design, sometimes produce seriousness and sorrow, and sometimes levity and laughter.

That this is a practice contrary to the rules of criticism will be readily allowed; but there is always an appeal open from criticism to nature. The end of writing is to instruct; the end of poetry is to instruct by pleasing. That the mingled drama may convey all the instruction of tragedy or comedy cannot be denied, because it includes both in its alternations of exhibition, and approaches nearer than either to the appearance of life, by shewing how great machinations and slender designs may promote or obviate one another, and the high and the low co-operate in the general system by unavoidable concatenation.

It is objected, that by this change of scenes the passions are interrupted in their progression, and that the principal event, being not advanced by a due gradation of preparatory incidents, wants at last the power to move, which constitutes the perfection of dramatick poetry. This reasoning is so specious, that it is received as true even by those who in daily experience feel it to be false. The interchanges of mingled scenes seldom fail to produce the intended vicissitudes of passion. Fiction cannot move so much, but that the attention may be easily transferred; and though it must be allowed that pleasing melancholy be sometimes interrupted by unwelcome levity, yet let it be considered likewise, that melancholy is often not pleasing, and that the disturbance of one man may be the relief of another; that different auditors have different habitudes; and that, upon the whole, all pleasure consists in variety.

The players, who in their edition[5] divided our authour's works into comedies, histories, and tragedies, seem not to have distinguished the three kinds, by any very exact or definite ideas.

An action which ended happily to the principal persons, however serious or distressful through its intermediate incidents, in their opinion constituted a comedy. This idea of a comedy continued long amongst us, and plays were written, which, by changing the catastrophe, were tragedies to-day and comedies to-morrow.

Tragedy was not in those times a poem of more general dignity or elevation than comedy; it required only a calamitous conclusion, with which the common criticism of that age was satisfied, whatever lighter pleasure it afforded in its progress.

History was a series of actions, with no other than chronological succession, independent on each other, and without any tendency to introduce or regulate the conclusion. It is not always very nicely distinguished from tragedy. There is not much nearer approach to unity of action in the tragedy of *Antony and Cleopatra,* than in the history of *Richard the Second.* But a history might be continued through many plays; as it had no plan, it had no limits.

Through all these denominations of the drama, Shakespeare's mode of composition is the same; an interchange of seriousness and merriment, by which the mind is softened at one time, and exhilarated at another. But whatever be his purpose, whether to gladden or depress, or to conduct the story, without vehemence or emotion, through tracts of easy and familiar dialogue, he never fails to attain his purpose; as he commands us, we laugh or mourn, or sit silent with quiet expectation, in tranquillity without indifference.

When Shakespeare's plan is understood, most of the criticisms of Rhymer and Voltaire vanish away. The play of *Hamlet* is opened, without impropriety, by two sentinels; Iago bellows at Brabantio's window, without injury to the scheme of the play, though in terms which a modern audience would not easily endure; the character of Polonius is seasonable and useful; and the Grave-diggers themselves may be heard with applause.

---

[5] Heming and Condell, fellow-players with Shakespeare. They furnished the materials for the First Folio, 1623.

Shakespeare engaged in dramatick poetry with the world open
before him; the rules of the ancients were yet known to few; the
publick judgment was unformed; he had no example of such fame
as might force him upon imitation, nor criticks of such authority
as might restrain his extravagance: He therefore indulged his
natural disposition, and his disposition, as Rhymer has remarked,
led him to comedy. In tragedy he often writes with great appearance of toil and study, what is written at last with little felicity;
but in his comick scenes, he seems to produce without labour,
what no labour can improve. In tragedy he is always struggling
after some occasion to be comick, but in comedy he seems to
repose, or to luxuriate, as in a mode of thinking congenial to his
nature. In his tragick scenes there is always something wanting,
but his comedy often surpasses expectation or desire. His comedy
pleases by the thoughts and the language, and his tragedy for
the greater part by incident and action. His tragedy seems to be
skill, his comedy to be instinct.

The force of his comick scenes has suffered little diminution
from the changes made by a century and a half, in manners or in
words. As his personages act upon principles arising from genuine
passion, very little modified by particular forms, their pleasures
and vexations are communicable to all times and to all places;
they are natural, and therefore durable; the adventitious peculiarities of personal habits, are only superficial dies, bright and
pleasing for a little while, yet soon fading to a dim tinct, without
any remains of former lustre; but the discriminations of true passion are the colours of nature; they pervade the whole mass, and
can only perish with the body that exhibits them. The accidental
compositions of heterogeneous modes are dissolved by the chance
which combined them; but the uniform simplicity of primitive
qualities neither admits increase, nor suffers decay. The sand
heaped by one flood is scattered by another, but the rock always
continues in its place. The stream of time, which is continually
washing the dissoluble fabricks of other poets, passes without
injury by the adamant of Shakespeare.

If there be, what I believe there is, in every nation, a stile
which never becomes obsolete, a certain mode of phraseology so
consonant and congenial to the analogy and principles of its
respective language as to remain settled and unaltered; this stile

is probably to be sought in the common intercourse of life, among those who speak only to be understood, without ambition of elegance. The polite are always catching modish innovations, and the learned depart from established forms of speech, in hope of finding or making better; those who wish for distinction forsake the vulgar, when the vulgar is right; but there is a conversation above grossness and below refinement, where propriety resides, and where this poet seems to have gathered his comick dialogue. He is therefore more agreeable to the ears of the present age than any other authour equally remote, and among his other excellencies deserves to be studied as one of the original masters of our language.

These observations are to be considered not as unexceptionably constant, but as containing general and predominant truth. Shakespeare's familiar dialogue is affirmed to be smooth and clear, yet not wholly without ruggedness or difficulty; as a country may be eminently fruitful, though it has spots unfit for cultivation: His characters are praised as natural, though their sentiments are sometimes forced, and their actions improbable; as the earth upon the whole is spherical, though its surface is varied with protuberances and cavities.

Shakespeare with his excellencies has likewise faults, and faults sufficient to obscure and overwhelm any other merit. I shall shew them in the proportion in which they appear to me, without envious malignity or superstitious veneration. No question can be more innocently discussed than a dead poet's pretensions to renown; and little regard is due to that bigotry which sets candour higher than truth.

His first defect is that to which may be imputed most of the evil in books or in men. He sacrifices virtue to convenience, and is so much more careful to please than to instruct, that he seems to write without any moral purpose. From his writings indeed a system of social duty may be selected, for he that thinks reasonably must think morally; but his precepts and axioms drop casually from him; he makes no just distribution of good or evil, nor is always careful to shew in the virtuous a disapprobation of the wicked; he carries his persons indifferently through right and wrong, and at the close dismisses them without further care, and leaves their examples to operate by chance. This fault the barbarity of his age cannot extenuate; for it is always a writer's duty to make the world better, and justice is a virtue independant on time or place.

The plots are often so loosely formed, that a very slight consideration may improve them, and so carelessly pursued, that he seems not always fully to comprehend his own design. He omits opportunities of instructing or delighting which the train of his story seems to force upon him, and apparently rejects those exhibitions which would be more affecting, for the sake of those which are more easy.

It may be observed, that in many of his plays the latter part is evidently neglected. When he found himself near the end of his work, and, in view of his reward, he shortened the labour, to snatch the profit. He therefore remits his efforts where he should most vigorously exert them, and his catastrophe is improbably produced or imperfectly represented.

He had no regard to distinction of time or place, but gives to one age or nation, without scruple, the customs, institutions, and opinions of another, at the expence not only of likelihood, but of possibility. These faults Pope has endeavoured, with more zeal than judgment, to transfer to his imagined interpolators. We need not wonder to find Hector quoting Aristotle, when we see the loves of Theseus and Hippolyta combined with the Gothick mythology of fairies. Shakespeare, indeed, was not the only violator of chronology, for in the same age Sidney, who wanted not the advantages of learning, has, in his *Arcadia*, confounded the pastoral with the feudal times, the days of innocence, quiet and security, with those of turbulence, violence and adventure.

In his comick scenes he is seldom very successful, when he engages his characters in reciprocations of smartness and contests of sarcasm; their jests are commonly gross, and their pleasantry licentious; neither his gentlemen nor his ladies have much delicacy, nor are sufficiently distinguished from his clowns by any appearance of refined manners. Whether he represented the real conversation of his time is not easy to determine; the reign of Elizabeth is commonly supposed to have been a time of stateliness, formality and reserve, yet perhaps the relaxations of that severity were not very elegant. There must, however, have been always some modes of gayety preferable to others, and a writer ought to chuse the best.

In tragedy his performance seems constantly to be worse, as

his labour is more. The effusions of passion which exigence forces out are for the most part striking and energetick; but whenever he solicits his invention, or strains his faculties, the offspring of his throes is tumour, meanness, tediousness, and obscurity.

In narration he affects a disproportionate pomp of diction and a wearisome train of circumlocution, and tells the incident imperfectly in many words, which might have been more plainly delivered in few. Narration in dramatick poetry is naturally tedious, as it is unanimated and inactive, and obstructs the progress of the action; it should therefore always be rapid, and enlivened by frequent interruption. Shakespeare found it an encumbrance, and instead of lightening it by brevity, endeavoured to recommend it by dignity and splendour.

His declamations or set speeches are commonly cold and weak, for his power was the power of nature; when he endeavoured, like other tragick writers, to catch opportunities of amplification, and instead of inquiring what the occasion demanded, to show how much his stores of knowledge could supply, he seldom escapes without the pity or resentment of his reader.

It is incident to him to be now and then entangled with an unwieldy sentiment, which he cannot well express, and will not reject; he struggles with it a while, and if it continues stubborn, comprises it in words such as occur, and leaves it to be disentangled and evolved by those who have more leisure to bestow upon it.

Not that always where the language is intricate the thought is subtle, or the image always great where the line is bulky; the equality of words to things is very often neglected, and trivial sentiments and vulgar ideas disappoint the attention, to which they are recommended by sonorous epithets and swelling figures.

But the admirers of this great poet have never less reason to indulge their hopes of supreme excellence, than when he seems fully resolved to sink them in dejection, and mollify them with tender emotions by the fall of greatness, the danger of innocence, or the crosses of love. He is not long soft and pathetick without some idle conceit, or contemptible equivocation. He no sooner begins to move, than he counteracts himself; and terrour and pity, as they are rising in the mind, are checked and blasted by sudden frigidity.

A quibble is to Shakespeare, what luminous vapours are to the traveller; he follows it at all adventures, it is sure to lead him out of his way, and sure to engulf him in the mire. It has some malignant power over his mind, and its fascinations are irresistible. Whatever be the dignity or profundity of his disquisition, whether he be enlarging knowledge or exalting affection, whether he be amusing attention with incidents, or enchaining it in suspense, let but a quibble spring up before him, and he leaves his work unfinished. A quibble is the golden apple for which he will always turn aside from his career, or stoop from his elevation. A quibble, poor and barren as it is, gave him such delight, that he was content to purchase it, by the sacrifice of reason, propriety and truth. A quibble was to him the fatal Cleopatra for which he lost the world, and was content to lose it.

It will be thought strange, that, in enumerating the defects of this writer, I have not yet mentioned his neglect of the unities; his violation of those laws which have been instituted and established by the joint authority of poets and of cricticks.

For his other deviations from the art of writing, I resign him to critical justice, without making any other demand in his favour, than that which must be indulged to all human excellence; that his virtues be rated with his failings: But, from the censure which this irregularity may bring upon him, I shall, with due reverence to that learning which I must oppose, adventure to try how I can defend him.

His histories, being neither tragedies nor comedies, are not subject to any of their laws; nothing more is necessary to all the praise which they expect, than that the changes of action be so prepared as to be understood, that the incidents be various and affecting, and the characters consistent, natural and distinct. No other unity is intended, and therefore none is to be sought.

In his other works he has well enough preserved the unity of action. He has not, indeed, an intrigue regularly perplexed and regularly unravelled; he does not endeavour to hide his design only to discover it, for this is seldom the order of real events, and Shakespeare is the poet of nature: But his plan has commonly what Aristotle requires, a beginning, a middle, and an end; one event is concatenated with another, and the conclusion follows by easy consequence. There are perhaps some incidents that might be spared, as in other poets there is much talk that only fills up time upon the stage; but the general system makes gradual advances, and the end of the play is the end of expectation.

To the unities of time and place he has shewn no regard, and perhaps a nearer view of the principles on which they stand will diminish their value, and withdraw from them the veneration which, from the time of Corneille, they have very generally received, by discovering that they have given more trouble to the poet, than pleasure to the auditor.

The necessity of observing the unities of time and place arises from the supposed necessity of making the drama credible. The criticks hold it impossible, that an action of months or years can be possibly believed to pass in three hours; or that the spectator can suppose himself to sit in the theatre, while ambassadors go and return between distant kings, while armies are levied and towns besieged, while an exile wanders and returns, or till he whom they saw courting his mistress, shall lament the untimely fall of his son. The mind revolts from evident falsehood, and fiction loses its force when it departs from the resemblance of reality.

From the narrow limitation of time necessarily arises the contraction of place. The spectator, who knows that he saw the first act at Alexandria, cannot suppose that he sees the next at Rome, at a distance to which not the dragons of Medea could, in so short a time, have transported him; he knows with certainty that he has not changed his place; and he knows that place cannot change itself; that what was a house cannot become a plain; that what was Thebes can never be Persepolis.

Such is the triumphant language with which a critick exults over the misery of an irregular poet, and exults commonly without resistance or reply. It is time therefore to tell him, by the authority of Shakespeare, that he assumes, as an unquestionable principle, a position, which, while his breath is forming it into words, his understanding pronounces to be false. It is false, that any representation is mistaken for reality; that any dramatick fable in its materiality was ever credible, or, for a single moment, was ever credited.

The objection arising from the impossibility of passing the first hour at Alexandria, and the next at Rome, supposes, that when the play opens the spectator really imagines himself at Alexandria, and believes that his walk to the theatre has been a voyage to Egypt, and that he lives in the days of Antony and Cleopatra. Surely he that imagines this may imagine more. He that can take the stage at one time for the palace of the Ptolemies, may take it in half an hour for the promontory of Actium. Delusion, if delusion be admitted, has no certain limitation; if the spectator can be once persuaded, that his old acquaintance are Alexander and Caesar, that a room illuminated with candles is the plain of Pharsalia, or the bank of Granicus, he is in a state of elevation above the reach of reason, or of truth, and from the heights of empyrean poetry, may despise the circumscriptions of terrestrial nature. There is no reason why a mind thus wandering in extasy should count the clock, or why an hour should not be a century in that calenture of the brains that can make the stage a field.

The truth is, that the spectators are always in their senses, and know, from the first act to the last, that the stage is only a stage, and that the players are only players. They come to hear a certain number of lines recited with just gesture and elegant modulation. The lines relate to some action, and an action must be in some place; but the different actions that compleat a story may be in places very remote from each other; and where is the absurdity of allowing that space to represent first Athens, and then Sicily, which was always known to be neither Sicily nor Athens, but a modern theatre.

By supposition, as place is introduced, time may be extended; the time required by the fable elapses for the most part between the acts; for, of so much of the action as is represented, the real and poetical duration is the same. If, in the first act, preparations for war against Mithridates are represented to be made in Rome, the event of the war may, without absurdity, be represented, in the catastrophe, as happening in Pontus; we know that there is neither war, nor preparation for war; we know that we are neither in Rome nor Pontus; that neither Mithridates nor Lucullus are before us. The drama exhibits successive imitations of successive actions, and why may not the second imitation represent an action that happened years after the first; if it be so connected with it, that nothing but time can be supposed to intervene. Time is, of all modes of existence, most obsequious to the imagination; a lapse of years is as easily conceived as a passage of hours. In contemplation we easily contract the time of real actions, and therefore willingly permit it to be contracted when we only see their imitation.

It will be asked, how the drama moves, if it is not credited. It is credited with all the credit due to a drama. It is credited, whenever it moves, as a just picture of a real original; as representing to the auditor what he would himself feel, if he were to do or suffer what is there feigned to be suffered or to be done. The reflection that strikes the heart is not, that the evils before us are real evils, but that they are evils to which we ourselves may be exposed. If there be any fallacy, it is not that we fancy the players, but that we fancy ourselves unhappy for a moment; but we rather lament the possibility than suppose the presence of misery, as a mother weeps over her babe, when she remembers that death may take it from her. The delight of tragedy proceeds from our consciousness of fiction; if we thought murders and treasons real, they would please no more.

Imitations produce pain or pleasure, not because they are mistaken for realities, but because they bring realities to mind. When the imagination is recreated by a painted landscape, the trees are not supposed capable to give us shade, or the fountains coolness; but we consider, how we should be pleased with such fountains playing beside us, and such woods waving over us. We are agitated in reading the history of Henry the Fifth, yet no man takes his book for the field of Agencourt. A dramatick exhibition is a book recited with concomitants that encrease or diminish its effect. Familiar comedy is often more powerful on the theatre, than in the page; imperial tragedy is always less. The humour of Petruchio may be heightened by grimace; but what voice or what gesture can hope to add dignity or force to the soliloquy of *Cato*.[6]

A play read, affects the mind like a play acted. It is therefore evident, that the action is not supposed to be real, and it follows that between the acts a longer or shorter time may be allowed to pass, and that no more account of space or duration is to be taken by the auditor of a drama, than by the reader of a narrative,

---

[6] Addison, *Cato*, V.i.

before whom may pass in an hour the life of a hero, or the revolutions of an empire.

Whether Shakespeare knew the unities, and rejected them by design, or deviated from them by happy ignorance, it is, I think, impossible to decide, and useless to enquire. We may reasonably suppose, that, when he rose to notice, he did not want the counsels and admonitions of scholars and cricticks, and that he at last deliberately persisted in a practice, which he might have begun by chance. As nothing is essential to the fable, but unity of action, and as the unities of time and place arise evidently from false assumptions, and, by circumscribing the extent of the drama, lessen its variety, I cannot think it much to be lamented, that they were not known by him, or not observed: Nor, if such another poet could arise, should I very vehemently reproach him, that his first act passed at Venice, and his next in Cyprus. Such violations of rules merely positive, become the comprehensive genius of Shakespeare, and such censures are suitable to the minute and slender criticism of Voltaire:

> *Non usque adeo permiscuit imis*
> *Longus summa dies, ut non, si voce Metelli*
> *Serventur leges, malint a Caesare tolli.*[7]

Yet when I speak thus slightly of dramatick rules, I cannot but recollect how much wit and learning may be produced against me; before such authorities I am afraid to stand, not that I think the present question one of those that are to be decided by mere authority, but because it is to be suspected, that these precepts have not been so easily received but for better reasons than I have yet been able to find. The result of my enquiries, in which it would be ludicrous to boast of impartiality, is, that the unities of time and place are not essential to a just drama, that though they may sometimes conduce to pleasure, they are always to be sacrificed to the nobler beauties of variety and instruction; and that a play, written with nice observation of critical rules, is to be contemplated as an elaborate curiosity, as the product of superfluous and

---

[7] Lucan, *Pharsalia*, III.138–140. "The course of time has not wrought such confusion that the laws would not rather be trampled on by Caesar than saved by Metellus." (tr. J.D. Duff.) Read "servantur."

ostentatious art, by which is shewn, rather what is possible, than what is necessary.

He that, without diminution of any other excellence, shall preserve all the unities unbroken, deserves the like applause with the architect, who shall display all the orders of architecture in a citadel, without any deduction from its strength; but the principal beauty of a citadel is to exclude the enemy; and the greatest graces of a play, are to copy nature and instruct life.

Perhaps, what I have here not dogmatically but deliberatively written, may recal the principles of the drama to a new examination. I am almost frighted at my own temerity; and when I estimate the fame and the strength of those that maintain the contrary opinion, am ready to sink down in reverential silence; as Aeneas withdrew from the defence of Troy, when he saw Neptune shaking the wall, and Juno heading the besiegers.[8]

Those whom my arguments cannot persuade to give their approbation to the judgment of Shakespeare, will easily, if they consider the condition of his life, make some allowance for his ignorance.

Every man's performances, to be rightly estimated, must be compared with the state of the age in which he lived, and with his own particular opportunities; and though to the reader a book be not worse or better for the circumstances of the authour, yet as there is always a silent reference of human works to human abilities, and as the enquiry, how far man may extend his designs, or how high he may rate his native force, is of far greater dignity than in what rank we shall place any particular performance, curiosity is always busy to discover the instruments, as well as to survey the workmanship, to know how much is to be ascribed to original powers, and how much to casual and adventitious help. The palaces of Peru or Mexico were certainly mean and incommodious habitations, if compared to the houses of European monarchs; yet who could forbear to view them with astonishment, who remembered that they were built without the use of iron?

The English nation, in the time of Shakespeare, was yet struggling to emerge from barbarity. The philology of Italy had been transplanted hither in the reign of Henry the Eighth; and the

---

[8] *Aeneid*, II.670.

learned languages had been successfully cultivated by Lilly, Linacer,[9] and More; by Pole, Cheke, and Gardiner;[1] and afterwards by Smith, Clerk, Haddon,[2] and Ascham. Greek was now taught to boys in the principal schools; and those who united elegance with learning, read, with great diligence, the Italian and Spanish poets. But literature was yet confined to professed scholars, or to men and women of high rank. The publick was gross and dark; and to be able to read and write, was an accomplishment still valued for its rarity.

Nations, like individuals, have their infancy. A people newly awakened to literary curiosity, being yet unacquainted with the true state of things, knows not how to judge of that which is proposed as its resemblance. Whatever is remote from common appearances is always welcome to vulgar, as to childish credulity; and of a country unenlightened by learning, the whole people is the vulgar. The study of those who then aspired to plebeian learning was laid out upon adventures, giants, dragons, and enchantments. *The Death of Arthur*[3] was the favourite volume.

The mind, which has feasted on the luxurious wonders of fiction, has no taste of the insipidity of truth. A play which imitated only the common occurrences of the world, would, upon the admirers of *Palmerin*[4] and *Guy of Warwick*,[5] have made little impression; he that wrote for such an audience was under the necessity of looking round for strange events and fabulous trans-

[9] William Lily (d. 1522), author of the Latin grammar used even in Johnson's day. Thomas Linacre (d. 1524) taught Greek to Erasmus and Sir Thomas More.

[1] Reginald, Cardinal Pole (d. 1558), called by More as learned as he was noble and as virtuous as he was learned (*Encyclopedia Britannica*). Sir John Cheke (d. 1557) made many Latin translations from the Greek. Stephen Gardiner (d. 1555), bishop and lord chancellor, encouraged the study of Greek at Cambridge.

[2] Sir Thomas Smith (d. 1577), wrote on the pronunciation of Greek as well as on the government of England. Bartholomew Clerke (d. 1590), professor of rhetoric at Cambridge, whom Haddon recommended to be Latin Secretary to Elizabeth after the death of Ascham. Walter Haddon (d. 1571) revised the Latin translation of the Book of Common Prayer. In Johnson's *Milton* he speaks of Haddon and Roger Ascham as "the pride of Elizabeth's reign."

[3] Malory's *Morte d'Arthur* had been printed five times before Shakespeare's death.

[4] *Palmerin of England*, a sixteenth-century chivalric romance.

[5] *Guy of Warwick*, a long fourteenth-century verse romance.

actions, and that incredibility, by which maturer knowledge is offended, was the chief recommendation of writings, to unskilful curiosity.

Our authour's plots are generally borrowed from novels, and it is reasonable to suppose, that he chose the most popular, such as were read by many, and related by more; for his audience could not have followed him through the intricacies of the drama, had they not held the thread of the story in their hands.

The stories, which we now find only in remoter authours, were in his time accessible and familiar. The fable of *As you like it,* which is supposed to be copied from Chaucer's *Gamelyn,*[6] was a little pamphlet of those times; and old Mr. Cibber[7] remembered the tale of *Hamlet* in plain English prose, which the criticks have now to seek in Saxo Grammaticus.[8]

His English histories he took from English chronicles and English ballads; and as the ancient writers were made known to his countrymen by versions, they supplied him with new subjects; he dilated some of Plutarch's lives into plays, when they had been translated by North.

His plots, whether historical or fabulous, are always crouded with incidents, by which the attention of a rude people was more easily caught than by sentiment or argumentation; and such is the power of the marvellous even over those who despise it, that every man finds his mind more strongly seized by the tragedies of Shakespeare than of any other writer; others please us by particular speeches, but he always makes us anxious for the event, and has perhaps excelled all but Homer in securing the first purpose of a writer, by exciting restless and unquenchable curiosity, and compelling him that reads his work to read it through.

The shows and bustle with which his plays abound have the same original. As knowledge advances, pleasure passes from the eye to the ear, but returns, as it declines, from the ear to the eye. Those to whom our authour's labours were exhibited had more skill in pomps or processions than in poetical language, and per-

---

[6] Thomas Lodge's *Rosalynde* (1590), based on the pseudo-Chaucerian *Tale of Gamelyn.*

[7] Colley Cibber (d. 1757), actor and playwright.

[8] Saxo Grammaticus, thirteenth-century Danish historian, in whose *Gesta Danorum* the Hamlet story appears.

haps wanted some visible and discriminated events, as comments on the dialogue. He knew how he should most please; and whether his practice is more agreeable to nature, or whether his example has prejudiced the nation, we still find that on our stage something must be done as well as said, and inactive declamation is very coldly heard, however musical or elegant, passionate or sublime.

Voltaire expresses his wonder, that our authour's extravagances are endured by a nation, which has seen the tragedy of *Cato*. Let him be answered, that Addison speaks the language of poets, and Shakespeare, of men. We find in *Cato* innumerable beauties which enamour us of its authour, but we see nothing that acquaints us with human sentiments or human actions; we place it with the fairest and the noblest progeny which judgment propagates by conjunction with learning, but *Othello* is the vigorous and vivacious offspring of observation impregnated by genius. *Cato* affords a splendid exhibition of artificial and fictitious manners, and delivers just and noble sentiments, in diction easy, elevated and harmonious, but its hopes and fears communicate no vibration to the heart; the composition refers us only to the writer; we pronounce the name of *Cato*, but we think on Addison.

The work of a correct and regular writer is a garden accurately formed and diligently planted, varied with shades, and scented with flowers; the composition of Shakespeare is a forest, in which oaks extend their branches, and pines tower in the air, interspersed sometimes with weeds and brambles, and sometimes giving shelter to myrtles and to roses; filling the eye with awful pomp, and gratifying the mind with endless diversity. Other poets display cabinets of precious rarities, minutely finished, wrought into shape, and polished unto brightness. Shakespeare opens a mine which contains gold and diamonds in unexhaustible plenty, though clouded by incrustations, debased by impurities, and mingled with a mass of meaner minerals.

It has been much disputed, whether Shakespeare owed his excellence to his own native force, or whether he had the common helps of scholastick education, the precepts of critical science, and the examples of ancient authours.

There has always prevailed a tradition, that Shakespeare wanted learning, that he had no regular education, nor much skill in the dead languages. Johnson, his friend, affirms, that *he had small Latin, and no Greek;*[9] who, besides that he had no imaginable temptation to falsehood, wrote at a time when the character and acquisitions of Shakespeare were known to multitudes. His evidence ought therefore to decide the controversy, unless some testimony of equal force could be opposed.

Some have imagined, that they have discovered deep learning in many imitations of old writers; but the examples which I have known urged, were drawn from books translated in his time; or were such easy coincidencies of thought, as will happen to all who consider the same subjects; or such remarks on life or axioms of morality as float in conversation, and are transmitted through the world in proverbial sentences.

I have found it remarked, that, in this important sentence, *Go before, I'll follow,* we read a translation of, *I prae, sequar.*[1] I have been told, that when Caliban, after a pleasing dream, says, *I cry'd to sleep again,* the authour imitates Anacreon, who had, like every other man, the same wish on the same occasion.

There are a few passages which may pass for imitations, but so few, that the exception only confirms the rule; he obtained them from accidental quotations, or by oral communication, and as he used what he had, would have used more if he had obtained it.

The *Comedy of Errors* is confessedly taken from the *Menaechmi* of Plautus; from the only play of Plautus which was then in English. What can be more probable, than that he who copied that, would have copied more; but that those which were not translated were inaccessible?

Whether he knew the modern languages is uncertain. That his plays have some French scenes proves but little; he might easily procure them to be written, and probably, even though he had known the language in the common degree, he could not have written it without assistance. In the story of *Romeo and Juliet* he is observed to have followed the English translation, where it deviates from the Italian; but this on the other part proves nothing against his knowledge of the original. He was to copy, not what he knew himself, but what was known to his audience.

---

[9] Ben Jonson's "To the Memory of my beloved, the Author, Mr. William Shakespeare." Jonson wrote "less Greek."

[1] Zachary Grey's *Notes on Shakespeare,* 1754. The Latin is from Terence's *Andria.*

It is most likely that he had learned Latin sufficiently to make him acquainted with construction, but that he never advanced to an easy perusal of the Roman authours. Concerning his skill in modern languages, I can find no sufficient ground of determination; but as no imitations of French or Italian authours have been discovered, though the Italian poetry was then high in esteem, I am inclined to believe, that he read little more than English, and chose for his fables only such tales as he found translated.

That much knowledge is scattered over his works is very justly observed by Pope, but it is often such knowledge as books did not supply. He that will understand Shakespeare, must not be content to study him in the closet, he must look for his meaning sometimes among the sports of the field, and sometimes among the manufactures of the shop.

There is however proof enough that he was a very diligent reader, nor was our language then so indigent of books, but that he might very liberally indulge his curiosity without excursion into foreign literature. Many of the Roman authours were translated, and some of the Greek; the reformation had filled the kingdom with theological learning; most of the topicks of human disquisition had found English writers; and poetry had been cultivated, not only with diligence, but success. This was a stock of knowledge sufficient for a mind so capable of appropriating and improving it.

But the greater part of his excellence was the product of his own genius. He found the English stage in a state of the utmost rudeness; no essays either in tragedy or comedy had appeared, from which it could be discovered to what degree of delight either one or other might be carried. Neither character nor dialogue were yet understood. Shakespeare may be truly said to have introduced them both amongst us, and in some of his happier scenes to have carried them both to the utmost height.

By what gradations of improvement he proceeded, is not easily known; for the chronology of his works is yet unsettled. Rowe is of opinion, that *perhaps we are not to look for his beginning, like those of other writers, in his least perfect works; art had so little, and nature so large a share in what he did, that for ought I know,* says he, *the performances of his youth, as they were the most vigorous, were the best.*[2] But the power of nature is only the power of using to any certain purpose the materials which diligence procures, or opportunity supplies. Nature gives no man knowledge, and when images are collected by study and experience, can only assist in combining or applying them. Shakespeare, however favoured by nature, could impart only what he had learned; and as he must increase his ideas, like other mortals, by gradual acquisition, he, like them, grew wiser as he grew older, could display life better, as he knew it more, and instruct with more efficacy, as he was himself more amply instructed.

There is a vigilance of observation and accuracy of distinction which books and precepts cannot confer; from this almost all original and native excellence proceeds. Shakespeare must have looked upon mankind with perspicacity, in the highest degree curious and attentive. Other writers borrow their characters from preceding writers, and diversify them only by the accidental appendages of present manners; the dress is a little varied, but the body is the same. Our authour had both matter and form to provide; for except the characters of Chaucer, to whom I think he is not much indebted, there were no writers in English, and perhaps not many in other modern languages, which shewed life in its native colours.

The contest about the original benevolence or malignity of man had not yet commenced. Speculation had not yet attempted to analyse the mind, to trace the passions to their sources, to unfold the seminal principles of vice and virtue, or sound the depths of the heart for the motives of action. All those enquiries, which from that time that human nature became the fashionable study, have been made sometimes with nice discernment, but often with idle subtilty, were yet unattempted. The tales, with which the infancy of learning was satisfied, exhibited only the superficial appearances of action, related the events but omitted the causes, and were formed for such as delighted in wonders rather than in truth. Mankind was not then to be studied in the closet; he that would know the world, was under the necessity of gleaning his own remarks, by mingling as he could in its business and amusements.

Boyle congratulated himself upon his high birth, because it

---

[2] Nicholas Rowe's *Life of Shakespeare*, prefixed to his edition, 1709.

favoured his curiosity, by facilitating his access.[3] Shakespeare had no such advantage; he came to London a needy adventurer, and lived for a time by very mean employments. Many works of genius and learning have been performed in states of life, that appear very little favourable to thought or to enquiry; so many, that he who considers them is inclined to think that he sees enterprise and perseverance predominating over all external agency, and bidding help and hindrance vanish before them. The genius of Shakespeare was not to be depressed by the weight of poverty, nor limited by the narrow conversation to which men in want are inevitably condemned; the incumbrances of his fortune were shaken from his mind, *as dewdrops from a lion's mane*.[4]

Though he had so many difficulties to encounter, and so little assistance to surmount them, he has been able to obtain an exact knowledge of many modes of life, and many casts of native dispositions; to vary them with great multiplicity; to mark them by nice distinctions; and to shew them in full view by proper combinations. In this part of his performances he had none to imitate, but has himself been imitated by all succeeding writers; and it may be doubted, whether from all his successors more maxims of theoretical knowledge, or more rules of practical prudence, can be collected, than he alone has given to his country.

Nor was his attention confined to the actions of men; he was an exact surveyor of the inanimate world; his descriptions have always some peculiarities, gathered by contemplating things as they really exist. It may be observed, that the oldest poets of many nations preserve their reputation, and that the following generations of wit, after a short celebrity, sink into oblivion. The first, whoever they be, must take their sentiments and descriptions immediately from knowledge; the resemblance is therefore just, their descriptions are verified by every eye, and their sentiments acknowledged by every breast. Those whom their fame invites to the same studies, copy partly them, and partly nature, till the books of one age gain such authority, as to stand in the place of nature to another, and imitation, always deviating a little, becomes at last capricious and casual. Shakespeare, whether life or nature be his subject, shews plainly, that he has seen with his own eyes; he gives the image which he receives, not weakened or

---

[3] Thomas Birch, *Life of Robert Boyle*, 1744.
[4] *Troilus and Cressida*, III.iii.224.

distorted by the intervention of any other mind; the ignorant feel his representations to be just, and the learned see that they are compleat.

Perhaps it would not be easy to find any authour, except Homer, who invented so much as Shakespeare, who so much advanced the studies which he cultivated, or effused so much novelty upon his age or country. The form, the characters, the language, and the shows of the English drama are his. *He seems,* says Dennis, *to have been the very original of our English tragical harmony, that is, the harmony of blank verse, diversified often by dissyllable and trissyllable terminations. For the diversity distinguishes it from heroick harmony, and by bringing it nearer to common use makes it more proper to gain attention, and more fit for action and dialogue. Such verse we make when we are writing prose; we make such verse in common conversation.*

I know not whether this praise is rigorously just. The dissyllable termination, which the critick rightly appropriates to the drama, is to be found, though, I think, not in *Gorboduc* which is confessedly before our authour; yet in *Hieronnymo,*[5] of which the date is not certain, but which there is reason to believe at least as old as his earliest plays. This however is certain, that he is the first who taught either tragedy or comedy to please, there being no theatrical piece of any older writer, of which the name is known, except to antiquaries and collectors of books, which are sought because they are scarce, and would not have been scarce, had they been much esteemed.

To him we must ascribe the praise, unless Spenser may divide it with him, of having first discovered to how much smoothness and harmony the English language could be softened. He has speeches, perhaps sometimes scenes, which have all the delicacy of Rowe, without his effeminacy. He endeavours indeed commonly to strike by the force and vigour of his dialogue, but he never executes his purpose better, than when he tries to sooth by softness.

Yet it must be at last confessed, that as we owe every thing to him, he owes something to us; that, if much of his praise is paid

---

[5] *Jeronimo,* anonymous play printed in 1605, or perhaps Kyd's *The Spanish Tragedy,* acted in 1592.

by perception and judgement, much is likewise given by custom and veneration. We fix our eyes upon his graces, and turn them from his deformities, and endure in him what we should in another loath or despise. If we endured without praising, respect for the father of our drama might excuse us; but I have seen, in the book of some modern critick,[6] a collection of anomalies, which shew that he has corrupted language by every mode of depravation, but which his admirer has accumulated as a monument of honour.

He has scenes of undoubted and perpetual excellence, but perhaps not one play, which, if it were now exhibited as the work of a contemporary writer, would be heard to the conclusion. I am indeed far from thinking, that his works were wrought to his own ideas of perfection; when they were such as would satisfy the audience, they satisfied the writer. It is seldom that authours, though more studious of fame than Shakespeare, rise much above the standard of their own age; to add a little to what is best will always be sufficient for present praise, and those who find themselves exalted into fame, are willing to credit their encomiasts, and to spare the labour of contending with themselves.

It does not appear, that Shakespeare thought his works worthy of posterity, that he levied any ideal tribute upon future times, or had any further prospect, than of present popularity and present profit. When his plays had been acted, his hope was at an end; he solicited no addition of honour from the reader. He therefore made no scruple to repeat the same jests in many dialogues, or to entangle different plots by the same knot of perplexity, which may be at least forgiven him, by those who recollect, that of Congreve's four comedies, two are concluded by a marriage in a mask, by a deception, which perhaps never happened, and which, whether likely or not, he did not invent.

So careless was this great poet of future fame, that, though he retired to ease and plenty, while he was yet little *declined into the vale of years*,[7] before he could be disgusted with fatigue, or disabled by infirmity, he made no collection of his works, nor desired to rescue those that had been already published from the deprava-

---

[6] John Upton, *Critical Observations on Shakespeare*, 1746.
[7] *Othello*, III.iii.265.

tions that obscured them, or secure to the rest a better destiny, by giving them to the world in their genuine state.

Of the plays which bear the name of Shakespeare in the late editions, the greater part were not published till about seven years after his death, and the few which appeared in his life are apparently thrust into the world without the care of the authour, and therefore probably without his knowledge.

Of all the publishers, clandestine or professed, their negligence and unskilfulness has by the late revisers been sufficiently shown. The faults of all are indeed numerous and gross, and have not only corrupted many passages perhaps beyond recovery, but have brought others into suspicion, which are only obscured by obsolete phraseology, or by the writer's unskilfulness and affectation. To alter is more easy than to explain, and temerity is a more common quality than diligence. Those who saw that they must employ conjecture to a certain degree, were willing to indulge it a little further. Had the authour published his own works, we should have sat quietly down to disentangle his intricacies, and clear his obscurities; but now we tear what we cannot loose, and eject what we happen not to understand.

The faults are more than could have happened without the concurrence of many causes. The stile of Shakespeare was in itself ungrammatical, perplexed and obscure; his works were transcribed for the players by those who may be supposed to have seldom understood them; they were transmitted by copiers equally unskilful, who still multiplied errours; they were perhaps sometimes mutilated by the actors, for the sake of shortening the speeches; and were at last printed without correction of the press.

In this state they remained, not as Dr. Warburton supposes, because they were unregarded,[8] but because the editor's art was not yet applied to modern languages, and our ancestors were accustomed to so much negligence of English printers, that they could very patiently endure it. At last an edition was undertaken by Rowe; not because a poet was to be published by a poet, for Rowe seems to have thought very little on correction or explanation, but that our authour's works might appear like those of his fraternity, with the appendages of a life and recommendatory

---

[8] Preface to Warburton's edition of Shakespeare, 1747.

preface. Rowe has been clamorously blamed for not performing what he did not undertake, and it is time that justice be done him, by confessing, that though he seems to have had no thought of corruption beyond the printer's errours, yet he has made many emendations, if they were not made before, which his successors have received without acknowledgment, and which, if they had produced them, would have filled pages and pages with censures of the stupidity by which the faults were committed, with displays of the absurdities which they involved, with ostentatious expositions of the new reading, and self congratulations on the happiness of discovering it.

Of Rowe, as of all the editors, I have preserved the preface, and have likewise retained the authour's life, though not written with much elegance or spirit; it relates however what is now to be known, and therefore deserves to pass through all succeeding publications.

The nation had been for many years content enough with Mr. Rowe's performance, when Mr. Pope made them acquainted with the true state of Shakespeare's text, shewed that it was extremely corrupt, and gave reason to hope that there were means of reforming it. He collated the old copies, which none had thought to examine before, and restored many lines to their integrity; but, by a very compendious criticism, he rejected whatever he disliked, and thought more of amputation than of cure.

I know not why he is commended by Dr. Warburton for distinguishing the genuine from the spurious plays. In this choice he exerted no judgement of his own; the plays which he received, were given by Hemings and Condel, the first editors; and those which he rejected, though, according to the licentiousness of the press in those times, they were printed during Shakespeare's life, with his name, had been omitted by his friends, and were never added to his works before the edition of 1664, from which they were copied by the later printers.

This was a work which Pope seems to have thought unworthy of his abilities, being not able to suppress his contempt of *the dull duty of an editor*.[9] He understood but half his undertaking. The duty of a collator is indeed dull, yet, like other tedious tasks, is

---

[9] Preface to Pope's edition of Shakespeare, 1725.

very necessary; but an emendatory critick would ill discharge his duty, without qualities very different from dulness. In perusing a corrupted piece, he must have before him all possibilities of meaning, with all possibilities of expression. Such must be his comprehension of thought, and such his copiousness of language. Out of many readings possible, he must be able to select that which best suits with the state, opinions, and modes of language prevailing in every age, and with his authour's particular cast of thought, and turn of expression. Such must be his knowledge, and such his taste. Conjectural criticism demands more than humanity possesses, and he that exercises it with most praise has very frequent need of indulgence. Let us now be told no more of the dull duty of an editor.

Confidence is the common consequence of success. They whose excellence of any kind has been loudly celebrated, are ready to conclude, that their powers are universal. Pope's edition fell below his own expectations, and he was so much offended, when he was found to have left any thing for others to do, that he past the latter part of his life in a state of hostility with verbal criticism.

I have retained all his notes, that no fragment of so great a writer may be lost; his preface, valuable alike for elegance of composition and justness of remark, and containing a general criticism on his authour, so extensive that little can be added, and so exact, that little can be disputed, every editor has an interest to suppress, but that every reader would demand its insertion.

Pope was succeeded by Theobald,[1] a man of narrow comprehension and small acquisitions, with no native and intrinsick splendour of genius, with little of the artificial light of learning, but zealous for minute accuracy, and not negligent in pursuing it. He collated the ancient copies, and rectified many errors. A man so anxiously scrupulous might have been expected to do more, but what little he did was commonly right.

In his reports of copies and editions he is not to be trusted,

---

[1] Lewis Theobald attacked Pope's edition in 1726 in *Shakespeare Restored*, and published his own edition in 1733. He made the most famous emendation in Shakespearean criticism, "a babbl'd of green fields" for "a table of green fields," Mistress Quickly describing Falstaff dying in *Henry* V. Pope made him the first hero of *The Dunciad*.

without examination. He speaks sometimes indefinitely of copies, when he has only one. In his enumeration of editions, he mentions the two first folios as of high, and the third folio as of middle authority; but the truth is, that the first is equivalent to all others, and that the rest only deviate from it by the printer's negligence. Whoever has any of the folios has all, excepting those diversities which mere reiteration of editions will produce. I collated them all at the beginning, but afterwards used only the first.

Of his notes I have generally retained those which he retained himself in his second edition, except when they were confuted by subsequent annotators, or were too minute to merit preservation. I have sometimes adopted his restoration of a comma, without inserting the panegyrick in which he celebrated himself for his atchievement. The exuberant excrescence of his diction I have often lopped, his triumphant exultations over Pope and Rowe I have sometimes suppressed, and his contemptible ostentation I have frequently concealed; but I have in some places shewn him, as he would have shewn himself, for the reader's diversion, that the inflated emptiness of some notes may justify or excuse the contraction of the rest.

Theobald, thus weak and ignorant, thus mean and faithless, thus petulant and ostentatious, by the good luck of having Pope for his enemy, has escaped, and escaped alone, with reputation, from this undertaking. So willingly does the world support those who solicite favour, against those who command reverence; and so easily is he praised, whom no man can envy.

Our authour fell then into the hands of Sir Thomas Hanmer,[2] the Oxford editor, a man, in my opinion, eminently qualified by nature for such studies. He had, what is the first requisite to emendatory criticism, that intuition by which the poet's intention is immediately discovered, and that dexterity of intellect which despatches its work by the easiest means. He had undoubtedly read much; his acquaintance with customs, opinions, and traditions, seems to have been large; and he is often learned without shew. He seldom passes what he does not understand, without an attempt to find or to make a meaning, and sometimes hastily makes what a little more attention would have found. He is

---

[2] Sir Thomas Hanmer's edition was published in 1744–43 [sic]. He was Speaker of the House of Commons.

solicitous to reduce to grammar, what he could not be sure that his authour intended to be grammatical. Shakespeare regarded more the series of ideas, than of words; and his language, not being designed for the reader's desk, was all that he desired it to be, if it conveyed his meaning to the audience.

Hanmer's care of the metre has been too violently censured. He found the measures reformed in so many passages, by the silent labours of some editors, with the silent acquiescence of the rest, that he thought himself allowed to extend a little further the license, which had already been carried so far without reprehension; and of his corrections in general, it must be confessed, that they are often just, and made commonly with the least possible violation of the text.

But, by inserting his emendations, whether invented or borrowed, into the page, without any notice of varying copies, he has appropriated the labour of his predecessors, and made his own edition of little authority. His confidence indeed, both in himself and others, was too great; he supposes all to be right that was done by Pope and Theobald; he seems not to suspect a critick of fallibility, and it was but reasonable that he should claim what he so liberally granted.

As he never writes without careful enquiry and diligent consideration, I have received all his notes, and believe that every reader will wish for more.

Of the last editor it is more difficult to speak.[3] Respect is due to high place, tenderness to living reputation, and veneration to genius and learning; but he cannot be justly offended at that liberty of which he has himself so frequently given an example, nor very solicitous what is thought of notes, which he ought never to have considered as part of his serious employments, and which, I suppose, since the ardour of composition is remitted, he no longer numbers among his happy effusions.

The original and predominant errour of his commentary, is acquiescence in his first thoughts; that precipitation which is produced by consciousness of quick discernment; and that confidence

---

[3] It was difficult for Johnson to speak of Bishop Warburton's edition partly from the dilemma that Warburton had praised Johnson's first writings on Shakespeare, and that, at the same time, Johnson disapproved of much of Warburton's work.

which presumes to do, by surveying the surface, what labour only can perform, by penetrating the bottom. His notes exhibit sometimes perverse interpretations, and sometimes improbable conjectures; he at one time gives the authour more profundity of meaning, than the sentence admits, and at another discovers absurdities, where the sense is plain to every other reader. But his emendations are likewise often happy and just; and his interpretation of obscure passages learned and sagacious.

Of his notes, I have commonly rejected those, against which the general voice of the publick has exclaimed, or which their own incongruity immediately condemns, and which, I suppose, the authour himself would desire to be forgotten. Of the rest, to part I have given the highest approbation, by inserting the offered reading in the text; part I have left to the judgment of the reader, as doubtful, though specious; and part I have censured without reserve, but I am sure without bitterness of malice, and, I hope, without wantonness of insult.

It is no pleasure to me, in revising my volumes, to observe how much paper is wasted in confutation. Whoever considers the revolutions of learning, and the various questions of greater or less importance, upon which wit and reason have exercised their powers, must lament the unsuccessfulness of enquiry, and the slow advances of truth, when he reflects, that great part of the labour of every writer is only the destruction of those that went before him. The first care of the builder of a new system, is to demolish the fabricks which are standing. The chief desire of him that comments an authour, is to shew how much other commentators have corrupted and obscured him. The opinions prevalent in one age, as truths above the reach of controversy, are confuted and rejected in another, and rise again to reception in remoter times. Thus the human mind is kept in motion without progress. Thus sometimes truth and errour, and sometimes contrarieties of errour, take each others place by reciprocal invasion. The tide of seeming knowledge which is poured over one generation, retires and leaves another naked and barren; the sudden meteors of intelligence which for a while appear to shoot their beams into the regions of obscurity, on a sudden withdraw their lustre, and leave mortals again to grope their way.

These elevations and depressions of renown, and the contradictions to which all improvers of knowledge must for ever be exposed, since they are not escaped by the highest and brightest of mankind, may surely be endured with patience by criticks and annotators, who can rank themselves but as the satellites of their authours. How canst thou beg for life, says Achilles to his captive, when thou knowest that thou art now to suffer only what must another day be suffered by Achilles?[4]

Dr. Warburton had a name sufficient to confer celebrity on those who could exalt themselves into antagonists, and his notes have raised a clamour too loud to be distinct. His chief assailants are the authours of *the Canons of criticism*[5] and of the *Review of Shakespeare's text*;[6] of whom one ridicules his errours with airy petulance, suitable enough to the levity of the controversy; the other attacks them with gloomy malignity, as if he were dragging to justice an assassin or incendiary. The one stings like a fly, sucks a little blood, takes a gay flutter, and returns for more; the other bites like a viper, and would be glad to leave inflammations and gangrene behind him. When I think on one, with his confederates, I remember the danger of Coriolanus, who was afraid that *girls with spits, and boys with stones, should slay him in puny battle;* when the other crosses my imagination, I remember the prodigy in *Macbeth*,

> An eagle tow'ring in his pride of place,
> Was by a mousing owl hawk'd at and kill'd.[7]

Let me however do them justice. One is a wit, and one a scholar. They have both shewn acuteness sufficient in the discovery of faults, and have both advanced some probable interpretations of obscure passages; but when they aspire to conjecture and emendation, it appears how falsely we all estimate our own abilities, and the little which they have been able to perform might have taught them more candour to the endeavours of others.

Before Dr. Warburton's edition, *Critical observations on Shakespeare* had been published by Mr. Upton, a man skilled in languages, and acquainted with books, but who seems to have had

---

[4] *Iliad*, XXI.99.
[5] Thomas Edwards, 1748.
[6] A *Revisal* [sic] *of Shakespeare's Text*, by Benjamin Heath, 1765.
[7] *Macbeth*, II.iv.12: "A falcon tow'ring in her pride of place."

no great vigour of genius or nicety of taste. Many of his explanations are curious and useful, but he likewise, though he professed to oppose the licentious confidence of editors, and adhere to the old copies, is unable to restrain the rage of emendation, though his ardour is ill seconded by his skill. Every cold empirick, when his heart is expanded by a successful experiment, swells into a theorist, and the laborious collator at some unlucky moment frolicks in conjecture.

*Critical, historical and explanatory notes* have been likewise published upon Shakespeare by Dr. Grey, whose diligent perusal of the old English writers has enabled him to make some useful observations. What he undertook he has well enough performed, but as he neither attempts judicial nor emendatory criticism, he employs rather his memory than his sagacity. It were to be wished that all would endeavour to imitate his modesty who have not been able to surpass his knowledge.

I can say with great sincerity of all my predecessors, what I hope will hereafter be said of me, that not one has left Shakespeare without improvement, nor is there one to whom I have not been indebted for assistance and information. Whatever I have taken from them it was my intention to refer to its original authour, and it is certain, that what I have not given to another, I believed when I wrote it to be my own. In some perhaps I have been anticipated; but if I am ever found to encroach upon the remarks of any other commentator, I am willing that the honour, be it more or less, should be transferred to the first claimant, for his right, and his alone, stands above dispute; the second can prove his pretensions only to himself, nor can himself always distinguish invention, with sufficient certainty, from recollection.

They have all been treated by me with candour, which they have not been careful of observing to one another. It is not easy to discover from what cause the acrimony of a scholiast can naturally proceed. The subjects to be discussed by him are of very small importance; they involve neither property nor liberty; nor favour the interest of sect or party. The various readings of copies, and different interpretations of a passage, seem to be questions that might exercise the wit, without engaging the passions. But, whether it be, that *small things make mean men proud,*[8] and

---

[8] *2 Henry VI,* IV.i.106: "Small things make base men proud."

vanity catches small occasions; or that all contrariety of opinion, even in those that can defend it no longer, makes proud men angry; there is often found in commentaries a spontaneous strain of invective and contempt, more eager and venomous than is vented by the most furious controvertist in politicks against those whom he is hired to defame.

Perhaps the lightness of the matter may conduce to the vehemence of the agency; when the truth to be investigated is so near to inexistence, as to escape attention, its bulk is to be enlarged by rage and exclamation: That to which all would be indifferent in its original state, may attract notice when the fate of a name is appended to it. A commentator has indeed great temptations to supply by turbulence what he wants of dignity, to beat his little gold to a spacious surface, to work that to foam which no art or diligence can exalt to spirit.

The notes which I have borrowed or written are either illustrative, by which difficulties are explained; or judicial, by which faults and beauties are remarked; or emendatory, by which depravations are corrected.

The explanations transcribed from others, if I do not subjoin any other interpretation, I suppose commonly to be right, at least I intend by acquiescence to confess, that I have nothing better to propose.

After the labours of all the editors, I found many passages which appeared to me likely to obstruct the greater number of readers, and thought it my duty to facilitate their passage. It is impossible for an expositor not to write too little for some, and too much for others. He can only judge what is necessary by his own experience; and how long soever he may deliberate, will at last explain many lines which the learned will think impossible to be mistaken, and omit many for which the ignorant will want his help. These are censures merely relative, and must be quietly endured. I have endeavoured to be neither superfluously copious, nor scrupulously reserved, and hope that I have made my authour's meaning accessible to many who before were frighted from perusing him, and contributed something to the publick, by diffusing innocent and rational pleasure.

The compleat explanation of an authour not systematick and consequential, but desultory and vagrant, abounding in casual allusions and light hints, is not to be expected from any single scholiast. All personal reflections, when names are suppressed, must be in a few years irrecoverably obliterated; and customs, too minute to attract the notice of law, such as modes of dress, formalities of conversation, rules of visits, disposition of furniture, and practices of ceremony, which naturally find places in familiar dialogue, are so fugitive and unsubstantial, that they are not easily retained or recovered. What can be known, will be collected by chance, from the recesses of obscure and obsolete papers, perused commonly with some other view. Of this knowledge every man has some, and none has much; but when an authour has engaged the publick attention, those who can add any thing to his illustration, communicate their discoveries, and time produces what had eluded diligence.

To time I have been obliged to resign many passages, which, though I did not understand them, will perhaps hereafter be explained, having, I hope, illustrated some, which others have neglected or mistaken, sometimes by short remarks, or marginal directions, such as every editor has added at his will, and often by comments more laborious than the matter will seem to deserve; but that which is most difficult is not always most important, and to an editor nothing is a trifle by which his authour is obscured.

The poetical beauties or defects I have not been very diligent to observe. Some plays have more, and some fewer judicial observations, not in proportion to their difference of merit, but because I gave this part of my design to chance and to caprice. The reader, I believe, is seldom pleased to find his opinion anticipated; it is natural to delight more in what we find or make, than in what we receive. Judgement, like other faculties, is improved by practice, and its advancement is hindered by submission to dictatorial decisions, as the memory grows torpid by the use of a table book. Some initiation is however necessary; of all skill, part is infused by precept, and part is obtained by habit; I have therefore shewn so much as may enable the candidate of criticism to discover the rest.

To the end of most plays, I have added short strictures, containing a general censure of faults, or praise of excellence; in which I know not how much I have concurred with the current opinion; but I have not, by any affectation of singularity, deviated from it. Nothing is minutely and particularly examined, and therefore it is to be supposed, that in the plays which are condemned there is much to be praised, and in these which are praised much to be condemned.

The part of criticism in which the whole succession of editors has laboured with the greatest diligence, which has occasioned the most arrogant ostentation, and excited the keenest acrimony, is the emendation of corrupted passages, to which the publick attention having been first drawn by the violence of the contention between Pope and Theobald, has been continued by the persecution, which, with a kind of conspiracy, has been since raised against all the publishers of Shakespeare.

That many passages have passed in a state of depravation through all the editions is indubitably certain; of these the restoration is only to be attempted by collation of copies or sagacity of conjecture. The collator's province is safe and easy, the conjecturer's perilous and difficult. Yet as the greater part of the plays are extant only in one copy, the peril must not be avoided, nor the difficulty refused.

Of the readings which this emulation of amendment has hitherto produced, some from the labours of every publisher I have advanced into the text; those are to be considered as in my opinion sufficiently supported; some I have rejected without mention, as evidently erroneous; some I have left in the notes without censure or approbation, as resting in equipoise between objection and defence; and some, which seemed specious but not right, I have inserted with a subsequent animadversion.

Having classed the observations of others, I was at last to try what I could substitute for their mistakes, and how I could supply their omissions. I collated such copies as I could procure, and wished for more, but have not found the collectors of these rarities very communicative. Of the editions which chance or kindness put into my hands I have given an enumeration, that I may not be blamed for neglecting what I had not the power to do.

By examining the old copies, I soon found that the later publishers, with all their boasts of diligence, suffered many passages to stand unauthorised, and contented themselves with Rowe's regulation of the text, even where they knew it to be arbitrary, and with a little consideration might have found it to be wrong.

Some of these alterations are only the ejection of a word for one that appeared to him more elegant or more intelligible. These corruptions I have often silently rectified; for the history of our language, and the true force of our words, can only be preserved, by keeping the text of authours free from adulteration. Others, and those very frequent, smoothed the cadence, or regulated the measure; on these I have not exercised the same rigour; if only a word was transposed, or a particle inserted or omitted, I have sometimes suffered the line to stand; for the inconstancy of the copies is such, as that some liberties may be easily permitted. But this practice I have not suffered to proceed far, having restored the primitive diction wherever it could for any reason be preferred.

The emendations, which comparison of copies supplied, I have inserted in the text; sometimes where the improvement was slight, without notice, and sometimes with an account of the reasons of the change.

Conjecture, though it be sometimes unavoidable, I have not wantonly nor licentiously indulged. It has been my settled principle, that the reading of the ancient books is probably true, and therefore is not to be disturbed for the sake of elegance, perspicuity, or mere improvement of the sense. For though much credit is not due to the fidelity, nor any to the judgement of the first publishers, yet they who had the copy before their eyes were more likely to read it right, than we who read it only by imagination. But it is evident that they have often made strange mistakes by ignorance or negligence, and that therefore something may be properly attempted by criticism, keeping the middle way between presumption and timidity.

Such criticism I have attempted to practise, and where any passage appeared inextricably perplexed, have endeavoured to discover how it may be recalled to sense, with least violence. But my first labour is, always to turn the old text on every side, and try if there be any interstice, through which light can find its way; nor would Huetius[9] himself condemn me, as refusing the trouble of research, for the ambition of alteration. In this modest industry I have not been unsuccessful. I have rescued many lines from the

[9] Pierre Huet (d. 1721), French scholar.

violations of temerity, and secured many scenes from the inroads of correction. I have adopted the Roman sentiment, that it is more honourable to save a citizen, than to kill an enemy, and have been more careful to protect than to attack.

I have preserved the common distribution of the plays into acts, though I believe it to be in almost all the plays void of authority. Some of those which are divided in the later editions have no division in the first folio, and some that are divided in the folio have no division in the preceding copies. The settled mode of the theatre requires four intervals in the play, but few, if any, of our authour's compositions can be properly distributed in that manner. An act is so much of the drama as passes without intervention of time or change of place. A pause makes a new act. In every real, and therefore in every imitative action, the intervals may be more or fewer, the restriction of five acts being accidental and arbitrary. This Shakespeare knew, and this he practised; his plays were written, and at first printed in one unbroken continuity, and ought now to be exhibited with short pauses, interposed as often as the scene is changed, or any considerable time is required to pass. This method would at once quell a thousand absurdities.

In restoring the authour's works to their integrity, I have considered the punctuation as wholly in my power; for what could be their care of colons and commas, who corrupted words and sentences. Whatever could be done by adjusting points is therefore silently performed, in some plays with much diligence, in others with less; it is hard to keep a busy eye steadily fixed upon evanescent atoms, or a discursive mind upon evanescent truth.

The same liberty has been taken with a few particles, or other words of slight effect. I have sometimes inserted or omitted them without notice. I have done that sometimes, which the other editors have done always, and which indeed the state of the text may sufficiently justify.

The greater part of readers, instead of blaming us for passing trifles, will wonder that on mere trifles so much labour is expended, with such importance of debate, and such solemnity of diction. To these I answer with confidence, that they are judging of an art which they do not understand; yet cannot much reproach them with their ignorance, nor promise that they would become in general, by learning criticism, more useful, happier or wiser.

As I practised conjecture more, I learned to trust it less; and after I had printed a few plays, resolved to insert none of my own readings in the text. Upon this caution I now congratulate myself, for every day encreases my doubt of my emendations.

Since I have confined my imagination to the margin, it must not be considered as very reprehensible, if I have suffered it to play some freaks in its own dominion. There is no danger in conjecture, if it be proposed as conjecture; and while the text remains uninjured, those changes may be safely offered, which are not considered even by him that offers them as necessary or safe.

If my readings are of little value, they have not been ostentatiously displayed or importunately obtruded. I could have written longer notes, for the art of writing notes is not of difficult attainment. The work is performed, first by railing at the stupidity, negligence, ignorance, and asinine tastelessness of the former editors, and shewing, from all that goes before and all that follows, the inelegance and absurdity of the old reading; then by proposing something, which to superficial readers would seem specious, but which the editor rejects with indignation; then by producing the true reading, with a long paraphrase, and concluding with loud acclamations on the discovery, and a sober wish for the advancement and prosperity of genuine criticism.

All this may be done, and perhaps done sometimes without impropriety. But I have always suspected that the reading is right, which requires many words to prove it wrong; and the emendation wrong, that cannot without so much labour appear to be right. The justness of a happy restoration strikes at once, and the moral precept may be well applied to criticism, *quod dubitas ne feceris.*[1]

To dread the shore which he sees spread with wrecks, is natural to the sailor. I had before my eye, so many critical adventures ended in miscarriage, that caution was forced upon me. I encountered in every page Wit struggling with its own sophistry, and Learning confused by the multiplicity of its views. I was forced to censure those whom I admired, and could not but reflect, while I was dispossessing their emendations, how soon the same fate might happen to my own, and how many of the readings

---

[1] "When in doubt, do nothing."

which I have corrected may be by some other editor defended
and established.

> Criticks, I saw, that other's names efface,
> And fix their own, with labour, in the place;
> Their own, like others, soon their place resign'd,
> Or disappear'd, and left the first behind.[2]          POPE.

That a conjectural critick should often be mistaken, cannot be
wonderful, either to others or himself, if it be considered, that in
his art there is no system, no principal and axiomatical truth that
regulates subordinate positions. His chance of errour is renewed
at every attempt; an oblique view of the passage, a slight misapprehension of a phrase, a casual inattention to the parts connected,
is sufficient to make him not only fail, but fail ridiculously; and
when he succeeds best, he produces perhaps but one reading of
many probable, and he that suggests another will always be able
to dispute his claims.

It is an unhappy state, in which danger is hid under pleasure.
The allurements of emendation are scarcely resistible. Conjecture
has all the joy and all the pride of invention, and he that has once
started a happy change, is too much delighted to consider what
objections may rise against it.

Yet conjectural criticism has been of great use in the learned
world; nor is it my intention to depreciate a study, that has
exercised so many mighty minds, from the revival of learning to
our own age, from the Bishop of Aleria to English Bentley.[3] The
criticks on ancient authours have, in the exercise of their sagacity,
many assistances, which the editor of Shakespeare is condemned
to want. They are employed upon grammatical and settled languages, whose construction contributes so much to perspicuity,
that Homer has fewer passages unintelligible than Chaucer. The
words have not only a known regimen, but invariable quantities,
which direct and confine the choice. There are commonly more
manuscripts than one; and they do not often conspire in the same
mistakes. Yet Scaliger could confess to Salmasius how little satisfaction his emendations gave him. *Illudunt nobis conjecturae
nostrae, quarum nos pudet, posteaquam in meliores codices in-*

---

[2] *Temple of Fame*, ll. 37–40, slightly misquoted.
[3] Joannes Andreas (d. 1480), Bishop of Aleria, a classical scholar, as was
Richard Bentley (d. 1742).

*cidimus.*[4] And Lipsius[5] could complain, that criticks were making faults, by trying to remove them, *Ut olim vitiis, ita nunc remediis laboratur.* And indeed, where mere conjecture is to be used, the emendations of Scaliger and Lipsius, notwithstanding their wonderful sagacity and erudition, are often vague and disputable, like mine or Theobald's.

Perhaps I may not be more censured for doing wrong, than for doing little; for raising in the publick expectations, which at last I have not answered. The expectation of ignorance is indefinite, and that of knowledge is often tyrannical. It is hard to satisfy those who know not what to demand, or those who demand by design what they think impossible to be done. I have indeed disappointed no opinion more than my own; yet I have endeavoured to perform my task with no slight solicitude. Not a single passage in the whole work has appeared to me corrupt, which I have not attempted to restore; or obscure, which I have not endeavoured to illustrate. In many I have failed like others; and from many, after all my efforts, I have retreated, and confessed the repulse. I have not passed over, with affected superiority, what is equally difficult to the reader and to myself, but where I could not instruct him, have owned my ignorance. I might easily have accumulated a mass of seeming learning upon easy scenes; but it ought not to be imputed to negligence, that, where nothing was necessary, nothing has been done, or that, where others have said enough, I have said no more.

Notes are often necessary, but they are necessary evils. Let him, that is yet unacquainted with the powers of Shakespeare, and who desires to feel the highest pleasure that the drama can give, read every play from the first scene to the last, with utter negligence of all his commentators. When his fancy is once on the wing, let it not stoop at correction or explanation. When his attention is strongly engaged, let it disdain alike to turn aside to the name of Theobald and of Pope. Let him read on through brightness and obscurity, through integrity and corruption; let him preserve his comprehension of the dialogue and his interest

---

[4] J.J. Scaliger (d. 1609), eminent classical editor. Salmasius (d. 1653), French scholar: "Our conjectures make us ridiculous and put us to shame, when later we come upon better manuscripts."

[5] Lipsius (d. 1606), Flemish editor of Tacitus: "Once we toiled over faults, now with corrections."

in the fable. And when the pleasures of novelty have ceased, let him attempt exactness; and read the commentators.

Particular passages are cleared by notes, but the general effect of the work is weakened. The mind is refrigerated by interruption; the thoughts are diverted from the principal subject; the reader is weary, he suspects not why; and at last throws away the book, which he has too diligently studied.

Parts are not to be examined till the whole has been surveyed; there is a kind of intellectual remoteness necessary for the comprehension of any great work in its full design and its true proportions; a close approach shews the smaller niceties, but the beauty of the whole is discerned no longer.

It is not very grateful to consider how little the succession of editors has added to this authour's power of pleasing. He was read, admired, studied, and imitated, while he was yet deformed with all the improprieties which ignorance and neglect could accumulate upon him; while the reading was yet not rectified, nor his allusions understood; yet then did Dryden pronounce "that Shakespeare was the man, who, of all modern and perhaps ancient poets, had the largest and most comprehensive soul. All the images of nature were still present to him, and he drew them not laboriously, but luckily: When he describes any thing, you more than see it, you feel it too. Those who accuse him to have wanted learning, give him the greater commendation: he was naturally learned: he needed not the spectacles of books to read nature; he looked inwards, and found her there. I cannot say he is every where alike; were he so, I should do him injury to compare him with the greatest of mankind. He is many times flat and insipid; his comick wit degenerating into clenches, his serious swelling into bombast. But he is always great, when some great occasion is presented to him: No man can say, he ever had a fit subject for his wit, and did not then raise himself as high above the rest of poets,

*Quantum lenta solent inter viburna cupressi.*"[6]

It is to be lamented, that such a writer should want a commentary; that his language should become obsolete, or his senti-

---

[6] Dryden, *Essay of Dramatic Poesy*, quoting Virgil, *Eclogue* I.25: "As cypresses rise above the hedgerow thorn."

ments obscure. But it is vain to carry wishes beyond the condition of human things; that which must happen to all, has happened to Shakespeare, by accident and time; and more than has been suffered by any other writer since the use of types, has been suffered by him through his own negligence of fame, or perhaps by that superiority of mind, which despised its own performances, when it compared them with its powers, and judged those works unworthy to be preserved, which the criticks of following ages were to contend for the fame of restoring and explaining.

Among these candidates of inferiour fame, I am now to stand the judgment of the publick; and wish that I could confidently produce my commentary as equal to the encouragement which I have had the honour of receiving. Every work of this kind is by its nature deficient, and I should feel little solicitude about the sentence, were it to be pronounced only by the skilful and the learned.

*Johnson began his* Life of Milton *in January 1779, finished it in six weeks, and published it in the second volume of his* Prefaces, Biographical and Critical, to the Works of the English Poets *in the spring of 1779. These volumes were not available apart from the whole set of sixty-eight volumes of prefaces and poems, but the lives were at once pirated in Dublin, and in 1781 they were revised and collected as* Lives of the English Poets. *The* Lives *represent Johnson's mature critical judgment, but, infused as usual with strong personal opinion, they were at once attacked. Reprinted from the first edition.*

# Life of Milton

The Life of Milton has been already written in so many forms, with such minute enquiry, that I might perhaps more properly have contented myself with the addition of a few notes to Mr. Fenton's elegant Abridgement,[1] but that a new narrative was thought necessary to the uniformity of this edition.

John Milton was by birth a gentleman, descended from the proprietors of Milton near Thame in Oxfordshire, one of whom forfeited his estate in the times of York and Lancaster. Which side he took I know not: his descendant inherited no veneration for the White Rose.

His grandfather John was keeper of the forest of Shotover, a zealous papist, who disinherited his son, because he had forsaken the religion of his ancestors.

His father, John, who was the son disinherited, had recourse for his support to the profession of a scrivener. He was a man eminent for his skill in musick, many of his compositions being still to be found; and his reputation in his profession was such, that he grew rich, and retired to an estate. He had probably more

---

[1] Elijah Fenton's "Life of Milton" was prefixed to his edition of *Paradise Lost*, 1725. Here and in several of the following notes we are indebted to G.B. Hill's edition of the *Lives of the Poets*, 3 v., Oxford, 1905.

than common literature, as his son addresses him in one of his most elaborate Latin poems. He married a gentlewoman of the name of Caston, a Welsh family, by whom he had two sons, John the poet, and Christopher who studied the law, and adhered, as the law taught him, to the King's party, for which he was awhile persecuted, but having, by his brother's interest, obtained permission to live in quiet, he supported himself by chamber-practice, till, soon after the accession of King James, he was knighted and made a judge; but, his constitution being too weak for business, he retired before any disreputable compliances became necessary.

He had likewise a daughter Anne, whom he married with a considerable fortune to Edward Philips, who came from Shrewsbury, and rose in the Crown-office to be secondary: by him she had two sons, John and Edward, who were educated by the poet, and from whom is derived the only authentick account of his domestick manners.

John, the poet, was born in his father's house, at the Spread-Eagle in Bread-street, Dec. 9, 1608, between six and seven in the morning. His father appears to have been very solicitous about his education; for he was instructed at first by private tuition under the care of Thomas Young, who was afterwards chaplain to the English merchants at Hamburgh; and of whom we have reason to think well, since his scholar considered him as worthy of an epistolary elegy.

He was then sent to St. Paul's School, under the care of Mr. Gill; and removed, in the beginning of his sixteenth year, to Christ's College in Cambridge, where he entered a sizer, Feb. 12, 1624.

He was at this time eminently skilled in the Latin tongue; and he himself, by annexing the dates to his first compositions, a boast of which the learned Politian had given him an example, seems to commend the earliness of his own proficiency to the notice of posterity. But the products of his vernal fertility have been surpassed by many, and particularly by his contemporary Cowley. Of the powers of the mind it is difficult to form an estimate: many have excelled Milton in their first essays, who never rose to works like *Paradise Lost*.

At fifteen, a date which he uses till he is sixteen, he translated or versified two Psalms, 114 and 136, which he thought worthy of the publick eye; but they raise no great expectations: they would in any numerous school have obtained praise, but not excited wonder.

Many of his elegies appear to have been written in his eighteenth year, by which it appears that he had then read the Roman authors with very nice discernment. I once heard Mr. Hampton, the translator of Polybius, remark what I think is true, that Milton was the first Englishman who, after the revival of letters, wrote Latin verses with classick elegance. If any exceptions can be made, they are very few: Haddon and Ascham,[2] the pride of Elizabeth's reign, however they may have succeeded in prose, no sooner attempt verses than they provoke derision. If we produced any thing worthy of notice before the elegies of Milton, it was perhaps Alabaster's *Roxana*.[3]

Of the exercises which the rules of the University required, some were published by him in his maturer years. They had been undoubtedly applauded; for they were such as few can perform: yet there is reason to suspect that he was regarded in his college with no great fondness. That he obtained no fellowship is certain; but the unkindness with which he was treated was not merely negative. I am ashamed to relate what I fear is true, that Milton was the last student in either university that suffered the publick indignity of corporal correction.

It was, in the violence of controversial hostility, objected to him, that he was expelled: this he steadily denies, and it was apparently not true; but it seems plain from his own verses to Diodati,[4] that he had incurred *rustication;* a temporary dismission into the country, with perhaps the loss of a term:

> *Jam nec arundiferum mihi cura revisere Camum,*
> *Nec dudum vetiti me laris angit amor;*
> *Nec duri libet usque minas perferre magistri,*
> *Caeteraque ingenio non subeunda meo.*

I cannot find any meaning but this, which even kindness and reverence can give to the term, *vetiti laris,* "a habitation from which he is excluded;" or how *exile* can be otherwise interpreted.

---

[2] Haddon and Ascham. See Preface to *Shakespeare*, p. 333, n. 2.

[3] William Alabaster (d. 1640) published *Roxana* in 1632.

[4] The lines to Milton's friend Charles Diodati were translated by Cowper: "Nor zeal nor duty now my steps impel/ To ready Cam, and my forbidden cell./ 'Tis time that I a pedant's threats disdain,/ And fly from wrongs my soul will ne'r sustain."

He declares yet more, that he is weary of enduring *the threats of a rigorous master, and something else, which a temper like his cannot undergo.* What was more than threat was evidently punishment. This poem, which mentions his *exile,* proves likewise that it was not perpetual; for it concludes with a resolution of returning some time to Cambridge.

He took both the usual degrees; that of Batchelor in 1628, and that of Master in 1632; but he left the University with no kindness for its institution, alienated either by the injudicious severity of his governors, or his own captious perverseness. The cause cannot now be known, but the effect appears in his writings. His scheme of education, inscribed to Hartlib,[5] supersedes all academical instruction, being intended to comprise the whole time which men usually spend in literature, from their entrance upon grammar, *till they proceed, as it is called, masters of arts.* And in his Discourse *on the likeliest Way to remove Hirelings out of the Church,* he ingeniously[6] proposes, that *the profits of the lands forfeited by the act for superstitious uses, should be applied to such academies all over the land, where languages and arts may be taught together; so that youth may be at once brought up to a competency of learning and an honest trade, by which means such of them as had the gift, being enabled to support themselves (without tithes) by the latter, may, by the help of the former, become worthy preachers.*

One of his objections to academical education, as it was then conducted, is, that men designed for orders in the Church were permitted to act plays, *writhing and unboning their clergy limbs to all the antick and dishonest gestures of Trincalos, buffoons and bawds, prostituting the shame of that ministry which they had, or were near having, to the eyes of courtiers and court-ladies, their grooms and mademoiselles.*

This is sufficiently peevish in a man, who, when he mentions his exile from the college, relates, with great luxuriance, the compensation which the pleasures of the theatre afford him. Plays were therefore only criminal when they were acted by academicks.

He went to the university with a design of entering into the

---

[5] Samuel Hartlib (d. 1670), author of works on education.
[6] *ingeniously: ingenuously* 1783

Church, but in time altered his mind; for he declared, that who-ever became a clergyman must "subscribe slave, and take an oath withal, which, unless he took with a conscience that could retch, he must straight perjure himself. He thought it better to prefer a blameless silence before the office of speaking, bought and begun with servitude and forswearing."

These expressions are, I find, applied to the subscription of the Articles; but it seems more probable that they relate to canonical obedience. I know not any of the Articles which seem to thwart his opinions: but the thoughts of obedience, whether canonical or civil, raised his indignation.

His unwillingness to engage in the ministry, perhaps not yet advanced to a settled resolution of declining it, appears in a letter to one of his friends, who had reproved his suspended and dila-tory life, which he seems to have imputed to an insatiable curi-osity, and fantastick luxury of various knowledge. To this he writes a cool and plausible answer, in which he endeavours to persuade him that the delay proceeds not from the delights of desultory study, but from the desire of obtaining more fitness for his task; and that he goes on, *not taking thought of being late, so it give advantage to be more fit.*

When he left the university, he returned to his father, then resid-ing at Horton in Buckinghamshire, with whom he lived five years; in which time he is said to have read all the Greek and Latin writers. With what limitations this universality is to be under-stood, who shall inform us?

It might be supposed that he who read so much should have done nothing else; but Milton found time to write the masque of *Comus*, which was presented at Ludlow, then the residence of the Lord President of Wales, in 1634; and had the honour of being acted by the Earl of Bridgewater's sons and daughter. The fiction is derived from Homer's Circe; but we never can refuse to any modern the liberty of borrowing from Homer:

> ——*a quo ceu fonte perenni*
> *Vatum Pieriis ora rigantur aquis.*[7]

---

[7] Ovid, *Amores*, III.ix.25: "from whom as from fount perennial the lips of bards are bedewed with Pierean waters." (Trans. Showerman. Loeb.)

His next production was *Lycidas,* an elegy, written in 1637, on the death of Mr. King, the son of Sir John King, Secretary for Ireland in the time of Elizabeth, James, and Charles. King was much a favourite at Cambridge, and many of the wits joined to do honour to his memory. Milton's acquaintance with the Italian writers may be discovered by a mixture of longer and shorter verses, according to the rules of Tuscan poetry, and his malignity to the Church by some lines which are interpreted as threatening its extermination.

He is supposed about this time to have written his *Arcades;* for while he lived at Horton he used sometimes to steal from his studies a few days, which he spent at Harefield, the house of the Countess Dowager of Derby, where the *Arcades* made part of a dramatick entertainment.

He began now to grow weary of the country; and had some purpose of taking chambers in the Inns of Court, when the death of his mother set him at liberty to travel, for which he obtained his father's consent, and Sir Henry Wotton's[8] directions, with the celebrated precept of prudence, *I pensieri stretti, ed il viso sciolto;* "thoughts close, and looks loose."

In 1638 he left England, and went first to Paris; where, by the favour of Lord Scudamore,[9] he had the opportunity of visiting Grotius,[1] then residing at the French court as ambassador from Christina of Sweden. From Paris he hasted into Italy, of which he had with particular diligence studied the language and literature; and, though he seems to have intended a very quick perambulation of the country, staid two months at Florence; where he found his way into the academies, and produced his compositions with such applause as appears to have exalted him in his own opinion, and confirmed him in the hope, that, "by labour and intense study, which," says he, "I take to be my portion in this life, joined with a strong propensity of nature," he might "leave something so written to after-times, as they should not willingly let it die."

It appears, in all his writings, that he had the usual concomitant of great abilities, a lofty and steady confidence in himself,

---

[8] Sir Henry Wotton (d. 1639), former Ambassador to Venice.

[9] Scudamore, the Ambassador to France.

[1] Hugo Grotius (d. 1645), author of the first great treatise on international law, *De Jure Belli et Pacis.*

perhaps not without some contempt of others; for scarcely any man ever wrote so much and praised so few. Of his praise he was very frugal; as he set its value high, and considered his mention of a name as a security against the waste of time, and a certain preservative from oblivion.

At Florence he could not indeed complain that his merit wanted distinction. Carlo Dati presented him with an encomiastick inscription, in the tumid lapidary stile; and Francini wrote him an ode,[2] of which the first stanza is only empty noise; the rest are perhaps too diffuse on common topicks; but the last is natural and beautiful.

From Florence he went to Sienna, and from Sienna to Rome, where he was again received with kindness by the learned and the great. Holstenius, the keeper of the Vatican Library, who had resided three years at Oxford, introduced him to Cardinal Barberini, and he, at a musical entertainment, waited for him at the door, and led him by the hand into the assembly. Here Selvaggi praised him in a distich, and Salsilli in a tetrastick; neither of them of much value. The Italians were gainers by this literary commerce; for the encomiums with which Milton repaid Salsilli, though not secure against a stern grammarian, turn the balance indisputably in Milton's favour.

Of these Italian testimonies, poor as they are, he was proud enough to publish them before his poems; though he says, he cannot be suspected but to have known that they were said *non tam de se, quam supra se.*[3]

At Rome, as at Florence, he staid only two months; a time indeed sufficient, if he desired only to ramble with an explainer of its antiquities, or to view palaces and count pictures; but certainly too short for the contemplation of learning, policy, or manners.

From Rome he passed on to Naples, in company of a hermit; a companion from whom little could be expected, yet to him Milton owed his introduction to Manso Marquis of Villa, who

---

[2] The Latin encomium by Dati and the Italian ode by Francini immediately precede the Latin section of Milton's *Poems*, 1645, as do the Latin verses by Selvaggi and Salsilli mentioned in the next paragraph.

[3] "Not so much about him, as over him." From Milton's preface to his Latin poems.

had been before the patron of Tasso. Manso was enough delighted with his accomplishments to honour him with a sorry distich,[4] in which he commends him for every thing but his religion; and Milton, in return, addressed him in a Latin poem, which must have raised an high opinion of English elegance and literature.

His purpose was now to have visited Sicily and Greece; but, hearing of the differences between the King and Parliament, he thought it proper to hasten home, rather than pass his life in foreign amusements while his countrymen were contending for their rights. He therefore came back to Rome, tho' the merchants informed him of plots laid against him by the Jesuits, for the liberty of his conversations on religion. He had sense enough to judge that there was no danger, and therefore kept on his way, and acted as before, neither obtruding nor shunning controversy. He had perhaps given some offence by visiting Galileo, then a prisoner in the Inquisition for philosophical heresy; and at Naples he was told by Manso, that, by his declarations on religious questions, he had excluded himself from some distinctions which he should otherwise have paid him. But such conduct, though it did not please, was yet sufficiently safe; and Milton staid two months more at Rome, and went on to Florence without molestation.

From Florence he visited Lucca. He afterwards went to Venice; and, having sent away a collection of musick and other books, travelled to Geneva, which he probably considered as the metropolis of orthodoxy. Here he reposed, as in a congenial element, and became acquainted with John Diodati[5] and Frederick Spanheim, two learned professors of divinity. From Geneva he passed through France; and came home, after an absence of a year and three months.

At his return he heard of the death of his friend Charles Diodati; a man whom it is reasonable to suppose of great merit, since he was thought by Milton worthy of a poem, intituled, *Epitaphium Damonis,* written with the common but childish imitation of pastoral life.

He now hired a lodging at the house of one Russel, a taylor in

---

[4] Manso's Latin distich is the first of the complimentary pieces in the Latin poems.

[5] Giovanni Diodati (d. 1649), Swiss Calvinist, translated the Bible into Italian. He was the uncle of Milton's friend Charles.

St. Bride's Churchyard, and undertook the education of John and Edward Phillips, his sister's sons. Finding his rooms too little, he took a house and garden in Aldersgate-street, which was not then so much out of the world as it is now; and chose his dwelling at the upper end of a passage, that he might avoid the noise of the street. Here he received more boys, to be boarded and instructed.

Let not our veneration for Milton forbid us to look with some degree of merriment on great promises and small performance, on the man who hastens home, because his countrymen are contending for their liberty, and, when he reaches the scene of action, vapours away his patriotism in a private boarding-school. This is the period of his life from which all his biographers seem inclined to shrink. They are unwilling that Milton should be degraded to a school-master; but since it cannot be denied that he taught boys, one finds out that he taught for nothing, and another that his motive was only zeal for the propagation of learning and virtue; and all tell what they do not know to be true, only to excuse an act which no wise man will consider as in itself disgraceful. His father was alive; his allowance was not ample, and he supplied its deficiencies by an honest and useful employment.

It is told, that in the art of education he performed wonders; and a formidable list is given of the authors, Greek and Latin, that were read in Aldersgate-street, by youth between ten and fifteen or sixteen years of age. Those who tell or receive these stories, should consider that nobody can be taught faster than he can learn. The speed of the best horseman must be limited by the power of his horse. Every man, that has ever undertaken to instruct others, can tell what slow advances he has been able to make, and how much patience it requires to recall vagrant inattention, to stimulate sluggish indifference, and to rectify absurd misapprehension.

The purpose of Milton, as it seems, was to teach something more solid than the common literature of schools, by reading those authors that treat of physical subjects; such as the Georgick, and astronomical treatises of the ancients. This was a scheme of improvement which seems to have busied many literary projectors of that age. Cowley, who had more means than Milton of knowing what was wanting to the embellishments of life, formed the same plan of education in his imaginary college.

But the truth is, that the knowledge of external nature, and of the sciences which that knowledge requires or includes, is not the great or the frequent business of the human mind. Whether we provide for action or conversation, whether we wish to be useful or pleasing, the first requisite is the religious and moral knowledge of right and wrong; the next is an acquaintance with the history of mankind, and with those examples which may be said to embody truth, and prove by events the reasonableness of opinions. Prudence and justice are virtues, and excellencies, of all times, and of all places; we are perpetually moralists, but we are geometricians only by chance. Our intercourse with intellectual nature is necessary; our speculations upon matter are voluntary, and at leisure. Physical knowledge is of such rare emergence, that one man may know another half his life without being able to estimate his skill in hydrostaticks or astronomy; but his moral and prudential character immediately appears.

Those authors, therefore, are to be read at schools that supply most axioms of prudence, most principles of moral truth, and most materials for conversation; and these purposes are best served by poets, orators, and historians.

Let me not be censured for this digression as pedantick or paradoxical; for if I have Milton against me, I have Socrates on my side. It was his labour to turn philosophy from the study of nature to speculations upon life, but the innovators whom I oppose are turning off attention from life to nature. They seem to think, that we are placed here to watch the growth of plants, or the motions of the stars. Socrates was rather of opinion, that what we had to learn was, how to do good, and avoid evil.

Ὅττι τοι ἐν μεγάροισι κακόν τ' ἀγαθόν τε τέκυται[6]

Of institutions we may judge by their effects. From this wonder-working academy, I do not know that there ever proceeded any man very eminent for knowledge: its only genuine product, I believe, is a small history of poetry, written in Latin by his nephew, of which perhaps none of my readers has ever heard.[7]

---

[6] *Odyssey*, IV.392: "What good, what ill / Hath in thine house befallen." (Trans. Cowper.)

[7] Edward Phillips' "compendious enumeration of the poets . . . from the time of Dante Aligheri to the present age," was appended to his edition of Buchler's *Thesaurus*, 1669. It contains the first praise of *Paradise Lost* in print.

That in his school, as in every thing else which he undertook, he laboured with great diligence, there is no reason for doubting. One part of his method deserves general imitation. He was careful to instruct his scholars in religion. Every Sunday was spent upon theology; in which he dictated a short system, gathered from the writers that were then fashionable in the Dutch universities.

He set his pupils an example of hard study and spare diet; only now and then he allowed himself to pass a day of festivity and indulgence with some gay gentlemen of Gray's Inn.

He now began to engage in the controversies of the times, and lent his breath to blow the flames of contention. In 1641 he published a treatise of *Reformation* in two books, against the Established Church; being willing to help the Puritans, who were, he says, *inferior to the prelates in learning.*

Hall Bishop of Norwich had published an *Humble Remonstrance*, in defence of Episcopacy; to which, in 1641, six[8] ministers, of whose names the first letters made the celebrated word *Smectymnus*, gave their Answer. Of this Answer a Confutation was attempted by the learned Usher;[9] and to the Confutation Milton published a Reply, intituled, *Of Prelatical Episcopacy, and whether it may be deduced from the Apostolical Times, by virtue of those testimonies which are alleged to that purpose in some late treatises, one whereof goes under the name of James lord bishop of Armagh.*

I have transcribed this title to shew, by his contemptuous mention of Usher, that he had now adopted the puritanical savageness of manners. His next work was, *The Reason of Church Government urged against Prelacy, by Mr. John Milton,* 1642. In this book he discovers, not with ostentatious exultation, but with calm confidence, his high opinion of his own powers; and promises to undertake something, he yet knows not what, that may be of use and honour to his country. "This," says he, "is not to be obtained but by devout prayer to that Eternal Spirit that can enrich with all

---

[8] Five: Stephen Marshall, Edmund Calamy, Thomas Young, Matthew Newcomen, and William Spurstow.

[9] James Usher is principally known for his *Annales Veteris et Novi Testamenti,* 1650–54, in which he worked out a chronology of the Bible; his dates are still often found in the margins of the Authorized Version.

utterance and knowledge, and sends out his Seraphim with the hallowed fire of his altar, to touch and purify the lips of whom he pleases. To this must be added, industrious and select reading, steady observation, and insight into all seemly and generous arts and affairs; till which in some measure be compast, I refuse not to sustain this expectation." From a promise like this, at once fervid, pious, and rational, might be expected the *Paradise Lost*.

He published the same year two more pamphlets, upon the same question. To one of his antagonists, who affirms that he was *vomited out of the university*, he answers, in general terms; "The Fellows of the College wherein I spent some years, at my parting, after I had taken two degrees, as the manner is, signified many times how much better it would content them that I should stay.——As for the common approbation or dislike of that place, as now it is, that I should esteem or disesteem myself the more for that, too simple is the answerer, if he think to obtain with me. Of small practice were the physician who could not judge, by what she and her sister have of long time vomited, that the worser stuff she strongly keeps in her stomach, but the better she is ever kecking at, and is queasy: she vomits now out of sickness; but before it be well with her, she must vomit by strong physick.—— The university, in the time of her better health, and my younger judgement, I never greatly admired, but now much less."

This is surely the language of a man who thinks that he has been injured. He proceeds to describe the course of his conduct, and the train of his thoughts; and, because he has been suspected of incontinence, gives an account of his own purity: "That if I be justly charged," says he, "with this crime, it may come upon me with tenfold shame."

The stile of his piece is rough, and such perhaps was that of his antagonist. This roughness he justifies, by great examples, in a long digression. Sometimes he tries to be humorous: "Lest I should take him for some chaplain in hand, some squire of the body to his prelate, one who serves not at the altar, only but at the Court-cupboard, he will bestow on us a pretty model of himself; and sets me out half a dozen ptisical mottos, wherever he had them, hopping short in the measure of convulsion fits; in which labour the agony of his wit having scaped narrowly, instead of well-sized periods, he greets us with a quantity of thumbring posies.——And thus ends this section, or rather dissection, of himself." Such is the controversial merriment of Milton: his gloomy seriousness is yet more offensive. Such is his malignity, *that hell grows darker at his frown.*[1]

His father, after Reading was taken by Essex, came to reside in his house; and his school increased. At Whitsuntide, in his thirty-fifth year, he married Mary, the daughter of Mr. Powel, a justice of the peace in Oxfordshire. He brought her to town with him, and expected all the advantages of a conjugal life. The lady, however, seems not much to have delighted in the pleasures of spare diet and hard study; for, as Philips relates, "having for a month led a philosophical life, after having been used at home to a great house, and much company and joviality, her friends, possibly by her own desire, made earnest suit to have her company the remaining part of the summer; which was granted, upon a promise of her return at Michaelmas."

Milton was too busy to much miss his wife: he pursued his studies; and now and then visited the Lady Margaret Leigh,[2] whom he has mentioned in one of his sonnets. At last Michaelmas arrived; but the lady had no inclination to return to the sullen gloom of her husband's habitation, and therefore very willingly forgot her promise. He sent her a letter, but had no answer; he sent more with the same success. It could be alleged that letters miscarry; he therefore dispatched a messenger, being by this time too angry to go himself. His messenger was sent back with some contempt. The family of the lady were Cavaliers.

In a man whose opinion of his own merit was like Milton's, less provocation than this might have raised violent resentment. Milton soon determined to repudiate her for disobedience; and being one of those who could easily find arguments to justify inclination, published (in 1644) *The Doctrine and Discipline of Divorce;* which was followed by *The Judgement of Martin Bucer concerning Divorce;* and the next year, his *Tetrachordon, Expositions upon the four chief Places of Scripture which treat of Marriage.*

This innovation was opposed, as might be expected, by the clergy; who, then holding their famous assembly at Westminster, procured that the author should be called before the Lords; "but

---

[1] *Paradise Lost,* II.719, paraphrased.
[2] Daughter of the Earl of Marlborough.

that House," says Wood, "whether approving the doctrine, or not favouring his accusers, did soon dismiss him."[3]

There seems not to have been much written against him, nor any thing by any writer of eminence. The antagonist that appeared is stiled by him, *a serving-man turned solicitor.* Howel in his letters mentions the new doctrine with contempt;[4] and it was, I suppose, thought more worthy of derision than of confutation. He complains of this neglect in two sonnets, of which the first is contemptible, and the second not excellent.

From this time it is observed that he became an enemy to the Presbyterians, whom he had favoured before. He that changes his party by his humour, is not more virtuous than he that changes it by his interest; he loves himself rather than truth.

His wife and her relations now found that Milton was not an unresisting sufferer of injuries; and perceiving that he had begun to put his doctrine in practice, by courting a young woman of great accomplishments, the daughter of one Doctor Davis, who was however not ready to comply, they resolved to endeavour a re-union. He went sometimes to the house of one Blackborough, his relation, in the lane of St. Martin's-le-Grand, and at one of his usual visits was surprised to see his wife come from another room, and implore forgiveness on her knees. He resisted her intreaties for a while; "but partly," says Philips, "his own generous nature, more inclinable to reconciliation than to perseverance in anger or revenge, and partly the strong intercession of friends on both sides, soon brought him to an act of oblivion and a firm league of peace." It were injurious to omit, that Milton afterwards received her father and her brothers in his own house, when they were distressed, with other Royalists.

He published about the same time his *Areopagitica, a Speech of Mr. John Milton for the liberty of unlicensed Printing.* The danger of such unbounded liberty, and the danger of bounding it, have produced a problem in the science of government, which human understanding seems hitherto unable to solve. If nothing may be published but what civil authority shall have previously approved, power must always be the standard of truth; if every dreamer of innovations may propagate his projects, there can be

---

[3] Anthony à Wood, in *Fasti Oxonienses.*

[4] James Howell, a Royalist, in *Epistolae Ho-Elianae: Familiar Letters.*

no settlement; if every murmurer at government may diffuse discontent, there can be no peace; and if every sceptick in theology
may teach his follies, there can be no religion. The remedy against
these evils is to punish the authors; for it is yet allowed that every
society may punish, though not prevent, the publication of opinions, which that society shall think pernicious: but this punishment, though it may crush the author, promotes the book; and it
seems not more reasonable to leave the right of printing unrestrained, because writers may be afterwards censured, than it
would be to sleep with doors unbolted, because by our laws we
can hang a thief.

But whatever were his engagements, civil or domestick, poetry
was never long out of his thoughts. About this time (1645) a
collection of his Latin and English poems appeared, in which the
*Allegro* and *Penseroso*, with some others, were first published.

He had taken a larger house in Barbican for the reception of
scholars; but the numerous relations of his wife, to whom he
generously granted refuge for a while, occupied his rooms. In
time, however, they went away; and the "house again," says
Philips, "now looked like a house of the Muses only, though the
accession of scholars was not great. Possibly his having proceeded
so far in the education of youth, may have been the occasion of
his adversaries calling him pedagogue and school-master; whereas
it is well known he never set up for a publick school, to teach all
the young fry of a parish; but only was willing to impart his
learning and knowledge to relations, and the sons of gentlemen
who were his intimate friends; and that neither his writings nor
his way of teaching ever savoured in the least of pedantry."

Thus laboriously does his nephew extenuate what cannot be
denied, and what might be confessed without disgrace. Milton
was not a man who could become mean by a mean employment.
This, however, his warmest friends seem not to have found; they
therefore shift and palliate. He did not sell literature to all comers
at an open shop; he was a chamber-milliner, and measured his
commodities only to his friends.

Philips, evidently impatient of viewing him in this state of
degradation, tells us that it was not long continued; and, to raise
his character again, has a mind to invest him with military splendour: "He is much mistaken," he says, "if there was not about this
time a design of making him an Adjutant-General in Sir William

Waller's army. But the new-modelling of the army proved an obstruction to the design." An event cannot be set at a much greater distance than by having been only *designed, about some time,* if a man *be not much mistaken.* Milton shall be a pedagogue no longer; for, if Philips be not mistaken, somebody at some time designed him for a soldier.

About the time that the army was new-modelled (1645) he removed to a smaller house in Holbourn, which opened backward into Lincoln's-Inn-Fields. He is not known to have published any thing afterwards till the King's death, when, finding his murderers condemned by the Presbyterians, he wrote a treatise to justify it, and *to compose the minds of the people.*

He made some *Remarks on the Articles of Peace between Ormond and the Irish Rebels.* While he contented himself to write, he perhaps did only what his conscience dictated; and if he did not very vigilantly watch the influence of his own passions, and the gradual prevalence of opinions, first willingly admitted and then habitually indulged, if objections, by being overlooked, were forgotten, and desire superinduced conviction, he yet shared only the common weakness of mankind, and might be no less sincere than his opponents. But as faction seldom leaves a man honest, however it might find him, Milton is suspected of having interpolated the book called *Icon Basilike,* which the Council of State, to whom he was now made Latin secretary, employed him to censure, by inserting a prayer taken from Sidney's *Arcadia,* and imputing it to the King; whom he charges, in his *Iconoclastes,* with the use of this prayer as with a heavy crime, in the indecent language with which prosperity had emboldened the advocates for rebellion to insult all that is venerable or great: "Who would have imagined so little fear in him of the true all-seeing Deity—as, immediately before his death, to pop into the hands of the grave bishop that attended him, as a special relique of his saintly exercises, a prayer stolen word for word from the mouth of a heathen woman praying to a heathen god?"

The papers which the King gave to Dr. Juxon on the scaffold the regicides took away, so that they were at least the publishers of this prayer; and Dr. Birch,[5] who examined the question with

---

[5] William Juxon, Bishop of London, chosen by Charles to administer the last rites on the scaffold. Thomas Birch originally favored the notion of a forgery in his edition of Milton, 1738, but later reversed himself.

great care, was inclined to think them the forgers. The use of it
by adaptation was innocent; and they who could so noisily censure it, with a little extension of their malice could contrive what
they wanted to accuse.

King Charles the Second, being now sheltered in Holland, employed Salmasius,[6] professor of polite learning at Leyden, to write
a defence of his father and of monarchy; and, to excite his industry, gave him, as was reported, a hundred Jacobuses. Salmasius
was a man of skill in languages, knowledge of antiquity, and
sagacity of emendatory criticism, almost exceeding all hope of
human attainment; and having, by excessive praises, been confirmed in great confidence of himself, though he probably had
not much considered the principles of society or the rights of
government, undertook the employment without distrust of his
own qualifications; and, as his expedition in writing was wonderful, in 1649 published *Defensio Regis*.

To this Milton was required to write a sufficient answer; which
he performed (1651) in such a manner, that Hobbes declared[7]
himself unable to decide whose language was best, or whose arguments were worst. In my opinion, Milton's periods are smoother,
neater, and more pointed; but he delights himself with teizing
his adversary as much as with confuting him. He makes a foolish
allusion of Salmasius, whose doctrine he considers as servile and
unmanly, to the stream of Salmacis, which whoever entered left
half his virility behind him. Salmasius was a Frenchman, and was
unhappily married to a scold. *Tu es Gallus*, says Milton, *et, ut
aiunt, nimium gallinaceus*.[8] But his supreme pleasure is to tax his
adversary, so renowned for criticism, with vitious Latin. He opens
his book with telling that he has used *persona*, which, according
to Milton, signifies only a *mask*, in a sense not known to the Romans, by applying it as we apply *person*. But as Nemesis is always
on the watch, it is memorable that he has enforced the charge of a
solecism by an expression in itself grossly solecistical, when, for
one of those supposed blunders, he says, *propino te grammatistis
tuis* vapulandum. From *vapulo*, which has a passive sense, *vapu-*

---

[6] Claude de Saumaise (d. 1653); a Jacobus was worth a pound.

[7] In *Behemoth*, 1682.

[8] "You are French [or a cock] and, as they say, too much belonging to
poultry [i.e., hen-pecked]."

*landus* can never be derived. No man forgets his original trade: the rights of nations, and of kings, sink into questions of grammar, if grammarians discuss them.

Milton when he undertook this answer was weak of body, and dim of sight; but his will was forward, and what was wanting of health was supplied by zeal. He was rewarded with a thousand pounds, and his book was much read; for paradox, recommended by spirit and elegance, easily gains attention; and he who told every man that he was equal to his King, could hardly want an audience.

That the performance of Salmasius was not dispersed with equal rapidity, or read with equal eagerness, is very credible. He taught only the stale doctrine of authority, and the unpleasing duty of submission; and he had been so long not only the monarch but the tyrant of literature, that almost all mankind were delighted to find him defied and insulted by a new name, not yet considered as any one's rival. If Christina, as is said, commended the *Defence of the People*, her purpose must be to torment Salmasius, who was then at her court; for neither her civil station nor her natural character could dispose her to favour the doctrine, who was by birth a queen, and by temper despotick.

That Salmasius was, from the appearance of Milton's book, treated with neglect, there is not much proof; but to a man so long accustomed to admiration, a little praise of his antagonist would be sufficiently offensive, and might incline him to leave Sweden.

He prepared a reply, which, left as it was imperfect, was published by his son in the year of the Restauration. In the beginning, being probably most in pain for his Latinity, he endeavours to defend his use of the word *persona;* but, if I remember right, he misses a better authority than any that he has found, that of Juvenal in his fourth satire:

> ——*Quid agas cum dira et foedior omni*
> *Crimine* persona *est?*[9]

As Salmasius reproached Milton with losing his eyes in the quarrel, Milton delighted himself with the belief that he had shortened Salmasius's life, and both perhaps with more malignity

---

[9] "What can you do? this sinister person is more hideous than any crime."

than reason. Salmasius died at the Spa, Sept. 3, 1653; and as controvertists are commonly said to be killed by their last dispute, Milton was flattered with the credit of destroying him.

Cromwel had now dismissed the Parliament by the authority of which he had destroyed monarchy, and commenced monarch himself, under the title of Protector, but with kingly and more than kingly power. That his authority was lawful, never was pretended; he himself founded his right only in necessity: but Milton, having now tasted the honey of publick employment, would not return to hunger and philosophy, but, continuing to exercise his office under a manifest usurpation, betrayed to his power that liberty which he had defended. Nothing can be more just than that rebellion should end in slavery; that he, who had justified the murder of his king, for some acts which to him seemed unlawful, should now sell his services, and his flatteries, to a tyrant, of whom it was evident that he could do nothing lawful.

He had now been blind for some years; but his vigour of intellect was such, that he was not disabled to discharge his office, or continue his controversies. His mind was too eager to be diverted, and too strong to be subdued.

About this time his first wife died in childbed, having left him three daughters. As he probably did not much love her, he did not long continue the appearance of lamenting her; but after a short time married Catherine, the daughter of one Captain Woodcock of Hackney; a woman doubtless educated in opinions like his own. She died within a year, of childbirth, or some distemper that followed it; and her husband has honoured her memory with a poor sonnet.

The first reply to Milton's *Defensio Populi* was published in 1651, called *Apologia pro Rege et Populo Anglicano, contra Johannis Polypragmatici (alias Miltoni) defensionem destructivam Regis et Populi.* Of this the author was not known; but Milton and his nephew Philips, under whose name he published an answer so much corrected by him that it might be called his own, imputed it to Bramhal;[1] and, knowing him no friend to regicides, thought themselves at liberty to treat him as if they had known what they only suspected.

---

[1] John Bramhall (d. 1663), Bishop of Derry.

Next year appeared *Regii Sanguinis clamor ad Coelum*. Of this the author was Peter du Moulin, who was afterwards prebendary of Canterbury; but Morus, or More,[2] a French minister, having the care of its publication, was treated as the writer by Milton, in his *Defensio Secunda*, and overwhelmed by such violence of invective, that he began to shrink under the tempest, and gave his persecutors the means of knowing the true author. Du Moulin was now in great danger; but Milton's pride operated against his malignity, and both he and his friends were more willing that Du Moulin should escape than that he should be convicted of mistake.

In his second Defence he shews that his eloquence is not merely satirical; the rudeness of his invective is equalled by the grossness of his flattery. "Deserimur, Cromuelle,[3] tu solus superes, ad te summa nostrarum rerum rediit, in te solo consistit, insuperabili tuae virtuti cedimus cuncti, nemine vel obloquente, nisi qui aequales inaequalis ipse honores sibi quaerit, aut digniori concessos invidet, aut non intelligit nihil esse in societate hominum magis vel Deo gratum, vel rationi consentaneum, esse in civitate nihil aequius, nihil utilius, quam potiri rerum dignissimum. Eum te agnoscunt omnes, Cromuelle, ea tu civis maximus et gloriosissimus,[4] dux publici consilii, exercituum fortissimorum imperator, pater patriae gessisti. Sic tu spontanea bonorum omnium et animitus missa voce salutaris."

Caesar, when he assumed the perpetual dictatorship, had not more servile or more elegant flattery. A translation may shew its servility; but its elegance is less attainable. Having exposed the unskilfulness or selfishness of the former government, "We were left," says Milton, "to ourselves: the whole national interest fell into your hands, and subsists in your abilities. To your virtue, overpowering and resistless, every man gives way, except some who, without equal qualifications, aspire to equal honours, or who envy the distinctions of merit greater than their own; or who

---

[2] Pierre du Moulin, son of a French Protestant theologian; Alexander More or Moir, son of a Scottish Presbyterian principal of a French College; the son was a professor at Amsterdam.

[3] In Johnson's translation, below, he avoids using Cromwell's name.

[4] "It may be doubted whether *gloriosissimus* be here used with Milton's boasted purity. *Res gloriosa* is an *illustrious thing*; but *vir gloriosus* is commonly a *braggart*, as in *miles gloriosus*." Johnson.

have yet to learn, that in the coalition of human society nothing is more pleasing to God, or more agreeable to reason, than that the highest mind should have the sovereign power. Such, Sir, are you by general confession; such are the things atchieved by you, the greatest and most glorious of our countrymen, the director of our publick counsels, the leader of unconquered armies, the father of your country; for by that title does every good man hail you, with sincere and voluntary praise."

Next year, having defended all that wanted defence, he found leisure to defend himself. He undertook his own vindication against More, whom he declares in his title to be justly called the author of the *Regii Sanguini clamor.* In this there is no want of vehemence nor eloquence, nor does he forget his wonted wit. "Morus es? an Momus? an uterque idem est?"[5] He then remembers that *Morus* is Latin for a mulberry-tree, and hints at the known transformation:

> ——*Poma alba ferebat*
> *Quae post nigra tulit Morus.*

With this piece ended his controversies; and he from this time gave himself up to his private studies and his civil employment.

As secretary to the Protector he is supposed to have written the declaration of the reasons for a war with Spain. His agency was considered as of great importance; for when a treaty with Sweden was artfully suspended, the delay was publickly imputed to Mr. Milton's indisposition; and the Swedish agent was provoked to express his wonder, that only one man in England could write Latin, and that man blind.

Being now forty-seven years old, and seeing himself disencumbered from external interruptions, he seems to have recollected his former purposes, and planned three great works for his future employment. An epick poem, the history of his country, and a dictionary of the Latin tongue.

To collect a dictionary seems a work of all others least practicable in a state of blindness, because it depends upon perpetual

---

[5] "Are you More or Momus? or is one the same as the other?" The following quotation is Ovid, *Metamorphoses*, IV.51, quoted from memory: "A tree which bore white fruit, and now bears black."

and minute inspection and collation. Nor would Milton probably have begun it, after he had lost his eyes; but, having had it always before him, he continued it, says Philips, *almost to his dying-day; but the papers were so discomposed and deficient, that they could not be fitted for the press.* The compilers of the Latin dictionary, printed afterwards at Cambridge, had the use of them in three folios; but what was their fate afterwards is not known.

To compile a history from various authors, when they can only be consulted by other eyes, is not easy, nor possible, but with more skilful and attentive help than can be commonly obtained; and it was probably the difficulty of consulting and comparing that stopped Milton's narrative at the Conquest; a period at which affairs were not yet very intricate, nor authors very numerous.

For the subject of his epick poem, after much deliberation, *long chusing, and beginning late,* he fixed upon *Paradise Lost;* a design so comprehensive, that it could be justified only by success. He had once designed to celebrate King Arthur, as appears from his verses to Mansus; but *Arthur was reserved,* says Fenton, *to another destiny.*

It appears, by some sketches of poetical projects left in manuscript, and to be seen in a library at Cambridge, that he had digested his thoughts on this subject into one of those wild dramas which were anciently called Mysteries; and Philips had seen what he terms part of a tragedy, beginning with the first ten lines of Satan's address to the Sun. These mysteries consist of allegorical persons; such as Justice, Mercy, Faith. Of the tragedy or mystery of *Paradise Lost* there are two plans:

| THE PERSONS | THE PERSONS |
|---|---|
| Michael. | Moses. |
| Chorus of Angels. | Divine Justice, Wisdom, |
| Heavenly Love. | Heavenly Love. |
| Lucifer. | The Evening Star, Hesperus. |
| Adam, Eve, } with the Serpent. | Chorus of Angels. |
| | Lucifer. |
| Conscience. | Adam. |
| Death. | Eve. |
| | Conscience. |

THE PERSONS

Labour,
Sickness,
Discontent, ⎱
Ignorance, ⎰ Mutes
with others, ⎰
Faith.
Hope.
Charity.

THE PERSONS

Labour,
Sickness,
Discontent, ⎫
Ignorance, ⎬ Mutes.
Fear, ⎭
Death,
Faith.
Hope.
Charity.

## PARADISE LOST

### THE PERSONS

Moses, προλογίζει,[6] recounting how he assumed his true body; that it corrupts not, because it is with God in the mount; declares the like of Enoch and Eliah; besides the purity of the place, that certain pure winds, dews and clouds, preserve it from corruption; whence exhorts to the sight of God; tells, they cannot see Adam in the state of innocence, by reason of their sin.

Justice, ⎫
Mercy, ⎬ debating what should become of man, if he fall.
Wisdom, ⎭

Chorus of Angels singing a hymn of the Creation.

### Act II

Heavenly Love.
Evening Star.
Chorus sing the marriage-song, and describe Paradise.

### Act III

Lucifer, contriving Adam's ruin.
Chorus fears for Adam, and relates Lucifer's rebellion and fall.

### Act IV

Adam, ⎫
Eve, ⎬ fallen.
Conscience cites them to God's examination.
Chorus bewails, and tells the good Adam has lost.

---

[6] "In a Prologue."

### Act V

Adam and Eve driven out of Paradise.

— — — — — — presented by an angel with

Labour, Grief, Hatred, Envy, War, Famine, Pestilence, ⎫
  Sickness, Discontent, Ignorance, Fear, Death, ⎬ Mutes.

To whom he gives their names. Likewise Winter, Heat, Tempest, etc.

Faith, ⎫
Hope, ⎬ comfort him, and instruct him.
Charity, ⎭

Chorus briefly concludes.

Such was his first design, which could have produced only an allegory, or mystery. The following sketch seems to have attained more maturity.

### Adam Unparadised:

The angel Gabriel, either descending or entering; shewing, since this globe was created, his frequency as much on earth as in heaven: describes Paradise. Next, the Chorus, shewing the reason of his coming to keep his watch in Paradise, after Lucifer's rebellion, by command from God; and withal expressing his desire to see and know more concerning this excellent new creature, man. The angel Gabriel, as by his name signifying a prince of power, tracing Paradise with a more free office, passes by the station of the Chorus, and, desired by them, relates what he knew of man; as the creation of Eve, with their love and marriage. After this, Lucifer appears, after his overthrow; bemoans himself, seeks revenge on man. The Chorus prepare resistance at his first approach. At last, after discourse of enmity on either side, he departs: whereat the Chorus sings of the battle and victory in heaven, against him and his accomplices: as before, after the first act, was sung a hymn of the Creation. Here again may appear Lucifer, relating and insulting in what he had done to the destruction of man. Man next, and Eve having by this time been seduced by the Serpent, appears confusedly covered with leaves. Conscience, in a shape, accuses him; Justice cites him to the place whither Jehovah called for him. In the mean while, the Chorus entertains the stage, and is informed by some angel the manner of the Fall. Here the

Chorus bewails Adam's fall; Adam then and Eve return; accuse one another; but especially Adam lays the blame to his wife; is stubborn in his offence. Justice appears, reasons with him, convinces him. The Chorus admonisheth Adam, and bids him beware Lucifer's example of impenitence. The angel is sent to banish them out of Paradise; but before causes to pass before his eyes, in shapes, a mask of all the evils of this life and world. He is humbled, relents, despairs: at last appears Mercy, comforts him, promises the Messiah; then calls in Faith, Hope, and Charity; instructs him; he repents, gives God the glory, submits to his penalty. The Chorus briefly concludes. Compare this with the former draught.

These are very imperfect rudiments of *Paradise Lost;* but it is pleasant to see great works in their seminal state, pregnant with latent possibilities of excellence; nor could there be any more delightful entertainment than to trace their gradual growth and expansion, and to observe how they are sometimes suddenly advanced by accidental hints, and sometimes slowly improved by steady meditation.

Invention is almost the only literary labour which blindness cannot obstruct, and therefore he naturally solaced his solitude by the indulgence of his fancy, and the melody of his numbers. He had done what he knew to be necessarily previous to poetical excellence; he had made himself acquainted with *seemly arts and affairs;* his comprehension was extended by various knowledge, and his memory stored with intellectual treasures. He was skilful in many languages, and had by reading and composition attained the full mastery of his own. He would have wanted little help from books, had he retained the power of perusing them.

But while his greater designs were advancing, having now, like many other authors, caught the love of publication, he amused himself, as he could, with little productions. He sent to the press (1658) a manuscript of Raleigh, called the *Cabinet Council;* and next year gratified his malevolence to the clergy, by a *Treatise of Civil Power in Ecclesiastical Cases, and the Means of removing Hirelings out of the Church.*

Oliver was now dead; Richard was constrained to resign: the system of extemporary government, which had been held together only by force, naturally fell into fragments when that force was taken away; and Milton saw himself and his cause in equal danger. But he had still hope of doing something. He wrote letters, which Toland has published,[7] to such men as he thought friends to the new commonwealth; and even in the year of the Restoration he *bated no jot of heart or hope,* but was fantastical enough to think that the nation, agitated as it was, might be settled by a pamphlet, called *A ready and easy Way to establish a Free Commonwealth;* which was, however, enough considered to be both seriously and ludicrously answered.

The obstinate enthusiasm of the commonwealthmen was very remarkable. When the King was apparently returning, Harrington, with a few associates as fanatical as himself, used to meet, with all the gravity of political importance, to settle an equal government by rotation; and Milton, kicking when he could strike no longer, was foolish enough to publish, a few weeks before the Restoration, *Notes* upon a sermon preached by one Griffiths, intituled, *The Fear of God and the King.* To these notes an answer was written by L'Estrange,[8] in a pamphlet petulantly called *No blind Guides.*

But whatever Milton could write, or men of greater activity could do, the King was now evidently approaching with the irresistible approbation of the people. He was therefore no longer secretary, and was consequently obliged to quit the house which he held by his office; and, proportioning his sense of danger to his opinion of the importance of his writings, thought it convenient to seek some shelter, and hid himself for a time in Bartholomew Close by West Smithfield.

I cannot but remark a kind of respect, perhaps unconsciously, paid to this great man by his biographers: every house in which he resided is historically mentioned, as if it were an injury to neglect naming any place that he honoured by his presence.

The King, with lenity of which the world has had perhaps no other example, declined to be the judge or avenger of his own or his father's wrongs; and promised to admit into the Act of Oblivion all, except those whom the Parliament should except;

---

[7] John Toland's *Life of Milton,* 1698.

[8] James Harrington, author of *Oceana;* Matthew Griffith; Roger L'Estrange, a Royalist and noted journalist.

and the Parliament doomed none to capital punishment but the wretches who had immediately co-operated in the murder of the King. Milton was certainly not one of them; he had only justified what they had done.

This justification was indeed sufficiently offensive; and (June 16) an order was issued to seize Milton's *Defence,* and Godwin's *Obstructors of Justice,*[9] another book of the same tendency, and burn them by the common hangman. The attorney-general was ordered to prosecute the authors; but Milton was not seized, nor perhaps very diligently pursued.

Not long after (August 19) the flutter of innumerable bosoms was stilled by an act, which the King, that his mercy might want no recommendation of elegance, rather called an *act of oblivion* than of *grace.* Godwin was named, with nineteen more, as incapacitated for any publick trust; but of Milton there was no exception.

Of this tenderness shewn to Milton, the curiosity of mankind has not forborn to enquire the reason. Burnet thinks he was forgotten;[1] but this is another instance which may confirm Dalrymple's observation, who says, "that whenever Burnet's narrations are examined, he appears to be mistaken."

Forgotten he was not; for his prosecution was ordered; it must be therefore by design that he was included in the general oblivion. He is said to have had friends in the House, such as Marvel, Morrice, and Sir Thomas Clarges;[2] and undoubtedly a man like him must have had influence. A very particular story of his escape is told by Richardson in his memoirs,[3] which he received from Pope, as delivered by Betterton, who might have heard it from Davenant. In the war between the King and Parliament, Dave-

---

[9] John Goodwin's Ὑβριστοδίκαι, 1649; Goodwin also escaped harm and died 1665.

[1] Gilbert Burnet, in his *History of My Own Times,* says "it was thought a strange omission if he was forgot. . . ." Johnson then paraphrases a remark from Sir David Dalrymple's *Memoirs of Great Britain,* 1771–73.

[2] Andrew Marvell, the poet, who had been Milton's assistant in the Latin secretaryship; Sir William Morice (d. 1676), Secretary of State under Charles II; Clarges was the brother-in-law of General Monk.

[3] *Explanatory Notes and Remarks on Milton's Paradise Lost,* by Jonathan Richardson Father and Son, 1734; as told Pope by the actor Thomas Betterton (d. 1710), who was a member of Sir John Davenant's company in 1661, and might, therefore, Johnson surmises, have heard the story from Davenant.

nant was made prisoner, and condemned to die; but was spared at the request of Milton. When the turn of success brought Milton into the like danger, Davenant repaid the benefit by appearing in his favour. Here is a reciprocation of generosity and gratitude so pleasing, that the tale makes its own way to credit. But if help were wanted, I know not where to find it. The danger of Davenant is certain from his own relation; but of his escape there is no account. Betterton's narration can be traced no higher; it is not known that he had it from Davenant. We are told that the benefit exchanged was life for life; but it seems not certain that Milton's life ever was in danger. Godwin, who had committed the same kind of crime, escaped with incapacitation; and as exclusion from publick trust is a punishment which the power of government can commonly inflict without the help of a particular law, it required no great interest to exempt Milton from a censure little more than verbal. Something may be reasonably ascribed to veneration and compassion; to veneration of his abilities, and compassion for his distresses, which made it fit to forgive his malice for his learning. He was now poor and blind; and who would pursue with violence an illustrious enemy, depressed by fortune, and disarmed by nature?

The publication of the Act of Oblivion put him in the same condition with his fellow-subjects. He was, however, upon some pretence not now known, in the custody of the serjeant in December; and, when he was released, upon his refusal of the fees demanded, he and the serjeant were called before the House. He was now safe within the shade of oblivion, and knew himself to be as much out of the power of a griping officer as any other man. How the question was determined is not known. Milton would hardly have contended, but that he knew himself to have right on his side.

He then removed to Jewin-street, near Aldersgate-street; and being blind, and by no means wealthy, wanted a domestick companion and attendant; and therefore, by the recommendation of Dr. Paget, married Elizabeth Minshul, of a gentleman's family in Cheshire, probably without a fortune. All his wives were virgins; for he has declared that he thought it gross and indelicate to be a second husband: upon what other principles his choice was made, cannot now be known; but marriage afforded not much of his happiness. The first wife left him in disgust, and was brought back only by terror: the second, indeed, seems to have been more a favourite; but her life was short. The third, as Philips relates, oppressed his children in his lifetime, and cheated them at his death.

Soon after his marriage, according to an obscure story, he was offered the continuance of his employment; and being pressed by his wife to accept it, answered, "You, like other women, want to ride in your coach; my wish is to live and die an honest man." If he considered the Latin secretary as exercising any of the powers of government, he that had shared authority either with the Parliament or Cromwel, might have forborn to talk very loudly of his honesty; and if he thought the office purely ministerial, he certainly might have honestly retained it under the King. But this tale has too little evidence to deserve a disquisition; large offers and sturdy rejections are among the most common topicks of falsehood.

He had so much either of prudence or gratitude, that he forbore to disturb the new settlement with any of his political or ecclesiastical opinions, and from this time devoted himself to poetry and literature. Of his zeal for learning, in all its parts, he gave a proof by publishing, the next year (1661) *Accidence commenced Grammar;* a little book which has nothing remarkable, but that its author, who had been lately defending the supreme powers of his country, and was then writing *Paradise Lost*, could descend from his elevation to rescue children from the perplexity of grammatical confusion, and the trouble of lessons unnecessarily repeated.

About this time Elwood the Quaker[4] being recommended to him, as one who would read Latin to him, for the advantage of his conversation; attended him every afternoon, except on Sundays. Milton, who, in his letter to Hartlib, had declared, that *to read Latin with an English mouth is as ill a hearing as law French*, required that Elwood should learn and practise the Italian pronunciation, which, he said, was necessary, if he would talk with foreigners. This seems to have been a task troublesome without use. There is little reason for preferring the Italian pronuncia-

---

[4] Thomas Ellwood (d. 1713); from Ellwood's autobiography, 1714.

tion to our own, except that it is more general; and to teach it to an Englishman is only to make him a foreigner at home. He who travels, if he speaks Latin, may so soon learn the sounds which every native gives it, that he need make no provision before his journey; and if strangers visit us, it is their business to practise such conformity to our modes as they expect from us in their own countries. Elwood complied with the directions, and improved himself by his attendance; for he relates, that Milton, having a curious ear, knew by his voice when he read what he did not understand, and would stop him, and *open the most difficult passages.*

In a short time he took a house in the Artillery Walk, leading to Bunhill Fields; the mention of which concludes the register of Milton's removals and habitations. He lived longer in this place than in any other.

He was now busied by *Paradise Lost.* Whence he drew the original design has been variously conjectured, by men who cannot bear to think themselves ignorant of that which, at last, neither diligence nor sagacity can discover. Some find the hint in an Italian tragedy; Voltaire tells a wild and unauthorised story of a farce seen by Milton in Italy, which opened thus: *Let the rainbow be the fiddlestick of the fiddle of Heaven.* It has been already shewn, that the first conception was of a tragedy or mystery, not of a narrative, but a dramatick work, which he is supposed to have begun to reduce to its present form about the time (1655) when he finished his dispute with the defenders of the King.

He long before had promised to adorn his native country by some great performance, while he had yet perhaps no settled design, and was stimulated only by such expectations as naturally arose from the survey of his attainments, and the consciousness of his powers. What he should undertake, it was difficult to determine. He was *long chusing, and began late.*

While he was obliged to divide his time between his private studies and affairs of state, his poetical labour must have been often interrupted; and perhaps he did little more in that busy time than construct the narrative, adjust the episodes, proportion the parts, accumulate images and sentiments, and treasure in his memory, or preserve in writing, such hints as books or meditation would supply. Nothing particular is known of his intellectual operations while he was a statesman; for, having every help and accommodation at hand, he had no need of uncommon expedients.

Being driven from all publick stations, he is yet too great not to be traced by curiosity to his retirement; where he has been found by Mr. Richardson, the fondest of his admirers, sitting *before his door in a grey coat of coarse cloth, in warm sultry weather, to enjoy the fresh air; and so, as well as in his own room, receiving the visits of people of distinguished parts as well as quality.* His visiters of high quality must now be imagined to be few; but men of parts might reasonably court the conversation of a man so generally illustrious, that foreigners are reported, by Wood, to have visited the house in Bread-street where he was born.

According to another account, he was seen in a small house, *neatly enough dressed in black cloaths, sitting in a room hung with rusty green; pale but not cadaverous, with chalkstones in his hands. He said, that if it were not for the gout, his blindness would be tolerable.*

In the intervals of his pain, being made unable to use the common exercises, he used to swing in a chair, and sometimes played upon an organ.

He was now confessedly and visibly employed upon his poem, of which the progress might be noted by those with whom he was familiar; for he was obliged, when he had composed as many lines as his memory would conveniently retain, to employ some friend in writing them, having, at least for part of the time, no regular attendant. This gave opportunity to observations and reports.

Mr. Philips observes, that there was a very remarkable circumstance in the composure of *Paradise Lost*, "which I have a particular reason," says he, "to remember; for whereas I had the perusal of it from the very beginning, for some years, as I went from time to time to visit him, in parcels of ten, twenty, or thirty verses at a time (which, being written by whatever hand came next, might possibly want correction as to the orthography and pointing), having, as the summer came on, not been shewed any for a considerable while; and desiring the reason thereof, was answered, that his vein never happily flowed but from the autumnal equinox to the vernal; and that whatever he attempted at other times was never to his satisfaction, though he courted his fancy never so much; so that, in all the years he was about this poem, he may be said to have spent half his time therein."

Upon this relation Toland remarks, that in his opinion Philips has mistaken the time of the year; for Milton, in his *Elegies*, declares that with the advance of the spring he feels the increase of his poetical force, *redeunt in carmina vires*.[5] To this it is answered, that Philips could hardly mistake time so well marked; and it may be added, that Milton might find different times of the year favourable to different parts of life. Mr. Richardson conceives it impossible that *such a work should be suspended for six months, or for one. It may go on faster or slower, but it must go on.* By what necessity it must continually go on, or why it might not be laid aside and resumed, it is not easy to discover.

This dependance of the soul upon the seasons, those temporary and periodical ebbs and flows of intellect, may, I suppose, justly be derided as the fumes of vain imagination. *Sapiens dominabitur astris.*[6] The author that thinks himself weather-bound will find, with a little help from hellebore, that he is only idle or exhausted. But while this notion has possession of the head, it produces the inability which it supposes. Our powers owe much of their energy to our hopes; *possunt quia posse videntur*.[7] When success seems attainable, diligence is enforced; but when it is admitted that the faculties are suppressed by a cross wind, or a cloudy sky, the day is given up without resistance; for who can contend with the course of nature?

From such prepossessions Milton seems not to have been free. There prevailed in his time an opinion that the world was in its decay, and that we have had the misfortune to be produced in the decrepitude of nature. It was suspected that the whole creation languished, that neither trees nor animals had the height or bulk of their predecessors, and that every thing was daily sinking in gradual diminution. Milton appears to suspect that souls partake of the general degeneracy, and is not without some fear that his book is to be written in *an age too late* for heroick poesy.

---

[5] Literally, "Strength returns to his poetry."
[6] "The wise man will be governed by the stars," quoted from Burton's *Anatomy of Melancholy*.
[7] *Aeneid*, V.231: "they are strong because they think themselves so."

Another opinion wanders about the world, and sometimes finds reception among wise men; an opinion that restrains the operations of the mind to particular regions, and supposes that a luckless mortal may be born in a degree of latitude too high or too low for wisdom or for wit. From this fancy, wild as it is, he had not wholly cleared his head, when he feared lest the *climate* of his country might be *too cold* for flights of imagination.

Into a mind already occupied by such fancies, another not more reasonable might easily find its way. He that could fear lest his genius had fallen upon too old a world, or too chill a climate, might consistently magnify to himself the influences of the seasons, and believe his faculties to be vigorous only half the year.

His submission to the seasons was at least more reasonable than his dread of decaying nature, or a frigid zone; for general causes operate uniformly in a general abatement of mental power: if less could be performed by the writer, less likewise would content the judges of his work. Among this lagging race of frosty grovellers he might still have risen into eminence by producing something which *they should not willingly let die.* However inferior to the heroes who were born in better ages, he might still be great among his contemporaries, with the hope of growing every day greater in the dwindle of posterity. He might still be the giant of the pygmies, the one-eyed monarch of the blind.

Of his artifices of study, or particular hours of composition, we have little account, and there was perhaps little to be told. Richardson, who seems to have been very diligent in his enquiries, but discovers always a wish to find Milton discriminated from other men, relates, that "he would sometimes lie awake whole nights, but not a verse could he make; and on a sudden his poetical faculty would rush upon him with an *impetus,* or *oestrum,* and his daughter was immediately called to secure what came. At other times he would dictate perhaps forty lines in a breath, and then reduce them to half the number."

These bursts of light, and involutions of darkness; these transient and involuntary excursions and retrocessions of invention, having some appearance of deviation from the common train of nature, are eagerly caught by the lovers of a wonder. Yet something of this inequality happens to every man in every mode of exertion, manual or mental. The mechanick cannot handle his hammer and his file at all times with equal dexterity; there are hours, he knows not why, when *his hand is out*. By Mr. Richardson's relation, casually conveyed, much regard cannot be claimed. That, in his intellectual hour, Milton called for his daughter *to secure what came*, may be questioned; for unluckily it happens to be known that his daughters were never taught to write; nor would he have been obliged, as is universally confessed, to have employed any casual visiter in disburthening his memory, if his daughter could have performed the office.

The story of reducing his exuberance has been told of other authors, and though doubtless true of every fertile and copious mind, seems to have been gratuitously transferred to Milton.

What he has told us, and we cannot now know more, is, that he composed much of his poem in the night and morning, I suppose before his mind was disturbed with common business; and that he poured out with great fluency his *unpremeditated verse*. Versification, free, like his, from the distresses of rhyme, must, by a work so long, be made prompt and habitual; and, when his thoughts were once adjusted, the words would come at his command.

At what particular times of his life the parts of his work were written, cannot often be known. The beginning of the third book shews that he had lost his sight; and the Introduction to the seventh, that the return of the King had clouded him with discountenance; and that he was offended by the licentious festivity of the Restoration. There are no other internal notes of time. Milton, being now cleared from all effects of his disloyalty, had nothing required from him but the common duty of living in quiet, to be rewarded with the common right of protection: but this, which, when he sculked from the approach of his King, was perhaps more than he hoped, seems not to have satisfied him; for no sooner is he safe than he finds himself in danger, *fallen on evil days and evil tongues, and with darkness and with danger compass'd round*. This darkness, had his eyes been better employed, had undoubtedly deserved compassion; but to add the mention of danger was ungrateful and unjust. He was fallen indeed on *evil days;* the time was come in which regicides could no longer boast their wickedness. But of *evil tongues* for Milton to complain, required impudence at least equal to his other powers; Milton, whose warmest advocates must allow, that he never spared any asperity of reproach or brutality of insolence.

But the charge itself seems to be false; for it would be hard to recollect any reproach cast upon him, either serious or ludicrous, through the whole remaining part of his life. He persued his studies, or his amusements, without persecution, molestation, or insult. Such is the reverence paid to great abilities, however mis-used: they who contemplated in Milton the scholar and the wit, were contented to forget the reviler of his King.

When the plague (1665) raged in London, Milton took refuge at Chalfont in Essex;[8] where Elwood, who had taken the house for him, first saw a complete copy of *Paradise Lost*, and, having perused it, said to him, "Thou hast said a great deal upon *Paradise Lost*; what hast thou to say upon *Paradise Found?*"

Next year, when the danger of infection had ceased, he returned to Bunhill-fields, and designed the publication of his poem. A license was necessary, and he could expect no great kindness from a chaplain of the Archbishop of Canterbury. He seems, however, to have been treated with tenderness; for though objections were made to particular passages, and among them to the simile of the sun eclipsed in the first book, yet the license was granted; and he sold his copy, April 27, 1667, to Samuel Simmons for an imme-diate payment of five pounds, with a stipulation to receive five pounds more when thirteen hundred should be sold of the first edition; and again, five pounds after the sale of the same number of the second edition, and another five pounds after the same sale of the third. None of the three editions were to be extended be-yond fifteen hundred copies.

The first edition was of ten books, in a small quarto. The titles were varied from year to year; and an advertisement and the arguments of the books were omitted in some copies, and inserted in others.

The sale gave him in two years a right to his second payment, for which the receipt was signed April 26, 1669. The second edition was not given till 1674; it was printed in small octavo; and the number of books was encreased to twelve, by a division of the seventh and twelfth;[9] and some other small improvements were

---

[8] *Essex: Bucks* 1783.

[9] *twelfth:* i.e., the tenth.

made. The third edition was published in 1678; and the widow, to whom the copy was then to devolve, sold all her claims to Simmons for eight pounds, according to her receipt given Dec. 21, 1680. Simmons had already agreed to transfer the whole right to Brabazon Aylmer for twenty-five pounds; and Aylmer sold to Jacob Tonson half, August 17, 1683, and half, March 24, 1690, at a price considerably enlarged.

The slow sale and tardy reputation of this poem, have been always mentioned as evidences of neglected merit, and of the uncertainty of literary fame; and enquiries have been made, and conjectures offered, about the causes of its long obscurity and late reception. But has the case been truly stated? Have not lamentation and wonder been lavished on an evil that was never felt?

That in the reigns of Charles and James the *Paradise Lost* received no publick acclamations is readily confessed. Wit and literature were on the side of the Court: and who that solicited favour or the fashion would venture to praise the defender of the regicides? All that he himself could think his due, from *evil tongues in evil days,* was that reverential silence which was generously preserved. But it cannot be inferred that his poem was not read, or not, however unwillingly, admired.

The sale, if it be considered, will justify the publick. Those who have no power to judge of past times but by their own, should always doubt their conclusions. The sale of books was not in Milton's age what it is in the present. To read was not then a general amusement; neither traders, nor often gentlemen, thought themselves disgraced by ignorance. The women had not then aspired to literature, nor was every house supplied with a closet of books. Those indeed, who professed learning, were not less learned than at any other time; but of that middle race of students who read for pleasure or accomplishment, and who buy the numerous products of modern typography, the number was then comparatively small. To prove the paucity of readers, it may be sufficient to remark, that the nation had been satisfied, from 1623 to 1664, that is, forty-one years, with only two editions of the works of Shakespeare, which probably did not together make one thousand copies.

The sale of thirteen hundred copies in two years, in opposition to so much recent enmity, and to a style of versification new to all

and disgusting to many, was an uncommon example of the prevalence of genius. The demand did not immediately encrease; for
many more readers than were supplied at first the nation did not
afford. Only three thousand were sold in eleven years; for it
forced its way without assistance: its admirers did not dare to
publish their opinion; and the opportunities now given of attracting notice by advertisements were then very few; for the means
of proclaiming the publication of new books have been produced
by that general literature which now pervades the nation through
all its ranks.

But the reputation and price of the copy still advanced, till the
Revolution put an end to the secrecy of love, and *Paradise Lost*
broke into open view with sufficient security of kind reception.

Fancy can hardly forbear to conjecture with what temper
Milton surveyed the silent progress of his work, and marked his
reputation stealing its way in a kind of subterraneous current
through fear and silence. I cannot but conceive him calm and
confident, little disappointed, not at all dejected, relying on his
own merit with steady consciousness, and waiting, without impatience, the vicissitudes of opinion, and the impartiality of a
future generation.

In the mean time he continued his studies, and supplied the
want of sight by a very odd expedient, of which Philips gives the
following account:

Mr. Philips tells us, "that though our author had daily about
him one or other to read, some persons of man's estate, who, of
their own accord, greedily catched at the opportunity of being
his readers, that they might as well reap the benefit of what they
read to him, as oblige him by the benefit of their reading; and
others of younger years were sent by their parents to the same
end: yet excusing only the eldest daughter, by reason of her
bodily infirmity, and difficult utterance of speech, (which, to say
truth, I doubt was the principal cause of excusing her) the other
two were condemned to the performance of reading, and exactly
pronouncing of all the languages of whatever book he should, at
one time or other, think fit to peruse, viz. the Hebrew (and I think
the Syriac), the Greek, the Latin, the Italian, Spanish, and French.
All which sorts of books to be confined to read, without understanding one word, must needs be a trial of patience almost beyond endurance. Yet it was endured by both for a long time,

though the irksomeness of this employment could not be always concealed, but broke out more and more into expressions of uneasiness; so that at length they were all, even the eldest also, sent out to learn some curious and ingenious sorts of manufacture, that are proper for women to learn; particularly embroideries in gold or silver."

In the scene of misery which this mode of intellectual labour sets before our eyes, it is hard to determine whether the daughters or the father are most to be lamented. A language not understood can never be so read as to give pleasure, and very seldom so as to convey meaning. If few men would have had resolution to write books with such embarrassments, few likewise would have wanted ability to find some better expedient.

Three years after his *Paradise Lost* (1670), he published his *History of England*, comprising the whole fable of Geoffry of Monmouth, and continued to the Norman invasion. Why he should have given the first part, which he seems not to believe, and which is universally rejected, it is difficult to conjecture. The stile is harsh; but it has something of rough vigour, which perhaps may often strike, though it cannot please.

On this history the licenser again fixed his claws, and before he would transmit it to the press tore out several parts. Some censures of the Saxon monks were taken away, lest they should be applied to the modern clergy; and a character of the Long Parliament, and Assembly of Divines, was excluded; of which the author gave a copy to the Earl of Anglesea,[1] and which, being afterwards published, has been since inserted in its proper place.

The same year were printed *Paradise Regained*, and *Sampson Agonistes*, a tragedy written in imitation of the ancients, and never designed by the author for the stage. These poems were published by another bookseller. It has been asked, whether Simmons was discouraged from receiving them by the slow sale of the former? Why a writer changed his bookseller a hundred years ago, I am far from hoping to discover. It is certain, that he who in two years sells thirteen hundred copies of a volume in quarto, bought for two payments of five pounds each, has no reason to repent his purchase.

When Milton shewed *Paradise Regained* to Elwood, "This,"

---

[1] Arthur Annesley, first Earl of Anglesey (d. 1686), who apparently had befriended Milton at the Restoration.

said he, "is owing to you; for you put it in my head by the question you put to me at Chalfont, which otherwise I had not thought of."

His last poetical offspring was his favourite. He could not, as Elwood relates, endure to hear *Paradise Lost* preferred to *Paradise Regained*. Many causes may vitiate a writer's judgement of his own works. On that which has cost him much labour he sets a high value, because he is unwilling to think that he has been diligent in vain; what has been produced without toilsome efforts is considered with delight, as a proof of vigorous faculties and fertile invention; and the last work, whatever it be, has necessarily most of the grace of novelty. Milton, however it happened, had this prejudice, and had it to himself.

To that multiplicity of attainments, and extent of comprehension, that entitle this great author to our veneration, may be added a kind of humble dignity, which did not disdain the meanest services to literature. The epick poet, the controvertist, the politician, having already descended to accommodate children with a book of rudiments, now, in the last years of his life, composed a book of logick, for the initiation of students in philosophy; and published (1672) *Artis Logicae plenior Institutio ad Petri Rami methodum concinnata:* that is, "A new Scheme of Logick, according to the Method of Ramus."[2] I know not whether, even in this book, he did not intend an act of hostility against the universities; for Ramus was one of the first oppugners of the old philosophy, who disturbed with innovations the quiet of the schools.

His polemical disposition again revived. He had now been safe so long, that he forgot his fears, and published a *Treatise of true Religion, Heresy, Schism, Toleration, and the best Means to prevent the Growth of Popery.*

But this little tract is modestly written, with respectful mention of the Church of England, and an appeal to the Thirty-nine Articles. His principle of toleration is, agreement in the sufficiency of the Scriptures; and he extends it to all who, whatever their opinions are, profess to derive them from the sacred books. The papists appeal to other testimonies, and are therefore in his opinion not to be permitted the liberty of either publick or private worship; for though they plead conscience, *we have no warrant,*

---

[2] Pierre la Ramée, French logician and opponent of Aristotelianism, killed in the Massacre of St. Bartholomew, 1572.

he says, *to regard conscience which is not grounded in Scripture.*

Those who are not convinced by his reasons, may be perhaps delighted with his wit. The term *Roman Catholick* is, he says, *one of the Pope's bulls; it is particular universal, or Catholick schismatick.*

He has, however, something better. As the best preservative against Popery, he recommends the diligent perusal of the Scriptures; a duty, from which he warns the busy part of mankind not to think themselves excused.

He now reprinted his juvenile poems, with some additions.

In the last year of his life he sent to the press, seeming to take delight in publication, a collection of familiar epistles in Latin; to which, being too few to make a volume, he added some academical exercises, which perhaps he perused with pleasure, as they recalled to his memory the days of youth; but for which nothing but veneration for his name could now procure a reader.

When he had attained his sixty-sixth year, the gout, with which he had been long tormented, prevailed over the enfeebled powers of nature. He died by a quiet and silent expiration, about the tenth of November 1674, at his house in Bunhill-fields; and was buried next his father in the chancel of St. Giles at Cripplegate. His funeral was very splendidly and numerously attended.

Upon his grave there is supposed to have been no memorial; but in our time a monument has been erected in Westminster Abbey *To the Author of Paradise Lost*, by Mr. Benson,[3] who has in the inscription bestowed more words upon himself than upon Milton.

When the inscription for the monument of Philips, in which he was said to be *soli Miltono secundus*, was exhibited to Dr. Sprat, then dean of Westminster, he refused to admit it; the name of Milton was, in his opinion, too detestable to be read on the wall of a building dedicated to devotion. Atterbury, who succeeded him, being author of the inscription, permitted its reception. "And such has been the change of publick opinion," said Dr. Gregory,[4] from whom I heard this account, "that I have seen

---

[3] The bust by Rysbrach was installed by William Benson in 1737.

[4] The inscription for the poet John Philips (d. 1709), was written by Francis Atterbury (d. 1732) objected to by Thomas Sprat (d. 1713), as reported to Johnson by a Dr. Gregory, probably David Gregory, Dean of Christ Church, Oxford, from 1756 to 1767.

erected in the church a statue of that man, whose name I once knew considered as a pollution of its walls."

Milton has the reputation of having been in his youth eminently beautiful, so as to have been called the Lady of his college. His hair, which was of a light brown, parted at the foretop, and hung down upon his shoulders, according to the picture which he has given of Adam. He was, however, not of the heroick stature, but rather below the middle size, according to Mr. Richardson, who mentions him as having narrowly escaped from being *short and thick.* He was vigorous and active, and delighted in the exercise of the sword, in which he is related to have been eminently skilful. His weapon was, I believe, not the rapier, but the back-sword, of which he recommends the use in his book on Education.

His eyes are said never to have been bright; but, if he was a dexterous fencer, they must have been once quick.

His domestick habits, so far as they are known, were those of a severe student. He drank little strong drink of any kind, and fed without delicacy of choice or excess in quantity. In his youth he studied late at night; but afterwards changed his hours, and rested in bed from nine to four in the summer, and five in winter. The course of his day was best known after he was blind. When he first rose he heard a chapter in the Hebrew Bible, and then studied till twelve; then took some exercise for an hour; then dined; then plaid on the organ, and sung, or heard another sing; then studied to six; then entertained his visiters, till eight; then supped, and, after a pipe of tobacco and a glass of water, went to bed.

So is his life described; but this even tenour appears attainable only in colleges. He that lives in the world will sometimes have the succession of his practice broken and confused. Visiters, of whom Milton is represented to have had great numbers, will come and stay unseasonably; business, of which every man has some, must be done when others will do it.

When he did not care to rise early, he had something read to him by his bedside; perhaps at this time his daughters were employed. He composed much in the morning, and dictated in the day, sitting obliquely in an elbow-chair, with his leg thrown over the arm.

Fortune appears not to have had much of his care. In the civil wars he lent his personal estate to the parliament; but when, after the contest was decided, he solicited repayment, he met not only with neglect but *sharp rebuke;* and, having tired both himself and his friends, was given up to poverty and hopeless indignation, till he shewed how able he was to do greater service. He was then made Latin secretary, with two hundred pounds a year; and had a thousand pounds for his *Defence of the People.* His widow, who, after his death, retired to Namptwich in Cheshire, and died about 1729, is said to have reported that he lost two thousand pounds by entrusting it to a scrivener; and that, in the general depredation upon the Church, he had grasped an estate of about sixty pounds a year belonging to Westminster Abbey, which, like other sharers of the plunder of rebellion, he was afterwards obliged to return. Two thousand pounds, which he had placed in the Excise-office, were also lost. There is yet no reason to believe that he was ever reduced to indigence. His wants being few, were competently supplied. He sold his library before his death, and left his family fifteen hundred pounds, on which his widow laid hold, and only gave one hundred to each of his daughters.

His literature was unquestionably great. He read all the languages which are considered either as learned or polite; Hebrew, with its two dialects, Greek, Latin, Italian, French, and Spanish. In Latin his skill was such as places him in the first rank of writers and criticks; and he appears to have cultivated Italian with uncommon diligence. The books in which his daughter, who used to read to him, represented him as most delighting, after Homer, which he could almost repeat, were Ovid's *Metamorphoses* and Euripides. His Euripides is, by Mr. Cradock's kindness, now in my hands: the margin is sometimes noted; but I have found nothing remarkable.

Of the English poets he set most value upon Spenser, Shakespeare, and Cowley. Spenser was apparently his favourite: Shakespeare he may easily be supposed to like, with every other skilful reader; but I should not have expected that Cowley, whose ideas of excellence were so different from his own, would have had much of his approbation. His character of Dryden, who sometimes visited him, was, that he was a good rhymist, but no poet.

His theological opinions are said to have been first Calvinistical; and afterwards, perhaps when he began to hate the Presbyterians, to have tended towards Arminianism. In the mixed questions of theology and government, he never thinks that he can recede far enough from popery, or prelacy; but what Baudius says of Erasmus seems applicable to him, *magis habuit quod fugeret, quam quod sequeretur*.[5] He had determined rather what to condemn than what to approve. He has not associated himself with any denomination of Protestants: we know rather what he was not, than what he was. He was not of the Church of Rome; he was not of the Church of England.

To be of no church is dangerous. Religion, of which the rewards are distant, and which is animated only by faith and hope, will glide by degrees out of the mind, unless it be invigorated and reimpressed by external ordinances, by stated calls to worship, and the salutary influence of example. Milton, who appears to have had full conviction of the truth of Christianity, and to have regarded the Holy Scriptures with the profoundest veneration, to have been untainted by any heretical peculiarity of opinion, and to have lived in a confirmed belief of the immediate and occasional agency of Providence, yet grew old without any visible worship. In the distribution of his hours, there was no hour of prayer, either solitary, or with his household; omitting publick prayers, he omitted all.

Of this omission the reason has been sought, upon a supposition which ought never to be made, that men live with their own approbation, and justify their conduct to themselves. Prayer certainly was not thought superfluous by him, who represents our first parents as praying acceptably in the state of innocence, and efficaciously after their fall. That he lived without prayer can hardly be affirmed; his studies and meditations were an habitual prayer. The neglect of it in his family was probably a fault for which he condemned himself, and which he intended to correct, but that death, as too often happens, intercepted his reformation.

His political notions were those of an acrimonious and surly republican, for which it is not known that he gave any better

---

[5] "He was more disposed to flee than to follow." Dominic Baudius, *Epistolae*, cent. II, epist. xxvii.

reason than that *a popular government was the most frugal; for the trappings of a monarchy would set up an ordinary commonwealth.* It is surely very shallow policy, that supposes money to be the chief good; and even this, without considering that the support and expence of a Court is, for the most part, only a particular kind of traffick, by which money is circulated, without any national impoverishment.

Milton's republicanism was, I am afraid, founded in an envious hatred of greatness, and a sullen desire of independence; in petulance, impatient of controul, and pride disdainful of superiority. He hated monarchs in the State, and prelates in the Church; for he hated all whom he was required to obey. It is to be suspected that his predominant desire was to destroy rather than establish, and that he felt not so much the love of liberty as repugnance to authority.

It has been observed, that they who most loudly clamour for liberty do not most liberally grant it. What we know of Milton's character, in domestick relations, is, that he was severe and arbitrary. His family consisted of women; and there appears in his books something like a Turkish contempt of females, as subordinate and inferiour beings. That his own daughters might not break the ranks, he suffered them to be depressed by a mean and penurious education. He thought woman made only for obedience, and man only for rebellion.

Of his family some account may be expected. His sister, first married to Mr. Philips, afterwards married Mr. Agar, a friend of her first husband, who succeeded him in the Crown-office. She had by her first husband Edward and John, the two nephews whom Milton educated; and by her second, two daughters.

His brother, Sir Christopher, had two daughters, Mary and Catherine, and a son Thomas, who succeeded Agar in the Crown-office, and left a daughter, living in 1749 in Grosvenor-street.

Milton had children only by his first wife; Anne, Mary, and Deborah. Anne, though deformed, married a master-builder, and died of her first child. Mary died single. Deborah married Abraham Clark, a weaver in Spital-fields, and lived 76 years, to August 1727. This is the daughter of whom publick mention has been made. She could repeat the first lines of Homer, the *Meta-*

*morphoses,* and some of Euripides, by having often read them. Yet here incredulity is ready to make a stand. Many repetitions are necessary to fix in the memory lines not understood; and why should Milton wish or want to hear them so often! These lines were at the beginning of the poems. Of a book written in a language not understood, the beginning raises no more attention than the end; and as those that understand it know commonly the beginning best, its rehearsal will seldom be necessary. It is not likely that Milton required any passage to be so much repeated as that his daughter could learn it; nor likely that he desired the initial lines to be read at all; nor that the daughter, weary of the drudgery of pronouncing unideal sounds, would voluntarily commit them to memory.

To this gentlewoman Addison made a present, and promised some establishment; but died soon after. Queen Caroline sent her fifty guineas. She had seven sons and three daughters; but none of them had any children, except her son Caleb and her daughter Elizabeth. Caleb went to Fort St. George in the East Indies, and had two sons, of whom nothing is now known. Elizabeth married Thomas Foster, a weaver in Spital-fields, and had seven children, who all died. She kept a petty grocer's or chandler's shop, first at Halloway, and afterwards in Cock-lane near Shore-ditch Church. She knew little of her grandfather, and that little was not good. She told of his harshness to his daughters, and his refusal to have them taught to write; and, in opposition to other accounts, represented him as delicate, though temperate, in his diet.

In 1750, April 5, *Comus* was played for her benefit. She had so little acquaintance with diversion or gaiety, that she did not know what was intended when a benefit was offered her. The profits of the night were only one hundred and thirty pounds, though Dr. Newton brought a large contribution; and twenty pounds were given by Tonson,[6] a man who is to be praised as often as he is named. Of this sum one hundred pounds was placed in the stocks, after some debate between her and her husband in whose name it should be entered, and the rest augmented their little stock, with which they removed to Islington. This was the greatest

---

[6] Thomas Newton, editor of *Paradise Lost,* 1749, and Jacob Tonson, the publisher (d. 1767).

benefaction that *Paradise Lost* ever procured the author's descendents; and to this he who has now attempted to relate his Life, had the honour of contributing a prologue.

━━━━━━━━━━

In the examination of Milton's poetical works, I shall pay so much regard to time as to begin with his juvenile productions. For his early pieces he seems to have had a degree of fondness not very laudable: what he has once written he resolves to preserve, and gives to the publick an unfinished poem, which he broke off because he was *nothing satisfied with what he had done*, supposing his readers less nice than himself. These preludes to his future labours are in Italian, Latin, and English. Of the Italian I cannot pretend to speak as a critic; but I have heard them commended by a man well qualified to decide their merit. The Latin pieces are lusciously elegant; but the delight which they afford is rather by the exquisite imitation of the ancient writers, by the purity of the diction, and the harmony of the numbers, than by any power of invention, or vigour of sentiment. They are not all of equal value; the elegies excell the odes; and some of the exercises on Gunpowder Treason might have been spared.

The English poems, though they make no promises of *Paradise Lost*, have this evidence of genius, that they have a cast original and unborrowed. But their peculiarity is not excellence: if they differ from the verses of others, they differ for the worse; for they are too often distinguished by repulsive harshness; the combinations of words are new, but they are not pleasing; the rhymes and epithets seem to be laboriously sought, and violently applied.

That in the early part of his life he wrote with much care appears from his manuscripts, happily preserved at Cambridge, in which many of his smaller works are found as they were first written, with the subsequent corrections. Such reliques shew how excellence is acquired; what we hope ever to do with ease, we may learn first to do with diligence.

Those who admire the beauties of this great poet, sometimes force their own judgement into false approbation of his little pieces, and prevail upon themselves to think that admirable which is only singular. All that short compositions can commonly attain is neatness and elegance. Milton never learned the art of doing little things with grace; he overlooked the milder excellence of suavity and softness; he was a *lion* that had no skill *in dandling the kid.*

One of the poems on which much praise has been bestowed is *Lycidas;* of which the diction is harsh, the rhymes uncertain, and the numbers unpleasing. What beauty there is, we must therefore seek in the sentiments and images.

It is not to be considered as the effusion of real passion; for passion runs not after remote allusions and obscure opinions. Passion plucks no berries from the myrtle and ivy, nor calls upon Arethuse and Mincius, nor tells of rough *satyrs* and *fauns with cloven heel.* Where there is leisure for fiction there is little grief.

In this poem there is no nature, for there is no truth; there is no art, for there is nothing new. Its form is that of a pastoral, easy, vulgar, and therefore disgusting: whatever images it can supply, are long ago exhausted; and its inherent improbability always forces dissatisfaction on the mind. When Cowley tells of Hervey that they studied together, it is easy to suppose how much he must miss the companion of his labours, and the partner of his discoveries; but what image of tenderness can be excited by these lines?

> We drove a field, and both together heard
> What time the grey fly winds her sultry horn,
> Batt'ning our flocks with the fresh dews of night.

We know that they never drove a field, and that they had no flocks to batten; and though it be allowed that the representation may be allegorical, the true meaning is so uncertain and remote, that it is never sought, because it cannot be known when it is found.

Among the flocks, and copses, and flowers, appear the heathen deities; Jove and Phoebus, Neptune and Aeolus, with a long train of mythological imagery, such as a college easily supplies. Nothing can less display knowledge, or less exercise invention, than to tell how a shepherd has lost his companion, and must now feed his flocks alone, without any judge of his skill in piping; and how one god asks another god what is become of Lycidas, and how neither god can tell. He who thus grieves will excite no sympathy; he who thus praises will confer no honour.

This poem has yet a grosser fault. With these trifling fictions are mingled the most awful and sacred truths, such as ought never to be polluted with such irreverend combinations. The shepherd likewise is now a feeder of sheep, and afterwards an ecclesiastical pastor, a superintendent of a Christian flock. Such equivocations are always unskilful, but here they are indecent, and at least approach to impiety, of which, however, I believe the writer not to have been conscious.

Such is the power of reputation justly acquired, that its blaze drives away the eye from nice examination. Surely no man could have fancied that he read *Lycidas* with pleasure, had he not known its author.

Of the two pieces, *L'Allegro* and *Il Penseroso*, I believe opinion is uniform; every man that reads them, reads them with pleasure. The author's design is not, what Theobald has remarked,[7] merely to shew how objects derive their colours from the mind, by representing the operation of the same things upon the gay and the melancholy temper, or upon the same man as he is differently disposed; but rather how, among the successive variety of appearances, every disposition of mind takes hold on those by which it may be gratified.

The *chearful* man hears the lark in the morning; the *pensive* man hears the nightingale in the evening. The *chearful* man sees the cock strut, and hears the horn and hounds echo in the wood; then walks *not unseen* to observe the glory of the rising sun, or listen to the singing milk-maid, and view the labours of the plowman and the mower; then casts his eyes about him over scenes of smiling plenty, and looks up to the distant tower, the residence of some fair inhabitant; thus he pursues rural gaiety through a day of labour or of play, and delights himself at night with the fanciful narratives of superstitious ignorance.

The *pensive* man, at one time, walks *unseen* to muse at mid-

---

[7] In his Preface to his edition of Shakespeare.

night; and at another hears the sullen curfew. If the weather drives him home, he sits in a room lighted only by *glowing embers;* or by a lonely lamp outwatches the North Star, to discover the habitation of separate souls, and varies the shades of meditation, by contemplating the magnificent or pathetick scenes of tragick and epic poetry. When the morning comes, a morning gloomy with rain and wind, he walks into the dark trackless woods, falls asleep by some murmuring water, and with melancholy enthusiasm expects some dream of prognostication, or some musick plaid by aerial performers.

Both Mirth and Melancholy are solitary, silent inhabitants of the breast that neither receive nor transmit communication; no mention is therefore made of a philosophical friend, or a pleasant companion. Seriousness does not arise from any participation of calamity, nor gaiety from the pleasures of the bottle.

The man of *chearfulness*, having exhausted the country, tries what *towered cities* will afford, and mingles with scenes of splendor, gay assemblies, and nuptial festivities; but he mingles a mere spectator, as when the learned comedies of Jonson, or the wild dramas of Shakespeare, are exhibited, he attends the theatre.

The *pensive* man never loses himself in crowds, but walks the cloister, or frequents the cathedral. Milton probably had not yet forsaken the Church.

Both his characters delight in musick; but he seems to think that chearful notes would have obtained from Pluto a compleat dismission of Eurydice, of whom solemn sounds only procured a conditional release.

For the old age of Chearfulness he makes no provision; but Melancholy he conducts with great dignity to the close of life.

Through these two poems the images are properly selected, and nicely distinguished; but the colours of the diction seem not sufficiently discriminated. His Chearfulness is without levity, and his Pensiveness without asperity. I know not whether the characters are kept sufficiently apart. No mirth can, indeed, be found in his melancholy; but I am afraid that I always meet some melancholy in his mirth. They are two noble efforts of imagination.

The greatest of his juvenile performances is the *Mask of Comus;* in which may very plainly be discovered the dawn or twilight of *Paradise Lost*. Milton appears to have formed very early that system of diction, and mode of verse, which his maturer judgement approved, and from which he never endeavoured nor desired to deviate.

Nor does *Comus* afford only a specimen of his language; it exhibits likewise his power of description, and his vigour of sentiment, employed in the praise and defence of virtue. A work more truly poetical is rarely found; allusions, images, and descriptive epithets, embellish almost every period with lavish decoration. As a series of lines, therefore, it may be considered as worthy of all the admiration with which the votaries have received it.

As a drama it is deficient. The action is not probable. A masque, in those parts where supernatural intervention is admitted, must indeed be given up to all the freaks of imagination; but, so far as the action is merely human, it ought to be reasonable, which can hardly be said of the conduct of the two brothers; who, when their sister sinks with fatigue in a pathless wilderness, wander both away together in search of berries too far to find their way back, and leave a helpless lady to all the sadness and danger of solitude. This however is a defect over-balanced by its convenience.

What deserves more reprehension is, that the prologue spoken in the wild wood by the attendant Spirit is addressed to the audience; a mode of communication so contrary to the nature of dramatick representation, that no precedents can support it.

The discourse of the Spirit is too long; an objection that may be made to almost all the following speeches: they have not the spriteliness of a dialogue animated by reciprocal contention, but seem rather declamations deliberately composed, and formally repeated, on a moral question. The auditor therefore listens as to a lecture, without passion, without anxiety.

The song of Comus has airiness and jollity; but, what may recommend Milton's morals as well as his poetry, the invitations to pleasure are so general, that they excite no distinct images of corrupt enjoyment, and take no dangerous hold on the fancy.

The following soliloquies of Comus and the Lady are elegant, but tedious. The song must owe much to the voice, if it ever can delight. At last the Brothers enter, with too much tranquillity; and when they have feared lest their sister should be in danger, and hoped that she is not in danger, the Elder makes a speech in praise of chastity, and the Younger finds how fine it is to be a philosopher.

Then descends the Spirit in form of a shepherd; and the Brother, instead of being in haste to ask his help, praises his singing, and enquires his business in that place. It is remarkable, that at this interview the Brother is taken with a short fit of rhyming. The Spirit relates that the Lady is in the power of Comus; the Brother moralises again; and the Spirit makes a long narration, of no use because it is false, and therefore unsuitable to a good being.

In all these parts the language is poetical, and the sentiments are generous; but there is something wanting to allure attention.

The dispute between the Lady and Comus is the most animated and affecting scene of the drama, and wants nothing but a brisker reciprocation of objections and replies to invite attention, and detain it.

The songs are vigorous, and full of imagery; but they are harsh in their diction, and not very musical in their numbers.

Throughout the whole, the figures are too bold, and the language too luxuriant for dialogue. It is a drama in the epic stile, inelegantly splendid, and tediously instructive.

The *Sonnets* were written in different parts of Milton's life, upon different occasions. They deserve not any particular criticism; for of the best it can only be said, that they are not bad; and perhaps only the eighth and the twenty-first are truly entitled to this slender commendation. The fabrick of a sonnet, however adapted to the Italian language, has never succeeded in ours, which, having greater variety of termination, requires the rhymes to be often changed.

Those little pieces may be dispatched without much anxiety; a greater work calls for greater care. I am now to examine *Paradise Lost;* a poem, which, considered with respect to design, may claim the first place, and with respect to performance the second among the productions of the human mind.

By the general consent of criticks, the first praise of genius is due to the writer of an epick poem, as it requires an assemblage of all the powers which are singly sufficient for other compositions. Poetry is the art of uniting pleasure with truth, by calling imagination to the help of reason. Epick poetry undertakes to teach the most important truths by the most pleasing precepts, and therefore relates some great event in the most affecting manner. History must supply the writer with the rudiments of narration, which he must improve and exalt by a nobler art, animate by dramatick energy, and diversify by retrospection and anticipation; morality must teach him the exact bounds, and different shades, of vice and virtue: from policy, and the practice of life, he has to learn the discriminations of character, and the tendency of the passions, either single or combined; and physiology must supply him with illustrations and images. To put these materials to poetical use, is required an imagination capable of painting nature, and realizing fiction. Nor is he yet a poet till he has attained the whole extension of his language, distinguished all the delicacies of phrase, and all the colours of words, and learned to adjust their different sounds to all the varieties of metrical modulation.

Bossu[8] is of opinion that the poet's first work is to find a *moral,* which his fable is afterwards to illustrate and establish. This seems to have been the process only of Milton; the moral of other poems is incidental and consequent; in Milton's only it is essential and intrinsick. His purpose was the most useful and the most arduous; *to vindicate the ways of God to man;* to shew the reasonableness of religion, and the necessity of obedience to the Divine Law.

To convey this moral there must be a *fable,* a narration artfully constructed, so as to excite curiosity, and surprise expectation. In this part of his work, Milton must be confessed to have equalled every other poet. He has involved in his account of the Fall of Man the events which preceded, and those that were to follow it: he has interwoven the whole system of theology with such propriety, that every part appears to be necessary; and scarcely any recital is wished shorter for the sake of quickening the progress of the main action.

The subject of an epick poem is naturally an event of great importance. That of Milton is not the destruction of a city, the conduct of a colony, or the foundation of an empire. His subject

---

[8] René Le Bossu, *Traité du Poème Epique.*

is the fate of worlds, the revolutions of heaven and of earth; rebellion against the Supreme King, raised by the highest order of created beings; the overthrow of their host, and the punishment of their crime; the creation of a new race of reasonable creatures; their original happiness and innocence, their forfeiture of immortality, and their restoration to hope and peace.

Great events can be hastened or retarded only by persons of elevated dignity. Before the greatness displayed in Milton's poem, all other greatness shrinks away. The weakest of his agents are the highest and noblest of human beings, the original parents of mankind; with whose actions the elements consented; on whose rectitude, or deviation of will, depended the state of terrestrial nature, and the condition of all the future inhabitants of the globe.

Of the other agents in the poem, the chief are such as it is irreverence to name on slight occasions. The rest were lower powers;

> ——of which the least could wield
> Those elements, and arm him with the force
> Of all their regions.

powers, which only the controul of Omnipotence restrains from laying creation waste, and filling the vast expanse of space with ruin and confusion. To display the motives and actions of beings thus superiour, so far as human reason can examine them, or human imagination represent them, is the task which this mighty poet has undertaken and performed.

In the examination of epick poems much speculation is commonly employed upon the *characters*. The characters in the *Paradise Lost*, which admit of examination, are those of angels and of man; of angels good and evil; of man in his innocent and sinful state.

Among the angels, the virtue of Raphael is mild and placid, of easy condescension and free communication; that of Michael is regal and lofty, and, as may seem, attentive to the dignity of his own nature. Abdiel and Gabriel appear occasionally, and act as every incident requires; the solitary fidelity of Abdiel is very amiably painted.

Of the evil angels the characters are more diversified. To Satan, as Addison observes, such sentiments are given as suit *the most exalted and most depraved being.* Milton has been censured, by Clark,[9] for the impiety which sometimes breaks from Satan's mouth. For there are thoughts, as he justly remarks, which no observation of character can justify, because no good man would willingly permit them to pass, however transiently, through his own mind. To make Satan speak as a rebel, without any such expressions as might taint the reader's imagination, was indeed one of the great difficulties in Milton's undertaking, and I cannot but think that he has extricated himself with great happiness. There is in Satan's speeches little that can give pain to a pious ear. The language of rebellion cannot be the same with that of obedience. The malignity of Satan foams in haughtiness and obstinacy; but his expressions are commonly general, and no otherwise offensive than as they are wicked.

The other chiefs of the celestial rebellion are very judiciously discriminated in the first and second books; and the ferocious character of Moloch appears, both in the battle and the council, with exact consistency.

To Adam and to Eve are given, during their innocence, such sentiments as innocence can generate and utter. Their love is pure benevolence and mutual veneration; their repasts are without luxury, and their diligence without toil. Their addresses to their Maker have little more than the voice of admiration and gratitude. Fruition left them nothing to ask, and Innocence left them nothing to fear.

But with guilt enter distrust and discord, mutual accusation, and stubborn self-defence; they regard each other with alienated minds, and dread their Creator as the avenger of their transgression. At last they seek shelter in his mercy, soften to repentance, and melt in supplication. Both before and after the Fall, the superiority of Adam is diligently sustained.

Of the *probable* and the *marvellous,* two parts of a vulgar epick poem, which immerge the critick in deep consideration, the *Paradise Lost* requires little to be said. It contains the history of a miracle, of Creation and Redemption; it displays the power and the mercy of the Supreme Being; the probable therefore is marvellous, and the marvellous is probable. The substance of the

---

[9] "Author of the *Essay on Study.*" Johnson, 1783. John Clarke's book was published in 1731.

narrative is truth; and as truth allows no choice, it is, like necessity, superior to rule. To the accidental or adventitious parts, as to every thing human, some slight exceptions may be made. But the main fabrick is immovably supported.

It is justly remarked by Addison, that this poem has, by the nature of its subject, the advantage above all others, that it is universally and perpetually interesting. All mankind will, through all ages, bear the same relation to Adam and to Eve, and must partake of that good and evil which extend to themselves.

Of the *machinery,* so called from θεὸς ἀπὸ μηχανῆς, by which is meant the occasional interposition of supernatural power, another fertile topick of critical remarks, here is no room to speak, because every thing is done under the immediate and visible direction of Heaven; but the rule is so far observed, that no part of the action could have been accomplished by any other means.

Of *episodes,* I think there are only two, contained in Raphael's relation of the war in heaven, and Michael's prophetick account of the changes to happen in this world. Both are closely connected with the great action; one was necessary to Adam as a warning, the other as a consolation.

To the compleatness or *integrity* of the design nothing can be objected; it has distinctly and clearly what Aristotle requires, a beginning, a middle, and an end. There is perhaps no poem, of the same length, from which so little can be taken without apparent mutilation. Here are no funeral games, nor is there any long description of a shield. The short digressions at the beginning of the third, seventh, and ninth books, might doubtless be spared; but superfluities so beautiful, who would take away? or who does not wish that the author of the *Iliad* had gratified succeeding ages with a little knowledge of himself? Perhaps no passages are more frequently or more attentively read than those extrinsick paragraphs; and, since the end of poetry is pleasure, that cannot be unpoetical with which all are pleased.

The questions, whether the action of the poem be strictly *one,* whether the poem can be properly termed *heroick,* and who is the hero, are raised by such readers as draw their principles of judgement rather from books than from reason. Milton, though he intituled *Paradise Lost* only a *poem,* yet calls it himself *heroick song.* Dryden, petulantly and indecently, denies the heroism of Adam, because he was overcome; but there is no reason why the hero should not be unfortunate, except established practice, since success and virtue do not go necessarily together. Cato is the hero of Lucan; but Lucan's authority will not be suffered by Quintilian to decide. However, if success be necessary, Adam's deceiver was at last crushed; Adam was restored to his Maker's favour, and therefore may securely resume his human rank.

After the scheme and fabrick of the poem, must be considered its component parts, the sentiments and the diction.

The *sentiments,* as expressive of manners, or appropriated to characters, are, for the greater part, unexceptionably just.

Splendid passages, containing lessons of morality, or precepts of prudence, occur seldom. Such is the original formation of this poem, that, as it admits no human manners till the Fall, it can give little assistance to human conduct. Its end is to raise the thoughts above sublunary cares or pleasures. Yet the praise of that fortitude, with which Abdiel maintained his singularity of virtue against the scorn of multitudes, may be accommodated to all times; and Raphael's reproof of Adam's curiosity after the planetary motions, with the answer returned by Adam, may be confidently opposed to any rule of life which any poet has delivered.

The thoughts which are occasionally called forth in the progress, are such as could only be produced by an imagination in the highest degree fervid and active, to which materials were supplied by incessant study and unlimited curiosity. The heat of Milton's mind might be said to sublimate his learning, to throw off into his work the spirit of science, unmingled with its grosser parts.

He had considered creation in its whole extent, and his descriptions are therefore learned. He had accustomed his imagination to unrestrained indulgence, and his conceptions therefore were extensive. The characteristick quality of his poem is sublimity. He sometimes descends to the elegant, but his element is the great. He can occasionally invest himself with grace; but his natural port is gigantick loftiness.[1] He can please when pleasure is required; but it is his peculiar power to astonish.

He seems to have been well acquainted with his own genius,

---

[1] "Algarotti terms it *gigantesca sublimità Miltoniana.*" Johnson.

and to know what it was that nature had bestowed upon him more bountifully than upon others; the power of displaying the vast, illuminating the splendid, enforcing the awful, darkening the gloomy, and aggravating the dreadful: he therefore chose a subject on which too much could not be said, on which he might tire his fancy without the censure of extravagance.

The appearances of nature, and the occurrences of life, did not satiate his appetite of greatness. To paint things as they are, requires a minute attention, and employs the memory rather than the fancy. Milton's delight was to sport in the wide regions of possibility; reality was a scene too narrow for his mind. He sent his faculties out upon discovery, into worlds where only imagination can travel, and delighted to form new modes of existence, and furnish sentiment and action to superior beings, to trace the counsels of hell, or accompany the choirs of heaven.

But he could not be always in other worlds: he must sometimes revisit earth, and tell of things visible and known. When he cannot raise wonder by the sublimity of his mind, he gives delight by its fertility.

Whatever be his subject, he never fails to fill the imagination. But his images and descriptions of the scenes or operations of nature do not seem to be always copied from original form, nor to have the freshness, raciness, and energy of immediate observation. He saw nature, as Dryden expresses it, *through the spectacles of books;* and on most occasions calls learning to his assistance. The garden of Eden brings to his mind the vale of Enna, where Proserpine was gathering flowers. Satan makes his way through fighting elements, like Argo between the Cyanean rocks, or Ulysses between the two Sicilian whirlpools, when he shunned Charybdis on the *larboard*. The mythological allusions have been justly censured, as not being always used with notice of their vanity; but they contribute variety to the narration, and produce an alternate exercise of the memory and the fancy.

His similies are less numerous, and more various, than those of his predecessors. But he does not confine himself within the limits of rigorous comparison: his great excellence is amplitude, and he expands the adventitious image beyond the dimensions which the occasion required. Thus, comparing the shield of Satan to the orb of the moon, he crowds the imagination with the discovery of the telescope, and all the wonders which the telescope discovers.

Of his moral sentiments it is hardly praise to affirm that they excel those of all other poets; for this superiority he was indebted to his acquaintance with the sacred writings. The ancient epick poets, wanting the light of Revelation, were very unskilful teachers of virtue: their principal characters may be great, but they are not amiable. The reader may rise from their works with a greater degree of active or passive fortitude, and sometimes of prudence; but he will be able to carry away few precepts of justice, and none of mercy.

From the Italian writers it appears, that the advantages of even Christian knowledge may be possessed in vain. Ariosto's pravity is generally known; and though the *Deliverance of Jerusalem* may be considered as a sacred subject, the poet has been very sparing of moral instruction.

In Milton every line breathes sanctity of thought, and purity of manners, except when the train of the narration requires the introduction of the rebellious spirits; and even they are compelled to acknowledge their subjection to God, in such a manner as excites reverence and confirms piety.

Of human beings there are but two; but those two are the parents of mankind, venerable before their fall for dignity and innocence, and amiable after it for repentance and submission. In their first state their affection is tender without weakness, and their piety sublime without presumption. When they have sinned, they shew how discord begins in natural frailty, and how it ought to cease in mutual forbearance; how confidence of the divine favour is forfeited by sin, and how hope of pardon may be obtained by penitence and prayer. A state of innocence we can only conceive, if indeed, in our present misery, it be possible to conceive it; but the sentiments and worship proper to a fallen and offending being, we have all to learn, as we have all to practise.

The poet, whatever be done, is always great. Our progenitors, in their first state, conversed with angels; even when folly and sin had degraded them, they had not in their humiliation *the port of mean suitors;* and they rise again to reverential regard, when we find that their prayers were heard.

As human passions did not enter the world before the Fall, there is in the *Paradise Lost* little opportunity for the pathetick; but what little there is has not been lost. That passion which is peculiar to rational nature, the anguish arising from the conscious-

ness of transgression, and the horrours attending the sense of the
Divine displeasure, are very justly described and forcibly impressed. But the passions are moved only on one occasion;
sublimity is the general and prevailing quality in this poem;
sublimity variously modified, sometimes descriptive, sometimes
argumentative.

The defects and faults of *Paradise Lost*, for faults and defects
every work of man must have, it is the business of impartial
criticism to discover. As, in displaying the excellence of Milton,
I have not made long quotations, because of selecting beauties
there had been no end, I shall in the same general manner mention that which seems to deserve censure; for what Englishman
can take delight in transcribing passages, which, if they lessen
the reputation of Milton, diminish in some degree the honour of
our country?

The generality of my scheme does not admit the frequent
notice of verbal inaccuracies; which Bentley,[2] perhaps better
skilled in grammar than in poetry, has often found, though he
sometimes made them, and which he imputed to the obtrusions
of a reviser whom the author's blindness obliged him to employ.
A supposition rash and groundless, if he thought it true; and vile
and pernicious if, as is said, he in private allowed it to be false.

The plan of *Paradise Lost* has this inconvenience, that it comprises neither human actions nor human manners. The man and
woman who act and suffer, are in a state which no other man or
woman can ever know. The reader finds no transaction in which
he can be engaged; beholds no condition in which he can by any
effort of imagination place himself; he has, therefore, little natural
curiosity or sympathy.

We all, indeed, feel the effects of Adam's disobedience; we all
sin like Adam, and like him must all bewail our offences; we have
restless and insidious enemies in the fallen angels, and in the
blessed spirits we have guardians and friends; in the redemption
of mankind we hope to be included; and in the description of
heaven and hell we are surely interested, as we are all to reside
hereafter either in the regions of horror or of bliss.

But these truths are too important to be new; they have been
taught to our infancy; they have mingled with our solitary

---

[2] Richard Bentley's edition of *Paradise Lost* was published in 1732.

thoughts and familiar conversation, and are habitually interwoven with the whole texture of life. Being therefore not new, they raise no unaccustomed emotion in the mind; what we knew before we cannot learn; what is not unexpected cannot surprise.

Of the ideas suggested by these awful scenes, from some we recede with reverence, except when stated hours require their association; and from others we shrink with horror, or admit them only as salutary inflictions, as counterpoises to our interests and passions. Such images rather obstruct the career of fancy than incite it.

Pleasure and terrour are indeed the genuine sources of poetry; but poetical pleasure must be such as human imagination can at least conceive, and poetical terrour such as human strength and fortitude may combat. The good and evil of eternity are too ponderous for the wings of wit; the mind sinks under them in passive helplessness, content with calm belief and humble adoration.

Known truths, however, may take a different appearance, and be conveyed to the mind by a new train of intermediate images. This Milton has undertaken, and performed with pregnancy and vigour of mind peculiar to himself. Whoever considers the few radical positions which the Scriptures afforded him, will wonder by what energetick operation he expanded them to such extent, and ramified them to so much variety, restrained as he was by religious reverence from licentiousness of fiction.

Here is a full display of the united force of study and genius; of a great accumulation of materials, with judgement to digest, and fancy to combine them: Milton was able to select from nature, or from story, from ancient fable, or from modern science, whatever could illustrate or adorn his thoughts. An accumulation of knowledge impregnated his mind, fermented by study, and sublimed by imagination.

It has been therefore said, without an indecent hyperbole, by one of his encomiasts, that in reading *Paradise Lost* we read a book of universal knowledge.

But original deficience cannot be supplied. The want of human interest is always felt. *Paradise Lost* is one of the books which the reader admires and lays down, and forgets to take up again.[3] Its

---

[3] After *again* "None ever wished it longer than it is." Added in 1783.

perusal is a duty rather than a pleasure. We read Milton for instruction, retire harassed and overburdened, and look elsewhere
for recreation; we desert our master, and seek for companions.

Another inconvenience of Milton's design is, that it requires
the description of what cannot be described, the agency of spirits.
He saw that immateriality supplied no images, and that he could
not show angels acting but by instruments of action; he therefore
invested them with form and matter. This, being necessary, was
therefore defensible; and he should have secured the consistency
of his system, by keeping immateriality out of sight, and enticing
his reader to drop it from his thoughts. But he has unhappily
perplexed his poetry with his philosophy. His infernal and celestial powers are sometimes pure spirit, and sometimes animated
body. When Satan walks with his lance upon the *burning marle,*
he has a body; when in his passage between hell and the new
world, he is in danger of sinking in the vacuity, and is supported
by a gust of rising vapours, he has a body; when he animates the
toad, he seems to be mere spirit, that can penetrate matter at
pleasure; when he *starts up in his own shape,* he has at least a
determined form; and when he is brought before Gabriel, he has
a *spear and shield,* which he had the power of hiding in the toad,
though the arms of the contending angels are evidently material.

The vulgar inhabitants of Pandaemonium being *incorporeal
spirits,* are *at large, though without number,* in a limited space;
yet in the battle, when they were overwhelmed by mountains,
their armour hurt them, *crushed in upon their substance, now
grown gross by sinning.* This likewise happened to the uncorrupted angels, who were overthrown *the sooner for their arms,* for
*unarmed they might easily as spirits have evaded by contraction,
or remove.* Even as spirits they are hardly spiritual; for *contraction* and *remove* are images of matter; but if they could have
escaped without their armour, they might have escaped from it,
and left only the empty cover to be battered. Uriel, when he rides
on a sun-beam, is material: Satan is material when he is afraid
of the prowess of Adam.

The confusion of spirit and matter which pervades the whole
narration of the war of heaven fills it with incongruity; and the
book, in which it is related, is, I believe, the favourite of children,
and gradually neglected as knowledge is increased.

After the operation of immaterial agents, which cannot be explained, may be considered that of allegorical persons, which have no real existence. To exalt causes into agents, to invest abstract ideas with form, and animate them with activity, has always been the right of poetry. But such airy beings are, for the most part, suffered only to do their natural office, and retire. Thus Fame tells a tale, and Victory hovers over a general, or perches on a standard; but Fame and Victory can do no more. To give them any real employment, or ascribe to them any material agency, is to make them allegorical no longer, but to shock the mind by ascribing effects to non-entity. In the *Prometheus* of Aeschylus, we see Violence and Strength, and in the *Alcestis* of Euripides, we see Death brought upon the stage, all as active persons of the drama; but no precedents can justify absurdity.

Milton's allegory of Sin and Death is undoubtedly faulty. Sin is indeed the mother of Death, and may be allowed to be the portress of hell; but when they stop the journey of Satan, a journey described as real, and when Death offers him battle, the allegory is broken. That Sin and Death should have shewn the way to hell might have been allowed; but they cannot facilitate the passage by building a bridge, because the difficulty of Satan's passage is described as real and sensible, and the bridge ought to be only figurative. The hell assigned to the rebellious spirits is described as not less local than the residence of man. It is placed in some distant part of space, separated from the regions of harmony and order by a chaotick waste and an unoccupied vacuity; but Sin and Death worked up a *mole* of *aggregated soil,* cemented with *asphaltus;* a work too bulky for ideal architects.

This unskilful allegory appears to me one of the greatest faults of the poem; and to this there was no temptation, but the author's opinion of its beauty.

To the conduct of the narrative some objections may be made. Satan is with great expectation brought before Gabriel in Paradise, and is suffered to go away unmolested. The creation of man is represented as the consequence of the vacuity left in heaven by the expulsion of the rebels, yet Satan mentions it as a report *rife in heaven* before his departure.

To find sentiments for the state of innocence, was very difficult; and something of anticipation perhaps is now and then discovered.

Adam's discourse of dreams seems not to be the speculation of a new-created being. I know not whether his answer to the angel's reproof for curiosity does not want something of propriety: it is the speech of a man acquainted with many other men. Some philosophical notions, especially when the philosophy is false, might have been better omitted. The angel, in a comparison, speaks of *timorous deer*, before deer were yet timorous, and before Adam could understand the comparison.

Dryden remarks, that Milton has some flats among his elevations. This is only to say that all the parts are not equal. In every work one part must be for the sake of others; a palace must have passages; a poem must have transitions. It is no more to be required that wit should always be blazing, than that the sun should always stand at noon. In a great work there is a vicissitude of luminous and opaque parts, as there is in the world a succession of day and night. Milton, when he has expatiated in the sky, may be allowed sometimes to revisit earth; for what other author ever soared so high, or sustained his flight so long?

Milton, being well versed in the Italian poets, appears to have borrowed often from them; and, as every man learns something from his companions, his desire of imitating Ariosto's levity has disgraced his work with the *Paradise of Fools;* a fiction not in itself ill-imagined, but too ludicrous for its place.

His play on words, in which he delights too often; his equivocations which Bentley endeavours to defend by the example of the ancients; his unnecessary and ungraceful use of terms of art, it is not necessary to mention, because they are easily remarked, and generally censured, and at last bear so little proportion to the whole, that they scarcely deserve the attention of a critick.

Such are the faults of that wonderful performance *Paradise Lost;* which he who can put in balance with its beauties must be considered not as nice but as dull, as less to be censured for want of candour than pitied for want of sensibility.

Of *Paradise Regained,* the general judgement seems now to be right, that it is in many parts elegant, and every-where instructive. It was not to be supposed that the writer of *Paradise Lost* could ever write without great effusions of fancy, and exalted precepts of wisdom. The basis of *Paradise Regained* is narrow; a dialogue without action can never please like an union of the narrative and dramatick powers. Had this poem been written not by Milton, but by some imitator, it would have claimed and received universal praise.

If *Paradise Regained* has been too much depreciated, *Samson Agonistes* has in requital been too much admired. It could only be by long prejudice, and the bigotry of learning, that Milton could prefer the ancient tragedies, with their encumbrance of a chorus, to the exhibitions of the French and English stages; and it is only by a blind confidence in the reputation of Milton, that a drama can be praised in which the intermediate parts have neither cause nor consequence, neither hasten nor retard the catastrophe.

In this tragedy are however many particular beauties, many just sentiments and striking lines; but it wants that power of attracting the attention which a well-connected plan produces.

Milton would not have excelled in dramatick writing; he knew human nature only in the gross, and had never studied the shades of character, nor the combinations of concurring, or the perplexity of contending passions. He had read much, and knew what books could teach; but had mingled little in the world, and was deficient in the knowledge which experience must confer.

Through all his greater works there prevails an uniform peculiarity of *diction*, a mode and cast of expression which bears little resemblance to that of any former writer, and which is so far removed from common use, that an unlearned reader, when he first opens his book, finds himself surprised by a new language.

This novelty has been, by those who can find nothing wrong in Milton, imputed to his laborious endeavours after words suitable to the grandeur of his ideas. *Our language,* says Addison, *sunk under him.* But the truth is, that, both in prose and verse, he had formed his stile by a perverse and pedantick principle. He was desirous to use English words with a foreign idiom. This in all his prose is discovered and condemned; for there judgement operates freely, neither softened by the beauty nor awed by the dignity of his thoughts; but such is the power of his poetry, that his call is obeyed without resistance, the reader feels himself in captivity to a higher and a nobler mind, and criticism sinks in admiration.

Milton's stile was not modified by his subject: what is shown with greater extent in *Paradise Lost*, may be found in *Comus*. One source of his peculiarity was his familiarity with the Tuscan poets: the disposition of his words is, I think, frequently Italian; perhaps sometimes combined with other tongues. Of him, at last, may be said what Jonson says of Spenser, that *he wrote no language*, but has formed what Butler calls a *Babylonish dialect*,[4] in itself harsh and barbarous; but made by exalted genius, and extensive learning, the vehicle of so much instruction and so much pleasure, that, like other lovers, we find grace in its deformity.

Whatever be the faults of his diction, he cannot want the praise of copiousness and variety: he was master of his language in its full extent; and has selected the melodious words with such diligence, that from his book alone the Art of English Poetry might be learned.

After his diction, something must be said of his *versification*. *The measure*, he says, *is the English heroick verse without rhyme*. Of this mode he had many examples among the Italians, and some in his own country. The Earl of Surry is said to have translated one of Virgil's books without rhyme;[5] and, besides our tragedies, a few short poems had appeared in blank verse; particularly one tending to reconcile the nation to Raleigh's wild attempt upon Guiana, and probably written by Raleigh himself. These petty performances cannot be supposed to have much influenced Milton, who more probably took his hint from Trisino's *Italia Liberata;*[6] and, finding blank verse easier than rhyme, was desirous of persuading himself that it is better.

*Rhyme*, he says, and says truly, *is no necessary adjunct of true poetry*. But perhaps, of poetry as a mental operation, metre or musick is no necessary adjunct: it is however by the musick of metre that poetry has been discriminated in all languages; and in languages melodiously constructed, by a due proportion of long and short syllables, metre is sufficient. But one language cannot communicate its rules to another: where metre is scanty and imperfect, some help is necessary. The musick of the English heroick line strikes the ear so faintly that it is easily lost, unless all the syllables of every line co-operate together: this co-operation can

---

[4] Ben Jonson in *Discoveries*, Butler in *Hudibras*, I.i.93.

[5] *Aeneid* II and IV.

[6] Giorgio Trissino's *Italia Liberata da' Goti*, 1548.

be only obtained by the preservation of every verse unmingled with another, as a distinct system of sounds; and this distinctness is obtained and preserved by the artifice of rhyme. The variety of pauses, so much boasted by the lovers of blank verse, changes the measures of an English poet to the periods of a declaimer; and there are only a few skilful and happy readers of Milton, who enable their audience to perceive where the lines end or begin. *Blank verse,* said an ingenious critick,[7] *seems to be verse only to the eye.*

Poetry may subsist without rhyme, but English poetry will not often please; nor can rhyme ever be safely spared but where the subject is able to support itself. Blank verse makes some approach to that which is called the *lapidary stile;* has neither the easiness of prose, nor the melody of numbers, and therefore tires by long continuance. Of the Italian writers without rhyme, whom Milton alleges as precedents, not one is popular; what reason could urge in its defence, has been confuted by the ear.

But, whatever be the advantage of rhyme, I cannot prevail on myself to wish that Milton had been a rhymer; for I cannot wish his work to be other than it is; yet, like other heroes, he is to be admired rather than imitated. He that thinks himself capable of astonishing, may write blank verse; but those that hope only to please, must condescend to rhyme.

The highest praise of genius is original invention. Milton cannot be said to have contrived the structure of an epick poem, and therefore must yield to that vigour and amplitude of mind to which all generations must be indebted for the art of poetical narration, for the texture of the fable, the variation of incidents, the interposition of dialogue, and all the stratagems that surprise and enchain attention. But, of all the borrowers from Homer, Milton is perhaps the least indebted. He was naturally a thinker for himself, confident of his own abilities, and disdainful of help or hindrance: he did not refuse admission to the thoughts or images of his predecessors, but he did not seek them. From his contemporaries he neither courted nor received support; there is in his writings nothing by which the pride of other authors might be gratified, or favour gained; no exchange of praise, nor solicita-

---

[7] William Locke (d. 1810), "whose taste in the fine arts," says Boswell, was "universally celebrated." (*Life,* IV.43.)

tion of support. His great works were performed under discountenance, and in blindness, but difficulties vanished at his touch; he was born for whatever is arduous, and his work is not the greatest of heroick poems, only because it is not the first.

*The* Life of Gray *was published in Volume X of Johnson's* Prefaces *(1781), and was reprinted in the same year in his* Lives of the Poets. *It was attacked at once, inasmuch as many of Gray's friends were still alive. Reprinted from the first edition.*

# Life of Gray

Thomas Gray, the son of Mr. Philip Gray, a scrivener of London, was born in Cornhill, November 26, 1716. His grammatical education he received at Eton under[1] Mr. Antrobus, his mother's brother;[2] and when he left school, in 1734, entered a pensioner at Peterhouse in Cambridge.

The transition from the school to the college is, to most young scholars, the time from which they date their years of manhood, liberty, and happiness; but Gray seems to have been very little delighted with academical gratifications; he liked at Cambridge neither the mode of life nor the fashion of study, and lived sullenly on to the time when his attendance on lectures was no longer required. As he intended to profess the Common Law, he took no degree.

When he had been at Cambridge about five years, Mr. Horace Walpole, whose friendship he had gained at Eton, invited him to travel with him as his companion. They wandered through France into Italy; and Gray's letters contain a very pleasing account of many parts of their journey. But unequal friendships are easily dissolved: at Florence they quarrelled, and parted, and Mr. Walpole is now content to have it told that it was by his fault. If we look however without prejudice on the world, we shall find that men, whose consciousness of their own merits sets them above the compliances of servility, are apt enough in their association with superiors to watch their own dignity with troublesome and punc-

---

[1] under: under the care of *in the 1783 edition, hereafter referred to as 1783.* Here and below Johnson has "Eaton," later corrected.
[2] brother: brother, then assistant to Dr. George, *1783*

tilious jealousy, and in the fervour of independance to exact that attention which they refuse to pay. Part they did, whatever was the quarrel, and the rest of their travels was doubtless more unpleasant to them both. Gray continued his journey in a manner suitable to his own little fortune, with only an occasional servant.

He returned to England in September 1741, and in about two months afterwards buried his father, who had, by an injudicious waste of money upon a new house, so much lessened his fortune, that Gray thought himself too poor to study the law. He therefore retired to Cambridge, where he soon after became Bachelor of Civil Law; and where, without liking the place or its inhabitants, or pretending³ to like them, he passed, except a short residence at London, the rest of his life.

About this time he was deprived of Mr. West, the son of a chancellor of Ireland, a friend on whom he appears to have set a high value, and who deserved his esteem by the powers which he shews in his letters, and in the *Ode to May*, which Mr. Mason has preserved, as well as by the sincerity with which, when Gray sent him part of *Agrippina*, a tragedy that he had just begun, he gave an opinion which probably intercepted the progress of the work, and which the judgement of every reader will confirm. It was certainly no loss to the English stage that *Agrippina* was never finished.

In this year (1742) Gray seems first to have applied himself seriously to poetry; for in this year were produced the *Ode to Spring*, his *Prospect of Eton*, and his *Ode to Adversity*. He began likewise a Latin Poem, *de Principiis Cogitandi*.

It seems to be the opinion⁴ of Mr. Mason, that his first ambition was to have excelled in Latin poetry: perhaps it were reasonable to wish that he had prosecuted his design; for though there is at present some embarrassment in his phrase, and some harshness in his lyrick numbers, his copiousness of language is such as very few possess; and his lines, even when imperfect, discover a writer whom practice would quickly have made skilful.

He now lived on at Peterhouse, very little solicitous what others did or thought, and cultivated his mind and enlarged his views without any other purpose than of improving and amusing him-

---

³ pretending: professing *1783*
⁴ seems to be the opinion: may be collected from the narrative *1783*

self; when Mr. Mason, being elected fellow of Pembroke-hall, brought him a companion who was afterwards to be his editor, and whose fondness and fidelity has kindled in him a zeal of admiration, which cannot be reasonably expected from the neutrality of a stranger and the coldness of a critick.

In this retirement he wrote (1747) an ode on the *Death of Mr. Walpole's Cat;* and the year afterwards attempted a poem of more importance, on *Government and Education,* of which the fragments which remain have many excellent lines.

His next production (1750) was his far-famed *Elegy in the Church-yard,* which, finding its way into a Magazine,[5] first, I believe, made him known to the publick.

An invitation from Lady Cobham about this time gave occasion to an odd composition called *A Long Story,* which though perhaps[6] it adds little to Gray's character, I am not pleased to find wanting in this collection. It will therefore be added to this Preface.

Several of his pieces were published (1753), with designs, by Mr. Bentley; and, that they might in some form or other make a book, only one side of each leaf was printed. I believe the poems and the plates recommended each other so well, that the whole impression was soon bought. This year he lost his mother.

Some time afterwards (1756) some young men of the college, whose chambers were near his, diverted themselves with disturbing him by frequent and troublesome noises.[7] This insolence,

---

[5] *The Magazine of Magazines,* February 1751, in which the poem bore Gray's name, whereas the separate publication, appearing a day earlier, was anonymous.

[6] which though perhaps . . . Preface: which adds little to Gray's character. 1783 (As the poem is not an integral part of the biography, it is omitted from this edition.)

[7] noises: noises, and, as is said, by pranks yet more offensive and contemptuous. 1783. Gray's house in London had been destroyed by fire, and he had consequently had a rope ladder installed in his rooms in Peterhouse. Some undergraduates early one morning "ordered their man Joe Draper to roar out fire. A delicate white night-cap is said to have appeared at the window; but finding the mistake, retired again to the couch. The young fellows, had he descended, were determined, they said, to have whipped the butterfly up again." (*Correspondence,* ed. Toynbee and Whibley, 1935, III.1220.) The master of the college offended Gray by calling the episode "a boyish frolic," and Gray "migrated" to Pembroke a day or two later. In a letter Gray said that he left "because the rooms were noisy & the People of the house dirty." (Ibid., II.458.)

having endured it a while, he represented to the governors of the society, among whom perhaps he had no friends; and, finding his complaint little regarded, removed himself to Pembroke-hall.

In 1757 he published *The Progress of Poetry* and *The Bard*, two compositions at which the readers of poetry were at first content to gaze in mute amazement. Some that tried them confessed their inability to understand them, though Warburton said that they were understood as well as the works of Milton and Shakespeare, which it is the fashion to praise.[8] Garrick wrote a few lines in their praise. Some hardy champions undertook to rescue them from neglect, and in a short time many were content to be shewn beauties which they could not see.

Gray's reputation was now so high, that, after the death of Cibber, he had the honour of refusing the laurel, which was then bestowed on Mr. Whitehead.

His curiosity, not long after, drew him away from Cambridge to a lodging near the Museum, where he resided near three years, reading and transcribing; and, so far as can be discovered, very little affected by two odes on *Oblivion* and *Obscurity*, in which his lyrick performances were ridiculed with much contempt and much ingenuity.[9]

When the Professor of Modern Languages[1] at Cambridge died, he was, as he says, *cockered and spirited up*, till he asked it of Lord Bute, who sent him a civil refusal; and the place was given to Mr. Brocket, the tutor of Sir James Lowther.

His constitution was weak, and believing that his health was promoted by exercise and change of place, he undertook (1765) a journey into Scotland, of which his account, so far as it extends, is very curious and elegant; for as his comprehension was ample, his curiosity extended to all the works of art, all the appearances of nature, and all the monuments of past events. He naturally contracted a friendship with Dr. Beattie, whom he found a poet, a philosopher, and a good man. The Mareschal College at Aberdeen offered him the degree of Doctor of Laws, which, having omitted to take it at Cambridge, he thought it decent to refuse.

What he had formerly solicited in vain, was at last given him

---

[8] praise: admire *1783*
[9] Joint productions (1760) of George Colman and Robert Lloyd.
[1] Languages: History *1783*

without solicitation. The Professorship of Languages[2] became again vacant, and he received (1768) an offer of it from the Duke of Grafton. He accepted, and retained it to his death; always designing lectures, but never reading them; uneasy at his neglect of duty, and appeasing his uneasiness with designs of reformation, and with a resolution which he believed himself to have made of resigning the office, if he found himself unable to discharge it.

Ill health made another journey necessary, and he visited (1769) Westmoreland and Cumberland. He that reads his epistolary narration wishes, that to travel, and to tell his travels, had been more of his employment; but it is by studying at home that we must obtain the ability of travelling with intelligence and improvement.

His travels and his studies were now near their end. The gout, of which he had sustained many weak attacks, fell upon his stomach, and, yielding to no medicines, produced strong convulsions, which (July 30, 1771) terminated in death.

His character I am willing to adopt, as Mr. Mason has done, from a nameless writer;[3] and am as willing as his warmest friend[4] to believe it true.

Perhaps he was the most learned man in Europe. He was equally acquainted with the elegant and profound parts of science, and that not superficially but thoroughly. He knew every branch of history, both natural and civil; had read all the original historians of England, France, and Italy; and was a great antiquarian. Criticism, metaphysics, morals, politics, made a principal part of his study; voyages and travels of all sorts were his favourite amusements; and he had a fine taste in painting, prints, architecture, and gardening. With such a fund of knowledge, his conversation must have been equally instructing and entertaining; but he was also a good man, a man of virtue and humanity. There is no character without some speck, some imperfection; and I think the greatest defect in his was an affectation in delicacy, or rather effeminacy, and a visible fastidious-

---

[2] Languages: History *1783*

[3] nameless writer: letter written to my friend Mr. Boswell, by the Rev. Mr. Temple, rector of St. Gluvias in Cornwall *1783*. (Johnson wrote Boswell in August 1782, saying that he had forgotten the name of the writer, which Boswell had evidently told him after seeing the first edition.)

[4] friend: well-wisher *1783*

ness, or contempt and disdain of his inferiors in science. He also had, in some degree, that weakness which disgusted Voltaire so much in Mr. Congreve: though he seemed to value others chiefly according to the progress they had made in knowledge, yet he could not bear to be considered himself merely as a man of letters; and though without birth, or fortune, or station, his desire was to be looked upon as a private independent gentleman, who read for his amusement. Perhaps it may be said, What signifies so much knowledge, when it produced so little? Is it worth taking so much pains to leave no memorial but a few poems? But let it be considered that Mr. Gray was, to others, at least innocently employed; to himself, certainly beneficially. His time passed agreeably; he was every day making some new acquisition in science; his mind was enlarged, his heart softened, his virtue strengthened; the world and mankind were shewn to him without a mask; and he was taught to consider every thing as trifling, and unworthy of the attention of a wise man, except the pursuit of knowledge and practice of virtue, in that state wherein God hath placed us.

To this character Mr. Mason has added a more particular account of Gray's skill in zoology. He has remarked, that Gray's effeminacy was affected most *before those whom he did not wish to please;*[5] and that he is unjustly charged with making knowledge his sole reason of preference, as he paid his esteem to none whom he did not likewise believe to be good.

What has occurred to me, from the slight inspection of his letters in which my undertaking has engaged me, is, that his mind had a large grasp; that his curiosity was unlimited, and his judgement cultivated; that he was a man likely to love much where he loved at all, but that he was fastidious and hard to please. His contempt however is often employed, where I hope it will be approved, upon scepticism and infidelity. His short account of Shaftesbury I will insert.

You say you cannot conceive how Lord Shaftesbury came to be a philosopher in vogue; I will tell you: first, he was a lord; secondly, he was as vain as any of his readers; thirdly, men are

---

[5] Mason, *Gray*, 1775, 403.

very prone to believe what they do not understand; fourthly, they will believe any thing at all, provided they are under no obligation to believe it; fifthly, they love to take a new road, even when that road leads no where; sixthly, he was reckoned a fine writer, and seems always to mean more than he said. Would you have any more reasons? An interval of above forty years has pretty well destroyed the charm. A dead lord ranks with commoners: vanity is no longer interested in the matter, for a new road is become an old one.[6]

Mr. Mason has added, from his own knowledge, that though Gray was poor, he was not eager of money; and that, out of the little that he had, he was very willing to help the necessitous.[7]

As a writer he had this peculiarity, that he did not write his pieces first rudely, and then correct them, but laboured every line as it arose in the train of composition; and he had a notion not very peculiar, that he could not write but at certain times, or at happy moments; a fantastick foppery, to which my kindness for a man of learning and of virtue wishes him to have been superior.

Gray's poetry is now to be considered; and I hope not to be looked on as an enemy to his name, if I confess that I contemplate it with less pleasure than his life.

His ode on *Spring* has something poetical, both in the language and the thought; but the language is too luxuriant, and the thoughts have nothing new. There has of late arisen a practice of giving to adjectives, derived from substantives, the termination of participles; such as the *cultured* plain, the *dasied* bank; but I was sorry to see, in the lines of a scholar like Gray, the *honied* spring. The morality is natural, but too stale; the conclusion is pretty.

The poem on the *Cat* was doubtless by its author considered

---

[6] From a letter to Stonehewer, August 18, 1758, printed by Mason.
[7] Mason, *Gray*, 335.

as a trifle, but it is not a happy trifle. In the first stanza *the azure flowers* that *blow,* shew resolutely a rhyme is sometimes made when it cannot easily be found. Selima, the cat, is called a nymph, with some violence both to language and sense; but there is good use made of it when it is done; for of the two lines,

> What female heart can gold despise?
> What cat's averse to fish?

the first relates merely to the nymph, and the second only to the cat. The sixth stanza contains a melancholy truth, that *a favourite has no friend;* but the last ends in a pointed sentence of no relation to the purpose; if *what glistered* had been *gold,* the cat would not have gone into the water; and, if she had, would not less have been drowned.

The *Prospect of Eton College* suggests nothing to Gray, which every beholder does not equally think and feel. His supplication to father Thames, to tell him who drives the hoop or tosses the ball, is useless and puerile. Father Thames has no better means of knowing than himself. His epithet *buxom health* is not elegant; he seems not to understand the word. Gray thought his language more poetical as it was more remote from common use: finding in Dryden *honey redolent of spring,* an expression that reaches the utmost limits of our language, Gray drove it a little more beyond common apprehension, by making *gales* to be *redolent of joy and youth.*

Of the *Ode on Adversity,* the hint was at first taken from *O Diva, gratum quae regis Antium;*[8] but Gray has excelled his original by the variety of his sentiments, and by their moral application. Of this piece, at once poetical and rational, I will not by slight objections violate the dignity.

My process has now brought me to the *wonderful wonder of wonders,* the two sister odes; by which, though either vulgar ignorance or common sense at first universally rejected them, many have been since persuaded to think themselves delighted. I am one of those that are willing to be pleased, and therefore would gladly find the meaning of the first stanza of the *Progress of Poetry.*

---

[8] Horace, *Odes,* I.35

Gray seems in his rapture to confound the images of *spreading sound* and *running water*. A *stream of musick* may be allowed; but where does *musick*, however *smooth and strong*, after having visited the *verdant vales, rowl down the steep amain*, so as that *rocks and nodding groves rebellow to the roar?* If this be said of *musick*, it is nonsense; if it be said of *water*, it is nothing to the purpose.

The second stanza, exhibiting Mars's car and Jove's eagle, is unworthy of further notice. Criticism disdains to chase a schoolboy to his common places.

To the third it may likewise be objected, that it is drawn from mythology, though such as may be more easily assimilated to real life. Idalia's *velvet-green* has something of cant. An epithet or metaphor drawn from Nature ennobles Art; an epithet or metaphor drawn from Art degrades Nature. Gray is too fond of words arbitrarily compounded. *Many-twinkling* was formerly censured as not analogical; we may say *many-spotted*, but scarcely *many-spotting*. This stanza, however, has something pleasing.

Of the second ternary of stanzas, the first endeavours to tell something, and would have told it, had it not been crossed by Hyperion: the second describes well enough the universal prevalence of poetry; but I am afraid that the conclusion will not rise from the premises. The caverns of the North and the plains of Chili are not the residences of *glory* and *generous shame*. But that Poetry and Virtue go always together is an opinion so pleasing, that I can forgive him who resolves to think it true.

The third stanza sounds big with Delphi, and Egean, and Ilissus, and Meander, and *hallowed fountain* and *solemn sound;* but in all Gray's odes there is a kind of cumbrous splendor which we wish away. His position is at last false: in the time of Dante and Petrarch, from whom he derives our first school of poetry, Italy was over-run by *tyrant power* and *coward vice;* nor was our state much better when we first borrowed the Italian arts.

Of the third ternary, the first gives a mythological birth of Shakespeare. What is said of that mighty genius is true; but it is not said happily: the real effects of his poetical power are put out of sight by the pomp of machinery. Where truth is sufficient to fill the mind, fiction is worse than useless; the counterfeit debases the genuine.

His account of Milton's blindness, if we suppose it caused by study in the formation of his poem, a supposition surely allowable, is poetically true, and happily imagined. But the *car* of Dryden, with his *two coursers*, has nothing in it peculiar; it is a car in which any other rider may be placed.

*The Bard* appears, at the first view, to be, as Algarotti[9] and others have remarked, an imitation of the prophecy of Nereus.[1] Algarotti thinks it superior to its original; and, if preference depends only on the imagery and animation of the two poems, his judgement is right. There is in *The Bard* more force, more thought, and more variety. But to copy is less than to invent, and the copy has been unhappily produced at a wrong time. The fiction of Horace was to the Romans credible; but its revival disgusts us with apparent and unconquerable falsehood. *Incredulus odi.*[2]

To select a singular event, and swell it to a giant's bulk by fabulous appendages of spectres and predictions, has little difficulty, for he that forsakes the probable may always find the marvellous; and it has little use, we are affected only as we believe; we are improved only as we find something to be imitated or declined. I do not see that *The Bard* promotes any truth, moral or political.

His stanzas are too long, especially his epodes; the ode is finished before the ear has learned its measures, and consequently before it can receive pleasure from their consonance and recurrence.

Of the first stanza the abrupt beginning has been celebrated, but technical beauties can give praise only to the inventor. It is in the power of any man to rush abruptly upon his subject, that has read the ballad of *Johnny Armstrong*.

*Is there ever a man in all Scotland—*

The initial resemblances, or alliterations, *ruin, ruthless, helm nor hauberk,* are below the grandeur of a poem that endeavours at sublimity.

In the second stanza the Bard is well described; but in the third we have the puerilities of obsolete mythology. When we are told

---

[9] Count Francesco Algarotti (1712–64), Italian critic.
[1] Horace, *Odes,* I.15
[2] Horace, *Ars Poetica,* l. 188: "Unbelieving, I hate it."

that Cadwallo *hush'd the stormy main,* and that Modred *made huge Plinlimmon bow his cloud-top'd head,* attention recoils from the repetition of a tale that, even when it was first heard, was heard with scorn.

The *weaving* of the *winding sheet* he borrowed, as he owns, from the northern bards; but their texture, however, was very properly the work of female powers, as the art of spinning the thread of life in another mythology. Theft is always dangerous; Gray has made weavers of his slaughtered bards, by a fiction outrageous and incongruous. They are then called upon to *Weave the warp, and weave the woof,* perhaps with no great propriety; for it is by crossing the *woof* with the *warp* that men *weave* the *web* or piece; and the first line was dearly bought by the admission of its wretched correspondent, *Give ample room and verge enough.* He has, however, no other line as bad.

The third stanza of the second ternary is commended, I think, beyond its merit. The personification is indistinct. Thirst and Hunger are not alike; and their features, to make the imagery perfect, should have been discriminated. We are told, in the same stanza, how *towers* are *fed.* But I will no longer look for particular faults; yet let it be observed that the ode might have been concluded with an action of better example; but suicide is always to be had, without expence of thought.

These odes are marked by glittering accumulations of ungraceful ornaments; they strike rather than please; the images are magnified by affectation; the language is laboured into harshness. The mind of the writer seems to work with unnatural violence. *Double, double, toil and trouble.* He has a kind of strutting dignity, and is tall by walking on tiptoe. His art and his struggle are too visible, and there is too little appearance of ease or[3] nature.

To say that he has no beauties would be unjust: a man like him, of great learning and great industry, could not but produce something valuable. When he pleases least, it can only be said that a good design was ill directed.

His translations of Northern and Welsh poetry deserve praise; the imagery is preserved, perhaps often improved; but the language is unlike the language of other poets.

In the character of his *Elegy* I rejoice to concur with the com-

---

[3] ease or: ease and *1783*

mon reader; for by the common sense of readers uncorrupted with literary prejudices, after all the refinements of subtilty and the dogmatism of learning, must be finally decided all claim to poetical honours. The *Church-yard* abounds with images which find a mirrour in every mind, and with sentiments to which every bosom returns an echo. The four stanzas beginning *Yet even these bones* are to me original: I have never seen the notions in any other place; yet he that reads them here, persuades himself that he has always felt them. Had Gray written often thus, it had been vain to blame, and useless to praise him.

*Although Johnson encouraged Percy to reprint poetry of the late Middle Ages and early Renaissance, he thought modern imitations ridiculous. The first of the following four poems is a general criticism of Thomas Warton's Poems of 1777, the second is a parody. The third and fourth attack Percy's version of the simple ballad style in his long original poem, The Hermit of Warkworth. Text of the first as recorded by Mrs. Thrale, the rest from Boswell.*

# Light Verse

## *Lines written in ridicule of Thomas Warton's Poems*

Wheresoe'er I turn my view,
All is strange, yet nothing new;
Endless labour all along,
Endless labour to be wrong;
Phrase that time has flung away,　　　　5
Uncouth words in disarray:
Trickt in antique ruff and bonnet,
Ode and elegy and sonnet.

## *Parody of Thomas Warton*

Hermit hoar, in solemn cell,
　Wearing out life's evening gray;
Smite thy bosom, sage, and tell,
　Where is bliss? and which the way?

Thus I spoke; and speaking sigh'd;　　　　5

——Scarce repress'd the starting tear;——
When the smiling sage reply'd——
——Come, my lad, and drink some beer.

## *Parodies of* The Hermit of Warkworth

The tender infant meek and mild
    Fell down upon a stone;
The nurse took up the squealing child
    But yet the child squeal'd on.

I put my hat upon my head
    And walk'd into the Strand,
And there I met another man
    Who's hat was in his hand.

## *A Short Song of Congratulation*

Johnson wrote only one personal satire—on Thrale's nephew,
Sir John Lade, whom he had not advised to marry, as he was
"not likely to propagate understanding." Sir John married a
prostitute and fulfilled Johnson's forecast in this poem by
squandering his fortune.

Long-expected one and twenty
    Ling'ring year at last is flown,
Pomp and pleasure, pride and plenty
    Great Sir John, are all your own.

Loosen'd from the minor's tether,                    5
    Free to mortgage or to sell,
Wild as wind, and light as feather
    Bid the slaves of thrift farewell.

Call the Bettys, Kates, and Jennys
    Ev'ry name that laughs at care,                  10

Lavish of your grandsire's guineas,
  Show the spirit of an heir.

All that prey on vice and folly
  Joy to see their quarry fly,
Here the gamester light and jolly      15
  There the lender grave and sly.

Wealth, Sir John, was made to wander,
  Let it wander as it will;
See the jocky, see the pander,
  Bid them come, and take their fill.      20

When the bonny blade carouses,
  Pockets full, and spirits high,
What are acres? What are houses?
  Only dirt, or wet or dry.

If the guardian or the mother      25
  Tell the woes of wilful waste,
Scorn their counsel and their pother,
  **You can hang or drown at last.**

# Letters

## *To the Right Honourable the Earl of Chesterfield*

February, 1755

MY LORD,

I have been lately informed, by the proprietor of the World, that two papers, in which my Dictionary is recommended to the publick, were written by your Lordship. To be so distinguished, is an honour, which, being very little accustomed to favours from the great, I know not well how to receive, or in what terms to acknowledge.

When, upon some slight encouragement, I first visited your Lordship, I was overpowered, like the rest of mankind, by the enchantment of your address; and could not forbear to wish that I might boast myself *Le vainqueur du vainqueur de la terre;*[1]— that I might obtain that regard for which I saw the world contending; but I found my attendance so little encouraged, that neither pride nor modesty would suffer me to continue it. When I had once addressed your Lordship in publick, I had exhausted all the art of pleasing which a retired and uncourtly scholar can possess. I had done all that I could; and no man is well pleased to have his all neglected, be it ever so little.

Seven years, my Lord, have now past, since I waited in your outward rooms, or was repulsed from your door; during which time I have been pushing on my work through difficulties, of which it is useless to complain, and have brought it, at last, to the verge of publication, without one act of assistance, one word of encouragement, or one smile of favour. Such treatment I did not expect, for I never had a Patron before.

The shepherd in Virgil grew at last acquainted with Love, and found him a native of the rocks.[2]

---

[1] Modified from Boileau, *L'Art poétique*, III.272.
[2] *Eclogues*, VIII.43.

Is not a Patron, my Lord, one who looks with unconcern on a man struggling for life in the water, and, when he has reached ground, encumbers him with help? The notice which you have been pleased to take of my labours, had it been early, had been kind; but it has been delayed till I am indifferent, and cannot enjoy it; till I am solitary, and cannot impart it; till I am known, and do not want it. I hope it is no very cynical asperity not to confess obligations where no benefit has been received, or to be unwilling that the publick should consider me as owing that to a Patron, which Providence has enabled me to do for myself.

Having carried on my work thus far with so little obligation to any favourer of learning, I shall not be disappointed though I should conclude it, if less be possible, with less; for I have been long wakened from that dream of hope, in which I once boasted myself with so much exultation,

My Lord,

Your Lordship's most humble,

Most obedient servant,

SAM. JOHNSON.

## *To the Right Honourable the Earl of Bute*

MY LORD,

When the bills were yesterday delivered to me by Mr. Wedderburne, I was informed by him of the future favours which his Majesty has, by your Lordship's recommendation, been induced to intend for me.

Bounty always receives part of its value from the manner in which it is bestowed; your Lordship's kindness includes every circumstance that can gratify delicacy, or enforce obligation. You have conferred your favours on a man who has neither alliance nor interest, who has not merited them by services, nor courted them by officiousness; you have spared him the shame of solicitation, and the anxiety of suspense.

What has been thus elegantly given, will, I hope, not be reproachfully enjoyed; I shall endeavour to give your Lordship the only recompense which generosity desires,—the gratification of finding that your benefits are not improperly bestowed. I am, my Lord,

Your Lordship's most obliged,

Most obedient, and most humble servant,

SAM. JOHNSON.

July 20, 1762.

## To Miss Susanna Thrale

July, 1783

DEAREST MISS SUSY,[3]

When you favoured me with your letter, you seemed to be in want of materials to fill it, having met with no great adventures either of peril or delight, nor done or suffered any thing out of the common course of life.

When you have lived longer, and considered more, you will find the common course of life very fertile of observation and reflection. Upon the common course of life must our thoughts and our conversation be generally employed. Our general course of life must denominate us wise or foolish; happy or miserable: if it is well regulated we pass on prosperously and smoothly; as it is neglected we live in embarrassment, perplexity, and uneasiness.

Your time, my love, passes, I suppose, in devotion, reading, work, and company. Of your devotions, in which I earnestly advise you to be very punctual, you may not perhaps think it proper to give me an account; and of work, unless I understood it better, it will be of no great use to say much; but books and company will always supply you with materials for your letters to me, as I shall always be pleased to know what you are reading, and with what you are pleased; and shall take great delight in knowing what impression new modes or new characters make upon you, and to observe with what attention you distinguish the tempers, dispositions, and abilities of your companions.

A letter may be always made out of the books of the morning

---

[3] Susy was thirteen at this date.

or talk of the evening; and any letters from you, my dearest, will be welcome to

SAM. JOHNSON.

## To Mrs. Thrale[4]

MADAM

If I interpret your letter right, you are ignominiously married; if it is yet undone, let us once talk together. If you have abandoned your children and your religion, God forgive your wickedness: if you have forfeited your fame and your country, may your folly do no further mischief.

If the last act is yet to do, I who have loved you, esteemed you, reverenced you, and served you, I who long thought you the first of humankind, entreat that, before your fate is irrevocable, I may once more see you. I was, I once was,

Madam, most truly yours,
SAM. JOHNSON.

July 2, 1784.
I will come down, if you permit it.

## To Mrs. Thrale

London, July 8, 1784.

DEAR MADAM,

What you have done, however I may lament it, I have no pretence to resent, as it has not been injurious to me: I therefore

---

[4] Johnson had been intimate with the Thrales for almost twenty years, and on Thrale's death in 1781, had been an executor of his will and a guardian of his children. That Mrs. Thrale was marrying at all would probably have disturbed Johnson, since he loved her, but that she was marrying her children's music teacher, an Italian and a Catholic, was more than he could bear. Hence this rough letter. Mrs. Thrale replied quietly, with dignity and affection, and Johnson's last letter to her shows him in control of his emotions. He died five months later.

breathe out one sigh more of tenderness, perhaps useless, but at least sincere.

I wish that God may grant you every blessing, that you may be happy in this world for its short continuance, and eternally happy in a better state; and whatever I can contribute to your happiness I am very ready to repay, for that kindness which soothed twenty years of a life radically wretched.

Do not think slightly of the advice which I now presume to offer. Prevail upon Mr. Piozzi to settle in England: you may live here with more dignity than in Italy, and with more security: your rank will be higher, and your fortune more under your own eye. I desire not to detail all my reasons, but every argument of prudence and interest is for England, and only some phantoms of imagination seduce you to Italy.

I am afraid however that my counsel is vain, yet I have eased my heart by giving it.

When Queen Mary took the resolution of sheltering herself in England, the Archbishop of St. Andrew's, attempting to dissuade her, attended on her journey; and when they came to the irremeable stream that separated the two kingdoms, walked by her side into the water, in the middle of which he seized her bridle, and with earnestness proportioned to her danger and his own affection pressed her to return. The Queen went forward.——If the parallel reaches thus far, may it go no further.—The tears stand in my eyes.

I am going into Derbyshire, and hope to be followed by your good wishes, for I am, with great affection,

Your most humble servant,<br>SAM. JOHNSON.

Any letters that come for me hither will be sent me.

*In the references, "Misc." is Hill's Johnsonian Miscellanies; all other references are to Hill's Boswell. Page numbers for the latter remain the same for Dr. L.F. Powell's revision, 1934–50.*

# Johnson Talking

**absurd.** When people see a man absurd in what they understand, they may conclude the same of him in what they do not understand. II.466.

**absurdity.** Let him be absurd, I beg of you: when a monkey is *too* like a man, it shocks one. *Misc.*, I.204.

**action.** Sir, you must not neglect doing a thing immediately good, from fear of remote evil;—from fear of its being abused. A man who has candles may sit up too late, which he would not do if he had not candles; but nobody will deny that the art of making candles, by which light is continued to us beyond the time that the sun gives us light, is a valuable art, and ought to be preserved. II.188.

What *must* be done, Sir, *will* be done. I.202.

**admiration.** Very near to admiration is the wish to admire. Every man willingly gives value to the praise which he receives, and considers the sentence passed in his favour as the sentence of discernment. III.411, n.2.

**amusements.** I am a great friend to publick amusements, for they keep people from vice. II.169.

**applause.** The applause of a single human being is of great consequence. IV.32.

A man who is used to the applause of the House of Commons, has no wish for that of a private company. A man accustomed to throw for a thousand pounds, if set down to throw for sixpence, would not be at the pains to count his dice. IV.167.

**attorney.** "He did not care to speak ill of any man behind his back, but he believed the gentleman was an *attorney*." II.126.

authors. Sir, it was like leading one to talk of a book, when the authour is concealed behind the door. I.396.

He is the richest authour that ever grazed the common of literature. I.418, n. 1. [On Dr. Campbell]

Authors are like privateers, always fair game for one another. IV.191, n. 1.

avarice. You despise a man for avarice, but do not hate him. III.71.

barrenness. All barrenness is comparative. III.76.

bawdy-house. Sir, your wife, *under pretence of keeping a bawdy-house,* is a receiver of stolen goods. IV.26.

beauty. Insipid beauty would not go a great way; and . . . such a woman might be cut out of a cabbage, if there was a skilful artificer. V.231.

belief. Every man who attacks my belief, diminishes in some degree my confidence in it, and therefore makes me uneasy; and I am angry with him who makes me uneasy. III.10.

belly. Some people have a foolish way of not minding, or pretending not to mind, what they eat. For my part, I mind my belly very studiously, and very carefully; for I look upon it, that he who does not mind his belly will hardly mind any thing else. I.467.

bishop. A bishop has nothing to do at a tippling-house. IV.75.

books. Mankind could do better without your books, than without my shoes. I.448.

What is written without effort is in general read without pleasure. *Misc.,* II.309.

boredom. Five hours of the four-and-twenty unemployed are enough for a man to go mad in. *Misc.,* I.301.

bores. He talked to me at club one day concerning Catiline's conspiracy—so I withdrew my attention, and thought about Tom Thumb. *Misc.,* I.203.

Boswell. If your company does not drive a man out of his house, nothing will. III.315.

brandy. He who aspires to be a hero must drink brandy. III.381.

bravery. Bravery has no place where it can avail nothing. IV.395.

cant. A man who has been canting all his life, may cant to the last. III.270. [On Dr. Dodd]

Clear your *mind* of cant. IV.221.

character. Derrick may do very well, as long as he can outrun his character; but the moment his character gets up with him, it is all over. I.394.

The greater part of mankind have no character at all. III.280, n.3.

**charity.** There is as much charity in helping a man down-hill, as in helping him up-hill. V.243.

**Chesterfield.** This man I thought had been a lord among wits; but, I find, he is only a wit among lords. I.266.

Chesterfield ought to know me better than to think me capable of contracting myself into a dwarf that he may be thought a giant. *Misc.*, I.405, n.2.

I have sailed a long and painful voyage round the world of the English language; and does he now send out two cock-boats to tow me into harbour? *Misc.*, I.405.

**Chesterfield's *Letters*.** They teach the morals of a whore, and the manners of a dancing master. I.266.

**chief.** He has no more the soul of a chief, than an attorney who has twenty houses in a street, and considers how much he can make by them. V.378.

**cities.** A great city is, to be sure, the school for studying life. III.253.

**clergy.** I have always considered a clergyman as the father of a larger family than he is able to maintain. III.304.

A clergyman's diligence always makes him venerable. III.438.

**comedy.** I know of no comedy for many years that has so much exhilarated an audience, that has answered so much the great end of comedy—making an audience merry. II.233.

**concentration.** Depend upon it, Sir, when a man knows he is to be hanged in a fortnight, it concentrates his mind wonderfully. III.167.

**conscience.** In questions of law, or of fact, conscience is very often confounded with opinion. No man's conscience can tell him the rights of another man; they must be known by rational investigation or historical enquiry. II.243.

**contempt.** No man loves to be treated with contempt. III.385.

**contradiction.** What harm does it do to any man to be contradicted? IV.280.

**conversation.** I never desire to converse with a man who has written more than he has read. II.48, n.2. [On Kelly]

His conversation usually threatened and announced more

than it performed; . . . he fed you with a continual renovation of hope, to end in a constant succession of disappointment. II.122.

A flea has taken you such a time, that a lion must have served you a twelvemonth. II.194.

Never speak of a man in his own presence. It is always indelicate, and may be offensive. II.472.

Questioning is not the mode of conversation among gentlemen. II.472.

Men might be very eminent in a profession, without our perceiving any particular power of mind in them in conversation.

It seems strange that a man should see so far to the right, who sees so short a way to the left. IV.19.

We had *talk* enough, but no *conversation;* there was nothing *discussed.* IV.186.

cordiality. Sir, he has no grimace, no gesticulation, no bursts of admiration on trivial occasions; he never embraces you with an overacted cordiality. IV.27.

country. They who are content to live in the country, are *fit* for the country. IV.338.

cow. A cow is a very good animal in the field; but we turn her out of a garden. II.187.

criticism. A fly, Sir, may sting a stately horse and make him wince, but one is but an insect, and the other is a horse still. I.263, n.3.

You *may* abuse a tragedy, though you cannot write one. You may scold a carpenter who has made you a bad table, though you cannot make a table. It is not your trade to make tables. I.409.

I would rather be attacked than unnoticed. For the worst thing you can do to an authour is to be silent as to his works. III.375.

Never let criticisms operate upon your face or your mind; it is very rarely that an authour is hurt by his criticks. The blaze of reputation cannot be blown out, but it often dies in the socket. III.423.

critics. He has a rage for saying something, when there's nothing to be said. I.329. [On Warburton]

Never mind whether they praise or abuse your writings; anything is tolerable, except oblivion. *Misc.,* II.207.

**cunning.** Cunning has effect from the credulity of others, rather than from the abilities of those who are cunning. It requires no extraordinary talents to lie and deceive. V.217.

**death.** It matters not how a man dies, but how he lives. The act of dying is not of importance, it lasts so short a time. A man knows it must be so, and submits. It will do him no good to whine. II.106.

I will be conquered; I will not capitulate. IV.374.

If one was to think constantly of death, the business of life would stand still. V.316.

**debaters.** Why, yes, Sir, they'll do any thing, no matter how odd, or desperate, to gain their point; they'll catch hold of the red-hot end of a poker, sooner than not get possession of it. *Misc.*, II.397.

**debt, national.** Let the publick creditors be ever so clamorous, the interest of millions must ever prevail over that of thousands. II.127.

**description.** Description only excites curiosity: seeing satisfies it. IV.199.

**despotism.** A country governed by a despot is an inverted cone. III.283.

**devil.** Let him go to some place where he is *not* known. Don't let him go to the devil where he *is* known. V.54.

**dictionaries.** Dictionaries are like watches, the worst is better than none, and the best cannot be expected to go quite true. I.293, n.3.

**dignity.** He that encroaches on another's dignity puts himself in his power. IV.62.

**dinner.** A man seldom thinks with more earnestness of any thing than he does of his dinner; and if he cannot get that well dressed, he should be suspected of inaccuracy in other things. I.467, n.2.

This was a good enough dinner, to be sure; but it was not a dinner to *ask* a man to. I.470.

**dirt.** By those who look close to the ground, dirt will be seen. II.82, n.3.

**dislike.** Nothing is more common than mutual dislike, where mutual approbation is particularly expected. III.423.

**dispute.** Every man will dispute with great good humour upon a subject in which he is not interested. I will dispute very calmly upon the probability of another man's son being hanged. III.11.

I know nothing more offensive than repeating what one knows to be foolish things, by way of continuing a dispute, to see what a man will answer,—to make him your butt! III.350.

**distance.** Sir, it is surprising how people will go to a distance for what they may have at home. V.286.

**distinctions.** All distinctions are trifles, because great things can seldom occur, and those distinctions are settled by custom. III.355.

**distress.** People in distress never think that you feel enough. II.469.

**dropped.** There are people whom one should like very well to drop, but would not wish to be dropped by. IV.73.

**drunkenness.** A man who exposes himself when he is intoxicated, has not the art of getting drunk. III.389.

He who makes a *beast* of himself, gets rid of the pain of being a *man*. II.435, n.7.

**education.** I cannot see that lectures can do so much good as reading the books from which the lectures are taken. I know nothing that can be best taught by lectures, except where experiments are to be shewn. You may teach chymistry by lectures.—You might teach making of shoes by lectures! II.7.

**endurance.** Where there is nothing to be *done* something must be *endured*. *Misc.*, I.210.

**Englishman.** We value an Englishman highly in this country, and yet Englishmen are not rare in it. III.10.

**epigram.** Why, Sir, he may not be a judge of an epigram: but you see he is a judge of what is *not* an epigram. III.259.

**exercise.** I take the true definition of exercise to be labour without weariness. IV.151, n.1.

**exhibitionism.** He wants to make himself conspicuous. He would tumble in a hogstye, as long as you looked at him and called to him to come out. I.432.

**fame.** Ah! Sir, a boy's being flogged is not so severe as a man's having the hiss of the world against him. Men have a solicitude about fame; and the greater share they have of it, the more afraid they are of losing it. I.451.

Sir, he is one of the many who have made themselves *publick*, without making themselves *known*. I.498. [On Kenrick]

Every man has a lurking wish to appear considerable in his native place. II.141.

flattery. Dearest lady, consider with yourself what your flattery is worth, before you bestow it so freely. IV.341.

You may be bribed by flattery. V.306.

flogging. There is now less flogging in our great schools than formerly, but then less is learned there; so that what the boys get at one end, they lose at the other. II.407.

food. A man does not love to go to a place from whence he comes out exactly as he went in. IV.90.

Frenchman. A Frenchman must be always talking, whether he knows any thing of the matter or not; an Englishman is content to say nothing, when he has nothing to say. IV.15.

friendship. If a man does not make new acquaintance as he advances through life, he will soon find himself left alone. A man, Sir, should keep his friendship *in constant repair.* I.300. Every heart must lean to somebody. I.515.

Always, Sir, set a high value on spontaneous kindness. He whose inclination prompts him to cultivate your friendship of his own accord, will love you more than one whom you have been at pains to attach to you. IV.115.

Most friendships are formed by caprice or by chance, mere confederacies in vice or leagues in folly. IV.280.

And this is the voice of female friendship I suppose, when the hand of the hangman would be softer. *Misc.*, I.331.

Garrick. No wonder, Sir, that he is vain; a man who is perpetually flattered in every mode that can be conceived. So many bellows have blown the fire, that one wonders he is not by this time become a cinder. II.227.

gaiety. Gayety is a duty when health requires it. III.136, n.2.

Solitude is dangerous to reason, without being favourable to virtue: pleasures of some sort are necessary to the intellectual as to the corporeal health; and those who resist gaiety, will be likely for the most part to fall a sacrifice to appetite; for the solicitations of sense are always at hand, and a dram to a vacant and solitary person is a speedy and seducing relief. *Misc.*, I.219.

genius. A man of genius has been seldom ruined but by himself. I.381.

Sir, a man cannot make fire but in proportion as he has fuel. He cannot coin guineas but in proportion as he has gold. V.229.

gestures. Action can have no effect upon reasonable minds. It may augment noise, but it never can enforce argument. II.211.

Giants' Causeway. Worth seeing, yes; but not worth going to see. III.410.

Goldsmith. He goes on without knowing how he is to get off. His genius is great, but his knowledge is small. II.196.

When people find a man of the most distinguished abilities as a writer, their inferiour while he is with them, it must be highly gratifying to them. II.235.

He was not an agreeable companion, for he talked always for fame. A man who does so never can be pleasing. The man who talks to unburthen his mind is the man to delight you. III.247.

No man was more foolish when he had not a pen in his hand, or more wise when he had. IV.29.

graces. Every man of any education would rather be called a rascal, than accused of deficiency in *the graces*. III.54.

grave. We shall receive no letters in the grave. IV.413.

great. A man would never undertake great things, could he be amused with small. III.242.

grief. All unnecessary grief is unwise. III.136.

Grief is a species of idleness. III.136, n.2.

hanged. Do you think that a man the night before he is to be hanged cares for the succession of a royal family? III.270.

happiness. If a bull could speak, he might as well exclaim,—Here am I with this cow and this grass; what being can enjoy greater felicity? II.228.

hate. Men hate more steadily than they love. III.150.

headache. Nay, Sir, it was not the *wine* that made your head ache, but the *sense* that I put into it. III.381.

heaven. A man who cannot get to heaven in a green coat, will not find his way thither the sooner in a grey one. III.188, n.4.

histories. This is my history; like all other histories, a narrative of misery. IV.362.

hypocrite. No man is a hypocrite in his pleasures. IV.316.

**ignorance.** A man may choose whether he will have abstemiousness and knowledge, or claret and ignorance. III.335.

**ignorant.** To help the ignorant commonly requires much patience, for the ignorant are always trying to be cunning. V.217, n.1.

**immortality.** If it were not for the notion of immortality, he would cut a throat to fill his pockets. II.359.

**impressions.** Do not, Sir, accustom yourself to trust to *impressions*. There is a middle state of mind between conviction and hypocrisy, of which many are conscious. By trusting to impressions, a man may gradually come to yield to them, and at length be subject to them, so as not to be a free agent, or what is the same thing in effect, to *suppose* that he is not a free agent. IV.122.

**inaction.** Rather to do nothing than to do good, is the lowest state of a degraded mind. IV.352.

**infidel.** If he be an infidel, he is an infidel as a dog is an infidel; that is to say, he has never thought upon the subject. II.95. [On Foote]

**ingratitude.** Why, Sir, a man is very apt to complain of the ingratitude of those who have risen far above him. III.2.

**intrepidity.** He has an intrepidity of talk, whether he understands the subject or not. V.330.

**ivory tower.** I hate a fellow whom pride, or cowardice, or laziness drives into a corner, and who does nothing when he is there but sit and *growl*; let him come out as I do, and *bark*. IV.161, n.3.

**jealous.** Little people are apt to be jealous. III.55.

**judge.** A judge may be a farmer; but he is not to geld his own pigs. II.344.

**kindness.** Getting money is not all a man's business: to cultivate kindness is a valuable part of the business of life. III.182.

**knowledge.** Sir, a desire of knowledge is the natural feeling of mankind; and every human being, whose mind is not debauched, will be willing to give all that he has to get knowledge. I.458.

A man must carry knowledge with him, if he would bring home knowledge. III.302.

If it rained knowledge I'd hold out my hand; but I would not give myself the trouble to go in quest of it. III.344.

**labor.** No man loves labour for itself. II.99.

**language.** [Chinese] is only more difficult from its rudeness; as there is more labour in hewing down a tree with a stone than with an axe. III.339.

**languages.** Languages are the pedigree of nations. V.225.

**law.** Let us hear, Sir, no general abuse; the law is the last result of human wisdom acting upon human experience for the benefit of the public. *Misc.*, I.223.

**lawyers.** Sir, a man will no more carry the artifice of the bar into the common intercourse of society, than a man who is paid for tumbling upon his hands will continue to tumble upon his hands when he should walk on his feet. II.48.

Lawyers know life practically. A bookish man should always have them to converse with. III.306.

**learning.** Their learning is like bread in a besieged town: every man gets a little, but no man gets a full meal. II.363.

In England, any man who wears a sword and a powdered wig is ashamed to be illiterate. III.254.

He has a great deal of learning; but it never lies straight. IV.225.

**lectures.** Sir, you have sconced me two-pence for non-attendance at a lecture not worth a penny. *Misc.*, I.164, n.5.

**letter writing.** A short letter to a distant friend is, in my opinion, an insult like that of a slight bow or cursory salutation;—a proof of unwillingness to do much, even where there is a necessity of doing something. I.361.

**levellers.** Your levellers wish to level *down* as far as themselves; but they cannot bear levelling *up* to themselves. I.448.

**liar.** As it is said of the greatest liar, that he tells more truth than falsehood; so it may be said of the worst man, that he does more good than evil. III.236.

**liberty.** The notion of liberty amuses the people of England, and helps to keep off the *taedium vitae*. When a butcher tells you that *his heart bleeds for his country*, he has, in fact, no uneasy feeling. I.394.

Every man has a right to liberty of conscience, and with that the magistrate cannot interfere. People confound liberty of thinking with liberty of talking; nay, with liberty of preaching. II.249.

How is it that we hear the loudest *yelps* for liberty among the drivers of negroes? III.201.

lie. If I accustom a servant to tell a lie for *me*, have I not reason to apprehend that he will tell many lies for *himself?* I.436.

Sir, don't tell me of deception; a lie, Sir, is a lie, whether it be a lie to the eye or a lie to the ear. *Misc.*, II.428.

life. Life is a pill which none of us can bear to swallow without gilding; yet for the poor we delight in stripping it still barer, and are not ashamed to shew even visible displeasure, if ever the bitter taste is taken from their mouths. *Misc.*, I.205.

Life is barren enough surely with all her trappings; let us therefore be cautious how we strip her. *Misc.*, I.345.

literary men. A mere literary man is a *dull* man; a man who is solely a man of business is a *selfish* man; but when literature and commerce are united, they make a *respectable* man. *Misc.*, II.389.

London. No, Sir, when a man is tired of London he is tired of life; for there is in London all that life can afford. III.178.

lords. Great lords and great ladies don't love to have their mouths stopped. IV.116.

love. It is commonly a weak man who marries for love. III.3.

[Love is] the wisdom of a fool and the folly of the wise. *Misc.*, II.393.

luxury. No nation was ever hurt by luxury; for . . . it can reach but to a very few. II. 218.

madness. With some people, gloomy penitence is only madness turned upside down. III.27.

mankind. As I know more of mankind I expect less of them. IV.239.

manners. When you have said a man of gentle manners; you have said enough. IV.28.

Sir, it is very bad manners to carry provisions to any man's house, as if he could not entertain you. To an inferior, it is oppressive; to a superior, it is insolent. V.73.

man of the world. One may be so much a man of the world as to be nothing in the world. III.375.

marriage. I would advise no man to marry, Sir, who is not likely to propagate understanding. II.109, n.2.

[After an unsuccessful first marriage, remarriage is] the triumph of hope over experience. II.128.

A man is in general better pleased when he has a good dinner upon his table, than when his wife talks Greek. *Misc.*, II.11.

*All* quarrels ought to be avoided studiously, particularly conjugal ones, as no one can possibly tell where they may end; besides that lasting dislike is often the consequence of occasional disgust, and that the cup of life is surely bitter enough, without squeezing in the hateful rind of resentment. *Misc.*, I.246.

melancholy. That distrust which intrudes so often on your mind is a mode of melancholy, which if it be the business of a wise man to be happy, it is foolish to indulge; and if it be a duty to preserve our faculties entire for their proper use, it is criminal. Suspicion is very often a useless pain. III.135.

memory. The true art of memory is the art of attention. IV.126, n.6.

merriment. Nothing is more hopeless than a scheme of merriment. I.331, n.5.

mind. To have the management of the mind is a great art, and it may be attained in a considerable degree by experience and habitual exercise. II.440.

misfortunes. If a man *talks* of his misfortunes, there is something in them that is not disagreeable to him; for where there is nothing but pure misery, there never is any recourse to the mention of it. IV.31.

money. A man who both spends and saves money is the happiest man, because he has both enjoyments. III.322.

morality. The morality of an action depends on the motive from which we act. If I fling half a crown to a beggar with intention to break his head, and he picks it up and buys victuals with it, the physical effect is good; but, with respect to me, the action is very wrong. I.398.

morals. If he does really think that there is no distinction between virtue and vice, why, Sir, when he leaves our houses, let us count our spoons. I.432.

Mrs. Macaulay. To endeavour to make *her* ridiculous, is like blacking the chimney. II.336.

narrowmindedness. A mind as narrow as the neck of a vinegar cruet. V.269. [On Lord North]

**nearsightedness.** Should I wish to become a botanist, I must first turn myself into a reptile. I.377, n.2.

**neglect.** All the complaints which are made of the world are unjust. I never knew a man of merit neglected: it was generally by his own fault that he failed of success. A man may hide his head in a hole: he may go into the country, and publish a book now and then, which nobody reads, and then complain he is neglected. IV.172.

**old age.** Contented with the exchange of fame for ease, [he] e'en resolves to let them set the pillows at his back, and gives no further proof of his existence than just to suck the jelly that prolongs it. *Misc.*, I.282.

There is nothing against which an old man should be so much upon his guard as putting himself to nurse. II. 474.

**painting.** Painting, Sir, can illustrate, but cannot inform. IV.321.

**patriotism.** Patriotism is the last refuge of a scoundrel. II.348.

**patrons.** General truths are seldom applied to particular occasions. ... Every man believes that mistresses are unfaithful, and patrons capricious; but he excepts his own mistress, and his own patron. I.381.

**please.** It is very difficult to please a man against his will. III.69.

**politeness.** It [politeness] is fictitious benevolence. V.82.

**politics.** We are not to blow up half a dozen palaces, because one cottage is burning. II.90.

Why, Sir, most schemes of political improvement are very laughable things. II.102.

**poor.** A decent provision for the poor, is the true test of civilization. II.130.

**poverty.** There is no being so poor and so contemptible, who does not think there is somebody still poorer, and still more contemptible. II.13.

**power.** Where bad actions are committed at so great a distance, a delinquent can obscure the evidence till the scent becomes cold; there is a cloud between, which cannot be penetrated: therefore all distant power is bad. IV.213.

**praise.** He who praises every body, praises nobody. III.225, n.3. Praise is the tribute which every man is expected to pay for the grant of perusing a manuscript. *Misc.*, II.192.

**preachers.** A man who preaches in the stocks will always have hearers enough. II.251.

**proverb.** He [a man] should take care not to be made a proverb. III.57.

**reading.** A man ought to read just as inclination leads him; for what he reads as a task will do him little good. I.428.

When I take up the end of a web, and find it packthread, I do not expect, by looking further, to find embroidery. II.88. [On Mrs. Montagu's *Essay on Shakespear*]

I am always for getting a boy forward in his learning; for that is a sure good. I would let him at first read *any* English book which happens to engage his attention; because you have done a great thing when you have brought him to have entertainment from a book. He'll get better books afterwards. III.385.

A man can tell but what he knows, and I never got any further than the first page. Alas, Madam! how few books are there of which one ever can possibly arrive at the *last* page! *Misc.,* I.332.

No man read[s] long together with a folio on his table: —Books that you may carry to the fire, and hold readily in your hand, are the most useful after all. *Misc.,* II.2.

**reason.** You may have a reason why two and two should make five; but they will still make but four. III.375.

**rebellion.** All rebellion is natural to man. V.394.

**recommendation.** Sir, it is such a recommendation, as if I should throw you out of a two-pair-of-stairs window, and recommend to you to fall soft. IV.323.

**religion.** Differing from a man in doctrine was no reason why you should pull his house about his ears. V.62.

**reputation.** You may be wise in your study in the morning, and gay in company at a tavern in the evening. Every man is to take care of his own wisdom, and his own virtue, without minding too much what others think. III.405.

**resentment.** Resentment gratifies him who intended an injury, and pains him unjustly who did not intend it. IV.367.

**retired tradesmen.** They have lost the civility of tradesmen, without acquiring the manners of gentlemen. II.120.

**rich.** Let me smile with the wise, and feed with the rich. II.79.

It is better to *live* rich than to *die* rich. III.304.

We are not here to sell a parcel of boilers and vats, but the potentiality of growing rich, beyond the dreams of avarice. IV.87.

**right.** Because a man cannot be right in all things, is he to be right in nothing? Because a man sometimes gets drunk, is he therefore to steal? III.410.

**rouge.** She is better employed at her toilet, than using her pen. It is better she should be reddening her own cheeks, than blackening other people's characters. III.46. [On Mrs. Macaulay]

**rudeness.** Sir, a man has no more right to *say* an uncivil thing, than to *act* one; no more right to say a rude thing to another than to knock him down. IV.28.

**sailors.** No man will be a sailor, who has contrivance enough to get himself into a jail; for, being in a ship is being in a jail, with the chance of being drowned. V.137.

**schools.** Placing him [a timid boy] at a public school is forcing an owl upon day. IV.312.

**Scots.** The noblest prospect which a Scotchman ever sees, is the high road that leads him to England. I.425.

Much may be made of a Scotchman, if he be *caught* young. II.194.

Sir, it is not so much to be lamented that Old England is lost, as that the Scotch have found it. III.78.

**scruples.** Whoever loads life with unnecessary scruples, Sir, provokes the attention of others on his conduct, and incurs the censure of singularity without reaping the reward of superior virtue. II.72, n.1.

**secrecy.** Depend upon it, Sir, he who does what he is afraid should be known, has something rotten about him. II.210.

**sense.** He grasps more sense than he can hold; he takes more corn than he can make into meal; he opens a wide prospect, but it is so distant, it is indistinct. IV.98. [On Mudge]

**serenity.** The serenity that is not felt, it can be no virtue to feign. IV.395.

**Shakespeare.** We must not compare the noise made by your tea-kettle here with the roaring of the ocean. II.86, n.1.

**shooting.** You may take a field piece to shoot sparrows; but all the sparrows you can bring home will not be worth the charge. V.261.

**singlemindedness.** That fellow seems to me to possess but one idea, and that is a wrong one. II.126.

**skill.** No man I suppose leaps at once into deep water who does not know how to swim. *Misc.*, I.165.

**sorrow.** There is no wisdom in useless and hopeless sorrow; but there is something in it so like virtue, that he who is wholly without it cannot be loved, nor will by me at least be thought worthy of esteem. III.137, n.1.

The poor and the busy have no leisure for sentimental sorrow. *Misc.*, I.252.

**spelling.** Never mind it, Sir; perhaps your friend spells *ocean* with an *s. Misc.*, II.404.

**statistics.** Round numbers are always false. III.226, n.4.

**stupidity.** Such an excess of stupidity, Sir, is not in nature. I.453.

**superiority.** No, Sir, I won't learn it. You shall retain your superiority by my not knowing it. II.220.

**talent.** He has not, indeed, many hooks; but with what hooks he has, he grapples very forcibly. II.57. [On Baretti]

**talking.** People may come to do any thing almost, by talking of it. V.286.

**tastes.** The lad does not care for the child's rattle, and the old man does not care for the young man's whore. II.14.

**tavern.** As soon as I enter the door of a tavern, I experience an oblivion of care, and a freedom from solicitude: when I am seated, I find the master courteous, and the servants obsequious to my call; anxious to know and ready to supply my wants: wine there exhilarates my spirits, and prompts me to free conversation and an interchange of discourse with those whom I most love: I dogmatise and am contradicted, and in this conflict of opinions and sentiments I find delight. II.452, n.1.

A tavern chair [is] the throne of human felicity. II.452, n.1.

**tenderness.** Want of tenderness is want of parts. II.122.

**threats.** I hope I shall never be deterred from detecting what I think a cheat, by the menaces of a ruffian. II.298. [To Macpherson]

**time.** He that runs against Time has an antagonist not subject to casualties. I.319, n.3.

**travel.** Jonas acquired some reputation by travelling abroad, but lost it all by travelling at home. II.122.

If a man comes to look for fishes, you cannot blame him if he does not attend to fowls. V.221.

**tricks.** Remember that all tricks are either knavish or childish; and that it is as foolish to make experiments upon the constancy of a friend, as upon the chastity of a wife. III.396.

**truth.** Hume, and other sceptical innovators, are vain men, and will gratify themselves at any expence. Truth will not afford sufficient food to their vanity; so they have betaken themselves to errour. Truth, Sir, is a cow that will yield such people no more milk, and so they are gone to milk the bull. I.444.

I would not keep company with a fellow, who lyes as long as he is sober, and whom you must make drunk before you can get a word of truth out of him. II.188.

Nobody has a right to put another under such a difficulty, that he must either hurt the person by telling the truth, or hurt himself by telling what is not true. III.320.

Every man has a right to utter what he thinks truth, and every other man has a right to knock him down for it. IV.12.

**tyranny.** There is a remedy in human nature against tyranny, that will keep us safe under every form of government. II.170.

**uncharitable talk.** Who is the worse for being talked of uncharitably? IV.97.

**understanding.** Sir, that is the blundering oeconomy of a narrow understanding. It is stopping one hole in a sieve. III.300.

Sir, I have found you an argument; but I am not obliged to find you an understanding. IV.313.

**unsettle.** They tended to unsettle every thing, and yet settled nothing. II.124. [Dr. Priestley's theological works]

**vanity.** All censure of a man's self is oblique praise. It is in order to shew how much he can spare. It has all the invidiousness of self-praise, and all the reproach of falsehood. III.323.

No man takes upon himself small blemishes without supposing that great abilities are attributed to him; and, . . . in short, this affectation of candour or modesty [is] but another kind of indirect self-praise, and [has] its foundation in vanity. *Misc.*, II.153.

**versatility.** Sir, a man may be so much of every thing, that he is nothing of any thing. IV.176.

**vex.** Publick affairs vex no man. IV.220.

**vice.** Madam, you are here, not for the love of virtue, but the fear of vice. II.435. [To Mrs. Fermor]

**vivacity.** Depend upon it, Sir, vivacity is much an art, and depends greatly on habit. II.462.

**wag.** Every man has, some time in his life, an ambition to be a wag. IV.1, n.2.

**watch.** He was like a man who resolves to regulate his time by a certain watch; but will not inquire whether the watch is right or not. II.213. [On Burnet]

**wealth.** The sooner that a man begins to enjoy his wealth the better. II.226.

Sir, the insolence of wealth will creep out. III.316.

**woman's preaching.** Sir, a woman's preaching is like a dog's walking on his hinder legs. It is not done well; but you are surprized to find it done at all. I.463.

**women.** Women have a perpetual envy of our vices; they are less vicious than we, not from choice, but because we restrict them; they are the slaves of order and fashion; their virtue is of more consequence to us than our own, so far as concerns this world. IV.291.

No woman is the worse for sense and knowledge. V.226.

**words.** Don't, Sir, accustom yourself to use big words for little matters. I.471.

**world.** This I would have you do, not in compliance with solicitation or advice, but as a justification of yourself to the world; the world has always a right to be regarded. II.74, n.3.

**writing.** No man but a blockhead ever wrote, except for money. III.19.

A man should begin to write soon; for, if he waits till his judgement is matured, his inability, through want of practice to express his conceptions, will make the disproportion so great between what he sees, and what he can attain, that he will probably be discouraged from writing at all. IV.12.

A new manner [of writing]! Buckinger had no hands, and he wrote his name with his toes at Charing-cross for half a crown apiece; that was a new manner of writing! *Misc.*, I.419.

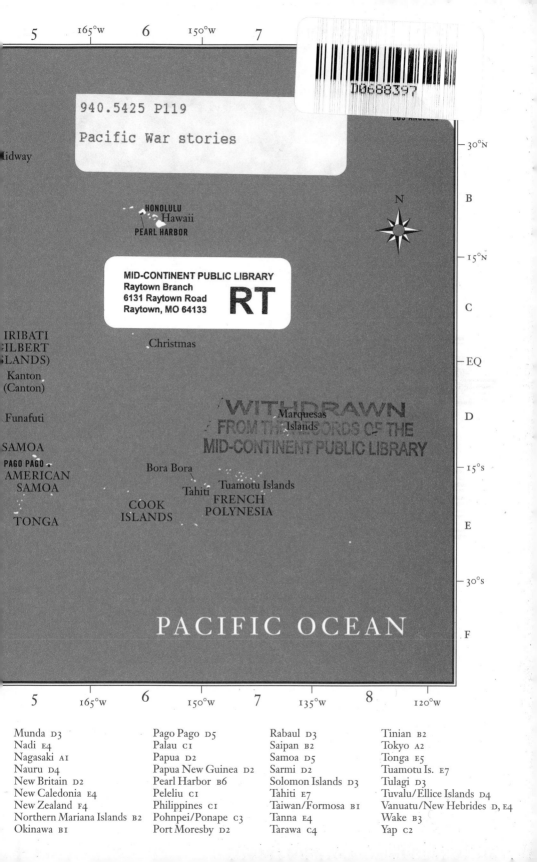

PACIFIC
WAR
STORIES

COMPILED AND EDITED BY
**REX ALAN SMITH
AND GERALD A. MEEHL**

# PACIFIC
# WAR
# STORIES

## IN THE WORDS
## OF THOSE
## WHO SURVIVED

ABBEVILLE PRESS
NEW YORK  LONDON

# DEDICATION

*This book is dedicated to Rex's wife, Wanda, for her patience and encouragement during his long hours of securing interviews and editing tape transcriptions thereof. It is dedicated also to Jerry's father, B-17 crew chief Paul Meehl; to Jerry's uncles, Al Hahn, Louis Meehl and Harlan Wall, whose stories from the Pacific he grew up hearing, and another uncle, Bill Durdy, who served in the Pacific but left almost no record of what he did or where he served; and especially to Jerry's wife Marla, not only for her considerable technical contributions, but also for her emotional support, greatly appreciated and highly valued, through projects past, present and future.*

PROJECT MANAGER: Susan Costello
EDITOR: Walton Rawls
COPYEDITOR: Marian K. Gordin
PRODUCTION EDITOR: Amber Reed

DESIGNER: Misha Beletsky
COMPOSITOR: Hall Smyth
PRODUCTION MANAGER: Louise Kurtz

First Edition
10 9 8 7 6 5 4 3 2 1

Library of Congress Cataloging-in-Publication Data
Pacific War stories : in the words of those who survived / [edited by] Rex Alan Smith,
    Gerald A. Meehl.—1st ed.
    p. cm.
    Includes index.
    ISBN 0-7892-0817-2 (alk. paper)
    1. World War, 1939–1945—Campaigns—Pacific Area. 2. World War, 1939–1945—Personal narratives,
American. 3. Oral history. 4. United States—Armed Forces—Biography. 5. Soldiers—United States—
Biography. I. Smith, Rex Alan. II. Meehl, Gerald A.
D767.P3344 2004
940.54'25'092273—dc22
[B]                                     2004052819

JACKET: *The strain of the intense fighting on the island of Peleliu in 1944 is etched on the face of this Marine.*

ENDPAPER MAP BY: *Michael Shibao*

PAGE 1: *U.S. troops storm ashore on the Philippine island of Leyte on October 20, 1944. This is the view that Fred Saiz and Dave Gutterman had as they landed on these beaches.*

PAGES 2–3: *Guam landing beach with Americans under fire crouching on the beach.*

# TABLE OF CONTENTS

## 8. THE WAR IN THE AIR, 1942–45

## 9. THE WAR AT SEA, 1942–45

# INTRODUCTION

A man in his eighties sits down at the table and carefully spreads out in front of him ten or so small black-and-white photographs. They have all now taken on a kind of amber hue, after some sixty-odd years, but their images are still sharp and clear. All the photos picture very young men, teenagers clowning for the camera, hats at jaunty angles, on beaches, in front of tents, palm trees always in the background. "I'm this fellow here." He points to one of the smiling lads in the photo closest to him. You look up from the old photo to the face of this amiable, distinguished, Pacific war veteran, and it's difficult to imagine that they are the same person.

Then, as arranged, he starts to tell his story, first what made him enlist in 1942, then the crazy things that happened while training Stateside for war, then being crammed into a converted Hawaiian cruise ship with thousands of other teenagers, crossing the Pacific with a sense of high adventure, and then further stories of wild times on leave in wartime Honolulu. Then he finds himself on another ship, this time going to invade an enemy island he has never heard of, an island few people even remember today. Then, in an uninterrupted stream, there are stories of terror, violence, and death, interspersed with bizarre and even humorous events. You marvel at how easily he can switch his narrative from a truly gruesome experience to one that is so funny he has trouble getting it out between fits of laughter. Ultimately he tells about hearing that atomic bombs had been dropped on Japan, and he confides that he felt a profound sense of relief when he learned that the war in the Pacific was finally over, that he would indeed survive the war. Then one last story, about another ocean voyage, on another ship, but this one is taking him home.

He stops for a moment, and you think the stories have ended, but it is just a pause. Perhaps unexpectedly, he has somehow tapped deep into a well-secured vault of Pacific war memories, and now they begin to resurface one after another. His face brightens again and again as more images of things that happened come into focus. "And I remember one time—and, you know, I don't think I ever told my family *this* story . . ." and he launches into a humorous, R-rated experience he had in Honolulu. Then another island combat anecdote. Then a story of a strange thing that happened to a friend of his on one of the islands. He will later say he's told you stories he hasn't related to anyone for a long time, and some of them he's never told since the war.

When they first came back, most Pacific war veterans didn't seem to talk much about what happened to them in the islands. They needed first to get on with their lives, and of course they knew that many other veterans had similar stories they could tell. What a vet had personally done, as just one individual embedded somewhere in the Pacific islands, might not have seemed all that spectacular, unique, or even interesting to others, at the time. Sometimes when tempted to tell their stories, the vets could see family eyes roll and hear a chorus of, "There goes dad again with his old war stories." But even with an interested audience, Pacific war veterans would seldom tell anyone about the bad things that happened. They figured war was tough for everybody in one way or another, and nobody would want to hear about the horrible things anyhow. However, half a century later, it dawns on some veterans that they actually did have a part in world history, and that what they did then was even fairly interesting. Since more people appear ready to give them an ear, many are now willing to share their experiences, willing to acknowledge that they did play a role, however small, in the outcome of the Pacific war.

Listening to a Pacific war veteran tell his stories is not a relaxing experience. You strain to imagine the scenes he is recalling, and you struggle to keep up, in your mind's eye, with the images he describes. But as you begin to relive with him his varied experiences, he is no longer an eighty-two-year-old man sitting across from you but a young man stationed on a South Sea island long ago, recounting events with an immediacy that also transports the listener to the Pacific. It's a form of time travel, and you are there on exotic Pacific islands, living hilarious events that happened on leave in Honolulu, experiencing horrific scenes of violence and death, feeling the discomforts of rain, heat, mosquitoes, and the oppressive humidity of the tropics, seeing stunning beauty in lush, island scenery, contemplating all those spectacular sunsets, enduring the boredom, waiting for something big to happen even on rear area islands.

As he talks, the face of the elderly man appears to merge with that of the smiling teenager in the photos. You no longer see the thinning hair and creased face but focus instead on a pair of eyes, the same eyes that saw everything he is describing, the eyes that have not aged, that are still as clear and blue at age eighty-two as they were at age eighteen. Those eyes recall all the Pacific islands he describes, all the events he witnessed, all the tragedy and humor of his experiences in the Pacific war. Yet, through his eyes you see but one part of WWII in the Pacific, a tremendous series of historic events staged and played out across one-third of the planet's surface. At the end of the interview, you look at the old photos again, and they seem familiar now. You don't see just old black-and-white snapshots anymore—the palm fronds are dark green, the tropical sky is brilliant blue, the beaches are searing white, and the uniforms are rumpled khaki against the tan, forever young faces.

It is this sense of time travel that we attempt to convey in *Pacific War Stories*. Having interviewed dozens of war veterans for our earlier book, *Pacific Legacy* (Abbeville Press, 2002), we sensed that some were aware that their island experiences had been overshadowed in the popular media by stories about the European theater of war, and we knew they wanted to be heard. But of all the eyewitness stories collected, we could only include a small fraction in *Pacific Legacy*. Nevertheless, we were determined to let them all have their say, before it was too late. So in this volume we have been able to present the firsthand war stories of more than seventy veterans, just as they recounted them to us, in as much detail as they remembered, with a level of clarity that is at once remarkable and fascinating.

Pacific war veterans are now all close to eighty years of age, or older, yet they still remember in spectacular detail what they did and saw during World War II. Their stories, in this volume, range from up-close and terrifying island combat, to perilous encounters at sea, to aching boredom on rear area islands, and include all the myriad feelings in between that comprise the vast scope, the color, and the vivid imagery within this rich tapestry of stories by veterans who put their lives at risk for their buddies and their country. The result, we hope, will provide those who weren't there a small sense of what it was like to have had a part in history, to have been out in the Pacific during World War II with a generation of brave and selfless individuals.

During the preparation of this book, Dave Levy, a PT boat skipper in the Solomons who served with John Kennedy, told us, "Everybody who was out in the Pacific has all kinds of stories of what they did during the war, and those stories are worth telling, of course. But what I find fascinating is how the war affected the course of our lives. I know my entire future was changed by my experiences in the Pacific with the Navy. Why don't you let the veterans finish their stories?" We agreed, and include an epilogue to many of the stories, so the veterans can reveal just how this war altered the trajectories of their later lives. For some, the impact was profound, either due to lingering effects of wounds suffered or because of horrifying memories that continued to resurface for years in nightmares and flashbacks. Some simply picked up where they left off and continued with what they had set out to do before the war. Others who could never resume their former lives headed off in entirely different directions, in careers perhaps energized by their Pacific war experiences.

But whatever the war veterans did after returning from the islands, all of them agree that their war experiences in the islands have become central elements in their lives. They have found that memories of what happened ten or even twenty years ago are not nearly so vivid as those harsh or humorous events on tropical islands recalled from sixty years ago.

The Pacific war veterans who have carried their memories deep inside them all this time are now, in this volume, ready to share their stories.

# PACIFIC WAR OVERVIEW

PAGES 14–15: *Island of Betio in Tarawa atoll,
scene of the first amphibious Marine landing on an atoll
in the Pacific war. The photo was taken in November,
1943, near the end of the 76-hour battle for this tiny island that took the lives of nearly 1,000 Marines and about
5,000 Japanese. The objective was the heavily defended
coral airstrip built by the Japanese. Invasion beaches
on the left side of the island were on either side of the long
pier stretching out to the left in the shallow water over
the reef. It was along this pier that Bob Sheeks and Vern
Garrett landed on the first day of the battle. Green Beach,
in the foreground, was where Bob Sheeks subsequently
came ashore on the second day of the battle.*

For America and her European allies, the Pacific war started on December 7, 1941, even though Japan had been fighting in the Pacific, on mainland China, since the 1930s. The Japanese attack on Pearl Harbor that day was part of a much larger operation that spanned much of the Pacific, with raids on Wake, Midway, Guam, the Philippines, and other islands. These attacks were, in part, intended to neutralize the American military, giving the Japanese time to expand southward and to secure critical natural resources such as oil fields in the Dutch East Indies (now Indonesia). The Japanese had feared that the American Navy, if not severely damaged, would respond with force to their expansion into the South Pacific. But if the American military could be disabled for several months, the Japanese reasoned, they could secure new territory without fear of immediate reprisal. It seemed more likely that America would have to negotiate some kind of settlement, since it would take time to recover from the attacks of December 7 and to build back their military presence in the Pacific.

Although the United States had guessed Japan's intentions to secure the natural resources of Southeast Asia for their Empire, the audacity of their attack on Pearl Harbor came as a real surprise. More than 2,000 Americans died on December 7, and numerous ships were sunk and damaged, with many more planes and facilities destroyed. But the two American aircraft carriers were not in Pearl Harbor that day and escaped damage. This proved to be a crucial element in the outcome of the Pacific war, since aircraft carriers would turn out to be the most important factor in the future success of the U.S. Navy.

At first the Japanese plan worked just as they had it figured. The attacks on December 7 across the Pacific did indeed neutralize the American military, and there was no early response to Japanese expansion southward into Southeast Asia. Meanwhile, British, Australian, New Zealand, and Dutch forces were overwhelmed by Japanese military superiority in

Malaya (now Malaysia), the Dutch East Indies (now Indonesia), and New Guinea (now West Papua and Papua New Guinea). And shortly after Pearl Harbor was attacked, the American garrison on Guam was overrun. Wake Island fell on December 23, after the out-manned American defenders, fighting with no help from outside, incredibly repulsed the first attempted Japanese landing. The large American military presence in the Philippines was wiped out as well. Following a few victories over the Japanese in battles to defend the main island of Luzon, the American and Filipino forces were doomed without logistical and further military support. After bitter fighting while holding out on the Bataan Peninsula southwest of Manila, the American and Filipino forces had to surrender in April of 1942. To move the defeated forces to POW camps, the Japanese decided to march them rather than transport them, and the Bataan Death March became one of the most notorious atrocities of the Pacific war.

By then only the heavily fortified island of Corregidor, in the mouth of Manila Bay, remained for the Japanese to conquer. The siege of Corregidor, gallantly portrayed in the American media, was a truly heroic effort by the defenders, but they, too, were doomed to surrender to the Japanese after the island was invaded in May of 1942. The Americans and Filipinos who surrendered on Corregidor were spared another death march, and were, for the most part, transported to POW camps. But all who surrendered faced years under horrific conditions in Japanese POW camps or under hard labor in the Philippines and Japan, and many did not survive.

But as bad as things were in the spring of 1942, the American aircraft carriers had escaped December 7 unscathed, and they were still capable of projecting military force in the Pacific. The first indication of what the U.S. could do with their carriers came in April of 1942. The U.S. intended to send a strong message to Japan that even while the fleet destroyed at Pearl Harbor was being rebuilt, there would be no respite for the Japanese. The plan was to actually bomb Japan, and from an aircraft carrier. However, getting small carrier planes close enough to bomb Japanese cities posed a great risk for the carriers. Surprisingly, someone had figured out that the B-25, a twin-engine Army Air Corps bomber, could take off from the deck of a carrier, and it had the range to allow the carrier to stay far enough away from Japan to avoid the Japanese Navy. However, the B-25 couldn't land back on the carrier, so it was decided that the bombers, after completing their mission, would fly on to China and land there. At special airstrips built in remote areas of Japanese-occupied China, the planes would land, quickly refuel, and then be flown farther south to a part of China not under Japanese control, where they'd be turned over to the Nationalist Chinese to use against the Japanese.

That this plan, outrageous as it seemed, was given the go-ahead provides a good idea of just how desperate the U.S. was to strike back in response to Pearl Harbor. Jimmy Doolittle, famous air racer of the 1930s, was chosen to lead this operation and train the air crews. Ultimately, sixteen specially modified B-25s were loaded onto the carrier USS *Hornet* in California, and it headed west toward Japan.

On the morning of the day before the planes were scheduled to launch, the *Hornet* was spotted by a Japanese ship, and its position was radioed to Japan. But instead of aborting the mission, they decided to launch the B-25s from that more distant point and take their chances on reaching China after bombing Japan. All sixteen B-25s lifted off from the *Hornet* and bombed Japan, and almost all the B-25s reached China. Incredibly, sixty-two of the eighty Doolittle Raiders were safely smuggled across China and made it back to the U.S.

The impact of the Doolittle Raid on Japan was profound. Though little damage was done, the fact that American planes had actually flown right over Tokyo and released bombs on a country thought secure from attack had a real psychological effect on the Japanese people. It was also a spectacular morale booster back in the U.S.—really the first bit of good news to come out of the Pacific since December 7.

The Doolittle Raid made the Japanese realize that they needed to finish the job they started on December 7 and destroy the American carriers while the U.S. Navy was weakened. They devised a plan to lure the American Navy out to fight, and they decided to do it by invading Midway Island, only 1400 miles from Honolulu, in June of 1942. They figured that a landing on an island that close to Hawaii would have to elicit a response from the U.S. Navy, and they were right.

Midway was probably a good idea from the Japanese point of view, since Japan still had a considerable advantage in terms of aircraft carriers and aircraft. For the Midway operation, they sent the same six aircraft carriers that had attacked Pearl Harbor, in addition to a vast armada of supporting cruisers, destroyers, and troop transports. Against them the Americans could only muster three carriers and a few other ships. On paper, the Japanese should have won an overwhelming victory. However, a key factor came into play that shifted the odds back to the Americans: the Japanese military code had been broken. Thus the Americans could foresee the movements of the Japanese fleet toward Midway. With this knowledge, the Americans were able to lie in wait and gain advantage from surprise. Still, the numbers were so lopsided that the Japanese should have won anyway. However, through a number of fortuitous actions the Americans ended up sinking four of the Japanese carriers, while losing only one of their own. Not only was the Japanese landing at Midway turned back, but Japan lost a majority of its capital ships, the carriers, as well as many experienced fighter pilots. Japan was on the defensive in the Pacific war from that point on.

But even with the stunning American victory at Midway, Japan was still in possession of many Pacific islands from which they had to be ejected. In early 1942 Japan had expanded not only southward into Southeast Asia, but eastward as well into the Solomon Islands in the western Pacific. This was viewed by America as a move to cut off communication with Australia and New Zealand, and thus make it even more difficult for the Allies to use those countries as staging areas for fighting the Japanese. The U.S. responded in two ways. First, a series of naval bases had to be constructed far enough south that ships could refuel and still make it to New Zealand and Australia. One of these bases was in French Polynesia, on the island of Bora Bora. Other bases were in Pago Pago, American Samoa, Fiji, New Caledonia, and the New Hebrides, and they were reinforced to keep the Australia/New Zealand lifeline open. The second step was to turn the Japanese back in the Solomons with military force. This would have to involve an island invasion, the first of wwii for the Marines.

Landings occurred in August of 1942 on the Japanese-held islands of Tulagi and Guadalcanal, across a body of water that came to be known as Iron Bottom Sound for all the ships that would be sunk there. Guadalcanal became the focus of the fighting since it was an island sufficiently large to support a number of airstrips. However, in 1942 the Japanese didn't take the American threat very seriously and deployed troops piecemeal to retake Guadalcanal. Contrary to what the Japanese expected, the Marines they faced turned out to be fierce adversaries. Conditions on Guadalcanal were terrible for both sides, with malaria becoming a factor for the first but not the last time in the Pacific war. Americans learned a lot about Japanese military culture when they discovered that the Japanese were determined to fight to the death, even commit suicide to avoid capture. The first banzai attack of the Pacific war was experienced on Guadalcanal. After a tremendous struggle under horrible conditions, the Marines and then the U.S. Army defeated the Japanese. As at Midway, this was a severe blow to the Japanese, the first of a string of defeats for them in island invasions that stretched to the end of the war. However, this also signaled what Americans would have to face—a determined and skillful foe who would fight to the death rather than surrender.

After Guadalcanal a debate arose in the U.S. military, and it centered on two dominant personalities. One was General Douglas MacArthur. He had been in command of the American and Filipino forces in the Philippines when the Japanese invaded at the end of 1941, and he had been ordered to be evacuated from Corregidor just before the final surrender. He was determined to avenge this humiliation by retaking the Philippines, and argued that the best way to defeat Japan was through New Guinea, the Philippines, Formosa, and then Japan. In his view, being a general, this would be mostly an Army operation with the Navy and Marines in support. However, the other person who had something to say about this was Admiral Chester Nimitz. It was his view that a highly mobile Navy and Marine force could go more directly to Japan through the Marshalls, the Marianas, and Okinawa, skipping over entire Japanese-occupied islands and cutting them off from sustenance in the process. In his view this would be mostly a Navy and Marine operation, with the Army in support. Franklin Roosevelt faced a difficult situation, with these two strong egos not willing to give an inch in either direction. What was finally worked out was a compromise that, in effect, satisfied both of them. MacArthur was authorized to take the Army through New Guinea and the Philippines toward Japan, and Nimitz was told to take the Navy and Marines through the central Pacific toward Japan. In military terms, this was described as a giant pincer movement that would ultimately strangle Japan. More accurately it satisfied the demands of two men who represented the interests and aspirations of the major services in the U.S. military.

In the end the reasons for this decision faded from significance because the strategy worked. But it took three years, many amphibious landings on islands no one had ever heard of, and thousands of deaths and injuries on both sides. The Army under MacArthur hopped up the north coast of New Guinea, taking more lightly defended areas and isolating the larger concentrations of Japanese troops. American allies Australia and New Zealand played key roles in the fight for New Guinea, supplying troops, materiel, and staging areas in their home countries. By November 1, 1943, Marines made landings on Bougainville, and later on Cape Gloucester on New Britain, to secure the right flank for the Army operations on the main island of New Guinea.

Meanwhile, Nimitz's first island invasion in the central Pacific was designed to be fairly simple. The Japanese had built an airstrip on a tiny islet that was part of Tarawa Atoll. The feeling was that after sufficiently intense air and naval bombardment, the Japanese defenders would be either dead or stunned by the shelling and the tiny island should be taken easily. However, there were two catches to this plan. First, the bombing and shelling of Tarawa didn't turn out as planned. It started spectacularly. The pre-landing bombardment of Tarawa in November 1943 was an awesome sight to behold for the Marines on the landing ships. Most were convinced that no living thing could survive such explosive mayhem inflicted on such a tiny islet. What they couldn't know, but would soon find out, was that the Japanese had ingeniously devised bunkers and shelters that protected most of their troops and guns from the bombardment. As a result, heavy fire surprised the landing waves as they went ashore on this supposedly devastated island.

The second catch involved the geography of the island itself. Tarawa was the first coral atoll the Marines had ever invaded. The fortified islet of Betio sat on a reef that extended several hundred yards out from the beach. The depth of the water over this reef varied from about a foot at low tide to over four feet or more at high tide. The Americans knew that the drop-front Higgins landing craft, designed for sloping sand beaches, were not really appropriate for coral atoll landings, and contracts had been let for a new generation of amphibious tracked vehicles, or amtracs. A number of these new amtracs were available for the Tarawa landing, but not enough to get all the invasion waves to the beaches. But it was thought that the depth of the water over the reef at high tide would be sufficient for the Higgins boats to reach the shore.

It turned out that the water covering the reef at high tide was *not* deep enough to allow the Higgins boats to get to the beach. So the first waves of Marines in the amtracs went right up to the beach and were immediately pinned down. But the Higgins boats of the later waves, bringing crucial reinforcements and supplies to the beach, hung up on the edge of the reef hundreds of yards out. All that could be done was to drop the ramps and dump the Marines into chest-deep water, with a three-hundred-yard wade in to the beach ahead of them, in the face of withering machine-gun fire. The carnage was unbelievable as the Marines were mowed down wading slowly across the reef. At one point, aborting the operation was considered, since so much was going wrong. But the Marines were tenacious and determined fighters. They hung on, slowly expanded the beachhead, and seventy-six hours later the battle for

Tarawa was declared finished, with the deaths of the last of the roughly 5,000 Japanese defenders. Fewer than twenty Japanese were captured alive. The cost for the Americans was significant. In just over three days of fighting to take one tiny island, over 1,000 Marines lay dead, many washing ashore on the beach to provide graphic photographic evidence of the cost of taking the island. War correspondents who witnessed this carnage were shocked. They did the simple calculation of the number of islands multiplied by the number of Japanese defenders and the number of American dead required to take these islands, and there was an uproar from the American public. The term "Bloody Tarawa" appeared in the media, and the eventual cost of the Pacific war started to come into focus for the American public.

But the strategy for defeating the Japanese was to be relentless, and more islands were invaded. With many more amtracs available and improved tactics for neutralizing Japanese fortifications learned from studying those on Tarawa, the landings at Kwajalein Atoll in January 1944 went better. Majuro and several other atolls were taken, but then the Navy and Marines faced the much larger and more heavily fortified Japanese islands of the Marianas—Saipan, Guam, and Tinian. These islands were considered by the Japanese to be part of their inner defense ring, and they were determined to hold them at all costs.

Meanwhile, MacArthur had control of the northern coast of New Guinea, and was ready to return to liberate his beloved Philippines. He intended to do this by invading the southern Philippines and driving relentlessly to the north, to eventually retake Luzon and Manila. To secure his right flank, he asked Nimitz if he could invade and capture a Japanese airfield on the island of Peleliu in the southern Palau islands. This would be a bit of a detour for the Navy and Marines, but it would facilitate MacArthur's return to the Philippines, and Nimitz agreed. Once again, it was thought that lessons learned from invasions of atolls in the central Pacific would stand the Marines in good stead in taking the relatively small, hilly island of Peleliu.

Then something happened that could have changed everything. Halsey's carrier planes, in making bombing raids on the central Philippines, reported that Japanese military strength there appeared to be weak. Halsey suggested that MacArthur directly invade the central Philippines and save months and thousands of lives in his drive to recapture Luzon and Manila. MacArthur jumped at this opportunity and started planning an invasion of the central Philippines near Leyte. If he wasn't going to invade the southern Philippines, the Peleliu invasion by the Marines became moot since the right flank argument was now irrelevant. But the invasion fleet had already sailed for Peleliu, and it would take immediate intervention by Admiral Nimitz himself to call it off. For reasons that only Nimitz knew, he decided to go ahead with the Peleliu invasion. It has been thought that he expected the battle to be fairly straightforward and didn't warrant calling the whole thing off. What happened was exactly the opposite. The gentle, rolling, vegetation-covered hills of Peleliu seen in pre-invasion photographs—once stripped of vegetation by the pre-invasion bombardment—turned out to be limestone cliffs that were honeycombed with fortified caves. The battle for Peleliu turned into a nightmare that lasted two months at a cost of almost 9,000 Marine and Army wounded and dead, and roughly 10,000 Japanese dead. To this day, Peleliu veterans are bitter about the decision Nimitz made to continue with an invasion that had become unnecessary.

Meanwhile, MacArthur landed at Leyte and started the difficult slog through the labyrinth of Philippine islands, all Japanese-held, in his drive to Luzon and Manila. He eventually achieved his goal and declared the Philippine campaign ended in June 1945, but at tremendous cost. When Japan surrendered a couple of months later, American troops were still fighting in parts of the Philippines, and the Japanese there were never fully defeated.

Major objectives of the Navy and Marine drive to Japan were the Mariana islands of Saipan, Tinian, and Guam. With those islands in U.S. hands, airfields could be built for the new B-29 Superfortress bombers, which could bomb Japan directly. However, the Japanese considered the Marianas part of their inner defense ring, and would fight to the death to keep those islands out of American hands. Marines landed on Saipan in June of 1944 and faced a fanatical and determined foe. Saipan was declared secure in July of 1944, but isolated resistance continued to the end of the war. Thousands of Japanese and Chamorro civilians had fled into the mountains when the Americans landed, and efforts to get them to surrender by American military forces and interpreters continued to the end of the war as well. Nearby Tinian was also invaded and secured, and there was an epic struggle to recapture the former American territory of Guam that went from July to August, 1944. Marine casualties soared, and thousands of Japanese died, but the occupation of Saipan, Tinian, and Guam signaled to the Japanese that the end was truly near as B-29s started bombing operations over the Home Islands in late 1944.

The B-29 bombing raids over Japan were arduous twelve-to-fourteen-hour round trips made even more dangerous by the fact that there was no emergency landing strip between the Marianas and Japan. If a B-29 was damaged or ran low on gas, the only alternative was to ditch in the ocean. In addition, an island halfway to Japan had Japanese airstrips and fighters based there that could intercept the B-29s on their way to and from Japan. This island's name was Iwo Jima, and it became clear that it was necessary to take Iwo. It, too, was a relatively small island, and with all the experience gained in other Pacific island landings the Marines were confident they could secure the island in a fairly predictable way. But once again things didn't go quite as planned. The Japanese had had time to construct the most elaborate and complicated network of caves and tunnels of any of their Pacific island possessions. With this tunnel network, they could house virtually their entire defensive force of 20,000 men and their weapons deep underground, immune to the American bombing and shelling. This set the stage for one of the most gruesome island battles of the Pacific war.

The Marines landed on Iwo Jima in February of 1945, and it became clear from the outset that the Japanese defenses had escaped the pre-invasion bombardment virtually intact. Marine casualties were high, but there was no alternative to proceeding with a series of frontal assaults against heavily fortified Japanese positions. The most famous photo of the Pacific war was taken by Joe Rosenthal when an American flag was raised on the summit of Mount Suribachi. This happened five days into the battle, but by no means did it mark the end of the fighting. The flag-raising only signified that the Americans had secured the very southern end of the island. The entire northern end still had to be taken, and it wasn't until late March that Iwo Jima was finally declared secure, at the cost of nearly 6,000 Marine dead and over 17,000 wounded. More than 20,000 Japanese died on Iwo. However, the taking of Iwo Jima served its purpose—the use of emergency landing strips there saved the lives of an estimated 20,000 airmen, and Iwo Jima–based Japanese fighters could no longer shoot down B-29s on their missions to Japan.

The final land battle of the Pacific war was for the island of Okinawa. This was considered to be the final steppingstone to the invasion of Japan itself. The Japanese realized this and, starting with the American invasion on April 1, 1945, put up a terrific resistance to the Marines and

*On September 2, 1945, General MacArthur (at micro-
phone) conducts the surrender ceremony aboard the USS
Missouri in Tokyo Bay as high-ranking Allied officers look
on. The first to sign the surrender document is Japanese
Foreign Minister Mamoru Shigemitsu. Behind him
stands General Yoshijiro Umezu, the Japanese Army chief
of staff, and other members of the Japanese delegation.*

*A Pacific War Overview*

Army troops sent ashore to secure the island. What resulted was a horrific eighty-two-day battle with nearly 7,400 American dead, more than 30,000 wounded. The civilian toll on Okinawa by far exceeded any other island battle in the Pacific, with a conservative estimate of 150,000 Okinawans killed. The Japanese dead totaled about 108,000. But now the stage was set for the final invasion of Japan, an event that was feared by every American serviceman in the Pacific.

Then something happened that none of those American servicemen expected. Two of a new type of explosive, something called an "atomic bomb," were dropped on the Japanese cities of Hiroshima and Nagasaki in early August 1945. The B-29s that dropped the atomic bombs flew from their bases on Tinian in the Marianas. Suddenly the Japanese surrendered, unable and unwilling to resist in the face of such terrifying new weapons. The American fleet sailed into Tokyo Bay, and on September 2, 1945, the Japanese signed the surrender documents on the deck of the Navy battleship USS *Missouri*. The Pacific war was over.

# CHAPTER 1

*Parts of the ship, flames, and bomb fragments
flew by us, reaching hundreds of feet into the
air. The ship's midsection opened like a blooming
flower, burning white hot from within. Our
entire magazine and forward oil storage had
exploded; tons of* TNT *and thousands of gallons of
fuel oil poured into the water. Black smoke
billowed into the sky as the oil caught fire.*
—Russell McCurdy, MARINES

FIRMAN BALZA, NAVY, USS *Maryland*, battleship

RUSSELL McCURDY, MARINES, USS *Arizona*, battleship

EVERETT HYLAND, NAVY, USS *Pennsylvania*, battleship

DEL ALDRICH, NAVY, USS *Ramsey*, destroyer-minesweeper

AL BODENLOS, ARMY, Schofield Barracks

HARVEY AND JEAN FRASER, ARMY, Schofield Barracks

WAYNE JOHNSON, ARMY AIR FORCE, Hickam Field

BILL AND RUTH COPE, ARMY AIR FORCE, Hickam Field

TOM LARSON, NAVY, Pearl Harbor

LENORE RICKERT, NAVY, Pearl Harbor, nurse

PAGES 28–29: *The forward section of the sunken battleship USS* Arizona *burns fiercely in this photo of Battleship
Row taken from astern of the ship on December 7, 1941.*

# "A DATE WHICH WILL LIVE IN INFAMY."
# PEARL HARBOR, DECEMBER 7, 1941

FIRMAN BALZA
NAVY

I joined a Naval Reserve division in Green Bay, Wisconsin, on October 21, 1940. I had turned seventeen on September 25 and had to be seventeen to get into the reserves. But then I decided to join the regular Navy, and I couldn't get my dad to sign for me, he wasn't too anxious for me to leave home and go into the regular Navy. Finally I said to him, "Now, Dad, look, if you don't allow me to go into the Navy, I'm going to go someplace. I'm not staying here. If I go in the Navy you will know where I am. If I go someplace else, you won't." So he says, "Now you have me between a rock and a hard spot. Under those circumstances I will sign for you to go into the Navy." I said, "Well, Dad, Mother can sign for me, but all I wanted was your permission." So he says, "I don't have much choice, do I?" I didn't answer that question, figuring that since he said I could go it was fine. So I joined the Navy on January 31, 1941, and I went to Great Lakes for training.

When I got out of training at Great Lakes, I was to report to the West Coast, so they put me on a passenger train, the Chippewa, all the way to the West Coast. I ate in the dining car ordered off the menu, had a Pullman berth, and a black man made up my bunk. I thought I had died and gone to heaven. That was great. I was only seventeen years old, and for a seventeen-year-old kid to be going across the country in that fashion was really something. I got to Seattle, and they put me on the ferry boat over to Bremerton. When I get there here's this great big piece of iron sitting in that dry dock. I had never seen so much iron stacked up in all my life. That big battlewagon had those great big 16-inch guns, and each gun was more than sixty feet in length, and I thought, "My God!" So that ship was the USS *Maryland*, and I boarded her on Easter Sunday, 1941.

They put me in the third division in the No. 3 Turret. There were four turrets with two 16-inch guns in each turret. We left the States after shakedown and went to Hawaii. They had moved the fleet out of the West Coast. Our home port had been Long Beach, and we sailed out of there in July of 1941. When we left the States there were about seven tankers laying in San Pedro Harbor there in Long Beach, waiting for the U.S. government to lift the oil embargo to Japan. So we as kids in the Navy knew that the U.S. was having some problems with the Japanese.

So we went into Pearl, and we got there in July 1941. You can't believe what Hawaii was like then. It was like I'd gone to heaven. You've never seen such a beautiful place in your whole life. And here you are, on this great big $90 million yacht in Pearl Harbor with a place to sleep and places to go ashore. But we only got what they called "Cinderella Liberty" then. That's a liberty that ends at midnight, because there weren't enough accommodations in Honolulu to put up all the sailors in the fleet or all the Army or Marine Corps that was there. So we could only go ashore until they turned the lights out, and we had to be back aboard ship by midnight.

On Saturday, December 6, I had the duty and I was aboard ship. Most of the guys had headed in to the beach on Saturday after inspection at 9:30 or 10 A.M. That morning we had Admiral's Inspection, and Admiral Kimmel came aboard and inspected us. We had what we called "AMI," Annual Military Inspection, and the big fleet admiral came on board and looked everybody over in the fleet that day. That night all the big, high muckety-mucks went down to Waikiki to the Royal Hawaiian and drank a lot of booze and danced and all that kind of stuff, and that's what they did on that Saturday night. But not me, I had the duty. But we didn't set watch at night. We didn't have anybody manning the antiaircraft guns or on patrol. All you did was you had to be there in case they needed you, and you didn't have anything else to do but go to bed. Actually we slept in hammocks. There were no bunks for us. The only people who got to sleep in bunks were the officers.

You get up early in the morning when you're in the Navy, about 5:30 A.M. Then you have breakfast about 7 or 7:30 A.M. Then after breakfast on December 7, a Sunday, it was time to go to mass. Being raised on the farm by my ma and pa, on Sunday you go to mass. There was no Catholic chaplain on the *Maryland*, so they had mass scheduled for 8:15 A.M. on the quarterdeck of the *Oklahoma*, which was tied up right next to us. Some of the guys had already gone over there, but I had to go into my gun compartment to change my shoes so I could go over on the gangplank to the

*Oklahoma.* But I never made it. If I had been a couple of minutes faster I would have been over on the *Oklahoma* when the attack started.

So I had changed shoes, and while I was there a couple of other guys had come up and we were talking before I headed over to mass. I was standing right near my battle station, the No. 3 broadside gun, which was a 5-inch gun on the starboard side facing Ford Island. I was talking to these two guys, a first class cook by the name of Rocky Hallsted, and a first class gunners mate who was in charge of that secondary battery I was on, Joe Klimcack. And we were talking about if the Japanese attacked Pearl Harbor and sunk a ship in the channel, all the ships in the harbor would be trapped and couldn't get out. And this was really spooky because exactly that almost happened just about an hour later. If they hadn't beached the *Nevada* over by Hospital Point, it would have blocked the harbor just like we were talking about.

So we were just standing there having this discussion, and all of a sudden a Jap Val dive bomber came flying right by us, over the top of the Naval housing on Ford Island, right over the administration building, and went over to the sea plane hangar on the end of Ford Island and dropped a big bomb in there and blew it up. Then all hell broke loose. The plane was well-marked, so there was no mistaking it was Japanese. It had big round red circles on the wings and fuselage, and that pilot was smiling at us as he went by. He was so close we could see his teeth. All I could say to Rocky Hallsted was, "It's the goddamned Japs!" Then we got the word over the loudspeaker, "All hands man your battle stations, and this is no shit!" and the guy blew the bugle for battle stations. I was right there outside my battle station, so I went into the gun compartment. But that gun couldn't be fired inside the harbor. You couldn't elevate those guns much above 15 degrees, because they were for surface bombardment and weren't set up for antiaircraft. So the order came in to take cover since we couldn't shoot our gun, but I thought that's kind of stupid. You have no place to go and no place to hide, so I figured I might as well do something. So I went into the midship casemate and I saw a petty officer in there sitting on the deck with his knees under his chin and I said to him, "Dutch, what do we do now?" And he says, "I'm not going anywhere until somebody tells me where I'm supposed to be going." So I sat down next to him, and I stayed there for just a few minutes, but I was antsy. So I said, "Dutch, I'm going to go up on the boat deck and see if I can give a hand to those guys on the antiaircraft battery." So I took off, and I don't know what Dutch did after that. I got up there to the No. 4 antiaircraft gun on the port side facing out to the harbor and overlooking the *Oklahoma*. This was a 5-inch gun set up for antiaircraft defense. We had eight of them on the boat deck. The next smaller gun we had after that was a 1.1, and the next after that was .50-caliber machine guns. There were no 20mm or 40mm.

Now sometimes you hear that some Japanese bombs fell on Honolulu. Well, that's the biggest crock in the world. You know as well as I do that the Japs didn't come all the way over there to bomb Honolulu, not when you have all the military stuff to bomb. But what was hitting Honolulu were antiaircraft rounds shot from our ships that weren't fused right. You're supposed to put the shell in a fuse pot setter, which sets the fuse time on it so it goes up a couple of thousand feet in the air and explodes. Well, I saw some guys take those shells right out of the can and hand them right to the loader. When he puts a shell in the gun and kicks it out and it's not fused, it's not going to blow up until it hits something. So those shells went all the way over seven miles and hit Honolulu, and that's who bombed Honolulu, the Navy did, and we did kill a few people that way.

Some of our guys had gone over early to the *Oklahoma* to visit friends they went through training with, so they could talk to them a while before mass, and some of those guys got caught over there. But we didn't lose any; they all made it off the *Oklahoma* before it rolled over, and they got back to our ship. It was only fifteen or so minutes into the battle when the *Okie* took four or five torpedoes. She was tied up to us with those big ten-inch hawsers and they snapped like store string, and she just rolled right over. It turned out the Catholic chaplain on the *Oklahoma* was a portly little fellow. And he was below on the second deck of the *Oklahoma* getting ready to go up and conduct the mass. When the *Oklahoma* rolled over, he was too big to get out of the porthole. But he stayed there in that compartment and helped all the guys he could to get out of the porthole, and he stayed right there in that compartment and he drowned. He got a Medal of Honor for that.

Even though at that time I was handling ammunition for a gun on the port side, and we were looking right out at the *Oklahoma* tied up next to us, I didn't actually see it roll over because it happened so fast. You see, I was on the boat deck handling ammunition for No. 4 antiaircraft gun, and I had to run forward underneath the barbette of No. 2 Turret of the big guns, where the ammunition hoist was located, to get more rounds. So on one of my trips toward the hoist, somebody hollered that the *Okie* was listing. By the time I got my round of ammunition off that hoist and came out from underneath there to bring it over to Gun 4, I looked out and the *Okie* had already rolled over. She rolled that fast. She was gone in a minute.

So I was running back and forth about sixty or eighty feet between the No. 4 Gun and the ammunition hoist. I'd get a round of ammunition and run it over to the gun, take it out of the can, and throw the can down through the sky port into the galley, where we threw all the empties to keep them out of our way. Then they'd put the round into the fuse pot to set the fuse, and shoot it about 2,500 or 3,000 feet into the air. The idea was to put a big iron umbrella over the ship so the Japs had to fly through that crap to get to us. So we were shooting as fast as we could.

On one of my trips there was a bunch of guys waiting their turn to get ammunition at the hoist when a bomb hit near the bow at the waterline, blowing out our forward air compressor and our forward switchboard, and the ammunition hoists stopped. No more ammunition came up because we lost our power and compressed air, which was used to ram the antiaircraft guns. There was a hydraulic cylinder on there, and you put a round on the loading tray and hit the lever and the air pressure took the projectile up into that gun, and the breech block came up and it fired, one after another. And we also lost two people down below decks when that bomb went in there, one guy on the switchboard and one on the air compressor. The bomb went in at the waterline and blew out about twenty frames of the bow inside. There was a great big hole in there, and you could probably drop my house in it, that's how big a hole it was inside there.

So there was no power for the hoist. Well, we made a human chain down the ladders all the way down to third deck, and we handed that ammunition up, one man to another, in a chain all the way up to the deck, and that's how we brought the ammunition up to the boat deck from the magazine. About this time the 1.1 antiaircraft guns needed help, and there were so many people there on that No. 4 Gun that we were stepping on each other. By that time we had people from the *Oklahoma* over there and others from the secondary batteries, so we had plenty of people to help.

On the 1.1s the ammunition came in a can, about five or six shells in a clip, and there were about six clips in each can. And you put one guy on one side on a handle and a guy on the other side on a handle to shoot that thing. But to get the ammunition cans to the guns, you ran up a vertical ladder in the superstructure to get to the flying bridge above the gun, and you had to drop the cans through a hatch in the deck down to the crew in the gun tub. So that's what I was doing the rest of the attack after I got off the 5-inch gun. All this time things were blowing up, bombs were going off, and ships all over the harbor were shooting as fast as they could. There was so much stuff blowing up around there you couldn't tell where it was coming from. The *West Virginia* behind us was burning from the waterline clear on to the foremast. The *Tennessee* was directly behind us and she was hammering away with everything she had. When the *Okie* coughed up and rolled over we put some cargo nets over the side so the guys in the water would have something to climb up on. It was about twelve to twenty feet from the waterline to the gallery deck, and ten to twelve feet from the waterline to the quarterdeck.

Japanese planes were strafing us from both sides of the ship. They would turn the machine guns on and wouldn't stop shooting until they got on the other side of you.

So to get ammunition to the 1.1s, you had to get up there on the flying bridge, and that whole flying bridge was closed in with glass, and you had to get down on your hands and knees and put the ammunition down through that hole in the deck. There was a guy by the name of Paul Buckman who was with me, and he was a kid who went through boot camp with me and was originally in the fifth division with me. We were paired up carrying these ammunition cans up there and putting them down through that hole for the gun. So he was there on his hands and knees putting that can in the hole. I had just turned and gone back into the superstructure to climb down to get another round, and I no more got inside the superstructure when I heard a tremendous loud sound of crashing and breaking glass and rattling noise. I turned around and went back out on the flying bridge, and the whole place was covered with broken glass. A plane had come in strafing from the starboard side and shot out all that glass. The shots went right over Paul Buckman's head where he was kneeling down. If he had been standing up, or if I had still been standing there a second earlier, we'd have been cut in half by those bullets from that plane. At the time it didn't really bother me, and I just immediately turned and went back into the superstructure and down the ladder. It wasn't until I got down to the bottom of the ladder to pick up another round of ammunition that I started to realize what had happened, and I started to shake so bad I had to hang on to the ladder to catch my breath. Then I realized Buckman was still up there, so I climbed back up to see what happened to him. And there he was, still on his hands and knees with all that broken glass around, and he was finishing up loading that round into that hole in the deck. That's the closest I came to getting killed on December 7.

My division officer Howard Crow got killed that morning. He was in the forward top on a gun director up there, which was his battle station, and he was up there with a guy by the name of Roberts, and Roberts saw the bomb hit the foc'sle and he hollered, "Duck!" Howard Crow ducked behind the director, but a piece of shrapnel came through that thin copper skin, hit the director, and glanced off and hit Crow right in the jugular vein. Roberts grabbed ahold of his jugular vein and tried to pinch it off, but each time his heart pumped, his life blood just went out of him. And Howard Crow died right in Roberts's hands. Howard was a kid from Texas, a nice young ensign, a nice young kid. And I learned later that he was supposed to get married that following Saturday, December 13. He was going to marry a little girl who had come out to Hawaii to marry him.

So, I was running ammunition up to that 1.1 right up until the attack stopped. Then I went around and helped clean up the mess. We had so many empty ammunition cans that we had dumped down into the galley that we couldn't get in there at all. It was filled right up to the brim, and we had to take all that out of there. They brought a barge up to the side, and we loaded that stuff off, and we loaded debris off. We put out some fires, we went and helped some of those guys on other ships, and we had fire and rescue working parties helping everybody we could, because the *Maryland* wasn't damaged that badly. We didn't have many casualties, and we only had five guys killed.

The only casualty I saw that day was Howard Crow. He was covered up with a mattress cover down in the laundry room. That's where they put him after he was killed. They lowered him down off the main mast with a hand line down to the signal bridge, and from there they hauled him down and put him in the laundry. I went down to see him. And there he was, laying underneath that sheet with just his hand showing. His hand looked kind of gray, like an old piece of rug, and that really shook me up. I was sick to my stomach for about three days after seeing that fine kid, seeing him and also seeing all the destruction and all the dead people floating around in the water. They would pick the bodies up out of all that oil and muck that was floating around and put them in a motor launch, and they hauled them over to Ten Ten Dock and handled them just like cordwood. They would take them by the arms and legs and throw them up into a pickup truck they had parked on the dock and take them away. My God, that was some horrible stuff to see.

So, we were trapped in our berth. We couldn't get out because when the *Okie* rolled over it pushed us up against the mooring quay. We had to blow the quay with dynamite so we could get out of there, get the front of the ship around, get a tug on it, and tow it out from behind the *Oklahoma*. So when they got us out they did the same thing with the *Tennessee*, which was tied up behind us, and they dragged her out from behind there. They took us over to the Navy Yard across the harbor, and they flooded aft and brought the bow up out of the water so they could get the hole up above the water. And then they put a patch on that, pumped the water out, and using ten-by-ten and eight-by-eight shoring timbers inside they shored that bow up where the big hole was. The plating on a battleship was an inch thick, and they were welding that patch on there with that thick steel.

We stayed in Pearl Harbor until December 20. We got under way with the *Pennsylvania* and the *Tennessee*, but we were the first ones out.

We were in various operations, up to the Aleutians during the Midway battle, and down to Christmas Island during the battle of the Bismarck Sea. Then we fired shots in anger in the Tarawa invasion; we were the flagship for that invasion. Then we went to Abemama in the Gilbert Islands. After that we came back to the States. A while later we went to Maui to La-haina Roads and picked up a big task force and went to the Marshalls to Kwajalein and bombarded Roi and Namur islands for the invasion there.

I stayed on the *Maryland* until 1944, just one week short of three years. Then I went home on leave, went back, and was teaching 20mm in a gun school in San Pedro and in San Diego. I ended up in Portland, Oregon, until April 15, 1945. I was assigned to a net tender, and we were supposed to go in on the invasion of Japan, but luckily we didn't have to go. I don't think I'd be here talking today if I'd have gone over there on that invasion. The net tenders were supposed to go in first and lay down a net and secure it, and the fleet would have pulled in behind it. My chances of surviving that would have been slim or none.

I went back to Pearl Harbor for the December 7 ceremony in 2003 and stood on the port gallery deck of the USS *Missouri*, which is docked now right where the *Maryland* was docked on December 7. The *Missouri* is facing the opposite direction to what we were on that day. The *Missouri* is in our old berth, Fox 5, the *Maryland* berth, and that's where we were when the Japs hit us. I stood there and looked out over Ford Island, and I had the moment of my whole eternity right there, because that's the spot where I was standing on the *Maryland* at 7:55 A.M. on December 7, 1941.

*"A Date Which Will Live in Infamy"*

# RUSSELL McCURDY

MARINES

I enlisted in the Marine Corps, and after basic training was assigned to the Marine detachment on the USS *Arizona*. Before December 7, the most notable thing that happened to me was being a member of a really good Whale Boat rowing team that we had on the *Arizona*. Our

ABOVE: *The USS* Arizona *Whale Boat team in the fall of 1941 in Hawaii. Russ McCurdy is in the front row at far right. Other team members, top row left to right, were Lawrence Griffin, Herbert Dreesbach, Marvin Hughes, John Baker, Eugene Brickley, Gordon Shive, and Burnis Bond. Kneeling, left to right, were Francis Pedrotti, Robert Erskine, Robert Dunnam, Donald Fleetwood, David Bartlett, and McCurdy. This all-Marine team from the* Arizona *won the play-off races and represented the ship in the fall fleet races. They finished runner-up and lost by only two feet to the Fleet Champions from the USS* Pennsylvania. *On December 7, 1941, all members of the team except Baker and McCurdy were killed on the* Arizona.

team was made up of members of the Marine detachment on the ship, and we started to compete. During the summer of 1941 we entered the Whale Boat competition with the Pacific Fleet.

I was proud to be part of that team, and we did really well in the races, and finished runner-up to the fleet champion team from the USS *Pennsylvania*. We almost beat them, too, losing by just two feet at the finish line.

A few months later we came up on Sunday, December 7. That morning at 0755 I was getting ready for liberty, getting cleaned up in the forward head. I had just come off the watch at about 0730, and I was getting ready to go into Honolulu to spend the day and have dinner with a local family. So, the first thing was that I felt a small thud like a water barge striking us. Then I felt another thud like that, and I wondered what was going on. I discovered later it was bombs exploding. I went up on deck and there were guys pointing up in the air at planes going overhead, and there were explosions over on Ford Island. Just after that, General Quarters sounded, and then machine-gun fire and our antiaircraft guns came into action. I ran back, and our Marine detachment had a quick muster, then we headed to our battle stations.

My battle station was on the mainmast some eighty-five feet above the water, where I was a gun director for the broadside guns. On the *Arizona* there were two gun director houses up on tripod masts, one forward, behind the No. 2 Turret, and one just aft of the center of the ship, right in front of the No. 3 Turret. What they called the mainmast was one of the tripod supports for the gun director house above, where I was headed. I followed Second Lieutenant Simonsen, USMC, who was one of our officers, up the ladder on the way to the searchlight platform, when halfway up I saw a large bomb go down into the quarterdeck below us on the starboard side. It exploded and debris flew up toward us. I took cover by leaning back and placing my body behind the tripod leg of the mast, waiting for the fragments and pieces of the ship to whistle past on both sides. The next second or so I proceeded on. Just as I stepped off the ladder onto the searchlight platform, there was Lieutenant Simonsen, and he was badly wounded. He had been right above me climbing up the tripod leg, but he had been hit and his chest riddled by shell fragments and machine-gun bullets. He died right there on the spot, and there was nothing I could do to help him. No one could have helped him.

At that point, it hit me that this was the real thing, and that I was suddenly indoctrinated into war. The attack was in full swing, but I still wasn't up at my battle station. So I continued climbing on up from the platform,

*"A Date Which Will Live in Infamy"*

up to the gun director house at the top of the mainmast, and the bombs and machine-gun bullets kept coming all the way up. I finally made it up to my control station where Major Shapley, Sergeant Baker, Corporal Nightingale, Corporal Goodman, Young, and several other Marines were stationed. We had a great vantage point, with full view of the entire harbor. It was a spectacular panorama, almost unreal to watch. The Japanese planes were swooping all around us, and I watched torpedo planes coming in low from across the harbor, heading toward Battleship Row. They'd drop their torpedoes and then pull out so close to us that the planes seemed only an arm's length away. They were so close, and the pullout speed was so slow, you could read their faces as they slid back their canopies as they went past us. I saw the USS *Oklahoma* roll over like a wounded, harpooned whale.

Then there was a really violent explosion in the front part of the ship, which caused the old *Arizona* to toss and shake. First the ship rose, shuddered, and settled down by the bow. This action gave the mast a quivering whiplash effect that turned our control station compartment into a dice box. We were shaken into a human ball, but none of us was injured. Parts of the ship, flames, and bomb fragments flew by us, reaching hundreds of feet into the air. The ship's midsection opened like a blooming flower, burning white hot from within. Our entire magazine and forward oil storage had exploded; tons of TNT and thousands of gallons of fuel oil poured into the water. Black smoke billowed into the sky as the oil caught fire.

Major Shapley was very calm and assessed the situation like he used to do with our Whale Boat team. Realizing that all director controls were knocked out and the ship was burning, he directed us to head below for further instructions. The wind was in our favor for the risky descent, and was blowing the fire and smoke toward the front of the ship. His calmness and skilled leadership gave me courage to remain calm and alert. We then proceeded down the ladder on the port side tripod leg. The heat was oven temperature, and the flames licked close by at times as the breeze from the after port quarter protected us and kept the fire and smoke blowing forward. The rails on the ladder were hot, and I got some slight burns on my hands as we kept our balance while moving down.

We got to the deck and it was chaos. There were charred bodies everywhere. The passageways were like white-hot furnaces. The wounded and burned were staggering out of the passageways from below, only to die up on deck because of their charred condition. Most were blind, and many had their clothes burned off. I noticed Lieutenant Commander Fuqua trying to comfort many men with his calm and cool manner. For this action and his excellent judgment throughout this ordeal he was awarded the Medal of Honor. One of the ship's cooks, a man who helped prepare the meals for our Marine Whale Boat team, was leaning against a bulkhead—one leg blown away, leaving just a bloody splintered stump. I saw a terribly burned guy on the deck, and when he spoke I recognized him as my first sergeant. He was lying there on the quarterdeck, burned beyond recognition. The only way I knew him was by his voice. He said, "Marines are Whale Boat champions." Then Commander Fuqua said to go ashore, and the sergeant said, "Swim for it, champions." He died a few minutes later en route to the hospital. Just a few minutes before, he had been fully dressed and directing us to our battle stations.

When Commander Fuqua directed the few Marines who survived the blast to swim to shore, Major Shapley and several of us Marines headed for the beach on Ford Island. The major led us through fire, oil, and debris, while bombs were falling and the underwater concussion waves struck us repeatedly. His encouragement guided us all through that swim to a pipeline one-half the distance to shore. While the major was giving words of encouragement to all of us, his strength was weakening, but he still assisted a struggling Marine who was exhausted by his effort to survive. For that, Major Alan Shapley was awarded the Silver Star for saving the life of Earl Nightingale. Now you know why my wife, Pearl, and I named our first child Alan!

I swam from the pipeline to the beach alone, arriving in back of Naval quarters. I headed through the back door of the fenced-in quarters, got inside, and the place was deserted. As I walked through I noticed oatmeal cooking on the stove. Someone had been fixing breakfast and had taken off. I thought, this isn't good to leave it here like this, so I took it off the stove and turned off the burner. Then I walked back outside and went on to Ford Island Headquarters. And that's where I stayed until Tuesday night. They first cleaned me up a bit, since I was kind of a mess with a lot of oil all over my hair and clothes, and then I helped with the wounded and assisted at the Armory with the machine-gun posts on top of one of the buildings.

After the attack was over, everyone was still very tense for the rest of the day Sunday, and then there was that awful show of firepower on Sunday night. Everyone started shooting and there was a complete dome of tracer bullets that took down several of our planes.

My only injuries throughout the entire ordeal were slight burns to my palms from the hot railing when I was climbing down the ladder.

But my hearing was affected when the *Arizona* blew up, and my ears were ringing for several weeks. It took many days to remove all the black oil from my hair, nose, eyes, and ears.

A lot of times people ask me, "Were you scared?" And the answer is, "Yes, I was scared!" And you're thinking, "Will I ever see home again? Will I see my family? How can I get out of this alive?" That's when you pray a lot and tell yourself to remember your Navy and Marine Corps training, stay calm and try to be like Major Shapley and Commander Fuqua. Those who have seen war carry unforgettable memories of their fellow men, and I will never forget those two and how they conducted themselves and how many other guys, me included, owe their lives to them.

After Pearl Harbor, I went to Marine Barracks, and then I was assigned to the Navy working in downtown Honolulu as a Navy mail carrier. The mail went from the Naval Communication Department in town to Naval Headquarters at Pearl Harbor. After one-and-a-half years, I was selected, along with 200 other Marines, to make up the only all-NCO class to attend officer training and become officers. We graduated 100 percent. I then went overseas and was assigned to the First Marine Division just in time for the Peleliu landing.

I was in the fourth wave coming in on Peleliu. I sat on the front of an amphibious tank taking depth readings to miss the shell holes in the reef as we came in to the beach. That was kind of crazy since I was exposed on the front of the tank, and there were things exploding all around us as we came in; but the machine gunners on the tank were exposed, too, and if we would have gone into one of those shell holes we'd have either drowned or been sitting ducks, and it would have been worse. A little later I was up on the airfield and was sent with a message back to the beach. I had to make it all the way back across the airfield, and it was like a checkerboard with shell holes, and I was under fire the whole way. And it was hot—direct tropical sun and no shade! I drank two canteens just on the way back, going from shell hole to shell hole. I made it out okay from Peleliu and was in the fourth wave on Okinawa and made it through that. I finally ended up in North China. I became a sole survivor when my brother, who was five years older than me, was killed a month before the war was over in Europe.

On December 7, 1941, the only survivors of our fleet runner-up Whale Boat team were Sergeant John Baker and me. Only fifteen out of the eighty-seven-man Marine detachment on the *Arizona* remained. After

Pearl Harbor, my first meeting with Major Shapley was in 1945 on Okinawa, when I was with the First Marine Division and he was a commanding officer of the Fourth Marines, Second Marine Division. We kept in touch after that. Shapley retired as a lieutenant general in 1962.

My first meeting with John Baker was on a small island off Guadalcanal in 1944. It turned out we were in the First Marine Division together. He then was a captain, and I was a lieutenant. We lost touch, and my next contact with him was when I wrote him in April 1974 about an article he wrote showing the 1941 *Arizona* Whale Boat team. He thought I had been killed on Peleliu, so I informed him I was very much alive! In the meantime, Baker had been informed by Dave Briner of my current address, and Baker wrote me in April 1974 setting the record straight. Our letters crossed in the mail, and he died in June 1974 before my letter was answered. Baker was the coxswain of our Whale Boat team. I maintained contact with Marines Earl Nightingale, Crawford, Cabiness, and Navy men Russ Lott, James William Green, Jim Vlach, John Anderson, and Richard Hauff. Shapley and Baker were Pearl Harbor Survivors Association members along with me, and most of the others I mentioned are also members, and most of us have met every ten years back at Pearl Harbor since 1966. Shapley died in 1973. James William Green died February 22, 1996, and his cremated remains were placed in USS *Arizona* on December 7, 1996.

I've had a lot of close calls and survived them all so far. I should have been killed on the *Arizona* on December 7, but I somehow made it through that. I was under fire at Peleliu and Okinawa and probably should have been killed a number of times at those places. And since the war I've had several heart surgeries and cancer, and I'm still alive. I've got good doctors! And I'm proud to report that at the fifty-fifth anniversary ceremony at Pearl Harbor, we had eleven *Arizona* survivors in attendance, including me.

EVERETT HYLAND

NAVY

**M**y brother was in the Marine Corps, a seagoing Marine with the USS *Indianapolis* detachment. And they were pretty big boys in those days. I figured that I'd somehow like to serve with him, but I could never make Sea School—I wasn't tall enough. He was over six feet, and I only hit five feet eight in those days. So I joined the Navy thinking I could somehow get with him eventually. When we both ended up in the Pacific Fleet, I put in a request to be transferred to the *Indianapolis*, and it never was approved. The only thing I could surmise was that he was in the Marines and I was a sailor, and that may have had something to do with the decision. They didn't tell a seaman second anything in those days, other than do this and do that!

So, I enlisted in November 1940. I went through boot camp in Newport, Rhode Island. They sent me to communications school in San Diego, and from there I went into the Pacific Fleet. I got assigned to the USS *Pennsylvania* in the summer of 1941. I went from San Diego to San Pedro on the USS *Crane*, and I was one of many passengers going to San Pedro to get on ships we had been assigned to. They were ready to move out, and we sailed for Pearl Harbor about a week after I got aboard.

We pulled into Hawaii that summer, and it was like I'd entered paradise! You know, you're eighteen years old and you're in a place you've only heard about. There used to be a radio program called *Hawaii Calls*, and I used to listen to it on Sunday afternoons. It would always start out, "From under the banyan on Waikiki Beach. . . ." And they broadcast this show live from the old Moana Hotel on Waikiki. So I'd always had this idyllic image of Hawaii, and to actually be there was like a dream. When I got there, I went out to Waikiki to see the Moana Hotel, but as a sailor you weren't allowed near those places. All I could do was look at the outside of the place. When I went back for the fiftieth anniversary in 1991, a buddy of mine, Coke McKenzie, and I were sitting on the veranda of the Moana and I said to him, "Fifty years ago if we'd have tried this they'd have kicked our butts right out into the middle of the street!"

When I went on shore leave in Honolulu, sorry to say, I was with the big boys, drinking. We used to hit Chinatown, that downtown area, and that was all there was to Honolulu then, it was pretty small. We used to hit some of the barrooms, but there wasn't too much to do. Some of the fellas would go out to Waikiki to the beach, and I went swimming out there a couple of times with them. But, believe me, this was good duty!

I was a radio striker, which, in lay terms, means a radio apprentice. I had learned Morse code, and I was allowed to stand a certain number of watches, but I was mainly a "go-fer." During GQ my battle station was the radio room, and the radio rooms in the old battlewagons were way down in the middle of the ship. Of course, in order to keep your watertight integrity, everybody's locked in. And I figured if we ever go to war, the last place in the world I want to be was locked down in the middle of the ship. I wanted to be topside, so if something happened I could get off. Not very good thinking as things turned out! So I volunteered for antenna repair, which put my battle station topside.

On Saturday, December 6, I was on the *Pennsylvania*, and we were in dry dock at the time. I really can't recall what I did that day, and it wasn't until fifty years later that I was able to piece together what happened on Sunday morning, December 7. We had a ship's reunion in Hawaii for the fiftieth anniversary of Pearl Harbor. I walked in wearing my name tag, and there were tables set up with about eight or ten fellows around each one. I sat down with my name tag and a fellow across from me started to cry. He was a radioman first, Ben Engelken, from Kansas, and on the morning of December 7 when he saw the antenna repair squad go topside—I was in that group—and he heard later that we were hit by a bomb, he assumed we all got killed. But I was the sole survivor and was sent straight to the hospital. Right after the attack he got transferred from the ship and never got the word that I survived, even though the others were all killed up there. But Ben told me that that morning, before general quarters sounded, he and I were getting dressed and getting ready to go to church somewhere.

So battle stations sounded, and I ran up the ladders to get to my battle station out on the deck. The fellows who had battle stations down below were coming down and passing me as I went up, and they were saying, "The Japs are attacking, the Japs are attacking!" But we said this all the time when we were out on maneuvers. So, I thought, yeah, yeah. But I got outside and they were right—the Japs were there, and they were attacking!

So the six of us assembled in a compartment on the starboard side on the main deck in the aft part of the ship, and first you had to make sure everyone was there. And then we each had a job to do. My job was to go down the full length of the starboard side of the ship and batten down the battle ports. These are the brass plates that fit over what some people call the "portholes." As I would go down the length of the ship I would take quick looks out, and so much was happening so fast it was hard to decide, remembering back, what I saw and didn't see. One of the things I thought I saw was people getting off the *Arizona* and going hand-over-hand on a rope over to the ship next to them. At the time I didn't know it was the *Vestal*. When I first started volunteering at the USS *Arizona* Memorial in the early nineties, I mentioned this to one of the rangers and he hadn't heard of that, so I shut up right away and figured this was all in my head. And then about four years ago our guest speaker was a fellow who got off the *Arizona* by going hand-over-hand to the *Vestal*; Don Sutton was his name. So I was right, and I did see that happening.

Though I was aware of Japanese planes flying around, the sky over the *Pennsylvania* wasn't filled with aircraft. But things were blowing up, and it was noisy and smoky. So, after I finished my job of battening down the battle ports, we assembled aft again, and there we were standing with nothing to do, and we were adjacent to the clipping room where the ammo comes up on elevators from the magazines down below. So we figured, why stand here, so we just fell into line and started running ammo out to the gun that was right on the fantail. You'd grab a shell, run it out to the gun, and hand it to Coke McKenzie. He was the third loader on the gun and a regular member of that gun crew. So according to the ship's log at 9:10 A.M., one of the Japanese planes dropped a bomb that hit right where we were running the ammo back and forth. And in that moment that bomb killed twenty-four people on the *Pennsylvania*. And there were five more killed from the crews of minelayers—I think two or three different minelayers—and they were killed on the *Pennsylvania* then, too. I don't know what they were doing on our ship, but they died there. Of the six of us on the antenna repair crew, five were killed. I was still alive, barely.

The next thing I knew I was flat on my face. I never really heard anything go off, but I realized all of a sudden we had been hit. My arms were out in front of me, and I could see all the skin was purple and peeled. That's when I said to myself, "My god, we've been hit." I stood up and wondered what had happened to the rest of the antenna repair crew and the gun crew, and that's when I noticed that my feet felt wet. I looked down, and I had blood spurting out a hole in my left leg. So, I had always been taught that if you're bleeding, you're supposed to apply pressure. So I put my finger on it to stop the bleeding, and my finger sunk right into the hole in my leg up to the second joint! I figured the heck with this noise, and that was enough for me.

I was fairly badly injured as it turned out. My right ankle was shot open, and I had a chip of bone out of the right shin. They say I got a bullet wound through the right thigh near my hip, but I don't know when I got that wound. My right hand was ripped open; I had five pieces of shrapnel in my left leg; I had a six-inch by eight-inch piece torn out of my left thigh; I lost part of my left elbow and part of my left bicep. I had on shorts and a T-shirt that morning, so everywhere I had skin exposed I had flash burns, which meant my legs, arms, and face. Interestingly enough, in my medical records, the Navy had all the wounds listed as "superficial." I found that out recently when I tried to get more compensation.

So, I heard some officer shouting, "Get that man down to sick bay." So they took me down below, and the sick bay for combat overflow was actually the old radio quarters where we lived. The first thing they did was sit me on the deck, and I'm thinking, "They left me alone." I don't know if they thought I was too badly hit to mess with, or whatever, but they finally came along and put me into a bunk. I remember a radioman whose battle station was right there, and as I remember it, his name was Osmond and I knew him fairly well since we worked in the radio room together. And I said to him, "Hey, Ozzie." So he stopped and he came over and looked at me, and he bent over and said, "Who are you?" And that's when I started to realize, holy mackerel, either there's something wrong with him or something wrong with me!

I was moved off the ship that afternoon, according to the log, and I was moved to a big Navy hospital right there at the Navy Yard, and they had me in there in the burn ward. And there's an interesting story about my stay in the burn ward. A year later I ran into my brother, and he told me that his ship, the USS *Indianapolis*, which had been out on patrol that day, had come back into the harbor about a week after the attack. When they docked, right away he went over to the *Pennsylvania* to look for me, but they had me on the "missing" list. He figured I had to be somewhere, so he started checking around and went over to the hospital. He finally found me, but he said the only way he identified me was by a tag that had my name on it tied on my toe. He said they had us all lined up there in the burn ward, and we looked like roast turkeys. I can't confirm this story with my brother, because he later got transferred off the *Indianapolis* and into a Marine combat unit, and he got killed on Iwo Jima.

But, you know, we had no dog tags at the beginning of the war; those came out a little later. So if you had your clothing taken off and if you couldn't talk, they had no way of identifying you. A few years ago I met a woman named Lenore Rickert, and she was one of the nineteen Navy nurses working in the Naval hospital on December 7. She worked the burn ward and took care of me. I told her the story about my brother and the tag on my toe. She got weepy-eyed, and she said, "When you boys were so far gone that we knew there was nothing we could do for you, we tagged you so we wouldn't lose your identity." They thought I was on my way out. My brother told me that the doctor told him that it was just as well I died, because if I did live I'd be blind and never walk again.

All this time I was out of it, and I didn't wake up until Christmas. A couple of years ago I met a guy who worked in the hospital at that time, and he said, "Not only did we tag you, but we moved you out of the ward so you wouldn't die in front of everybody." He said there was a separate building outside somewhere, and they rolled us out and put us out there. Apparently it was bad for the morale to die in front of the other patients!

The first thing I can remember happening when I was conscious again of what was going on around me, was that there were food carts going by. And I mentioned to a corpsman who I noticed next to me, "They certainly feed well in here." I had no idea where I was. And he said, "That's Christmas dinner." And then I realized I had been out from December 7 until Christmas, and that's when I started remembering what was happening to me.

Because of my burns, they couldn't do much surgery to get shrapnel out or fix bones up. And by that time infections had set in, so I guess I was kind of a mess. They moved me out of the hospital at Pearl fairly soon. I think I was in the second group to be moved back to the mainland. They put me on the old passenger liner, the *Lurline*. They took us back to San Francisco, and from there on a ferry boat they took us up to Vallejo Naval Hospital, and that was somewhere around New Year's. I was there for about six months, and after that they sent me to Brooklyn Naval Hospital for physical therapy. I guess they were emptying the West Coast to make room for new casualties coming in.

My father died when I was one year old, and my mother brought my brother and me up. She came west when I was still in Vallejo. Even though I was listed as missing that time my brother came to try and find me a week after the attack, apparently they got it sorted out because the telegram they sent my mother was that I was wounded. So, she had moved to California to be closer to me. But then I got sent to New York, and not long after that I got sent back on duty. I'd been in hospitals for nine months. When I got out I had pretty much healed—when you're young you bounce back fast! With the work they did on my face, you really can't tell I had been burned except I do not have any lips.

I got assigned to the Atlantic Fleet to the light cruiser *Memphis*, and I was on that ship for about six months. Then I got transferred off that and spent the rest of the war on the beach, assigned to shore duty at the Naval Air Station in Charleston, South Carolina.

After I got out of the Navy, I got married and became a science teacher. At some point I got divorced and then retired from teaching in 1983. After that I got involved with working for a courier company out of Los Angeles. I had the best time of my life! I was living on 747s and flying all over the world for nine years. The company handled mostly Asia, but I used to end up in Eastern Europe once in a while, too.

I decided to go to Hawaii for the fiftieth anniversary of the Pearl Harbor attack in 1991. I was staying at a hotel in Waikiki, and there was an attractive Japanese woman sitting at this tour desk in the lobby. She was working for the second largest tour company in Japan at that time. Every morning I'd go down and see this cute little Japanese lady, and I used to stop and talk with her. My buddy who was with me, Coke McKenzie, took some pictures of us, and I told her, "If you give me your name and address, I'll send you a copy of these photos." She had to think about that one! But she gave me her address and I heard from her. I sent her the pictures, then made a trip to Hawaii and stayed a week and met her son, and got along well with him. Then I took her on a trip to San Diego to meet my mother and my daughter. In fact my mom just died about six years ago at age ninety-six. But my daughter said, "Dad, don't let this one get away." So I put my toothbrush in my pocket, moved to Hawaii, and got married to Miyoko.

Some people think it's kind of odd that I am married to a Japanese lady since the Japanese darned near killed me on December 7. And you know, I didn't have a great love for those people when we were fighting them. But many years after the war I met a Japanese person who introduced me to Japan and Japanese culture. So, when I met Miyoko I didn't have any animosity for the Japanese any more. Now we live in Hawaii, and I volunteer at the USS *Arizona* Memorial on weekends. I get to meet a lot of people and tell them my story. I hope it makes their visit to the memorial more meaningful, to hear from me and the other Pearl Harbor Survivors what it was like on December 7. Hawaii isn't what it was when I was first here in 1941, but it's still a great place to live, and I enjoy my life here now.

# DEL ALDRICH
NAVY

I joined the Navy in 1939, and I was on the USS *Ramsey* in Pearl Harbor. It was one of the old four-piper destroyers launched in 1918, an old four-piper tin can. But it had become a mine layer by the time I got on it. I wasn't an electrician yet, but I was striking for it. At that time I was mess cooking, when the December 7 attack started. I had just taken a load of food to the aft quarters, back where they ate below deck, and this was about 8:00 A.M. I was working out of the galley, which was on the main deck right amidships. I'd just gone down carrying a load, and I was yelling at the guys, "Here it is. Come and get it or I'll throw it out."

About the time I got down below, there was a bunch of explosions. The guys who already had gotten out of the sack were saying "Oh, God, somebody's sure practicing awful early this morning." We knew there was something going on, but we didn't know yet what it was. So then I went on up to get another load of food, and I looked over and there's the old battleship *Utah* rolling over. So I turned around and yelled down the hatch, "BOMBING." And then I started to run. I didn't know what the hell was going on, and I didn't look up in the air right then. You know this is maybe two minutes after the first bomb. About that time the General Quarters siren went off.

The first ones the Japs dropped over on our side of Ford Island were torpedoes, and those Jap torpedo bombers came in real low, right over the top of us. We were all lined up there, a whole row of mine layers tied up one to another, and those planes came right over us.

And I'm looking across at the *Utah*, and there wasn't any smoke or fire, it was just rolling over at her berth. So I'm running forward on the open deck and I look up and there's a Jap plane coming right over the top or our mast, just as low as he can get and still clear it, and he's looking for Del Aldrich! He sees me running and he opens up, and, well, he was a little late because his machine gun bullets landed out in the water behind us. But there I was, just twenty years old, and he's shooting at me and I'm running!

So as we realized that the Japs were attacking us, we started to open up with every gun we had. We had lost our sights in rough seas for this old 3-inch antiaircraft gun on the foc'sle, when a deck locker had washed right over the side with the sights for this gun in it. It never got replaced because it was a real old gun anyway, and nobody thought much about using it. And this friend of mine was a gunners mate, and he was real excited and ran up there and decided he was going to shoot this gun. So he was throwing those 3-inch shells into the breech, closing it, and running around and pulling the lanyard, and away it'd go. Well, he didn't set the fuse or anything, and those shells would just go up in the air and come down somewhere and explode when they hit the ground. If you don't set the fuse for a certain altitude, that's what they do. And that's how we shelled Honolulu!

Everybody got to their battle stations, and we had one boiler under steam because we had ready duty, and we were the second ship out of the harbor that morning. We just dropped the lines and started to head out. And as we were maneuvering, that's when we saw one of those Japanese two-man subs in the harbor. The *Curtis* was trying to depress that 4-inch gun that she had aft, and she could only go so low, but she was shooting at it anyway. Then the *Monahan* tried to ram it, and went right over the top of it. Everything in the harbor on that side of Ford Island was shooting at that sub. All you could see was just a little bit of the conning tower. You could see that it was a sub and you knew it had no business there.

So, anyway, we were the second ship out of the harbor. We must have gotten out of there in fifteen minutes. We went right out in front of the harbor and started patrolling for submarines with sound gear. A bunch of us were sitting on the deck handling .50-caliber ammunition. I saw a forty-year-old man, one of our most experienced guys, he was sitting on the deck and his hands were shaking so bad he couldn't move the clips of .50-caliber ammunition. And I'll tell you what, he wasn't shaking any worse than me—it was mutual! We were so wound up we would just shake. And I also know I was scared as hell!

After that we were standing off Pearl Harbor and just patrolled back and forth for a solid week. The next Sunday we went back into Pearl Harbor, and we hadn't really gotten a good idea of how bad it was because we had left so fast. But what I really remember was all the smoke, and this was one week later. So we came in and got provisions and fueled up and got a load of mines. We came right back over to where we were berthed on December 7, and of course there was the *Utah*, belly up. Some of us got to go ashore briefly, and I went over to Aiea for something. They had this big desk made of planks, and that's where they were trying to keep track of how many had been killed. It was a body count station, and this was where they were running the bodies through. We noticed that on their list it was up to 2,000 dead, and I said, "Jesus Christ, can that be right?" I didn't think that many could have been killed, but they were.

So we got back on the *Ramsey* and headed for the South Pacific. We were out for about two months. We had quite a cruise down there in the South Seas. We started out in Samoa, first to American Samoa, to Pago Pago, and then to British Samoa. Then we went over to Fiji, the New Hebrides, and New Caledonia, and we were laying mines in all those harbors.

When we got back to Pearl Harbor after our two-month South Seas tour, I was transferred temporarily off the *Ramsey* to a BOQ on shore, and they sent us over to help out on the damaged ships. So I got assigned to the *Maryland*. I walked on board, and it was sitting very low in the water. I think she was touching bottom, and they were trying to raise her and had us doing work to help out. They had a lot of guys they pulled off other ships to help out with the salvage.

We have a little organization called the Naval Mine Worker Association. We have reunions and stuff, and we have a newsletter. It was an offshoot of the Pearl Harbor Survivors Association, which was formed in 1958, and it's really a going proposition. They have a darned good newsletter, so I've stayed in touch with a lot of the guys over the years. The Pearl Harbor Survivors Association is a lot easier to explain to people than the Naval Mine Worker Association. Most people don't know anything about what we did out there in the Pacific during the war.

OPPOSITE: *Al Bodenlos at Schofield Barracks, Hawaii, just prior to December 7, 1941*

## AL BODENLOS
ARMY

I enlisted in the Army on July 7, 1940, at Cleveland, Ohio. From there I went to Fort Hayes, in Columbus, Ohio, and later to Fort Ord and went through really rigid basic training. There, from my record, they found out I had a musical background, so they assigned me to the bugle section. There were about eight or ten bugles there.

I got to Schofield in Hawaii in July of 1941 and I was put in charge of fifteen buglers. I was bugle master of the 804th Engineer Aviation Battalion. I was still based at Schofield Barracks in December 1941, and it was a great base. They had a round building where they had the boxing matches and the hula shows, right there on the base. Entertainers would come out every week and put on hula shows for us soldiers, singing, dancing, and otherwise, with their ukuleles and guitars. They also had a roller-skating rink out there. I used to love to roller skate! I had my own roller skates, and we had a lot of things we did right at Schofield. We heard very little of the war in Europe in those days, in early 1941.

And you wouldn't believe how idyllic Hawaii was before the war. We used to go out to Waikiki to the two big hotels out there on the beach, the Moana and the Royal Hawaiian. The Royal Hawaiian was quite a place. Out on Kalakaua Avenue they had some little cottages you could rent for a buck a night. And down the beach a ways was a real neat bar. It was a circular rotating bar and went around and around. It's where the police station is now on Waikiki Beach. Of course I never drank much, but once in a while we'd go in there. If we couldn't get a room at the Royal Hawaiian, or the Army-Navy YMCA was full, we would just walk down to Kapiolani Park, down toward Diamond Head at the far end of Waikiki, and sleep right on the grass. Well it was warm, you were never cold, and nobody bothered you. I wouldn't do it today! But that's what we did. And there were some old banyan trees—they're still there—and one of them you could walk into, in there among all the roots and vines hanging down. There was this old Hawaiian gal, she must have been in her fifties—she seemed old to us then—and we called her mama. She was servicing the boys inside that banyan tree, right there in the park!

So I used to get my buglers out there in the morning for reveille, and we would play marches in harmony and they were beautiful. And the commander liked it, and my CO said that we should put together a drum and bugle corps. So on December 6, I got leave and was sent into Honolulu to buy instruments. I bought the instruments, had the receipts for them, and I got overnight liberty. So that evening a couple of buddies and I went out to Waikiki to watch a hula show. First we went to the Moana, but there wasn't much going on there. But someone said there was a hula show next door at the Royal Hawaiian, so I went over there and watched for a while. They had set up out on the beach for the show. But that evening what I really wanted to catch was the battle of the bands at the old Army-Navy YMCA. There were bands from all the battleships, and the bands were putting on a concert. The USS *Arizona* band had been in the competition, and the band from USS *Pennsylvania* won that night. The next morning the *Arizona* band was back on their ship and down below passing ammunition, and that's where they died.

But that band competition was something. The place was packed, so many guys had gone to watch the bands. I couldn't get a bed in the YMCA, so I slept on a cot in the annex. That night I was looking forward to a beautiful Sunday the next morning. I was planning on going swimming at Waikiki, and maybe later to a bar.

So I got up the next morning, December 7, and while I was shaving we heard what we thought was maneuvers, and the announcer on the PA said, "All military personnel report back to your stations immediately." And we thought, "Oh, boy, they're calling maneuvers for us." So we rushed across the street to the Black Cat Café for a quick cup of coffee and a hot cake, which we ate in about five minutes, and it cost about 10 cents. Then I went out and got on the shuttle bus to Schofield. The driver was an ethnic-Japanese guy. As the bus headed out toward Pearl Harbor we could see planes flying around up ahead and big columns of smoke, and we could hear explosions in the distance, and you could see the planes diving. It was quite a scene as the bus drove on that road right by Pearl Harbor. The attack was going on as we drove past. Planes were flying around and ships were blowing up. Somewhere near where the *Arizona* Memorial Visitors Center is today, an MP stopped the bus and pulled out the Japanese driver and arrested him on the spot! This guy hadn't done anything—he was just driving the bus! So we had to get away from the bus because the Japanese planes were swooping down after they dropped their bombs, and with their machine guns they were shooting anything in sight. The MP said to get away from the bus because if it was hit it would blow up.

Meanwhile the attack was still going on and Japanese planes were zooming right over us. We all took cover in a ditch by the road and watched the show. The Japanese planes were coming in real low right over us on their strafing runs of the harbor, and I swear I could see the faces of the pilots. I could see a ship had turned over—I found out later it was the *Oklahoma*—and the *Arizona* was burning and putting out a huge column of black smoke. The breeze was at our backs and was blowing all the smoke out to sea, so we had a real good view. The harbor was just aflame.

After a while they found another driver from somewhere, so we got back on the bus and headed to Schofield. By then my outfit was deployed at Wheeler and the other bases, because we were an aviation engineer outfit attached to the Seventh Air Force at Wheeler Field. And when we went by Wheeler we could see our engineers filling craters in the runway even as the attack was still going on! They were also pushing the damaged and burning airplanes off the runways with their bulldozers. The 804th was the very first Army ground force in action that morning. We got a great citation for being in action right away, about seventy minutes after the initial attack. The only other comparable one was an engineering outfit in the Philippines, and they got a similar citation.

So my duty then, because I was bugle master of the battalion I automatically became a courier, so I rode a motorcycle delivering messages to the different bases. That was my function that started on Sunday morning and continued for two days. When I got to Wheeler with my first message they were still bombing and shooting. That night, I had to get on a truck going from Schofield to Wheeler, which was almost right next door, and the driver asked me to lay on the right fender because on the right side of the road was a drop off, and of course they had to keep the lights off the truck because of the black-out order. So I was the guide on the right bumper, getting that truck down that narrow road and by that drop off. I was panic-stricken because I thought, God, if that damned truck goes off the edge I'll be killed, because the truck would roll on me as it went down the hill. That was probably the most scared I was the entire day of December 7 until that evening when it all sunk in!

I don't believe we got any sleep all that night, because there were rumors of invasion on the windward side of the island. And we were ready for anything, with our rifles and helmets on. We were waiting for them!

So I spent the next two days delivering messages, and then I spent half the third day literally passed out because of exhaustion. After that I was at Schofield for almost a year.

Then I was shipped to Canton Island, in an engineering outfit again. Our group worked on the desalinization unit. Canton was out in the middle of nowhere in the Pacific with no fresh water, so they needed this "desal" plant. I was there for sixteen months, from late 1942 to early 1944. There really wasn't that much to do there except swim in the lagoon. We had movies. We had a little rec room with a Ping-Pong table. We had those great big records of radio programs, Bob Hope and all those. They'd send those to us and we would listen to them. You could have beer or soft drinks when they had them. Our dress was khaki shorts and white T shirt, sandals and dark glasses, which I never wore, which is probably why I had cataracts. The duty was good and I figured I was out of harm's way. But there were no women there! Right when I was ready to come back, then they brought some nurses over. Well, you know who got ahold of them—the officers! We never saw a gal over there except from a distance right at the end.

I was back at Honolulu for a while, and then back out to Tinian, Guam, and Saipan. I ended up in air-sea rescue at Okinawa after the war ended.

For years I wiped everything out from the war, and my family never asked me one thing about it. I found later they thought it would upset me. I just wiped it out of my mind. I didn't think about it. I didn't join the Pearl Harbor Survivors until 1990 because I didn't even know they existed until a friend of mine was at the convention center, and he said, "You know, Al, you can get a free Pearl Harbor license plate." Well, it wasn't free but that's when I joined the Pearl Harbor Survivors, and that brought everything back to light again. I got involved in speaking at schools and universities and I tell the story of Pearl Harbor. And of course there were the acquaintances I had in the *Arizona* band. I became friends with them because of our musical background—remember I was a bugler—and I never saw them again. They're still there on the *Arizona* and in my heart.

## HARVEY AND JEAN FRASER
ARMY

On December 7, 1941, at Schofield Barracks, Hawaii, I had been relieved as a company commander in the Third Engineer Battalion, Twenty-forth Division, and reassigned to Camp Beauregard, Louisiana. Scheduled to leave on December 8, we had sold our car, and all our furniture was packed and down at the dock. And on this Sunday morning my wife, Jean, and I were sleeping late on cots in our now-empty house at Schofield.

We were awakened by the sound of airplanes getting louder and louder, but we didn't think too much of that because our house was right next to the edge of Wheeler Army Air Base. Then, the next thing we knew there was a loud crash that shattered the glass in our windows! We jumped out of bed thinking one of our planes had crashed right near us. Then we looked out and saw airplanes with the Rising Sun on 'em and knew they were Japanese! They were firing their guns and flying right up our alley heading for the barracks of the Third Engineers. They were so goddam low you could see the pilots' faces and their white neckerchiefs. I ran to get my pistol, but then remembered I had turned it in and didn't have any antiaircraft to fight back with. They were bombing the airfield right across the way from us, but the big crash had been from a bomb that missed the field and exploded in the general's front yard, just across the street from us.

I said, "Jean, you'd better stay here. I gotta go over and report to the battalion." Then I went and reported to this colonel, and he said, "You're going to take over your old company." So I raced over to my old company, and, Jesus Christ, it was pure pandemonium! Now, I'd been relieved, and they'd appointed a new CO, but because I was seasoned in the job, I became the senior company commander.

Things were confused as all hell, and about that time there came hordes of Air Corps people from Wheeler. They'd already been bombed over there, and a lot of them killed and their airplanes burned up. "We want to borrow rifles," they hollered! "We don't have any weapons!" We did have some extra rifles in the supply room, so I told the supply sergeant, "Give 'em the goddammed guns and ammo. They are gonna go out to shoot airplanes." I am sure they didn't hit any, but we gave 'em about fifty Springfield rifles and ammo. The way it was in the old Army, boy, you *never* let a weapon go without a receipt. But I told the sergeant, "The hell with the receipts! We're at war!"

So they went out and shot at planes but didn't bring the rifles back. Then, before I was due to leave Hawaii the Army said, "You've got to find all those rifles or you're gonna *buy* 'em! So we advertised in every paper in the Hawaiian Islands saying, "ALL RIFLES WITH THESE SERIAL NUMBERS MUST BE RETURNED!" And can you believe it, before we left Hawaii in August I had all the rifles back but nine.

We had spent two or three years building bunkers at Wheeler so that in case of attack their airplanes would be protected, but the Army's commanding general was so fearful of sabotage by local Japanese that he ordered the planes to be all bunched in the open in front of the hangars where they could be guarded. The result was it took only one or two bombs to set them all on fire, and they melted and fell down like dead people. Little piles of junk all perfectly lined up.

We didn't know where to go, because we had never had our alert stations defined under the new division set-up. So, we didn't move out for two or three days. In the meantime, the colonel said to me, "Harvey, we gotta have slit trenches over there in the residential areas. I want a whole bunch of slit trenches over there. You get all the earth-digging machines you can and start diggin' those trenches!"

I said, "Colonel, you remember the last time you had me dig slit trenches? I cut the cable to Honolulu and goddamned near got court-martialed for it."

"Damn you!" he said, "I want you to dig slit trenches!"

So we got the ditch diggers and started. We put trenches by all the houses, and we also cut the electric line, the cable between Schofield Barracks and Honolulu, and the water line. We had trenches—some of the 'em filled with water—and we were out of communication with Honolulu and had water running a foot deep down the main street of Schofield Barracks. And I caught holy hell for it.

*"A Date Which Will Live in Infamy"*

That night, God almighty, it was terrible! People didn't know what the Japanese might have out there. They did know they had been able to come with all those airplanes and shoot our airfields and Pearl Harbor all to hell. And if they could do that they just might have troop transports out there, too. There were rumors all over the place that the Japs were landing at Ewa, Barbers Point, even Diamond Head. So, I'm tellin' you it was worth your life to go out! People were shooting at anything that moved! They were especially ready to shoot at anything that flew, and if I'd have been a pilot, I'd *never* have taken an airplane up that night. At Pearl Harbor our antiaircraft gunners actually did shoot down five of our own airplanes coming in from their carriers out at sea.

That night the colonel called me to set up machine guns right outside the CP instead of up on top where they used to be. Then he got into the nearest cellar and called the company commander and said, "We're never going to make it through the night! The Japanese are landing at Kahuku!" Well, I doubted that very much, but I told him, "All right, Colonel, goddammit, if they do come in here we'll get together and fight the sunzabitches!"

Then he'd say, "I smell gas!" and run and ring the gas alarm. And that caused some more pandemonium. Pretty soon everybody had a gas mask on but the first sergeant and me and some private. And I'm running up the stairs hollering, "Take those goddamn masks off! There ain't any gas."

A couple of days later I was ordered to take my company out to the North Shore in the Haleiwa area to support the Twenty-first Infantry Regiment, commanded by Colonel Doc Cook.

Then by late August when it had become obvious that Hawaii was not going to be invaded, my original orders for change of station were reactivated. We came back to the States on the *Republic* in an eight-ship convoy that included the battleship *Tennessee*, which had been bombed and shot up at Pearl Harbor and was being returned to the Bremerton Navy Yard for repair, refitting, and modernization.

From the States I was sent to Europe, and that is where I spent the rest of the war and wound up as a brigadier general. Then, as my final career, I wound up spending nine years as president of a small—but one of the finest—engineering schools in the entire country, the South Dakota School of Mining and Technology.

# WAYNE "JIM" JOHNSON
ARMY AIR FORCE

The government was going to start registration for the draft. So me and a bunch of the boys who were hanging around a little mom and pop grocery store decided we'd join up with the National Guard. What I wound up as was a waiter in the officers' mess. Well, I complained about that, so we had an old mess sergeant who told me to go see the sergeant-major up at division headquarters, to see if I could get a transfer. He rattled off a bunch of rigmarole to me, but what it came down to was that the only option I had was to take foreign duty. That was Panama, Philippines, or Hawaii, and I decided Hawaii would be about the best place to be. Then they told me I could put in for Officers' Candidate School, but I told them, "I've had enough of you suckers—I don't want any of that."

Well, finally the papers came through for Hawaii, and in San Francisco I got aboard an old Army transport. We came to Honolulu, and I saw Diamond Head and all that and I felt elated. It was a beautiful-looking place, and we all thought that was swell, and the island smelled so good.

They had me over at Bellows Field on the windward side of the island for a little while. I was there about a month-and-a-half, until October 31, 1941, and I remember that date quite clearly, because I had a couple of real sore arms. The night before I'd been in to Honolulu and I got tattooed—a big eagle on one side and a great big palm tree and a hula-hula girl on the other. The next morning I could hardly wear a shirt! I'd try taking it off, then the sun would burn on me, and that was worse. I had those duffel bags and laundry bags to carry down and put on the bus, and it was just misery.

When we got to Hickam Field I thought I was in heaven. Everything was nice, newly painted, and there were great big barracks open to the air.

That barracks was a big thing—a nine-wing building three stories high. It had a mess hall that would seat 2,000 people. All we had was Venetian blinds and screen wire on the windows and great big overhangs to keep it cool. I was up on the third floor. Chow was good—cafeteria style.

Well, the first thing I know after we get there, they lined us up and said, "There's two things you have to do in this man's Air Corps here— you've got to pull a month of guard duty and pull a month of KP." Well, I wanted to get the worst over first, so I volunteered for a month of KP.

I'd just finished my month-long KP assignment on Saturday, December 6. This fellow I knew had a private airplane license, and he was going to take me and another fellow out and fly us around first thing on Sunday, December 7. So we got up early that morning, shaved and showered and put on our clean uniforms, and went down to breakfast. After breakfast we were waiting around on our bunks there for the bus to Honolulu, so we could drop off at John Rogers airport. So, we were sitting there, chit-chatting and taking life easy waiting for the bus, and about that time we heard a pretty loud bang. Well, we didn't think too much about that because a day or two before some people with firecracker cherry bombs had set them off a ways down in our same wing, and in a hollow building like that it made quite a bit of noise. And at the same time we heard these airplanes flying, but we didn't think too much of that either because carrier plane pilots were always flying in to Pearl Harbor for the weekend. So, we heard two or three of those bangs go off, and then we heard some more go off, and they were closer. We looked out of the window and saw some airplanes down west of us where they had Air Corps Supply. That was a big civilian repair and work place for the airplanes. And out there, about 300 or 400 feet up in the air zooming past, was an airplane with the rising sun painted on the wing. Well, that just didn't jibe with what they'd told us at our big Thanksgiving dinner, about how we didn't have to worry about attack because we were so invulnerable that nobody would try it. Well, when I saw that rising sun I knew somebody had lied to me! We knew, of course, that we were having trouble with Japan, and when we saw that meatball on that airplane we knew we were into it.

I was on the second floor at that point, which I figured wasn't too much protection, so we all decided to get out of that place. We went downstairs and stood on the steps, and we saw two or three more Zeros fly over, and we could see bombers up in the sky over Pearl Harbor. They looked to be up about three or four thousand feet. There's a big parade ground there to the north of Hickam Field barracks, I guess about a city block square, and we took out across that thing, about fifty or sixty of us. On the other side was a bunch of old wooden barracks, and we ran down around them and looked back and could see they'd done a lot of damage up there at Air Corps Supply. Big black smoke was billowing up.

I guess all that consumed about twenty-five to thirty minutes. Then there was the question of what the heck are we going to do? Now, just over to the west of us was the fire station and a kind of brig. Just about then they hit that brig and fire station and did quite a bit of damage. There were quite a few casualties. Well, if I'd chosen guard duty first instead of KP, that's where I'd have been, and I'd have been killed or injured for sure.

So we were hiding down there among those wooden buildings and we weren't doing any good, so we decided to go back and get into the armory and get some rifles and gas masks and pistols and so forth, and ammunition. A bunch of us headed back—thirty of us or better—back to the barracks to get in the armory for our section, down on the first floor. Well, it had a steel door and the door was locked. Most of the noncoms and anybody else in authority who had keys had taken off for the weekend, so we got down there and tried that door—five or six of us—and we didn't budge it. Finally the whole bunch of us got together and we just rammed that door open by using a group of bodies as a battering ram. The guys up front, and I was one of them, we got pretty well squashed.

We got rifles and ammunition and bandoleers of 30.06 ammunition. Back outside I looked up and these Jap planes were still coming across once in a while, and I said, "We can stand right here and if we all fire up at them as they go by somebody's liable to hit one of them." But we never did hit one.

Meantime some other guys got into the armory and got some .30-caliber air-cooled machine guns, and I think one .50-caliber, and they went out on the parade ground and set up the darn things. They'd had more training on such things than we'd had. About that time, here came the sergeant. He said, "I want thirty guys to fall out here right now. We're going to go over to the headquarters building for guard duty. We'll march over in formation, and the first guy that breaks and runs, I'm going to shoot." We formed up in two columns and started across the parade ground west of the headquarters building, when here came some Jap planes again, machine-gunning all the way across that field. We all scattered like quails and hit the dirt, and the sergeant didn't shoot a one of us!

After things kind of quieted down, they assigned a group of twelve or

*"A Date Which Will Live in Infamy"*

fifteen of us to take 4x4 trucks and go down to the commissary and get GI cans—brand-new ones—and they sent us to fill the cans at the swimming pool and then haul the water to the hospital. We made about six trips doing that. The reason was they didn't want to take any chances on saboteurs having poisoned the water supply. We had all those Japanese-Americans working there, and we didn't have any way to know where their loyalties were. And those cane fields there, people could slip around and hide in there pretty well if they wanted to. There were all kinds of suspicions and rumors going on, and they weren't taking any chances.

So, after we got squared away following the attack, I stayed in the Army Air Corps until I finally ended the war in the Air Transport Command, flying cargo all over the Pacific.

## BILL AND RUTH COPE
ARMY AIR FORCE

BILL: I graduated in 1938 from a small Methodist college in northeastern Ohio called Mount Union. I was a three-letter man.

I got a job with the state after I graduated, but it wasn't much and the pay was bad. One day a flyer came through and made the Army Air Corps sound romantic and travel-oriented, plus it sure was more money. It was a good thing I had a college degree because that was one of the requirements, and I joined. Pretty soon I was in flight school, and I was surprised when they washed out about half of my class in 1940 for various reasons.

In June of 1941 I finished flight training, and as a brand-new second lieutenant I got a dream assignment: bomber pilot at Hickam Army Air Base in Hawaii. It was wonderful! Hawaii at that time before the war was so quiet and serene—just beautiful. We did flying training in the mornings and hit the beach in the afternoon! My training began in the old B-18 twin engine bomber built by Douglas. That plane was slow and would have been a sitting duck for Japanese Zeros. We could only crank it up to 130 mph, and we had no guns.

ABOVE: *Bill and Ruth Cope in Hawaii, 1941.*

So there I was in Hawaii, driving a convertible that wasn't paid off, and we get word of some girls coming in on the *Lurline* from California. So of course off we went to the dock.

RUTH: I had just graduated from Cal Berkeley. I had been in the drama department. Gregory Peck was a classmate of mine and a friend—the drama department was really small then. We could tell he had talent and would make something of himself. For years people kidded me and wanted to know why in the world I picked Bill over Gregory Peck! But I don't regret it anymore—Gregory has died and Bill is still here, so I guess I made the right choice!

So these pilots were there to meet us at the dock when we got off the ship. There were five of us girls from Cal. I had a friend from Montana who was stationed at Hickam, and he alerted the rest of them to our arrival. Bill had this convertible and we spent a lot of time together during the two-week vacation. At the end of the two weeks I told the other girls I was going to stay in Hawaii. This came as a shock to them. They all had new jobs and boyfriends to get back to. But I had lost my parents in 1938 and there was no one to tell me not to do it, so I stayed.

BILL: There I was, a pilot with a convertible. What could she do?!

RUTH: Bill was stationed out at Hickam and I got a room in a boarding house in Honolulu. He would lend me his car and I would drive it back to town, and he would stay out at the base. It took him a month to ask me to marry him. We were married on Thanksgiving weekend, November 26, 1941.

BILL: On my first date with Ruthie, I was madly in love with her, of course, but I had this ego thing with girls, and I had this convertible, so on our first date I parked and I said to her, "I love you, take off your knickers." And she wouldn't do it!

RUTH: I think I was the first one who ever turned him down! Bill always tells everyone I married him for his convertible. That may have been true, but then I found out it wasn't even paid for!

BILL: So of course I wanted to marry her—it was love at first sight. I proposed to her on the terrace at the Hickam officers club. I finally said I'd like to marry her but I couldn't afford it. I was paying for a car and uniform. So she said, "Well, I have $1000 in cash—will that help?" I said, "That'll do it!" We were married in what passed for the chapel in the officers club.

They had a little altar at one end of a room with slot machines at the back. All the lieutenants were playing the slot machines while we were up there getting married. Then we had the reception out on the terrace at the officers club. The officers club, terrace, and the room we were married in are still almost exactly like they were in 1941. No more slot machines though.

We moved into our quarters at Hickam, a two-story building, and our unit took the two levels on one end of it. Our windows looked out at Pearl Harbor in the distance. You could see the ships in the harbor then because at that time Hickam was a new field and there were no trees yet. When you drive by that building today, and it's still there and looks exactly like it did when we lived there, the trees are all big now, and you can barely see across the street!

On December 6 I had the dubious honor of being Officer of the Guard with orders to inspect the Hickam flight line before and after midnight to see that all the planes were lined up wing tip to wing tip, with guards on duty to keep an eye out for saboteurs. This was the sad story for military aircraft over almost the entire island. There were a few fighters that were dispersed to northern Oahu, and a few pilots from Wheeler Field got up there and were able to take off, and they shot down eight enemy aircraft. One of these guys is my close friend Col. Rasmussen, from flying cadet days. He was our best man. We still see each other, and he ended up being quite a watercolor painter in Florida.

So, I had gone off duty at midnight of December 6. The next morning Ruth and I were still in bed reading the paper when we heard loud explosions from Pearl Harbor. I said the Navy must be practicing close today. Then I looked out our second-story window—and remember we could see all the way to the harbor—and I could see explosions and ships burning. None of this made any sense, and we were sitting there wondering who, what, and why. Then one of the enemy planes came zooming over real low, coming at us from the direction of the harbor, and flew right over our quarters. As it went over we could see the Rising Sun on the fuselage. I yelled out, "My God, it's the Japs!" As we looked out the window we could see the *Arizona* rise up out of the water as it exploded.

RUTH: So Bill jumps up out of bed and is running around getting his uniform on. Usually when he would go over to the base on duty he was in uniform with a tie on. That morning he just threw his uniform on and was heading down the stairs to the door when I yelled at him, "Come back, come back!" And he said, "What do you mean come back?" And I said, "You forgot your necktie." I don't know what I was thinking. He just turned around and I'll never forget the look on his face. He was probably thinking, "How did I ever get involved with this dumb-o?" Then he ran out the door. That's the last I saw of him for the rest of the day.

So there I was alone, and the raid was going on, and the only thing I could think of to do was to start vacuuming! This seems ridiculous now, but that's what I did. But then the power went out, and that was it for the vacuuming. Then the phone rang and they wanted me to report to the base hospital. I told them I wasn't trained for hospital work—not that I was trying to get out of anything, but to let them know I wasn't really qualified to do anything in a hospital. So, they say, "Can you wash dishes?" and of course I knew how to do that, so that's what I did the rest of December 7—I washed dishes in the Hickam base hospital. Since the power was out, their big automatic dishwashers weren't working and the dishes were piling up and somebody had to do something with them.

BILL: I ran over to the flight line, which wasn't that far away from our quarters. As I got close, a flight of enemy high-level bombers dropped bombs on the hangers and aircraft that were around there—big explosions everywhere. What I would normally do when I was coming off Officer of the Guard—I had come off duty at midnight the night before—was that I would go to the Operations Building the next morning and report off duty. So that's what I figured I'd better do. I go in there and the only one in the office was a crusty old lieutenant colonel sitting at a desk. There was debris from the bombed building falling on his head, and explosions all around. He was just sitting there, frustrated and mad, and looking for someone to take it out on. I smartly saluted and said, "Lt. Cope reporting off duty, sir!" And he just exploded! He yelled, "Get the hell out of here!" And that's exactly what I did.

But back outside the field was complete chaos. No one knew what to do. We had no plans for how to respond to this type of assault. Everyone was just wandering around looking for something to do. We all agreed we needed guns of some sort, but no one could find the key to the armory. All of the airmen who were authorized to drive had gotten into the motor pool, jumped into just about every vehicle in there, and were wildly motoring around the base. I stopped one truck driver and asked him where he was going. He said, "I don't know, but every one else is going!"

Finally someone got into the armory, and later that day an airman posted a pom-pom type antiaircraft gun outside my window and was pom-pomming into the air. I opened the window and said, "What are you shooting at?" He yelled back at me and said, "I don't know—everyone else is shooting." But this had fatal consequences. Later that evening Navy aircraft were coming in from one of our carriers to land on Ford Island. Thinking they were enemy aircraft, a few of them were shot down by our own antiaircraft guns.

So, after December 7 the base was a mess and we had no planes to train in, and it was very frustrating. But a few of the old B-18s were still more or less in one piece. They were patched and wired together, and we finally started flying search missions.

RUTH: I finally saw Bill again late in the evening of December 7. We were more worried about Bill's family and my aunt and uncle in Montana and that they'd be wondering what had happened to us. After December 7 they were talking about evacuating all the wives back to California. But then I got a job with the WARDS. This was a group of military wives and civilian women, and we plotted radar sightings of all aircraft around Oahu Island. The intention was to avoid shooting down our own aircraft by tracking and identifying every aircraft that was in the air around Oahu. We worked up at Fort Shafter. This was top secret work, and I couldn't even tell Bill much about what I was doing.

BILL: After December 7 we started getting more of the new B-17s. They were great planes. I wouldn't be here today except for the durability of the B-17. During the Battle of Midway we flew our B-17s up to Midway and gassed up and then went out looking for the Jap fleet. But they were taking evasive action and were headed for home. We didn't have much luck bombing them because our bomb sight was designed to aim on a fixed target, such as anchored ships or buildings. I had an engine go out and came home on three.

RUTH: But if they had taken Midway, you wouldn't have had any place to re-fuel.

BILL: Yeah, if they had taken the island I wouldn't have had any place to land. I didn't have enough gas to get home.

RUTH: I found out I was pregnant the weekend of June 6, 1942, and I remember it because it was the week of the Battle of Midway. I plotted Bill out in the Battle of Midway. He never got to see where I worked. It was all top secret. He said, "I'm going to be out of town for a few days and I can't tell you where I'm going." And I couldn't tell him I knew where he was going! The timing came out perfectly because he took off for New

Caledonia about the time I headed back to the States and was getting ready to deliver our first daughter.

World War II strengthened our marriage. We became an Air Force family—career Air Force. We were in the military. We had everything go wrong that could have gone wrong for us. We had just been barely married when we were separated in June 1942. If you really wanted an excuse to see that the marriage was going wrong, that would have been it. But we stayed together and we're still together.

BILL: She was in the hospital in the States having a baby, and they asked her how long her husband had been overseas. And she says, "Over a year." And they said, "Ohhh? Oh, really! He's been gone over a year and you're having a baby now?"

RUTH: I didn't say that I had been over in Hawaii with him nine months earlier!

BILL: In 1942 the Japs had starting building an airfield on Guadalcanal in the Solomon Islands. So we flew our B-17s from Hickam to Fiji, and then on to New Caledonia. I was bombing Guadalcanal from New Caledonia, and then a little later we moved to Espiritu Santo in the New Hebrides. The Seabees would go ahead of us and carve out runways in the coconut groves. We didn't have much in the way of supplies. Sometimes we would sleep under the plane wings, poured gas into the tanks by hand, ate powdered eggs and powdered milk. I didn't get malaria. But I hoped I would—I let the mosquitoes bite me! I figured they'd send me home!

RUTH: When he came back home he weighed 125 pounds though.

BILL: Remember I said we had trouble hitting ships with bombers because of the fixed bombsight? Well, I ended up hitting a Japanese ship by mistake. Here's how it happened. The Japs brought four transports down "The Slot" with supplies for their troops. They anchored off the part of Guadalcanal they controlled and were off-loading to small boats that would take the supplies in to the beach. A request came to our squadron of B-17s to come from our base in Espiritu Santo to bomb these transports. We flew up there—it took several hours to get there from Santo— and we were coming in over Iron Bottom Bay to hit them. I was flying on my squadron commander's wing, and my bombardier was supposed to watch and drop our bombs when the lead plane dropped. It was called pattern bombing. As we got near the target, we saw that the transports were being protected by what looked like battleships, cruisers, and destroyers and they were throwing up a lot of ack-ack. We were getting some hits, and then a half a dozen Zeroes came at us head-on, and they were firing at us. I knew my bombardier was firing at the Zeroes with his nose gun and I was afraid he wouldn't dump our bombs at the right time. So I called down and said, "Get ready to get those bombs away." All he caught was "bombs away." He thought we were in trouble, so he dumped our bombs. They ended up hitting what looked like a battleship and seriously damaged it. Our Navy later finished it off. Of course, I couldn't see what had happened under us to our bombs. When we got back to base, I was apologizing for dropping early when some of the pilots behind us came in and were congratulating me for hitting the battleship! It was all by mistake, but we hit it! This got no publicity because there was no media in the area at the time.

Most of the time we were flying search missions for the Navy to try and spot the enemy carrier forces. Eight- and nine-hour flights, and come back and hope we could find our island. Finding the island was a greater worry than Zeroes. The Zeroes were hesitant to attack us because of the ten .50-caliber machine guns we had on the plane. They didn't know we couldn't hit anything.

After thirty-five missions in the Solomons' combat zone, I returned to the States and received a Distinguished Flying Cross and two Air Medals. The rest of the war I had operational and inspection jobs.

Bill stayed on and made a career in the Air Force. In 1948 he participated in the Berlin Airlift. Bill and Ruth enjoyed their years in the Air Force in spite of the many moves. They feel the experiences enriched their lives and those of their two daughters.

And Ruth did see Gregory Peck again. "After twenty-five years I ran into Gregory Peck at a fundraiser in Fresno, where we happened to be stationed at that time. And he said, 'Oh, Ruthie, the years have treated you so well.' I don't know what he told his French wife—he told her in French who I was, but I don't know what he said about me." Bill and Ruth ended up moving back to Hawaii where it all started for them, and they volunteer at the *Arizona* Memorial at Pearl Harbor.

OPPOSITE: *Tom Larson (right) and*
*William Lynch in front of the Royal Hawaiian*
*Hotel, Honolulu, December, 1941.*

## TOM LARSON
NAVY

A fter two years of college at the University of Minnesota, I was restless and wanted to see the world. A Rover Eagle Scout, I decided to make a vagabond journey around the world and traveled all over Europe with my rucksack. I ended up getting out of there, working my way back on a cargo ship in 1939, just four months before the Germany invaded Poland and started the war in Europe. I worked passage home and joined the Naval Reserve. By August 1940, I'd spent time on several ships and had taken a Naval Reserve cruise on the battleship *New York*. I went through the V-7 program and was commissioned an ensign in the Naval Reserve in September 1941. They sent me out to San Diego, and I did some training in naval intelligence and was assigned to the destroyer base.

Then I got a very interesting assignment. I was to be the executive officer on a beautiful 115-foot pleasure yacht the Navy had acquired, named *Elvida*. Its Navy designation was "YP-109." The YP stood for "yard patrol." The Navy wanted the yacht sailed to Hawaii, where it would patrol the Hawaiian Islands. The other officer assigned to YP-109 had been in the Navy several months longer than me, and he was the reserve ensign in command. We had a crew of fifteen men to sail this thing to Pearl Harbor, after we had made a few trial runs off the coast of

California. My assignment sounded like a dream: sail a yacht to Hawaii, deliver it to Pearl Harbor, and return on a Navy ship to the destroyer base in San Diego. It didn't quite turn out to be that simple!

We sailed from San Diego on November 25, 1941, and accompanied a tanker, the *Ramapo*. A couple of days later we hit a big storm that made us all miserable. Only four of us on the boat didn't get seasick, but the other ensign, from Hollywood, was in the sack all the way to Hawaii, seasick. But we finally pulled into Pearl Harbor the afternoon of Friday, December 5. After reporting to the section base commander, I remained aboard the yacht while the other ensign went into Honolulu for shore leave.

The next morning, Saturday, December 6, I reported to the section base commander, expecting to get information on doing some patrolling of the Hawaiian Islands in the YP-109, and on which ship I would catch a ride back to San Diego. Instead I was handed orders to report for duty the next morning, December 7, to CINCPAC (Commander in Chief, Pacific), at the submarine base at Pearl Harbor, for duty as a communicator! I was supposed to be trained to use an electric coding machine. That meant no cruising the islands in the yacht and no return trip to San Diego for a while. That afternoon I went over to the staff communications office of CINCPAC to meet my new boss, and then I moved into the BOQ close to the submarine base. For a BOQ it was pretty plush—a three-story building surrounded by palm trees, and I started contemplating some hikes up into the mountains I could see from Pearl Harbor. I was standing there late that afternoon, and a perfect rainbow spanned the mountains. This was looking to be pretty good duty, and I went to bed early that night because I had to report for duty first thing next morning.

So I got up bright and early on Sunday morning, December 7, ready to report for my first day of new duty at 8 A.M., but polite naval custom was to report a bit early to relieve the night watch, so I wanted to get over there about 7:45 A.M. I got dressed in my best tropical white uniform, and met up with Lieutenant (j.g.) Herb Fairchild to walk over to work. I remember it was a beautiful morning, and the tropical air was fragrant. There were all these beautiful tropical trees, and we were strolling slowly toward the submarine base at Pearl Harbor where CINCPAC had its headquarters.

As we were walking along, I noticed some small, low-flying, single-winged planes above us and to our left. I thought maybe they were doing maneuvers, but that seemed odd for a Sunday morning. As we continued to walk along, there was a large tropical tree ahead of us. One of the planes flew right overhead, and I waved at the pilot. Just as he went over, leaves from that tree fluttered down. I didn't think anything of it until later, and it was only then that I realized he'd been strafing. The bullets going through the tree had knocked the leaves loose, and that's why they were fluttering to the ground. None of this was registering at the time though. I did notice guys all around us running for shelter. More planes flew low right overhead, heading toward Ford Island where the battleships were moored. Now I noticed the sounds of gunfire, .50 caliber and antiaircraft. One of the planes flew very low over us, and I could see a large, red rising sun insignia on the wings, and just as I realized that, the plane burst into flames and plunged straight down into the water nearby!

We were still heading to work, and as we rounded the corner of the sub base headquarters building more men were running for cover into the building. I thought this was all unusual, but it hadn't dawned on me yet what was actually happening. I still thought I was seeing some kind of elaborate American military maneuvers! The only thing I remember thinking was how unusual that they were doing this on a Sunday.

We went into the building and up to the second floor to report to work. Somebody there yelled at us that we were at war, and the Japanese were bombing us. Unbelievable! I was in a state of shock! I remember my only feeling was one of complete surprise. So there I was reporting for my first day of duty, and everyone was running around and no one was there to train me what to do. Suddenly a lieutenant shoved a clipboard into my hands and told me I was now the "officer messenger plugger." This didn't make any sense to me at all, so he quickly told me that I was to deliver freshly decoded messages to various staff officers. Though I was mainly just delivering messages, they were all top secret and urgent, and this work needed to be done with great haste.

So I started running around delivering decoded messages to the offices of the top commanders of the Pacific fleet, all there in that building. Among them was the overall commander, Admiral Kimmel, and I went into his office many times that morning with messages. He was middle-aged, lean, and was known for his fiery temper. Later on in movies they made about the Pearl Harbor attack, they always depicted Kimmel as cool and collected and reacting calmly to the attack. But it was exactly the opposite! I'd go in there with a message that contained more bad news, and he'd read it and start ranting and raving and cursing loudly. He was red-faced and flustered and highly agitated, not the cool and calm person of the movies! I couldn't blame him. Those messages brought him news of the battleships sinking, the planes and hangars at Ford Island being blown up, and various other facilities being bombed and strafed.

Of all the staff officers I delivered messages to that morning, and there were many, I remember Admiral Kimmel the most vividly. He knew he had to take the blame, and he did. He was the only one on his staff who was fired. When Nimitz came to relieve him after the attack, the rest of his staff stayed on, but he was sent home.

If there wasn't a message to deliver right away, I would run upstairs and go out on the roof and watch the attack for a few minutes. It didn't dawn on me that there was any danger, and I didn't experience any fear. I'd just stand there and watch the Japanese planes flying overhead, and look over at Ford Island where all the battleships were sunk or damaged. There were huge columns of black smoke pouring out of all the ships, there were explosions, ships were burning, and some of the Japanese planes were being shot down and exploding into the water. There were loud explosions, and the firing of the guns from our ships was echoing over the harbor. I'd watch all this for as long as I thought I could stay away, then I'd run back down and resume delivering messages. But periodically throughout the attack, I got chances to go up on the roof to watch the attack in progress. I guess I was kind of in a state of shock. It was hard to comprehend what I was seeing.

Later that day, some of the young officers who had been rescued from the sunken battleships, some still with oil on their clothes, were brought over and reassigned to our staff. All had harrowing stories to tell. One had been able to escape from a porthole when the *Oklahoma* rolled over. He said there was an officer behind him who was too big to fit through the fairly small porthole opening, and there was no choice but to leave him behind to drown. A few who showed up at our building had been lucky and had been ashore on liberty for the weekend. They had rushed back to Pearl Harbor and wanted to do anything they could to help.

I ran messages all day, and finally got back to the BOQ that evening. It was only then that it finally sunk in that we were at war. Everyone was restricted to base—no hikes in the mountains for me! That night there were sporadic explosions and gunfire. Everyone was tense. Rumors were racing around, and one was that the Japanese were on the way to make a landing on Oahu. During the night there was a big crash, and an antiaircraft shell went right through the ceiling and floor of the room next to me. There was more shooting of machine guns during the night, and I had a genuine fear of getting hit by stray bullets. I got down in a corner of my room thinking that I'd be safer there. I was terrified! We were issued side arms in case the Japs invaded. I heard later that some of our planes coming in that night were shot down by our own antiaircraft guns.

The next morning I went to work and felt really jittery. I hadn't slept well at all, and I felt uneasy all day at work. If there was any loud noise, I'd jump. I was still doing the same kind of work, delivering messages, because no one in the communications office could take the time to train me for the work I was there to do. The flow of messages had slowed, so I had time to go up and spend more time on the roof. I talked to the machine gun crews up there, and we looked out at the mess in the harbor. The *Arizona* was still smoking heavily, and they had work crews with hydraulic drills over on the upturned hull of the *Oklahoma* trying to get guys out who were trapped inside.

During that day after the attack, I got a chance to talk to a lot of the sailors who had been on the ships that were damaged or sunk. They had many amazing and horrible stories, and they were telling these stories one after another.

Finally on December 11 I had a chance to go over and see the yacht I'd sailed on to Hawaii, the *Elvida*. I barely recognized her—she had been painted by the crew—but they were all still there and okay. A bomb had dropped nearby but no one had been hurt and the yacht was untouched. Then I hitchhiked over to Hickam Field, which was right by Pearl Harbor. The place was a mess! Some of the buildings were in ruins, many men had been killed when the big barracks building was bombed, and a lot of our planes were destroyed on the ground.

I continued in my assignment with CINCPAC at Pearl Harbor for another seven months, finally getting trained properly in communications. About a month after the December 7 attack, Kimmel was relieved and then Nimitz arrived. He was a wonderful guy, a German from Fredericksburg, Texas, and he appreciated having young reserve officers like me around. I was in and out of his office many times. He was always nice, and sometimes offered me coffee.

I spent eleven months at the naval base at Tulagi in the Solomons. While I was on Tulagi we'd go over to the PT base to drink torpedo alcohol mixed with lime juice and look for souvenirs from downed Jap planes. I ended up on the *Lexington* in Tokyo Bay with the Seventh Fleet when the Japanese surrendered.

---

I got out of the Navy and resumed my academic career at Berkeley. Before that I was on a six-month expedition to a remote area of Guatemala. I got a B.A. in anthropology from Berkeley., I'd heard about an expedition the University of California was putting together, so I signed on for it. I always liked travel and had many adventures during my life, but one of the best was the university's Southern Africa Expedition in 1947–48. I wrote a journal during that expedition, and something interesting happened every day. I wrote a book about that expedition that will soon be published. I ended up getting a Ph.D. in anthropology from the University of Virginia. I got married, started a family, and began taking them along with me on my travels. I studied at Oxford, and then I got a teaching position in South Africa at the University of Witwatersrand, and we moved the whole family down there. During teaching breaks, I'd go to Botswana to study the Hambukushu people. I'd first gotten interested in them in 1950, and I've made a total of eight expeditions from 1950 to 1994 to study them. From my time in the Pacific during the war, I went back a number of times to the islands and got interested in what had gone on at Bora Bora during the war. There were a lot of relationships between the U.S. military personnel stationed there and local women, and I have been working on following up what happened to the offspring of those relationships. I published one small book on the wartime history of Bora Bora, and I'm working on another. In the last few years I've published or re-published five books about my experiences in Africa. I also recently published a book about my experiences on Tulagi during the war called *Hell's Kitchen: Tulagi 1942–43*.

OPPOSITE: *Lenore and Bud Rickert shortly after getting married in 1945.*

## LENORE RICKERT
NAVY

I attended the Orange County Nursing School. At that time to get into the Navy, after basic nursing training you had to go on and get more training. So I went up to Oakland and trained for another year before applying for the Navy. I joined the Navy rather than the Army because in the Army you did only bedside nursing. In the Navy you also taught the corpsmen, so that when they were on ships they would be able to do the nursing. It was the teaching aspect that appealed to me.

So they sent me to Pearl Harbor in 1940 for a two-year duty assignment. I was assigned to the eye-ear-nose-and-throat wards, three of them, at the Navy hospital on Hospital Point. It was very low key there at that time. I was working in the wards and also training corpsmen. If they passed certain tests they could become Navy corpsmen. Over the weekends only about a fourth of the nurses were on duty, and they'd have a lot of wards to take care of. Hawaii at that time was very very nice! I was glad to get assigned there because I'd heard a lot about Hawaii and was tickled to death I got a chance to go.

While I was on the wards there at Pearl Harbor, this Marine had three different surgeries, two of which he didn't need at all, just to get back in the

79

ward that I worked on. On the weekends we had captain's inspection, and everything just had to be perfect in the ward. The little stands beside the patients' beds could only have three changes of underwear, a toilet bag with toothpaste and toothbrush and that kind of thing, and that was all that was allowed. Well, this fellow comes up to me, and I'm already wondering why he'd been there three different times for surgeries he really didn't need, and he came over with a portable typewriter. So while I was waiting for the captain to come down for inspection, I'm standing by the window. He says, "Miss Terrell, what am I going to do with this?" And it's a portable typewriter in a case. So I said, "You're going to have to drop it out the window." And he did! So that got me, because it smashed all over the ground outside! But then he passed inspection—his unit beside the bed was okay! But that really got my attention. His name was Bud Rickert.

We nurses weren't supposed to go out with servicemen. In fact, nurses at that time weren't supposed to have any contact with males at all. If you did it, you did it very secretly. But of course there were a certain number of nurses who had boyfriends.

In Hawaii where the cruise ships come in at Honolulu Harbor there is a landmark called the Aloha Tower. Well, down below that there was a basement, and they had units in there that you could rent. So he rented one and put a set of civilian clothes there. I was the only nurse who had a car, so mine was kind of the community car. When I'd go to bed at night on the second floor of the nurses' quarters, I would tie a string around my toe and drop the end of it out the window. The nurses who wanted to borrow the car would pull it, and I would get up and come down and take them over to meet their boyfriends. It was a Ford coupe, and coupes then didn't have a back seat—only just a little ten-inch space behind the front seat, so there wasn't much room to haul many people around! But I would squeeze in as many of them as necessary!

The Marine Corps base was attached to the Navy hospital grounds; there was just a fence between them. We could talk over the phone because nobody could tell who I was talking to. So we would arrange to meet, and he would tell me when he was going to be relieved. I would go down and flash my lights off and on as I drove down that long fence, and he'd come out of the bushes and jump in the car with me. Once in a while he'd have somebody who wanted to go to town with him, so he would just bring him along. It would be like we didn't know each other at all, that I was just giving him a ride. So after we had dropped off any others who came with him, then I would drop him off down there at the Aloha Tower. He would change into his civilian clothes, and then we'd go out for a picnic.

There was a Chinese couple who cooked for us in the nurses' quarters, and they would always pack picnic lunches for me. So we would go around on the other side of the island where nobody was, have a picnic, and spend whatever time we had together. There was a lighthouse right over on the far side of Diamond Head, and there were landscaped grounds with no one around, and that's where we'd go a lot of times. We couldn't go together to Waikiki or in Honolulu because we couldn't risk being seen together. So after our picnics, I'd bring him back and drop him off at the Aloha Tower. He'd change back into his uniform, and then I'd take him back to the Marine base.

We were having a great time, but then he got orders to ship out to Wake Island. That was hard, and I was pretty upset. This was before December 7, so he was there on Wake when the war started, and when Wake fell he was a POW. Most of the fellows captured by the Japanese were shipped to Japan, but he was in the group they kept on Wake. He was there until later in the war when they found out he had worked as a newspaperman and could write. Then they took him to Tokyo where he was supposed to write scripts for a soap opera that Tokyo Rose would broadcast over the radio to American troops in the Pacific. And that saved his life, because not long after they shipped him to Tokyo, they executed the American POWs on Wake. I got five postcards from him while the Japanese had him as a POW on Wake. I think they came through Greece somehow. The cards were all a year to a year and a half old, and they were all blacked out except the date, "Dear Lenore," and "Love, Bud," and that was it, period. But that was better than what they allowed the other POWs to do in Japan. They never got to send any word out that they were all right.

So anyway I was on duty on Sunday morning, December 7. Right across the water from us was the seaplane base, but those planes would never fly over the hospital. So that morning I was waiting for the captain to show up to make rounds, and I heard a plane flying real low. I'd never heard a plane that low over by us at the hospital, so I ran over to the window and down comes this plane with a huge red circle on the side. I could see the pilot and I could see he was Oriental, but I didn't know what that big red circle was. It went right by the window real close, headed down, and the pilot waved to me and I waved to him. Then the plane crashed right there, right down to the ground just outside the window! Later on, one of the corpsmen cut a piece of aluminum from that plane and made a watchband for me. He even etched palm trees and things on it.

Immediately after that plane came down I heard bombs going off. I looked over toward Ford Island and could see things blowing up, and I knew we had a problem. When the captain came to the ward he said the Japanese were attacking. The wards were full, and our patients all got up right away when the attack started and ran down to the water to see if there was anything they could do there. Just near the hospital were some docks and ships, but when they got there the water was on fire, so they couldn't do anything. By this time new patients were starting to come in, and they were burned from being thrown off the ships and into the water where there was burning oil. They were terribly burned.

There was a man in the ward who had had eye surgery the day before, and both of his eyes were covered with gauze patches. He pulled the spread off his bed, put it on the floor, and laid down on it because he figured someone else would need his bed, and we did. I rushed over to the nurses' quarters the minute the attack started, because some were still sleeping and some were at the Catholic church, which was a couple of blocks from the hospital. So I got over there, rounded everybody up, and told them to get back to their wards, because we had patients all over the place.

So when our old patients returned to the hospital, they wanted to help. And these were patients who had had tonsillectomies or nose operations or things like that, and they wanted to help with the people who were being brought in. We had all these burn cases with huge, horrible blisters that had to be cut off, so I would ask patients who had been in the ward the night before, "Can you cut flesh?" If they said they could, I'd give them scissors. If they said they couldn't, we'd give them a big bucket full of water with about six drinking tubes, and they'd go around and give these burn victims water. They all wanted water. They wouldn't be screaming or yelling, but they'd just lie there and gasp, "Water . . . water . . . water." So those guys just went up and down the wards giving water to the burn patients.

And cutting burn blisters was pretty gruesome. These were big blisters, some six inches high and over large patches of skin. That all had to be cut off. After the blisters were cut off, we painted the raw flesh with something, but I can't remember what it was. And we had so many patients to take care of I think it was five days when I didn't go to bed at all. In the morning after working all night, I'd go over to the nurses' quarters and take a shower and then come back and be at the hospital all day and all night.

Before December 7, we'd put in requests for supplies once a week, and we were lucky if we got half of what we asked for. So I thought, oh, gads, we'd never have enough equipment or supplies. But everything just came rolling out on that morning. We didn't have to write requests or anything; we just had to send somebody over and say we needed something and out it came, right now. So we were able to keep up with what we needed to treat the patients.

As all these sailors were being brought in with burns, some were dying right there in front of us, and that was pretty traumatic. But you couldn't let it bother you too much. We just had too much to do. I'd never worked with burn patients before, and it was bad. But those guys were just wonderful. As much as they were suffering, they were just glad to be alive. They would do anything you asked them. We were doing a triage as the burn patients came in. I would try to put the more severe cases close to the front, because the ones in bad shape needed most care. I think the pain was so much they didn't feel it, because they didn't complain. All the while the attack was going on we could hear bombs going off and explosions, but I never looked out the windows. I was too busy dealing with the burn patients that were flooding into the hospital. The doctors knew what to do and they told us, so I became an expert on burns very quickly!

We had these burn patients lined up in the wards, and we had their clothes off. They didn't have any dog tags or wrist bands so we tied tags on their toes with their names. That's the only way we had of identifying them. And they just lay there with their raw burned skin, and we treated them as best we could.

After the attack was over, we got into a kind of routine in the burn wards. The worst cases were flown back to the Mainland, and we attended to the rest. Shortly after the attack I heard that Wake was attacked, and of course I was worried about Bud. And then when Wake finally fell a few weeks later, I didn't know what happened to him until about a year later I started getting these postcards from him. They had a date on them, so I knew he was at least alive.

I stayed there at Pearl Harbor for another year to finish out my two-year assignment. After that I went back to San Diego, and they sent me down there to talk to women's clubs and things like that, because I had been at Pearl Harbor and could tell my story and they would buy war bonds. But I didn't like that, so I asked for a transfer and they sent me to New Caledonia. We didn't know where we were going. I was told to report to San Francisco, and when I got there they said I'd be told what ship to go on. We had no idea where we were going. When we got there, none of us had ever heard of New Caledonia. There were two Navy hospitals in New Caledonia. Navy ships came in there, and if they had casualties who needed more care than what they could give them on the ships, they'd leave them with us.

The captain of the hospital we were assigned to was there on the dock to meet the ship. We lined up, and he asked which one of us was the most senior. It had taken about a month to get there, but we had never really talked about how long each of us had been in the service. We finally determined who the most senior nurse was, and she was a real tall red-headed girl. The captain wasn't that tall, so then he asked who was next in line as far as seniority was concerned. Turned out I was the next most senior. So right away the other woman was sent on to Australia some-where, and I stayed there in New Caledonia and became chief nurse.

The hospital and our quarters were long buildings, and the captain had fixed up the chief nurse's quarters, which had its own shower and its own private toilet. The other nurses had to go up the hill to a shared toilet. While I was there, the president's wife, Eleanor Roosevelt, came out to visit us in New Caledonia. And you know, she was a wonderful woman. She went from bed to bed to bed to bed, and she said she would like to have the addresses of the men she saw. Quite a few of the patients were still there a few weeks later, and they heard from home that Mrs. Roosevelt had contacted the families of everyone and told the parents that she had talked with their sons and that they were doing well. But while she was there, she got to use my toilet since it was the only private toilet around there! She thought that was great, not having to go up the hill!

In New Caledonia there was social life for some of the nurses, but I didn't have any because I was still hoping my love life was still alive, and I was hoping that some day we would get together again. My assistant nurse and I got along well and we did a lot together. There was only one car for the hospital, and that was the captain's car, and he would let me use it any time I wanted to. And I was driving around the island one day and found a tree right at the edge of the water, and it had roots that went out into the water. I stopped and looked at it, and then realized it had oysters hanging on the roots that went into the water. So I pulled them out. My assistant loved oysters and was able to fix them up with sauce and eat them. She loved those oysters! But that tree was the only one I found that had oysters on it. My assistant ended up marrying a man she met there in New Caledonia. I would arrange for her to be able to use the car so they could go out and get away from the rest of us. That way she was able to keep the relationship going.

So after my two years in New Caledonia, I went back to the West

Coast. And you know, all I have to do is live one day at a time, because things have always worked out for me in unbelievable ways. When I got back from Noumea I got sent to Long Beach to sell war bonds and get blood donations. I went around to all the different plants where mostly women were working, the aircraft plants and so on, and I did that for about three and a half months. Then I went to the captain and said, "You know, this is not what I joined the Navy for." He said, "I know you haven't been the happiest about your work, but we have never sold this many bonds or gotten this much blood than since you've been here. But I understand how you feel, so I will see that you get transferred." So he got me transferred to Bremerton, Washington, and this was right as the war was ending. I arrived at Bremerton the day the Pacific war was over. So no one was around at the base and everybody was out celebrating. There was no room in the hotels, and people were out in the streets. I reported in to the hospital, and they said, "We got a call from Washington, D.C., for you to go to the airport." So I said, "What's at the airport, and where is it?" And they said, "All we were told was that you were to go to the airport as soon as you checked in."

So I went out to the airport and I'm standing around, and there were no planes on this field and no one around, but I can see a man clear across the field coming toward me and he's in a Marine uniform. And I'm looking at him and he's walking toward me. And as he got closer, I suddenly realized who it was, and I couldn't believe it—it was Bud, my boyfriend from Hawaii who had been captured at Wake. At the end of the war he'd been in Tokyo working on the scripts for the Tokyo Rose radio show. When the Japanese were getting ready to sign the surrender documents, Governor Stassen was sent over to Tokyo, and he had something to do with organizing the capitulation papers. And while he was there he met this Marine, and so Stassen put him in the plane with him and brought him back with him, and the plane landed in Bremerton. So there he was in Bremerton, coincidentally where my new assignment was. That's the way life has been for me. I don't have to make decisions, they're made for me! So when he came walking up to me I couldn't believe it. He's six feet tall and was standing there weighing 117 pounds and looking terrible, but at the same time he looked great to me! He came right up to me and put his hands on my shoulders and said, "We've got so much catching up to do." And I thought, "What he's been through, if he can have this kind of spirit, he'd be all right for a husband!"

So we decided to get married that very day and went down to get a license. During the war, some women were marrying more than one man so they could get their stipends from the government. When the authorities found this out, then they started checking up. You couldn't get a wedding license until they had checked that you didn't have three or four of them already. We had to go to the judge there in Bremerton, and he wanted to know why we wanted to get married, you know, that sort of thing, and we told him about our story and Bud being a POW and just getting back, and that judge couldn't sign the papers fast enough!

Then I said I didn't care what church it was, but I wanted to get married in a church. We found out that the ministers were all somewhere at a conference, and we could only find one minister. I said, "I don't care what church it is, I just want to be married in one." So we got married in a Lutheran church, and the executive officer stood up with us. And this all happened on the day Bud got back. So I knew it was meant to be. Luckily Bud came back okay, and he wasn't sour or bitter or anything, even after all he went through. Everything just worked out right. These things were just supposed to be!

When I got out of the Navy after the war I didn't belong to any veterans' organizations or anything. I stayed in touch with some of the nurses I had served with, but I never thought too much about that time period. Then for the fiftieth anniversary of the Pearl Harbor attack in 1991, they decided they were going to honor some of the women who had been at Pearl Harbor on December 7. The first thing they did was invite us nurses over for a Memorial Day ceremony in May 1991. I gave a talk at the memorial service, and I guess they must have liked it because they invited me back for the December 7, 1991, ceremony. They wanted me to give the same talk about my experiences the day Pearl Harbor was attacked. Well, about two weeks before we were set to leave for Hawaii, I get word that the president, the elder Bush, was going to attend. So instead of me giving my speech, they wanted me to introduce him. I said okay, so when we got there they sat down with me and went over what I should say to introduce him, and that's what I did. Afterwards I wanted to see the old hospital, but we had been told before that it had been torn down. However, on that trip they took us over there, and the hospital is now some top secret facility, with the windows blacked out and everything, but it's the same building and it's still there. And by chance at the ceremony I met a burn victim I treated on December 7, Everett Hyland.

*"A Date Which Will Live in Infamy"*

Yes, I saw the movie *Pearl Harbor*. They flew seven of us nurses who had been at the Naval hospital on December 7 over to Hawaii for the premiere. They set up a screen on the deck of a brand-new aircraft carrier in Pearl Harbor, and we all sat out there with a lot of VIPs and watched the movie. At first I didn't think much of it. First of all, none of us nurses had our hair down like the nurses in the movie. Either your hair was short, or if you had long hair you had to braid it and put it up under your cap. You couldn't show any hair, and in that movie they had hair down to the middle of their backs! They showed some nurses going to pieces in the movie, and I don't know about that. As far as I know all the nurses did what they were supposed to do. I didn't hear of anybody who came apart because of that, and I didn't see anybody who didn't do their job like they were supposed to. So at first I didn't like the movie much, but afterwards when I saw young people watched it, at least they found out roughly what happened on December 7, and they learned that at least something went on there at that time. Maybe it's good that they made the movie so that it would appeal more to those young people.

My experiences in WWII definitely affected the rest of my life, no question about that. I think it made me appreciate everything that is good. You know, a good day, good people, good experiences. It certainly broadened my outlook. It put a whole new set of things I wanted to accomplish in front of me and affected the way I wanted to live my life. I want to get the most out of it. I try to do that very definitely, and it's 2004 and I'm ninety years old now, and I think I've accomplished that.

# CHAPTER 2

*"On the Bataan Death March I saw many guys trying to help comrades in distress, but it wasn't the guys that were in distress who were killed. It was the guys who were trying to help them."*
—John Bruer, ARMY

ALAN HANCOCK, ARMY, Bataan Death March

IRVING STROBING, ARMY, Corregidor

JOHN BRUER, ARMY, Bataan, Corregidor

PAGES 88–89: *U.S. and Filipino troops, grim-faced and exhausted after the ordeal of the siege on Corregidor, surrender to the Japanese outside the west entrance to the Malinta Tunnel in this captured photo taken on the afternoon of May 6, 1942.*

# THE FALL OF THE PHILIPPINES: CORREGIDOR AND THE BATAAN DEATH MARCH 1941–42

ALAN HANCOCK
ARMY

I was with Headquarters Company, Thirty-first United States Infantry before the war. I had left and gone to the Philippines from Fort Sam Houston, Texas.

Well, there we were in the Philippines and the Japs invaded, and we ended up out on the Bataan Peninsula, where things went from bad to worse. We ran out of food and we ate our horses—these were from the Twenty-sixth Cavalry—and then we got into carabao, the water buffalo, and the wild pigs the Filipinos had. We had to take these from the Filipinos. We'd go out and talk a man out of one. We'd tell him the government had to have it, and we'd give him a receipt for it signed "Tom Mix," "Buck Jones," or anything else. After the war I found out that some of those people kept those pieces of paper and took them back to the government after the war. They'd have one of those wild hogs weighing 160 pounds or so that we'd taken and given them a receipt for, and they'd collect a thousand dollars for it because by that time they decided it had become a registered Berkshire!

At the surrender I went in to Mariveles. There was a construction site there where they were working on those submarine beds. I got there, and that night they blew up one of our ships that had all the 500-pound bombs on it. Huge explosion! I spent the night there, woke up the next morning, and we were completely surrounded by a Japanese naval landing party, same thing as our Marines, all of them six-footers.

We'd been advised that General King had gone over to surrender, but we didn't know if the Japanese would accept it. When we walked out of there that morning, surrounded by that Japanese naval landing party, we didn't know if they were going to shoot us—kill us on the spot—or what.

Really and truly, if we had known what we were going to have to go through I don't think any of us would have surrendered, general or not.

So they put us into the Death March, and I made it—all the way to San Fernando. That's where they put us on the narrow-gauge railroad. Another guy and I were having malaria—running 106–107 degrees temperature, and we were lucky in that Monday, Wednesday, Friday were my days to have fever and Tuesday, Thursday, and Saturday were his. So we were able to drag each other along, and we got into this barrio near Camp O'Donnell. Then we walked the last two or three miles into that camp. And I remember when I got in that night—I'd managed to carry a little money with me—I bought a can of corned beef for a hundred-and-fifty bucks and a package of Lucky Strike cigarettes for a hundred-and-fifty bucks. Somehow there were always people around somewhere who had such things. Like, while I was in O'Donnell, I got a hold of a little bitty jar of Armour's Star Fixed-Flavor bacon. It had four slices of bacon in it, and I got two of those little game-chicken eggs—the eggs of their fighting-cock breed; they're like a banty. So I had two eggs and four strips of bacon, and I fried them in my mess kit. Now, there were about eleven thousand people in that prison camp, and people offered me as much as a thousand dollars a bite, but what good would a bite do anybody? Or money, either, for that matter. So, my buddy and I ate it.

We ate snakes, and we got into rats in prison camp, and everything else. When we first surrendered and made the March, we didn't get anything to eat. Then when we'd get rice, it'd have husks and worms in it, and for about the first week we'd pick them out, but after that we quit picking them out.

What kept us survivors going was determination—the determination that "I am going to live."

Eventually they moved a great many of us to Japan. They figured that the prisoners they left in the Philippines would die. This was General Homma's attitude. He didn't want to take prisoners. He wanted to kill us all off, because he knew that if you have prisoners you've got to take care of them.

So I got shipped to Japan, and I was in the Fukuoka main prison camp, the largest prison camp in Japan.

The people in this country, they don't realize that never, while we were in prison camp, did we cease to fight the Japanese! When we worked in the coal mine we sabotaged it so it would stop production for six weeks. I've had people ask me, "Why did you surrender?" And, hell, I didn't.

I was in the main camp at Fukuoka, and my job was to boil bandages. We had to reuse them. They were cloth of any shape, form, or fashion that we could use. I had two of those huge rice cook-pots, and I had the only fire outside the Japanese kitchen. Then one day they came around and told us we all had to go into the barracks and close the doors from the inside until they came back. Well, I mentioned my fire would need to be tended— they're deathly afraid over there of a fire getting loose—so they agreed that I, and I alone, would be allowed to go back and forth outside so as to tend to my fire, which was directly across the street from my barracks.

This, I did. And of course every time I'd go out to tend my fire I'd sneak a look under my arm to see what they were doing. Well, they were all lined up, heads bowed, and their officer in front of them. And at this ceremony, or whatever it was, they were listening to a radio, and when it was over you could tell by their faces that their balloon had busted. Within a matter of fifteen minutes after this thing had ended and they broke up, we could tell by their long faces that something was wrong, but we didn't know what. Then, when they went to change guards I was over tending my fire, and this one guard was right on top of me before I saw him. Normally this would have been big trouble for me, because we had to bow to them as they approached us. If we didn't, they'd beat us. We could not salute them, we had to bow to them; they called it *kedi*, and the higher the rank the deeper the bow. In other words, you could bow your head, but if he was a high-ranker you had to bow from the waist. Well, I tried to bow to him, and the sonofabitch saluted me! And I thought, hey, something is wrong here! So he went on and had a consultation with the guard he was relieving, and I said to myself, I'm going to find out something. I'll take a chance on getting the shit beat out of me. So, this time I deliberately watched, and when the guard that had just been relieved walked right by me, I didn't bow, but when that sonofabitch got close, he saluted me, too!

Man, I beat a path over to the barracks. I said, "Hey, the goddam war is over! When a Jap salutes me it's got to be over." Well, I found out later in talking to one of the Japs who spoke pretty good English—a graduate of the University of Seattle—that the Emperor told them in his speech that the lowest American outranked the Emperor. So that was the reason they were saluting me. Shortly after the second Japanese guard had saluted me, these Japanese doctors came out. I had my fire right beside their dispensary. And one of those doctors who came out had his hands behind his back, kind of dry-whistled, walked around with a long face, and said, "Ver' soon you be happy." So I asked him, "Is the war over, and are we going to get to go home?" And he said, "I not privileged! I not privileged!"

Captain Walter Kosteki, who later became a colonel, he was the American doctor, and the Japanese at the camp surrendered to him. They didn't pay any attention to English colonels or anybody else. They paid no attention to anybody but Americans, and the Americans were god. The Japanese there surrendered to the Americans. Captain Kosteki immediately moved out, went downtown, and took over a hospital for our bad patients. He'd make telephone calls back to the base, and he got a lot of our really sick guys down there to the hospital in town. Then we ran the Japs out. Six of us went down and took rifles from them, and we ran them out of camp. We had to threaten to walk the Japanese lieutenant through the camp barefooted to get him to leave. We went out to the caves where we had buried food for them and brought it back for us. We went to the brewery and got a truckload of beer and ice and so forth.

Basically speaking, our people were interested in eating, as you can imagine.

I finally ended up coming out of there on a C-47 down to Kanoye and over to the island where we had a typhoon—Okinawa. Finally got out of there on a B-25 and landed at Clark Field, then rode a C-47 down to Nichols Field, and from there went to the Twenty-ninth Replacement Depot. That was at Lipa, Batangas. We POWs had built the airfield there. That was the first airfield we built for the Japs in the Philippines after we were captured. So I was at Lipa twice: once as a POW building the airfield, and then there at the replacement depot heading home.

I am the immediate past-commander of the Thirty-first Infantry Regiment Association, Inc., chartered in the state of Arkansas. I'm a life member of damn near every veteran's organization there is, and a life member also of the Confederate Air Force. I live alone, I'm quite a student of history, and I guess I saw a bit of it.

# IRVING STROBING
ARMY

enlisted in the Army in 1939. I was nineteen years old and a strapping 119 pounds! But when I got out of the Jap prison camps at the end of the war I only weighed 98 pounds. The thing was, I didn't have much weight to lose! I was in the Signal Corps and was first trained as a "pigeoneer." That meant I worked with messenger pigeons. This was a holdover from the old days before reliable radio communication when they had to use messenger pigeons to communicate with the front-line troops. They did this a lot in WWI. So, in the Signal Corps we used all forms of communication, from radios to pigeons! I got trained on Morse code and could key messages very quickly. We all could.

I was looking forward to going overseas and was excited to hear I was being posted to the Philippines. This seemed very exotic to me. I was just a kid from Brooklyn and here I was heading out to the Pacific. I finally arrived in the Philippines in May 1940 and was stationed first on Corregidor Island out in Manila Bay. The Philippines was considered good duty at that time. It was a tropical climate and totally different from anything I had ever seen. It took a while to get used to the heat and humidity, but after a while it was quite comfortable. Everything was just open to the breeze, and it would cool off at night enough to sleep. I couldn't get over the tropical vegetation. It was all bright green and seemed to just burst out of the ground. Things could grow anywhere! Corregidor was a beautiful island. A lot of it was like a big, manicured tropical park. The lawns were all trimmed and were immaculate. Everything was landscaped meticulously, with big trees and paved sidewalks and large old buildings on the base. But after we surrendered and the Japanese had bombed and shelled it for months, you wouldn't even think it was the same place. Those stately old buildings were just bombed-out shells, the trees were just splinters, and landscaping was totally destroyed. The place ended up looking like a moonscape. But before the war it was really a paradise.

I lived in the Topside Barracks with the Fifty-ninth Coast Artillery guys. There were big day rooms, like rec rooms, in the barracks. There were Ping-Pong tables, couches, and chairs. You could listen to the radio or read or write letters there. A large movie theater was next door to the barracks, and it was very popular. It was one of the few places to go at night. They always liked to come up with funny announcements before movies. Like before a good Western, there would be an announcement: "A five-man detail will be sent around after the movie to pick up spent brass cartridges!"

After that I was assigned duty as a radio operator in Manila on a transmitter using Morse key. I also had duties at Camp John Hay in Baguio up in the mountains on Luzon. On December 7, 1941, which was December 8 in the Philippines, I was roaming around Manila on a three-day pass. When we got word the Japs were bombing the airfields all leaves were canceled, and I went back to duty on the radio transmitter. After that we were very busy all the time trying to coordinate communication between the units in the field and other command headquarters in the Philippines and in Hawaii. Then the Japanese landed on Luzon, and it was just a matter of time before they got to Manila.

At 10 P.M. on December 31, 1941, the Japanese had entered the outskirts of Manila, and we were ordered to blow up our transmitter and report to pier 1 down on the waterfront, right next to the Manila Hotel, to catch a boat to be taken out to Corregidor. So we did as we were ordered, blew up our transmitter, and went down to the pier. It took a while for the boat to show up to take us to Corregidor, so we were just sitting there on the pier, kind of feeling sorry for ourselves, and it didn't help that we could hear the music coming from the big New Year's Eve party at the Manila Hotel next door. That was the fanciest hotel in the city, and the people at the party were wealthy Filipinos and a lot of U.S. Army and Navy officers and their wives. They were all dressed up and were partying and carrying on like nothing out of the ordinary was going on! Those were the kinds of things that were happening—crazy things, people acting like everything was okay, or maybe just ignoring how bad things were, or they didn't want to admit how bad things were. Here we were evacuating the city with the Japs right on our tail, and they were still having a big fancy New Year's Eve party at that beautiful old hotel. We just sat there on that pier and listened to the music and laughter coming out of that hotel and could barely even talk to each other. Later that night we finally got the word to move over to pier 3 where we caught a boat for Corregidor.

The first thing that happened when I got to Corregidor was that I smashed my right hand in a car door. Of course, this is the hand I used to key the Morse code, and it was a serious injury for a radio operator like me. It turned out I healed up okay, but this injury to my keying hand was in my records. I didn't know it then, but smashing my hand in that door probably saved my life. Later, when the fighting on Bataan really got going, they shipped the "best" operators over there to maximize the communications capability during the fighting. Well, they looked at my records and saw this injury to my right hand, and that was enough to disqualify me from that assignment. All the radio operators who were shipped over there either were killed or ended up in the Death March. And thank God I missed out on that because I had had a broken hand!

At first things weren't too bad on Corregidor. In fact, after the chaos and confusion and strangeness of Manila, on Corregidor it seemed like nothing had happened. We were getting bombed on occasion, but not much at first. Our radio unit got right to work. We ended up being assigned to the Malinta Tunnel at the back of lateral 12. The Malinta Tunnel was originally built as a road and trolley tunnel through Malinta Hill to connect the two ends of the island, and it was about 200 yards long. At some point they had dug branch tunnels out from the main tunnel. They called these "laterals." There were quite a few of them, and some were long and had a few bends in them, like the hospital lateral which had its own exit out the side of the hill. That's where I set up a transmitting station, just outside the entrance to the hospital lateral, so I could get a good signal and I could transmit to Honolulu. That's how we kept in touch with the outside world.

As the situation deteriorated, we got more people moving into the laterals. There were administrators in MacArthur's lateral, and he had a desk in there. General Moore also had his own lateral as island commander for his staff. But most of the other laterals were used for storage, except for the hospital lateral, of course, which kept getting more and more crowded as time went on. Most of the men on Corregidor were outside at the gun batteries or on the island defenses. This is something that people don't understand. They think all the Army was jammed into the shelter of the Malinta Tunnel, but only a small fraction was in there.

The siege of Corregidor went on for quite a while, or so it seemed to us. We settled into a routine like you do anywhere, even though our circumstances were pretty dire! I used to sleep out on a ridge outside the west entrance to the tunnel. There was a nice breeze out there, and I could duck into the tunnel if there was a bombing raid or if shelling started. There was a kitchen set up outside the west entrance to the tunnel. In the morning I'd come down from my ridge, stop by the kitchen for a bowl of oatmeal, pick up a couple of sandwiches, and head into the tunnel for work. The latrine was also located outside the west entrance, and there was a machine shop out there, too. In fact, the ridge I slept on overlooked the machine shop; it was right above it. There weren't many vehicles on the island that were driving around that I saw. Mostly there were ambulances that came to the tunnel, and some drove right down to the hospital lateral.

Sometimes I slept in the air shaft at the back of our lateral. But during the shelling it was dangerous because of falling rock in there. We shared lateral 12 with the finance office, and we were at the back. There is a picture you see all the time of the finance office guys, and I was just in back there with the signal section, but you couldn't see us. Most of our transmissions were inter-island, but we could communicate with Honolulu, like I told you, and with Port Darwin in Australia. We were probably as up to date with what was going on in the outside world as anyone else on the island. And it didn't look good, I'll tell you that! It was pretty clear to us that nothing was coming in to the island, and the big brass got out, which was appropriate, I suppose. They also got out people who had special skills, and I wasn't one of those, unfortunately.

Some days I'd see MacArthur on his daily walk before he was evacuated. He was always walking around outside, and because of this, I guess, the PR was that he was fearless. But the odds were in his favor of not getting hit. Corregidor was a fairly big island and the shelling couldn't hit everything. But our man was Wainwright. He would sit down and talk to you like a grandson, like he was a member of your family.

After the fall of Bataan and especially near the end, the shelling was pretty much incessant, and everyone had to hunker down and keep under cover. Then the Japs landed on the island, and it was just a matter of time. I was there in the back of lateral 12 on the transmitter keying messages, and then someone said the Japs were right outside the

*The Fall of the Philippines*

tunnel, and I sent what became known as the last message from Corregidor: "I can hardly think. Can't think at all. . . . The jig is up. Everyone is bawling like a baby. They are piling dead and wounded in our tunnel. Arms weak from pounding key long hours, no rest, short rations. Tired. I know how a mouse feels. Caught in a trap waiting for guys to come along and finish it. . . ."

Of course, this kind of personal message (of which the above is only a part) was against all regulations, but at that point what were they going to do to me?

Then that was it. It was all over and we surrendered. Someone said a Jap tank was coming up the road to the tunnel, and we all figured he would just drive down the main part of the tunnel and turn the turret from side to side and shoot down the laterals and kill us all. So I went way to the back of lateral 12 and tried to take cover. But then they said the tank wasn't coming, and we were called out into the main tunnel for the surrender formalities, and some Jap officers appeared. Let me tell you, it was a shock to see them after being shelled and bombed and chased by them for months. And I just thought to myself, well, there they are, the hated Japs. They were short and kind of strutted into the tunnel and shouted some commands. An interpreter told us we had to kneel, and I was tapped on my shoulder by a saber, and then we were filed out the west entrance. There were a whole lot of us standing there just outside the tunnel overlooking the North Dock, and nobody was saying a thing. It was just total silence. We could see General Wainwright go down to the dock to be taken to Manila for the formal surrender. He got into a boat with some of the Japs, and as they pulled away from the dock we all saluted, all together, no one told us to, but we all just stood there silently and saluted, and most of us were crying.

After the surrender I don't think the Japs knew what to do with us. We weren't confined or anything for a couple of days. They didn't have any food for us, so we were allowed to scrounge for food back around the barracks areas and mess halls. Then I was pulled out with some other guys and taken to an area where there were Japanese wounded. Each of us had to attend to one Japanese guy. I had to take care of this guy who was assigned to me, wipe his brow, give him sips of water, and so on. We were ordered to do this, but there wasn't any brutality. It was like they wanted us to help them out, and I didn't really mind it. This went on for two or three days. Then they took us back with the others and things changed. We were rounded up and taken down to the Ninety-second Garage area.

This was a seaplane base with a big concrete tarmac and a ramp down to the ocean to launch the planes. There were a couple of big hangars, and they were just skeletons from the bombing and shelling. They herded us out there onto the concrete and there was not a bit of shade, and we were just left out there. The area was surrounded by Japanese guards, so we couldn't go anywhere. We just had to sit out there on the concrete in the sun, and it was miserable. After being so hot all day, at night we all got chilly, and a lot of us were sunburned so that made the chill at night worse, We used any bits of cloth or scraps of sheet metal for shade, and we just sat out there for a week or two without much food or water. This was our first experience with what we were going to become very familiar with, which is how badly the Japanese treated prisoners.

So we were finally loaded into a rusty old freighter and hauled to Manila and unloaded on the beach there. Then they paraded us around the city for a while on the way to Bilibid Prison in Manila, where they kept us for about two weeks. Then they transported us to the Cabanatuan camp.

I was only at Cabanatuan until November of 1942 when they shipped me to Japan. I arrived at Honshu on November 27, 1942. The Japanese had me do all kinds of things. I helped build a dock, and I worked at a rock quarry and a steel mill. The worst thing was the brutal guards. There was just no reason for the things they did and the way they treated us.

I was liberated in 1945, and I stayed in the Army until 1949. But my years as a POW never really left me, and I had a lot of health problems. The most serious was that I was disabled by TB and ended up in a TB-ward in Denver. I was laying there and all the guys in this TB ward got to talking, and it turned out that probably 90 percent of us in there had been POWs. I ended up working as an air traffic controller and am a member of the American Defenders of Bataan and Corregidor. Those are the only guys who I can really talk to about what happened during the war. They've been there, and, you know, really there's no way anyone can imagine what it was like except for them. After all my experiences, people always ask me what I think about the Japanese. To this day I don't hold a grudge toward the Japanese in general, but I can never forgive those brutal guards.

# JOHN BRUER
ARMY

I enlisted in June 1941, just a few months before Pearl Harbor, and I went to chemical warfare school in Maryland. Then from there I was sent down to Savannah, Georgia, which was where the Twenty-seventh Bomb Group was located. This was in the late summer or early fall of 1941. I got shipped out to the Philippines, so I ended up there at the time of Pearl Harbor. I was in chemical warfare, on detached service to the Twenty-seventh Bomb Group in the U.S. Army Air Corps, and I was based at Nichols Field, on the outskirts of Manila.

The Philippines was good duty. At that time, the American was king, and the Filipino people were terrific people. Peacetime service was good in the Philippines. It was an education because it was an altogether different way of living than what we were used to in the States. When we first got to the Philippines it was just like opening the pages in a geography book. It was just like you've seen, you know, houses up on stilts with water underneath, and everybody had two or three pigs that they stuck under the house. Out in the barrios that's the way it was. The cities were modern.

If you were on leave you could have a good time in Manila. There were a couple of big cabarets. On one side of Manila was the International Cabaret, and on the other side was the Santa Ana Cabaret and the Santa Ana race tracks. When you're at liberty, you go off and explore those places, you know? There was a lot of good music and dancing, and of course, there was all kinds of booze, American booze, and it was all tax-free. The exchange rate back then was two to one, and you could buy Camels, Chesterfield, Lucky Strike cigarettes if you were a smoker. You could get them for ten centavos a package. That would be about five cents

American money, tax-fee. There were a lot of women, too, lots of nice girls. In Manila there were a lot of people who were part Filipino, and probably part French and Portuguese, a mixture. Just beautiful people.

When things went bad, it went bad in twenty-four hours—on Monday, December 8 there, which was December 7 in Hawaii. It was quick. After we ate breakfast on that Monday, that was the day, around 10:30 or 11:00, that they struck Clark Field. Being at Nichols Field, we were close enough. After that happened, right away after they struck Clark Field, the mobilization started. We were on battle status then, and we picked up and traveled around for a while, but we had nothing to fight with. We had a lot of airplanes there, but they weren't complete planes. I mean if we had the fuselage and had the wings, we didn't have any motors. If we had the fuselage and the wings and the motor, we didn't have the landing gear. The whole port area was just one mass of shipping crates with parts of airplanes. The Americans were starting to build up the Philippines, but back in those days everything was dependent on being shipped by sea. They never would ship complete units.

At Nichols Field we had P-40 fighters, and B-17 and B-18 bombers. The common attack plane was the A20E. It was a twin-engine plane, very fast and maneuverable for the day. But the planes were all eventually destroyed, and I ended up fighting as infantry on Bataan. Everybody did at the end. After that all started, it didn't make any difference what you were, a Marine, a sailor, a soldier, we all ended up being infantrymen. We knew things were pretty grim, that we probably wouldn't get any help. We knew they were fighting in Europe, but truthfully, we didn't think we would just be completely abandoned. We still had hopes, even after the retreat into Bataan. We'd sit around, if we had a chance, and look out to sea. You just kind of had hopes, just figured that any day an armada of rescue ships would sail into Manila Bay, but it never happened.

I ended up at the southern tip of Bataan at a little place that had once been quite a place, Mariveles. That's where I got captured the first time. Well, then they started the Bataan Death March. And you know, that Bataan Death March, it was the most brutal thing you could imagine. I saw so many people slaughtered for absolutely no reason. Even just after a couple of days guys would get weak, and if you were near them, why, you'd try to help them. But all of a sudden you'd get to thinking that's probably not the right thing to do. I saw many guys trying to help comrades in distress, but it wasn't the guys that were in distress who were killed. It was the guys who were trying to help them. Absolutely brutal.

*The Fall of the Philippines*

I've often thought, was that the nature of those Japanese, or were they duped? I'm serious, because I can't see how any human being can be that savage. But the Japanese army was that same way. A two-star private could beat the hell out of a one-star private, and the one-star private could beat the hell out of the private that didn't have any stars. That was their whole damn system.

So on the Death March we were going through an area where I had been on patrol a number of times, so I kind of knew where I was. It was the second or third night I was on that Bataan Death March, and I was talking to this guy. I'd never seen him before in my life, but he'd been trotting along behind me, so we just decided we were gonna make a break for it. When it got dark and the Japanese started to run up and down the road with kerosene lanterns, we watched for our chance and just slipped off the road into the rice paddies. We had to make it across maybe a quarter to half a mile of rice paddies, and then you get to the edge of a jungle. We thought we could get in the jungle and hide. Well, we did that. It took us a day or so to go through the jungle and up over a slight rise and get down to the seashore. I knew that getting across to Corregidor would be the only way to save my life. Corregidor was a U.S. military island, heavily fortified, and it sat out there by itself in the mouth of Manila Bay. It was right across from Bataan where we were. We could see Corregidor out there, but how could we get across all that water to get to it?

You know the Filipinos were great fishermen, and they had what they called "*bancas*," fishing boats made out of hollow logs. They had outriggers on those things so they could handle them easily between the islands and handle the sea. Well, whenever you were along the seacoast in peacetime, you'd see these goldang bancas from these fishing villages. When there'd be a little wind, they'd break loose and wash up on shore. They'd never come after them, and we used to see them abandoned on the beach all the time. So my idea was, if we could get to the seashore, we might be able to find one of those damn things.

Well, we got to the seashore in a couple of days, but you know, there was not a single banca to be found. There was just nothing. We finally came across a log, and we kind of rolled that out to the water. That would float. Then we scrounged around—you couldn't go out in the middle of the day because it was too hot, just early mornings and in the evenings—and finally found a couple of pieces of driftwood, or boards, that would kind of serve as paddles, and we decided that we would try that log. We'd go out and paddle along, staying relatively close to the coast, like in the early morning, and then come in to the shade, and go out again in the evening. You could see Corregidor off in the distance, but, oh, my God, from Bataan it looked like about the head of a pin, a long ways away. And we were starting to figure that we'd never make it because it was too far.

But anyway, this one evening we were paddling along and just about ready to give up for the day. The searchlights on Corregidor had been on for about fifteen or twenty minutes and they were scouring the skies for invading planes. Every once in a while they'd shoot a beam down across the water because Japanese submarines were known to be in the area. That was common knowledge because the Japanese had already taken the mainland, Manila, and Bataan, and next they were out after Corregidor. Anyway, the beam of light came across the ocean, and we didn't think anything of it. Well, then, pretty soon off in the distance you could see a boat, and it started to kind of circle us. So we figured, well, geez, the jig is up. We didn't know but what it might be Japanese. It went on for about half an hour. It was a fast boat. It would circle us and come in and then finally we could see it was a pretty good-sized boat. It started coming closer, coming closer, and then finally we could see on the back end of the boat that there was a small American flag fluttering. Well, geez, it was a damned American PT boat! They'd spied us from the North Mine Dock on Corregidor. They thought that it was probably a periscope of a submarine or something, so they came out to investigate.

That PT boat was armed with guns and what looked like fifty-gallon oil drums strapped to the sides. Those were actually depth charges, and, boy, they were ready for battle. They got up close to us. They had binoculars, so they could see it was two guys sitting on a log. Then they came and pulled us off the log, and not a word was spoken. These guys reached out over the boat, pulled us off the log, threw us in the boat, and wrapped us in big old gray blankets, and then she turned gung ho back to the North Mine Dock on Corregidor. When we got to Corregidor they turned us over to the medics. We were hospitalized on Corregidor for dehydration and from the effects of the sea and the sun. We were just burned to a frazzle. I was hospitalized for ten days to two weeks and was anxious to get up on my feet again. I was in the hospital down in the Malinta Tunnel. They had a complete hospital in there.

I finally got out of there, and I contacted Colonel Romer, who was in the tunnel, head official of who was left in Chemical Warfare Service. He said, "I got a good job for you." I said, "That's good; I'd like to do something." He said, "Take from four to six hours a day. I'm going to send you down to the acid plant at the North Mine Dock. You'd be kind of valuable down there." They made sulfuric acid for submarine batteries, so I helped out there. Well, then, these submarines would come in, mostly in the night, American submarines, and their batteries would be checked. I didn't have to do that, but they'd add acid to the batteries and get them ready. So that's where I was. It was easy work, a nice bunch of guys to work with, plenty of coffee, and it was something to do.

Then finally Corregidor fell. The Japanese paid dearly to take Corregidor. They had Manila, that's true. They had Manila Harbor, but when they decided they were gonna take Corregidor, they started coming out there by the bargeload, figuring they could just step on Corregidor and take it, but that wasn't true. The guns on Corregidor sunk bargeload after bargeload of Japanese right off the coast, and they'd probably have 200, 300, 400 men on one barge. But when they finally got onto Corregidor the jig was up because there was no place to go, so those of us that were left there just simply had to surrender.

The Japanese came into the Malinta Tunnel where I was, and everybody just threw down any weapons they had, just threw them in a pile. We were herded out of the tunnel, and we lived outside for days on this big concrete tarmac by the seaplane base, and that was miserable.

Finally they hauled us off of Corregidor. They took us off in ships we had to wade out to and climb up rope ladders to get on. They were kind of cattle boats or horse boats. Then they sailed us over toward Manila and stopped just offshore of Dewey Boulevard and anchored. We had to get off down the rope ladder in water up to my armpits, and then you had to wade to shore. That was right onto Dewey Boulevard, which was a glorious place in peacetime Manila. After we got ashore there, the group that I was with, they took us to the state prison, Bilibid Prison. They marched us through the streets to get there. We were at Bilibid Prison for four or five days with nothing to eat but raw onions, that was all there was. From Bilibid, they loaded us on railroad cars and hauled us up to Cabanatuan Prison Camp.

I've spent the last fifty, sixty years trying to forget what happened in the Philippines after the surrender. I first went to Cabanatuan No. 2, and I can't tell you the dates we were there. You see we had no calendars, no paper, no pencils, no anything to keep track, no watches, no nothing. Finally when camp No. 2 was decimated and they figured there weren't enough of us left anymore, then they moved us all down to Cabanatuan No. 1, and I was there until I went on a work detail up to Japan. They put out a call, and another fellow and I figured that any-place would be better, and that we could just at least get out of the trop-ics. We volunteered for a work detail and had no idea where we were going, but we ended up going to Japan, the island of Kyushu. We worked in a coal mine. Weather-wise it was better than the Philippines, but you worked seven days a week, twelve to fifteen hours a day, four or five thousand feet underground with coal miners.

Our treatment wasn't much better in Japan than it was in the Philip-pines. It was, well, brutal, to say the least. When I first got into the Army and was in good shape, my average weight was from 194 to 196 pounds. When I got out of prison camp I weighed 112. I was lucky to have sur-vived, very lucky. There were a lot of guys that I always figured were stronger and in better shape than me, but they didn't make it. I saw a lot of guys who would just give up, and in ten days they'd be gone.

I was in Camp Seventeen, near a city called Amuta , and the Japanese didn't believe in letting us form groups. I mean when you were above ground and out of the coal mine, why, if you would gather in groups of more than two or three or four, somebody would get the ax. They were absolutely opposed to that, and we were stripped of our leadership. We had no officers. They were all taken away for that very reason. You were just simply on your own. We lived in units, about forty fellows to a unit, but that was just for work purposes and going back and forth to the mine. As far as fraternization, and even to sit around to have bull ses-sions or something, well, you didn't have time because you were either underground working in the coal mine or trying to get a little sleep, a little rest, and that was life.

I don't think about Japanese people now. I guess they're all right though. But I'll tell you about one episode with the Japanese. Of course we had to learn to speak Japanese, not fluently, but we had to be able to understand in order to express ourselves. Down in the coal mine there was this Japanese fellow, an older man, probably in his early sixties, and he was a son-of-a-b' when it came to work. But you know, when you'd get off in a lateral on a detail in a mine, with probably two or three American prisoners, and if you would get him off by himself all alone, he would let you sit down and rest for a minute or two., Then he would start talking with you. He'd say, "*Mati, mati* —wait." He'd go on, "Just wait, some day this war will be over and you'll go home, and when the war is over and you go home, my five sons will come home, too." That guy was a beast to work for, but he had to be that way because he had to account to the Japanese army for what he could get out of us. Yet when he'd get off alone and, I suppose, maybe get in a little sentimental mood or something like that, then he'd tell us to be patient. So there was a bit of humanity in some of them. By and large, most of them, as I say, they were just like the Japanese army, they were indoctrinated that we were prisoners and we were their slaves.

The hard part of it was, I was tall, six foot two, and a pretty good size man. Well, the average Japanese is about five foot two or four, you know, short, and the bigger you were the more delight they had in beating on you. Well, in front of the guard house they had what we called "the chopping block," a big block of wood. The Japanese would bring you up to the chopping block, and if they were going to read you off or beat you up they'd jump up on top of the chopping block, so then they'd be four or five inches taller than the Americans. Anytime you got called to the chopping block, you knew that you were in for it. Guys that would lose their heads and try to fight back, they'd end up being used immediately for bayonet practice, you know, and killed that way. So if they had you there at the chopping block, you couldn't react. You just had to be totally passive. There was nothing you could do, you just had to take it. I had a couple of broken jaws and broken noses, stuff like that, but I mean, what are you going to do? That's the way it went.

We were right across the bay from Nagasaki, and I saw the atomic bomb go off. I saw the whole thing but didn't know what it was. It was a real clear morning. Our camp had been bombed out by the Americans because they were getting ready for the invasion. We were on the island of Kyushu, so American planes were coming in off the aircraft carriers and starting to prepare for their drive on Tokyo. So about 60–70 percent of our camp was just simply burned down.

We'd work in the mine; then when we'd come back after daybreak in the morning, just for our own good we'd do what we called "camp duty." Everybody that had worked all night in the mine, before you'd lay down to get any rest, you'd do a little camp duty, a little clean-up work to try to keep our camp as livable as it could be. Well, this particular morning I was outside; I'd come off the mine and was doing camp duty. It was a beautiful clear blue morning, and we heard heavy airplanes, but that wasn't out of the ordinary because we'd hear planes every once in a while. We figured they were heavy planes because you could tell by the engine noise. You couldn't see them since they were so high up. Then all of a sudden the ground just kind of shook like a tremor. I didn't think anything of that because small earthquakes were common. Well, then we looked out across the water and, all of a sudden, we saw this huge white mushroom cloud rising up in the air across the bay over at Nagasaki. Well, geez, I thought they must have hit something hot in Nagasaki. Nagasaki was kind of an industrial town as far as we could learn, so we figured the American bombers probably hit a refinery or something hot to make a cloud that large.

After that happened, there was a lot of jabbering among the Japanese guards. In all the Japanese guard houses there'd be three or four of them talking together. Within a day or so, I had worked through the night as I usually did on my shift, and I was getting back to camp shortly after daybreak. The shift that went over to relieve us passed by because, going back and forth to the mine, the two shifts would pass. So the shift that was supposed to relieve us, well, they were only gone about an hour and a half and they came back. They said they got over to the mine and didn't even go underground. They just got over there and sat around a little bit, and the soldiers brought them back. There was no more work at the coal mine. We thought right then that there was something funny going on. This had never happened before. Then, the next day at daybreak, all of a sudden there were no more Japanese. They were gone! When daybreak came in the morning there wasn't a Japanese guard to be seen, so we were just on our own. We found out later this was because of the atomic bombing at Nagasaki, but we didn't know anything about that bomb or the bomb dropped earlier on Hiroshima. We didn't know anything about that because we had no newspapers or anything.

The Americans knew we were there by that time because, earlier, when they were coming over and bombing and burning out our camp, we wouldn't take cover. We'd just lay out on the ground on our backs and wave our arms at them, hoping they'd recognize us because the camp wasn't marked. So they finally figured out that we were Americans. Then when they come back on their strafing runs in the daylight, they'd fly over our camp and wave their wings at us, so they knew we were there. After the Nagasaki deal and the Japanese had left, one morning at daybreak we heard heavy planes close, and so we looked up and there were two big B-17s flying right over our camp. All of a sudden, a tool kit came down, and it had a couple of wrenches in it. There was also a note in the tool kit. It said we were to clear a space because they were gonna drop parachute supplies to us. So we cleared a space the best we could. Then another plane flew in, with "p o w Supplies" written on the wings, and the bomb bays opened and the parachutes started to fall. There were shoes, G I shoes, fastened together with wire in big bundles. A bundle of shoes must have been twenty feet by twenty feet. Just all shoes, G I shoes, assorted sizes. Then they'd parachute skids out, packed with cases of food and cases of bandages and medicine and coveralls, clothes, underwear, tobacco—cigarettes and pipe tobacco and pipes—and food. Then we had to gather that stuff up and kind of sort it out and apportion it out, and at last we started having something to eat. There was canned meat, too, and canned potatoes and vegetables.

Then guys started getting itchy about getting out of prison camp. We knew that eventually we'd be liberated because they knew we were there, so it was a matter of waiting. A fighter plane flew over one day and dropped a package, and in it was a note that said they'd set up a temporary airfield at Kagoshima, that's the southern-most city on the island of Kyushu. Guys started to say, "If the Americans are on the southern tip of the island, instead of waiting for them to come to get us, let's go and find them." So two or three groups of five to seven guys started out. One day a plane flew over, and it dropped a note out that was from a guy by the name of Ward Redshaw. He'd been in a group that had headed out to Kagoshima. So these flyboys, they flew over our prison camp, and this Redshaw wrote a note telling us that they'd gotten down to Kagoshima and that the Army Air Corps was flying them out.

So, finally, a group I was with, there were five of us, kind of figured why not take a chance? By that time we had new G I clothes and knapsacks. So we packed up some rations and chocolate bars and stuff that had been dropped to us, and we took off and just headed south. Some of the Japanese trains were still running, so we figured we'd just get on the damn train. If it was heading south, we'd just ride south until the train stopped. Anyway, we spent two or three days like that. We knew we were getting close because we could talk enough Japanese to civilians along the way, and they'd kind of direct us. So we were walking along, it was getting dark, and we were thinking we'd better stop for the night, and, geez, three Japanese soldiers came toward us, riding bicycles. They rode up to us and stopped. They weren't armed, but they were Japanese military, and we didn't know what they would do with us. Before, the civilians had all been very friendly and helpful. So these soldiers seemed like they wanted to help, too, and they persuaded us that they knew where the Americans were. They told us to come with them, that they'd take us to where the Americans were. So they got off their bicycles, pushed them, and walked with us. We walked, I guess, maybe thirty to forty-five minutes, and we came to an old two-room Japanese schoolhouse. That's where these Japanese soldiers were from.

We went in there and sat down. Everybody sat on the floor; there were no such things as chairs. The first thing you know, they brought a great big wooden bucket full of hot tea, and we had food left in our knapsacks, so we figured, well, no use to fight them, just take a chance and see if they were on the level. So we broke off a little chocolate and bribed them along a little bit. Well, they had a telephone there, and after we sat there maybe forty-five minutes to an hour, all of a sudden we could hear trucks, and by golly, two big Army trucks had pulled up with American soldiers. They were the first Americans we'd seen in a long time who weren't POWs. They were from this airfield we were trying to find. Those guys didn't understand Japanese and didn't know how many of us there were, so they sent two trucks, and there were only five of us! So three of us got on one truck and two got on the other, and they drove us to this temporary airfield. There they put us in a squad tent and fed us some food. The next morning at daybreak, a sergeant came into the squad tent and said, "Come on, fellas, wake up. Get up. Get dressed. We're gonna have some coffee and bread, or you can even have pancakes if you want them. We're gonna have a little breakfast and we're gonna fly you out of here." So we got up and had breakfast and then got in an airplane. I think it was a B-17. We had to sit in the bomb bays; they just had some planks in there to sit on, and they flew us to Okinawa.

A couple of officers came up, asking us our name, rank, and serial number because they figured they had to have some records on us. There wasn't anything on us, nothing. "Well, where have you been?" they asked. We told them we'd been prisoners of war and we'd been up on the island of Kyushu and at Omuta near Nagasaki. Geez, when they discovered how close we were to Nagasaki, everybody scattered! We didn't know what had happened, but we found out later they thought we were radioactive. All of a sudden guys in white coverall suits and masks showed up, and we didn't know what these little boxes they were carrying were, but it turned out they were Geiger counters. They started combing us over, between our legs and up and down our backs and under our arms and around our heads with these goddamn Geiger counters. Well, then, the next thing, they took us off to this area where they said, "Take off all your clothes—everything! Your knapsack, everything you've got and throw it in a pile." We stripped down just as naked as naked could be, and there was a building there with showers. They had us go through there, and then we had to scrub down with the old brown GI soap and take a good shower with that. Well, after we got through with the shower, a couple of guys came in with masks on, and they had these kind of like potato sprayers, and they started spraying us with some kind of a mist. Then they threw in towels so we could dry ourselves. By that time a small truck had driven up, and they had all new clothing issued for us, new clothes and shoes and everything. All this time we didn't know why they were doing this, other than they said we might be contaminated. We didn't know what radiation was. We didn't know anything about atomic business or that sort of thing. We didn't know beans. Then they flew us from Okinawa to Manila. At Manila they had a repatriation camp set up there. There were a few guys there, but from our particular area we were kind of the first ones there.

We landed at Clark Field. That's when we first saw that a lot of the craters were still there. It was kind of spooky returning to the Philippines, especially to Clark where I had spent some time. Then they took us down to this hospital camp, and they had complete clinics set up there. So we had to go to sick bay twice a day, every morning and every afternoon. By this time we had started to kind of find out a little bit about the atomic bombs, and as the days went by we found out more.

We were at this hospital camp on the outskirts of Manila about a month, and I started to gain weight back. Of course our biggest interest was to get back to the States. They were supposed to fly us back on hospital planes, but the people that were wounded, the amputees and that sort of thing, had priority. So I found another fellow that I'd kind of buddied up with, and we found out it would be another five or six weeks before our turn would come up to go back to the States.

We went to downtown Manila one day. Of course I'd been there in Manila before the war, before Pearl Harbor, and I knew that all the action when I was a soldier there, down in the port area, was Pier Five. There used to be a lot of good places for servicemen to go down there, so that's where we went. Well, geez, it was all gone. Everything was different, but we got into a little bar there. A lot of sailors were in there. We got to talking with them. They'd only been there a day or two. They were off a ship, the *Admiral Ford*, and it was a brand-new ship. They'd been to Europe on this ship, and then they'd brought some occupation forces from Europe through the Suez Canal and to Manila. The ship was scheduled to sail out from Manila and was heading for San Francisco. At San Francisco the ship was to be decommissioned, and it was to go back to the big shipping line there, the Matson Line, that owned it. It was the maiden voyage of this brand-new ship. They were telling us about their ship, and that it was all air conditioned and everything. So my friend and I got to thinking, why can't we get on that godamn ship and go home, go back to the States? So, when we got back to the hospital camp we went to the transportation office to see the major we had talked to. We told him that we'd been downtown and this *Admiral Ford* was in there and it was heading back to the States, and if there was any chance we could get passage on that ship and get going we'd rather do that than wait to fly back. "Oh, no, you can't do that, fellas. You're in no shape for that, because you know that will be roughly about a three-week journey. I don't think that would be good." Well, we wanted to go anyway.

The next morning we went back to the transportation office again, because we didn't have much time to spare. That ship was ready to leave, and we finally talked the transportation office into letting us go. The next day the ship was leaving, so they put in a call for us and took us down into Manila in a command car, and we got on the *Admiral Ford*.

We didn't see land from the time we left Manila until we saw the western shore of North America. They let us off at Tacoma and took us to Madigan General Hospital at Fort Lewis. I was there for a while, and in early October I got shipped to Illinois to Vaughn General Hospital, Maywood, Illinois. I did get home to Eau Claire for four or five days at Thanksgiving, but I was in the hospital in Illinois until May of 1946.

For the whole war I was listed officially as missing in action. No one knew I was a pow, I was just "missing." I didn't have any contact with my family until I got to the hospital camp in Manila, and there I was able to put in a transoceanic call. It took a couple, three hours to get through, but I sat and waited it out, so I just had a chance to tell both my mother and father that I was alive and I was doing okay, and I would be home as soon as I could. They were pretty relieved to hear that. I was discharged then the following May.

I was a pow in Japan about three years. There were pilgrimages or tours to go back, and I was contacted. Different people would pay my way if I wanted to go back, but even if I could pay my own way I have absolutely no desire to go back. It was a miserable experience, a miserable part of my life. Let's just say that I've managed to overcome it.

*The Fall of the Philippines*

Up to this point I've had two heart attacks, but generally I have been okay health-wise, even though some former POWs have had a lot more problems. But I was wounded on Bataan. I've still got three or four Japanese slugs in my right hip and a piece of metal in my right shin that they were thinking of taking out, but there was a chance that if they disturbed it I might end up with a stiff ankle or something like that, so it was better to leave it there. Through the years I know it's there, but it hasn't bothered me too much. I had problems with nightmares though. Still do. Every once in a while something crops up, you know. It can be things from combat or from the camps. A vision creeps in every once in a while, but I'm not complaining. I'm just lucky I made it, lucky I'm back.

When I got back, nothing was like it was when I left, and I kind of had to start over; but I've made it. As I say, I'm eighty-five years old now [in 2003], and I'll be eighty-six next month, and I'm still able to get around, and I have to say, I'm lucky. I've had a good life. When I sit and kind of think back about it now, had it not been for that period, things probably would have been different.

I thought at the time, given everything that was happening, there was only one word, "survive." That's the only word that comes up. At the time, conditions being what they were, and my physical condition, that was the utmost thing. I guess with all of us, there's a lot of things we've done that if we knew the outcome we wouldn't have done. But if you don't know the outcome, you do what you think is best at a particular time. Sometimes it turns out and sometimes it doesn't turn out; like in my case, after I did what I thought was best, I did a lot of suffering, but damn it, I'm here.

# CHAPTER 3

*"The original plan was that we would take off and bomb Japan late in the day, fly all night, and land at dawn the next morning at a temporary field they'd built in China, in an area occupied by the Japanese."*

—Bill Bower, ARMY AIR FORCE

BILL BOWER, ARMY AIR FORCE, B-25 pilot

PAGES 114–115: *The B-25 bomber piloted by Jimmy Doolittle lifts off from the deck of the USS* Hornet *on the way to bomb Japan on April 18, 1942.*

OPPOSITE: *Bill Bower (second from left) and his B-25 crew pose on the deck of the USS* Hornet, *spring 1942.*

# THE DOOLITTLE RAIDERS BOMB TOKYO, APRIL 1942

BILL BOWER
ARMY AIR FORCE

Our outfit had been flying the new B-25 bomber for a whole year, so we were a pretty hot bunch. We got the first ones right off the manufacturing lines.

They had asked for volunteers, and of course we volunteered, but we didn't know what we were volunteering for. We just knew that we wanted to get out of that seedy base in Oregon and go do something else.

We didn't know where we were going, but it was somewhere special—we knew that. Since they had selected the top crews in the squadron, we knew something rather interesting was in the works, and we wanted to be in on it. We had known something was up, because we'd flown to Minneapolis to have the planes modified, adding extra tanks and stripping them of all the extra gear.

We didn't know for sure, but our mission pretty much had to be in the Pacific, since we needed to use long-range tanks, but I don't recall that we ever spent much time worrying about where we were going. At that stage of life, I was in my early twenties, things were pretty much day to day.

We didn't find out officially where we were going, for sure, until we got onboard the carrier *Hornet*, but they couldn't really have kept that type of secret from us, couldn't have kept us in the dark totally. So we each had a pretty good idea where we were off to. But we didn't sit around the bar and talk about it. We had other things to talk about.

I didn't much enjoy being on the *Hornet*. It was pretty dull business. They spread us Air Corps guys out all over the ship. I was given a berth right up in the prow, right by the anchor chains. There were four of us assigned to this one cabin, to divvy up the three bunks in there. When I got there, one of the Navy guys found other accommodations and slept on the floor somewhere, so I could sleep in his bunk. He didn't have to do that, but they were good to us.

There wasn't much humor onboard. It was a pretty tight ship. The farther we went west, the more tense it became. We all realized that this was the real thing. We were tense in that we'd been told that if we were discovered in Japanese waters and couldn't take off as scheduled, they'd dump the airplanes over the side and make a run for it. But it was obvious they weren't going to dump them. We were going to go no matter what.

We studied a lot, and we had a guy on the ship who had been a Navy attaché in Tokyo just before the war. We'd have classroom sessions, and he lectured us each day. We'd ask questions, and he'd answer questions about the Japanese and Japan, about what the place looked like and what he'd seen. I have a clear memory of that, of asking questions about places in Japan. One day they presented a list of targets, and we got to choose what we wanted to bomb. I ended up picking a factory near Yokohama. Somebody said it belonged to Ford Motor Company. I thought that was a pretty good deal, because I drove Fords!

So the day for launching the mission was fast approaching, but the morning before we were scheduled to lift off they spotted a Japanese picket boat, and the jig was up—they knew where we were. So we had to

*The Doolittle Raiders Bomb Tokyo*

leave a day early or not at all. I was lying around in my bunk and didn't hear the call to quarters up where I was. All of a sudden Jack Hilger came in and got me up. I think he did so because my plane was ahead of his on the deck and he wanted to make sure I showed up. By the time Jack got to me, they had all the hatches secured for battle stations, and we had to go back through all those hatches, one after another, about 400 feet back from the bow before we could get up on deck. I didn't have time to put on my flight suit—I just ran out of there in what I had on. We got up on deck, and there was no doubt or hesitation about going, no one thought it was a suicide mission.

The original plan was that we would take off and bomb Japan late in the day, fly all night, and land at dawn the next morning at a temporary field they'd built in China, in an area occupied by the Japanese. As far as I can remember, we had no knowledge of any other friendly fields in that whole area of China. Where they built this air strip just happened to be isolated from where the Japanese operated. So they had this temporary field where they positioned enough fuel to give each one of us enough to get out and fly down to Kunming, which still was not occupied by the Japanese, and that was the plan. We'd just land, fuel up right away, and get out of there.

But there we were firing up our planes in the morning a day early and more than 400 miles farther away from Japan than our fuel supposedly allowed to get to China safely, and thinking we'd get to Japan in the middle of the day. I didn't reflect much about how it would work out. We had to go, and quitting was not an option. I knew I was going to go. There wasn't any doubt about that, no hesitation. But in terms of people thinking of it as a suicide mission, I don't believe any of us ever felt that's what it was. We were competent and pretty highly trained. If you understand how to fly an airplane, there was no doubt that we could go ahead and handle any conditions or weather they could put us through.

There was a submarine right in the middle of Tokyo Bay that was giving us a weather report, so we knew going in pretty much what our winds were going to be. Bill Pound, my navigator, had that information, and we discussed it en route. But we didn't talk much about anything initially. We just loaded up and went.

My plane was named "Werewolf," but I didn't have anything painted on it. I was the twelfth plane off the *Hornet*. There were two lines painted on the deck for us, because our wingspan was seventy-seven feet and the deck was only seventy-five feet wide. One line was the nose wheel line, and I had to keep the nose wheel right on it so the wing wouldn't hit the control island of the carrier. There was a swell running, and a guy gave us a signal to go when the deck was just starting to come up, so that when we were lifting off the deck we were high on the wave. I didn't have any problems at all taking off. There was a thirty-knot head wind, plus the carrier was going twenty, so all you needed was another thirty knots or so on the takeoff roll. I watched the eleven planes in front of me take off with no problem, so by the time I got up there I was confident I could do it. We'd been trained to do short take-offs, but doing it for the first time on an aircraft carrier was interesting! I got into position, locked the brakes, gunned the engines, and waited for the guy to give me the signal to go. It turned out the takeoff was easy.

After takeoff, I circled around and came back over the ship to get the exact heading and check the compass. Since we were taking off one after another and heading out right after takeoff, we were pretty much in single file. I flew all the way to Japan right down on the deck to avoid detection, and we were all by ourselves. I never saw another B-25 on the way. We were right above the ocean. And it was a nice day. Beautiful weather!

Evidently we were north of our course when we got to the Japanese coast, so we turned south and came down the coast, still right down on the deck. We could see people on the ground very clearly, and I was impressed with the countryside. It was a beautiful country, green, well manicured, and neat. There didn't seem to be any clutter anywhere. We started climbing a little bit, to about 700 feet, and all of a sudden we flew right over an airfield. We went right over it at the same altitude as the planes in the traffic pattern. They didn't seem to notice us, and we flew on.

As we got close to Yokohama, things looked exactly like what the briefings on the *Hornet* said they would look like, though all we had gotten was a verbal description. The barrage balloons were there, and we flew right through them. So once we got over the target about noon, it was like, "Well, there it is and it looks just like they said it would." We had climbed a bit by then so we were at about 1,500 feet when we released the bombs. Then we had only one thought: get out of there!

We went right back out over the ocean, so we didn't see land again until we touched it after we bailed out in China, and then we didn't really see it before we got down because it was dark. It was just pitch dark.

We couldn't tell if we were over land or anything. No lights. We were in the clouds, and it was dark. Our navigator had some good fixes, but for the last three or four hours we were in solid weather. We were climbing gradually, trying to get above it, but it was real deep. Once it got dark, we were at about 10,000 or 11,000 feet, and we decided we'd just fly straight ahead by dead reckoning, since we knew we were going to be over land. We flew toward the area where the airstrip we were supposed to land on was. We didn't really know how far we had flown, but we figured that when the red lights came on indicating we were out of gas, we'd jump. When we were getting ready to bail out, the bombardier popped his chute somehow, so we had to repack it, which was difficult under those conditions. He had caught it on something when coming out of the nose. So I bailed out last, and floated down in the dark—couldn't see a thing. I took with me my pistol and a pack of cigarettes, and I still have that pistol. When the parachute jerked open, that pistol slid down my leg and cut my toe. I pulled it back up and strapped it back on. My father carried that pistol in World War I.

All of a sudden I was on the ground. I landed right by a tree, but missed it okay. I remember it was wet and I was within fifty or seventy-five feet of a sharp cliff. It was near midnight, eleven o'clock or so, and we ended up being close to the temporary field we were supposed to land on. A lot of the planes had made it to that area, including Doolittle's. In fact we went down right near Doolittle. But some of the fellows had decided they couldn't wait, and they put down on the beach right when they got to the coast of China, which was sort of a silly thing to do. Lawson and Hoover tried to go in near shore. But one of our guys, Farrell, he got a lot farther into China than any of the rest of us did. How he got clear into there, damned if I know, and he was the last man off the *Hornet*! It turned out that a tailwind pushed us farther into China than we would have been otherwise.

I got out of my parachute, and it was rough country. Everyone on my crew survived the landing, and we quickly got together. It was hard walking for a couple of days, but we finally got to where people started to help us, and they assembled us in a cave. That was within a week, I think. We were all back in that cave area. From then on we were in the hands of friendly Chinese. We went out as a group, went on a train, and then we commandeered a bus. A Dutch priest knew the way and could speak the language and got us food. We went from warlord to warlord, I guess. It was well coordinated. We finally got to Chungking, and they served us a dinner with Madame Chiang-kai Shek. Then they put us up in her compound before they flew us out all the way back to the States. All this time I was wearing the same clothes I had on when I took off from the *Hornet*. They got pretty rank! We went a long way to get out of China, 1,500 miles.

People ask me about what we thought of Doolittle. Of course he was a hero to all of us because of his reputation as an air racer in the 1930s. But when we met him we just immediately got the feeling that here was a real competent and capable individual. So there wasn't a blind response to Doolittle that we'd do what he ordered. He never took away your power of reason. He'd just set the example, and it wasn't difficult to follow that example. So, we knew if he was going to go we were going to go, and we could make it. And he conditioned us to the point that we knew we were capable of operating as well as he could operate. He instilled in us the sense that at least we had that competence.

After I got back to the States, I was sent out to Europe flying B-25s. For about a year and a half, we were 300 miles behind the enemy lines in Italy, on the island of Corsica. The Germans were to the south of us in Italy, down at the Rapido River, Monte Cassino, and Naples, and we were above Rome. In fact, our organization in Corsica is the story of *Catch-22*. The bomb wing there included the 340th Bomb Group, and that was Joseph Heller's group. He was a crew member on a B-25. Our leader, General Bob Matt, was really a flamboyant character, a wonderful person and a great leader, and I think he's incorrectly and cynically depicted in this book. He really was a helluva leader. But I can pick out some of the people I knew in that book. Actually, you can find them in any organization.

On the Doolittle Raid, out of eighty crewmen on the sixteen planes, one died on the parachute jump into China, four either drowned or died in landing accidents, and eight were captured in Japanese-occupied China. Two of those were executed, one died during captivity, and four were released at the end of the war. The crew that landed in Russia didn't get out of there until a year later, when they managed to escape. Most of us ended up doing much more dangerous flying in Italy, and a number of our group were either killed or captured over there. At the time the raid seemed exciting to us, but we didn't think it was too big a deal. We didn't concentrate too much on what they ended up calling the Doolittle Raid. It was only in later years that there was a lot of interest built up. We have been getting together for years now. It's influenced our whole lives. We are a pretty tight family.

I think that the war treated me fairly kindly. I went from a second lieutenant to colonel in less than four years. That was just four years and two months from the time I was commissioned. I was flying the whole time. So things kind of went my way. I stayed in the Air Force after the war and retired in the late sixties. Some of the guys I knew got out right after the war and flew for the airlines, but I stayed in, and I don't regret it.

# CHAPTER 4

*"When we got ashore, we were told to dig fox-holes before taking care of any personal needs, because Jap planes or ships were expected at any minute."*

—Robert Mahood, MARINES

ROBERT MAHOOD, MARINES, Guadalcanal

CARL ALBRITTON, ARMY, New Guinea, Philippines

DAVE BOWMAN, MARINES, Peleliu, Okinawa

PAGES 124–125: *One of the early Pacific island battle-grounds, Bloody Ridge on Guadalcanal, is shown here after the Japanese were turned back in September, 1942. Japanese and American bodies had been removed before the photo was taken. This open ridge was the logical place for the Japanese to attack since it was the only path to the American airstrip, Henderson Field, not covered by inhospitable jungle. Marine commander Colonel Mike Edson's final fall-back position, which was tenuously held throughout repeated Japanese charges straight into the Marines' machine gun fire, is in the foreground.*

# ISLAND COMBAT BEGINS AT GUADALCANAL, TARAWA, PELELIU, NEW GUINEA, 1942–44

## ROBERT MAHOOD

MARINES

After graduating from high school, I had a short stint in the California National Guard, and then I enlisted in the U.S. Marine Corps on August 11, 1939. In the spring of 1941 I was finally transferred to the Second Separate Engineer Company, Twenty-second Marine Regiment, in California. We had a few weeks of intensive training before we boarded the SS *Lurline*, and we headed out across the Pacific for Samoa in July of 1942.

We got to Pago Pago, American Samoa, and it was the most beautiful sight I had ever seen. The harbor seemed like a "C"-shaped crater of an old volcano, with steep sides rising almost vertically from the harbor. Everything was bright green. There were a few white buildings scattered along the shore and many thatched-roofed huts in sight. There was a small airstrip to one side of the harbor entrance, stretching through an old coconut plantation and composed of packed coral. Once in the harbor we were besieged by scores of dugouts and outrigger canoes filled with Polynesian boys hawking curios and fresh fruit. A number of them were diving into the water alongside the big liner to retrieve American coins tossed overboard by some of the nearly 4,000 Marines aboard.

We left Pago Pago at noon, and we were sorry we weren't allowed to get off and explore the island. After a few hours at sea we arrived at another island, Upolu, in British-mandated Samoa, and came into Apia harbor. This island had a lower silhouette than Pago Pago and seemed a lot larger. There were only a few natives in the harbor, and it seemed there was a lack of wartime urgency in the town of Apia. It was a beautiful colonial setting with many white stucco, two-story buildings along the waterfront. The most impressive sight was the neatly planted rows of coconut palms for as far as the eye could see.

We were boated to the lone public pier and then trucked to some buildings near the harbor entrance. They were metal-roofed, two-story wood frame buildings known as "Quarantine Houses." This was where new arrivals were housed for a period of time to see that no infectious diseases were introduced into the local population. There were no indoor toilets and only one cold-water spigot for each building, but compared to where some of the other Marines were housed, I felt like we were staying at the Hilton!

We took our meals at the island racetrack where the bulk of the Twenty-second Marines were encamped. The natives were very friendly and went out of their way to make us feel welcome. There seemed to be a birthday party at some place on the island every night, and we were always invited to join in the ceremonies. At each party, a suckling pig was cooked in a deep pit filled with hot stones, along with fruit and vegetables, and it was all covered with wet banana tree leaves. I can still recall the delicious flavor and aroma of the food we ate. After the meal, a guitar or ukulele would magically appear, and we were treated to wonderful native Samoan songs and dances. To make us feel welcome, they always played their version of "You Are My Sunshine" or "Deep in the Heart of Texas."

By the end of August we had boarded the USS *Crescent City*, a Navy transport bound for Guadalcanal. We first stopped in Pago Pago and stayed overnight in the harbor. Then we headed to Tonga and pulled into the harbor at Tongatapu late in the afternoon. The big aircraft carrier USS *Saratoga* and the USS *South Dakota* were there, both having been hit by torpedoes. So we knew we were getting close to where things were happening. Our next stop was Espirito Santo in the New Hebrides, but we stayed only a day because they were nervous about Jap air raids.

We left there and finally got to Guadalcanal on September 18, 1942, to join the First Marine Division. They had been fighting for a little over a month when we got there. We unloaded unopposed on Red Beach where they had first landed. The tension was high, and we could see from our landing craft evidence of shore fire and bomb damage. Shortly after landing operations began, an SBD Navy dive-bomber came winging in for an approach to Henderson Field, and it seemed that the whole fleet began to fire at him. The plane was hit, the pilot tried to make a landing on the beach, but he didn't quite make it and crashed about 100 feet offshore. I was in a landing craft on our way to the beach and passed alongside the area where the two airmen were being pulled out of the sinking plane. They were taken to the beach by another boat, and I over-heard one of the downed airmen loudly cursing the Navy, the Marine Corps, and the whole United States. I think the other one died in the crash. There was a Marine in my boat who had loaded his BAR and was preparing to join the hundreds of people shooting at the plane when I told him it was one of ours. I had to scream at him to keep him from fir-ing. He seemed very annoyed at not being able to shoot. He jammed his rifle butt down on the deck of the boat and that caused it to discharge three rounds of automatic fire, just missing his head!

When we got ashore, we were told to dig foxholes before taking care of any personal needs, because Jap planes or ships were expected at any minute. Around midnight I was just finishing washing up when I heard a loud bang and looked up in the sky to see a sickly green parachute flare from a star shell illuminating the whole area. We learned that it was from a Japanese submarine or destroyer, and they began shelling our beach position. So this was it, my first encounter with the Japs, and I was scared stiff! It was kind of a shock when you realized this wasn't practice or training, these were real Jap shells trying to kill us. I could smell the burned powder in the air and heard voices yelling in all directions. I took a flying leap into the nice, safe foxhole I'd dug earlier, only to find it oc-cupied by one of the company's lazier types who had not bothered to dig his own. I was both infuriated and scared. It was the worst case of mixed emotion I ever experienced. My anger subsided, and fear took over as the shelling got closer and closer, and we huddled there together, arms un-consciously holding each other in some sort of futile protection. That moment of fear we shared seemed to bond us into some vague brother-hood for the rest of the time we served together. I don't recall that we had any casualties from that first taste of war with the Japanese.

The next day I noticed, in addition to our own trucks and Jeeps, a number of Japanese trucks and staff cars being driven around by Marines. At the mess line, to supplement our corned beef or Spam, we were served steaming plates of rice, which had been captured from the Japanese. Some had weevils in it.

We finally set up our camp just east of the Lunga River delta, and we operated out of there for the next three months. One of our first projects as engineers was to set up sandbag reinforcements around the division headquarters of General Vandergrift, which was just south-west of Henderson Field next to a low ridge. That afternoon we heard the siren for "condition yellow," meaning unidentified aircraft approaching, then "condition red," enemy aircraft approaching, and "condition black," enemy bombing in progress. This prompted a mad scramble for shelter. I looked up and saw a group of silvery specks in tight formation, just ahead of a highway of white smoke puffs made by our antiaircraft batteries. Then I heard the whistling of falling bombs as I groveled into the hard coral bottom of the newly sandbagged staff office, along with about twenty-five other Marines. Three bombs straddled the ridge area where we were—they were just that close— and other bombs continued to fall right onto Henderson Field. I noted more than one person with urine-soaked trousers that day, including my own. After the bombers passed over, I saw medical corpsmen haul away a field-grade officer who had gone into uncontrollable shock. Another officer was practically in tears, not from fear but because one of the daisy-cutters had ripped through a beautiful piece of leather luggage in which he had placed two souvenir magnums of Japanese sake wine, which were also destroyed.

We continued our engineer projects around Henderson Field while the fighting continued just inland of where we were. In early October, after a lot of firing and shelling up by the front lines, we got word that the Japanese had made a big push and had been turned back, and that the Marines had counted 1,500 dead Japanese. One of the other engineer battalions took bulldozers up there, dug a big trench, and buried the sons of heaven.

During this time wild rumors would sweep through the Marines, and these sure had an effect on morale. We heard things like the Japanese were using women navigators in their bombers, a "fact" supposedly sworn to by some eyewitnesses who had seen them in plane wreckage. Then we were devastated by news that Walter Winchell and Deanna Durbin had been killed in an airplane crash, which of course turned out to be untrue. One rumor that made us leery of Army units was that Shirley Temple had been raped by some soldier. A lot of these rumors were going around the island just before the big sea battles and troop landings by both the U.S. and Japanese in mid-October 1942.

On October 12, 13, and 14 we really got hit hard by the Japanese. The first day started with an unusually heavy air raid. That night, several enemy warships bombarded Henderson Field with some heavy-caliber naval guns for several hours. They tore up the airfield, killed and wounded several of our guys, and damaged some of our aircraft. The Marine Corps lost several pilots who had just arrived to reinforce the original fighter squadron on the island. By morning we had few planes left in flying condition.

Then we saw five enemy transports near Cape Esperance, and we realized they had been unloading troops and supplies all night, but they were out of range of any guns we had on the island. Around noon, nine SBD dive-bombers had been patched and repaired into some kind of flying condition, so they could at least take off with a load of bombs to try and get the transports before they could pull away. While they were climbing for altitude, a lone PBY Catalina flying boat appeared from the southeast and made a low-level torpedo run at the transports. The PBY dropped the one torpedo it carried and turned sharply to come back toward Henderson Field. The torpedo scored a hit near the bow of a transport, but then two Japanese Zero fighters appeared out of nowhere and gave chase to the PBY. We were all watching this scene, and we were silently urging on the big, slow PBY as the Zeros closed the gap between them. The Zeros started firing bursts, and pieces flew off the tail surfaces of the PBY as it passed over the beach where we were working. Just as it looked like the Japanese pilots were about to shoot it out of the sky, our antiaircraft opened up after the PBY flew by us, catching the Zeros in a withering hail of bullets. First one and then the other blew up in bright orange fireballs, and they fell into the trees near the airfield behind us. Someone told me the pilot of that PBY got the Medal of Honor.

Meanwhile, the SBDs had begun their dive-bomb run and scored several hits on the Jap transports, which were scrambling to get under way. Just then we heard the "condition yellow" signal and looked west to see if there were more Jap planes on the way. I saw a formation of planes, but I thought they looked familiar. Almost everyone on the beach was running for cover, but I yelled that the planes were B-17s. They were a beautiful, familiar sight for me, since I was raised in Seattle where they were first made. So everyone came back out to the beach, and we watched as the bombers adjusted their course and lined up on the Japanese transports. They released their bombs at very high altitude, but some of their load found targets, and there was much fire and smoke. One ship was run aground, two were sunk in the area, and two were sunk the next day.

We finally got our turn on the front lines. On our first night, dug in up there on a low grassy ridge surrounded by jungle, our whole company was jittery. We heard Jap voices in the jungle below. Captain Brewer called for mortar fire to drop in front of our lines in a parallel pattern in the hope that we would kill a few Japs in that patrol down there. The mortar battery was east of us two ridges over. Well, the mortar shells started dropping, but not in front of us in a parallel pattern. They began to climb the hill in a tangent, and shells started to fall in our lines. One made a direct hit on one of our foxholes. It blew one of the guys to pieces and severed the leg of another. These guys were from our original company, so several of us were asked to gather up the parts and pieces of the one who had been killed. We placed them in a Marine blanket and buried it in a shallow grave right there on top of the ridge. Captain Brewer read a few words over the remains.

Everything was real tense after this death. The war seemed to be closing in on us fast. Shortly after dark we heard a single shot. It was followed by another shot that seemed closer. Then the air was filled with shots being fired, and some sounded as close as twenty feet away. I tried to raise my head up, expecting to see a Jap charging right at my foxhole, but it was too dark to see anything. I heard something roll into my foxhole and, thinking it was a grenade, I jumped out of my hole and hit the dirt and waited for the explosion. Nothing happened, so I figured it was a dud or a rock that had rolled in, so I crawled back into the hole. I would rise up quickly and fire a shot from my 1903 Springfield rifle in the general direction of where I figured the Japs were coming from, thinking if we laid down enough fire that would stop them. About then I heard someone yelling, "Cease fire, cease fire!" One of our guys was coming down the line yelling to cease fire until all the firing stopped. For my money that Marine deserved a medal for bravery in personally stopping the uncontrolled firing by us engineers who had just wasted over 2,000 rounds of ammunition firing at shadows. Any stray shot could have hit him. The captain was very angry and ordered combat fire discipline training for every day that we stayed at the front.

We finally moved off the front lines and back to our beach area. At last we were able to get cleaned up and bathe in the ocean, and we ate a lot of chow. One of our guys was bathing in the surf when all of a sudden a Japanese torpedo came out of the ocean and slid right past him and stopped about thirty feet up on the beach from the water's edge. Turned out it came from a Jap submarine that torpedoed our supply boat.

One night I witnessed a naval battle offshore out in Iron Bottom Sound. I found out later they called it the "Second Battle of Savo Island." I can say I have never witnessed a more awesome sight. We could see salvos of hot shells in threes moving across the night sky in big arcs to hit or miss unseen targets. The battle seemed to last for hours, and all of us beach defense guys sat on the front edge of the gun emplacements and watched the spectacle. There were from two to six vessels burning at different times all through the night. We sent out rescue craft the next morning to pick up survivors. Many of both sides were found, but few Japanese were brought in. Some of the Naval personnel had gaping shrapnel wounds, severed limbs, or they were burned, with oil covering their bodies. They were all in various stages of shock. I counted over fifty American bodies lying on the beach in neat rows. These were the guys who had been recovered by our rescue teams and were either dead when found or died on the way to the beach. We could see two or three ships out there that morning, still burning or lying dead in the water. One of these was one of our six-turret cruisers.

Finally in mid-December 1942, we loaded up on the Navy troopship USS *Hunter Liggett* and left Guadalcanal. What a relief! They took us to Brisbane, Australia, and after a few weeks we got transferred down to Melbourne. A couple of days after we got there I was admitted to the Army hospital with a very bad ear infection. After a few weeks they sent me to a rest camp near Frankston for observation. Finally in early March 1943, an Army doctor told me my ear perforation was permanent, and he was sending me back to the U.S. classified as unfit for combat duty. I didn't argue. I got shipped back to San Francisco as one of 125 American wounded or medically unfit, and that was the end of my combat experience in the Pacific war.

I stayed in the Marines and retired in 1967 as a first sergeant after serving in Korea and Vietnam. I will always be proud that I was a Marine.

# CARL ALBRITTON

ARMY

I went into the service on October 7, 1942, and shipped out to the Pacific on the SS *Matsonia*, an ocean liner they'd converted into a troopship. We were going from Hawaii on to New Guinea. Besides the Navy crew, our entire regiment was on it, probably about 9,000 men, all three battalions.

I was in New Guinea and later the Philippines, but it was pretty much the same routine for us medics. The medical officer stayed there in the Aid Station, and they had phones. We also had twelve litter men, four for each company. But when you got five or six knocked down in, say, thirty minutes, then you'd have to improvise litters and use the natives. We hired a slew of them to help us with the litters!

So the litter men would carry the wounded and dead down when they couldn't get an ambulance to them, and we were in a lot of terrain where this happened. In one place it was two-and-a-half miles to the closest vehicle! I was actually an assistant ambulance driver for a while. If we ran out of litters, you had to improvise some way or another, and sometimes you'd get two poles and take a couple of jackets and pull those jackets nice and tight over the poles, right in through the sleeves, and you'd have a pretty good litter.

So anyway, we had twelve first aid men, and by that I mean field men, medics, and that is what I ended up doing. But of the twelve of us, they gave three medics to each company, and each company consisted of three platoons for combat. I stayed with Company A all the way through.

We found out right off that the worst of it was that they gave us those big radio packs to carry our stuff in. We took them because we were carrying blood plasma and all the stuff you had to carry, and it all wouldn't fit into the bags we did have. So these radio packs were like big backpacks, but sometimes we'd get mistaken for radio men! Usually we'd take along several units of blood plasma, all sorts of bandages, all kinds of tape, scissors, compresses, morphine Syrettes, and lots of sulfa powder.

If a man had lost a lot of blood, most of them would be in shock. So we'd take his rifle and stick it into the ground with the bayonet on, or if they didn't have a bayonet we'd use a tree limb or something. And we'd hang the blood plasma bottle above him, string the tube down from it, and get the needle going into the arm, usually.

So we'd be going along and someone would get shot and then you'd hear, "Medic!" And if it was out in the open you had to work and wish. If there was some cover around, like a tree or even big weeds, that was better, but even then you could expect the Japs to fire at you. You were just hoping it all worked out. But a lot of times we had to go right out into open fields. And we had tags, and when you had someone hit you'd write on the tag the approximate time, where the wounds were, if you gave him morphine, what bandage you used, and so on. You'd write all this down and tie the tag onto them. It didn't take too long, maybe thirty seconds or so. Shrapnel made the worst wounds—big, jagged, torn up wounds. A bullet would make a clean wound.

I never saw anyone flip out and go out of their head, but a lot of them would just drift off. That's the way it would usually happen. They wouldn't scream or yell or anything, they'd just mentally drift away. You could look in their eyes and tell it. I guess we lost about ten or twelve like that. We'd just send them back to the rear to the hospital. There wasn't anything I could do with them. Only about two or three of them came back to the outfit. The rest of them didn't ever come back.

We were out on patrol one time in the Philippines, and the lieutenant decided we were going to stop for the night in some high grass. He said, "Boys, I think it'll be all right. Just lay down here in this grass." The second platoon was dug in on top of the hill. And about one or two in the morning, the Japs set up two of their little old mortars, and they started pumping them into us! Some would explode but a lot were duds, and we could hear them hit the ground. I was face down with my legs spread, and something hit right near one foot. I yelled out, and one of the guys near me says, "Doc, are you hit?" And I looked back and yelled, "I've lost a foot!" I'd looked back and saw my shoe off to one side, and I thought my foot had been blown off. But then I could see my foot and the shoe next to it, and I realized it was a dud shell that had knocked my shoe off.

While I was figuring this out the guy had come crawling over to help, and he saw my foot and the shoe and he said, "Oh, hell!" So he's there with me, and I realized I had been hit in the neck. He said, "Your foot's bleeding a little bit, but it looks like it's in one piece. But take a look at me, would you?" He stripped his jacket off, and there were holes all over his back—you could stick your finger in some of them, lots of them! He was as bloody as a hog. So I started talking to him, "Well, you've got a few here, and there's one down there." And he was carrying on, and I knew he was in bad shape. I got him bandaged up and he said, "Man, I wonder if I'm going to get out of here." And I said, "We'll have to wait until daylight. If you start out now, it'd be sudden death! There's no way to get anyone back." That shelling was bad.

So this guy laid next to me there all night, and I knew he was hurting. I said, "I'm going to give you a shot." He said, "Well, I wish you would if it would help me." I gave him one, and I took one myself. And he got to laughing at me, and we laughed the rest of the night!

When it was daylight I walked him down a bit and I knew he was sore. He had shrapnel in his back and legs, great big slugs in him. I don't know how many he had in him, so I said, "Now you aren't walking anywhere." But he wanted to. It was about a half mile to the medics' tent, and he wanted to walk. He said, "Get me up so I can walk." I said, "I got one little slug and you got forty or fifty it looks like. I can walk but you can't!" I made him get on a stretcher, and they carried him down. I was walking along there by the side of him, and he said, "Hey, Doc, you're not even limping on that peg leg!" He was making fun of me, you know, for thinking I'd had my foot blown off. And I said, "I'm going to kill you before you get to the hospital!"

They got us into the hospital, and the doctor, a major, said to me, "Well, you don't have too much to worry about. That piece went in but it will work out through the closest bone." And that's just what happened—that little piece of shrapnel worked its way out about ten or eleven years later. He said, "Yeah, that shrapnel will work out, but we have to keep you here for a while." And I said, "I feel guilty. It's sore but I feel okay, and I'm guilty. My buddies are up there fighting my fight. My friends are all up there." And the doctor said, "Well, you'll get back up there soon enough." And I said, "I just get the feeling my friends are up there fighting for my family, and I'm supposed to be doing that." But that's the only time I was ever in the hospital.

So I'm laid up there in the hospital, and this dentist friend of mine comes up to me and says, "Your wife's going to get a telegram that you were wounded. Her and your mother are going to go crazy before they hear it from you. The telegram will be sent, and your Purple Heart will be right behind it." And I said, "I don't want one!" There were a lot of us who didn't want one because we thought it was a jinx. But I felt better when I found out it meant five points added to my total, so I'd probably get to go home sooner. Well, the next morning I was running a high temperature and I felt pretty bad. And this dentist came to see me and said, "Well, let me scratch a line or two for you." They knew I had a little girl at home, you know. I went by the nickname of "Pappy" as soon as they found out she'd been born. I was "Pappy" at age twenty-four! We had one guy who was thirty-two, and he was "Old Folks"!

So this dentist sat down there on the side of my cot and wrote a nice little letter to my wife. It dawned on me that she could tell it wasn't my handwriting, and that would scare her to death anyway! But we got that letter right out airmail, and it beat the telegram. This old boy who delivered the telegram, he came up to her door, and she knew by the expression on his face that he didn't know she'd already gotten the letter saying I was okay. All he could tell was that it was a telegram from the War Department. He started in by saying, "I hate to deliver these. It makes my life hard." So she said, "Oh, he's already written me a letter saying he's okay." And he said, "I wish they'd all do that!"

But the dentist told me, "You get that wife of yours a letter in your own handwriting as soon as you are able. She knows this first one isn't in your handwriting, and she's probably worried that you are injured worse than we said you were, so you get her a letter quick."

At the end of the war I got on a hospital ship coming back. It was an old rusty Liberty ship, but they had converted it into a hospital ship. We got on that ship, and they were bringing the ones on with malaria and stuff like that, and they were awfully sick. But then they brought in about eight or ten ambulance loads of guys who were bad off mentally, and we had to lead them across the gangplank, you know, eight or ten deep, and onto the ship. They took them right down and put them in the hold, and some were violent. They didn't know where they were, and they weren't putting it on. I mean, you could tell by their eyes that they weren't putting it on! And I was always glad I didn't end up like that.

*Carl Albritton*

## DAVID BOWMAN

MARINES

O n my seventeenth birthday, May 1, 1940, I went to join the Marine Corps. Because of a heart murmur, they said, "You're unfit for military service." So on my eighteenth birthday I signed up for the draft. Everybody had to sign up for the draft, and shortly after that I was called up. I was about to be inducted into the Army, and I said to this medical officer, "What happened to that heart murmur I allegedly had these many years?" He said, "You have a heart murmur?" He whipped out his stethoscope, checked me out, and promptly labeled me: "unfit for military service." So they reclassified me 4-F, and I figured I would never be in the military. I really felt bad about it because my two brothers were in the Marine Corps. In 1943 I was called up again, and this time I didn't open my peep when I went through the physical. Well, no one said anything about a heart murmur, and they accepted me. This was shortly after my birthday in May 1943, when I was nineteen years old.

ABOVE: *Dave Bowman stands at parade rest after being named "Honor Man," number one in his class at boot camp, 1943.*

I kept my mouth shut and went through boot camp, so they sent me to the First Armored, which was just forming. We were scheduled, supposedly, to go to Tarawa, but we didn't go for some reason. That was in November 1943. By then the Fourth Division was training at Camp Pendleton, and when the Fourth Division went overseas, the First Armored went with it. My first invasion was when we hit the Marshall Islands, at Roi-Namur, which was part of Kwajalein Atoll. That was my first combat. The first time you get into combat, at least from my perspective, you don't realize the gravity of the situation. It was us against them. Of course we lost people, but it wasn't as grave as the situation at Peleliu. That first time in combat, it's kind of like cops and robbers or cowboys and Indians. The second time is a little more sobering, the third is more sobering, the fourth is like, hey, get me get out of this! But I've always believed that wars should be fought by young people who don't really know what they're getting into. You take an old head that's been around, and he's already concerned with covering his own body! An older guy won't take risks. He's doing more thinking and wondering what he's doing there. Young guys could give a damn—it's all full speed ahead!

With our tanks we were basically fire support. They'd have some trouble somewhere, and we would have to go over there and shoot at whatever was the problem. We moved through there pretty rapidly. Our objective in this type of unit was to pick up the fire power when the naval fire lifted, and when the strafing from naval fighters moved up. We were amphibious tanks, and we were supposed to pull out when they got land tanks ashore, but that never happened. Course, we had pretty good ordnance aboard. We had sand bags around the front of the bow and so forth, so if anything hit us it would detonate as opposed to going through the metal.

After Roi-Namur, we went to Guadalcanal, and then we were with the Third Division. Shortly after that they sent us to Pavuvu, which is a little island in the Solomons not far from Guadalcanal. They had fixed up this island just for training and re-outfitting Marines. We started preparing for Peleliu there, and we got a bunch of new guys. The Third Armored was formed about July of 1944, and we hit the beach at Peleliu on September 15, so few of us knew each other. We were training on Pavuvu in the neighborhood of two-and-a-half months, but that's not a hell of a lot of time to work with each other before going into combat. We ended up going to Peleliu with the First Marine Division.

Our amphib tanks had letter designations. The H stood for the Headquarters Company Battalion. So the tank labeled "H1" was the one the commanding officer rode in, "H2" had the executive officer, and "H3" had the next officer in rank. At any rate, the crews of those three units had the top officers in the battalion.

For the Peleliu invasion, we were loaded on an LST. They dropped us off about two or three miles from the beach, and then we lined up and formed a line of departure. There were probably sixty amphib units lined up heading for the beach. Since I was the tank commander I was up looking out the top hatch on the turret. As we approached the beach, there were huge, mushroom-shaped, coral boulders, and we had two or three of our tanks that got bellied up, high-centered, on these things. As we got closer we were hearing things hitting off the outside of the tank. All hell was breaking loose above us, and I pulled down into the turret so that just my head was sticking up. But we had two weapons on the outside of the tank, side-by-side .30-caliber machine guns, and these guys were basically exposed from the shoulders up. They had a metal shield around their machine guns, but they were exposed. I didn't stay down in the turret too much because it gets hotter than hell in there. We had what I guess you'd call a periscope, but it was more like a little mirror you could look out ahead with down in the turret, but they weren't too effective. It was easier to just kind of sit low in the turret and peek out the top hatch.

When we got to the beach, the objective was the airstrip, which was a couple hundred yards in from the beach. So we drove right out of the water and up and over the beach and all the way to that paved coral strip. But when we got there we found we were alone. There was nothing else to do but drop back. We pulled back to where the other tanks were. I don't know why they were just sitting there, just inland from the beach, because everybody's objective was this airstrip. Later in the afternoon we went back up there, but initially we were the only ones there.

The Japs had huge mines all over the beach, and I don't know why we didn't trip any of them. I understand that one of our tanks, before it reached the beach, hit one of those tethered marine mines, those big balls with horns on them. Of course it blew everything out of the water, and the tank just disintegrated. I guess, in reality, it's a matter of luck if you come through or not. Yes, a lot of it is luck.

About noon of D-Day, September 15, I was sent to carry a message to the command post, and I went into that area where "Push Push" Puller was, that's what we called "Chesty" Puller. He was famous for being a fire-breathing blood-and-guts Marine, and he just threw his guys into those cliffs behind that beach they came in on. It turned into a slaughter.

The Japs were in caves up in those cliffs, and they just mowed down the Marines as they tried to advance. When I got over into that area looking for the CP, there were all those dead Marines stacked up around there. It was terrible. I remember seeing one guy, he was killed by concussion from a shell, and his nostrils were blown up like twin balloons. I'll tell you, it was a frightening thing to see all these dead guys, they were the first regiment on the original landing on September 15. They were all still lying where they were hit, they hadn't been touched by human hands. Later they had a division graves registration team come around, but by the time they got to all the dead, and collected dog tags and so forth, a lot of those bodies had completely deteriorated.

When I was carrying that message to the command post, I saw this big blond-headed kid, alone, standing guard on a 37mm gun that they had left behind for whatever reason. So I said, "Hey, don't you know they're looking down here and they're seeing this damn artillery piece and they'll be after it to knock it out, and if you're standing here stargazing you're gonna get hit too! You better get under cover over there and you can still see your piece from there." Well, he didn't think too much of that, so when I came back by there about an hour later, he was just in pieces, and so was the 37mm. It was all shot to pieces because, you see, every bit of that terrain was preregistered. The Japs knew exactly what elevation and what windage and the distance, and they could fire at preregistered spots. We finally figured out that all these stakes stuck in the coral, that looked like they were part of native crab nets, they were aiming stakes that the Japs had put out there to preregister on. When some of our guys or a tank or gun got close to one of those stakes, the Japs would just open up, knowing they would hit anything near those stakes. So we wised up and flattened down all those aiming stakes, and of course after that we had a lot less casualties. Your life, more or less, depends on your ability to adapt to a situation and clue yourself in, because if you don't, you don't remain among us for long.

You know, when we were up on the airstrip and pulled back, well, actually we went back close to the beach. We pulled in beside two or three tanks. The one we pulled up beside had taken a hit right over the radioman/assistant driver's position, and that Marine had had his head blown off, and just part of his skull was remaining. His brother was close by, and they wouldn't let him go see his brother. It was about noon, so my crew, we opened up some vittles and sat there and ate. I mean, it's tough, somebody died, but it wasn't gonna interfere with our meal. The rest of the crew from that tank were all out on the beach, but of course the dead guy was still in the hatch down below. It didn't bother us to the point where we were upset by the death. We were just happy it was them and not us. I guess it's the best way to be. Nothing's gonna save them, they're dead. I would have a different perspective even later in the war, and today, but at that time, hey, that's the breaks. You live, you die. You couldn't let it get to you very much.

So the afternoon of D-day we had this Japanese tank charge. We saw them coming. They were heading at us from the far side of the airstrip, and we were just off the airstrip close to the beach. They just suddenly appeared, but we just shot them up and stopped every one of them. They were all knocked out because their light tanks were about like our half-tracks. You could shoot through them with a .30 caliber. That night we were on the inside of the airstrip and, therefore, we were silhouetted against those burning tanks. Several of the Japs had tried to get out of their tanks but died before getting out, and they were half hanging out of hatches in those tanks in various positions. I remember this one dude, he would rise up. I mean it was really a macabre sight to see, but of course, this was his dead body responding to the heat from this burning tank. But as bad as this was to have to look at all night, our big concern was that we were being silhouetted. All the Japs up on top in those cliffs behind the airstrip and all those adjoining caves could see us down there. However, we'd been told to stay there, and of course, like any Marine, you're given orders, you do it, you carry it out.

All that night the nearest tank we knocked out couldn't have been more than fifty yards from where we were set up. That's not very far, in the dark it looks a hell of a lot closer. We could smell those stinkin' little greasy bastards burning. That's a hell of an odor, burning flesh.

But the next morning, and this was the second day, in preparation for continuing our attacks, our ships started shelling, and when the shelling started, that's what did my gunner in. That's when he flipped out. The terrain literally shook, and everything off shore, all the ships, everything behind us was firing, and those 16-inch rounds from the battlewagons looked like barrels going through the sky. You could see them, they were slow moving, and then, "Wham, wham, wham, wham!" and everything up ahead and around us was exploding.

I can really understand why Earl went bonkers, because he had been through that before when his ship was shot out from under him. He was in the Marine detachment on the *Vincennes*, and his ship was sunk early in the war up by Guadalcanal. He floated around in the bay for eight hours with a big hunk of his buttocks shot away. So, they finally pulled him out of the drink and put him in the hospital for quite a while and then, and this is what I couldn't understand, they sent him back into combat with us. He'd already had that very traumatic experience and about died, and then here he was again under fire on Peleliu. When Earl went over the crest, we'd been there all day on D-day, all night of the 15th, and this was the morning of the 16th. He just started wildly firing a .30 caliber—just everything, everywhere. He was just crouched down, inside the turret of the tank, and he was yelling and firing the .30 caliber. I was in the turret also, and I couldn't get him to stop. I was yelling at him but it was like he had gone into another place mentally. He was yelling, and I guess he was reliving the sinking of the *Vincennes*. We got Earl out of there and I never saw him after that.

When he left, we had other fish to fry. I never heard from him until after the war. I really thought he was dead. I finally got a letter from him in 1993, and he had painted a picture of our tanks in the water offshore at Peleliu at the line of departure, just before we started in to the beach. He painted it from a photo he had found of our tank there in line, and you can see Earl and me up out of the hatch at the top of the tank. I always felt bad about him. The Marines should have never sent him back into combat.

So our ships were shelling the area right in front of us on that second day, and then we started in with fire support like we had done at Roi-Namur. The difference was, and this is what made Peleliu so terrible, these cliffs ahead of us were full of caves, and it was a hell of a thing to get those Japs killed in those caves. Some of these caves had big doors and the weapons were on rails. They'd run 'em out and fire off a few rounds and then roll right back in, and the doors would shut. You could see right where they were, and I watched Navy dive-bombers go in. It looked like they laid direct hits, but apparently it didn't faze 'em because a little while later the doors would open and here the guns would come out and shoot again. When you see all of this horrific bombardment you think no human life could survive, but they do, they crawl out of them holes.

There was this tiny little island just about 300 yards off the western shore of Peleliu called Ngesebus, and there were a bunch of Japs over there in bunkers with artillery that was harassing the Marines as they tried to move up the west side of the island. So they put together a little amphibious invasion of Ngesebus, and our amphib tanks were in on this. They shelled this little island for quite a while before we went in, and that got some of the Japs, but there were still plenty of them over there. At Ngesebus, in the last twenty minutes of that operation, we had sixty casualties. That's pretty damn sobering. My tank, the old H3, was surveyed after that operation, and by surveyed I mean it was shot up so bad we couldn't use it anymore—it was just junk.

So, we went over in the morning and were clearing out this little island, but right at the end we ran into some pretty active opposition. There was a pill box, a pretty sturdy operation, and the Japs were firing through slits. We ran our tank right up on it, and the bow of the tank was raised right in front of those slits so they couldn't see out. Before we could fire that damn 37mm, our entire gyro went out. Then we couldn't move the turret and were just sitting ducks. This was right during that last twenty minutes when guys were getting shot all around us, and we had to knock out this position. So we had to operate the turret by hand to swing it around, and believe me, that was a pretty hairy moment. We didn't know if they had heavy caliber weapons in that bunker, because if so they could fire right through the bottom of the tank, because we were tipped up in front of the firing slits. But we got the turret cranked around by hand and were able to fire sideways and knock this thing out. But right when we were high-centered in front of that pill box, the ranking NCO in charge was on my tank, and he had been at Pearl on December 7, so he'd been in the Marine Corps a while. But I guess he thought we were all going die right there, because he just went bonkers; he fell out on the deck at the bottom of the tank just crying like a baby. You hate to see a grown man cry, especially a Marine Corps sergeant who's supposed to be a leader of the troops. I don't know whatever happened to him after that. He left us, so they might have surveyed him, too. Anyway, when we came back to Pavuvu they put me in charge of the armored section of those tanks. I became NCO in charge of those men.

Anyway, my tank, H3, was surveyed, so I was given this machine gun and a crew and assigned perimeter defense. So we set up where they told us to go, and there was a dead Marine right next to our position. And I mean he smelled bad because he was rotting away. At Peleliu, bodies ballooned the first day, and after about three days they burst, and these huge blow flies were everywhere. When you opened a can of meat and vegetable stew or C ration, you had to fan it while you ate it, because otherwise blow flies would take it away from you.

When they put us on the machine gun, my part of the campaign for Peleliu was pretty well over. We were lucky, because a lot of our guys, after

144                                          *Island Combat Begins at Guadalcanal*

they lost their tanks, they made litter bearers out of them. Can you imagine climbing up through all that crap and carrying a litter with somebody on it? That must have been hell. I'm glad I never had any of that duty.

So, I was there in charge of this machine gun squad, and our time was consumed primarily with trying to figure out how to move that dead body without permission from graves registration. But we never moved him. I'd watch his remains at night, and believe me, this dead Marine was almost totally disintegrated. He was right next to my foxhole; I could reach out and touch him. I would watch his remains at night whenever a star shell went off overhead. Frequently in the darkness we relied on star shells from 60mm mortars or from Navy vessels to light up the area so we could see if any Japs were crawling around. The shells would burn brightly overhead and lasted about three, four, or five minutes. They'd float down slowly on a parachute. It's kind of an eerie feeling and sight because you've been straining your eyeballs to see any movement out in front of you, and then there's this weird bright white light from the star shells, and here was this decomposing body, a Marine, right next to me.

Admiral Halsey wanted Admiral Nimitz to back off on the operation at Peleliu, not even invade it in the first place. I didn't know that until later. We had heard that the reason we were hitting Peleliu was that we were 500 miles off of Mindanao, and that MacArthur wanted Peleliu neutralized before he made his famous return to the Philippines. But I have since heard that Halsey decided that there wasn't any point hitting Peleliu. They found out right before we invaded Peleliu that MacArthur could just go right into Leyte and we could bypass Peleliu, just like they did with Truk. As it happened, for whatever reason, Nimitz didn't go along with it. He wanted the island hit. Other Peleliu veterans feel bitter about this because Peleliu was really a hellhole and so many guys died. When you think it maybe was totally unnecessary, that's just kind of hard to think about.

I was at Peleliu from D-day on September 15 to almost Thanksgiving. It was way up in November and we were getting shipped back to Pavuvu. There were twenty or twenty-five of us Marines that got assigned to go aboard a merchant vessel. I guess this ship had brought in supplies to Peleliu from somewhere, and instead of going back empty they wanted it to drop us off in the Solomons on its way back to Australia.

After the five Sullivan brothers went down on the *Juneau*, the Navy passed the word that no more brothers would do duty together. Well, as it happened, Sergeant Major Holmes, aka Smilin' Jack, who never cracked a smile, was trying to engineer a transfer. A guy in the Seventh Regiment had a friend in the Third Armored, and they wanted to get together with each other, so this guy in the Third Armored put in for a transfer to the Seventh Regiment. The transfer went through, so they sent him across. We were on Pavuvu, and the division at that time was somewhere else, so they sent him across the bay to the Seventh Regiment, and they sent a guy from that unit to the Third Armored to replace him.

Well, when the sergeant major saw the service record for this guy— he'd had a desertion rap somewhere in his background that he had beat— the sergeant major was just fit to be tied; he didn't want a man like that in the Third Armored. When I found out what unit this guy came from, I told the sergeant major, "I've got a brother over there in that unit!" My brother was there, and he was a BAR man, and I used to see him going through our area, carrying that BAR, which with all the equipment must have weighed twenty-five pounds. He was my older brother, Charles, and he was kind of a little dude, but he still lugged that BAR around. When I told the sergeant major about my brother and wondered if we could get him in our outfit, he got on the horn to division, and they talked to the Seventh Regiment, and he said, "You got a guy over there named Bow-man?" "Yeah." "I'm going to send this deserter back to you, and you send me that guy Bowman." That's how my brother came to be in my outfit, and he had it really made, because he went from being a gravel-grinder carrying a BAR to an armored unit. But when he got to our outfit, they didn't have a job for him.

So Dr. Weiss was our battalion doctor, and my brother became his Jeep driver. I have to believe that my brother came from a praying mother, be-cause at Okinawa the Seventh Regiment had a 120 percent casualty rate. In other words, their replacements replaced replacements, and they really got shot up pretty bad. So, by getting my brother into the Third Armored, we saved him from a worse fate. I often wondered what happened to that dude that wanted to be with his buddy, because it's very doubtful he got out unscathed; I mean, like I say, the Seventh Regiment really got shot up.

So when we hit Okinawa, the First and Sixth Divisions went north. The Seventh, the Seventy-seventh, the Ninety-sixth, and the Twenty-seventh Army Divisions hit to our right flank. We went in at Yontan and then went all the way north, and I think in about two weeks we secured our end of the island. I was still in the Third Armored, and we were at-tached to the First Marine Division at that point.

When we hit the beach, our commanding officer was John

Williamson. He was unhappy that when we got to the line of departure, D company, supposedly on our left flank, was a no-show. So he told me to go find that commanding officer and have him get on the horn to him. I could have been the first man on the beach at Okinawa, because I bailed off the bow of the H1 and took off. I was worried about those guys landing behind me, just cutting down everything ahead of them, shooting and not looking, just shooting. I was concerned about the Marines behind me and not the Japs in front of me! Anyway, later that morning I ran into Ernie Pyle. I didn't know who the hell he was at the time, but I was told later. It was about noon on Easter Sunday morning, and of course, a couple of weeks later Ernie Pyle got hit on an adjacent island.

At Okinawa Colonel Williamson had a kidney stone, and I think they took him to Guam. Major Parker became the commanding officer, and the executive officer moved up, took over H1 and my crew. This guy, his name was LaFrancois, had been a Marine gunner, which was a rate comparable to a warrant officer. But this guy was a captain by this time, and he had been a Marine gunner with Edson's group when they made the Makin raid from a submarine. The scuttlebutt had it that Captain LaFrancois wrote the story that was published in the *Saturday Evening Post* called "Gung Ho," and Hollywood made a movie with Randolph Scott, so LaFrancois got a lot of press and prestige. I remember him calling us out before we moved. He said, "Men, we're going to be the first in Naha, and we're all going to be wearing medals." Well that went over like a lead balloon! None of us wanted to be wearing medals, you know?

Right about that time we had a guy step on a land mine, and he was in a column of Marines, just walking along, and "boom." His legs were blown off, and the guy behind him had his guts blown out, and the guy in front got hit pretty seriously too. In the Marines all chaplains were Navy personnel. Our chaplain was a Catholic priest, a monsignor, and Alex Rheaume, who was our corpsman, ran right over there to these guys and was hollering, "Get the chaplain." So the chaplain came over and wanted to know if this boy who just had his legs blown off was a Catholic. And Rheaume, he was a chief pharmacist mate, an enlisted man, a naval corpsman, and the chaplain was an officer, but Rheaume, who was a catholic, really exploded. He said, "It doesn't make any difference whether he's Catholic or not! Obviously he's dying, say something to him." Later on, this major who was at Peleliu, he heard about it, and this major said, "Look, you will conduct Protestant services

*David Bowman*

147

along with your Catholic service, and you will conduct Jewish services if I tell you to." Well, it wasn't long before we didn't have a chaplain. We went through the rest of the war without a chaplain.

So the guy who stepped on the mine died. The guy behind him who had his guts blown out, I'm told that they literally picked his guts up and stuffed them back in the cavity, mud and all, but the guy survived. I don't know what happened to the third guy.

We never really had much to drink but we came across some sake, and this other guy and I were drinking it one night, and I knew something was troubling him. So I asked him about it, and he voluntarily told me about a situation where he had gone into this cave with a friend of his looking for souvenirs. They split up when they got in there and went down separate passages, or so they thought. So, he went one way, and his friend went the other. But this cave came back and rejoined, and he didn't know that. He came around this corner in the cave and there was movement there, so he opened fire. He went over to look at the body and found out he just killed his friend. He drug him out to the mouth of this cave so his friend would be found by the graves registration people, but then he took off back to his unit and kept his mouth shut. In his cups, he was telling me about it, wanting sympathy, I guess, but I told him, I said, "Well, let me tell you, the guy's dead, his family has been notified, they may have even spent the $10,000 insurance that they got from the government, and nothing you do now is going to bring him back. So let me suggest to you that we just forget about this. I didn't hear a word of what you just told me, and I'm not going to say anything about it. I would suggest to you, don't you ever say anything about it." Thinking back on it, maybe I should have said something about it, but I felt like it wasn't appropriate. I can imagine that a family, on hearing that their loved one was souvenir-hunting and got killed out of his own stupidity, that would take all the luster off his life. All they knew was that he was "killed in action." So I figured it wasn't my place to take that away from them.

I got hit on June 12, 1945, and I think Okinawa was declared secure about June 19 or 20 of 1945, so it was just before the end of the battle. I was pretty lucky to go all the way through to that point, because I had several exposures to direct fire. At that time I was a platoon leader for several of our tanks, H1, H2, H3, and several other throw-ins that they didn't know what to do with. Every morning I'd call the roll, and there would be about thirty-five to forty men, I guess, and I'd have to find tasks to keep 'em busy. We had made a series of landings up and down a

*Line of departure preceding the first wave, Marine am-
phibious tanks head toward Peleliu on September 15,
1944. The island at upper right is obscured by smoke from
the pre-landing bombardment. Dave Bowman, commander of tank H3, is silhouetted at the top the tank turret
in the right foreground. His gunner, who broke down 24
hours after this photo was taken, is to Dave's right at the
top of the turret.*

cove on the coast. Our tank had gone through a slot in a seawall and was
up on a hill, and I was going back down to check something out on the
shore. I was running down this seawall, and we came under a mortar
barrage. This was real sudden, these mortar rounds just started exploding all around me, and one must have hit real close because I was literally lifted up in the air off the sea wall and cartwheeled head over heels
and down a hell of a drop, ten or twelve feet. I landed real hard, and I still
don't know exactly how, but I must have landed on my knees from the
problems I had later. I guess I was dazed. Our corpsman, Rheaume, had
seen me from an adjacent area and came running down there and took
care of me. A piece of shrapnel had blasted a chunk out of my skull, and
you can still feel the dent in my head from that. Well, at that time it was
a bloody mess, and I had no idea how bad it was. Rheaume calmed me

*David Bowman*

down and patched me up. So that seemed like the most serious injury, but I knew there was something wrong with my legs. You know I got a hernia from lifting an ammo case on Peleliu. Well, I thought, dammit, I've had a recurrence of that hernia. But something was different because there was pain radiating from my knees up as opposed to my groin down. So Rheaume gave me some codeine, I think, though I'm allergic to codeine today. That kept me going, and we finished up our operation that day. A few days later the battle was over. But my knees were really bothering me, and it turned out my knees were injured much worse than I originally thought. And this really started a lot of problems for me later on with my knees.

There were two events in World War II that scared the bejabbers out of me. I never was particularly apprehensive. I had crawled out of the sack on the morning of a landing onboard ship, had gone through several battlefield breakfasts, had gone down to the tank deck on an LST, and fired up the tanks in there with all the noise and exhaust fumes, and those big LST doors would open and you drive right out into the ocean, and you go to the line of departure and head for the beach under fire. I mean, this was commonplace, and I just did it and didn't think much about it. But at Peleliu we had gotten ashore and out of our tank, H3, and we were spread out, and we came under mortar or artillery fire. Each time those projectiles detonated, there was a yellowish smoke that came from them. We thought that was odd, but it wasn't until somebody got it in his mind that he smelled gas that we got worried. We could smell something like chlorine gas, and suddenly someone shouted out, "Gas! Gas!" None of us had any gas masks, so my heart sunk to my bowels, and a terrible cold feeling swept over me. My thoughts were, "Give your soul to God 'cause your ass belongs to Tojo." Like I say, that was very frightening. I told a shrink about this once, and he wrote it up. This was after the war. He said, "Mr. Bowman thought he was in imminent danger of a gas attack, but there was no gas attack." Well, that's true. There wasn't. But like I say, it smelled like gas, and that voice coming out of the smoke . . . "Gas! Gas!" And of course, we'd all heard horror stories of WWI, and none of us had gas masks, and you could smell chlorine, very pronounced. This shrink, in giving his observation, it was easy for him to say, "but there was no gas attack."

That was one. The other was when we were close to Naha on Okinawa in kind of a recessed part of the coast, like a small bay. Anyway, we were bivouacked on this point, and it was about dark when all of a sudden all hell broke loose. Later, we found out there were 350 Japs in boats trying to sneak behind us to make a landing. Navy patrol craft picked up on them and started firing direct fire at these small boats carrying these Japanese troops. Only thing was, we were right on the beach in that direct fire. I was lying on my back and I could see these tracers, 40mm tracers, going past right in front of my nose, right above my head. I was trying to make myself as flat as possible, to the point I thought my toes may get shot, so I was trying to dig my heels in deeper. My first thought was, my birthday was May 1, and just when I was about to become a man I was about to be gelded! I was worried about getting my baltics shot off by a 40mm. The Navy finally got word to lift fire, and then we hopped to it and my battalion was instrumental in mopping up those Japs, and like I say, there were about 350. But that feeling of lying there as flat as I could and having those tracers going right above my nose, well, that really got to me.

After I got blown off the sea wall, I continued to have problems with my knees. I had my first knee replacement surgery in 1979. That one only lasted about five years; then I had the second one. Both knees were messed up. The upshot of it was that I had five procedures in ten months, and I believe that's what triggered my diabetes, which ended up disabling me so I couldn't work.

I also had problems with nightmares after the war. As a matter of fact, ten years after the war I walked into a VA facility in New Orleans and asked to see a psychiatrist. When I came back from the Marines I was having nightmares, and I just had a kind of rage inside of me. I was drinking and having marital difficulty. So I told this guy that I was just mad at the world. And he said, "Well, we better keep you here." So they kept me for three months. They gave me daily medication and nocturnal medication, and then they gave me the "sparky" treatment, electroshock. Then I started looking around and saw all these guys with bulkhead stares. In the Navy all walls are bulkheads, and an empty stare is a bulkhead stare. The realization hit me that the doctors were taking care of their problems this way—just zapping their brains. This was how they were treating what's now called post-traumatic stress disorder. But the realization hit me that prefrontal lobotomies were their way of taking care of these people that couldn't forget, and hey, there but for the grace of God go I.

At the VA hospital, the words they used to describe me were "aloof to my fellow patients," and I guess I was. I knew that I was rational, and I could see that many of them were irrational. We were on a locked ward, but I never lost touch with reality. I never heard voices. But I was angry. Years later, of course, all my symptoms, the nightmares and anger, are classic symptoms of post-traumatic stress disorder. But they had never heard of it then, and a lot of guys in that ward were suffering from it like I was. But the reaction of the doctors at that time was that they were dealing with schizophrenia, and a lot of us got that label. Nowadays, there is a lot better knowledge and treatments for post-traumatic stress disorder.

After they gave me all this sparky treatment, they said I was becoming confused. Well, hell, anybody they put a jumper cable to your head, it's gonna confuse you! After three months they let me go, and I wanted to just get the hell out of there. The only way they'd let me out is if they wrote me up as schizophrenic. I knew damn well I wasn't schizophrenic, and there was no schizophrenia in my family, but I didn't give a damn and just wanted out of there so I said, sure, just let me out.

After I got out of the VA and got back my job—I was a gasoline transport driver hauling aviation gas—it just scared the bejabbers out of the Standard Oil Company that they had a diagnosed schizophrenic driving for them. So they asked for my resignation. I said, "Okay, I don't want to work for people that don't want me here," so I resigned. I also broke up with my wife at that time.

Anyway, many many years later when I was disabled to the point I could no longer work—this was in 1993—I went back to the VA to get this schizophrenia off my record. The VA gave me an appointment with three psychiatrists, and I was interviewed by all of them at different times of the day. The three thought the "schizophrenia" diagnosis was totally wrong, that I suffered from classic post-traumatic stress disorder, and they recommended my records be changed. Now this was in the nineties, after Vietnam and after a lot of research had been done on post-traumatic stress disorder.

So finally, I got documentation from the VA that I wasn't ever schizophrenic. But in my estimation the VA really owes me for ruining my life. After I got reevaluated in the nineties, the VA said, "We will make every effort to obliterate this from the file." Well, they did, I guess, but it was too late to change things that happened before.

After I got out of the VA hospital in 1956 and got divorced, I remarried. I married a little French girl from Louisiana, and after we came to Colorado, she had cancer and only lived about two or three years after we were married. I remarried again, and Bernadette is my third wife. We've been married almost thirty years.

So my experiences in the Pacific had quite an impact on my life, and just about all that happened to me after the war I can trace back to those experiences. But I believe that I was a good Marine. The fact that I made sergeant in under two years was not the usual thing. It's kind of funny that both of my older brothers, who had been in the Marine Corps longer, I ended up outranking and was their sergeant when we did duty together for a short time in Japan right after the war! Yeah, as I look back on it now, I was a good Marine.

CHAPTER 5

> *"These guys, the Marines, God love 'em, they'd fight until they couldn't fight anymore. They'd fight with broken arms, gunshot wounds, shrapnel wounds, and things like that. I'd patch them up and tell them to go back to the ship and they'd say, 'I'm all right,' and they would just keep fighting."*
>
> —Vern Garrett, NAVY

VERN GARRETT, NAVY, corpsman, USS *Yorktown*, carrier,

and Marine invasions: Tarawa, Guam

ROBERT CLACK, NAVY, corpsman, USS *Yorktown*, carrier

STERLING CALE, NAVY, corpsman, Pearl Harbor, Guadalcanal

DAVE GUTTERMAN, ARMY, medic, New Guinea,

Philippines, Japan

PAGES 154–155: *A corpsman administers morphine to a dying Marine who was hit by sniper fire moments before on Peleliu.*

OPPOSITE: *Vern Garrett (left front) and members of the medical unit at Eniwetok late in the war. Dr. Kirsch is at left in back row.*

# COPING WITH CASUALTIES:
# MEDICS AND CORPSMEN, 1942–45

## VERN GARRETT
NAVY

enlisted in the Navy, but I had a little bit of a push. I knew some guys on the local draft board very well, and they said, "Well, you're going to go pretty quick." So, I beat them to the punch. You know, I had the opportunity to join the Navy and I wanted to join. So, I enlisted in Indianapolis and went to Great Lakes for boot camp. So, there I was in boot camp, and we had an officer come up and he says he was going to do a head count. And we were lined up there and he went down counting us off, "Two, four, six, eight, ten, twelve. Okay, now you guys are going to the medical department." And that's how I became a Pharmacist Mate! So, I went from there to medical school at the University of Chicago. We went seven days a week, eight to ten hours a day, for about six months. The training was like what we would do if certain things happened. For example, if a guy was shot, then what would we do, and that was what we were trained to do. What to do with shock wounds and things like that. We did everything except an appendectomy. And I came out as a pharmacist mate.

From there I went to Norfolk, Virginia, and then I got on the USS *Yorktown* in 1943. I was on the original crew. First we did a shakedown cruise. Then we headed out to the Pacific. When we got to Pearl Harbor they hadn't moved anything. All the ships were still sunken there, and we had a hard time getting that *Yorktown* in there.

I was on the *Yorktown* for about six months. It was like a big hotel. We had twenty-six doctors on the *Yorktown*, and a crew of, I think, it was like 2,500. I was an operating room technician, so I'd help out in the operating room. There were some movies they showed the medical staff on the *Yorktown* that they made at Guadalcanal showing trauma wounds and how to deal with them. In our previous training we hadn't seen much blood, but I saw plenty of blood later. I had emergency training and got assigned to a rescue team. When planes came in all shot up and crashed, we'd pull the pilots and crew out.

So, if you've seen the movie *Fighting Lady*, I'm the guy who goes to that wrecked plane and pulls the pilot out. The pilot's name was Crommelin. He was a commander. That was on the Mili Island raid. It was 650 miles from Tokyo, and this was in 1943. He caught a 20mm shell in the cockpit, and it exploded in there and filled him full of shrapnel. One of the other pilots winged him in, you know, talked him in while flying next to him. His plane was all shot up. So, I think we picked about twenty or thirty pieces of shrapnel out of Crommelin. The plane wasn't burning that bad, but it was shot full of holes. I remember that. My other job was helping out in the OR. It was mainly gunshot wounds, shrapnel, and burns, injured pilots.

When the *Yorktown* got back to Pearl Harbor, I got off and they were going to transfer about three or four of us guys to the fleet Marines, and one of them was me. We didn't know where we were going to go. We talked to an old chief pharmacist mate who did a lot of transferring at Pearl Harbor, and he says, "You don't want to go where you're going to go!" That's when we heard we were heading out into the Pacific with the Marines on some island invasion. We had no idea where we were going, but we found out when we got on the ship that it was Tarawa.

Tarawa was terrible. They really bombed that place. It was great fireworks, I'll tell you. And they bombed that little island for days. They bombed it so much we thought it would be a cakewalk going in. So, the way it worked for us pharmacist mates was that we showed up and were assigned to a company, so that there was one pharmacist mate for every 100 Marines. I went in on a Higgins boat with my company of Marines I'd been assigned to. I really didn't know any of them. But as I was trying to climb down the cargo net to get onto the Higgins boat, I was carrying a forty-pound pack of medical supplies, plus my backpack, so I was carrying maybe sixty pounds, and you had to climb down that cargo net and those are big ropes, and your hands are barely big enough to hold on to them, and I just slipped and fell. I don't know how I landed, but my arms were bruised and I banged my teeth on the steel edge of the Higgins boat. Fortunately there was no blood, just pieces of teeth knocked out. I've got that as a memory of Tarawa! It's lucky I didn't knock my brains out.

So, I got down in that Higgins boat and, you know, going in, you had fear, but we didn't panic for some reason or another. They dumped us way out there and we had to wade in. And then I got shot going in, just a minor wound, a flesh wound. So, I had to find someone else to patch me up, but it wasn't bad, really wasn't much more than a Band-Aid wound. It is difficult to describe all the things that went on at Tarawa. Sometimes when I think about Tarawa it becomes a big blur. When somebody got shot they'd yell for the corpsman, and that was me. Then I'd have to go patch them up, put bandages on, or compresses. That was what we were trained to do. My job was to keep them alive right after they were hit, stop the bleeding if I could. There was always a lot of blood.

So, the first guy I patched up was a back wound, believe it or not. We were wading in and got next to the pier and this guy somehow got shot in the back. So, I patched him up and had him wait there next to the pier until we got enough wounded to make a load to take them back out to the ship. I don't remember many specifics, but I do remember another guy I patched up on Tarawa. He was shot in the stomach. I looked him up after the war. So, we were pinned down there next to that pier right on the beach, and we couldn't go very far; we were all kind of bunched up there right by the pier. And guys were getting shot and I was patching them up right there.

These guys, the Marines, God love 'em, they'd fight until they couldn't fight anymore. They'd fight with broken arms, gunshot wounds, shrapnel wounds, and things like that. I'd patch them up and tell them to go back to the ship and they'd say, "I'm all right," and they would just keep fighting.

Those guys would do that! I was nineteen, and we had some seventeen-and eighteen-year-old kids in there. They just wouldn't give up. That's the Marine Corps; they instilled something in those kids. But I was Navy and I didn't have that kind of training. The thing is, the pharmacist mates were in and out of there and I never got to know anyone real well. They shipped me back to Pearl again after Tarawa. I stayed there about two months, and then I headed to Eniwetok, and then Saipan, Tinian, and Guam. I was in a lot of landings. But you can do that when you're young! On all these islands, we'd bury the dead Japanese face down. The reason for that is, if you bury them face down they go straight to hell, or so they say. We did that on every island we were on. We'd bury them face down. And that tells you what we thought of the Japanese.

Later the Japanese used wooden bullets, and they were bad because they would splinter when they hit the body. If we saw one of those wounds, we wouldn't even touch them. They were sent right back to Pearl Harbor. We'd try to get them to a MASH unit.

I think I would have liked to have stayed on the *Yorktown*. Sometimes you wonder why did you live that long, or how did you do that. I was lucky. The only time I was hurt was on Tarawa, and that was minor.

I got out of the Navy in March of 1946. I was discharged after about three and a half years. The duty on the *Yorktown* was great. All those landings with the Marines, that was rough duty, but it was necessary and I was trained for it. I didn't go into the medical profession, but I have two kids who are doctors. I had nightmares after the war for maybe four or five months. I'd dream of people getting killed. I remembered faces. I had nightmares about people screaming for mercy. You know, people were screaming for mercy all the time, and it's like your hands are tied or something. They'd want to be put out of their misery, and there was nothing I could do for them. They were begging for mercy to die because the pain was so excruciating. There were times that there was bleeding I couldn't stop. We would just shoot them with morphine and let them die. We patched them up as best we could to try and stop the bleeding. But sometimes it's like trying to stop a hole in a dike. We'd sprinkle some sulfa powder on the wound and try and patch them up.

For years I tried to get ahold of a doctor I worked with, Dr. Kirsch, but I never could find him. I've often wondered if my experiences in the war affected the rest of my life. It's the bad stuff you never forget. You can't tell anybody, and you don't feel like telling anybody.

## ROBERT CLACK
NAVY

On February 14, 1943, I was notified that I was to go aboard the USS *Yorktown* for duty. I left the Navy Medical Center at Bethesda, Maryland, where I had been training, and on the same day reported at Newport News Naval Base for temporary duty until the completion of construction of the *Yorktown*. I then got two weeks of leave at home, and came back to the ship on March 11. For the next two weeks I went aboard ship every day and explored the whole thing. It was a beautiful, brand-new, huge ship. I had been trained to be on a damage control party. If there is a crash on deck, we had to get out there and try and save the air crew.

We came back into port for a short time, and I got liberty. There were some other big ships anchored nearby. We finally got under way and made our way over to the Pacific through the Panama Canal. When we got to Pearl Harbor we had difficulty maneuvering in the harbor due to the remains of the sunken ships and the salvage operations.

We weren't there long. One day we watched a lot of the ships in the harbor getting under way, and we figured something was on, since we knew they weren't going back to the States. Finally we went to General Quarters the next morning for getting under way. When we were secured from General Quarters (about 9:30 A.M.) I went out on the fantail to watch Pearl Harbor, Honolulu, and Diamond Head slowly slipping out of sight. Then I went back up on the flight deck to watch the island of Oahu growing smaller and smaller until it disappeared.

We were in company with the *Essex, Cowpens,* and *Independence.* Next morning we went topside and saw a whole fleet of ships in formation. We were thirty-seven in number. There were six carriers. In addition to the three already mentioned, there was also the *Yorktown*, *Lexington*, and *Belleau Wood*, along with seven cruisers and twenty-four destroyers. Rumors, called scuttlebutt, were many and all different, but it was believed by most that we were headed for Wake Island, and finally we got the word confirming this. The message went out to all the crew, "We are to attack Wake Island October 5, 1943, at dawn." I had to admit I was somewhat apprehensive. This was going to be our first action. We got word to cover all bedding, mattress and pillows, with fireproof covering. They told us to be ready for action in a minute's notice. All hatches not absolutely necessary for passage were "dogged" watertight.

We sent our planes out, the ships bombarded the place, and I wondered if there was much left of the island when we were through with it. We didn't have many problems with battle damage, and our damage control crew didn't have to do anything. I felt this was lucky since I was expecting the worst. I was relieved when all the pilots got back okay.

We headed back to Pearl, and in mid-November 1943 we sortied out of the harbor again. Ships of every description—transports, LSTs, cargo ships, tankers, destroyers, battleships, and cruisers—filed out with us. We stood on the flight deck at parade rest, and the band played "Aloha Oe" and "Anchors Aweigh." The mooring detail cast off the last line, and the tugs strained against the hull to help us maneuver out of the harbor. Finally we were under way again, and the *Lexington* followed us shortly thereafter.

After we secured from routine GQ, we saw several ships of the force of which we were a part. As usual we started guessing where we were going, but the late scuttlebutt said it was the Marshall and the Gilbert Islands. After three uneventful days of smooth sailing we were finally given the "Dope." We were part of a force of 224 ships—consisting of carriers, battleships, cruisers, and destroyers—1,100 planes, 3,000 troops, and about 5,000 Seabees.

When we got deep into enemy waters, again all hands covered bedding with flameproof covers. "H" Division hands, me included, were entrusted to check all first-aid stations for any shortages. I helped check life belts throughout the ship. Preparations were being made for the worst.

The first islands we hit were Mili and Jaluit. We pounded these tiny islands all day and burned every building on Mili. Our pilots said they shot up the enemy aircraft before they got off the ground. They also said they knocked out several gun emplacements, one oil storage tank, and three oil trucks. On Jaluit they said they sank one medium tanker and blasted airfields and installations. We lost one plane, and the *Lexington* lost two.

Marines then landed on Tarawa. They were covered by a battleship and the *Enterprise's* task force. Troops landed on Makin Atoll, and our aircraft bombed and strafed in support of that landing. Reports later in the day said our operation on Makin was successful with rather weak opposition. But we heard the Tarawa landing was heavily opposed.

Our task force kept the Japs from repairing their airstrips on Jaluit and Mili, and we patrolled a large area between Truk, which scuttlebutt said was the "Japanese Pearl Harbor," and our landing operations. The other task forces had similar areas to patrol, and together we formed a complete blockade against any operations from Makin to Tarawa. We were in Jap submarine waters, and that was our most dangerous threat most of the time.

In the middle of the afternoon one day, we heard on the ship's PA system, "All hands to battle stations. Prepare to repel air attack." We lost no time getting to our stations. Then the loudspeaker said that enemy planes were only sixty-five miles away—Zeros and bombers.

At this particular time the *Lexington* had the interceptor patrol up, and we and the *Cowpens* immediately launched fighter aircraft. A few minutes later the Jap planes were reported at forty miles away and coming in. At thirty-five miles away *Lexington* fighters intercepted them and shot down about nineteen of the forty with the loss of only one plane. The enemy planes were running the other way before our fighters got to the scene.

I was on damage control party duty, and for an hour or two we sat around reading, alternating on the headphones, or walking around to keep awake. About 6:30 Jim came up to relieve me from the damage control party, and a fellow walked up asking for something for a toothache. I had to go down to sick bay for duty then anyway, so I took him down into the dental office. I gave him something for his toothache and he left the office. Overhead, F4F Wildcats from another carrier were circling. In the low weather they had lost their way and requested permission to land, and we had said yes.

The last F4F came in for what appeared to be a beautiful landing, but for some unknown reason its tail hook never caught a landing cable. It bounced over both barriers and into the planes spotted forward and then burst into flames as her gas tanks exploded. This scattered liquid fire over several men and threatened every plane spotted on the flight deck—and maybe the whole ship. It was pretty dark by this time. TBFS and

SBDS, probably thirty in all, were in the danger zone. Those planes had full gas tanks and 500- or 1,000-pound bombs. Firefighters were on the alert for such things and were throwing water, CO2, and Fomite in the area almost as soon as it was hit. Our flight deck was afire, we were in easy range of Jap planes, and our .50 caliber ammunition started exploding.

I heard about all this later, of course, since I was below decks. As I left the dental office I was aware of an unusual stir around the sick bay and hurried back there. A seaman bearing an unconscious figure came down the ladder area into the dressing room where Dr. Gard had him placed on a portable table. His eyes were bulging out and the veins of his forehead were distended. I recognized him as a former stretcher-bearer from my dressing station crew. It is doubtful he knew what was going on, but he was making a last subconscious struggle for air. Dr. Gard pulled his tongue out and lifted his chin while Turner gave him a couple of strokes of artificial respiration. I went for the resuscitator and stood by to assist. His neck was half again its normal size, and the swollen tissue was filled with fluid from ruptured blood vessels. We used the resuscitator, but he died shortly afterwards. The machine worked fine, but oxygen is of no help if the heart ceases to beat. It turned out the man's neck was broken.

I went back to the dressing room to see if I could help out there. The first thing I saw was four dead bodies. One man had a mangled arm and chest—apparently he had died instantly. Two were burned beyond all recognition. A tattoo, recognized by his buddies, was the only means of identifying one. The other we identified by blood type. This proved to be comparatively easy since his blood group was relatively rare, and the process of elimination matching with surviving crew members led to his identification.

This one accident proved to be deadly. There were a total of five men killed, and fifteen to twenty had injuries of various degrees of seriousness. Four planes were shoved overboard, having been burned and warped until they were of no further use but just in the way.

I had spent several minutes finding men to help identify the others, and trying to keep those who were just curious out of sick bay. Then the GQ sounded and over the PA we heard, "Repel air attack." I was upset, and since I had been on duty in sick bay, as far as I knew the flight deck was burning, making us a perfect target and unable to launch aircraft for fighter support. However, they had put the fire out in two minutes flat, and the air attack never matured.

Next day I heard many intimate stories of just what took place on the flight deck that night, stories from men who were in the midst of it all and, by fate, remained uninjured, and stories from men who saw their buddies burned to death and were unable to help. According to his buddies, one fellow, the worst burned, had a money belt around his waist containing $800. No trace of it was found.

But back at Pearl, for the second time since we came to the Pacific, *Yorktown* was picked by the admiral as a place for the reading of several citations. We all went up to the flight deck in our best whites with new haircuts and shoeshines and stood at attention while the awards were handed out. Last but not least of those awards was the Distinguished Service Cross awarded to our skipper, Captain J. J. (Jocko) Clark, for meritorious execution of orders in carrying out attacks on a number of islands. The *Yorktown* had been in all but one carrier action since August, and we'd never been hit by the enemy. Our planes had scored very high, and we were considered the number-one carrier out there. The *Essex* and the *Lexington* were a month or so senior to us, but we all went into action together. The *Enterprise* and *Saratoga* were good; they were veterans of the entire war to that point. They pioneered carrier warfare out there and deserved a lot of credit. But we were still number one, and it was great being part of that crew!

## STERLING CALE
NAVY

I went into the service in 1937, right out of high school. I wanted to get into "lighter than air" training, and they were just starting the dirigibles then. So I joined the Navy and got assigned to Lakehurst, New Jersey. The day I got there the *Hindenburg* came in from Germany, and I stood there and watched the damned thing blow up and burn. I was supposed to be helping pull it in, but I had just got there. I was too late to join the ground crew, so I was standing there watching. After that disaster, the Navy canceled the dirigible program and sent me all the way back to the West Coast, to San Diego and hospital corps school. I didn't have any choice, they just assigned me to be a hospital corpsman. I didn't mind it because I had always been interested in medical studies. I had been a Boy Scout and Eagle Scout, and we had had first aid training and all that sort of thing. So they trained me to be a hospital corpsman for six months. We trained on everything from A to Z—anatomy, physiology, first aid, minor surgery, and all the stuff that goes with it.

I graduated second in my class, and they asked me, "Where do you want to go, Cale?" And I said, "Well, I'm from Illinois so I'd like to go back there." They said, "Well, we only had one position for Illinois, and the number-one guy in the class took Illinois. But you're second, so you have your choice for world-wide assignments." So I thought, Jesus Christ, being from Illinois and the Midwest, the most water we ever had there was Lake Michigan and the Mississippi River. I had read somewhere about Hawaii out in the middle of the Pacific, so I said, "Oh, hell, send me to Hawaii!" That's about as far away as I could get. So they sent me to Hawaii, and I arrived on my birthday, November 29, 1940, as a brand-new hospital apprentice second class. I was stationed down in the old Naval hospital in Pearl Harbor. I took the course for surgical technician while I was there, and I was assigned to the officers' ward. In June, 1941, I was transferred for duty to the U.S. Naval Dispensary at Pearl Harbor.

On Saturday, December 6, I worked that evening. I was on night duty in charge of the pharmacy and the laboratory. By that time I was a second class pharmacist mate, and they had me on duty at night to take care of the sick or anyone that got hurt in the Navy Yard. I got off duty at 6:30 A.M. on December 7, and after a while I left the hospital. I started walking down the street about a quarter of a mile to the receiving station, where we had to sign in with the master-at-arms, because all the pharmacist mates lived off the post. So I signed in with him and came out, and I noticed planes flying around. Planes maneuvered every month, and the reservists and National Guard would train and have an attack on Pearl Harbor. So, I noticed the planes that morning, but I didn't pay that much attention to them because I thought they were ours. Then I noticed they were dive bombing Ford Island and the battlewagons and were actually firing weapons, so I figured this wasn't a mock attack. I saw one of them turn off to the right, and I saw the rising sun on the fuselage and the wings. I thought, "Hell, those aren't our planes, those are Japanese planes!"

So I rushed back over to the receiving station, took the fire ax, and started breaking down the door into the armory. I handed out those old peashooters, the Springfield rifles, to anyone who came by. But I didn't take one for myself, because pharmacist mates weren't supposed to have weapons. And later I got written up for a court-martial for handing out those rifles. After the attack was over, and late in the day when I came back there, the master-at-arms says, "Don't go anywhere. You're on report." I said, "For what?" And he said, "For breaking into the armory." So I said, "We aren't supposed to protect ourselves?" He said, "It's all right to protect yourself, but this is peacetime, and you can't break into the armory in peacetime when war hasn't been declared." But it turned out that the president declared war the next day, and they dismissed the charges and gave me some sort of award, and a carton of cigarettes!

So anyway, right after I had broken into the armory and handed out the weapons and ammunition, I went on down to Ten-Ten dock. I was just standing there observing when I heard a loud droning sound of aircraft engines coming from in back of me. So I looked around to the east and couldn't see anything because the sun was right in my eyes. But suddenly seven or eight torpedo bombers came in very low out of the sun and flew right over me, over my right shoulder, heading across toward Battleship Row. I could see them drop their torpedoes, and five or six of them were heading to the USS *Oklahoma*. I could see that there was going to be trouble and injuries, and I figured I'd better get over there. So I rushed down to Officers Landing and jumped into a launch and tried to get to the *Oklahoma*. But I never did get there. The *Oklahoma* exploded right in front of us, turned turtle, and sank in seven minutes before we could even get across to the ship. So I spent the next four or five hours in the water pulling guys out and getting them into the launch. I had started to take frogman training and had the medical portion completed already. I was a second class diver and was studying the underwater demolition portion. So I got into the water, swimming around looking for survivors. There was a lot of burning oil on the water, so I'd dive down underneath, swim around, come up, take a breath, see somebody in the water, go back down underneath, and try to pull them over to the launch. I think I picked up some thirty-five people. We were just trying to save lives. Some of them, when we got to them, weren't alive any more. Some were badly injured. Some were okay. Luckily I didn't get hurt. We'd pull these guys out and take them ashore to the hospital if they needed medical treatment.

So this went on for several hours. After that I went back over to the receiving station, and that's when they told me they were writing me up for a court-martial for unauthorized distribution of firearms. Then the master sergeant gave me one of the old Springfield rifles and told me, "Don't let anybody in or out who doesn't belong here." I said, "Okay." So, I'm standing there on guard duty and the medical officer came down, and he comes up to the front door and I snapped to attention and saluted him. He said, "Cale, what are you doing here?" And I said, "Well the master-at-arms says nobody in or out who doesn't belong here." Then he said, "Cale, pharmacist mates don't carry weapons. You carry first-aid kits! I'll have a little job for you later on."

Well, the little job he had for me later on was being in charge of the burial detail on the USS *Arizona*. This was a really difficult assignment, because I had become close to some of the guys on the *Arizona*. We had gone through basic training at Great Lakes together, and some of them were my closest friends in the service. Even later when I was a corpsman on Guadalcanal, I didn't really get to know any of the Marines when we'd go on patrol, because I was assigned to a different group every day. So, I reported down there on the Friday after the attack with half a dozen people, and we had hip boots and gloves clear up to our elbows, and we started to take off bodies. I went aboard the *Arizona*, and the back part of the ship was still just above the water. Suddenly I became sick. I'd never been on a battlewagon before, and as I came aboard it was slightly rocking back and forth. I also saw ashes blowing off the ship. Those were ashes of people who had been burned to death, and I wondered how I was going to pick up ashes of some of these burned people. That's the first time I'd ever been sick like that in my life. It was partly from the ship motion and the smell, but partly because I wasn't able to do anything, and it was human beings' remains being blown off the ship in the breeze.

So we went onboard and started to find bodies. There was one coming out of a hatch. I saw his helmet coming out of the hatch, so I went to pick up the helmet and there was no head. I opened up the hatch, and there's the rest of the body inside, but there was no head. So we picked up that man and put him in a seabag and sent it up to Red Hill, which was the emergency burial place for the Pearl Harbor dead. I was keeping meticulous notes. Every time I picked up a body I thought if I kept a good record of where we found them, they could tell who the person might be because he may be near his duty station. We found a whole bunch of bodies in the fire control tower. There was a ladder that went up there, and they were stacked in there like sardines—solid charcoal about three feet tall. And we'd have to try and spread them apart. An arm may come off or a leg may come off or a head may come off. And we'd just try and get one whole person and put it into a seabag and send them to Red Hill. I guess they were trying to get away from the fire and climbed up there.

So, we could get down as far as the second deck in the back part of the ship, pulling off bodies. And that was very gruesome duty. I worked on that detail for about a week. Most of the rest of my crew were seamen. I just happened to have been put in charge. I realized that some of the bodies we were recovering may have been guys I knew. But at that time we didn't have dog tags. We didn't get those until after Pearl Harbor. But on December 7 no one had anything like that, so it was impossible to really identify the bodies, they had all been burned so badly. The ones down in the water, the fish had already started to feed on. Some of them had some things in their pockets, like a little knife or something, but it wasn't enough to identify them. So I never knew if I took some of my friends off the ship for burial.

Toward the end of this duty I reported back in to the master-at-arms, and he said, "I'm sorry Cale, but it looks like you're headed for a court-martial again." So I said, "What did I do this time?" He said, "You're keeping a war diary." I said, "But I'm not keeping any war diary. I'm taking meticulous notes on where we find the men and how many there are and how many we sent up to Red Hill." He said, "Yeah, but you can't keep a war diary in a time of war. And you can't tell how many men are going and where they're going." I said, "There must be some kind of a circumstance where this is allowed, because we are taking off bodies, and these people can't do any harm to anybody. They're not going to fight again." But the master-at-arms said, "Yeah, but that's the Navy regulation, and you broke it." So they called me over, took my notes, said it was a war diary, and had them burned. I told the commander, "What the hell is going on? I'm in charge of a burial detail doing my duty. Don't call me in because I'm keeping a war diary. It's a war all right, but this is no diary. Those were my notes." "Let it go," he said. "What caused it?" I asked. He says, "The chief warrant officer down at the dispensary reported you for doing this." So I went down there and asked this chief, "Why did you do that?" He says, "You haven't given me any alcohol lately." I was in charge of the pharmacy and laboratory, and every once in a while I'd give him a pint of 180-proof medical alcohol. After they finally found out what this was all about, they gave me another award, and another carton of cigarettes! And I still don't have any court-martials in my record.

Shortly after that they assigned me to the First Marine Division, the Fifth Regiment. I'd never been on any duty like that, and they told me I'd learn fast. So they put me in a vehicle and took me over to the Marine camp, which wasn't too far from Pearl Harbor. Shortly after that we shipped out to invade Guadalcanal. I landed with the Marines there in August 1942. I didn't know what to think. I hadn't been briefed or anything on what was going to happen. I didn't know what happened in the field. I was trained in trauma wounds, as well as what they called "death and medialogical matters," which is how to handle dead bodies. But I never had any field training. There were some other people who came with us from the States, and they had to show me what to do. I only had my whites with me, from working in the hospital, so I had to dye them in coffee grounds to get them khaki. So I was wearing a coffee-grounds khaki uniform as a hospital corpsman in the Marines.

I would usually go out with a platoon on patrol. In my pack I had gauze compresses, plasma, blankets, so a wounded guy could be covered up and wouldn't go into shock, and we always had a lot of sulfa powder.

The first time I went out with a platoon somebody got shot, and they started yelling, "Doc, corpsman!" You run out and try to help, and that's when you may get shot. And getting shot at was quite a bit different from anything I'd experienced before. I never got the feeling anyone was shooting at me at Pearl Harbor. The first guy that I had to deal with on Guadalcanal was already dead. Many times when you went out to fix somebody up he was already dead. All you could do was put him over on the side, take his dog tags, and remember where you put him so you could pick him up on the way back if you were continuing the patrol. We'd either send the wounded back with somebody, or we'd pick them up on the way back.

When I'd get called over to someone who'd been shot, the first thing to do was to find out what happened, to figure out the nature of the wounds. A lot of times they'd be bleeding underneath their uniforms, and you couldn't tell what kinds of wounds they had unless you got to him and his arm was blown off or his leg was blown off, or he got shot in the head. But he may have a sucking wound in the chest, a hole in his lungs, and he'd be having a hard time breathing, then you'd try and patch the hole up so he wouldn't be losing his air. But if there was bleeding from underneath the uniform, you would have to cut the uniform off of them. You'd cut the pants leg down the seam and split it open, or cut open their shirt. The first thing was to try and stop the bleeding. If you could, you'd try to put on some kind of tourniquet between the wound and the heart. Then you'd sprinkle a lot of sulfa powder over the wound area, patch them up, give them a shot from a morphine Syrette, and bind their wounds. Some of them went back to duty, and some of them you'd have to call for a stretcher to haul them back to the first-aid tent.

But these Marines were really tight with each other; you know, there is that "Semper Fi" stuff in the Marine Corps. They all had trained together, and everybody looked out for the other people. So when one of the Marines would get shot, his buddies would get real concerned and try to help. I was an outsider, but for them the corpsman was the main person who could save their lives, and they'd protect the corpsmen against anything. In that way the corpsman was the best buddy they had! There wasn't anybody else who was going to come out and patch them up when they got shot.

The conditions were very miserable on Guadalcanal. It was very hot and rainy, and especially hot and humid at night, and there were lots of mosquitoes. We all took those great big orange malaria pills, which turned us yellow. Even though we were taking the pills, a lot of guys got malaria anyway. People would get a lot of bites. It was so hot at night that some of the guys would strip down, and then the mosquitoes would bite them. I kept my clothes on to try to minimize the bites, and we had some mosquito repellent you could rub on your body. But the problem was that for some skin areas that were exposed, like your neck, you would perspire and dilute the repellent, and that's where the mosquitoes would bite.

I was on Guadalcanal for a month or two. Then one day I got orders to report for duty to Illinois! This was a pretty big shock, and of course I thought this was great, first because I'd get off Guadalcanal, and second because I was from Illinois, and that's where I had wanted to go in the first place. I went back through Hawaii and had to spend some time there. They did all kinds of testing on me to make sure I didn't have malaria or any other diseases. While I was there, on December 12, 1942, I got married to a woman I'd met when I was stationed there before the war. And then we moved to Illinois, and I never got back to the Pacific during the war.

While I was based in Illinois, my wife thought it was too cold. She was from Hawaii and wanted to go back there. So I requested a transfer, and it took six different assignments before I got back to Hawaii, but we finally got there in 1947.

I have never had problems with bad dreams or nightmares from my various experiences. I often wonder, geez, I've seen people in bad shape at Pearl Harbor, and people shot and dying at Guadalcanal, and I don't dream about it. I just don't think about it. I've never been back to Guadalcanal, and I've never wanted to go back. And I've never wanted to go back to Korea or Vietnam either.

I've always liked living in Hawaii. I met my wife there, I got married there, and I've lived there since the late 1940s, except when I had assignments to Korea or Vietnam. But in all that time of living in Hawaii, I never went over on the USS *Arizona* Memorial, because I knew my friends from basic training had been killed on that ship. When I came back from Vietnam in 1974, that's the first time I went over to the Memorial and looked at the list of names of the dead they have there. I went down the list and thought, "I knew that guy, and that guy, and that guy. . . ."

# DAVE GUTTERMAN
ARMY

I was from the Bronx, and it was getting kind of lonely after the war started, since most of my friends had already left for the service. I was ready to go, but I was still in high school. So I got drafted into the Army right out of high school, and I had basic at Fort McClellan in Alabama, which was quite a change for a boy from the big city. After basic training, our commanding officer lined us up and said, "Well, you guys did pretty good, and from here you'll be going off to hell's kitchen." And that's just about what happened. We piled onto a troop train, and one morning we woke up in Fort Bliss, Texas. We see guys in boots and breeches, and horses, so we said, "What the hell is going on?"

I found myself in the First Cavalry Division, Seventh Regiment. That was Custer's old command—his last, as it happened. They started right away teaching us to ride horses, since we were a cavalry outfit. They took us out to corrals, and we were trained how to ride horses. I really enjoyed it, but the first time I got on a horse I was wondering if I was going to stay on or get knocked off—one or the other. Being a city boy from the Bronx, it took me a while to learn how to ride a horse, but I liked it.

I ended up as a medical corpsman, an aid man. The way this happened was that one day they lined us up and said, "Any volunteers?" And then they said, "You, you, and you." And that's how I ended up as a medic. It wasn't bad, but in combat it got kind of rough at times, because you have to go out there and get the wounded. We did carry side arms, but when you are out there under fire you're ducking, and you aren't thinking about using a side arm. You're just trying to get the wounded guy out as fast as possible.

We finally got shipped out to Australia and landed in Brisbane. We got there in June or July of 1943, which was winter there in Australia, and it was cold! We were in a camp outside of town and got jungle training there. Australia was a very nice country, and I enjoyed it there. We'd get leave and go to town, and that's where we first tasted Australian beer. And holy cow, the goddamned beer was warm! But once I got to drinking it, I liked it. I think you got drunk faster on that warm beer. There were a couple of dances we went to, and the Australians were very personable. I think the Australians liked us. We had no problems. And in combat, those Australians were tough. We stayed there for a while, and then they shipped us to New Guinea.

We landed at Oro Bay in New Guinea. This wasn't a combat landing, the beach already had been secured. There we did more jungle training, night training in the jungle, and we were there for about another month. Then we went into our first combat in the Admiralty Islands, just north of New Guinea. We went down the cargo nets and into the landing craft. They were bobbing and weaving, and I was kind of scared getting over into those goddamned landing craft. You wonder if you are going to make it or not. I know that there were a few broken legs, where guys slipped and fell off those cargo nets. But you have a job to do, and you have to get down with the rest of the guys. You don't want to chicken out, but you're still scared. You just try not to show it.

So that was our first combat landing, and you think, "This is the real thing, buddy!" Actually, that first landing was fairly safe, they weren't shooting back much there, not like later. Our objective was the Momote airfield. Some other troops ahead of us took the airfield, so we moved inland, but we started to get a couple of guys knocked off. Then you know that this is the real thing, and that's when you start worrying and sweating it out, and you're scared. We were advancing on a muddy road, and every so often you would see wounded guys getting carried back from action ahead of us. Those troops had their own aid men, so I wasn't involved yet in picking up wounded. We were going up the road in a double column, and every so often the column stopped when there'd be mortar fire or something. At this point you don't really know if you're going to chicken out; you don't know that until you actually get called to go after a wounded guy. So we started to get hit, and they were calling for an aid man, and just for a moment you hesitate, geez, do you want to go out there and risk getting hit yourself? But you go, and you just kind of dodge up to where the guy is, and you're scared as hell. I was just hoping I wasn't going to get clobbered too. You try to talk to the guy and tell him he's okay and it's not too bad, just relax, maybe give the guy

*Coping with Casualties*

a cigarette. If he was in pain you'd shoot him with a morphine Syrette, which was like a quarter grain of morphine, or something like that. If he was bleeding you'd try and tie him off. You'd open that big package of gauze compresses and patch him up. Sometimes you'd go out alone, and sometimes the stretcher-bearers would follow. If they didn't follow you but you needed them, you'd holler for stretcher-bearers, and soon a couple of guys would come running out with the stretchers.

There was another spot in the Admiralties called Manus Island that we landed on. It was another island in that group, but it was just a thick jungle. The objective there was an airstrip at Lorengau. After we took it, you should have seen what they did to it. They made it a playground! The Seabees turned it into a big base. It was amazing what those guys did.

After the Admiralties we rested a little while, and then we hit the Philippines. Our first landing in the Philippines was on Leyte, at Tacloban. It got kind of rugged for a while there. Then we got on LSTs and landed at Lingayen Gulf, where we saw a few of those kamikazes. Some of our ships got hit. After we landed, the Filipinos really welcomed us; they liked us. They were all yelling, "*Mabuhay*," which means hello. Then we headed down toward Manila. I watched Manila burn, and we liberated the city. Then we ended up fighting in the mountains.

Near the town of Enfante we had our first experience with a banzai attack. It was at night, and you're already scared as hell. It was just before dawn when we heard a lot of howling and screaming out in front of our positions, and suddenly there was a bugle blown and here they came. We threw everything but the kitchen sink at them. They broke through a little, but it wasn't too disastrous, though it was really scary. I was back at the CP about that time, just a little behind the frontline foxholes. We were hoping they wouldn't break through completely. The Japs were crazy that way, and it seemed like they didn't care for their lives.

We left the Philippines at the end of July, and then we were getting ourselves ready to invade Japan. I didn't expect that I'd live through it if we made that landing. So I was certainly glad they dropped those atomic bombs. That's a hell of a thing to say, but that's the way I feel.

I made it through without a scratch, but I was pretty sick a couple of times. I was in the hospital once with the crud, you know, jungle rot. I got it and I couldn't move! Then I got malaria and went to the hospital. It turned out that when I came down with it and headed to the hospital, the outfit took quite a beating that night. I was lucky and never had a recurrence of malaria.

One time we went out on a thirty-day patrol, about a dozen of us, with just a radio, looking for Japs. On the way back, as we were finishing that patrol, we saw a barge about a 100 yards away from us, and there were Army guys guarding it. There was a big canvas cover on it, but part of that cover was flapping in the wind. We took a closer look and said, "Goddammit, that whole barge is loaded with beer!" So we kind of drifted over toward those guys and said, "Hey, how about some of the beer?" We had picked up some souvenirs, some Jap hats and a couple of rifles and stuff like that, and we traded them for about a half-dozen cases of beer. That night when we got back to camp, we had a real good time!

With a buddy of mine, who ended up being my best man, we were in a combat situation where at one point we were pinned down, grenades being thrown and all that, when suddenly the guy gets hit by a grenade fragment. His wife got a telegram after that, and she was all excited that he got wounded. But it was just a little scratch on his ass, and she thought he was dying! We were all laughing about that at the time. But he got a purple heart for that.

I received a silver star for two incidents that happened on the same day. We were in combat in the Philippines, and we were out on patrol. We were going through the jungle, and these guys were out front about twenty-five or thirty yards, the point men, and all of a sudden the Japs opened up. There was Jap machine-gun fire, crossfire, and our men got hit, and they were calling, "Medic!" I hesitated for just a second—you're afraid to go out there yourself—but I crawled out there. You have to go out after the guys that are hit, and you're right in the line of fire. Naturally you're scared as hell, but you have to go out there. I crawled out to those guys, and I patched them up as best I could, and the Japs were shooting at us. I had to drag them back one at a time to where the stretcher-bearers were, and they got them back to the rear. Then it got quiet for a little while, but there was more firing nearby, and there was a call for a medic. There wasn't a medic around where those guys got hit, so they called on me, and I volunteered to go over there. I went after them, and there were three guys hit up there. So it was the same thing, I had to crawl out there, patch them up, and drag them back to get them out of the line of fire. It was kind of hard when they are shot up. You're trying to give them plasma and anything else they need, and this wasn't easy because there were a couple of Jap snipers taking potshots at us. And again I got them to where the litter-bearers could get them to the rear. This took a little while, because I had to patch them up and then try to drag them back to the litter-

*Coping with Casualties*

bearers, and then the Japs were shooting at them, too. The litter-bearers didn't get hit; they were kind of lucky, and I guess I was kind of lucky, too. You say a prayer here and there. I heard later those guys lived. I didn't get the medal until I got home, and then they finally sent it to me.

We landed in Japan on the day the surrender was signed in Tokyo Bay. That day they wanted us dressed in khaki uniforms, which we were. But still we had our weapons, just in case. They said something about expecting problems from an outfit called the Black Dragon Society, so just in case, we went in fully loaded. We landed and marched through their streets, and they were subdued. As you were marching by, you'd look at the houses and you'd see people kind of taking sneaky looks through curtains, watching us. It was a good feeling we didn't have to battle them. When we landed, my only feeling about the Japanese was that we defeated the bastards. But after being there about a month it wasn't that bad. The Japanese people were subdued and nice and friendly. There was one little incident where one of the Japanese got a little wild, and one of our guys had to shoot him, but just in the arm or leg. They took him to the hospital, and he was okay. He got a little crazy; that's about it. We were in a Jap naval barracks there that we took over for a while. Then it became very boring there. And then we heard we were going to go home on points. I was there until October 1945. I went home on the USS *Hershey*.

In general, I enjoyed Army life, but once we were ready to get out, it was like, let's get the hell out of here, let's go. But it was an adventure. One of the high points of the war for me was that I made it through. If I had to do it again, I would.

# CHAPTER 6

*"We were doing work that nobody else could do, coaxing valuable information from prisoners that could save American lives."*
—Henry Fukuhara, ARMY

BOB SHEEKS, MARINES, Japanese language officer,
Tarawa, Saipan, Tinian

DAN WILLIAMS, MARINES, Japanese language officer,
Saipan, Tinian, Iwo Jima

HARRY FUKUHARA, ARMY, Nisei interpreter, New Guinea,
Philippines, Hiroshima

PAGES 178–179: *Japanese Language Officer Bob Sheeks assists a Japanese civilian in making surrender appeals using a jeep-mounted loudspeaker during the Tinian campaign in 1944.*

OPPOSITE: *Bob Sheeks, kneeling in foreground, broadcasts surrender appeals through jeep-mounted loudspeakers to cliffs in background on Tinian where Japanese military and civilian personnel are hiding.*

# COMMUNICATING WITH THE ENEMY: INTERPRETERS, 1942–45

## ROBERT B. SHEEKS
MARINES

I was born of American parents in Shanghai in 1922 and grew up there, until age thirteen. My father and my mother moved to Shanghai not long after the First World War, and he worked there as a business executive. We lived in the French Concession, a well-to-do section of the city where affluent American and European families resided. My mother died when I was ten years old, and in 1935 my father, brother, and I returned to the U.S.

After grabbing Manchuria, Japanese forces attacked at Shanghai in 1932 to quell anti-Japanese demonstrations, boycotts, and also some Chinese civilian and military armed resistance. Japan later labeled the action "The Shanghai Incident," but it was very real, extremely brutal warfare.

It was in 1932 that I saw evidence of Japanese military atrocities in Shanghai. These had been profusely and gruesomely illustrated in newspaper photographs, but I also was an eyewitness to something Japanese soldiers did. One day Dad drove us to the evacuated residence of a British family in the Northern Shanghai suburb of Hongkew. We had learned that our friends had fled from Shanghai and taken temporary refuge in Hong Kong. We had visited their beautiful, large home and broad gardens before and began looking around. The house had been looted and was a mess. Then, in the back garden, we saw something horribly revolting. Two servants, still there as caretakers, had been tied onto poles by the Japanese and then literally grilled to death.

The torturers had built fires in the garden, trussed their victims like hogs, and roasted them to death. Japanese soldiers did things like that. Why? Well, our Chinese friends had an explanation. The Japanese thought the Chinese servants would know where money or other valuables had been hidden. They figured the servants would do anything to escape pain and when tortured would reveal everything. So the Japanese persisted. As a result, I carried for years a heavy load of hatred of Japan and believed that Japanese by nature were cruel and bestial. One might stomach their arrogance, but not their needless torture of helpless Chinese people. After we resettled back in the States and while I was going to junior high school in California, on my bedroom dresser I kept a death shrine. There was a hate picture of the Japanese Emperor and the Crown Prince, which I had clipped from a magazine. I hoped to kill them some day.

Harvard accepted me and granted scholarship support, so off I went to college. Right after Pearl Harbor, the Office of Naval Intelligence in Washington compiled lists of people with any Asian language background, Japanese preferred. I had a little Chinese language ability, and no Japanese. But the Navy needed recruits and was scraping the bottom of the barrel. They were even taking people who had studied Egyptian hieroglyphics, because it was thought they would be good at learning other languages or doing code work. A U.S. Naval officer, Commander A. E. Hindmarsh, came to Harvard looking for candidates to send to the Navy Japanese Language School.

He was a Harvard graduate and had been in charge of the Navy's Japanese language school at Pearl Harbor, which was being relocated to the University of California at Berkeley. So Commander Hindmarsh recruited me at Harvard, and also some of my friends and classmates. That is how we ended up at Berkeley learning Japanese a month after Pearl Harbor was attacked. I was there only half a year before the Navy relocated the language school to the University of Colorado. This was done so that our Japanese-American instructors would not be sent to internment camps. On the West Coast, Japanese-American families were being rounded up and sent voluntarily, or otherwise, to inland locations for the duration of the war.

So there I had been at Berkeley, now at Boulder, immersed in Japanese language training. I had carried a burning, quite poisonous hatred of things Japanese since leaving Shanghai. But who was now training us but

Japanese Americans. They were among the finest, most admirable people I had ever met, thoughtful, cultured, kindly, excellent teachers, and doing more for the war effort than I ever had done. In spite of the fact that they had relatives dispossessed and sent into grim camps, having lost all their family property and savings in California and other West Coast states, they were training us future "warriors" to go out and fight people of their ancestry. When we were shown confiscated Japanese movies at CU for our language training, and after I read about Japanese history and culture, the exposure and contact began to heal my warped, poisonous childhood emotions. Long before the war ended, I became an admirer of many elements of the Japanese character and culture. I began to think, well now, except for those militaristic totalitarian types the Japanese aren't bad. Soon I was able to keep hating Tojo and the Emperor and the Japanese military, but certainly not all Japanese people.

Our Japanese language course was intense, and we had to learn fifty new words a day. The load accumulated fast. We had four hours of class every day and were expected to put in eight hours a day minimum of study, perhaps even ten hours. We had exams every Saturday, all day long, and we were expected to know everything we had learned, cumulatively. We were supposed to be able to read, write, and speak, but there was too much to learn so quickly. We were under such pressure that, of our small class of thirty-five or so we later had two suicides. I heard that among trainees from other graduating classes, there were suicides later in the war. After we graduated, we pretty much went in different directions. I was assigned to Camp Elliot, outside of San Diego, where I was to brush up on terminology suitable for Marine combat operations. The Navy school had provided almost nothing that pertained to fighting on land, so at Camp Elliot we were taught the Japanese for words such as "mortar," "grenade," "howitzer," etc.

The Marine Corps then sent me to the Second Marine Division, which was being reinforced in New Zealand, with a shipload of replacement recruits on the SS *Lurline*, a former luxury liner that used to carry tourists to Hawaii. The ship zigzagged for safety, making its way across the Pacific to Wellington via stops in Samoa and Melbourne. Marines on board were replacements for casualties at Guadalcanal and to increase the size of the Second Division.

We stopped briefly in Samoa, for one day and one night. But while there I saw a little bit of Pacific island culture. I had been assigned to Shore Patrol, wearing a big "SP" armband and on alert for "any trouble," meaning drunken rowdiness. I had never done any police duty or anything like it. We were checking to see if any sailors or Marines were too drunk or boisterous, or offending the Samoans. Mostly it was a matter of liquor. I don't know what I would have done if I had run into a major problem. I took a short break from SP patrolling to witness a "*taupo*" festival, honoring an especially distinguished village maiden, who is treated like a queen.

It was beautiful. At the ceremony, in a Polynesian-style thatch meeting house, the Samoans were very serious and dignified. The atmosphere was churchly, the women dressed in full-length sarongs. There was a big community kava bowl, from which drinks were dipped. Men looking like chiefs would stand up and give talks. There was beautiful choral singing, and some swaying dance to the music. One of the elders saw that this young kid in uniform was genuinely interested in the event, so he kindly explained to me what it was about. I have thought I would like to return to Samoa someday to see and hear such a ceremony again.

We went from Samoa to Melbourne, and then on to Wellington. At that season, Wellington was cold and wet, and we had to march over slippery and wet hills. It was winter there, August, and we were living in tents. Later I got lucky and was provided room space in a regular farmhouse.

I knew a little about the next invasion before it happened, but I didn't know any specifics about Tarawa. Only when we were on our way there were we told that the target was Tarawa. The ship I was on, the *Monrovia*, was the second-level command ship, and the Marine commander onboard was General Leo Hermle. When we arrived at Tarawa, bombardment had already started. We were to land on this tiny island called Betio, just an islet that was part of Tarawa Atoll. Everybody aboard the *Monrovia* thought no Japanese could survive the intense aerial bombardment and naval shelling of Betio, because the whole little island was a mass of smoke and flame. U.S. planes were dive-bombing and strafing. We thought they were eradicating and evaporating the entire island. That went on and on.

Soon it dawned on us that indeed somebody was left alive on the island when they started shelling us, and their big shells were coming in close to our ship! The Navy decided they didn't want to have ships sunk and withdrew, delaying the landing, leaving landing craft circling and waiting. Then more planes, more bombing, more shelling. Again we thought certainly nobody could survive. It was amazing. When we looked at the tiny island, with all its palm trees shattered, it looked more

*Communicating with the Enemy*

like the surface of the moon. But we had a few old battle hands like Colonel Edson, who said, "You'll be surprised. There'll be plenty of resistance." No one believed him, but we began to feel a bit nervous.

Soon the interrupted landing restarted, and the boats and amtracs headed in to the beach. Some of the first guys got in okay because the Japanese were holding their fire until more troops were wading in and the beach got crowded. Then they let us have it. We couldn't evacuate casualties immediately, but later, at Saipan, returning boats came back right away with wounded. At Tarawa, everybody went in and nobody came back right away. So those of us still onboard ships didn't really know what was happening. We could hear a lot of firing going on, so we could surmise that the Japanese were still very much alive and it wasn't just us shooting them. We were not getting radio reports, other than bad news that boats were being sunk, and that casualties were high.

It was then that I started to see a few guys returning from landing attempts, one with the side of his face shot off, one missing a hand. On the beach, all hell had broken loose and communications weren't working too well. We heard blurted voices saying they need water and plasma and ammunition. People were kind of in shock.

General Hermle, on my ship, was second in command of the division and the landing operation, but part of the force was held in reserve onboard ships. The situation was so serious that it seemed essential that some group go in and find out what was going on. Hermle volunteered to lead this group, and it was really something for a general to do that.

I was ordered, but had volunteered, to be part of his group. We loaded up and went in in our Higgins boat, one of the wooden landing craft with a drop-front ramp. It was hit by bullets, and the coxswain was shot in the muscle under his arm, so he couldn't steer very well. He was really bleeding, but he kept saying, "I'm all right, I'm all right!" We wanted to be sure to get to shore and not be stuck on the reef. A nearby amtrac, an amphibious tractor that had discharged its people was headed back to the ships. We flagged it down, and General Hermle commandeered it for our use. We all transferred into it from the boat. It was somewhat safer because at least it was metal, not plywood. The amtrac took us to the seaward end of the long main pier.

When we got there, General Hermle said to me, "Sheeks, go in and see if you can get a prisoner and find out what's going on." In retrospect it seems ludicrous, but if you are a kid and a general tells you something like that, you just say, "Yes, sir," and do it. The general stayed in the amtrac because he was in charge of communications and had to report back to the command ship. He kept reporting constantly what he could see, but of course he couldn't see much of anything! He was too far away and there was smoke and haze.

We were under rather heavy fire, so I went wading and crawling toward shore under the pier in the chest-deep water. It was an awful mess down there, full of wounded guys who had drifted in. They were hanging onto the pier's coconut log pilings to survive, guys scared out of their wits taking refuge. Others were trying to keep from drowning if the tide rose. Here I was, still with my shiny little second lieutenant bars on, and these guys were saying, "Lieutenant, Lieutenant, help us."

You weren't supposed to wear insignia into battle, but I needed to show authority since I was only twenty-one years old and looked even younger. Anyway, I tried to make some encouraging remarks. With one other Marine, I attempted to get up and crawl along the top of the pier. We half crawled, and half walked hunched over. When we were shot at, we jumped back down into the water and stepped back under the pier again. Even crawling on top of the pier was easier than trying to move forward in the water among the pilings.

We had been issued morphine Syrettes and used them all up on the wounded in greatest pain. While somebody went back to get a corpsman, I continued on my mission with several guys wading and crawling toward shore. We naively believed we were going to grab a Japanese prisoner to find out what was going on! I mean the assignment was really pathetic.

Soaked from head to toe with saltwater and grime, I got about two-thirds of the way in along the pier, which must have been at least a couple of hundred yards long. I got to a gap in the pier where a large shell had hit it, and there was a lot of firing right there at the gap. Of course we were scared, but also it seemed pointless to continue crawling toward shore, since obviously I wasn't going to be able to catch a prisoner. So we went back out to the far end of the pier, somewhat sheltered from the firing. By this time it was late in the day, getting dark, and we were bone tired. It was the farthest point from the beach, and we thought we might get some sleep. During the whole Tarawa battle it seems to me that I got only a couple hours of decent sleep, trying to nod off on hard coral gravel with firing going on, soaked with salty seawater, fearful of snipers. It was a relief when night was over. But then came the fiery hot sun. You are groggy the whole hot tropical day, dozing if and when possible.

On the second day I caught a ride on a passing landing craft out to a

*Communicating with the Enemy*

headquarters battleship, thinking I would catch up with General Hermle and try to report what I had been able to see at the pier. Unable to find him, I grabbed a few hours sleep on deck. When you are so short of sleep you don't really crave anything else. After that nap, I could move around on my own, because duty for me was not so organized. I didn't have any companions in this language racket until later the second day. At that time, I went back onto the island, having learned that Green Beach, on the west end, was okay for landing. So we did an end run, but the tide had gone out, and the reef water was really shallow.

On shore it was a big problem finding where everybody was. Finally I ran into a couple of our senior Japanese language officers, Captains John Pelzel and Eugene Boardman. They were in a terrible place, bogged down in a taro pit. Japanese snipers were in the tops of palm trees firing at them, but we couldn't see them. At least one was firing directly at us, and somebody finally shot him. The sniper had been quite close, about thirty or forty feet away, in one of the few palm trees that hadn't been completely blasted by bomb and shell explosions. We should have been more suspicious earlier.

It seemed impossible to capture live prisoners. From then on our efforts were aimed at retrieving maps and documents from the bodies. I thought some of them were alive, just wounded, you know. I imagined one of them was moving and had survived, but he hadn't. It was pretty hard to find any live enemy. In these firefights nobody was giving up. Some of the Japanese we later did take prisoner had been stunned by grenades, so Marines were able to drag them alive out of emplacements. Toward the end of the battle, we did get a number of Korean laborers who surrendered themselves. They knew about putting hands up, but they didn't have white flags, and they didn't really know how to surrender. The Japanese military had never been told that surrender was a possibility, and they never imagined surrendering. But as you can imagine, if you are a Korean labor battalion guy and aren't thinking you are a samurai, you're more likely to surrender than the regular Japanese military types. Some of the Japanese troops committed suicide to avoid capture. They either blew themselves up by hand grenade, or put a rifle under their chin and pulled the trigger with a toe.

There were strange gushing noises at night, especially off of Green Beach. It turned out to be great schools of fish coming in to feed on the bodies and body parts. They weren't sharks, just fish. You could hear fish jumping and splashing. The bodies would wash around, and fish would swarm in to feed on them.

By the time the battle was over on the fourth day, we were gathering together what few prisoners we had. MPs were bringing them along to the beach. I tried to quickly interrogate the ones who were dying to see what they knew before they died. Eventually several batches were pulled together, and I was ordered to take them out to a ship that was standing by. I was to accompany them back to Pearl Harbor, interrogating them all the way enroute.

I learned a lot from Tarawa. I became aware of a major obstacle to capturing prisoners alive: How could you possibly communicate with the enemy when you could hardly hear yourself think during the fighting? War is really noisy! One time I was near Dave Shoup, who really made a name for himself as a powerful combat leader at Tarawa. We were talking loudly among ourselves, there was firing going on, and Colonel Shoup made a memorable remark. He did not say the war was getting on his nerves or that it was dangerous. He complained only about the noise. He said, "God, how can a man think with all this noise going on!" You never consider noise as the worst part of war, but for Shoup it disturbed his thinking.

For communicating with the enemy during battle, even if you had a loudspeaker it probably would be useless. If you had a good situation you could try shouting, but shouting in a foreign language is not easy. If you have a loudspeaker, you could stay farther back, behind an obstacle, and your voice could still be heard. At Tarawa I couldn't really speak to anybody. In the first place if you got up and tried to shout you might not survive. So you needed a loudspeaker to project your voice. I thought if I had been able to talk to some of the Japanese before we killed or captured them, we might have got some more prisoners, and capturing them might have been much simpler.

The other thing I learned at Tarawa was that the Japanese did not know how they were supposed to surrender. They had no familiarity with our customs involving surrender, like using white flags. In fact, the Japanese didn't think surrender was even an option. The top brass had indoctrinated the troops that no Japanese in all of history had ever surrendered! They believed that anyone who gave up was no longer Japanese, not a citizen any more, could never go home, would be a disgrace to family and Emperor and Japan as a nation. This was driven into them. There were no instructions about what to do if they did happen to be captured. So you could see what we were up against, and it didn't really dawn on us early in the war that the Japanese mentality was so very dif-

*Communicating with the Enemy*

ferent from ours. We really needed somehow to let Japanese troops know that survival and surrender were feasible, that some troops had already surrendered safely, and that the idea was not unthinkable. I pondered this matter while going back from Tarawa to Hawaii with our Japanese and Korean prisoners. We had something like sixteen or eighteen prisoners, none of them of high rank, no officers. They didn't have much information, so we didn't get much out of them.

In Hawaii I was assigned temporarily to the CINCPAC headquarters of Admiral Chester Nimitz at Pearl Harbor. I lived in a BOQ in Honolulu with some language officer colleagues who were also at Pearl Harbor. The office I worked in was right next to where decoding was done. We non-specialists weren't allowed in there although we were Intelligence officers doing classified work. Even where my desk was located was walled off from others, because I was working on stuff they thought should be highly classified. I helped to write reports, illustrated books really, about Japanese military buildings on fortified islands. I prepared two volumes about Betio Island, using Japanese maps and captured structural drawings, and photographs we had taken.

Then, by chance, I met a spectacularly beautiful gal at the wedding of a friend. She was in the wedding reception of my friend George Ewart, an English-Chinese Eurasian lad from Shanghai, who had just married a Chinese-American girl named Gladys. Much to my delight, when I was introduced to the glamorous girl we started conversing. She was about twenty and looked like a supermodel. I learned that she was of Portuguese/Chinese/Hawaiian descent. That was my exposure to cultural anthropology. It turned out she was a singer and dancer in a musical review restaurant in Honolulu. The place had an awful hybrid name, "La Hula Rhumba." She invited me to visit the restaurant as her guest. It was a large night club right in the main part of Waikiki that served dinners, fancy and expensive. She was a leading showgirl and performed very graceful, slow hula dances while singing in Hawaiian. She was marvelous to watch: tall, slim, curvaceous, long black hair, wonderfully decorative. I realize that I should have suspected there would be a husband or equivalent boyfriend around someplace, but there had been no sign or mention of one at the wedding reception. I should have asked George or Gladys Ewart about her marital status, but perhaps I did not really want to know.

That girl was so beautiful and seemed so available. Of course, I was very available and unmarried. We enjoyed drinks and conversation together at the reception and agreed it would be nice if we could see each other again soon. We certainly did so, almost immediately, and began an affair that was surreptitious in accordance with her preference. It had to be surreptitious because, I was told, she was still living at home with her old-fashioned parents. When we went out together, she always wanted it to be lunchtime, rarely for an early dinner, because of her evening hours at La Hula Rhumba. That went on for weeks and then months.

Suddenly one day, around noon, I was startled to get a personal phone call from her at my office. She said, "I have to see you immediately." I asked if it could wait until evening, after my office hours. She said it was very urgent and could not wait. You can imagine that the first thing that sprang into the mind of an amorous young man was, "My God, she's pregnant!" But that wasn't the reason for the urgency. No, that wasn't it at all. I rushed from Pearl Harbor to downtown Honolulu to meet her at a coffee shop. She immediately began explaining, "I've got to apologize, and, Bob, I have three things to tell you. First, I'm married. Second, my husband has found out about us. And third, he wants to kill you!" Just like that! I felt like I had been shot right between the eyes.

When I regained calm, I said, "Do you mind if I ask you a question?" She said, "You are going to ask me why I didn't tell you I was married." I replied, "No, that isn't my first question. My first question is, how did he learn about you and me?" Then another shock. She said, "I told him." She explained, "The two of us were having an awful, fighting argument about something. I told him that our marriage was hopeless, and blurted out that I was in love with a Marine officer. I said it to hurt him. He already knew who you were through your mutual friend George, but nothing about our relationship. One time he had seen us lunching together, but I had explained we were just friends, had met at the wedding, and had run into each other at lunch time. Today he talked with George Ewart about you and wanted to know how to find you. He told George, 'Your Marine friend that my wife met at your wedding is having an affair with her.'" I said to her, "It doesn't surprise me that he's upset!"

She and I discussed what we were to do, and we agreed not to see each other for a while. The next few days were full of apprehension. We did not meet in person, but did speak by phone. Suddenly fate stepped in. Out of the blue, orders came for me to rejoin my division at Kamuela on the Big Island of Hawaii, where it was stationed at the huge Parker Cattle Ranch, preparing for the next campaign. Suddenly I was on my way out of Honolulu. It was a relief to be going off to war.

*Communicating with the Enemy*

That girl was so lovely, it was hard to believe her beauty was entirely natural, but it was. I knew I could not forget her, but I also realized that her husband might be waiting to kill me in Hawaii. That memory also haunted me through all the rest of two more years in the Pacific, through the invasions, all the dangers, and everything. Of course I was in much more imminent danger during battle, but the threat of being killed by a jealous husband in Hawaii remained in my mind, especially as I would be going back through Honolulu sooner or later if I survived the war.

During my time in Hawaii, we devised things like a so-called "Surrender Pass," which had instructions in Japanese (also English) about surrender procedures, use of white flags, etc.

I was able to get a variety of leaflets printed by the *Honolulu Advertiser* newspaper, as their contribution to the war effort. We made bundles of about five hundred leaflets each, delivered them to friends who were pilots and aerial artillery spotters, and they dropped them from small, light aircraft at prearranged locations. We feared that most might be used as toilet paper by the enemy, but some did get through. Mostly the texts were about Japan losing the war, about surrendering, etc. It was an improvised, amateurish project, but later seemed to show some results.

There were no official funds available, and the only financial source we could come up with for propaganda supplies and equipment was the division's recreation budget. So we diverted recreation funds to pay for loudspeaker equipment to use for voice beaming to Japanese soldiers in fortified emplacements and caves.

The whole idea at the time seemed outlandish to most Marines, as everyone was convinced that no Japanese would ever surrender. I wasn't that sure myself that any of these things would achieve important results. However, by the time we were loading up for the Marianas campaign, I was pleased that we had cartons of wrapped leaflets ready for dropping, and hand-held, battery-powered megaphones, and jeep-mounted loudspeakers powered by small electric generators. We requested that the Division Command have all this stuff off-loaded early in the landing.

The other major part of this effort was to try to convince Marines that it was important to take Japanese prisoners alive, in spite of the risks involved. I went around to various units to talk about the value of intelligence information, how it can save lives, and how much better it is to know in advance where the enemy is instead of finding out the hard way. Few believed this, and most were very skeptical, especially the tough, pre-wwii "old breed" sergeants. I was always trying to convince Marines that it was in their best interest to try to take prisoners, and for language personnel to try to talk Japanese into coming out of caves and surrendering.

Such efforts were difficult, but at Saipan and Tinian we were more successful than I would ever have thought likely. In spite of tough talk, a lot of Marines were quite cooperative and even kindly toward prisoners, both civilian and military. When they saw the miserable condition of refugees they tried to help them, gave them water, and bandaged them up. Most Marines were kind guys, basically.

On many occasions I found myself in the odd position of trying to save the enemy from my own people. One of my regrets is that I did not have the foresight to prepare more Jeep-mounted loudspeaker equipment with power enough to be heard well at a distance. I had only one such unit, with power provided by a small gas engine generator strapped onto the back seat of the jeep The generator would stop in heavy rain, and sometimes fail at a crucial moment.

I landed on Saipan early in the afternoon on D-day, going straight in to the beach, which was fairly steep and getting badly mortared at the time. We went over the side of the amtrac and slid down onto the beach. Then it turned around and left. Some vehicles to the right had been hit and were still smoking, so we were lucky there. I knew approximately where we were, and I knew about where we were supposed to set up the D-2 position. With me was Navy JLO Otis Cary, the Japan missionary lad. The Navy had sent along an old Korean man from Hawaii, brought there for Navy Civil Affairs duty to talk to the Koreans on the island. There was also another Navy language officer, Bill Decker. We were just plopped down on the sand and getting ready to go inland. Some Marines right near us were crawling inland, when two of them jumped into a ready-made hole. I don't know if it was a shell-hole, or what, but it was just fifteen feet in front of us. We saw them going forward and jumping in there to take temporary shelter. Just at that moment a Japanese mortar shell went right in that hole. There was an explosion and these two guys just evaporated. We couldn't see any sign of them. They were disintegrated, just mixed in with the sand and vegetation and scattered all over the place. Otis Cary, Bill Decker, and the Korean were terrified. This was the real thing, and it was right in front of their eyes. I had been at Tarawa so the shock was minimal for me.

I stayed on the beach until dark, after the others had returned to the ship, and then crawled and walked inland, finally locating the D-2 and headquarters area, which was really just some coral rocks, some foxholes, and pandanus trees. In the night we had a mortar attack. The next day a few Japanese tanks came rumbling down from a nearby valley. We were not affected, but altogether it was enough to keep us awake. The mosquitoes seemed especially fierce and numerous. We would chew tobacco to get enough spit to rub on mosquito bites to stop the itching. We thought it kept the mosquitoes away, but mostly we would get under a poncho and smoke a cigarette to get some relief from the mosquitoes.

After the main fighting was over and we were getting into the mopping-up phase, we would go to a likely area and clean it out. We would try and get the Japanese to give up because they were hiding all over the place. I would try to get some results using the loudspeaker. I had my hand-held battery-operated megaphone, and I would say set phrases like, "*shimpai shinaide*" ("don't be afraid") and "*te o age*" ("put your hands up"). Sometimes there was time to try to say more, like, "The war is over, we have water for you, many people have given up already." So then sometimes someone would answer. Sometimes there was nothing, but maybe you would hear a sound, or they would make a noise as they were getting ready to detonate something, and usually you would have a little bit of warning, and then all of a sudden, boom! But I always tried to talk the Japanese out of the caves first, and if there was no result or no response then the demolitions guys would take over. They often thought I was really just delaying their work.

We declared the island "secured" sometime in July. So when I would go out on daytime mopping-up patrols and night recon and security patrols, our job was to try and capture somebody. You might have to kill them if they were trying to penetrate our lines. Anyway, I could hear people, so I knew they were there. I would ask those who surrendered, usually civilians, how many more civilians are out here? Do you know of any troops? What units? What routes do they take moving around? After that time on patrols and mop-ups we got something like seven or eight thousand, and there were still more out there. I don't know how many we ended up with totally in the POW and refugee camp, but probably well over ten or twelve thousand. These included Japanese, Koreans, Chamorros, and Carolinians from Truk.

It is hard to believe that three divisions of our troops, sixty thousand men, going across a narrow little island, almost walking hand in hand, could not sweep out all those hiding in the hills. But the Japanese and the others could and did hide; they could even infiltrate back and forth at night. Months after the war, there was that Captain Oba, with his soldiers not just surviving but doing fine! It's still a mystery.

Soon after Saipan was secured, *Time* magazine came out with an article written by Robert Sherrod. It had a question headline, "Suicide for 20 million?" implying that all the Japanese in Japan might fight to the last man, woman, and child. At the time I was writing a short article about Saipan and what had happened to the civilians. I especially wanted to correct the impression that based on what had happened on Saipan we were up against a mass suicide of everybody in Japan. Of course it's very dramatic if you see one or two hundred people, including whole families, jump off a cliff one after another. It makes you think the world is coming to an end. But the world was not coming to an end; it's one or two hundred people jumping off a cliff. There's a difference. So the way I wrote the article, I took a little sideswipe at Sherrod and *Time* magazine for writing something that possibly could be misleading.

Anything that anyone writes on active military duty has to go out through a censor. The division censor called me in and said, "Hey, Sherrod's a great friend of the Marine Corps and we don't want to publish criticism of him like this, do we?" I replied, "Well, I'm not writing it about him. I'm writing it about facts compared to the impressions he is giving the American public about war with Japan." He said, "I think you better cut out all of this section." So I said I would, or otherwise the article wasn't going to get published at all. I modified the text and it was later published.

Except for some time spent during the Tinian campaign and a diversionary operation at Okinawa, I was on Saipan for fourteen months. Believe it or not, while we were at Saipan and getting ready for the invasion of Japan, we were still getting people out of caves. Not many, but I would say several every few days.

At Tinian, Colonel Dave Shoup sent for me because he was curious about a Japanese warrant officer who had surrendered but was helping us get other Japanese out of caves. He had gone back into several caves to help me. On his second day he went into a cave to talk some Japanese into surrendering and they shot him, shattering his arm. He came out badly bleeding, so I got him patched up and gave specific instructions at camp to keep him separate from other military prisoners. Later I think somebody suspected what he had done and roughed him up a bit. So Shoup wanted to talk to this guy.

I had a distinct impression that Shoup was kind of an uneducated guy, very rough and tough. What I didn't realize or appreciate at the time was that he was mentally very inquisitive and alert. He wanted to go see this guy he had heard about and wanted to psychoanalyze the prisoner, to learn why he would help us. But the way he went about it was crude. The first thing Shoup said to me when we were in the tent with the prisoner was, "So, now Sheeks, find out, ask him, why is he a traitor?" Of course this went against all my training, which was aimed at trying to be subtle enough to get information out of people. I didn't translate it directly, but made it sound like, "My colonel wants to know why you want to assist us?" My Japanese was not very fluent so it took me quite a few words to explain things and what it was that the colonel wanted to understand. That talk went on for quite a while. The Japanese guy responded patiently and quietly, explaining his thoughts and background, and reasons for helping to rescue people. Colonel Shoup got impatient and wanted to know what he was saying. Then Shoup went on with other questions. I guess he was suspicious of the Japanese warrant officer. I wasn't. He was an older gentleman, a decent guy, sensible, he wanted to save some lives, he didn't want to see civilians die needlessly. He was quite helpful to me. I was trying to interpret what Shoup was saying accurately. The warrant officer didn't understand any English but he got the tone of Shoup's questions. Eventually he said to me, almost like an uncle, "I know this is not easy for you, and I can see you are having difficulty with your superior officer, but you do understand my situation so why don't you just explain it to him. You know what to say."

So I tried, but Shoup kept asking more and different questions. The Japanese man gave calm, sensible answers. But Shoup was very impatient. Finally Shoup said to me "Okay, Sheeks, let's go." And on the way back in the Jeep, I will never forget it, Colonel Shoup shook his head and said, "We'll never know what makes these Nips tick!" I realized that I knew what made the Japanese officer tick, but I didn't know what made Shoup tick! Colonel Shoup was super-thorough in his role, which was to secure the island as rapidly and efficiently as possible by military means. The Japanese warrant officer happened to be an intelligent, humanistic person, keeping his dignity in a situation of utter and devastating defeat. It was a total mismatch of minds, with no communication. Language was not the barrier.

It was very gratifying to be awarded the Bronze Star for the work I had done to facilitate the surrender of Japanese troops and civilians during the Saipan and Tinian campaigns. You know, most Marine officers are decorated for killing the enemy. I think I may be one of very few Marines in WWII who got a medal for saving enemy lives!

By mid-1945 we were gearing up for the Okinawa campaign. I was on a transport with the Second Marine Division waiting in reserve at Okinawa. The high command decided they didn't need a reserve division, so they sent us back to Saipan. The landing was April 1, and I think I got back to Saipan on April 8. As that was my birthday, I thought that survival was a great birthday present—I didn't need cake!

From Okinawa I returned with the Second Marine Division to Saipan, where we were to prepare for the assault on Japan proper. I had accumulated a great many service points by then and was long overdue for home leave. I was supposed to get a month in the U.S. So I was on a Navy PBY from Saipan to Hawaii, sleeping on the floor. It was uncomfortable, but I didn't mind. I was headed for home. Not a cloud in the sky, except I had to transit Honolulu.

This return to Hawaii had been on my mind since I left the year before. To say the least I was concerned that there was an angry husband waiting for me. Remember, he had told his wife that he aimed to kill me. So all the way from Saipan to Honolulu, what was I thinking about? Should I even let my pal George know that I was there? I decided I was going to call him immediately when I arrived and ask about that couple.

I got to Honolulu and right away reached George by phone, and he insisted that I come on over for dinner. He asked me, "Do you remember that girl and her husband?" And I said, "Well, yes, I do. Much more than slightly." Of course I remembered them. How could I forget? George then told me something I could never have imagined. He said, "You know, it's a funny thing. They had been having a terrible time, hadn't been getting along with each other. Their marriage was almost breaking up, and then you came along. Now they talk about you fondly, and they feel that in a strange way you had helped them to get on with their lives together. They refer to you as her 'second honeymoon,' and they wanted to meet you if you ever came to Honolulu." Her second honeymoon! And this after all my many months' worry. Of course I was tremendously relieved, but told George, "Well, I don't think I had better see them." And George said, "I think it would be okay if you want to." "No," I told him, "I think I had better leave things just as they are." So here I had lived with an uneasy conscience, plus fear, thinking I might have to sneak in and out of Hawaii. Then it turns out I was a "second honeymoon" that saved a marriage! Life really can be so unpredictable.

*Communicating with the Enemy*

I was in Hawaii for only about a week, then shipped out on a baby flat-top named the USS *Makassar Strait*. It was exiting from the Pearl Harbor channel when many guns began firing. It was announced on the ship's PA system that the war had ended, that two atomic bombs had been dropped on Japan. All of us on board wondered, "What the hell is an atomic bomb?" The main thing for us was that the Japanese had decided to surrender. The ship still had to zigzag and keep lights out all the way to San Pedro, California, because there still could be Japanese submarines that hadn't gotten the word or wouldn't accept that their war was over. By the time I arrived back in the U.S. the war really was over and folks were tired of it. I had looked forward to being a returning Marine and talking about the campaigns, but most Americans were already bored by the subject of warfare. They wanted to talk about gasoline rationing and all their wartime problems.

I went to Washington D.C., where I saw General Watson, our ex-commandant of the Second Marine Division, now Commandant of the Marine Corps. I told him that I wanted to go with the Marines to China if possible, or at least to Japan. He asked what my longer-term plans were, and I said I wanted to stay in the Marine Corps for the next few years. He then asked what had been my vocation. I told him that I had only been an undergraduate student at Harvard. He very kindly advised me that I could get back into the Marine Corps at any time, and that I should first go finish up at Harvard. Then if I really wanted to be in the Marine Corps, I would have plenty of years to serve as a Marine. I said, "Yes, sir." I never went back to duty in the Marines, but I was active in the Marine Corps Reserve for the next twenty years, with the rank of major.

I ended up working in Asia. I continue to do consulting work in Taiwan, and I'm now eighty-one years old. It is unlikely that I would have worked in Asia all those years after the war if I hadn't been a JLO. The Japanese language training completely changed and determined the path of my life. When I went back to Harvard after the war, I studied government, dropping entirely my prewar major of biology, then ended up getting a degree in what was called "Far Eastern Studies," not as good a word as "Asian," but in those days they thought of that area of the world as the "Far East." Afterward, I completed a two-year masters degree program at Harvard in China Regional Studies, and I have lived and worked in various parts of Asia ever since.

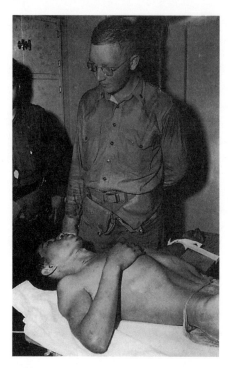

## DAN WILLIAMS

MARINES

**K**ore wa nan desu ka? This question, "What is this?" was like a mantra for each of us when we started the Navy Japanese Language School course at the University of Colorado in Boulder. It was the fourth sentence on page one, Lesson One, Book One, of the six-volume "Standard Japanese Readers" authored by N. Naganuma. There was not a word of English in the whole six volumes, only Japanese characters, and we were there to learn the Japanese language. This awesome challenge seemed to be underscored by an order stamped onto the flyleaf of each textbook: the book was to be returned ". . . if and when the recipient leaves the Naval Service."

Even before Pearl Harbor the Navy knew that Japanese-speaking Navy and Marine officers were needed. A few officers were sent to Japan, Harvard, UC/Berkeley, Hawaii, and other places for Japanese

ABOVE: *The moment of Dan Williams' first Japanese language translation experience on board ship the day before the Kwajalein landing in 1944. He is interrogating a wounded Japanese prisoner who has just been picked up from a small boat.*

Language training. There were even semi-official classes in Washington and other USN installations, including the USMC detachment on American Samoa.

In mid-1941, a Navy Japanese Language School was organized at UC/Berkeley, operated by members of UC's newly enhanced Japanese language faculty, under the leadership of Professor Florence Walne. In overall command was USN Lieutenant Albert Hindmarsh, to whom the Navy had granted extraordinary authority to create and operate every phase of this greatly needed and highly specialized Japanese Language training facility.

Initially, "BIJ" ("born in Japan") candidates were sought in this new and complex recruitment effort, then "BIC" ("Born in China") people, with the idea that the latter might know some of the Chinese characters used in both languages. These were usually the children of American missionary, business, or other families who had lived in those countries. Even though most of us had not been born in China or Japan but had lived there, as in my case, we were accorded the BIJ or BIC label. And in total, we were a small number. The Navy recruited students for the Japanese language courses that were then being given in about eight U.S. universities. Those with skills in different languages and others with demonstrated academic learning abilities were sought in order to meet growing demands.

My parents were missionaries to China, my father the Mission's treasurer and business manager, and we were living in Shanghai in 1931 when the Japanese invaded Manchuria, ignoring League of Nations disapproval. We were there in early 1932 when Japanese navy landing forces entered Shanghai and for two months battled the outgunned Chinese Nineteenth Route Army, inflicting heavy casualties among Chinese civilians and property destruction. Japanese atrocities in Manchuria and Shanghai, including a few we had witnessed, dominated our family conversations and those of all "foreigners" living there. We schoolboys were indelibly impressed by biplane fighter dogfights, visible from our classroom windows, between the few Chinese and overwhelmingly many Japanese aircraft, as well as the constant sounds of artillery bombardment, but particularly by our totally unauthorized visits to the sandbagged defensive machine gun positions of our "invincible" U.S. Marines and those of the British, French, and local international Shanghai Volunteer Corps forces guarding the International Settlement and the French Concession of Shanghai. The Japanese were not then ready for an all-out invasion of China, so they left Shanghai in that spring of 1932, and things returned to normal. Until 1937, the year considered by the Chinese to be the beginning of WWII, when the Japanese returned to stay and to conquer China, the Japanese continued local harassment of Chinese and made threats to the Chinese and to foreigners.

In 1936, my family returned to the U.S. for a one-year furlough, and I traveled separately through Manchuria (then called "Manchukuo" by Japan), across the Trans-Siberian Railroad and via Europe. A Japanese visa was necessary to transit the Chinese port of Dairen (now "Dalian"), occupied by the Japanese as a "treaty port," and I also needed a Manchukuo visa (obtainable only from a Japanese office in Dairen) to visit that puppet state. It was "ruled" then by Henry Pu-Yi, known to students of Asian history and to movie goers as the leading character of *The Last Emperor.* I observed and learned much about Japan and the Japanese as I wandered around Dairen, Harbin, and other parts of Japanese-occupied Manchuria.

My father returned to China in 1937 and my mother and sister in 1938, the latter to return to the States in 1941 at the urging of the State Department. My father and hundreds of other Americans, British, Dutch, and other foreigners believed that they had an obligation to their jobs and to the Chinese to stay, so they remained in Shanghai, and were interned by the Japanese in 1942. My father was one of 1,300 business and professional, crew member, missionary, and miscellaneous detainees at the "Pootung (now Pudong) Civil Assembly Centre," a site now occupied by Shanghai's very visible TV tower, across the Huangpu River from Shanghai's famous Bund. He was repatriated in December 1943 on the second exchange voyage of the Swedish ship *Gripsholm.* Many other Americans and other foreign nationals remained interned by the Japanese at camps in China until VJ Day in 1945.

Meanwhile, at the University of Alabama, I eagerly consumed all available news on Japan and China and was undoubtedly one of the few students there with any interest in the Far East or knowledge of its languages, peoples, and culture. Interestingly, UA now has probably the largest university center for Japanese interests in our southeastern states. I graduated with a bachelors degree in 1941 and completed my masters in 1942, the latter shortly after receiving a letter from then Navy Lt. Albert Hindmarsh at the Navy Department in Washington. How that letter came to me, down South and somewhat out of the loop, what "networking" might have been going on, remains a mystery, but its arrival forever affected my future. A very few mornings later, after an overnight but direct ride on the streamlined "Southerner" train, I arrived in Washington, D.C., at the agreed time. At the Navy Building, two Marine guards conducted me to Lieutenant Hindmarsh, who greeted me cordially, showed me his one-sentence orders from the Chief of Naval Operations, and said, "Do you know any Japanese?"

I replied that I knew a few words, numbers and the chant of a Japanese food vendor I had often heard in the Hongkew district of Shanghai, where most Japanese then lived. Then he asked, "What about Chinese?" After writing a couple of the very few Chinese characters I knew, I heard him say something to the effect of, "Okay, you're in. We need you. Would you be interested?" I signed promptly, and in the following month, June 1942, arrived at the University of Colorado at Boulder, the new location of the Navy Japanese Language School. Because of the ethnic Japanese instructors who were Nisei, that is, born of Japanese immigrant parents in America and thus American citizens, the school had been moved intact from Berkeley to Colorado because of the Presidential Order to remove everyone of Japanese ancestry away from the West Coast. Most were "resettled" into internment camps, such as Tule Lake and Manzanar in California, and many others, but our Nisei instructors were given permission to live and teach in Boulder. They were our friends, were totally committed to the nation's war effort, and were as determined to teach us thorough and comprehensive Japanese as we were to learn it.

Even though we were members of the Armed Forces, we were enrolled as University of Colorado students and could and did wear civilian clothes. As future intelligence officers, our backgrounds were investigated rather intensively by the FBI and Naval Intelligence, a process that did produce a few dismissals of recruited JLS students. The school schedule was intense, total immersion in Japanese in order for us to become proficient in speaking, reading, and writing Japanese as quickly as possible. Each day, we usually had four hours of classes, about six hours of study, some *undo* (physical exercise), followed by a three-hour "final" type exam every Saturday morning. We did enjoy diversions like campus dances, hikes, skiing, theater on and off campus, and other local reconnaissance.

Our classes consisted usually of five to seven students, so there was time for some individual instruction. We learned more than 3,500 characters, plus the Japanese *kana*, and a vocabulary sufficient to read a newspaper, with some dictionary help. Listening to Radio Tokyo at night on my Zenith short wave radio, the only one in the dorm, became a measure of our growing Japanese comprehension. Before graduation, each student had to memorize a chapter on Japanese national defense, the *Kokubo*, and endure an oral final evaluation by a faculty committee. Our Navy-commissioned graduates went to Navy indoctrination schools and then were assigned to overseas or Washington intelligence center duty, sea duty, or specialty duties. Those volunteering for Marine commissions, and I was in that group, got a few days leave, and then reported to a section of USMC Camp Elliott, San Diego, called Green's Farm for two months of infantry training. There were many square miles of hills and other space for our practice firing of all types of weapons, day and night combat problems and exercises, and general USMC troop training. Upon completion, I was assigned to the new Fourth Marine Division at Camp Pendleton, CA, to the D-2 (Intelligence) Section and was soon joined by eleven Boulder classmates, who were assigned to R-2, or regimental, intelligence sections or to our D-2 group.

After some practice invasion landings on beaches near Oceanside, CA, and on an island offshore called San Clemente, our entire Fourth Marine Division departed San Diego and sailed directly to Kwajalein Atoll in the Marianas for our first actual battle. We took Roi and Namur islands (for some reason code-named "Burlesque" and "Camouflage") at the north end of the atoll where the Japanese had built airfields, while the Seventh Army Division took the Kwajalein island airfield at the south end. During the battle, in a destroyed concrete command center, some of our Marines discovered Japanese code books, readily identifiable by their red canvas-bound steel covers that made them easily sinkable in the sea. These highest priority intelligence prizes, which I was able to see contained only letters, numbers, Japanese *kana* and characters, were taken with greatest dispatch and secrecy by special PBM flying boat to Admiral Nimitz's code-breaking unit at Pearl Harbor. Nothing was more decisive in the planning and conduct of the Pacific war than the continued success of the Navy's FRUPAC (Fleet Radio Unit Pacific) Japanese code-breaking operation, guarded with supreme secrecy, at Pearl Harbor. No other code books were found in any of our division's four Pacific island invasions.

Although I interrogated several prisoners during the Roi-Namur battle, my first and most memorable interrogation occurred just prior to the invasion. When the Navy captured a local fishing and patrol boat, a Japanese seaman was wounded and brought aboard our ship, the USS *Appalachian*, for medical treatment, and I was asked to talk to him. My first genuine Japanese language interrogation, other than classroom exercises, was like a first solo in flight training. Since there is no one to help, if you do not know all you need to, you are out of luck. Using medical terms learned in Boulder, I had no trouble asking him about his injuries and describing what the doctors would be doing. Before his surgery began, in my halting Japanese, I obtained information on his Kwajalein assignments.

After Roi-Namur, our division was at its base camp on Maui. During much of the time that followed, I and other USMC language officers were temporarily assigned to JICPOA (Joint Intelligence Center Pacific Ocean Area) at Pearl Harbor for daily Japanese language experience that was most helpful in maintaining conversation and reading skills.

Prisoners of war were generally enlisted men of all ranks, but there were officers who had been doctors, dentists, businessmen, and teachers, and they were glad to be away from Japan's militarist control. Japanese army line officers were very different, reflecting their "divine *bushido*" commitment, and in battle usually chose suicide rather than surrender. The few POW line officers we saw were usually those incapacitated by wounds, which allowed capture. Not only were they less cooperative in interrogation, but, as we found out on Saipan, these officers often killed military or civilian comrades who were trying to surrender and accept our offers of food, water, cigarettes, and ultimate repatriation to Japan.

In our next operation, the landing on Saipan in June 1944, I came ashore in one of the earlier waves and spent the first night dug into a foxhole, with enemy artillery shells exploding all around. My pack was at ground level and was struck by a piece of hot shrapnel. It sizzled through part of my Japanese dictionary inside, which provided some unintended protection. Hundreds of Japanese military and civilian personnel retreated to caves near Marpi Point on Saipan, from which some of our JLOS, using amplifiers and printed instructions, tried to talk them into surrendering. Many did, but some, prevented by their officers from doing so, were either killed or committed suicide. Participating in the taking of Saipan were our Fourth Marine Division on the east, the Second Marine Division on the west, and the Twenty-seventh Army Infantry Division in the middle.

One night, I was with a reconnaissance patrol well behind our battle lines, and we decided to spend the night on a more easily defended hilltop between ravines. We were attacked twice by roaming Japanese, who were eliminated promptly by our watchful Marines on the perimeter. Then, about 2:00 A.M., while I was on watch, a lone Marine arrived. It was none other than longtime Shanghai childhood friend and fellow Boulder JLS student Bob Sheeks, now a Japanese language officer in the

Second Marine Division. I had not seen him since his Boulder graduation more than two years before, and we began a fascinating exchange of combat intelligence experiences. I recall that during our three-hour conversation, before Sheeks returned to his unit, we witnessed the first time a Japanese plane had been shot down over Saipan at night by one of our new, radar-equipped, P-61 "Black Widow" Army Air Corps night fighters, a comforting event for us.

During the previous afternoon, our patrol had approached the entrance to a concrete bunker of the type the Japanese used for command centers, a possible location of code books, I thought. Soon after my call out, an unarmed Japanese sergeant came out with his hands up and said in perfect English, "My name is George, and I am from Honolulu." He said we could safely enter the bunker, as there were only women inside. To my amazement, the only occupants were dejected and miserable looking Asian "comfort women," about whom I had then never heard, forced to service the Japanese army. George, a Nisei in his early twenties, told us that he had been visiting Japan from his home in Honolulu at the time of Pearl Harbor, was drafted into the Japanese army, and that his current duty was being in charge of those "comfort women."

After we finished taking nearby Tinian, our division regrouped on Maui, and, for us Boulder graduates who had just been promoted to USMC first lieutenants, we again had Pearl Harbor intelligence center duty. But soon we once more loaded ourselves on Navy transport ships for a few practice maneuvers prior to the invasion of Iwo Jima. Simultaneously, the Fifth Marine Division embarked from its camp near Hilo on the Big Island for the same invasion, and both units were granted a very few days of liberty in Honolulu. Even though the Japanese on Iwo Jima knew from almost ceaseless sea and air bombardment that we were coming, when a notepad with Iwo Jima notations was discovered in a phone booth in Waikiki, the Navy decided that it would flood the fleet with information booklets on the Japanese-held island of Ponape, as a deceptive move. We intelligence officers were asked to become experts on Ponape and held briefing meetings. Booklets on Ponape were "mistakenly" dropped widely, fooling no one along the way, even though our Marines had not yet been told the name of our next target island.

At sea later, when the Marine units had been told that Iwo Jima was our destination, our briefing sessions were as incomplete as the intelligence information on which they were based. We the invaders were fooled. Since no one had been on the island, we assumed from aerial photos showing defensive pillboxes around the three airfields that Iwo Jima was like other Japanese-held islands and that its defenses could be erased by naval gunfire and aerial bombing. Nobody imagined that the island's tunnel network was as deep as London's deepest subways, and that its occupants were as impervious to our preliminary bombardment as Londoners were to the Nazi blitz. There was no way of knowing that many tunnel entrances on Iwo concealed heavy weapons zeroed in on the very beaches on which the invading Marines would land. POWs later told me that as long as the Japanese defenders remained in the tunnels, they were uninjured by our millions of dollars' worth of wasted naval gunfire and aerial bombs.

One of my unforgettable memories comes from early in the morning of the Iwo Jima landing. Before the sun had risen down at the ocean surface, I looked up and saw, way above us, a clear sky full of silver shapes flying north, illuminated by the sun at their altitude, B-29s headed for Tokyo. Down below, battleships and Navy carrier bombers were pounding the island, to no avail we later realized. The noise of that bombardment, and of Navy landing craft maneuvering to take aboard the first waves of Marines, was so great and the B-29s were so high that they seemed to be floating silently up there in the sunlight.

So then it was time for the landing, and everyone was on deck watching. The amtracs, the LCVPS, LCMS, and other landing craft delivered their first waves of Marines to their designated beaches without problems. Some observers began to think that Iwo's defenders had been pulverized by all of the preliminary "softening up." Suddenly, the Japanese began shelling the beaches that were by now jammed with Marines, blasting personnel and equipment, interrupting all landing plans. Very quickly, shot-up Marines, covered with coarse black sand, were brought back to our ship, and placed on beds, including mine.

Then our time came to leave the ship, climb down the cargo nets into the landing craft, reach the beach, and climb up from the beach on the soft, coarse, black volcanic sand to the first airfield level. There we found an empty, half-covered, Japanese gun emplacement. It was still smoldering and smoky, but offered protection from anything except a direct hit. We dug in there for a while, then decided that it was a good location for prisoners, so I stayed there the entire time I was on Iwo except when out on patrol.

At one point a prisoner mentioned his familiarity with the Japanese headquarters and staff and volunteered to deliver a letter to his commander, General Kurabayashi, from our commanding general, offering an honorable surrender. At General Clifton Cates's direction, I typed the letter in English on our general's stationery, gave it to the Japanese volunteer, who, after reassuring us again of his close association with his headquarters people, entered the underground passage system. Evidently, his was not a welcome message. There was no reply, and we never saw the messenger again.

Certainly, one of the most memorable events of the battle for Iwo Jima was the flag-raising. I was less than a mile away, with a perfect view. When the flag went up, there were immediate calls, "Hey, the flag is up!" Actually, I am censoring here, since Marines repeatedly use a particular adjective, the "F word," in this type of situation. What I actually heard was, "Hey, the f——g flag is up, and the f——g island hasn't even been secured yet!" Everyone clapped and cheered, and that of course was the raising of the first flag. Later, we noticed more activity atop Mount Suribachi, and another, larger flag was raised, replacing the first, smaller one. The second raising was the one pictured in the famous photo by Joe Rosenthal. A month later, the battle for Iwo Jima still was not over.

I was on Iwo for about a month and a half. After that, our Fourth Marine Division returned to Maui, and we USMC language officers were again assigned to JICPOA at Pearl Harbor to glean intelligence from captured Japanese POWs and documents. We were all involved in discussions of the forthcoming invasion of Japan, with a possible detour by our division to retake Wake Island. During that time in Honolulu, I also took a refresher course in Chinese at the University of Hawaii.

VJ Day in August of 1945 was a stupendous event. It meant that we would not be engaging in bloody and costly Iwo Jima–type battles in an invasion of Japan. It affected the lives of millions of Americans and others, but was not entirely a surprise to me. A BOQ roommate, a USN communications officer at Pearl Harbor, had mentioned to me the contents of several messages exchanged with the Japanese concerning cessation of hostilities. At the moment the news broke, I was returning to Pearl Harbor from Waikiki where I had been on a dinner date with a woman Marine lieutenant, and I was driving us in her USMC Jeep. As we approached the Iolani Palace and Kamehameha's statue on King Street in downtown Honolulu, I could see pandemonium and a mob of joyous servicemen pouring toward us and upsetting anything movable along the way. A discretionary right turn took us inland to Moanalua Drive, a parallel route to Aiea Heights overlooking Pearl Harbor, and then we saw an incredible sight. Every ship in the harbor and many land installations seemed to be firing tracer bullets, rockets, and anything else that would explode, so that the whole sky was lighted by fireworks—all live ammunition, of course. It was a never-to-be-forgotten sight.

Quite promptly after the Japanese surrender and the end of World War II, our Fourth Marine Division was ordered back to Camp Pendleton, CA, for demobilization, except for three of us Boulder JLOs who had lived in China. We were ordered to join the USMC occupation of three cities in North China. I was stationed at Tientsin (now Tianjin). One day I was confronting Japanese civilians assembled with their bed rolls in a Japanese school gym, telling them that we would protect them from those in the local Chinese population who wanted to kill them. I assured them they would get food and water, no internment, and a return to Japan as soon as possible. A few asked me, "When can we get out of here and get back to normal? Our businesses are suffering." I said, "I think you are talking to the wrong guy. Your Japanese army came in, looted and wrecked our home in Shanghai, interned my father, took our car, and made the first floor of our house a machine gun nest." I was perturbed and went on and on. They were silent.

I had witnessed Japanese atrocities in China before WWII and hated the individuals involved, but I felt no animosity toward all Japanese. Memories of the past did not affect my wartime duties with POWs. The defeated army and navy personnel I dealt with were disciplined and respectful. The unique experience at "USNTS JapLang" (the Japanese Language School) at CU/Boulder, the commitment and friendly teaching skills of the Nisei and other faculty members, and the personalized Japanese language training we received was a combination that evolved for that time and place, and might never be repeated anywhere. It provided me with the opportunity to be a part of the "can-do" Marines I had long admired, increased my lifelong familiarity with and interest in the Orient, and makes particularly pleasant any contact I now have with Japanese. My periodic trips to China and university and business contacts there still continue. Perhaps no American is truly an expert on the essentially significant events and people of Asia, as we are only students, but for most Boulder grads, gaining that desired understanding remains a constant challenge.

Thirteen years after VJ Day, I was northbound for Hiroshima on a train from Kyushu, and discussing the nuclear bombing of our destination city with two fellow Japanese passengers. Both told me that our atomic ending to the war was beneficial to the Japanese people in two ways: it freed them from two decades of mistreatment by their military-controlled government, and it saved possibly two or three million Japanese and American lives that would have been lost in an invasion of Japan. Their certainty in expressing their first reason surprised me. Their second reason might have included them and me. Later, on a Pan-Am flight—when there was a Pan-Am—from Tokyo to Guam, on a very clear day, our 747 flew over Iwo Jima. The irony was that I was looking down on that island where so many Marines had died fighting the Japanese, sitting on a plane filled with Japanese newlyweds headed to their honeymoons on Guam, another island we had to take from them and where there were many more American casualties.

Would it be true to say that if many Americans today were asked, "What was and is the importance to the U.S. of Iwo Jima and Guam?" that most of them would have no idea of just where those islands are or that the U.S. ever had anything to do with them?

OPPOSITE LEFT: *Members of the Fukuhara family in Hiroshima in 1937, from left, Harry (age 17), Pierce (age 15), their mother Kinu, and Frank (age 13). Older brother Victor (age 23) had already been drafted into the Japanese army and was serving in Manchuria. Victor returned to Hiroshima by August of 1945, was exposed to the atomic bomb blast, and later died from the effects of radiation.*

OPPOSITE RIGHT: *Two of the Fukuhara brothers in Kobe, Japan, October, 1945, Frank (age 21) and Harry (age 25) at the 172nd Language Detachment, 33rd Infantry Division*

# HARRY FUKUHARA

ARMY

I f you can, picture standing on the platform of the Hiroshima city railroad station in early October 1945. That's where I was on the morning of October 2. I was probably one of the earliest members of the U.S. Occupation Forces to see Hiroshima after the atomic bomb had been dropped. I couldn't believe what I saw. But I was there unofficially. I had driven twenty-four hours continuously from Kobe to get there on a personal mission to find my family, if they were still alive. But to understand why I was there, I must explain my background.

I was born in Seattle, Washington, in 1920. My parents were Japanese who had immigrated to the U.S. from Hiroshima. My father died in 1933 from a prolonged illness. That same year, my mother took the family, three brothers and a sister, back to her home, to Hiroshima. I didn't want to go. I was thirteen years old, I didn't speak Japanese, and I was leaving the U.S., the only home I knew. I came back to the U.S. almost as quickly as I could, right after I graduated from high school in Hiroshima in 1938. I was working my way through college in Los Angeles as a houseboy and gardener. That is what I was doing when the Japanese attacked Pearl Harbor on December 7, 1941.

I was interned along with more than 100,000 other Japanese and Japanese-Americans. I was shipped to the Gila River Internment Camp in Arizona. In November 1942, I volunteered from Gila River for the U.S. Army. I trained at the Military Language School at Camp Savage, Minnesota. You are probably wondering why I volunteered for the Army after having experienced mistreatment and incarceration by the American public and the government. People ask me that all the time. As time has passed and I reflect back on what I have learned and experienced, some of my feelings and impressions have changed. But some of the basic beliefs and feelings have remained the same. So let me try and explain this.

I was one of twenty-six *Niseis* who volunteered from Gila River Internment Camp on November 23, 1942. I'm sure we all had our different reasons because of different backgrounds. But what we shared, although we didn't say so openly, was our strong feeling of patriotism and loyalty to our country. Some of us were *Kibeis*, born in the U.S. and raised in Japan. We had lived in both countries and were able to compare. Being of Japanese descent, we had an even stronger desire to prove our allegiance to this country, and that was prevalent among all of us who were volunteers. But this was not a universal feeling in the camp. I volunteered when it was not the popular thing to do from within the confines of an internment camp. But I felt strongly that it was the time when I must make a decision for better or for worse, and to back up my decision with action. Some *Isseis*, first-generation Japanese immigrants, thought I should know better because I had lived in Japan. But I never regretted joining the Army, although there were times during the war that I wished I were somewhere else!

The day Pearl Harbor was bombed, the woman I gardened for fired me on the spot. A neighborhood store owner refused to sell my sister and me groceries. He said he didn't want "Jap business." My Caucasian neighbors turned me in as a curfew violator and said they were doing their patriotic duty. These are the types of things we faced after Pearl Harbor.

The popular saying during that time was, "A good Jap is a dead Jap." Nothing good or favorable was said about *Niseis*, us second-generation Japanese-Americans, despite the fact that we were born American, ate hot dogs, played baseball, and celebrated the Fourth of July. But our citizenship was ignored, our inalienable rights violated, and we were interned. With the help of the American media, we became bad Japanese, not good Americans. Maybe if there had been more Asian-American journalists, public opinion would not have reached such levels of hysteria.

However, during this very difficult time, two things affirmed my belief in this country—the U.S. military and an elderly couple, Mr. and Mrs. Clyde and Florence Mount. I was the Mounts' houseboy, and I could have been considered as just an employee. But they offered to help me avoid internment by adopting me or providing refuge in their Ohio family home. Unfortunately that didn't work out, and I went into the camp. But they drove hours to visit me, defying public sentiment and using precious rationed gas. When I went into the Army, they displayed a star in their

*Communicating with the Enemy*

window, which at that time signified that a member of their household was serving in the U.S. military. They really took me in as one of their own.

And in a way, it was that way with the military. It was not really a very democratic environment, but we encountered very little of intended discrimination, at least nothing like what we had experienced on the outside. As Military Intelligence Service soldiers, we were treated with respect and dignity. The U.S. Army needed us, and we rose to the challenge. We were doing work that nobody else could do, coaxing valuable information from prisoners that could save American lives. Our mission was to serve as interpreters, interrogators, and translators with combat units fighting against the Japanese Imperial Army. We were Nisei Army linguist soldiers trained to use our Japanese language capabilities to support our fighting forces by providing timely and useful information against an enemy we knew very little about.

I ended up in the Pacific for almost two-and-a-half years, starting from Australia and participating in General MacArthur's island-hopping strategy to return to the Philippines. I took part in three enemy landings and five military operations in New Britain, New Guinea, Morotai, and Luzon. I suffered from battle fatigue and was hospitalized several times with malaria. By the end of the war I was physically and emotionally exhausted. In August of 1945 I was on the island of Luzon in the Philippines. My unit, the U.S. Thirty-third Infantry Division, had successfully taken Baguio City. We had returned to the lowlands to regroup, retrain, and prepare for the final showdown. This was going to be a really fearsome assault on Japan, a massive amphibious landing that would have dwarfed the Normandy invasion. It would have literally turned the tide red with blood.

But then I heard the atomic bomb had been dropped on Hiroshima. I am often asked how I felt when I heard the bomb had been dropped on the city where my family was living. At first it didn't have much meaning. Like other soldiers, I had never heard of an atomic bomb. I knew nothing about it. But each day more information was disseminated, and I found out more. One of my duties was to explain to the Japanese p o w s what had happened. I told them that a new bomb called the atomic bomb, equivalent to thousands of tons of T N T, had been dropped on Hiroshima on August 6 and that one single explosion had completely wiped out the entire city of Hiroshima and that it had been erased from the surface of the earth. I told them no living thing had survived and that all human and animal life were nonexistent. I also told them that no vegetation, plant life, or trees, would grow there, and people would not be able to live there for at least 100 years due to radiation. When I told them that, they just sat there, totally silent. Either they did not believe me or else the information was beyond their comprehension. To tell you the truth I didn't want to believe it myself.

For the first few days I kept thinking, why? Why did they drop it on Hiroshima? There were other better targets, such as Tokyo, Yokohama, and Osaka. Then I tried to rationalize that my mother had probably moved out and was living with relatives in the countryside where it would be safer and food more plentiful. I figured my brothers would be away from home attending college or drafted into the Japanese army. But my thoughts returned to the original assumption, that if they were in Hiroshima they could not have survived the blast. The more I thought about it, the more depressed I became. My thinking degraded to the point that I blamed myself—that they had died because I had volunteered to fight against them.

Shortly after that I was given the choice of going home or going to Japan with the Thirty-third Division as part of the Occupation. This was a very difficult decision for me—I was torn. I was afraid that it would be futile to look for my family, and that whatever I found would make me very bitter. But I decided that I needed to go, and so I signed up for the Occupation.

I arrived in Japan in mid-September 1945. I had explained the situation to my division commander, Major General Clarkson, and he gave me permission to go to Hiroshima. My Jeep driver and I finally made it to Hiroshima after three attempts. My driver was a nineteen-year-old young soldier from Michigan. He was blond, blue-eyed, and about 6 feet 3 inches tall. He was scared because we had passed through areas where our military had not yet traveled and villages where returning Japanese soldiers were drunk and wild. When we went into police stations and railroad stations to ask our way, I told him to act like an officer and I would be his interpreter. After all that driving, almost twenty-four hours straight, we finally reached the outskirts of Hiroshima just as dawn was breaking. We made our way into the ruined city to Hiroshima city railroad station platform. I was astounded at what I saw. I could see all the way across to the other side of the city, a distance of several miles. It was eerie and lifeless. There was no movement or noise.

After a while I saw a few men around bonfires. When I asked for directions, they acted like zombies and did not even look up to see who was talking to them. I thought they were the only ones who had survived.

Finally we found the house where I had lived seven years before. I told the driver to stay with the Jeep, but he didn't want to be left alone. The two of us, he armed with a rifle and me with my .45-caliber pistol, knocked on the door of my house. It seemed like a long time when finally two emaciated-looking elderly women appeared at the door. It was my mother and my aunt, but neither said a word. They just stared at the tall soldier standing next to me. I had rehearsed what I was going to say, but when they both stood there looking scared I just said, "Mom, I'm home" in Japanese. My aunt recognized me before my mother did. When she did, she broke down. Her first words that tumbled out were, "What are you doing here? How did you get here? Where did you come from?" We were finally welcomed into the house.

When we went in I noticed the splintered glass embedded in the walls. The back of the house, facing the epicenter of where the bomb exploded, was etched with the shadows of the trees and shrubs that themselves had been scorched into skeletons. My older brother, Victor, was lying on the floor upstairs. My mother told me he had been on his way to work when the bomb went off. He was dying but I did not know it then. My mother said he had showed up several days after the bombing. He had difficulty talking and could not recall what had happened. I tried to get him hospitalized in Hiroshima, but there was no room. I had him moved to Kobe where I was stationed, but he died within a year.

My two brothers, Pierce and Frank, had just returned home a few days before my arrival. Both had been drafted into the Japanese army. I found out years later that both had been assigned to suicide units near the beach where my Thirty-third Division was supposed to have landed on Kyushu, as part of the final invasion that was to end the war in the Pacific. Only Truman's decision to drop the atomic bomb had avoided all that bloodshed.

Looking back on it now, sometimes I think it was fortuitous. My older brother died from the atomic bomb, but my two younger brothers, both Japanese soldiers, and myself, an American soldier, are alive today because of it. Plus my mother. One life for four. Maybe they were not bad odds amid the misfortunes of a great war.

For years, by virtue of a silent mutual agreement, we avoided talking about what happened to our family in Hiroshima. The only balm for the tragedy has been time—a full half-century and more. It's been that long since my brother died, and nearly thirty-five years since my mother died. Until she died she was plagued by unexplainable illnesses. I can talk about what happened in Hiroshima now, more than half a century later. I believe that talking about it now, with a purpose, is the medicine I need.

# CHAPTER 7

*"John F. Kennedy was the only one who wanted to go back into combat after he'd lost his boat. And, you know, they would normally send them home, but he wanted to stay there and get another boat."*

—Dave Levy, NAVY

DAVE LEVY, NAVY, PT boat skipper, Solomons, Philippines

AL HAHN, NAVY, PT boat motor machinist mate, Philippines

PAGES 214–215: *Dave Levy at the controls of PT 59 in early 1943. Guadalcanal is in the background. Dave later turned this boat over to John F. Kennedy after PT 109 was rammed and sunk. In this boat Kennedy pulled off a daring evacuation of some trapped Marines from under the noses of the Japanese.*

OPPOSITE: *On Tulagi in the Solomon Islands in 1943, Dave Levy, twenty-two-year-old skipper of PT 59, stands second from left along with fellow PT boat skippers and a Solomon Islands native. The flag was plucked from the water the night the Japanese evacuated Guadalcanal in early 1943. Shortly after this photo was taken, Dave sent the flag back to his twelve-year-old cousin, Teddy Amdursky, who still has the flag today.*

# MANNING THE PT BOATS, 1942–45

DAVE LEVY
NAVY

I n 1941, right out of Syracuse University, with a degree in political science, I volunteered for the Marine Corps Officer's Training School. A colonel from the Marines, an Annapolis graduate, had come to Syracuse, and he put us in the order that he wanted to choose us. I was number five, and the four ahead of me were all football players, tough, physically fit guys. There was a lot of feeling against Jewish kids in the college, and I thought that's why he made me number five. I was mad as hell. Those four guys all went to Guadalcanal, and all of them ended up being killed.

I decided my next best bet was the Navy, but I couldn't get into the

Navy's Officer's Training School because they required math, and I had no math in college. I went to the University of Rochester and took a summer course in math, and then I got in. I was in the Navy by September 1941.

I decided I wanted to get into small boats. I was looking for destroyers, since I heard the bigger ships were very tough and required etiquette, social things, and you had to dress up. So I volunteered for the torpedo school at Newport, Rhode Island, figuring destroyers had torpedoes on them and that this would get me into destroyers. I went to torpedo school with no idea of getting into PT boats. I didn't know what the hell I was getting into.

All the hotshot kids were trying to get into PT boats, but I just happened to be at the right place at the right time—or the wrong place. A lot of the guys who volunteered for PT boats had sailing experience. There also seemed to be a lot of Ivy Leaguers, and a lot of football players. I was in the first class out of there, and I was twenty-one years old.

In the town of Newport, when I was first there, there was a fellow who owned a bar, a Mr. Hogan. And I went out with Mrs. Hogan. And all the guys were saying "Hogan, they're after you, they're after you." They called me Hogan. And that lasted during the whole war. A lot of friends looked me up in the service and they'd say, "Is Mr. Levy here?" The answer was, "Well, we don't have a Mr. Levy, but we have a Mr. Hogan." It stayed with me. I couldn't get rid of it. When Jack Kennedy, with whom I served in the Solomons, met me in Rochester after the war, he said to my wife, "Ohhh, Mrs. Hogan. How are you?" My wife was okay with that since she knew the story.

I don't know what it was about the PT boats that appealed to all these Ivy League guys. Most of them had gotten in early. Jack Searles and his brother were a couple of years older than us. But the rest of them graduated about the same time I did. They thought PT boats were fun, they were small and you could be the skipper. Those were the same reasons I suppose I volunteered, because I didn't want to get on a big ship and have all the regulations.

We shipped out from Panama and headed across the Pacific on a transport ship with our PT boats onboard. This was about late summer 1942, and the Marines had just invaded Guadalcanal and Tulagi in the Solomons. We unloaded the boats at New Caledonia, and then they towed us up to the Solomons, two PT boats behind each destroyer. When they towed us to Guadalcanal, I was in the boat the couple of days

*Manning the PT Boats*

it took. We had to steer to keep from hitting each other. That was from Noumea all the way up to Guadalcanal.

I'd never heard of Guadalcanal, since nobody then was talking about it much. When we got there we immediately were towed over to Tulagi, which is across Iron Bottom Bay from Guadalcanal. Tulagi was a fairly small island, and the Marines had cleared it out before we got there, and it became our PT boat base. They let us off there, and we didn't see the Navy for a long time after that.

It was mid-September of 1942 when I got to the Solomons. The Marines had invaded Guadalcanal in August, so I was there close to the beginning. One PT boat squadron was there ahead of us, and they were pretty beat up when we got there. They had lost boats, so we had more crews than boats. We went on patrol every other night, and I shared my boat with another crew. Luckily my boat, the 59, stayed together all the time, but we were there on a shoestring. We barely had enough fuel to keep going, and we didn't get anything much to eat. We ate Spam for two-and-a-half months. Nothing came in. Ours was Squadron 2 and the other was Squadron 3. There were supposed to be twelve boats in a squadron, but we had fewer than that because of the losses. Those first two squadrons were the only thing there in the Solomons until December or so.

I never realized, when we were there, that we were the only thing between the Japs and New Zealand and Australia. I never had a feeling for the overall picture, and I never had a feeling for why we ate Spam for two months. The Navy was having plenty of problems, and they weren't helping us very much. We were the only thing left there, just us and the Marines on the shore. I didn't really realize how important the airfield was. It was the whole answer to Guadalcanal. Had we lost that airfield, it would've been all over, and the Japs would've been on their way to Australia.

One of the nights I had off, Jack Searles took my boat out. We had broken the Jap code, and our intelligence people had figured out exactly where and when a Japanese general was coming into Guadalcanal on a submarine. So Searles was sent out there with my boat. The submarine came up at that location at that time, and they fired their torpedoes at it and blew it up. This was one of the real notable things that happened there in the early going. Searles got the Navy Cross for that.

We always saw planes flying around during the day, ours and theirs. We picked up our pilots when they went down, and a lot of planes went down off that airfield on Guadalcanal. Some ran out of fuel coming back if they went too far north. They would go to Bougainville to bomb, run out of fuel, and they'd try to crash land on the reefs, particularly the torpedo planes. I saw a whole squadron go down within maybe fifty or sixty miles of the field on Guadalcanal. There was so much of that, so many mistakes.

In the Solomons our PT boats were no match for a Japanese destroyer. If the Japs could see you, you were hit. They got you. The Japanese navy and army were experts. We didn't realize it at first, but they had been at war for six years and they were good. Their destroyers just raised hell with our whole Navy. They sank our cruisers one after another. And their torpedoes were good. They worked. We were using World War I torpedoes that weren't very good. Every night we'd go out and we'd report some Jap ship was hit or sunk, but it wasn't necessarily so.

When we were on patrol, I had to know what was going on immediately ahead of me. And I was on the radio listening and talking all the time, and I was always telling everyone else what I was doing. We were effective because we were there, not because we did so much. But we showed. We were the Navy that showed. They had to be thinking of us as a possible threat. A lot of times they had to get the hell out of there, because they didn't want to deal with us.

There was one guy who was on my boat for a little while—Red Riley, we called him. He was a reddish-blond Irish kid, and he was my Exec for a few weeks. And then he went to another guy's boat and was killed almost immediately. I knew him quite well, but we didn't talk a hell of a lot about something that happened to someone we knew. They were just gone, and we wrote them off and didn't do much about it. We just shut it off. I never looked at the empty cots or all that stuff that you see in the movies. If someone got hurt, we'd take them over to Guadalcanal, and they'd fly them out. Tulagi was a lousy place to try and treat the wounded. If they didn't fly you out, you were dead.

Once a bomb landed, oh, maybe a hundred feet from my boat. And it could have done a pretty good bit of damage if it had come a little closer, even without hitting me. I was shot at a lot of times. But when you're shot at and missed, you don't pay that much attention to it.

One time we were out on patrol and were sent to check out a PT boat that had been destroyed. Its remains had washed up on the beach. It was hit and ended up there, and I took a photo of it. Frank Freeland was the skipper, and he got killed, along with a lot of his crew. He was hit by destroyer gunfire, which did a pretty good job on that thing. We were sent to see if we could retrieve anything useful out of it, but we didn't find anything.

*Manning the PT Boats*

PT boats were not designed for what we used them for. We lost an awful lot of people to small-arms fire in going up against Japanese barges in the Solomons. The Japanese would move all their people in small barges. And they'd have, maybe, thirty guys with small arms in each barge. We'd come up to them and all hell would break loose. We lost a lot of people trying to sink those barges, and we were not equipped for it. We had machine guns and 40mm cannon on the back of the boat, but PT boats stood up from the water, maybe, six feet, and we had 3,000 gallons of high octane gas aboard. And we had depth charges and torpedoes. PT boats were such easy targets, standing up like that in the water. Their barges were almost flat with the water, and you've got all that gunfire. It was just a stupid thing to use PT boats for that purpose, and it was done during the whole war. It was worse in Hollandia, in New Guinea and that area. In the Philippines it was the same. There was no sense in it. I don't know why they didn't figure out some kind of a gunboat with some kind of armor on it and put it down in the water so that it wasn't such a big target. It was ridiculous.

I saw a lot of those barges, and that problem really started in the Solomons in 1942. We even tried to figure out how to put some armor on our boats out there, which was impossible. We were trying to make concrete or steel panels, but nothing really worked. We had a lot of losses, but I was lucky. I had guys leave my boat and get killed on another boat. I had a chief petty officer on my boat who thought I was taking too many chances, and he got off because of that. I really didn't think I was taking any more chances than anyone else.

Most of the time we were doing nothing. We slept during the day so we could stay awake at night. The Japanese only came down with their ships in the dark of the moon, because they were afraid of our aircraft. So we had only, maybe, ten days in a month when they would come down. The rest of the time we were out on patrol, but didn't expect anything. I used to turn on our main radio and listen to music from San Francisco. There were beautiful nights out there in the Pacific, with the stars and moon out, and there were little tropical islands all around that you could see for miles. We knew the Japs wouldn't come out on those nights. We could relax, or I'd go to sleep in the back of the boat.

Torpedo alcohol played a big part in what was happening. It was 180-proof, pure grain alcohol, and it was fuel for the torpedoes. But when we didn't have to go out on patrol, the kids used to drink that goddamned stuff by the glassful, usually with grapefruit juice. One night in early 1943 there was a truckload of that stuff in 55-gallon drums on Tulagi being transferred from a supply ship to the boats, and the truckload got lost. And can you imagine how many people got drunk?

Then they decided they were going to stop us from drinking it by putting gasoline into it. And the kids just determined that they could make stills and distill it. That's how we got the gasoline out. I had the most beautiful still in the world on my boat, but I didn't know it. It was under the floorboards. My crew used all the best materials to build it. They had stills going all the time. I would make inspections and miss the still. I knew something was going on since they would share it with me, but I didn't bother them.

When the crew got a little rambunctious, we took care of it. When they had alcohol from the torpedo tubes and everything else going, there was bound to be some trouble. I was on a first-name basis with the crew, but I kept somewhat of a distance. I thought you had to. You'd figure that way I didn't know what they were doing, but I did know. They just called me "Skipper," and I got along great with everybody in the service.

I had a machinist mate on my crew who was an older man, maybe thirty-six years old, and his name was Homer Facteau. He was a little short guy, but he absolutely knew how to handle machinery and handle the young guys on the boat. They looked up to him. He had spent his life in the Adirondack Mountains, at Saranac Lake, taking care of speedboats. So he had a real feeling for the PT boats and what it took to put them together and keep them going. He was the most valuable guy I ever had. All the younger guys would do anything he told them. They looked up to him. Sometimes we had to change engines, and he'd change them over in one night. He'd have those kids working, and that boat was ready the next morning. He was marvelous. As a result, we had the fastest boat in the squadron.

The PT boats were loaded with officers from Princeton and Harvard, and all those Ivy League schools. I had never had a lot of contact with those people before, but I got to know most of them one way or another. What happened was that so many of these Ivy League guys knew each other. So they had a head start on us. You know, like in our Squadron, Searles knew Nicoloric, and they knew maybe ten guys in PT boats. And they all had played sports together. So you had to sort of fight their club a little. Not that they made the rest of us miserable, but all their friends had the inside track, and I started on the outside but finally got into their group. In the end it didn't make any difference. But some guys never made it into that group. The reason I made it is that I was in the

Solomons almost before anybody else. And they all looked up to me because I had lived through that. But it was like a club for them, and this club did a lot to enhance the members' reputations, and I never went for that. Some of these guys got the Silver Star while they were in Washington, just because they knew the right people. Some of that "old school" stuff was sickening. Sometimes we cooked on the boat. We had a mess cook but he was trained to be on a big ship. He was a nice guy, but I don't think he liked the action. We had a lot of Spam, and there wasn't much to cook. We had a PT boat tender there, the *Jamestown*, and the crews sometimes ate on the *Jamestown*, which was a huge yacht of somebody's that they converted into a tender. They had it all camouflaged with a lot of tree limbs and things to make it hard to pick out from the air. The night the Japanese left Guadalcanal, they came in with destroyers to pick up as many of their guys as they could. We knew they were going to leave because we had their code. The Navy thought that they were going to take their men around to another part of Guadalcanal—on the back side. So they put us out on the back side of the island and let the Japs get on their ships. And we had lost so many PT boats by then, they didn't want us to directly attack their ships. So we went to the back side of Guadalcanal and the Jap planes bombed us, but we didn't get hit. The next morning, as it got light, we headed back around toward Tulagi, and we went past where the Japs had been loading their guys on destroyers off the northwest coast of Guadalcanal.

The destroyers were all gone. They'd had to leave in a hurry as it got light, because they were worried about getting attacked and sunk by our airplanes. As we got there, we saw all kinds of Japanese in the water. The destroyers just left them behind, left them floating there in the water. I picked up thirteen of them and sat them up on the bow of my boat, and we took them back to Tulagi. I thought it was sensible, that maybe we'd be successful in getting information from them, but the Marines were mad as hell when I got them there. And they took control. They took those Japs off our boat, and I don't know what happened to them. But it was amazing to be out there just floating around among all those Japs in the water and picking them up. There must've been 500 of them out there floating around. We didn't shoot any Japs in the water. They'd had it, and they weren't going to fight.

When the Japanese pulled out, we found a Japanese officer's boat and brought it back to cruise around in. There were also flags in the water, and I picked one up. It was with some other stuff, packs they had just thrown into the water. So I sent that flag to my cousin, who's now a doctor in Washington.

Around this time I had leave in New Zealand, in the second group that went down there. I decided to climb the highest mountain in New Zealand, Mount Cook, down on South Island, but I didn't get to the top. At four o'clock in the afternoon I got up to where there was a stone hut, and I was so tired I just went to bed and walked down the next day. I got back to Auckland a day late and didn't realize it. I got back on the day I was told to, but the ship had left, and I missed it. The commander of our base was so upset I missed the ship that he kept me in Tulagi two weeks longer than I was supposed to be, at the end of my tour.

After I got back they sent us up to the Russell Islands, a ways west of Guadalcanal. When we first went ashore, everything was very peaceful. There wasn't anything to do, so I decided to take a nap. I was sitting in a plantation front yard, napping, and I look up and there's two native soldiers in shorts. They looked at me, and I was a little startled. They didn't know who the hell I was. They were surprised because the Japs had just left. They didn't expect to see any Americans, and there I am taking a nap.

Sometime after that, Jack Kennedy showed up, just when I was ready to go home. I had been there a year. I met and talked with him for about a month when we were at Tulagi. Sometimes we called Kennedy "Shafty," because he liked to say "shafted again." Another friend of Kennedy's was Lenny Thom. He was a college football player from the Big 10, a great big guy and a lot of fun, a nice guy. He always had a joke. They moved from Tulagi up to where Kennedy lost his boat, and I was there when that happened. Kennedy never talked much about it. He always felt that he had screwed up. But he did a wonderful job of saving the people off his boat. And, you know, he was a good swimmer, even with a horrendous back, and he really saved two guys.

It happened on a dark, dark night. I don't think he was at the wheel, and I don't think they saw the destroyer before it cut them in two. This kind of collision was very unusual, the only one I know of. A lot of boats went aground because the charts were so lousy that you never knew where you were, but a PT boat colliding with a Jap destroyer, that was a unique event. I heard from a guy who was in another boat very close to Kennedy that night. He said it was so black and dark you couldn't see a damn thing, and he said that he never blamed anybody for it. It could happen to anybody. His name was "Little" Robinson.

I talked to Kennedy about it later, and he was not proud of the whole thing. As a matter of fact, we kind of kidded him about it, and I joked that he was a "great Naval hero." So then he started to kid me back, and we were both calling each other "great Naval heroes." None of us gave a damn about being a hero, all we wanted was to get back home. He was the only one who wanted to go back into combat after he'd lost his boat. And, you know, they would normally send them home, but he wanted to stay there and get another boat.

I was going back to the States about that time, so they assigned Kennedy my boat, the 59. And in that boat he had his other adventure, where he got into a tight place and evacuated some trapped Marines. He did that in my old boat with my crew. He thought that would make his name for wartime achievement, but it was the ramming and sinking of the 109 that did it for him, and that always irked him a little. Kennedy came to Rochester after the war, where my wife and I lived, to make a speech, and so we went to hear it. He spotted my wife and me in the audience, and he wrote a note to us that said, "To the wife of a great Naval hero and my friend." And that's how we used to kid each other.

Kennedy was an interesting character. He had spent time in Europe, in London, at the School of Economics, when his father was the ambassador to England, and he really had a pretty good idea of world affairs. None of the rest of us knew anything. And he would say to me, I'll always remember, "You people," he said, "are all soft on Communism, aren't you?" And by that he meant Jewish people were soft on Communism, since I was Jewish. He was kidding me, of course, and we laughed about it. I was with him when his older brother got killed. And he had a brother-in-law that got killed, and he was the only one left in the family that was in combat.

I got sent back to the States in time for Christmas 1943. When I left, one good souvenir I got was the aluminum plaque off the 59 that said "Commissioned on . . ." and so forth. I took that home with me, and I still have it. Later I had a duplicate made and sent it to Jack Kennedy when he was president, because he had the 59 after I did. I think it might be in his library in Boston.

I flew from Guadalcanal to Hawaii in PBYs, and had to stop at a number of islands en route—it's a long ways from the Solomons to Hawaii. Then I flew from Hawaii to the States on a big Pan Am China Clipper flying boat. I was able to sit down at a table and eat in that thing. I couldn't believe it. After being out in the Solomons eating Spam, there I am sitting on the Clipper eating a fine dinner. That was first-class treatment.

After a little break in San Francisco, I got assigned to Newport as an instructor on PT boats. When Kennedy came back a little later, they sent him to the Newport Naval Hospital. After that, he got assigned to join us at Newport. There were a number of us combat veterans there training the new guys, and we had a house on the beach at Newport. We asked Kennedy to get us some scotch, since his old man was importing it, and he sent a truckload of Haig and Haig Pinch to that house. They stacked up the cases in the kitchen, and you couldn't see out the windows. After that, what happened in that place, you couldn't believe. It was a party all the time, and Kennedy was right there in that group with us. And the girls used to come from all around. They'd come in carloads, because we were the party house. And the worst people in this party house were our married guys. They were horrendous! We would do training during the day and party every night.

During this time we had a guy who was supposed to have impregnated a girl when he was training down in Panama. We called him "Louie Lopez" because in Panama he talked like a Spaniard. This woman claimed that he had impregnated her, so they sent Kennedy down there to look at the kid and talk to the woman. And Kennedy said, "This kid's the spitting image of Louie." And that's all we needed to know.

I was back in Newport for a long time, a year and a half, and then they decided to send me back out to the Pacific, to the Philippines. The PT boats really had a chance of doing some good when they were in the Philippines, but things didn't go well. The whole Navy was down there fighting the Japanese navy, but the commanders screwed up and put the PT boats where they were facing the large ships of the Japanese navy. When they had some trouble, they blamed it on the fact that the officers and crews weren't well trained. So the idea was that they were going to take a bunch of us who had PT boat experience in the Solomons and send us over there to help the crews in the Philippines. By the time we got ready to go out there, the war was practically over. But I had my orders and went on over to San Francisco, where I partied big time while waiting to board the *Matsonia*. By the time I climbed onboard that ship, I was pretty well partied out and slept most of the way to Hawaii.

The next leg of the trip, from Honolulu to the Philippines, was on the *Hollandia*, which was a cruise ship they'd turned into a troop transport. I threw away all my clothes before I got on the ship, because I knew I could get clothes when I got there, and I went aboard with two seabags full of whiskey. I was really in business with that whiskey. I traded for everything. I got to Hollandia and traded for a

Jeep. Then I got a guy to take me out to a barge that was full of beer, and I got 300 cases of Rainier beer for my whiskey. I kept on using that as trading material.

There was a Navy nurse onboard ship who found out she was pregnant. She wanted to get an abortion out there in the Pacific, and she heard maybe I could arrange it with my whiskey to trade. I asked around and had the liquor to trade for it, but I decided it wasn't a good idea. It ended up two dentists were going to do it. I called it off, and she didn't get the abortion. They sent her home.

Then I ended up in the Philippines until the end of the war, near Leyte. I was in Squadron 23 when I went back out there. We had Higgins PT boats, and they were not anywhere near as good as the Elco boats we had in the Solomons. I was second in command of the squadron there, and we didn't do much of anything, just a lot of exercises. We were set to go north for the invasion of Japan.

At the end of the war I was entitled to go home right away, but I stayed for awhile and set up the procedure for how to scrap the PT boats. We had the crews loosen all the nuts and bolts, so that when we got a boat under a big crane we could pick up the engines and stuff. Everything was supposed to be loose enough so that we could do it in a hurry. We could scrap maybe ten boats in a day, or fifteen. Once we'd gotten the engines and other heavy stuff out of them, we pushed them up on the beach and burned them. The ones that were newer, we put them out on buoys, maybe a hundred or so. But the rest of them we burned, about 300 boats. I didn't think anything about it. You'd think I'd have some kind of emotional attachment to those PT boats, but I didn't care. I just wanted to go home.

We burned them because we had to be careful. There were Chinese in business in the Philippines when we were there, and they would do things like buy whole sawmills shipped over for our use. The whole goddamned thing would come in crates, and somebody would sell it to them. It would end up on the mainland of China, and we didn't want the boats to get in the hands of people in illegal businesses.

I did one further thing in the Philippines, which made me want to go into law. The war was over and I was ready to come home, but I volunteered to do some legal work to see what it was like. I was chosen by the admiral to investigate a crime, a stabbing in a whorehouse in the Philippines. An Army guy got stabbed, cut up pretty bad, in a big brawl near Leyte. He didn't know who did it. So I was supposed to find out. I took a Navy yeoman and went to the place and questioned everybody, maybe ten people. I took their testimony and was supposed to report to the admiral. It just kept running through my mind: who did what to whom? And I got more confused the deeper I got into it. There happened to be a black Navy mess guy involved, and the admiral was sure that he did it, but I couldn't prove it. At the end I put in the report that I just couldn't find out, and I didn't tap the black guy. The admiral, a Southern gentleman, was sure the black guy did it. So he wrote me a bad fitness report as a result. It was the first and only bad one I had in the service. And I challenged it. I said what I did and how I did it, and I had all the testimony and wasn't able to determine who did what to whom. I answered the questions about that fitness report, and they expunged the whole thing from my record. So that was my start at being a lawyer.

At the end of the war I was in a fog. I didn't know what was happening. I didn't really feel comfortable until I got home. I visited an aunt in San Francisco, and she started giving me all this stuff about being crazy from combat. And I didn't like it, so I left, because I didn't think I was crazy. Maybe I was.

So when I got back to Syracuse I started law school immediately. I got back in December 1945, and I was in law school in January and was graduated in two years. I went summers and got out in record time. I got paid to go to law school from the GI Bill.

After the war, Jack Kennedy asked me if I'd help him run for president. At the time I had just started to go into practice, and it looked like his campaign was going to take two years. I didn't want to spend two years doing that, so I said no. He asked the same question of another guy he'd met before the war in Europe, who was out there in the Solomons with us as an intelligence officer, a guy named Byron White. "Whizzer" White, the football star from Colorado, wasn't that friendly, and he didn't want to talk much to anybody when we were on Tulagi. He was kind of a cold fish. We got the Japanese code, and White was sent to tell us what was happening, without us knowing his source. So he kept away from us; that was part of his job.

Kennedy talked Byron out of his law practice and into helping him run for president. Kennedy won, of course, and Byron got appointed assistant attorney general. And then when there was a Supreme Court opening, Kennedy got him in there. So I guess I blew my chance to be a

Supreme Court justice. But I don't have any regrets. I had a great career in law. But it was nice of Kennedy to ask me. I had gotten along with him very well and I respected him. I thought he was quite a guy.

What bothered me about the war and still bothers me is that everybody thinks it's glamorous and everybody thinks it's efficient. It's the least efficient type of any activity I've ever been a part of. And if you're a thinking person and you're out there in those islands and you're seeing what's going on, you can't understand it. We were doing what we were told to do and we did it. But I didn't know that it was such an important event.

I never smoked, but I lost two wives who smoked. I had malaria and dengue fever. I got dengue fever in Guadalcanal and got rid of it fairly easy. But I was sick as hell with malaria. I got that in the Philippines. I was taking Atabrine and I still got malaria, and it lasts for a lifetime. But I was lucky after the war because I never had any trouble with nightmares. Maybe that's because I had this bad attitude. I mean, I treated the whole thing like it was a joke. The only trouble I've had was hearing, and I still have problems with that. I lost 30 percent of my hearing from the noise of the engines on the boat, and gunfire I guess. As a lawyer, when I'm trying a case I use hearing aids. But I'm able to get along without hearing aids most of the time. I hate them, so I don't wear them. But if I go to a PT boat convention, everybody's wearing hearing aids.

The war really changed my whole life. Before I went to the Pacific, I wasn't real motivated, and I didn't really know what I was going to do in life. But after my experiences in the Navy, I came back with a real sense of self-confidence. I'd had to get along with all types of people, and I'd had to run a PT boat and have that responsibility. I'd taken that boat and my crew out in stressful situations under fire and I was able to do it. I think I was pretty good at it, and that builds your self-confidence. The only way I got that range of experience was being on PT boats in the Navy. I got out of the Navy and just felt like I had the confidence that I could do anything, and let's get to it. Some of the PT boat guys I knew have gone back to the Solomons, but not very many. I mean, most of them feel like I do, the hell with that place. I don't want to ever see it again. The jungle and climate were terrible, and who the hell wants to go back and see it. But I'll never forget what happened to me out there in those islands. My life was never the same, and the war in the islands changed me for the better. I have had an enjoyable and successful life practicing law. I go to the office in the mornings, and I'm now eighty-five. I still ski, and I fish all over the world.

## AL HAHN
NAVY

I heard about Pearl Harbor when I was in Longmont, Colorado, and I was working for a doctor there. I was over at one of his neighbors, and he said, "Say, did you hear what happened to the United States naval fleet?" "No, I didn't hear a thing." And he said, "The Japanese bombed them at Pearl Harbor." "Pearl Harbor," I said, "where is that? Never heard of it." "Well," he said, "that's a naval base in the Pacific." "Well," I said, "Why did they do that?" Well, of course, he didn't know. We decided that they kind of wanted to declare war on the United States. I was a senior in high school at that time; I had four or five months to go before I graduated, and that's the way I heard about the United States getting into war and about Pearl Harbor. Then I went to school the next day, and they had a big assembly and talked about it a little bit, and by this

ABOVE: *Al Hahn in the engine room of* PT *161 in the Philippines in early 1945. Two of the three Packard V-12 engines are visible in this photo. Al controls the clutch levers that engage the engines on commands from the skipper in the cockpit just above the engine room on the main deck.*

time I think Congress had declared war on Japan. That's how I got acquainted with it.

I had to finish high school first before I could enlist, and so I did. While I was in high school I was taking a course to learn how to be a machinist. During the month of May they sold the entire machine shop to the government, so that ended my classes. I lacked about two weeks, but the teacher said, "Oh, well, that's good enough. You just about completed it." I kind of liked it and wanted to pursue that and learn a little bit more, so I got a job working at the Silver Engineering Works in Denver. I worked there until October 1942, but then I decided that there was too much excitement going on in the world to keep working in a defense plant during the entire war. So a neighbor kid and I, we both graduated together, we decided we were going to enlist. So we did, we joined the Navy.

I'd never even seen the ocean. So this friend of mine and I, we both joined the Navy, joined together. We left Denver in, let's see, we joined in November of '42, then we headed up to Idaho—Farragut, Idaho. We went through boot camp in Farragut. Everybody used to talk about all of the terrible things at boot camp, but I thought it was like a vacation! I enjoyed it, you know, I just thought it was a good place to live, lots of friends, good food, and there's always something to do and a lot of excitement and everything. I couldn't see anything wrong with boot camp.

The recruiting officer had said, "Okay, you want to be a machinist. We can just work that out and you can go to a machinist school." So I applied for a machinist school, but I think that the people who were assigning all of this stuff, they didn't know the difference between a machinist and a motor machinist. Well, there's a world of difference between them, but they sent me to a motor machinist school, and then I went to Ames, Iowa, to Iowa State University.

When I went to high school I was a very poor student. I didn't have the slightest interest in school. I was interested in all kinds of other things, but school was not one of them. I did so poorly, you know, I graduated at the bottom of my class. Maybe not the very, very bottom, but close to it. But anyhow, when I got to Ames, Iowa, they had a sort of motivational factor that if you graduated within the top 10 percent you could get an advancement. I got to thinking, you know, I didn't think I was really as dumb as my high school record indicated. I thought, I'm gonna shoot for it, see if I can get in the top 10 percent. So I knuckled down and studied pretty good, and I graduated sixth out of 120 guys. I was number six! So I was in the top 10 percent real easy and I got my rate that I was looking for. Then at the same time they were having a recruiting session for PT boat personnel, and they only took guys that had a good record. They said if they were in the upper 10 percent, or something like that, they could apply for PT boats if they wanted to. It was all voluntary. Of course, I was just beginning, so I didn't really know what a PT boat was, but we talked around on campus there and different people began to tell me that they were a pretty nice little boat. They were fast, and they do this and that and everything, and the more we talked the more interested I got. So I decided I was going to apply for that, and I did. I applied for it and I got it. Then I went to Melville, Rhode Island.

There at Melville we began to study aircraft engines, because that's what they had, Packard V12s. While I was in Ames, Iowa, we were studying diesels. That meant that what I learned in Ames was okay for the principle of the thing, but it didn't specify the details or even the difference between a diesel and an aircraft engine. We were trained to be familiar with all the other parts of the PT boat. You would have to become familiar with the entire boat, but that was more as a matter of generality. For example, we all had to learn how to drive the boat.

We really became pretty much like a family on our boat, officers and enlisted men. The only real difference was the officers knew what was going on most of the time, and the rest of the crew didn't know anything! They'd say, "Well, there's no need for you to bother yourself with all of this kind of stuff." What I'm really saying is, especially when we got into the war zone and they were planning strategy, they would go up to the headquarters and get briefed on what they were going to do, and they'd come back to the boat and they never told us anything. They'd just say, "Well, we're going on a mission tonight. Everything ready?" You know, that was really the only difference between them and the enlisted men, because most of the time the officers were just part of the gang.

The skipper who ran the boat was a first lieutenant, and there were two officers on each boat. We'd usually have an ensign and a lieutenant (j.g.). The boat is built for twelve more or less. I was on a Higgins boat in the Mediterranean and an Elco boat in the Pacific, and there were about twelve of us, but that varied a little bit. Sometimes we'd take on a couple of extra personnel, like during an invasion.

We slept on the boat all the time. The enlisted men were sleeping in one area and the officers were in another area. The enlisted men slept in the very bow of the boat, except where the bow comes to a point. We had what we called a locker there that we threw all our sea bags and stuff in, just threw them in and filled it up. Then right behind that there was room for twelve people in there, and then behind that was a chart room, chart house, and the officers' quarters were right underneath that. They just had a little bitty spot, just for two people. It was about like an ordinary bathroom in a house.

We had a bathroom, but it was so tiny that we only used it in extreme emergencies! Most generally when we'd go out on patrol we went out at night, and in the morning we'd come in. We were always tied up at a dock at the PT base, and at the base they'd have a chow hall and showers, a bathroom and those facilities, and this is what we used except for sleeping. When we'd come in off of a patrol, we'd eat breakfast at the base. Then usually the next thing for me to do would be to fuel the boat. We'd fill her back up so we had 2,000 gallons of 100-octane gasoline. The refueling area wasn't real close to our dock. For safety purposes they kept it maybe like a quarter of a mile away. We'd go over there and fill her up. That was my job. I was down in the engine room all the time. The engine controls, like engaging the clutches and throttles, were run by hand by me. On the Elco boat in the Pacific I had a seat right on top of one of the three engines, and there were long handles for clutches to engage the engines. At minimum it would take two of us, one in the engine room and one at the wheel up on deck, to really drive the boat. I was just about always in the engine room, and I was looking at an instrument panel in front of me that relayed instructions from the skipper on the bridge right above. You not only had instruments that'd tell you what each engine was doing in several different categories, but also signals from the bridge about, you know, forward, reverse throttles, and so forth. We had throttles down there and they had throttles up above, and it was kind of a combination right there.

First I was assigned to the Mediterranean on a Higgins PT boat, and we saw a lot of action, and we had a lot of our guys hit. Every one of our crew got wounded except two, and of the two who didn't get wounded one was our executive officer and the other was me!

In October of '44 I came home for a leave, a long one. Then I went back to Boston, and it was in December that I got word I was getting shipped out to the Pacific. I left Boston and I think it took us five days by train to go to San Francisco, and there I got on the *Matsonia*. It was a luxury liner in peacetime, but they converted it to a troop ship. It was a nice ship and all that, but it wasn't much like a luxury cruise or anything.

It was pretty well crowded, but they had a lot of nurses on a different deck up above. Of course they'd stay there in their quarters and we stayed in ours. At least I didn't see any hanky panky going on, but we were enlisted men anyway and that was out of the question since the nurses were officers. There was, well, what you might call speculation about those nurses, but I don't think anything ever happened! Anyhow, we dropped them off in Hawaii, at Honolulu.

Then we went to New Guinea. When we crossed the equator, they had what they called a Neptune Party. This was to initiate those of us who had never crossed the equator before. The ones who had gone through this before were called Shellbacks, and those of us who hadn't were called Pollywogs. Unfortunately for me, I was in a cabin with mostly Shellbacks. In fact, most of the guys on that ship were Shellbacks, so they really had it in for us Pollywogs. The first thing that happened was they stripped us naked and had us crawl through a gauntlet, which was a long line of guys on each side, and it was a swat line. Each one of those guys had a wooden slat they had pried off some packing crates. So as we crawled down through this double line, these guys were beating us on the butt. That was bad enough, but what made it really difficult was that at the end of the line were a few guys with a fire hose, and they were spraying that thing full force at us as we tried to crawl out of this line. So that meant it was a struggle to just get through the line, and all the time we were getting beaten with these wooden slats. I couldn't sit down for a week!

For some of the Pollywogs, they blindfolded them and had them walk the plank, which was a board out over a tub filled with water, but they thought they were walking a plank out over the side of the ship into the ocean since they couldn't see. They'd scream and holler when they went over that plank and hit the tub of water, and thrashed around thinking they were in the ocean. But when they got the blindfolds off they saw they were still on deck, and all the Shellbacks really laughed at that. I was lucky and didn't have to do that. After this was all over we got issued Shellback cards, and I carried mine in my wallet for years. You never want to lose it, so in case you cross the equator again you don't have to go through another initiation. Right now my Shellback card is in a safety deposit box!

So we finally got to a place called Hollandia on the north coast of New Guinea. I was there for just a little while, oh, maybe a week. Then by this time I was already assigned to a PT boat squadron, to squadron nine. From Hollandia they took us up to Samar near Leyte in the central Philippines. It was a brand-new base, and it was a main PT boat base for the Philippines.

From there I got assigned to PT-161, and that was the boat I rode in the Pacific all of the time I was there. I was probably the second or third replacement "motor mac" for that boat because that was such an older organization. The original crew, they probably weren't even in the Navy anymore by the time I got there.

I was maybe a little apprehensive of moving in with that crew because I was just a new guy on their boat. But I got a pretty warm reception because I already had this experience in the Mediterranean, and everybody was pretty curious to know what was going on in the Mediterranean. So by the time I told them a few of those stories, well I was one of the gang.

It took me about five minutes to make the transition from the Higgins PT boat I was on in the Mediterranean to the Elco boat in the Pacific. I mean, they're basically the same, maybe a little different arrangement, but you pick that up in a minute or two. I was based on an island off of Mindanao called Basilan. It's about twenty miles from Zamboanga. Actually it was a little island off of the island of Basilan. Just a little tiny one. You know a big ocean wave could roll over the top of it, so that was where we were based.

We'd trade little things with the Filipinos, cartons of cigarettes or something. Actually this friend of mine and I, we bought a boat. It was one of those dugout canoes, a double outrigger. I think we bought it for a carton of cigarettes and a couple of t-shirts and a pair of dungarees; I think that was about all we paid for this boat. It was a brand-new one, just carved out, a beautiful little boat. We got it and we used to sail it around when we had days off. But when I went off to the invasion of Borneo, one of the base force guys got it, and he used to sail it over to Isabella Island, you know, and get to drinking sake. His squadron commander wanted to put a stop to that, so he burned our boat while we were gone. All we could see when we got back was a little pile of ashes! That really upset us, but there was nothing we could do about it.

Well, I'll tell you, in the Pacific I didn't see as much action as I did in the Mediterranean. The only activity I really saw in the Pacific was during the invasion of Borneo. It was probably in February of 1945. Our job during that invasion was first of all to patrol the area, and if we possibly could we'd shoot up things like petroleum storage. If we saw any gas tanks and stuff like that we were supposed to blow them up. And we did blow a few of them up. The only real enemy engagement that I experienced at that time was when we were sent to shoot up a Japanese army camp up one of these big rivers. I guess it was someplace between five and eight miles up the river in Borneo. I don't even know the name of the river. Nobody was ever worried about whether I knew any of this stuff or not; they just said this is where we're going. We had some native guides and they would sit on the bow of the boat with their feet hanging over the end. They would point toward the deepest part of that river, this way or that way, and we kept on going. We had another boat right behind us. We got up there and sure enough there was this big Japanese army camp, and the plan was that we were supposed to surprise them, shoot for maybe two minutes with all our guns, and then get out of there. On each boat we had one 40mm, one 37mm, two sets of twin 50s, two sets of twin 30s, and that's a lot of firepower right there. Then you multiply that by two because there was another boat right behind us. When we first went in there, we quick turned around in the river so we were headed in the right direction to make a getaway. Then we fired away just like we were supposed to. Finally we figured, well, we did as much damage as we can, and we're going to take off.

So we took off, our boat did, and wham, some of the Japanese were still sitting behind their machine guns, and they hit the other boat right there down by the engine room. They put 50 or 100 holes in it, and anyhow their engines conked out on them. I never could figure out how they could conk out all three of them, but they did. We got this urgent call on the radio that they're dead in the water, and they were yelling, "Come and get us." Well, you know, we didn't really like that kind of an assignment, but okay, here we come. We turned around in the river and we went back. But now you have to keep all the Japanese away from their guns; they didn't return fire very much as long as you were firing. They were ducking for cover. We pulled up and were firing, and the other boat still had their guns going. The engines were dead but the guns were still okay. So they are firing and we are firing all the time, and we had to turn around again in the river to rig a tow. We tied a line onto the other boat and started to take off. Well, we were in such a big hurry we kind of gunned it a little too much and snapped the line. Well, it takes a long time to stop, go back, turn around, tie on again, and all the time we had to keep these guns going.

By this time though we started running out of ammunition. We had a lot of ammunition down in the bottom of the boat, but up there on deck where the guns were, they were empty. About half the crew had to give up their gun positions and start moving their ammunition up, and this darn ammunition was heavy. They were pushing it up, and pretty soon their arms were getting played out. They just ran out of power. They were yelling, "We need some fresh help." What they were thinking of doing was taking some of the guys that had been shooting, putting them down, and taking these guys that were lifting and put them behind the guns, and this executive officer said, "By golly, let's get Hahn up here; he could push some of that ammunition up for you." He called the engine room and sent another engineer down there who was all exhausted. He said I was supposed to go up there on the deck and he was going to be in the engine room. So I went up there and I wanted to know what I was supposed to do. The exec said, "Get down there and start pumping up this ammunition." Well, just about the time I was ready to jump down there, here comes a gunner's mate off of the 40mm. He said, "I can't fire the 40mm anymore. It's too hot. It's gonna blow up." And the exec said, "Well, what's the difference? If you don't fire it, the Japanese are going to be killing you, so you might as well die right behind the gun no matter how hot it is." Well, this guy was kind of panicking. I don't know what to tell you, but he just fell apart. So the skipper said to him, "Get down there and push up this ammunition." So he sent him down there and he asked me, "Can you fire the 40mm?" I said, "I've never fired it, but I know how." So he put me on the 40mm. That's the only time I fired a gun in the entire Navy.

I wasn't worried whether the gun would blow up or not. There was just too much going on around there to even think about it. As fast as they'd bring this ammunition up, well, I'd empty it. All I know is when we were shooting out there we knocked down about all of the coconut trees that were in this area. You know there were a lot of coconut trees standing there, but that 40mm, if you hit a coconut tree it was a goner. The trigger was on the right foot pedal. It took two guys to fire it; one guy, he would aim it in the right direction, and the other guy would aim it up and down. I did the up-and-down and I had the trigger. You'd just push that lever down with your foot and it would fire. There were all these tents and everything around there in that camp, and I could see what I was shooting at real well. With this 40mm you'd have sights on it and you'd pretty much go by the sights. When you put a clip in, a clip had four shells in it, and you could shoot all four shells in two seconds if you wanted to. It was kind of like bang...bang...bang...bang. You know, maybe one shell every two seconds. Something like that, because somebody had to feed 'em into it. It took two guys to feed 'em in—if they had all the shells there. We had to wait until they brought them up from the locker, so you have to go a little slower. We really shot up the place. I could see my shells hitting and exploding and dirt and debris would fly, and we hit a lot of things.

The guns were so hot that as soon as the shell went in there it went off. In about half a second it would heat up and explode. Most of that stuff is kind of like a blur because we were all firing as fast as we could. Finally we got the second tow rigged and pulled them out of there and back around a bend in the river so we could quit shooting. Nobody on either boat got hurt; well, I shouldn't say nobody, since we had one guy who collected the Purple Heart for this: On the way out, this guy had a Thompson submachine gun, and he was out shooting it too. Well, that was just about as effective as shooting little BBs! But anyhow, that's what he was doing, he was standing up there on the deck firing that thing, and one of the Japanese shot and hit him. He thought he was shot clear through the neck. What happened was when he was shot he grabbed his neck and looked at his hand and he saw all this blood and he passed out!

Because too much other stuff was going on nobody had time to mess with him until we got around the bend and back down the river a ways. Then they looked him over and said, "Well, what's the matter with you?" He kind of came to and said he was shot through the neck. They looked at his neck, and there was a little blood there. They wiped the blood off and the skin was barely broken, there was just a little scratch there, and it didn't look too bad. So they told him he wasn't shot through the neck at all. So he said, "Well, where's all this blood coming from?" They looked closer, and it turns out he was shot through his ring finger. When the bullet hit his finger, it knocked his hand back. The force of the bullet was so hard that his hand came off the Thompson and he hit himself on the neck with his own hand. The force of his hand hitting his neck was kind of painful there, and he thought he was shot through the neck. So his finger was bleeding, and when his hand hit his neck his fingernail scratched the skin a little bit, see? So they were all laughing and told him he didn't have any hole in his neck; the problem was his finger! Well, he looked at that and thought that's not too serious. Then he was okay. But he got a Purple Heart for that. I was up on deck shooting the gun and saw him go down, but I was watching the boat behind us and hoping the towline wouldn't break again. So even though all this firing was going on, they were still shooting back, there were still some of them popping bullets back at us.

One day the guys on my crew were telling about what happened to them in the days gone back. They mentioned this one officer, they called him a ninety-day wonder, from back east, one of those wealthy families. I don't know if anybody knew his name or not; I didn't recognize the name or anything. They told about this guy going off on his own and getting his boat cut in two, jeopardizing the life of the crew, even one or two guys were killed on account of that. Then after I came home and got married, and about fifteen years later, why, there's this guy running for president, and come to find out he used to be on PT boats. I found out his was the boat that was cut in two, and I finally put it all together that this was old John Kennedy!

The 157 boat was the one that had picked Kennedy up, and it ended up in the Philippines where I was. People knew the story and that the 157 had picked up him and the surviving members of his crew. I got a picture of it. That was a pretty old boat by then because it would have been in the Solomon Islands right at the beginning of the war. Those boats saw activity at different places, and it would have been a three-year-old boat by that time. And my boat, the 161, was the same age. But really, even though we were in the tropics, the boats stayed in surprisingly good shape, though there was quite a bit of mildew. We'd be assigned to a base right next to a jungle or something, and there were a lot of insects flying around at night. Whenever possible we'd go out and anchor maybe a half a mile or a quarter mile away from the shore and there were no insects. Then we'd sleep on the boat down in our berths below decks. You'd think it would be too hot to sleep down there, but surprisingly, around the equator, it wasn't as hot as I thought it might be. I don't know why it is, and there was high humidity too, but we were always close to the water. I think that the ocean itself, if you're near the surface, it has a cooling effect, and I never really suffered from the heat down there around the equator.

Towards the end of the war our job was to go through the islands and pick up all of these prisoners. They had isolated these prisoners on these islands. The Japanese couldn't get to them and these guys couldn't escape, so they were just prisoners on the islands without anybody to guard them. They were hard up for food and medical and all of that. We would just gather them up and take them to Zamboanga.

About this time the war ended, and the way we found out about it was kind of amusing. The way it was, see, all the PT boats have a policy that when a crew leaves a boat there's supposed to be two people to stay aboard. One of them has to know how to handle the ship, as far as the steering mechanism goes, and the other one has to be the engineer who knows how to start the engines, put them in gear, all that stuff. This one particular night we were over in this little town of Isabella off of Basillon. We just went there about a day earlier, and we were supposed to get three brand-new engines in our boat. Our engines had so many hours on them that it was time to replace them. We were getting ready for the invasion of Japan, which I heard at one time was supposed to take place maybe in November or December. So we went up there and took all the bolts off of the engine room hatch covers. The next day we were supposed to lift that hatch up; you needed a crane to do that because it was pretty heavy. Then that would expose all the engines, and we could remove them and put the new ones in.

So evening came and the crew wanted to see some movies, so okay, who's gonna stay aboard? Well, I don't know whether I volunteered or whether it was my turn, but anyhow, I stayed aboard to be the engineer on the boat, and our radioman, he was going to be the guy who knew how to pull the boat out from the dock if necessary—emergency stuff. So the rest of the crew headed to the movies, and we stayed there on the boat and wanted to listen to the radio. I never could hear those darn radios, there was so much static and stuff, but him being a radioman, he was able to pick up the radio broadcasts a little better. We were just kind of hanging around on the boat, and he was down there fiddling around on the radio. Then he pokes his head up on deck and says, "Say, you know, I've been picking up some news and it kind of sounds like the war might be over." "Well, what happened?" I said. This was a complete surprise. We're getting ready for an invasion, and here you hear the war is over. So he said, "I'm gonna tune in a couple more different frequencies and see if I can pick up something else." Well, pretty soon he stopped and said, "You know, the United States set off a couple of very strange and very powerful bombs. They dropped them over in some places in Japan and killed a lot of people. It's a kind of a bomb that we had never used before." So I said, "Well, what kind of a bomb is that?" And he said, "I don't know but it's supposed to be very, very powerful. I'm gonna keep listening." So pretty soon he came back up and said, "There's more reports and excitement out there that the war is over."

And we were looking down about a mile away, and we could see some tracer bullets going in the air. That was our old base where we normally would be. We figured they must have discovered this too and were celebrating by shooting their guns in the air. So we were wondering how we were going to let the other guys from our crew know the war was over. We couldn't go get them because we had to stay on board, and they were over at the movies. This was at an outdoor theater, which really wasn't a theater at all, just a sheet hung up from the trees. So he said, "I know what we can do. We have a mortar, so let's set it up and get their attention." I didn't know how to set it up. I wasn't acquainted with that stuff, being an engineer. But he got that mortar and he got a plate that went on the deck and everything, and then he got out the star shells. He started dropping them in this mortar. They'd go up and explode right over the guys who were watching the movie a ways away, and it was like the Fourth of July; these star shells went off like fireworks and lit up everything. So the guys on our crew couldn't understand what on earth happened to us. They thought we lost our mind. They came running back, thinking we were under attack or something, and they were yelling, "Hey, what's the big idea?" So we told them, "The war is over!"

Then the celebrations began. The next day I noticed our quartermaster was running a new flag up on the flag mast because the old ones get so tattered from being whipped around in the wind. I thought I'd like to have a souvenir of this event, and I asked him. I said, "You've got some more of these flags on stock down there?" "Yeah," he said, he had a little supply. I said, "That's the one I want because that was flying on our boat the day the war ended. I want to take it home." He just handed it to me and put a new one up there. I've still got it to this day. I thought it would be nice to have it.

This bomb was so new and different to us, we didn't understand it, and didn't know the consequences. We never heard a thing about radiation and all of that, and it took a little while for that to sink in, but it didn't make an impact about whether we felt it was a moral thing to do or not. We didn't examine any of that. We decided that the war was over and that's good enough for us, no matter what.

We waited around there a couple of more weeks for some kind of an assignment, and they said everybody's going home. Then we took the whole squadron, and the last thing they did, and I don't know why they did it, but we were all loaded up, we had all the base force people on the boat, and a lot of material, luggage, and all that stuff. Then the squadron commander sent a crew in there to douse all those tents and buildings and everything with gasoline and set them afire. That's what he did. All the natives were waiting; they knew the war was over too. They were waiting to occupy those tents and everything. I thought it was a very senseless thing to do, to burn all that. Those natives were shaking their fists at us and everything. I thought it was terrible, but anyhow, that's the way we left that base: in flames. Then we went up to Samar, and as soon as we got there—the engines still hot—we had orders to pull the engines out of the boat. I remember opening up our $CO_2$, a big tank, you know, that they put out the fires and stuff with? I sprayed it on the engines, just to cool them off, and it cooled them off quite a bit!

Then we went down and started dismantling the engines. The next day they came and pulled the engines out and dropped them in a dump truck and took them along the shore of the island and just dumped them—all the engines out of all those boats—they dumped them in a big pile on the beach just a little ways in the jungle. Then the hulls, they put them another place, set gasoline afire to them and burned them. There again, I don't know why they just didn't give them away to those Filipinos. They could have used the boat hulls for housing if nothing else. There was nothing sentimental about the boats from a practical point of view, but we thought that it was a lot of foolishness to just destroy them. They should have just gone ahead and given them to somebody who could use them. As far as I know, those engines are still there.

I got on an LST, and it took us thirty-three days to cross the Pacific. That's when we stopped at Pearl Harbor. They wanted to pick up some supplies. They wanted a volunteer. I said, I'm gonna go ashore here, and I jumped on this truck, drove into this base, threw on a few packages, jumped in the truck, and was back on the ship. I suppose I had my feet planted on Hawaiian soil about ten minutes. To this day that's all the time I've ever spent in Hawaii.

When the war was over I was ready to go home. I just figured, you know, I didn't join the Navy for a career. I was more interested in helping win the war and doing my part.

But my hearing was damaged being down there with those engines. I didn't even notice it at the time, but one of the other crew members brought it to our attention. He said, "Why do the motor macs talk so loud?" He was talking to guys from another crew, and they said, "Well, our motor macs, they're the same way; they talk loud." They passed it around and they found out that all these guys that spent a lot of time in the engine room were loud talkers when they were playing poker. You know everybody talks kind of quiet, except these guys. They talked loud. Well, the motor macs didn't realize they were talking loud because they could hear their own voice, and it didn't sound very loud to them because their hearing was affected. Then we began to notice, to pay a little attention to our ears, and I noticed my left ear didn't work very good. I was fully unaware of it, and my right ear seemed to be pretty good. Then when I got discharged, they wanted to know if I had any disabilities because of the war. I was so happy that I came back alive that I figured what the heck is a little hearing loss? That doesn't amount to anything compared to your life, so I thought I got by pretty good. So I didn't complain. I thought if I complained they'd keep me there for two or three more days. I said I have nothing to put down, but then after that I used to do almost all my hearing through my right ear.

I sometimes think about fear, and what was it like to face the enemy fire and all that, and how fearful did I get? But it appears it doesn't work quite that way. When you become involved in combat, fear doesn't even enter the picture. It's excitement. And you get intensely excited, you know? It seems like it takes away the fear. You get so excited that you can't calm down for a long time. It isn't really fear; you're just really cranked up like you had way too much caffeine.

You know, to tell you the truth, I think I've been that way ever since. After the war I always have had a sort of a difficult time relaxing. I don't know what's the cause of it, maybe it's in my genes. I don't know, but I get involved or excited pretty easily. If I have an exciting evening I can't go to sleep. I think there's a lot of people like that anyhow so maybe I'm not any different from anybody else, but excitement has been kind of my problem. I mean keyed up. It was after the war when I began to notice it. I don't remember being that way when I was a kid before the war. In fact, when you're riding PT boats, they kind of have a policy that if you ride a boat for six months and you're in any action, they say that's enough. You don't need to ride any longer. You've taken your chances and you came through it, and they'll find somebody else to take your place.

I had this opportunity to get off the boat when I was in the Mediterranean. I got to thinking, you know, you get on the base force and it's just like a civilian job, from 8 to 5, and I thought, oh, that isn't any fun at all. It just seemed so drab and so monotonous. I decided I didn't want that. I'd rather ride the boats because it's kind of like riding a motorcycle; it's more exciting, more fun. They'd go more places. I kind of think I became addicted to the darn boats. I just kind of loved it. I can't explain it, but it was hard to leave the boats behind.

*Al Hahn* 243

# CHAPTER 8

187
FIRE
EXTINGUISHER
LITTLE
BING CROSBY
TO
SEVENTH AIR FORCE
TO
TOJO

*"Suddenly, I heard something hit the plane and turned to look out the left waist gun window, and there was thick black smoke trailing out of the left engine. It turned out that ground fire had hit the prop governor and part of the engine had been shot away."*

—John Beddall, ARMY AIR FORCE

JOHN BEDDALL, ARMY AIR FORCE, B-25 radio operator and gunner, Marshalls

A.C. KLEYPAS, ARMY AIR FORCE, B-24 radio operator and gunner, New Guinea, Philippines

JIM ROSENBROCK, ARMY AIR FORCE, P-38 and P-51 armorer, New Guinea, Philippines

JOHN VINZANT, ARMY AIR FORCE, B-29 pilot

FRED WOLKEN, ARMY AIR FORCE, C-47 troop carrier pilot, New Guinea, Philippines

DON VAN INWEGEN, ARMY AIR FORCE, B-29 tail gunner

BILL MASHAW, NAVY, Naval Air Transport Service pilot

LOUIS MEEHL, ARMY AIR FORCE, gunner

PAGES 244–245: *A Seventh Air Force B-24, "Little Hiawatha," parked on the coral airstrip on Funafuti in November, 1943. Ground crew members and an officer stand behind a bomb with the inscription "Bing Crosby to Seventh Air Force to Tojo."*

OPPOSITE: *John Beddall (front row center) poses with members of his B-25 crew, back row from left, Lt. Bryant, Capt. Bus Knight, Joe Csizmadia; front row from left, Pete Downs, Beddall, and a pilot from another plane. Photo was taken on Makin Atoll in front of the B-25 "Broad Minded."*

# THE WAR IN THE AIR, 1942–45

## JOHN BEDDALL
ARMY AIR FORCE

I enlisted in April 1941, from Idaho. I had some friends who thought it would be a great idea if we all joined the Army Air Corps together. I wasn't quite eighteen so my parents had to sign for me. I went home, and when I told them my mother started crying, but my dad said, "It'll probably do you some good." So he agreed to sign for me. Well, it turned out that none of my friends enlisted, for one reason or another, so I went in alone.

During training I got the request I wanted, to be a radio operator on a bomber, and the location I wanted, which was Tucson, Arizona. So I ended up being a radio operator/gunner on B-25s. I shipped out first to

Honolulu where we did training. We were doing fully loaded short takeoffs and we thought they were going to put us on a carrier.

Then I was based for ten months out in the Pacific, and I was based on Makin Atoll. We were flying bombing missions to targets in the Gilberts and Marshalls. I flew a total of fifty missions. On my fifth mission we were sent over to bomb the Japanese-held atoll of Maloelap where they'd built an airstrip on one of the islets called Taroa. We'd come in real low on these missions to bomb and strafe, so we were right at coconut height. I was shooting things up on the ground with the right waist gun as we zoomed over the airstrip, and all the other guns on the plane were firing. Suddenly, I heard something hit the plane and turned to look out the left waist gun window, and there was thick black smoke trailing out of the left engine. It turned out that ground fire had hit the prop governor and part of the engine had been shot away. First the propeller started windmilling faster and faster until the engine seized up, and then the propeller just stopped turning. Since the prop blades were flat to the wind, they created a lot of wind resistance. It's amazing that my pilot was able to keep control of the airplane with one engine shot out so close to the ground.

So there we were, a long way from home, out over the ocean with only one engine. My pilot, and he was a great one, was Bus Knight. He was a University of Nebraska football star, and he played in the 1941 Rose Bowl game. So, he was nursing our B-25 along on one engine running wide open, barely above the surface of the ocean. Over the intercom he told me to throw anything heavy overboard to see if we could gain some altitude. Taking the waist guns out of their mounts was normally a two-man operation, but since the engineer was still in the tail gun position, I did it by myself. I put my foot up on the frame of the open waist gun window to brace myself, reached out with one hand and grabbed the barrel of the machine gun as far out as I could reach, and with the other hand yanked mightily on the butt end of the gun. It pulled right out of its mount, and I pitched it into the water. The adrenaline was really flowing! We were so close to the surface that the spray was flying up from the ocean, and my foot got wet when I put it up on the frame of the open waist window. I did the same with the other waist gun, and then started to pull up the two steel armor plates in the floor. Each was about three feet long, one foot wide, three-quarters of an inch thick, and about 200 pounds in weight. But the adrenaline was pumping and I yanked the first plate up from the floor, got it up on the waist window frame, slid it out of

*John Beddall's B-25, with one engine shot out, has just braked to a stop on the nearly completed coral runway on Majuro Atoll. The plane, piloted by Bus Knight with Col. Solomon Willis flying as co-pilot, was the first American aircraft in WWII to land on a Japanese mandated Pacific island taken back from the Japanese. This was an honor being prepared for Admiral Nimitz and the Navy, but fate intervened on behalf of the Army Air Corps. Seabees and other naval personnel crowd around the plane.*

the plane, and into the ocean it went. I was just starting to get the second one when Pete suddenly came up behind me from out of the tail gun position, grabbed me, and yelled that if I threw out that plate it would cut off the tail! Of course it wouldn't since the tail of a B-25 was above the level of the waist gun windows and I had just thrown one big plate out with no problem. So I just grabbed him, bodily threw him back toward the rear of the plane, and finished throwing out the other armor plate. I never talked to him after that, and he never flew another mission.

On our maps the closest atoll with an airstrip we could land on was Majuro. Well, the Marines had just taken that atoll from the Japs, and the Seabees were sprucing up the Jap runway to get it ready for a Navy plane to be the first to land on an atoll that had been forcibly taken from the Japanese. But we had an emergency and we had to come in and land.

Another of our B-25s, named "Luscious Lucy," had been flying beside us to make sure we made it. The pilot buzzed the runway to get the Seabees out of the way, and then we came straight in and landed okay.

But there was a complication. Admiral Nimitz was commander of the Navy fleet, and when the runway was finished he was going to take off from a carrier, circle the atoll, and land on Majuro as the newsreel cameras rolled. That would make him the first American to land on a pre-war airstrip that had been owned by the Japanese. So here we come, an Army Air Force B-25, and landed on the runway before Nimitz could have a chance. So that ended the celebration they intended to stage for Nimitz landing on Majuro, and the Navy wasn't real happy about this! They sent four Navy captains over right after we landed to inspect our plane. They figured four captains would outrank any officers that could have been on our B-25, and normally that would have been the case. But on that mission, our colonel, Solomon Willis, was flying in the right seat with my pilot, his good friend Bus Knight. So it was a stand-off, with Col. Willis being of equal rank with the Navy captains. We lined up in front of our B-25, and the Navy captains lined up in front of us. They could see right away that we had a legitimate reason for the emergency landing, and they didn't really know what to say. They felt they needed to say something, so one of the captains sees me, an enlisted man, lined up next to Col. Willis. We were right under the machine guns in the nose of the plane. So this captain comes up to me and says, "Aren't you going to clean those guns?!" I just moved a little closer to Col. Willis and said, "No, sir!" Col. Willis stood his ground and defended me from the Navy. We had to abandon our plane right there at Majuro since they didn't have any repair facilities.

So until they could fly us back to Makin, the enlisted men, me included, were put up in a tent on Majuro, while the officers on our crew were taken out to a ship. But to eat dinner, they came and got us and took us out to that ship, and I'll never forget that meal. Here I had been eating powdered eggs and minimal food like that for weeks, and in front of us in the chow line was what seemed like a feast, and there was two of every category: for potatoes they had baked and mashed, for meat they had pork chops and beef, and so on. I couldn't believe how good the Navy ate!

After that our crew was sent to Honolulu for R and R. We were catching rides on planes headed that direction, and on one leg we were in a B-24 that was being ferried back. We were taking off from Kwajalein, and on our take-off run I noticed that we had gone past the last runway marker and were still on the ground. I started to get worried that this pilot was going to run us right into the ocean off the end of the runway. Well, we got to the end of the runway and the pilot just raised the landing gear, but the plane stayed at the same altitude. This didn't seem like a good situation! The left wing dipped a little bit as I was looking out at the palm trees whizzing past, and then we were over the ocean, still right on the deck. But that pilot got the plane straightened out, and we started climbing real slow and made it to Honolulu.

When we got there, I headed out to a recreation center that had been set up next to the Royal Hawaiian Hotel. It was a low building with card tables, pool tables, and—this was the best part—fridges with bottles of cold milk. We all wanted to drink milk—it had been so long since we had tasted it. I would just pull a bottle out of the fridge and drink that ice cold milk, and it tasted so good!

Back at our base Col. Willis had this little dog named "Pistol Head." He used to whistle to it, and the little dog would come running. Pistol Head was kind of the squadron mascot, a great little dog. Well, one day Col. Willis was driving a Jeep back from the officers club. It flipped over and he was killed. This came as a blow to the squadron, a real tragedy. After that the dog just kind of moped around. He kept thinking Col. Willis was going to come back. Well, one day one of the guys was joking around and saw the dog hanging around. So this guy imitated Col. Willis's whistle. The dog perked right up, thought his master was back, and came running, but couldn't find Col. Willis. That was about the cruelest thing I ever saw—that dog was so disappointed—you could just see it searching around for its master because he thought he heard the whistle. That still chokes me up to think about it.

Our missions were usually around four hours round trip. We bombed Jap bases on a lot of little atolls in the Gilberts and Marshalls, and also Ponape. We were told to never be taken alive. If we were over a Jap island and were hit and couldn't make it, just push the controls over and nose it in. We heard the Japs killed enlisted men outright and tortured and then executed the officers. We think this is what happened to Capt. Colley and his crew. His plane crashed near the shore of an island, and we saw four of the five crew make it out onto their raft. A PBY went out to pick them up, but the Japs beat them to it. We never saw or heard from those guys again. Ten years after the war they were officially pronounced dead.

---

I think my experiences in the Pacific affected me, and of course I'll never forget what happened. In 2002 my wife, Hazy, and I did a cruise around the Pacific islands with a lot of other veterans. We stopped at a couple of the atolls I was on during the war. As we went along I learned all about what the others did, and it was interesting to hear all the different types of experiences they had. I was only in one small bit, flying out over the atolls and islands, and some of those guys had a lot more dangerous jobs. But I did my part, I did what I was trained to do, and I survived. I volunteer at the Mesa wing of the Commemorative Air Force. I have a notebook with photos of B-25s and some of the islands we bombed, and we have a B-25 there in the hangar we are restoring. People look at the plane, and I show them the photos in my notebook and tell them about my experiences. I think it helps them to relate to the Pacific war if I'm there and they are looking at the B-25 and can hear a little bit about what we were doing out there.

OPPOSITE: *Wartime photo of A.C. Kleypas.*

*The War in the Air*

## A.C. KLEYPAS
ARMY AIR FORCE

I got drafted in a funny way. When I got out of high school I was eighteen years old, and that was in 1942. I had another brother who's two-and-a-half years older than I am. I got a draft notice so my mama went with me to the Draft Board and I said, "Hey, what are you doing drafting *me*? I've got an older brother at home and he wasn't drafted." The guy there says, "Is that right? Well, what's his name?" Sure enough they had lost my brother's records, even though he had his draft card and everything. So anyway, they looked at me and mom and said, "Well, one of ya'll's gotta go right now. Either you or your brother can go, but one is going now." I looked at my mama, and I didn't want to say it, but I said, "I'll go." My brother stayed at home an extra year.

I wanted to get in the Air Corps, so I took a bunch of tests and got in. They sent me to radio school, basic training, in South Dakota, then all over, including Yuma, Arizona. I finally ended up in California, and they shipped us overseas out of San Francisco. I ended up being a radio operator on B-24s. And on a B-24 the radio operator was also a gunner.

So we flew a brand-new airplane across the Pacific, and made a lot of stops along the way. I remember one was at Christmas Island and another was Guadalcanal. They were still shooting there at nights. Then we flew out the next day, and we landed at Townsville, Australia. I forget how long we stayed there, probably two or three days. But it was there we had to give up our brand-new airplane. We were just flying it across the Pacific so somebody else could get it.

From Townsville we got on a ship, a little old stinkin' boat, smelled like goats. Took us three days and we went to Port Moresby, New Guinea. There were about three or four airfields where they operated out of there. We used to go down and bomb the Celebes, some islands way off to the west. Anyway, we did a lot of missions out of New Guinea. Another place we flew out of was right across from Biak Island on the north coast. It was a little island by the name of Owi. This little island was just airstrip from water to water. It was nothing but just a coral island like all these islands were. And we used to take off there and fly long missions, most of them were ten or eleven hours over water all the time, and we bombed a lot of different islands. We even went over to Balikpapan on the island of Borneo. That was a long mission for us, and let me tell you something about our two missions over there. You know, you heard about the Japanese and the kamikazes, and how they'd fly their planes into our ships? Well, on that Balikpapan mission, that's the first time they kamikazed an airplane in the air that I knew of. They took fighter planes and tried to fly them into ours, and if one rammed a B-24 with a crew of ten, then it took ten American lives for one Japanese. That's not bad, is it? That happened over Balikpapan, and that was where all the Japanese oil fields were.

Their planes would come at you, and you couldn't really shoot them. The chance you'd shoot one of those planes down was one in 50 or 75 or 100. It's not as easy as they make it look in the movies. It's the real thing and it's a lot harder. A lot of times they'd just come up from the bottom of the formation and try to ram us.

We were making the first bombing mission from Angaur to bomb some town in Formosa. We were taking off the first day, and our lead man, the big boss himself, got a little bit off on the side of the strip and hit a plane over there and cut the end of the wing off, and they crashed. We were the next to take off and we got about half way down the runway, and we had to stop. We were carrying 1,000-pound bombs, and the bombs from that lead plane that just crashed started going off, so we had to cancel the whole mission. It was raining, it was raining real hard. One of the guys on that crew, the radio operator, was a real good friend of mine. In fact, part of the crew I usually flew with was on that plane including my copilot. See every now and then they would split us up. So those guys died and I didn't. I still have trouble with that.

But our planes were close to crashing all the time. We took off at Owi one time and were so loaded down we couldn't get off the runway. And the copilot was screaming at the pilot, "Pull it up!" I was standing right behind him. We cleared the end of the runway and we were over the ocean right away, but we hadn't gained any altitude. We just put the landing gear up, and we were about six feet off the water, loaded with all those bombs, and we couldn't gain any altitude. If there would have been a six-foot wave, we would have hit it and crashed!

So when I had flown probably twenty missions, we went over to Palau because we couldn't land at Leyte. They had the invasion of the Philippines up there in Leyte, and they also had a strip up in Palau. We were supposed to go up there and land on that strip and operate out of that strip. When we'd move, all the base moved. They would put them on the LSTs, you know, our tents and our cookstoves and the people that were on the ground that maintained the planes, they would all get on the LSTs and go up there. Well, they landed up there, but we took off with the planes and couldn't land there. So they diverted us, and we went over and landed at Angaur, which is in the Palau islands. We had no food or anything, and we had to bum our food. We lived on K rations there for a long time. We had to dig our own well for water. We had it rough there for a while.

After we finally got away from there, we went over to Samar in the Philippines. We used to fly from there, and once they captured Manila they moved us to Clark Field, and we flew out of there. That's when we did a lot of bombing up at Taiwan, and they really had the antiaircraft guns up there.

When we went over there to Palau the Seventh Air Force was based there. They had all new airplanes, had everything so fine, and here we were a bunch of crumbs. We didn't have anything. Some of our planes had 100 missions on them. We had come up from the lowest place you can get, down in New Guinea. You never see our planes on film or anywhere because there was never a report. Nobody ever took pictures or anything, because no press would ever go there. We never had anything filmed, no war correspondents. None of them wanted to go there it was so bad, so we got no coverage and no one knew where we were, and people still don't know anything about what we did. Who knows that American planes bombed the Celebes? No one's even heard of the Celebes, and that was true during the war and right up to now!

I had several close calls. We had a lot of times when we'd come back with three engines. I'd have to put out a Mayday alert call on the radio in that case. They would give us a direct shot and locate us and track us all the way in case we lost another one, because we couldn't go on two engines. We were coming in on three engines one time and fixing to land, and we didn't have much of a control tower to keep track of the landing pattern. We were just about on the ground, and all of a sudden there was another plane that pulled out right under us. We almost had some kind of major crash because we didn't have any power to maneuver with only three engines. We had a lot of close calls like that. We'd get a lot of holes in the airplane, engines shot out, but no major crashes. I never parachuted out or anything like that. But I would have jumped out several times if we would have been up higher. I told a guy once, "I'm getting out of here," and looked down and we were about 100 feet off the ground. Ain't no way that's gonna work!

On my missions I made sure I took my parachute and my flight jacket, my survival kit and my escape kit. But really, if you got shot down, you didn't have a chance. They'd kill you. We bombed Formosa up there one time. They call it Taiwan now. We had some planes shot down. I know we killed thousands of people. We dropped magnesium fire bombs. They'd come in big clusters. When you dropped them they just looked like confetti falling. When they hit the ground they'd go off, and you can't put them out unless you put them in a bucket of sand or something. That place was one massive ball of fire when we left.

We lived in tents on dehydrated food, powdered milk, and powdered eggs. We used to have a good breakfast. We could get hotcakes out of that mixture, along with gallon cans of strawberry preserves. We ate good food, but fresh meat or anything like that? We never had any. We had what we called bully beef, which came from Australia. It was corned beef. I thought it was fun. I was nineteen, twenty years old. I didn't know any better!

If you flew a ten-hour mission it took you about fifteen hours all told. We'd get up at 3:00 in the morning and go to briefing. We'd get something to eat, get this, get that, get in the plane. When you got back you'd do it all again, but in reverse. You'd have to go to debriefing if there was anything important. If there wasn't anything important happened, a lot of times they'd let us enlisted men go, and they'd just talk to the pilot and copilot.

I was out at our swimming pool one day a couple years ago and my wife Shirley hollered at me. She said, "Hey, somebody's on the phone." And it was Memorial Day, so I picked up the phone and this guy says, "Hey, have you ever flown on a B-24?" And I said, "I know who you are." I said, "You were my engineer, weren't you?" I hadn't seen him since 1945. He found me over the internet, and so we've been corresponding ever since. He lives in North Carolina. He's my age. He stood

*A.C. Kleypas (center) and two buddies pose in front of one of his squadron's B-24s on Owi Island, near Biak on the north coast of Papua New Guinea*

up there and he'd tell the pilot when the gear was down. We took off one time, and it wasn't a bombing mission. We had to fly a lot of times when we didn't get credit for flying, see. A lot of times we went on missions just to test airplanes, test the engines. When they'd change engines we had to go do a little reconnaissance run, take up new people, and so forth. Anyway one time they sent us somewhere on New Guinea to pick up a load of black powder. Now what we were doing with black powder I don't know. They don't tell us, they just say go get it. So we landed on another one of those metal strips down there, and loaded the cases of black powder. When we started taking off we lost an engine, No.4 engine, and here we had this load of black powder. We barely got airborne and we came around to do an emergency landing, trying to get back down on that air strip. Well, that old copilot—he's dead, he got killed later on—he feathered that prop. Well, to feather the prop you pushed a button in and then turned it loose. Well he pushed it in but then held it down. That old engineer knocked him off of that thing because it goes through the props and it goes right back in. Well, if you don't feather the prop at such a resistance, the thing turns and it just shakes your plane up. Then as we were coming down, the landing gear wouldn't come down. The engine that had quit also had the hydraulic pump on it that lowered the landing gear, and the hydraulic pump was out because the engine was out. So somebody looked out and said, "Hey, we ain't got the landing gear down!" Well, here we go up and around again, wide open and trying to get enough altitude to make another turn and come around again to make a landing. We had to crank the wheels down by hand, and finally came in and landed. That was a close call.

When we bombed Corregidor the Navy had shelled it already, and there was nothing there but just bare rock. It was just so bombed it was just a wasteland. When we moved from New Guinea and went up to the Philippines, it was like we were going to the Waldorf Astoria! We got those natives over there to build us a frame out of bamboo. Then we would put our tents on top of it, and we had us a nice place. Things were looking up, really uptown. And they would wash our clothes for us. They started out at about fifty cents and ended up about five dollars. You know how those things go, don't you? One of them comes and says, "Me wash your clothes, fifty peso." And the next one comes, "Well, I'll give you a dollar, here take that." Then somebody else would give him two, and it'd keep going up in price.

I was living in tents the whole time I was in the Pacific. I never spent a day anywhere except in Army tents, and usually we took our raincoat and put it across the bar that held our mosquito nets. Of course the tents always leaked and it rained all the time, so the raincoat would keep the water off. It was like camping out for over a year. We flew during the day all the time. I never flew a night mission.

The way we knew we were flying a mission was that there was this bulletin board, I guess you'd call it, and if you were on a mission they'd have your name on there and what time you were leaving. We didn't know where we were going or anything. We'd get up the next morning and we'd go to the briefing and they'd tell us where we were going. We'd go by the lunch place and pick up a box of cold, beat-up sandwiches, and they'd always give us some kind of an artificial drink made out of grapefruit juice. We had canned grapefruit juice and stuff. Everything we had was canned. So we took lunch with us since we'd be gone ten, twelve hours. We would leave when the sun was barely coming up or earlier. We'd get back before the sun went down most of the time. I had a seat because I sat next to this radio. The waist gunners didn't have seats. They'd just sit in the back, sleep, whatever. I was up with the pilot and copilot. We were just this far apart anyway; there was just a little partition between us. We'd test our engines every time before we'd take off. We had to get twenty-nine inches of mercury and 2,700 RPM. If we couldn't turn that on four engines we couldn't go.

On takeoff I was supposed to get my back up against something to brace in case we crashed, but I would watch. I'd look over the shoulders of the pilots. If we didn't have 100 miles an hour when we passed the control tower, which was usually located in the center of the strip, then we were in trouble and we would never make it. So I was looking to see if we had 100 miles an hour halfway down the strip. I wanted to see if we were gonna make it. Me and the engineer would always stand there right behind them on the takeoff. A lot of times we'd just have to turn around and go back because we just couldn't take off, couldn't make that. The biggest danger was failing on takeoff.

I could never do it now. You were just scared to death all the time. Then you gotta worry about getting to the target because we always flew over the water, and there was no rescue for us. If you had to go in, a B-24 doesn't ditch very well. They didn't hold together very good because the bottom, the bomb bay, was made out of like a roll-up garage door. And you had a big catwalk going down the middle of the bomb bay. You had to take your parachute off to walk down through there. That's how tight it was. Well, that usually just caved in, and if you hit very hard it would break that plane in half. Everybody used to call the B-24s "flying cremators."

One of the worst flights I ever had was when we went through a hurricane and we didn't know it. See, we didn't get good weather forecasts. Supposedly we got them from the Navy, but half the time the Navy wasn't there either. That storm we flew into was the most horrible thing. I guarantee you, we'd hit downdrafts and would lose 500 feet just like that. The pilot and copilot would put their feet against the dashboard and pull back on that yoke with all they had to try to pull it out of a dive. It was raining so hard the water was coming in every crack in that airplane. It was coming in there like you were pouring it with a sprinkler. That was the worst weather I've ever seen. I guess it was a typhoon. We were in it about thirty minutes, and we had no radar.

When we were flying in tight formation and we'd hit bad weather, how do you know where everyone else is? You can't see a thing, so what you'd try to do, you'd try to spread out. We would fly out to these places on all these long missions, and we would never fly totally all the way in formation because you'd burn up all your gasoline. So we'd kind of all fly on our own out to a rendezvous point, and then we'd start circling out there at a given time, and try and get into formation. Every now and then someone wouldn't make it. They just wouldn't show up, and sometimes that was it, we'd never see or hear from them again—just vanished over the ocean somewhere.

When I came home I was full of scabies. Do you know what scabies are? It's like mildew got to you. It'd just eat you up, being in that constant heat and humidity down in those islands. Right after I got back I was a little nervous there for a while. I wouldn't talk about it. I never talked about it. And after I got out of the Air Corps, I didn't ever want to fly again. The last time I got out of that B-24 at the end of the war, I said that was it—no more flying. For thirty years I would not fly. We finally took a trip to Las Vegas on an airplane, and this was thirty years after the war, and I was scared to death. But during that first flight I asked the stewardess if I could go up and talk to the pilot. She told me no. They won't let you in that cockpit, but he came back there and talked to me. He said, "When we land I'll let you come up front and I'll tell you about everything." Well, I was wanting to get off then! It was mostly just, I guess, tension, and I didn't want to get back in an aircraft. So many times I'd get up in a B-24 out over the Pacific during the war and I'd look down, and it's so far to fall, you know, I just felt very uncomfortable. I could tell, flying on those B-24s, by listening to every sound if something was wrong. Every sound, every little thing, if something didn't sound right you'd know it. You'd fly up there, you'd hear those engines, you'd know if they were running smooth. There were so many times that planes didn't come back, just disappeared over the ocean, and I knew how easy it was for that to happen, so I always was listening for trouble. After the tension on all those flights, worrying about the plane and whether we'd come back, that's why I didn't want to ever fly again. But once I got over that, and it took thirty years, now we fly all the time.

## JIM ROSENBROCK
ARMY AIR FORCE

I went into the service in 1939 at Lowrey Field in Denver, but we stayed in tents at Stapleton, which ended up being the major airport for Denver after the war. There wasn't much there before the war. When they got a barracks built at Lowrey we moved into there.

On December 7, we had been in downtown Denver to a show or something, and we got back to the base and they said the Japs had bombed Pearl Harbor. Everybody was upset and ready to go, and so was I. But we had to wait. They wouldn't let you go. I kept putting in for going overseas to fight. I got tired of the States. When I got out into the Pacific, I was glad I got in the Air Corps, because those guys in the infantry had it rough.

I finally went overseas in 1942. We were on a German ship. We were packed in there, I'll tell you. They told us we would never get sunk by a submarine, that we didn't have to worry about it because we could outrun them. We didn't believe that! It was a big troopship they'd confiscated from the Germans somewhere. Man, oh, man, we had a bunch on there. I was never seasick, but boy, some of those guys, they were seasick from the time they got on to the time they got off. That was terrible! We left from Frisco, and first we went to New Guinea. We waited there to get assigned to our outfits. When I got assigned, then they shipped me to the

Dutch East Indies. My outfit was the Ninth Fighter Squadron, the "Flying Knights." I was an armorer, and I was trained to fill the planes with .50-caliber machine-gun bullets. At first we had P-38s, and a little later on we had P-51s. The P-51s were a little different, but we had civilian technicians who would come out and tell us how to do it.

Major Bong was in our outfit. He was one of the hotshot pilots, and he won the Medal of Honor. He shot down forty enemy planes, I think it was. We ended up at Leyte in the Philippines. We ground crew guys didn't have a whole lot to do with the pilots; they pretty much stayed to themselves. Most of them were real young guys, but they were real nice. That's one thing about the pilots, they were real nice fellas. They had an officers club. The officers had the whiskey and the beer and everything. If we enlisted men were lucky, we got about a six-pack of beer a month. That was our limit! And then, we had a plane that flew from the Philippines to Australia, and they would bring back fresh eggs for the enlisted men, and that was great!

We were living in tents, up off the ground with bamboo floors. They had local guys that made the tents and got them up off the ground with bamboo. It rained a lot, man! But overall I didn't mind the tropics. It wasn't too bad. At first it was rainy and kind of humid and everything, but after a while I got used to it. I didn't mind it. I kind of liked it out there in the Pacific.

We'd have trouble with Japanese bombing raids at night. At Leyte we had an artillery outfit—antiaircraft—right behind us, and when they'd cut loose we'd jump out of bed and get in our foxholes and they'd be full of water. When you were digging foxholes, you'd go down two or three feet and you'd hit water, so all our foxholes had water in the bottom of them. They'd have big searchlights, and there'd be antiaircraft fire. Every few shots was a tracer, and you could watch the tracers go up to where the Jap planes were flying. One time the Japs had gotten ahold of one of our cargo planes and they loaded up a bunch of Jap troops in it. They were going to pretend to be a friendly plane and then land and attack us. So, they were coming into the airstrip at Leyte and they gave the wrong signal, the wrong code, and, well, that was the end of them. Our antiaircraft guns shot them down, blasted them. That didn't take long. They didn't land, they didn't get a chance. So we went over to where the plane crashed and collected those bodies and loaded them onto one of the Philippine ox carts and took them to a big hole and dumped them.

There wasn't much around Leyte, just our camp and sand and water, and that was it. For recreation we had movies, and we had a ball team and played teams from different squadrons. Out team was mostly enlisted men. We played fast-pitch softball, and that's where I learned how to pitch. Most of it was softball, not much baseball. Some of the major league ball players were over there once for exhibition games. We'd also play poker at night in the tents. We'd sit there by candlelight and play poker.

My cousin, Mel Rosenbrock, he was over there. He was in the Army. I got to see him. Somebody wrote and told me he was coming over there and I found out some Army guys had just gotten there, so I asked around and located him and got to see him. He was in the infantry. He had just come in right near our base, and I was lucky I got to see him. We got into the service at different times and were always in different places, so it was just a fluke that we ended up on Leyte at the same time. It was great to see him, and we had someone take a photo of us when we got together there at Leyte.

In Leyte I got sick—I got yellow jaundice. Oh, man, I got sick, I'll tell you. You turn real yellow. Your whole body turns yellow, and that was more yellow than I already was from taking the Atabrine. We took that to keep from getting malaria, and that turned us yellow, too. After I was in the hospital for a few days, I got word our outfit was going to move. And the doctors said, "You can't go. You'll have to catch up to them." But you know, trying to catch up with an outfit in the war is pretty hard to do. So I told the doctors I was going, and they said, "Well, you can go but you can't do anything." So I went and laid around and that was it. But I was lucky. I recovered pretty fast. My cousin Mel had malaria. But they told us we had to take Atabrine every day, and I did, and I never got malaria. But I did get jungle rot, right on the side of my foot. Oh, man! I had a big hole in the side of my foot. Some guys, they'd get jungle rot so bad they'd get sent home. I saw one guy with jungle rot so bad on his hands the skin was gone, and it was just raw meat on the back of his hands. That was bad stuff.

Christmas day of 1944 I was still at Leyte and we were all expecting a lot of holiday mail from home. So, I was driving a truck down there to get the mail, and I slid the thing right off this muddy little road and into a ditch. So there I was trying to get this truck out, and I had to get another truck to pull it out, and I ended up missing mail call. That really got to me, to miss mail call on Christmas. Well, later, I finally got my holiday mail and there was a package from my parents with a pair of slippers. And

I opened this package and looked inside the slippers and there was a wad of newspaper up in the toe of one of them. Well, come to find out later my mom had wrapped a watch in the newspapers and stuffed it in the toe of one of the slippers. What had happened was that censors were opening mail all the time, and one of them must have stolen the watch that was in that slipper. So I got the slippers and the wad of newspaper, but I never saw that watch! This was the problem with mail being opened the way they did for security. You'd get things stolen out of packages.

Then we loaded up and went to Okinawa. One of the sorriest things that happened there was that we had a ship coming in bringing in our beer, and the Japs sunk it, and there went our beer. Oh, boy. We were all pretty upset about that!

We were supposed to hit Japan. We were all torn down and ready to go, and they dropped the bombs and the war ended. We had a ball team, fast-pitch softball, and the day we found out the war was over we were out playing ball. I came in and the guys told me my name was up on the board, that I had enough points to go home. Man, I couldn't believe it. And I left the next morning. They had a couple of ships that had just come in. They had brought some troops over and they were real fast ships. So they told us to be ready the next morning, and away we went. We didn't stop at all, just came straight back. It didn't take us long. Going over it took us thirty-one days, and that was a long ride, but going back it took less than half that. We landed in Washington State near Seattle and we were there for about two days, and then they shipped us to Denver, to Fort Logan for discharge.

After I got to Fort Logan I got my discharge right away. They asked me if I wanted to stay in and I said no. But I should have stayed in. I had six years in at the end of the war, but I was fed up with it. I had had enough with the military. But now I kinda wish I'd have stayed in. It would have been a good retirement. But now it's too late!

I still don't care for the Japanese. When we went to Hawaii a few years ago and we went to the USS *Arizona*, there were some Japanese tourists who threw flowers and laughed, and I just couldn't take that. I wouldn't mind going back to Leyte and the Philippines but I don't know if it's safe over there now. I don't know if I would recognize anything there anyway.

*The War in the Air*

# JOHN W. VINZANT
## ARMY AIR FORCE

I joined the Army Air Corps on December 12, 1942, because otherwise I would probably have been drafted into the infantry, and I just flat didn't want to have to walk. I had roughly five months of flight training in AT-6s. I soloed in 27 hours, and when I left I had about 130 hours of flying time.

Following that, we went to Vance Air Base at Enid, Oklahoma. And there we were trained in twin-engine B-25s. Then we were moved into four-engine training in B-17s and B-24s. At test time I think we were pretty well slotted for our future assignments. We didn't know what they were preparing us for, but apparently they did. I suppose by this time we should have been impressed by what we were doing, but we were so damned young that we just took it as a matter of course, because we thought we were geniuses.

Then we were sent to Barksdale Air Base in Louisiana, where we spent five or six months in transition into B-29s. At this point we were all pretty egotistical about what we were doing. Training there was intense, and we were the first group of B-29 pilots to go through there. By this time we had had so much training that none of us had any problems to speak of in adapting to the B-29. The first B-29 crews were assembled at Lincoln, Nebraska, and this was done before we went to Barksdale. We had an eleven-man crew: a bombardier, two pilots, a flight engineer, a navigator, a radioman, left and right waist gunners, a tail gunner, a central fire control gunner, and a radar operator.

In May of 1945 we were finally sent overseas. We flew to Hickam Field, then to Johnston Island for refueling, a couple of more places I don't remember, and then finally to North Field on Guam, where we left the airplane. From there we were taken in a C-46 to Saipan where we were given another airplane. Guam, Saipan, and Tinian—worthy locations of the five B-29 Wings: two on Guam, two on Tinian, and one at Isely Field on Saipan.

We started flying actual missions in July 1945. Some people had a lot of trouble with the B-29, but I have to say I never did. As for the famous jet stream effects, they told us about it but we never experienced it. When I got there, missions were being flown at between twenty-two and twenty-seven thousand feet, and that range was well below the jet stream. Most of my missions were to the southern and middle islands of Japan. We needed to be out on the flight line a good two hours before takeoff, for we had a very long checklist to run through, with the co-pilot calling off the items. But the man who had the longest checklist was the flight engineer. The pilot did not respond to all the items on the checklist, but the flight engineer did. Unlike the B-17 or the B-24, the B-29 had only the basic flying instruments on the front panel. The flight engineer had a huge instrument panel of his own to watch over.

A round-trip bombing mission over Japan lasted about fifteen to sixteen hours. It made for long hours of boredom until we got northwest of Iwo Jima and started getting the flight together for the final run over Japan. For maximum firepower protection against enemy fighters we flew in very much the same box formation that was developed by General LeMay for the Eighth Air Force bombing missions over Germany. But by the time I began flying missions, the Japanese air force was so short of gasoline that we met almost no resistance by enemy fighters. Every once in a while we would see one a long way out, but a direct attack by fighter aircraft never occurred in any of the missions I was on.

The Japanese antiaircraft fire was pretty good, but they never hit my aircraft with anything heavy. We were hit by smaller pieces of flak that sounded, as it's often been said, like hail on a tin roof and made holes in the plane but never hit any of the crew or changed the way the airplane flew.

The last mission we flew was on August 14, 1945, five days after the dropping of the second atomic bomb, and our particular target was the Osaka Army Arsenal. What we had been trained for was to provide bombing assistance for the actual invasion of Japan, which was to have occurred in November. But a reason for this particular mission was that the Japanese seemed to be dragging their feet on the business of actually agreeing to surrender. So to encourage them to get on with it, General LeMay set out to organize what he thought would be a range of 1,000

B-29s over Japan. He actually got 834 in the air, but there were 6 that either turned back or landed on Iwo Jima. The result was a final raid over Japan of 828 B-29s.

We were still in the air on the way back from that raid when we got word that the war was over. Figuring we would try to get down as soon as possible to celebrate, we were ordered to fly carefully and far apart, so as not to endanger each other in a rush for the runways so as to begin partying. And for about three days that's just what we did. We got drunk and partied.

After that we flew missions of mercy. I flew four of those—three over Japan and one to Taiwan. They were to prisoner of war camps. Our airplanes were loaded with 55-gallon barrels full of clothing, food, medicines, and newspapers, and we dropped them by parachute accompanied by instructions, "We know where you are. Stay where you are. Don't leave the camp." B-29s from all three islands—Guam, Tinian, and Saipan—were busy flying those mercy missions.

I left to come home in mid-February. All the troops coming home were sent from Saipan on troop transports. From that area it was about seventeen days by ship to California. Finally, in March, I got back to Camp Chaffee in Arkansas, which was near my home in Augusta, Arkansas. In June I was back at the University of Arkansas and was graduated in 1950. That was the summer the Korean War started, and in October I was called back into service and was flying airplanes again.

I was separated from service in June 1953 and started medical school that September. I have to say I enjoyed my time in the service, feel I made a worthwhile contribution to my country, and learned a lot about organization and self-discipline. What I learned certainly did help me to become qualified to do what I had always wanted to do: spend the rest of my working life as a practicing physician.

# FRED WOLKEN
ARMY AIR FORCE

I was with the Fifty-fourth Troop Carrier Wing, Thirty-ninth Troop Carrier Squadron. I flew C-47s, the old Gooney Birds, to islands all over the western Pacific, at one time or another, but mostly in the Philippines. We flew in all kinds of adverse weather conditions, and many times our airstrip at Laoag, on the extreme north of Luzon in the Philippines, would be socked in and we couldn't land there. We'd have to back off, and we'd come back out over the water, and there was an island that was only about ten or twelve feet above sea level out there offshore. The Navy had just blown all the trees off that little island, cleared it off, and we could come in there and land. Many times we couldn't get back to our landing strip at Laoag. It was back in a pocket up against the mountains, and the clouds would kind of set in there. So we'd come into that other strip on that little island offshore. I don't know what we would have done otherwise. There wasn't anyplace else to land around there.

I think my closest call was when I tried to take a picture of a bridge. There was a bridge up there in northern Luzon that I wanted to photograph from the air, and it was kind of tucked in near the coast, and the mountains were right up against the coast. I said to my copilot I wanted to take some pictures of that bridge, so I needed to sit in the right seat. I said to him, "Hell, you've been over here longer than I have," so he got into the left seat, the pilot's seat. So here we come down this coastline and I said, "We'll go out and make a turn," because I was sitting on the right side as copilot, and as we flew down the coast the bridge was out the left side. We were coming out of this turn so I could get a good picture of the bridge out the right-side cockpit window, and I said, "Now get your wing down so I can get a good picture." Well, the damn fool gets his wing up, and I said, "Hell, I can't get a picture of the bridge that way." So I said, "Make another circle."

And we get way out there off the coast, a mile and a half or whatever it takes to make that circle, and he spotted a gap in the coastal mountains. He figured he could fly us through that gap and over to the other side, and I could take the picture as we went over the coast. So he said, "Do you think we can go through that gap?" I kind of thought a minute, and I said, "Yeah." I'd been on the other side and knew it was possible, but I told him, "It might be a little bit rough, so pull up just a little bit as you start through it." Hell, those mountains went up probably to 2,000 feet or so, and we were down pretty low so I could get my picture.

Anyway, here we come straight in toward that gap. And I'm sitting there taking pictures. And he said, "You got it?" I was waiting to get as close as we could to the bridge, for the best angle, before we flew through the gap. About that time I snapped it and we were just about to start through the gap. And he started to pull up a little bit but he was too low, so he started to try a turn, and I thought, Jesus Christ, we're not going to make it. We were headed right into the side of the mountain. So I got on the controls, put high RPM on those props and full power, and we did a steep bank. The thing was, he was starting the turn, and once you commit you couldn't turn back. I banked that thing on full power and I swear the wing tip scraped the rocks on that mountain as we turned past it. When we got back to the base and landed, I walked out there and looked at that wing expecting to see damage. I don't see how it could have missed those rocks.

Well, I went over and I chewed his butt out. I said, "Jesus Christ. You've got no business sitting in that left seat. No wonder you're supposed to be permanent copilot."

Damn, that was a close call. Looking at those mountains straight ahead and going into that turn, I thought of home and the folks and everybody in just a split second. Boy, I thought I was dead. That scared the hell out of me.

I got malaria, and I came down with it when I went on leave to Australia. If you were going to get malaria I guess it hit me at the right time. Australia was as good a place as any to get it!

## DON VAN INWEGEN
ARMY AIR FORCE

I was a tail gunner in B-29s, and we were based on Tinian. When General LeMay first arrived he had a reputation as a real tough no-nonsense person. He had already made a name for himself in the bombing campaign in Europe.

When we got the word of that first Tokyo firebombing mission, this came as a real shock to us. Up until then we had been doing high-altitude precision bombing like they had been doing in Europe. But for this raid, all that went out the window. We were to go at night and go in low, at 6,400 feet, and set the city on fire with incendiaries. The idea was that the Jap's war production was taking place not only in big factories and plants, but in small businesses and even private homes. This meant going after the civilian population. I didn't think much about it at first, and I don't think anyone else did. We were most worried about going in so low, and trying to get there at night, and whether we could make it back okay.

Those firebomb raids on Japan were really a sight to behold. Just the scale of the operation was incredible. Three planes at a time would take off from Tinian from three of the parallel runways at North Field. We headed straight out from the island. You couldn't turn until you were well away from the island since there were planes on either side of you. Also, we'd have to go out to the planes in the late afternoon. Those planes had been sitting out there in that tropical sun all day, and they were like ovens inside. We'd wait until someone got in there to start the engines. You'd be soaked instantly once you got inside. Once they got two engines started and got the air circulation going, it took a while to get it comfortable inside.

So we took off in the evening, at 8:15 P.M. for the Tokyo mission and flew all the way there and back alone. It was about a seven-hour trip each way, and that's a long time in a B-29! As we got close to Japan, we could see the glow from the fires started by the planes in front of us. Well, I mean the guys up front could—I was looking out the tail. As we got over the city, the plane started getting buffeted by the thermals from the fires below. It was really a rough ride! We had a couple of planes in our group do slow rolls, and not on purpose! They would be flipped by the turbulence of the updrafts from the fires. Can you imagine that, a B-29 rolled over by thermals from fires! Amazing. They said some of the wing roots of those planes were bent and they were sent back to Boeing for analysis. Those wings took a lot of punishment under the best of conditions. The wings of a B-29 bent upwards when you first lifted off the runway as they took the weight of the plane and the bombs. Then at "bombs away" they'd straighten out again, and the plane would almost be sprung back to normal. We'd be pressed down into our seats by the upward acceleration when the bombs left the plane.

So we dropped our bombs on Tokyo and turned back out to sea. It was still pitch dark, and the only thing I could see as I looked out my tail-gunner window was the city burning in the distance. It seemed like I could see the light from those fires for a long time. Finally I radioed the navigator and asked how far away we were from Tokyo. He said about 150 miles, and I could still see the glow from the fires on the horizon from that far out!

A few days later on Tinian they announced that for every man who flew that mission, that he had accounted for so and so many dead Japanese. A lot of guys started cheering, but my initial reaction was, what a crime. I have to say that it was an individual thing. The announcement was meant to fire us up, but it backfired on me. But the Japs started it, and that's war, and it's terrible. That's all there is to it.

After the war I was active in my bomb group veterans' organization, and I returned to Tinian fifty years later to arrange for a marker to be erected at North Field where we flew from. The runways are all still there, but they tore down all the buildings. In fact, everything is pretty well overgrown except for those big runways. It's kind of odd to go there and still see them, and think about all the times I took off and how glad I was to land on them again coming back from those long missions!

# BILL MASHAW
NAVY

I had a roommate in college who was trying to get a flying class together. He needed one more person, and I told him I didn't want to do it, but if he couldn't find anyone else I probably would; so he got me into it. I took up flying with that class under government sponsorship, and with that I made a commitment to go into the service after the course. The result was that I got to choose if I went into the Navy Air Corps or the Army Air Corps. I must have been nineteen or twenty and in my second year of college at Southern Arkansas University. I grew up in a family in Arkansas where we didn't even have a family car, so I learned to fly before I had a driver's license for a car.

The war had started during my sophomore year at Southern Arkansas University. On December 7, 1941, we were all gathered around a radio in a professor's room on our floor of the dormitory. He was our history prof. We had a National Guard unit there that was activated almost immediately. I was lucky I hadn't joined them, because I was playing football and didn't have time to work out with them. So I took the CPT, Civil Pilot Training, and had primary and secondary training, and then waited to be called. I was called up in December, on Christmas Eve of 1942, and chose Navy. Then I went to preflight school at the University of Georgia, and primary flight training at Peru, Indiana, and down to Pensacola, where my girlfriend and I finally got married. I met her through my roommate at college, and she was going to Purdue then, but I was afraid I'd lose her so I married her. I was committed but she wasn't, so I had to take her out of circulation! And we've been married for sixty years.

So, I went through flight training at Pensacola and was trained as a carrier pilot flying the SBD dive-bomber. Just as my squadron was being called to go out to the Pacific, they kept me there as an instructor. So, I didn't go out with the guys I trained with, and I think about half of my buddies who went out flying off carriers never made it through the war. While I was an instructor there at Pensacola we had a number of big-time athletes come through. One was Ted Williams, the baseball player. He was a student of mine and he came through pilot training. I knew him well because I had given him a number of flight instruction lessons. It turned out that I was the guy who gave him his final flight to determine whether he got his wings or not. I remember that after the flight—and he passed it with no problem—we went and parked the plane under a tree and ate pecans and talked about baseball. I really admired him because he was in there to go to war. He didn't want to play on the baseball team there. He said he didn't get into the military to play baseball, and that they had already taken that away from him. He was pretty bull-headed about that, and they would have kept him there if he'd have played baseball for the Navy, but he wanted to go overseas.

We had a lot of training accidents in Pensacola, and I had some good friends killed there. They were learning to be navigators with a little plotting board in their laps while flying those planes, and if you didn't figure right you could easily go 180 degrees in the wrong direction. And that's what caused some accidents there. They'd be out over the Gulf, and instead of coming home they'd go the other way, and that would be it. You wouldn't see them again.

One of the most dangerous things I did there involved training some English pilots who had come over. These guys weren't afraid of anything, and they were pretty careless. I remember practicing night carrier landings sitting in the back seat of an SBD with them flying those planes, and I got scared plenty good! Night carrier landings are the toughest flying of all, because you have seven flare pots on each side and that's all the lighting you have, and you were trained in the Navy to land the plane in the first 300 feet. But to come in and land without any other point of reference except for those flare pots, that was the toughest thing of all.

They trained you to get out of a sinking plane if you went in the drink off a carrier. They had a thing called a "Dilbert Dunker." Dilbert is the Navy's idea of a dumb pilot, and he was always doing the wrong things, like landing with the gear up and things like that. For this Dilbert Dunker, you would go down a slide in a mock-up cockpit into the water and it would flip over and then you had to get out. They figured if you could get out of that thing—and it wasn't easy—you could get out of an SBD in the ocean.

One day another friend of mine and I checked out a couple of SBD dive-bombers to go for an overnight flight to Shreveport, Louisiana, and back. But it was really so I could go see my girlfriend. This was before we were married. We gassed up in Shreveport and flew to Arkansas where my girlfriend was, and we landed those planes on a little cow pasture airport that didn't even have blacktop. We'd circled the house where she lived, and her mother had seen the planes and come out to the field to look at them. I asked her mother if she wanted a ride and she said yes, so we put her in the backseat and I took her for a ride. And they'd have kicked me out of the Navy for that if they'd have found out! Then we put on an airshow in my little hometown about sixty miles away. We flew up there and put on an aerobatics show like they'd never seen! They had this little two-story schoolhouse on the hill, and I was flying right by the second-story windows waving at my old schoolteacher. It shows how immature you are at that age. It was dumb! I would have ruined my whole career if they'd have found out about it back at Pensacola. I was glad I flew around that small town where I knew people, because the superintendent of schools said he didn't care who it was, he was going to report us. But my little brother heard it and told my parents and they talked to a few people, and the school board had a meeting and told the superintendent not to report those guys. We didn't do any harm. If I hadn't known anyone in the town, that superintendent would have reported me for sure.

After a while as an instructor I asked to be put into multi-engine training, because it looked like the war was going to be over before too long, and I thought if I had multi-engine I might want to be a commercial pilot. So I took multi-engine training, and that's what I went overseas with. I was flying out of Honolulu all over the Pacific islands picking up hospital patients. I was flying a four-engine plane, the C-54, which was the same as a civilian DC-4. I was based at John Rogers Field on Oahu, a Naval Air Station right next to the commercial airport. I lived in barracks on the base. Hawaii was great. We'd check every morning to see whether we had to fly or not. If we didn't we'd go out and do something. I had just taken up golf a year or two before and I remember going to the Wailai Country Club, and they'd let us play that club with no fees or anything. Waikiki was awfully nice. The Navy took over those hotels and converted some of them into hospitals and some for recreation. We also played a little baseball. But I was flying most of the time. We were in the Naval Air Transport Service, or NATS. So even though I was trained and ready to go as a carrier pilot, my active duty in the Pacific was as a transport pilot.

My most exciting excursion was when I went into Okinawa while it was still under attack. We hauled out a load of mental cases, psychological breakdowns, so we had to haul them back. That was a rough flight, and those guys were in bad shape and heavily sedated. We'd bring these guys back to Hawaii to hospitals. We went to islands all over the Pacific. I remember Guam and Kwajalein and Samar in the Philippines. We also landed at Johnston Island. That island was just about all airstrip, and the reef was real shallow all around it. The runway was so short that if you didn't make a good landing you'd go into the ocean, and there were a lot of wrecked airplanes in the shallow water all around that island. If you had an accident, the deal was that you were stationed there from then on. You didn't want to end up living on Johnston Island, so that was a real inducement to make a good landing there!

I was a teetotaler, but everyone down in the islands on duty wanted something to drink. So we would pick up a stash of bourbon and take it with us out of Hawaii, and you could swap it for most anything out in the islands—it was really valuable! But the main thing we got out of it was good food. We'd land on some island and talk to the cooks at the Officers Club and make a deal for their best meal for a fifth of bourbon. Otherwise they'd just feed us sandwiches or worse. And they didn't have much freshwater to bathe in on those islands, so we could get a freshwater bath for a fifth of bourbon. And that tells you how much we liked freshwater baths in the tropics! Brackish water isn't much fun for bathing.

The range of a C-54 aircraft wasn't that great, and we'd usually fly eight hours at a stretch at most. Because of that we had to land at a lot of islands to refuel. If need be we could fly up to eleven hours, but we usually just flew eight. We were very aware of the "point of no return," or the equal-time point. That's where you get halfway there and have to decide whether to keep going or to go back.

Something that bothered me a lot was that I'd been trained as a combat pilot and had to learn how to bail out of an airplane, but on these transports we didn't even wear parachutes. That's because you couldn't get out of that C-54 anyway. And we were defenseless with no guns, but we were flying through enemy territory sometimes. Plus, you were depending on your navigator to find these little islands from hundreds of miles away with very crude navigational devices. If you got in bad weather and couldn't find a star for navigation, you didn't know where you were. So the real scare was whether you were going to get to the next island, and if you had to fly through any kind of weather.

I had one real close call with the weather. We left Samar in the Philippines headed for Guam, and we flew right into some real rugged weather. I remember we lost altitude from 21,000 feet down to 7,000 feet without any control. We were just being tossed around inside the clouds. When we finally got control again we were trying to figure where we could be, and we didn't know. We knew we were going to run out of gas if we couldn't find Guam. We were talking this over, and just then we saw a little flash of light through the clouds. So we said, "Let's go down and see what that is." We thought we were a good hour and a half from Guam, but we got down low to where we had seen that light, and that was Guam! If we hadn't seen that little flash of light we would have flown right over Guam and on for another hour and a half, and we'd have had to ditch in the ocean. There was no way we'd have gotten out of that.

Several times we would lose one of the four engines when we were between islands way out over the ocean, and that was always scary. But the really frightful thing I felt was that we were defenseless, and we couldn't bail out of the plane. Ditching it in the water was the only way to get out of it. We had guys in our group who ditched C-54s, and some got out and some didn't. We also had a lot of times when guys would take off and head out for some island, and you'd never hear from them again. They'd just vanish.

When we were hauling wounded we usually would have a couple of nurses back there taking care of them. They would try to keep the guys under sedation and under control; that was the main thing. We sometimes had problems with the patients. Some were difficult to control, and it was uncomfortable. The planes had no heat in them, so they'd get cold. The nurses would try and give them blankets to keep them warm. Sometimes there would be a lot of noise coming from back there in the plane, some yelling, and that was commonplace, you know, groaning or yelling from the pain or from anxiety. For the mental cases they would sedate them real big time. But I mostly stayed up in the cockpit—that was my job—and the nurses took care of the wounded in the plane.

I guess of all those islands I liked Guam the best. It was well-populated and a huge American base. That was the place I saw an old Marine buddy from Pensacola who was in a Corsair fighter squadron. We met up and had fun together. He and his wife had known me and my wife, and we had been real close at Pensacola. He was my only real buddy from the military that I kept in close contact with after the war, and I was in touch with him until he died a couple of years ago.

I never was a committed flyboy. Flying an airplane wasn't something I had grown up always wanting to do. I found it exciting and I enjoyed it and I sure thought it was better duty than something else, but I'm not much of a military guy. With my crews out there in the Pacific, I always made a gentlemen's agreement with them to show military bearing when anyone else was around, but when we were together, just us on the crew, we were all good old boys.

My best buddy—a kid from the same little town as me, went through every grade of school with me, played ball with me—he got in the Army Air Corps, and I got word while I was out in the Pacific that he had been killed over Germany. From that day on I was ready to come home. I don't know why that affected me so much, because I had seen a lot of bad situations, but they were people I wasn't that close with. But once it was George, that hit me. So I figured I had enough of flying. After things ended in August of 1945, from then on we knew we were on borrowed time out there. The mechanics weren't doing work as good as they had when the war was still going on. We seldom ever took a trip without losing an engine after the war ended. As a matter of fact, I came home from Honolulu on a ship. I didn't even fly back. I felt my luck had all run out. I'd had enough. I got out of the Navy when I got to California. They were giving three of us physicals before we got out, and neither of the other two could give a urine sample so I loaned them one. That was my last good deed in the Navy!

I think the biggest thing I got out of the Pacific war was the GI Bill. When I got out I got to go to a good law school at Columbia University in New York City. And I grew up. After all this time I think I could still get into an SBD and fly it. They had an airshow over here a while ago and they had an SBD. I took a look at it, and it looked real familiar. I didn't fly a plane for quite a while after the war, until I was flying back to see the Indianapolis 500 one year with a guy, and he let me fly the plane for a while. And it's amazing, it's like the old thing about riding a bicycle. You take the controls and it's the same kind of touch. It comes right back to you.

## LOUIS MEEHL
ARMY AIR FORCE

**A**fter the war started, my brother, Paul, was drafted into the Army Air Corps and was with the Eighth Army Air Force in England. As the sole remaining son in our family, I had a deferment because we had a dairy and were considered essential to war production, and I guess my dad figured I was essential to the dairy. But the longer I stayed at home, and the more my friends were leaving to go into the service, the lonelier it got. I got to looking around, and pretty soon all that was left were the 4-Fs and the draft-dodgers. People would look at me and wonder what was wrong with me and why I was still at home. I finally decided I had to get into the service, and this didn't make my folks very happy, especially my dad, but I just had to go. So I enlisted in the Army Air Corps. They made me a gunner and sent me to the Pacific. I flew on A-20s in the 417th Bomb Group, B-24s in the 90th, and B-25s in the 38th. I was on islands all through the western Pacific, New Guinea, the Philippines, the Ryukyus, and even up to Japan later on.

It was after the war had ended, and we'd moved up to an airstrip on a little island called Ie Shima, right next to Okinawa. It was the island where Ernie Pyle was killed. We were living there in the usual primitive conditions that we'd put up with on all the islands we'd been based on—tents, C and K rations, nothing to do but fly missions. The airstrip there was right near the beach; well, the island was so small that everything was near the beach, and our tents of course were close to the coast.

We got word a storm was coming, and the pilots flew our squadron's planes off somewhere. The rest of us on the flight crews and the ground crews were left behind to fend for ourselves. The wind started blowing, the rain was coming down, and we were trying to hold on to our tents to keep them from blowing over. Well, it turned out this storm was a typhoon, what we call a hurricane in the States, and the wind blew stronger and stronger, and the rain was being driven horizontally. What a storm! I'd never experienced anything like it. After a while, we couldn't hold the tents up anymore. First one of the tents blew down, then another, and pretty soon all the tents were down, and we were outside in the weather. There was no other shelter—our bombing and the Navy's shelling when we'd taken the island had flattened all the trees, and it was just bare sand and rock. And the wind just kept blowing harder!

Next thing we knew the tents and everything inside them started to blow away, right off the island and out into the ocean. We just couldn't hold on to them under those conditions—the wind just ripped anything out of your hands if you tried to hold on to it. So after the tents and everything were gone, all we could do was huddle together and try to protect ourselves. It was like we were just a bunch of wet, cold sheep huddled together, and the wind kept blowing even harder. We'd rotate the guys on the outside of our huddle toward the middle because the rain was being blown so hard it hurt when it hit you. We all took our turns on the outside of the group being stung by that wind-driven rain. Some of us had bruises from that rain afterwards.

This seemed to go on for hours, and the whole time we just stayed there huddled together. When the wind and rain finally started to let up, it dawned on us that everything we had was gone. I had a lot of photos from all the islands we'd been on, some souvenirs, and of course the rest of my clothes and personal effects, and they were just gone. Our planes came back, and they flew in some more tents for us, but later when I shipped back to the States I didn't have much more to take home with me than the clothes I had on the day the storm started!

OPPOSITE: *Wartime photo of Louis Meehl*

# CHAPTER 9

*"The kamikaze hit us with sixteen different waves over a period of five hours—so many that the destroyers' radar couldn't even keep track of them all."*

—Bill Lewis, NAVY

RUSSELL FRINK, NAVY, USS *Fletcher*, destroyer, Solomons

WYLIE DAVIS, NAVY, USS *Chicago*, cruiser

PERRY MAX JOHNSTON, NAVY, LST 958

OZ LEVERENZ, NAVY, destroyer crewman

BILL LEWIS, NAVY, LCSL captain, Okinawa

CLARENCE COOK, NAVY, armed guard, merchant ships

BILL POND, NAVY, USS *Tulagi*, carrier, deck crew

CLARENCE "DUDE" STORLA, COAST GUARD, LST 831

GEORGE THOMA, NAVY, USS *Sperry*, submarine tender

MIKE DEBOLT, NAVY, USS *Portland*, cruiser

LEO DORSEY, NAVY, carrier fighter pilot

"EX-CHIEF PETTY OFFICER," NAVY, Underwater
Demolition Team [name withheld by request]

JIM LOCKHART, NAVY, submariner

PAGES 280–281: *Aircraft carriers at Ulithi Atoll on December 8, 1944, from front,* Wasp, Yorktown, Hornet, Hancock, Ticonderoga, *and* Lexington. *Today, the* Yorktown *survives as a museum ship at Patriot's Point, South Carolina, and the* Hornet *is on display near Oakland, California.*

# THE WAR AT SEA, 1942–45

RUSSELL FRINK
NAVY

joined the Navy partly because of *The Saturday Evening Post.* As a boy I was an avid reader and became fascinated by a series of *Post* stories about a tramp steamer and its captain, and especially the illustrations of his ship riding the sea. The rest of it was because of my father—his stories of the sea—and the time when I was fifteen that he took me aboard a boat off the California coast. When that boat got out on the open sea, I got a thrill from feeling it seem to come to life. And I was hooked.

So, as soon as I was graduated from high school I hurried out to join the Navy, and on September 18, 1940, was signed up for a six-year hitch. First came boot camp and its efforts to make a sailor out of me. Then an assignment to the battleship *Colorado* where I first learned Navy life and got a taste of Navy discipline.

In late July 1941 the *Colorado* entered the Bremerton (Washington) Navy Yard for a refitting so massive that her crew could not live aboard. Consequently, on December 7 I was on leave and at home with my folks in the mining town of Mystic, South Dakota. Coming back from a Sunday afternoon visit to my girlfriend I happened to stop in at the railroad depot. The agent there was all excited and hollered at me, "Hey, Frink! Didja hear? The Japs have bombed Pearl Harbor!"

First thing the next mornin' I was on a train back to Bremerton and burnin' mad. To think the Japanese would pull off such a rotten stunt when we were supposed to be at peace! And on Sunday, mind you! And as a dedicated Navy man, I felt really sick about all those ships shot up or on the bottom at Pearl Harbor. At the same time I had a deep feeling, Hey! I don't know whether I'll make it through this or not, but I know the United States is gonna make it. There's just no way them guys can take us no matter how many of our battleships is sittin' on the bottom at Pearl Harbor.

And I'll never forget how that feeling got reinforced as I was changing trains at Billings, Montana. There were a lot of cowboys there—on their way to volunteer—and, man, they were mad enough to eat those Japs up! It was great to hear the pals of some bronc-stomper give him a big hoopla as he climbed into that car headed for war. And that Western way of saying good-bye—so sharp and brisk and, yet, you could tell it meant so much inside—that was a real plus for my morale.

As for how I got on destroyers: I used to see those majestic great gray ladies—the battleships—come walkin' into the harbor. Next would come the cruisers. Then the destroyers would file in through the channel looking so cocky and sharp and charming that you'd just want to spank 'em on the fantail, and I fell in love with 'em.

After the war started and the United States began turning out destroyers just like it did guns and shells, they were searching through the fleet for men to man them. And, what sailor in his right mind wouldn't put in for that?

When I got word I'd been accepted for the destroyer program, I was standing watch in the *Colorado*'s aft engine room while we and other battleships were hiding in fog banks off the Aleutian Islands. That was when what later turned out to be the Battle of Midway was shaping up, but at the time it was thought the Japanese would go after the Aleutian Islands instead, and so we were there waiting for them to try it.

When we came back it was to Long Beach, California, and Bing Crosby and other stars were out there with yachts offering to take men ashore. I saw Humphrey Bogart as he came alongside with his fancy little putty-putt boat offering to take guys to the beach.

There, I found I was being assigned to the *Fletcher*, one of the first of the new destroyers to come out and the first of her class, so I said good-bye to the *Colorado* and was sent to Goat Island Receiving Ship at San Francisco. After about ten days of chomping at the bit I got my travel orders to New York and went down to the ferry dock where you went to go cross-country from San Francisco.

I was sent to the Brooklyn Navy Yard, and then I got to go aboard the *Fletcher*! Now, they call destroyers "Cans," as short for "Tin Can." But every sailor knows better. It's really "Can" for "Can Do," and don't you forget it!

Before I even seen my living quarters (and still wearing my "blues," yet!), I went down in the engine room to see what kind of engine I'd be playing with. And, boy, it was something to see! With both engine rooms on the *Colorado* we could put out 28,500 horsepower. But here I was looking at an engine that was little by comparison but put out 30,000 hp! And that was not to mention the after engine room!

I was assigned to the forward engine room—which is the control room—where later on I was to have the privilege of being throttleman when on a full power run forward the captain suddenly called for emergency full astern. All throttlemen live for that day, and I was to get to do it! Anyway, I got to touch all these goodies and to see what an impressive power plant I'd be standing watch on.

After some action in the Atlantic, we went through the Panama Canal (the first time for me, and that's quite a thing to go through, that Canal) and on to Bora Bora. And you could not imagine a more idyllic place. You haven't lived 'til you've been to Bora Bora! Then we headed out to Noumea, New Caledonia. Us and a sister ship, the *O'Bannon*. She was the first of the new 2,100-ton *Fletcher*-class destroyers, after us, to come off the ways. We were number 445, she was 450, and there was quite a bit of rivalry between us.

We had to approach the channel to the harbor at Noumea through a minefield, and pretty soon, chug, chug, chug, here came an old man in a little power boat. He was hollering something like, "Ahmlaaalallllaaaa," and kept it up until we got the drift that we'd got into the minefield. Since we hadn't hit any mines this far, we backed out safely by following our own wake, then waited for a local destroyer to lead us in. When we got in there, we saw what looked like wrecks swinging on rusty anchor chains. And we couldn't believe it! This was our Pacific Fleet!

As was usual we nested up with some other destroyers. Many of the old can men on the *Fletcher* knew guys on those cans. And, man, they were really talking. They had been in that first battle of Savo Island where the cruisers *Quincy*, *Vincennes*, and *Astoria* went down, and, oh, man, we learned what we were in for!

From there, they moved us up to Espiritu Santo (code named "Button") in the New Hebrides, where we were given the job of escorting one of these old converted tankers that they put a flat top on to make an aircraft carrier. They were taking planes to Henderson Field at Guadalcanal, but things were so hot there that they didn't dare bring her closer than two hundred miles out. They headed this converted carrier into what little breeze there was, gave her as much speed as she could take, and started launching planes. She was just jam-packed with planes, and some of the first ones to take off would lose altitude, and you'd see sheets of gasoline come off them as their pilots made a desperate attempt to jettison enough weight to stay above the water. And we'd go right over the top of 'em. A few didn't make it but most did, and we learned later that they'd touched down okay at Henderson Field.

The day we came into Noumea I made Machinist Mate, Second. TA DA! Now my General Quarters station would be on the lower level but in the aft engine room, and I'd be standing my regular watches on the lower level in the forward engine room.

In the first part of November we became part of the escort screening a large convoy coming to supply the guys on Guadalcanal with stuff they needed to be able to stay there. On November 12 they were unloading, and we and the *O'Bannon* and a bunch of cruisers and other ships were offshore out in the bay when there was an air attack warning. Everybody went to GQ. Here came the Japanese aircraft. And for the first time our GQ was for real. I was the last guy down the hatch to the aft engine room and I remember thinking as I dogged it behind me, "Oh, I sure like that blue sky!"

Even when we weren't in combat you couldn't get guys from topside to come down, even for a cup of coffee. To save their lives they wouldn't come down there.

The *Fletcher* carried 600 pounds of steam superheated to 875 degrees, and if you took a hit or anything else should happen down there to release that steam, a lot of guys could get boiled. But in action I felt safer down there than topside. The Spanish have a word, *querencia*, meaning that place in the bull ring from which the bull goes forth. And he will keep returning to his *querencia* because it is the place in the ring where he feels safest. And at General Quarters you need to have your own *querencia*. You may have to talk yourself into it, but it is essential that you have it. Mine was the engine room, and once I had it I wouldn't have been caught dead in one of them topside gun tubs, just as them dinghies up there wouldn't have been caught dead below decks!

Anyway, I dogged down that hatch and went down the ladder. I was kinda uptight. I knew Jap planes were on their way in and I'd have to give all of them pumps all the TLC—Tender Loving Care—they'd need. I'd have to be watching and sometimes adjusting pressures on the fire pumps, bilge pumps, the fire main pressure pumps, and also make sure the water and feed-water booster pumps kept doin' just exactly what they were supposed to do.

You can't see out from the engine room, but down there the ship speaks to you and tells you a lot about what is happening when you are in action. The turns of the propellers tell you the speed you are making. The heeling over of the hull tells you the ship is turning and how sharply and which way. The sharp "Wham!" of the 5-inch guns—they're our main battery guns and can shoot seven miles—announces that you are in a surface fight. When them 40mm cut in—and their sound will lay your ears back some—you'll know you're being attacked from the air. And what'll really put your ears flat against your skull is when the 20mm antiaircraft guns cut in. And the sound of a torpedo hitting your ship somewhere! Well, imagine that you are a kid walking along a railroad siding and pick up a big rock and throw it against an oil tanker. BOING! It's a ringing sound. Now add about ten decibels to that BOING! and imagine you are hearing it from inside that tanker, and you've got it.

Anyhow, on that afternoon all those guns were cutting in and the ship was really moving. I mean it was making time and heeling over in the turns. We shot down two airplanes in that action, one of them American. The American had been told not to be where he was, but when them Marine fighters got on somebody's tail they just wouldn't let go. They had been warned not to follow them down low and toward a ship. If they were coming head on or at some funny angle the gunners wouldn't see their identifying insignia, and too many ship's gunners weren't all that hot at instant silhouette recognition anyhow. When they saw a plane coming in low and right at 'em, they were gonna shoot at it.

Fortunately the Marine pilot survived our attentions. He managed to fly to the beach and set his plane down on it. He suffered a couple of broken legs, they said, but it could have been a lot worse.

Finally, the guns quit shooting and everything calmed down. We come out of that fracas with no damage, but one of the transports got a nice big hole in the side of it. Didn't sink. They unloaded it later on, and I saw a forty-five-foot Navy launch go right in that hole to get stuff needed by the boys on the island.

About eight o'clock we turned around and went back down Sea Lark Channel. Meanwhile the Japs were comin' in. A little before midnight we went to GQ, and our column of ships started to go down "The Slot" between two columns of Jap ships. The *Fletcher*, being so new, had the latest and best radar, so we were supposed to be the lead ship. But somehow in the maneuvering we wound up as the last ship in the column, and as things were to turn out that was the best thing that could have happened to us. Torpedoes hit the can in front of us and blew it up so quick and complete that we sailed right over where she'd been and never scraped anything.

Topside a couple of damage control engineers spotted the wake of a Japanese Long Lance torpedo coming straight toward us. We'd all been warned to get off our feet in a situation like that, otherwise shock from the explosion was likely to shatter your ankles and drive 'em up your butt. So they got off their feet . . . but there was no explosion. The fish was running so deep it passed underneath and never touched us—went right under where I was standing in the engine room.

Having been in the engine room I didn't know nothin' about all that 'til the next day. What I did know then was a desperate jangle from the engineer order telegraph. Those ol' reduction gears started a moanin', and all of a sudden we were laid way over to port in a hard right-hand turn. A bunch of black-powder smoke from torpedo-launching charges come down through the ventilators, and I knew we were on a torpedo run.

Pretty soon things became such a shambles it was a wonder ships weren't ramming each other. The destroyer *O'Bannon*, which by now was up front, actually did have to back down to keep from hitting a Japanese ship, then wound up so close to a Jap battleship that it couldn't depress its guns enough to hit her.

The bridge talker reported salvos from the main battery of the battleship *Hiei* were walking up our wake. They weren't just over-and-under ranging shots. They were coming right up our wake, and no way could we keep ahead of 'em.

Destroyers have a special emergency burner that the firemen can put underneath the boiler to make more smoke to add to that from the fantail smoke generators, and they put them there now. We were makin' a *lot* of smoke, and with those shells getting too damn close the captain made a hard right turn and managed to get us back into the smoke. Pretty soon when we stuck our nose out to see if we could find some useful work, the *Hiei* was still there and had us dead to rights. We ducked back into that smoke before she could hurt us and managed to get out of that madhouse.

Most of this action took place after midnight when it had become Friday the 13th. The *Fletcher's* number was 445, which adds up to thirteen. We had thirteen officers aboard. There were thirteen guns in the main and secondary batteries. Every time we went into battle, I wore exactly the same dungarees and thought the same thoughts. Now we know it'd be crazy to believe that kind of superstitious stuff could have any effect on anything, but of all the American ships in that fuss only the *Fletcher* and the cruiser *Helena* remained unhurt. We had one shrapnel hole in the forward stack, and that was all. Having been in the engine room I didn't see any of that action as it happened, but when daylight came I saw the results, and it was a mess.

We heard that destroyers *Cushing*, *Laffey*, *Monssen*, and *Barton* and the cruiser *Atlanta* had all been sunk. The cruiser *San Francisco* was off to our port with a big hole in her starboard bridgeway. There was almost nothing left of her port bridgeway where, we were told later, an armor-piercing shell had killed everyone in there, including Admiral D. J. Callaghan.

I think it was the destroyer *Sterett*, a little 1,500 tonner, that was at our side. Holes in her sides had been plugged with mattresses, and you've never in your life seen so many mattresses stickin' out of the hull of a ship.

By now we had run out of torpedoes and out of ammunition, and in company with other surviving ships headed for "Button" (Espirito Santo) at the best speed we could make. The cruiser *Juneau* was part of our company. She had taken a torpedo and was down by the head quite a ways, but making good time—probably eighteen to twenty knots.

I had come up to the second level for a cup of coffee and just opened the hatch when, "Boom!" A great pillar of smoke boiled up from the water, and the *Juneau* was there and then she wasn't. Debris came splashing down, and one of the splashes was an entire 5-inch gun turret with men inside. And if you can believe it, some of 'em got out! When it was going down in the water they got out! We heard later that out of her crew of over a thousand men, all but ten were lost. Among them were five brothers named Sullivan, resulting in a rule that never again could brothers be allowed to serve in the same military unit.

At "Button" we come alongside the destroyer *Aaron Ward*. She was shot up something unbelievable! I happened to look up at the afterdeck house, and there was a 40mm gun up there. You know those tin seats that look like something off a farm tractor or something? That's what the one at that gun looked like, only this one had had a big hole shot right up through its middle, and I thought "Oh, brother! That gunner must have cashed in real sudden."

We were back at Guadalcanal in time for the November 30 night battle off Tassafaronga. A Japanese flotilla had come in to resupply their troops, and we were a part of Task Force Sixty-seven comin' in to prevent it. We came in battle column, and because of the *Fletcher*'s superior radar we were in the lead. Then came destroyers *Maury* and *Drayton*; then cruisers *Minneapolis, Honolulu, New Orleans, Pensacola*, and *Northampton*; then destroyers *Lardner, Lamson*, and *Perkins* all in line astern.

Our radar picked up the Jap ships at 7,000 yards (four miles) off the port bow. Our captain reported to the cruisers and asked permission to fire torpedoes. They refused him, saying the distance was too great. Four minutes later he did get permission, and we and the *Perkins* and *Drayton*, and, I believe, the *Maury*, launched our ten each. Then we destroyers were sent to the north to leave the cruisers a clear field for shooting at the enemy. And the cruisers took some bloody noses from it! The Jap cans let all us American cans get past, then they come out launching their torpedoes.

They hit the *Minneapolis* with two. They hit the *New Orleans* with one, setting off magazine explosions that blowed off her entire bow from between the No. 1 and No. 2 Gun Turrets. They hit the *Pensacola* with one that flooded her after engine room. But it was the *Northampton* that got the worst of it. She took hits setting off explosions so huge that guys who were near her on the *Honolulu* said it had brought tears to their eyes. Our guys who saw it from topside said her after section blazed up with fire; then pretty soon her stern sank into the water, her bow rose in the air, and she slid out of sight.

We cruised the area picking up her survivors and got so many that when they formed a chow line along the port side of the deck house their sheer weight gave us a port list. Our cooks had to cook nonstop just to get 'em fed.

On February 11 we were part of a task force going someplace—and in those days that meant up The Slot at Guadalcanal—when the cruiser *Helena* reported that her scouting plane had spotted a submarine and had marked the place with a smoke pot. We were ordered by the squadron commander to break off from the task force and investigate. We went and, sure enough, according to the guys topside, we saw the smoke pot and at the same time our sonar guys began picking up reflections. Guided by the sonar our captain went after it and dropped a full pattern of eight depth charges.

Anyhow, after that set detonated we made a 180-degree turn and went back and dropped another set. Pretty soon we heard and felt shock waves from two deep explosions and knew that sub was on its way to the bottom. A few minutes later we heard and felt the shock wave from another huge explosion, a deep, heavy WHUMP! that shivered the ship. It made us all wonder if somehow those cotton-pickers had put a torpedo into us someplace. We all looked at each other kind of wild-eyed, dust and paint chips and stuff came down off the overhead frames, but no damage reports were coming over the telephone or sound system. We knew it had to have come from that sub, but why? Ships around us felt it heavily, too, but neither they nor us were ever able to figure out its cause. No question but that it had come from the sunken submarine, but could it have been carrying a load of explosives? Or, as some of our submariners suggested, could it have been an explosion of hydrogen gathered in the battery compartment? We'll never know.

To sum up, in November '43, we were involved in the invasion of Tarawa. After that mess they sent us back to convoy some hurt ships to the States. We spent ten days in Frisco and then come back out again and to New Guinea by way of Guadalcanal, and we went through the New Guinea campaign from end to end.

In February '44 we were sent to escort three oil tankers up from Funafuti to the Marshalls for the invasions of Kwajalein and Eniwetok. We didn't like that at all. They plowed along at what seemed like zero knots, and, even if we were zigzagging like crazy, it was boring to keep down to their speed.

I'll never forget when we went to General Quarters convoying those tankers, and the guy on the bridge phone for the engineers was the chief water tender. Somethin' was in the air, but the twelve-to-four watch passed and nothing happened. I'm on the throttles in the forward engine room. The telephone talker is right alongside me when he called the bridge and says, "I want to know what the hell is goin' on." He must have said it kinda nervous, because this chief answers, "Awwww, hell, you're just as safe as if you were in your mother's arms."

Then, just at that moment, BOOOM!!!!!! One of the Jap planes dropped a bomb that missed a tanker, but just barely, and that wasn't quite the punctuation mark we wanted for that chief's remark.

We went through the entire Philippines campaign, went to Puerto Princessa in Palawan, then went down past Tawitawi to Borneo. By this time it was the summer of 1945, and the old *Fletcher* was getting pretty battle-worn. Our deck house didn't even have many rivets left, and when we darkened ship we had to shut off inside lights. And we couldn't keep the water-feed pump pressure up right. And so on and so on. So, we were sent back home to the Terminal Island Navy Yard. And for us that was the end of the war.

When people ask what I got out of my service I have to say that it gave me a great sense of pride to have served. I thought it was a wonderful experience. I wouldn't have missed it for the world. Actually, I wouldn't mind doin' it again, though maybe I'm a little more crazy than most guys.

In a destroyer engine room, especially when in combat action, you have to be able to cope with the unexpected and, often, do it suddenly. And out of this I developed a "can do" feeling and confidence in my ability to cope with situations as they arose.

After the war I worked for a time in my father's sawmill at Mystic, South Dakota. After that I worked for a time in the Homestake goldmine at Lead, South Dakota.

Meanwhile I was serving in the National Guard, where I was sent to electronics school. From that I was able to make a career at Boeing Aircraft Company in Seattle. Now I am retired and back home where I was born and raised in the beautiful mountain setting of Mystic, in the Black Hills of South Dakota.

I've had a good life, much enriched both psychologically and in opportunity by my Navy service, and at heart I will be a Navy man until I die.

# WYLIE DAVIS
NAVY

I got into the Navy in the summer of 1940, when President Roosevelt announced on the radio one night a new program for reserve officer's training by the thousands, the V-7 program. I just graduated from college, and I was also in the Army National Guard, a rifle company. I was getting a little nervous about that being nationalized, and I didn't want to be a buck-assed private in the Army. No ROTC had been available to me, and my mother had refused to let me go into the Army Air Corps flight training at age twenty when I wanted to do that. The war clouds were getting pretty dense at that point in the summer of 1940, which was right after the Nazis overran France. And, you know, even at my age, just barely twenty-one, it seemed to me that our entry into the war was inevitable. I just questioned the timing, and I didn't foresee the way we'd get into it.

So I went down immediately and started looking into the new program, and within thirty days I was in the Navy for four months training, first month aboard a ship and three months of intensive academic training, and I got a commission and went straight to the Pacific Fleet. I was in about a year before the attack on Pearl Harbor, assigned to the USS *Chicago*, a cruiser based at Pearl.

On December 5, 1941, we left for Midway with the *Lexington*. We went out there to deliver some airplanes, and were quite close to Midway when we got word of the attack on Pearl Harbor. My recollection is that the night before I had had watch, maybe the mid-watch, and it was Sunday morning and there was a light schedule at sea. So I had just hit the deck, and I think I was shaving or something, when we got the word on the PA system, "Repeat, this is not a drill. This is not a drill."

Well, they called us to General Quarters at that point, because they didn't know where the Japanese fleet was.

We chased all over the central Pacific looking for the Japanese force, and we were lucky as hell we didn't find it. They had a lot of carriers, and we would have been eaten alive. The *Lexington* eventually became a formidable fighting carrier, but at that point practically all the planes were obsolete. So we would have been sitting ducks if we had run into those folks. The general assumption was that they had approached from a more southern route. So we went looking for them to the south, and fortunately they were north.

When we finally got back to Pearl a week later, things were still smoldering. It was extremely depressing, like a graveyard. I will say this though, and maybe it was because of my youth, but at that point I never did get very depressed about death. Even on a few occasions when people I knew in the immediate area were killed, that didn't depress me as much as the possibility of defeat, and the fact that we were getting our asses whipped. That's what depressed me more.

So we went into Pearl, and I think we were there just two nights. I spent one night ashore. There was a family I knew there, and I had a girlfriend whose parents were nice people, and they put me up for one night. And I never saw them again. I never have been back to Pearl since.

We went on toward the Marshall Islands and on down to Suva in Fiji, and headed to the Coral Sea from there. At the Battle of the Coral Sea, it was my first sighting of any Japanese force, May 7, 1942. Our Task Group, under an Australian admiral in the HMS *Australia*, was probably seventy-five miles from the carrier force. And the Japanese were about the same distance. It was essentially just a long-range carrier battle, just like Midway—on a smaller scale. There wasn't any surface engagement. Early in the afternoon on May 7 we were cruising along and we got some aircraft radar contact, and all of a sudden at a fairly low altitude—not more than 1,000 feet—a number of Japanese fighters flew right over us! Big red meatballs on their wings. It raised your blood pressure a little bit. The feeling of excitement at that instant was more than fear, you know. It was like the feeling you get at the beginning of a big football game. And you could hardly believe that for the first time there is this enemy in a position to really shoot at you. But the fighters just took off quickly. I don't know what they were doing there, looking for a carrier probably. Or, what is more likely, they were flying support for a torpedo plane attack, which came shortly thereafter. But we never saw the fighters again. They probably just took off for higher altitude, having spotted us.

About thirty or forty minutes later we got these aircraft on radar, and generally it was out starboard at low altitude. It was eight to twelve planes, and they turned out to be a new type of aircraft nicknamed the "Betty." We got the first picture of them ever taken. The ship's photographer was standing right next to me. One came in from the starboard quarter, and the airplane passed over the ship at not more than thirty feet off the water strafing from his tail gun. And I could see that pilot's eyeballs! We got that picture, and it became a standard recognition photograph throughout the Navy. It was a beautiful airplane, aerodynamically sleek, twin engine. And it was fairly fast, but most of them were shot down. They had to fly through some intense automatic-weapon fire, 40mms, and I don't know how anybody could fly through that.

So when they came in we took high-speed evasive action. Fortunately we were already cruising fairly fast, and I think at one point we got up to thirty-three knots. We saw several torpedo wakes within twenty yards of the ship, but they missed everything. Most of the Japanese planes were shot down, but maybe two or three escaped. As I recall, we lost two men from the strafing, who were buried at sea the next day. I didn't go because I was on watch, but I saw the ceremony from the bridge. I knew one of the guys that was killed. Both were hit very close to where I had been at my battle station. These guys were group members on the 5-inch guns, which were all around where I was on each side of the ship.

So after the action at Coral Sea, we headed to Australia. And the next episode I was involved in had to do with a Japanese midget submarine. It was in Sydney Harbor, and we were still in this Australian Task Force. So we went with the Australians and other ships on leave and recreation to Sydney and Brisbane, back and forth, more or less. Still in and out of the Coral Sea. In the meantime all the other ships had taken off for Midway except us. And, incidentally, we knew that the Japanese were probably going to attack Midway. We knew that the code had been cracked. It was like everybody was getting ready for a big football game. They just took off, the *Lexington* and the *Yorktown*, which was badly shot up. But we stayed behind. And we had a marvelous three or four days of leave and recreation in Sydney.

The people I was running around with, they were what you would call "quail hunting," including me. As a group we rented a flat over in King's Cross, which was a notorious place. And we didn't fool around with hotels. We would send an emissary out on the streets during the "brown out" with a whiskey bottle and invite everyone in sight for a drink. It was like the Pied Piper. Talk about your shore leave. But, in any event, we were one night ashore and then one night aboard, which was probably the only thing that saved our lives from that kind of thing. We needed a rest. But this was our last night in Sydney. And I happened to be aboard. The captain was ashore at some big party, and this was the captain who later committed suicide. Incidentally he was the same man who inspired *The Caine Mutiny*. Wouk had served with this guy in the Asiatic Fleet, on the old *Blackhawk*, before we got him. Same guy. Miserable son-of-a-bitch. But, any event, he was ashore, and I had the "sky control watch," which meant, in that situation, one 5-inch gun manned on each side of the ship, and two 40mms manned, one on each side of the ship. Everything's quiet, and there's supposedly not a Japanese within 2,000 miles south of the Solomons. We're way up in the harbor, and there was a net at the harbor entrance.

We were moored to buoys at both ends of the ship, with half the crew and the captain ashore. This was about ten o'clock at night. Half moon, bright moonbeam, clear sky. I'm in charge. I had a telephone talker on each unit awake. The rest of them could sack out on the deck if they wanted to. I had a younger junior officer, an ensign, who was in charge of the 40mms, but under my direction. And I got a call from another ensign, a friend of mine, who was officer of the deck. He said, "We just got an alert at the harbor entrance, so be advised." We got those all the time, but I checked to be sure my crew was awake, the gun crews. And I checked my searchlight crews to be sure they were awake. Now I'm up in the center of the ship, not the battle stations. This was what we call the Flight Deck, where we launch the airplanes.

So I'm chatting with this ensign about the good times we'd had ashore, girls, etc., when suddenly I look out into the channel, and at first I thought it was a buoy in the moonbeam that I'd never noticed before. Then I saw a wake behind it, and you know buoys don't leave wakes. This is not a runaway buoy, it wasn't just a periscope, it was a whole conning tower. I said, "That has got to be a submarine conning tower, and there aren't any known U.S. submarines in here, and if there were they wouldn't be operating half-submerged." So the first thing I did was scream, "Action starboard," which means get ready to shoot. We got the searchlight ready. I didn't want to shoot until I was sure. And you know, I thought, well, maybe it was some kind of motor launch. For the only time in my life I drove a searchlight, so I got to open up right on target. They were kind of primitive, I mean the gear was, but the operator opens right on that bugger, and there is no question about it. It's a conning tower. And I yelled, "Commence firing!" to the 5-inch guns and also the 40mms. Then the 5-inch gun refused to fire electrically. It misfired. And I remember saying, "Keep the son-of-a-bitch off," which meant go to the manual percussion. They did, and by the time we fired the gun was depressed against the shield, so you couldn't lower it down to where we could hit the sub. And the sub was so close that the shell went right over him, ricocheted off the water, and went up into the middle of town somewhere! I learned later it took a chunk out of an apartment house, but fortunately it didn't hurt anybody.

Then we got one of the 40mms going. "Bam . . . bam . . . bam . . . bam," with these tracers ricocheting wildly off the water and going all over the place, but the sub submerged and disappeared. The rest of the harbor traffic, they were coming to a screeching halt. The ferry boats were thinking, "Let's get outta here." But everything quieted down. Not a sound. And they finally got ahold of the captain at this party, and he came back to the ship. He was back within thirty minutes. Things were still quiet. And none of the senior officers had really seen that submarine. None of them! The officer of the deck and I had seen it, and other antiaircraft control officers had seen it, and all the enlisted men on the gun crews, of course, had seen it, but since none of the senior officers had seen, it the captain didn't believe we had seen a submarine.

The captain called me up to his cabin and chewed me out. He said, "Davis, have you ever seen a submarine? Any kind of submarine? Other than a toy in your own little bathtub?" The sarcasm. He was mean. And I said, "Captain, as a matter of fact, yes. Now, granted, I don't have much experience in the Navy, but it so happens that before you joined the ship, before the attack on Pearl, we did operate in and out of Pearl for several weeks with U.S. submarines. I not only saw them, I went aboard one as a visitor. And in addition to my training, of course, I know a conning tower when I see one. The only conceivable question in my mind was whose was it? And it couldn't have been ours."

So he says, "Davis, I think we let you go ashore too often. I think you're hallucinating." I said "Captain, I guess there's nothing I can do about it, but that's the way it was. There is just no question about it" And he said, "Well, you're dismissed. You will hear from me further." I could see myself getting court-martialed, and at this point I didn't know whether the 5-inch shell that ricocheted off into town had hurt any-body, you know? And that's to say nothing about those 40mms that went God knows where all over the place.

So I was no sooner out of his door when we get this explosion close by. "BOOM!" It was pretty loud. Well, it turned out to be a torpedo that had blown up a shallow-draft ferryboat of some kind that was moored about fifty yards forward of us, with a bunch of Dutch sailors sleeping aboard. And it killed most of them. That Japanese submarine had finally fired. And by then we had a petty officer who was up on one of those buoys getting ready to cast off, in case we had to get under way. And about this time that guy yelled, "GOD DAMN. SHIT. GET ME OFF OF THIS THING!" It seems that another torpedo had almost hit his buoy. And he said later, "It was so close I could SPIT on it. I didn't know whether to jump or what. I just stayed on the buoy, and it missed by three yards at most. And it ran up on the beach and didn't explode." They only had two torpedoes, I guess. One at each end. Two-man subs.

So at this point the captain was convinced that something was wrong. He still wasn't convinced that it was a submarine. So we get under way. Half the crew's still shacked up or passed out ashore. And as we're going out the harbor entrance another Japanese submarine is coming in fully surfaced, and the captain finally was concerned. "I'll be goddamned, " he says. And we're out there shooting at this guy with .45s. They finally sank four of them there in the harbor with depth charges. FOUR of them. In fact one of them is still on exhibit in a Sydney park. Well, I was the guy who started all the ruckus! Just happened to be at the right place at the right time. Looking at the moonbeams, you know? It was a wild night. The next time I saw the Japanese was at the Guadalcanal operations in August.

So then we headed up to the Solomons, and we were in the first Bat-tle of Savo Island, the first night action when the *Quincy*, *Vincennes*, and *Astoria* got sunk. And the *Canberra*, which was steaming just ahead of us, also got sunk. That was worse than Pearl Harbor in my opinion. That was a real disaster. And again, it was inexcusable. It was because of mis-takes made by our skipper. They hauled him in on the carpet. Admiral King finally got him to Washington, and that was an interesting story. Kept him waiting in his office every day for a week before he finally called him in. King was a rock-hard target. The right man for his time. But apparently he really put it to this guy. They never court-martialed him, but they threatened him with it and sent him to Key West, or wherever it was that the guy killed himself. They were down on him for turning away from the enemy. But at that point it couldn't have had any significant effect on the outcome of the engagement. The *Canberra* had already been blown out of the water, and when we turned away, the *Quincy*, *Vincennes*, and *Astoria* were already completely ablaze. They were doomed ships.

But in any event he did not pursue the enemy as he should have. As a matter of fact we had them in an enfilade position at fairly short range. His excuse was that he couldn't possibly identify the enemy, but everybody else on the ship, including me, had them identified. We knew we were catching hell out there. But that was his cowardice, even though the thing was practically over at that juncture

The real responsibility for that disaster lay in our being where we were when the Japanese came down, because they had been picked up by spotters in New Georgia earlier the preceding afternoon. My gunnery officer, this guy who later had his ribs broken in the director, said "Well, Wylie, we were talking about this report, and three Japanese cruisers were spotted." He says, "They'll be coming in here about two o'clock in the morning." They were there at 2:05 A.M.

And we were just there sitting there. We weren't even at battle stations. We happened to be closer to Savo Island, and the *Quincy*, *Vincennes*, and *Astoria* were farther up "The Slot" to the north. The Japanese task force came around Savo Island the same way we came around when we took the Marines in there two days before. They opened up with star shells. They had some aircraft in there too, and artillery—gunnery star shells. They illuminated the area. The Japanese opened up with the 5-inch .38s, the light cruisers.

First we heard the gunfire. Then the star shells went off, and all of a sudden everything's lit up and you could see all these ships charging around. Seconds earlier it was pitch black, and you didn't know what was out there. It was sort of eerie.

Well, when the thing started I had just come off watch at midnight, and I was very tired. We'd been at battle stations most of the time for two days, and there were a lot of aircraft attacks after we had put the Marines ashore. The Japanese were there with air attacks all the time. Torpedo planes, dive bombers, everything. So we were tired, and I had finally gone to sleep. When the gong sounded General Quarters, I didn't know where I was two hours later. You know, I was groggy. But of course I had my clothes on. I just put on my shoes and was running up a ladder just behind the captain's cabin to go across the catapult and get to my rear battle station. And I'm halfway up that ladder when a torpedo tore our bow off. It was a TREMENDOUS explosion. It almost knocked me off the ladder, and at that point I was paralyzed for awhile. And this was the Battle of Savo Island off Guadalcanal.

That's the only time I can recall in my experience when I was momentarily paralyzed from fear, and also from being groggy I guess. It was just for a few seconds, you know, but it seemed interminable. Well, then I get up topside and it's pitch dark, and then all of a sudden there's the illumination. The star shells. And tracers are flying everywhere. So I get up there, and then I've got to decide which catapult to run across. I was closer to the starboard catapult, and shell fire was coming from the port side, so I ran across the starboard catapult. This was very fortunate, because right then a shell hit the port catapult, opening up the neck of our executive officer, who was standing below it. It didn't kill him, but it almost did. It exposed his jugular vein. I mean, you could see it. He later recovered. Wonderful guy. So I get across and go to my battle station. In the meantime the Japanese had roared on past and were shooting the hell out of the *Quincy*, *Vincennes*, and *Astoria*. The *Canberra*, which was just ahead of us in the column, had been raked and was sinking within 300 yards of us. But the only major damage we got was the torpedo that took the bow off. Fortunately it was just the extreme tip of the bow and didn't result in much flooding.

After we went back and got a major overhaul, then we returned to the Pacific and got sunk. The way this started, we were put into a task group to go back to the Solomon Islands. The mission of this task group, apparently, was to prevent or at least harass the Japanese and make it as costly to them as possible to evacuate Guadalcanal. And they knew we were in the process of doing it, and that's what we were up there for. We were approaching The Slot; I think we had actually sighted Savo before that evening. But certainly we were within fifty miles of it. As I say, we were steaming in this fairly tight formation and we pick up these bogies, and the next thing I knew one of them practically took the foremast off. I was still up there, and it flew right over my head. It had dropped a fish. That one missed us, and it was poor aim on his part. In the meantime I got replaced and went back to my battle station. And we were still steaming along without taking evasive action. This all happened within five minutes. More planes were picked up. They came in two or three waves. I guess the first wave missed completely. The second one and the third one got four torpedo hits on our ship.

*The War at Sea*

I got to my battle station, and one torpedo hit right under there, and that was just two-thirds of the way aft. It was a violent explosion, and I was lifted off the deck. It's a very potent weapon, 2,000 pounds of TNT. When it hit there was a tremendous column of water over us. I remember one kid couldn't swim and didn't have a life jacket. He got a little hysterical for a few minutes. He thought the ship was going down immediately, which I did too at that point. There was so much water coming over, just from the explosion. But fortunately none of the people around me got hurt. A lot of us were knocked down. And we took two torpedoes almost dead amidships, and a fourth one farther back.

No other ship was hit. It's just miraculous we didn't go down within minutes, but fortunately there weren't any fires of any significance. And we didn't have any explosions of ammunition. The ship was just flooded. Casualties were all engineering people. But we came so close that it was just miraculous we were able to keep it afloat.

So everything got dark, and the *Louisville* took us in tow that night. We had no power at all and were being towed back south. The next morning a seagoing tug took over the tow from the *Louisville*, and we knew we were leaving an oil slick all over the ocean. And we knew the Japs were coming back. We lost about eighty people out of a crew of 1,100. That's a lot of people. But the Japs knocked the hell out of two engine rooms.

So the next day, we were in tow at not more than two or three knots and leaving a slick. And we assumed they would be back. The question was when. And they came back about one or two o'clock in the afternoon. And we got two more torpedoes. Same thing. Same old Bettys. Of course at that point we were dead in the water. And the tug got the hell out of there, and we didn't blame him. So the ship took about twenty minutes to go down completely. That was plenty of time for people to abandon ship.

I stepped over, and I was in the water not more than fifteen minutes before I got picked up in a big raft. We were listing at least 20 degrees at this point, which seems a lot steeper than it is. But, any event, I wasn't in the water very long. My chief concern at that point was the oil slick catching fire, and sharks. Fortunately there was no fire, and we didn't get any sharks or returning Japanese. But I had that oil in my fingernails for weeks. An old destroyer picked me up. There were several ships around, and they picked us all up. And that turned out to be the end of my career as a seagoing sailor. After that I went into flight training.

I then spent seven months of my active duty up in the Aleutians flying PBYS. I had some exciting episodes up there, but it was all related to bad weather and the aviation risk with that.

There's a certain equanimity you get from your training, and confidence in what you can do with that training, and a youthful exhilaration that almost compensates for the fear. At least it tends to balance it out. It isn't that you don't feel fear, but you don't normally get paralyzed from it. You're able to function.

All of my combat action at sea was jammed into less than a year. It's amazing. I was in the Navy on active duty for five and a half years, and my time in combat went from May 7, 1942, to January 30 the following year, and that was it. I had a lot of other exciting times. Looking back on the time I spent on ships, and it wasn't that long really, there were things that I liked that were really unique that I've never experienced anywhere else. Whether it's realistic or not is beside the question, but you get a sense of being home after you've been aboard ship for a while. I always felt secure from everything when I got back aboard ship. That was home, with an intensity I never felt as a child in my home. I think it was because I realized that it was a hazardous world I was living in at that juncture, and I knew it was all the time. So, no matter where you work, most of the time aboard ship you're so used to it that you feel at home and you feel comfortable with it.

I used to enjoy the mid-watch. It was quiet; it was hushed; and the captain in ordinary situations leaves and is sacked out. He might have been right behind you in the pilot, but nevertheless the captain was not there; and you felt a feeling not only of comfort and satisfaction, but of being in command, which is something, especially for a younger officer. So you're the one in charge of this huge fighting machine, with all those people depending on you, and so on. And you felt like that more on the mid-watch than at any other time, because there were just no other people around. I'll never forget times like that.

# PERRY MAX JOHNSTON
NAVY

n the Pacific war I sailed on LSTs, first as a pharmacist mate and later as an ensign. Wanting to beat the draft, I volunteered for the Navy just after I received my master's degree in Zoology. From North Texas State University, I went directly over to the recruiting station in Dallas. They took a look at my application and said I could qualify as a pharmacist mate. So they started me out as a pharmacist mate third class, thanks to my master's degree. Well, as a refugee from the draft, so to speak, I felt fortunate that I would be in the Navy and not the infantry, so I signed on.

I picked up my ship in New Orleans, and we used to watch the LSTs come down the river there, and everybody would say, "Well, that's a one-way trip to Hades if you get on one of those." And then, lo and behold, I got assigned to one! It was LST 245, which was not a very big ship. Designed specifically to transport things that can be easily unloaded out the front, it had two huge doors that opened outward from the bow, so the whole front end of the ship was open. There was a ramp right inside those doors that would go down between the open doors. Most times we had vehicles down there on what we called the tank deck, and the vehicles could drive down the ramp right out the front. If we had amphibious vehicles we'd lay offshore, and they could drive right into the ocean and head into the beach from there. Other times we'd pull up to pontoons they'd have built out from the beach.

Even though I started out as an enlisted man on that LST, the captain of my ship insisted that even pharmacist mates stood deck watches. So, in addition to whatever watch situation I had in the sick bay, they also had me standing deck watch, you know, up on the con. On occasion I was actually steering the ship. Of course it did get you out from below decks, and the air was a little fresher and everything. I think I had started out down on the third level, on a rack of bunks, and eventually worked myself up higher in the ship, though the Navy is never democratic. We went from New Orleans to Guantanamo, Cuba, and then through the Panama Canal, and once we left Panama the next landfall was Bora Bora. Now that was a beautiful island. It was a good place to get off the ship, and we had a little shore leave. Then we continued on westward, passing the International Dateline on November 12, 1943, and then we went to Suva in the Fijis. After that we went to Australia, and then up to Cairns, which is on the northeast side of Australia, just inside the Great Barrier Reef area. Then we went to Manus Island in the Admiralties.

A little bit after that I left the 245, because I had applied for a commission, with the recommendation of my commanding officer. I got a summons stating that Pharmacist Mate First Class Perry Johnston was to report to the commanding officer of the Seventh Fleet, who was then on the AGC 2, an amphibious task group command ship. So they sent me over in a small boat, an LCVP, which was the only small boat we had on an LST. I went over and was surprised that I wasn't going to see the admiral himself, but I saw a lesser functionary. He advised me that my commission application was in order and that I was to be detached from the 245 and returned to San Francisco.

So I left the ship and started back to the States. Part of my transportation was by aircraft, and at one point we landed in the Philippines. I was getting into a boat to be taken over to a staging area where they were sending people back, and I looked up and who's standing there looking back at me but my brother! I was an enlisted man and he was an officer, and it was just an amazing coincidence that we ran into each other. And so we had an opportunity to visit. He was a communications officer attached to the Seventh Fleet and was on his way to another assignment. We chatted for most of that evening, but we had to do all kinds of things so that I could go over to the officer barracks where he was staying. But we had a good visit, the first time I'd seen him in about three or four years.

When I finally got back to San Francisco, I went to Treasure Island and got my formal commission, and then I was sent to Hollywood Beach, Florida. I would call it the ensign's attitude adjustment course! My wife, whom I married in 1942, came down there, and we lived in Hollywood Beach.

I didn't have any idea I'd get reassigned to another LST, but that's what happened. Of course I was already very familiar with LSTs, so it was merely a matter of moving upstairs from the below-deck crew quarters to the main-deck officers' quarters.

An LST sort of wallows as it goes across the ocean. It wasn't uncommon in heavy seas that as the ship crossed over the crest of a wave the bow would drop down, ramming into the trough, and then the tank deck would just ripple. I think that's what kept those ships going, the fact that they could ripple. They were not so rigidly constructed that they just broke in two when they hit the troughs between waves. And of course LST 958 survived the big typhoon in Okinawa in 1945, and that was really something.

First, the wind started blowing, and we had word that the typhoon was on its way. At this point I was a deck officer, so I stood deck watch. We were ordered to get under way so rapidly that some of the repair crew working on our vessel had to leave with us. It was late afternoon, and the sea was running heavy coming into the bay. We cleared the entrance to Buckner Bay, and we steamed around out there into the open ocean. (Actually an LST doesn't steam, it motors.) Anyway we got out, were given a certain course to follow, and were ordered to meet the storm head-on, because with LSTs if you got broadside to the waves in a heavy storm they might just roll the ship over, and everything with it. We actually passed through the eye of the typhoon but then caught it again on the other side. And during the storm both the big bow doors were lost, and it was wild! There were heavy seas and high winds, and spray was coming over the bow of the ship as it lumbered along and tried to maintain a heading. I was scared shitless. There was nobody out there but us, and we were awfully lonesome. We were getting radio messages from other ships that they were in distress and so on, and we couldn't do anything about it. We could have been next.

This went on all night long, running the engines full speed and keeping the ship headed into the wind and waves, just trying to hold position so we weren't turned broadside to the swell and rolled over. You can't see anything, and the only thing you can hear is the wind and the waves, but you know what your compass is saying, that you're on a certain heading, and you're trying to maintain the engines. We were pretty much at maximum power, and when we'd come over the crest of one of those big waves the screws were coming out of the water. They'd come out and you'd get a lurching followed by a slapping, and then they'd dip back under. It was like taking an electric beater out of a cake mix.

When you'd come up on the wave you'd see the wave up in front and there you are. You'd climb up it, and then the ship would go over the crest, then you'd go into the trough, and slap and pop, and you'd look forward and there the old deck would be rippling, and you'd look aft and the stern would be coming up, and you'd wonder if the thing was going to break in two. And on that particular night, as I said before, we lost both bow doors. There was the ramp behind the bow doors, but it wasn't particularly watertight. We had to do all kinds of things to keep going, like using pumps to keep the ocean out of the ship. It was incredible but the bow doors had just been ripped right off! And the only thing that was keeping the sea out was the tank deck ramp.

I think this typhoon was a maximum of twenty hours before the seas calmed down and we could get on back to base.

The next day, when we could fully assess the damage, we saw that the storm had swept away almost anything that had been on the main deck. Some of the gun emplacements were gone. The davits where the small boats had been were just like somebody had taken them and twisted them back.

After the storm we took the 958 back to Hawaii without the two big bow doors. We got into where the tank ramp was, at the front of the ship, and completely welded it shut to make it more secure. But that tank ramp was never meant to be the bow of a ship—it was flat against the ocean we were trying to move through, and we had to push a lot of water, but we did make it back to Hawaii. And so I guess it was a fortunate ship.

I got out of the Navy after the war and went back to school. My academic career was kind of like the Navy for me, because in the Navy I worked up from enlisted man to officer, and in college I went from my master's in zoology before the war to a Ph.D. after the war. I ended up as a professor of Zoology at the University of Arkansas.

# OZ LEVERENZ
NAVY

I was from Wisconsin, but I was working in Texas when I enlisted in the Navy's V-7 Officer's Candidate program. I was gonna be drafted, but I preferred to be in the Navy. I liked boats. However, the real reason I joined the program was that I thought I was smart enough to get a commission. They put me in the V-7 class at Northwestern University starting September 15, 1941.

On December 7, I was home on a seventy-two-hour pass, and my future wife Peg and I were out riding in the beautiful Wisconsin countryside. We had planned to be married in July, but once I went into the Navy program we realized we would have to wait until I was commissioned. It was about three o'clock when we heard the news from Pearl Harbor, and we were just stunned.

The V-7 cadets all had to be back at eight o'clock that Sunday evening, and when we were called to assembly, Captain Wygant, who had been brought back from retirement to head the school, gave us about a fifteen-minute talk. It was packed with emotion about what we had to prepare ourselves for, and that the war wasn't going to be over in a hurry. He concluded with a prayer for those who had died at Pearl Harbor, saying, "No greater love hath any man!" That's how he ended, and I'll never forget it!

I don't think I was afraid. The war was a helluva long distance away, and with all the necessary training in between there wasn't time to be afraid. We knew that war was grim. Still, we'd been jolted from relatively mundane lives into a kind of adventure, and we were regarded by people as heroes just by being in uniform.

When I finished Midshipman's School I stood fairly high in my class and had some choice in the type of duty I would have. Destroyers sounded good, sounded macho, the fighting fleet, a ship of the line, and all that, and so I asked for and got destroyers. But they didn't yet have enough to go around, and I had to wait for new construction. In the meantime they sent me to torpedo school in Rhode Island. The day after graduation Peg and I were married. I had my ensign's stripe, and in the dead of winter we reported to Newport, Rhode Island, on our honeymoon.

I reported to the USS *Gherardi*, DD637, a brand-new 1,630-ton Bristol Class destroyer commissioned in September 1942. The skipper, a man by the name of Captain J. W. Schmidt, was one of the finest men I've ever known. He took a liking to me and taught me ship handling, and to me ship handling was the compensation for being at sea!

This was probably the fastest destroyer ever built. Our chief engineer was a Scotsman, John McGinnis MacKenzie, who had been chief engineer of the liner *America*—which later became the *West Point*. And Mac was a marvelous engineer! With the result that on our full-time trials, we made 423 turns per minute in that destroyer, which is the equivalent of 42.3 knots (over 48 miles per hour)! We ran those trials on the way from the Philadelphia Navy Yard to Boston. We had a fairly smooth sea, but I was seasick as a dog. I wanted to crawl off that ship at Boston and die!

I was torpedo officer and assistant gunnery officer. And one time the captain looked at me and said, "Oz, you go down to your bunk. You're so God-damned green, you're makin' *me* sick!" After a week or so I was able to function, but I was still God-damned sick! And so were most all of the landlubbers on the ship!

For our first war service the *Gherardi* was assigned to the North Atlantic Patrol. I don't think I ever got as scared in combat as I did in some of those storms where the waves were higher than the ship. We also took part in the North African and Sicilian campaigns, and the landings in Italy.

We arrived back in August 1943, and I was ordered to new construction on the West Coast, the USS *Cassin*. This was a reconstruction of the destroyer *Cassin* that was so heavily damaged in the attack on Pearl Harbor. In fact it was so damaged that about the only thing left of the original was the nameplate. They should have abandoned it and not built another 1,500-tonner. They were impractical, and as a result, we got all the crappy jobs in the Pacific that nobody else wanted.

The ship wasn't gonna be ready right away, so they sent me to fire control school, where I was going to become a gunnery officer. I went to the school for a month and then returned to put the *Cassin* in commission—as gunnery officer! The executive officer was supposed to have done this, but he had come down with mumps and was out of things almost through-out the shakedown. All this, and I was still a lieutenant junior grade! Later on I was promoted to full lieutenant. But, you know, Navy promotions were based on time-in-grade with virtually no merit promotions. But that didn't mean you couldn't have the responsibility. And serving in two jobs wasn't bad for me. I was a good gunnery officer. In fact, I was good enough with a rifle that on every ship I served on I was the mine-killer. We always sank mines with an M-1 Garand rifle, and when they saw one they would call, "Leverenz, report to the bridge with your rifle!"

We put the ship into commission out at Mare Island.

We shook-down at San Diego and got out to Hawaii in April 1944, and then we were heading west. We were to escort the battleship *California* from Pearl out to Eniwetok, and while we were waiting for her to get ready they sent us out for a couple of nights of full radar practice shoots. Commodore Roland Smoot, for whom we had a lot of respect, came along to observe. They'd have a seagoing tug tow a radar target, which was a screen about fifteen feet high and maybe twenty feet long. They'd tow it along at a good speed, and we'd shoot it full at night by radar alone. The tow vessel is only 1,500 feet ahead of the target and at a distance of 10,000 yards, or about six land miles. And, well, our radar wasn't working right. The image was jiggling all around, and we couldn't tell the tow vessel from the target vessel. When we came in on the firing round the captain said to me, over the phone, "Commence firing."

I said, "Captain, we can't fire right now, we're having difficulty with our fire control radar."

He said, "God damn it, I said commence firing!"

I said, "Captain, we are endangering lives on the tow vessel if we commence firing!"

He said, "That's an order!"

I stuck my head out of the gun director, and he was right down about ten feet below me. I said, "All right, if you want to kill twenty-two men like happened just last week on this same kind of exercise, you can come up here and do it yourself! I ain't a-gonna do it!" And I climbed out of the director and came down from the bridge.

Commodore Smoot looked at me and never said a word, and I knew I was within my rights. But the captain said, "Report to your quarters! You're under suspension!" So, I went, and I don't know just what tran-spired then, but I was told that the commodore recommended to the captain that we abort the exercise.

Well, I rode all the way out to Eniwetok reading *Navy Regulations* and some novels, catching up on my sleep and this sort of thing. The captain never talked to me, and I assumed I was gonna get a General Court for disobeying orders. But those sailors killed only a week before in the same kind of situation told me what I'd done was right.

When we got out to Eniwetok we were gonna sortie with a fast-carrier task force that had thirty-six destroyers in its screen. And, what do you know, our captain was the senior destroyer skipper and, under the screen commander, would be in command of it. By that time, I was a full lieutenant, and I heard him over the ship's address system, "Lieutenant Leverenz, report to the bridge!"

I came up to the bridge and the captain said, "Oz, take the conn. I've got responsibilities in addition to our ship, and I need a good ship handler."

I said, "Captain, I can't do that."

"What the hell do you mean, you can't do that?"

I said, "Well, under *Naval Regulations*, I'm suspended from all duties!" He said, "We'll talk about that some other time!"

I said, "I'm under suspension, under your orders, and I'm putting myself in a bad position if I do anything wrong."

"All right!" he said. "Suspension is lifted! Take the conn!"

I was just tickled to death, and I never heard about it again.

Then came the Saipan campaign. We didn't do much there, but we did at Tinian, which followed right after Saipan was secured. The Marines landed there on August 24 and ran into trouble with enemy soldiers hidden in caves. The *Cassin* was given the job of helping them out with artillery. Some Marine gunnery officers who knew the territory came aboard to help me pick the caves to shoot into.

We were only about 1,000 yards offshore, and so first, before we would shoot into a cave, our Japanese interpreter would call out in Japanese over a bullhorn, "Come out, and you won't be hurt. You'll be treated under the Geneva Convention." But it didn't faze 'em a damn bit! The Japanese soldiers would *not* come out, nor would they let any civilians out either. But with those soldiers slipping out every night to kill Marines, we had no choice but to shoot into the caves.

In early October we were sent with three heavy cruisers, the *Salt Lake City*, *Chester*, and *Pensacola*, and seven other destroyers to make a raid on Marcus Island. This operation was a little scary. Marcus was only some 500 miles from Japan, and we were given no air cover. Instead they gave us a bunch of balloons to release. We got up there at night and were to release these balloons, so if they had radar on the island the Japanese would think we had aircraft! I don't know who thought that one up or who they thought they were fooling, but we released them over the island. We got back counter-battery fire, and a helluva lot of it! That island was just covered with guns! They had guns, I'd estimate, up to 6-inch, but they were not that accurate. And so we bombarded them quite a bit, but how much damage we did I don't know.

The captain of the destroyer *Downes* was going in to clean out the boat basin. Going in to 6,000 yards—that's three miles—and that was pretty God damn close under those big guns! I was up in my seat in the Fire Director looking into the boat basin through the range finder. And I called down to the captain and said, "Captain, there isn't a God damn thing in that boat basin! I can't even see anything as big as a rowboat!" The captain called the *Downes* and said, "Commander, our range finder can't see anything in the boat basin!"

He answered, "We're goin' in to clean out the boat basin!" So we both went in with our guns blazing. Every time I looked over at the *Downes* she was just a sheet of fire, and we must've looked the same way! We were shooting at every flash we saw of counter-battery fire. We got in to 6,000 yards, and there wasn't anything in the boat basin. Then as we started going out, a shell hit about 300 or 400 yards outboard of us. Then a shell hit about 300 or 400 yards inboard of us. I said, "Captain, you'd better start zigzagging, because they've got us straddled!" He started, and the next shell hit right where we had been!

When the invasion of Leyte and the Battle of Leyte Gulf came along we weren't much involved in it. We were off to the south with Admiral McCain's Task Force 38 screening his aircraft carriers while they attacked a Japanese fleet in Sulu and Sibuyan seas moving toward Leyte.

We bombarded Iwo Jima in early December, several months before it was invaded, and we never had a shot fired back at us. However, some planes did take off from Iwo. A couple of torpedo bombers and a couple of fighters came at the task force. I don't know who shot 'em down, but with everybody shooting at 'em, they just disappeared.

Then we went down to Guam and were tied up beside the destroyer *Ellet* when orders came through naming me her executive officer. The *Ellet* was an old destroyer, and quite a famous one. She had been one of the escorts of the *Hornet* when they took off for the Doolittle Raid. We put the *Ellet* in good shape, but still we were an old ship and junior in the squadron, so we got all the shitty jobs, like being on harbor patrols when everybody else had liberty, and all that kind of stuff. Then because the *Ellet* had been out there all during the war, we were sent back to the States. I'd understood I was to be given command of the *Ellet*, and I had always wanted my own command, but on the very day we arrived at Mare Island the first atom bomb was dropped. Then when they were repairing the engines they accidentally dropped one on the concrete dock, and I knew then that the *Ellet* would never go to sea again.

So I told the captain I wanted to get out, and he said, "Have you seen your new orders? I am commander of the squadron of Fleet Mine-sweepers, and I have asked for you to be Division commander. How does that strike you?"

And I said, "I still want out."

So, I went to Great Lakes and was released. I then went to work for the Arthur Andersen Company and stayed with them until I retired.

I am proud of my service, and proud of what I did. Aside from occasional bouts of fear, I think the worst of it was being away from home so long, and the boredom. Someone once said life in the Navy in wartime consists of alternately being scared to death and bored to death. I think that is a good description, but I wouldn't take anything for having been a part of it all.

## BILL LEWIS
NAVY

After graduating from Rapid City High School I attended the South Dakota School of Mines for one year, then received an appointment to West Point but flunked the physical. I had a malocclusion—a couple of my molars didn't touch just right. So the second year at the School of Mines I wore tooth braces. Then I changed my mind about West Point and instead attended the Naval Academy.

I graduated from the academy on the seventh of June 1944. Then I was sent to a training school for the operation of LCSLS (Landing Craft Support–Large). Basically they were gunboats, 158 feet long and 300 gross tons, crewed by sixty-five enlisted men and six officers, and armed with rocket launchers, 20mm, 40mm, and .50-caliber antiaircraft guns, and a 3-inch gun up in the bow. The LCSLS were no speedboats and could cruise at only about eleven knots.

In August I was appointed captain of LCSL 121 and sent to Boston to put her in commission. In December we went down to Chesapeake Bay for our shakedown cruise. Then we headed for Pearl Harbor by way of Key West and the Panama Canal.

On April 13, 1945, we departed Pearl Harbor and went out to Eniwetok in the Marshalls, then to Saipan, and then to Okinawa. The trip to Okinawa wasn't too eventful, but it sure got eventful after we arrived there. We went into Buckner Bay, got resupplied, came alongside an ammunition ship and loaded up with ammo, and a few days later we were sent out to our first assignment.

At Okinawa the Japanese had begun sending swarms of suicide planes—the kamikazes—against our Navy, with such grim results that some fifteen or so warning stations had been established at distances ranging from about forty to seventy miles offshore. They were called RP (Radar Picket) stations, and their primary job was to detect and warn the fleet of incoming kamikazes. Their usual makeup was three or four destroyers plus four LCSLS. The destroyers did the radar detecting so well that the Japanese made them prime targets for attack by overwhelming swarms of kamikazes. And that's where the LCSLS like mine came in. We were nothing more than floating gunboats, sometimes called the Mighty Midgets because, according to at least one authority, we had more firepower for our size than any other ships in the Navy. So we were sent out to help the destroyers survive by adding our firepower to theirs.

We had been in Buckner Bay no more than a week when we were given our first assignment: to join LCSL Flotilla Four at RP 15, which was the northernmost radar picket station between Okinawa and Japan. And only a couple of days after that—on the night of May 23, 1945, we were hit, and I mean really hit. According to a later report the kamikaze hit us with sixteen different waves over a period of five hours—so many that the destroyers' radar couldn't even keep track of them all. But all we knew at the time was that they were swarming in like bees. I don't know how many other ships got hit, because we were too busy with problems of our own. We and the three other LCSLS were steaming in a diamond formation about a half-mile apart, with us in the rear, when a diving suicide plane crashed right short of us. It didn't hit us, but the bomb it was carrying exploded so close to our port side that it sprayed us with shrapnel that killed two of our men and wounded six others. Also it blew a big hole in our side and damaged our steering gear, but fortunately it was far enough forward that it didn't damage the engine room, and we didn't lose power. One bad thing about those night attacks was that the phosphorescence of your wake would point like an arrow to your ship, and all a kamikaze had to do was follow it.

I was up in the conning tower when the thing blew, and the impact threw me from one side of the conning tower to the other, where I crashed into the captain's chair and got my rear end severely bruised. I was the senior skipper in our division, so the doctor was aboard my ship. Later he looked at my damage and said, "I am going to give you a citation for a Purple Heart."

I said, "No Way! Fifty years from now when my kids ask me how I got my Purple Heart, I'd have to tell them I got it for a big bruise on my butt."

The next morning we were detached because of our dead and wounded, and also needing repair, and proceeded back to Buckner Bay. On the way we came under attack again, and I think we shot down two kamikazes. But however it was, when we returned we were given credit for six enemy planes shot down.

At Buckner Bay we turned over our dead and wounded and then went alongside a repair ship to get patched up. First, though, we had to go alongside an ammunition ship and offload all the ammo we had. Leaving the repair ship I was up in the conning tower and saw discolored water dead ahead. I knew it could mean trouble and told the officer of the deck, "Come left." Then I proceeded to leave the tower. But somehow his signal down to the helmsman had gotten screwed up. When you go down the steps from there you are facing aft, so I saw our stern was swinging in the wrong direction. I ran into the pilot house and told him, "Engines back full!" but it was too late. By that time we had run up on a coral reef. When the tide went out we were sitting up there high and dry as if we were in dry dock. Well, we had been at sea ever since Boston, which was about three months ago, so we took advantage of it to clean out our strainers and perform other hull maintenance.

The fleet commander had put in a recommendation that night for me for the Silver Star. Then on the next morning he saw us upon that reef and sent in a letter of admonition. I didn't get the Silver Star; I got the Bronze Star with a combat V. I was told by one of my friends on Admiral Turner's staff that the reason was that the letter of admonition and the recommendation for a Silver Star arrived at the same time. A classmate of mine who happened to be his flag lieutenant said the admiral tore them both up and said, "Let's give him a Bronze Star."

When the tide came in we floated right off that reef with no bottom damage at all. Then we proceeded back out to the picket station where we suffered a couple more air attacks, but nothing dramatic happened to us at all. However, on the evening of June 11, while we were out there, LCSL 122, skippered by a classmate and good friend of mine, Dick McCool, got hit pretty badly. She was attacked by two kamikazes at the same time. One was shot down just before it got to her, but the other one crashed into the starboard base of her conning tower, and its bomb went on through the ship and exploded on the port side. Dick was on the conning tower when it hit. He had shrapnel wounds and bad burns, but he managed to get over the portside rim of the conning tower, grab hold of the receptacle for the running lights, then drop down to the other deck. By this time the ship was very much on fire, but he went below and pulled out a couple of his sailors from stations down below decks. Another LCSL came alongside and took off the wounded, and we came alongside and helped to fight fire.

Dick got the Medal of Honor for his action that night. I later saw a copy of his citation. It said in part: "Although suffering from shrapnel wounds and painful burns he proceeded to the rescue of several men trapped in a blazing compartment, subsequently carrying one man to safety despite the excruciating pain of additional severe burns. Unmindful of all personal danger, he continued his efforts without respite until aid arrived from other ships and he was evacuated."

After the war we were up in Tokyo Bay and given the job of running around the harbor taking liberty parties from the big ships up to Tokyo and bringing them back, and that's how I met my wife. We were picking up this liberty party from the cruiser *Columbia*, and on the way back the naval aviator that had the observation aircraft on the cruiser was onboard, and I was talking to him about wanting to go into aviation. He said, "We've got a great group of nurses coming over from one of the hospital ships and we're going to have a little dance on the fantail, so why don't you stay alongside and join us."

So I sent a message to Flotilla Command that we had some kind of a generator problem and would have to remain alongside the *Columbia* until we could get it fixed. So we remained alongside, and, to make a long story short, I went to the party with him and met an Army nurse who was there. She was assigned to a hospital in Tokyo, so I would run up to Tokyo every now and then to see her. Finally, before I left Tokyo to come back, we got married. It was a whirlwind romance. We met in the fall and we got married in January. Then she left and was sent back to the States. For our honeymoon, the Army gave us a free week in the honeymoon suite of a big luxury hotel up on Mount Fuji.

When I left I was commander of Task Force something or other—I don't remember the number. I was the senior skipper of the LCSLS that were returning. We went from Tokyo down to Guam, Guam back to Hawaii, and from there back to Long Beach. I left the ship in Long Beach.

Then I went into aviation training and became a Navy pilot. When I got out of the Navy I went to work for North American Aircraft as what they called a Sales Engineer–Pilot. I was supposed to give demonstration flights for the customers and handle the sales of the airplanes to them. Then I left flying and went fully into the marketing. When I retired I was head of North American's International Operations, which handles the sales of all their aircraft overseas. I got to travel all over the world, met a lot of good people, and I loved it.

## CLARENCE COOK
NAVY

I was in the Navy, in the armed guard, assigned to man the guns on civilian Merchant Marine cargo ships. A lot of people don't know that Navy gun crews were on Merchant Marine ships all during the war. I was in a 5-inch gun crew on the *Hastings*, a Victory ship, which was a cargo ship. They made hundreds of Liberty and Victory ships during the war, and these ships kept the war going. They were hauling cargo all over the world.

I made two trips across the Pacific on the *Hastings*. The Merchant Marine crew was a rough bunch, but the captain and the officers were good. Those of us in the armed guard kept to ourselves on the ship. We had our own quarters near the back of the ship, and we ate by ourselves also. We had an unfortunate incident on the *Hastings* where one of the cooks tried to molest a little guy, an oiler in the engine room. The captain was really angry and said this just couldn't happen on his ship. So, we got to Eniwetok and the captain wanted to get rid of this cook, off-load him. The Navy officers there on the island said that if they took him he would probably be killed. They said that they only had one palm tree left after the invasion, but that it would probably fit him. So the captain told this cook that if he bothered anyone he would be shot, and the cook didn't cause any more trouble!

On our first trip across the Pacific, we loaded in San Francisco a mixed cargo of some ammunition and some beer, but they didn't tell us which hold the beer was in! They also loaded some cots and a lot of vehicles,

ABOVE: *Wartime photo of Clarence Cook, USN.*

Jeeps and trucks. They loaded them with ramps up onto the deck. Of course, that made us very top heavy, but that didn't seem to stop them. We went across the Pacific and stopped just briefly in Hawaii. We anchored right across from the old *Arizona*, and a lot of her superstructure was still sticking out above the water. I got shore leave and took a bus out to the Royal Hawaiian Hotel at Waikiki. I got a Coke at the Red Cross tent out there and had a look at the hotel. What a place! The Navy was in there, and the submarine guys had taken a lot of it over. I tried to get into the bar but it was full and I couldn't get in.

Then we continued on to the Philippines and stopped somewhere near Leyte. They brought barges out to start unloading the vehicles with a big crane. When the first Jeep they unloaded got down to the barge, an Army guy there unbolted the windshield and just pitched it into the water! I guess they didn't like windshields on their Jeeps.

On our second trip we loaded ammunition and had a straight run to Okinawa, no stops, and we were zigzagging all the way. We were joking that all the zigzagging was in case we blew up we wouldn't take any other ships with us. We were really a floating bomb. We didn't actually go to Okinawa but to a little island nearby. We unloaded on this island, but there was no dock. There was an airstrip though, and they said this was the island where Ernie Pyle was killed. I found out later it was Ie Shima. Barges came out and unloaded the ammo. We had to watch for scrap and floating boxes in the water, and every morning we'd shoot anything like that we saw. Otherwise the Japanese would hide themselves and come floating out on that scrap and climb up the anchor chains. It took us ten days to unload all that ammo, and LSMs made smoke to hide us from Jap airplanes. We had trained on our guns to defend the ship, but we were under orders not to shoot at any planes because they could follow the tracers down to the *Hastings* under the smoke screen.

One day a Zero was snooping around and one of the smoke-making LSMs opened fire with a 20mm machine gun. Well, hell, the plane could easily avoid the fire from one machine gun, and it came swooping in low under the smoke and saw us. The captain of the 3-inch gun crew couldn't resist and had his crew open fire. They made a clean hit and blew the Zero out of the sky. It was like it was there one minute and then—poof—gone in a big explosion. It was quite a shot! We thought for sure they would catch hell for breaking orders about not shooting, but the commanding officer of the Navy armed guard didn't say anything about it.

After that, parts of the plane came floating by the ship. There was part of a wing, a piece of canvas like from a seat belt, and, can you believe it, a parachute—from a suicide plane! There were also these little antipersonnel bomblets. Some of our Navy guys went over the side and got the stuff out of the water to keep the sides of the ship clear of debris, so the bombs wouldn't go off. Then they put the bombs on the barges to be taken ashore. We never did get over to Okinawa itself, but we could hear firing in the distance and see the light of flamethrowers at night.

On our way back from Okinawa we headed for Samoa, and that involved crossing the equator, which meant the famous Neptune Party to mark the crossing of the equator. If you had never been across the equator before, you were a Pollywog, and you had to be initiated into King Neptune's Realm of the Bounding Main. Everyone on the ship who had already been across the equator and initiated, they were called Shellbacks. So, the way this worked was that the Shellbacks made life miserable for the Pollywogs. I was a Pollywog, and they were going to make me miserable!

The first thing was that the Pollywogs were smeared with thick, sticky bunker oil. Then they cursed at us and read our violations that we deserved punishment for. One of my main violations was that I was from Texas, and this really made me a target. The Shellbacks decided I needed to be punished for this, and they ruled I was to be thrown overboard. I was blindfolded, and they hauled me up some ladders to what seemed like a high point on the ship. All this time I figured they were just trying to scare me so I went along with it. But then they made me stand on the edge of something and pushed me off—I flew right into the air and hit the water! I couldn't believe they had actually pitched me over the side! I ripped off the blindfold and realized they had rigged a float cover filled with seawater on the deck below a gun tub. They had pushed me off the edge of the gun tub and into this thing on the deck filled with water. It scared the shit out of me since I thought they had really pushed me overboard. There was a lot of laughing, of course, but I didn't find it very funny. So, after this, all of us Pollywogs got a diploma stating that we were now Shellbacks. On later trips I got to do the initiating, especially when we took some Army guys back later in the war.

So, then we pulled into Samoa. It had been quite a while since we had seen females of any type, so we were looking forward to seeing some real island beauties when we got to Samoa. We pulled into Pago harbor and it looked like a tropical paradise. There were huge green mountains all around the bay, palm trees along the shore, and some white beaches.

There was a naval hospital there, and the governor's house was on a hill overlooking the bay. The docks were up along one side of the bay, and as we got close to the docks we could see people on the pier. We saw what looked to be topless island women in wraparound skirts, and they seemed to be waving their skirts at us. We all started cheering. It was like a dream come true. But then as we got closer to the dock, what we thought were topless Samoan maidens turned out to be Samoan men! They weren't wearing shirts, but they were wearing wraparound skirts all right. It turns out both men *and* women wear these types of skirts they call lava-lavas on Samoa. The men were actually in a band playing tunes to welcome us. I guess that shows you how long we had been at sea without women, to mistake a bunch of Samoan men in a band for topless women!

The water in Pago harbor was crystal clear and beautiful. I could look over the side and see way down deep into the water where these big fish were swimming around. We got shore leave, and the first thing that happened was that I was almost killed on the dock. A Jeep-load of Marines, drunk on something the locals called "tuba," were racing around like idiots and just about ran me down. I had to jump out of the way at the last minute or I would have been a casualty right there in Samoa!

From Samoa we went on to Panama City. But then they reassigned me from the *Hastings* to an old merchant marine oiler, and back out across the Pacific I went, still a member of the Navy armed guard and still on a civilian ship. Our captain on that oiler was a real alcoholic. Nobody ever saw him until we docked at San Pedro, and two of the Merchant Marine officers had to help him down off the ship.

After that I was assigned to a Navy ship—finally. In all my time in the Navy I had never been on a Navy ship! It was an LSM and it had a Navy crew. We were supposed to take it up to San Francisco for decommissioning. Just after we left San Pedro and got into open water, a seam opened up right near the rudder, and the ship started taking on water. All hands had to muster that night to man the pumps, and we pumped water out of that ship all the way to San Francisco. We finally got it there where it was decommissioned, and that was the end of the war for me.

## BILL POND
NAVY

I was on the USS *Tulagi*, an escort aircraft carrier, and when we left the States we headed out to Pearl Harbor. Five days and four nights with that ol' carrier thumping along at flank speed—twenty-two knots—and carrying twenty-four new F6F Hellcat fighter planes. That sea was just as smooth as a table top, and yet I was the sickest son-of-a-gun you ever seen. There's just something about that long, slow, rolling motion that'll get to you.

We got to Pearl Harbor in late November 1943. There was a lot of oil still on the water, and they were still working at sweeping it up. They were using boats that looked like small skiffs with some sort of a paddle deal attached, and they were continually going around the harbor sweeping off that oil as it came up.

I saw the sunken *Arizona* and thought about the men who went down with her. Hope nobody would try to salvage it, I thought. "As it is, it's like a shrine to those people down there, and there ain't no sense in disturbing them. Leave 'em down there." And I believe in that!

I went ashore in Pearl Harbor, and that is where I got my tattoo. I might add, I don't think that I was stone cold sober when I had it done!

When the Americans returned to the Philippines, we supported the landings in Lingayen Gulf. That's where the Japs first began hitting the fleet with those Kamikaze suicide planes.

There was a couple of cruisers in with us, the *Minneapolis* and the *Louisville*. And I was looking right at the *Louisville* when she got hit.

Scared?—I was the scaredest rascal you've ever seen in your life. But when those Kamikazes come in and people were hollering, "Dive for cover," I said, "Hell, I can't see nuthing that way, and I want to see what's going on." The old guys who had been through it before, man, they was hunkered down in there. But I'd only just turned eighteen and didn't have any better sense, so I stood up and saw them Japanese planes coming in like flies. And when one of 'em would get hit, it'd go all to pieces like it was made of balsa wood.

Then one hit the *Louisville*'s bridge. God! I was looking right at it when it happened. I seen that. He come in from the right-hand side and made a swing around. I don't know what his idea was. I couldn't understand why he didn't just want to come straight in. But, he had that bridge in mind, and he was boring in to hit it, and he did. It turned the *Louisville*'s bridge into a great ball of fire, and I think it killed about twenty-two or twenty-three men, but the *Louisville* didn't even slow down. Like most all Navy ships she had an alternate steering system, and so even though there was probably nobody left alive in the bridge she was able to keep right on going.

That scared the hell out of me, but what made me think about it more than anything else was their wounded. Evidently their sick bay wasn't near as big as ours, so later in the day they transferred some of them over to us by breeches buoy. They'd sling them on those lines strapped in those wire-basket stretcher things.

They was burned. God! They was *cooked*. Looked like their clothes was cooked into 'em, and they just looked like fried meat. I don't know how in the world any of them ever come out of it.

I didn't remember much about the rest of it after that. But if I remember right, the Kamikazes finally broke off from us about three o'-clock in the afternoon. They were tenacious little devils. They didn't yet know how to live, for as we learned later, they were just kids, too young to be flying them planes. Young as sixteen years old, and all juiced up with glory propaganda.

Didn't any of 'em come too close to us, and we was told not to shoot unless we seen something to shoot at. It was a matter of saving ammunition. We used to say, "We have ammunition to burn," but the officers would say, "Don't shoot unless you've got a target in sight."

I can't understand why the Kamikazes wasn't paying much attention to us. I think there was three or four made a pass at us, but that was all. They was mostly going for the outlying vessels. They probably thought they could knock them out and then take us over. But we had a good bunch of men on them outlying ships.

I think the thing I loved most was when I was transferred into the "A" Division! I *loved* that. I was put in charge of refrigeration and steam heat.

When you was out at sea they didn't allow anyone but the officers to shower with fresh water. The rest of us had only brackish or saltwater showers, and that ol' saltwater was rough on the skin! So was the saltwater soap. But, in the "A" Division, now that's where we had it made. Those ships had the finest water-distilling systems, and we operated a lot of that stuff! We knew how to tie into the lines, and so, tucked in behind some supply racks down there, we had ourselves a freshwater shower!

I think there were seventy-two in our division. Our quarters were several decks down, all of us in the same compartment. We slept in pipe-stand bunks stacked five bunks high. All we had was the island. All our ventilation came down through ducts from the island up above. The place was hot, and to say it smelled like a goat pen would be putting it mildly!

I washed my clothes in the sea like so many other men did. We'd tie 'em up in a secure bundle at the end of a long line and hang them over the side and let them drag through the sea for a while. It was a pretty good system, and it did get them clean.

Man, I'll tell you, I used to go out and sit on the flight deck at night and just watch the sea go by. I've done that so many times! It'd turn phosphorescent where the screws had stirred it up and leave a long, glowing trail of our wake behind us.

And the flying fish: I used to wonder how they could sail through the air and hit through just the top of a wave and fly out of the other side and sail on to go through the top of the next one.

As for how I look back on it now, I remember it as rather uneventful for the most part. They used to say that in the Navy you're either bored to death or scared to death! And you were bored to death a lot more than scared to death, because we didn't have that much going on! We was in that one major action. I got three or four stars for that . . . just that one battle. The rest of it was all patrol duty. As far as the experience is concerned, it was a great experience. I wouldn't have missed what I saw for a million dollars. Like so many other guys, it helped me to grow up. And if able, and they needed me, would I go back in there again? Hell, yes!

# CLARENCE "DUDE" STORLA
COAST GUARD

I learned how to be a machinist of sorts, and then I went out to the West Coast, where I was working at the Bremerton Navy Yard, across Puget Sound from Seattle. This was in the first part of 1942, and I was boarding at a place where the landlord was in the Coast Guard. I got to know about the Coast Guard from him and was told that it was tougher to get into than the Navy. But I didn't want to go into the Navy. At that point I was deferred by working in a defense place, but I didn't know how long I'd be deferred. And I didn't want to be in the Army, particularly the Infantry. So one night, some of us were playing poker and drinking all night, and I don't know what happened. We got patriotic or something, and we took the ferryboat across to Seattle and enlisted in the Coast Guard right then and there!

So I went to boot camp in a place called Port Townsend. And they had tough boot camps, tougher than the Navy from what I understand. You had to learn to do a little bit of everything. You had to learn to signal, both the semaphore and lights, and learn to handle small boats.

Then I was sent to Portland, Oregon, and assigned to what they call Captain of the Port, which is mostly guarding docks. We were big buddies with the Russians then, and a lot of Russian ships were coming in, particularly some of those that had been beat up in the Murmansk run, and I was guarding some of those. I carried a .38 and a big, long billy club. It was good duty, but I felt I wanted something else. So after a few months, someone advised me to go to school. I was just a seaman second by that time, but I wasn't aboard a ship. I wanted sea duty, I guess. So I went to Seattle and took a bunch of tests. I remember the officer said to me, "You ever been to college?" I said, "No." None of my people had ever been to college. He says, "Well, on this reading comprehension test you got the highest grade ever to go through the Thirteenth Naval District." I said, "That's good?" Well, I always had done a lot of reading. So he says, "Boy, you could go to any school you wanted to." So, he named off some schools and said, "There's one open in New York City: Water Tender." "That's for me," I says. I didn't know what a water tender was, but I knew what New York City was!

So, they sent me there. And it turned out it was for steam machinist. Well, I already knew some outside machine stuff. The Navy water tenders were the guys who ran the stills—the evaporators. And so I ended up getting the water tender rate and later first class fireman. I was always a good seaman, but I didn't take any crap from anybody, and they didn't like that insubordination. I threw an officer over the side once, or at least threatened to. You get a lot of smart asses in the service. They think that just because they got rank they can do anything, and I don't take crap from anybody.

Then we were going to go over to Europe, and we went down to Pier 92. I don't know what happened, but they changed the orders for a small group of us and sent us down to Algiers, Louisiana, right across from New Orleans, to a Naval repair base.

There was an LST that had been commissioned in Pittsburgh, and they'd taken her down the rivers there to New Orleans and to Algiers, and it was going out. I think I was scheduled to go out on a patrol frigate, but some other water tender got in a fight and was thrown in the brig, so they needed a water tender in a hurry. I volunteered and ended up on LST 831, an all–Coast Guard ship. And we took off for Theodore, Alabama, which was an ammo depot. We loaded that LST to the gunnels with ammo of various kinds, powder and shells, and you could barely crawl from one end of that ship to the other. It was a great big floating bathtub, and it was really loaded. They said, "Okay, you're taking this out to the Caroline Islands." And so we had nobody with us, no convoy, no nothing. If we get there, fine. If we don't, they only lost one ship.

So we take off for the Panama Canal, and I don't know if they knew what we were carrying. We went through the canal and came back up the West Coast to San Diego. Our skipper walked around with six-guns, and he thought he was kind of strong. He was a wiry fellow. When he got up in the morning—usually he slept up on the signal bridge on a little cot—he'd go up the mast to the crow's nest and survey his little empire, and then he'd come down hand-over-hand on a cable, down to the signal bridge. So I got up there one night and greased the cable real good with a mix of this graphite grease stuff.

Well, the next morning the captain got up as usual, went up to the crow's nest, looked around, and then swung over to go hand-over-hand down the cable. Well, he hit that cable, and he went down like greased lightning, and at the bottom he hit and bounced! But it helped to break the boredom and monotony, you see.

So, we'd do anything just to break the monotony. A lot of the people would sleep. Some of those guys got so they could sleep almost all the time they weren't on duty or eating. I worked out. I had the machinist carve me out some weights. I also read a lot. And I'd write. I'd write these long letters home, and the officers would pass them around. I was a good writer, I guess, college material and didn't even know it. And so they asked me if I wanted to be a correspondent. You know, just to write up lies to send home.

So, I'd take a photographer, and he'd take a picture of a guy at whatever island we pulled into, and I'd ask, What's your name? What's your hometown? And then you'd put words into his mouth: "Don't worry about me, Mom," and all that. One time I got carried away and wrote it up the way I saw it. Guys going over the side, scared, counting their rosary, officers having to force them over, crying some, you know, all about these kids. I wrote it all up. The skipper called me in and said, "Who do you think you are? Hemingway?" So I had to go back to what's your name, what's your hometown, and so on. That's when we became publicity ship of the flotilla.

We were at Okinawa on D-Day. Then we'd go back to the Philippines, and to Saipan. During the first part of the war we hauled around Marines, but later soldiers, mostly. We took Marines in on D-Day at Okinawa. We had amtracs and stuff topside. Jeeps and trucks. Once we even had a little Piper Cub that a Marine sergeant flew. At Okinawa, it was Easter Sunday and April Fool's Day. First day of April 1945. And I knew we were going in the next morning because I overheard the officers. So I told this little Marine sergeant—he was a short, husky guy like I was and a weight lifter—and he flew this little reconnaissance artillery spotter plane, and so he says, "God, I got this bottle of rum in my plane box." So, I went down to the galley and got some fruit juice, and we sat in a Jeep, which was chained topside, and I felt no pain that next morning when I went onshore driving an LCVP! I'd drive that thing in to the beach, sometimes as cox'n and sometimes I was manning a little 30mm on it.

Sometimes our LST would go right up on the beach and open the doors and unload, but not always. You see, at Okinawa we laid offshore and opened the bow doors and ramp, and the amtracs went into the water out there and drove in. In fact, they laid down smoke, did a feint, and then people walked ashore. There was tough fighting later. We stayed a quarter-mile off the beach in our LST.

But, at any rate, here we were, beached up there at Okinawa. And we'd been unloading supplies and so on. This was at least our second time at Okinawa. And it was all secure, and there were all kinds of amphibious craft lined up and down. And I looked down the beach and I see a little LCI there, which was carried on a larger ship. I was up in the con with the skipper, and I says, "My God, there's my brother." And he says, "Are you sure?" I said, "I knew he was in the Navy, but I didn't know he was here." I mean, it was quite a coincidence, you know?

And so he says, "Take a photographer and go over there and get a picture, and we'll have a nice story out of this." So I went over, and it was hot as hell out on that beach. And I still have the picture that went back Stateside, my brother and me there on Saipan. What a coincidence that was.

We were under attack by Kamikaze planes a lot. I remember shooting at Kamikaze planes, because they'd usually come in the early morning when it was barely getting light, or at night when it was getting dark.

But what our people didn't realize was that there were also Kamikaze swimmers and Kamikaze speedboats. We captured one of those speedboats, took the ammo out of it, and the skipper used it for a gig. Sometimes we'd station people at night around the edge of the ship with BARS with orders to shoot anything that moves. Of course, we laid down smoke a lot, too.

But there would still be raids coming over. I remember going to sleep topside after it got dark. We weren't supposed to do that, but it was hot down below—so hot you couldn't touch the bulkhead, sometimes. I'd sneak up and sleep in the gun tubs, and I'd see those planes come over and then the searchlights would catch them, you know, like spiders in a web, but I'd hunker down and go to sleep.

I didn't like the service in terms of the bureaucracy and in terms of the stuff you had to put up with, which was so silly sometimes. Just someone showing off their power. When I was broken the last time, the skipper caught me reading on watch. There wasn't anything to do. It was the middle of the night. He said, "What are you reading?" And I said, "I'm reading *Caesar's Commentaries* in the Latin." I'd had two years of Latin in my little old country town. "Ahh, dirty stories," he says. And

I guess they were, *Caesar's Commentaries* in Latin. But he was impressed. He was educated, and most of the people onboard weren't. I was self-educated, in a way, and I'd read more than almost anybody aboard.

And so he would order me to stand watch with him during the night, so he would have someone to talk to. But I didn't want to talk to him, just because he ordered me. So he'd say, "Storla, would you mind standing watch with me tonight?" And then we'd finally get to talking. I remember one time during the day, it was kinda hot and we were standing there, and there were some seamen down there chipping paint, which was a never-ending task aboard ship. They were working just hard enough to be technically defined as working. And he says, "Look at those lazy Joes. They'll never amount to anything." I said, "Well, why should they? They have nothing to look forward to. Why should they knock themselves out?" And he said, "Awwww, that's just the way they are." I said, "Tell them that when they finish that section there, they can have the day off." You know, they can't get too many rewards at sea, except maybe sack time. Free time. Being on a ship is like being in prison, in a way. So he said, "Aw, it won't work. They'll just sleep." But he sent the bo'sun down there, and the bo'sun told them the plan. Pretty soon we looked back down there and, "Chip, chip, chip, chip, chip." The paint chips were flying! And those guys finished that section in record time! The skipper was so mad that I was right. And right there I learned something. Later on I taught Industrial Sociology for a long time, after I got my doctorate, and I did some consulting for companies. And this is a basic sociological truism, that you catch more flies with syrup.

We'd pick up this mutton—greasy mutton from Australia—and that was enough to make you sick. We didn't get much fresh stuff. We looked forward to "Pogey bait," which was candy, and "Gedunks," which was ice cream made from powdered milk. And there was "Horse coffee" and "shit on a shingle." I still like it. Most people don't. Our food was so bad that we would steal K-rations and C rations from the Army as delicacies.

I remember sitting out on nice warm tropical nights when it was calm and the water would be fluorescent. We'd be blacked out most of the time because there were enemy around. But one time I was sitting there on the fantail talking with a few of the guys, and surprisingly not too much about women. We had some Army guys aboard, and this Army guy comes out while we're talking. He's naked and he's got a Bible in his hand, and he looks over and says to us, "Good evening," and then he steps over the rail and jumps right down into the ocean, just like that!

We reported it right away, but we were in convoy and there was nothing we could do. They wouldn't stop because we were in convoy, and if they tried to find him the next day he'd have been long gone. In addition to that guy, on another trip we had a couple of guys who went berserk and had to be carried down and tied to their bunks.

When we were anchored off Saipan I was real happy to see those B-29s taking off early in the morning. And they'd take off and get in formation, and much later we'd hear them straggling back. But I was glad to see them taking off to bomb Japan, because at least the war was getting closer to the end.

We used to listen to Tokyo Rose on the radio. She'd play some songs we hadn't heard before. Often the first time I heard songs that really became popular was Tokyo Rose playing them. We got a kick out of her; we enjoyed her. She helped our morale.

We had movies on the ship. Sometimes the same one over and over! We'd get *Tall in the Saddle*. I saw that damned movie so many times I couldn't believe it. We'd find another ship and go alongside and throw a line over and transfer movies.

I remember one time we were coming back from some island pretty empty, and the skipper now had his own Jeep—well, actually, we'd stolen it from the Army and had it down on the tank deck. Somehow it got loose. The ship was wallowing around, and that Jeep was running around on its own, and we were trying to run and grab it. It would come at you. It's like it had eyes!

After the war we made it all the way back across the Pacific. We got back to the States, went to 'Frisco, and later took the ship through the Canal and decommissioned her in Orange, Texas.

After the war this buddy of mine from the ship and I hung around together for awhile, and we were working in San Francisco. And I finally said, "I'm going to go to college, use the GI bill, and see what college is like." He said, "I don't want to go to college." He says, "I'll stick around and work and help you." I said, "No, you better take off, Butch." His name was Butcher. I've never heard from him since. Hell of a nice guy. We were really good buddies.

I went through five different majors. First I went into journalism. People were teaching me how to write for newspapers, and I never worked for a newspaper. Then I went into English. That was when the "new criticism" was on, and they didn't want to talk about the milieu of the writer, just the internal work, and I thought that was dumb. I was interested in the social setting of literature, and literature is still one of my first loves. Sociology and literature are my hobbies. I really wanted to be a writer.

You develop a certain camaraderie with the people you serve with on the ship. You didn't get along with everybody, necessarily, but you had to tolerate each other because it was a little world, you see? You were self-contained pretty much. And you swore that you would be buddies to the death and that you would look each other up, but it didn't work out that way. I tried looking up a few people after the war, but the situation was too different. I went to Des Moines and looked up this guy—he was a water tender, too, and he was married. And I said, "Hey, Robbie, you remember that night in Copa Solo?" And he stopped me, "Shhhhh," because his wife was there.

We weren't like the guys in Europe who had it bad a lot of times. But still, they were in "civilization" and we were on one tropical island after another, and nothing looked even vaguely familiar. Sometimes we'd go ashore and have a couple of cans of warm beer, but there was nothing there. Even Manila wasn't much, and Tokyo wasn't much, so we didn't even have a real liberty. But I did talk to some Chamorros in the Marianas, even though we weren't supposed to fraternize. And I talked to quite a few Filipinos in Panay and Tacloban. I was curious about their way of life and so on. Most of the guys aboard ship just called them a bunch of "gooks," you know?

And I often think this has had something to do with me going into sociology and anthropology. I ended up teaching anthropology in Wisconsin, and I was always curious about the different people and cultures I saw in the Pacific. You see, I was a green country kid from Minnesota, and out there on those islands were people with quite different ways of life, even though I didn't have a chance to see too much of it. And if I hadn't been in the Coast Guard during the war, that wouldn't have happened to me. I mean, I wouldn't have gone around the world. One reason I went back to LSU for my doctorate was because I'd been stationed at Algiers, Louisiana, and I used to go over to New Orleans. I wanted to get away from those cold winters, and besides, you see, I had the GI bill from being in the service. That GI bill was worth it alone.

# GEORGE THOMA
NAVY

I was on North Atlantic patrol before the war started, in Battleship Division Three, onboard the USS *New Mexico*. I think we were about 300 miles off the coast of England when the officer of the deck got on the horn and shouted down, "The Japanese have attacked Pearl Harbor." I was sitting next to a chief petty officer who said, "Boy, that guy is in real, real trouble." The impregnable Pearl Harbor? He really thought the guy was kidding. He said, "The Japanese couldn't attack Pearl Harbor." And then all of a sudden, on comes the skipper, and he told us all about it. So we immediately turned around and headed back.

Shortly after that, I went around to the Pacific and was assigned to a beautiful ship, the submarine tender USS *Sperry*. Right after Pearl Harbor, about the only fighting ships in the Pacific were the submarines, and the *Sperry* would have to service them to keep them out there.

When the guys got off patrol, we'd have ice cream and fruit and apples and everything else down there for them. We would have extra submarine crews and everything else that went onboard submarines. We'd keep those long periscopes in crates on deck. We had a torpedo shop and also a huge machine shop below decks. They did everything on that ship. It was absolutely incredible. But those damn torpedoes never worked very well. They discovered later that the torpedoes were running too deep.

I got to the Pacific in June of 1942. We got to Hawaii, and the contrasts I saw were incredible. The first thing in my mind about Hawaii was all the advertising I'd seen, hula girls and palm trees and beautiful things like that. There was no question about it, the hills of Hawaii looked beautiful as we came in. And then you started getting into the channel that goes into Pearl, and all of a sudden you saw the overturned *Oklahoma*. It just made me sick, because there were still guys trapped in there. It just made me feel that this is what I'm here for. This is what the real game is. And it made me mad as hell. Man's inhumanity to man. I could never understand that. And I still don't to this day. And no matter how many times I'd go ashore, I would just have that lousy feeling.

And I can remember that when I got to Pearl we were put on some detail, because the harbor wasn't very well cleaned up yet. This was April or May of 1942, and I can remember working by the *Shaw*. I remember that terrible odor. It was the first time I ever smelled dead human beings, and it was awful, absolutely terrible. I said to myself, "My God. Those were people."

So the first chance I got after we hit Pearl, I took a bus tour around the island, and I took photos out the bus window. God, I liked Hawaii. I thought that it was pretty sharp. When Artie Shaw was in Pearl Harbor, I used to sing with the Shaw Band. I had played in a trio with Louie Armstrong many years ago, with Louie's first wife, Lil. I was a drummer. She was a pianist. I knew Gene Krupa. I knew all those great musicians.

So we left Hawaii and headed farther out into the Pacific, and I fell in love with the Pacific. I thought this was an absolutely tremendous place. I used to watch that water, and the flying fish. And at nighttime I'd look out at the sky. You can't believe that the sky is so gorgeous, the stars and everything. Then when you'd look at your wake, you'd see the phosphorescence, all these little lights in the water glowing behind you. This was a contrast to those giant black North Atlantic waves that could just consume you. I liked those Pacific nights on deck. They were incredible. I've seen the Southern Lights, and I've seen the Southern Cross. I've been "Down Under." When I was in Majuro I would go swimming in that warm water, and I would put those goggles on and look down at that coral and couldn't believe what I was looking at. It was just a whole new world for a guy who grew up living in the city of Chicago.

So we're cruising along out in the middle of the damn ocean, and they decide they're going to have this great big "crossing the 'Line' ceremony," you know, an equator-crossing ceremony, a Neptune party. And I'll never forget standing next to the rail with the engineering officer, and he said to me, "Can you believe they're stopping the ship for that ceremony? There could be a million Japanese submarines out there." We were all alone you know. We never traveled anywhere but all alone. We never did go with an escort. So I said, "That's scary as hell." He said, "You bet it is."

So they put a swat line together, and I had to go through that line. And, let me tell you something, they had taken those damn canvas sleeves and filled them with sand and soaked them in saltwater and gotten them hard as everything, and they hit you with them. And I said to myself: Will I ever get to that fo'c'sle? I know what I'll do. I'll run as fast as I can damn near run, and, boy, they wouldn't let you do that. So I had to go all the way through again, with those guys beating me. But there was a guy who didn't want to go through the ceremony, so we hid him. They found out later, and the crew held a kangaroo court and charged him with violation of Naval tradition. Verdict: Guilty. So they shaved his hair, and he had to wear a sign that acknowledged his guilt for five days. They were tough.

So we finally got to Noumea in New Caledonia, and then to Brisbane, Australia. A fellow there stopped us and said, "Why don't you two guys come home. We'll fix you something to eat and get to know you." We said, "Geez, that'd be super." So we did. And this family took us in, which was just super. They were wonderful people, wonderful people. We had a New Year's Eve dance there, and I set that sucker up. I got the hall; I got the band; I got the girls; I got the whole ballgame. Just set that baby up. It was great!

We ended up back at Midway. We were servicing submarines at Midway. A buddy of mine and I set up a little business there. We called it Thoma-Epstein Enterprise, Inc. Our motto was, "We'll do anything that is legal." We wrote letters for the guys. They'd come to us and say, "I feel like I don't know that girl back home anymore, and I gotta send her a letter and tell her about that." And I'd sit down and write a letter for him. I think our fee was a buck or some dumb thing like that.

Then there was the time we put on the "*Sperry* Scandals" in 1944. Lyle Epstein and I said, hey, let's write a show, let's do something great, and boy did we put a show on! There was a whole program we called "*Sperry* Scandals," and we had skits and we had the whole ballgame. We put out an ad in the little newspaper there, the *Midway Mirror*: "Help Wanted: Actors Comedians Dancers Singers with the *Sperry* Scandals. Dates for tryouts will be announced later." We put that in there and we got everybody—every guitar, every ukulele came out. We had the show right onboard ship, back on the fantail where we had the movies. Here's a review from the *Midway Mirror*: "Sperry Scandals: A Big Hit. The *Sperry* Scandals and Lyle Epstein and George Thoma deserve the highest praise for their organizing and writing the entire show." Then we had guys come from other ships, and we put it on a couple of times.

I'll tell you what. I've got a lot of super feelings about the *Sperry*. It was absolutely incredible. I just loved it. When one of those subs came in off a patrol she'd come up to the *Sperry*. They'd just tie right up to the *Sperry*. Remember we could put one alongside another. First thing that happens is that we've got a little ship's band onboard, and we have that band out there to play for those fellows. Then we had ice cream ready, and we had fresh fruit ready for that crew when they got off that submarine. And those guys'd come onboard and they'd eat that ice cream. And they'd eat those apples and eat those oranges, and it was just absolutely incredible. And the skipper would get off that submarine with a list of all the things that were wrong or needed fixing. And then the relief crew and the water mechanics and the machinists and everybody else'd pile onboard that submarine and repair her. And they'd put her back into service.

The crew would live aboard the *Sperry*, or on Midway, where they'd go to a part of the island called "Gooneyville." When that relief crew repaired that submarine they'd take it out. They'd take it back out on a shakedown cruise to be sure everything was all right. And then they would bring her back in, and then it'd be ready to go out on the next patrol.

So we had gone from California to Pearl and out to Midway and over to Brisbane and back to Midway, maybe a couple of times, and to Majuro for a while, and when I left that ship to come back to the States, we were in Majuro. I flew back. The first time I was ever on an airplane in my life. I was recommended for shore duty.

And I tell you, when I got to California I met the woman's editor from the *San Francisco Chronicle*, and did she show me San Francisco. It was just an incredible experience. It really was. She was an absolutely marvelous person, and I went to every author's cocktail party. We used to go to the Top of the Mark, and everything was on the house.

Wars are nasty things and are absolutely wasteful and absolutely insane, but for us, as the kids we were, there are certain aspects of them that were life's great adventure. We never dreamed that we would be in those places doing those things, and you really learned how to get along with other people.

# MIKE DeBOLT
NAVY

*Mike DeBolt was assigned to one of the 5-inch gun mounts on the cruiser USS Portland, known to her crew as "Sweet Pea." He kept a detailed diary from the time he reported aboard at Pearl Harbor in December 1943 until the end of the war, when the Portland hosted the surrender signing of the Japanese contingent at Truk. In between, the Portland was involved in the invasions of Kwajalein, Peleliu, the Philippines, and Okinawa, in addition to routinely fending off attacks from Japanese aircraft. The ship had many close calls, but while Mike was aboard, Sweet Pea suffered no serious damage. Mike was a witness to one of the last great naval surface engagements of the Pacific war, the Battle of Surigao Strait in the Philippines. His references to "GQ" denote "General Quarters," when all hands were called to report to their battle stations. The following pages from his diary describe the Battle of Surigao Strait as he experienced it.*

Tuesday, October 24, and Wednesday, October 25, 1944: Tuesday morning we had reveille at 0330 [3:30 A.M.], ate chow and then had GQ. There was a very small raid by Japanese aircraft at daybreak. At 0750 GQ again. A big raid was reported to be coming from the northwest. Our fighters went out and intercepted the enemy planes. They shot down six. Some got through and went for the transport area [the ships unloading supplies for the landing at Leyte]. They scored a hit on a Liberty ship and sunk one LCI. One transport shot down 3 Jap planes. We were tracking a Val but he never came closer than 17,000 yards. At 1130 we had GQ again and there was another raid, seven more large bogies [groups of Japanese planes]. Our fighters intercepted all raids and knocked down 12. The Jap planes never came close to us, but the transport area sure received hell. We made black smoke from the stack. One

Jap plane crashed into an LCI. The total number of our ships put out of commission so far is ten.

After securing from GQ, about 1330 we received word from the task force commander over the loudspeaker: "A surface engagement is very imminent." Word was passed, "All divisions make preparations." There was constant chatter about the whole deal. Scuttlebut was flying everywhere on the number and class of enemy ships, potency and so forth. I heard there could be six battleships, three cruisers and seven destroyers.

We went alongside and tied up to an ammunition ship to get armor piercing shells. All the time we were bringing aboard ammo (400 rounds of 5" also), the men stood by the lines with axes ready to cut them so we could take off in a hurry if enemy planes came in. During the time we were tied alongside, the PT boats went past, heading for the entrance to the gulf to intercept the Jap fleet. Toward the end of our work, the enemy planes came in. GQ sounded when they were 25 miles away. You should see the speed at which the battle stations are manned! Your heart seems up in your throat. I thought we never would get away from that ammo ship. A destroyer on the other side zoomed right away. Just as we got away the other ships started firing at the Jap planes coming in. This all happened toward dusk. The planes were headed for the transport area again. They never really came close to us. Three came real close once, but we didn't see them in time. It was quite a scene. The sky was full of air bursts, men were lowering 8" shells in magazines, ammo was on the deck, men were chopping holes in empty powder cans and throwing them over the side. You couldn't have the empties lying around because of splintering if we were hit. Four of the float planes from our cruisers came in right at that time, and they were almost mistaken for the enemy. They were actually fired upon. I bet those pilots were really worried. After the raid was over, we figured that two Vals, one Sally, and one Zero were destroyed.

We were all thinking about the upcoming surface engagement, and it was interesting to note the feelings and talk among the men. The old salts who had been in surface engagements before were very worried and jittery. One man kept playing solitaire constantly. It was common to see a fellow light up a cigarette, lay it down, and light up another immediately without knowing it. Everyone was joking and laughing. Death seemed to be a joking matter. It was very odd that way. You'd hear words like, "Hey, you better collect all your debts!" "Who has your address book after you're gone?" "I'll take care of your gal!" "Who has any extra life belts?" "Hey, keep a constant bearing on that land over there because we might have to swim for it!" "I think I'll establish a one man beachhead over there; where's the No. 2 motor whaleboat?"

Us new men, never seeing surface action before, were not quite as worried. We felt rather adventurous and wondrous about the whole matter. I personally figured there was no sense in worrying. I couldn't help what happened. Death is absolutely one thing that doesn't worry me in the least. Practically all men had a butterfly feeling in their stomachs. Some guys got real hungry (chow time had been disturbed because of the heavy air raids). I was eating once when they fired off our port side guns at incoming enemy planes. One guy said he had been constipated for three days. He heard the news about our impending surface engagement and presto—like a goose! It was the first time I'd seen men with helmets and lifebelts real close by.

I had the 8 to midnight watch, and when I went off watch there wasn't too much dope on the situation. I hit the sack and went dead asleep. I was awakened at 0200. People were yelling, "They're coming!" I put on my helmet and life belt and went up on deck to watch the action. Our force first picked up the enemy ships at 0130 at 60,000 yards (30 miles). Our PT boats kept us informed on the enemy movements, like when the Japanese force came up the channel, how many there were and how large. We could see it on the horizon when our destroyers first struck the Japanese ships. They made three torpedo runs on the enemy ships. They must have sent 170 torpedoes at them. The Japs shot numerous starshells and also trained searchlights looking for our destroyers. We could see the lights and the firing, and it was terrific.

After our destroyers had made their raids, we started on our run. We were executing the old naval maneuver "crossing the T." There were six cruisers in line and we were second in formation. Farther back of us were our five battlewagons. They were hidden close to the island more or less. All of our guns fired to starboard first. It seemed as though we were the last to start. We heard the word, "Cans [destroyers] have withdrawn from area to get out of our range." Battleships opened up first at 26,000 yards, shooting over our heads. We opened up at 0353 at 16,000 yards. I have never seen or hope to see such another spectacle. It was amazing. No less than 150 shells were all in the air and converging in one area on the Jap ships. The shooting was deadly. We fired nine-gun salvos, and shifted targets after a few salvos. After the first run, we turned around and came back firing to port. We were by no means doing all the firing. The Japs straddled us [shells exploding just in back and just in front as they find the range]. In Navy fire this is considered a hit because the next salvo would have been right on us, but something delayed it. Projectiles were flying and whistling overhead. I hit the deck many a time on my hands and knees. I saw one Jap shell splash only 50 yards off our starboard beam. The only way I was able to see this was that it just so happened that a ship in back of us fired right then, and the flash from their guns illuminated it so I could just see the splash. It felt like I could reach out and wash my hands with the splash. All enemy ships were dead in the water and ablaze after our second run.

After it got a little light we steamed out the channel, only five cruisers, to polish them off. There were two distinct groups of ships on fire. The one we made a run on must have been their two battlewagons. One was burning from bow to stern. It looked just like a big barn fire. I don't see how a man could come out alive. We came back up the channel, turned around and went back again. I could see a Jap destroyer that wasn't too bad off. Parts of the stern and bow were shot away, so our two light cruisers made a run on it, sending it to the deep 6. I saw eight distinct fires. All were Japanese ships burning on the horizon.

Later our destroyers went over to pick up survivors. They were allowed to pick up 400 men. At first the Japs refused the lines, but later changed their minds. One Jap warrant officer said their two big battleships blew up simultaneously.

## LEO DORSEY
NAVY

I enlisted in the Navy as a cadet in December 1942, knowing I had to do something or be drafted. At that time you could still sign up as a cadet, and if you washed out you were back as a civilian, which most people didn't realize. They put a stop to that right afterwards.

I went through primary training flying the old Stearman biplane at Norman, Oklahoma, and then I went to Corpus Christi, Texas. Corpus turned out more Naval pilots than Pensacola did. Most people think of Pensacola as being the big place, but Corpus Christi was huge, and they turned out a lot of pilots. At Corpus we flew the old Vultee Vibrator, and then the SNJ. Then just before we got our wings we had a little time in the old SBD dive-bomber. We thought we were pretty hot pilots when we got in that SBD! That was one of the better airplanes they had when the war started, but it really wasn't worth a damn at that point.

We flew gunnery in the SNJ out over the gulf, and it got so you really felt at home in it. We used to fly instrument hops in the SNJ. The instructor would be in the back seat flying the instruments, and you'd be in the front. There was an outlying field there, right along the Gulf. They'd all land down there, park the airplanes, and sunbathe a little bit. We were coming in to land there one time and this instructor was flying it. He buzzed the field and pulled up, did a Chandell, dropped the gear, came down and was going to land, but he was going too damn fast. I could see that. He touched down about the middle of the runway, decided he wasn't going to make it, poured the coal to it, and was heading right toward the Gulf. There were a bunch of bulrushes and stuff there, but what he didn't know was that there was a big woven wire fence in the middle of all of them. The landing gear caught on that, and, boy, we just cartwheeled almost right into the Gulf, ending up upside down. It knocked him out, and since I kept my seatbelt loose I came down right on the back of my neck. I finally poked a hole in that little old canopy, got out of it, and got him out. If it would have caught fire we'd have been dead, because we were there quite a while before we got out.

There wasn't a whole lot that separated instructors and students at that point. He really didn't have but a few more hours in the SNJ than I did. Once you get your wings they may make you an instructor right away, which happened to him, I guess. Of course he was unhappy as hell.

We went right from the SNJ into the Corsair fighter, and I made my first carrier landing in a Corsair. You put in for your choice, but you never knew if you'd get fighters or not, which was what I wanted. This one friend of mine was dating a WAVE who worked in the personnel office, and he said, "Don't worry about it. We can get you assigned to fighters," and damned if they didn't! I always wondered if she had anything to do with it or not. I'd like to find her again and thank her anyway. That was early 1945.

We practiced on land doing short takeoffs and landings before we did it on a carrier. We did all that at Cecil Field in Jacksonville. I was pretty confident that I would be able to do it once I got on a carrier. I was too damn dumb to know any different, thinking back on it. I guess when I landed the first Corsair on the carrier I probably had less than 200 hours total. On the Corsair you didn't have much forward visibility; you had to kind of bank it around as you came in. That was the only trouble with the Corsair. I hated to wear goggles, but you needed to because you had to open the cockpit and stick your head out to see around that big nose. You were always looking at the LSO, the landing signal officer. He would stand out there on the deck with paddles in his hands and give you signals on what corrections to make as you came in.

I did my first carrier landing on a carrier that had been converted from a cruiser, out in the Gulf of Mexico. The only thing different from what we practiced on land was that they had a lot narrower deck. You felt like the wings were hanging over the side. But even that was big compared to some of those jeep carriers that Kaiser was turning out. They were really midgets.

Then we ended up flying the F8F Bearcat for a while, because it came out right at the end of the war. It was designed specifically to fight the Kamikazes because it climbed like crazy; it was just a little airplane, real small. It had a big R2800 engine, and it held the record for zero to

10,000 feet for a long time. You could take off and just point her up and she'd really go.

I got out to the Pacific in the late spring of 1945. I went out on a ship to Pearl Harbor, where we were supposed to have what they called an operational readiness inspection, to make sure you were up to par. But they were in a hurry to get everything out there, and we didn't do much on that.

So I got assigned to the carrier *Antietam*, still flying the Corsair. That was one of the newer, big Essex-class carriers. We were flying mostly around Hawaii. They called it submarine patrol, but it was mostly just practice. They realized then that they had all the stuff they needed out there. Man, they had carriers massed because they thought we were going to have to invade Japan. That's what I thought I was going to be doing, and that's what everybody thought. Then I got assigned to the USS *Randolf* as a replacement pilot, still flying the Corsair. There were a lot of squadrons that were low on guys. You never knew where you were going to end up. We headed out from Hawaii, and I'm not sure where we went. We didn't put in at any islands; we were out at sea all the time. And when they dropped that bomb, the first one didn't scare the Japanese much, but then there was the second one, and the war ended.

I signed up to stay in one year after it was all over because I figured that even though the airlines were hiring like crazy, they wanted all those multi-engine bomber pilots, you know. I stayed in until the end of 1946, then got out and went to the University of Denver. I was in my senior year when the Korean war broke out, and they recalled the whole squadron. I was back on the *Antietam* again, still flying Corsairs. They sent us over to Korea.

I got out in 1954. I went back and finished my degree, and then in the spring of 1955 I went to work for the airlines. I stayed there until I reached the age of sixty in 1983, and you had to quit then.

I had my eightieth birthday last summer [2003], and my wife bought me an hour's flying time in a Stearman like the one I'd trained in. A guy up north of Grand Junction has one with a bigger engine, and, man, it felt great to be out there again with your head in the breeze and the stick in there in a biwing airplane. It all came back to me; it was just like I was eighteen years old again.

## EX-CHIEF PETTY OFFICER
NAVY

I enlisted in the Navy in September 1943. They gave me a chief petty officer rating to come in, and I volunteered for that.

Then I started my training program. I was supposed to be in the Seabees. But the Navy was organizing Naval Combat Demolition Units (NCDU) and recruiting volunteers. They had us all come into a big auditorium and talked to us about the need for this and what they wanted and so forth. I met some of the needs they were looking for. I was a fair swimmer, and I had explosives experience from handling them in the construction industry.

They convinced me that I would be needed very badly, so I volunteered for that service, even though I realized it would be more dangerous than being in the Seabees. Later I went through training in Virginia, deep-sea diving, SCUBA, re-breathers, and that was the first thing we had to do in shallow water up to seventy or eighty feet deep. As the weather got colder and we could not work in the St. James River they moved us down to Ft. Pierce, Florida, which was a special training program for Naval Combat Demolition Units, and the Scouts and Raiders. I went through that program, which ended up developing into what they call the SEALS today. I was in one of the first units organized, and we were the guinea pigs.

Later, after we completed what they called "hell week" and went through the training, this was in December 1943, we were sent to Honolulu and over to Waimanalo on the Windward Shore of Oahu, and that's where our base was. Part of our training was climbing those damned mountains up and down and also doing demolition work out there in the water. We were only there for a couple of weeks, but I did get leave in

Honolulu. You couldn't believe Honolulu at that time. Hotel Street down there was nothing but houses of prostitution from one end to the other. You couldn't believe it. Those buildings were built right to the edge of the sidewalk, with stores on the bottom and living quarters on the top floors. But what they were was whorehouses. As you'd walk down that street, at each place where the door opened to head upstairs, I'm telling you the truth, sometimes there would be 500 men standing in line to get upstairs to visit a girl. And there were hundreds of these places.

I guess they decided we were uncivilized-type people, and they transferred us over to Maui and put us just as far away from humanity as they could. After they got us over there we went through continuous training. About that time they changed our name to Underwater Demolition Teams, or U D T. All this took place in about forty-five days from the time I left the States. Each unit was seven men, and a group of units made up a team, consisting of 120 or 130 men in each team.

We hadn't known it, but we had been training for the invasion of Roi–Namur while we were on Maui. I'd never heard of Roi–Namur before in my life, or Kwajalein or the Marshall Islands or anything; never heard of them. Our mission was to clear the beaches of any man-made or God-made obstacles that would prevent the Marines from landing.

There was a small island off the southwest tip of Roi–Namur, and the object was to get some Marines on that little island so they could set up artillery and mortars and bombard Roi–Namur. So we went in to that small island southwest of Roi–Namur on the night of January 29, the night before the invasion on the thirtieth. We paddled to the beach in our rubber boats and made sure there were no obstacles that would prevent the Marines from landing. We didn't really find many obstacles, because most of those obstacles were on the ocean side.

We scouted the island, which was pretty much uninhabited, and the Marines landed and set up their artillery and shelled the heck out of Roi–Namur. The rest of the Marines landed on Roi in the morning. The Marines had their own demolitions people, but they were strictly on land. We had to handle anything in the water. But if something needed to be blown up, we blew it up! However, my combat experience didn't last too long. The Marines took only two days to secure Roi–Namur. They wiped it out and cleaned it up. They were the damnedest fighting machine you ever saw in your life.

The Japs had all the warheads for their torpedoes stored in one big concrete blockhouse, and all of a sudden the thing just blew up. They say it was the largest explosion in the Pacific during the war, other than the atomic bombs. When that thing blew, it hurled people and concrete 500 yards out into the ocean. Nobody knows what caused the explosion. Some of our people may have blown it up, or one of the battleships may have thrown a big 16-inch shell in there and hit this building, or planes may have dropped a bomb, but somehow or other the explosion occurred. If you go out there on the island today, there now is a hole that must be about ten acres across, and thirty-five or forty feet deep, but it's a saltwater lake, and that's the crater that explosion left. I saw the explosion. I was on Roi, and the explosion was over on Namur. I went over later and saw where it blew up.

A couple of days after that I went down to the southern end of the atoll to the island they called Kwajalein. The whole atoll was Kwajalein, and this one island was also called Kwajalein. That is the island where the airport is today. They wanted someone down there to do a piece of work for the Army. The Army had invaded Kwajalein. My team went down there, and that's where I was injured. I was down about seventy-five or eighty feet in my SCUBA gear working on disabling some mines, and there was an explosion. One minute I was down there working on those mines, and the next thing I knew I was aboard a hospital ship. When that thing blew, the concussion knocked me out and injured me pretty badly.

When I woke up on this hospital ship, they were taking me to an Army hospital on Maui, because I was working with the Army on Kwajalein. All this time I was trying to tell them I belonged to the Navy. After a while they came in and said, "Hey, you belong to the Navy, so we are going to transfer you over to Aiea Naval Hospital on Oahu." I had internal injuries from the concussion of that underwater explosion. I was there for quite some time, and this was in February 1944 when I got back there. Then in June they put me on the old passenger liner *Lurline* and transferred me to San Francisco and put me in a Naval hospital in Oakland. Later they transferred me down to a hospital in San Diego. I was getting to where I was able to get up and get around, but they wouldn't let me out by myself. I would lose consciousness. I would bend over to tie my shoes and I'd black out; that type of thing.

So finally in October they said they'd done all they could do for me, and they asked if I'd like a discharge. All this time I hadn't seen my daughter who was born in April 1944, so I said, "Hell, give me my discharge. I'll take it and go home." So they discharged me in October 1944, and I went home to see my wife and daughter in Atlanta. I still had periods of blacking out, and it was two or three more years before I ever got straightened out. But everything finally worked out.

Like I said, my daughter was born when I was in the hospital recovering from injuries received on Kwajalein. She was less than a year old when I first saw her. She grew up and got married, and she and her husband accepted a job on Kwajalein twenty-three years ago, and they have been out there ever since. They just love it. He is an electrical engineer, chief engineer for the Kwajalein missile range, and chief of instrumentation. Their youngest son was born on Kwajalein.

When my daughter and her husband first moved to Kwajalein, they couldn't get me permission to visit the island for a long time. It was a closed island because they had a lot of secret stuff going on out there with the missile range. But she knew she had a connection to Kwajalein through me, so she wanted to get me to visit out there. Finally, in the mid-eighties, they got permission for me to visit. The first time I went back I couldn't visit Roi–Namur, but later on I was able to go there. I recognized things, everything's still there, and it's such a small island. There are the Japanese blockhouses and those guns they had pointing out to sea, and they're still pointing out to sea. Roi and Namur used to be separate islands real close together, and now they've bulldozed sand in between them and they're one island. My son-in-law has about a thirty-foot boat, and we were able to go to the spot where I was injured, out in the lagoon just offshore of Kwajalein. I know exactly where we were when I was injured.

One of my sons went out to Kwajalein five years ago on a job. He worked a year and returned to the States. They rehired him, and he and his wife have been out there nearly two years now and they love it. So my daughter and one son are both working there now. I went to the ceremony for the sixtieth anniversary of the invasion in January 2004 with my other son who works in Boulder, Colorado. We stayed with my daughter and son-in-law while we were there. A most enjoyable visit.

I really don't know how this happened, that my kids have ended up working and spending so much time on the island where I was injured during the war. Whether it was because my kids grew up hearing about Kwajalein from me, or if it's just coincidence, I don't know. But that little island has really become a big factor in our lives.

## JIM LOCKHART
NAVY

I blackmailed my dad to let me go into the Navy when I was seventeen. He wasn't going to let me go that young, but I said, "You know, if you were seventeen years old and your country was in trouble, you wouldn't let a little thing like your dad stop you, and I'm not going to let it stop me." That was probably the Thursday or Friday after December 7, and my dad went down with me on Monday to talk with a recruiter. I'd already had it set up that he was going to sign, and they said, "When do you want to go, Wednesday or Friday or next week?" So I said, "How about Wednesday?"

In boot camp they gave us a sheet to fill out to request what type of service you want to do. I made up my mind that I didn't want to get all shot to hell in this war. And, by golly, I figured I'd just take submarine service. They gave you three choices, and I put down "submarine sea duty" for all three of them. And I got submarine sea duty. But they start you out on a relief crew, and you get to go over the side and scrape the hulls and the sanitary tanks and all that before you actually get on a crew.

When you get done with those duties, then you are qualified for a submarine crew. Being on a submarine crew, a real asset was that when you went overseas you got 20 percent sea pay, and being on a submarine gives you 50 percent more, so I got 70 percent more pay than other seamen.

The *Yorktown* was in San Francisco, and they loaded us aboard for its shakedown cruise, and they transported us to Hawaii. This would have been September 1943. They put me on a relief crew on a submarine tender called the *Griffin*. I was having girl trouble there, so I put my name down for the first submarine that was leaving Hawaii. Another guy put his name down, too, and they took him and left me. He shipped out on the *Gudgeon*, which went down on the next trip, and it took him with it. So I figured, how lucky can you get?

So about a month later they sent us to Brisbane, and then around the southern part of Australia to Fremantle, and I was still on the *Griffin*. We were on the relief crew tending the submarines. They'd come in, and we'd refit them and send them back out. All of a sudden I find myself assigned to the USS *Aspero*, No. 309, and by then it was 1944. We had a little shakedown cruise and stopped at Darwin there in northern Australian to top off our fresh vegetables. We had a very successful patrol. We fired all twenty-four of our torpedoes, and we sunk about five or six ships. After we fired them all, there wasn't anything to stay out there for, so we came back and dropped off all the fuel we didn't use at Darwin. Then we went back down to Fremantle.

My job on the sub was a gunners mate striker, but when we were submerged I was assigned to the after torpedo room. When we were trying to sink a ship, it was the most boring thing you can imagine as you wait down there to get in position to fire your torpedo. They don't know you're there yet, but you know they're there. We also had torpedoes that operated on sound, and they were electric torpedoes that didn't make a wake. They'd home in on sound. They'd take forever to get there, but when they got there they'd be effective.

We had a person in each compartment with headphones on, and anything that goes out over that circuit we pick it up, so we know when we are ready to fire our torpedoes. They got six tubes in the forward torpedo room and four tubes aft. We always had the torpedo tubes loaded, but you'd pull the torpedoes out on a regular basis and reservice them and put them back in.

When we were tracking a target, we'd wait until they'd fire the forward torpedoes, and then we'd get instruction to fire the aft torpedoes. They have to have enough men to do the main job, and there isn't anything to keep them all busy during other times, so all you can do is sit and wait, and it's boring as hell.

We had block and tackle to load the torpedoes into the tubes. The only thing that's done in the torpedo room is that when they say, "Fire one," you hit the hand-powered fire knob with the heel of your hand and the torpedo would fire out of the tube with compressed air. It would all start with the forward torpedo room. And you'd hear the instruction, "Make ready the forward tubes." And then, "This is going to be a firing run." So when they get to where they have it figured out they are going to fire and the angle on the bow and so forth, that all comes over the intercom, and then you hear, "Fire one." You can feel the whole sub lunge. After they fire all that they are going to fire, you get a report, and I still make use of that today. Somebody will ask, "How are you doing?" And I say, "Hot, straight, and normal," which is the report the sonar guys give the conning tower, that the torpedoes were running hot, straight, and normal.

When the torpedoes hit, you could hear them. But then the Jap destroyers would come over and try to get you. Then we would seek out a layer of water where there would be a big temperature contrast with the surface; you get enough of that between you and the destroyer, and they can't pinpoint you. The guy on the sonar can hear the screws of the destroyers going over you. When they started depth-charging, you could tell how close they were because it would go, "Click . . . whoom!" The click was the detonator, a higher pitched sound that travels faster than the "whoom." And when it gets down to where you can't hear that click, they have you zeroed in. And then they're just beating the hell out of you. On that first war patrol I don't think they ever got close enough that we couldn't hear the click of the detonators. Nobody ever got all shook up, because you could hear the detonators, and you knew they weren't close.

That first war patrol was pretty good indoctrination for me. We got depth-charged, but they were never that close, and I felt safe. We could go down deep, 400 or 600 feet, and they can't get us, and the more water you get between you and them the safer you are. Sometimes we'd be able to get in a layer of water where the Japs would think we were deeper, and they'd set the depth charges deep. Then we could hear them hit the deck and roll off along the side, but they didn't explode. They were set to go off too deep. But when you heard one of those hit the deck, you had time to say your Hail Marys!

On the surface our flank speed would be about twenty-two or twenty-three knots. Submerged we'd usually go only about three knots. You could go faster than that, but your batteries wouldn't last long. In the sequence of a day, we'd ride underwater in the daytime, and when it got dark we surfaced and recharged our batteries. But when the sun came up, we'd dive again.

On that second war patrol we were in the China Sea pretty close to Lingayen Gulf, and we picked up a convoy. We'd sunk some of their ships, and they got us nailed in; they drove us down in shallow water in that bay. And as we proceeded in there we went after this one ship, but it was empty. I don't know why the skipper went out on a limb to sink an empty ship, but he did. I guess because it was there. And it looked like it was going to be duck soup, but it didn't turn out that way. We had a hell of a time getting away from them. At one point we were down long enough that when you wanted to strike a match to light a cigarette, the match wouldn't burn. We were that short on air. They kept us down all day, and then they had us on their sound gear and that kept us down all night, and then all the next day. We were hard up, getting depth-charged that whole time. We had some powder you could shake out on a sheet, and it would take the carbon monoxide out of the air and enrich the oxygen. That helped a little bit. But they were right on top of us, pounding us into the mud. It got to the point that if we surfaced they were going to shoot the hell out of us, but they were going to kill us if we didn't, because sooner or later they were going to get a depth charge on us.

So we tried to maneuver and turn around so we could get back out of that bay. We hit a reef and our bow came up a little bit. So we went "all back two thirds" on the engines to get off of that reef. And all of a sudden we got our stern in another reef behind us. We couldn't go ahead and we couldn't go back, so we had to go up. We pumped our auxiliaries to sea; we put a bubble in bow buoyancy, and that didn't work. Nothing worked. So we blew all main ballast, safety and negative, the whole thing, and we were still hung up. So then the captain turned the screws over, shook it back and forth, and finally we came up like a cork. And then we had to flood all those tanks to get back down. As we were doing it, we were trying to turn around, and when we got up to the surface we found out that we couldn't open the main induction intake to fire up the diesels. Behind the conning tower you have a main induction air intake about four feet by six feet to suck the air in for the diesel engines. We'd had so many depth charges that they bent the stem on the valve that opened the main induction, and they couldn't get it open. We were in dire need to get power out of the diesel engines to get the hell out of there. So the captain said, "Dog all watertight doors open between the conning tower and the engine room, and we'll take a suction through the conning tower hatch." And if you tried to walk through that door with four of those engines going flank speed, pulling in all that air, it would just pull you right over on your face.

So, in the process, we got turned around in this bay and aimed in the right direction to come out. I got called up to the conning tower with my binoculars in case they wanted me to go up on lookout. The captain told the quartermaster, "You go up and take the aft lookout, I'll take the forward lookout." The quartermaster started up through the hatch, and he yelled back down, "Captain, there's an airplane out there." So the captain said, "Let me know when he starts to dive." So the quartermaster went up there, and right then he said the Jap plane was diving. So the captain said, "Clear the bridge, dive, dive." He pulled the hatch shut, and just as he did that plane dropped two bombs on us, one on the port side and one on the starboard side, and it just shook the hell out of us. I mean, he didn't probably miss us ten feet on either side. But it knocked out the main bus tie to the motors, and we didn't have any power, so the lights went out. Everybody grabbed battle lanterns, and they went and reset the bus ties, and we got power back on. But we didn't get hit directly, and we got out of that bay. They had destroyers and destroyer escorts chasing us all the way out to sea, but we made it out. That's the only time the captain broke out the booze. The captain said everybody could have a drink!

When we got out of there, we went up the coast and waited for that transport ship, and we got that sucker when he came out of that bay. We never messed with destroyers. It just wasn't worthwhile. They were so maneuverable, they'd see your torpedoes coming and could get the hell out of the way.

When you finally get in position to fire at a target, the first order is, "Open the outer doors." That just takes the cover off the outside, and then you're ready to fire. All you have to do is put the information through the computer up in the conning tower. Then you wait for the order to fire. The computer sets the course and direction of the torpedo. It will take whatever bearing you have set in it. You can fire in almost any direction that way, no matter which direction the sub is facing. The detonator on a steam torpedo is the same as on an electric torpedo, and it was an impact detonator.

I ran into a guy once who was a POW captured on Bataan, and the Japs used him to man their ships. One time we had just one torpedo left, and we wanted to spend it right. There was a whole convoy, so we went down and we stayed down until that convoy got right over us, and we surfaced smack in the middle of it, so they couldn't shoot at us or they'd hit each other. Our skipper decided he was going to ram one of the Jap ships and the bullnose went into the side of the Jap ship and bounced off. And this guy I met, he told me, "I saw an American submarine, and those submarines were our worst enemies. I watched a submarine trying to ram our ship, and I could have jumped from the ship I was on down to the bow of the submarine, and I'd have been home free." So I said, "Why in the hell didn't you?" And he said, "I'd have caught it from both ends!" And I asked him when and where, and he said in the China Sea in October 1944, and he told me about where it was. I said, "Hell, that was us!" After that our skipper picked out one of the ships and fired our last torpedo at it, and then we went down and let the convoy go by and then went home.

We weren't supposed to go down deeper than 600 feet, but we got blown down farther than that. If they start hammering on you, you just keep going down. With the momentum of something as heavy as a submarine, sometimes you'd run by forty or fifty feet before you could get going another direction. You put a bubble in bow buoyancy to get your bow up, and then you put your screws to work pushing her up. You blow the water out of the bow buoyancy tank, and that gives you positive lift on the bow.

I went out on two war patrols, and each was about sixty or seventy days.

When I got back to Pearl Harbor, it was time to change out crews, and I got changed out. When I went to the sub base in Pearl Harbor, I went down and found somebody on the *Gilmore* who didn't want to go to sea any more, and I didn't want to stay on shore, so we swapped. And he happened to be in the Tenth Division in Ships Service, so I took his job and I was making ice cream and selling it to the crews. The *Gilmore* went to Brisbane and then up to the Philippines, and that's where we were when the war was over, in Subic Bay.

You might say that a kid of seventeen is a long ways from being mature. I grew up in the Navy. I thank God for it, because I never would have survived if I hadn't had some kind of structure put in me, and, boy, in submarines they give you structure! It probably affected decisions that I made in one area or another that I didn't consciously know where it came from, but it's all part of it. It's given me a sense of self-sufficiency . . . and when to lie and when not to!

# CHAPTER 10

*"We were ready for the Japanese. With all that monotony of manning the guns day after day, you really began to wish for a target."*
—Charles McNeal, ARMY

FRED GILES, NAVY, Bora Bora

DOUG McEVOY, NAVY, Midway

REX ALAN SMITH, ARMY ENGINEERS, Canton,
Funafuti, Guam, Philippines

CHARLES McNEAL, MARINES, Samoa

ROBERT PHELAN, ARMY, rear area islands

CARL HAMILTON, NAVY, Seabees

PAGES 352–353: *U.S. Navy Seabees haul a load of sand from an outlying small island toward the main island of Bora Bora where Fred Giles was stationed.*

OPPOSITE: *Wartime photo of Fred Giles.*

# LIFE IN THE REAR AREA ISLANDS, 1942–45

FRED GILES
NAVY

had obtained my Amateur Radio Operator (HAM) license at the age of fifteen, so when WWII broke out I joined the Navy and entered the Naval Radio Service. We were all studying like crazy because they kept telling us that radio transmissions would be extremely important. It came down to a friend and me as to who would finish number one in our class. Well, it turned out he beat me, and he was number one. But these are the ironies of life—he was sent right off to the Pacific and ended up on Guadalcanal. And I ended up on, of all places, Bora Bora! It turned out that second wasn't so bad after all!

The Navy was putting together a big operation to open an island Naval base in the central South Pacific, and they were looking for an island that was in friendly territory and had strategic value. Since the Japanese were charging across the western Pacific, they wanted to pick an island that would be safe and that could be used as a transshipment and refueling point for ships traveling from the West Coast of the U.S. to Australia, New Caledonia, and New Zealand. French Polynesia was the obvious place to build a base, but the French on the main island of Tahiti were leaning toward the Vichy side of the fence and there were some questions about building a U.S. base there. It turned out that there were enough French who were sympathetic to the Allies to work out a compromise. They said we could build a base, but it couldn't be on Tahiti. It had to be on a little island out of the way called Bora Bora.

I didn't know any of this until much later, of course. At the time I just got my orders that I was to be part of something they called Operation Bobcat. We loaded up on a few ships and headed out into the Pacific. When we pulled up at this island, I thought it looked like every picture I had ever seen of Paradise. There was a huge green mountain right in the middle of the island, and a coral reef out from shore a ways that encircled the entire island except for just one pass for ships to come inside. It was a natural naval fortress. The water was unbelievable. It was warm and so clear that from the railing of the ship we could look right down and see all kinds of sea life swimming about, with forests of multicolored coral everywhere.

We had to build the base from scratch. It was a lot of work, it was hot, and a lot of things didn't work at first. We even had to build roads to haul our big guns around to higher parts of the island. We put up these big coastal defense artillery guns on ridges overlooking the lagoon entrance. There were six or eight of them altogether.

My job was to run the short wave radio installation. We built the radio shack a little ways out from the base and up on a hill. I had a great view from up there, and had the place to myself most of the time.

All this time while we were getting the base set up, there were locals around. They were awe-struck by the number and size of our ships and the sheer size of our occupation. But most of all, they loved the movies. Of course we young guys couldn't help but notice that many of the local Polynesian girls of Bora Bora were very beautiful. And they were friendly! A lot of the guys started dating the local girls. There was one that my commanding officer was after, and she was incredibly beautiful. I found out later that she did not like him, but he pushed himself on her anyway.

Well, one day I was down in the village, Vaitape, and I saw her walking along. So I went up to her and tried to talk to her. She wanted nothing to do with me! I guess she was still upset about her experience with my commanding officer. She told me she didn't want to have anything to do with Americans ever again, and walked away. But I wasn't going to give up. I saw some of her girlfriends and asked them what her name was. They told me, "Her name is 'Tuta.'" So the next time I was in town I was asking around, "Where is Tuta?" And every time I asked this, the locals would burst out laughing. I couldn't figure out what they thought was so funny. So I kept going around, "Where is Tuta? Where is Tuta?" and there was even more laughing. Finally one old man took me aside and said in broken English, "You know, Tuta means 'shit' in Tahitian." I felt so embarrassed, but at least I knew why they were laughing at me! And of course, they all knew whom I was trying to find all along; it's a small island.

So this kept up for a while—me looking for her and she avoiding me. Finally, one day I saw her in town and I snuck up from behind her. She had this amazing long, wavy, jet-black hair down her back, down past her waist, and I came up and pulled on it and asked her what her real name was. For some reason, she turned around and started talking to me. She said later she was surprised by what a nice guy I was! I guess I had her fooled! No, really, we got along great and we started dating. And I tell you, I was smitten! Turns out her name was Tetua, not Tuta.

So, anyway, Tetua and I started to date, and a lot of nights we would sneak up to my radio transmitter shack since it was up on that hill in the breeze with that great view and we could be alone. But the transmitter in that shack was a big piece of equipment, and in those days there were a lot of tubes in that thing. They gave off a lot of heat when it was turned on. Some of the Navy photographers figured that my radio shack would be a great place to dry their prints, and they would hang them out to dry using the heat from the transmitter. You see, it was so humid all the time that when they developed prints, they had a hell of a time getting them to dry. So these guys started coming up to my radio shack to do their photography work. Then, for some reason, they started to come up sometimes in the evenings when Tetua and I were there and we didn't understand why. Usually we would see them coming and Tetua would sneak out the back. Sometimes they would try and come up there and catch us, and they'd drive up with the jeep lights off. I found out later that they were actually under direct orders of the commanding officer, because he was furious that Tetua had spurned him and that she wanted to be with me instead. You see, my CO wanted to court martial me because the reconnaissance photos the photographers were drying in my radio shack were classified, and that was going to be his excuse to get back at me for dating Tetua.

After a while I figured out another way to see Tetua. I bought a little native outrigger canoe that I hid down by Faanui Bay. This was outside the Naval Base. I would get in that canoe in the evening and paddle around to the village of Vaitape. I figured I was safe in the canoe because the commanding officer had no jurisdiction on the open water, and those guys couldn't find me out there in the lagoon paddling anyway. I would get to the village and spend my time there with her. The people I thought were her parents, who were actually her real parents' cousins, thought it was a great idea for us to be dating. Initially, they were encouraging her to date me even while she was trying to avoid me. The Bora Bora natives liked their daughters to date us Navy guys because we would bring the families gifts, and get them flour and sugar and coffee and things they found really hard to get otherwise. Plus I was told that they liked getting anglo blood into the family, and that this went way back in their culture. The Tahitians were inherently aware of the dangers of inbreeding because of the smallness of their islands.

Well, pretty soon Tetua was pregnant. We had a little daughter and we named her Turia, and things were going great there on Bora Bora. I thought I had found paradise! I was a long way from the fighting on this amazing tropical island, with this beautiful Polynesian woman and our little daughter. But then the war started winding down, and one day I got orders to ship out to New Caledonia off in the western Pacific. This was really devastating, but I was determined to get back as soon as possible, and I told this to Tetua. She didn't believe me. She was sure I would never come back, and wrote this off as another bad experience with an American. So the first chance I got in New Caledonia, I shipped two 100-pound sacks of flour and two 100-pound sacks of sugar to Tetua and her family. These were scarce resources on Bora Bora, and I knew it would be a big deal when they saw I cared enough about them to send flour and sugar. Apparently this did the trick and convinced Tetua and her family that I was serious about getting back.

Sadly, in the end, none of the guys that had girlfriends and children ever went back. There were about 6,500 men on Bora Bora, which resulted in almost 100 children. Out of those 6,500 men, I was the only one that returned to his girlfriend and child.

wwii ended and I got back to the States and got out of the Navy. First thing, I went right back down to Bora Bora. It was great being there again with Tetua and our daughter, but I needed to find some way of earning a living, and there wasn't much going on there at Bora Bora. So we moved to Tahiti and I opened a little radio repair shop. Pretty soon we had a second daughter, and we named her Maeva. Things were going okay for us, but a back injury I sustained while in the Navy came back to haunt me and I had to return to the States for medical care. It looked like I would have to be there a while for treatments, and I figured it would be best if we all could be together in the States, so I tried to work out how to do that.

But getting Tetua out of Tahiti and into the U.S. didn't turn out to be easy. There was a rule at that time that you had to be 51 percent white to immigrate, or you had to be directly related by blood. We could get our daughters into the U.S., but Tetua was Polynesian and couldn't meet the criteria. This was a big problem. Because of my health I couldn't live in Tahiti, but Tetua couldn't get into the U.S. And then we faced the question of what should we do about our daughters? I suggested we get the girls into the States first. They could go because they were born American because of me. Then we would work on Tetua, but there was no guarantee that the U.S. would ever let her in. This was a big deci-

*Life in the Rear Area Islands*

sion, and we finally decided, or actually Tetua decided, that she would send the girls with me to California, and that it was best for the girls to be raised in the U.S. regardless of her feelings or chances! I knew that she was completely and totally heartbroken, but she wanted the best for her children. She figured that it could very well be that when the girls left it would be the last time she would see them, or me for that matter.

But then we all got to work to try and figure out a way to get Tetua into the U.S. It turned out that someone remembered that her maternal grandmother's maiden name had been "Hamblin," a good Caucasian-sounding name, and that her great-grandfather had been English. So somehow in Tahiti they cooked the books through various family connections to make the case that Tetua was 51 percent white. I'm still not sure how they did this, but it ended up that Tetua was eligible to immigrate. She joined me and the girls in British Columbia where Tetua and I were officially married. Then we went back to San Francisco where we found Naval housing at Hunters Point. Then we had a son, and we named him Fred Jr. Shortly after the birth of our son, we moved to Alleghany, California, a tiny isolated gold-mining town of 150 people in the high Sierras, deep in snow country in the Tahoe National Forest. There we operated a hard rock gold mine for almost fifteen years! What a change for Tetua! But that is a whole other story!

We go back to Bora Bora and Tahiti quite a bit because of all the relatives down there. It's funny how things work out. When I joined the Navy and was in radio school, I'd never even heard of Bora Bora. But that island affected the rest of my life, and I have a wife and children and grandchildren to show for it.

ABOVE: *Photo of Tetua and daughter Turia taken on Bora Bora during the war.*

## DOUG McEVOY
NAVY

I received a draft notice to report for induction thirty days before I was going to graduate from high school in the spring of 1942. But my principal was on the Draft Board, and he said if I was there for twelve years I was going to be there for graduation. So they gave me a sixty-day deferment, and I didn't go in until thirty days after I graduated. This was the year after Pearl Harbor. I showed up for induction with a group, and they were drafting into all the services. Everybody was picking which service they wanted, and I picked the Army. The guy at the desk stamped "Navy" on my papers. So I said, "I'm sorry, but you made a mistake." And he said, "No, I didn't. We're taking every third one in line for the Navy whether you want it or not." So that's how I got into the Navy—by accident!

I started out doing my training at Great Lakes, Illinois. Then they were going ship me to New London, Connecticut, for aviation metalsmith school. But my orders, when they were cut, sent me to San Diego to welding school. So I went to San Diego and went through arc welding, gas welding, and underwater welding. This took about three months. After that I didn't think I was really an expert, but I could weld. And then I got a ten-day leave out of San Diego, and it took *three* days to get back home to Detroit. I had a day or two there, and when I got back to San Diego they shipped me to Pearl Harbor on the aircraft carrier *Hornet*. When I got to Pearl Harbor there were still sunken ships sticking above the water, or partly above the water.

So, I was there in Hawaii for about a month before I got shipped to Midway. During that time I was working on ships in dry dock at Pearl Harbor. I was a shipfitter. When you were in transit, you got all the stuff that wasn't real pleasant to do, like working at the bottom of the dry dock scraping barnacles!

I got to go into town on leave while I was there and I was disappointed. I was expecting a little South Seas village but Honolulu was a modern town; they even had electric buses. I was looking for grass huts! I really didn't have much social life in Honolulu. I was too young to drink. I was eighteen or so. But I ended up working a lot with an Oriental magician that I was paying to teach me magic. I was always interested in magic tricks, and I got to talking to him one day when I was in town. I was showing him some of the things I knew, and he was showing me things a lot better than anything I knew!

So, I learned magic when I was in Honolulu. I did magic the rest of the time I was in the service. I also did card tricks. I guess that was an unusual skill to learn in Honolulu! I also carried my ice skates with me the whole time I was in the Navy, and amazingly enough I went ice skating in Hawaii. They had a little ice rink in a town outside Honolulu called Waiwa. That's another thing not many sailors did in Hawaii.

So, then the word came down that they needed shipfitters for the submarine base on Midway, and I got sent out there. I'd heard about Midway mainly because I had a real good friend who was killed on one of the ships in the Battle of Midway. I'd never heard much about the island itself, though. I got there, and I thought the island looked pretty small! I was supposed to be there for about nine months and I ended up being there for more than a year, because they wouldn't release us until they got replacements, and they never got replacements. I was there when Roosevelt died, on VE Day, when they dropped the bombs, and on VJ Day. The only way I got off Midway was when the war ended.

We didn't have much to do. There was a lot of gambling and fights going on, some pretty brutal fights, really. Some of the guys sent there were kind of rough. Some were sent there as a kind of punishment, or other units didn't want them. In fact, Eddie Peabody had a huge band in Honolulu, and they cut the band in half and gave half the band to Ray Anthony. The story I heard is that he and his fellow musicians came in one morning intoxicated and played reveille or taps with an eight beat, and they shipped them out to Midway as punishment. They were only out there for about three months, but they performed for us while they were there. Every Saturday night they would play, and that was great.

After a while I started resenting being stuck there. It wasn't real pleasant, there wasn't much to do, and because of that, I think, there were actually murders that took place there on Midway. There was an inside shipfitters shop, where I was, and it was in a building on the base; and there was an outside shipfitters shop out on the pier, and they would work on the submarines right where they tied up. And my friends were in the outside shop, and if they would dive into the water in the morning and pull a body out they would get the day off. They would occasionally find bodies of American sailors in the water. These guys were evidently killed in fights over gambling debts, or that's what my friends thought.

One night I was on the twelve-to-four A.M. watch. When a sub would pull in and would have to be worked on, they would send all the submariners to this place on the island called Gooneyville, and they would stay there until they were ready to go back out on their submarine. The story we got was that this one fellow was writing a letter, and another guy put his foot on the bunk and was jiggling it, and he told him to stop two or three times and the other guy didn't, so he took a gun and shot him. I was at the other end of the island, and the officer of the day came down and picked me up to go over there since they had gotten word there was a problem. So we went down there, and they had arrested the guy who had done the shooting, and we were trying to get a statement out of a guy who witnessed it. He was so intoxicated that we walked him up and down the barracks four or five times, but we couldn't get him conscious enough to talk.

Another thing that my friend from the outside shop told me was that some guy had won a lot of money gambling, but then he just disappeared. We had a little 8 1/2 by 11 news sheet that they published every day, and they were asking in the paper if anyone had seen this guy. And this was a small island, but no one had seen him. They finally found him tied to one of the pillars under the pier. We figured that he had been killed for his money. You see, they all went to this beer hall where they gambled. That was on the main submarine base, just behind our chow hall. I went there a couple of times, but I didn't really drink that much and I usually gave the other fellows my beer tickets.

Our main form of entertainment was that we had a different show every night, a movie. After we worked all day we would go back to the barracks, get cleaned up, go over to the chow hall and eat, and then come back. We had about an hour or so when we kicked around the barracks, then we'd go back over to the chow hall where they showed the movies. We'd play pinochle until the movie started, to pass the time, but that wasn't gambling, that was just cards.

I was pretty sick of Midway by the time the war ended. You were away from home, and I was just a young kid then. I wanted to get off the island, so I volunteered for duty anywhere else other than Midway, even to go into combat, but they said that they couldn't get a replacement for me so they wouldn't even process the paperwork.

The subs would come in, and the crew would be off the ship when we started working. Primarily I did stuff that was rebuilding things off the subs. One time I was injured pretty badly trying to fix a coffeepot off a sub. One of their coffeepots had gone bad, and I was going to make a new bottom for it. I brought it to the shop, and I was sweating off the bottom when that molten metal went down and hit the concrete and came back up through the big coffeepot and hit me in the eye. It closed my eye and matted it shut. They thought I would lose my sight but I didn't. I have a little tic in that eye now, but nothing that interferes with vision. I was in the underground hospital for about three days. You know, the hospital was underground there on Midway. There was only a sick bay aboveground on the base.

I had a girlfriend at home during the whole period I was on Midway, and we wrote letters back and forth, so mail call was a pretty big deal. We had a seaplane, a Catalina flying boat, that used to land in the lagoon, and it brought the mail in from Pearl. Sometimes when the water was real calm inside the reefs they would have to send a PT boat out to zigzag in front of the plane to roughen up the water so the plane could take off. I guess if the water was too calm, it would be like the seaplane would be almost glued to the surface. It needed a little rougher water to be able to break the surface of the water to take off.

Finally the war ended and I left Midway on a sub tender, back to Pearl and then back to California.

So, after all those letters, when I got back after the war I got married to my girlfriend. We were married just nine days short of thirty-four years when she passed away. We were actually childhood sweethearts. When I got off the ship in California coming back from Midway, I got a thirty-day leave and went home and got married. Then I had to report back to California, and I had my wife with me then. I was supposed to go back overseas again, but I got seasick every time I was on any kind of ship. I remember one time when I was on a Liberty ship I was the only one who was seasick. I even got seasick on the aircraft carrier on the way to Hawaii, and on the sub tender on the way home, and it's a floating industrial city. So, I wasn't much of a seagoing sailor.

So, they were going to ship me out, and my bus broke down that was taking me to my ship. I headed back to the base and had to wait for the bus to get fixed. At that time my aunt back in Detroit was running the insurance company of the skipper of that base, and she had told me to stop in and see him if I got there. I really didn't want to go up there and see him since I was just a second class shipfitter. But since the bus had broken down, and I had two hours on the base and nothing to do, I thought I'd go up and say hello to him and keep everybody in Detroit happy. So, I went over to his office, and the first thing he said was, "You just got married, didn't you?" And I said, "Yeah." And it turned out he knew all about it because my aunt had apparently talked to him. And he says, "How long are you going to be here?" And I said, "Another hour or so." So he said, "Can you think of any reason you shouldn't go overseas?" And I said, "Yeah, I have chronic seasickness." So he picked up the phone and took me off the ship and gave me duty on the base. And that was a great deal! Because when you are seasick, first you are afraid you are going to die, and then that's the only thing that keeps you going, the hope that you will!

So I was only in California for a couple of months, and then I got discharged at Camp Shumaker in California. My wife and I spent all our money, for on the way back to Detroit we went via Florida. So we finally got home and I had no money and needed a job.

I started out on that first job reporting to work with a pliers, and then I was welding and then doing sheet metal work and then drafting and then I was in charge of the whole place! I went on to other jobs, but, for that first job, if I hadn't had my Navy welding and sheet metal experience, I would never have made it to superintendent. So I guess the Navy did affect the course of my life in that way.

A while after my first wife died I got remarried, and my wife Doris and I split time between Denver and Phoenix. We go on cruises now, and this is interesting because I found a way around my seasickness. Now I wear this little bracelet; it's like two elastic bands with a little half-round button, and I press that button against my wrist, and I don't know what it does but it takes care of the motion sickness. So at least I have overcome that part of my Navy experience.

I think I would like to go back and see Midway now. I haven't wanted to go back in the past. When I was younger I had no desire at all to ever see that island again!

But I think now it would be interesting to see it again.

## REX ALAN SMITH
### ARMY ENGINEERS

I t was a sleepy Sunday noontime at Stallings Drugstore in Rapid
City, South Dakota, when I heard about the attack on Pearl Harbor. I was having an after-church cup of coffee with friends, and in
the background a radio was playing soft Sunday music. Then, suddenly we heard:

"Ladies and Gentlemen, we interrupt this broadcast to say that the
Japanese have bombed the American naval base at Pearl Harbor!"

We were shocked as we gathered around the radio to listen for further details, and we were very angry at the Japanese for the sneak attack.
We kept assuring each other, however, that it would take "our boys" no
more than six months to give those sneaky Japanese a military spanking
they would never forget.

At the time I was a draftsman for the Soil Conservation Service but
would be transferred over to the Army Corps of Engineers as part of
a crew surveying what would become a base for advanced training of

ABOVE: *Rex Alan Smith in the pilot house at the controls
of the dredging ship* Kingman, *under way in Manila Bay
in early 1945.*

365

B-17 bomber crews. (Known first as Rapid City Army Air Base, it would become, years later, Ellsworth AFB.)

I remained there as a draftsman until about November when the base had become operational. And it was about then that there appeared from somewhere an optional order for me to transfer to the U.S. Engineers in Honolulu. I took that opportunity. Probably I would have been drafted later, but I was eager to get out quickly to where things were happening. In fact, I was thrilled. I had traveled a bit—once to Pierre, South Dakota, once to Greeley, Colorado, and even once on a train to far-off Omaha, Nebraska—but as a South Dakota ranch kid I never expected to see much more of the world than that. Now here I was, on my way to faraway exotic, romantic Hawaii!

I left Rapid City on November 12, 1942, and would not see it again until December 1945. My travel orders put me on a bus to Cheyenne, then on a Pullman to the Oakland Ferry and eventually San Francisco.

In San Francisco they put me up in the Drake-Wiltshire Hotel, which I immediately decided must be one of the world's finest. Then I waited. There were more men waiting to go overseas than ships.

Finally I received orders to report immediately to Oakland Outer Harbor for embarkation. That would have been in late November 1942.

The ship was the *Frederick Funston*, a transport making her maiden voyage and still smelling of fresh paint. She was so crowded by the need to get more men overseas that there were even stands of pipe-frame bunks on her shelter deck, and I wound up in one of them. The deck above provided a roof over my head, but otherwise our deck was wide open to the weather, and until we entered tropical waters the weather was cold. I had two blankets, but could have used four. We were told to use our life preservers as our pillows, to have them handy in case of need. They were canvas over blocks of hard, dry cork and were as comfortable as sacks of rocks. But, at age twenty-one it was still an adventure.

I don't know just what I expected Honolulu to be, but what I found was a city crowded with servicemen in the daytime and totally dead at night. There was an early curfew, and God help you if you were caught violating it. At this point I was not in the Army at all. I was a purely civilian employee of the Corps of Engineers. But as time passed that distinction would gradually become blurred.

The Army had taken over Honolulu's prestigious Punahou School for the duration of the war, and I was assigned to the Civil Engineering Division in Dillingham Hall. Soon I became bored with it. Civilian or

*Life in the Rear Area Islands*

not, I wanted to get out to where the war was. I'd been hearing about an Engineers project way out in the Pacific at a place called Canton Island, a tiny atoll on the perimeter between islands the Japanese had taken and those still held by us. Eventually I received a transfer to Canton—an event that was to change the course of my life.

Canton was right on the equator. It had almost no vegetation, only one palm tree on the entire island, and its surface was white coral. In appearance it was like living on a snow bank. It had a shallow lagoon so studded with coral heads that at low tide it looked much like a lake drying up, and it provided our only recreation. We spent most of our spare time swimming and diving in its balmy waters looking for sea shells, admiring the beauty of the coral heads studded with colorful clams, and watching the fish.

The Engineers at Canton were commanded by Lt. Col. J. J. Kestley. I was assigned as a draftsman, and before long I had graduated to also doing some airfields surveys. Then I progressed to making soundings and drawing up weekly charts of a ship channel being dug from the sea to the lagoon by the Engineer seagoing hopper dredge *Pacific*. I got to know the guys on the dredge, and I became fascinated by the art of ship handling.

At about that time, the Navy wanted Col. Kestley down at Funafuti Island, an atoll in the Ellice Islands, to supervise the deepening of a channel from sea to lagoon, and he offered me the chance to go along as sort of his "right-hand man." I took it and again wound up doing soundings, charting the channel, and under the colonel's direction generally supervising the job.

The Navy had us quartered on the Navy survey ship *Sumner* until she was sent somewhere else, then on the destroyer tender *Cascade*, and finally on the ammunition carrier *Sangay*. We were there to deepen Te Bua Bua, an old natural channel that the Navy wanted deep enough for battle-damaged ships, riding low in the water, to be able to come into the lagoon for repairs. Although the *Pacific* was too small to dig to the required thirty-five-foot depth, we had her there to start the job while waiting for the arrival of the much larger *Alexander MacKenzie*.

It was on the *Sumner* that the line between my civilian status and the military first began to become a bit blurred. My quarters were in "Officers Country," I took my meals in the officers wardroom, at a Purple Heart award ceremony I was invited to stand in formation with the ship's officers, and eventually I was even assigned to a General Quarters station.

And it was while I was on the *Sumner* that the Japanese, making a surprise air raid, missed an opportunity to possibly change the course of the war. I was awakened by General Quarters clanging in the alleyway, and when I swung out of my bunk and my feet touched the deck I could already feel faint tremors from distant explosions. I got my pants on and out into the alleyway just in time to see the watertight door being dogged down from the other side. Not being enthusiastic about remaining trapped in a watertight compartment during a bombing, I looked around and spotted a little screen ventilating hatch overhead. I climbed up some pipes on the bulkhead, pushed it open and wound up on deck almost among the feet of a very surprised 5-inch gun crew.

We learned later that the Japanese planes had come in behind a flight of our returning bombers and so were not detected by radar. It was a bright moonlight night, and on this particular evening there was plenty to be seen. Half of the Tarawa invasion fleet had assembled in the Funafuti lagoon: battleships, cruisers, destroyers, transports loaded with troops, cargo ships, and other kinds of vessels all lying perfectly exposed in the moonlight. But apparently the Japanese had been ordered to come down and just strike the airfield, and they were people who did not deviate from orders. Consequently, the only bombs going into the lagoon were those missing their target. When that became apparent, the commodore (or whoever was in command of such things) signaled from the submarine tender *Sperry*, "To All Ships, do not open fire unless I do." And nobody did fire—excepting one. We could see far down the lagoon our dredge *Mackenzie* spraying the sky with showers of 20mm tracers. They were too far away from the action and the range of their guns was far too short for them to be doing any good, but they were shooting anyway.

One string of bombs exploded in the water not far from us, but obviously by accident. As for the damage done to the airfield, I never saw an official report, but according to scuttlebutt they had blown up a radio station, destroyed fourteen airplanes, wounded two men, killed a dog, and put the airstrip out of business until eleven o'clock the next morning. But think of what they might have done! As it was, the Battle of Tarawa would be won, but just barely and at terrible cost, and any damage to its support fleet might have been enough to tip the balance the other way.

A few days later we were informed that the aircraft carrier *Independence* had taken a torpedo at Tarawa and was limping back to Funafuti. Well! That's just what we had been digging the channel for! I spent all that day making final soundings and most of the night preparing a channel chart to be flown or taken by destroyer out to the *Independence*. Then we went down to Te Bua Bua to see her coming in—and she didn't. Surrounded by her destroyer escort she came over the horizon moving toward us much like a mother hen surrounded by her chicks. Then she changed course, went around the island, and came through Te Ava Fuagea, a tortuous natural channel that had always been there. Damn! We had been working like beavers and had fired hundreds of tons of dynamite to get the channel ready for this sort of thing, and the *Independence* didn't even use it.

As I recall, it was late in December when Colonel Kestley was called back to Honolulu. He was replaced by Major H. H. Helmboldt, who also became captain of the *MacKenzie*. Directly behind the *MacKenzie*'s bridge were two identical sets of living quarters. Major Helmboldt moved into the captain's quarters on the portside, and at his request I moved into the visiting officers quarters on the starboard. And this, I thought, was a pretty weird thing. I seemed to be both a civilian employee of the Army Corps of Engineers and also a quasi-officer. On the various Navy ships I had been given officers quarters, ate in the officers wardroom, and in all respects was treated as an officer. Here on the *Mackenzie* it was the same.

My quarters were also the magazine for the 20mm antiaircraft guns on the wings of the bridge. My desk was a piece of plywood laid across two stacks of 20mm magazines, and magazines were also stacked across the cabin bulkhead so that when I went to sleep at night I'd be looking at the painted noses of tracers looking back at me.

In late January Funafuti again became a marshaling point for a large part of the fleet, this time for the invasion of Kwajalein and other Marshall islands. By mid-February those islands had been secured, no damaged Navy ships had needed our Funafuti channel, and I was transferred back to Honolulu.

For a time I had a job with a title far beyond my age, and, according to some, duties beyond my capability. Both the *Pacific* and the *Mackenzie* had been put to work dredging Honolulu Harbor, and I found myself at age twenty-three with the exalted title of Superintendent of Hopper Dredging. That didn't last too long, but for a while I had the job plus a cabin cruiser and crew for my personal transportation. While I had it, the job was a great learning experience.

When the job was taken over by someone with more years and qualifications, I was transferred to the mechanical engineering department, and once again I wound up as a draftsman.

In October the *Dan C. Kingman*, a sister ship of the *Mackenzie*, showed up, and because of the manpower shortage she had arrived with a short crew, which was now filled out with parolees from the Oahu prison. She was to be sent to some forward area pretty close to the action, because those going on her were to receive hazardous duty pay plus "Rank of Assimilation" cards stating that in the event of capture by the enemy they would automatically become full-fledged members of the Army.

I began to keep a diary, and the first entry says:

November 19, 1944: "Last night I was given an Aloha party at my old friends the Foxes' in Waikiki. I'm a big boy now, but when they gave me the Hawaiian Farewell—putting their arms around me and singing "Aloha Oe"—I seemed to get something in my eye.

"At 0910 this morning we pulled away from Pier 2-A, and then stood outside the harbor all day while destroyers, aircraft carriers, battleships, and cruisers followed by Liberty and Victory cargo and troop transport ships all passed us. Then our own convoy of the small and slow was formed: a de-magnetizing ship, a minesweeper, two seagoing tugs, a submarine chaser, and us—at 2,500 gross tons by far the largest vessel in the bunch.

"At 1600 we began kicking up a whole six knots, course 174 degrees, medium swell, scattered cumulus, light breeze."

November 20: "Our yesterday's civilian captain, now wearing a lieutenant commander's leaves, has, as I hear it, spent most of his life sailing dredges up-and-down San Francisco Bay, and I know that neither he nor any of his officers have ever been in a forward war area. But he obviously has read enough novels to know what is expected of him, and he measures up well: Secret orders—we are not to know where we are going until we get there—firm jaw, responsible bearing, measured tread, and his eyes—although a bit watery—have become steely blue. By his very bearing he makes it clear that he is the Captain, by God, of a Ship in a War, by God, and it is not his fault it happens to be a dredging ship whose deadliest weapons are not fired from guns but served from the galley.

"Anyway, I had thought to bring a boat chart along and now the quartermasters and engineers are secretly informing me of our speed and courses, and I think my dead reckoning will keep track of where we are."

December 1: "Atoll sighted on starboard beam at 1630. According to my dead reckoning it should be Mejit. However, since I have had no navigation checks since seeing Johnston Island seven days ago, I could have been all wrong. So I asked the chief mate if it was Mejit. And that was a mistake. He grew red in the face and started shouting, demanding

*Life in the Rear Area Islands*

to know how in hell I could know that and accusing me of having somehow snooped into his navigation records. Well, I was feeling pretty good about having hit our position right on the button after seven days of dead reckoning. So I didn't let him know about my chart, and I continued to keep it through the rest of the voyage."

December 10: "Since Kwajalein, we have been in a new convoy that requires us to maintain eleven knots speed. The *Kingman* was built for power, but low-speed power, and the diesels pound and strain to keep our position in the formation. The skipper and the chief engineer are at it again—the captain, red-faced and angry, insists that the engineer will, by God, give us enough revolutions to keep up. The chief, also turkey-necked and angry, insists that if we do not ease our giddy pace our engines may bloom like flowers and spread parts from here to Fiji."

December 13: "According to my dead reckoning, here today, Guam tomorrow."

December 14: "At dawn it could be seen at about fifteen miles. At 0730 we could see Rota to the north. The Japanese still hold it but it is no longer a threat. At 1100 we slid past the cliffs of Guam's Arote Point. We could see shell scars, but the cliffs are still beautiful. There is much broken Japanese shipping in the harbor, and especially noticeable is one long hull lying keel up with her bottom out of the water. A lot of captured Japanese landing craft are being used as shuttle boats and are charging around the harbor everywhere."

Our work there was pretty dull and monotonous but with a few bright spots. For instance:

December 27: "At 2300 last night I heard the old man holler, 'Smeeth! To the bridge!' When I got there the tower on Arote Point was signaling with a red light. The old man asked, 'what are they saying?' And I said, 'Condition Red.' He asked what that meant. I answered, 'Air attack imminent.' And he went nuts. He ran into the wheelhouse hollering, 'Stop her, Mr. Barnes! Goddamit, Mr. Barnes! Stop her I say!' Second officer Barnes was startled and not a little confused, but he recovered well. He rang 'drag up,' threw both screws in full reverse, picked up the bullhorn, and began hollering, 'Bos'n to the foredeck! Bos'n to the foredeck!' Shorty showed up in nothing flat, and on Barnes's command knocked out the anchor chain stops. The chains roared out, rust flew, and we were at anchor. So now what to do? Unlike the *Mackenzie* we had no guns, gunners, or battle stations. But the captain figured he ought to observe the situation somehow, so he hit the fire alarm.

"Finally one lonely 'bandit' showed up, very high, and with everyone in the harbor and on shore shooting at it, tracers were flaming up all over the sky. On the *Kingman* they were shooting too—with every fire hose we had."

One day I was walking along the deck, and from right under my feet there came an enormous Wham! The entire ship shuddered from the impact of something, but what? In this secure harbor it couldn't have been a torpedo or gunfire or a bomb. What it turned out to be was that the water jacket on one of our diesel engines had sprung a leak into a cylinder, and the huge piston had come up and hit it with an impact so great that it actually bent a four-inch diameter piston rod. The chief engineer needed a drawing made of the rod to be flown back to Honolulu for making a replacement. The old man remembered that I had been a draftsman, and thus began my emancipation from the drag tender business.

When the rod job turned out all right, the old man decided he would like another structure built on top of the pilot house and gave me the job of designing and drawing up the plans for it. I didn't have the qualifications for designing something to withstand the stresses of a ship rolling on the sea, but he didn't know that, and besides, the thing never got built anyhow. But while I was working on it, the *MacKenzie* arrived at Guam, and its captain asked our captain if he would transfer me to the *Mackenzie* for training as a third mate. The old man wouldn't transfer me, but the very request seemed to convince him that I was worth more than he had thought I was.

From Guam we were sent to Leyte in the Philippines, but we never knew why. All we did was sit out there in Pedro Bay, which was already about 600 feet deep, and there wasn't much we could do to improve that. So we waited, and while waiting we learn that the *Kingman* was to be gradually converted to an all-Army crew.

From Leyte we were sent to Manila. Coming in, I saw something that really depressed me. The Army had just taken the island fortress of Corregidor with a massive drop of parachute troops on the island's flat top. But as we came by we saw the steep cliffs of its sides white with the parachutes of men who had missed the top, and I thought, how awful it must have been to come down so hard onto those cliffs and the trees sticking out from them.

There were sunken enemy ships all over the place, and we wound up anchored by a sunken destroyer. Having always been as curious as a puppy I hurried to recruit some other guys and a boat operator to go over there and look at the thing with me. After it was sunk it must have been used as a hideout by Japanese snipers. And I would guess it had been Filipino guerrillas who finally took them out. The bridge structure had been burned, but sticking out of it was a wooden two-by-four from which dangled, by a rope around its neck, the body of one Japanese soldier, and the body of another lay on the foredeck.

Back on the *Kingman* we reported what we had seen and went to chow. Then I joined the old man and a few others on the fantail to enjoy the evening breeze. Suddenly, from the galley, which was only a little way forward from the fantail, there came a terrible stench. The captain went in to investigate, and I heard him shriek, "T'row it out! T'row the goddam t'ing out! T'row it over the side, and I mean now!"

What had happened was that we had aboard an old World War One re-tread sergeant who, it turned out, had always wanted a skull, and now he had one. He had taken one of the Japanese heads from the destroyer and was now cooking the flesh away in one of the galley cooking pots. Needless to say, he never finished the job. Public opinion was against it.

We were put to digging ancient mud out of Manila's Inner Harbor, and in the process brought up enough historic cannonballs to have armed the Spanish Armada. Once we even brought up a dainty cup and saucer that had miraculously survived their trip through the drag-pipe, the huge pump, and the steel distribution boxes.

By the time we arrived there the fighting had moved well out of the city, but even so, the first time I went ashore I found myself stepping over the body of a Japanese soldier on the dock. And it was on that trip that a couple of us came across what had been the Japanese central bank. The building had been blown open, and in its vault we found ourselves walking across a carpet of Japanese occupation money, and money was stacked in cases against the walls. It was worthless, of course, but just the same we stuffed our pockets with it. When we got back to the ship, other men said they wanted to go and do the same. Next day I took some of them over there, only to find a Navy shore patrolman guarding the door. He said, "You can't go in. Last night they took fourteen booby traps out of there." Well! Yesterday we were the boobies, and it was just by dumb luck that we hadn't gotten ourselves blown up.

After the booby traps were cleared out, the place was open to anyone to carry out as much money as he wanted. And even then there was so much of the stuff that to clear the building they were burning it in the alley. Then somebody got a great idea: "Let's send it to the Navy hospital at Guam as souvenirs for the men there." And that is what they did.

We had started at Leyte to let men off and replace them with Army, and continued it at Manila until eventually the electrician Rex Oldfield and I were the only civilians left aboard, and we were "assimilated"—he as a second lieutenant and I as a warrant officer.

It was well after the A-bombs had been dropped and Japan had surrendered that my warrant officer appointment finally came down. Meanwhile, the *Kingman* had continued dredging and I had continued to serve as third mate. But now I was faced with a hard decision. Had I known then what I know now, probably I would have taken that commission, because I did dearly want to become a legitimate member of the Armed Forces. On the other hand, I had not seen my home for almost three years, nor even the United States, and I didn't know but what it might be another two years before I could. In the service then you got to go home only after you had earned a certain number of "rotation points," and the points depended on your time served overseas, but my three years there with the Corps of Engineers did not count—I had no points.

So, on September 13 I reluctantly wrote a letter declining the appointment. On September 22 I reluctantly left the *Kingman* for quarters ashore in the GENED (General Engineer District) Officers Club while awaiting transportation home. Rex Oldfield came with me because he, too, had become concerned about the extra time he might have to spend overseas if he accepted his commission.

Then we discovered we were orphans. We didn't know if we were getting paid anymore. We had no way to get in touch with our office in Honolulu, so we wandered around trying to get travel orders on our own. Finally we got a set and had just gotten comfortably settled down in a nice compartment on a homebound Liberty ship when the old man called for us and said, "I am sorry, but these papers are not in order!" So, it was back to the beach again.

We ended up walking miles across Manila, trying one office after another. At last we got another set of orders, only to have the ship we were to sail in damaged by collision with another ship. After the passing of some sixty years I can't remember exactly how we got the Navy involved in this problem. But however it was, the captain of the destroyer *Kalk*, which was about to sail for Pearl Harbor, told us there were a couple of bunks in his chiefs quarters that we could have.

To make a long story a little shorter, we got into Pearl Harbor on November 15 and were picked up at Pearl City by an Engineer weapons carrier sent to take us to the Engineer camp at Red Hill. But we had enough of camps for awhile and told the driver to take us instead to the Alexander Young, a fine hotel downtown. Then we went out and had a wonderful dinner of fried oysters, fresh vegetables, fresh milk, and a malted milk.

Then I went into furious action. I was determined to get home for Christmas. There was a transport leaving on the nineteenth, and I worked desperately at getting my Engineer affairs straightened out and my possessions gathered and packed so as to make it. And I did make it, but just barely.

November 19, 1945: "It happens that my old friends Charlie and Mabel Fox are going home on this same vessel, and at 5 o'clock we were standing on the fantail of the transport *Evangeline* watching the harbor slide by. The ship is loaded with home-going servicemen, and as we passed through the harbor things got pretty noisy when the ships there are all began saluting us by sounding . . . ___ ' (V for Victory) on their whistles and horns."

Passing Diamond Head I felt a little depressed to think I might never see Honolulu again. But there was a superstition that if in passing Diamond Head you threw a lei overboard and it drifted toward shore you would return. Friends seeing us off had given us leis, so I did throw mine overboard and it did drift toward shore. (And although it would take fifty-seven years for it to work, it did! In December 2002, I returned to do something I never dreamed I would be privileged to do—join my co-author Jerry Meehl in signing copies of our book *Pacific Legacy* at the exact place where the Pacific war had begun: Pearl Harbor.)

My experiences in the Philippines during the war directly affected and probably even molded my future life. There, a Captain Trinidad, who had been the skipper of a Philippine inter-island steamer sunk by the Japanese became a part of the *Kingman* Filipino "Shadow crew"—a device used to help the Manila Filipinos get back on their feet after almost four years of vicious oppression and plunder by the Japanese. We spent a lot of time on the bridge together. He invited me to his home, and he and his family became my fast friends. In spite of their war-depleted resources they even gave me a big birthday party, and Mrs. Trinidad entered into correspondence with my mother.

They, in turn, introduced me to the Agcaouilis, who lived next door. We, too, became the best of friends. Felix Agcaouili was a prominent attorney who had as one of his clients a Major Ferdinand Marcos, who later was to become president of the Philippines. Marcos had formed a partnership with Brigidio Cifra who had large timber concessions on the island of Mindoro. Somewhere along the line Agcaouili and Marcos came up with the idea that I should become American representative for sale of their furniture-grade logs. I didn't know a damn thing about that kind of business or, for that matter, any other kind of business. However, I had read so many Horatio Alger books as a boy that I figured it didn't matter very much—all it took was determination.

I moved to Chicago, set up shop, and actually did sell a shipload of their logs. Man! I was walking tall! My commission would have been $14,000, and in 1946 that was *money*! But right after that I came down to breakfast one day and saw the headline, "Philippines Embargo Hardwoods." And that was the end of that.

I finally ended up in the insurance business, and actually insurance turned out all right. I spent more than thirty happy years in the service of a wonderful company, in a career that if not distinguished was satisfying and good. Then quite by accident I wound up in the writing business. At the urging of a friend I wrote an article on inflation for the *Life Association News*. It caught the eye of a *Readers Digest* editor who asked if I could do anything else. The result was *Let Not This Sparrow Fall*, the story of one of my flying experiences, and it appeared in the June 1973 *Digest*. This led to a book, *Moon of Popping Trees*, published by Reader's Digest, and later the text for *One Last Look*, the story of the Eighth Air Force in World War II, and *The Carving of Mount Rushmore*, both published by Abbeville Press.

I found that I love research, and I like being published. But I do hate writing. For me, at least, trying to do it so that people will read it is the most exasperating drudgery I have ever known. But I do it anyhow, to tell stories that I think should be told of things I think should never be forgotten. For instance *Pacific Legacy*, written with co-author Jerry Meehl, was published by Abbeville as a memorial to those in the Pacific war who fought and died for their country and whose sacrifices must never be forgotten.

# CHARLES McNEAL
MARINES

**W**hen I enlisted, it was kind of like that old cadence song, "You had a good home but you left." I had always wanted to be a baseball player, and somebody said to me, "They have a lot of sports in the military service." In 1940 people knew a war was coming, and they were building up the glories of being in the service, back there in 1940. This old boy in Farmington, Arkansas, he'd been around, he'd been everywhere, and he said, "What you want to get into is the Marine Corps—now there's an outfit!"

I was sent to Camp Lejeune, North Carolina, for boot camp training, and it was tough. It was drill, drill, drill. They kept us busy all the time, sometimes until midnight. Some guys couldn't take it and were sent home. I was determined I was going to make it, and I did. They were forming the Seventh Defense Battalion, and I wound up in the artillery. I didn't choose it. They just sent me over there and I was in it. I wound up on those six-inch naval guns, and since I weighed 200 pounds and was pretty athletic, my job all the time was carrying shells.

We sailed from San Diego on the transport *William Biddle*. I got seasick when we sailed out of the harbor and stayed sick all the way to Hawaii, but I had to work in the mess hall anyway.

When we arrived at American Samoa we had cases of measles aboard. Measles are deadly to the native people out there, and so we were put under quarantine. At first we were quarantined aboard ship, but then they let us off and into a roped-off compound. And we had to stay there three weeks after the last man had measles. It was really a boring time, sitting on that ship and then in that compound.

Here is a letter of mine, dated one month to the day before Pearl Harbor, that my mother saved:

377

*Dear Folks*, I don't have anything to write but the mail leaves today. I have been setting here about fifteen minutes trying to think of something to write but I guess there isn't anything. It is raining today. I am a mess cook and we have got the mess hall cleaned up for tomorrow's inspection. It is a good job and I might ship over for another month. It is better than working under the hot sun. This is the ultimate of boredom and there is no hint of war.

My mother had a grocery store in Farmington, Arkansas. I sent her a picture from Samoa during this time before the war, and she put it up in the window. Other people seeing it began bringing in pictures of their boys in service. When I got home from the Pacific that window was solid pictures.

On December 7, there in American Samoa, I had garbage detail. Every Sunday morning we hauled off the garbage. Getting the barrels, lifting them, and splashing them around, there wasn't any way to do it except to just get it all over you. And the part that really hurt was hauling off the officers' garbage. They allowed them to bring their wives down there—I just hated that, but I did it anyway. I didn't hesitate to just get it all over me. Then, it was probably eight o'clock when I went to the head, and I was setting there on it when defense call sounded.

When defense call sounds, you run down and get your rifle and get your gear. To do that you run through some tents there, and that was the ammunition dump. It wasn't even underground. Instead of just running through there and then going up to our guns, they kept hanging these bandoleers of ammunition on us. Well, you can imagine what it would be like if you had a bunch of ammunition out in peacetime, you'd be shooting each other and shooting at everything else. So now it seemed odd that all of a sudden they were loading us up with all this ammunition, live ammunition, for our Springfield rifles, which is what we had.

Then we marched. These guns were up on each point of the hill. But the sergeant, instead of just marching us up the road, he spread us out, and then somebody said that Pearl Harbor had been attacked. Well, we didn't believe it. But anyway, we went up and we sat on the guns all day, and we stayed there. So for several days I had all this garbage on me, and no baths or anything like that up there! It was several days before we could begin to go down and clean up and get some stuff, soap and whatever else you might need. Now, if you can imagine the size of that hill, whatever you took up there you carried on your back.

Anyhow, finally we got to go down and take a bath, but from then on we lived on the guns. You'd go down and man them before daylight; then about noon you'd go and play cards. Then just before dusk you'd go down and man the guns again. Then at night after dark you'd go back up to the quarters.

We were ready for the Japanese. With all that monotony of manning the guns day after day, you really began to wish for a target. At that time we may not have had more than 150 effectives to defend that whole is- land, but we wanted the Japs to come anyway. Finally they did come, and started shooting at us—and that's the kind of shooting that's loud! They did it most all of one night. It was naval fire, either one or two sub- marines or surface ships. You're asleep, then all at once there is this loud noise. We thought it was our own three-inch guns shooting at some- body. They were shooting down into the harbor area, apparently trying to blow up radio stations and whatever else they could shoot up there. They were lobbing them over those mountains, and the terrain was such that there was only one place where they could do it, and it was on the reverse side from where we were.

Now, we could have shot at them there, if we'd had anything for con- trol. We had put up an observation post over here so that we could fire at that point, but that night there was no communication. Apparently they had cut the wire. It lasted minutes, or an hour, then it was over with. I remember thinking, "Now if everybody will do just what they are supposed to do, we can whip them," but actually, probably that sub- marine or whatever it was could have come in and took us over.

Later we found a rubber boat—I didn't find it, because we were up there on top of that hill—but anyhow they'd landed and apparently came ashore, looked around, spied on us or whatever, then left.

During this time, right after the war started, you'd stay down there on those points by yourself—we were lookouts, one on each gun, one here and one fifty yards up the hill. One night this sergeant came down—by then we didn't know if you went down you may or may not come back up again that night. He didn't say if he was coming back or not, he just went down. We didn't stand four-hour watches, we just stayed on half the night until somebody would come at midnight, and you were scared. Well, I didn't know he was coming back and I heard something. I kind of slipped over there, but didn't hear anything else. Then I heard it again, and then a third time. I knew there was some- thing down there. Then here came this figure lunging up this hill right at me. Boy! I pulled my .45, and when he heard that bolt slam back he hollered, "Metzger!" That was his name. Man, that scared me. I couldn't even speak because I'd almost shot that man. I'd have hated to kill him, because he was the one who knew how to run our raisin-jack still! But he should have told me he was coming back, and not just come charging back up there.

After a period of time, when the Marines had got enough men through boot camp and trained, they sent a brigade down there to Samoa. We looked out in the harbor one morning, and there was the *Mariposa*, the *Monterey*, and the *Lurline* sitting out there waiting to unload. They were loaded with a brigade.

Then we were sent over to another island, British Samoa, over to Apia harbor. We had a great big old house there. It had belonged to a French doctor, but the military had taken it over and our whole battery moved in there. This was where some American Marine outfits got final training before going on to Guadalcanal or wherever. The Twenty-second Marines came through there, and the Seventh Marines. When those outfits came through I volunteered to go with every one of them, to go into combat and get out of the boredom of Samoa. And they all turned me down. Then there were some guys who were going up to take their flight physicals, and they said, "Mac, here's something you can volunteer for." And I said, "What the hell. Okay, what is it?" And they told me it was for flight school. Twelve of them were turned down, but two of us passed.

A little later I went to sick bay with the "mu mu," which is elephantiasis, and it starts with a mosquito bite. Your arms and other parts swell up, so I was in the hospital to come home. They told me there was no cure for it over there, but if I got back in the States it go would go away by itself. Then they came to me one day and said I could stay in the hospital and go home that way, or my outfit was going home and I could go home with them. So I said I would go back with the outfit. So I came home in March of 1943. I'd been out there in the islands for two years.

They sent me to Camp Lejeune, North Carolina. You'd have six months in the States before being reassigned overseas. It was boredom. We went to those little old towns in North Carolina and drank that bootleg whiskey. I couldn't get a whiskey ration. I went into the sergeant and asked for one, and he said, "How old are you?" I said, "Twenty," and he said, "You are not old enough to drink!"

After about ninety days I got hold of two buddies and said, "Let's go overseas again." I talked them into it, and we applied and the orders came through. But my orders didn't come. I went into the sergeant major again, and he said, "Oh, you're going to Boston to flight school." So I got into flight school, and that's where I spent most of the rest of the war.

Let me give you my views on the Marine Corps. They will take a boy eighteen or nineteen years old, and they will change him into a Marine. The first thing they're going to do is to try to break him down. And in boot camp if he does crack they will send him home. It is incessant pounding. Close-order drill hour after hour, until midnight sometimes. Then you go and pack your gear and do this and do that. Busy every second and always under the eye of the drill instructor. After about three weeks of that you begin to believe that you really are what they often call you—a simple shithead. Then they take you to the rifle range. Now, a Marine's rifle is his most important possession. They teach you to shoot for about three weeks, day after day and hour after hour. They put you in positions they want you to be in, and if your body doesn't want to go that way they will bend it that way. But also you develop a comradeship and a fellowship with the other men going through the same thing. And you develop the idea that you're a Marine and able to do whatever you have to do with very little equipment. By the time you leave boot camp, you have been put back together as a Marine and you're proud of it, and you discover that your drill instructor is proud of you, too. And you will remain a Marine for the rest of your life.

## ROBERT PHELAN
ARMY

I was in the Army and trained as a radar operator. We formed up in California and shipped out on a vessel called the *Sea Pike*. When we started from the coast of California that morning it was nice and warm and the sea was calm, but by afternoon when we were out in open water the wind came up from the north, the sea got rough, and by nightfall I don't know how many people were sick. There were 2,750 of us on that ship, and except for maybe the crew, I'd say that 95 percent were sick at the same time. I don't know whether anybody ever ate or not. I never saw or tasted of food for over twenty-four hours, and I was vomiting over and over and over again. There wasn't anything in me to come up, but I kept vomiting anyway. But after I got over that I never was sick again. We had some more rough water before we got to New Guinea, but I never had any more trouble.

Well, they got us over there and transferred our group to an LST, and we ended up going ashore on an island called Morotai, right next to a bigger island named Halmahera. It turned out that it wasn't anything out of the ordinary. I was prepared, and I was expecting almost anything. We knew our job, and the best information they had on Halmahera was that it was a big, long island and heavily defended. The Japs had airfields and fighter planes and coastal defenses and everything. Now, around in behind them was the little island of Morotai, and the best information we could get was that there was only a small force of Japanese on the island. They had started an airstrip there at one time. They had cleared off some of the palm trees and had made a preliminary start on an airstrip, and then they had discontinued it. But they had a small force of men on the island.

A short time before we invaded, a submarine went from Australia up to the waters between Morotai and Halmahera. They intercepted a native in a canoe. They took him on board and got a statement from him, and he described from his own personal knowledge the force that the Japanese had on the island of Morotai. He said they had no coastal defenses or anything like that. So they told us all of that in detail. The Japs knew we were coming, there was no question about that, but they thought we were going to hit the big island of Halmahera and take their airfield and, bang, bang, bang, go from there.

So our unit slipped in behind and hit this island of Morotai. We had rocket ships and destroyers and cruisers, and, sometime before daybreak you could see the flashes of all the guns. What I didn't know about at that time was the big battleships; they had started from a different point and a different direction, and when we opened up on Morotai they opened up the big guns on Halmahera. So that didn't give the Japs any time to leave Halmahera and come around and interfere with us. So our forces fired everything they had. They had told us as much as they knew about what to expect, and none of us had any fear that I know of. They called us to breakfast that morning at 2:30 A.M., and for a change we had steak! We had eaten dehydrated stuff for so long! They had moved us from the tip of New Guinea in four days by LST, and they had trucks on the deck of this LST. So as soon as I finished breakfast I went out and climbed up on top of the highest truck that I could find, so that I could see. I just wanted to see everything that went on, so I stayed up there the whole time while they were bombarding the shore.

After that was over they pulled in close to shore, and we went down a landing net into water about waist deep and waded ashore. General Douglas MacArthur was down the shore just a little ways, but someone carried him in, he didn't wade! But anyway, so far as I know, not a shot was fired at us from anywhere on shore. I never saw a shot fired there and I never heard of one being fired. It was just a routine affair, and we didn't think anything about it, hardly.

We got our radar set up that day just as soon as we got ashore. We had a big truck and a big generator that furnished the power, and then it was hooked in to searchlights. You could turn it on automatic and the searchlight would follow exactly where the radar pointed. Or the operator could take it over any time he wished and operate it manually. When he tracked an enemy plane with the searchlight on it, as soon as he released the manual control it'd snap back to automatic control, and the radar would make the light track the plane.

We started unloading our equipment and getting it in operating order, and we worked as hard as we possibly could getting organized and set up. We got through just before dark that night, and soon after dark the first Japanese plane came over. I don't know what type of plane he was, but we picked him up on radar just like that. A minute or so after we got him on radar, they turned the searchlight on and he was in the beam, just like a butterfly. And the antiaircraft guns brought him down right quick.

We only stayed on Morotai about four days. Out four-and-a-half miles away toward the big island of Halmahera there was a little coral atoll; they called it an island but it was just a coral spot, and they moved our unit out there, out in the bay on this little old coral reef called Sem-Sem. We ended up staying more than a year on that tiny island, and during that year I got off that island one time. They let me go back to the island of Morotai for a day or two toward the end of the war. All that time there were about twenty or so of us on this little island less than a mile long and less than a quarter-mile wide at the widest. It had a higher spot on each end, and in the middle it came down to where at high tide the water washed across—so we were really on two little knolls, and each was only a few feet above sea level. We were on duty day and night. If the red alert was sounded from the mainland or anywhere, we got up immediately and were in action. On Thanksgiving night and on Christmas night—that would have been in 1944—we never got one wink of sleep either night. Just as fast as one air raid was over and the all-clear was sounded—before we could even get undressed—another raid would start and the red alert would go on again. Those two nights were the worst we had. On that Thanksgiving night, over at the airfield on Morotai we lost forty-eight big bombers on the ground, loaded with gasoline and explosives. I never did hear the number of fighter planes and things like that that were lost, but it was bound to be tremendous. With the bombs dropping, those airplanes were exploding, and our little coral island four-and-a-half miles away was just a shakin'.

There was no freshwater on Sem-Sem. They had to bring it to us on barges. They put it in empty gasoline drums, and a whole lot of the time it seemed like they didn't even rinse the gasoline out of those barrels. You could still see it floating on top of the water, and taste it. That was the only thing we had to drink or cook with or take a bath with in over a year. When the war finally ended I sure was glad to get off that tiny little island!

## CARL HAMILTON
NAVY

I was captain of the football team my senior year in Lepanto, Arkansas. We had a six-man football team there. I had been to a movie on that Sunday afternoon, December 7, and this friend of mine said, "Carl, they've bombed Pearl Harbor!" So we went down to the drugstore and stood around there, and half-a-dozen of my buddies came in, and we talked about it and decided why don't we just go into the Navy. The next day everybody was a little hotter about it, so we called a recruiting officer in Jonesboro, and he came over. We had the whole football team there to sign up. It was the first football team as a group to join the Navy. Well, then we had publicity from all over the United States. They ran pictures of us and talked about us on newscasts. The Navy was taking advantage of this, a whole football team enlisting. It turned out I was colorblind, so the recruiting officer helped me memorize the colorblind test because they didn't want to lose the captain of the team. It'd make better Navy publicity if they could get us all.

So then we went to Little Rock. Well, I had this leg I'd gotten torn up in football about two or three months prior to that. We were going through the physical, and we were all run through the tests in there naked. Then this old doctor wanted us to jump up on a bench, then jump down. He was watching me all the time, because he saw my leg was swollen. Well, when I jumped that leg locked up on me, and I fell right there on the damn floor. So he came over and said, "Well, Carl, I'm going to have to send you home. You come back and see me in a couple of years after you get well." And out of the whole damn group of ten or twelve of us, I was the only one who failed. And that was the hardest thing that ever happened to me in my life. So I went home—all I could do was go home—and the rest of the guys went on. Incidentally, we never lost one member of that football team, not a one. Every damn one survived.

So I went back, and now I was not satisfied in school anymore, so I went to this trade school over in Paragould, Arkansas, and took a course in welding. Then, I went to the shipyards in Mobile, Alabama, but I had to wait there for my eighteenth birthday so I could go to work. From there I went to Memphis, and that was when I finally got to where my leg was strong enough to pass the physical and I could join the Seabees.

I really enjoyed being in the Seabees. I was probably one of the youngest men in my battalion. At the time I went in they wouldn't accept you if you didn't have a trade. But I was a welder, and I had worked for a company in Memphis building landing barges. We had six weeks of boot training and then we had an additional six weeks under the Marine Corps.

When we shipped out to the Pacific, we went over on the *President Polk* to New Caledonia. And immediately they put me in the transportation pool. I didn't know how to drive a truck, and especially not one of those big old army trucks. We were driving on those little old narrow roads down to the supply depots and back, and we were hauling bombs and that sort of thing. I stayed in that transportation unit until we went to Guadalcanal, and there again I was running a truck. That would have been in August of 1943. I drove a dump truck there, and we worked a little bit on the airstrip there, Henderson Field.

I was in the Seventy-third Seabee Battalion, Company A. The companies were not specialized—we had all various talents in every one. After a while I was taken off trucks and worked with the chief as a grade foreman, spotting grades on roads and airfields, which meant that after the engineers had laid out their stakes for a road or whatnot I was to see that the dozers and dump trucks made their cuts and fills to match the stakes.

Then I worked operating a bulldozer in a coral pit. When we built airfields and roads, they were just as good as airfields and roads anywhere. Sometimes we'd have crews out dredging coral right off the reefs. Other times, like on Guadalcanal or Peleliu, we could find older coral right near shore and we could dig it out of there. But however we got it, we'd haul that crushed-up coral over to where we were working, spread it around and grade it, and then steamroll it until we had a compacted, flat, smooth surface. Then we'd load up water trucks down at the beach with seawater, and they'd haul it over to the airstrip and run up and down the length of that runway watering the coral with seawater. That crushed-up coral was

ABOVE: *Carl Hamilton helped build this blinding white coral airstrip at Munda in the Solomon islands in 1943. These Corsair fighters (of the type Carl saw shot down by friendly fire at Munda, and later flown by Leo Dorsey) have just landed on the recently completed airstrip.*

still alive, and those little microscopic coral animals in there would grow together with that seawater keeping it moist, and it would set up like concrete after a few days. It would be just as solid and slick and smooth as paving. These airstrips would end up being bright white, and that was quite a bit different from the asphalt or even the concrete runways we built in the States. If we got an air raid and bomb craters, or if we got potholes, we could just patch it up with more crushed coral, water it down with seawater, and it would be as good as new. That coral was amazing stuff. We could build roads and even some foundations the same way. So for all those runways and roads we built, it was all local material, and we didn't need to depend on anything coming in from the outside.

But most of the time, for the Quonset huts or other buildings we were putting up, concrete would work better for the slabs we'd build them on. So whatever concrete that would come in, we'd survey and lay out where they wanted things, pour the slabs, and then put the Quonset huts up on those slabs. Those Quonset huts went together just like a jigsaw puzzle. We'd unpack the parts and lay them out and just put them together. We built some docks, but not many. We were usually moving too fast to make anything very permanent. Instead of docks they used lighters, which were steel pontoons buckled together. They'd go out to the cargo ships and get loaded up and bring things right to the beach.

The first invasion I was in on was at Munda, New Georgia, on up in the Solomons chain. We went in on LSTs. We landed on a little island offshore, and then we crossed the bay in small amphibious vehicles they called "ducks." And that's when the action was still going on at the beach. The Marines were already going in, and they were in front of us. I think when I went in it was about the middle of the day. I don't think I was afraid, I don't think I had any fear, but there were a lot of thoughts going through my mind, like, "Where am I going? What's going to happen?" You didn't really have time to be afraid because you were busy all the time, and moving. And it was so danged muddy—we were in mud up to our knees when we hit the beach.

We didn't get fired on when we were landing. We were firing at them with our artillery, and we had our observation planes directing our fire. The Marines had the Japanese driven back a mile or two. We shot down one of our own planes, and that was the second plane in our history to be shot down by our own artillery. He was an F4U, a Corsair fighter, flying low. We were lobbing those mortar shells in, and one of them hit his wing and knocked the plane down. But even though he was low he somehow got out, and his chute had just opened when he landed in a tree. A couple of guys from our outfit went over and got him out of the damn tree, and I guess he was okay.

When I got to the beach, my buddy and I took a Jeep back to where we were going to set up a little temporary camp at the airfield. The Japs had started to build a coral airfield there. Our job was to immediately get that airfield set up so planes could land. We started out in that darn Jeep and got maybe a quarter of a mile when the Jeep mired down in mud up to the doors, and we spent the better part of that day trying to winch it out.

So we got that airstrip at Munda repaired and expanded and built more taxiways and roads with coral and set up Quonset huts and got things arranged into a nice base there.

Our next invasion was Peleliu. They brought that First Marine Division in there, and God, they were tough fighting boys. Of course those

Japanese were dug into those coral tunnels, and they couldn't get them out. It was just a maze of tunnels through those coral hills.

We had a lot of confusion on the beach when we into Peleliu. If you can imagine all these hundreds of men going in and the shelling from battleships and cruisers going on, and all you can see is all this firing and smoke. We were still on the ship, just far enough in to be out of rifle range. There were some rifle bullets that did hit the ship, and one or two guys got hit. Then the Marines started in as the first wave. After that they started dumping those danged pontoons off the LSTs, and we were in the water towing those things in and buckling them together to make a floating jetty. Eventually we built a big causeway where they could unload the tankers and so forth.

Then we moved right on in, and within two or three days the Marines had got the Japs pushed off the airfield into the hills a quarter of a mile beyond, and we started filling the holes in the runway. There again, like on Munda, the Japs had built a small coral airstrip, and our job was to get it operational and then expand it. Our bombers had made craters in the airstrip, and the Japs had filled the holes in with coconut logs. But that made them mushy, so we had to go in with shovels and drag buckets or whatever and dig out those craters and then fill them with good coral, which would be solid. I think it took us about two or three days to fix up that airstrip. We had to start taking coral out of a hill near the shore, where we found our source. And we used up most of that hill.

Our planes taking people to the Philippines, to Tacloban or to Luzon, would land at Pelelieu. The men would stop at the transient camp and wait until there were aircraft available to take them on to the Philippines. There was an island just across from Peleliu called Angaur where the bomber base was. They landed all the big planes over on that base. We carried equipment back and forth over there, but we never set up our camp there. The Seabees set up a good permanent-type camp on Peleliu, and we lived quite comfortably there after we got things together.

I hit the States right when the war ended. I had been overseas about twenty-eight months and had enough rotation points to come home for ninety days leave. So I got on board the train and came back to Arkansas. I had been home in Lepanto about two days when they dropped the first atom bomb. And I thought it was so great that we finally had something that would stop that war.

# CHAPTER 11

*"When the Japs came looking for who was broadcasting over the radio, they could never find me. They knew they had taken all the Europeans, and I don't think they really seriously thought an islander could be doing anything useful with a radio."*

—Falavi, COAST-WATCHER

FALAVI, COAST-WATCHER, Beru, Gilberts

KIMIUO AISEK, Truk

JORGE CRISTOBAL, NAVY, Pearl Harbor, Guam

PAGES 390–391: *These Solomon islanders, working as scouts for the U.S. Marines, have just returned to camp after leading a Marine patrol on a long trek into the jungle in April, 1943.*

# WAR AS ISLAND NATIVES SAW IT, 1942–45

FALAVI

COAST-WATCHER

I was attending the Kennedy School on Vaitupu when I was recruited as a coast-watcher to help out two New Zealanders on Beru in the Gilberts [now Kiribati]. I got polio when I was fifteen, and I was a cripple. I couldn't walk. But I was keen, and the New Zealanders taught me all about the radio. I watched them make their reports, and I helped count airplanes flying over and watched out for Japanese ships going by. Then one day the Japanese came to Beru. The two New Zealanders took off into the bush. But the Japs knew they were there because they had been able to track the radio signal.

So we were all gathered up in the village, and the Japs said they would kill one islander every hour until the New Zealand coast-watchers gave themselves up. Someone found them in the bush and told them, so they came in to the village and turned themselves in. They didn't want to see us suffer on their account. In addition to the New Zealanders, the Japs rounded up all the Europeans on Beru. There were about fifteen total including two nuns. The Japanese told us they were taking them all to Tarawa, and they were never seen or heard from again.

Before they left, the Japs made the New Zealanders bring out their radio, and they smashed it all up. After they left, I collected all the pieces and put it back together. I had paid attention to their lessons about the radio and how it worked, and I was able to get it working again after a while. I turned it on and started to contact the people the New Zealanders had been reporting to. I first called the Americans on Funafuti, and they didn't believe me. They knew the New Zealanders had been taken by the Japanese, and they thought it was a Japanese trick, that I was doing this with the direction of the Japs. I kept telling them what hap-

393

pened and that I was telling the truth, but they never believed me. I finally raised the Americans in Hawaii and told them what happened and convinced them I was telling the truth. So they said okay, please start reporting just the way the New Zealanders had been doing, and I was to tell them about all the Jap planes and ships going by Beru. But they told me I was in great danger. They said the Japs came for the New Zealanders because they could track the radio signal to Beru, and they warned me that they would do the same thing again and come after me.

So I got my friends to help me. I would make a report on the radio, and then they would pick me up, and pick the radio up, and move me and the radio into the bush or to another part of the island. When the Japs came looking for who was broadcasting over the radio, they could never find me. They knew they had taken all the Europeans, and I don't think they really seriously thought an islander could be doing anything useful with a radio. I think they came just because their officers told them to, and they thought it was a nuisance and just wanted to break the radio again. But I kept broadcasting, and they kept looking for me, but they never found me thanks to my friends who kept moving me and the radio around Beru. Those Japs never did catch on!

I broadcast for the two months before the Tarawa invasion, and told the Americans all about the Jap planes and ships I saw heading to and from Tarawa. The Americans were very grateful, and thanked me over and over again for doing this for them. They said it was a great help in getting ready for the Tarawa invasion. I didn't mind doing it. I was glad to help.

When the British came back to Beru after the war they knew about what I had done, the coast-watcher work, and they awarded me the King George Medal. I think people here respected me for what I did, and every time there is an American or British visitor they are brought to me, and I talk to them and tell them about what happened during the war, and how we outsmarted the Japs!

# KIMIUO AISEK

The Japanese ran Truk when I was growing up. I took three years of Japanese in school, and worked for them. I spoke Japanese, and many people my age who grew up during that time—the "Japan Time"—speak better Japanese than English. With the Japanese administration, everything was under control. We islanders were ordered to keep everything clean and neat, and the island has never looked so good again. Today we don't have that kind of discipline, and you can see that things are not so neat now.

I was seventeen years old in 1944 and was working for the Japanese navy at the Dublon base. I drove a small boat back and forth from a dock in Dublon Town to the Japanese cargo ships. It was a good job, and I was well treated. Things were still good on Truk for us then.

One day in 1944 the American planes came and bombed the Japanese ships and sank many of them. I was scared, but I stood on shore and watched it all, and I saw where the ships sank. This is when things started to go bad on Truk. After this the Japanese were very angry, and their treatment of us changed. What was the worst for us was not the American raids where they sank ships, but the later bombing raids by the big bombers way up high. They dropped bombs right across the island. The bomb explosions covered the island of Dublon, and almost everything was destroyed. A lot of the Japanese supplies were destroyed, and many of our gardens were ruined. Pretty soon the Japanese started running out of food, and they asked us islanders to give them more food from our gardens. But our gardens were ruined, so we didn't have much food to give. This started the really bad times, when food was very scarce and the Japanese were more and more desperate to have food and they took it from us. They were going hungry and we islanders were going hungry.

I heard things about the Japanese. There was a Japanese surgeon, a captain. After American pilots were captured in the raids, they were taken to the Japanese hospital to recover. But this captain did things to them, medical experiments. A couple were bayoneted to death, and others were beheaded. I heard about this during the war from Japanese friends of mine who didn't approve of these things. The Japanese captain was arrested by the Americans after the war and was hanged after a war crimes trial. I heard he denied his guilt right up to the end.

After the surrender, the Americans came to Truk and told the Japanese military and civilians they had to be shipped home to Japan. Many didn't want to go. They had lived for many years on Truk, and had friends there. Some Japanese men had married Trukese women. They were given a choice—either leave by themselves or take any children they had, but the Trukese wives must stay on Truk. After they left most were never heard from again. But every now and then, in just these recent years, some older Japanese tourists come back and start asking questions. They want to see the old Japanese town on Dublon. I take them and they can't believe their eyes. There used to be a nice little town over there, neat and clean. Now nothing's there but jungle and a few roads. The ruins of the old hospital are still above the town, and one of the old fuel tanks by the docks is still there. It's rusted now and empty, and it is still there only because it was empty when the Americans bombed and it didn't explode like the rest. There are also a couple of the old piers, and I can still see the pier where I docked my boat when I was driving it back and forth out to the Japanese ships. Some of these Japanese weep when they see that almost nothing is left of their little town. Some of these Japanese men will ask questions about certain Trukese families, and Trukese women, and what happened to them. Most are dead now, but some of the kids are still around. It's all very sad.

I saw where a lot of the Japanese ships went down during the raids. When we started scuba diving at Truk, I went out and found where the ships were. We started to get more and more sport scuba divers coming to Truk, and they all wanted to see the sunken ships. I took tourists out to the ships for years, and made more dives and located more of the Japanese ships. Many are getting covered with coral now, but the tourists still come. They say Truk is one of the most famous scuba diving locations in the world. I'm glad I didn't go to the bomb shelters during the raids. If I had, I would have never seen where the ships sank, and I wouldn't have known where to look for them for the scuba divers.

*War as Island Natives Saw It*

# JORGE CRISTOBAL
NAVY

I graduated from high school in 1934, on Guam. After graduation my father, a very industrious businessman, decided he'd send me to Japan so I could learn the porcelain trade from the Japanese. I was just past seventeen years old and didn't have much of an inkling of what I wanted to do, but then my father asked me if I wanted to go to Japan. Not knowing a word of Japanese, I thought it would be hard for me, because I would first have to learn the lingo. But I figured there would be some institute in Japan where I could learn Japanese. So I left Guam in 1935 with my mother.

For almost a year I attended a school of basic instruction and chemistry and everything else, but I wanted to find out where I could learn better Japanese. I went to Waseda University, where there was an international language institute. I was in school with about sixty-seven people from all over the world, all learning Japanese. Our instructors were two graduates of Washington State University, first-generation Japanese-Americans, *Nisei*, and they were very good teachers. I started from the beginning, and in almost eleven months I learned Japanese.

I left there after the Sino-Japanese war started. A friend of mine said to me, "I think it would be a good idea if you moved out of Japan. This is going to be a big war between China and Japan." At that time I was writing letters to Guam in Japanese, and my father had a friend of his translate the letters for him. My father was very surprised with how much I'd learned. But I told him I had to come back because of the Japanese war with the Chinese.

I left Japan in September 1938 and arrived at Guam about a month later. I was hoping to continue my studies in Hawaii. But my father said,

"Remember you have brothers and sisters, and I have to send them to school, too. Maybe you should get a job here on Guam and make some money and then use that money to get to where you want to go." So I went to a trade school in carpentry for about a year. The Chamorros—that's what we call ourselves on Guam—were accepted by the United States government for service in the Navy, and we could be mess attendants aboard ships. So I thought, why not? That was something I could do to improve my life and see more of the world and learn more, so I took a chance, went for my physical examination, and joined some other Chamorros in the U.S. Navy as mess attendants, and that's about as far as we could go.

They qualified me physically and mentally, and they transferred me to Treasure Island in San Francisco Bay. After a few weeks of training, my orders came through to report to the battleship USS *Maryland*. A lieutenant by the name of Jablonski taught us everything about being mess attendants. He found out I had a good knowledge of English. He wanted me to take care of Commander Baker, the executive officer of the battleship. I had to learn a lot of things about being in the Navy: taking care of my bed, washing dishes, cooking, but these are things you would like to learn as you grow up anyway.

I was on the USS *Maryland* in 1939. In 1940, in the middle of August, they said I should present myself to the commanding officer of the USS *California*, another battleship. So I said, "What the heck is going on here? I was just learning how to get along on the *Maryland*." He said, "Captain Bunkley asked for you by name." I didn't know how he got my name, but I found out later.

He asked me, "Do you know how to brush shoes?" And I did. "How about white shoes?" "I do that, too, sir." "How about ironing a white coat?" "I do that, too, sir." So we finally satisfied one another that I'd get along very well. I took all my bags, and at that time we used hammocks; there were no bunks. So I got transferred over to Captain Bunkley's area on the *California*. But they must have found out that I knew some Japanese language, because that was an important thing, and I think maybe that's why they transferred me over there.

I was very studious about things with the Navy, a little bit at a time. I was a mess attendant, but I was also in the supply group, and we were assigned to the third deck down below the water line. That was my battle station. We'd load up ammunition from the magazine, and it would be hauled up on the conveyors to the guns on deck. Most of those guys were Negroes—blacks—so they taught me how to handle those things. They were pretty good people. We had to help one another.

At that time we belonged to Battleship Division One, and we were sent to Hawaii. Before December 7, we had gone on a two-week, northern Pacific battleship exercise, and we got back to Pearl Harbor on December 5, about five o'clock in the evening.

I was just hanging around the ship that weekend. On Sunday morning I was up on the main deck getting ready to go to mass when I heard some bombing. I ran into an officers-country guard, a Marine, and I asked him, "What's going on, sir? Is there supposed to be a fire alarm or something?" He said, "Well, it's just training on Sundays." Most of the senior officers were gone for the weekend, but two lieutenant commanders were aboard ship. All of a sudden there was an explosion, and one of the officers said, "The Japanese are bombing us now!" I said, "What?" He said, "Close all the portholes you possibly can." Then I saw a Japanese Zero airplane go by to bomb Ford Island. And I thought, this is not a game. Then they said over the loudspeaker, "We are at war with Japan!" I thought, my God, what is going on now? I found out later that Guam was cut off, that they had been attacked by the Japanese that day, too. Then there were ships blowing up, the *Arizona* blew up, and there were fires on the water. The oil on the water was burning and coming toward our ship.

Most of us stayed up on deck because we took torpedoes and water started coming in below decks. We couldn't go to our battle stations down there below decks, so I stayed up on the main deck and tried to take cover under the 16-inch guns. I felt sorry for the Marines, because one of the torpedoes landed right underneath their area, and the armory was right there. That torpedo blew up and killed those Marines. So the torpedoes hit, and the ship started sinking, settling into the sand of the harbor bottom. I watched the whole attack right from the main deck—the planes coming over and the bombing and fires and everything. And I was thinking, all it would take would be for one bullet to ricochet from the deck into me. And all three of us Chamorros on the ship were right there, and we didn't know where to go. I only had on my shorts and T-shirt, and we were running all over the place trying to fight the fire floating in on the water, and it was a mess.

Nobody was in a clear state of mind at that moment. One of the officers told us to bring up all the potatoes from below. He said, "We don't want to waste them!" I said, "You're thinking of potatoes at this time?

What the heck is going on?" I didn't go down, but a couple of the mess attendants did, and those potatoes were in big wooden crates, each weighing more than 120 pounds. And you should have seen those guys coming up with those crates of potatoes! They were trying to save those potatoes! I guess there's a little bit of humor in this, but it wasn't a laughing matter when you think of it. I don't know what happened to those potatoes.

So I was there on the deck watching the attack, trying not to get shot, and helping out any way I could. Some of the men tried to swim over to Ford Island, but the officers called them back again, so they swam right back to the ship. I went back to the fantail toward where the captain's quarters were, and there was a Marine standing guard there. He said, "If I were you I'd stay away from that damned place; it's liable to blow up." Right underneath that area was the ammunition, and if another torpedo would have hit there I wouldn't be here now.

Burning oil was coming toward us, and some tugboats came over and tried to push the oil away. The ship that was behind us, the *Oklahoma*, capsized, and we couldn't see anything but bare steel of that hull back there. There were men trapped in there, and they had to be cut out. They were lucky to get out alive. And on that day, December 7, there were twelve Chamorros from Guam killed at Pearl Harbor.

I stayed aboard ship after the attack. I was an obedient sailor and couldn't leave the ship without orders. So a couple of officers on land came over and gave us some clothing to wear. About four or five of us remained aboard ship with the officers, and we stayed up on the bridge since it wasn't safe to go back to our quarters. The captain had a sea cabin up there with a bathroom. I don't know where we got the water from, but we could take a marine bath. And they brought us something to eat from Ford Island.

So after a while an officer came over and said there were four captains at Makalapa that needed help. He gave me some clothing, a toothbrush and toothpaste, soap and what not, and a pair of shoes; so three of us went over there to help those captains. Makalapa is right across from the submarine base laundry, so you could imagine I'd walk back and forth three times a day with the laundry, and I wasn't the only one. But we were just glad to still be there.

So after a while I got a message that I had to report to "Regal." The officer there said, "Are you Cristobal?" And I said, "Yes." He said, "You are now going to be assigned to the staff of Vice Admiral Ghormley in New Zealand, and you'll be sailing to New Zealand on the *Regal* with the admiral and his staff." That ship, the USS *Regal*, had never been moved for years, and it could only steam at seven knots! The admiral was aboard ship, and they wanted me to be there, too.

We went from Pearl Harbor all the way down to New Zealand. First we stopped by Johnston Island and picked up a New Zealand family, a telephone technician and his family. We stopped at Samoa briefly, and then we went over to New Caledonia. Every day when we were on ship we had to wear our life jackets. We could only take a bucket full of water every day; that was rough!

We got to New Caledonia, and it was a French island. They were very hospitable, gave us food and water to clean up. Then we went down to New Zealand and it was cold! We got there close to the middle of 1942. We moved to another ship, the *Argonne*, and it became our flagship. The admiral stayed there and I was his mess attendant.

The Guadalcanal battle was really on the go at that time. The ships would sail, Marines were invading, and the admiral was a very gentle guy; he wasn't a brutal guy. So after that he started having heart trouble, and then Admiral Halsey came and took over. Halsey was a pure warrior! And I became his mess attendant. Admiral Wilkinson was there, too, and he said he didn't want me to go any place else, that I was liable to get my head shot off. We got good housing in New Zealand. So Halsey called me in when we moved into this house, and he said, "Cristobal, from now on you are my housemate." And I was working for him at all times. I couldn't be too far away from him. I liked him because he respected me as a human being. But he was a very strict man. He kidded me a lot, and I kidded him back. Then we moved to New Caledonia and stayed there for a while, then back to New Zealand. We didn't stay in one place for too long.

Some time later, Halsey said, "Cristobal, do you want to go to Guam?" So I smiled and said, "Yes, I probably would. That's where my family is." So he said, "I'm going to have you transferred to the Third Marine Division as an interpreter." He told me the Marines were about to invade Guam and take it back from the Japanese. He knew I spoke Japanese, and I could translate for the Chamorros also. He knew I was worried about my family, and he wanted to give me a chance to go home and find them.

They assigned me to headquarters First Battalion, Ninth Regiment, Third Marine Division. I went in on the third wave landing at Asan Beach, and I was right there in the middle, looking like a Marine. I was wearing a helmet and everything was Marine for me! I went down that rope ladder from the ship to get into the amtrac, and I had a carbine with me. It was light to carry, and it could fire eleven shots without reloading. We were getting shot at, and two guys in my same amtrac got killed right next to me. So I called to God, "Please spare me. I haven't seen my family all these years, and I am finally at home now." I couldn't explain my feelings as I went ashore, but I went right in there with the rest of them. I crawled right up there, and three or four guys followed me there in between Asan and Piti. Of course, I was very familiar with that whole area. I was working as a native scout for the Marines, talking to the local people, and helping the Marines move through those areas I was familiar with.

I was there for three weeks, and I hadn't been able to find my family. I saw some Chamorros I knew, and they'd say, "Jorge, we've seen your family, but it was four or five days ago." And that was a little bit too long. I was worried about them.

You're not going to believe this, and every time I talk about it my hair stands on end. I was with a Marine patrol up in the hills, and we were slowly moving up looking for Jap stragglers. The master sergeant was up in front, and he was a real gung ho happy Marine. He saw someone up ahead, and I saw him, too. He was ready to open fire, and I said, "Hold it, hold it!" He said, "Why, I'm going to kill that so-and-so Japanese." And I said, "No, wait a minute. That guy isn't armed." I thought it was a Chamorro, and I had to stop him from shooting. So we walked up to this person slowly—you're not going to believe this; it's hard for me to even tell it now, but that was my father! I hollered out, "That's my father!" and I ran up and just dropped down on my knees in front of him. And he looked at me and said, "Son, I thought you had joined the Navy!" I was there in front of him dressed just like one of the Marines, and I guess my face had changed a little bit, too. So I said, "Well, now I am fighting with the Marines." The rest of my family was nearby, and we had a big family reunion up there. I couldn't believe I had found them.

We arranged for some trucks to come up and get them because there were a lot of other Chamorros around there, too. They were taking a rest because they were walking to the other side of the island. They had been told to go to Agat, and to do this they were crossing over the center of the island, over the mountains. They were told they could find shelter there at Agat because the Seabees were building a camp for them. So I arranged for the trucks to take them to the camp, and then they were safe.

Later they sent me over to Sasebo, Japan. Then they called me up to Tokyo, and I became a war crimes commission interrogator. They had about three or four of those Japanese language officers in there doing the same thing. I was translating Japanese for the courts commission.

I was a year and a half in Japan. An admiral in Washington got me transferred back to Guam, and I stayed there for about nine months. Then my transfer came through to San Diego and then to Jacksonville, Florida, and I stayed in the Navy there working for Admiral Perry. At that time I was head mess attendant, and they gave me light duty. While I was there I went to a university in Florida and took banking and investment in my spare time. So an investment company in Florida hired me to work in my off hours, and I stayed in that job for three years. I bought a couple of homes while I was there, and made some money on them. I finally retired from the Navy on December 31, 1961, as a chief petty officer. I was discharged with WWII Pacific Ocean marks of distinction and honors. Then I went back to Guam and got into investing in housing and construction, and I've been living on Guam ever since.

Before the war my parents had a Japanese friend in Guam, a lady. And for the two years I was in Japan before the war I had been writing my father in Japanese, because I wanted to prove to him that I was learning the language very well. So I mailed two or three letters to my dad, and I told him to have their friend translate the letters for them. So this woman was a blabbermouth Japanese in Guam, and after the Japanese invaded she turned me in as a spy. She said, "These are the parents of Jorge Cristobal who went to Japan before the war. And I think he was a spy when he went to Japan to learn the language." And from then on the Japanese were watching my family. In those days the Chamorros on Guam were their enemies. So my parents had to be very careful during the Japanese occupation.

So people ask me if I have any hatred for the Japanese because of them invading Guam and not treating my parents well, or that they bombed me at Pearl Harbor, or that I fought them with the Marines. But I have never had any animosity for the Japanese whatsoever, even during the war. Well, we're all humans anyway in the first place, and I never tried to hate anybody else. And anyone who thinks they hate me and tries to talk bad about me doesn't know me very well!

# CHAPTER 12

> *"The military police were particularly active, and if you said something [bad about the war] that someone overheard, you could be in much worse shape than if you were bombed by the Americans."*
>
> —Akira Kasahara, Tokyo

PAUL KURODA, Tokyo

AKIRA KASAHARA, Tokyo

PAGES 404–405: *American B-29s return to North Field on Guam after a bombing raid over Japan. To the Japanese, the B-29s became an uncomfortably familiar sight as the fire bombing raids intensified in early 1945.*

# THE VIEW FROM JAPAN, 1942–45

PAUL KURODA

I heard about the attack on Pearl Harbor in my house by radio early in the morning. This was Monday morning in Japan, and I was getting ready to go to work. I took the commuter train and went to my lab at the University of Tokyo. I think, in a way, when I realized that it had finally come to this, that in some ways I was relieved. Before that, I had seen so many soldiers and horses and so on moving around downtown Tokyo—going somewhere but nobody knew where. We felt something was going to happen very soon, but we had no idea that Japan was going to attack Pearl Harbor.

When I heard that news, of course I got scared. That was very scary. Immediately I expected a counterattack. You know, American planes could have easily attacked us from the Philippines. And so we were very scared. But nothing came out of it, no counterattack. Then for several days we got good news after good news—all the American ships wiped out at Pearl Harbor. Also the British Far Eastern fleet was sunk, their ships *Repulse* and *Prince of Wales* went down. So I must say that for a while all the Japanese became very much excited. Even the people who had been against the war really became sort of for it. That lasted for several months, I think, until the April 18, 1942, Tokyo raid by Colonel Doolittle.

People ask me if that came as a shock, but I wasn't really surprised by it. I had thought the Americans would counterattack before that. I saw Doolittle's planes flying overhead. It was a beautiful day, and the raid was a nice show for me, because I was seeing for the first time the American B-25s. They did some damage, but it wasn't serious at all. Compared to the raids that began in 1944 it was nothing.

Then, in May and June of 1942, we heard about the Battle of the Coral Sea and the Battle of Midway. So, for about six months prior to that, I think all Japanese were very happy. The Battle of Midway the government really tried to cover up. They announced it as a victory, but their explanations didn't sound quite right. I had a friend who was aboard one of the ships. He got back alive, and he told me all about it and how terrible it was.

But things really got bad when the B-29 raids started in late 1944. I remember vividly the air raids of November 27, 1944. I don't remember the total number of airplanes—I read later that there were about 270, I think. These were B-29s, and they were planes we hadn't seen before. That was scary—having B-29s overhead, more than 200 of them. That was rather scary. I was doing an experiment in my lab at the time, and I think I am the only person in Tokyo who did my business as usual without going into the shelter. This story is well known among my friends who are American scientists, because when we are together we talk about such things. I think I am the only scientist who has gone right on with research experiments when B-29s are flying overhead and dropping bombs. I'm rather proud of that. I thought, "Maybe I am about to make some great discovery, and so I can't die tonight." That's the sort of feeling I had!

I stayed on in Tokyo through all the terrible fire-bomb raids in 1945. But after the war, science in Japan almost came to a stop, so I decided to go to the United States to continue my research. I ended up becoming a nuclear physics professor at the University of Arkansas.

# AKIRA KASAHARA

n 1941 I was fifteen years old and halfway through middle school. I was well aware of the Japanese conflict in China that started in the early 1930s, and when I got to middle school it was really at the height of militarism. We had military training, but it was considered athletic exercise. Toward the end of the fourth year of middle school, I was taught how to use a rifle. In senior high school, there was military reserve training. We lived in Tokyo, and my parents didn't talk about the war at first. But a few years later when the bombing started, my father said, "I cannot leave the city, but if the rest of the family wants to move with their belongings to the countryside, that's okay, but I can't do it." He was active in the military reserves, and because of that he felt that he couldn't leave.

On December 7 when Pearl Harbor was attacked, it was December 8 in Japan, a Monday, and I was in school. Since the war had been going on in China for so long, it wasn't a big shock. People were anticipating that something else was going to happen, because we knew the diplomatic situation with the U.S. was becoming difficult. I was too young to make judgments, but I remember that initially most people were really excited. It sounded like things were going very well until we heard about the Battle of Midway. The Japanese media made it sound like it wasn't all that bad, but we knew we couldn't trust the media because it was controlled by the government.

But I remember what was later called the Doolittle Raid in 1942. The American bombers came right overhead. You could see bombs dropping out, and we were all very surprised. The American planes I saw were flying low, and they seemed quite large, bigger than the other planes we had seen over Tokyo. Afterwards, not much was mentioned about the bombing in the newspapers, but everyone was talking about the American planes and knew about the bombing.

When I got to senior high school, we only had classes one day a week. The rest of the week, including Saturdays, all the students worked in factories, and the teachers, too. There was also one day for military drill. I was working at an iron press factory just in the outskirts of Tokyo. We would get big chunks of iron, and then we'd put them into a press that would make them into plates. About a year before the end of the war, we noticed that we had more and more idle time because of waiting for the material to be delivered. At that time, even before the bombing started, I realized that the war wasn't going well for Japan because they weren't able to deliver the iron to us like they had before. Obviously we knew we couldn't trust everything we read in the newspapers, but we were hesitant to discuss the situation or say anything negative about the war.

But we were just sitting around at the factory waiting for materials to come in, and what else could you do but talk about things. Some of my friends there were very vocal and active pacifists and said more than others about how they thought we were losing, but then they were arrested. We realized that if someone overheard anyone talking about things going badly for Japan in the war, they'd be turned in and arrested. So after that I didn't talk about the war. You had to be careful.

There was a military draft, and draft age was nineteen. I went through my physical and would have had to go into the military except I got a deferment because I was a science student. I think medical students also got a deferment. But, of course, a lot of my friends had to go into the military.

My brother got old enough to start smoking legally at age twenty-one. He got a ration, and so I started smoking even though I was underage. Later I got a cigarette ration. Everything was rationed. If you joined the army, you could receive a special package of cigarettes from the Emperor as a reward!

The air raids before 1944 were sporadic and infrequent and didn't really bother us, but when the B-29 raids started in 1944, and we saw so many planes flying overhead, we knew something had changed for the worse. But even though I saw the bombers dropping bombs, as long as they don't drop them on your head you don't worry too much. I think that is the psychology of survival. It's kind of strange. No one really got angry at the Americans when the bombing started, but neither did it really increase our will to fight. We didn't get angry at the Japanese government

*The View from Japan*

either. The military police were particularly active, and if you said something that someone overheard, you could be in much worse shape than if you were bombed by the Americans. So that's the choice you have, and when you come into a situation where there is no solution, you just don't think about it. We were in a situation where we couldn't do anything but try to survive, so nobody was really angry. Number one, we couldn't go anyplace. Number two, we couldn't do anything to stop our country from fighting, so what option do you have? It was a very helpless feeling. All you can think about is how to live under these circumstances, how to survive.

I finished high school and started university in 1945, and I moved to the countryside and lived with relatives. The individual departments in the University of Tokyo made their own decision whether to relocate to the countryside, and my department decided to move. I think the campus had some fire damage, but it was not bombed. Some parts of Tokyo weren't bombed or burned. Most of the destruction occurred downtown.

Our family house burned during the big firebomb raid in March 1945. I happened to be home that night with my parents, my two sisters, and one of my brothers. My other brother had been drafted and served in China for a while, but he got sick and they sent him back, and he was somewhere else in Japan.

First we could hear the planes coming overhead, but we couldn't see them because it was dark. Then air raid sirens went off. The bombing was taking place downtown, and since our neighborhood was distant from there we didn't immediately go to our designated evacuation area. Then you could see the big fires started by the bombing, and I saw a B-29 get shot down in the distance. It went down in a long bright streak in the darkness. But as the downtown fires intensified, the flames propagated and started burning toward us. They were getting closer and closer, and we were finally told we had to evacuate. We had a preassigned place to go, and we realized that our house was going to burn and there was nothing more we could do. So we grabbed our things and left. To get to our evacuation location, we had to go through an area that had just burned. I saw a lot of people who had been burned. There was a bomb shelter where people had gone, and they were killed down in that shelter, either from the heat or lack of oxygen. I saw people dying. There weren't many medical people around, but I did see a few fire engines.

My father had made a shelter in our backyard, not for us but for some of our belongings. He dug out a hole and made a concrete shelter. We figured we were probably safe from the bombs, but fire is what we were most worried about. We thought we could escape to our evacuation area, but we couldn't carry all our belongings with us, so that is why we had the shelter. I put a lot of books in the shelter, and I still have some that are burned around the edges. Even though they were in the shelter, the heat burned the edges. It's kind of interesting what you preserve in a situation when you think everything will be totally destroyed. I have a feeling that people are basically optimistic. They never think this is the end of the whole thing. You believe you are going to survive somehow, so you try to keep whatever it is you have, to the extent possible. That's the reason I felt those books were important. I didn't even know if I was going to use them after the war. I simply felt that it was important for me to keep those books. I wasn't thinking about that at the time, but I wondered afterwards why I kept those particular books. I think it was because I had hope for the future, that I would want to have them in the future, and that there would be a future.

So it was a frightening night, with so much of Tokyo burning—huge fires—and I think it was especially traumatic for older people. My father was about fifty-five or so, and I think it was hard for him. If something like that happened to me now, it would really affect me! But I was young, and it seemed to me at the time that we were just going to deal with things as they happened.

We got to our evacuation area, in a park, and a relief group was there to help people. People were talking about all the areas of Tokyo that were burning. I remember the fires and evacuating, but I can't remember where we stayed that night. It must have been in that park, and it wasn't just that night but for the next few days. The fires burned for a while, and then you couldn't touch anything in the burned-out areas because everything remained hot, so we couldn't really go anywhere. Finally a few days later we went back to look at our house, and it was totally destroyed, burned. We dug out our possessions from the shelter and moved outside of Tokyo to live with relatives.

Downtown was totally destroyed where there were commercial areas, but uptown, where the wealthy people lived, it didn't burn. I don't know if that was intentional or not. After that raid I went back to the university, and my department already had moved to the countryside. That's where I heard about the atomic bomb being dropped on Hiroshima.

Even when the Japanese military went into Manchuria and Korea, we were told there was some kind of logic to it, and the Japanese people kind of understood why we were doing it even if they disagreed. We had had

*The View from Japan*

a war with Russia, and the government said we needed a buffer zone between us and Russia. So to create this buffer zone, the military went into some areas of China. Since China was not well united at that time and kind of weak as a country, the Japanese were afraid China might easily be taken over by the West and bring our enemies very close to us. So to avoid that, the government said the only way to survive was to exert influence over China. In the thirteenth century the Mongolians tried to invade Japan through Korea, so the government thought the Russians could easily do the same, and that's why they said they had to annex Korea. So at least up until Pearl Harbor, there was some kind of logic for the actions of the government. Before Pearl Harbor, I always thought we were on reasonably good terms with the Americans, even though there was diplomatic tension. But when all the government propaganda changed, and suddenly America became our enemy after Pearl Harbor, I guess some people believed it, but others wondered about it. It didn't seem to make much sense to me to expand the conflict beyond China.

I understood that the reason the Japanese Navy built all their ships was not for battle, but to keep from fighting. They said that having a strong defense system discouraged Western forces from invading. Before the war, when the Japanese military went down into Indochina for the oil, the Navy thought the Americans would be afraid that we were getting too close to the Philippines. That's why the Navy tried to stop the military expansionists. The Navy didn't want to have a war at that time. They wanted a strong military to be able to deter Western influences and to be able negotiate better with other countries. So the Navy had that philosophy all the way. The Navy didn't want to attack Pearl Harbor. That was dictated by the military planners. But once you have a situation where military expansionists come into power, it's very difficult to go against that policy. If you object or question the government, you are branded unpatriotic and a traitor. So once the decision had been made to attack Pearl Harbor, the Navy knew what they were getting into, but they wanted to do their best once it was started. They were military professionals. It is not just a question of good or bad, or what for—once it's done it's done.

I have heard after the war that Americans feared that every Japanese civilian would have fought to the death, even using bamboo spears. And, indeed, there was talk in Japan before the war ended that we would all fight. There wasn't much discussion, because we knew we couldn't really discuss things like that or question them because you'd be arrested. But many of us realized that this was crazy, you know, bamboo spears? What would you want to die like that for? It was a joke! You couldn't have said that at the time, but obviously it was strange. So, I think, maybe some people were worried about the Americans invading and may have fought like that, but many wouldn't when they saw there was no point. I wasn't worried, because I was outside of Tokyo, a long ways from where the Americans would be invading.

But what I did worry about was Hiroshima. Clearly this was a new type of bomb. I had taken a university physics course, so I knew what it was, and the other science students knew what it was. From physics we knew that this was being worked on and that those types of bombs might exist. We saw then that something had to be done. We knew we couldn't fight against that. But what I didn't know, and a lot of people didn't know, was the radiation effects. A young Japanese scientist named Ted Fujita—I met him later when he became internationally known for his research on tornadoes—he went to do the survey at Hiroshima right after the explosion. He went right to the epicenter when radioactive material was still there, and he didn't know anything about the radiation risk. But what he really was proud of was that he calculated the altitude of the bomb when it exploded from the shadows objects cast from the heat and radiation. Other people did this calculation later, and I heard that his initial estimate was not far off from the others.

I think the Japanese feeling was that if that was the only bomb, and if it didn't happen any more, we could take it. But when the second one exploded, we knew we couldn't continue. It wasn't a question of morality. I think that to some extent it is correct to say the bomb ended the war. But at the same time, if someone asks me if the bomb was needed to end the war, probably not, because things were already so bad. But the thing is, someone has to decide to end it, someone on the Japanese side. They could have stopped before, but the bomb became the trigger.

Then we all listened to the Emperor's address on the radio telling us we'd lost the war. I felt relieved. I also had a great deal of hope that things would be normalized. Toward the end of the war it had gotten so crazy, I couldn't imagine things getting worse. For example, one of the craziest things that happened during the war was that every time the Emperor's picture appeared in the newspaper, we had to cut out the photo and bring it to school because an image of the Emperor was sacred. You had to cut it out of the paper so the picture wouldn't be damaged when you threw the newspaper away. I don't know what they did with all those newspaper pictures of the Emperor students cut out. Even though we had been told the Emperor was a god, there are some things that just strike you as crazy, and that was one of them. You think, "Why does this have to be done?"

In fact I never remember being told in elementary school, in the 1930s, that the Emperor was a god, but suddenly just before the war with the U.S. started, that's the time the government really began to tighten down. They started to push the Emperor as god, and that business of cutting out the pictures was the craziest example of what started to happen. But you know you can't always fool kids. I remember asking my teacher one time why we had to cut out the pictures of the Emperor and bring them to school. And she said, "It's not a question of 'why,' it's just something you have to do." And once we were told that, we never asked again, but that didn't stop us from questioning it ourselves.

So that day of the Emperor's broadcast, I was really surprised by what he sounded like. We had never heard his voice before. He spoke kind of slowly and sounded strange. I think we understood he sounded different because of the way people treated him and because of his isolation from everyone else.

After the Emperor's radio address, I heard that American ships were coming into Tokyo Bay for the surrender. I didn't go down to the shore to look at the ships, but I think some people did. But then the war was over, and I was relieved. And of course nothing worked, a lot of the infrastructure had been destroyed, like electricity and water plants.

After the war when the American occupation troops came in, people didn't know what to expect. I don't think we hated the Americans, we just didn't know about them, except for the government propaganda during the war. But very soon, even in the first few days after the Americans came, things started to turn around for the better, so we thought maybe the Americans weren't so bad. Trains started moving, and we started to get electricity and water back, so the infrastructure came back fairly quickly, and I don't know how they were able to do that. But then things were really bad for the economy. We had terrible inflation, there were shortages, and the rebuilding was a massive task.

One of the things the American occupation forces did when they came into Tokyo was to set up a library. They really worked hard to win us over, to win our hearts. During the war we couldn't read any American or English journals or publications, but there were books in the library on all kinds of subjects, including science. That was the first time

I ever saw the *Journal of Meteorology*, and as it turned out I ended up making a career in meteorological research.

At this time the traffic was totally jammed. There were no stoplights working, and the attitude of the people toward the Japanese police was not to listen to them, since they had treated people so badly during the war. So the American military police had to come in and do traffic direction, and that's the only thing that kept traffic moving. They did a great job with the traffic, and things like that won the people's hearts.

I never saw MacArthur in person, but of course he was a very prominent figure. Some people were saying he was a god. The Emperor was powerful and a god, but MacArthur was even over the Emperor, so he must be a god! But I think MacArthur did very well. He was quite diplomatic.

Some Japanese were against the Emperor after the war, since they blamed him for how badly the war had gone. And there was a quite active Communist movement to try and abolish the Emperor system. But I think MacArthur recognized this movement was directly related to the Communists, so he made an effort not to tear down the social system, since he knew the Emperor was a key to keeping order in the country. A lot of people still respected the Emperor system, and I didn't have any negative feeling about the Emperor. However, it didn't take me long, during the war, to figure out who was really running the system, and it wasn't the Emperor. It was a group of militarists. In fact, in the whole history of Japan, the Emperor was used by various people as a figurehead to unite the country, and not necessarily to hold absolute power. And that was the way all of Japanese history was.

So the people knew the Emperor didn't have any real power, but there was historical continuity. People were comfortable to have that arrangement, even though they knew others were using the Emperor for their own ends. So the question is, who uses the Emperor and what do they do to achieve their goals? When MacArthur used the Emperor to stabilize the country, there was a precedent in Japanese history for doing that. Then he brought in some new systems we had never seen before, but he blended the new things with some elements of our old system, like the Emperor. That's why I think that if you totally tear down a country's system, it's difficult to replace it entirely with something new. People have to develop their own system if it is truly self-government.

My father ended up going back and rebuilding his house, but he rebuilt it on another lot nearby. He didn't own the land we were living on, so he rebuilt on another lot, a smaller lot. I can't remember exactly how that worked, how he was able to rebuild the house when there were so many shortages and a lack of construction materials. I think he did it gradually over time as things became available. I was still living with relatives in the country. I continued in university and finished my undergraduate degree in 1948. Then I went to graduate school and got a qualifying degree, which was like a master's degree, and then my Ph.D.

I traveled around a bit after the war, even though traveling was quite difficult. I took one trip to make meteorological measurements in Hokkaido during a total solar eclipse. We got help from the American occupation headquarters to let us use a sleeping car on the train for all of us who were going to Hokkaido. So we had good weather, saw the eclipse, and were able to make our measurements. Science was popular, and people were interested in helping, like that American library with scientific publications in it.

I got married in 1952 and came over to the U.S. in 1954. In those days invitations to get positions in the U.S. were so instantaneous! When I wrote a letter asking about the availability of U.S. positions, I got a letter back right away. There were post-doctoral positions open, and if I wanted to come they'd send me all the paperwork, and that was amazing! It wasn't so easy to get a visa to come to the U.S., but in those days there was a fairly strong incentive for the U.S. Embassy to get Japanese to come to the States to study. So it took time, and I had to go through all the health checks and so on, but it was pretty easy. I expected it would be hard for me to live in the U.S. since I was coming from a defeated country, but it turned out that people in the U.S. were very friendly to me. One year later my wife joined me and stayed. It was a wonderful opportunity. I've been an atmospheric scientist in the U.S. ever since.

# CHAPTER 13

> "It was rough fighting the Japanese in the Admiralties. There was an Imperial Marine Division in there, and they were one of the top units in the Japanese military."
> —Fred Saiz, ARMY

JIM MILLIFF, MARINES, Bougainville, Guam

HARLAN WALL, ARMY, Philippines

FRED SAIZ, ARMY, New Guinea, Philippines

MILO CUMPSTON, MARINES, Iwo Jima

BILL HASTINGS, MARINES, Iwo Jima

JOE WOODS, MARINES, Saipan, Iwo Jima

PAGES 418–419: *U.S. Fifth Division Marines are pinned down on the porous coarse volcanic sand beach on Iwo Jima, February 19, 1945.*

OPPOSITE: *Jim Milliff (standing at far right) and fellow Marines on Guadalcanal shortly after surviving their combat experience on Bougainville and prior to the invasion of Guam. Standing from left: Chester Lawson, Frank Brandemhil, George Walters and Milliff; kneeling from left, Edward Spielbush and Elbert Ross Underwood.*

# THE FINAL PHASE OF ISLAND COMBAT, PHILIPPINES, SAIPAN, GUAM, TINIAN, IWO JIMA, OKINAWA, 1944–45

## JIM MILLIFF
MARINES

I went down to enlist on December 8, 1941. One of those "Pearl Harbor Avengers," I was going to join the Navy, but a friend of mine talked me into the Marines. He had been turned down by the Marines in the morning on account of his teeth, so he went and got his teeth fixed. He said, "Let's just see if we can pass the exam." And, boom, we were in! But they didn't take us until December 19, because they were signing guys up at the rate of a thousand a day, and the Marines were only used to handling 200 per day.

Before I went overseas, the captain said nobody goes to officer's school. But they'd give us tests, and every time we'd take a test I'd come in first. I guess that shows you how dumb the rest of them were. And so he kept saying that nobody goes to a military school, but with my test scores I thought I would have a chance. I was a private first class, and we had a brand-new NCO from the reserves. I used to box a little, so I said to him, "This is your chance to show how tough the Marine Corps is." And then this corporal referred to my ancestry in an inferior light, so I hit him. Actually I just shoved him. And for that I went to the brig for twenty days on bread and water. That also ended any chance I had of being an officer. But then, I'm here, and a lot of those guys that were good officers aren't here!

The two biggest ocean liners in the U.S. at that time were the *America* and the *Washington*, and I went across the Pacific on the *America*. We didn't go in convoy because that thing could go twenty or thirty knots. It could run away from the Japs, and it had a 5-inch gun on board. The skipper on that thing had been the skipper on one of the ships at Pearl Harbor, and every time there'd be reports of Japanese in the area, we had to sit out on deck with this 5-inch gun. I was in the ballroom up on the promenade deck. There were about six berths in a stack, and the stacks of bunks were so crammed in there you could barely move. But since I was a sergeant, I took the top bunk so nobody could climb down on top of me. But when we got out in the Pacific we just stayed out on the deck.

We went to New Zealand, to a little town just north of Auckland. We trained there for a while, and then we shipped out for Bougainville, and we landed at Empress Augusta Bay. You know, we'd pulled up offshore of this island, and you're sitting there out on the ocean, and it's a beautiful, sunny day, eight o'clock in the morning. And you're standing there, looking around to see what you can see. And these little plops are hitting the water, you know? All of a sudden, it dawns on you, "Hey! They're shooting at us!" There's nothing you can do.

It was really rough, you know. We went in on landing crafts at Bougainville, and we lost a lot of them. The Coast Guard was bringing us in. So we did the run in to the beach, and then you hop out of the amtracs. That's a scary thing, too, because you're about a good seven feet in the air, and you have to jump out onto the beach with the Japs shooting at you. And you're thinking that every one of the enemy is aiming right at you.

But when we did go inland on Bougainville, it was like one big swamp. So, there we were in a swamp, and all we had ever learned to do in training was dig in, but in that swamp you had to do the reverse and build up little islands out of the muck. We were in this swamp for a while, but they

*The Final Phase of Island Combat*

kept moving us up. Finally, there's a hill in front of us. We were on the front lines, and all of a sudden here come the Seabees to bulldoze that hill down out there in front of us. And we said, "Hey! Do you guys realize that this is the front lines?" "Oops!" So then they went back, and they said, "You'd better move those Marines forward." So they moved us forward, and we were there for sixty days on the front lines in the jungle and didn't come back that whole time. What they finally did was build a perimeter to keep the Japs away from the airstrip they had built there, and then they brought the Army in to relieve us, the Americal Division, I think it was. They held that perimeter for the rest of the war. They never took them off Bougainville. So then they brought us back to Guadalcanal, and we get down there and there's a whole big military city, a great big city with a beautiful, massive airport and the whole business.

The next operation we were in on was the invasion of Guam in 1944. We landed at Asan Point, Third Marine Division, Ninth Regiment. We came in on "Blue Beach." We went up across the beach and dug in. There were high cliffs ahead of us beyond the beach to the right and left. So, I told the guy ahead of me, "When you're gonna move, let me know." They were shooting at us, and we were laying low in holes we made for ourselves in the field behind the beach at the foot of these cliffs. And so when he decided he was going to move, he started throwing rocks at me to get my attention. Well, I dug deeper—I thought I was receiving fire! Pretty soon the word comes back from our colonel. He wants a machine gun up there. Well, I'm a machine gunner, so I go up there with another machine gunner, and we get fire and my gunner gets killed. And another bullet goes right by me and hits the colonel. So we didn't have to see any more of that colonel. And we had our ammunition dump along there, too. The Japs blew it up, and we lost about 120 men that day.

Then a guy said to me, "There's a Jap in there," and he pointed to a cave in the cliff. So, there's a Marine I knew coming by with a flamethrower, and I said, "Hey, there's a Jap in there." And so he turned the flamethrower in there. Seven Japs ran out, and we shot them. Then the next day, they brought the Seabees in, and they just mined that whole cliff and all their caves and blew it up. They brought a war dog with them. And the war dog and his leader, they went around the bottom of the cliff and checked the caves. And if the dog goes "GRRRRR," then the Marines start scrambling. A war dog is a messenger and he smells out the enemy. He does all kinds of work. We used them first on Bougainville. And they're really like humans. They crack up if they get too much work.

They got a rank, too. I said to the guy, "What rank's your dog?" He says, "Sergeant." And I said, "What're you?" He says, "I'm a corporal." His dog outranked him.

So, we got past that first set of Jap positions, and there was a hill up behind them farther up from the beach. We came up there and the Japs had this hill, but it looked real familiar. It was just like this place where we had trained on maneuvers in California called Murphy Canyon. So we all looked at one another and said, "Murphy Canyon." The captain says, "Murphy Canyon. First Platoon on the right, Second Platoon on the left, and the Third Platoon in the middle." And when the machine guns started firing, everybody charged just like in training. We took that hill and only lost one man. And you could see it from the harbor. One of the chief surgeons was out on the ship—he was from my hometown. And somehow he found out from guys coming back that I was in there in that deal, and so he wrote a big, glowing letter back home about what a wonderful outfit we were.

And then we turned and took a pass to the right. And then they took us farther down to the right to take a little island just off the coast, Cabras Island, I think it was, and we rode over on amtracs and jumped out. We went in there and I thought, well, we're going to lose the whole company here. And we jump out of the amtracs and there's a great big pillbox staring at us, a big, black hole, you know? So, bam, bam, bam, bam, and we are all shooting at it. And I yell, "Down men, let's sneak around." We sneak up to it, and of course, it's empty.

Sure the Japs were terrible and did a lot of bad stuff, but sometimes we were just as bad as they were. I had a guy in the outfit that would knock the teeth out of dead Japs, and he had this whole jar full of gold teeth. But the only thing that most of us took were the flags, mainly, and some valuables. We discouraged that gold teeth business because it was just, you know—things can get worse and worse.

We finally got inland a ways and we had dug in on the slope of one of the hills. Capt. Dave Lewis put the Company on a Third Watch, which meant that every third foxhole had a Marine on watch. No matter what the watch, you only slept off and on during the dark hours in combat. I was in a foxhole with two other Marines, Alcorn and Hobson, with our light machine gun. We always found a two-forked stick and put it in front of the foxhole, so when we awakened at night, we knew which direction was front. It had been the kind of day where it rained and then the sun would come out, you know, off and on. And that night the moon

*The Final Phase of Island Combat*

was out, and we could look down this hill in front of our foxhole and there was a little road down there a ways.

And I looked and I saw about ten or twelve Japs coming up that road in the moonlight. Well, I reached back to get my weapon to kill them, but the Marine who had stood the last watch in the hole had wrapped all our weapons in a poncho to keep them dry from these passing showers, so I couldn't get a weapon out real easily. So, I thought, well, I'll lay quiet, because I knew if I turned around and rummaged around trying to get out a weapon, they would see me and might shoot me.

Well, one of them was coming up pretty close, so I figured I'd lay quiet, and after he goes by I'll unwrap my rifle and shoot him. Well, he didn't go by. He saw me and he came at me with this big Samurai sword, and he was going to behead me with that thing. I had seen those sabers, and in training we'd been taught that even though you didn't have your weapon, you still weren't unarmed, you had your hands. I planned that when he swung the saber down, I would deflect the blade with my left hand. I am right handed, and if I lost the left hand it wouldn't be so bad for me. So it worked out just like I planned. I deflected the blade with my left hand, caught the back of the blade with my right hand, yanked him off balance, kicked him with my right foot, stuck my left foot in his belly, rolled onto my back in the foxhole and lifted him up in the air on my foot so the Marines in another foxhole could shoot him.

And I'm doing all this thinking, and I could hear somebody yelling. A Marine in the far foxhole started shooting with his .45 and hit the Jap. One of the bullets, evidently, ricocheted off the parapet and went into my right hip. But I didn't know it at the time. I had this tight feeling in my hip, but I thought I'd got kicked in the fight. And then, I hollered "Cease fire!" And I kicked the Jap off my foot. Well, he goes up in the air, and the guy starts shooting all over again. So, I yell again to cease fire, and he stopped firing. I looked at this Jap and he was kind of breathing, so I let him have one out of my .45, and that was that. But all during this, I could hear some guy yelling. At the end I realized my mouth was open, so when I shut my mouth the yelling stopped. It was me—I was the one who had been yelling! It was like I was two people, the trained me who is fighting off this Japanese guy like I'd been taught, and the real me who is scared to death!

When daylight came we called for a corpsman, and we discovered that I couldn't walk. The corpsman, Hills was his name, cut the right pant leg off. I told him to stop, that I needed those pants. He said, "You're through with this war, Marine, you don't need them, because there's a bullet lodged in your right hip."

They took me back there to the field hospital, and they had some antiquated X-ray machine. I didn't know how bad I was hit, you know. I knew that my hands were cut pretty bad, because that was where I'd grabbed the saber.

They noticed I had an entrance wound in my hip, but they couldn't find the bullet. They said they could see where it had gone in, but it didn't come out. Well, if it didn't come out, it must be in there somewhere. So, while I was in the hospital the Japs had broken through, and in the hospital they gave all of us weapons. We had to stay there in the hospital but be ready to defend ourselves. Luckily the Japs didn't get to our hospital and the breakthrough was turned back.

I was in the hospital just for a short time, and the hole where the bullet went in healed over, so they sent me back to my company. And I said, "What about the bullet?" And they said, "Well, we can't find it." And that's when I said, "Well, it didn't come out." They didn't know what to do, so I went back to my outfit.

I got back, and next thing we were marching down the road when the lieutenant halts us and says, "Left face." And we left face and he says, "This is our campsite." And it was a jungle. We said, "How are we gonna put tents in here?" He said, "Clear it." We said, "How're we gonna do it?" And he says, "You got bayonets!" So, pretty soon, you heard, "Fire in the hole!" Guys are getting down and BOOM! They were blowing up trees. They were blowing up everything. I looked out as we got things cleared off and there was a beautiful beach. So, we built the camp there.

After a while I went over to the hospital to see them again, and I said, "Now, look. There's a bullet in here somewhere, because I can't walk right, and the thing must be right up against the joint." And so they took another X-ray and said, "Oh, yeah, there it is." They still had that piece of antiquated equipment, but this time they aimed it right. So I said, "What're we going to do about it?" And the doctor said, "Oh, that's inoperable. They may take that out when you get back to the States, sometime. But for now go back to your outfit."

So back I went. They were making sweeps of the island, and I was assigned duty as a police sergeant. I stayed back and kept the camp clean with a detail. And that was my job. So, pretty soon they brought in guys who had been over any length of time, and they were going to be sent home. The captain said, "Okay now, I've put down the names of the

*The Final Phase of Island Combat*

men that have been good performers out here. And we're gonna send them home first in the order they're drawn." They just drew the names. So the first guy drawn was a guy named Quick, whose brother had been killed. The next was me. My mother had just died and I had a bullet in my hip. And so I got sent home on that.

So when I got home I found out that after I was wounded, for some reason, they had sent a letter to my folks that I'd been killed. But I was already home when the letter got there—I beat it back. And the notice was in the Oakland *Post Inquirer*, and it's gone and I'm still here. But when I came home I was probably never in better shape in my whole life, 190 pounds and no fat. My dad took a look at me, because I was yellow from taking Atabrine for malaria, and he starts shoving the food down. I went back to the base, and people that I'd served with didn't even recognize me. My dad had said, "You get that bullet out of there, and you do it right now. Don't wait."

So in late 1944 when I headed back I was assigned to duty up on Bainbridge Island, Washington. And that was interesting, too, because that's where they were breaking the Japanese codes, only I didn't know it. There were 100 sailors, 78 Marines, and 500 WAVES—and that means 500 women—on this base. And, you know, you get to think you're a lady's man with those kinds of odds. They always told us it was a high-frequency radio school, and all we were there for was in case there was sabotage, but we were really there to guard the code breakers. It was a beautiful duty because if you wanted to go into Seattle, that was fun, but why go to Seattle—you had everything at the base there. Bowling alleys and WAVES and everything.

While I was there I went to the hospital over at Bremerton. They brought in this commander of the hospital, who was a captain. And he sat down and said, "Well, okay, sergeant. Now, how'd the bullet get in there?" So I told him. Pretty soon they go out and they bring in somebody and it was Gregory Peck. He was visiting the hospital, and he wanted to hear about it so I was telling him, and he shook my hand. He was a big, tall guy and visiting with the USO or something.

So the doctors all got together and they said, "Well, we'll call you." I went back to my base, and after a while I got a call. I went back over there and there was this Dr. Kowalski. He looked like Groucho Marx. He looks at me and says, "Oh, yeah, sergeant, I remember your bullet in the right hip." So I says, "Think you can get it out?" "Yeah, I can get it out." And I said, "They told me that it was inoperable." Well, he got in there and it was rough. He had to take the whole hip apart to get it out, because the bullet was rammed in there. And he told me later, "You know when you were overseas and that first guy told you that stuff about it being inoperable? He was right!" But Dr. Kowalski got it out and he gave the bullet to me. I have it at home. It's an American .45, so all of my hospital reports had to say, "Not self-inflicted," because it was an American bullet.

I got the Purple Heart, and they also gave me the Silver Star there in Bremerton for that little incident with the Jap officer and his sword. I didn't know anything about getting it, but it had been written up by my lieutenant. The commanding officer they had in the Marine barracks was a minister in civilian life. He had been a Marine in World War I. So he gets us all lined up there and he calls, "Sergeant Millgriff." He was mispronouncing my name so bad I didn't even know that he was talking about me. Pretty soon, the old Marine gunny says, "He needs you! GET OUT THERE! March out there!" So, I marched out there, and the first I knew I was going to get the Silver Star was when they presented it to me.

So I got the Jap's sword and his pistol. I still have the sword. I gave the pistol to my brother Bill to hold for me because I was moving around. And Bill walked in his sleep, and he lost the pistol. He thinks he may have done something to it when he was sleepwalking. But he never found the pistol. It was a beautiful pistol. He felt bad about it, but he doesn't know what happened to it. And, of course, I still have the scars on my hands. They've faded now, and you can barely see them. Over the years I must have told that story of the Jap that charged me with his sword a hundred times, but people keep wanting to hear it.

I'm still in touch with a lot of the guys I served with. I'm active in the Yolo County Marine League, and the Golden Gate Chapter of the USMC 3rd Division Association. I try and go to the reunions, and I even edited our newsletter for a while. Just about all of us who are still around got wounded at one time or another, either on Bougainville or Guam or Iwo. Getting wounded on Guam may have saved my life, since a lot of my friends in my unit got killed on Iwo.

OPPOSITE: *Harlan Wall (far right) and his gun crew near Clark Field, Philippines, in early 1945. Harlan comments, "This photo shows a group of sad G.I.s who thought the war would never end."*

*The Final Phase of Island Combat*

## HARLAN WALL
ARMY

I n Colorado we had a great football team in high school. We were playing in the state high school championship game on Friday, December 5, 1941, and we won. We were state champs! Our local newspaper was just a weekday paper, but we were all excited about getting to see the write-up in the papers on the following Monday. On Sunday the folks were having a birthday party for my younger brother, Don; his birthday was December 7, so we didn't have the radio on. That evening we went down to the church, where we were having a fund raiser for the young people. I'll never forget Russ Rosenbrock, he came in and he said, "Are you ready to get your gun?" And I said, "Gun? What for?" "Well, didn't you hear?" And I said, "No, what happened?" "Oh, the Japs bombed Pearl Harbor." All I could say was, "Oh, my!"

So then that was all anyone could talk about. The Monday paper came out the next day, and I think coverage of our game barely made it in at all! The Japs stole our thunder! So that made me mad at them right then and there!

Right after I graduated from high school in the spring of 1942, I tried to join the Navy. But they wouldn't take me because they said I was color-blind. I didn't even know it. I came home after taking the test and

I told mom that I didn't pass. And she says, "Oh, that's impossible. How couldn't you have passed? You're healthy." So I said, "Yeah, I'm healthy, but I'm color-blind." "You're what?" "Color-blind." They didn't have the foggiest notion that I was color-blind. I can tell colors, it's just different shades when there are two colors real close together, and I can't separate them. I can read most of them, but several of them I can't. But my grandpa was color-blind. And he was very color-blind. There was no doubt! He had this beautiful blue car. It was just a beautiful blue. And he always called it "coffee brown"! And my brother Les is color-blind.

So I ended up getting drafted in 1943. The Army didn't care if I was color-blind. I had tried to join the Navy, but when I spent all that time on the ships going across the Pacific, boy, was I glad I never got in the Navy. Oh, was I glad! Being out on the ocean on a ship was not for me! I ended up being assigned to the artillery.

Then we got shipped over to New Guinea to Finschhaven for what they called staging. Our big guns followed us; they weren't on our troop ship. I remember we loaded up in San Francisco and pulled out in the afternoon. It was a cold and cloudy day, and it was raining a little bit, just a light drizzle. A lot of us were out on the deck, and they had the Notre Dame–Army game on the PA system. I was all absorbed in it. That was the year Army had a real good team, they had Blanchard and Davis. And we were all out there on deck listening to the game and watching the Golden Gate Bridge go overhead. Then we were out in the ocean and the bridge got smaller and smaller, and then you couldn't see it at all. There were a bunch of guys sitting around listening to the game, but they kind of kept disappearing. I was absorbed in it. When I finally looked around, here the guys were, hanging over the rail! They had a latrine out on deck and they had, oh, I don't know, probably about a dozen commodes lined up on each side, and there guys were hanging their heads in the commodes. One guy was fishing his false teeth out! I didn't really have a problem with getting seasick, but I didn't like being on that ship, and I spent a lot of time out on deck.

We had a Neptune party for when we crossed the equator. Because it was a big ship and there were so many of us, they couldn't initiate all of us, so we had representatives to go through the ceremony. It was mostly sergeants and officers, but we all got our Shellback cards. I still have mine.

When we got to New Guinea there were still some Japanese, but they were back in the hills. The ones that were left were just trying to survive because they were bypassed in the island-hopping campaign. Because we were staging there, we were still training, mainly target practice.

One day we figured we'd like to rig up a platform we could swim off of. So we got some scrap and some weights and built a platform down there on the shore. It was a pretty steep hill down to the ocean, so we fixed it up so that we had this nice little platform to swim from. And that water was so clear and warm, that's some of the best swimming I've ever seen. And then one day a big storm, I think it was a typhoon, it came by and the wind and waves were really something. After the storm, we went down to see if our little platform was still there, but the wind and waves had tossed it right out of the water and halfway up the slope from the shore! So that was the end of our swimming set-up there. But we were getting ready to leave about that time anyway.

So they shipped us out and we went on a Liberty ship from New Guinea to the Philippines in convoy. We weren't in convoy from the States to New Guinea, but we were in convoy going from New Guinea to the Philippines. That was in 1944.

The fight for Manila was over, and we were the first troops to come in to Manila Harbor. There were a lot of sunken ships there. In fact, there was only one pier open at that time. We were scheduled to come in and were about six or seven hours late. So they put another ship in where we were supposed to dock, and it hit a mine and blew up! They figured that mine had broken loose and floated in there and "boom"! So they towed that ship out. I don't think it sank but it was damaged pretty badly. So they towed it out and we pulled right in.

After we unloaded in Manila we were just in the outskirts, and we knew we were going up to the front. We were getting our guns ready because they had come in the hold with us on the Liberty ship from New Guinea. We were checking our guns out and it was after dark. We were working on the guns, and all of a sudden, "ping—ping—ping—ping," you know, bullets whistling by, and some of the guys were all upset. I said, well, we just as well get used to this because we'll probably have a lot more. I wasn't too concerned because it was dark and they'd be lucky to hit you!

Very soon after that we were sent right up to the front near Laguna de Bay, or close to it. They had a bunch of Japanese cornered there, or not really cornered since they were still fighting. But they were trying to escape across this bay there at night, in boats or barges or anything to cross the bay. The reason they brought us in originally was because we had radar, and we were to blow them out of the water when they would get on their boats.

We were attacked quite often. They would come in and they would try and blow up the guns. That's when we were in our foxholes defending ourselves. We didn't go out after them, but we sure tried to keep them out. I was shooting an M1. The officers had carbines, but everyone else would have M1s. They would come in after dark. At our gun emplacement we had four machine guns at the corners, .50 caliber, then we had outposts in between depending on the terrain so you could cover all the areas coming in. For our artillery, we had four 90s in a gun emplacement. I was a gun commander on the 90s on a gun crew.

But then the Japs would try and infiltrate at night. You wouldn't see them as a rule. You knew they were out there because they were shooting at you. And you would just fire back. The idea was to just put as much fire power out there as you could. Just cover the area. They would try and sneak in. What they did was they would have a pack and they would load it with explosives, probably ten or twelve pounds of explosives in there. And what they would try to do was that if they could get close enough they'd drop a hand grenade in there and swing the pack and throw it and try and knock a gun out. That's what they were after. So we'd have to make sure they didn't get close enough. About the closest they got was about thirty or forty yards. You couldn't see them at night. We wouldn't shoot flares up. We just tried to lay down as much fire as we could. Rifles, machine guns, hand grenades. We'd all just start shooting, just firing away. And in the morning there would be bodies out there.

We heard about guys taking gold fillings out of the teeth of the Japanese bodies, but I never saw anyone do that. But wars bring out the worst in people. One morning there were a couple of dead Japs out there, and this one guy, he looked at them and he pissed in their faces. You know, just a stupid thing. War is a terrible thing, it brings out the worst in people. This was a guy from our unit, a good friend of mine. So I asked him, "Why did you do that?" And he says, "I don't know." Guys would go through the bodies looking for souvenirs. But I didn't do it. I couldn't bring myself to do something like that. I wasn't that cruel, I guess. I have never been a great souvenir person in the first place, and I just didn't care about it.

We had one guy crack up during this time. Well, one night we were under attack and he just curled up down in the bottom of his foxhole and started crying. After the firing stopped we couldn't get him to snap out of it. We tried talking to him, but it was like he couldn't hear us and he just kept crying. It was really strange. He just couldn't take it and just kind of snapped, I guess. So the next morning they took him away and I never saw him again. I never heard what happened to him.

After a while they sent us up near Clark Field. We were set up there to guard the airfield. The Japs tried to sneak in there and blow up airplanes. In fact they did get in there a few times. When the Air Corps wanted help, they got it! We were with the Forty-third Division up at the front, and the old general up there was raising Cain because the Air Corps took us away to Clark Field, but it didn't matter. We were also doing regular artillery support fire.

In our four-gun artillery position a Jap came out of the brush one day and walked toward where we were, and he had his hands in the air like he wanted to surrender. One of the guys in my crew had his M1 trained on him as he walked toward us. When the Jap got close, all of a sudden he reached behind his head and pulled out a pistol. So our guy shot him five times before he hit the ground, and he was dead. It was a close call, and we all thought that was the end of it, but when we walked out there and had a look at that Jap pistol, he had pulled the trigger of the thing but it had misfired. If it had gone off he would have shot our guy. That really shook him up.

I was in the Philippines when they dropped the bombs. What a relief! You know, it was crazy. It just looked like that war would go on forever. It was the most depressing thing because you couldn't see an end to it. We just knew we'd have to invade Japan. In fact, we were set up guarding these airstrips, and they had brought some infantry units in and they were training at that time and they had their bullhorns and they were marching. They were staging for the invasion of Japan. And then when the war was over, that was when they told us that we would have gone in on the second wave on Honshu Island. We were scheduled!

Our captain called us in after it was over and said, "Well, I want to tell you what we missed." They had this plan. We had an LCT that we were assigned to, the number and everything. We were going in. But we were artillery and weren't going in on the first wave, we were going in on the second wave. They were going to invade Honshu first and set up landing strips there. And they were going to do this in November. See, that wasn't far away. We were close! We just shuddered when we heard that. Ohhhh! Then you wonder why we applauded Harry Truman for dropping that bomb. When we heard about that bomb we just cheered. It killed 200,000 people and you cheer, and that's terrible. But we knew it was over, and they couldn't withstand that. We didn't know we only had two bombs, but neither did they. We knew with that kind of a weapon they couldn't withstand it and they had to give up. It would have been bloody, and think of all the Japanese that would have been killed. It was a drop in the bucket, the people killed by the atomic bomb, compared to what would have been killed if we would have invaded.

So the war was over and we were all really anxious to get back home. At that time they were already thinking about integrating the military, and there were black troops out in the Pacific. There was a guy in my group who was from Louisiana, and he heard they were going to put blacks on the ship with us going back to the States. This was something he really didn't want to hear. He said, "If they put blacks with me on that ship, I'll refuse to get on." So we got down to the pier to get on the ship to go home, and we saw these blacks getting on. And when we were assigned our berths, they mixed the blacks in with the whites, which was really the first time they had done this in the military as far as I know. Most of us were okay with this, but I ran into my friend and he was complaining that they had put a black right in the same compartment with him and some other guys. But there he was on the ship and we were heading home, so I asked him, "Hey, I thought you said if there were blacks on the ship you wouldn't even get on, and now you're sharing a compartment with blacks."

"Well," he said, "I don't like it, and if I really didn't want to get home so bad I would have never gotten on this ship." So he wasn't so negative on blacks that he couldn't deal with it if he could go home! We were guessing that is why they did that, putting blacks in with the whites on the ships going home. They figured that the white guys would be so eager to get home they would put up with anything, and this was the first step in integrating the military. It turned out that everyone got along on the ship just fine. We were all desperate to get home! It took us fifteen days to get from Manila to San Francisco, and we didn't stop anywhere on the way, we rolled right along.

I'm still in touch with a few of the guys I knew in the Army, and I have a few things I brought back from the Pacific, some wooden bullets the Japanese used at the end when they ran out of lead, some occupation money from the Philippines, and some photos. That's about it. I never thought about staying in the Army—I got out. It was a no-brainer!

When I got back I did have some trouble with nightmares for a little while. Well, nothing serious, but whenever I heard a backfire or a loud noise at night, any kind of a banging noise when I was sleeping, that would give me a shock. You know we would sleep with our rifles by our side at the front, and at the first sign of any kind of trouble, a shot or anything, the first thing you'd do you would grab your rifle before you were even awake. I remember after the war if I'd hear a loud noise I'd wake up at night and reach for my rifle, and it wasn't there. And, ohh, that's not a good feeling! You break into a cold sweat for about half a second before you fully wake up and realize you weren't in the Philippines but at home. So I had these things happening for a little bit, but not for long, because it wasn't like some guys who were really in for a long time and saw a lot of action. Some of those guys had a rough time getting over it. When we got back from WWII, they had no mercy. They said, "Well, the war's over, now let's get back to work. You have to get back in." And there were some guys who had trouble, and some of them turned into alcoholics and so forth.

I had some problems with my hearing after the war. We'd sometimes put cotton in our ears when we were firing the guns, but I don't think that did much good. A lot of the time the gun would go off and it didn't bother me much, but every once in a while it would be different and it really would affect my ears. I'd have ringing in my ears for a while. But no one really thought about ear protection like they do now.

A lot of guys went to school on the GI Bill. And my younger brother Les, he'd say, "You dummy! You could have had four years of college for nothing!" But I figured I'd wasted enough time in the Army. I really didn't know what I wanted to do in school anyway, and I always wanted to farm to begin with, that's just what I wanted to do. I've never regretted farming. That's what I was interested in, and I've always liked it.

## FRED SAIZ
ARMY

When I was nineteen I joined the Civilian Conservation Corps. As soon as I turned twenty-one I had to sign up for the draft, and it wasn't long before I got my notice. I was drafted into the Army in March 1941, and they sent me to Fort Bliss, Texas, to the First Cavalry Division. I was with them until I got out, that same group. While I was at Fort Bliss they bombed Pearl Harbor, and then we knew we were in it! So they sent us home for a week. We had maneuvers in Louisiana the summer of 1942, and then they sent us to Australia. We trained in Australia about ten or fifteen miles north of Brisbane, up in the mountains. We built a camp over there, and we trained for about a year before we were ready for New Guinea.

When we got to New Guinea—the first place we went—the landing had already been made, and we just went in as a mop-up operation at Oro Bay. Then from there we went into the Admiralty Islands, and that was

ABOVE: *Fred Saiz shortly after boot camp in 1942. On 31 January 1945, General Douglas MacArthur issued the order "Go to Manila! Go around the Japs, bounce off the Japs, save your men, but get to Manila! Free the internees at Santo Tomas! Take the Malacanan Palace (the presidential palace) and the legislative building!" The next day, the "flying column," as the mobile unit came to be known, jumped off to slice through 100 miles of Japanese territory. Fred was a member of this high risk "flying column" that was able to overcome or go around all obstacles in its path and rescue the internees.*

rough. We had our first combat landing there, and there were several islands we fought on. We first landed at Los Negros, and then at Manus, and then a couple of smaller islands. When we went in there we were on LSTs until we got close to the island, and then we got into landing craft from the LSTs. On the landing craft, they would let the front end down when we got to the beach. That first landing under fire was something. I was thinking I just wanted to find a hole! But we kept on going. What had happened, the battleships had shelled the hell out of the beach and the area right behind, and the airplanes had bombed it just before we landed. The Japanese had moved back, so it wasn't too bad getting in to the beaches. We didn't really get shot at too much until we got inland, and you just keep shooting back. We were well trained and knew what to do.

We had been together so long we were just like a family. We protected each other, but it made it hard when we had casualties. You'd take care of them as best you could, and then you'd keep on going. But it was hard when guys started getting shot. One time a mortar shell landed right next to where the mortar platoon was. I was in a hole nearby, and the mortar shell hit right where those guys were. I went over to pick one guy up, and his guts were all gone. A big piece of shrapnel had torn him apart. I put my hands underneath to turn him over, and there was nothing underneath. It was sickening, and he was one of my buddies, which made it real hard. But you just have to keep on going. You try to help the ones that are alive.

It was rough fighting the Japanese in the Admiralties. There was an Imperial Marine Division in there, and they were one of the top units in the Japanese military. They were big, and they were good fighters. When we were fighting the Japanese, morning and night was all the same, you'd just stay awake all the time. I'd maybe sleep a little bit in the foxhole while my buddy was on guard, and then we'd switch and I'd keep a lookout while he tried to sleep a little bit. The Marines were in Guadalcanal way before we got into New Guinea, so we had a lot of good information from them about how the Japanese fought. We kind of knew what to expect, that they would probably fight to the death, and that we'd have banzai attacks.

The first thing they warned us about was not to sleep in a hammock, because the Japs would cut you to pieces. We had these hammocks that we'd string from one tree to another, and they had a zipper lining so the mosquitoes wouldn't get in to you. They were comfortable, especially when it was raining. But that was a death trap. The Japanese would be watching out for that from the jungle, and they would come in at night with their bayonets and butcher you if you were in one. So we were warned about that. Then what we'd do was put our hammocks up, dig our hole, form a fire line, and we'd wait for them. And that's how we survived.

Another thing we learned from the Marines that probably saved my life was to dig three foxholes just a short distance apart for each machine gun. Then when the Japs were attacking, you would first shoot from one hole, and then quickly go over to the next and shoot from there, and then switch to the third. The reason was that if you stayed in the same hole, the Japs would zero in on you. We figured we only had about two or three minutes that we could stay and shoot that machine gun out of one hole before we had to move. And that's exactly what happened one time. I was shooting my machine gun from one hole, and I'd just gone over to the next hole when a Jap hand grenade came flying into the hole I'd just left. It blew up, and if I'd have been in there I'd have been killed.

Sometimes the Japanese would be dug into holes and bunkers, but a lot of the time we would have to patrol looking for them, and we'd have to spot them. We patrolled a lot, and this was all in the jungle, and that was quite a bit different from what we were used to from training in the States. But you know, we got used to it. You adapt to it, you know the terrain, you know what you're expected to do, and you just watch your step, and you watch everybody's back.

We had the same guys all the way through, the ones we started with back in the States. I was a rifleman and machine gunner, and I had the same sergeant for my squad all the way through, although we lost some of our guys in these various operations. There were 230 men in our troop when we went overseas. When we came back there were only 108 from the original ones that went.So as we went along we got replacements. When you get replacements you have to train them, and you have to work with them and keep training them. There was one incident that happened in the Admiralties that involved replacements. We'd just about finished clearing out those islands, but there was another island across from where we were camped. They sent us on a patrol up there with about twelve replacements, and we were to train them on how to go on patrol. Well, we encountered some Japanese over there, and they kind of pinned us down on a ridge, so we stayed overnight that night. But we had also taken a desk sergeant with us. He wanted to go on patrol to see if he could kill a Jap, so he went with us.

That night we were pinned down and couldn't get back to our camp by the beach. We couldn't do anything more about it that night, so we set guards around and dug in to spend the night. We'd fight our way out the next morning. This was more than the desk sergeant had bargained for. About midnight he got worried and went to check on one of the guards, who was one of the replacements. The guy on guard had heard that the Japanese would sneak up on you, and you'd have to be very careful. So he heard footsteps behind him, turned around, and shot the sergeant, shot him through the right shoulder. We bandaged him up as best we could, but he needed medical attention back at the camp.

So that night I had to go down to where the camp was and tell them what had happened, to arrange to get that sergeant out of there. So I snuck off this ridge, and it took me about two or three hours to get down there. I was alone because you had a better chance of sneaking out of that situation in the dark by yourself. So I snuck out and went down the trail in the dark to our camp to arrange for a stretcher and a radio. It took me a while since it was dark, and I got back to the camp about 4 A.M. They called for a PBY flying boat to come and pick the sergeant up the next morning, assuming we could get him down off the ridge and back to the camp. So we took a stretcher and started heading back in the direction of where he was. By the time we got back up close to that ridge it was about eight or nine in the morning, and the guys were coming down with him. The Japs had left overnight, and our guys started down with him right at dawn. They had made a stretcher out of their jackets and bamboo poles, and they were bringing him down, which was pretty rough. When we met up with them, we put him on the regular stretcher and took him the rest of the way down to the camp. The plane came in and picked him up, and he lived. They ended up giving me a Bronze Star for that.

So here was a guy who wasn't trained for combat, but he wanted to kill a Jap and almost got himself killed! He was a desk sergeant in the orderly room, and he never had even carried a gun! So it was bad judgment for him to be up there in the first place, in a combat situation. Then it was inexperience on his part to get up and walk around at night when we were all looking for the Japs to infiltrate our lines, like they always did. You never got up and walked anywhere at night! And then it was inexperience on the part of the replacement who shot him. That's why we had to train the replacements. Otherwise they could get themselves and the rest of us in trouble.

I think we were in the Admiralties for about a year. After we cleared those islands we stayed there for quite a while. And from there we went in on the Leyte landing in the Philippines. I was right in the first wave. We hit Tacloban there by the airfield. We went right through Tacloban and on from there. After we cleaned that island, we jumped over the San Jacinto Strait and went over to Samar. It was just a little strait that we could cross in boats and on bridges. So we crossed over there, and the Japanese were fighting pretty much the same way, out of the jungles. It was the same tactics they'd used in the Admiralties. They were going hit-and-run, and they'd come in at night or they'd ambush you on the trails.

From there we came back to Leyte, loaded up on ships, and went to Lingayen on Luzon and landed there. And from there we went straight into Manila. We made a wild dash to Manila. They wanted us to get in as quick as we could. We bypassed everything, and we just kept on going. We had tanks, Jeeps, and half tracks, and I was riding in a Jeep most of the time. We were trying to get to Manila as quick as we could, because our assignment was to get to Santo Tomas and liberate the American civilians being kept prisoner there. We were afraid that if we waited, the Japs would start killing them. We knew exactly where they were. We got the intelligence information and knew right where to go.

We encountered a lot of resistance along the way, and the Japanese would kind of hold us down for a while, but we kept on moving. So we went straight in there to Santo Tomas, which I guess had been some kind of college, and we knocked the wall down with the tanks, and there were all the American civilian prisoners in their little huts all over the backyard there. There was a big backyard behind the main building, and the buildings and grounds were behind this big wall. When we hit the wall the Japanese guards got out of there. Those prisoners were happy to see us! They were skinny and starved.

So we stood around there for a while waiting for more troops to come in, and then we kept on moving. What we had to do next was to take Manila, and that was house-to-house fighting. That was an altogether different kind of combat from anything we had done before. We hadn't been trained to fight house-to-house, and we just had to figure it out as we went along. We had been trained as jungle fighters. A lot of times we'd hit some resistance, and we'd call for artillery to help us, and they'd fire point blank at the buildings. And the Japanese resisted all the way.

There were a lot of Philippine civilians killed in Manila during that fighting. Luckily most people got out of the way and ran out, and the city was almost deserted. But of the ones that stayed, a lot of them got killed. Sometimes the Japanese would use the Philippine civilians as human shields when they were trying to get away. The Japs would grab

*The Final Phase of Island Combat*

them and drag them in front of them. We couldn't shoot at the Japanese when they had civilians in front of them.

Crossing the Pasig River was pretty rough. It was the main river that flowed right through the city, and it was a big, wide river. We fought at the old post office, and we tore that place up. It was a big old building about five or six stories high right by the river, and we had to go through there. We were fighting floor-to-floor inside the post office, because the Japanese were holed up in there. There was also a church nearby that got bombed. The front end of the church got blown up, but the altar and everything stayed put. Everything was just perfect except the front end of the church.

So we got through Manila and kept on going, on north of the city to Taytay and other towns north of there, until we cleaned out that whole area and had it pretty well under control. After that we went to a rest camp maybe eighty miles or so outside Manila, and we camped there for a while. Then we started training there for a landing in Tokyo Bay. We were trained and ready when they dropped the bombs to end the war. We didn't know what was really happening until the Japanese started giving up, and then we got word the war was over and the Japanese were surrendering.

They said the guys who had more than 85 points could come back to the States. I think most of our division had more than a 100, so we got replaced right there in Luzon, and they sent us to Manila to wait for a ship to take us back to the States. We came straight back on a casualty ship. We had to help the guys who were in casts, and all that, and we were like nurses until we got to the States. We didn't make any stops, and we came straight back to San Francisco. I got out of the Army about a week later. They put us on a troop train that got us into Denver, to Fort Logan, and I got discharged there.

I came close to getting killed a lot of times. All of us did. I still have a little piece of shrapnel in my back that they never took out. An artillery shell exploded close to me. There was a big chunk of that shell that they took out of my back, but they left the little piece in there. The shell fragment hit a tree first, so it didn't go in too deep, but that was the worst wound I ever got. That was in the Philippines at Leyte. There was a field hospital not too far from the front lines, so after I got hit I went down there, and the doctor pulled the fragment out and put some sulfa in the wound and bandaged it up. I just laid there for a while talking to him, and the next morning I went back to my outfit.

One time I was making my way up a hill through the jungle and there were a lot of holes where Japanese could have been, so I was walking up there with my machine gun just spraying back and forth. Then the gun jammed, so I stopped to try and fix it and was looking down at the machine gun and working on it. All of a sudden, out of the corner of my eye, I saw a Japanese soldier running at me. He had a rifle with a bayonet on the end of it, and he was charging right at me. I didn't have time to do anything but throw the machine gun at him as he lunged at me. That knocked his bayonet to one side, but then he just brought up the butt end of his rifle and hit me right in the forehead with it, just under the brim of my helmet. That sent me flying backward and onto the ground, but before that Jap could finish me off, some of the guys in my squad, who were right behind me, shot him. I still have a knot on my forehead to this day from where that Jap hit me with his rifle butt.

A lot of times we could see the Japanese as they came at us. They'd make banzai charges at night, and that's how they'd come at you. We'd be ready for them, dug in since we knew they'd be coming. We had our fire lines, and everyone had a certain area to fire at, and all that ground was covered with flying bullets when they'd come in. It was all pretty well organized. But it was hard to stop all of them, and we had Japanese that got pretty close, right up to our lines before they got shot. They'd come right in to you. I think the closest they ever got to me was about ten feet away, but we'd always get them before they got to us. Sometimes the Japs would run out of bullets, and they'd come at you with a bayonet on the end of their rifles. A lot of the time their supply lines had been cut, and they would run out of ammunition. So they had to fight with whatever they had, and it was mostly knives and bayonets. That's why they'd fight more at night than in the daytime. We'd never run out of ammunition, and we'd shoot as fast as we could to make it hard for them to get up close to our lines. We'd use artillery support a lot, and we had the Army Air Force, too. We could call in artillery or air strikes to where the Japanese would be, and the Air Force would strafe them to soften them up for us.

Almost all the Japanese carried flags on them, and these were white with a red ball in the middle and lots of Japanese writing on them. So if we had a night attack, there would be bodies laying around in the morning, and every time we killed one of them we'd search their pack and take what they had. We got a lot of souvenirs, and we'd sell them to the Navy. The Navy would buy anything! They wanted souvenirs real bad. We'd even trade souvenirs for whiskey or whatever they had. We had a lot of samurai swords, but we had to leave them there. We couldn't bring anything like that home with us. They said that some of the officers were able to ship them home, but we couldn't. So I brought back one of those Japanese flags. My kids and grandkids had it framed for me, and it's hanging on the wall in my barbershop today.

We took Atabrine all the time for malaria, so we all turned yellow. We were all just as yellow as could be! But when I got discharged and came back to the States and stopped taking Atabrine, I came down with malaria after the Atabrine got out of my system. I had malaria for probably twenty years. This happened to a lot of GIs. I had lived in Rocky Ford, Colorado, and then moved to Boulder, and I found a doctor who was from Austria, Dr. Weicker, and he's the one who cured me. He was very familiar with malaria, started giving me some treatments, and pretty soon I started getting better.

I was in pretty good shape when I got back from the Pacific, except for that malaria thing. But I lost my hearing, and I still can't hear very well today. I guess that came from all the noise of the artillery shells and gunfire. And when I got back I had some trouble with nightmares, though my wife Kate can tell more about that than I can! I'd have bad dreams and she'd try to wake me up and straighten me out. She says I'd be making strangling noises and thrashing around with my arms, and that really worried her. She'd have to be careful in waking me up because I'd be swinging my arms around. I'd dream the Japanese were coming at me at night with their bayonets. In the Pacific we knew they were coming and we'd stop them, but in my dreams they'd get to us, and that's kind of scary. I had those dreams for a long time. Sometimes I'd go for a long time without dreaming, and then all of a sudden I'd have a nightmare. I'm eighty-five years old [in 2004], and I just had one about three months ago.

When I was nineteen in the Civilian Conservation Corps, I started cutting hair. Then when I turned twenty-one and went into the service, I cut hair at Fort Bliss for three or four guys from my outfit. And when I went overseas, I took some hand clippers, and I cut hair overseas. Every time we were in rest camp, I'd cut my friends' hair with hand clippers. Then when I came back I didn't know what else to do, so I went to barber school and got my barber's license. I came up to Boulder in the spring of 1946, and I have been cutting hair there ever since.

## MILO CUMPSTON

MARINES

About 1943 someone asked General Vandegrift, commandant of the Marine Corps, what kind of Marines he had. He said he had two kinds: the kind overseas and the kind going overseas. So they organized another division, and I was in it: C Company, Fifth Engineer Battalion, Fifth Marine Division.

And we had extensive training at Camp Lejeune, North Carolina. This particular unit was the Twenty-second Combat Team, and it was made up of people that could do anything. If you wanted a bridge built, they could build a bridge. If you wanted welders, if you wanted automobile mechanics or tank drivers, or you wanted riflemen, machine gunners, demolition experts, mine disposal—whatever it entailed, that unit was capable of doing it.

We wound up at Camp Pendleton at Oceanside, California. And there we went into further training. Of course mostly it was field training there, night marches and such.

Well, we left there and went to Hawaii. Aboard ship we had five or so cases of polio. It was a Danish ship called the *Sommelsteich*, and I think it had Dutch officers and Javanese crew. And this was in mid-1943. Since there was polio aboard ship, they changed their plans for us. We made port in Hilo, down on the "Big Island" of Hawaii. They put us on narrow-gauge railroad cars, and we went clear around the island to the north end, where they dumped us all off. They hauled us from there down to the beach, and then we had to walk about four or five miles with all our gear to where they set us up. We were there for a month or six weeks in quarantine, because they didn't want the polio to spread.

So the Navy brought in all our supplies—tents and all kinds of stuff.

We had some bulldozers in there, and we knocked down palm trees back about 50–75 feet from the beach, which formed a kind of cove. They wanted us to work a little bit, so we made a beautiful beach out of it there to keep us occupied. And we set up our quarters there. In years since, our cove is now where there's a big Hilton Hotel or Sheraton, and they use that beach. When we got there it was nothing but lava rock and sand. But we did find a couple of temples, too, Hawaiian temples that, while not abandoned, were not in use.

Well, from there we went up to the Parker Ranch, up to a place called Camp Tarawa. And we trained at this camp. And then we did further training over at a place called Mountain View. It was a jungle training camp that sits on the side of the Kilauea volcano. There was very thick undergrowth in there.

So one day word came down that we were going to ship out. We went over to Saipan and then headed north for a four-day run to Iwo Jima. That was the first we knew about it. And when we got to Iwo we never saw such ships like that in our lives. Battleships and destroyers just making it like Indians circling round a wagon train. That's what they were doing at that island, bombarding the hell out of it.

I never had any feelings other than, let's go in and get the thing done. I can't think of anyone not really wanting to get on that island and get this thing over with, because it was only going to be a two-day operation. And I was there for thirty-five days.

Of course we'd all been trained and brainwashed and everything else, and we even had courses in Japanese. We learned to speak a few Japanese phrases. One that I remember distinctly was "*Hadaka nene array.*" It meant, "Take off your clothes. Strip." If you caught prisoners, you'd keep them out there at a distance in case they had a grenade on them or under the armpits, and we'd have them strip to make sure they weren't carrying grenades or weapons.

You waited your turn to get on the landing craft, and we climbed down cargo nets on the side of the ship and into the landing craft. Hell, we were just waiting to get in there and see who is dead and who wasn't. We got into the boats and just circled offshore for quite a while. Some guys got sick. There's always someone sick, puking in the landing craft. But you could look over the side of the landing craft and see Iwo very plainly. And the battleships were banging away at Mount Suribachi. We were underneath their line of fire. Those shells going overhead made a wiggly, swishing sound. You'd hear a gun blast out back of you from some ship, and then something would go over, "shooowwooowwooo," like that, and then you'd hear, "Boom!" kind of deep and muffled. But when we went into the island there was no firing right on the beach where we landed. I couldn't understand why the earlier waves couldn't get in to Green Beach. They said we were the first ones to land there, but there was a lot of evidence that they had tried earlier. We landed and got right up to the second terrace.

And these terraces were beach terraces, steep volcanic sand and hard to get up. Most of our people were in demolitions, which was my assignment. We were there to take out things like pillboxes and blow up caves. We had explosives, shape charges, and packs of C2 and Compound X.

C2 comes in sticks about 2 x 2 x 10 or 12 inches long. There's usually four of them in a pack, and that made up a satchel charge. It was like a backpack you could strap over your shoulder and carry. We used to use the full bags, but if you didn't need a full charge you'd just pull out one stick. You'd punch a hole into it, it was malleable, and put a fifteen-second delay cap and fuse in there, make a ball out of it if you wanted to, strike the fuse, count off about ten, and then throw it. You'd get a hell of a lot bigger explosion than you would from a hand grenade. Then for the C2 you could set the primer cord and wrap the C2 around it. Then you could light the primer cord and the whole goddamned thing would blow.

We also had blocks of TNT. Or you could have shaped charges. We'd blow caves with that stuff. We'd tie these together with primer cord with caps in there, and one would set off another. We'd blow the area right above the cave entrance, and the explosions would cover up the entrance.

The guys in the infantry would carry a stick of C2 with them in their hip pocket. When they got ready to heat a can of pork 'n' beans with a K ration there, they'd take three little pebbles and set them on the ground, put a piece of C2 about the size of your little finger between them, open up the can and set it on the pebbles, light a match, and get that little bit of C2 to burn. The intense heat from that would warm up your can of pork 'n' beans and even bring it to a boil! They figured this out themselves, and we had a hell of a time keeping the infantry away from the explosives we needed to use, because they cooked with it!

We started hitting resistance after we got up the second terrace. And we just dug a hole and stayed there. In this sand, you'd sink clear up to your damn knees, it was so porous. And walking was the big problem, you know? I remember we got the shit shot out of us there up on the second terrace. They started laying a barrage in there on us. There were

*The Final Phase of Island Combat*

a couple of fellows that were shot right away. Mortars started to come in, and I don't know if there was small arms or not, but mortars were the first thing. A lot of people were injured that way.

In fact, right in our area there was a pillbox. We had a Marine gunner in charge of us at the time, Gunner Howell, and I had a friend named George Herman who was an armored 'dozer operator. So we had this pillbox down there, and Gunner Howell told us not to go near it because it was booby-trapped. Well, George, with his bulldozer, he could knock down anything. So George went in and rammed the shit out of the pillbox with his bull-dozer, and all of a sudden, "BOOM," the pillbox blew up. And it also blew that bulldozer upside down. So George crawled out of it, and he's bleeding. Well, what we had in the dozers for protection was sandbags. They were laid along on the floor plates to protect from shrapnel ricochets. Well, when that thing went off it blew that sand up under his arms and his chin, little pieces of sand, you know? Which would give you an idea of why he was bleeding profusely. It was only just superficial wounds, but there was a lot of blood coming out. "Christ, what's wrong with him?" we asked. Well, he was picking sand out of himself for a *long* time. But he was crying, snot was running out of his nose, and he said, "That son-of-a-bitch." He said, "You tell Gunner Howell that I've neutralized that goddamned pillbox!"

When you spend the night under combat circumstances, you stay awake. First of all, there's shooting all night, since we were bombarding them all night. You dig the hole for your foxhole, and there was so much sulfur in there that sometimes when it would rain it'd burn you. You know, if you mix sulfur with water you get acid. And some guys had burns over their arms and legs and back and their asses. There were lots of guys that were evacuated because of burns from sulfur.

Almost everybody's awake at night. There's two of you in a two-man hole, and there was one of you awake all the time. We had K rations to eat, and I don't know when in the hell it was that we had our first real meal. I was there over two weeks before I had my clothes off, my shoes and socks and everything. After we secured Suribachi we turned and went up the island to the north. Part of the forces that went across island turned and went up.

But we were in the area around the first airstrip we took, Motoyama No. 1, and while we were there the first B-29 to land on Iwo came in and skidded along the runway there. And this was while the fighting was still going on. The Japs held the north end of the runway, and we had the south end. We were fighting to clear the whole thing when that B-29 all of a sudden comes in for an emergency landing. He landed in our territory, came to a stop in Japanese territory, and quick-turned around and taxied back to our territory!

Another thing we did as part of our demolitions work was clear mine fields. You'd take your combat knife, your K-bar, and you'd get down on your knees and gently probe the very surface layer, just ease it into the sand at a shallow angle and move over it. We'd have a row of guys doing this, and each guy would have about three feet in front of him he'd be probing, and the guys on the outside of the line would have ribbons where they would mark the edges of where we'd cleared.

I had a crew disposing of those land mines we'd cleared. Normally we would defuse them and set them aside. Well, some of the guys on this disposal crew were kind of crazy. They'd pick the mines up by hand, go over to a little cliff there, and they'd throw them over, trying to get them to go off. What a bunch of nuts!

Right near the end we had the Japs bottled up in a pocket way up in the north of Iwo Jima. One of my corporals, Al Abotellio, had a lot of anti-personnel mines left over, and if you don't use the damned mines you've got to account for them, which was a real nuisance. You have to turn them back in and say why you didn't use them, and all that kind of bullshit. So we went down, and Al set out a mine field just to get rid of these damned things.

Well, shortly after he laid those extra mines out in an area he figured no one would be going into, the Japanese decided to make a counterattack and sneak into the middle of our area. It wasn't a banzai charge. They did this deliberately to start confusion and panic. They did this before dawn, so we didn't know what was going on, and we were asleep in our tents up on the higher ground. Then these mines started to go off in the wee hours of the morning. We didn't know what the hell happened. We thought maybe a chicken got into them or something. All we wanted to do was to get rid of the damned mines anyway, so if they were blowing up that was okay with us. So comes the dawn and there were about thirteen or fourteen dead Japanese out there. They had run into the mine field when their main force pulled out and was going back in a different direction, back to where some Air Corps and other rear-area types were fighting them. There ended up being over 200 Japs killed, but they also killed a number of our pilots, some Marines, and some other support people. So our little mine-field inadvertently helped play a role in stopping their attack!

And that was the last of it. That day we went down past the cemetery to the west beach and went aboard ship. I was really tired. I was excited and everything, you know, because I got off the island alive, but we had to climb up those cargo nets to go aboard, and normally those nets were easy to climb. But the closer I got to the top the more tired I got. And when I finally got on the deck of that ship, I felt totally exhausted. Maybe it was because of the feeling of safety on the damned ship. I didn't need adrenaline any more, and I was just wrung out.

The Japanese were afraid of us Marines more than the Army or the Navy. According to the Japanese, to be a Marine you had to kill your mother and father. That's what the Japanese told us when we got to Japan. I went into Japan, and we carried shoulder holsters and .45s, but we didn't carry any visible weapons. It was late summer, and it was sweaty and hot, but we didn't have any problems with the Japanese.

# BILL HASTINGS
MARINES

I was a corporal with the Fifth Amphibian Tractor Battalion, assigned to the Fourth Marine Division. At Saipan, I landed on Red Beach 2 in my amtrac, and I was told to stay there and follow the orders of some infantry lieutenant. Once we unloaded and were there for a few minutes, he says let's go, and we drove right down the beach, down by the sugar mill. We were the first and only ones to travel for at least a mile-and-a-half along that beach, and we were under fire the whole way. So, anyway, we went down there and there's that sugar mill in ruins, and we were helping out any way we could since we had nothing else to do. We were under heavy shelling, and we had an artillery attack, and we were helping with the wounded.

But of course mortars and stuff were landing all around, and there was one mortar that landed very close, killing the lieutenant as I was standing there talking to him. He saved me because he took everything from that mortar explosion, and I was saved because I was standing on the other side of him. The first three times I got wounded on Saipan were rather trivial, but the fourth one stopped me. A piece of shrapnel went in the back of my leg high, and didn't come out. It protruded through the skin in front of my leg. It traveled a good distance because it went in high and ended up low.

Three or four days later, aboard the transport, the doctor took it out. They measured it, and it was a half inch by three-quarters of an inch. It was a piece of shrapnel that went clear through my leg. It just tore up the muscle, but luckily it didn't hit bone. I could still walk, but I knew I shouldn't be walking. I found that when a guy gets wounded and no bones are broken, you don't hardly even feel it for about three or four hours. I was evacuated out to the ship before I even began to feel the pain. I went back to Pearl Harbor to the hospital, and then I went back to Saipan. We got new equipment and new replacements, and then we were ready to go to Iwo Jima.

On Iwo we hauled the Twenty-fourth Regiment in to the beach. I came ashore in the fourth wave. I think it was around 9:30 or so. We unloaded the troops and went back out and brought ammunition in on the second trip. I landed way on the far right of the invasion beaches. We came up and swung around and went up by a big rock formation called Turkey Knob. There was a big concrete blockhouse up there about two or three stories high. It must have been about sixty feet square. I can't swear to that, but as I remember back it was about that. I saw a 16-inch naval shell hit that damned blockhouse, and it didn't do a thing. It exploded, but it didn't hurt that blockhouse a bit.

We had 129 LVTs in our battalion, and after the first five days we only had 9. We'd land okay and unload, and then we'd go back out to the LST, and from there we were told, okay, go to someplace else, get this ammunition or that ammunition or something, and take it back in to the beach. So we did that a few times, and by then most of the day was over. So, on our last trip out to the ship we didn't go back in because the beach was getting so cluttered that they didn't want us to add to the clutter. Then they told us to stand by because we may have to go in tomorrow to get the guys out. They were seriously thinking of withdrawing, pulling them off. But they didn't.

So the next day we got more ammunition and hauled that in, and brought wounded out, and we could do that as long as our tractor was still in one piece. Our tractor kept going for about three days, and then we got two 37 mm hits. One went through the oil reservoir, and that obviously put us out of business. Amazingly it ran for quite a while after we were hit, but the smoke was pouring out. If it could have been fixed we would have fixed it, but it just finally stopped, and we got out with our machine guns.

After we got out of the tractor we became infantry. We had three machine guns, and from that point on that's what we did. Some people ask, "You were trained to handle an amphibious tractor. How could you suddenly be in charge of a machine gun squad?" Well, all Marines are trained on everything. In theory, every Marine could do just about every other Marine's job. I handled flamethrowers, bazookas, everything.

We had a hell of a time on that island. After you don't sleep for three or four days at a time, you're too numb to get scared; you're just numb.

You then respond from training, your mind is gone, everything is gone, but you are still doing your job as a result of your training. No way could you sleep because they'd jump in the foxholes with you. They were good infiltrators at night and, I mean, you sleep, you die! That's all there was to it. I went four days without sleep. We were physically fit, but we were numb and groggy. On other islands you could pair off and one guy could sleep while the other kept a lookout, but not on Iwo Jima. I must say that I had a lot of respect for the Japanese troops before, but right there those guys were good, dedicated—they were real warriors.

So the fighting was almost the same every day. We'd start moving forward, and then someone would get shot. So where did the shot come from? Then you just cover each other, you just know you have to get up to that certain point where you get fired on. Then the word is passed, "Give this guy some cover, he's going to go up." So everybody around there that had something to shoot was shooting, not indiscriminately, because we only carried eighty rounds of ammunition; we had to measure it off. Say you come up to one cliff with a hundred or so caves. Where's the shooting going to come from? So, you concentrated on the one cave you were interested in. The others, if somebody gets shot they just get shot. You'd try to get in any way you could, side, front, just any way to get there.

When the flags went up on Suribachi, I saw them both from where I was, even the small one they raised first. Of course, in those days I had 20-15 vision. The guys I was with didn't say a word; well, in the first place, we were up where we would have been shot if we'd have made a loud noise, but we all felt, well, I don't know, a thrill, a sense of pride, patriotism, but it wasn't an exuberant jump up in joy and holler kind of deal.

One day I was creeping forward and I saw a Japanese soldier run into a wooden doorway to a cave, and he closed it behind him. I took a big lump of C4 explosive, and I have to admit I hadn't worked with it much, and I didn't know how much to put on this door. So I took a hunk of it and plastered it on the door, wired it up, got back, and blew it up. And I'll tell you that was quite an explosion! It was pretty obvious that I didn't really need that much C4 to do the job. It was a much bigger explosion than I'd expected.

So the dust and smoke is clearing, and Japanese money started to flutter down from the sky. I guess that there was a safe or a strongbox behind that door to that cave, and when I blasted the cave it blew open that safe, and it must have had the payroll for the whole island inside. Those

Japanese bills were blown all over the island. I picked up a few of the bills and I still have them, and that's about the only souvenirs I kept from Iwo.

So, I made it all the way through to the end, and my only wound on Iwo was that I got knifed lightly. I went into a cave, stepped over some bodies, and one I stepped over was still alive. He got up behind me, and I was just able to see him move out of the corner of my eye, my peripheral vision, you know, just in time for me to swing around. He hit my hand with his knife, but I had a .45 in my other hand, so I won and he lost.

What can you say? It's got to be luck or something. But I don't attribute mine to luck. Because after all, you really don't have any luck. I remember it to this day that about the fourth or fifth day on Iwo I'm laying on the beach. It took us three days to get from the beach to that airfield. And I'm on this beach and artillery shells are crossing right overhead, and way into the middle of the night it got to worrying me that they were going to collide right over my head. You know, what a stupid thing to worry about. But it got to bothering me, and I really got scared. All of a sudden—I didn't ask, it just came—a big booming voice from up there someplace said, "You are chosen, do not fear," and I relaxed, and I haven't been afraid since. I'm not a nonreligious person, I'm just kind of in the middle. But after that, every time we were asked to do something, which was constantly, nobody would want to do it unless I was with them. They thought I was going to come through. I still have this feeling. For some reason, I can't explain it, but whenever we were asked to do something they would say, well, Hastings has to go with us. And when I got all the way to the end, and I was one of the few guys who hadn't been carried off that island dead or wounded, I left there and never wanted to see that place again.

Well, I said I never wanted to go back, but—and it wasn't my idea—I ended up going back to Iwo for the fiftieth anniversary trip, and I'll tell you, I didn't like being there. A couple of my buddies called and asked me to go with them, guys who I had been with there, and I says, bullshit, why do you want to go back there for? Well, okay, they wanted to go back, so I said, okay, I'll go with you. And I must say I only went because the guys wanted me to be there with them. I would never have gone back on my own. And immediately, as soon as my friend made the call and I said yes and hung up the phone, I started having flashbacks. Every day, once or twice a day, something would just happen or I'd see something bad, something I'd seen on Iwo. It could be at home or anyplace else, and, boom, I'd get a flashback. It would be a flash of something dangerous or somebody getting killed, or something like that. And this was fifty years later. In fact I hadn't had problems for years until the subject came up to go back to Iwo.

I did have problems for about a year when I first got back from the Pacific. It was like bad dreams, or loud noises or something like that and I'd duck into the gutter or into a doorway, you know, just crazy things. I went immediately into college, and they kept having beer parties and stuff, and, boy, I would go. While I'd be there, I would have a sudden feeling that I've got to get out of there, these people are jammed up too much, they're too close together, and it kind of ruined it. You know, you'd get ten or fifteen guys bunched up together on Iwo and you'd get a mortar on top of you. So I got to Iwo for the fiftieth and I had a few flashbacks that day. None of the other guys I went with on that trip had this happen to them. The flashbacks slowly faded after I returned from the Iwo trip, and about a year later they were gone.

People ask me if it wasn't depressing being in such a bad place with so many bad things happening. But it didn't depress us. We had a job and knew what to do, and we were trained to do it, and we were in a war.

But then some of the guys who were there did stupid things, and it would have been just as well if they had stayed home. I remember one guy, he had two kids and a wife, and he was a replacement in our unit. He stayed on the LST while the rest of us went ashore with the gear. After three or four days he says, "I want to go in to the beach." "What the hell for?" was the reply. "I want to get some souvenirs," he says. "You just stay right where you're at and we'll bring you all the souvenirs you want." So he says, "No, it won't be like getting them myself. I want to get some for my kids." Well, there was no talking him out of it, so he rode in with one of the guys to the beach. Lo and behold, he wasn't there ten minutes before one of those big 16-inch rockets hit that tractor, and nobody ever found a piece of that tractor or anyone that was on it. They were just vaporized. So he got killed and he wasn't even supposed to be there! Now that's the kind of thing that depressed me, not the actual combat but the stupid and senseless things that happened. I'm glad I'll never see that island again.

OPPOSITE: *Joe Woods (kneeling at right front) and other survivors of the Iwo Jima battle, "all cleaned up" just before they left Iwo, 1945.*

## JOE WOODS
MARINES

I was in an amtrac heading into the beach at Iwo Jima, and you have a strange feeling that this is very serious. You see, the best fighting man on earth is nineteen years old. He doesn't have any life experience. So you have an attitude that this is like a football game except that the ones who lose, lose real big. I was apprehensive. It was scary when we landed because there were a lot of people getting killed. When I hit the beach there, I got in a shell hole. There was a big shell hole maybe 20, 30, 50 yards inland from the beach. There were eighteen guys in our field party, our firing party. We were there for a while taking cover while we were being shelled, and a big shell hit on my side just outside the shell hole, and the shrapnel from the explosion sprayed the other side, and got fourteen of them—nine of them were killed and five were wounded, and the four on our side were more or less OK. I just had a concussion where I couldn't hear for about an hour. So if I hadn't been in the sheltered part of the shell hole I would have been killed or wounded like those other fourteen. The funny thing about it was I couldn't hear for an hour or so, so I couldn't run the radio. When my hearing started coming back, there was ringing in my ears and I still have the ringing in my ears, from that explosion.

So during combat you see people killed, and you get hardened to it. I don't say you get used to it, but you get hardened to it and you go on doing what you're trained to do. You can have a few nightmares. The first few nights on Iwo we were just at the end of the air field. We were up at the end of that in a sort of a quarry. We would try to keep star shells lighting the terrain up at night, and the star shells sounded just like bombs anyway. There were caves around there, and one of them was only 50 feet away from where I had set up my radio. The way we'd do it was that somebody keeps watch all night and you keep the star shells going. Every 45 seconds a star shell would go up and that kept the area lit up. All of a sudden a Japanese guy came up out of that cave. He was so close that when he came up, this friend of mine shot him, and the dead Japanese guy fell on me. And that was scary! If I had to tell you one thing I was during my tenure in the Marine Corps, it's that I was scared!

Right near the end of the battle, I sat down and wrote a letter to my folks:

Iwo Jima, Volcano Is.
March 14, 1945

Dear Mom and Pa,

Now that I have some stationary, some ink and something to say, I've decided to write a letter to you, giving you some idea what has been going on here and what I've been doing. First of all, I'd like you to know that the island is secured except for a few pockets of resistance in the northern sector. A lot of Japs have gone to stay with their ancestors, but we've found that the only good Nips are the dead ones. By now the Japs are sensing uneasily that Pearl Harbor was a mistake.

As I said before, this island was the best defended in the Pacific because of the fact that it has natural caves and underground tunnels. We've found

*The Final Phase of Island Combat*

blockhouses that were three stories underground. There is a network of catacombs here that enables the Japs to walk underground and come up in back of the lines and shoot at us from the rear. These are systematically being blown up or caved in by our demolitions squads.

To give you an idea of how we bypass seemingly unoccupied caves, there was a Jap sick bay in a cave just a stone's throw from where I'm sitting now, and there were twenty live Japs in there. Two Marines went down and gathered up all their rifles and ammunition and persuaded (by means of an interpreter) seven of them to come out of the place they were in. The other thirteen said they were going to commit suicide, so we threw 150 lbs of TNT in there to save them the trouble. It's a wonder any of them came out. They usually choose death to surrender, but the Japs on this island have been fighting in China, some of them, and they are a little wiser than the others. They usually kill themselves with a bayonet, but we did find a few that hung themselves. They're a lot more afraid of us than we are of them. Those guys that we did capture turned, in complexion, from yellow to white because every Marine was in favor of sending them to their ancestors. It's a strange feeling you get when you're here in combat. The more Japs you see dead, the better you feel, and you can even look at the most horrible sights and never bat an eyelash. Maybe it's because they seem more like animals than men. You should see some of this stuff they eat, rice and a lot of stuff that looks like chopped onion. They drink this stuff called sake. It's supposed to be like beer but none of the Marines touch it. It's usually booby trapped or poisoned. No wonder these Japs are so small, and their teeth and eyes so bad. They almost all wear thick rimmed glasses (I have two pair I'll send home) and they look the same as in the movies. The only thing, the movies don't make some of these sights as bad as they really are.

The last few days I've been out looking for a few souvenirs. I went up to a little village that the Japs left in a hurry and I found a couple of bayonets and scabbards. I have one which I'll send home. I was looking for a Jap raincoat in a quartermaster dump they had, but they were either full of holes or too small. I had to settle for a rubber suit that one of these big Jap imperial marines must wear. I found a dispatch case with some Jap picture postcards in it which I'll send. I also have a couple of Jap war bonds, a flashlight, a hat, and a lot of other junk that is worth saving.

Their rifles have been collected because of infiltration through our lines. We don't want them to pick up anything they can use as a weapon. A few of my buddies have flags that the Nips wear around their waists or in their helmets. But the Japs I've come across either smelled so bad you didn't want to search them or they didn't have a head, never mind a helmet. When a Marine shoots a guy, he's dead, and there's usually no doubt about it. Lately, up in the northern part of the island, they've been getting a lot of hand-to-hand combat. The Japs charged a tank with long sticks with bayonets and grenade launchers on the end of them. Last week three Marines were in a hole when eight Japs jumped in on them with knives. The Marines got them all (with knives) and, but for a few cuts, they were OK themselves. One of the guys we know was telling us what happened to him. He was creeping up on a pillbox full of Japs. He put his head over a little ridge, and about a foot in front of his face was a Jap 37mm gun. It was lucky nobody saw him, and a couple of minutes later a buddy wiped it out with a flamethrower. Then, after he passed this, a mortar shell landed in back of his heel but it was a dud.

The snipers have knocked off the shooting, but every once in a while you'll hear a zing. That's when we duck. We had a radio watch one night and bullets were bouncing off the rock right next to us. In the morning we found twenty-eight Japs in a hole about fifty yards away who were doing the shooting.

Now as we look down on the beach on which we received such a pounding the first week of the campaign, it looks as calm as Waikiki but not so inviting. As I look back at the day I landed, I wished to heaven I were in the Navy or someplace where I could move to another position on a ship or a plane if they started firing at me. We had to lay on the beach with the ocean at our back, and the only way to go was forward. We had to take it and give back twice as much. I've found it much better to look at a place such as this from the sea or from the air than to land on it and find out for yourself just what and whom you're fighting. I now consider myself a Marine and I'm proud that they let me wear the uniform, because now as never before I realize that it is all they say it is. A girl asked me wouldn't I like to be a sailor and sail all over the place. I've probably had more time at sea than half the sailors in the States now. Well enough of this SEMPER FIDELIS stuff.

Today I received another letter from you with a newspaper clipping showing the mass being celebrated aboard ship. That wasn't our ship but that was the convoy I was in.

When I was on my way here I wrote Frank a letter telling him I was on my way to combat, so he just didn't want to let *you* know. I'd sure like to be with him on the West Coast. That Hollywood Canteen is quite the place, and if you were a serviceman and went there you wouldn't be asking me what attracts us.

It's the same place you saw in the movie *Hollywood Canteen* and everything's free, and movie stars serve you and they have top bands there. John Garfield and Bette Davis run it. One Sunday I went in there and saw Jimmy Dorsey and band, Dinah Shore, Danny Kaye, Lana Turner, Raymond Massey, Gene Tierney, and people like Helen Broderick, Basil Rathbone, Frank Morgan, etc., working behind the ice cream bar, while on the dance floor people like Carole Landis, Dorothy Lamour, Leslie Brooks, Gloria DeHaven, Jean Parker, Martha O-Driscole, June Allyson, etc., etc., wait for you to dance with them. Then you ask me what attracts us. Just a minute, I'm drooling.

I'll take a week of commando training too if I can have the weekend in Hollywood. I hope he stays there for a long time. If he does get shipped out, tell me right away will you? He'll probably write anyway, and maybe he'll be stationed someplace, sometime, where I can see him.

Oh yes, I'm going to join the Veterans of Foreign Wars soon. That's a good thing to belong to.

Well, I guess this is enough for awhile. I hope you're all feeling well. Goodbye, God bless you, and write soon.

> Au revoir.
> Your son,
> Joe

My wife and I were able to go to Iwo Jima for the 50th anniversary trip. Something like 700 Iwo veterans and their wives and families went on that trip. I had a goal on that trip. I had written that letter to my folks and I went back and found that spot and I sat there where I first wrote it and read it aloud. I hoped that would give me some kind of closure to my experiences there, and I think it did. Iwo certainly affected the rest of my life. I was so close to death, and being a young person, you have every reason to live and you're healthy, and it could be taken away so fast. I really decided not to worry about anything anymore because things couldn't get worse than that. That's the whole attitude I took away from that place.

# CHAPTER 14

*"One time one of those Jap planes was heading right toward our ship. He looked like he'd picked us out of all of the rest of the ships around us, and you could even see his smile and everything. He was that close."*

—Dale Killian, COAST GUARD

JIM SPRIGGS, NAVY, USS *Laffey*, destroyer

BOB KARR, NAVY, USS *Laffey*, destroyer

LARRY DELEWSKI, NAVY, USS *Laffey*, destroyer

DALE KILLIAN, COAST GUARD, LST 170

PAGES 460–461: *A Japanese kamikaze aircraft disintegrates under a hail of intense anti-aircraft fire from the USS Yorktown.*

OPPOSITE: *Wartime photo of Jim Spriggs.*

# FACING THE KAMIKAZE, 1944–45

JIM SPRIGGS
NAVY

I was with the *Laffey* from the time it was launched in 1944. I was drafted in 1943. I got my "greetings," so I reported for induction and went to Huntington, West Virginia, another fellow and myself. And they gave us a choice, Army, Navy, Marines, or Air Corps. And this buddy of mine says, "What are we going to do?" And I said, "Well, I'm going to go into the Navy." And he said, "Sounds good to me."

I was on the commissioning crew of the *Laffey*, but I broke my leg and missed the shakedown cruise. So we were over on the Normandy invasion, but we were only over there for about twenty-nine days. Once they got far enough inland they didn't need us anymore. So we hauled tail to the United States, got a new radar, and went through the Panama Canal and over to the Philippines.

Most of the time I spent in the after engine room as a machinist mate. My berth was one deck down from the top deck in the aft part of the ship. When you went down the ladder into the compartment, at the bottom of the ladder, on the right, the center bunk was mine. You can still go down to that compartment on the *Laffey* today and see where my berth was, but on the ship now they have it set up as a display area.

We had a real good ventilation system, so we were able to sleep down in our berth even in the tropics. It got warm, but it wasn't unbearable. The vents were about 12 or 14 inches in diameter, and they put pressure in there and the air moved real good. They also had an exhaust fan so the turnover was pretty fast. We had freshwater showers almost all the time. Very seldom did we have saltwater showers, only when the evaporators were down for a short time.

Really and truly I enjoyed life aboard ship. Sometimes when we were out to sea, when things were quiet out there, there was nothing more peaceful than being out there and watching the sun go down, or watching the sun rise.

When we got up by Okinawa, we knew it would be grim, but we knew we had a job to do and that's part of it. At 8 A.M. on April 16, 1945, I was waiting in chow line. The line was long, so to pass the time we were watching some very large fish that were swimming alongside of the ship. I think they were sharks. I thought to myself, I wouldn't want to be in the water with that bunch, not realizing that in a very short time, it was probably the safest place to be!

When GQ went off, I went to my battle station in the after fire room. We didn't have a working annunciator, so we made steam based on the sound of the guns firing. Now, if the 5 inch was firing the enemy planes were quite a distance out. If the 40 mm guns start firing, they're a little closer, and if the 20 mm start firing, we better get our tail in gear, and that's how we made steam. We knew from the sound of guns what was going on. The smaller caliber the guns firing, the faster we knew we had to go! Pretty soon we heard *all* the guns firing, and we knew we were under heavy attack. We got up as much steam as we could so the ship could do evasive action. But then bombs and planes started hitting the ship, and we knew things were bad.

Most of the Japanese planes had a 500-pound bomb on them, and when they'd hit the ship there was a "ka-wham," and the ship would bounce up and down, and reverb through the ship. I wasn't so concerned with my own safety as I was with the shipmates who were on deck. In fact, I was too busy to think about it other than to wonder who got hurt.

During all that was happening, I went across the shaft alley to put a bilge pump on the line to pump water. As I was going past the No. 3 boiler, the first class water tender said, "Kick that so-and-so." It so happened that the fellow who was operating the burners had frozen with fear, and the water tender couldn't get him to move. I gave him a good kick in the posterior. That did the job, because he was so mad that all he could think of was returning the favor.

The first Japanese plane that hit us caused our rudder to jam hard left. The only way we could maneuver to try to get the planes that were diving on us to miss was to change speeds or reverse direction to throw the pilots' aim off. We also tried to make smoke from the boilers so the ship could get under it and the pilots couldn't see us well enough to fire on the ship. With all the changes going on, it kept all the people in the No. 2 fire room very busy making sure we kept up the steam pressure for whatever was needed to save our ship.

While we were under attack, I had a set of powered phones on for part of the time. I could listen in on what was happening topside. I would then relay information to other people down there, and sometimes we could get a little jump on what we needed to do.

So the ship was hit again and again and took on water. We had water from the after engine room bulkhead on back to the stern, which was about a third of the ship. The fantail was just about under water, and my berth was under water and I lost everything. I got out on deck about fifteen minutes after the attack finally ended. Others were taking care of the wounded and so on, so my main concern was keeping the ship afloat! You know, what could I do to keep it from sinking? So we used cutting torches to stabilize things. We welded plates on the inside and outside of the ship, whatever we could. I had a friend on the ship who grew up in the oil fields, and he was an excellent welder. So he and I worked mostly in our compartment. We'd cut out damaged material and weld new stuff back in and do all kinds of things.

After the attack, a ship came alongside to help us. I think they took our wounded off. I didn't know how bad Jack Ballenger was wounded, so I sent him a pair of dungarees with a dollar in the pocket. That's supposed to be a good omen for a stricken shipmate. Jack was wounded in the right leg and buttocks and his right hand was crippled.

As we had no steering, the other ship would try to keep the *Laffey* from turning while we went forward on the port screw and backed down on the other one to try to make forward progress. When the other ship bumped us, it felt as if the *Laffey* was going to capsize. We were waterlogged and the after compartments were flooded. It didn't feel as if we were going to right ourselves. I think that was when I was the most scared.

This operation failed and we had to wait on a tug to tow us. Since my berth was under water, I strung a hammock from the No. 3 mount, that was all mangled up, over to a gun tub just to the side, and we "hotsacked." That means, when you get out it's still warm and somebody else gets in. Sometimes it rained and I got wet a few times. It'd wake you up in a hurry.

It took twenty-four hours to get to Buckner Bay on Okinawa. By this time I'd been up about thirty-six hours straight, so I just went down into the engine room and fell asleep. So while I was down there they held a muster to see who was missing in action and so forth, and I didn't attend the muster because I was asleep. So later on that day I woke up and went up on deck and there was this yeoman from Minneapolis named Vernon Straus, and Vernon, he and I were always good friends. You know on a ship you pick out some people you get along with, and he was a red-headed little guy and a great friend. So he says, "Where have you been?" I said, "Well, I went down to the engine room and fell asleep." "Well," he said, "we held a muster and you're listed as missing in action." And I said, "Hell, I'm here!" He tried to get it stopped but he couldn't, so I was officially listed as missing in action.

Back in Okinawa, it had taken the better part of a week to patch the ship together so that we could get under way for home. I can't remember the exact day we got under way. It was a somewhat sad occasion when we did set sail, because we were leaving so many shipmates and good buddies behind. I don't think there were many of us who didn't breathe a sigh of relief that we were leaving Okinawa.

On the way back to the States, somewhere between Ulithi and Pearl Harbor, one of the patches on the port side came loose. We started taking on water. Since we were by ourselves, we asked for assistance from a group of fleet tankers that were about twelve or fourteen miles away. They ignored us and kept on going west to where we had just come from. We managed to control the leak and made it to Pearl, where we went into dry dock for repairs. That was a good thing, because we hit a pretty bad storm before we got to Seattle. We'd have probably sunk then!

When we arrived in Seattle, I was on the first leave party for thirty days leave, so I didn't have time to send a telegram to my folks. It was all I could do to get my tickets together and catch a train. When I got home and got off the train I looked my dad up. My dad was a bus driver, and he worked the afternoon shift and I knew where he was. He was very surprised to see me since the telegram from the Navy saying I was missing in action had just arrived a few days before I did! So when he got off his shift that night I went home with him since we lived out in the country. And when I walked into the house, my mom just looked at me and said, "Well, I got the telegram two days ago but of course I didn't believe it." So she wasn't really shocked to see me because she just didn't believe the telegram that I was missing in action. I almost beat the telegram home anyway!

After the ship was on display near Seattle, they fixed it up and I went back out on the *Laffey*. We went back to Pearl Harbor and did plane guard duty for carriers while they were training new pilots.

Just recently I got a call one day from a lady in New Hampshire, and she says to me, "Are you Oliver J. Spriggs?" And I says, "Yes." "Were you aboard the USS *Laffey*?" "Yes." So there was a dead silence at that point. And then she says, "Well, I had an uncle who was killed on the *Laffey*." So I said, "What was his name?" And she says, "Laverne Hazen." That's one of the names on our roster, and he'd been killed. And so I said, "Why sure, I knew him." And again there was a dead silence for a little while. And she said, "Well, you know my mother was his sister, and their mother, my grandmother, she never got over her son's death; she never had closure because they never sent a body back. The only thing she had was the telegram from the Navy saying he'd been killed in action." So we talked an hour or an hour and a half, a long time. And she said, "All these years we have been trying to find somebody who knew him, and we are going to be at your next reunion." She must have seen it probably on our web page. So her mother came with her and she is eighty-four years old, and we met those people at the reunion. And this lady, the sister of the fellow who was killed, I talked to her probably an hour, but I didn't tell her the whole story. But, really, the reason they never sent a body back was that there was no body left. It was a direct hit. There were two other good buddies of mine who were killed at the same time. They were on a 20 mm gun on the fantail. There were three 20 mm mounts on the fantail, and one of those Japanese planes just plowed right in there and blew up. There was nothing left.

Well, I knew Laverne Hazen real well. His bunk was probably ten feet from mine, and we stood watches together all the time. And really and truly, I have trouble even now dealing with that when I talk about it—or any of them for that matter. My shipmates during that time were closer than my own family. Because we went through a lot with each other in such a way. That may sound ridiculous, but it's true.

## BOB KARR
NAVY

was with the *Laffey* from the beginning, when it was launched, and I had been on the ship for the Normandy invasion, and then out to the Pacific. First we were in the Philippines and had encountered kamikazes there, so we kind of knew what to expect. I was assigned to Mount 43, which was a quad-40. It was right behind No. 2 stack on the starboard side. We heard that we were going on picket duty and we pulled alongside the ammunition ship to unload our empty shells and take on more ammo. We all felt that our time of testing was near at hand.

Our first day out there on station, Saturday, was rather quiet. We had moved north to relieve the ship that had been on picket station No. 1. We heard of a few bogeys around but none came close to disturb us.

Sunday was much the same. G.Q. was before sunrise, and we kept a constant lookout from sunrise to sunset for any bogeys that might appear. It was really a pleasant day.

Monday, G.Q. again was called at sunrise. And then it all started at approximately 8 A.M. I heard over the headphones that a large number of bogeys were on the radar screen. They were approaching us from the north. The skipper already had alerted the engine room and we were on the move.

On Mount 43, we all began to scan the horizon. It wasn't long before we spotted a faint outline over Mount 3 to the stern of one or two bogeys scouting out the ships awaiting them. Then I heard on the headphones, "Bogeys approximately nine miles." They closed to about seven miles, then retreated.

Now the word came over the headphones that as many as fifty bogeys were in our vicinity. We now were up to full speed and moving away from the previous sightings. On the horizon aft of Mount 3, the bogeys appeared. Mount 3 commenced firing, and soon we saw smoke as one of the bogeys went spiraling into the sea. But then there was an onslaught of planes from many directions.

We in Mount 43 spotted a plane about 100 feet off the water, coming in on the starboard beam. It was too close for the 5-inch guns, and they already had targets, so it was up to Mounts 41 and 43 and Mounts 21 and 23 to stop this plane. As it bore down ever closer, we could see the pilot trying desperately to make his target, and we were firing at it as fast as we could.

Our guns were down level with the sea, and the bullets from the 20s and 40s began to shred the plane as it got closer, and the *Laffey* began turning to port. When the plane was only 100 yards away, it slowly rose up and then plunged into the sea. Those of us in Mount 43 let out a yell of victory. That was short lived.

Almost immediately, another bogey came in from the starboard bow quarter. We fired a few bursts. The plane passed over the ship and our gun cut out as we swung past the No. 2 stack. The plane continued on a swooping quick turn out over the port side and back toward the stern at a steep angle and hit Mount 44, which was diagonally across from us on the other side of the ship. But as it hit, the plane cartwheeled over Mount 23 and those of us in 43, spewing gasoline and starting fires, and there was flying debris everywhere as the plane blew up.

Right before the plane crashed, my crew could see it would hit us, so they jumped over the gun tub and down underneath to the main deck. But I had headphones on and a helmet on top of that so I couldn't get loose or I probably would have jumped down to the deck and out of the way also. So, I stayed on the gun with my headphones as the plane cartwheeled right over the top of me. About all I could do was dive down under the gun and try and get some protection from the plane that was disintegrating into pieces as it crashed into and over the ship. My pointer, K. D. Jones, and I both dove under the gun. Pieces of the plane were flying over and around us, and the generator out of the engine of the plane ended up in the gun tub with us.

The fires set off the 40-mm ammunition stored around Mount 44. The gun covers on Mount 43 were burning, so it was time to get out of there. As I crawled on my stomach around the gun tub and toward No. 2 stack, exploding ammo kept whistling by. I went to the gunner shack under Mount 41 to collect my thoughts and to thank God that I was still alive. I then moved down to the main deck amidships. Every time a plane would come at the ship, there were other crew members who had taken cover there, and they would run back and forth to get on the opposite side of the ship from where a plane looked like it would hit. I figured this wasn't a great place to be.

About this time I saw Jake Snyder and Larry Delewski filling and carrying clips of 20-mm ammo to Mounts 20 and 21. So I helped them, and I made one trip to Mount 21 and was just going in to pick up one for Mount 20 when Lt. Runk told me to go to the bridge and tell Commander Becton that the aft steering room was flooded and the rudder jammed. I carried the message to the bridge then returned to pick up a clip of 20-mm ammo for Mount 20. All this time the attack was going on in full swing, with Japanese planes zooming down at us, guns firing almost constantly. Planes were hitting the ship and there were explosions from near misses. It was pretty chaotic.

I was intent on carrying ammunition to help out the various gun mounts that were still firing and didn't even see a Japanese plane come zooming low right over the ship. It clipped the radar mast, and an American Corsair fighter that was right behind it also clipped the mast, and both crashed into the ocean off to the side of the ship.

Just as I was on my way back down the ladder after taking the clip forward, I saw a big explosion as a bomb hit right close to the ship. Shrapnel from that bomb killed Stanley Wismer in Mount 20 and fatally wounded Joe Mele who was in the handling room of Mount 2. As I touched the main deck, right by where the bomb exploded, I heard this voice behind me saying, "Please help me." There stood Fred Burgess on one leg, the other had been torn off above the knee by shrapnel from the bomb. This was a very difficult thing to see. He was one of the gun crew on Mount 20 and he was trying to get out of the way as that bomb hit. I caught him as he collapsed, and laid him on the deck. There wasn't really anything that I could use for a tourniquet, so I got ahold of a guy's shirt and tied it on his leg. We carried him into the wardroom to be cared for, but they couldn't do much to save him because he had lost too much blood. After I came back out, I found Wismer lying on the main deck. I gave him artificial respiration, but soon one of the officers came by and said he was gone.

I went back to see if Jake and Larry were still loading ammo. Someone stopped me and asked if I could help Zupon. He had been up in one of the forward gun mounts. A piece of shrapnel had ripped away part of his shoulder, and someone had to keep pressure on the artery to slow the bleeding. I stayed with him until help came and he was transferred to a waiting vessel.

By this time the attack was over, and word was passed to jettison all loose gear to lighten the ship. We were down under water at the stern. I went back to Mounts 43, 44, and 23 and disposed of all loose material, including the Japanese generator that had landed in the gun tub with K. D. Jones and me.

But through all this I didn't get a scratch. I've never quite figured that out. The one time I figured I should have gotten hit was when I was crouched down in the gun tub just after that first plane hit. The ammo from the gun was going off in every which direction. You couldn't know where they were coming from. I was lucky I wasn't hit.

That night, I lay down in the Mount 43 gun tub, using my life preserver as a pillow, and I slept all night long—I didn't wake up until morning. We were totally given out. My usual sleeping quarters were under six feet of water near the stern of the ship. I had been standing watch the night before and had only slept about three hours or so, so I was really beat.

I've got some souvenirs, some pieces of shrapnel, and a 7-mm bullet from a strafing Japanese plane that hit the ship. Thankfully the skipper was able to maneuver the ship to keep most of the damage to the stern. All of the crew at the stern, from the No. 2 stack on back, took an awful beating, but it did save the ship. The idea was that if we were under attack, to turn the stern to the attack.

We got the ship back to Seattle, and it went on display with descriptions of where the planes had hit, where people had been killed, and so on. Thousands of people came down to tour the ship, and members of the crew were standing by to answer questions. One of the ladies who came aboard to tour the ship started talking to me, and she offered to take me for a car ride. And I ended up marrying her! I guess that affected my life a little bit. If the *Laffey* had never been attacked, I would have never met my wife! I guess it worked out. So I came back to Seattle with my wife and have been living here ever since. I haven't really had any problems with nightmares, but I often think of the fellows who were killed. A lot were personal friends, and I knew them very well. We had been together for almost two years. But a lot of us survived, and I believe God's protective hand was upon us that day.

## LARRY DELEWSKI
NAVY

I was part of the original crew of the *Laffey*. I was the gun captain of Mount 3. That was an enclosed gun turret with two 5-inch guns near the back of the ship. I usually slept inside the gun mount itself on corrugated steel. I kept a blanket in a little storage area in the mount where there were tools, and that's where I kept my blanket. I spent many a night in there because it was not only close to my duty station, but with the living conditions on board ship our bunks were stacked three high in the lowest part of the ship, with a very small overhead. My bunk was the middle bunk. If I was in my bunk and put my fingers to my nose I could touch the guy above me. So it was more comfortable in the gun mount.

ABOVE: *The USS* Laffey *is down by the stern after being attacked by 22 Japanese kamikaze aircraft on April 16, 1945. The mangled remains of the two 5-inch guns in Mount 3 near the stern, one canted up at a severe angle, are the result of one of the kamikazes that crashed into the mount and exploded, ripping open and destroying the mount, killing six and severely wounding six members of the gun crew, and ejecting gun captain Larry Delewski out the far side. After the attack, Jim Spriggs strung his hammock from this shattered gun mount and slept outside, since his berth, below deck in the aft part of the ship, was under water. Bob Karr's battle station, the gun tub of Mount 43, is visible on the starboard side just behind the number two smoke stack.*

We had an experience at Ormoc Bay in the Philippines before we got to Okinawa. One of the destroyers, the *Hughes* was badly damaged by kamikazes, and the *Laffey* was sent to take her in tow, which we did. And then a seagoing tug came and took over the tow, and then we tied up alongside and moved along with this other ship. We had first-hand experience of our doctors and our medical people going aboard and helping out. We saw the results of a direct hit up close while the fires were still being fought with their hoses and our hoses as well. So we knew exactly what kamikazes could do.

After that we got sent out to Picket Station 1, which was approximately seventy miles north of Okinawa. The *Laffey* was part of an umbrella of U.S. warships spread out in position to pick up incoming Japanese planes on radar and to protect the larger ships of the fleet farther south. Once the planes were contacted, the communication team, on temporary duty from its carrier-based fighter squadron, would notify their home base from on board the *Laffey*. Fighter planes would be launched to intercept the incoming planes. The Japanese came to realize that they were not doing the kind of damage they hoped to do because of this early warning system. They decided they had to get rid of this picket line.

Two basic kamikaze techniques were used. Sometimes a lone raider would sneak in low to the water to do the damage. At other times the pilots might use a mass attack. They chose the mass attack technique for the morning of April 16, 1945, when we were on duty on Picket Station 1. In all, some eighty planes appeared on picket line radar screens that morning. Of these planes, twenty-two chose to dive at the USS *Laffey*.

Some people ask me if we knew what we were getting into, and the answer is yes. This is because on April 12, just prior to joining the picket line, the *Laffey* had entered the U.S. anchorage at Karama Reto adjacent to Okinawa. We went in there to reload ammunition and to refuel. We also got our mail that day. And we got two replacements, part of the normal rotation of personnel, one of which was assigned to my gun, and it turned out he lasted three days.

At Karama Reto, when we anchored, what we saw was a graveyard of destroyers and small ships at anchor, some with the front blown off, some with the back blown off, some with the top blown off, you name it. This damage was a result of confrontations with kamikazes on the picket line. These ships had been hit from every possible angle. It was all very real. No, we were not blind and we were not stupid. We knew where we were headed and what could happen. There was no question in anyone's mind that this was serious business. We knew we had to be at our best. But we were to learn that even at our best, when twenty-two planes dive at a single ship in less than eighty minutes some were bound to get through.

So when we got our assignment to Picket Station 1, it wasn't like we just went out there and got attacked immediately. The first day it was quiet, and the second day was quiet, but it was the morning of the third day when we had trouble.

My battle station on that morning was as captain of Mount 3, the same as it had been on D-Day and at Cherbourg in Europe. It was the same station I had manned on all *Laffey* operations, whether with the carriers on a raid of Japanese cities or with a bombardment group in support of an invasion of Mindoro, Luzon, Mindanao, Iwo Jima, or Okinawa. So, the first thing that morning I was waiting in line for breakfast, and I was halfway down the chow line, still on the main deck and hadn't gotten to the ladder that would have taken us down to the mess hall. So when the enemy planes were detected in our area, general quarters was sounded. At that point, you forget about breakfast!

Yes, my gun crew was experienced and well practiced. We had no trouble firing both guns of the mount every three seconds to take advantage of the latest fuse setting. This rate of fire was especially important when firing at incoming aircraft.

As G Q sounded we all got into the turret, and I was looking for targets. My normal position as mount captain during antiaircraft action was in an open hatch on the top of the mount. This was my lookout position. I saw a Japanese plane off to starboard, and we were aiming in that direction when another Japanese plane slammed into the port side at the main deck level just under a cluster of five torpedoes forward of our mount. The plane hit the after "head" at the main deck level exploded and came apart. Because our turret was turned away, one of the plane's wings hit the back of the mount, and this caused a terrible fire in this after main-deck area, including the back of Mount 3 above the main deck and in the ammunition handling area below. We had what I call a two-story fire. The fire was in the gun turret and down in the handling room because the gun mount consisted of the enclosed turret mount above the deck and the handling room directly below the mount. The fire spread from the burning gasoline that was in the wing of the plane that hit us. As it turned out, this hit would be critical because the heat of the fire in the after deck-house warped the closing device for my top look-out hatch.

Once the fire was under control, the hatch could only be opened a few inches. It no longer was useful as a lookout position.

When we got the fire under control my orders were to switch to local control and pick my own targets. I couldn't use my top hatch any more, and that's why I then had to partially hang out the hatch on the side of the mount to find targets. This hatch was on the port side in relation to the ship, but that was the right-hand side of the gun mount since our guns faced to stern.

The area most damaged by this first plane was part of the after deck-house, which included some officer's quarters and the crew's head. This combination shower, sink, and toilet area, while needed, was not vital to the ship's fighting ability.

Right after we were back in business, my first target came in from the stern slightly to starboard. So I spotted the target by eye and told Calvin Cloer roughly where it was. He was the pointer. He made the guns elevate and depress, and he closed the electrical firing circuit when on target. Jim LaPointe was the trainer. He made the gun traverse horizontally. Once they picked it up on their screen with cross hairs in the middle, which is like a simple sight, they would center on it themselves. There was one person responsible for elevation, and one person responsible for training the gun from side to side. With great teamwork they locked onto the target. So we aimed and fired and shot that plane right out of the sky!

More Japanese planes were coming at us, so we helped the 40-mm crews of the quad-forties on top of the after deck-house to bring down their chosen targets. Then I was in the process of choosing the next target for Mount 3. Because the top hatch was no longer of use, I was hanging halfway out the portside hatch. I was looking out and spotted a Japanese plane that was to port, and we were in the process of training around to that target. I can still remember yelling to "Frenchy" LaPointe to train to a bearing of 135 degrees for the next target. While the mount was turning, another plane came in from the starboard side and made a direct hit on the left side of the gun mount, the opposite side to where I was leaning out the hatch. The plane hit, and there was a terrific explosion. The enclosed gun mount was blown apart, and everyone in the mount was either killed or suffered from internal injuries from concussion. But I was blown out of the hatch by the concussion, and I flew out and over the deck in the direction of the front of the ship. I became a projectile!

The force of the explosion was great enough to drive the left-hand gun so it was pointed almost straight up into the air, in a position at least

70 degrees above the right-hand gun. These guns normally move and remain in tandem. One whole side of the turret was missing, and that was 1-inch thick steel.

In all, six men died in Gun Mount 3 that day. Another six who did survive went to hospitals for anything from a couple of months to as many as twenty months, with severe internal injuries from the concussion and burns.

I have often said that my guardian angel was with me that day. If the mount had turned a degree or two less, I'd have been blown over the side and into the sea. If the mount had turned a degree or two more, I'd have been blown into that still-burning mass of twisted metal that had formerly been the head area. As it turned out, when I regained consciousness I was draped over a K-Gun, which is a depth charge launching device some fifteen feet forward of Mount 3 on the main deck. And amazingly, my injuries were minimal. I had some pieces of shrapnel in my back, which they later picked out and cauterized, and I had some burns above the collar on my neck.

When I opened my eyes the first thing I saw was this communications officer, Commander Runk, throwing a dud over the side. This was an unexploded projectile that was on the Japanese plane, and he just heaved it overboard. The Japanese used makeshift bombs made from stockpiled projectiles from cruisers and other ships that had been sunk.

So, my first reaction was to get back to Mount 3. The first thing when I got back there, I found Chester Flint pinned in the starboard hatch to the turret by parts of the kamikaze's motor. I tried to free him, but he died in my arms. This was very difficult. You must realize we lived closely together, and I was very close to the guys on my gun crew. We were a tightly knit team. So I knew Chester very well. We not only had General Quarters together, but we stood the same watch. Chester came from an area where there weren't too many people who could read. There were occasions where he wanted to send his girlfriend a gift and I'd write to my mother and she'd mail his girlfriend a gift, and then he'd pay me. And he died in my arms.

On the starboard side there were 20-mm guns right below the bridge, and next thing a Japanese plane hit right over there. A young man who lived no more than fifteen miles from where I live now in Pennsylvania was one of the people killed there. This man who was killed, Wismer, it was only a short time before that that he and a man by the name of Ketron, switched positions at Wismer's request. Wismer didn't like the idea of being in Gun Mount 1 with everything closed in, and when there is any kind of weather they really batten things down. And he got tired of being cooped up in the turret. You know, there are thirteen people in there in that small space of the mount, and that's close quarters, and he got tired of that business, and actually got permission from the people up the line including the gunnery officer to switch assignments with Ketron. And Ketron was equally tired of being out in the weather. And that simple switch determined their fates. Wismer is on the list of fatalities, and Ketron and I just talked the other day.

Do not think for a minute that the attacks were random or haphazard. The first attacker went for the bridge and the radar antenna. The next one was sure to dive into the stern to jam the rudder. Once the crew had to wait to see them and could no longer steer, the ship could become a sitting duck. But not the *Laffey*. Sure, our radar was gone and the rudder was jammed and almost every compartment aft of the stacks and engine rooms was flooded, but *Laffey* still made steam and continued moving—in a circle, but we were moving.

So, there wasn't much more I could do there except go to the bridge and report that Mount 3 was out of action. I was told to take over Mount 2 just forward of the bridge. The man who had charge of Mount 2, Warren Walker, had gotten some shrapnel wounds and had gone down to see the medics. I had some shrapnel in the back of my neck, which some shipmates picked out. Later the wounds were treated along with some neck burns. Mount 2 was under the control of the fire control people, so at that point it's just a matter of making sure it's loaded properly and on time. The actual aiming and fuse setting is done by the fire control people. We were still under attack and Japanese planes were still hitting the ship; I could feel the impact and hear it. And we were firing all the time at planes that were coming at us. Although there was no particular damage to Gun Mount 2, a piece of shrapnel went right through the watertight hatch, and right into the stomach of one of the crew, a guy named Mele, and he only lived a few minutes. That hatch is just two sheets of aluminum on that watertight door, and it just came right through there and got him.

After the attacks were over I went on back to my area, back around Mount 3, and did what I could to help the damage control party. Their assignment was to know every compartment in their area and where every available source of water would be for fighting a fire. We had all undergone a lot of fire-fighting studies and training.

On that day the USS *Laffey* lost thirty-two men. Another seventy-one were wounded. Mine is only a small part of the story. There are dozens of individuals who could tell similar stories about their experiences on the

*Larry Delewski*

*Laffey* and other ships that served on radar picket duty off Okinawa. There were actually four destroyers hit that same day, and at one point I heard we had as high as eighty enemy planes on our radar screen. Almost 200 men were killed, and another 300 or so were wounded in that one day.

Later in the day on April 16, 1945, seagoing tugs came alongside the *Laffey*. Lines were put over to help keep us afloat. Pumping did little good because of holes in the bottom. People ask, how did you get holes in the bottom of the ship when the enemy planes and bombs were striking the ship above the waterline? Well it's because the Japanese had taken big shells from ships that had been sunk, and put fins on them, and made them into crude bombs. So when they dropped one of those on the ship from above, it penetrated the main deck and the decks below and kept going right out the bottom of the ship. And that's how we got holes in the bottom. The ship was taking on water from those holes so that the main deck was only a couple of feet above the water in the stern before we could temporarily plug those holes.

We were moved to a shallow-water anchorage where underwater welders patched the hull so *Laffey* could be pumped out. Once *Laffey* was pumped out and the rudders freed, the ship was steered manually. It was a long way back to Guam, Hawaii, and eventually Seattle.

After the war was over I did have some nightmares and other problems. As a matter of fact, to this day don't walk up on my blind side or to the side of me. I can be sitting and watching a TV show, and if somebody comes up on the side I'll jump. That's part of the enduring thing from the *Laffey*. In Seattle, when she was once again ready for sea and was heading for Bikini Atoll, the captain called me in and told me he wasn't taking me along this time, that he thought I had had enough. So I was transferred to the Naval Hospital in Seattle where I proceeded to tear up a few pillows and things in my sleep. I was having nightmares. When my wife and I were first married, we didn't dare have an alarm clock. She'd get down on the side of the bed and reach in with one hand and shake me to wake me up. She never knew what I would do. It doesn't happen too often any more.

My experiences on the *Laffey* affected the rest of my life. One of my prayers that day during the attacks on the ship was certainly that if I was spared I would try and do something worthwhile with my life. I made up my mind right then that if I was spared I was spared for a reason, and I ended up teaching special education for twenty years. I did it and I felt like it was right.

*Facing the Kamikaze*

## DALE KILLIAN
COAST GUARD

The draft was right on me, so I went and signed up in the Coast Guard. I volunteered for sea duty. We shipped out to the Southwest Pacific and went across in a cargo ship, an AKA. We got to Hollandia, New Guinea, and there's where we got our LST. It was quite interesting, and Hollandia was quite a base. We'd go back there for supplies and take a big company of either Marines or Army and make an invasion on up the coast. We must have done about ten or twelve invasions up there. Then we headed to the Philippines, and then we made one over in the Dutch East Indies, over at Morotai.

On an LST there's an upper deck and then there's a lower deck, and we'd fill that upper deck and the lower deck with troops, vehicles, or whatever you had for a landing. We unloaded everything out the big bow doors that would swing open when you got to the beach. A ramp would let down and you'd roll things right on to the beach. There was an elevator there in the bow, and you could lower things down from the upper deck and roll it right out on the beach.

I had sixteen months' duty over there, and it passed pretty quick. We had a Frenchman that was a skipper for a long time, and he was out of New Orleans. He was pretty rough, but he was a brave soul. He'd take our ship and more or less stick his neck out, as well as his crew's. One night we were in convoy off the coast of New Guinea somewhere. We'd unloaded up the coast and were heading back empty, with just the crew on board. So it's the middle of the night and one of our LSTs got torpedoed. In those situations the convoy would usually go on in a group, because it was dangerous to stay behind to help a ship that had been hit, to leave the protection of the other ships. But our captain said, "Well, we're going to stay behind and help this ship." There was one other LST that stayed back with us to help. There must have been fifteen to twenty ships in the convoy, but two of the LSTS stayed back, and one LST towed the ship that had been hit. One of the destroyers also stayed back with us and tried to protect us. Of course everyone thought the skipper was pretty brave, because we would have been a dead target for more torpedoes.

When that LST got hit, I didn't hear the explosion, but I heard GQ going off. On our ship the GQ alarm was a bell, and it would be like, "Ring, ring, ring, ring," a real solid ring, real fast. My GQ station was in the front of the ship near the big gun, a three-inch gun. There was one in the front and one aft. I wasn't on the gun crew, but I was up there just to help the gunners mates. So I was up there at my GQ, and we stopped to help the other ship. It had been hit but it wasn't burning, it was listing. Some of the crew of this ship that had been hit were thrown into the water, so I got orders to man the small boat, the LCVP, and I went out and picked up a couple guys that had their life jackets on. It was dark, of course, and it wasn't real easy to find them. But they were hollering, and even though it was a danger to have any light, we had a flashlight we used to see them. The LCVP was noisy, so I'd have to throttle down and listen for them yelling and then go in that direction.

One of them had been doing guard duty in the aft gun turret, and he just got thrown right into the ocean by the explosion. Luckily he had his life jacket on. You talk about a guy happy to be picked up! He was smiling, and after I picked him up he said that when the torpedo hit, it threw him so doggone high in the air he thought he'd never hit the surface! And when he plunged into the water he thought he'd never come back up.

After I picked those guys up and they were alive, I had a kind of a feeling of accomplishment. My mission had really been taken care of, I'd saved some lives; so I wasn't near as enthusiastic after that as I was before. I was ready to go home. I had a sort of sense of completion of things.

We had two or three attacks by those suicide Jap planes. There were several times when we got real scared, because you could see that it's a suicide plane and it's heading right your way. Of course a lot of times they'd tell you, "Hit the deck!" and we'd lay down, but you'd keep watching. I remember one time one of those Jap planes was heading right toward our ship. He looked like he'd picked us out of all of the rest of the ships around us, and you could even see his smile and everything. He was that close. All the guns were turned loose on him. He was firing away, too, but just be-

*Facing the Kamikaze*

fore he got to the ship he turned right a little bit through all this ack-ack, and he was weaving right through it and didn't seem to get hit for some reason. And he turned and headed off down toward a destroyer, and that destroyer got him just like that. This was at Lingayen Gulf. It was really scary. Of course everybody was scared, but we never did get hit.

There were five boys in my family, and I had a brother in the Army and one in the Navy and I was in the Coast Guard. While I was overseas one thing that was real distressing to me was that I lost my brother in Europe. At that time we had a very compassionate skipper. He was a different skipper from the Frenchman. But I never will forget that he wrote my mother the nicest letter, but it was a pretty trying time there for awhile. And it wasn't too many months afterwards that I was able to come home.

But mainly boredom was the problem, and a lot of people tried to pass it off by reading a few books and magazines. Some of them would just do a lot of extra sleeping. I'd do some reading and try to pass it off that way.

After I came back from sea duty I was stationed up at the Coast Guard base in Seattle. Of course, the war in Europe had just gotten over as I was coming back, and we kind of thought we might have to go back and invade Japan. But then they dropped the bombs and that was that. I stayed in touch with my shipmates for years, and we've had a few reunions. I made three or four of them.

But war is for young people. They can take things like that. I think there was something about being a young man out there in the Pacific that probably helped me mature more, and to assess values a lot better. So I guess it had a lot of good effects. It's a rough experience as you go through it, but I'm glad I went through it. And I've always been proud to have played a small part in the war. I think our generation can take some pride in what we did out there in the Pacific during wwii.

# CHAPTER 15

*"I can still feel the apprehension of coming off that gangplank to step foot on Japan. I was the fifth officer in line coming off that gangplank, and there were seventy-five or a hundred Japanese standing there."*

—Ken Guenther, ARMY

HOADLEY DEAN, ARMY, advance party into Japan

KEN GUENTHER, ARMY, Philippines, Hokkaido

PAGES 482–483: *Hiroshima, October 1945. This is the view that greeted Harry Fukuhara when he returned to find his family.*

# THE SURRENDER, AND ENTERING JAPAN, 1945

HOADLEY DEAN
ARMY

**W**hen the war got going, I wrote to the Army: "I have had four years of ROTC and I can't see very well, but there has to be something I could do for my country. I'm ready to be called back to duty. "Six months later I got orders to report to Camp Dodge, Iowa, the Des Moines Reception Center.

I worked through the Seventh Service Command Headquarters in Omaha. But I wanted to go overseas. Then, in January 1945, I finally received orders to go overseas, by air to Luzon Island in the Philippines.

We landed at Clark Field on Luzon so soon after it had been taken back from the Japanese that we weren't sure whether or not it had become fully secured. We were there only a week or two before orders came down for us to get our stuff ready because we were being sent to the Philippine island of Leyte. We landed on a sandy beach just outside the town of Tacloban and were assigned to the Fourth Replacement Depot. When I walked into my assigned tent, lo and behold, there was one of my Alpha Tau Omega fraternity brothers from the University of South Dakota!

At the replacement depot I wound up doing just what I'd done Stateside, except that now the daily requests were from combat units asking for so many riflemen or machine gunners or cooks, or whatever. I will never forget how distressing that job could be at times. Here I was sending guys fresh from the States straight into combat. Down on the island of Mindanao, the Americal Division was suffering very severe casualties and would send messages like, "You gotta send us 500 riflemen, because we got wiped out yesterday." That made me feel both like God and really depressed—with the power and responsibility to order 500 guys to go replace 500 who'd been shot, and knowing damn well a lot of them would get shot, too!

Oh, my God, the heat in the Philippines! We would often have to tie cloths around our heads to keep the sweat from dripping onto our papers. We'd quit work about 11:00 in the morning, go over to the mess hall and eat, and then go to our tent and lie there until two or three o'clock in the afternoon, because in the middle of the day it was just too hot to work. It was just stifling! Yes! I remember the heat!

Around the first of August 1945, we could tell there was something going on. You can always tell in the military, because that's when people become more close-lipped and have a different attitude. And sure enough, they came in and said, "Pack up all your stuff to go aboard ship!" So, we got it all ready, boarded the ship, and at sea were told that we were going to the China coast, because the Sixth Army was going to invade Japan from there.

While we were on our way, we heard about the dropping of the atom bombs, and that caused considerable apprehension! What does it mean? What's this gonna mean to us? You see, at that point we didn't know all the facts. We knew those bombs were powerful, but we didn't realize how powerful. Then when they told us that instead of going to China we were now proceeding directly to Japan, we thought that these new power-bombs had simply advanced the invasion date and that we still would have to fight our way in.

Then we got word that the Japanese had surrendered, but even then I was afraid. I knew that in every battle in the war so far, the Japanese troops had chosen to fight to the death rather than surrender or be captured. In the recent battle for Okinawa, where they had to have known they would lose in the end, they still fought so ferociously as to make it one of the bloodiest battles in World War II. So, now, how were they going to respond to the first foreign conquerors in Japan's entire history about to set foot on their home soil?

When the Japanese sent a pilot out to help guide our ship through the rocks and such and into the harbor of Yokohama I felt a lot better, but when we got off the ship each of us was carrying a .45 caliber pistol and a carbine rifle.

We unloaded directly onto the pier and into trucks. While loading up I saw the Japanese eyeing us and still wondered whether some of them were about to start shooting. But, surprise! Unbelievably, they not only didn't look like picking a fight or even hating us, but some of them even

*The Surrender, and Entering Japan*

appeared happy to see us! Big crowds of them lined the streets as we drove along. They were silent, but if you can believe it, some of them actually gave us the "V for victory" sign, and I even thought I heard one of them say, "Hello, G.I. Joe."

We rolled out on the road from Yokohama to Tokyo and stopped at Zama Military Academy, which they told us was the old West Point of Japan. There they put me and the other officers into some old Japanese barracks, and we went about setting up the Fourth Replacement Depot. We were attached to the Sixth Army, which was the one that did the invasions, but now they changed the designation to Eighth Army, which would be the one that administered the Occupation of Japan. And we became the replacement depot and deployment center charged not only with sending replacements to various military units in Japan but also with sending people home to the States.

I spent about six months in that job and then was rotated home and received my discharge.

After I came home I served in Washington as assistant to U.S. Senator Harlan Bushfield and then U.S. Representative Harold Lovre. Back in South Dakota, I was made manager of the Black Hills and Badlands Association, a tourist promotion group. With some partners I founded a stock brokerage and real estate firm in Rapid City, and served as campaign manager for Joe Foss, my old college friend and Medal of Honor winner, in his successful run for the governorship of South Dakota. Among other posts, I have served as South Dakota Highway Commissioner, a director of Frontier Airlines, a director of the National College in Rapid City, and president of the Mount Rushmore Memorial Society.

The world has been good to me since the war, and I have to say I owe much of it to the maturing experience of having been thrust as a green country kid into what amounted to an executive position in the Army, and to the human relations experience I gained there in dealing with the stream of men who passed through my office.

# KEN GUENTHER
ARMY

went to the University of South Dakota, and that's where I got my
ROTC commission as second lieutenant and was called to action in
1942. Our corps headquarters, IX Corps, ran the Desert Training
Center where they were teaching all the tank crews how to chase
Rommel across North Africa, and we had 400,000 troops under us. I
was the Special Services officer, on the staff of the general, and I was the
only staff member who wasn't a West Point graduate.

It was all a Regular Army thing in those days. From there we ran the
Louisiana Maneuvers, and then we went to Fort McPherson at Atlanta
and handled all the troops in Georgia, Alabama, and the whole South—
training them. From there we went to Hawaii—this would be late 1943
or early 1944—where we started planning the invasion of the main
coast of China. We were at Schofield Barracks, that's where our headquarters was, and we stayed there and did our planning. And then we
went to the Philippines, to Leyte.

We had a helluva great general in Hawaii when we shipped out to
Leyte. General Ryder headed the Thirty-fourth Infantry Division that
led the attack on Anzio. Also, he was a former commandant of cadets at
West Point. He liked me, I guess, for the reason that I was an athletic
guy and he was too, and he'd played first base on that team where Omar
Bradley and Eisenhower played. When we were getting ready to leave
Hawaii he said, "Ken, you know MacArthur hates booze. He doesn't
like any liquor in his command whatsoever. He's dead set against it."
And he says, "We gotta get around that. We're going to the Philippines,
to Leyte." So, he says, "I want you to go and get some medical chests,
those metal chests with Red Cross on them. Get as many as you can get.

Get with the medics and see how many of those you can find. Then go to the Officer's Club and have them order liquor, and fill every one of those chests with as many bottles of liquor as you can, and mark on the chests, "Medical Supplies." I got "Southern Comfort," "Three Feathers," and "Ten High," and I filled a hundred, at least, of these footlockers with the Red Cross on them. We took this booze to the Philippines with us. Anyway, that's the kind of general old General Ryder was.

The real battle for Leyte was over when we got there. However, we were there soon enough afterwards that we took several captives—dug them out of caves and things of that kind. Some of them were still hiding out there. But anyway, that's my memory of Leyte—digging those guys out of the caves, and doing our planning.

And by that time it had changed. Instead of China we were going to invade Japan. We were to be the Strike Force Command. We had two Army and one Marine division assigned to us. These were the units that were gonna hit the beaches.

In the invasion, we were to lead the strike. We were to be in charge of the corps over the division to hit the mainland of Japan in southern Kyushu. What I was involved with was Special Services—the morale of the troops—to provide what little amenities you could in a battle like that, and see that they had plenty of supplies of that nature, that there were chaplains available, the humanistic side, the recreation side of what the hell we are going to do with these people when we get them over there.

A lot of these troops, like the Seventy-seventh, had fought their way from island to island coming across that damned Pacific Ocean, and they were getting a little tired of it. So, they needed something to spruce them up. You had to fire them up again, and this was very important. We had every big-name entertainer, from Bob Hope to Spencer Tracy, everybody coming over there to try to get the troops pepped up while we were doing this planning. The fighting in the Philippines was about over then, and we were waiting to do this next step, so the troops had a lot of time on their hands. We had to do something to keep them happy.

So then we got orders to leave Leyte and steam toward Kwajalein and assemble our armada for the eventual invasion of mainland Japan. Kwajalein was to be our staging area.

Forever burned in my memory, if I live to be as old as Methuselah, is that morning as our command ship is approaching Kwajalein. I can see it now just like it had happened this morning: The sun is coming up and we're steaming toward it. And here, as we come over the horizon were these hundreds and hundreds of masts of ships. Our armada fleet, the invasion fleet, spread out before us as far as you could see, silhouetted against the sun coming up, and it's a scene I'll never forget. It just was—I'm quivering now, even thinking about it—an unbelievable sight. That silhouette, that sun coming up over that ocean, and seeing that enormous power, the ships, the aircraft carriers, everything spread out there before you. It was just awesome.

So then we joined them, anchored, and waited, but Old Harry dropped the Bomb shortly after we got there. When I heard about the A-bombs, it was shocking and even unbelievable. We had no idea there was a weapon like that. But mostly, I think I felt relief—tremendous relief—thinking "Oh, my God! Now we don't have to go through this." We knew that in such an invasion we were in for trouble. Intelligence knew they were expecting us at any time, and were expecting us about where we were going to be. So, yes, the news was terrific. I don't remember dancing for joy, but I probably did. As a lifelong Republican I never voted for Harry Truman, but today he's one of my favorite presidents!

When the Japanese gave up, our part of the armada was diverted to Hokkaido, the northern island. And another thing that—like Kwajalein—I'll never forget and I can still feel, was the apprehension of coming off that gangplank to step foot on Japan. I was the fifth officer in line coming off that gangplank, and there were seventy-five or a hundred Japanese standing there. We had all checked our .45s at our sides before we came down that ramp, and we all had the feeling: "What's going to happen? We've been fighting these people for four years, and now, hell, we're walking on their homeland." So maybe some kook there might take a shot at you, and in modern days you'd really be afraid. It was late in the afternoon, starting to get dusk, and we thought "Holy Toledo!" and were looking both ways at the same time to see what was going to happen. But they were so submissive and sullen and quiet. The apprehension was sure there, but they turned out to be very cooperative with everything we asked them to do.

And at IX Corps headquarters, we became the military governors of the island of Hokkaido. We had the Kurile Islands that we were in charge of, too, and while you were standing on them you could see the Russian mainland on a clear day, and they didn't like us that damn close. So we had Russian officers come join our headquarters. They ate with us, and I'll never forget how they'd sit over in their corner talking and drinking that vodka—they had more bottles of vodka than we had glasses of water on our table—and they'd eat those breakfasts of cold fish and cold tomatoes and drink that vodka.

After we got settled down in Hokkaido, we took our whole corps headquarters staff and went down to the exact area of the beach that our troops were to hit. And I'll guarantee you, the invasion would have been murder. The Japanese had concrete emplacements two- and three-feet deep with machine guns and all types of cannon pointed exactly where we were coming in, just as if they had read our battle plan. We all agreed when the general said, "My God! This would have been even worse than we thought!" We'd have softened it up with air and sea bombardment, of course, but even so it would have been absolute slaughter on both sides. It was unbelievable! Just like they'd had our map! I walked it. I went into some of those dugouts and concrete emplacements, so this is not secondhand—I was there, and it was unbelievable.

We had developed a casualty figure of 50,000 in our briefings, as I recall. And then we saw it would have been even worse than we expected. Anyway, we were thankful we didn't have to do it, and those who want to ban the bomb and wish it had never been dropped can sit around with their teacups in the Waldorf-Astoria or somewhere and talk about it, but to have been there and had to go through it—Well, probably I wouldn't be here today.

So now we had all these troops that had worked hard at winning the war. "Ken, we've got to keep these guys busy. We've got to have things for them to do."

Number one: Close all the red-light districts and have all the girls tested. Then open them wide again. And here was another number one: There was a great fine-beer brewery in Hokkaido where they made their beer with a rice base—and it's the best beer I ever drank—but anyway, they had no more metal left to make bottle caps. So the general says: "Ken, your first job is to contact Schlitz and Budweiser and every brewery you can and get all the beer caps over here that you can immediately. We'll make arrangements for the Air Corps to fly a special plane with beer caps so these guys can have some beer. We gotta keep these guys entertained, and no way can they have beer until we get bottle caps." So a week later when a plane came in with beer caps, we opened up the brewery, and everybody was happy!

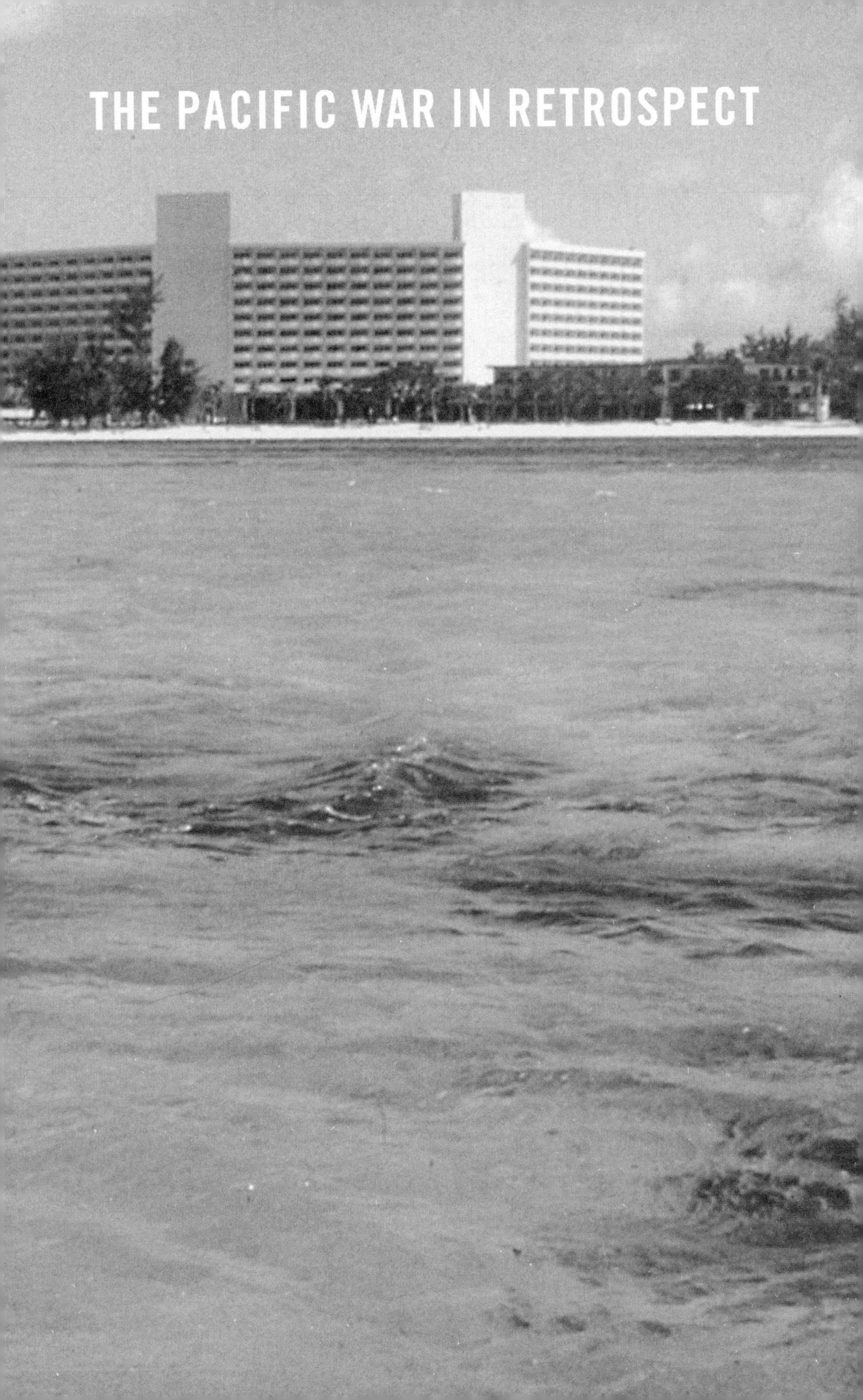
THE PACIFIC WAR IN RETROSPECT

PAGES 492–493: *This U.S. tank still sits in the shallow water offshore where it was put out of action during the 1944 invasion of Saipan.*

# THE PACIFIC WAR IN RETROSPECT

I t has been more than six decades since Japan's infamous attack on Pearl Harbor marked the beginning, for America and her allies, of a devastating war in the Pacific. On December 7, 2003, at the annual commemoration of the attack, it was noted that the youngest member of the Pearl Harbor Survivors Association was eighty, and the oldest was well past ninety. But there were still plenty of lively octogenarian Pacific war veterans attending the public ceremony at the USS *Arizona* Memorial Visitors Center, and even more Pearl Harbor Survivors at the private ceremony on the Memorial itself, straddling the sunken hulk of the USS *Arizona*. Back over at the public ceremony, a contingent of Japanese Pacific war veterans was in attendance, including Yuji Akamatsu. On the morning of December 7, 1941, at the controls of a torpedo bomber, he took off from the Japanese aircraft carrier *Kaga*, on his way to attack Pearl Harbor. Sixty-two years later, on December 7, 2003, he returned to Pearl Harbor at ground level, having last seen it skimming twenty feet above its calm waters and dropping his torpedo on a track to the USS *Nevada*. The American Pearl Harbor Survivors had mixed feelings about seeing him sitting there in his wheelchair, exuding a weakened version of his former torpedo pilot persona, but still smiling and shaking hands and signing programs. Several of the American veterans went over to greet him, through his interpreter, and shake his hand. Others didn't want to get near him. "I don't have anything to say to that guy," one Pearl Harbor Survivor stated gruffly, while a few others around him nodded in agreement. Over half a century has passed, but the memories for these former warriors are still very close to the surface, and their emotional reaction to the Pacific war has dimmed little in the intervening years.

It is this intensity of emotion that emerged over and over again in the interviews for this book. It is veteran Jorge Cristobal, a Guam native who left the island to join the U.S. Navy before the war, pausing tight-lipped for several seconds after relating how, on patrol after the invasion of Guam, he stumbled across his father in a jungle, after not having seen him since before the war. He barely was able to save his father from being shot by a fellow Marine, who mistook the man for a Japanese straggler. It is John Beddall stopping in mid-sentence and having to look down to mask his reaction to the story he was telling about how, after his beloved squadron commander's death, another airman cruelly deceived the CO's little dog into believing his master had returned by mimicking his familiar whistle. And it is the intensity of the mental images that have stayed with some Pacific war veterans their whole lives, which only emerge at night. It is Navy corpsman Vern Garrett still dreaming of terribly wounded and dying Marines screaming for mercy, begging to be put out of their misery when he could no longer do anything for them. It is Fred Saiz still seeing vivid images in his sleep of Japanese charging through the jungle toward his position, but, unlike his real experiences, when he always stopped them short of his foxhole, the Japanese make it through in his dreams.

Indeed, the memories and experiences from the Pacific war will live as long as the veterans from that generation live. After that, recorded or written accounts, like the ones presented here, will be all that remain. And, of course, the islands will still be there, the physical reminders of the war in the Pacific. Those islands carry with them the many ironies that have emerged over the years from that war. Consider that of all the battleships sunk and severely damaged at Pearl Harbor, the two deemed unworthy of salvage efforts, the USS *Arizona* and the USS *Utah*, are the only battleships from the December 7 attack that survive to this day. All the others were scrapped shortly after the war ended, removing them from sight forever. Visitors to Pearl Harbor today can peer down into the water and still view these old battlewagons, or what remains of them, in their final resting places on either side of Ford Island. Or, contemplate that on the site of one of the most heavily fortified Japanese strongholds on Saipan, the beachhead where, before they killed all the Japanese defenders, the U.S. Marines had such great difficulty in landing, there now stands, on that same dazzling, white sand invasion beach, a luxurious Japanese tourist resort hotel.

It would seem that after this many years, there wouldn't be much left from a transient war that briefly visited remote tropical islands for a matter of several years or, in some locations, just several months. The combatants came from faraway countries, and the local island populations had little vested interest in their aims. They were either moved out of the way or got out of the way on their own, though some, like Kimiuo Aisek, had to work for the Japanese, and others, like Falavi, actively assisted the Allies. The islands were deemed important mainly for their strategic value as sites for airstrips. But much remains that veterans can still find when they go looking for physical links to their memories. Bill and Ruth Cope can point to their quarters at Hickam Field where they were startled early on a Sunday morning by bombs falling on Pearl Harbor. The low two-story building is unchanged from when they lived there in 1941. "Only now there are more trees, and you can't see the ships at Pearl Harbor like we could that morning," recalls Bill. The island of Guadalcanal, where Pearl Harbor survivor Sterling Cale was sent in 1942 as a corpsman with Marines fighting desperate battles there, and where Bob Mahood stood onshore and watched ships burning and sinking in Iron Bottom Sound, is still an epicenter of fighting and unrest. Ethnic and tribal conflict in 2000 turned Guadalcanal into a dangerous place once again, and in 2003 Australian troops made the first combat landing on Red Beach since the U.S. Marines stormed ashore there in August 1942. The Australians were called in by the Solomon Islands government to help rein in the spreading chaos then enveloping the island country.

Across Iron Bottom Bay from Guadalcanal, the island of Tulagi, where Dave Levy skippered a PT boat in the early, desperate days of the war when, in the Solomons, PT boats were about the only craft the Navy left there for fighting, has reverted to a quiet backwater fishing port. A few concrete foundations of old Quonset huts and some rusting refueling pipes are all that suggest that the roar of powerful Packard V-12 PT boat engines once echoed across the bay. Farther up in the Solomon Islands chain, the massive coral airstrip at Munda, the handiwork of Seabees like Carl Hamilton, is still used as an airstrip, little changed from when Carl and the others put finishing touches on its packed coral surface. In fact, coral airstrips on islands across the Pacific, an incredible testament to the construction skills of the Seabees and Army engineers as well as to the durability and strength of the natural coral material that went into making them, survive in a number of different manifestations. They are either still used in original condition or have been resurfaced and lengthened to accommodate modern jet aircraft bearing tourists to islands like Bora Bora where Fred Giles, USN, met a lively and beautiful island woman named Tetua, marking the start of a life together for them.

More ironies abound the farther west one travels in the Pacific. Former Japanese stronghold islands like Guam, Saipan, and Tinian, wrested from Japan's grasp by Americans in scenes of violent combat experienced by Jim Milliff, Bob Sheeks, and Dan Williams, have developed into posh Japanese tourist resort havens. The American WWII presence on Saipan and Tinian is mostly evident from the huge airstrips built for the B-29s flown by airmen like Don Van Inwegen and John Vinzant on their long missions to bomb Japan. These same airstrips are now used to fly in Japanese tourists from Nagoya and Tokyo. The beaches at Leyte, where MacArthur came ashore to begin taking back the Philippines and where soldiers like Fred Saiz and Dave Gutterman came in under fire, have reverted to resort use mainly by tourists from other parts of the Philippines. Few Americans visit the twice-life-sized gilded statues of MacArthur and his landing party, erected on the beach at Leyte where he made his long-awaited return. Corregidor, the island MacArthur was driven from at the beginning of the war, where John Bruer retreated after escaping the Bataan Death March, and where Irving Strobing sent his last radio message as the island fell to the Japanese, is now an ecotourism and historical park complete with hiking trails and camp sites. The Malinta Tunnel, where the crowded hospital was strung out through its long laterals, and where MacArthur's headquarters was jammed into another of the laterals to be sheltered from Japanese shelling, is now toured by visitors who learn of the battles for Corregidor from a "sound and light show," with dioramas set up in the laterals depicting scenes from the troubled island's history. The shattered, bomb-perforated old concrete buildings from the prewar American base remain for passing hikers and mountain bikers to ponder. Numerous U.S. and Filipino monuments dot the island where Americans surrendered early in the war and then parachuted in at the end of the conflict to take it back.

There are islands that are difficult to visit today, although most Americans wouldn't bother visiting them even if it were easy. Midway, center of the vortex of the naval battle that was the turning point of the Pacific war, where Doug McEvoy and others in his unit later were effectively confined for nearly two years endlessly servicing submarines with no hope of transfer, was turned over to the Department of Interior after the Navy moved out in the 1990s. It started operating as an ecotourism resort and national wildlife refuge in 1996, but closed again to tourists in 2002. Tarawa, the capital of the island nation of Kiribati, is remote but at least has limited air service. However, not many Americans bother to visit the little islet in Tarawa Atoll called Betio, now an overcrowded commercial center. Huge, shell-scarred concrete bunkers built by the Japanese are interspersed with local housing, and the final, rusting remains of American amphibious landing craft are slowly dissolving on the reef where in 1943 U.S. Marines were gunned down on their way in to the beach. This tiny island is where Bob Sheeks first realized the problems of communicating with Japanese in the midst of battle, and where Vern Garrett patched up his first wounded Marine.

The most difficult island to visit in the Pacific is Iwo Jima. You would be hard-pressed to find an American today who knows that Iwo Jima, where Milo Cumpston ducked Japanese sniper fire as he cleared mines, where Bill Hastings was "lightly knifed," and where Joe Woods took time out from combat to write a letter to his folks, is now a Japanese military island off limits to all outsiders. Only by virtue of a special fiftieth anniversary Iwo Jima veterans' tour arranged with the government of Japan could Joe Woods return to the exact spot where he wrote it, fifty years earlier, and read that letter aloud.

For all the sailors who traversed the vast expanses of the tropical Pacific, only a few can still visit the ships they served on. The second USS *Yorktown* (the first was sunk in the Battle of Midway), where Robert Clack and Vern Garret were pharmacist mates, is now a museum ship at Patriots Point near Charleston, South Carolina. The USS *Laffey*, the destroyer singled out near Okinawa for attack by twenty-two Japanese kamikaze planes, is anchored just behind the *Yorktown*, and she was only narrowly saved by her crew from scrapping after the war. They had saved her once before at Okinawa when five kamikaze aircraft crashed directly into the ship, three others ravaged *Laffey's* decks with bombs, and three more exploded nearby as they were shot down and hit the water. Jim Spriggs, Bob Karr, and Larry Delewski will carry memories of that day to their graves. Meanwhile, when they can find time and if they are able, they turn up at Patriots Point once a year to do volunteer maintenance on their old ship. There are a few WWII vintage submarines that have been preserved, like the *Bowfin* at Pearl Harbor, and visitors can still visit these museum pieces. But for submarine veterans like Jim Lockhart, these relics are living parts of his memory, and he can vividly recall, when attacked by Japanese depth charges, regularly timing the delay between the click he could hear of a detonator and the subsequent explosion, to calculate just how close to death he and his sub mates were.

One Pacific island is easy to visit and is dominated by Japanese war memorials. Okinawa, where Dave Bowman was blown off the sea wall, has many monuments to the Japanese war effort, perhaps fitting since Okinawa is part of Japan, but some think the scale of suffering and death by Americans who fought there is disproportionate to their modest memorials. Japan's two most-visited war-related sites, at least by Americans, are Hiroshima, where *Nisei* Japanese language interpreter Harry Fukuhara returned to find his family after the war, and Nagasaki, the city John Bruer saw destroyed from his POW camp across the bay. Both cities have excellent museums that cover not only the facts of the atomic bombs' effects on their citizens, but also the ongoing issues with atomic weapons that carry into the twenty-first century, and how they have affected all of humankind, not just the populations of Hiroshima and Nagasaki.

The Japanese remember the war as ending with the atomic bombs, but for Americans a prominent symbol of the Japanese surrender is the battleship USS *Missouri*. Since 1999, visitors to Pearl Harbor can stand at the exact spot where Douglas MacArthur presided over the surrender ceremony on the deck of the *Missouri* in 1945. The ship is anchored roughly where Firman Balza watched the USS *Oklahoma* when it was torpedoed and capsized on December 7, 1941. The bow of the *Missouri* points directly at the USS *Arizona*, where Russell McCurdy narrowly survived explosions and fire on December 7. The two ships are said to be like bookends, symbolizing the beginning and the end of the Pacific war for the U.S.

The remaining survivors and eyewitnesses to that great conflict, now in their eighties and beyond, have lived long, full lives. Yet, what they usually remember most vividly are not the humorous stories of time spent on remote tropical islands, the boredom, the heat, the mosquitoes, the dazzling white sand beaches. What haunts them to this day are memories of those who didn't return, of friends who died young, who didn't get to live to see the age of eighty. In the minds of the survivors, those friends remain in their memories, to use the popular term, "forever young," but in a tragic, sad kind of way. An epitaph that recalls those memories of friends lost on faraway Pacific islands appeared at a cemetery on the scarred, tiny island battlefield of Betio in Tarawa Atoll:

"To you who lie within this coral sand, we who remain pay tribute to a pledge that, in dying, thou shalt surely not have died in vain. But when again bright morning dyes the sky, and waving fronds above shall touch the rain, we will remember."

*The Pacific War in Retrospect*

## ACKNOWLEDGMENTS

The authors thank long-time editor and friend Walton Rawls for his considerable editorial expertise, Marian Gordin for her skillful handling of the manuscript formats, project manager Susan Costello for her support and encouragement, Andrea Clyne and Sue Finley for their expert transcription of numerous voice tapes, and Pacific war veteran descendents Sue Littlepage, Joanie Kleypas, Terry Goodwin, Fred Giles Jr., and Jeff Reaves, whose assistance was of great help in completing their parents' contributions to this book. We acknowledge the USS *Arizona* Memorial National Park Service Oral History Collection and Daniel Martinez for contributions to Russell McCurdy's account that supplemented an interview on December 10, 1996.

# INDEX

Page numbers in *italics* refer to illustrations

# PICTURE CREDITS

Cover: NA 80G-48358. Endpapers: Michael Shibao. 1: NA 111-SC-341675.
2–3: NA Marine Corps 88167. 14–15: NA b-65141AC. 26: NA 80G-700777 28–29:
NA 80G-32424. 39: USS Arizona Memorial. 55: Al Bodenlos. 66: Bill and Ruth Cope.
73: Tom Larson. 79: Lenore Ricker. 88–89: NA 111-SC-334296. 114–115: NA 80G-
41197. 117: Bill Bower. 124–125: NA 80G-16322. 138: Dave Bowman. 149: Dave Bowman. 154-155: NA 127-GW-734-96102. 157: Vern Garrett. 178-179: Bob Sheeks. 181:
Bob Sheeks. 198: Dan Williams. 208 L, R: Harry Fukuhara. 214–215: Dave Levy. 217:
Dave Levy. 230: Al Hahn. 244–245: NA 65226 A.C. 247: John Bedall. 249: John Beddall. 252: A.C. Kleypas. 257: A.C. Kleypas. 260: Jim Rosenbrock. 277: Louise Meehl.
280–281: NA 80G-294131. 317: Clarence Cook. 352–353: NA 80G-12717. 355: Fred
Giles Jr. 359: Fred Giles Jr. 365: Rex Alan Smith. 387: NA Marine Corps 60459.
390–391: NA Marine Corps 54377. 404–405: NA 59056 A.C. 418–419: NA 80G-
48557. 421: Jim Milliff. 429: Harlan Wall. 436: Fred Saiz. 455: Joe Woods. 460–461:
NA 80G-415001. 463: Jim Spriggs. 472: U.S. Navy. 482–483: NA 80G-373264.
492–493: Gerald Meehl.